WITHDRAWN

Under the Editorship of

**EDWARD McCHESNEY SAIT**

POMONA COLLEGE

# American Constitutional Development

### SECOND EDITION

## By CARL BRENT SWISHER
THOMAS P. STRAN PROFESSOR OF POLITICAL SCIENCE
THE JOHNS HOPKINS UNIVERSITY

HOUGHTON MIFFLIN COMPANY

The Riverside Press Cambridge

COPYRIGHT, 1954, BY CARL BRENT SWISHER
COPYRIGHT, 1943, BY CARL BRENT SWISHER
ALL RIGHTS RESERVED INCLUDING THE RIGHT
TO REPRODUCE THIS BOOK OR PARTS THEREOF
IN ANY FORM 𝕏 The Riverside Press
CAMBRIDGE, MASSACHUSETTS
PRINTED IN THE U.S.A.

# CONTENTS

29509

# PREFACE TO SECOND EDITION

ELEVEN EVENTFUL YEARS have passed since the publication of the first edition of this book. That edition was written in the constitutional perspective of the New Deal of the 1930's and of the national defense period which followed, and was published in the midst of the period of World War II. Only brief reference was possible to the constitutional problems raised by the war itself. The story of the war was not yet complete, and it was too soon to see it in the perspective of history.

As far as the major portion of the book is concerned, the perspective of the time in which it was written seems not inappropriate today. Although the New Deal lost its novelty, much of its program was integrated permanently into our governmental pattern. Although World War II became a thing of the past, national defense activities continue as a major preoccupation. For all the changes here and there, we are still committed to a vast amount of federal control over agriculture, industry, and labor. We are still committed to defending ourselves at whatever cost in a world grown vastly more dangerous to us, and to the economic and political adjustments which defense requires. Constitutional development, in other words, is still dominated by concern for survival and maintenance of welfare, whether the threatened ills be economic or military.

Since the first thirty-six chapters dealt with largely completed events and were written in this perspective, it has been necessary to change them only by redrafting pages and parts of pages here and there, leaving the basic structure essentially unchanged. The major modifications have come at the end of the book, with the tieing in of constitutional events which had not occurred or were not seen in their total setting at the time of publication in 1943. The last three chapters have been largely or completely replaced by four new ones. The new ones deal with the constitutional issues of economic control, the constitutional issues of war, crises for liberty, and the unfolding of judicial behavior in the period of the Roosevelt-Truman Supreme Court. No more than the first edition does the second attempt the rounding out of the constitutional story. American constitutional development is a continuing process. It will go on with the continuing dynamics of a powerful society, adjusting itself to the inevitabilities of new situations as they arise. The story is perennially continued, new chapters waiting only for the constitutional events dictated in combination by the course of past development and the interplay of novel happenings. There is always more to come when the passage of time has made the writing possible.

The author has a sense of continuing obligation to the original editor, the late Edward M. Sait, and to the other people to whom acknowledgments were made in the first edition. Many students have aided in the working out of ideas and the conception of arrangement of materials for the new chapters. Mrs. Eva Redfield Rubin read and made helpful criticisms of early drafts. Mrs. Edna L. Fulton has ably done the necessary secretarial work.

CARL BRENT SWISHER

THE JOHNS HOPKINS UNIVERSITY

# PREFACE TO FIRST EDITION

FOR THE CONVENIENCE of readers, a statement of the scope and purpose of this volume has been incorporated in the Introduction which immediately precedes the first chapter. My task at this point, therefore, is limited to giving a brief account of the origin of the book and making grateful acknowledgment for the assistance of many people. The volume rests in part upon projects which were completed before plans for this particular study were made. They include the writing of two biographies of members of the Supreme Court, the organization of a course in American constitutional development at Columbia University in the early nineteen-thirties, and two years of fruitful experience at the Department of Justice. The present volume was outlined in 1937 and 1938 in oral and written conversations with Russell M. Story and with Edward M. Sait, the editor of the series in which this book is included.

I am indebted to the many persons who aided in shaping the book and improving it as to style, accuracy, perspective, and emphasis. Professor Sait followed the preparation of the book from beginning to end, and is entitled to high credit for its better qualities. Carl McFarland read two-thirds of the chapters and criticized them in detail. Robert E. Cushman made important suggestions for the revision of a third of the manuscript and read part of the galley proof. James Hart scanned the entire manuscript. V. O. Key, Johannes Mattern, and Malcolm Moos read substantial blocs of material. My wife, Idella Gwatkin Swisher, followed the book from its inception to the final stages of publication. Many other people, including both colleagues and graduate students, read chapters or parts of chapters and aided in working out particular problems.

Still others assisted in various ways. Librarians in the Social Sciences at the Johns Hopkins University, Margaret Lough and Beatrice Blakslee, cooperated generously. Mary Ellen Brown helped with research and stenographic work. Lilly E. Lavarello did much of the typing and helped to make the index. The Social Science Research Council made an award to cover the cost of final revision and preparation of the manuscript for the press.

CARL BRENT SWISHER

THE JOHNS HOPKINS UNIVERSITY

# INTRODUCTION

"WE MAY WELL WONDER in view of the precedents now established," said Charles E. Hughes in 1920, "whether constitutional government as heretofore maintained in this Republic could survive another great war even victoriously waged."[1] The conflict known as the World War had ended as far as military hostilities were concerned, but was not yet officially terminated. Most of the war statutes were still in effect, many of the emergency organizations were still in operation, and the pent-up emotions of the American people, now denied their normal military outlet against the enemy, were turned against so-called radicals, nonconformists, and other unpopular groups in the United States. The war had brought invasion of the rights of property and regimentation of individual lives to a degree never previously experienced by American citizens. Much of the regimentation of property soon came to an end, and gradually, in spite of the fears of Mr. Hughes and others, the traditional safeguards of civil liberty became effective once more. The country experienced a nominal "return to normalcy." Beneath the surface, however, apart from the war and in spite of professions of Presidents Harding, Coolidge, and Hoover in favor of more business in government and less government in business, the decade of the nineteen-twenties witnessed a renewed and less spectacular extension of peacetime regulatory power over the rights of property. The business collapse of 1929 outlived protestations that the economic order was fundamentally sound and belied the prophecy that prosperity was "just around the corner." The crisis, characterized by a member of the Supreme Court as "more serious than war," culminated in the program called the New Deal. That program included regulation of property in some respects more

[1] *New York Times*, June 22, 1920.

drastic than during the earlier war period, regulation sanctioned by the Supreme Court only after the administration came near winning a struggle to "reform" the Court itself.

Before the New Deal program had moved far enough into history for unbiased appraisal, the flames of war again engulfed much of the world. During World War II the outer reaches of governmental power over life, liberty, and property moved far beyond those of World War I and the New Deal period. If "constitutional government as hitherto maintained in this Republic" had faced an uncertain future a quarter of a century earlier, the earlier uncertainty now appeared infinitesimal in contrast with that upon the horizon. Commitment to participation in the newly organized United Nations marked a fundamental change in the pattern and scope of the power of the federal government even in time of peace. Before conditions of peace could be approximated so that the new status of American democracy could be appraised, the development of the "cold war" with the Soviet Union and of military conflict in Korea brought about a vast program of rearmament with accompanying bureaucratic expansion and extension of governmental power.

So it is that in the 1950's the threat to democratic government remains ominous and the measure of damage already done stands unascertained. In a high degree the solution of the problems of the future lie in conditions of the future about which men can only speculate. Even so, the roots of the civilization and of the constitutional system of the United States go deep into the past. Established principles of law, the wellspring of custom, the tradition of meeting particular problems in particular ways, the inherited conviction that rights must be preserved, the devices of administration entrenched in statute, administrative orders, and judicial decisions — all carry over into the determination of future conduct. To a degree, therefore, the time most fitting for restudy of the past is the time when the future is most uncertain. The experiences which have molded our institutions are not devoid of current significance because they took place in times gone by, amid conditions different from those of today. Differences of conditions, indeed, add at times to their relevance in the search for perspective.

This volume represents a restatement of significant facts in American constitutional history, in the hope that a fuller knowledge and better understanding of those facts will contribute to a better understanding of the problems of today and tomorrow. It is in the main a factual presentation, organized with such breadth of vision as could be brought to the task. Opinion and evaluation creep inevitably into the selection and organization of materials, and into the language of the writer, but the purpose has been not to indoctrinate the reader with a point of view, but to portray for readers of varying points of view the swelling tide of American constitutional development as it has flowed down through the years.

The tendency in other works in the field has been to expand accounts of the origin of the Constitution and changes which took place down until the post-Civil-War period and to deal only in brief summaries with the period thereafter extending down to the present day. Many authors have dealt fully with the relevant portions of English history and with those phases of the British constitution which crept inevitably into our constitutional system in spite of widespread antagonism to the common law and other characteristics of the mother country. They have given us detailed histories of the colonies, showing the evolution of characteristics which molded the institutions of the several states and at some point shaped the pattern of the federal system. They have drawn from the inadequate records of colonial experience accounts of early unsuccessful efforts toward the establishment of inter-colonial union, efforts which paved the way for the final achievement. Histories of the period of government under the Articles of Confederation and of the adoption of the Constitution and the establishment of the new government have been written in great detail. The constitutional controversies of the first third of the nineteenth century, especially those involving slavery and the Civil War but including others, have been presented from many angles.

Important as is the study of origins and early history, however, the development of the Constitution of the United States has not been a mere matter of origin and application during the first century of its existence. The unfolding of constitutional powers has continued at an accelerating pace. Differences which may have appeared originally to be but differences of degree have become so great as to amount to differences of kind. The Constitution of the nineteen-fifties is much further from the Constitution of the eighteen-seventies than was the latter from the Constitution as orginally applied.[2] For readers concerned with problems of today and tomorrow, the history of the Constitution must leave no gap between the much-discussed period of early decades and the happenings of the present hour. The period

2 For discussion of meanings attached to the word "constitution," see chapter 1.

of Theodore Roosevelt and William Howard Taft rivals or exceeds in importance that of Andrew Jackson and Martin Van Buren. The first World War had an impact upon our constitutional system no less great than that of the Civil War. The evolution of governmental controls for corporate enterprise and the judicial rationalizations of sweeping extensions of governmental power are far more important today than the earlier bitter controversies over the constitutional issues of slavery. The New Deal and the coming of the second World War shook our institutions to their very foundations. The need for discussion of recent constitutional development is no less great because the history of yesterday cannot be embalmed in settled interpretation until the perspective of tomorrow has been achieved. No implication is intended that the distant past may be ignored or neglected. Every period must be re-examined from time to time in the light of new experience. The present account of the early decades of American constitutional history is to some extent such a reinterpretation within the limits of the space allotted.[3] It has seemed best, however, to expand the traditional account of the post-Civil-War period and to reserve approximately half the volume to continue the account of American constitutional development after the turn of the twentieth century.

The method of interpretation varies in terms of efforts to show, not merely the nature and scope of the Constitution in particular periods, but also the causes of changes and the manner in which they were brought about. Ample use is made of decisions of the Supreme Court,[4] because of the fact that the judicial battle-line marks oftentimes the periphery of permitted constitutional expansion. The outlines of the Constitution are molded amid the clash of conflicting philosophies on the Court. Yet judicial decisions alone provide an inadequate basis for an understanding of constitutional development. The attitudes of the people or of politically influential groups determine whether or not attempts will be made to expand or curtail the operations of constitutional government in particular directions. The area of conflict may therefore be found oftentimes in Congress rather than in the judiciary. The negative decisions of Congress have as

---

[3] The centuries of English history lying back of the origin of the American constitutional system must be passed with but a reference. Study of such history, recorded in the works of many authors, will amply repay the reader interested primarily in the development of the American Constitution.

[4] For a brief discussion of source materials, see the bibliographical note at the end of this volume.

much to do with shaping the contours of the Constitution as do the enactments which it makes in new fields. The fact that Congress chartered no national bank between 1836 and the Civil-War period, for example, is of comparable importance with decisions of the Supreme Court in earlier years holding that Congress had the power to establish such a bank. Except in time of war or other major crisis, legislative steps of constitutional significance have seldom been taken without prolonged debate. Such debate and the maneuvering connected with it play a prominent part in many of the following chapters.

The executive branch of the government, like Congress and the judiciary, plays an important part, both positively and negatively, in the development of the Constitution. Such presidents as Martin Van Buren, James Buchanan, Benjamin Harrison, and Calvin Coolidge played parts which were largely negative or which sought to restrain the contemporary course of constitutional expansion. Thomas Jefferson, Andrew Jackson, Abraham Lincoln, Woodrow Wilson, and Franklin D. Roosevelt enlarged the powers of their office and established precedents for the exercise of broader powers by their successors. In a very real sense they, like the participants in the Constitutional Convention of 1787, were makers of the Constitution.

Within the executive branch of the government a limitation upon constitutional development has come into view, particularly in recent years, apart from the personality, ability, and program of the President. It lies in the ability or inability of the administrative mechanism to perform the tasks assigned to it. Both in private industry and in government, experience has shown that huge organizations tend to bog down in bureaucratic lethargy. Even though Congress enacts measures conferring new powers, the President approves them, and the Supreme Court gives its sanction, all will be to no avail if the task prescribed is too difficult for performance or if it adds too much of a burden to an already overburdened administrative machine. Although constitutional development is not primarily a matter of administration, the development of machinery and methods is so related to it as to require periodic attention to the organization and reorganization of the government for the performance of governmental functions.

The following chapters, therefore, reproduce in various ways the interplay of administrations, the Executive, Congress, and the courts, to show the processes by which the Constitution is adapted to the needs of the people as the needs arise and as demands for change are made. Even though situations may never completely reproduce themselves, it is believed that the volume illuminates the events of the past in such a way as to promote a deeper understanding of the events of today and the probable events of tomorrow.

......................................................................................................................................

# CHAPTER 1

# THE CONSTITUTION IN EMBRYO

THE TERM "United States" is a symbol deeply grooved in the minds of all Americans. It takes its color largely from the contemporary scene. It signifies an area stretching from the Atlantic to the Pacific and from a well-defined Canadian border to an equally well-defined Mexican frontier. It connotes a highly industrialized nation, with industry and industrial organization extending even to the details of agricultural production. It symbolizes more than one hundred and fifty million people, most of whom believe with satisfaction or take for granted the fact that they live in the wealthiest and most powerful country in the world, under a system of government substantially better than any elsewhere in operation.

## THE BRITISH COLONIES IN AMERICA

For an understanding of constitutional origins, however, it is necessary to blot out much of the contemporary picture, and to substitute for it one that is very different. It is necessary to remember that the first United States were but thirteen in number. They had been called, and had called themselves, not states, but colonies. As colonies they had been established largely for the utilitarian purpose of promoting the welfare of the mother country. They extended southward in one tier, from Maine (then part of Massachusetts) only to Georgia, and westward, as a rule, only to the Appalachians. All of them either bordered upon the Atlantic Ocean or had open routes of transportation to the Atlantic by rivers and bays.

This tier of thinly settled colonies carried on commerce largely with the mother country. They had some commercial relationships with the colonies of other nations, particularly in the West Indies, but they traded with each other only to a slight extent. They conducted foreign trade and most intercolonial trade in slow-moving sailing vessels. No good roads had been constructed, either among or within the several colonies. Stagecoach lines operated in few sections, and the riding was rough. Men who traveled between distant points usually did so by horseback. Railroads were as yet beyond the horizon of the future. Although Benjamin Franklin had astounded his neighbors by bringing sparks of electricity out of the clouds, the telegraph, the telephone, the radio, the machinery of electric power, and the use of atomic energy were beyond the wildest imaginings of the people. The speed of horses and sailings vessels measured the speed of communication and transportation.

The major interest of the British Empire and of most British subjects in planting colonies on the American continent had lain, not in the establishment of new societies which would eventually become independent, but in creating posts for the accumulation of raw materials and the promotion of the trade of the Empire. It was assumed that the colonies would remain a part of that Empire. The colonies fulfilled their imperial purpose in so far as they led to profitable trade, yielded coveted raw materials, and held the rich resources of the new country against the predatory efforts of other nations.

Although many thousands of immigrants in the colonies came from various parts of continental Europe, the settlers were predominantly Englishmen, and, until near the time of the separation from Great Britain, continued to think of themselves as Englishmen. They included, however, large numbers of people who would be disturbing factors in any society. Many who crossed the sea primarily in search of wealth were more adventuresome than the rank and file of their brethren left at home. They developed an originality and independence not consistent with traditional forms of governmental and social regimentation. Religious dissenters constituted important elements in the population of certain colonies — and religious dissent in those days usually signified traits of nonconformity and strength of will likely to resist regimentation by a government three thousand miles across the sea. Indentured servants, who courageously submitted to a form of temporary slavery in return for the opportunity to establish themselves in a new country, made up part of the population. So also did convicts and persons politically out of favor with the government at home, who likewise brought a heritage of independence not characteristic of the rank and file of the society from which they came.

Because of these factors, including great distances, slowness of transportation, and the independent characteristics of the colonies, the mother country found its colonies hard to govern. The difficulties multiplied with time. Although the colonists were predominantly English and thought of themselves as Englishmen, they remained on the American continent generation after generation, developing ties and loyalties in the new country and losing more and more their personal contact with the mother country. For want of that contact, patriotic relationships tended to break down. Slowly but inevitably patriotic sentiments attached themselves to colonial homes, and withered away in relation to the mother country.

### THE CONSTITUTIONAL HERITAGE

Whatever their reasons for leaving their ancestral homes, the English colonists in America brought with them a constitutional heritage which molded colonial governmental institutions and continued in a high degree to guide those of the United States. The word "constitution," as used in connection with government, has many meanings. In the narrow sense of the term it is now used to characterize the documents which comprise the basic laws of the United States, each of the several states of the Union, and of a number of other governments. This use had its origin in the United States, and is therefore relatively recent. The royal charters granted at the time of the establishment of some of the colonies resembled the charters given by the British government to its great exploring and trading companies, but also constituted something in the nature of fundamental laws. The Virginia charter, for example, which was granted in 1606, dealt, not merely with property and commerce, but also provided that British subjects and their children in the several British colonies and plantations in the New World should "have and enjoy all liberties, franchises, and immunities, within any of our other dominions, to all intents and purposes, as if they had been abiding and born, within this our realm of England, or any other of our said dominions." [1]

The Mayflower Compact, drafted in 1620, was probably the first basic law or constitution worked out by the people to be governed. [2] The Fundamental Orders of Connecticut, adopted in 1639, was another. [3] In the several colonies the varied charters, compacts, and orders which defined the basis of government accustomed the colonists to the conception of a basic law or constitution laid out in a formal

[1] *American Historical Documents,* Harvard Classics, XL (1910), 58.
[2] *Ibid.,* p. 62.
[3] *Ibid.,* p. 63.

written statement.    When the colonial governments had to be revised
at the time of the separation from the mother country, it is not surprising that a written constitution was drafted sooner or later for each
of the free and independent states.    The Articles of Confederation
performed the same function for the Union to the extent of their
powers, and were supplanted by the more adequate Constitution
drafted in 1787.

Broadly speaking, however, the word "constitution" refers, not
merely, or perhaps not at all, to a written basic law, but to the fundamental principles which determine the structure and operation of
government.    In his *Treatise on Constitutional Limitations* Thomas
M. Cooley, long regarded as a leading authority on constitutional
matters in the United States, stated that a constitution was sometimes
defined as "the fundamental law of a state, containing the principles
upon which the government is founded, regulating the division of the
sovereign powers, and directing to what persons each of these powers
is to be confided, and the manner in which it is to be exercised."    He
thought an equally complete and accurate definition would be "that
body of rules and maxims in accordance with which the powers of
sovereignty are habitually exercised." [4]    In this sense every people
which is politically organized has a constitution, however much it may
differ from the constitutions of other politically organized societies.

At the end of the colonial period the word had additional significant connotations.    The British constitution was a product of centuries of evolution.    Many of the important steps in the process were
in the nature of taking power from the King and prescribing orderly
procedure as to the subject matter usually under the control of Parliament.    The evolution of this restrictive phase of the English constitution is usually assumed to have begun with Magna Charta in 1215
when King John was forced to make certain concessions to the rights
of Englishmen, concessions thereafter enforced against his successors.
Through declarations of rights, bills of rights, petitions, remonstrances,
and other devices additional restraints were imposed on the King
down through the centuries.    Some of them, it is true, merely shifted
power from the King to a Parliament of the landed and mercantile
class, but they were brought forth — partly at least — in the name of
liberty, and basic rights were extended to all the people.    In addition
to connoting the political organization of the English people, there-

---

[4] Thomas M. Cooley, *A Treatise on Constitutional Limitations* (7th ed., 1903), p. 4.

fore, the constitution signified also the preservation of the rights of men against violation by government.[5]

By the end of the seventeenth century, substantial and permanent results had been achieved in some fields, as in the instance of persons accused of crime, who were accorded the protections involved in grand jury and trial jury procedures and in many other devices to prevent arbitrary action. Religious liberty varied in terms of the ruling English sovereign and dominant political groups, and in terms also of the varied religious denominations. Economic liberty and economic opportunity also varied in terms of many factors. The attitudes of sovereigns and of the dominant groups in Parliament determined the extent and manner in which the Empire sought to expand colonial enterprises and foreign trade. Adam Smith illuminated a rift in economic philosophy at the time by his study entitled *An Inquiry into the Nature and Causes of the Wealth of Nations.* Smith advanced the theory that the wealth of nations would be promoted by the abandonment of rigid governmental controls and the promotion of free economic enterprise. He opposed the restrictions of the old mercantilist system, assuming that the competition of businessmen would promote the operations of business and industry and enhance prosperity as a whole. He gave voice to a rising sentiment for throwing off governmental shackles upon business, on the assumption that economic liberty would be more productive of wealth than co-ordination under government control.

The process of curtailing royal absolutism was rationalized and justified by resort to various contract theories as to the origin of government and the original allotment of authority to the monarchs. John Locke, in his *Two Treatises of Government,*[6] published in the latter part of the seventeenth century, had contributed greatly to the advancement of the American Revolution by his use of the theory of social contract. He defended the right of a people to break the contract whereby they permitted the sovereign to rule over them if the sovereign violated the terms of his contract. The ideas advanced by Locke became an integral part of the thinking of those Englishmen

[5] So deeply engrained was this conception of the constitution that the newborn American states, in drafting their own constitutions, included bills of rights as integral parts. When the federal Constitution was drafted, giving limited powers to a federal government, the people were so accustomed to this practice that they insisted upon amendments to include a bill of rights in spite of the fact that, according to the language of the Constitution itself, the federal government possessed, not all powers except those reserved, but merely those which were granted by it.

[6] The title appears in later editions as *Two Treatises on Civil Government.*

who were pushing the Crown of England more and more into the position of a figurehead, and became the commonplace lines of argument of the Englishmen in America who sought at first merely to restrain the power exercised over them by the mother country, and then finally sought to achieve complete independence.

As the British acquired territorial possessions throughout the world, the English constitution expanded into the constitution of an Empire. Although the constitution, as it related to colonies and colonial possessions, was pragmatic and not clearly defined, general experience with the management of colonies demonstrated the validity of certain principles. While the colonies were established predominantly to promote the welfare of the mother country or of certain groups or classes in the mother country, it proved advantageous to manage the colonies, not merely through governors appointed by the Crown and through legislation enacted by Parliament, but through the aid of local assemblies as well. The use of local assemblies seems to have been based, not upon a scrupulous desire to protect the rights of Englishmen wherever Englishmen might reside, but rather upon lessons of experience. Matters of local government in colonies lying far from the mother country raised unfamiliar problems and could be handled more efficiently by men on the ground, who knew local problems, than by statesmen at home. From expediency, therefore, the delegation of authority to the colonies for the management of local affairs became one of the established principles of the constitution of the British Empire. Likewise from expediency, the colonists approved of the principle and chose to regard the right of self-government as a fundamental political right which could not be denied. This fact is important in connection with the strife between Parliament and the colonies which led to the Revolution. The colonists or their Revolutionary leaders ultimately agreed to uphold the theory that the legislative power of Parliament was limited to the mother country, and that legislation for the colonies could be enacted only by the respective colonial legislative assemblies. Whether or not the theory was correct — and it is one on which authorities differ [7] — its adoption marked an important step in the movement toward colonial independence.

Government by local bodies tended to develop local sentiment and feelings of local independence at the expense of the unity of the

[7] See Charles H. McIlwain, *The American Revolution* (1923), and Robert L. Schuyler, *Parliament and the British Empire* (1929).

Empire. The colonists proved unco-operative in matters not immediately involving their own interests. Varying degrees of strain existed between the governors appointed by the Crown and the assemblies elected by local residents. In the seventeen-sixties, after the winning of the French and Indian or Seven Years' War, Parliament attempted to revamp the scheme of colonial government. In theory, at least, it sought to co-ordinate the several sections of the Empire to make the parts take their place as servants of the whole. Parliament sought especially to compel the colonies to restrict their trade to the closed system of the Empire, thereby cutting off profitable trade with other nations, and it sought to collect from the colonies taxes to cover the expenses of the operation of the colonial system.

Colonists resented the threat to their livelihood involved in efforts to cut off certain profitable lines of trade outside the mercantile system of the Empire, and in the prospect of the enforcement of other controls still more drastic. As for taxes, the colonists had all the dislike of people everywhere for the payment of taxes. Furthermore, although the new country was rich in raw materials, the dearth of money added to the weight of the burden of taxes levied. It is not surprising that the colonists resisted the innovation of levies made in London, and that they hit upon the argument of "no taxation without representation" as a device to justify resistance. They did not seek representation in Parliament in order that taxes might be levied upon them by a body in which they had representatives. Presumably they knew the practical impossibility of maintaining representatives in Parliament who would exercise any influence worth mentioning. Their desire was not to secure representation, but to avoid taxation.

New colonial legislation by Parliament provoked heated debate throughout the colonies concerning the authority of Parliament over them. The debates settled nothing as far as the legal question was concerned, but they did a great deal to focus the attention of colonial leaders upon the issues of empire, and to stimulate among the colonies an awareness of themselves as political entities with interests antagonistic to those of the mother country. The period of slightly more than a decade which preceded formal separation from the mother country constituted a period of intensive education in preparation for independent political life. Ideas were threshed out, competent leaders put aside their personal affairs and concentrated upon the affairs of state, and the psychology of the people adapted itself to what appeared to be the inevitable transition.

It is doubtful whether at this time any government in England, however skillful and diplomatic in its methods, could have extended its control over taxation and greatly regimented commerce in the colonies. The London government which attempted to do these things was anything but skillful and diplomatic. It met colonial disobedience with reprisals. When it made concessions, as in the repeal of the obnoxious Stamp Act, it did so in such a manner that good will was not restored. When a band of Bostonians dumped a cargo of tea into the harbor in protest against British taxes, the government made a martyr of the city and the colony of Massachusetts by blockading the port against commerce, suspending the colonial charter, and resorting to military rule. Guarantees of rights, such as jury trial and the writ of habeas corpus, were suspended in certain cases, thus giving further cause for the charge of gross persecution. Among other punitive measures, Parliament sanctioned search without formal warrant wherever smuggled goods were suspected of being hidden. The quartering of British soldiers in colonial homes was authorized. When, at Lexington, on April 19, 1775, British soldiers fired on a group of colonists, killing eight and wounding others, they touched off the flames of revolution.

The thirteen colonies, in spite of their common origin, had until this time shared few interests except as antagonisms to common enemies — the Indians and the French — were involved. Sporadic "congresses" of colonial representatives had been held, largely for the purpose of presenting a united front to these enemies. The congresses had provided a limited amount of experience in co-operation, and there was some talk of a permanent union, particularly in connection with the "Albany Plan" proposed by Benjamin Franklin in 1754. But neither the government at London nor the colonies themselves were sufficiently interested in co-operative action to bring about formal steps toward union. The strife over taxation and the regulation of commerce, however, created a new and stronger bond among the colonies. The Stamp Act Congress, which met in New York in 1765, provided early evidence of that bond. More important evidence was provided by the meeting of the first Continental Congress in Philadelphia in 1774, the forerunner of congressional assemblages which continued to meet until the ties of formal union were established.

The Continental Congress, which consisted of delegates variously chosen by dissatisfied groups in twelve of the thirteen colonies, was an extra-legal body.  It did not assemble to make laws for the colonies or to promote a revolution.  It included men who had already given much time to discussion of the grievances of the colonies through what were known as "Committees of Correspondence."  Most of the delegates sought some means of restoring peaceable relations with the government at London and of keeping the colonies within the Empire without acknowledging the authority asserted by Parliament.  They and the people to whose grievances they listened complained of the violation of their rights under the British constitution.  A much-considered memorial from residents of a colony in Massachusetts denounced the gross infraction "of those rights to which we are justly entitled by the laws of nature, the British constitution, and the charter of the province." [8]  Benjamin Franklin drafted for the Congress a resolution stating that "there is a manifest *defect* in the constitution of the British Empire in respect to the government of the colonies upon those principles of liberty which form an essential part of that constitution."  The colonists desired the establishment of a political union, Franklin's statement continued, not only among themselves, but with the mother state, "upon those principles of safety and freedom which are essential in the constitution of all free governments and particularly that of the British legislature." [9]  In an "address" to the people of Great Britain, Congress stated that "the legislature of Great Britain is not authorized by the constitution to establish a religion, fraught with sanguinary and impious tenets, or, to erect an arbitrary form of government, in any quarter of the globe." [10]  Later, in December, 1775, the second Continental Congress adopted a report opposing "the claim and exercise of unconstitutional powers, to which neither the Crown nor Parliament were ever entitled.  By the British constitution, our best inheritance, rights, as well as duties, descend upon us: We cannot violate the latter by defending the former." [11]

In the meantime, in April, 1775, the so-called Battle of Lexington had taken place, and armed strife had begun.  Although members of the Congress continued for a considerable period to labor for the restoration of peace without severance from the Empire, their functions came to be more and more the management of a colonial military struggle with Great Britain.  They adopted Articles of War, provided for the organization and equipment of an army, issued paper money to finance military operations, and in other ways con-

[8] *Journals of the Continental Congress* (34 vols., 1904-1937), I, 33.
[9] *Ibid.*, I, 48.          [10] *Ibid.*, I, 83.          [11] *Ibid.*, III, 410.

ducted themselves as a combined legislature and executive of an independent nation. Every new incident of conflict drove deeper the wedge separating the New World from the Old. Men who had hitherto acknowledged the sovereignty of the King over the colonies, while merely denying the authority of the British Parliament to legislate for them, began to demand formal and permanent severance from Great Britain.

The adoption of the Declaration of Independence, on July 4, 1776, was a culminating step in a long series, all of which moved in the direction of a separation between the American colonies and the nation under whose supervision they had grown to their existing state of maturity. The Declaration, eloquently phrased by Thomas Jefferson, was a justification of the Revolution in language similar to but more highly polished than that already used by Jefferson himself and other Revolutionary colonists on many occasions. It stated the doctrine that men possessed inalienable rights and that governments derived their just powers from the consent of the governed. By the presentation of a long list of grievances, Congress sought in the Declaration to demonstrate the fact that the despotic rule of the King had been such an abuse of his powers as to leave to the people no recourse but to take from him the authority over them which had hitherto been recognized. The accumulation of accusations to justify revolution was directed, not at Parliament, but at the King. The King having grossly abused his powers, and the people of Great Britain having refused to heed the pleas of the colonists, no alternative was left to them but to reject all his claims of authority. The document concluded as follows:

WE, THEREFORE, the Representatives of the United States of America, in General Congress, Assembled, appealing to the Supreme Judge of the world for the rectitude of our intentions, do, in the Name, and by Authority of the good People of these Colonies, solemnly publish and declare, That these United Colonies are, and of Right ought to be Free and Independent States; that they are Absolved from all Allegiance to the British Crown, and that all political connection between them and the State of Great Britain, is and ought to be totally dissolved; and that as Free and Independent States, they have full Power to levy War, conclude Peace, contract Alliances, establish Commerce, and to do all other Acts and Things which Independent States may of right do. And for the support of this Declaration, with a firm reliance on the protection of Divine Providence, we mutually pledge to each other our Lives, our Fortunes and our sacred Honor.

The separation from the mother country marked the transition of the American settlements from colonies into states. History recorded it as a dramatic movement in behalf of human liberty. The controls of monarchy were broken off, and governmental power was thereafter exercised exclusively by governments organized at home and operated by people who knew intimately the problems with which they had to deal. The victory for liberty was extended in that, from time to time over a period of ensuing decades, the United States abandoned restrictions on political rights which continued to apply in Great Britain and which stood in the way of the establishment of a broader democracy.[12]

Apart from the question of liberty achieved by throwing off the shackles of British domination, the significance of the Revolution lay in the fact that it punctuated the beginning of an independent nation, a nation destined to be too populous, too wealthy, and too powerful to suffer even a slight degree of governmental control from the distant shores of another continent. The language of the revolutionaries may be interpreted to show that they foresaw the future development of a great nation. How much they actually foresaw of the developments of the distant future is a matter for speculation, but clearly their instincts pointed in the direction in which the developments took place. At the very least — and in this case the least means a great deal — they are entitled to full credit for having been right.

## THE BEGINNINGS OF CONSTITUTIONAL ORGANIZATION

Formal separation from Great Britain made necessary the reorganization of government in the colonies, which had proclaimed themselves free and independent states. Varying types of governmental organization and varying degrees of order had been preserved in the several colonies during the years immediately preceding the Declaration of Independence. Revolutionary organizations had grown more and more powerful, and were ready to take over the reins of government wherever they had not already done so. Under the encouragement of the Continental Congress most of them drafted constitutions

[12] A slower movement in the same direction was also initiated in the mother country, however, and it continued to persist. As far as liberty with respect to labor was concerned, indeed, Great Britain did away peaceably with the institution of slavery before the United States accomplished the same result amid the catastrophe of a civil war. Canada and other British colonial possessions maintained unimpaired governmental relationships with Parliament and with the Crown, and achieved nevertheless forms of democracy which gave protection to human rights not inferior to that provided in the United States.

which provided for governments similar to those of earlier years. The colonial governors, the representatives of the King, were of course missing from the new picture. In their places the constitutions provided for new executive officers, but, no doubt because of the earlier experience with governors appointed by the King, the authority of the new officers was greatly restricted. The legislative bodies, on the other hand, the successors of the colonial assemblies which as representatives of the people had stood high in popular estimation, were given or assumed broad powers. Yet many constitutions restrained governmental authority by bills of rights which echoed the contemporary opposition to arbitrary exercise of governmental powers and reasserted the doctrine that government existed only with the consent of the governed.

Until the establishment of the state governments, the Continental Congress was the principal organization providing leadership in the struggle for independence. Now the state governments began to acquire prestige above that of Congress. They possessed affirmative powers, while the Continental Congress was largely advisory, lacking power of compulsion over either the states or the people. Congress could make plans for the conduct of the war and it could make requests for money, men, and equipment, but it had no authority or power to take them if the requests were unheeded. Some central authority was needed for the efficient conduct of the war, and some permanent plan of union had to be devised.

In July, 1775, Benjamin Franklin submitted to Congress a document called Articles of Confederation and Perpetual Union, which was referred to in the text as a constitution.[13] Serious consideration of a federal constitution began in June, 1776, along with the preparation of the Declaration of Independence. So many difficulties stood in the way that results came slowly. The over-all difficulty was the fact that the colonies had not yet developed awareness of important common interests, except those temporary interests involved in waging war against a common enemy. Every state was jealous of the delegation of authority to a government which it would be unable to dominate. The particular difficulties included inability to agree upon bases for representation for voting, for the allotment of taxes, for the selection of men for military service, and for the proper division of other duties, rights, and responsibilities. Because of the many grounds for disagreement, the inevitable tendency was to allot to the

[13] *Journals of the Continental Congress*, II, 198.

Union the absolute minimum of authority necessary for performance of functions which could not be performed adequately by the state governments.

On November 15, 1777, Congress voted to accept a compromise document which, like that proposed by Franklin, was called Articles of Confederation and Perpetual Union. It created a confederacy called the United States of America. It provided that each state should retain its sovereignty, freedom, and independence, and every power, jurisdiction, and right not expressly delegated to the Union government of the United States, and characterized the Union as a League of Friendship.

Since the document was drafted by the Continental Congress, it is not surprising that the principal agency of government provided was a similar Congress with a range of powers similar to those which the Continental Congress had been seeking to exercise. Under the Articles each state selected annually, and provided support for, from two to seven delegates in Congress; but whatever the number of delegates chosen, each state had only one vote. Congress exercised war powers and powers over foreign affairs, and had jurisdiction over disputes among the states with respect to territory. Only with the assent of at least nine states, however, could Congress exercise many important powers, including those of warfare. The Articles authorized Congress to appoint a committee of the states to manage affairs of the Union while Congress was in recess.

As the long period of controversy with Great Britain had an effect in shaping the new state governments, so also it had an effect in determining the powers to be conferred upon Congress. The people continued to resist exercise of the taxing power and control of commerce by a distant government. As the colonies had denied the power of Parliament to tax them, so the states denied the power also to Congress — even though that body consisted of representatives or delegates from the several states. In providing for the payment of the expenses of the Union, Congress determined the share of the several states according to the value of land in each state, but it was given no power to compel payment. As a reflection, no doubt, of colonial hostility to commercial regulations established by Parliament, the Articles gave to Congress no power to regulate commerce.

These deficiencies of power and the requirement of the assent of at least nine states for the exercise of important powers, and the failure to provide for a definite executive or for the development of an efficient executive organization within Congress, constituted lamentable weaknesses in the Articles of Confederation. Nevertheless, to characterize the government provided for under the Articles as "the whole vicious scheme," [14] as was done by a reputable historian at the centennial of the Constitution, is to ignore the circumstances under which the Articles were adopted. They represented the first formal act of permanent union. They were drafted at a time when the colonists were intensely conscious of the tyranny implicit in any government powerful enough to dominate them. Had the Continental Congress proposed at this time the establishment of a strong central government, the states probably would have rejected the plan. There is every reason to believe that the Articles of Confederation, with all their defects, represented the best that could be done at the time toward the establishment of permanent union. They constituted an important step in the development of the Constitution of the United States.

The Articles of Confederation did not become operative until 1781, when the Revolutionary War was near its end. Ratification by state legislatures had been delayed by a controversy over western lands, some of which were claimed by more than one state. It was contended that these lands ought to be the property, not of certain states, but of the confederacy as a whole. The claimant states finally cleared the way for ratification by ceding or agreeing to cede their claims to the United States, whereupon the action of Maryland completed the process of ratification. But, oddly enough, the subject which had delayed the technical formation of the Union now aided in binding it together once the Union had been formed. When the war was over, the states had no common enemy in the military sense to hold them together, but they held property in common — property capable of yielding revenue to replenish the empty United States Treasury into which the several states made payments with great reluctance and after much delay, if they made them at all. The land served, furthermore, to fix the eyes of the nation upon possibilities of future greatness. It was tangible evidence of the possibilities of the future in which optimistic Americans believed.

### GOVERNMENT UNDER THE ARTICLES OF CONFEDERATION

The Articles of Confederation and the governmental machinery in operation from the time of the organization of the Continental Con-

[14] John Fiske, *The Critical Period of American History, 1783-1789* (1888), p. 99. For an entirely different approach see Merrill Jensen, *The Articles of Confederation* (1940).

gress down to the establishment of the new government in 1789 have created difficulties of classification for precise legal minds. The Articles declared that each state retained its sovereignty. They referred, not to laws made by Congress, but to "determinations of the United States in Congress assembled." They spoke of the Union as a Confederacy. In view of these facts, and of the absence in Congress of the power of coercion or taxation or regulation in important fields, some students have failed to find any element of sovereignty in the Union government operating under the Articles of Confederation, or even sufficient authority to dignify it with the title of government.

Another line of reasoning distinguishes between the internal sovereignty of the states and external sovereignty in the relation to foreign powers and finds that, as to the latter, the states were never sovereign and that, with the separation from Great Britain, sovereignty passed directly, not to the states, but to the Union. Writing a Supreme Court opinion in 1795, within the period of his own recollection of the Revolutionary struggle, Justice Paterson outlined the activities of the Continental Congress and discussed the position of the government in the international field:

> Congress raised armies, fitted out a navy, and prescribed rules for their government: Congress conducted all military operations both by land and sea. Congress emitted bills of credit, received and sent ambassadors, and made treaties. Congress commissioned privateers to cruise against the enemy, directed what vessels should be liable to capture, and prescribed rules for the distribution of prizes. These high acts of sovereignty were submitted to, acquiesced in, and approved of, by the people of America. In Congress were vested, because by Congress were exercised with the approbation of the people, the rights and powers of war and peace. In every government, whether it consists of many states, or a few, or whether it be of a federal or consolidated nature, there must be a supreme power or will; the rights of war and peace are component parts of this supremacy. . . . As to war and peace, and their necessary incidents, Congress, by the unanimous voice of the people, exercised exclusive jurisdiction, and stood, like Jove, amidst the deities of old, paramount, and supreme.[15]

[15] Penhallow v. Doane, 3 Dallas 54, 80-81 (1795). "The truth is," Justice Paterson continued, "that the states, individually, were not known nor recognized as sovereign, by foreign nations, nor are they now; the states collectively, under Congress, as the connecting point, or head, were acknowledged by foreign powers as sovereign, particularly in that acceptation of the term, which is applicable to all great national concerns, and in the exercise of which other sovereigns would be more immediately interested; such, for instance, as the rights of war and peace, of making treaties, and sending and receiving ambassadors." Ibid., p. 81.

Justice Sutherland restated the theory in an opinion delivered in 1936:

> As a result of the separation from Great Britain by the colonies, act-ing as a unit, the powers of external sovereignty passed from the Crown, not to the colonies severally, but to the colonies in their col-lective and corporate capacity as the United States of America. Even before the Declaration, the colonies were a unit in foreign affairs, acting through a common agency — namely, the Continental Con-gress, composed of delegates from the thirteen colonies. That agency exercised the powers of war and peace, raised an army, created a navy, and finally adopted the Declaration of Independence. Rulers come and go; governments end and forms of government change; but sovereignty survives. A political society cannot endure without a supreme will somewhere. Sovereignty is never held in suspense. When, therefore, the external sovereignty of Great Britain in respect of the colonies ceased, it immediately passed to the Union.[16]

These opinions rationalize the fact that a government had sprung into being and continued to function over a considerable period with-out anything in the nature of a written fundamental law to guide it. If the definition of Judge Cooley is accepted, that a constitution is "that body of rules and maxims in accordance with which the powers of sovereignty are habitually exercised," [17] then it may be said that the United States had a constitution even before the adoption of the Articles of Confederation and that those Articles were merely descrip-tive of the constitution already in operation. It might be said that even the Articles were an incomplete description of *the* Constitu-tion, since in later years the most significant acts under the Confed-eration were not authorized by the Articles at all.[18] The establishment of a bank, for example, and the provision for the disposition of west-ern lands could be justified only by very broad interpretation of a document which provided that each state should retain its sovereignty and every power not expressly delegated to the United States in Con-gress assembled.

The government as established by the Continental Congress and as

---

[16] United States *v.* Curtiss-Wright Export Corporation, 299 U.S. 304, 316-317 (1936). For further discussion of the case, see chapter 38. See also Rufus King in Jonathan Elliot (ed.), *Debates in the Several State Conventions on the Adoption of the Federal Constitution . . . Together with the Journal of the Federal Convention . . .* (5 vols., 1836-1845), V, 212-213. George Sutherland, *The Internal and External Powers of the National Government,* Senate Doc. No. 417, 61st Cong., 2d sess. (1910).

[17] *A Treatise on Constitutional Limitations,* p. 4, quoted above.

[18] See Homer C. Hockett, *The Constitutional History of the United States,* I (1939), 157.

prescribed in the Articles of Confederation proved to be seriously defective at many points. Congress succeeded in remedying some of the defects.[19] Through a process of experimentation, for example, it established machinery which partly compensated for the absence of an executive and of executive machinery. The Congress had originally attempted to perform the functions of managing foreign affairs, and war, navy, and treasury matters, through committees chosen from its own membership. The work of these committees took so much time, however, and their organization proved so imperfect for the performance of their functions, that Congress found it necessary to draw on outside personnel and to establish in each field boards which were responsible to Congress. It was then found that boards without responsible heads failed to operate with the necessary efficiency and speed. In response to criticism both from within and from without, Congress took the next logical step and provided for "secretaries" at the head of the several departments.[20]

Before the Articles were superseded by the present written Constitution, departments had been established in the fields of foreign affairs, war, navy, treasury, and post office. They became so much a part of the established machinery of government that the framers seem to have taken for granted their continuation in some form under the Constitution. The departments were often unable to operate effectively, but the fault lay not so much in the form of departmental organization adopted as in the absence of congressional power over taxation and other vital subjects.[21]

Congress expanded the scope of its powers in several fields. In 1781, in an attempt to secure a currency which would be sound and

[19] For a study of the work of the Congress see Edmund C. Burnett, *The Continental Congress* (1941).

[20] For discussion see Jay Caesar Guggenheimer, "The Development of the Executive Departments, 1775-1789," at pp. 116-185 of J. Franklin Jameson (ed.), *Essays in the Constitutional History of the United States* (1889). See also Charles C. Thach, *The Creation of the Presidency, 1775-1789* (1922).

[21] In this field, as in others, the reader must avoid the error of giving terms as used in earlier years the content which they hold today. Reference to the executive departments established by the Continental Congress should not call to mind pictures of the vast governmental establishments now covering many acres of ground in the city of Washington. The Department of Foreign Affairs, for example, the forerunner of the modern Department of State, was stowed away on the second floor of a musty little two-story wooden building. In climbing the rickety stairs representatives of foreign countries were said to have been obliged to bow their heads to keep their formal headdress from coming in contact with the ceiling. (Guggenheimer, *op. cit.*, pp. 163-164.) Other departments were similarly lacking in grandeur. They provided the necessary core, however, for the development of the more complex and more powerful institutions of later years.

of uniform value throughout the colonies, it chartered the Bank of
North America. The exercise of this power was defended by James
Wilson, later a member of the Supreme Court of the United States,
on grounds similar to those taken by expansionists after the adoption
of the Constitution. He argued that any power which could be exercised only on a national scale must belong to Congress, since it was
beyond the competence of the states and could not, therefore, be
among the powers reserved by them.[22] The action of Congress in
assuming authority to establish the bank resulted in so much criticism
that the bank sought a firmer foundation by securing a new charter
from the state of Pennsylvania. The action of Congress, however,
was the forerunner of the establishment of the Bank of the United
States shortly after the adoption of the Constitution.

In providing for the disposition of western lands ceded by the states
to the United States, Congress again went beyond the scope of its
prescribed powers. Just as many Englishmen had regarded the colonies as existing chiefly for the purpose of exploiting the resources of
the New World for the benefit of the mother country, so many
Americans regarded the West principally as a field for American
exploitation. The settlement of the West was similar to that of the
Atlantic seaboard, however, in that large numbers of residents were
persons who for some reason or other had been discontented in their
eastern homes and had moved westward to start anew. They were
concerned with the development of their own homes and not with
the exploitation of the resources of the country for the benefit of
people of the eastern states. The conflict of attitudes persisted down
through the years until the entire West had been admitted to statehood. In the controversy over western lands which preceded the ratification of the Articles of Confederation, Congress promised that the
lands ceded should, upon adequate settlement, be so organized as to
afford settlers all of the rights possessed in the original states. Arrangements to carry out the plan were made by Congress in 1787 in the
famous "Northwest Ordinance." It made provision for dividing up
the territory north of the Ohio and east of the Mississippi River and
for establishment of colonial, or rather "territorial," governments. It
became the basis of a territorial system for the lands of the United
States in some respects similar to the colonial system of Great Britain.
The enactment of the ordinance was one of the outstanding achievements of the Continental Congress.

[22] Hockett, *op. cit.*, I, 177-178.

In general, however, the period between the end of the Revolution and the adoption of the present written Constitution was one of governmental ineffectiveness as far as the Union was concerned. Congress was unable to secure from the states the money needed to pay the national debt and current expenses. Such painful economic readjustments were taking place that the states found payment of their own debts and expenses extremely difficult. Some of them resorted to issuing additional paper money, and saw it depreciate in value along with that previously issued by the states and by Congress for war purposes. Congress had no machinery for maintaining the soundness of its own obligations or for coercing the states into adherence to sound fiscal policies.

Merchants engaging in foreign trade, who had resented bitterly the efforts of Great Britain to prevent them from trading with other countries, now paid for their nominal freedom the price of exclusion from the ports of the British West Indies and of costly discrimination in ports across the sea. Other nations likewise refused to trade with American merchants on satisfactory terms. Congress had the theoretical power to make treaties, but it lacked effective power to enforce obedience to them, since it was authorized neither to exclude nor to tax commerce coming into the ports of any state. The infant industries built up in some of the states during the war operated at the mercy of established industries abroad, for Congress had no power to levy protective tariffs and the states could not be expected to act unanimously in such a cause.

The import duties levied by the states created conflicts between the states. Some states — New York particularly — greatly lightened the burden of internal taxation by collecting substantial levies from foreign commerce. New Jersey was embittered by the fact that both New York and Pennsylvania collected import duties on goods intended for sale in New Jersey, duties which were eventually paid by the residents of New Jersey. North Carolina suffered similarly from action taken by Virginia and South Carolina. The states collected duties, not merely on goods from abroad, but on those brought in from other states as well. Virginia, with an eye particularly to the commerce of Pennsylvania and Maryland, provided for the confiscation of vessels which failed to pay duties. Restrictive laws applied to importations by land as well as by sea. Pennsylvania collected toll on large numbers of items imported from other states.[23] Some states

[23] Albert J. Beveridge, *Life of John Marshall* (4 vols., 1916-1919), I, 310-311.

enacted similar tariff measures for the combined purpose of raising revenue and giving protection to home products. If the legislation achieved these ends to some extent, it achieved also the undesirable results of interfering with the development of interstate business and of creating antagonism among the states.

Lines of conflict were developing among groups within most of the states as well as among the several states. The pressure of hard times accentuated the conflict of interests between debtors and creditors. Qualifications for voting excluded from the suffrage those who had no property. The debtor elements among landholders and the holders of some other forms of property were sufficiently numerous to win control in some of the state legislatures. They effectively opposed the taxation which would be necessary to pay the debts of states and put government obligations on a sound financial basis.

In some states they secured the enactment of measures of various kinds to relieve the burdens of debtors. In other states, where they were unable to obtain control of the legislatures, they engaged or threatened to engage in outright rebellion. The Shays Rebellion of 1786 in Massachusetts aroused terror among creditors and holders of substantial property and people in the several states whose property interests depended upon the preservation of order. The whole fabric of economic organization upon which the survival, not merely of governments, but of the people themselves, was assumed to rest seemed to be breaking down.

In the midst of the trying conditions after the close of the Revolutionary War, Congress provided ineffective leadership. The able citizens of the several states who had made up the membership during the war crisis returned to their private affairs or moved to other government positions. Their successors, lacking both power and prestige, could do little to remedy the ills of the country. Attempts were made to secure amendments to the Articles of Confederation which would give to Congress revenue powers as well as other powers that were badly needed; but amid the jealousy and diversity of sentiment which prevailed the necessary unanimous action was impossible to secure.

Experience with government under the Articles of Confederation demonstrated the need for certain fundamental changes if order was to be maintained and business and commercial relationships preserved and promoted. The federal government needed the power to raise revenue without the intervention of the states. In order to maintain satisfactory relations with foreign countries, it needed the power to regulate foreign commerce. In order to promote industry and commerce at home, it needed the power to levy import duties and to take over from the states the regulation of interstate commerce. It needed the power to break down and prohibit commercial barriers among the states, to deal with the national and state debts, and to prevent the forcible satisfaction of debts by depreciated paper money or by the tender of other property less acceptable to creditors than coin. It was believed that these and related measures would restore order, promote industry and commerce, and redound to the benefit of all classes of people. These considerations provide the background for the story of the adoption of the new Constitution.

# CHAPTER 2

# THE WRITTEN CONSTITUTION

MOST FUNDAMENTAL POLITICAL CHANGES are brought about only after long periods of agitation and discussion. The movement toward a new constitution, providing for a closer integration of the Union and giving substantial powers to the central government in the United States, was no exception. It began even before the formal adoption of the Articles of Confederation, with suggestions from Alexander Hamilton and others for a constitutional convention to provide for a government which would be something more than a league of states. It grew with the disclosure of the inadequacy and ineptitude of government conducted by means of a congress of delegates from the states, with the voluntary co-operation of the states constituting the principal source of support.

Numerous attempts were made to secure the adoption of individual amendments to the Articles of Confederation. To become effective, however, such amendments had to be adopted unanimously by the thirteen states, and in no instance could all of the states be persuaded to act together. The jealousy and distrust which prevailed among them were such that comprehensive constitutional revision, when finally undertaken successfully, was achieved, not by directly announcing the full purpose, but in oblique fashion, with emphasis upon the promotion of commerce among the states.

Since the task had to be approached indirectly, the promotion of commerce provided a logical medium. The landholders and merchants of the time were engrossed in the development and improvement of arteries of commerce. Companies were being organized in many of the states to remove obstructions from rivers and to build locks and canals where navigation was not otherwise feasible. The inconsistency of spending large sums of money for the removal of natural barriers to navigation and erecting at the same time political barriers against trade was apparent even to the most provincial businessman.

Maryland and Virginia found it necessary to co-operate for the improvement of navigation on the Potomac River, which for a long distance marked the boundary line between the two states. They made an agreement between themselves in spite of a restrictive provision in the Articles of Confederation to the effect that "no two or more states shall enter into any treaty, confederation or alliance whatever between them, without the consent of the United States in congress assembled, specifying accurately the purposes for which the same is to be entered into, and how long it shall continue." The fact that it was necessary either to violate the Articles of Confederation or to await sluggish action by a suspicious Congress indicates the virtual impossibility of securing united action where it was needed. The agreement worked out by commissioners of Virginia and Maryland, who met at the home of George Washington in March, 1785, dealt with a number of causes of friction and provided for uniform import duties and for the regulation of commerce and the currency in the two states. The action, in other words, ran counter to the tendency which was pulling the several states apart and creating friction over taxation of imports, discriminatory commercial regulations, and the issuance of paper money which in some states was made legal tender in spite of its depreciated value.

The legislature of Maryland suggested that Pennsylvania and Delaware be invited to join in the agreement. James Madison, an active sponsor of the movement in the Virginia legislature, brought about an arrangement whereby the several states were invited to send delegates to meet at Annapolis, Maryland, in September, 1786, to discuss the commercial problems of the several states. The convention was not to be a formal constitutional convention, and it had no connection with Congress; yet the correspondence of many of the persons interested shows concern far beyond the mere regulation of commerce. They had in mind fundamental constitutional change.

Although delegates to the Annapolis Convention were appointed in at least nine states, only five states actually participated. Those in attendance saw the problem as so broad as to require consideration by all of the states, and they agreed that a solution lay, not merely in making common commercial regulations by interstate agreements, but in comprehensive action to cure "important defects in the system of the federal government." Instead of attempting to work out additional interstate agreements, therefore, or of debating the issues involved, the convention adjourned after making a report recommending that a convention of deputies from the several states be called to meet in Philadelphia the following May, to investigate and prepare a plan for remedying the defects of the government.

The movement for the convention at Philadelphia was strongly supported by political and business leaders throughout the country. Congress, to which the report of the Annapolis Convention had been sent, fell in line. Pursuant to the Articles of Confederation, it issued a call for a convention to be held at Philadelphia in May, 1787, "for the sole and express purpose of revising the Articles of Confederation and reporting to Congress and the several legislatures such alterations and provisions therein as shall when agreed to in Congress and confirmed by the states render the federal Constitution adequate to the exigencies of government and the preservation of the Union." [1]

### THE CONSTITUTIONAL CONVENTION

Although the Constitutional Convention was scheduled to meet on May 14, 1787, it was not until May 25 that a sufficient number of delegates arrived to make a quorum. The formal work of the convention was done between that date and September 17, when a draft of the proposed Constitution was signed. Fifty-five delegates attended at some time, but the average attendance was only about thirty. They included prominent leaders from the several states. George Washington, who, because of his military leadership during the Revolution and because of his wealth, his integrity, and his reputation as a man of affairs, was regarded as the outstanding citizen in the entire country, was chosen as the presiding officer of the Constitutional Convention. Benjamin Franklin, another of wide reputation, also attended in spite of the feebleness of old age. Prominent among the more active members of the convention were Gouverneur Morris and James Wilson, of Pennsylvania, James Madison and George Mason, of Virginia, Roger Sherman, of Connecticut, and Elbridge Gerry, of Massachusetts.

The proceedings of the convention were kept secret. Direct evidence of their nature consists principally of inadequate notes made for a formal journal of the convention and the invaluable, but also inadequate, notes preserved by James Madison and other members. These materials, edited by Max Farrand in recent years as *The*

---

[1] For the report of the Annapolis Convention and the call for the Constitutional Convention see Allen Johnson (ed.), *Readings in American Constitutional History* (1912), chapter XI.

*Records of the Federal Convention,*[2] show the persistence of conflicts and adjustments on innumerable points. They show disagreements between large states and small ones, between North and South, between agricultural and mercantile interests, and along many other lines.

Most of the numerous studies of the work of the convention were based primarily upon these records until, in 1913, Charles A. Beard, a distinguished American historian, utilized a fresh approach by analyzing the property holdings of the members of the convention.[3] He discovered a remarkable degree of correlation between property holdings and the support of governmental changes calculated to preserve or add to the value of property. He demonstrated how the ratification of the Constitution had been supported by people with the same property interests as the members of the convention responsible for drafting it, while opposition came from various groups, such as debtors, whom state legislatures would be barred from relieving and holders of real estate who would have to pay higher state taxes because state governments could no longer be supported mainly by state duties on imports. Although the Beard analysis provided a healthy antidote for the pompousness of much previous historical writing — thereby offending some fellow historians and others who failed to comprehend his purpose — it did not provide, and evidently was not intended to provide, a complete substitute for analysis based on factors other than those exclusively economic. The very starkness of the economic interpretation, when presented alone, tends to distort the picture and to create the erroneous impression that the founding fathers are to be condemned on moral grounds because of the influence of their property interests. On the other hand, the neglect of the economic approach has led at times to the characterization of the founding fathers as virtual demigods handing down to the people of the United States a perfect document in the form of a new Constitution.[4]

Some of the basic economic issues fail to stand out clearly in the records of the convention because the members were in broad agreement concerning them. The movements for the improvement of navigation and promotion of interstate commercial relationships, and

[2] 3 vols., 1911; rev. ed., 4 vols., 1937.

[3] *An Economic Interpretation of the Constitution of the United States.*

[4] This distorted impression arose in part also from the tendency to ignore the influence of English and colonial history in determining the character of the work of the founding fathers.

for the holding of the conventions at Annapolis and at Philadelphia, had been engineered and promoted chiefly by men engaged in commerce in some form.  The delegates at Philadelphia had interests broader than the problem of interchange of goods across state lines, but all were concerned in some fashion with promoting the stability of property and improving the conditions of business.  The advocates of cheap money, the spokesmen of debtor classes, the sponsors of state legislation weakening the obligation of contracts, were not present in the Constitutional Convention at Philadelphia.  It was not necessary to take time on the floor of the convention to refute ideas which these persons would have expounded had they been present.  Prominent statesmen who were opposed to the creation of a powerful central government such as would be necessary to achieve the economic results desired by most members of the convention refused to participate.  Patrick Henry, of Virginia, "smelled a rat," as he expressed it, and refused to be a delegate.  Richard Henry Lee, of the same state, the man who had proposed both the Declaration of Independence and the Articles of Confederation, likewise refused membership.  Other persons were for various reasons out of sympathy with the purposes or with the proceedings of the convention, and either rejected appointment initially or failed thereafter to attend. As far as their broad economic point of view was concerned, the delegates who worked at the task and created the draft of the Constitution which was proposed to the states were in substantial accord on matters of trade and property.

In spite of this relative unanimity of attitude on broad economic issues which rendered debate unnecessary, some illustrative comments appear in the records of the convention.  The members feared the political power of profligate and unfortunate people as expressed through the state governments.  When, for example, on a day early in the convention, Governor Edmund Randolph, of Virginia, presented the plan of government worked out by James Madison and others, he deplored the development of too much democracy in the states.  He thought the chief danger of the times arose from the democratic parts of the state constitutions.  None of the constitutions, he contended, had sufficient checks against democracy.  The feeble senate of Virginia, intended to operate as such a check, was a phantom.  Maryland had a more powerful senate, but recent events in that state showed that it was not powerful enough.  Checks established in the constitutions of New York and Massachusetts, although constituting yet stronger barriers against democracy, seemed insufficient.[5] Similar comments made throughout the period of the convention revealed the same attitude. The delegates were intent upon shackling the as yet undisciplined forces of democracy to such an extent as to protect property and trade.

Homogeneity of broad economic views nevertheless left room for sharp differences among the delegates as to the method of achieving desired ends. Representatives of small states objected to changes that would reduce the relative influence of their states in the federal government by basing representation upon population instead of upon statehood as under the Articles of Confederation. Most delegates from the large states, on the other hand, contended that representation should be based upon population, and argued that the effectiveness of the government would depend upon its possession of power directly over the people rather than merely over the states as political units. The arrangement whereby members of the lower house of Congress were to be selected on a population basis while the Senate was to have equal representation from each of the several states was one of the important compromises of the convention. The provision that senators were to be selected, not by vote of the people, but by the state legislatures, was adopted in the interest of economic stability, for the Senate, thus indirectly selected, was expected to act as a check upon the popularly elected House of Representatives.

The separation of the "departments" was brought about in the Constitution by a number of factors. Whereas the government under the Articles of Confederation had been modeled largely after the Continental Congress, which had drafted the Articles and which had been in high repute at the time it did so, the government under the new Constitution embraced many of the principles and forms of organization which had been developed in the constitutions of the several states. Familiarity with state practice and disillusionment with Congress as the sole agency of government, quite as much as belief in a doctrine, brought about resort to the separation of powers. The Constitution, therefore, provided not only for a Congress but for an executive and for courts. Thus, three main branches or "departments" were recognized and given powers — in place of the single agency of Congress under the earlier Articles.

Although the experience of Congress had demonstrated the need for an efficient executive branch of the government, it did not demon-

[5] Farrand, *op. cit.* (1911 ed.), I, 26-27.

strate the kind of executive organization likely best to serve the needs of the country. The experience of the states, in which the executive had thus far been held in check, threw little light on the subject. Questions as to whether the Executive should be single or multiple and questions as to power, term, and mode of selection provoked heated debate. They were settled by compromise and not in terms of the interests of any particular class, section, or economic group.

The need for a federal judiciary which would make possible the uniform application of law throughout the country was apparent. Questions as to the tenure of judges and the kind of courts to be established gave rise, however, to sharp differences of opinion. Beyond giving a power of veto to the President, the convention was unable to work out any specific arrangement for a check upon the legislation enacted by Congress. The problem of checking state legislation inimical to the federal government was so difficult that the convention approached it indirectly through the provision that the federal Constitution, laws, and treaties should be the supreme law of the land and should be binding upon the judges in every state. Here again the differences of opinion were not along class lines. They were the products of sectional jealousies which operated within state lines, and of differences of opinion as to how given results might be achieved.

So numerous were the compromises which had to be accepted by each member of the convention that none was wholly satisfied with the product. A majority of the delegates, however, felt that the adoption of the Constitution as phrased was the only alternative to the breakdown of the Union. Because it seemed the best that could be achieved, they gave it their full support.

THE PROVISIONS OF THE CONSTITUTION

The first three of the seven articles of the proposed Constitution dealt in sequence with the legislative, executive, and judicial departments of the government to be established. The first article provided that all legislative powers granted by the Constitution should be vested in a Congress consisting of two houses. The House of Representatives was to consist of members chosen every second year by the people of the several states. The convention avoided difficult questions as to property qualifications for voters by providing that in each state the qualifications should be those of persons allowed to vote for members of the most numerous branch of the state legislature. Each state was to have at least one representative, but thereafter representation was to be based upon population. A compromise provision required that direct taxes levied by the federal government should be measured in each state by the population in that state [6] and that in the measurement of population three-fifths of "all other persons" — that is, slaves — were to be included.

The Senate consisted of two members from each state, chosen, not directly by the people, but by the legislatures. Senators served six years, in contrast with representatives, who served only two years. They had to be at least thirty years of age, in contrast with the twenty-five-year age limit for representatives. The Vice-President of the United States presided over the Senate. The House of Representatives had the sole power of impeachment, while all impeachments were to be tried before the Senate. Each house had the power to determine its own rules and regulations and the qualifications of its members.

A provision in the interest of the large states, whereby all bills for raising revenue were to originate in the House of Representatives, was weakened by the proviso that the Senate might propose amendments as with other bills. The President might veto legislation, but Congress could override the veto by a two-thirds vote.

By the eighth section of the first article numerous powers were conferred upon Congress. First came ample powers of taxation, with the provision that all duties, imposts, and excises should be uniform throughout the United States. The language unfortunately left room for a century and a half of controversy as to the scope of the purposes for which money might be collected. Congress could borrow money, coin it, regulate its value, and punish counterfeiting. Congress received the tremendously important power to regulate commerce with foreign nations, among the states, and with the Indian tribes, which restricted the power of the states in the same field at least to the extent that they could not enact commercial regulations in conflict with those of Congress. The question as to their power to regulate such commerce in the absence of federal legislation remained for the courts in future years. Congress received broad war powers and other important powers in enumerated fields without the requirement of more than a majority vote for the enactment of legislation as under the Articles of Confederation. Finally, Congress was

[6] To prevent the selection of subjects of direct taxes, as, for example, slaves or land or farm products, in such a way as to bear excessively on the property of any section.

authorized "to make all laws which shall be necessary and proper for carrying into execution the foregoing powers, and all other powers vested by this Constitution in the government of the United States, or in any department or officer thereof."

Certain legislative prohibitions were laid upon Congress and upon the states. The importation of slaves could not be prohibited until 1808. The privilege of the writ of habeas corpus [7] could not be suspended unless the public safety required it in case of rebellion or invasion. Bills of attainder [8] and *ex post facto* laws [9] could not be passed. Exports could not be taxed — a provision insisted upon by the exporting states of the South. Uniformity of treatment had to be granted to the ports of the several states in the regulation of commerce. Money could be drawn from the Treasury only in consequence of appropriations made by law. Titles of nobility could not be granted, and the receipt of gifts by any federal officer from any king, prince, or foreign state was restricted.

The limitations upon the powers of states also dealt with such matters as bills of attainder and *ex post facto* laws and titles of nobility, but they went much further. Among them were provisions calculated to restrain the excesses of democracy deplored by most members of the Constitutional Convention. No state was to coin money, emit bills of credit, or make anything but gold and silver a tender in payment of debts, or pass any law impairing the obligation of contracts. The enforcement of these provisions would prevent thereafter losses to creditors resulting from inflation of currency and from varied restrictions upon the collection of debts. One of the serious causes of friction among the states was eliminated by the provision that, except for inspection purposes, no state could tax either imports or exports. The states were forbidden to enter into treaties or alliances. Without the consent of Congress they could not enter into any agreement or compact with other states or with foreign powers, nor could they keep troops or ships of war in time of peace or engage in war unless actually invaded or in imminent danger.

Article II vested the executive power in the President. Members of the convention had varied all the way from those who favored an

---

[7] Whereby a person held by a government official could secure immediate judicial inquiry into the legality of his detention.

[8] "A bill of attainder is a legislative act, which inflicts punishment without a judicial trial." Cummings *v.* Missouri, 4 Wallace 277, 323 (1867).

[9] Laws punishing acts not criminal when committed, or increasing penalties for offenses after their commission.

executive to serve during good behavior to others who feared the lodgment of power in the hands of one person even for a short period of time and thought that a multiple executive would be the proper solution. The Constitution provided that he should hold his office during the term of four years and did not prohibit election for addi. tional terms. Various modes of selecting the President had been advocated. Some favored election directly by the people, but to most members of the convention this arrangement was too democratic. Choice by one or the other or both of the houses of Congress was advocated, as were various other methods. The convention compro. mised upon a college of electors selected by each state equal to the total number of senators and representatives from the state. Each of the electors had two votes. The person receiving the high. est vote of the college, if that constituted a majority, was to be Presi. dent and the person receiving the next highest vote was to be Vice. President. In the absence of a majority the House of Representa. tives, each state delegation having one vote, would elect the President; and in case of a tie for second place the Senate would elect the Vice. President. Benjamin Franklin, who greatly feared the development of a monarchy, thought the Executive ought to serve from patriotic motives and without compensation.[10] The Constitution provided merely that the President should receive compensation which should neither be increased nor diminished during the period for which he had been elected.

In addition to conferring upon the President a general grant of executive power and a broad command to "take care that the laws be faithfully executed," the Constitution made him commander-in-chief of the army and navy and of the state militia when called into the federal service. It empowered him to grant pardons and re. prieves for offenses against the United States except in cases of im. peachment. It lodged in him the power to make treaties with the advice and consent of the Senate, two-thirds concurring. With the advice and consent of the Senate he was to appoint ambassadors, other public ministers and consuls, judges of the Supreme Court, and other officers whose appointment was not otherwise provided for. Appointments of inferior officers could be made, however, by the President alone, the courts of law, or the heads of the departments. The President was directed to give Congress information on the state of the Union and to recommend measures which he deemed necessary

[10] Farrand, *op. cit.* (1911 ed.), I, 81-85.

and expedient. He might convene Congress in special session. The President, Vice-President, and all civil officers of the United States could be removed from office on impeachment for and conviction of treason, bribery, or other high crimes and misdemeanors.

Article III of the Constitution vested the judicial power of the United States in a Supreme Court and such inferior courts as Congress might establish. In leaving to Congress the establishment of the system of inferior courts, the Constitutional Convention avoided many of the problems about which the members were unable to agree. Attitudes as to terms of service for judges varied all the way from those who thought that terms should be short to others who favored life appointment. The methods of selection proposed included popular election, a proposal supported by Franklin for appointment by members of the bar, and selection by the President. The compromise worked out provided that judges should be appointed by the President with the advice and consent of the Senate, and should hold their offices during good behavior at a compensation which should not be diminished during their continuance in office.

The Constitution carefully defined federal judicial power to put in the hands of the federal courts jurisdiction which, if exercised by the state courts, might impede the equal enforcement of federal laws. It gave the Supreme Court original jurisdiction in certain types of important cases — that is, cases might be brought directly before the Supreme Court without the necessity of beginning in lower courts and moving up to the Supreme Court through the process of appeal. Otherwise it gave the Supreme Court appellate jurisdiction with such exceptions and under such regulations as Congress should make. It provided that the trial of all crimes, except in cases of impeachment, should be by jury in the state where the crimes had been committed. It limited the definition of treason to levying war against the United States, or adhering to their enemies, or giving their enemies aid and comfort; and conviction of treason could be secured only on the testimony of two witnesses to the same overt act or on confession in open court. In this manner the convention guarded against the abuses of punishment for treason which in earlier years had prevailed in Great Britain.

The other four articles of the Constitution dealt with a great variety of matters. Article IV required each state to give full faith and credit to the public acts, records, and judicial proceedings of every other state. It declared the citizens of each state to be entitled to all the privileges and immunities of citizens in the several states. The convention avoided a definition of citizenship, however, with results that were disastrous many decades later when the question of citizenship of Negroes aided in precipitating the Civil War. Persons held to service or labor who escaped from one state into another were required to be delivered up on claim of the party to whom such service or labor might be due; this clause provided the basis for the highly controversial fugitive-slave legislation of later years. A person charged with crimes in one state who fled to another state was to be delivered up for removal on demand of the executive authority of the state from which he had fled; but the Constitution did not answer the question as to how a reluctant state executive was to be coerced into obeying the constitutional provision. When near the eve of the Civil War the Supreme Court passed upon the question, it held that no such coercion was possible under the federal system, and that the obligation to surrender the fugitive was but a moral obligation without benefit of coercive sanction.[11]

The Constitution authorized Congress to admit new states to the Union and to make rules and regulations respecting the territory or other property belonging to the United States, but said nothing about the power of Congress to prescribe the conditions under which new states were to be admitted. The question was left unsettled as to whether restraints could be placed on new states which had not been placed over the old. The Supreme Court later held that, once admitted, a new state was in a position identical with that of the other states and that Congress could enforce no discriminating restrictions against it.[12] The Constitution protected the states already in existence by provision that new states should not be carved out of old ones or be created by the junction of states or parts of states without the consent of the respective legislatures. The United States guaranteed to every state a republican form of government and protected it against invasion and, on its application, against domestic violence.

Article V dealt with the amending process. The Articles of Confederation had provided for amendment only by agreement in Congress and subsequent confirmation by the legislatures of all the states. Experience had demonstrated that amendment under this provision was virtually impossible. As a result, the Constitutional Convention worked out somewhat easier methods of amendment — proposal by

[11] Kentucky v. Dennison, 24 Howard 66 (1860).
[12] See Coyle v. Smith, 221 U.S. 559 (1911), and cases cited.

Congress, on the vote of two-thirds of each house, and ratification by the legislatures or conventions of three-fourths of the states. Only in the instance of the Twenty-First Amendment has Congress provided for ratification by state conventions instead of legislatures. Congress must call a convention for the proposal of amendments on application of the legislatures of two-thirds of the several states, and amendments so proposed must be submitted to the states for ratification in like fashion as amendments proposed directly by Congress. This latter method, however, has never been used. The article gave protection to the small states by the provision that no state, without its consent, should be deprived of its equal suffrage in the Senate.

Article VI bound the United States under the Constitution to honor all debts and obligations incurred before the Constitution was adopted. It provided that the Constitution and the laws made in pursuance of it, and the treaties made under the authority of the United States, should be the supreme law of the land in spite of anything in the constitutions or laws of any of the states. Legislative, executive, and judicial officers, both of the United States and of the several states, were to be bound by oath or affirmation to support the Constitution of the United States.

The seventh and last article of the Constitution consisted of a single sentence providing, "The ratification of the conventions of nine states shall be sufficient for the establishment of this Constitution between the states so ratifying the same." The article deviated from the amending process laid down in the Articles of Confederation both by authorizing ratification by conventions instead of legislatures and by calling for the establishment of the Constitution upon ratification by only nine of the states instead of by all of them. The article thus emphasized the extent to which the Constitutional Convention had gone beyond its instructions from Congress, which had called the convention "for the sole and express purpose of revising the Articles of Confederation and reporting to Congress and the several legislatures such alterations and provisions therein as shall when agreed to in Congress and confirmed by the states render the federal Constitution adequate to the exigencies of government and the preservation of the Union." Many provisions of the Articles of Confederation had been incorporated into the new Constitution, but it was essentially a new instrument representing changes hardly less revolutionary than those which had taken place with the separation from Great Britain.

THE RATIFICATION OF THE CONSTITUTION

A draft of the proposed Constitution was signed by thirty-nine of the fifty-five delegates who at some time attended the convention, representing twelve of the thirteen states. Rhode Island had not been represented at any time. The draft of the Constitution was sent to the president of the Congress with a letter from George Washington as president of the Constitutional Convention. The proposed Constitution and the letter were laid before Congress, together with resolutions of the Constitutional Convention to the effect that the Constitution should be referred to conventions in the several states. The Constitution was attacked in Congress by Richard Henry Lee, of Virginia, who urged the addition of various provisions before it should be ratified. Congress compromised by sending it to the states for action without itself passing upon the document at all. This compromise, although contrary to the amending provisions prescribed by the Articles of Confederation, prevented the consumption of time by debate in Congress and cleared the way for action by the states.

Since debates in the Constitutional Convention had been held behind closed doors, little or no information had been given to the public concerning the proceedings. The public was, therefore, unfamiliar with the issues and the controversies which had resulted in compromises in almost every sentence of the Constitution. The issues were threshed over again in private discussions, in the press, and in public assemblies. Some of those who had signed the Constitution were handicapped in their defense of it because of private agreement with many of the criticisms. They could defend it only as the best document that could be worked out under the circumstances, and they argued that the survival of the Union depended upon its adoption.

Three men, Alexander Hamilton, James Madison, and John Jay, made the most systematic and the most celebrated defense of the Constitution in a series of articles signed "Publius," first published in New York to influence sentiment in that state. They expounded the defects of the Articles of Confederation and the need for fundamental change in the government, and explained the proposed Constitution in detail. The articles were reprinted for use in other states and were brought together in a volume called *The Federalist*. That book, which appeared thereafter in many editions, was and still is one of the most distinguished works in political science produced in the United States. It was propaganda for the adoption of the Constitution, it is true, and it presented only one side of the picture; but it was a carefully marshaled aggregation of sound arguments for establishing a strong central government.

Various groups and interests opposed the adoption of the Constitution, and their opposition took various forms. Debtor classes and small property holders, who had profited by what the conservative Federalists regarded as too much democracy and who had not been represented in the Constitutional Convention, were represented in the state legislatures which provided for the ratifying conventions, and in the ratifying conventions themselves. Their opposition is apparent in the analysis of votes on the Constitution, although they seem usually to have lacked leaders with the ability to phrase persuasive objections in terms of class issues. In order to pacify them, the Constitution was defended in some conventions as an instrument of democracy, but many representatives of the debtor groups remained unconvinced.

Jealousies among the states and the desire to preserve more of the independence of each of the states than could prevail under the new Constitution provided both genuine grounds of opposition and emotional arguments for opponents who had some other basis for antagonism. This may have been true of Patrick Henry, for example, who as governor of Virginia had been head of a great commonwealth which would lose part of its political identity under the new Constitution. Apart from the subject of local patriotism, however, he was concerned lest the federal government should injure the western part of the state by making a treaty with Spain surrendering the right to the use of the Mississippi River.

Point by point, the provisions in the Constitution were criticized. There was little argument in the state conventions that the new federal government would be too weak to perform the required functions, but much was said about the dangers which lay in its strength. It was feared that the presidency was but a stepping-stone to monarchy, particularly in view of the fact that the Constitution contained nothing to prevent the re-election of the same man term after term. It was feared that Congress, the recipient of broad authority, would become the instrument of arbitrary power.

The proposed Constitution was criticized because it contained no bill of rights, such as was to be found in most of the state constitutions, and no statement that powers not specifically granted to the federal government were reserved for exercise by the states. It is true that provisions such as those included in bills of rights were interspersed at various points in the Constitution. Among them were prohibitions against the suspension of the privilege of the writ of habeas corpus and against the enactment of bills of attainder and *ex post facto* laws. The trial of crimes was to be by jury and was to be held in the state in which the offense was committed. No religious test was to be required as a qualification for office. Other provisions familiar in state constitutions were not included, however. The document contained no guarantee of freedom of religion, or of the press, or of assembly. It contained no guarantee of the right to keep and bear arms or of protection against the quartering of soldiers. It offered no protection against unreasonable searches and seizures. Many procedural safeguards were omitted, including protection against double jeopardy and against criminal prosecution without the preliminary step of indictment by grand jury, protection against excessive bail, excessive fines, and cruel and unusual punishments, and there was no guarantee of jury trials in civil cases.

Hamilton devoted one of his *Federalist* articles to the subject. The truth was, he declared, that the Constitution was itself in every rational sense and to every useful purpose a bill of rights.

> The several bills of rights in Great Britain form its constitution, and conversely the constitution of each state is its bill of rights. And the proposed Constitution, if adopted, will be the bill of rights of the Union. Is it one object of a bill of rights to declare and specify the political privileges of the citizens in the structure and administration of the government? This is done in the most ample and precise manner in the plan of the convention; comprehending various precautions for the public security, which are not to be found in any of the state constitutions. Is another object of a bill of rights to define certain immunities and modes of proceeding, which are relative to personal and private concerns? This we have seen has also been attended to, in a variety of cases, in the same plan.[13]

So insistent was the demand for amendments to the Constitution guaranteeing these several items of protection that a number of state conventions ratified the Constitution only after the Federalist leaders gave assurance that they would bring about the ratification of amendments immediately after the setting up of the new government. Part of the strategy of the critics of the Constitution was to insist that a second constitutional convention be called to consider amendments

[13] *The Federalist* (Lodge ed., 1895), No. LXXXIV, pp. 538-539.

prior to the establishment of the new government.[14]  The advocates of
adoption of the Constitution realized that holding another convention
at this time would probably result in failure of the whole movement
for a stronger government.   They agreed, therefore, to submit and to
bring about the adoption of the desired amendments for the preservation of civil rights as soon as the new government was put in operation.   With this assurance, enough reluctant delegates cast votes in
favor of the Constitution to create the majority necessary for ratification.   Even so, two states, Rhode Island and North Carolina, remained outside the Union for some months.

The success of the movement for the creation and adoption of the
new Constitution may be regarded as a stupendous achievement
brought about by the skill of men of great ability and integrity, without going to the extreme of considering it a perfect document, as was
once the custom.   As the framers themselves knew and admitted, it
was an imperfect instrument adopted to weld resisting states into "a
more perfect Union."   Like the Articles of Confederation, it marked
a step in the development of the American constitutional system.
Further stages were to be marked by successive enlargements of the
Constitution, usually by interpretation, occasionally by formal amendment.   Events of the years ahead, rather than merely the deeds of the
founding fathers, were to make it the charter of freedom, the symbol
of democracy, and the source of power and strength which it became.

[14] See Edward P. Smith, "The Movement Towards a Second Constitutional Convention
in 1788," in J. F. Jameson, *Essays in the Constitutional History of the United States*
(1889), pp. 46-115.

# CHAPTER 3

# THE CONSTITUTION IN OPERATION

ON JULY 2, 1788, when the requisite number of nine states had ratified the new Constitution, Congress appointed a committee to examine the ratifications and report a measure for putting the Constitution into operation in pursuance of the resolutions of the federal Constitutional Convention.[1] The committee proposed that the first Wednesday in the ensuing December be the day for appointment of presidential electors, that the electors assemble on the first Wednesday in January, and that proceedings under the Constitution be commenced on the first Wednesday in February. It did not, however, fix upon a seat for the new government;[2] and for more than two months, within which time two additional states ratified the Constitution, Congress wrangled periodically over this question. Many delegates regarded New York, where Congress was then assembled, as too far north of the center of the country. Baltimore, chosen by a preliminary vote, was later abandoned.[3] Support for Philadelphia and Lancaster in Pennsylvania, both prominent contenders, was inadequate. Not until September 13 did Congress finally decide that "the present seat of Congress" should be the place for commencing proceedings under the Constitution.[4] Because of the time lost in debate, Congress found it necessary to postpone each of the several stages whereby the new government was to come into being. It provided that presidential electors should be appointed on the first Wednesday in January, to meet a month later, and that proceedings should be instituted on the first Wednesday in March.

## ESTABLISHMENT OF THE GOVERNMENT

The friends of the Constitution knew that the mere adoption of the Constitution would constitute a hollow victory unless they fol-

[1] *Journals of the Continental Congress* (34 vols., 1904-1937), XXXIV, 281.
[2] *Ibid.*, pp. 303-304.  [3] *Ibid.*, p. 386.  [4] *Ibid.*, p. 523.

lowed it up by determining the choice of personnel of the government and the adoption of measures in harmony with their purpose.    They suspected the opponents of the Constitution, now known generally as Anti-Federalists, of planning to elect to office men of their own beliefs in order to defeat the purposes of the Constitution.    George Washington wrote long political letters expressing his concern about the choice of personnel and urging the selection of good Federalists. The thinking of Alexander Hamilton and other Federalist leaders operated along the same line.[5]    They were eminently successful.    The list of officials chosen to federal office immediately or subsequently appointed included more than half of the members of the Philadelphia Convention.    Twenty-six of the thirty-nine men who signed the Constitution found a place in the new government.[6] Other Federalists, who had not been in the Constitutional Convention, but who had done service in the state ratifying conventions or elsewhere, likewise appeared among the new federal officials.    Some members of the Anti-Federalist group were also chosen, it is true, but they were definitely in the minority.

The eleven states which had ratified the Constitution chose presidential electors pursuant to the resolution of Congress.    The resolution said nothing about the mode of making the choice.    A number of different methods were used.    In some states the electors were chosen directly by the legislatures; in others they were elected by districts or at large.    New York lost its vote on this occasion through a disagreement in the legislature as to the best method of choosing electors.    At succeeding presidential elections the tendency for some years was toward the choice of electors by legislatures.    Later the method was adopted of choosing them at large in terms of nomination by political parties.    On the first Wednesday in February, 1789, the electors, who had been chosen a month earlier, met in their respective states and voted for two persons, at least one of whom was not a resident of the same state with themselves.    Certified lists of the votes were sent to the president of the Senate, who opened them in the presence of both houses.

The tabulation of the votes and the announcement of the election of the President and Vice-President were delayed because of the failure of the new Congress to assemble on time.    Although the date set for commencement of proceedings under the new Constitution

[5] See Charles A. Beard, *Economic Origins of Jeffersonian Democracy* (1915), pp. 89-92.
[6] *Ibid.*, pp. 104-105.

was Wednesday, March 4, 1789, senators and representatives from only five states were present on that day. It was not until April 1 that a quorum was formed in the House of Representatives, and it was not until April 6 that the requisite number of senators appeared. On the latter day the Senate notified the House of Representatives that it had elected a presiding officer for the sole purpose of opening the certificates and counting the votes of the electors. The House was invited to meet with the Senate to perform that function. Votes had been cast by sixty-nine electors, each of them giving one vote for George Washington. The other votes divided among nine candidates with a total of thirty-four for John Adams. Washington, therefore, was elected President; and Adams, Vice-President. On April 30, nearly two months after the date set for the initiation of the government, Washington appeared to take the oath of office. The chancellor of the state of New York administered the oath of office, since there was as yet no federal judicial officer.

Every step taken by the newly established government agencies was important in that it set a precedent for action in the years ahead. Because of this fact and because of the relation of early decisions to the prestige of the new government, some of the leaders were morbidly conscious of the possibilities involved in every move. What methods of communication, for example, would be proper for the two houses of the Congress of a great nation in dealing with each other? What term should be used in addressing the President, the head of a great nation? How should Congress communicate with the President? What forms should the Senate observe when receiving the President to give advice and consent as to treaties? Should the Vice-President sign bills as the Vice-President of the United States or as president of the Senate? These appeared to be grave constitutional questions for legislative and executive officers of the time. Although they doubtless had less actual relation to the future prestige of the government than many persons anticipated, some of the decisions had effects upon important matters of procedure under the Constitution for many decades.

The painful self-consciousness felt by many of the legislators is illustrated by the following report of the committees of both houses as to the proper mode of intercommunication:

> When a bill or other message shall be sent from the Senate to the House of Representatives, it shall be carried by the secretary, who shall make one obeisance to the chair, on entering the door of the

House of Representatives, and another on delivering it at the table into the hands of the speaker. After he shall have delivered it, he shall make an obeisance to the speaker, and repeat it as he retires from the House.[7]

John Adams, who as Vice-President of the United States was also president of the Senate, had spent many years in foreign capitals and in diplomatic activities. He was much impressed with the necessity of observing the proper forms of etiquette down to the last detail. In spite of the fact that the Constitution forbade the granting of titles of nobility, he thought that high government officials, and particularly the President of the United States, should have titles of distinction. So insistent was he upon this point that one senator derisively applied to him the title of "Rotundity,"[8] while another nicknamed him "Bonny Johnny."[9] In one of his frequent lectures to the Senate on matters of etiquette and diplomacy, Adams remarked that an agent appointed to a foreign court would have titles calling him "The Most Illustrious, The Most Powerful," and whatnot. Since the agent was appointed by the President, the President himself must be something that included all the dignities of the diplomatic corps and something greater still. "What will the common people of foreign countries, what will the sailors and the soldiers say, 'George Washington, President of the United States'? They will despise him *to all eternity*."[10]

In addition to Adams, many people in both houses of Congress were concerned about the question of titles. Both houses appointed committees to consider and report on the matter. The Senate committee reported in favor of "His Highness the President of the United States of America and Protector of the Rights of the Same."[11] The House of Representatives decided to use merely the title appearing in the Constitution, that of "President of the United States," and the Senate reluctantly fell into line.

The delivery of presidential messages was at first weighted down with an impossible burden of ceremony. The constitutional basis for such messages was found in Article II, Section 3, of the Constitution, which provides that "he shall from time to time give to the Congress information of the state of the Union, and recommend to their consideration such measures as he shall judge necessary and expedient." The first message of President Washington was a combined

---

[7] *Annals of Congress*, 1st Cong., 1st sess., 23-24.
[8] *The Journal of William Maclay* (1927), p. 29.
[9] *Ibid.*, p. 246.        [10] *Ibid.*, p. 26.        [11] *Ibid.*, p. 25.

inaugural address and annual message to Congress.  Pursuant to formal procedure worked out for the occasion, he took the oath of office in the presence of both houses assembled in the chamber of the Senate, after which he delivered an address in the verbose language of diplomacy.  Thereafter, each of the two houses prepared a formal address in reply and called upon the President and read it to him, whereafter he, in turn, having been informed as to what was expected, read a previously prepared formal reply.  The text of his reply to the Senate indicates the character of the interchange:

> Gentlemen: I thank you for your address, in which the most affectionate sentiments are expressed in the most obliging terms.  The coincidence of circumstances which led to this auspicious crisis, the confidence reposed in me by my fellow citizens, and the assistance I may expect from counsels which will be dictated by an enlarged and liberal policy, seem to presage a more prosperous issue to my administration than a diffidence of my abilities had taught me to anticipate.  I now feel myself inexpressibly happy in a belief that Heaven, which has done so much for our infant nation, will not withdraw its providential influence before our political felicity shall have been completed, and in a conviction that the Senate will at all times co-operate in every measure which may tend to promote the welfare of this confederated republic.  Thus supported by a firm trust in the great Arbiter of the universe, aided by the collective wisdom of the Union, and imploring the divine benediction on our joint exertions in the service of our country, I readily engage with you in the arduous but pleasing task of attempting to make a nation happy.
>
> GEORGE WASHINGTON.[12]

In spite of criticisms from the less pretentious and more democratic officers of the government, this ponderous mode of interchange was continued until the administration of Thomas Jefferson, who did away with it by the simple expedient of sending written messages to Congress without making a personal appearance at all.  His example was followed until the administration of Woodrow Wilson, who resumed the delivery of messages to joint sessions of the two houses of Congress.  The subsequent interchanges, however, were not resumed.

The Senate, and particularly its presiding officer, Vice-President Adams, was much concerned over the procedure to be followed when

[12] *Annals of Congress*, 1st Cong., 1st sess., 38.

the President called on the Senate for advice and consent in the mak‑ ing of treaties.   Where should the President sit?  If he was given the chair of the presiding officer, where should the Vice-President sit? What part should the latter officer play in the proceedings and how was the proper dignity of the Senate to be preserved?  In preparation for the first formal meeting for consultation, it was decided that President Washington should have the chair of the presiding officer of the Senate and that Vice-President Adams should take a seat with the senators.   Motions for action concerning the several provisions of the treaty, however, were to be put, not by Washington, but by Adams as president of the Senate.   The meeting was conducted so formally that everybody was thoroughly dissatisfied.   Senators proved unwill‑ ing to discuss the several provisions of the treaty in the presence of the President, who in turn was highly impatient when senators asked the opportunity to consider the treaty at leisure and in private before acting upon it.[13]  The President returned at a later date to complete action on the matters then pending, but he did not attempt again to use the Senate as an advisory body in the drafting of treaties.   Ad‑ ministration leaders thereafter first worked out the details of treaties in collaboration with the other nations parties to them and then sent them to the Senate for formal action of approval or disapproval.

The unfortunate method of conducting the first meeting between the President and the Senate in exercise of the power to make treaties, therefore, had the effect of eliminating one of the devices provided by the Constitutional Convention for co-operation between the two branches of the government.   The field remained an area of conflict down through the years.   When Presidents drafted treaties without taking the Senate into their confidence, the Senate, jealous of its own prerogatives, frequently showed its authority by refusing to give its sanction or by insisting on amendments; and this procedure required the reopening of negotiations with the representatives of other parties to the treaty.   No serious attempt was ever made to restore the Senate to the contemplated character of an advisory body to the President. In the making of treaties, however, a number of Presidents have found it expedient to appoint senators to international conferences out of which treaties might grow and to take Senate leaders into their confi dence in the drafting of treaties later to be submitted to the Senate for action.   These expedients have aided in securing senatorial co-

[13] For an account of the proceedings see *The Journal of William Maclay* (1927), pp. 125-130.

operation. In summary the attempt of the founding fathers to impress the people of the United States and of foreign countries by elaborate procedure in various fields, which they evidently thought characteristic of the country from which the United States had broken away, did much to prevent the initial establishment of flexible machinery adapted to the needs of the new government.

## THE EXECUTIVE DEPARTMENTS

During its first session, Congress passed acts to establish the Department of State, the Department of War, and the Treasury Department. When acting under the Articles of Confederation, Congress had found it necessary to maintain government agencies in these fields, and their continuation was taken so much as a matter of course that the Constitution did not provide directly for their establishment, but referred to them indirectly on one occasion by a mention of "each of the executive departments," and on another occasion by permitting Congress to vest appointments in the "heads of departments." The old Department of Foreign Affairs continued to function in some fashion until Congress on July 27, 1789, passed an act establishing a new department with the same name.[14] It was to be headed by a Secretary, who was directed to perform duties in the field of foreign affairs as instructed by the President of the United States. A chief clerk, appointed by the Secretary, had charge of the records of the department when the office of the Secretary was vacant.

Although no one opposed establishment of a Department of Foreign Affairs as provided in the statute, debate on provisions as to appointment and removal, originally included in the bill, showed a confusion as to the position of executive officers in the government. Under the Constitution, the President, by and with the advice and consent of the Senate, was to appoint federal officers, except that Congress might vest the appointment of inferior officers in the President alone, in the courts of law, or in the heads of departments. Nothing was said about the removal of officers except for the provision that the President, the Vice-President, and all civil officers of the United States should be removed from office on impeachment for and conviction of treason, bribery, or other high crimes and misdemeanors. In proposing the establishment of a Department of Foreign Affairs, James Madison included language to the effect that there should be an officer "to be called the Secretary to the Department of Foreign

[14] 1 Stat. 28.

Affairs, who shall be appointed by the President, by and with the advice and consent of the Senate; and to be removable by the President." [15]   A congressman moved to strike out the words having to do with appointment, saying that the Constitution itself prescribed the method, and that the inclusion of the language in the act would seem to be conferring power which was already there.   Debate showed that other persons thought the Secretary was an inferior officer, and that his appointment therefore might at the discretion of Congress be placed in the President alone.   The words of the bill were calculated to guarantee participation by the Senate.

The controversy on this point spread to a more serious controversy over the provision that the Secretary was to be removable by the President.   Some congressmen thought it clearly within the intention of the Constitution that all executive officers appointed by the President should be removable by him alone, even though the appointment had been made with the advice and consent of the Senate. Others thought that an officer appointed with senatorial participation could be removed only with the concurrence of the Senate, and that the appointment continued indefinitely even after the expiration of the term of the appointing President.   That, indeed, seems to have been the impression of Alexander Hamilton as one of the authors of *The Federalist*.[16]

Madison, a co-author of *The Federalist* and now a member of the House of Representatives, disagreed with the interpretation of Hamilton and with the arguments of those of his colleagues who believed that an executive officer could be removed only by impeachment or by joint action of the President and the Senate.   He argued that it was the intention of the Constitution that the President should be responsible for the executive department.   If responsibility was to be placed upon him, it was necessary that he have control of personnel to the extent of ridding himself of persons unsatisfactory to him.[17] The issue was debated at length over a considerable period by Madison and by other persons who took varying positions on it.   Congress ultimately eliminated from the bill the language providing for appointment of the Secretary and for his removal, and indicated merely by inference the right of the President to remove the Secretary in a section giving the chief clerk the custody of the records of the depart-

---

[15] *Annals of Congress,* 1st Cong., 1st sess., 385.
[16] See *The Federalist* (Lodge ed., 1895), No. LXXVII, pp. 476-477.
[17] *Annals of Congress,* 1st Cong., 1st sess., 479-482.

ment whenever the principal officer should be removed by the President.[18]

Apart from the controversy over appointments and removals, the Department of Foreign Affairs was established with little difficulty. Some weeks later, after deciding not to organize a Home Department, Congress changed the name of the Department of Foreign Affairs to Department of State and gave it certain additional functions, including the keeping of the seal of the United States and the recording of newly enacted statutes.[19]

The War Department was established with but little debate.[20] Congress gave the Secretary for the Department of War jurisdiction over such military and naval affairs as the President might entrust to his care. As in the instance of the Secretary for the Department of Foreign Affairs, later called the Secretary of State, the statute made an indirect reference to his removal by the President. It was not until 1798 that a Department of the Navy was organized.[21]

The establishment of the Treasury Department gave rise to a great deal of debate. As in the case of the management of war and of foreign affairs, it had been found necessary during the Revolutionary War to establish a finance department with a single individual at its head. Robert Morris, of Pennsylvania, held that position until after the close of the war, when criticism of his administration and the unwillingness of Congress to follow his advice led to his resignation. Thereafter, instead of appointing another Secretary, Congress returned to the use of a board for the management of financial affairs. Some of the members of Congress under the new Constitution wished to continue the use of a treasury board rather than resort to a department headed by one man, arguing that the responsibility was too great to be left in the hands of a single individual. Most people,

[18] Madison's interpretation was accepted widely but by no means unanimously. Until 1926, authorities differed concerning the power of the Senate to interfere with the removal power of the President. In that year, by a vote of six to three in a decision supported by a detailed historical analysis on the part of Chief Justice Taft, himself a former President, the Supreme Court adhered to the position taken by Madison. It found the power to remove executive officers essential to the performance of the executive duties which the Constitution laid upon the President. (Myers v. United States, 272 U.S. 52 [1926].)

The whole controversy resulted from a vagueness in the language of the Constitution which might easily have been eliminated by those who drafted it. In this instance, as in many others, however, the vagueness was caused in part by the necessity of compromising on various points. It was sometimes easier to secure the adoption of vague provisions than of others which were clear and exact. Once adopted, they lent themselves to conflicting interpretations and gave rise to years of controversy.

[19] 1 Stat. 68.          [20] 1 Stat. 50.          [21] 1 Stat. 553.

however, were convinced that a board would lack the necessary vigor, enterprise, and co-ordination.   They wished to bring about the organization of a department which would not merely collect and expend revenue in a ministerial fashion, but would also provide Congress with plans for the management of the financial system of the country. These advocates of a strong department supported a bill to provide for an agency which would be, not an instrument of the President, as were the State and War Departments, but quite as much an instrument of Congress, making reports to that body rather than to the President.

Critics of the plan for a strong department were particularly concerned about a provision in the bill which directed the Secretary of the Treasury to digest and report plans for the improvement and management of the revenue and give information to either branch of Congress in person or in writing, as might be required, respecting all matters referred to him by either house.   Members of the House of Representatives stressed the fact that the Constitution lodged in the House the initiation of bills to raise revenue and that this measure threatened to transfer that power to the Secretary of the Treasury.[22] By a large majority, the House of Representatives adopted an amendment directing the Secretary of the Treasury to digest and *prepare* plans rather than report them.[23]   A smaller number of persons in the Senate were concerned about the same problem.   An unsympathetic commentator remarked as follows:

> A puerile debate arose, whether the Secretary of the Treasury should be allowed to exhibit his reports and statements to the legislature.   The champions of liberty drew their swords, talked blank verse about treasury influence, a ministry, violation of the privileges of the House by giving him a hearing from time to time.   They persevered so long and so furiously, that they lost all strength, and were left in a very small minority.[24]

As a sequel to this debate, Alexander Hamilton, Secretary of the Treasury, let it be known at the beginning of the second session of Congress that he was ready to appear before the House of Representatives to make a report on the public credit which the House had asked him to prepare.   The House, evidently fearful of the precedents involved, decided that the report should be submitted in writing rather than orally.   The question arose on other occasions as to the

---

[22] For the opposing point of view see *Annals of Congress*, 1st Cong., 1st sess., 617.
[23] *Ibid.*, p. 631.     [24] *Works of Fisher Ames* (Seth Ames ed., 2 vols., 1854), I, 56.

admission of the head of an executive department to the floor of the House, but none was ever permitted to appear.[25] The development of the committee system in Congress made possible a partial substitute for the appearance of executive officers before the houses. They now appear regularly before the appropriation committees and frequently before other committees to testify concerning proposed legislation affecting matters within their jurisdiction.

Although the statute establishing the Treasury Department [26] allotted duties directly to the Secretary of the Treasury instead of leaving them to the delegation of the President, it made the same indirect reference to the removal of the Secretary as in the instances of the Secretaries of State and War. This power of removal gave the President control over the functions to be performed by the Secretary. The power of the Secretary was further limited in that, whereas in other departments the principal officer was given full charge of the entire department, some functions of the Treasury Department were allocated to a comptroller, a treasurer, an auditor, and a register, who had duties independently prescribed and who were not under the control of the Secretary.

Nevertheless, the office of Secretary of the Treasury became for a time one of the strongest in the government. It was made so partly by the importance which the organization of finance had in the establishment of the new government. An additional factor, however, was the leadership of Alexander Hamilton, the first occupant of the office. He was appointed to the office after it had been rejected by Robert Morris, who had held the corresponding office during the Revolution.[27]

The establishment of a new Post Office Department was regarded as of lesser importance. Postal administration had been in charge of a Postmaster General since 1775. Congress enacted temporary measures dealing with postal matters until the permanent organization of the department in 1794. It was not until 1829, however, that the Postmaster General was invited into cabinet meetings with the heads of other departments. In the meantime, Congress kept a measure of direct control over postal affairs by requiring direct reports on certain matters.[28]

[25] See Mary L. Hinsdale, "The Cabinet and Congress: An Historical Inquiry," *Report of the Proceedings of the American Political Science Association* (1905), II, 132-133.

[26] 1 Stat. 65.      [27] William Graham Sumner, *Robert Morris* (1892), p. 109.

[28] Lloyd Milton Short, *The Development of National Administrative Organization in the United States* (1923), pp. 102-103.

THE JUDICIARY

The account of the establishment of the judicial branch of the government is an intricate story. It is often neglected because it involves technicalities of legal organization and procedure which are mysteries to the layman. It is of major importance for an understanding of the federal system, however, and neglect results inevitably in a blurred conception of the governmental structure. Difficulties arise in part from a confusion between the province of the Constitution and of the Judiciary Act as to judicial power. The former contained the broad authorization of the power to the federal government. The latter represented the compromise decision of Congress as to how much of the power authorized by the Constitution the federal judicial system should actually exercise, and as to the machinery to be used. Concerning judicial machinery it is helpful to remember that Congress sought to establish a judicial hierarchy by which cases of lesser importance would be decided by lower federal or state courts, while more important cases would go directly or indirectly to the Supreme Court. Entanglement with state judicial systems inevitably created difficulties. The fact that constitutional amendments affecting judicial powers were under discussion added to the confusion. In spite of all the difficulties, however, Congress established a reasonably efficient judicial system which operated as a powerful branch of the government. The following paragraphs enlarge upon the story.

Agreement in Congress on the outlines of the judiciary branch was less general than on the executive. One reason for the difference lay in the fact that, whereas the development of executive departments had begun under the Continental Congress, there was then no federal judiciary worthy of the name. Differences of opinion in the Constitutional Convention and in the state ratifying conventions over the federal judiciary had been sharp, furthermore, and many of the amendments to the Constitution urged as necessary in a bill of rights were proposed in connection with the exercise of judicial powers.

The Constitution left the details and much of the outline of the federal judicial system to determination by Congress. It provided for a Supreme Court, but did not state the number of members or the period during which it should be in session. It prescribed the limited "original" jurisdiction of the Supreme Court — that is, jurisdiction in cases begun in that court — but left to Congress the determination of its jurisdiction in cases appealed from other courts. It left to Congress the establishment of inferior courts, but did not command the establishment of such courts, apparently leaving to the discretion of Congress the decision whether or not much of the federal judicial power should be exercised by the courts of the several states rather than by federal courts.

The so-called Anti-Federalists in Congress sought to minimize the power and the extent of the federal judiciary. They advanced their arguments both in connection with the proposed Judiciary Act, which was before Congress for many weeks during the summer of 1789, and in connection with the series of amendments to the Constitution advocated by Madison and other Federalists in fulfillment of their promise, made in the ratifying conventions, that amendments would be proposed.[29] Anti-Federalists in both houses of Congress attempted to prevent the establishment of inferior federal courts except for the exercise of admiralty and maritime jurisdiction, leaving to the state courts the exercise of most of the federal judicial power. When these attempts failed, the Anti-Federalists insisted on curbing the power of the federal courts wherever possible. The Federalist leaders, on the other hand, sought to establish a complete system of federal courts for the exercise of all jurisdiction that might arise in any manner under the Constitution, laws, and treaties or under the authority of the United States. The result of the struggles was a series of compromises, both with reference to the Judiciary Act and the several proposed constitutional amendments.

The Judiciary Act fixed membership of the Supreme Court at a Chief Justice and five associate justices, who would hold two sessions of the Supreme Court each year. Some Federalist leaders favored a larger membership, whereas the opponents of a complete federal judicial system believed that even six judges were more than were needed. The total number of six was agreed upon because it was divisible into groups of two judges each, who in the intervals between the terms of the Supreme Court were to join with district judges in holding circuit courts in each of the three circuits which were established by the same act.

The statute provided for a district court, to which a district judge was to be appointed, in each of the eleven states which were then members of the Union and in the territories of Maine and Kentucky. Each district judge held annually four sessions of his court

---

[29] For the best study of the adoption of the Judiciary Act of 1789 see Charles Warren, "History of the Federal Judiciary Act of 1789," *Harvard Law Review*, XXXVII (November, 1923), 49-132.

and in addition sat with two justices of the Supreme Court to make up the circuit court whenever it met in his district. In the limited number of cases which might be appealed from the district court to the circuit court, however, the statute provided that no district judge should vote in any case of appeal or error from his own decisions, but he might assign the reasons for his decision.[30]

Important paragraphs of the Judiciary Act dealt with the jurisdiction of the several federal courts. Cases involving admiralty and maritime jurisdiction and cases of lesser importance in other fields were allotted to the district courts, which stood at the foot of the judicial hierarchy. The circuit courts were designed to perform the greater part of the federal judicial business apart from admiralty cases. They handled, not merely most cases arising under federal statutes, but also cases under state laws involving persons who were citizens of different states. Federal jurisdiction in the latter was given because of the fear that a citizen of one state would not receive justice in the courts of another. As for the Supreme Court, the Constitution provided directly that it should have original jurisdiction in certain cases. Its jurisdiction in cases appealed from other courts, which would constitute the major portion of its work, was also described in broad outlines, but was left subject to regulation by Congress. The Judiciary Act prescribed the types of cases which might be appealed from district courts to circuit courts and from district courts, circuit courts, and state courts to the Supreme Court.

The right of appeal from state courts to the Supreme Court in cases involving federal questions, although opposed by critics of centralization of power, was a prerequisite if harmony and order in the interpretation and enforcement of federal law were to be preserved. The only workable alternative would probably have been the requirement that all cases involving federal questions should be tried originally in federal courts rather than in state courts. The Anti-Federalist group opposed this alternative, and succeeded in preventing its adoption. The state courts were allowed to retain jurisdiction concurrent with that of the federal courts in suits between citizens of different states and in many types of cases involving the enforcement of federal laws. Congress, in later years, passed statutes vesting additional areas of fed-

---

[30] 1 Stat. 73, 75. A perennial difficulty of situations in which the same judge sits both on a higher and a lower court is the problem of his hearing appeals in cases in which his mind is already made up and his position has been publicly declared. It provided an argument against having circuit duties performed by Supreme Court justices.

eral jurisdiction in state courts. They included suits by the United States for penalties and forfeitures, cases under customs and internal-revenue and excise statutes, and the prosecution of crimes against the United States. It is said that this voluntary surrender of federal judicial powers to the states ceased only when the state courts themselves proceeded to hold that Congress had no constitutional power to impose such jurisdiction on state tribunals and officials. The controversy became important in connection with the disinclination of the northern states to allow the use of their courts and officials for the enforcement of the federal fugitive-slave law. Procedure which had been worked out as a concession to the advocates of state rights had then to be abandoned because of the opposition of persons — slave-owners of the South — who were also exponents of state-rights doctrines.[31]

Although the Federalists in Congress compromised in their desire to have the federal judiciary exercise all the judicial power that could have been conferred upon it under the Constitution, the compromise was expressed in the judiciary statute alone rather than in the proposed amendments to the Constitution. None of the ten amendments adopted, the so-called Bill of Rights, impaired substantially the functioning of the federal judiciary. They did, however, assert certain fundamental rights of the American people as against the federal government, and they prescribed constitutional procedures by which the judiciary was to be governed. They made use of warrants, properly safeguarded, a necessary preliminary to searches and seizures. They made indictment by grand jury a necessary preliminary to criminal trial except in certain specified instances. They forbade putting any person in jeopardy twice for the same offense and compelling any person in any criminal case to be a witness against himself. In language which took on new meaning after the Civil War, when it was inserted in the Fourteenth Amendment as a prohibition against the states, the Fifth Amendment provided that no person should be deprived of life, liberty, or property without due process of law. Private property could not be taken for public use without just compensation to the owners.

Congress had great difficulty in drafting a satisfactory provision to require that persons accused of crime should have the right of trial by a jury drawn from the vicinity of the crime. An amendment was finally agreed upon calculated to achieve that end and to

[31] See Warren, *op. cit.*, pp. 70-71.

guarantee other requisites of a fair and impartial trial. Excessive bail, excessive fines, and cruel and unusual punishments were forbidden. The right of jury trial was guaranteed in civil cases where the value in controversy exceeded twenty dollars.

The Judiciary Act provided for certain officers whose functions crossed the line between the executive and judicial branches of the government. A marshal was to be appointed in each district to execute the orders of the court and he was empowered to appoint deputies to aid him. An attorney for the United States was to be appointed in each district whose duty it was to prosecute criminal cases and all civil actions in which the United States should be concerned. Finally, the act provided that

> there shall also be appointed a meet person, learned in the law, to act as Attorney General for the United States, who shall be sworn or affirmed to a faithful execution of his office; whose duty it shall be to prosecute and conduct all suits in the Supreme Court in which the United States shall be concerned, and to give his advice and opinion upon questions of law when required by the President of the United States, or when requested by the heads of any of the departments, touching any matters that may concern their departments. . . .[32]

As originally drafted, the bill provided that the district courts were to appoint the district attorneys and that the Supreme Court should appoint the Attorney General. The language was changed, however, so as merely to provide, in the passive voice, that the officers should be appointed. The result was that the selection of personnel passed into the hands of the President and the Senate.[33]

The position of Attorney General had its predecessor in the colonial and state governments, and, still farther back, in the official with the same title in England.[34] It is to be noticed that the Attorney General was required to conduct litigation only in the Supreme Court. For many years that task was light, as was also the task of giving advice to the President and the heads of departments on legal matters. It was not until the time of the Civil War that the Attorney General was given important responsibility for supervising the work of district attorneys, and it was not until 1870 that Congress created the Department of Justice to be headed by him. His salary was fixed in 1789 at fifteen hundred dollars, in contrast

---

[32] 1 Stat. 73, 93.    [33] See Warren, *op. cit.*, pp. 108-109.
[34] Homer Cummings and Carl McFarland, *Federal Justice* (1927), p. 11.

with thirty-five hundred dollars for the Secretary of the Treasury and the Secretary of State and three thousand dollars for the Secretary of War. It was expected that the Attorney General, like the chief law officers in the several states, would add substantially to his income by continuing his private practice. He did so for a great many years, and it was not until the appointment of William Wirt to the office in 1817 that the Attorney General was required to maintain his residence at the seat of government.

## THE CABINET

In the government of England and in the colonial and state governments, the principal executive officer was usually supported by some kind of advisory council. It varied in form from government to government and from period to period, but, generally speaking, it brought to the executive the best judgment of men of ability and prestige and tended to stabilize and improve public administration. The Constitutional Convention considered from time to time the provision of such a council for the President, but for various reasons no action was taken. The lack of an executive council or privy council or cabinet was stressed by critics of the Constitution to show its inadequacy in the form in which it was proposed to the states.

Although the Constitution made no direct provision for a council, there were at least three possibilities for the exercise of the functions of such an agency. One possibility was in connection with the Senate, which at that time consisted of only twenty-six men and was therefore not so large as to be unwieldy. The Constitution encouraged co-operation between the President and the Senate by providing that the Senate should give advice and consent in connection with appointments and with the making of treaties. The painful experiences of the President and the Senate in the effort to work together on the only occasion on which such co-operation was attempted, however, destroyed any hope that the Senate would ever function as an effective advisory body to the President.

Another possible advisory body was the Supreme Court. The practice of calling upon judges for advisory opinions reached far back into English history and it had prevailed in the colonies. The Constitutional Convention rejected a proposal to authorize the President to call for opinions of the Supreme Court upon important questions of law,[35] but Washington and members of his cabinet consulted in-

[35] H. B. Learned, *The President's Cabinet* (1912), p. 129.

formally on many matters with Chief Justice John Jay in such a way as to indicate a growing co-operative relationship. In 1793, however, when the administration was faced with certain difficult questions of international law in connection with the interpretation of treaties, the President, through Secretary of State Thomas Jefferson, asked the Supreme Court if he was free to request the opinion of the Court upon legal questions which had to be solved, but which could not be brought up in a judicial manner. A long list of questions was submitted with the inquiry.

The Court replied that it had no power to give advisory opinions. As for the lines of separation between the three departments of the government, it said,

> these being in certain respects checks upon each other, and our being judges of a court in the last resort, are considerations which afford strong arguments against the propriety of our extra-judicially deciding the questions alluded to, especially as the power given by the Constitution to the President, of calling on the heads of departments for opinions, seems to have been *purposely* as well as expressly united to the *executive* department. We exceedingly regret every event that may cause embarrassment to your administration, but we derive consolation from the reflection that your judgment will discern what is right, and that your usual prudence, decision, and firmness will surmount every obstacle to the preservation of the rights, peace, and dignity of the United States.[36]

The opinion, courteously expressed though it was and wise as it may have been, all things considered, established a barrier which prevented the President from using the Supreme Court in an advisory capacity. The President turned finally, therefore, as he had already begun to turn, to the third and last possibility for an advisory council, the heads of the several departments. The Constitution provided that he might call upon them for opinions in writing upon any subject relating to the duties of their respective offices.[37] As a matter of fact, since they were appointed by him and since it was agreed that they were subject to removal by him, and while in office were to perform functions under his direction, except in the case of the Secretary of the Treasury, he had full authority to make use of their advice without any constitutional provision on the subject. During his first

[36] Charles Warren, *The Supreme Court in United States History* (rev. ed., 2 vols., 1926), I, 110-111.
[37] Article II, Section 2, Paragraph 1.

administration President Washington began to refer matters to the Secretaries of State, War, and the Treasury, to the Attorney General, and on occasions to the Vice-President and to the Chief Justice. Gradually the practice developed of calling the first four into session for discussion of matters of state. The Vice-President and the Chief Justice were left behind. The Secretary of the Navy was added with the creation of his office in 1798. The Postmaster General was included in the cabinet in 1829. In later years the heads of other departments were invited into the group as new departments were created and given full-fledged status. In this manner the cabinet evolved as a creature of custom rather than of law. Unlike the Senate, its membership was of the President's own choosing. Unlike the Supreme Court, its membership was subject to removal by him. The President shared with the cabinet interests which were not shared with the Senate or with the Supreme Court. The executive officers, therefore, on the whole constituted the logical choice of the available groups for use as an advisory council.

In spite of the general use made of the cabinet, no President has ever found it necessary to rely upon it for advice to the exclusion of that of other persons. Although the appointment of members of the cabinet is a prerogative of the President, his choice is often determined less by his own desires than by the necessity of making political concessions to sections or groups within the country. In any event, the head of a department may prove a disappointing choice without being so bad as to justify removal. Andrew Jackson relied more heavily upon what was called his "kitchen cabinet" than upon his official family. Franklin D. Roosevelt began his administration with a so-called "brain trust" that was reputed to be more influential than the heads of the departments. Other Presidents have relied extensively upon particular individuals — as, for example, the reliance of President Wilson upon Colonel House — and all of them have resorted more or less frequently to outside advice. Since its establishment, however, the cabinet has remained a stable and usually, no doubt, at least a moderately influential advisory group.

••••••••••••••••••••••••••••••••••••••••••••••••••••••••••••••••••••••••••••••••••••••••••••••••••••••

# CHAPTER 4

# THE PROGRAM OF THE NEW GOVERNMENT

THE NATURE OF THE CONSTITUTION during the first decade of its existence can be gleaned in part from the language of the document. A survey of the administrative structure evolved for its operation throws additional light on the subject. The vitality and the essential purpose of the Constitution, however, can be fully understood only in terms of the program or programs worked out and put into operation by the dominant group of statesmen. Activities in a number of fields were important, but those connected with finance and with foreign policy warrant special attention.

In terms both of time and of importance the financial program came first. If the nation was to have credit standing either at home or abroad, it was necessary that the new government repair at once the financial calamities of the old. The nation could not put its house in order merely by providing henceforth for current and future expenditures. It had also to find some means of retiring the debt of the Revolutionary period. That debt was long overdue; and the condition of government credit was indicated by the fact that obligations were badly depreciated and could often be bought at small fractions of their face value. Full redemption was required, not merely on grounds of sound fiscal policy, but by the language of the Constitution as well. The first paragraph of Article VI provided, "All debts contracted and engagements entered into, before the adoption of this Constitution, shall be valid against the United States under this Constitution as under the Confederation."

The debts of the several states incurred during the Revolutionary period were in much the same position as the national debt. A few states had made substantial payments, but most of them had not done so; and the obligations of the states, like those of the federal government, were selling at small fractions of their face value. There was no legal connection between the debts of the states and of the United

States, but in terms of the financial welfare of the country the connection was obvious. Both types of debts would have to be retired, or faith in their redemption would have to be re-created, before the country could operate on a sound financial basis. If the states had been unable to pay their debts prior to the adoption of the new Constitution, payment would be even more difficult now, since they had lost their power to collect duties on foreign and interstate commerce. The federal government, which now had broad powers of taxation, seemed likely to be the only medium through which the credit of the states as well as of the federal government could be restored.

The program adopted was worked out largely by Alexander Hamilton. He seems to have conceived it even more broadly than the mere restoration of the credit of the state and federal governments and the provision of adequate revenue. Quite aware that a strong central government was as yet a matter of constitutional theory rather than of fact, he devised financial mechanisms by which the creditors of the state and federal governments would be given a stake in a government capable of raising adequate revenues, both by duties on imports and by excise taxes laid within the country. With economic ties he bound private financial interests to the support of the government. He had in mind, likewise, the establishment of import duties that would be protective of the industries of the country as well as a source of revenue. The conflict over his program solidified the Federalist party, weeded certain eminent statesmen from its ranks, and gave a point of attack to the opposition party.

Although there were several predictions of the dissolution of the Union during the controversy over the program, the time had passed when substantial groups openly advocated the defeat of the Constitution. Instead, both the friends and the opponents of that general measure sought to use it for their own purposes. Both parties professed loyalty to the Constitution while insisting upon interpretations of it which best served their ends. Before the first term of the First Congress had expired, some statesmen were resorting to tactics employed ever since — using constitutional arguments against proposals to which their real opposition rested on other and perhaps less lofty grounds.

### FOREIGN COMMERCE AS A SOURCE OF REVENUE

One of the first measures debated, and the second measure to be enacted by the First Congress, dealt with "duties on merchandise imported into the United States."[1]   On April 9, 1789, referring to the notorious deficiency in the Treasury of the United States, James Madison introduced in the House of Representatives a resolution calling for duties on certain items of import and for tonnage duties on vessels engaged in the carrying trade.[2] With this proposal began the struggles which have characterized tariff controversies from that day to this. Men argued as to whether duties should be levied merely for revenue or whether they should be high enough to give a certain amount of protection to American industry. Congressmen who favored high duties generally were opposed to those which bore particularly upon their own constituents. Representatives of the shipping interests of the North urged the imposition of high tonnage duties on the competing ships of England and other foreign countries in order to promote their own business. Representatives of people in the South, who made use of northern or foreign ships and had to pay freight on their products or purchases, opposed tonnage duties, which they regarded as taxation levied upon them for the benefit of the North.

As always, the duties laid by the first measure were worked out by compromise. Although they were not high in terms of modern standards, they were to some extent protective both of American manufactures and of American shipping.[3] The legislation marked the beginning of the American protective system, a system of taxation on imports so scaled as to raise prices in the United States on the goods imported and make possible the successful competition of American manufactures.

### SUPPORT OF THE PUBLIC CREDIT

The tariff and tonnage measures constituted the first step in the direction of a sound fiscal system. The measure to establish the Treasury Department was not enacted until September 2, 1789, shortly before Congress adjourned. No additional action was taken in the field at that session except to ask the Secretary of the Treasury to prepare for submission to the House of Representatives at the ensuing session a report concerning adequate provision for the support of the public credit. In addition to giving information about the federal government proper, he was asked to apply to the governors of

---

[1] Stat. 24.        [2] Annals of Congress, 1st Cong., 1st sess., 107-108.

[3] See F. W. Taussig, The Tariff History of the United States (5th ed., 1910), pp. 14-15; William Hill, "The First Stages of the Tariff Policy of the United States," Publications of the American Economic Association, VIII (November, 1893), No. 6.

the several states for statements of their public debt and of the amount of loan-office certificates or other public securities of the United States which were in the state treasuries.[4]

Secretary Hamilton responded on January 9, 1790, with the first of his celebrated documents on public finance, known as the *First Report on the Public Credit*.[5]  As to the debt owed by the federal government, Hamilton found its present state of depreciation a national calamity.  He urged the refunding of the debt at its face value into new securities, which, because of the provision for adequate federal revenue, would maintain their value thereafter and would circulate as money, meeting in part the need of the country for an adequate circulatory medium.

Intricate problems of justice were involved in the funding of the public debt.  Many patriotic people who had subscribed to public loans during the period of the Revolution had been unable to hold their securities until such time as the government might redeem them, and had sold them at greatly depreciated prices. These securities had fallen more and more into the hands of people who were able to speculate in them.  From the time of the drafting of the Constitution, many Federalist leaders had had in mind the refunding of the debt at its face value; and knowledge or suspicion as to the funding plans had increased speculation.  The securities had risen rapidly in value, adding to the wealth, not of the people who had made loans to the government in time of crisis, but of those who had been shrewd enough to buy them at the right time.  Even among the members of Congress who were responsible for the financial program of the government, considerable quantities of government securities were held or were acquired in anticipation of the rise in value to be brought about by new legislation.[6]  Although the issue had not yet been formally discussed in Congress, the argument was already being advanced that speculators ought not to be allowed to profit either at the expense of the original holders of the securities or of the taxpayers of the country.  It was contended variously that only the amounts received by the original holders should be paid by the government, or that the amount paid in excess of that received by the original owners should

---

[4] *Annals of Congress,* 1st Cong., 1st sess., 939.

[5] *The Works of Alexander Hamilton* (Lodge ed., 9 vols., 1885-1886), II, 47-106.  The report appears also in *Annals of Congress,* 1st Cong., 3d sess., 2041-2082.

[6] Charles A. Beard, *Economic Origins of Jeffersonian Democracy* (1915), pp. 135-136, 165 ff.

be paid to the original holders rather than to the present owners of the securities.

Using a series of arguments based on justice, policy, and expediency, Hamilton insisted that the face value of the securities should be paid to the present holders. One of his arguments was based upon the constitutional provision that the debts contracted under the Articles of Confederation should be as valid against the United States under the Constitution as under the Confederation. This, he said, amounted to a constitutional ratification of the contracts respecting the debt in the form in which they existed under the Confederation. Under this standard there could be no doubt that the rights of the assignees and original holders must be considered as equal.[7]

Hamilton asked, not merely for the funding of the federal debt hitherto incurred, but for the assumption and funding of the debts of the states as well. That subject had likewise been much discussed in advance of formal consideration by Congress; and he sought to answer the arguments of his opponents. His arguments, which were based on the economic welfare of the country and on reasoning as to the best financial methods of liquidating the state as well as the federal debt, sounded persuasive. He made no attempt, however, to show positively that the Constitution authorized the federal government to assume responsibility for the payment of the debts of the states and to raise revenue for that purpose. The most that can be said in favor of his strategy is that he was thinking in terms of economic statesmanship rather than of constitutionality in the legal sense. Although, for political reasons, the fact was not stressed, the assumption of the debts by the federal government was the only way of assuring their payment. There is apparently no constitutional means by which the federal government can force a state to pay its debts.[8] In addition to giving assurance that state debts would not be repudiated altogether, their assumption by the federal government gave the holder of securities a stake in the federal rather than in the state governments and aided in strengthening the new Union at the time when its firm entrenchment was a part of the strategy of the Federalist leaders.

The assumption of state debts would justify expansion of the federal

[7] Hamilton, *op. cit.*, II, 62.

[8] See Roswell Page, "The West Virginia Debt Settlement," *Virginia Law Register* (N.S.), V (August, 1919), 257, 278; T. R. Powell, "Coercing a State to Pay a Judgment," *Michigan Law Review*, XVII (November, 1918), 1-32. See also Virginia *v.* West Virginia, 246 U.S. 565, and Lawrence B. Evans, *Cases on American Constitutional Law* (4th ed., 1938), note, pp. 261-262.

revenue system.   This expansion was also desired by Hamilton and other Federalists at the time when precedents for the exercise of federal power were being established.   He proposed, accordingly, not merely the collection of duties on imports, but excise taxes within the country as well, beginning with taxes on the manufacture of liquor. Furthermore, the management of his broad financial schemes called for aid in the form of banking machinery which was not then available.   Hamilton gave notice that in a subsequent report he would present a plan for the establishment of a national bank.

## THE "CONTINENTAL" DEBT

Hamilton sought the privilege of presenting in person his *Report on the Public Credit*.   Whether he was merely desirous of emphasizing the points made in his report, or whether in addition he sought to establish the precedent of personal appearance of the Secretary of the Treasury before a house of Congress, the records do not show.   In any event, the House directed him to submit his report in writing and did not ask him to appear in its behalf.[9]   The funding of the debt incurred by the Continental Congress and by the Congress operating under the Articles of Confederation began soon after the report was received.

Charles A. Beard's study entitled *Economic Origins of Jeffersonian Democracy*, like his earlier work, *An Economic Interpretation of the Constitution of the United States,* has done much to demonstrate the hard-headed economic strategy of the founding fathers.   He shows that the most vigorous advocates of the funding of the debt at its face value were themselves owners of federal securities who, like anyone else who held them, would profit by the operations of the Hamilton system.   Some people held them as a patriotic duty, or as an expression of confidence in the new government; others undoubtedly were mere speculators.   As a practical matter, the one group could not be served without profit to the other.   Few people in Congress favored the opposite alternative of repudiating the national debt or any part of it, but a considerable number sought to prevent speculators from enriching themselves by timely purchases of government securities. Under the leadership of James Madison, who in connection with this issue began his separation from the Federalist leadership, they sought to devise some scheme whereby the debt funded at its face value would be distributed equitably between the present holders and the

[9] *Annals of Congress*, 1st Cong., 2d sess., 1079-1081.

original holders who in a time of national crisis had taken the risk of lending money to the government.

Madison's motion to this effect was debated at length and was criticized by the Hamiltonians on many grounds. Their principal constitutional argument was that such a distribution of payments would punish the speculators who had already acquired their government securities and that it therefore fell within the definition of an *ex post facto* law, which the Constitution forbade Congress to enact.[10] Madison replied that this was a civil matter and not a criminal action at all. The definition of *ex post facto* law did not extend to all retroactive legislation, but only to that which dealt with criminal matters.[11] Although this contention as to the narrow meaning of the *ex post facto* clause was sound enough to be upheld a few years later by the Supreme Court,[12] the proposal was defeated.[13] Members of Congress continued to say, with Madison, that without discrimination between original holders and present owners "we shall be raising monuments of gratitude, not to our officers and soldiers who fought for us, but to those who speculated on our securities";[14] but the movement to reimburse only the present holders proved irresistible.

ASSUMPTION OF STATE DEBTS

The funding of the national debt at its face value was agreed to by majorities in both houses only after heavy battle. The question of the assumption of state debts resulted in strife that was even more bitter. A number of congressmen opposed assumption for the simple reason that their own states had paid substantial portions of their own debts, and yet, under the proposed arrangement, they would have to join in paying the debts of other states. This was particularly true in the case of Virginia. Madison tried vainly to secure an arrangement which would not discriminate against his own state. His opposition drove him still farther from the camp of the leading Federalists. He denied that the Constitution required the assumption of state debts. The subject had been discussed in the Constitutional Convention, he said, but no action had been taken.

While Congress was debating issues of the public credit, Thomas Jefferson, who had recently returned from Paris where he had served for some time as American minister, came to New York to take up his duties as Secretary of State. For a time he watched from the side-

---

[10] *Ibid.,* pp. 1257, 1271.    [11] *Ibid.,* p. 1311.    [12] Calder *v.* Bull, 3 Dallas 386 (1798).
[13] *Annals of Congress,* 1st Cong., 2d sess., 1344.    [14] *Ibid.,* p. 1339.

lines the battle over the assumption of state debts. No doubt he was fully aware of the state and sectional issues involved and of the speculation in government securities which prevailed wherever investment capital was available. He preferred that the states should pay their debts by levying their own taxes in their own way, he said, but he saw "the necessity of yielding to the cries of the creditors in certain parts of the Union; for the sake of the Union, and to save us from the greatest of calamities, the total extinction of our credit in Europe." [15] He was greatly pleased to learn of the vast improvement in the credit of the United States in Amsterdam, with the prospect of the completion of funding arrangements for the debt.[16]

He was also greatly interested in another controversy in Congress which seemed to have no particular relation to the assumption of debts. The subject was the location of the national capital. Congress continued to wrangle over that subject. It was generally expected that the capital would be moved to some point south of New York, but a sufficient majority could not be secured to locate it at Philadelphia or Baltimore or at other points in the central states. Georgetown, on the Potomac, the border between Virginia and Maryland, was being seriously considered. The Virginians, realizing, no doubt, that this was the southernmost position which had any chance of being chosen, were strongly in favor of Georgetown. Jefferson remarked avidly that locating the capital there would "vivify our agriculture and commerce by circulating through our state an additional sum every year of half a million of dollars." [17]

Hamilton, to whom Jefferson had not yet developed the antagonism of later years, seems to have consulted with Jefferson, who, although an executive rather than a legislative officer, was highly influential with the Virginian delegation. Hamilton is said to have promised the location of the capital on the Potomac after an interim period of ten years at Philadelphia if Jefferson would use his influence to bring about the assumption of state debts.[18] Whatever the details, it is clear from the records that both Jefferson and Madison consented to the compromise which had been worked out. They fell into line reluctantly, however, and their repressed resentment concerning the assumption of state debts added to the vigor of their opposition to other phases of Hamilton's financial program.

[15] *The Writings of Thomas Jefferson* (Library ed., 20 vols., 1903), VIII, 43-44.
[16] *Ibid.*, p. 46.    [17] *Ibid.*, p. 53.
[18] Claude G. Bowers, *Jefferson and Hamilton* (1925), pp. 64-67.

A NATIONAL BANK

The next segment of that program was presented on December 13, 1790, shortly after Congress had assembled for another session, in the form of a "report on a national bank." [19]  A national bank, he argued, would give three principal advantages to the government.  First, it would augment the active or productive capital of the country.  Secondly, it would facilitate the efforts of the government to obtain pecuniary aid, especially in sudden emergencies.  Thirdly, it would facilitate the payment of taxes.  There were at present, he said, only three banks in the United States, none of which was equipped to perform the necessary functions.  He therefore proposed the establishment of a new national bank with the power to open offices or, in modern terminology, branches wherever its officers should think fit within the United States.

Hamilton's proposal was warmly supported by the financial interests of the country.  It co-ordinated well with the funding of the public debt and the assumption of state debts for payment by the federal government.  A measure to carry the proposal into effect passed the Senate with little difficulty.  In the House of Representatives, however, it met serious opposition.  James Madison broke with his leading co-author in the writing of *The Federalist,* and challenged the constitutionality of the establishment of a national bank. [20]

In spite of Madison's opposition, the bill passed the House of Representatives by a vote of 39 to 20.  It was sent to the President for his approval.  He, having heard of the constitutional arguments against the bill, consulted with Madison and with the Attorney General, Edmund Randolph, and the Secretary of State, Thomas Jefferson. Randolph and Jefferson agreed with Madison that the bill was unconstitutional.  The Jefferson argument is the more important.  Jefferson contended that the power to establish a national bank was not among the express powers given by the Constitution, and he denied that the power "to make all laws necessary and proper for carrying into execution the enumerated powers" could be legitimately interpreted to support such a measure.  Even if the bank was found expedient for the performance of the enumerated functions, he denied that it was necessary for their performance.  He thought it must be necessary as well as convenient if it was to be constitutional.  The veto power of the President, he said, was the shield provided by the Constitution to protect against invasions by Congress.  It was to protect the

[19] *Annals of Congress,* 1st Cong., 3d sess., 2082-2112.    [20] *Ibid.,* p. 1951.

right of the executive, of the judiciary, and of the states and the state legislatures.   The present was a case of a right remaining exclusively with the states.   The right involved was one of those intended by the Constitution to be placed under its protection.

Jefferson was cautious, however.   As if seeking to avoid the establishment of a barrier between himself and his chief should the President decide against him, he closed his opinion with the following paragraph which has constitutional significance in its own right, apart from the subject of the bank and the doctrine of implied powers:

> It must be added, however, that unless the President's mind on a view of everything which is urged for and against this bill is tolerably clear that it is unauthorized by the Constitution; if the pro and the con hang so even as to balance his judgment, a just respect for the wisdom of the legislature would naturally decide the balance in favor of their opinion.   It is chiefly for cases where they are clearly misled by error, ambition, or interest, that the Constitution has placed a check in the negative of the President.[21]

With the opinions of the Attorney General and the Secretary of State before him, the President turned to Hamilton for his opinion on the subject of constitutionality, which he had not discussed in his report to the House of Representatives.   Hamilton now wrote a long opinion rebutting the arguments of the other two officials and defending the constitutionality of his bill.   As a shrewd Federalist, he argued in terms of logic and principles of government, rather than in terms of the intentions of the men who drafted the Constitution. The Constitution gave implied powers, he contended, as well as express powers, and the former were as effectually delegated as the latter.   He added "for the sake of accuracy" that there was another class of powers which might be properly denominated resulting powers; that is, powers which would be a result from the whole mass of powers of the government and from the nature of political society.   He contended that the power to establish a corporation, in this case a banking corporation, was clearly implied.   He denied that a power which was necessary within the meaning of the Constitution had to be one without which a given function could not be performed at all.   The word necessary, he said, often meant no more than needful, requisite, incidental, useful, or conducive to.   With this definition in mind, he had no doubt that a national bank was necessary for the performance of a number of essential governmental functions.[22]

[21] Jefferson, *op. cit.*, III, 153.
[22] For Hamilton's opinion see *The Works of Alexander Hamilton* (D. C. Hamilton ed., 7 vols., 1850-1851), IV, 104-138.

Hamilton debated the question from all angles, laying out in some cases almost word for word the material to be used by Chief Justice Marshall in 1819 in upholding the power of Congress to charter a bank.[23]    The President signed the bill, apparently convinced by Hamilton's argument.    The bank was established and it performed its function for the period of twenty years during which its charter was scheduled to run.    Its constitutionality was never directly challenged in the courts.    It was only after the establishment of its successor some years after the charter of this bank had expired that a case was taken to the Supreme Court and the opportunity was given to Chief Justice Marshall to read Hamilton's argument into the constitutional law of the country.

### THE REVENUE SYSTEM

The "Act to incorporate the subscribers to the bank of the United States" was approved February 25, 1791.[24]    On March 3, following, another measure was approved which constituted an important segment of Hamilton's program.    It revised the duties laid upon distilled spirits imported from abroad and provided for the collection of duties on spirits distilled within the United States.[25]    The importance of the measure was not merely in the immediate provision of additional revenue, but in the establishment of a precedent for raising revenue by the collection of duties or, as they were more commonly called, excise taxes, on the production of commodities within the United States.    From the point of view of strategy it was well to establish the precedent of collecting excise taxes, even though for the time being it might have been possible to raise the needed revenue by duties on imports alone.

The measure was important, furthermore, because the excises provided for were collected initially from farmers in certain sections of the country rather than from merchants or from manufacturers in the modern sense of the term.    Because of transportation difficulties, many western farmers were able to market grain only in the compact form of liquor.    Always restless under authority, they were enraged at interference with their mode of livelihood by the new scheme of taxation.    Instead of submitting peaceably, they tarred and feathered and otherwise mistreated collectors sent out by the government.    The administration recognized this first important challenge to its author-

[23] See McCulloch v. Maryland, 4 Wheaton 316 (1819).
[24] 1 Stat. 191.                    [25] 1 Stat. 199.

ity. The President called for volunteers, organized a small army, and, accompanied by Hamilton, moved westward from Philadelphia, then the capital of the United States, into Pennsylvania to suppress what was called the Whiskey Rebellion.

The rebels were dispersed, order was restored, and the revenue was collected thereafter without particular disturbance, save always for illicit manufacturers who continued to inhabit some of the wilder and more mountainous regions. The precedent of enforcing the law in the face of resistance did much for the firm entrenchment of the federal system. The taxing of western farmers, however, and the somewhat ruthless enforcement of law against them, had the effect of deepening the separation between the farming and debtor groups, on the one hand, and financiers, merchants, and manufacturers, on the other. It aided in solidifying the ranks of what was to be known as Jeffersonian Democracy.

Other taxing measures revealed the same economic cleavages and led also to discussion of the important question of the difference between direct and indirect taxes. Direct taxes were required by the Constitution to be apportioned among the states according to population. Indirect taxes, instead of being measured by the population of the states, were to be applied uniformly without reference to state lines. It seems to have been generally understood that taxes on land and poll taxes were direct. Members of Congress questioned whether these were the only ones that might be so classified, or whether some of the proposed excise taxes were also direct. If they were direct, the burden would have to be divided according to population, whereas, if they were indirect, the burden would rest upon the subject taxed without reference to the distribution of population.[26] In 1794, Congress enacted a measure laying duties "upon carriages for the conveyance of persons."[27] It provided for the collection of duties at certain rates upon carriages kept for personal use or for hire, with the exception of carriages chiefly employed for husbandry or for transporting goods, wares, merchandise, produce, or commodities. As phrased, it bore most heavily upon wealthier groups in the country, since in those days the people who kept carriages merely for pleasure and personal transportation were relatively few. When the measure was under consideration in the House of Representatives, Madison, who was becoming a consistent opponent of Hamilton and his program,

[26] *Annals of Congress*, 3d Cong., 1st sess., 652-653.
[27] 1 Stat. 373.

objected to the tax on carriages as an unconstitutional measure.[28]  Although his argument was not reported, there is reason for believing that his opposition was based, not upon concern for wealthy tax-payers, but upon dislike of excise taxes in general.[29]

In any event, a suit was instituted soon afterward in the United States circuit court in Virginia for the avowed purpose of testing the constitutionality of the tax.   Trial by jury was waived, and the parties to the suit seem to have agreed upon a highly fictitious state of facts. Under the Judiciary Act the circuit court could take jurisdiction in the case only if at least two thousand dollars was involved.   The tax on one carriage of the type owned by the litigant seems to have been sixteen dollars.   The statement of facts averred that Hylton, the person involved, kept the ridiculous number of one hundred and twenty-five carriages for his own private use.   That number of carriages, with a tax of sixteen dollars on each, raised the amount to the necessary two thousand dollars.[30]

Judges in the circuit court divided on the constitutional question. The agreement in the circuit court had provided that if the decision was against Hylton, the judgment could be discharged by the payment of sixteen dollars.   Hylton lost his enthusiasm for the litigation, and preferred to pay the sixteen dollars rather than incur the additional expense of an appeal to the Supreme Court.   The government, in order to have the question properly settled, felt it advisable to pay counsel to argue both sides of the question in the higher court.[31]  The Attorney General, arguing in defense of the constitutionality of the tax, was supported by special counsel in the person of Alexander Hamilton, who had recently resigned as Secretary of the Treasury. He was in ill health, but he was speaking in defense of his financial program, and one of the judges reported that he spoke with astonishing ability.[32]

Although the Supreme Court consisted of six justices when the membership was full, the case was argued before only three justices — Iredell, Paterson, and Chase.   Justice Wilson did not participate because he had been a member of the circuit court in the decision of the case below.   Justice Cushing was ill.   The new Chief Justice,

---

[28] *Annals of Congress,* 3d Cong., 1st sess., 730.          [29] See, for example, *ibid.,* p. 622.

[30] See the statement of the case, Hylton *v.* United States, 3 Dallas 171 (1796).

[31] See Charles Warren, *The Supreme Court in United States History* (rev. ed., 2 vols., 1926), I, 147-148.

[32] *Ibid.,* p. 148.

Oliver Ellsworth, took his seat after the date of the argument and was not qualified to participate in the decision.

Each of the three justices wrote an opinion in the case, according to the custom of the time. They were obviously bewildered by the question as to what constituted a direct tax within the meaning of the Constitution. Justice Chase even remarked that he believed some taxes might be both direct and indirect at the same time. All concurred, however, in upholding the tax as an indirect tax.[33]

The variously phrased conclusions of the justices that direct taxes within the meaning of the Constitution were limited to capitation taxes and taxes on land represented the position of the Supreme Court for almost a century. It left the way open for the collection of such excise taxes as the federal government saw fit to levy as long as they were uniformly applied. The decision was, therefore, a substantial victory for Hamilton and his financial system. It was only in connection with the income-tax controversy of the eighteen-nineties that the Court, by a bare majority, classified income taxes as direct taxes which could be levied only in terms of the rule of apportionment.[34]

## THE CONTROL OF FOREIGN AFFAIRS

The establishment of the prestige of the new government in foreign

---

[33] 3 Dallas 174.

[34] In 1798, when the country was badly in need of funds in preparation for possible war with France, Congress added a direct tax to the existing forms of revenue and provided for its apportionment according to population among the sixteen states then comprising the Union. (1 Stat. 597.) The sum of two million dollars was to be raised on the basis of an assessment of lands, houses, and slaves. The measure was resented by farmers and added to the unpopularity of the Federalists, who were responsible for it. A rebellion against collection of the tax, reminiscent of the Whiskey Rebellion, occurred in one section of Pennsylvania. (See John B. McMaster, *History of the People of the United States* [8 vols., 1883-1913], II, 434-438.) The rebellion was put down, but the experience with the direct tax did not recommend it as a satisfactory form of raising revenue. The Republicans tried it during the War of 1812, but there was obvious inequity in measuring a tax on property partly by population rather than by the amount or value of the property taxed. This and other reasons discouraged the use of direct taxes with the result that duties on imports and excises were the principal forms of federal revenue until the taxation of income began to compete with them.

The carriage-tax decision was important in another respect. It was the first case in which the Supreme Court weighed carefully the constitutionality of an act of Congress. On this point Justice Chase remarked, "As I do not think the tax on carriages is a direct tax, it is unnecessary, at this time, for me to determine whether this Court constitutionally possesses the power to declare an act of Congress void, on the ground of its being made contrary to, and in violation of, the Constitution; but if the Court have such power, I am free to declare that I will never exercise it but in a very clear case." (3 Dallas 175.) The institution of judicial review was not yet clearly established, but its possibilities were being seriously weighed and it needed only a clear case and a persuasive statement to make it a part of the permanent equipment of the government.

affairs was a delicate task. Thomas Jefferson, as Secretary of State, had to struggle to avoid embarrassing involvements, even with France, the former ally of the United States. Referring in 1790 to a possible war between Spain and England, he predicted that France would also become involved. "In that case," he said, "I hope the new world will fatten on the follies of the old. If we can but establish the armed neutrality for ourselves, we must become the carriers for all parties as far as we can raise vessels." [35] On another occasion he wrote that "there will be war enough to insure us great prices for wheat for years to come, and if we are wise we shall become wealthy." [36]

War broke out between England and France in 1793, but the hopes of the United States for peaceful enrichment were speedily dashed. The British government declared subject to seizure the ships of all neutrals trading with the French West Indies. Vessels, cargoes, and seamen were captured by the British in large numbers and impressed into their own service. The United States seemed helpless in the situation, unless it went to war in defense of its commercial interests, and the prospect of success in such a war was not bright. There was much friction between the United States and Great Britain on other grounds. Many of the states during the Revolutionary War had eagerly confiscated or sequestered debts owed by their citizens to subjects of the King. The treaty of peace with Great Britain, signed in 1783, provided that no legal barrier was to stand in the way of the collection of debts owed to British subjects. Most of the Americans had refused to pay, however, and the creditors were unable to use the state courts for bringing suit. Because these debts remained unpaid, the British retained possession of trading posts in the West, which by the treaty they had agreed to surrender, and continued to take from that section of the country large quantities of valuable furs.

The Federalists knew that the United States was not equipped financially or otherwise to participate in another war. As between England and France, furthermore, the sympathies of many of them were deeply linked with England, and they were bitterly hostile to the bloody régime now governing France under the symbol of Liberty, Equality, and Fraternity. The Anti-Federalists, on the other hand, or the Republicans, as they were coming to be called, sympathized predominantly with France. Amid noteworthy debates between Hamilton and Jefferson as to the scope of presidential powers over foreign affairs, Washington, in spite of treaty obligations to

[35] Jefferson, op. cit., VIII, 61.    [36] Ibid., p. 64.

France, issued what was in effect a proclamation of neutrality.    He
sent Chief Justice John Jay to England to work out a treaty dealing
with commercial problems generally, the carrying of contraband, the
debts owed to British subjects, the occupancy of the trading posts in
the West, and other points of friction between the two countries.

The Republicans were opposed originally to the attempt to work
out a treaty with Great Britain.    They were enraged when Jay returned with a treaty which has been called "the most humiliating
compact into which America ever entered." [37]    The British representatives felt that they had the upper hand and they refused to make
any important concessions.    The United States was defeated on almost every important point.    The British, by contrast, secured the
right of free navigation and trading on the Mississippi; an agreement
that the United States would pay all debts due from American citizens
to British creditors; the freedom of all American ports to British
vessels, with a pledge to lay no further restrictions on British commerce; and other privileges which were regarded by many Americans
as deeply humiliating.    By means of the treaty, war with Great
Britain was averted and orderly relationships between the two countries were provided for, even though at the expense of the claims of
the United States.    Little more could be said for the treaty when it
was brought back for the approval of the Senate and of the country.

The publication of the treaty brought a nation-wide storm of protest.    Jay was burned in effigy in town after town.    Hamilton was
stoned in New York when he tried to make a speech on the subject.
President Washington was attacked with almost equal bitterness, but
he presented the treaty to the Senate for action.    Jefferson, who in the
meantime had resigned as Secretary of State, opposed the treaty and
saw the issues working toward a firmer consolidation of the Republican party, of which he was to be the head, while Hamilton issued a
series of public letters [38] defending the treaty both on grounds of policy
and constitutionality.    The Senate approved it after some two weeks
of secret debate.

The treaty was signed by the President on August 12, 1795, but the
controversy over it raged for almost another year.    In March, 1796, a
motion was offered in the House of Representatives to ask the President to lay before the House a copy of the instructions given to John

---

[37] Albert J. Beveridge, *The Life of John Marshall* (4 vols., 1916-1919), II, 114.
[38] "Camillus," *The Works of Alexander Hamilton* (Lodge ed., 9 vols., 1885-1886), IV,
371-524.

Jay when he was sent abroad to make the treaty, together with the correspondence and other documents relative to it.    The motion was supported by the enemies of the treaty and opposed by its friends. Questions were asked as to whether the purpose of the motion was to institute impeachment proceedings, but the proponents declined to give their reasons.    The motion was debated over a period of weeks. Its focus was quickly shifted, however, to the question of the constitutional power of the House of Representatives with reference to the making of treaties.

The making of the treaty threatened the prerogatives of the House of Representatives in at least two respects.    It provided for the regulation of commerce between the United States and Great Britain, for example, whereas the Constitution provided that Congress should have the power to regulate commerce with foreign nations.    The treaty, in this respect and in others, was regarded by some as an unconstitutional usurpation of legislative power.    In the second place, the treaty provided for the ascertainment of pre-Revolutionary debts due from Americans to British subjects and for the payment of those debts by the United States.    The Constitution provided that no payments should be made from the Treasury of the United States except pursuant to appropriations made by law.    If the treaty was binding on all parties, it put the House of Representatives under an obligation to vote appropriations which the members might not be willing to authorize.    Could members of the House be coerced in this matter or had they a right to refuse to pass the necessary legislation, even though their refusal would have the effect of defeating the treaty? The question was extremely important; for, unless some limit to the treaty-making power could be found, it would be possible for the President and the Senate virtually to supplant the authorized form of legislation by Congress wherever a treaty with a foreign power could be agreed upon.    On the other hand, the Constitution clearly gave to the President and the Senate the power to make treaties, and it provided that treaties, along with the Constitution and laws, should be the supreme law of the land.    Failure to carry out a treaty would constitute a violation of public law and public morality.

Madison aligned himself with the enemies of the treaty.    His analysis of the treaty-making power narrowed that power far below the level claimed for it by the Federalists.    If the treaty power alone, he said, could perform any one act for which the authority of Congress was required by the Constitution, it might perform every act for which the authority of that part of the government was required. Congress had the power to regulate trade, to declare war, to raise armies, to levy taxes, to borrow and appropriate money, and to perform other functions.  If by treaty, as paramount to the legislative power, the President and the Senate could regulate trade, they could also declare war, they could raise armies to carry on war, and they could procure money to support armies.  According to the doctrine now maintained, the United States, by means of an alliance with a foreign power, might be driven into a state of war by the President and Senate, contrary both to the sense of the legislature and to the letter and spirit of the Constitution.

He rejected the contention that a treaty was paramount to all other acts of government.  He took the position that, while the President and the Senate had the power of making treaties, Congress was under obligation to exercise its own judgment in the matter of giving sanction and co-operation in instances where the Constitution had given express and specified powers to the legislature.  The House, in its legislative capacity, he said, must exercise its reason.  It must deliberate, for deliberation was implied in legislation.  If the Constitution put the House under obligation to carry all treaties into effect, it would no longer exercise a legislative power.  It would be the mere instrument of the will of another department, and would have no will of its own.[39]

The debate on the constitutional question ranged widely over the subject.  When the House returned to the question before it, that of asking the President to submit copies of instructions, correspondence, and other documents relative to the treaty excepting such as might not properly be disclosed, the resolution was passed by a vote of 62 to 37.[40]

The President responded with a flat refusal in a document which constituted an important precedent.  The nature of foreign negotiations required caution, he said, and their success must often depend on secrecy.  One reason for vesting the power of making treaties in the President and the Senate had been to limit knowledge of negotiations to a small number of people.  It would establish a dangerous precedent to admit a right in the House of Representatives to demand and to have as a matter of course all the papers respecting a negotiation with a foreign power.  The papers asked for could not relate

[39] For Madison's address see *Annals of Congress*, 4th Cong., 1st sess., 487-495.
[40] *Ibid.*, p. 759.

to any purpose under the cognizance of the House of Representatives except that of an impeachment, which was not mentioned in the resolution.    He had never doubted that the power of making treaties was exclusively vested in the President by and with the advice and consent of the Senate, and that every treaty so made and promulgated became the law of the land.    Every House of Representatives, he said, had therefore acquiesced in that interpretation.    He offered what he considered ample evidence to support it.    He concluded:

> As, therefore, it is perfectly clear to my understanding that the assent of the House of Representatives is not necessary to the validity of a treaty; as the treaty with Great Britain exhibits in itself all the objects requiring legislative provision, and on these the papers called for can throw no light; and as it is essential to the new administration of the government that the boundaries fixed by the Constitution between the different departments should be preserved — a just regard to the Constitution and to the duty of my office, under all the circumstances of this case, forbid a compliance with your request.[41]

The Republican members of the House were enraged at the President's blunt refusal of their request.    Madison wrote angrily to James Monroe:

> I have no doubt that the advice, and even the message itself, were contrived in New York, where it was seen that if the rising force of the Republicans was not crushed, it must speedily crush the British party, and that the only hope of success lay in favoring an open rupture with the President.[42]

The House compressed its indignation into a resolution saying that the House of Representatives did not claim any agency in making treaties, but that, when a treaty stipulated regulations on any of the subjects submitted by the Constitution to the power of Congress, it must depend for its execution, as to such stipulations, on a law or laws to be passed by Congress.    It was the constitutional right and duty of the House of Representatives in all such cases to deliberate on the expediency or inexpediency of carrying such a treaty into effect, and to determine and act thereon as in their judgment might be most conducive to the public good.    It was further resolved that it was not necessary to the propriety of any application from the House to the Executive for information which might relate to any consti-

[41] *Ibid.*, pp. 760-762.
[42] *Letters and Other Writings of James Madison, Fourth President of the United States* (4 vols., 1884), II, 97.

tutional functions of the House that the purpose for which such information might be wanted or to which it might be applied should
be stated in the application.[43]

On the whole, the President came off best in the exchange. His
language may have been more abrupt than was necessary, but he
established the precedent of withholding from Congress information
which he recognized no constitutional obligation to give.

Legislation in support of the Jay Treaty was reluctantly enacted,[44]
but its enforcement did not settle the constitutional question as to the
power of the House of Representatives with reference to the making
of treaties. Debate on that question continued down through the
years. It came to be recognized that, whatever the moral obligation
involved, Congress was under no constitutional obligation to enact
legislation in support of treaties already made, or to avoid the enactment of legislation in conflict with such treaties. Purely legislative
powers were exercised through the process of making treaties, but the
fears of Madison and others that Congress might be superseded by
the President and the Senate were justified only to a limited extent.
In 1920, the Supreme Court held that a treaty based on the authority
of the United States might give constitutional support to an act of
Congress regulating the killing of transient wild birds, even though
a statute without the benefit of such a treaty might be unconstitutional as an infringement of the powers of the states.[45] That decision
opened the way to an expansion of legislation through the making
of treaties should the government see fit to use it.

## WARE v. HYLTON

The outcome of the struggle in 1795 and 1796 over the Jay Treaty
was pro-federal, pro-Executive, and pro-Federalist. In the latter year
the Supreme Court handed down a decision as to the scope of the
treaty-making power, which in the minds of the people aligned the
Court with the Federalists in Congress as proponents of a strong central government. The case involved an attempt to collect debts incurred by Virginians to creditors in England prior to the Revolutionary War. During the war the legislature of Virginia had passed
an act sequestering British property and providing that debts to
British subjects should be discharged by the payment of the money

---

[43] *Annals of Congress,* 4th Cong., 1st sess., 771-772, 782-783.
[44] McMaster, *op. cit.,* II, 280-281; *Annals of Congress,* 4th Cong., 1st sess., 1291.
[45] Missouri *v.* Holland, 252 U.S. 416 (1920).

due into the loan office of Virginia.   Under this statute large sums were turned over to the state.   The treaty of peace with Great Britain provided that creditors on either side should meet with no legal impediment to the recovery of the full value of bona-fide debts previously contracted.   The treaty seemed to restore the rights of British creditors which had been impaired by the Virginia war measure.

During the period of the Articles of Confederation, the creditors were unable to secure any satisfaction in the state courts, the only courts available for litigation of this kind.   The Constitution adopted in 1789, however, declared that treaties, along with the Constitution and statutes, should be the supreme law of the land, and provided for the establishment of a system of federal courts with jurisdiction in controversies of this and of many other kinds.   As soon as the courts were established, a number of suits by British creditors were immediately instituted.

Ware *v.* Hylton [46] was a test case brought in the United States circuit court in Virginia.   Prominent among counsel for the debtors was Patrick Henry, from the beginning a bitter opponent of the Constitution.   Associated with him, oddly enough, was John Marshall, who in later years derived fame, not from arguments such as those urged in this case in behalf of state rights, but from his strong defense of nationalism as Chief Justice of the United States.

The lower court divided on the issue, and the case was appealed to the Supreme Court.   In that Court, Justice Iredell, one of the five justices then sitting, merely recorded the opinion in behalf of the Virginia debtors which he had delivered in the circuit court.   The other four, each of whom wrote an opinion, agreed that Virginia had had the right to sequester British property during the war, but held that the treaty of 1783 was paramount to the Virginia sequestering act and that British subjects, therefore, had a right to recover the debt from the original debtors, even though equivalent amounts had been paid by the debtors to the state of Virginia.   The four justices recognized the moral obligation of Virginia to reimburse the debtors, but under their decision the obligation of the debtors to the British creditors was legal and binding, whether or not the state reimbursed them.

This decision in favor of British creditors, handed down at the time of the controversy over the unpopular Jay Treaty with Great Britain, deepened the bitterness of debtors and anti-English and pro-

[46] 3 Dallas 199  (1796).

French groups in the United States toward the Federalists, who seemed to dominate the central government, including even the Supreme Court. Apart from the controversies of the hour, however, the decision established an important precedent in demonstrating the subordination of state laws to treaties made by the United States.

# CHAPTER 5

# FEDERAL TURMOIL

FEDERALIST LEADERS in all branches of the government took advantage of the vagueness of constitutional terminology to extend federal powers over the states and over the rights of individuals. States and individuals, in turn, used the same vagueness of terminology to demonstrate the absence of federal authority over them. In spite of some improvement in business conditions, the years between 1789 and 1801 constituted a period of turmoil, and of resistance to the process by which the states were being knitted into a single sovereign unit. Most of the constitutional controversies involved the growing rift between Federalists and Republicans. As the Federalists sought to broaden the scope of federal activities, Republicans developed state-rights doctrines to combat the program of expansion.

## PRIVATE COLLECTION OF DEBTS FROM STATES

Even though the federal government relieved the states of their Revolutionary War debts, thereby insuring that these debts would be paid, some states demonstrated low ethical standards concerning the fulfillment of other obligations. They resisted particularly the efforts of British subjects to collect debts declared valid by the Jay Treaty, and showed a general lack of interest in fulfilling obligations to citizens of other states.

The states protected themselves in part by refusing to be sued in their own courts. The only way to get access to them was through a federal court. Under the Constitution and the Judiciary Act the Supreme Court was the only federal court that could possibly have jurisdiction in a suit against a state by a citizen of another state or by a citizen or subject of a foreign state. The Constitution extended federal judicial power to cases and controversies between a state and a citizen of another state, and between a state and a citizen or subject of a foreign state. It provided also that the Supreme Court should have original jurisdiction in suits to which a state was a party. No one doubted that a state could bring such a suit, but many people contended that the Constitution did not impair the sovereignty of the states to the extent of permitting individuals to sue them without their consent.

Before the adoption of the federal Constitution, Hamilton, Madison, and John Marshall all seem to have expressed the opinion that the Constitution did not authorize suits against a state by a private individual without the consent of the state.[1] The language of the Constitution did not necessarily carry this restriction, and soon after the federal judiciary was organized a number of suits of the kind were instituted against particular states. The suits offended the dignity of the states and provoked great indignation, which was heightened, no doubt, by the fact that in some instances the debts involved were owed to British creditors.

Executors of a British creditor brought one such suit in the Supreme Court against the state of Georgia in a case known as Chisholm v. Georgia.[2] The state sent a written protest denying the jurisdiction of the Court, and refused to argue the merits of the case. Edmund Randolph, not as Attorney General but in his private capacity, appeared for the plaintiff. After Randolph had delivered his argument, the Court obligingly expressed a willingness to hear any member of the bar who might care to speak in opposition, but no volunteers appeared.[3] Five justices wrote opinions. Only Justice Iredell thought that a state could not be sued in a federal court without its consent. The other four decided against the Georgia contention, clearing the way for such suits against states as citizens of other states might see fit to bring. The lower house of the Georgia legislature reflected the rage of that state when it passed a bill providing that any federal marshal or other person who executed any process issued in this case should be declared guilty of felony and should suffer death, "without benefit of clergy," by being hanged.[4] Similar hostility to the decision was expressed throughout the country, and influential persons and state legislatures called for a constitutional amendment to eliminate the effects of the decision. As a result, Congress proposed, and the states ratified, the Eleventh Amendment, pro-

[1] See Andrew C. McLaughlin, *Constitutional History of the United States* (1935), p. 301, note 4.
[2] 2 Dallas 419 (1793).
[3] Charles Warren, *Supreme Court in United States History* (rev. ed., 2 vols., 1926), I, 95.
[4] *Ibid.*, p. 100.

viding that "The judicial power of the United States shall not be construed to extend to any suit in law or equity, commenced or prosecuted against one of the United States by citizens of another state, or by citizens or subjects of any foreign state."

Attempts were made by subterfuge in later years to secure access to the federal courts for suits against states. Since it was still possible for one state to sue another, six creditors of the state of Louisiana who were citizens of New Hampshire assigned debts to New Hampshire, evidently to have that state make the collection for them. The Court held that New Hampshire was not a real party to the suit, and that the Court, therefore, did not have jurisdiction.[5] In another instance, however, the owners of certain bonds issued by North Carolina, which were in default, donated the bonds to South Dakota. South Dakota brought suit in the Supreme Court to collect on the bonds. The Court decided in its favor, holding that in this case the state was the real party, and was therefore entitled to sue.[6] On the whole, the losses resulting from inability of individuals to sue states have not been great. Whether on grounds of improved ethical standards or of business expediency, the states have usually fulfilled their clear obligations. The elimination of friction may well have justified enactment of the constitutional amendment.

ALIEN AND SEDITION ACTS

The four measures known as the Alien and Sedition Acts, which were passed by Congress in June and July, 1798, had their background in the strife between the Federalists and the Republicans, and in the conflict between a group of vociferous sympathizers with France and a group of equally vociferous sympathizers with Great Britain. The French government had been irritated by the Jay Treaty between the United States and Great Britain. For that and other reasons the two countries drifted rapidly toward a state of war. The publication of the famous X Y Z papers, disclosing the treatment of American representatives in Paris and the bullying and high-handed attitude of French diplomats toward the United States, served temporarily to unify the American people and to give support to war preparations. The Federalist leaders in Congress, having for once almost a free hand because of this sentiment, brought about the enactment of measures to increase taxes, and to lay direct taxes on

---

[5] New Hampshire v. Louisiana, 108 U.S. 76 (1883).

[6] South Dakota v. North Carolina, 192 U.S. 286 (1904).

houses, lands, and slaves, and other financial measures, including authorization to borrow money for the emergency. Congress also provided for building up the navy and for the creation of a Navy Department.

Unfortunately the Federalist leaders did not stop with measures of this kind. For many years they had writhed under the venomous criticism of the Republican minority in Congress and the castigations of the Republican press. They had resented the efforts of French propagandists to embroil the United States with England. Some of them had been hostile to the heavy inflow of Irish immigrants, enemies and critics of England, who were aligning themselves with the developing Republican party. The crisis in the form of a probable war with France seemed to the Federalists to provide an excuse and the occasion for rough treatment of their several enemies.

The first of the restrictive measures to be passed was an amendment to the Naturalization Act.[7] It provided that the minimum period of years which must be spent in the United States before citizenship could be conferred should be extended from five years to fourteen years. It provided in addition for the registration both of aliens already in the United States and of those who might subsequently arrive. The attitude of some of the Federalist leaders is indicated by provisions proposed, but not included, in the bill as passed. Robert Goodloe Harper, then of South Carolina and later of Maryland, urged that the time had come to declare that nothing but birth should entitle a man to citizenship in this country.

> He thought this was the proper season for making the declaration. He believed that the United States had experience enough to cure them of the folly of believing that the strength and happiness of the country would be promoted by admitting to the rights of citizenship all the congregations of people who resort to these shores from every part of the world.[8]

Harrison Gray Otis, of Massachusetts, offered a resolution to the effect that no person who was born an alien and who had not yet become a citizen of the United States should hereafter be capable of holding any office of honor, trust, or profit under the United States. The Otis resolution failed of adoption. It is not clear whether the reason for its failure lay in opposition to its provisions or in the belief that it was unconstitutional, since arguments were made that a con-

[7] 1 Stat. 566.    [8] *Annals of Congress,* 5th Cong., 2d sess., 1567-1568.

stitutional amendment was the only proper means for enacting provisions of this kind.[9]  The requirement of fourteen years of residence, however, reflected the sentiments of a majority of the members of Congress.  It became effective, and remained so until the five-year provision was restored in 1802.[10]  The second statute in the group, known as "An act concerning aliens," [11] authorized the President to order the departure of all aliens whom he should judge dangerous to the peace and safety of the United States.  Aliens convicted of disobedience of such orders were to be imprisoned for a term of not exceeding three years and barred thereafter from acquiring citizenship. The only recourse of the alien ordered out of the country was to attempt to prove to the satisfaction of the President that no injury or danger to the United States would arise from his continuing in residence.  If convinced, the President might then grant him a license to remain.  The President might, as a condition of allowing him to remain, require him to give bond for good behavior.  Aliens ordered out of the country were given the right to remove or dispose of their property, but even so, the discretionary power of the President to interfere with their rights and liberties was sweeping.  His judgment alone, or his whim, or the judgment or whim of the person whom he chose to carry out the provisions of the act, would determine the fate of all aliens residing in the United States.  In view of the bitter prejudices of the Federalists against certain alien groups, it was a reasonable assumption on the part of the Republicans that gross discrimination would result.  Perhaps because of the intense criticism directed against it, little attempt was made to enforce the act, although its mere existence no doubt had a restraining effect upon the conduct of aliens in the United States.  The act was limited to two years, and was not renewed.

The third measure was entitled "An act respecting alien enemies." [12] It provided that, when the President issued a proclamation of the existence of war with any foreign nation, "all natives, citizens, denizens, or subjects of the hostile nation or government, being males of the age of fourteen years and upwards, who shall be within the United States, and not actually naturalized, shall be liable to be apprehended, restrained, secured and removed, as alien enemies."  The President was empowered to issue rules and regulations governing the disposition of such aliens.  This statute was generally regarded as less sweeping in its invasion of private rights than were the others.  It contained

[9] *Ibid.*, pp. 1570-1571.     [10] 2 Stat. 153.     [11] 1 Stat. 570.     [12] 1 Stat. 577.

no limit as to time, and was not thereafter repealed. It remained in effect, and constituted the basis of regulations concerning alien enemies which were issued during the first World War, more than a century after its enactment.[13]

The fourth and most drastic of the measures was called "An act in addition to the act, entitled 'An act for the punishment of certain crimes against the United States.' "[14] It was known familiarly, however, by the more adequately descriptive title of "The Sedition Act." It was introduced in the Senate by James Lloyd, of Maryland. As introduced, it contained drastic provisions which did not survive. One section was said to have declared that every Frenchman was an enemy to the United States, and that to give him aid or comfort was treason, punishable with death. Another provided that any person who justified France or defamed the government of the United States should suffer punishment by imprisonment or fine.[15] Such provisions were too drastic for the more far-sighted of the Federalist leaders. Alexander Hamilton feared that some of them might result in civil war. "Let us not establish a tyranny," he said. "Energy is a very different thing from violence. If we make no false step, we shall be essentially united, but if we push things to an extreme, we shall then give to faction *body* and solidity."[16]

The bill passed the Senate after it had been shorn of the specific references to France and certain other drastic provisions. Its sponsors in the House of Representatives justified the measure by pointing to current utterances of the press denouncing the handling of the foreign policy of the United States and attacking the alien bill. The *Aurora*, a Republican paper published in Philadelphia, had been a particularly vigorous critic. Quotations from the pages of the *Aurora* were utilized to demonstrate the necessity for a sedition act. Said one advocate of the sedition measure:

> The gentleman (Mr. Livingston) makes his proclamation of war on the government in the House on Monday, and this infamous printer (Bache) follows it up with the tocsin of insurrection on Tuesday. While this bill was under consideration in the Senate, an attempt is made to render it odious among the people. "Is there any alternative," says this printer, "between an abandonment of the Con-

---

[13] See chapter 26.          [14] 1 Stat. 596.

[15] John B. McMaster, *History of the People of the United States* (8 vols., 1883-1913), II, 389.

[16] Hamilton letter to Oliver Wolcott, June 29, 1798, in *The Works of Alexander Hamilton* (Lodge ed., 1886), VIII, 491.

stitution and resistance?" He declares what is unconstitutional and then invites the people to "resistance." This is an awful, horrible example of "the liberty of opinion and freedom of the press." Can gentlemen hear these things and lie quietly on their pillows? Are we to see all these acts practiced against the repose of our country, and remain passive? Are we bound hand and foot that we must be witnesses of these deadly thrusts at our liberty? Are we to be the unresisting spectators of these exertions to destroy all that we hold dear? Are these approaches to revolution and Jacobinic dominations to be observed with the eye of meek submission? No, sir, they are indeed terrible; they are calculated to freeze the very blood in our veins. Such liberty of the press and of opinion is calculated to destroy all confidence between man and man; it leads to a dissolution of every bond of union; it cuts asunder every ligament that unites man to his family, man to his neighbor, man to society, and to government. God deliver us from such liberty, the liberty of vomiting on the public floods of falsehood and hatred to everything sacred, human and divine! If any gentleman doubts the effects of such a liberty, let me direct his attention across the water; it has there made slaves of thirty millions of men.[17]

The measure passed both houses in spite of strenuous Republican opposition, although the majority in the House of Representatives was small. As passed, it provided punishment for attempting in any of a variety of ways to prevent the enforcement of the laws of the United States. The second section provided punishment for making false, scandalous, and malicious statements against the government of the United States, or either house of Congress or the President, with intent to defame them or bring them into contempt or disrepute, or to stir up the hatred of the people against them or bring about sedition in any of its various forms. Persons prosecuted under the act were allowed to plead the truth in their own defense, but truth was oftentimes hard to discover. The press would indeed be muzzled if it could make no statement or implication other than those which it could prove in a court of law. The act, if it were enforced to the fullness of its provisions, was broad enough to bar virtually all criticism of any agency of the federal government.

### THE VIRGINIA AND KENTUCKY RESOLUTIONS

The Alien and Sedition Acts enraged Republicans all over the country, as well they might, for they were directed primarily at Re-

---

[17] *Annals of Congress*, 5th Cong., 2d sess., 2098.

publicans and sympathizers with France. Republican leaders saw in them, however, not merely a menace to their freedom to criticize Federalist administration, but also a point of vulnerability in the Federalist armor. They believed that the Federalists had gone too far. Jefferson, Madison, and others took full advantage of their opportunity. Jefferson was then Vice-President of the United States — having received but three electoral votes less than the total received by John Adams, who became President. Because of the office, he felt himself restrained from campaigning openly against Federalist measures and policies. Secretly, however, he led a campaign of attack against the sponsors of the Alien and Sedition Acts and aided in the phrasing of significant doctrines in opposition to the further centralization of power in the federal government. Unknown to the public, he prepared the first draft of the so-called Kentucky Resolutions [18] which were adopted by the Kentucky legislature, November 16, 1798. Madison prepared somewhat similar resolutions, which were adopted by the Virginia legislature on December 24, 1798.[19] Similar sentiments were expressed again by the Kentucky legislature approximately a year later in another set of resolutions.[20] The Virginia Resolutions opened with the statement that the general assembly of Virginia was firmly resolved to maintain and defend the Constitution of the United States and the constitution of the state against every aggression, either foreign or domestic. The assembly found that the powers of the federal government resulted from a compact to which the states were parties. The states, it said, had the right to interpose in a case of a deliberate, palpable, and dangerous exercise of powers not granted by the compact. It declared the powers provided for in the Alien and Sedition Acts to be palpable and alarming infractions of the Constitution, and subversive of the general principles of free government.

The Kentucky Resolutions likewise declared that the several states were united by compact. The federal government, they said, was not made the exclusive or final judge of the extent of the powers delegated to itself. On the other hand, each party had an equal right to judge for itself as well of infraction as of mode and measure of redress. The Resolutions argued at length the question of constitutionality, enumerating the powers over crimes given in the Con-

---

[18] Jonathan Elliot (ed.), *Debates in the Several State Conventions on the Adoption of the Federal Constitution* (5 vols., 1836-1845), IV, 540 ff.

[19] *Ibid.*, p. 528.          [20] *Ibid.*, p. 544.

stitution and arguing that the omission of statements as to other similar powers was to be interpreted as meaning that the Constitution did not intend to give them. Since the Constitution gave no specific authority to exercise many of the powers provided for in the Alien and Sedition Acts, they took the position that the federal government could not constitutionally exercise such powers.

The legislatures of Virginia and Kentucky sought to secure the concurrence of the legislatures of other states in the several resolutions. A number of legislatures in the northern states which were dominated by Federalists pointedly rejected the doctrines expressed. Legislatures in the southern states, which might have been expected to be more in sympathy with the resolutions, took no positive action.[21] In terms of doctrine, the resolutions were important because of the assertion of the powers of the states to check encroachment by the federal government. Jefferson and Madison seem to have had nothing in mind as concrete as the nullification doctrines of Calhoun a third of a century later, but they planted the seeds from which the later nullification doctrines grew. The importance of the resolutions was not limited to the statement of doctrine, however. They were a part of the propaganda of the growing Republican party against Federalist domination. The propaganda, together with other factors, brought about the overthrow of the Federalists in the election of 1800, and the entrenchment of Republican leaders in federal office. Large numbers of petitions were submitted to Congress protesting against the Alien and Sedition Acts and urging their repeal. Concerted but unsuccessful efforts were made to secure the repeal of the two measures, but they continued in force until 1800 and 1801, when the Alien Act and the Sedition Act, respectively, expired by their own provisions. The controversy, however, aided in drawing public attention to the measures and added to their unpopularity.

## ENFORCEMENT OF THE SEDITION ACT

Critics of the administration accepted the drastic provisions of the Sedition Act as a challenge. In newspapers, pamphlets, and placards they poured out defiant criticism. Federalist leaders collected evidence of violations to secure convictions in the federal courts. The

[21] For discussion see Frank Maloy Anderson, "Contemporary Opinion of the Virginia and Kentucky Resolutions," *American Historical Review*, V (October, 1899 — July, 1900), 45-63, 225-252; Ethelbert Dudley Warfield, *The Kentucky Resolutions of 1798* (1894); and Herman V. Ames, *State Documents on Federal Relations: The States and the United States* (1907), No. 1, pp. 16 ff.

judges themselves participated with varying degrees of enthusiasm in the campaign to weed out sedition. It should be noted that the work of federal judges had importance beyond the mere handling of cases over which they had jurisdiction. Most or all of the judges were firm believers in the federal system, and they were in a sense missionaries of that system, who carried the gospel of federalism to people otherwise largely ignorant of the system of federal laws. In the minds of most of the judges, patriotism, loyalty to the federal government, and obedience to the Federalist leaders of the country were inextricably intertwined. Their charges to grand juries consisted, not merely of exposition of the laws, but of the principles of the Federalist party as well. By their Republican opponents, therefore, they were accused of delivering political harangues throughout the country.[22] A number of the judges called for diligent enforcement of the Sedition Act; and, under Justice Samuel Chase, of Maryland, a member of the Supreme Court who handled a number of sedition cases in the United States circuit courts, procedure was grossly unfair. In most instances, the method of selecting jurors was such that Federalists were called to serve in the trials of offenders who were for the most part Republicans.

Jefferson had suggested that one of the purposes of the sponsors of the Sedition Act was to reach Albert Gallatin, the powerful critic of the Federalists in the House of Representatives. But under the Constitution, a man could not be prosecuted for his utterances on the floor of the House; and Gallatin seems to have been discreet elsewhere. Matthew Lyon, however, spoke freely outside the House. He had charged President Adams with continually grasping for power and having an unbounded thirst for ridiculous pomp, foolish adulation, and selfish avarice. He brought about the publication of a letter from another man which referred to "the bullying speech of your President, and stupid answer of your Senate." "We wondered," said the letter, "that the answer of both houses had not been an order to send him to a madhouse. Instead of this the Senate have echoed the speech with more servility than ever George III experienced from either House of Parliament."[23] Lyon was indicted for sedition, and was convicted. Said Justice Paterson:

> As a member of the federal legislature you must be well acquainted
> with the mischiefs which flow from an unlicensed abuse of govern-

[22] See Warren, *op. cit.,* I, 165 ff.
[23] Francis Wharton, *State Trials of the United States during the Administrations of Washington and Adams* (1849), pp. 333-334.

ment and of the motives which led to the passage of the act under which this indictment is framed. No one, also, can be better acquainted than yourself with the existence and nature of the act. Your position, so far from making the case one which might slip with a nominal fine through the hands of the Court, would make impunity conspicuous should such a fine alone be imposed.[24]

Lyon was therefore imprisoned for four months and fined one thousand dollars. He was handled in a contemptuous and brutal manner and thrown into a filthy jail.

The experience made a martyr of him in the eyes of his constituents and of Republicans throughout the country, and they rallied to his support. He was re-elected to Congress while in jail, and Republican friends raised the amount of his fine. He returned to Philadelphia in triumph to resume his seat in the House of Representatives.

On Lyon's return, Representative James A. Bayard, of New Jersey, introduced a resolution that he be expelled from the House — he

having been convicted of being a notorious and seditious person, and of a depraved mind, and wicked and diabolical disposition, and of wickedly, deceitfully, and maliciously, contriving to defame the government of the United States, and having with intent and design to defame the government of the United States, and John Adams, the President of the United States, and to bring the said government and President into contempt and disrepute, and with intent and design to excite against the said government and President the hatred of the good people of the United States, and to stir up sedition in the United States, wickedly, knowingly, and maliciously written and published certain scandalous and seditious writings or libels.[25]

John Nicholas, of Virginia, and Albert Gallatin spoke in Lyon's defense. Forty-nine persons voted for the resolution and forty-five against it. Since a majority of two-thirds was necessary in order to expel a member, however, Lyon was permitted to retain his seat.

For a violent attack on President Adams and his administration James Compton Callender was brought to trial in the United States circuit court in Virginia under Justice Samuel Chase. The justice abused counsel for Callender and intimidated witnesses in a scandalous manner, and Callender was convicted.[26] In many other cases the judges or Federalist officials demonstrated a zeal for persecution

---

24 *Ibid.*, p. 337.        25 *Annals of Congress,* 5th Cong., 3d sess., 2959.
26 Albert J. Beveridge, *Life of John Marshall* (4 vols., 1916-1919), III, 36 ff.

of Republicans under the Sedition Act which added to the hatred felt for them by Republicans throughout the country.[27]

Part of the constitutional significance of the enactment and enforcement of the Alien and Sedition Acts lay in the fact that the unpopularity of the measures contributed to the overthrow of the party in power and to the installation of another party with somewhat different principles and aspirations. The Sedition Act had further significance in that, because of its invasion of freedom of speech and freedom of the press, it came to be regarded as a gross abuse of constitutional rights. Yet, in stirring up hostility against the enforcement of such a measure, it probably helped to preserve civil liberties during the years ahead. It should also be remembered, however, that unanimity of sentiment against such legislation is apt to prevail in times of comparative peace when there is no fundamental cleavage within the political order. During the Civil War the government found ways of dealing with seditious activities without the adoption of a new Sedition Act. During the first World War, a Sedition Act was adopted which was in some respects more far-reaching than that of 1798. It was enforced with more decorum than the act of 1798, but with a high degree of ruthlessness.[28] In the face of possible involvement in another war, Congress, in 1940, enacted another measure which gave broad powers for the curtailment of freedom of speech and of the press.[29] The enactment of this measure attracted no attention comparable to that received by the Sedition Act of 1798.

[27] For the most important cases see Beveridge, *op. cit.* For others of lesser importance see Frank Maloy Anderson, "The Enforcement of the Alien and Sedition Laws," *Annual Report of the American Historical Association* (1912), pp. 115 ff.

[28] For discussion see Carl Brent Swisher, "Civil Liberties in War Time," *Political Science Quarterly*, LV (September, 1940), 321-347.

[29] 54 Stat. 670.

# CHAPTER 6

# GROWTH OF FEDERAL JUDICIAL POWER

THE SUPREME COURT OF THE UNITED STATES was slow in acquiring prestige. During the first decade of its life it heard relatively few cases, most of these being of no great general importance. John Jay, the first Chief Justice, was better known for his diplomatic achievements than for his work as a jurist. He resigned in 1795 to accept the governorship of New York. John Rutledge, of South Carolina, was nominated as Jay's successor at a time when the Senate was not in session. Four months after he had taken his seat, the Senate refused confirmation. Oliver Ellsworth, of Connecticut, was then appointed. He served until September 30, 1800, when he resigned. Although he had participated so effectively in the enactment of the Judiciary Act as to be regarded as the author of that measure, he likewise brought no great distinction to the office of Chief Justice or to the Supreme Court in general.

## THE FIRST DECADE

The failure of the Court to achieve immediate distinction was due, not merely to the infrequency of important judicial controversies and to the judicial qualifications of the Chief Justices and other personnel, but also to the manner in which the decisions of the Court were announced. In deciding important cases it was customary that each judge write an opinion. This procedure inevitably blurred the lines of decision. It is seldom that two judges arrive at the same decision through identical lines of reasoning. Even when the lines of reasoning are much the same, the modes of expression are apt to be strikingly different. The fact that no single judge was given responsibility for writing the opinion of the Court as a whole deprived the public of the illusion of unity in the interpretation of law, which is created when the Court accepts the opinion of a single spokesman. The public learned of the decisions of the Court, therefore, but it was treated with opinions only of individual judges. The consequent obscurity of official reasoning through as many opinions as there were judges was eliminated only when John Marshall, of Virginia, appointed Chief Justice shortly before the retirement of President John Adams, took upon himself the task of writing most of the important opinions of the Court. Marshall initiated the change himself without the aid of any change in statute or any formal rule of the Court. It did not mean that his brethren were necessarily silent in all cases, but, except on the infrequent occasions in which the writing of important opinions was formally assigned to them, their opinions stood in the subordinate position of concurring opinions or of dissent. The voice of the Court, usually the voice of Marshall himself, was heard through the official opinion. It was to the efforts of Marshall, over a period of more than a third of a century, that the establishment of the prestige of the highest tribunal in the land was largely due.

One reason for the resignation of Chief Justice Jay and for his refusal to accept the position again when it was offered to him in 1800 was the requirement that Supreme Court justices travel throughout the country for work in the circuit courts. Other men found positions on the Court unattractive for the same reason. The transportation difficulties alone were discouraging. The work on circuit, furthermore, required a knowledge of local law which few men could be expected to possess. The circuit-riding requirement was criticized from the very beginning, and periodic attempts were made to do away with it during the entire century in which it was in operation. Criticism was levied, not merely in terms of the excessive burden laid upon members of the Supreme Court, but also on the ground that these judges should have time to remain at the capital of the country and add to their knowledge of federal jurisprudence. The opposing argument was that many of the cases appealed to the Supreme Court arose out of local law and that a knowledge of such law could be acquired most effectively through participation in the work of the lower courts.

Early in 1801 the circuit-riding requirement was temporarily abolished. Congress passed an act [1] limiting the duties of Supreme Court justices to the single tribunal. The membership was to be reduced to five when the next vacancy occurred. The work of the circuit courts was to be performed by duly appointed circuit judges. Had

[1] 2 Stat. 89.

the new arrangement not become entangled with party politics, it might have survived.   The movement for change initially was not a conscious partisan movement, but rather was an attempt to promote the efficient operation of the federal judiciary.   When in the early months of 1801 the proposed measure came up for final consideration, however, the elections of 1800 had sounded the death knell of the Federalist party.   The judiciary, on the other hand, filled with men appointed for life, was a Federalist stronghold.   Over Republican opposition, the lame-duck Federalist Congress was able to create sixteen circuit judgeships, to which President Adams promptly appointed sixteen Federalist politicians.

Republican leaders were enraged at this use of the judiciary to take care of politically discredited Federalists.   Many of them were opposed generally to the strengthening of the judiciary, furthermore, because of the bias against Republican dissent displayed in the conduct of many cases.   The Jeffersonians regarded their own accession to power as a revolution which was incomplete to the extent to which the federal judiciary was permitted to stand in their way.   In a number of instances early in Jefferson's administration, federal judges, including some of those recently appointed by President Adams, showed a clear disposition to interfere with the new administration.

Republicans in Congress countered by sponsoring a measure to repeal the act providing for the new federal judgeships.   The remaining Federalists in Congress argued that the sixteen judges recently appointed could not constitutionally be deprived of their offices through a repeal of the statute.   Article III, Section 1, of the Constitution provided that "the judges, both of the Supreme and inferior courts, shall hold their offices during good behavior, and shall, at stated times, receive for their services a compensation which shall not be diminished during their continuance in office."   The Federalists contended that the judges could be removed against their will only by impeachment.

The Constitution did not direct the establishment of any particular federal court except the Supreme Court, and it did not prohibit the abolition of any court which Congress might see fit to establish.   The Republicans approached the subject, therefore, from the point of view of the tribunals — that is, of the circuit courts established by the act of 1801 — and not from the point of view of the offices of particular judges.   They passed the measure abolishing the newly established circuit courts and returning the Supreme Court justices to circuit duty without making any provision for the judges who had been disestablished.[2]

Knowing that a serious question of constitutionality was involved, the Republicans brought about the enactment of another measure to prevent or postpone consideration of the question by the Supreme Court. The new measure provided that the Supreme Court should henceforth conduct only one term of court annually, and put off for a period of fourteen months the first ensuing session.[3] Within that period the Supreme Court justices returned to their circuit work. Although an attempt was made to secure a Supreme Court decision on the constitutionality of the repealing act, the Court avoided the question.[4] It was probably fortunate for the judiciary that the controversy was permitted to die down. Power for the time being was in the hands of the administration rather than those of the Court.

Having eliminated the newly appointed judges, the Jefferson administration moved next against those long in office. It brought about the impeachment of a federal district judge, John Pickering, who had been guilty of gross misconduct in court, evidently as a result of insanity. Conviction was secured in spite of the fact that insanity was not listed along with high crimes and misdemeanors for which an official might be impeached. The next step was one of the most dramatic controversies in American history, the impeachment trial of Samuel Chase, a member of the Supreme Court, for his mode of handling sedition cases and other cases on circuit. The prolonged battle in the Senate ended in acquittal by a narrow margin. The result blasted the hopes of those Republicans who contemplated sweeping Federalists from the judiciary.

## MARBURY v. MADISON

It was in the midst of the series of conflicts between the Jefferson administration and the judiciary that the case of Marbury v. Madison arose and was decided. The case, indeed, which may be regarded the first of outstanding permanent importance to be decided by the Supreme Court, was a part of that conflict. The attention which it received in contemporary discussion was in terms of the strife between the administration and the judiciary rather than in terms of the doctrine announced in the case, namely, that the Court had the power to declare acts of Congress null and void when in conflict with the Constitution.

[2] 2 Stat. 132.          [3] 2 Stat. 156.          [4] Stuart v. Laird, 1 Cranch 299 (1803).

The statute involved was an act concerning the government of the District of Columbia.[5]  The act provided that the President should appoint such number of discreet persons to be justices of the peace as he should think expedient.  They were to continue in office for five years, and their compensation was to be in the form of fees.  The act was passed on February 27, 1801.  The President, who was to retire from office a week later, immediately appointed forty-two justices of the peace, and the appointments were immediately confirmed by the Federalist Senate.  The commissions were made out and signed by the President and returned to the Department of State for delivery to the persons appointed.  That department was in charge of John Marshall, who, although he had already been appointed to the position of Chief Justice, continued as Acting Secretary of State until the end of the Adams administration.  In the transition from one administration to another, the State Department failed to deliver some of the commissions.  When President Jefferson took office, he ordered commissions sent to some of the persons appointed, but withheld others, clearly regarding the appointment of such a large number of justices of the peace as an effort of his predecessor to do political favors for Federalists.[6]

The offices involved were relatively unimportant.  They were temporary, and the fees were small.  Had it not been for the conflict already raging between the administration and the judiciary, history would have made no record of the failure to deliver the commissions.  Under the circumstances, however, four of the would-be justices of the peace petitioned the Supreme Court for a writ of mandamus to compel the Secretary of State, now James Madison, to deliver their commissions.  The application was made in December, 1801.  Chief Justice Marshall issued a rule to Madison, ordering him to show cause at the next term of the Supreme Court why the writ of mandamus should not issue against him.  At the term of Congress then in session the act was passed postponing the next term of the Supreme Court, so that it was not until February, 1803, that the Court again convened.

The essential facts as to the commissions were known to a number of persons intimately connected with the litigation, including Attorney General Lincoln and Chief Justice Marshall.  Difficulties were

[5] 2 Stat. 103.
[6] For the underlying story and for an account of the case in the Supreme Court see Charles Warren, *The Supreme Court in United States History* (rev. ed., 2 vols., 1926), I, chapter II. and Albert J. Beveridge, *The Life of John Marshall* (4 vols., 1916-1919), III, chapter III.

incurred, however, in getting the facts into the legal record. Madison proved unco-operative. The recollection of the Attorney General was conveniently faulty. John Marshall was now a member of the deciding tribunal, rather than a witness in the case. The Senate refused to certify that it had participated in the appointment.[7] Madison disregarded the order of the Court that he show cause why the writ of mandamus should not issue. Through affidavits, however, and through the unwilling testimony of subordinate officials in the State Department and other persons who were summoned, enough legal evidence was secured to establish the facts to the satisfaction of the Supreme Court. It was believed that the Court would order Madison to deliver the commissions. It was likewise believed that Madison, taking orders from Jefferson in the matter, would refuse. The prestige of the Supreme Court faced a gloomy prospect. At the very least, it would suffer from such an impasse. The expected decision might very probably result in the impeachment of Chief Justice Marshall and perhaps other members of the Court. If, on the other hand, the Court failed to issue the order, the result would have the appearance of a Republican victory. Marshall refused to be impaled on either horn of the dilemma. In his opinion in Marbury v. Madison[8] he put Jefferson in the wrong, and then, by a gesture which appeared to be one of self-restraint, he held that the powers of the Supreme Court were so limited by the Constitution that a writ of mandamus could not issue from the Court in the exercise of its original jurisdiction.

Since the opinion of the Court was written by Chief Justice Marshall, with no dissenting or concurring opinions, the Court stood as a unit, or appeared to do so. The Chief Justice approached the decision by asking three questions. First, had the applicant a right to the commission? Second, if he had a right and that right had been violated, did the laws of his country afford him a remedy? Third, if they did afford him a remedy, was it a mandamus issuing from the Supreme Court?[9]

In answer to the first question, the Court came to the conclusion that the appointment was made when a commission had been signed by the President, and that the commission was complete when the seal of the United States had been affixed to it by the Secretary of State. In the case of officers not removable by the President, the

---

[7] See *Annals of Congress*, 7th Cong., 2d sess., 37.
[8] 1 Cranch 137 (1803).          [9] *Ibid.*, p. 154.

right to the office was then in the person appointed, and he had the absolute unconditional power of accepting or rejecting it.  Since these steps had been taken with reference to the appointment of Marbury, to withhold his commission was "an act deemed by the Court not warranted by law, but violative of a vested legal right." [10]  The reasoning was based, not upon the specific language of statutes, but upon broad common-sense interpretation of the Constitution.  The language was persuasive, or would be persuasive to those having no emotional interest in the situation, but it was nevertheless so general in character as to be vulnerable to those who held opposing convictions.

The answer to the second question, whether the laws of the country afforded Marbury a remedy, was likewise reached, not by a close study of federal statutes, but by an interpretation evidently based on the principles of the common law.  Said the Chief Justice, "The government of the United States has been emphatically termed a government of laws, and not of men.  It will certainly cease to deserve this high appellation if the laws furnish no remedy for the violation of a vested legal right." [11]  Having made this assumption, which was based on no constitutional or statutory provision, he examined the case to see if there was anything in it to exempt it from the general rule, and he found nothing.  He found that an act of the head of a department was examinable in a court of justice when the act was ministerial in character; that is, when its performance was a duty laid upon him by law without the placement of discretion in his hands.  Marbury had a legal title to the office and he had a consequent right to the commission, "a refusal to deliver which is a plain violation of that right, for which the laws of his country afford him a remedy." [12]

In dealing in this manner with two of the three questions which he had posed for himself, the Chief Justice moved toward a head-on collision with the Jefferson administration.  He now took up the third question, whether Marbury was entitled to the remedy for which he applied.  He broke that question into two parts.  The first part dealt with the nature of the writ of mandamus.  Going back to Blackstone's *Commentaries*, he demonstrated the fact that the writ was the proper instrument for the protection of legal rights such as that here denied.  This conclusion led to the other part of the question, namely, whether the writ of mandamus could issue out of the Supreme Court.

[10] *Ibid.*, p. 162,          [11] *Ibid.*, p. 163.          [12] *Ibid.*, p. 168.

The inevitability of a clash with the Jefferson administration now seemed clearer than ever. Section 13 of the Judiciary Act of 1789 provided that the Supreme Court should have power to issue writs of mandamus "in cases warranted by the principles and usages of law, to any courts appointed, or persons holding office, under the authority of the United States." [13] The Secretary of State was clearly a person holding office under the authority of the United States. The Court was authorized to issue the writ in this case, unless the law was unconstitutional and therefore incapable of conferring the authority. In this connection the Chief Justice raised a question to which little or no attention had been given by counsel or by the political factions interested in the case. The Court was acting in this case, not as an appellate tribunal, but as a court of original jurisdiction. Section 2 of Article III of the Constitution listed types of cases in which the Supreme Court was to have original jurisdiction. It stated that in all other cases within the judicial power of the United States the Supreme Court should have appellate jurisdiction, with such exceptions and under such regulations as Congress should make. There was doubt as to whether the power of Congress to make exceptions applied both to the original and the appellate jurisdiction of the Supreme Court or only to the latter. Marshall concluded that it applied only to the latter. The description of the original jurisdiction of the Supreme Court in the Constitution, he reasoned, was complete. Congress had no power to add to that jurisdiction. Among the items listed in it he did not find power to issue writs of mandamus. The relevant provision of the Judiciary Act, therefore, was not authorized by the Constitution.

This line of reasoning enabled Marshall to escape from the political dilemma and gave him the opportunity to expound the principle which made the decision significant long after the political controversy was forgotten. "The question," he said, "whether an act, repugnant to the Constitution, can become the law of the land, is a question deeply interesting to the United States; but, happily, not of an intricacy proportioned to its interest." [14] The Constitution, he said, was either a superior, paramount law, unchangeable by ordinary means, or it was on a level with ordinary legislative acts and, like other acts, alterable when the legislature should please to alter it. He had no doubt that our Constitution, set up to establish a government of limited powers, was of the former type, and that an act of

[13] 1 Stat. 81.          [14] 1 Cranch 176.

Congress repugnant to the Constitution was void. It was emphatically the province and duty of the judicial department to say what the law was. If two laws were in conflict, the Court must decide on the operation of each.

> So if a law be in opposition to the Constitution; if both the law and the Constitution apply to a paramount case, so that the Court must either decide that case conformably to the law, disregarding the Constitution; or conformably to the Constitution, disregarding the law; the Court must determine which of these conflicting rules governs the case. This is of the very essence of judicial duty.[15]

It was clear to the Chief Justice that in establishing the judiciary the Constitution intended that the judges should look to the Constitution as well as to the statutes in searching for the law. It was to be a rule for the government of the courts as well as of the legislature. It would be immoral to impose the oath of office upon them if judges were to be used as instruments for violating what they swore to support.

Since the case was not one in which the Court could, under the Constitution, exercise original jurisdiction, the Court did not attempt to compel the Secretary of State to deliver the commissions. The prestige of the Court was enhanced rather than impaired. The Republicans, who cared quite as little about the commissions and quite as much about the political issue as did the Federalists, were enraged at the strategy of the Chief Justice in writing an opinion to demonstrate the illegality of their action before reaching a reluctant conclusion that the Supreme Court had no power to do anything about it. They found no merit in Marshall's thoughtful discussion of the appointing process.[16] They argued convincingly that all discussion of the powers and the conduct of the executive department could have been and should have been avoided. The only point necessary to be decided was that the writ could not issue from the Supreme Court in this case, because the Court had no power to issue writs of mandamus in the exercise of its original jurisdiction. Since the Court had no jurisdiction, all discussions of the merits of the case were irrelevant. They were *obiter dicta,* and were therefore without merit as a statement of existing law.

---

[15] *Ibid.,* p. 178.

[16] For a modern appraisal of the power of the President in connection with appointments see W. W. Willoughby, *The Constitutional Law of the United States* (3 vols., 1929), III, 1506-1507, and United States *v.* Smith, 286 U. S. 6 (1932).

When the decision was announced, in February, 1803, little public attention was given to the discussion of the power and duty of the Court to pronounce null and void, and refuse to enforce, legislation in conflict with the Constitution. The power of judicial review had been exercised many times in the state courts. Its possibilities had been mentioned by judges in the Supreme Court and other federal courts. Statesmen not connected with the judiciary had recognized the probable existence of this judicial power, and its announcement by the Supreme Court occasioned no particular surprise. The current political situation was not one in which Congress was enacting sweeping legislation which was likely to be challenged by the Court. Judicial review operated in a negative direction only. The party in office was supposed to be opposed to the expansion of the powers of the federal government. Few statutes sponsored by the Jefferson administration and enacted by the Republican Congress were likely to be so broad as to be deemed unconstitutional by a Federalist judiciary. As a matter of fact, although a number of acts of Congress were appraised by the Supreme Court in terms of the Constitution, more than half a century passed before the Supreme Court held another one unconstitutional. From 1803 to 1857, when the Dred Scott case [17] was decided, no judicial restraint was laid upon the legislative power of Congress. It was only after the federal legislative power began to be exercised more broadly that the judiciary began to place its veto upon legislative measures.

RIVALRY BETWEEN STATE AND FEDERAL JUDICIARIES

The growing power of the Supreme Court under the leadership of John Marshall, the clashes between the Federalist judiciary and the Republican administration, and the Republicanism of certain state courts and their natural aspirations for independence of federal control, led to clashes between federal and state judiciaries. It will be recalled that, when framing the Judiciary Act, Federalist leaders in Congress sought to place all federal judicial power in the hands of the federal courts. The Anti-Federalists, or Republicans, on the other hand, sought to limit the activities of the federal judiciary to a narrow field and leave the exercise of most federal jurisdiction in the hands of the state courts. The statute adopted was a compromise between the two factions. More power was given to the federal judiciary than the Republicans desired, but an area of federal juris-

[17] Dred Scott v. Sandford, 19 Howard 393.

diction was left to state courts, and the right of appeal to the Supreme Court of the United States was given in cases decided by state courts which involved the interpretation of the federal Constitution, laws, or treaties.

One of the most eminent state courts of the early decades of the nineteenth century was the court of appeals of Virginia. It was presided over by Judge Spencer Roane, an able jurist and an entrenched political leader who was said to have been Jefferson's choice for Chief Justice of the United States. Unfortunately for the aspirations of both Jefferson and Roane, Chief Justice Ellsworth had resigned early enough to permit John Adams to appoint John Marshall to that position, and no method was found for ousting him. As the jealous head of a rival institution, Roane offered the first state challenge to the power of the Supreme Court to review cases previously decided in a state tribunal. As in the Marbury case, the political questions involved were uppermost in the minds of contemporaries, but the legal question was of paramount importance for the years to come.

Like much of the litigation of the period, the case grew out of a dispute over land titles.[18] The land involved was called the Northern Neck of Virginia, which had been granted to Lord Fairfax by Kings Charles II and James II. The state of Virginia made a claim to the land during the Revolutionary War, and, after the death of Lord Fairfax in 1781, it based a further claim on the ground that an alien could not inherit land in the state. Lord Fairfax had sought to pass the land to his nephew, Denny Martin, a British subject, but the state, ignoring Martin's claim, granted part of the land to David Hunter. Parts of the land were sold by the various claimants, John Marshall and his brother, James M. Marshall, being among the purchasers from the Fairfax heir. Litigation over the title dragged through the courts for many years. Finally, in 1810, the court of appeals of Virginia demolished the Fairfax title and upheld the rights of the Hunter estate.

A writ of error was sued out in the Supreme Court of the United States. Because of his interest in a part of the property which would be affected by the decision, Chief Justice Marshall took no formal part in the case. Two other justices were absent. By a vote of three to one the Supreme Court reversed the decision of the Virginia court, holding that the treaty with Great Britain, drafted in 1794, protected

---

[18] For accounts of the case see Beveridge, *op. cit.,* II, 206-208, and Warren, *op. cit.,* I, 443-453.

the Fairfax estate against confiscation by the state.    The opinion was written by Justice Joseph Story, nominally a Republican from Massachusetts, who had already imbibed most of the Federalist principles of John Marshall.[19]

The Supreme Court issued a mandate, directing the court of appeals of Virginia to carry out the decision.    Angered at the temerity of the Supreme Court in issuing orders to them, the Virginia judges called upon the bar of the state to argue the question whether or not they should obey the mandate.    After an argument of six days, the Virginia court held that the federal Judiciary Act was unconstitutional in so far as it extended the appellate jurisdiction of the Supreme Court to that court.    Republican leaders applauded, and re-echoed the defiance.

The case of the claimants under the Fairfax title was in the hands of John Marshall's brother.    He immediately took the case to the Supreme Court again by means of another writ of error.    This time the emphasis was not on questions of title, but on the constitutionality of the exercise of the power of the Supreme Court to review a decision of the highest court of a sovereign state.    Justice Story again delivered the opinion of the Court.[20]    He rejected arguments based on the sovereignty of the state and on conceptions of the Constitution as the product of a compact among sovereign bodies.    In language similar to that used later by Daniel Webster and other great Federalists, he declared:

> The Constitution of the United States was ordained and established, not by the states in their sovereign capacities, but emphatically, as the preamble of the Constitution declares, by "the people of the United States."   There can be no doubt that it was competent to the people to invest the general government with all the powers which they might deem proper and necessary; to extend or restrain these powers according to their own good pleasure, and to give them a paramount and supreme authority.   As little doubt can there be that the people had a right to prohibit to the states the exercise of any powers which were, in their judgment, incompatible with the objects of the general compact; to make the powers of the state governments, in given cases, subordinate to those of the nation, or to reserve to themselves those sovereign authorities which they might not choose to delegate to either.   The Constitution was not, therefore, necessarily carved out of

[19] Fairfax's Devisee *v.* Hunter's Lessee, 7 Cranch 603 (1813).
[20] Martin *v.* Hunter's Lessee, 1 Wheaton 304 (1816).

existing state sovereignties, nor a surrender of powers already existing in state institutions, for the powers of the states depend upon their own constitutions; and the people of every state had the right to modify and restrain them, according to their own views of policy or principle.   On the other hand, it is perfectly clear that the sovereign powers vested in the state governments, by their respective constitutions, remained unaltered and unimpaired, except so far as they were granted to the government of the United States.[21]

With these principles in mind, he examined Article III of the Constitution to determine the appellate jurisdiction of the Supreme Court.   Writing at great length, he justified the exercise of power by that Court to review cases decided by the highest courts of the states in prescribed cases involving the interpretation of the federal Constitution, federal statutes, and federal laws.   Doubtless fearing that the Virginia court of appeals would again refuse to execute the mandate, the Supreme Court sent it this time, not to the court of appeals, but to the lower court in Virginia in which the case had originated.

From the point of view of a legal statement, the opinion of Justice Story left little more to be said in defense of the power of the Supreme Court to review decisions of the state courts.   Republican leaders, however, continued to denounce what they regarded as the encroachment of the federal judiciary upon the prerogatives of the states.

The position of the Supreme Court needed to be restated in a case in which John Marshall would not be restrained from participating because of a personal financial interest.   Marshall had great prestige in spite of the denunciation to which the Republicans subjected him. He had a capacity for the clear and persuasive statement of constitutional principles which Story did not possess.   The occasion for an opinion by Marshall arose, or was engineered, in the case of Cohens v. Virginia,[22] decided in 1821.[23]   The Virginia legislature had enacted a law forbidding the sale of lottery tickets in the state, except those from lotteries authorized by the laws of the state.   Cohens violated the law by selling tickets of a lottery sponsored by the District of Columbia. He was convicted.   The offense was petty, and for that reason no appeal could be taken to a higher court in the state.   Cohens' counsel took the case to the Supreme Court of the United States, arguing that the lottery was authorized by an act of Congress which provided for the government of the District of Columbia, and that the state law,

[21] *Ibid.,* pp. 324-325.          [22] 6 Wheaton 264.
[23] For accounts of the case see Beveridge, *op. cit.,* IV, 342-371, and Warren, *op. cit.,* I, 547-563, 657-659.

being in conflict with the federal law, could not constitutionally be enforced.

Before hearing arguments as to whether the act of Congress authorized the sale of District of Columbia lottery tickets in Virginia, the Court heard arguments exclusively on the jurisdictional question whether the case could legitimately be brought before it.   On this point Chief Justice Marshall wrote an opinion which his biographer has called "one of the strongest and most enduring strands of that mighty cable woven by him to hold the American people together as a united and imperishable nation." [24]   Marshall asserted that the appellate power of the Supreme Court over the judgment of a state court was opposed chiefly on arguments drawn from the supposed total separation of the judiciary of a state from that of the Union and their entire independence of each other; but the hypothesis of complete separation between the state and federal governments was not supported by the Constitution.   He reasoned as follows:

> That the United States form, for many and for most important purposes, a single nation, has not yet been denied.   In war, we are one people.   In making peace, we are one people.   In all commercial regulations, we are one and the same people.   In many other respects, the American people are one; and the government which is alone capable of controlling and managing their interests in all these respects, is the government of the Union.   It is their government, and in that character they have no other.   America has chosen to be, in many respects, and to many purposes, a nation; and for all these purposes, her government is complete; to all these objects, it is competent. The people have declared, that in the exercise of all powers given for these objects it is supreme.   It can, then, in effecting these objects, legitimately control all individuals or governments within the American territory.   The constitution and laws of a state, so far as they are repugnant to the Constitution and laws of the United States, are absolutely void.   These states are constituent parts of the United States.   They are members of one great empire — for some purposes sovereign, for some purposes subordinate. [25]

In a government so constituted, he thought it not unreasonable that the judicial power should be competent to give efficacy to the constitutional laws of the legislature.

> We think that in a government acknowledgedly supreme, with respect to objects of vital interest to the nation, there is nothing incon-

[24] Beveridge, op. cit., IV, 343.      [25] 6 Wheaton 413-414.

sistent with sound reason, nothing incompatible with the nature of government, in making all its departments supreme, so far as respects those objects, and so far as is necessary to their attainment.    The exercise of the appellate power over those judgments of the state tribunals which may contravene the Constitution or laws of the United States, is, we believe, essential to the attainment of those objects.[26]

Rephrasing his argument time and again, the Chief Justice concluded by saying that the Court was unanimously of the opinion that the objections to its jurisdiction were not sustained.    The case was then argued on the merits.    In writing the opinion of the Court, the Chief Justice posed two questions:  (1)  Did the statute purport to authorize the sale of lottery tickets in states where such sale might be prohibited by law?  And  (2)  Was the law constitutional?  The second question would have to be answered only if the first was answered in the affirmative.    He reached rather quickly the conclusion that the act of Congress had not intended to authorize sales such as that which Cohens had made.

The judgment of the lower court was therefore affirmed.  The appeal had been without avail as far as Cohens was concerned.    Yet it had given Chief Justice Marshall an opportunity to proclaim and publish a long essay on the nature of the federal Union and the power of the federal judiciary.    It was a powerful utterance in the struggle between nationalism and localism which raged throughout the period in which Marshall was Chief Justice.    Marshall was attacked in the Republican press through editorials and through a series of articles written by his rival, Judge Spencer Roane.    Thomas Jefferson was among his most resentful critics.    It is safe to say that none of the Republican leaders was convinced or pacified by the opinion of the Supreme Court, even though in this case there was no ultimate interference with the enforcement of the state law.    Yet Marshall's statement and restatement of the principles of federalism, as he saw them, laid the groundwork for a system of constitutional law which was to exist long after the contemporary controversies were forgotten.    Under his leadership the federal judiciary was so entrenched in a position of power that the vicissitudes of civil war and social and economic struggle in the decades to come were unable to bring about more than a temporary disturbance.

[26] *Ibid.,* pp. 414-415.

••••••••••••••••••••••••••••••••••••••••••••••••••••••••••••••••••••••••••••••••••••••••••••••••••••••••

# CHAPTER 7

# THE PRESIDENCY AND THE UNION

SINCE THE OFFICE OF PRESIDENT was wholly new, the early occupants had no tradition to follow. Even though an entire article of the Constitution was devoted to the Executive, the character of the presidency was determined in large part by the men first chosen to it. No one can confidently predict what the office would have been like during the early decades of government under the Constitution had George Washington not been selected as the first President. His writings and the record of his activities do not indicate that he had either the brilliance or the learning variously displayed by Hamilton, Jefferson, Madison, and perhaps others. He lacked the qualities of colorful popular leadership demonstrated in later years by Jackson, Lincoln, and the two Roosevelts. When he took the office, however, he possessed the confidence and veneration of all groups and all sections of the country. He was the symbol of a nation united. If he lacked some of the qualities of constructive statesmanship, he knew how to use the abilities of other men who in specialized fields had keen minds, or great facility for expression, or possessed more of the techniques of political strategy than himself. He perhaps made little contribution to the science of government; yet under his hand the ship of state held steady while the machinery of the new government was being established.

Washington seems to have had no desire to serve beyond a single term. Toward the end of his first term he had Madison prepare for him a draft of a valedictory or farewell address in which he outlined the principles to which he thought the nation should adhere. He was persuaded to accept the office for another term. During that term the strife between sections of the country, between the developing political parties, and between the friends, respectively, of France and England, so divided the country that no policy sponsored by the President, however carefully administered, could escape bitter attack.

Much of the halo about the name of Washington was dispelled amid strife.   Determined that a second term should be his last, he asked Hamilton to take over the task of completing the draft of a farewell address begun four years earlier by Madison, who had now moved definitely into the ranks of partisan critics of the administration.

The address was made public, not on the date of his retirement from office, but on September 17, 1796,[1] prior to the presidential election of that year.   He explained his retirement, not on any ground of policy in opposition to his third term, but on the ground that his services, rendered for eight years at a real personal sacrifice, were no longer needed by the country.   He devoted many pages to a plea for unity among the American people.   He deplored what he called the spirit of party, whether in internal or foreign affairs.   He warned particularly against sectional divisions within the country and against "permanent alliances with any portion of the foreign world."   He warned against hasty changes in the Constitution.   "In all the changes to which you may be incited," he urged, "remember that time and habit are at least as necessary to fix the true character of government as of other human institutions."[2]

Whatever the effect of the address, the nation failed to avoid partisanship in the election of Washington's successor.   The campaign was a bitter struggle.   For the presidency, the majority of the Federalists favored John Adams, who had served two terms as Vice-President; and for Vice-President they favored Thomas Pinckney, of South Carolina.   Hamilton and other Federalists lacked enthusiasm for Adams, however, and sectional jealousy played into the struggle. The Anti-Federalists, or Republicans, favored Thomas Jefferson for the presidency and scattered widely as to the vice-presidency, giving a considerable amount of support to Aaron Burr.   Party lines were not yet completely formed, and the result was one which could not well have occurred at subsequent elections.   Adams was chosen to the presidency with seventy-one electoral votes.   The next largest number of votes — only three less than those accorded to Adams — went, not to Pinckney, however, but to Thomas Jefferson, the leader of the Republicans.   The ensuing administration was in the hands of a Federalist President and a Republican Vice-President, with division in the Federalist party as to the support to be given to the President.

[1] United States President, *A Compilation of the Messages and Papers of the Presidents* (20 vols., 1917–?), I, 205.
[2] *Ibid.*, p. 210.

The new President, taking office with a prestige in no sense comparable with that of his predecessor, had to stand or fall in terms of his own ability as a statesman and politician.  The division among the Federalists, the unwise enactment of certain legislation such as the Alien and Sedition Acts, and other factors, left him badly discredited at the end of a single term.  By 1800 the lines of the two political parties were clearly established.  Each of the presidential electors chosen as Republicans cast his vote for the two Republican candidates, Thomas Jefferson and Aaron Burr.  The Federalists cast their votes for John Adams and Charles Cotesworth Pinckney, of South Carolina, with the exception of one vote cast for John Jay, of New York.  There were seventy-three Republican electors as against sixty-five Federalist electors, but the balloting resulted in no election because of the fact that Jefferson and Burr each had the same number of votes.  The Republicans had contemplated electing Jefferson as President and Burr as Vice-President, but the election drew no distinction between them, and the final decision was left with the House of Representatives.

The House of Representatives was to choose the President from one or the other of the two Republicans, Jefferson and Burr, but the participating voters were both Federalists and Republicans.  The Republicans in the House voted for Jefferson; the Federalists divided, a considerable number of them voting for Burr.  As the Constitution required, the formal vote was taken, not by individuals, but by states.  In a long series of ballots, eight states were for Jefferson, and six for Burr; but, since the delegations from two states were equally divided, Jefferson failed to secure the support of the required majority of the states.  It seemed for a time as if the House were in permanent deadlock.  The time for the inauguration of the new President was approaching.  There was no constitutional or statutory provision for the government of the country in the absence of both the President and Vice-President.  Federalist representatives continued to support Burr for the presidency, with the result that neither Burr nor Jefferson could secure the votes of a majority of the states.  Finally, however, perhaps partly because they recognized the seriousness of the situation and partly because Burr refused to pledge himself to conduct the presidency as a Federalist, enough Federalist representatives withheld their votes to permit Jefferson to secure a majority.  Jefferson was elected, therefore, on the thirty-sixth ballot.

THE TWELFTH AMENDMENT

The electoral college seems never to have functioned exactly as the framers of the Constitution intended. In no election did the electors in the several states constitute, as was originally intended, a deliberative body exercising their own best judgment as to persons who were to be President and Vice-President. They were chosen to express the will of their constituents rather than to exercise their own discretion. It had been assumed that on some occasions the votes of the electors would concentrate sufficiently upon particular candidates to result in an immediate election, but it seems to have been expected that on many, and perhaps most, occasions the electoral college would exercise somewhat the functions of a nominating convention, and that the House of Representatives would choose the President from the five candidates receiving the highest number of votes in the electoral college. The machinery failed to anticipate the development of political parties, in terms of which electors would be chosen to vote for party candidates, with the result that, no matter how large the vote of the party, its two candidates would receive the same number of electoral votes, and the election of President would devolve upon the House of Representatives. The machinery likewise failed to anticipate the operation of political parties in Congress and the possible defeat of the will of the people by the efforts of the minority party to defeat the intentions of the majority as to which of the two candidates should be President and which should be Vice-President.

As a result of the election of 1796, at which a Federalist was chosen as President and a Republican as Vice-President, a constitutional amendment had been proposed to the effect that each elector, instead of casting two votes for President, should vote separately for President and Vice-President. No action was taken on the proposal. After the battle which resulted in the election of Jefferson, a similar amendment was introduced. The first Congress of Jefferson's administration lacked a sufficient majority of Republicans to sanction a constitutional amendment without the help of Federalist votes. The Federalists showed no disposition to be helpful. The Republican majority of the next Congress, however, was large enough to carry a constitutional amendment if all acted together. The Senate passed the amendment by a two-thirds vote of the members present, but the number of votes cast for the amendment was not as much as two-thirds of the total membership of the Senate. The validity of the action of the Senate was challenged on the ground that the Constitution required a vote of two-thirds of the total membership, but the contention was rejected. The question of the meaning of the constitutional requirement of a two-thirds vote was not passed upon by the Supreme Court until 1920, when in connection with the Eighteenth Amendment the Court held that the requirement was a vote of two-thirds of the members present — assuming the presence of a quorum — and not a two-thirds vote of the entire membership present and absent.[3]

In spite of the strength of the Republicans, the amendment faced strong opposition. Many members believed, as Washington had advised, that until the Constitution was well established it was unwise to make changes unless they were absolutely necessary. The Federalists were opposed to the amendment because it was sponsored by Republicans. There was general opposition, furthermore, on the ground that it would destroy the dignity of the office of Vice-President. Hitherto, election as Vice-President had meant that the candidate had been the second choice of the country for the presidency. Under the constitutional amendment the incumbent would be elected directly as Vice-President with the expectation that he would become President only in the improbable event that the office of President should become vacant. An unsuccessful attempt was made, indeed, to secure the elimination of the office of Vice-President altogether. It was argued that the office was not needed, and that some other officer of the government could be designated to assume the duties of President should the latter office become vacant.

In view of the development of the two-party system, it seemed likely that few elections of President would be thrown into the House of Representatives should the amendment be passed. Since the small states possessed undue strength in the election of President when the choice was made in the House of Representatives, where each state had one vote regardless of its size, there was some opposition to the amendment on that ground. Small states were also critical of the amendment, furthermore, because of the requirement that the House make its choice from not more than three of the highest candidates on the list in contrast with the provision for five in the original Constitution. It was argued that if only three candidates were to be considered, it was most probable that only men from the large states would be chosen, and that the election of a President from a small state would be virtually impossible. Both houses accepted the

[3] Rhode Island v. Palmer, 253 U.S. 350 (1920).

amendment, however, with the provision that the choice should be made from the persons, not exceeding three, having the highest number of electoral votes. Actually the machinery for election by the House of Representatives has been a matter of little importance because of the fact that since the date of the enactment of the Twelfth Amendment only one President, John Quincy Adams, has been chosen in this manner.

The amendment was accepted by both houses of Congress and was speedily ratified by the requisite number of states, so that it might become operative for the election of 1804. It successfully adjusted electoral machinery to the operations of a two-party system. Its failure in one instance — the election of 1824 — resulted from the temporary breakdown of the two-party system and the temporary development of a number of small factions so that no candidate received the requisite majority.

The device of separate voting for President and Vice-President meant a degradation of the latter office from the position originally contemplated. According to the plan first adopted, the Vice-President was to be a man of presidential capacity who would occupy the lower rather than the higher office merely because another man had received more electoral votes. He would be in a real sense an assistant President. Under the provisions of the Twelfth Amendment the man in the vice-presidency never had at any time during his candidacy any prospect of becoming President except in the improbable event of the death of the occupant of that office. He was chosen with the probability in mind that his most important functions would be presiding over the Senate and participating in social functions. The nomination was made, at times, merely as a reward for past political services. On occasion, as in the instance of Theodore Roosevelt, it was hoped that the nomination would sidetrack a man whose activities were embarrassing the leaders of his party. Men eager to be President often scorned acceptance of the lesser office. In spite of the occasional allotment of important functions by the President, the Vice-President remained an official largely cut off from important participation in public affairs.

Although from the beginning the electors functioned largely as automatic representatives of the will of the people rather than as deliberate agents, little or no consideration of the advisability of abolishing the electoral college altogether and choosing the President and Vice-President directly by popular vote was given in connection with the adoption of the Twelfth Amendment.  The question has been considered from time to time in more recent years, and constitutional amendments to eliminate the cumbersome mechanism have been introduced, but the need and desirability of such a change have not been sufficiently apparent to overcome political lethargy in the matter.  Vested interests have developed around the traditional machinery, and the need for change will have to become more obvious than it now is before support can be won for a constitutional amendment on the subject.[4]

### THE JEFFERSON ADMINISTRATION

The transfer of governmental powers to Jefferson and to the Republican party brought new trends.  In his inaugural address Jefferson sought to minimize the differences between the two parties.  "We have called by different names brethren of the same principle," he said.  "We are all Republicans, we are all Federalists."[5]  Differences in policy soon proved real and important, however.  Persons imprisoned under the Sedition Act were liberated.  The measure providing judges for the United States circuit courts was repealed.  Impeachment proceedings against arrogant and incompetent judges were successful in some instances and had a general restraining effect.  The requirement of fourteen years of residence in the United States before an alien could become a citizen was reduced to the previous period of five years.  The internal taxes which Alexander Hamilton had sponsored to establish a precedent and extend federal control as well as to raise revenue were abolished.  Yet rapid reduction was made in the national debt, the existence of which some Federalists had regarded as quite as much a blessing as an evil.  Procedures were simplified and exaggerated pomp and ceremony were discarded.  To get rid of the empty ceremonial interchange between the President and Congress, Jefferson put an end to the practice of making personal appearances before Congress.  His messages were delivered in writing and gave no occasion for a formal reply.  The Federalists delivered scathing criticisms of Jeffersonian innovations, but the trend continued and it soon became clear that the eclipse of the Federalist party was permanent.

A shift in the position of the Republican party from one of criticism

[4] For a discussion of the adoption of the Twelfth Amendment see Lolabel House, *A Study of the Twelfth Amendment of the Constitution of the United States* (1901).
[5] *Messages and Papers of the Presidents*, I, 310.

and restraint to one of positive responsibility modified considerably the principles of the Republican leaders. Hitherto they had challenged the extension of federal power and had stressed the authority of the states to act as co-interpreters of the federal Constitution in opposition to encroachment by the federal government. They had appraised the Constitution as the product of a compact among the states and as therefore subject to restraint by the states. When the federal government was in their hands, however, their doubts as to the extension of federal power to carry out the functions deemed to be necessary began to clear away. Except in opposition to the federal judiciary, which for a time continued to be dominated by Federalist leaders, they had little to say about the rights of the states as against the authority of the federal government. The Federalist party, on the other hand, became less and less nationalist and more and more sectional and particularistic in its policies. For example, talk of secession in the United States from 1800 until well along in the eighteen-twenties, which represented the extreme anti-nationalist position, was predominantly the product of Federalists rather than of Republicans. The Federalist party continued to be made up of much the same financial and commercial interests as before. The Republican party continued to include the great mass of debtor and landed interests in the United States. The two parties fought over the tariff, the Bank of the United States, territorial expansion, relations with foreign countries, and other matters. The continuing conflicts of interest are illustrated here in terms of the purchase of the Louisiana territory from France and of the embargo levied during Jefferson's second administration in an attempt to solve the problem of commercial relationships with Great Britain and France.

## THE PURCHASE OF LOUISIANA

Even prior to the time of the adoption of the Constitution, the status of the Mississippi and of the port of New Orleans was a matter of vital importance to a large section of the United States. A part of the opposition of Patrick Henry and others to the adoption of the Constitution was the fear that a strong national government dominated by the North and East might make and enforce treaties with Spain by which the United States would be denied access to the Mississippi outlet. The more distant sections of the country had no desire to see the commerce of the South and West drained away in the direction of the southern port. The possibilities of agricultural and commercial development of the Southwest, however, depended largely upon the availability of local transportation.

Early in Jefferson's administration he learned of rumors about a transfer of New Orleans and perhaps of the Floridas from Spain to France, which was then dominated by Napoleon Bonaparte. Jefferson sent Edward Livingston and James Monroe to negotiate for the possible purchase of New Orleans and the Floridas. Communication between the United States and representatives abroad was extremely slow, and the American agents found themselves in a situation in which they had to act hastily. The outcome was that they exceeded their instructions and arranged for the purchase, not of the Floridas, but of New Orleans and the whole of Louisiana. The area negotiated for was approximately equal to that of the entire United States as it stood before the purchase. The treaty provided that

> the inhabitants of the ceded territory shall be incorporated in the Union of the United States and admitted as soon as possible according to the principles of the federal Constitution to the enjoyment of all rights, advantages, and immunities of citizens of the United States, and in the meantime they shall be maintained and protected in the free enjoyment of their liberty, property, and the religion which they profess.[6]

Spain and France were to have special concessions in the use of the ports of the ceded territory for a period of twelve years. The amount to be paid was approximately fifteen million dollars.

Jefferson did not doubt the desirability of the arrangement made by his envoys, but he was in an embarrassing position as far as constitutional questions were concerned. He and Madison, his Secretary of State, had made themselves the leading critics of broad interpretation of the Constitution during the period of Federalist control. Yet, when his first administration was hardly half over, the two men were sponsoring a treaty to double the area of the United States and provide for the government of the newly acquired territory, without the support of any clause in the Constitution specifically authorizing the acquisition of new territory. Article IV, Section 3, of the Constitution provided for the admission of new states and gave Congress the power to make rules and regulations respecting the territory or other property belonging to the United States, but the section was believed

[6] Article III of the treaty with France, in Hunter Miller (ed.), *Treaties and other International Acts of the United States of America* (1931), II, 498, 501.

to refer only to territory belonging to the United States at the time the Constitution was adopted.

The treaty was signed at Paris on April 30, 1803. On July 16, Jefferson called a special session of Congress to meet on the seventeenth day of October to deal with "great and weighty matters claiming the consideration of the Congress." [7]   While waiting for Congress to assemble, he wrote to John Breckinridge, a member of the Senate, that the treaty must of course be laid before both houses because both had important functions to exercise respecting it.   He thought Congress then would see their duty to their country in ratifying the treaty and paying for the territory, so as to secure a good which would otherwise probably never again be in their power.   But, he added:

I suppose they must then appeal to *the nation* for an additional Article to the Constitution, approving and confirming an act which the nation had not previously authorized.   The Constitution has made no provision for our holding foreign territory, still less for incorporating foreign nations into our Union.   The executives, in seizing the fugitive occurrence which so much advances the good of their country, have done an act beyond the Constitution.   The legislature in casting behind them metaphysical subtleties, and risking themselves like faithful servants, must ratify and pay for it, and throw themselves on their country for doing for them unauthorized, what we know they would have done for themselves had they been in a situation to do it.   It is the case of a guardian, investing the money of his ward in purchasing an important adjacent territory; and saying to him when of age, I did this for your good; I pretend to no right to bind you: you may disavow me, and I must get out of the scrape as I can: I thought it my duty to risk myself for you.   But we shall not be disavowed by the nation, and their act of indemnity will confirm and not weaken the Constitution, by more strongly marking out its lines.[8]

Jefferson wrote to the Attorney General and to others about a constitutional amendment which would give to the United States the same powers with respect to Louisiana that it had with respect to other territory.   Because of the fear that France would withdraw from its bargain, and perhaps for other reasons, Jefferson urged that little be said publicly about the constitutional question.   He wrote to the Attorney General:

I quote this for your consideration, observing that the less that is said about any constitutional difficulty the better; and that it will be

[7] *Messages and Papers of the Presidents*, I, 345.

[8] *The Writings of Thomas Jefferson* (Library ed., 20 vols., 1903), X, 410-411.

desirable for Congress to do what is necessary, *in silence*. I find but one opinion as to the necessity of shutting up the country for some time.[9]

To Wilson C. Nicholas, who apparently believed that the United States already had the power to acquire territory, he again expressed his own doubts in the matter and his dislike of broad construction:

When an instrument admits two constructions, the one safe, the other dangerous, the one precise, the other indefinite, I prefer that which is safe and precise. I had rather ask an enlargement of power from the nation, where it is found necessary, than to assume it by a construction which would make our powers boundless. Our peculiar security is in the position of a written Constitution. Let us not make it a blank paper by construction. I say the same as to the opinion of those who consider the grant of the treaty-making power as boundless. If it is, then we have no Constitution. If it has bounds, they can be no others than the definitions of the powers which that instrument gives. . . . I think it important, in the present case, to set an example against broad construction, by appealing for new power to the people. If, however, our friends shall think differently, certainly I shall acquiesce with satisfaction; confiding that the good sense of our country will correct the evil of construction when it shall produce ill effects.[10]

Albert Gallatin, who was now Secretary of the Treasury, Madison, and others of Jefferson's advisers who had been advocates of strict construction of the Constitution during the period of Federalist domination were now able to persuade themselves that the Constitution should be interpreted broadly to justify the acquisition of Louisiana without taking the trouble to secure the adoption of a constitutional amendment.

Their lack of concern about the principles to which they had paid heated tribute before they came into power has not been unique in American history. Traditionally the critics of governmental powers have been people who lacked the opportunity to determine the exercise of that power. It is true that Jefferson, Madison, Gallatin, and others had held political office in earlier years when they developed the Republican opposition to Federalist principles, but they had been a minority group within the government. Now they had responsibility for the development of policy. Having the votes at hand with which to secure the measures they thought desirable, they allowed constitutional qualms to be suppressed. Jefferson followed the

[9] *Ibid.*, X, 412; see also X. 417-418. and XIX, 135.  [10] *Ibid.*, X, 418-420.

advice of those men around him who thought it unwise to entangle themselves in unnecessary difficulties by seeking a constitutional amendment to authorize the doing of something which might be done by conveniently stretching the language of the Constitution. The treaty was submitted to the Senate on October 17, 1803, without an accompanying resolution for a constitutional amendment. The Senate debated the treaty behind closed doors and gave its sanction on October 20 by a majority which greatly exceeded the requisite two-thirds and which for the most part followed party lines.[11]

Since action by both houses of Congress would be necessary to carry the treaty into effect by appropriating money to pay for the territory and making provision for its government, Jefferson had given some thought to the immediate submission of the treaty to the House of Representatives as well as to the Senate. His advisers warned him against inviting controversy in this manner; and the treaty was not made available to the House of Representatives until after the Senate had acted upon it. Although in connection with the proposed legis-lation members of the House raised embarrassing questions about the making of the treaty, including questions of constitutionality, it was now too late for such questions to have any effect upon ratification of the treaty.[12]

The United States had no machinery for governing the newly ac-quired territory. The Senate speedily passed a bill authorizing the President to take possession, and providing that, until Congress should establish a temporary government, the powers exercised by the offi-cers of the existing government should be vested in such persons and should be exercised in such manner as the President of the United States should direct. Federalists criticized this proposed blanket adoption of machinery which, for all they knew, might be wholly dic-tatorial in character and in conflict with the principles of the govern-ment of the United States. Republicans, under the leadership of John Randolph, joined in the criticism to the extent of insisting that the act apply only to the period during which the present Congress was in session.[13] Before Congress adjourned, it enacted a detailed measure for the establishment of a territorial government.[14]

---

[11] *Ibid.*, X, 425, and Everett S. Brown, *The Constitutional History of the Louisiana Purchase* (1920), p. 13. For a summary of Senate debates on the treaty prior to ratifica-tion see *William Plumer's Memorandum of Proceedings in the United States Senate, 1803-1807* (1923), ed. by Everett S. Brown, pp. 3-14.

[12] Brown, *The Constitutional History of the Louisiana Purchase* (1920), chapter IV.

[13] *Annals of Congress*, 8th Cong., 1st sess., 498 ff.; 2 Stat. 245.    [14] 2 Stat. 283.

Congress enacted other measures to provide for the payment for acquired territory,[15] and for the regulation of imports into the territory, as provided by the treaty.[16] In connection with the several measures the varied questions, constitutional and otherwise, concerning the acquisition and government of foreign territory were discussed. Some of the Federalists, it seems, had no doubt about the ability of the United States to acquire territory, but thought that the territory should have been taken by force rather than by purchase. Others, who recognized the power to acquire territory, objected to the provisions in Article III of the treaty that the inhabitants of the territory should be incorporated into the United States and should enjoy all the rights, advantages, and immunities of citizens of the United States. Territorial acquisitions, they thought, should be in the nature of newly acquired possessions which were subject to exploitation by the possessor without the rights which inhered in membership in the nation itself. The enactment of the measures to pay for the territory and to establish a government for it resulted, not from the solution of these theoretical questions, but from the decision of administration leaders that the prescribed steps should be taken.

Had the discussion of constitutional questions as to the power of the federal government to acquire and govern territory been conducted in more recent years, much would have been said about previous decisions of the Supreme Court and perhaps about probable future decisions if proposed measures were enacted. Although the Marbury case, with its assertion of the power of judicial review, had been decided by the Supreme Court as recently as the February term of 1803, little was said in the congressional debate on the acquisition of Louisiana about the part which the Court might play in connection with the constitutional questions being discussed. One exception was the comment of Senator William Plumer, of New Hampshire, a Federalist who had voted against ratification of the treaty, but who thought that, since the treaty had been ratified, Congress ought to enact legislation to carry out its provisions. He admitted that cases might "arise respecting the rights of individuals under this treaty in the courts of law, in which the constitutionality of the treaty may be questioned. And there may be cases in which it may become the duty of the judges, if that is their opinion, and if the nature of the case require it, to declare the treaty to be repugnant to the Constitu-

[15] 2 Stat. 245, 247.
[16] 2 Stat. 251.

tion." [17]  For the most part, however, congressmen indicated no aware ness that there was a tribunal apart from Congress which would have the last word in the determination of constitutional questions.

It was not until 1828, in connection with the government of Florida, which had been purchased in 1819, that the Supreme Court passed upon the question of the power of the United States to acquire and govern territory.  Chief Justice Marshall, speaking for a unanimous Court, declared succinctly that "the Constitution conferred absolutely on the government of the Union the powers of making war and of making treaties; consequently, that government possesses the power of acquiring territory, either by conquest or by treaty." [18]  Having acquired the territory, the United States governed it by virtue of that clause in the Constitution which empowered Congress "to make all needful rules and regulations, respecting the territory, or other property belonging to the United States."  Apart from this constitutional provision, he thought it possible that the power to govern territory which lacked the status of statehood might result necessarily from the fact that it was not within the jurisdiction of any particular state and was within the power and the jurisdiction of the United States.  "The right to govern may be the inevitable consequence of the right to acquire territory." [19]  Whatever the source of the power, the possession of it was unquestioned.

The question raised in connection with the Louisiana Purchase about the power of the United States to acquire title to territory and to govern territory which for physical or other reasons could not easily be incorporated into the United States proper remained undetermined by the Supreme Court for nearly a century.  It had to be dealt with finally in connection with the government of insular possessions acquired as a result of the Spanish-American War.

THE BURR CONSPIRACY

American statesmen held various sentiments as to the areas which ought to be incorporated into the Union.  Some wished to include, not merely the original thirteen states and the territorial possessions held at the time when independence was declared, but also the Lou-

[17] *William Plumer's Memorandum,* p. 32.

[18] The American Insurance Co. *v.* 356 Bales of Cotton, 1 Peters 511 (1828).

[19] *Ibid.,* p. 543.  The case was also important for the discussion of the status of territorial courts and for the differentiation between courts established pursuant to Article III of the Constitution and "legislative" courts established pursuant to powers granted elsewhere in the Constitution.

isiana Territory, Mexico, and the Floridas. Others, however, felt that the Union, even in its original dimensions, was too extensive and too diverse in its interests to survive unbroken. There seems never to have been a time in the early decades of American history under the Constitution when the secession of one section or another was not considered a real possibility. In discussing the prospective ratification of the treaty for the acquisition of Louisiana, Jefferson remarked that the Federalists of the East saw in this acquisition the formation of a new confederacy embracing all the waters of the Mississippi on both sides of it, with a consequent breaking-off of the western portion of the existing Union. He did not think such a prospect assured, but, on the other hand, he did not greatly dread it. He thought it no menace to the welfare of the eastern states that their western border should adjoin another nation inhabited by their sons. "If they see their interest in separation," he wrote, "why should we take sides with our Atlantic rather than our Mississippi descendants? It is the elder and the younger son differing. God bless them both, and keep them in union, if it be for their good, but separate them, if it be better." [20]

Plans for the establishment of a western empire were developed by no less a personage than Aaron Burr, Vice-President of the United States during Jefferson's first administration.[21] Burr's political career had been doomed since the time he had killed Alexander Hamilton in a duel. His western expedition was clearly intended to re-establish himself and to rebuild a reputation. The records do not clearly show the emphasis which he placed on the secession of a part of the United States on the one hand and the conquest of Mexico on the other. Rumors began to reach Jefferson as to the organization of a military expedition. On January 22, 1807, at the request of the House of Representatives, Jefferson submitted to Congress such account of the expedition as he had been able to bring together along with the report that two of Burr's emissaries were under arrest and were being brought eastward for trial.[22]

Jefferson stated that another of Burr's emissaries had been liberated

[20] *The Writings of Thomas Jefferson* (Library ed., 20 vols., 1903), X, 409-410.

[21] For accounts of the Burr Conspiracy see Albert J. Beveridge, *The Life of John Marshall* (4 vols., 1916-1919), III, chapters VI-IX; Henry Adams, *History of the United States During the Administrations of Jefferson and Madison* (9 vols., 1889-1891), III, chapters X-XIX; *Reports of the Trials of Aaron Burr* (2 vols., 1808). See also *Annals of Congress,* 10th Cong., 1st sess., 386-778.

[22] *Messages and Papers of the Presidents,* I, 400-405.

by habeas corpus. On the day after the message was delivered to Congress, the Senate speedily passed a bill to suspend for three months the privilege of the writ of habeas corpus in cases of persons charged with treason, misprision of treason, or other high crime or misdemeanor. The Senate sent the bill to the House "in confidence" and urged its speedy enactment. The House rejected it indignantly by a vote of 113 to 19.[23]

The two prisoners, J. E. Bollman and Samuel Swartwout, had in the meantime been denied release on habeas corpus by the United States court in Washington by a divided vote, the judges differing along party lines. An appeal was taken to the Supreme Court. It was evidently in an attempt to prevent the Supreme Court from ruling on the matter that the Senate passed the suspension bill mentioned above, which the House thereafter rejected.

Justice Johnson, a Jefferson appointee, stating that he had the support of one of his brethren who was prevented by indisposition from attending, contended that the Supreme Court had no power to issue a writ of habeas corpus. Chief Justice Marshall and a majority of the Court, however, found that the Court did have the power. The purpose of the inquiry was to determine whether or not the prisoners, Bollman and Swartwout, should be held for trial on a charge of treason, in levying war against the United States. The opinion of the Court, written by Chief Justice Marshall, was an important constitutional statement on the interpretation of treason. Like many of his leading opinions, however, it had significance beyond the legal question immediately involved and beyond the interests of the persons immediately affected. It reflected somewhat the abiding hostility between the Jefferson administration and the Supreme Court, particularly as it was expressed in the attempt to deny jurisdiction to the Supreme Court in this case by suspending the privilege of the writ of habeas corpus. The opinion was written also with the fact in mind that Aaron Burr himself was soon to be brought to trial in a federal court on the charge of treason. It told Jefferson what kind of facts he would have to prove if he was to secure a conviction.

Article III, Section 3, of the Constitution provided that "treason against the United States shall consist only in levying war against them, or in adhering to their enemies, giving them aid and comfort." To constitute that specific crime, said Marshall, war must be actually

<hr>

[23] Beveridge, *op. cit.*, III, 347-348.

levied against the United States. The definition did not extend to mere conspiracy to levy war.

In language that was to embarrass him later, however, in what appeared to be his effort so to interpret the law as to avert the conviction of Burr, he added that it was not necessary that an individual actually appear in arms in order to be convicted of treason. On the contrary, he said:

> if war be actually levied, that is, if a body of men be actually assembled for the purpose of effecting by force a treasonable purpose; all those who perform any part, however minute, or however remote from the scene of action, and who are actually leagued in the general conspiracy, are to be considered as traitors. But there must be an actual assembling of men for the treasonable purpose, to constitute a levying of war.[24]

In language which may have constituted an indirect reprimand to Jefferson, Marshall declared that crime which had not ripened into treason need not for that reason escape punishment. Congress was competent to provide punishment for such offenses.

> The framers of our Constitution, who not only defined and limited the crime [of treason], but with jealous circumspection attempted to protect their limitation by providing that no person should be convicted of it, unless on the testimony of two witnesses to the same overt act, or on confession in open court, must have conceived it more safe that punishment in such cases should be ordained by general laws, formed on deliberation, under the influence of no resentment, and without knowing on whom they were to operate, than that it should be inflicted under the influence of those passions which the occasion seldom fails to excite, and which a flexible definition of the crime, or a construction which would render it flexible, might bring into operation. It is, therefore, more safe as well as more consonant to the principles of our Constitution that the crime of treason should not be extended by construction to doubtful cases; and that crimes not clearly within the constitutional definition should receive such punishment as the legislature in its wisdom may provide.[25]

He found no support for a charge of treason against the prisoners. As to their obvious culpability in engaging in an enterprise against the dominions of a power at peace with the United States, that was an offense no part of which had been committed in the District of

---

[24] *Ex parte* Bollman and *Ex parte* Swartwout, 4 Cranch 75, 126 (1807).
[25] *Ibid.*, p. 127.

Columbia, and the trial could not be held in that district.    The prisoners were therefore discharged.

While Republican leaders talked hotly of impeachment for Marshall, arrangements were made to bring Burr to trial in the United States circuit court at Richmond over which Marshall presided.    The several steps in the trial provided occasion for a series of opinions by Marshall in which he rephrased and elaborated his statements made in the habeas corpus case concerning the nature of treason.    The political maneuvers involved in the trial were such that Jefferson was dragged virtually into the position of prosecutor, with much of his prestige apparently depending upon conviction of Burr.    Jefferson's political opponents, on the other hand, including not merely Federalists but a dissident Republican faction led by John Randolph, maneuvered for Burr's release.    In the face of implied threats of impeachment, Marshall criticized the administration because facts had not already been assembled to prove a case of treason as defined in his opinion in the Bollman and Swartwout case.    He admitted Burr to bail when the administration sought to keep him incarcerated.    He offended the dignity of the President with a subpoena to appear at the trial and present certain materials in evidence.    Jefferson ignored the subpoena, but he was enraged at what he regarded as an indignity done to the President of the United States.

The trial was a political battle, with the principles and procedures of law as the implements of warfare.    The administration was defeated, and Burr went free.    In his ensuing annual message to Congress, Jefferson presented the materials of the trial.    He said:

> You will be enabled to judge whether the defect was in the testimony, in the law, or in the administration of the law; and wherever it shall be found, the legislature alone can apply or originate the remedy.    The framers of our Constitution certainly supposed they had guarded as well their government against destruction by treason as their citizens against oppression under pretense of it, and if these ends are not attained it is of importance to inquire by what means more effectual they may be secured.[26]

In response to Jefferson's plea for legislative support, Senator William B. Giles, of Virginia, introduced a bill to define the crime of treason.    The bill listed a series of acts, including some of those which had been committed by Burr and his associates, and applied

[26] *Messages and Papers of the Presidents*, I, 417.

the penalty for treason to persons aiding in the doing of any of the acts, "although not personally present when any such act is done or committed." [27] The definition extended even to assembly "forcibly to resist the general execution of any public law" of the United States. Had the measure been enacted, it would have provided serious embarrassment for southern advocates of nullification in the years to come. The bill passed the Senate after speeches were delivered criticizing John Marshall and the federal judiciary, but it did not pass the House. As for impeachment proceedings against Marshall, the government became so involved in problems of international relations that it had little time to give to conflicts between the Executive and the judiciary. Jefferson's second term was nearing its end, furthermore, and concern which might otherwise have been felt for the humiliation of the President by a political opponent in another branch of the government could not be given too much attention in view of the fact that the presidency would soon be occupied by another man. As for the threat of secession in the South, which had been involved in the Burr conspiracy, it faded into the background in comparison with other threats of secession by the commercial states of the Northeast.

RESTRAINING AMERICAN COMMERCE

Most of the important activities of the American government during the first decade of the nineteenth century were involved with the military or diplomatic strife of European powers. Through the purchase of Louisiana the United States acquired an acrimonious boundary dispute with Spain and otherwise aroused ill-will which lasted for a number of years. The land hunger of those Americans who sought the acquisition, by force or otherwise, of both Florida and Mexico was a constant source of danger.

Most of the difficulties in commercial intercourse were in relation to France and England. Those nations, engaged in a bitter war, gave no thought to neutral rights, and sought to destroy all commerce which might benefit the enemy. Hundreds of American merchant ships, laden with goods bound directly or indirectly to one or the other of the belligerents or their possessions, were seized or destroyed, largely without reference to principles of international law. Several thousand seamen on American merchant ships were captured and impressed into the British service. Impressment was justified

[27] *Annals of Congress*, 10th Cong., 1st sess., pp. 108-109.

by the contention that the seamen captured were British subjects. Legal rights in the matter were confused by the fact that many of the persons involved had been British subjects, but had been naturalized or were in process of naturalization in the United States. Great Britain at that time refused to recognize the right of any subject to renounce his allegiance — a position similar to that then taken by the United States concerning its own expatriates.

It was true at that time, as in certain centers it is true today, that large numbers of influential people who in every legal sense of the word were Americans lived sentimentally with one foot on European shores. They were far more concerned about the outcome of the war in Europe than about the preservation of the integrity and the prestige of the United States. They were hot partisans of Great Britain, on the one hand, or of France on the other. This partisanship, running true to tradition, was largely in terms of the alignment of Federalists on the one hand and Republicans on the other, although in certain areas, Virginia for example, where the Federalists had little power, a rift was developing among the Republicans in terms of the European conflict.

Great as was the provocation arising from French violation of American rights, that arising from British activities was greater. Jefferson's sympathies were predominantly with France. He sought to solve problems of relations with Great Britain through a treaty dealing with the points in controversy, but a treaty negotiated by James Monroe was so humiliating in its provisions that Jefferson refused to bring about its ratification. Republicans who were less anti-British than was the rank and file of party leadership showed signs of grouping themselves around Monroe as the successor to Jefferson in the presidency. Jefferson's own choice was Madison, and he sought to avoid a party rift which might defeat his plan. In his annual message to Congress in December, 1806, therefore, he sought to shift the emphasis of his administration from foreign to domestic affairs. He called attention to the fact that the current stream of revenue was reducing the public debt as rapidly as contracts for payment allowed and was at the point of creating a surplus. He asked what should be done with this surplus. It was derived largely from duties on imports. Should the duties be lowered and give advantage to foreign over domestic manufacturers? In general he thought not. He believed that the people of the United States who paid most of the duties would prefer its continuance and application to the great purposes of the public education, roads, rivers, canals, and such other objects of public improvement as may be thought proper to add to the constitutional enumeration of federal powers. By these operations new channels of communication will be opened between the states, the lines of separation will disappear, their interests will be identified, and their union cemented by new and indissoluble ties.

He supposed a constitutional amendment would be necessary

because the objects now recommended are not among those enumerated in the Constitution, and to which it permits the public money to be applied.[28]

Even with the recommendation of a constitutional amendment, the program represented a sweeping change of ground for the Republican leader who had opposed federal centralization in the hands of Federalist leaders. The collection of money by the federal government for expenditure in the states, so that "the lines of separation will disappear," was a conception broad enough to have been sponsored by Hamilton himself.

Long before enough revenue had accumulated to enable Congress to enter upon Jefferson's domestic program, new controversies forced the attention of the government back to foreign affairs. In June, 1807, the British attacked for the first time an armed vessel of the United States. The American frigate *Chesapeake* was attacked by the British *Leopard* and sailors alleged to be British subjects were forcibly taken. For a time the whole United States, including Federalists and Republicans alike, was in an uproar. Had the nation been equipped for war, war would almost inevitably have occurred. The United States had almost no army, however; its harbors were without adequate defenses; and the condition of the navy was not much better. The alternatives left open seemed to be war, an embargo on all American shipping, or meek acquiescence in whatever depredation Great Britain found it convenient to commit.

In the preceding year, as a mode of coercion to be used against Great Britain, Congress had passed an act to prohibit the importation of certain goods from Great Britain.[29] The act was poorly enforced at best, and operated as little more than an invitation to smuggling. Congress found it expedient from time to time to authorize the suspension of the act. As the crisis became more serious, however, Jeffer-

[28] *Messages and Papers of the Presidents,* I, 397-398.     [29] 2 Stat. 379.

son seems to have concluded that the lesser of evils was a sweeping embargo on all commerce between the United States and foreign ports. "I deem it my duty to recommend the subject to the consideration of Congress," he said in a special message, "who will doubtless perceive all the advantages which may be expected from an inhibition of the departure of our vessels from the ports of the United States." [30]

Congress acted speedily. Within a few hours after the reading of Jefferson's message, the Senate passed an embargo measure, which was probably drafted by the President, and sent it to the House.[31] The vote was 22 to 6. The House took more time, debating the issue behind closed doors, and finally passed it by a vote of 82 to 46.[32] Henry Adams has characterized this as probably the most dexterous of Jefferson's feats of political management. "On his mere recommendation, without warning, discussion, or publicity, and in silence as to his true reasons and motives, he succeeded in fixing upon the country, beyond recall, the experiment of peaceable coercion." [33]

Some arguments on the ground of constitutionality were no doubt delivered prior to the enactment of the measure, but the secrecy of the debates prevented their publication. The arguments were rephrased and expanded in subsequent debates which were influenced by experience with the embargo measure.[34] It proved an almost impossible task to keep the American people from trying to ship their surplus products to foreign markets.[35] The area along the Canadian border was in a state of virtual insurrection. In spite of the closest supervision, loaded vessels escaped from Atlantic ports. Under pretext of engaging in coastal trade, vessels slipped away to trade with foreign countries. Jefferson issued vigorous orders as to the checking of all vessels seeking the right to sail, and owners and communities over which hung the shadow of misconduct found it next to impossible to get clearance from ports under any circumstances. The shipping interests in New England, whether Federalist or Republican, reacted with bitter hatred for the President. The Republican faction in the House of Representatives, which was led by John Randolph, attacked the embargo on both constitutional and economic grounds.

The constitutional argument was not well defined on either side. The Constitution gave no direct power to levy an embargo, but such

[30] *Messages and Papers of the Presidents*, I, 421.　　[31] Henry Adams, *op. cit.*, IV, 173.
[32] *Ibid.*, IV, 175.　　[33] *Ibid.*, IV, 176.　　[34] For the statute see 2 Stat. 451.
[35] For a discussion of the enforcement of the embargo see Henry Adams, *op. cit.*, IV, chapter XI.

action had been taken in times past as an implication of the power to regulate foreign commerce. Since the Federalists had hitherto assumed the right to exercise this power, it was not easy to attack it now. Republicans had no difficulty in rephrasing old Federalist arguments, but there was no denying the fact that in interdicting all American commerce with foreign countries the administration had assumed power unprecedented in its breadth. As a dissenting Republican, John Randolph stated the argument in opposition to the embargo by saying that, although such a measure might be enacted for temporary enforcement, it could not be made permanent as in this case. The power, he said, "may be an implied power, from the power to regulate commerce; but regulation is one thing and annihilation is another. As the Constitution prohibits us from laying a duty on exportation, *a fortiori* we ought to be prohibited from restraining it altogether." [36] The argument was not so persuasive, however, as to have any great influence.

Another important constitutional question was raised before Congress adjourned. Realizing that, during the recess of Congress, events might take place which would render the suspension of the embargo desirable, the Senate passed a measure authorizing the President to suspend it at his discretion. Federalists and other administration critics attacked the measure on the ground that it provided for an unconstitutional delegation of legislative power to the President. The question was analyzed as follows by Philip Barton Key, a Federalist who had occupied briefly one of the judgeships in the United States circuit courts which were created at the end of the Adams administration and abolished soon after Jefferson came into power:

> To suspend or repeal a law is a legislative act, and we cannot transfer the power of legislating from ourselves to the President; it is not a transferable power. Such an act is a flagrant violation of the Constitution in its letter, object, and spirit; it is tearing up the limits of the Constitution, and converting its prescribed bounds into legislative discretion. If to suspend or repeal a law be a legislative act, as it manifestly is, then, if we are competent to transfer one act of legislation, we are equally so to transfer all, and it undeniably follows that we have as much right to grant the President a power to make laws as to repeal laws. Let it not be said, it is too great an absurdity to suppose such a case. I resist the doctrine *in limine*. I say the Constitution never left such a discretion to be used by us. If it has, **no**

[36] *Annals of Congress,* 10th Cong., 1st sess., p. 2049.

distant day determines our liberties, and legislatures will be found hereafter courtly and servile enough to devolve the power on the President, and ease themselves of the burden of legislation.[37]

The argument was answered by George W. Campbell, a Republican from Tennessee, who showed that the measure did not give unrestricted authority to the President to suspend the embargo, but merely provided for suspension if certain circumstances occurred, such as peace in Europe or the suspension of hostilities or changes in methods affecting neutral commerce. The President, therefore, would not himself be repealing a law, but would merely be executing the measure now under consideration.[38]

The measure was passed[39] without such illumination of the constitutional question as would provide a guide for future years in discussions of the constitutionality of the delegation of legislative power. The question arose thereafter in many congressional debates and in many judicial decisions. In spite of the frequency of the discussions, it was not until 1935 that the Supreme Court held an act of Congress unconstitutional because of the delegation of legislative power.[40] Even after that decision, there remained a considerable area of uncertainty regarding the power of Congress to delegate authority to make decisions which seem legislative in character.

The enforcement of the embargo resulted in a controversy embarrassing to the administration in a case tried in the United States circuit court in Charleston, South Carolina, before Justice William Johnson of that state, whom Jefferson had appointed to the Supreme Court. An amendment to the original Embargo Act authorized United States collectors to detain, pending a decision by the President, any vessel ostensibly bound with a cargo to some other port of the United States whenever in their opinion the intention was to violate or evade any of the provisions of the Embargo Act.[41] The matter of detention was left clearly dependent upon the opinions of the collectors as to the destination of the cargoes. Violations of the law were so extensive, however, that collectors were informed that the President considered unusual shipments, particularly of flour and other provisions, as sufficient cause for the detention of the vessel. A number of ships were detained in the port of Charleston because of this order issued by the President, through the Secretary of the

---

[37] *Ibid.*, 10th Cong., 1st sess., p. 2125. See also pp. 2211 ff.    [38] *Ibid.*, pp. 2142-2143.
[39] 2 Stat. 490.    [40] Panama Refining Co. *v.* Ryan, 293 U.S. 388 (1935).
[41] 2 Stat. 499, 501.

Treasury, to the collectors. The owner of one of the vessels, which was loaded with rice and cotton, petitioned the court for a writ of mandamus to direct the collector to issue a clearance to the vessel for a trip to Baltimore. The collector acknowledged his belief that the port of Baltimore was the real destination of the vessel, but he felt bound by the order of the President, which seemed to leave him no discretion. "The officers of our government," said Justice Johnson, "from the highest to the lowest, are equally subjected to legal restraint; and it is confidently believed that all of them feel themselves equally incapable, as well from law as inclination, to attempt an unsanctioned encroachment upon individual liberty." [42] He found that under the statute action was to be based upon the opinion of the collector and not upon the discretion or judgment of the President or the Secretary of the Treasury. The mandamus was accordingly ordered.

This decision by a judge who was a Jefferson appointee was hailed with great delight by all enemies of the administration and of the embargo, and the opinion was published in newspapers all over the United States.[43] It was hailed as evidence of the extent to which the Jefferson administration was invading the liberties of the people. The Attorney General prepared for the President an official opinion to the effect that the court had no power to issue the writ of mandamus in this case. Jefferson took the unusual step of seeing that this opinion was circularized throughout the United States to counteract the influence of the opinion of the court, and to indicate the policy which the administration might be expected to follow.[44] Justice Johnson then published a reply to the opinion of the Attorney General, indicating that "a bias is attempted to be given to public opinion by the overbearing influence of high office, and the reputation of ability and information, [so that] the ground is changed; and to be silent could only result from being borne down by weight of reasoning or awed by power." [45] Collectors thereafter were in a difficult position. If they disobeyed the President, they might lose their office. If they ignored the judicial interpretation of the law, they might be liable to suit for damages. In modern times it might seem odd that the issue was not taken to the Supreme Court. The explanation doubtless

[42] Gilchrist v. Collector of Charleston, Federal Cases No. 5420, p. 356.
[43] Charles Warren, *The Supreme Court in United States History* (rev. ed., 1926), I, 326-327.
[44] *Ibid.*, pp. 329-330, and **Federal Cases No. 5420**, pp. 357-359.
[45] Federal Cases No. 5420, p. 359.

lies partly in the fact that that tribunal was dominated by Marshall, who was Jefferson's political enemy.

The question in the South Carolina case was not one of constitutionality, but of interpretation of a statute. The legal effect of the decision could, therefore, be eliminated by a new statute placing discretion as to the clearance of ships in the hands of the President rather than of the collectors. At Jefferson's request such a measure was introduced at the ensuing session of Congress and was passed to the accompaniment of hostile criticism of the judiciary.[46]

In the autumn of 1808, the United States district court for Massachusetts passed directly upon the constitutionality of the embargo. The measure was intensely unpopular throughout New England with both Federalists and Republicans, and particularly with Federalists. The judge himself was a Federalist. Yet he adhered to the early doctrines of his party as to the broad interpretation of federal powers, and held the legislation to be constitutional. He held that the measure was not unconstitutional as going beyond regulation to the point of prohibition itself, and that the commerce power might be used, not only for the advancement of commerce, but also for the promotion of other objects of national concern.[47]

Perhaps because they knew already Chief Justice Marshall's conceptions as to the breadth of federal power, the opponents of the embargo did not appeal the decision to the Supreme Court. The Court seems never to have passed upon the constitutionality of an embargo in a case in which such a measure was directly involved. The experiences of the Jefferson period, however, and experiences with embargoes which preceded it and which followed during the War of 1812 did much to establish the firm belief that such a measure was constitutional. In 1827, in deciding a case involving another phase of the commerce power, Chief Justice Marshall spoke of the "universally acknowledged power of the government to impose embargoes."[48]

The decision of a federal court that the embargo was constitutional did nothing to allay the hostility of its opponents. The economic loss due to the cessation of the foreign transport business was tremendous. The loss of foreign markets for American goods cut off a vital stream of revenue. Since the pressure of the embargo fell most heavily on the northeastern states, it gave weight to the arguments of

---

[46] Warren, *op. cit.*, I, 339-340; 2 Stat. 506, 509.
[47] United States *v. The William*, Federal Cases No. 1670; Warren, *op. cit.*, I, 342-350.
[48] Gibbons *v.* Ogden, 9 Wheaton 1, 191 (1827).

those leaders who talked more and more openly of secession. After Madison had been chosen as Jefferson's successor, but before he took office, the opposition brought about a repeal of the embargo measure and the substitution of a provision for non-intercourse with France and Great Britain, which could be suspended by the President on the restoration of amicable relationships with those countries.[49]　A year and a half later, Jefferson described the repeal and its outcome in the following language:

> The Federalists, during their short-lived ascendency, have nevertheless, by forcing us from the embargo, inflicted a wound on our interests which can never be cured, and on our affections which will require time to cicatrize.　I ascribe all this to one pseudo-Republican, Story. He came on (in place of Crowninshield, I believe) and staid only a few days; long enough, however, to get complete hold of Bacon, who, giving in to his representations, became panic-struck, and communicated his panic to his colleagues, and they to a majority of the sound members of Congress.　They believed in the alternative of repeal or civil war, and produced the fatal measure of repeal.　This is the immediate parent of all our present evils, and has reduced us to a low standing in the eyes of the world.　I should think that even the Federalists themselves must now be made, by their feelings, sensible of their error.　The wealth which the embargo brought home safely has now been thrown back into the laps of our enemies, and our navigation completely crushed, and by the unwise and unpatriotic conduct of those engaged in it.[50]

The repeal of the embargo publicly discredited the program by which Jefferson sought to preserve the dignity and the property of the United States and to keep the country at peace by the virtual prohibition of all foreign commerce.　He had expected that the withdrawal of the United States from the field of foreign trade would force Great Britain to make concessions.　The movement failed.　It failed likewise to draw the states more closely together and to promote the prosperity of the country by stimulating internal commercial relationships.　The suppression of commercial business brought about by the embargo did have an important effect, however, in stimulating migration westward and in the settlement of the western states.　In a sense, therefore, by merging in new states population from the rival states of the East, he did prepare for a more distant cementing of

[49] 2 Stat. 528.
[50] *The Writings of Thomas Jefferson* (Washington ed., 9 vols., 1853-1854), V, 529.

the bonds of union, save as issues between the North and the South, connected particularly with the subject of slavery, refused to be buried even in the new states of the West.

## THE WAR OF 1812

Throughout most of Jefferson's two administrations and the first administration of Madison the United States stood constantly at the brink of war. The Federalists were opposed to war with Great Britain, both because of their sympathies with that country in its struggle with France and because war, like the embargo, would be destructive of American commerce. They used, in addition, the argument against the centralization of power in the federal government which Republicans in earlier years might have been expected to use. Philip Barton Key, in the House of Representatives in 1809, said:

> We are an agricultural people, a peaceful people. The bond of our union was mutual defense. We are not constituted with active powers for offensive operation; but we are all-powerful for defensive measures. In a state of war, armies will become necessary; and even when necessary, they are always dangerous to republics. Their shield and safety is a well-regulated militia. I have no doubt, if war is declared, that we shall raise a great force; and if we do, it is war that will jeopardize the independence of the several states.[51]

The experience of more recent years has demonstrated the validity of the principle stated by the Federalists. The conduct of the Civil War brought about great centralization of power in the hands of the federal government and of the President. The experience of the first World War was far more sweeping. The successful conduct of the War of 1812 would probably have required drastic centralization of authority in the hands of Madison. Unfortunately, although he was a great scholar in the field of political science, a great constitution-maker and legislator, he had not the mind or the personality for highly personalized leadership in a time of crisis. At no time did he have a united nation behind him. He lacked the ability to bring about national unity.

The weakness of Republican war leadership was indicated at every turn. In spite of the length of time during which war had been imminent, the Republican leaders had not brought about the unanimity of popular sentiment which is always necessary for the support of

[51] *Annals of Congress*, 10th Cong., 2d sess., p. 1355.

a major war. The country possessed a war faction, a faction bitterly opposed to war, and a great mass of people who had no particular interest one way or the other. Furthermore, although there had been ample time to provide the necessary equipment for fighting, the equipment was hopelessly inadequate. Neither the army nor the navy was organized, trained, or equipped for effective combat. The military organization was honeycombed with politics and incompetence, which was matched only by the civilian organization in Washington. Although he made some changes, Madison struggled through the war period without gathering about him an efficient body of administrative assistants. He neither achieved nor sought to achieve the dominant influence over Congress which is necessary for the efficient management of a war. The votes in favor of a declaration of war indicated the lack of unity of sentiment in that body. The vote of the Senate was 19 to 13 in favor of the declaration, while the vote in the House was 79 to 49.[52]

Having been trained in the principles of Republican economy, the House of Representatives at first indignantly refused to restore internal revenue taxes to provide the funds needed by the government. It eventually acquiesced reluctantly in the levying of those taxes and in other revenue plans including the levying of a direct tax. A national bank was badly needed. The Bank of the United States, which had been chartered in 1791 as the result of the efforts of Hamilton, was no longer in existence, its charter having expired in 1811. The Republicans had prevented the renewal of the charter of this Federalist institution. Gallatin recommended the renewal of the charter, but Congress refused to carry out the recommendation. It was not until 1816, when the chaos of post-war finances made such a step essential, that Republican leaders, including the President, gave their support to the establishment of a second Bank of the United States.

For an army the government relied in part upon the militia of the several states. The Constitution provided that Congress should have power "to provide for calling forth the militia to execute the laws of the Union, suppress insurrections and repel invasions."[53] Pursuant to an earlier act of Congress,[54] delegating to the President the power to

---

[52] This is the vote recorded on the measure as passed by the House before submission to the Senate for approval. No record is given for the vote of concurrence in the Senate amendments. (See *Annals of Congress*, 12th Cong., 1st sess., pp. 1637, 1682.)
[53] Article I, Section 8, Clause 15.  [54] 1 Stat. 424.

call forth the militia, calls were made upon the several states. Some of the states co-operated reluctantly and others refused outright. It was argued in some instances that there was no violation of the laws of the Union and no insurrection or invasion, and that the federal government had no right to call out the state militia. The general court of Massachusetts announced an opinion that only the states had the power to decide whether or not conditions existed which justified the use of the state militia by the federal government.[55] Other New England states took the same position.[56] The constitutional question did not reach the Supreme Court until 1827, when the Court held, in an opinion written by Justice Story, that the authority to decide whether the exigencies contemplated in the Constitution had arisen was vested by the Constitution and statutes exclusively in the President, whose decision was conclusive upon all other persons.[57]

Heated debates took place in Congress over the raising of an army by conscription. In spite of denunciations of such a measure as unconstitutional and as a threat to the Union itself, a conscription bill passed the Senate. It passed the House also, but with amendments which the Senate refused to accept. It therefore failed to become a law, largely perhaps because the war was already near its end. In view of the bitter opposition to conscription, the results which would have flowed from the enactment of such a measure defy prediction. As to its constitutionality, however, the question was settled more than a century later by a decision of the Supreme Court based on the conscription measure of the first World-War period. The Court held such a measure to be within the powers of the federal government.[58]

The opposition of the New England states to the continuation of the war resulted in the famous Hartford Convention of 1814. The resolutions passed by the convention recommended that the legislatures of the several states enact measures to protect their citizens from the operation of unconstitutional acts of the federal government and in various ways sought to strengthen the position of the states in the Union. The convention did not advocate secession from the Union. It was a gathering of dissenters, however, held in a time of war, when dissent could not easily be tolerated. The war ended soon afterward, but the convention came to symbolize the resistance to the

[55] Herman V. Ames, *State Documents on Federal Relations* (1906), No. 2, pp. 13-15.

[56] For discussion see Andrew C. McLaughlin, *A Constitutional History of the United States* (1935), pp. 350-351.

[57] Martin *v.* Mott, 12 Wheaton 19 (1827).

[58] Selective Draft Law Cases, 245 U.S. 366 (1918).

efficient conduct of the war, which, in spite of a few victories toward the end, brought humiliation to the people of the United States and to their government.  It helped to identify the Federalist party as the party of disloyalty, and speeded the final steps of its disintegration.

Amid the chaos which followed the war there was need for strong measures such as the Federalists of another generation would have advocated.  Although some of the measures were enacted, they were sponsored, not by Federalists, but by the stronger leaders of the Republican party.

### INTERNAL IMPROVEMENTS

As mentioned above, the Republicans, in spite of their dislike for old Federalist institutions, found it necessary, in restoring financial order after the war, to establish a new Bank of the United States. That agency will be discussed in another chapter in connection with Supreme Court decisions bearing upon the constitutionality of the legislation.  The long period of restraint upon foreign commerce had provided opportunities for the building-up of small industries in the United States, which now clamored for protection against foreign competition.  Their pleas were answered by a tariff measure containing many protective provisions.  The measure marks the beginning of a rapid rise in barriers against foreign trade for the benefit of home industries.  Jefferson and his immediate successors were not industrialists, but their policies had much to do with the growth of industry in the United States.

Now that the war was at an end, the nation turned again to the building of roads and canals, which made possible the development of commerce and the use of products of sections of the country hitherto inaccessible.  Congress had not yet accepted Jefferson's invitation to participate extensively in that work.  In his annual message to Congress in December, 1816, Madison included the following sentence:

> And I particularly invite again their attention to the expediency of exercising their existing powers, and, where necessary, of resorting to the prescribed mode of enlarging them, in order to effectuate a comprehensive system of roads and canals, such as will have the effect of drawing more closely together every part of our country by promoting intercourse and improvements and by increasing the share of every part in the common stock of national prosperity.[59]

[59] *Messages and Papers of the Presidents*, II, 561.

Before it adjourned, Congress passed a measure providing funds

> for constructing roads and canals, and improving the navigation of water courses, in order to facilitate, promote, and give security to internal commerce among the several states, and to render more easy and less expensive the means and provisions for the common defense.[60]

Congress took no steps, however, toward securing a constitutional amendment to authorize the expenditure of federal funds on such projects.

Madison vetoed the bill.   Alluding to the power of Congress to provide for the common defense and the general welfare, he expressed the opinion that it did not extend to measures of this kind.   If that provision were broadly interpreted, it would give to Congress a general power of legislation instead of the defined and limited one hitherto understood to be given by the Constitution.   The result would be that the constitutions and laws of the several states in all cases not specifically exempted would be superseded by laws of Congress.   Such a view of the Constitution, furthermore, he argued,

> would have the effect of excluding the judicial authority of the United States from its participation in guarding the boundary between the legislative powers of the general and the state governments, inasmuch as questions relating to the general welfare, being questions of policy and expediency, are unsusceptible of judicial cognizance and decision.[61]

James Monroe, who was inaugurated as President the day after Madison's veto message was delivered, demonstrated enthusiasm for internal improvements, but added a caution that the government must proceed always with a constitutional sanction.[62]   In his first annual message he again lauded the creation of public improvements, but added that

> a difference of opinion has existed from the first formation of our Constitution to the present time among our most enlightened and virtuous citizens respecting the right of Congress to establish such a system of improvement.   Taking into view the trust with which I am now honored, it would be improper after what has passed that this discussion should be revived with an uncertainty of my opinion respecting the right.   Disregarding early impressions, I have bestowed

[60] *Ibid.*, II, p. 569.          [61] *Ibid.*, II. 570.          [62] *Ibid.*, II, 577.

on the subject all the deliberation which its great importance and a just sense of my duty required, and the result is a settled conviction in my mind that Congress do not possess the right.

He therefore suggested that Congress submit to the states a constitutional amendment which would confer the power in question.[63] A resolution providing for a constitutional amendment was introduced, but was not adopted. It was opposed, not merely by those who objected to the extension of federal activities, but also by those who believed that the Constitution already gave the necessary power and that support of the constitutional amendment would be a dangerous admission that this and other broad powers were not given by the Constitution.[64] Congressmen who believed that the federal government had some power in this field differed as to extent, some arguing that Congress did appropriate money for roads, canals, and river improvements, but could not engage in the actual construction.

Monroe finally came to the conclusion that Congress had the power to appropriate money for public improvements which were general in character rather than local. He defined the power narrowly, however. In 1822 he vetoed an act for the preservation and repair of the Cumberland Road which gave the power to enforce the collection of tolls by penalties, and so encroached, he believed, upon what are now called the police powers of the state. In connection with his veto message he submitted a lengthy document stating his views on the general subject of public improvements.[65]

More than a century passed before the Supreme Court delivered its pronouncements upon the power of Congress to appropriate money for the general welfare.[66] Without judicial determination of the question the subject was highly important throughout the decade of the eighteen-twenties and afterward. There had been as yet little development of corporation law in the United States, and experience had not yet been developed for the handling of large-scale projects by means of funds brought together by private corporations. The failure to enact a constitutional amendment giving unquestioned power to the federal government, and the reluctance of many legislators to engage in broad spending of federal funds on such projects, left the way open for the development of corporate enterprise in this field.

[63] *Ibid.*, II, 587.

[64] Homer C. Hockett, *Constitutional History of the United States*, I (1939), 350-352.

[65] *Messages and Papers of the Presidents*, II, 711 ff.

[66] United States *v.* Butler, 297 U.S. 1 (1935); Charles C. Steward Machine Co. *v.* Davis, 301 U.S. 548 (1937).

### THE PRESIDENTIAL TERM

With the experience of administration after administration the office of President took on its relatively permanent form. In some respects its powers were expanded widely, and in others they were limited. The action of the several Presidents established the tradition that no occupant of the office should serve more than two four-year terms, a tradition which survived for more than a century and a half. Washington seems to have had no real desire to be President at all. He accepted a second term reluctantly and refused altogether to accept a third term. His reasons, as given in his Farewell Address, were personal reasons rather than conceptions of public policy. John Adams was retired by the voters at the end of one term. In a letter to John Taylor, written after his election to a second term, Jefferson let it be known that he would not again be a candidate. His opinion originally, he said, was that the President should have been elected for seven years and should have been ineligible thereafter. He now thought that service for eight years with the power of removal with the people at the end of the first four was a better arrangement. He said:

> The danger is that the indulgence and attachments of the people will keep a man in the chair after he becomes a dotard, that re-election through life shall become habitual, and election for life follow that. General Washington set the example of voluntary retirement after eight years. I shall follow it, and a few more precedents will oppose the obstacle of habit to anyone after a while who shall endeavor to extend his term. Perhaps it may beget a disposition to establish it by an amendment of the Constitution. . . . There is, however, but one circumstance which could engage my acquiescence in another election, to wit, such a division about a successor as might bring in a monarchist. But this circumstance is impossible.[67]

Madison, with all his eminence as a statesman, was too colorless to arouse any demand that he serve beyond two terms. The same was true of Monroe. Had either of them been a powerful popular leader with a desire to continue in office, the tradition might well have been shattered before it was established. As it was, the desire to continue any President in office beyond two terms was felt so rarely that the tradition lasted until a popular sense of its justification had virtually disappeared. It died of old age in 1940 at the hands of a skillful popular leader in a time of foreign war.

[67] *The Writings of Thomas Jefferson* (Ford ed., 10 vols., 1892-1899), VIII, 339.

The presidency was vitally affected by the vicissitudes of the two-party system. As long as Federalists provided successful opposition for Republicans, the election of the President, once candidates were nominated, functioned much as it has done in later years. During the period between the end of the War of 1812 and the administration of Andrew Jackson, however, party organization was in chaos. The Republican party broke into factions, largely because it had no effective opposition, and it was not until after a great deal of sectional strife that new party alignments were established. One of the important political results was that electoral votes in 1824 were divided among a considerable number of influential candidates. No candidate having received a majority, the election was thrown into the House of Representatives. The administration of John Quincy Adams provided a focal point for the hostility of the group which successfully supported Andrew Jackson for the presidency in 1828. The eight years of the Jackson administration tended to solidify opposition by the Whigs, the successors to the Federalists. For some years thereafter the Whig party fulfilled the function of an opposition party, usually in the minority.

A tradition of nomination by party caucus in Congress seemed for a time in the process of formation. Congressional partisan control was bitterly criticized, however, by factions in the party which happened not to be in control in Congress. The vicissitudes of party machinery during the chaotic period of the eighteen-twenties probably had much to do with the shift to the system of nominating by national party conventions, even though the system did not get well under way until the eighteen-thirties.

Along with the congressional caucus went another arrangement that for a time seemed likely to entrench itself as an important tradition. Jefferson had served as Secretary of State under Washington. Madison had served as Secretary of State under Jefferson. Monroe had served as Secretary of State under Madison. John Quincy Adams had served as Secretary of State under Monroe. The succession seemed far more than a coincidence. The chain of circumstance was broken when Henry Clay, Secretary of State under John Quincy Adams, failed of election in competition with Andrew Jackson. Jackson was succeeded in the presidency by Martin Van Buren, who for a time had been his Secretary of State. James Buchanan, who became President in 1857, had been Secretary of State under James K. Polk. But since that time no man who has held that particular cabinet office has ever become President.    If a tradition may be said to have been developed at all, it was probably broken in 1824.    John Quincy Adams was elected, not on the basis of popular nomination or the vote of presidential electors, but as a result of compromise in the House of Representatives.    The nomination of Van Buren was due, quite probably, not to the fact that he had been Secretary of State, but to the fact that he was the choice of Andrew Jackson.    It was believed for a time that Cordell Hull, Secretary of State under Franklin D. Roosevelt, might be the candidate of his party in 1940 to succeed Roosevelt.    The prospect was eliminated by Roosevelt's decision to seek a third term.    In view of Roosevelt's attitude toward the public-utility magnate who opposed him as the Republican nominee, the circumstance may perhaps be likened to that under which Jefferson admitted that he might be willing to serve another term; namely, the prospect of being succeeded by a monarchist.

Only for a brief period did the vice-presidency give some promise of providing training for future Presidents.    Adams and Jefferson both held that office before their election to the presidency.    Only one other Vice-President, however, Martin Van Buren, was subsequently chosen to the presidency without having in the meantime become President by virtue of the death of his predecessor.    Six Vice-Presidents — Tyler, Fillmore, Johnson, Arthur, Theodore Roosevelt, and Coolidge — did succeed to the higher office because of the death of Presidents.    Other than through this route of succession, however, serving as Vice-President has offered no prospects for the holding of higher office.

# CHAPTER 8

# THE OBLIGATION OF CONTRACTS

NEXT TO POLITICAL AND RELIGIOUS LIBERTY, the acquisition of property loomed large in the minds of American pioneers.   Land, houses, and the necessary equipment constituted the primary forms of property. Closely related were the devices of transportation and trade, such as horses and wagons and ships.   Apart from the direct utilization of natural resources, the processes of trading for profit provided the principal mechanisms for acquiring property.   Trade depended on good faith in the performance of contracts, since non-performance would result in loss of property and profits.   The founding fathers had this fact much in mind when they grouped in Article I, Section 10, of the Constitution a series of prohibitions against undue interference with rights of property.   The section read in part as follows: "No state shall . . . coin money; emit bills of credit; make anything but gold and silver coin a tender in payment of debts; [or] pass any . . . law impairing the obligation of contracts."

In the Constitutional Convention and in the ratifying conventions these several clauses seem to have been considered pretty much together.[1]   Their purpose was to check abuses in the form of laws depreciating the currency for the relief of debtors, requiring acceptance of land or other commodities in lieu of gold and silver, and otherwise endangering property rights resting upon and guaranteed by contracts.   The founding fathers seem to have been concerned exclusively with state laws impairing the obligation of private contracts. They did not discuss the applicability of the contract clause to contracts made by the states themselves, nor did they discuss in any significant manner the breadth of the definition of the word "contract." It was left to the Supreme Court, under the guidance of John Marshall, to develop the contract clause into an instrument for the regi-

---

[1] For analysis see Benjamin F. Wright, *The Contract Clause of the Constitution* (1938), chapter I.

mentation of states in connection with their own contracts and to interpret broadly the meaning of the word "contract" so as to extend control beyond the scope usually given to it.　In a series of decisions ranking in importance with any others in American constitutional history, Marshall used the contract clause to prevent the repeal of legislative grants, to prevent the withdrawal of tax exemptions, to prevent the impairment of a charter granted by a state, and to prevent the relief of debtors under certain circumstances by state insolvency laws.　The several cases, summarized in the following pages, illustrate the fact that much of the nationalism of John Marshall was not nationalism in the sense that he desired the extension of federal control over private enterprise, but only in the sense that he sought to make the federal judiciary an instrument for the protection of private rights against interference by the states.

### GRANTS OF LAND MADE BY STATE LEGISLATURES

The melodramatic speculation in the stock market indulged in by the people of the United States in the nineteen-twenties had its counterpart in the early years of American history in speculation in land. Undeveloped land existed all along the western border.　Population was increasing rapidly and was characterized by a steady movement westward.　It seemed inevitable that the virgin lands of today should provide homes for the settlers of tomorrow.　The owner of these lands had only to await the process of settlement to see their value increase many times over.　Speculators, acting individually and through land companies, bought up large tracts and promoted settlement, making or hoping to make huge profits in the process.　The wealth of many families was garnered in this manner.　Speculators were undeterred by the fact that some of their number overreached and so impoverished themselves.　Robert Morris, sometimes called the financier of the Revolution, maneuvered himself into a debtors' prison. James Wilson, a member of the Constitutional Convention and later an associate justice of the Supreme Court, fled from his home to escape his creditors.　Like unregulated speculation in stocks, speculation in land was frequently tainted with fraud.

The first great contract case arising out of speculation in public land arose in connection with the disposition of much of the area now included in the states of Alabama and Mississippi.　The land was claimed by the poverty-stricken and thinly settled state of Georgia. A huge section of this territory was first sold to speculators in 1789.

They were unable to pay for the land, however, and the transaction fell through.[2] The invention of the cotton gin in 1793 added tremendously to the potential value of the land. In 1795, speculators, organized into four land companies, swooped down upon the Georgia legislature, involved nearly all of the legislators in their plan by allotting lands to them or making other awards, and secured the enactment of a measure to dispose of the entire area for five hundred thousand dollars. Justice James Wilson and a member of the United States Senate were prominent among the lobbyists. The land companies made extensive sales to other speculators all over the United States.

The news of the corruption of the legislature and, presumably, also news of profits being made out of the sale of the land, quickly reached the people of Georgia. They elected a new legislature, which repealed the granting statute to the accompaniment of a melodramatic display of righteous indignation. Purchasers of land involved consulted their lawyers about the validity of the rescinding act. One of the lawyers, in turn, consulted with Alexander Hamilton. In an opinion written in 1796, Hamilton argued that the rescinding act was void because of violation of the contract clause of the Constitution, following lines of reasoning later taken by Chief Justice Marshall. The legislature had revoked a grant, previously made for a valuable consideration, to the prejudice of third parties presumably innocent of fraud or corruption. Such a revocation contravened the first principles of natural justice and social policy. In addition to these general considerations, he argued, the language of the contract clause was the equivalent of saying that no state should pass a law revoking, invalidating, or altering a contract. A grant, whether made by a state or an individual, was virtually a contract that the grantee should hold and enjoy the thing granted. If the terms of the Constitution were taken in their larger sense and given effect according to the general spirit and the policy of the provision, he thought that the revocation of the grant by the act of the legislature of Georgia might justly be considered as contrary to the Constitution of the United States. He thought that the courts of the United States would be likely to pronounce it so.[3] Robert Goodloe Harper, who was involved in the

[2] Albert J. Beveridge, *The Life of John Marshall* (4 vols., 1916-1919), III, 553-554. For a detailed account of the several transactions and the litigation discussed herein see *ibid.*, chapter X.

[3] Wright, *op. cit.*, p. 22.

litigation both as a purchaser and as counsel, made extensive use of the Hamilton opinion, presenting the argument finally before the Supreme Court of the United States in the famous case of Fletcher *v.* Peck.[4]

Counsel opposing the claims of persons who had purchased land granted by the Georgia statute of 1795 stressed the fraud involved in the enactment of the statute as a cause of its invalidity. This case, however, involved, not the original purchasers, but third parties who had no legal notice of the fraud, and the Supreme Court refused to inquire into the matter of fraud. Said Chief Justice Marshall: "It may well be doubted how far the validity of a law depends upon the motives of its framers, and how far the particular inducements, operating on members of the supreme sovereign power of a state, to the formation of a contract by that power, are examinable in a court of justice."[5]

This attitude on the part of the Court may have suggested to observers a moral callousness highly inconsistent with the sensitivity of the Chief Justice concerning the rights of the so-called innocent third parties. The attitude had importance, however, far beyond the reaches of this case. It indicated the probability that the federal courts would not in future cases invade the processes of state governments in search of misconduct which might have a bearing upon the validity of state laws. It exempted the states from judicial interference which would have followed inevitably upon the acceptance of the principle that it was the duty of the Court to inquire into the details of the enactment of state legislation in order to determine its validity.

Marshall's opinion, like that of Hamilton, is shot through with evidence of belief in principles of natural justice which are to be used as guides in the interpretation of the Constitution. The basic principle set forth is the inviolability of private property as far as invasion by government is concerned. As Marshall saw it, the principle of the rescinding statute on the other hand, was that a legislature might, by its own act, divest the vested estate of any person for whatever reasons it might deem sufficient. He admitted that in the matter of general legislation one legislature was competent to repeal any act which a former legislature was competent to pass and that one legislature could not abridge the powers of its successor. But if the act done was in the nature of a contract, he argued, a succeeding legislature could not undo it: "The past cannot be recalled by the

[4] 6 Cranch 87, 123 (1810).    [5] *Ibid.,* p. 130.

most absolute power. Conveyances have been made; those convey-ances have vested legal estates, and, if those estates may be seized by the sovereign authority, still, that they originally were vested is a fact, and cannot cease to be a fact." [6]

He assumed that the nature of society and of government prescribed some limits to the legislative power. Although all legislative power was granted to the legislature, he doubted whether the act of trans-ferring the property of an individual to the public was in the nature of a legislative power. "The validity of this rescinding act, then," he reasoned, "might well be doubted, were Georgia a single sovereign power." [7] It is to be noted that he did not rest this doubt upon any provision of the constitution of Georgia or of the Constitution of the United States. It was based upon his conception of "the nature of society and of government."

Having proceeded thus far in terms of what might be called higher-law principles, the Chief Justice now turned to the contract clause of the federal Constitution. Georgia was not a single sovereign power. The state was a member of the American Union, and that Union had a Constitution which all acknowledged as supreme and which imposed an impassable limit to the legislatures of the several states. Among other things, it declared that no state should enact any law impairing the obligation of contracts. He asked two questions: "What is a con-tract? Is a grant a contract?"

A contract, he answered, was a compact between two or more parties. It was either executory or executed. An executory contract was one in which a party bound himself to do or not to do a par-ticular thing. A contract executed was one in which the object of the contract had been performed. Both types of contract contained obligations binding on the parties. A grant was a contract executed, the obligation of which still continued. It would be strange, he said, if a contract to convey was secured by the Constitution, while an absolute conveyance remained unprotected.

If a grant by a private party was covered by the contract clause, was a grant by the state excluded from the operation of the provision? Was the clause to be considered as inhibiting the state from impairing the obligation of contracts between two individuals, but as excluding from that inhibition contracts made with itself? He found no such distinction in the words of the Constitution. If contracts made with the state were to be exempted, the exemption must arise from the

[6] *Ibid.*, p. 135.  [7] *Ibid.*, p. 137.

character of the contracting party. Whatever respect might have been felt for the state sovereignty, it was not to be disguised, he said, that the framers of the Constitution viewed with some apprehension the violent acts which might grow out of the feelings of the moment, and that the people of the United States, in adopting that instrument, had manifested a determination to shield themselves and their property from the effects of those sudden and strong passions to which men were exposed. The restrictions on the legislative power of the states were obviously founded in this sentiment. The Constitution of the United States contained what might be deemed a bill of rights for the people of each state. He concluded:

> It is, then, the unanimous opinion of the Court that, in this case, the estate having passed into the hands of a purchaser for a valuable consideration, without notice, the state of Georgia was restrained, either by general principles, which are common to our free institutions, or by the particular provisions of the Constitution of the United States, from passing a law whereby the estate of the plaintiff in the premises so purchased could be constitutionally and legally impaired and rendered null and void.[8]

Justice Johnson wrote a concurring opinion which further illustrated the extent to which the decisions of judges in this period were determined by beliefs as to fundamental principles of government rather than by the language of constitutions or laws. He wanted it distinctly understood that his opinion was not based on the contract clause. He had serious doubts as to the meaning of that clause. He did not hesitate to declare that a state did not possess the power of revoking its own grant, "but I do it on a general principle, on the reason and nature of things; a principle which will impose laws even on the Deity."[9]

CONTRACTS IN THE FORM OF EXEMPTION FROM TAXATION

In 1812, two years after the decision in Fletcher v. Peck, the Supreme Court decided the case of New Jersey v. Wilson,[10] in which it held that exemption from taxation prescribed in a grant of land made by a state was a contract which could not be impaired, even after the land had been sold by the original grantee. The case was one in which the colonial legislature of New Jersey had bought up and granted certain lands to the remnant of the tribe of Delaware

---

[8] *Ibid.*, p. 139.          [9] *Ibid.*, p. 143.          [10] 7 Cranch 164.

Indians in return for which the Indians released their claim to certain other lands.   In 1801 the Indians moved to northern New York.   The land which had been granted to them was sold soon afterward and the state of New Jersey sought to tax it.   The new owners challenged the constitutionality of the tax.

The exemption from taxation, said Chief Justice Marshall for the Supreme Court, was certainly a contract clothed in forms of unusual solemnity.   "The privilege, though for the benefit of the Indians, is annexed, by the terms which create it, to the land itself, and not to their persons.   It is for their advantage that it should be annexed to the land, because, in the event of a sale, on which alone the question could become material, the value would be enhanced by it." [11]   He admitted that New Jersey might have insisted on a surrender of the privilege of exemption from taxation as a condition on which the sale of the property should be allowed.   The state had not insisted on this condition, however, and had given its consent to the sale of the land with all its privileges and immunities.   The purchaser succeeded to all the rights of the Indians.   He was entitled to the benefits of their contract.   This contract, said the Chief Justice, was certainly impaired by a law which would annul this essential part of it.

The opinion of the Court was unusually brief for a decision establishing a principle of such great importance.   The Chief Justice made no mention of the questions of public policy involved in permitting a state legislature to withhold segments of property within the state from the exercise of the taxing power in future years.   He and his colleagues concerned themselves exclusively with the question of the impairment of vested rights of private parties, without reference to other aspects of public policy.[12]   The decision was never overruled. The Supreme Court in future years did insist, however, that the intention to grant exemption from taxation should be so clearly expressed as to leave no doubt in the matter.[13]   The land involved in the New Jersey case, as a matter of fact, subsequently lost the right of exemption.   Beginning in 1814 the land was regularly assessed for taxation.   In spite of the decision, the owners acquiesced in the taxation for a period of some sixty years.   When, after the end of that period, the power of the state to tax was challenged, the Supreme

[11] *Ibid.*, p. 167.          [12] See Wright, *op. cit.*, pp. 36-37.
[13] For cases see *The Constitution of the United States of America*, Annotated, Senate Doc. No. 232, 74th Cong., 2d sess. (1938), pp. 342-346.

Court held that the right of exemption from taxation had been lost as a result of acquiescence in the exercise of the power over this long period of years.[14]

## THE CONFISCATION OF CHURCH PROPERTY

A vital question in the interpretation of the contract clause was the extent to which the rights of corporations chartered by the state were protected from interference.   The question was approached, but not fully answered, in the case of Terrett v. Taylor,[15] decided in 1815. Before the Revolution the Episcopal Church had been the established church in the colony of Virginia.   By the operation of Virginia statutes and the common law, certain lands became vested in the Episcopal Church.   A Virginia statute of 1776, in the language of Justice Story, "operated as a new grant and confirmation thereof to the use of the church." [16]   It was subsequently asserted by the Virginia legislature, however, that this statute was inconsistent with the bill of rights and the constitution of the state, which guaranteed freedom of religion, and was therefore void.   In 1801, the legislature asserted the right of the state to all the property of the Episcopal churches in the state and authorized overseers of the poor to seize and sell certain lands and appropriate the proceeds to the use of the poor. Justice Story in the opinion for the Court said:

> That the legislature can repeal statutes creating private corporations, or confirming to them property already acquired under the face of previous laws, and by such repeal can vest the property of such corporations exclusively in the state, or dispose of the same to such purposes as they may please, without the consent or default of the corporators, we are not prepared to admit; and we think ourselves standing upon the principles of natural justice, upon the fundamental laws of every free government, upon the spirit and the letter of the Constitution of the United States, and upon the decisions of most respectable judicial tribunals, in resisting such a doctrine.[17]

Oddly enough, Story did not state upon what "letter" of the Constitution the decision rested or upon what "decisions of most respectable judicial tribunals."   Presumably, he must have had in mind the contract clause and the cases of Fletcher v. Peck and New Jersey v. Wilson, but he did not cite them.   Since the property was never actually given by the state, but the title merely confirmed in the church by

[14] Given v. Wright, 117 U.S. 648  (1886).
[15] 9 Cranch 43.          [16] Ibid., p. 50.          [17] Ibid., p. 52.

the laws of the state, it would have been no easy task to find a contract in any state law, even though Justice Story did characterize the statute of 1776 as "a new grant and confirmation" of the land. The Court may have relied less heavily on the letter of the Constitution than on its "spirit" and on what Justice Story called "the principles of natural justice" and "the fundamental laws of every free government." At any rate, like Chief Justice Marshall, or even more than Marshall, Story was ever ready to rely upon principles of natural justice as the key to the meaning of the Constitution. This tendency to make use of natural-law concepts has been revealed from time to time throughout the entire history of the Supreme Court. It existed with greater starkness in the early years, however, than in more recent times, when the Court avoids the old terminology and talks instead in such terms as due process of law, reasonable, unreasonable, arbitrary, capricious, suitable, unsuitable, fair, and unfair, in working out the application of the Constitution.[18]

The decision concerning the power of a state to take over church property, at any rate, added another support to the structure being built in decision after decision by the Supreme Court. That structure represents one of the most important achievements of the Marshall régime.[19]

## CHARTERS AS CONTRACTS — THE DARTMOUTH COLLEGE CASE

In 1819, the Supreme Court decided the Dartmouth College case,[20] one of the most important cases decided in all its history. It determined the fact that in constitutional law charters of private corporations were contracts which could not be impaired by the states granting them. It gave stability to the rights of corporations which could not have been achieved in any other way. The decision preceded the time when the laws and traditions of corporate enterprise made it possible for corporations to engage safely in large-scale enterprise and when participation of the federal government in the management of internal improvements was still being discussed. The Dartmouth College decision, coupled with the development of a more adequate

[18] For discussion see Charles Grove Haines, *The Revival of Natural Law Concepts* (1930). See also Edward S. Corwin, "The 'Higher Law' Background of American Constitutional Law," *Harvard Law Review*, XLII (December, 1928), 149-185, 365-409.

[19] See Edward S. Corwin, *The Twilight of the Supreme Court* (1934), chapter II; "The Basic Doctrine of American Constitutional Law," *Michigan Law Review*, XII (February, 1914), 247-276.

[20] Dartmouth College *v.* Woodward, 4 Wheaton 518 (1819).

body of corporation law in the several states, had much to do with the fact that economic development in the United States took place largely through privately owned corporations rather than through activities of the federal or state governments.

The decision had to do with the charter, not of a business corporation, but of a college, which had been granted in the name of the King of England in 1769. The facts which gave rise to the case are extremely complicated and not particularly relevant to an account of American constitutional development. It is enough to say briefly that a virtual feud arose between factions connected with the management and operation of the college. The people of the whole state took sides. The division rested initially on matters of religion and ultimately on considerations of party politics. The Republican party was in power in the state. The Republican legislature enacted a law modifying the charter of the college, reorganizing the board of trustees, rearranging the management of the institution, and changing the name from Dartmouth College to Dartmouth University. The old board of trustees brought suit against the secretary of the college, who had aligned himself with the new administration, for the recovery of the college charter, records, seal, and other items.[21]

The case was argued before a New Hampshire court of three Republican judges — one of them, incidentally, Levi Woodbury, was many years later appointed to the Supreme Court of the United States. The court, through the able opinion of Chief Justice William M. Richardson, decided against the college.[22]

"A corporation considered as a faculty," said the justice, "is an artificial, invisible body, existing only in contemplation of law."[23] Corporations were of two kinds, public and private. Private corporations were those which were created for the immediate benefit and advantage of individuals. To this class belonged all companies incorporated for the purpose of making canals, turnpike roads, and bridges, and also banking, insurance, and manufacturing companies. Public corporations, on the other hand, were created for public purposes. The corporators had no private beneficial interest, either in the franchises or in the property. In this group were included coun-

---

[21] The case has been widely discussed. See for example discussions and citations, Beveridge, op. cit., III, chapter V; Charles Warren, The Supreme Court in United States History (rev. ed., 2 vols., 1926) I, chapter XI; Wright, op. cit., pp. 39-46.

[22] Dartmouth College v. Woodward, 65 N.H. 473 (1817); Edward S. Corwin, John Marshall and the Constitution (1919), pp. 154-172.

[23] Ibid., p. 627.

ties, towns, and parishes. He found that Dartmouth College was established for religious and educational purposes for the benefit of the public, and not for the benefit of the trustees or other individuals. It was, therefore, a public corporation. The justice was of the opinion that the charter of a public corporation did not constitute a contract protected against impairment by the contract clause of the Constitution, but even if it was such a contract, he was of the opinion that the action taken in this case had not been such as to constitute impairment.

The case was appealed to the Supreme Court. The opinion of Justice Story in Terrett v. Taylor had made it clear that the Supreme Court would not protect from impairment the charter of a public, as distinguished from a private, corporation. Daniel Webster, who with others had been counsel for the college in the New Hampshire court, had the task of demonstrating the fact that the college was not a public corporation, but a private charity, or, as he expressed it, an eleemosynary corporation. Having established the private status of the corporation, it was then necessary to show that the charter had been impaired by the act of the New Hampshire legislature.

It was no easy task, in any event, to demonstrate the fact that the charter of the college contained all the necessary elements of a contract. Webster shrewdly avoided reliance merely upon the logic of the law. He dramatized the dangers which surrounded all educational institutions if no means was found to protect them from political interference by the legislature. Arguing more profoundly, he sought to demonstrate that the act of the New Hampshire legislature was a violation of fundamental principles of government. "It is not too much to assert," he declared, "that the legislature of New Hampshire would not have been competent to pass the acts in question, and to make them binding on the plaintiffs without their consent, even if there had been, in the constitution of New Hampshire, or of the United States, no special restriction on their power; because these acts are not the exercise of a power properly legislative." [24] Apparently he conceived of government in terms of some ideal which divided functions into legislative, executive, and judicial, and which was superior to and binding upon the federal and state constitutions, whatever the provisions of the latter. The effect of the legislation, he continued, was to take rights and property from one and to give them to another. "This is not the exercise of a legislative power. To justify

[24] Dartmouth College v. Woodward, 4 Wheaton 518, 558 (1819).

the taking away of vested rights there must be a forfeiture; to adjudge upon and declare which is the proper province of the judiciary." [25] Having by these and other devices elaborated his argument that the legislation was a violation of political morality, thereby securing the mental attitude toward the case which he desired, he proceeded to demonstrate that the charter of the college was a contract which was being impaired by the legislation, in violation of the contract clause of the Constitution.

Joseph Hopkinson, who participated with Webster in the argument of the case, likewise sought to demonstrate the fact that the college was a private and not a public corporation.

> It is true [he said] that a college, in a popular sense, is a public institution, because its uses are public, and its benefits may be enjoyed by all who choose to enjoy them; but in a legal and technical sense, they are not public institutions, but private charities. Corporations may, therefore, be very well said to be for public use, of which the property and privileges are yet private. Indeed [he continued in language significant for an understanding of the contemporary attitude toward corporations], there may be supposed to be an ultimate reference to the public good in granting all charters of incorporation; but this does not change the property from private to public.[26]

The assumption, however fictitious, did prevail at the time that the most private of corporations was supposed to reflect a legislative conception of the public good. Corporation charters were granted pursuant to special acts of the legislature and conveyed special privileges and oftentimes monopoly rights, from which it was assumed that some return would accrue to the public good. It was only in later years that corporations for private purposes came to be formed under general rather than special laws and the conception of public good almost completely disappeared.

Chief Justice Marshall wrote the opinion of the Court. After stating briefly the procedure by which the case had reached the Court, he continued with language which readers of his cases in subsequent years have come to recognize as spelling in advance the doom of the legislation involved:

> This Court can be insensible neither to the magnitude nor delicacy of this question. The validity of a legislative act is to be examined; and the opinion of the highest law tribunal of a state is to be revised:

[25] *Ibid.*      [26] *Ibid.*, pp. 616-617.

an opinion which carries with it intrinsic evidence of the diligence, of the ability, and the integrity with which it was formed. On more than one occasion this Court has expressed the cautious circumspection with which it approaches the consideration of such questions; and has declared that in no doubtful case would it pronounce a legislative act to be contrary to the Constitution. But the American people have said, in the Constitution of the United States, that "no state shall pass any bill of attainder, *ex post facto* law, or law impairing the obligation of contracts." In the same instrument they have also said, "that the judicial power shall extend to all cases in law and equity arising under the Constitution." On the judges of this Court, then, is imposed the high and solemn duty of protecting, from even legislative violation, those contracts which the Constitution of our country has placed beyond legislative control; and, however irksome the task may be, this is a duty from which we dare not shrink.[27]

There is irony in the fact that he began reading the opinion and his statement about the irksomeness of the duty of passing upon a state legislative act while obviously ignoring the effort of William Pinkney, one of the counsel for the university, who wished to move a reargument of the case in the hope of convincing the Court that the New Hampshire legislation was not unconstitutional.[28]

Webster and his colleagues had done their work well. Resorting to a device not infrequently used by lawyers and judges in difficult cases — the device of assuming that which they ought to prove — Marshall stated that "it can require no argument to prove that the circumstances of this case constitute a contract. . . . Surely in this transaction every ingredient of a complete and legitimate contract is to be found."[29] These statements have been persuasively challenged by modern students,[30] but they were not challenged at the time by any member of the Supreme Court.

Using almost verbatim the words of Judge Richardson, Marshall declared, in language requoted many times in years to come, that "a corporation is an artificial being, invisible, intangible, and existing only in contemplation of law."[31] Examining the characteristics of corporations in general and of the Dartmouth College Corporation in particular, he came to the conclusion that the latter was a private and not a public corporation, that its charter constituted a contract, and that the contract was unconstitutionally impaired by the legislation

[27] *Ibid.*, p. 625.  [28] Beveridge, *op. cit.*, IV, 260-261.  [29] 4 Wheaton 627.
[30] See Wright, *op. cit.*, pp. 43-45.  [31] 4 Wheaton 636.

in question.   Revealing, as it were, a confusion arising out of Webster's discussion of fundamental principles of government, Marshall admitted that prior to the Revolution Parliament was all-powerful and was in a position to annul corporate rights, even though such an act might give a shock to public opinion.   Yet, he continued, "the contract would at that time have been deemed sacred by all.   What has since occurred to strip it of its inviolability? Circumstances have not changed it.   In reason, in justice, and in law, it is now what it was in 1769." [32]   Having admitted that Parliament was all-powerful in the matter, he found that "in reason, in justice, and in law," the contract was still "sacred" and possessed "inviolability."   Clearly there is an intermingling of conceptions of law as emanating from government and of law as emanating from a source superior to any earthly government which effectively closes the channels of thought and reasoning.

In a concurring opinion Justice Story revealed the same obsession for higher-law principles.   "It is a principle of the common law," he said, "which has been recognized as well in this as in other courts, that the division of an empire works no forfeiture of previously vested rights of property.   And this maxim is equally consonant with the common sense of mankind and the maxims of eternal justice." [33] Among others he cited his own opinion in Terrett v. Taylor as illustrating the point.   If compelled to answer, both justices might have admitted that they had no authority to decide cases exclusively on the basis of "the common sense of mankind" or "the maxims of eternal justice," but, believing firmly as they did in such maxims and principles, they used them freely as guides to the interpretation of constitutions and laws emanating from worldly sovereigns.   For an understanding of the judicial process and of the development of American constitutional law, therefore, a knowledge of the political and social philosophy of the judges is quite as important as a knowledge of the detailed provisions of legal documents.

Whatever one may think of the logic by which the decision in the Dartmouth College case was reached, that decision firmly entrenched in constitutional law the fact that a charter of a private corporation is a contract which may not be impaired by state law.   The principle gave protection to vested rights in corporate property and encouraged the growth of corporate enterprise.   Serious abuses resulted, in that the creators of corporations lobbied through politically minded and

[32] *Ibid.*, p. 643          [33] *Ibid.*, p. 707.

often venally minded legislatures charters containing broad grants which in the public interest ought never to have been authorized and sought protection thereafter in the contract clause of the Constitution. The remedy lay in the more careful drafting of charters and in their authorization by general law rather than by separate acts by the legislature, and also in the tendency adopted by the Supreme Court after the end of the Marshall régime of scrutinizing carefully and interpreting narrowly the rights conferred.   In spite of legislative and judicial checks, the principle of the inviolability of corporate charters has remained a principle of paramount importance in American constitutional law.

## STATE BANKRUPTCY LAWS

The year 1819 witnessed the decision of another important contract case, that of Sturges v. Crowninshield,[34] in which the contract clause of the Constitution was used to curb the effect of state bankruptcy laws in releasing debtors from the obligation to pay their debts.   Disturbances which preceded and followed the War of 1812 resulted in widespread financial disorder.   The banking system of the country, which will be discussed in an ensuing chapter, was in a particularly chaotic condition.   As a result of pressure from debtors and of growing hostility toward imprisonment for debt and other legal arrangements for the punishment of failure to meet obligations, many of the states had enacted broad bankruptcy or insolvency laws. Debtors who fell into difficulties resorted blithely to the relief which the laws provided, and creditors were left without adequate protection for their rights.   The Constitution gave Congress the power to enact uniform laws on the subject of bankruptcy,[35] but did not prohibit the enactment of such laws by the states in the event that Congress failed to exercise its prerogative.   There was no federal law on the statute books during the period under consideration.   The debates throw little light on the question whether the framers of the Constitution intended the contract clause to restrain the power of the states over bankruptcy.   In view of the broad interpretation given to the contract clause in case after case, however, it is not surprising that a creditor, suffering from the operation of a state bankruptcy law, appealed to the Supreme Court for the protection of his constitutional rights under the contract clause.

In writing the opinion of the Court, Chief Justice Marshall dis-

[34] 4 Wheaton 122.          [35] Article I, Section 8.

cussed the New York law which was involved in relation to two clauses of the federal Constitution.    He held first of all that the fact that the Constitution gave to Congress the power to enact bankruptcy laws did not destroy the right of states to enact such laws if Congress failed to exercise its powers.    He held in the second place that a state law enacted after a contract was made violated the contract clause of the Constitution in so far as it sought to relieve the debtor from the obligation to pay his debt.    This did not mean that the contract clause stood as a bar to all state bankruptcy legislation.    Without violating the contract clause, for example, a state could abolish imprisonment for debt and otherwise change what is known as the legal remedy.    It reached and exceeded the limit of its power when it sought to annul the obligation of the debtor.

To all appearances members of the Court were in full agreement about the case, presenting a united front to the bitter criticism of debtor classes.    Eight years later, however, in connection with the decision of another case, it was discovered that the Court had been divided as to the general principle to be applied.    All of the justices, it seemed, were agreed that a state bankruptcy law which did away with the obligation of contracts in existence at the time when the laws were enacted violated the contract clause.    Some of the justices wished to go farther and hold that the Constitution was violated by laws which sought to relieve debtors of obligations incurred through contracts made even after the bankruptcy statute had gone into operation.    It was not necessary to decide the principle as broadly as that in order to decide the Sturges case, however, since in that case the contract was made before the bankruptcy law was passed, and the Court maintained an appearance of unanimity by stating only points on which all justices were agreed.

In his opinion in the Sturges case, Chief Justice Marshall made the following statement: "A contract is an agreement in which a party undertakes to do, or not to do, a particular thing.    The law binds him to perform his undertaking, and this is, of course, the obligation of his contract." [36]    When in 1827 the case of Ogden v. Saunders [37] was argued before the Supreme Court, it was discovered that Marshall's language was less clear than it seemed.    There was difference of opinion as to whether the words "the law" as used by Marshall referred merely to the statute of the state having jurisdiction over the contract, which, of course, would include bankruptcy laws,

[36] 4 Wheaton 197.          [37] 12 Wheaton 213.

or whether they referred to principles of higher law or of natural justice or of moral law which were supposed also to be operative. There was difference, furthermore, as to whether the obligation of the contract arose out of the law or merely out of the agreement between the parties.

The Ogden case involved a contract made after the applicable bankruptcy statute was enacted. Four justices, writing separate opinions, took positions which were, in effect, that "the law" applicable to the situation was governed by the specific enactments of the legislature and not principles of higher law. They held that the obligation of a contract was a legal obligation, which derived its force, not from principles of morality, but from the provisions of state laws applicable to contracts. A contract made after a bankruptcy statute was enacted, therefore, was made subject to the provisions of that statute as well as others that were relevant, and the rights of the creditors were limited by it. The law, in effect, became a part of the contract. The application of the remedy given by the bankruptcy statute did not impair the obligation of the contract, since the obligation from the beginning was limited by the provisions of the statute.

Three justices — Marshall, Story, and Duvall — dissented from this position of the majority of the Court. They took the position that the contract clause restricted bankruptcy legislation applicable to future contracts as well as those which had been previously made. An act of the legislature, argued Chief Justice Marshall, did not enter into the contract and become one of the conditions stipulated by the parties. Contracts derived their obligation from the act of the parties, not from the grant of the government. The original obligation, created, not by state law, but by the parties, was protected by the Constitution. The obligation was impaired by any law which lessened it.

In spite of his efforts to present his argument clearly, the Chief Justice again confused conceptions of law and morality. To the majority of the Court, the obligation of a contract was the legal obligation to carry out its provisions. That legal obligation was determined by the laws of the state having jurisdiction. To Marshall, however, the obligation of a contract was the commitment made by the parties, whether or not the state provided the means for enforcing it. The obligation, or the duty to fulfill the contract, was a moral conception, a conception of natural justice, which was not dependent upon state law. His reasoning led to the stern doctrine that, whatever the change in the economic situation of the parties to a contract, nothing could be done by a state to relieve a debtor from the accumulation of his obligations. The doctrine was too stern for the times. The majority of the justices, under the pressure of changed social attitudes, were more lenient, and, in effect, allowed the states to modify as to the future the extent of the claims which creditors might make.

The situation involved in the use of bankruptcy laws to relieve debtors from their commitments had much in common with the enactment of what is called social legislation in recent years. The legislation was no doubt the product, in part at least, of the political efforts of debtor groups. It seems to have represented, however, a growing sensitiveness as to the predicament of the economically unfortunate who were caught in the toils of legal obligations to more prosperous members of society. The newly acquired protection was abused in that people freely involved themselves in debt, assuming that, if their economic ventures failed to pay, they could escape from their burden of debt by means of bankruptcy and be free to start over again. The American people have never moved backward in this field, in spite of some abuses. The operation of state laws was suspended when the federal government entered the field with uniform legislation, but the protection to debtors has been preserved and extended as social conscience, political pressure, or conceptions of a better economic order have made themselves felt.

The defeat of Chief Justice Marshall in the Ogden case [38] marked the end of the rapid expansion of the contract clause as a curb upon state legislation. The decision represented his first defeat in the determination of a constitutional question. It marked the climax of his economic conservatism and the beginning of a trend away from the economic principles which he had sought to entrench in American constitutional law. It would, perhaps, be inaccurate to say that Marshall had grown more conservative with the years. A high degree of consistency is apparent throughout his opinions. While his position remained unchanged, however, the social and economic attitudes of the people began slowly to reflect new trends. Yet the slowness of

[38] Technically Marshall was not defeated as to the Ogden case. It involved a further question as to whether a state law could relieve a debtor from the claims of a creditor in another state made in a federal court or in a court of another state. Justice Johnson, who had been with the majority in upholding state bankruptcy laws as applied within the respective states, joined Chief Justice Marshall and Justices Story and Duvall in holding that a state bankruptcy law could not operate beyond the limits of the state.

this movement should be emphasized. Marshall was venerated and trusted by large numbers of people as long as he remained at the head of the Court. As later chapters will show, it remained for Justice Story, whose philosophy was closely identified with that of Marshall, to lament bitterly the passing of the old order and the coming of a new one in which he felt that he had no part.

Although subsequent decisions set limits to the principles announced by Marshall in connection with the contract clause, his basic contribution has endured. Grants made by a legislature are not subject to repeal unless provisions for repeal are included in them. Exemptions from taxation which are clearly given by contract are not subject to repeal. With certain exceptions as to police power and eminent domain, charters of private corporations cannot be altered or repealed unless the right of modification or repeal is reserved. The contract clause remained extremely important for the protection of vested rights against state legislation until after the Civil War, when gradually the use of the due-process clause of the Fourteenth Amendment became an even more important instrument for the same purpose. In spite of the shift of emphasis from the contract clause to the due-process clause, the former, largely as a result of the work of the Supreme Court in the Marshall period, remains an instrument of no small importance.

••••••••••••••••••••••••••••••••••••••••••••••••••••••••••••••••••••••••••••••••••••••••••••••••••••••••••

# CHAPTER 9

# THE BANK OF THE UNITED STATES

"THE BUSINESS OF THE UNITED STATES is business," declared President Calvin Coolidge during the nineteen-twenties. This apparently commonplace statement expressed a fundamentally important truth, not merely for the decade in which it was made, but for most of the course of American history. Down through the years the people concentrated upon the acquisition of property by profitable interchange of goods and services. The welfare of business required sound money and credit guarded by law. The regulation of coinage, the currency, and the banking system have involved some of the most intricate problems of constitutional government. At the time of the adoption of the Constitution, the United States had little coin, little precious metal in any form, and no paper money of uniform value throughout the country. The era of the conduct of interchange by means of checking accounts in banks was still far in the future. Most of the early banks were state institutions. Their operations were inadequately regulated by law and the value of their notes lacked stability. For this and other reasons the federal government entered the field with an institution of its own creation.

It will be recalled that the first Bank of the United States was chartered in 1791 for a period of twenty years, largely as a result of the efforts of Alexander Hamilton.[1] He justified the establishment of a national bank in terms of the "necessary-and-proper" clause of the Constitution. The authorizing statute was adopted over the protests of Thomas Jefferson, James Madison, Edmund Randolph, and others, who contended that the establishment of a bank was not authorized by the Constitution. Jefferson remained permanently hostile to the bank, but it performed services for the government during the period for which it was chartered, and Congress from time to

[1] See chapter 4.

time enacted measures supporting it. Constitutional questions were not again raised until time for the renewal of the charter.

The services rendered to the federal government and to the country were important. The bank and its branches scattered throughout the country provided safe places of deposit for the revenue collected by the government. The notes of the bank provided a medium of exchange generally acceptable everywhere, in contrast with the notes of state banks, which varied in value from institution to institution and in terms of the distance from the issuing bank. Because of the general acceptability of the notes of the bank, they provided a convenient medium for the transfer of funds from one section of the country to another. Without such a medium of exchange, transfers could be made only by the difficult process of moving gold or silver. The bank aided government financing by making loans from time to time when the uneven flow of revenue failed to provide funds for necessary expenditures. The bank seems to have been well managed, and it apparently did not attempt to mold public opinion, or to shape the policies of Congress, or to interfere with presidential or congressional elections, as did its successor many years later. Albert Gallatin, as Secretary of the Treasury, fully recognized its value, and urged the renewal of its charter.

In spite of the services which it rendered, the bank faced much opposition. A great deal of the stock was owned in England. Although only citizens of the United States could be directors of the bank, substantial profits flowed out to the foreign stockholders. The people of the United States felt at that time the same hostility toward foreign creditors which the debtor West has always felt toward creditors in the East. The bank was regarded as an instrument by which the resources of the United States were drained away to foreign creditors. Furthermore, although control of the bank was in the hands of citizens of the United States, those citizens were largely Federalists. In the eyes of many Republicans this fact alone was enough to justify condemnation of the bank.

The Bank of the United States had competitors and influential opponents, furthermore, in the large number of state banks which had been established since 1791. These banks sought the privilege of serving as government depositories, and hoped to see their own bank notes circulate widely in place of those of the national bank. The state banks were chartered under poorly drafted laws, the extent of their note issues and loans was not properly prescribed, and many of them grossly abused their privileges. The Bank of the United States, through the periodic presentation of state bank notes for payment in specie, operated as a helpful check upon the activities of state banks. They fretted under this form of control, however, and perhaps realized the extent to which it might be abused if the Bank of the United States sought to exercise arbitrary power. The state banks, therefore, either openly or indirectly, took the lead in opposing the recharter of the Bank of the United States. They used arguments against foreign ownership and Federalist control, and revived again the question of the constitutional power of Congress to charter a national bank.

Individual politicians shifted positions as to the bank in terms of political expediency. William H. Crawford,[2] of Georgia, and John C. Calhoun, of South Carolina, who represented a region where state rights were exalted, nevertheless favored the renewal of the charter of the bank, which was opposed by their political rivals. Daniel Webster, an ultimate defender of the rechartered bank against the attack of the Jackson administration, initially opposed the establishment of the bank. James Madison, who in 1791 had argued that Congress had no power to establish a bank, ultimately found such an institution so necessary as to require the suppression of his constitutional scruples.

Crawford declared that the right to create a bank was exercised because the collection of revenue and the safekeeping and easy and speedy transmission of public money was more perfectly secured by the erection of a bank than by any other means that could be devised. A bank, therefore, was necessary and proper to enable the government to carry into complete effect the right to lay and collect taxes, imposts, duties, and excises.[3] He would not say that the existence of the government absolutely depended upon the operations of a bank, but only that a national bank enabled the government to manage its fiscal concerns more advantageously than it could do by any other means. In the selection of means to carry into effect any constitutional power, a sound discretion must be exercised. What was proper at one time might be extremely unfit and improper at another. "The Constitution, in relation to the means by which its powers are to be executed, is one eternal *now*. The state of things now, the precise point of time when we are called upon to act, must determine our choice in the selection of means to execute the delegated powers."[4] The

[2] *Annals of Congress*, 11th Cong., 3d sess., 134.    [3] *Ibid.*, pp. 140-141.    [4] *Ibid.*, p. 142.

opposition to the bank, he contended, was based upon avarice, combined with the love of domination.  Some of the states had created their own banks, and wished to compel the federal government to use them as depositories.  Many individual members of state legislatures were stockholders in state banks and were motivated by avarice in their attacks on the national bank.  He declared that the love of power on the part of certain of the states influenced them to send instructions to Congress to vote against the bank.

Crawford was speaking at a time when the responsibility of members of Congress to the governments of the states was a matter of disagreement.  In general, it was assumed that United States senators were subject to instruction by the legislatures which elected them, whereas the members of the House of Representatives were responsible only to the people, and might, therefore, receive requests but not commands from the legislatures.  The following resolution of the general assembly of Pennsylvania indicates the kind of formal pressure used by the legislatures upon Congress, and the distinction made between senators and representatives:

> That the senators of this state, in the Senate of the United States, be, and they are hereby, instructed, and the representatives of this state, in the House of Representatives of the United States, be, and they hereby are, requested, to use every exertion, in their power, to prevent the charter of the Bank of the United States from being renewed, or any other bank from being chartered by Congress, designed to have operations within the jurisdiction of any state, without first having obtained the consent of the legislature of such state.[5]

Henry Clay would not say how far a representative was bound by the instructions of his constituents, but he found something ominous in the fact that resolutions of legislatures were being thrown into the background and their interference regarded as officious, whereas a great deal of attention was being given to delegations of self-created societies.  "If it be improper for states to obtrude upon Congress their sentiments, it is much more highly so for the unauthorized deputies of fortuitous congregations." [6]

THE SECOND BANK OF THE UNITED STATES

Efforts to secure the renewal of the charter of the first Bank of the United States failed by a narrow margin, and the bank closed its

[5] *American State Papers*, **VIII**, *Finance*, II, 467.
[6] *Annals of Congress*, 11th Cong., 3d sess., 210-211.

doors. In the process of liquidation large sums of money were returned to the British stockholders, just before the outbreak of war between the United States and Great Britain. The war threw a heavy strain upon the finances of the country, the state banks suspended specie payments, and their notes circulated at depreciated figures, varying in terms of institutions and the distance from the banks of issue at which the notes were offered. Because there was frequently no other money available, the government had to accept state bank notes in the collection of its revenue, but, because those notes lost much of their value when moved from the vicinity of the issuing bank, the government was able to transfer money from one section of the country to another only at the expense of a high depreciation cost. In these and other respects, the government paid a heavy penalty for failure to renew the charter of the bank. Many attempts were made to secure the establishment of a similar institution, but government officials were unable to agree upon it. When, in January, 1815, an act to incorporate a bank was passed, President Madison vetoed it. He waived the question of constitutionality as precluded "by repeated recognition under varied circumstances of the validity of such an institution in acts of the legislative, executive, and judicial branches of the government, accompanied by indications, in different modes, of a concurrence of the general will of the nation." [7] However, the bank provided for, he believed, was not such as would revive the public credit, provide a national medium of circulation, and aid the Treasury by making necessary loans.

Another attempt was made, with John C. Calhoun exercising powerful leadership in the House of Representatives. He avoided the constitutional question, saying that it had already been so much discussed that all had made up their minds on it. He was concerned with whether or not the United States ought to establish a bank. He asserted that the depreciated state of the currency was a stain on public and private credit and injurious to the morals of the community. The state of the circulatory medium was opposed to the principles of the federal Constitution. That instrument gave Congress the power to regulate the currency of the United States. That power was being exercised, not by Congress, but by banking institutions no longer responsible for the correctness with which they managed it. Gold and silver had entirely disappeared. There was no money but paper money, over which Congress had no control. He found that the

[7] *Messages and Papers of the Presidents*, II, 540.

establishment of a national bank, which itself would pay specie, would be the proper mode of re-establishing a sound currency under the constitutional supervision of Congress.[8]

So great was the need for financial reform that most of the Republican party, except for the faction led by John Randolph, supported the establishment of a national bank. Henry Clay left the speaker's chair to recant his errors of some years earlier and to give his support.[9]

The opposition was left largely to the Federalists, led by Daniel Webster.[10] It was ineffective in both houses. Congress passed "an act to incorporate the subscribers to the Bank of the United States," [11] and on April 10, 1816, Madison signed the measure. Arrangements were speedily made for the establishment of the parent bank at Philadelphia and the several branches at various points throughout the United States.

Since the financial ills of the times were blamed in part on abuses committed by state banks, it was not to be expected that these banks would welcome the establishment of a national institution intended to act as a check upon them as well as to provide competition. The Bank of the United States conducted itself so as to arouse even more hostility than might have been expected. Instead of acting conservatively, and coercing state banks into doing the same by refusing to accept their notes or by calling on them for specie in payment of their notes when they expanded too rapidly, the national bank began its career by lending too heavily itself. It soon found itself in a position where it had to contract its loans. In doing so it had to call on state banks, which were already embarrassed, for the redemption of their notes. The hostility of state banks resulted in hostile legislation of one sort or another in many states. The constitution of Indiana, adopted after Congress had chartered the second bank, prohibited any bank chartered outside the state from doing business within its borders. The constitution of Illinois forbade the establishment of any but state banks. The legislature of Tennessee enacted a law providing that any bank not chartered under its authority must

[8] For a summary of Calhoun's address see *Annals of Congress*, 14th Cong., 1st sess., 1060-1066.

[9] Henry Adams, *History of the United States*, IX (1891), 117; *Annals of Congress*, 14th Cong., 1st sess., 1189-1195.

[10] For a summary of Webster's address see *Annals of Congress*, 14th Cong., 1st sess., 1091-1094.

[11] 3 Stat. 266.

pay fifty thousand dollars each year for the privilege of banking within the state. Kentucky laid an annual tax of sixty thousand dollars each on two branches of the Bank of the United States. Ohio placed a tax of fifty thousand dollars each on two branches. Georgia also placed a special tax on branches. Maryland provided for collection of taxes on the notes issued by the Baltimore branch, and, in lieu of such taxes, authorized the branch to make an annual payment of fifteen thousand dollars.[12] The obvious purpose of the several state laws was to make it impossible for the Bank of the United States to function as Congress intended. It was essential that the rights in the matter be determined by the Supreme Court, the tribunal with final authority.

McCULLOCH v. MARYLAND

The case of McCulloch v. Maryland,[13] decided at the 1819 term of the Supreme Court, along with the other important cases of Dartmouth College v. Woodward and Sturges v. Crowninshield, arose out of an attempt to collect penalties from the Baltimore branch of the Bank of the United States for refusal to pay taxes as prescribed by the Maryland law. The case was presented before the Supreme Court by an array of eminent counsel, which included Daniel Webster on the side of the bank whose charter he had previously opposed. Chief Justice Marshall wrote the unanimous opinion of the Court. He dealt with the case in terms of two questions, the power of Congress to charter the bank, and the power of the state to tax it. He began ominously with the statement that "no tribunal can approach such a question without a deep sense of its importance, and of the awful responsibility involved in its decision."[14]

As to the power of Congress to incorporate the bank, Marshall agreed that it could scarcely be considered an open question. The power had been exercised by the first Congress elected under the present Constitution. "The bill for incorporating the Bank of the United States did not steal upon an unsuspecting legislature, and pass unobserved."[15] It was fully debated at that time; the original act ran its course and was permitted to expire; the government was embar-

---

[12] For a summary of the hostile state laws see Beveridge, *Life of John Marshall* (4 vols., 1916-1919), IV, 206-208; Charles Warren, *The Supreme Court in United States History* (rev. ed., 2 vols., 1926), I, 505-506.

[13] 4 Wheaton 316. For discussion of the decision see Beveridge, *op. cit.*, IV, chapter VI; Warren, *op. cit.*, I, chapter XII.

[14] 4 Wheaton 400.        [15] *Ibid.*, pp. 401-402.

rassed thereafter for want of an institution of the kind, and the measure creating a new bank was enacted. "It would require no ordinary share of intrepidity to assert that a measure adopted under these circumstances was a bold and plain usurpation, to which the Constitution gave no countenance." [16]

Counsel for Maryland had contended that the Constitution must be construed, not as emanating from the people, but as an act of sovereign and independent states. They took the position that the powers of the federal government were delegated by the states, who alone were truly sovereign, and that these powers must be exercised in subordination to the states. Marshall rejected this contention, arguing that the powers of the federal government flowed directly from the people. "The government of the Union," he said, ". . . is, emphatically, and truly, a government of the people. In form and in substance it emanates from them. Its powers are granted by them, and are to be exercised directly on them, and for their benefit." [17] Marshall knew, of course, as did every other statesman who lived through the period of the adoption of the Constitution, that only a small fraction of the people had participated in any way in the adoption of the Constitution, and that group and class interests had had a great deal to do with the shaping of the document. In the decision of this case, however, he was concerned, not with questions of divisions among the people, but with the juristic question as to whether the power of the federal government flowed directly from the people or flowed through and was curbed by the sovereignty of the several states.

If any one proposition could command universal assent, he concluded, it might be expected to be this, "that the government of the Union, though limited in its powers, is supreme within its sphere of action." [18] He set out to discover, therefore, whether the Constitution brought the establishment of a bank or creation of a corporation within the sphere of action of the federal government. He did not find the power among the enumerated powers of the government. He reasoned, however, that the power to establish a bank could be implied from other powers which were specifically granted. It was "necessary and proper" to the exercise of powers conferred. In order to be necessary and proper, he argued, absolute indispensability was not required. A thing might be necessary, very necessary, absolutely or indispensably necessary. A sound discretion as to the exercise of

[16] *Ibid.*, p. 402.          [17] *Ibid.*, pp. 404-405.          [18] *Ibid.*, p. 405.

the powers conferred was left to Congress. In working out his standard of interpretation of implied powers, the Chief Justice phrased the
following eloquent statement:

> Let the end be legitimate, let it be within the scope of the Consti-
> tution, and all means which are appropriate, which are plainly
> adapted to that end, which are not prohibited, but consist with the
> letter and spirit of the Constitution, are constitutional.[19]

He rejected the contention that the creation of a corporation so ap-
pertained to sovereignty as to be a function only of the states. He
said:

> In America the powers of sovereignty are divided between the gov-
> ernment of the Union and those of the states. They are each
> sovereign, with respect to the objects committed to it, and neither
> sovereign with respect to the objects committed to the other.[20]

The doctrine of implied powers was not new at the time when the
decision was handed down. Alexander Hamilton had asserted it
clearly in connection with the establishment of the first national
bank. Members of Congress had discussed it in that and in other
connections. Marshall had phrased it in a Supreme Court decision
as early as 1805.[21] Yet the opinion in McCulloch v. Maryland, both
because the controversy was widely known and because of the fullness
of the statement, came to be regarded as the basic case in American
constitutional law for the statement of the doctrine of implied powers.

The Court decided both that Congress had the power to establish
the bank and that it might establish a branch in the state of Maryland. The Chief Justice then moved to the next question, whether
Maryland might tax that branch without violating the Constitution.
In discussing the issues, Marshall treated the case as if it represented
a bona-fide instance of taxation by the state for revenue purposes,
rather than an indirect attempt to hamper the operations of the bank.
He reverted to the principle that the Constitution and laws of the
United States were supreme and controlled the constitutions and laws
of the respective states. From this principle he deduced corollaries
that a power to create implied a power to preserve, that a power to
destroy, if wielded by a different hand, was hostile to and incompatible with the powers to create and preserve and that, where this
repugnancy existed, that authority which was supreme must control.[22]

[19] *Ibid.*, p. 421.        [20] *Ibid.*, p. 410.
[21] United States *v.* Fisher, 2 Cranch 358 (1804).        [22] 4 Wheaton 426.

He insisted on discussing the issues in terms of absolutes. "We are not driven," he declared, "to the perplexing inquiry, so unfit for the judicial department, what degree of taxation is the legitimate use, and what degree may amount to the abuse of the power." [23]  He found that the question of the power of a state to tax a means employed by the government of the United States in pursuance of the Constitution was controlled by propositions that "the power to tax involves the power to destroy," and that "the power to destroy may defeat and render useless the power to create." [24]  This line of reasoning led inevitably to the conclusion that the Maryland law was unconstitutional, without reference to the question as to whether the statute was really a revenue measure.

Marshall's proposition that "the power to tax involves the power to destroy" and the reasoning based upon it have been used for more than a century as a curb upon state taxation affecting instrumentalities of the federal government. Yet the results have been criticized. In a dissenting opinion, written in 1928, Justice Holmes spoke disparagingly of

> certain dicta of Chief Justice Marshall which culminated in or rather were founded upon his often-quoted proposition that the power to tax is the power to destroy. In those days it was not recognized as it is today that most of the distinctions of the law are distinctions of degree. If states had any power it was assumed that they had all power, and that the necessary alternative was to deny it altogether. But this Court, which has so often defeated the attempt to tax in certain ways, can defeat an attempt to discriminate or otherwise go too far without wholly abolishing the power to tax. The power to tax is not the power to destroy while this Court sits.[25]

The decision in McCulloch v. Maryland brought a storm of criticism. By contrast with their lack of concern about the Dartmouth College case, which had equally important implications for the future, people in all parts of the nation felt themselves vitally affected by the decision. The controversy over the bank had penetrated to all sections of the country. Newspapers, lawyers, judges, state legislatures, and others voiced indignant criticisms. Judge Spencer Roane, of Virginia, published anonymously a series of articles attacking Marshall's opinion. Marshall published anonymously a series of articles

[23] *Ibid.*, p. 430.          [24] *Ibid.*, p. 431.
[25] Panhandle Oil Co. *v.* Mississippi *ex rel.* Knox, 277 U.S. 218, 223 (1928). See also Justice Frankfurter's discussion of McCulloch *v.* Maryland in Graves *v.* New York *ex rel.* O'Keefe, 306 U.S. 466, 488-489 (1939).

in reply.   In Virginia and Ohio the legislatures went on record as opposing the federal encroachment on the powers of the states represented by Marshall's opinion.   Decisions on the constitutionality of state bankruptcy laws and on the power of the Supreme Court to review decisions of state courts when federal constitutional questions were involved aided in creating the background of hostility.   Local interests in state banking, in laws for the relief of debtors, in slavery, and in opposition to the protective tariff joined in the chorus of denunciation.[26]

## OSBORN *v.* BANK OF THE UNITED STATES

The controversy over the Bank of the United States was too violent to be terminated by a single decision of the Supreme Court.   The reiteration of the opinion of the Supreme Court was needed, as well as discussion of related constitutional issues.   Some state officials largely ignored the opinion in McCulloch *v.* Maryland.   In Ohio, steps were taken to enforce a law requiring the payment of a prohibitive tax of fifty thousand dollars a year on each branch of the bank.   To forestall prohibitive action by the federal court in the state, certain state officials seized one hundred thousand dollars in the vaults of the branch of the bank in Chillicothe, only to be met with a court order directed to the auditor and others preventing the payment of the money into the funds of the state pending judicial determination of the rights involved.   After hearing argument in the case, the United States circuit court directed that the one hundred thousand dollars, with interest thereon, be returned to the bank.   The decision came up for review by the Supreme Court in the case of Osborn *v.* Bank of the United States.[27]

After discussing important jurisdictional questions, Marshall reexamined the question of the power of Congress to incorporate a bank and provide for its operation.   Referring many times to McCulloch *v.* Maryland, he reiterated and elaborated upon the doctrines announced in that case.   He found a way to answer indirectly the attacks made upon the Court for its earlier decision, declaring that the courts did nothing of themselves, but were the mere instruments of the law:

> That department has no will, in any case.   If the sound construction of the act be, that it exempt the trade of the bank, as being

[26] For discussion of the attacks upon the Supreme Court see Beveridge, *op. cit.,* IV, 309 ff.

[27] 9 Wheaton 738 (1824).

essential to the character of a machine necessary to the fiscal operations of the government, from the control of the states, courts are as
much bound to give it that construction as if the exemption had been
established in express terms.    Judicial power, as contradistinguished
from the power of the laws, has no existence.   Courts are the mere
instruments of the law, and can will nothing.   When they are said
to exercise a discretion, it is a mere legal discretion, a discretion to be
exercised in discerning the course prescribed by law; and, when that is
discerned, it is the duty of the court to follow it.   Judicial power is
never exercised for the purpose of giving effect to the will of the
judge; always for the purpose of giving effect to the will of the legislature; or, in other words, to the will of the law.[28]

For all of Marshall's disclaimer, however, his realistic critics undoubtedly continued to look upon him and his tribunal, not as passive
instruments of the law, but as effective agents of the proponents of
nationalism.   Nevertheless, as far as action by the Supreme Court was
concerned, the decision settled the question of the constitutionality
of the Bank of the United States.   The Court was unanimous as far
as the broad constitutional question was concerned, although Justice
Johnson dissented on jurisdictional grounds.

In one important respect Marshall's opinion in the bank cases
differed from most of his other outstanding opinions.   Most of his
contributions to American constitutional law were handed down in
connection with decisions invalidating laws in conflict with the Constitution.   He is regarded as a great nationalist.   Yet only in the
bank cases was his task that of upholding the exercise of a positive
power by Congress.   Even in these cases, he was not supporting the
exercise of broad federal powers over rights of property.   He was
merely upholding an act of Congress which gave broad powers to a
financial institution of an essentially private character even though
the federal government owned one-fifth of the stock and appointed
one-fifth of the directors.   There is little to indicate that he would
have favored the enactment and enforcement of federal laws for the
regulation of private enterprise, or laws providing for the operation
of business enterprise directly by the government.   He was a nationalist in the sense that he used the federal judiciary and the federal Constitution to curb the interference of the states with vested rights in
many forms.   He read into the Constitution his conceptions of natural
justice and of the fundamental nature of free government, conceptions
which were essentially laissez-faire in character.

[28] 9 Wheaton 866.

THE NATIONAL BANK IN NATIONAL POLITICS

After the date of the Osborn case, only occasional controversies arose about the possible unconstitutionality of the establishment of a national bank by the federal government, yet the use or non-use of such an institution for federal purposes greatly affected the character of the constitutional structure of the nation. After a period of initial fumbling, which deepened the hostility of many state banks and many businessmen affected, the Bank of the United States was carefully managed under the direction of an able financier, Nicholas Biddle.[29] It became a powerful and prosperous institution. It gave to the federal government the many types of aid expected of it. Its notes provided a currency of relatively uniform value throughout the country. It aided in the collection and transfer of revenue from one section of the country to another. It operated to some extent as a check upon the undisciplined activities of the growing number of state banks. The hostility of state banking interests, however, never fully subsided. Apart from immediate financial interests, furthermore, many people viewed uneasily the growing power of the institution. In comparison with the corporations of the present day, the Bank of the United States was a relatively insignificant institution. In comparison with the institutions of its own time, however, it stood alone in the range of its potentialities. It was linked with the government and was a valuable agent of the government, but if it chose to do so it might hamper the operations of the government or, conceivably, through the manipulation of finances, it might bring the federal government under its own control. These possibilities began to be realized and discussed in the early eighteen-thirties when bank officials and friends began to talk of the renewal of the charter, which was to expire in 1836. Andrew Jackson, who became President in 1829, was known to distrust all banks. Many persons connected with his administration were known to hold state-rights philosophies. Some of them had close connections with state banks, which resented the control over them exercised by the national bank and were envious of the privileges enjoyed by that institution and its branches of serving as depositories of federal funds.

Uneasiness about the possibility of securing a renewal of the charter speeded the efforts of the bank toward that end. Strife over the

---

[29] For a well documented though biased history of the bank see R. C. H. Catterall, *The Second Bank of the United States* (1903). The interpretation followed herein is that presented in the relevant chapters of *Roger B. Taney* (1935) by Carl Brent Swisher.

issue developed among the members of the administration. When it began to appear that the President was hostile to the renewal of the charter, the friends of the bank united with the Whig party, which was building a leadership in such men as Henry Clay and Daniel Webster, to force action just prior to the presidential election, when it was thought that the President would either have to accept the measure or submit to defeat at the polls as the result of a veto. With the assistance of Attorney General Roger B. Taney and other opponents of the Bank of the United States, Jackson drafted a vigorous veto message which was both a constitutional document and a political address, phrased persuasively to capture the attention of the people of the United States.

The message did not deny that the bank had produced some benefits to the country, but characterized it as the instrument of a class and of a section by which other classes and other sections were made to pay tribute. Attention was called to the fact that more than one-fourth of the privately owned stock was held abroad, with the result that a heavy proportion of the profits of the bank went to the benefit of foreign capitalists. Most of the stock owned in the United States was held in the middle and the eastern states. This section, therefore, received tribute from the debtor areas of the South and West. The present stockholders had received great profits from the monopoly grant of banking privileges under the federal government. There was no reason why the monopoly grant of these payments to individuals should be renewed.

The message included an argument by Taney that the Supreme Court had not passed upon the constitutionality of the present Bank of the United States in all its aspects, but had merely decided that Congress had the power to establish a bank. The Court had found itself unable to determine the several questions bearing upon the constitutionality of this particular institution, such as whether its monopoly privilege was constitutional or whether it was "necessary and proper" that the bank have a capital of as much as thirty-five million dollars. These were matters into which the Court was not equipped to inquire. The President, on the other hand, in exercising his constitutional function of passing upon newly enacted legislation, was under obligation to consider them. Furthermore, even if the Court had considered the whole ground, the President, in dealing with proposed legislation, was bound to follow his own judgment on the subject of constitutionality. The opinion of the judges had no more authority over Congress than the opinion of Congress had over the judges; and the President was restrained by neither in exercising his judgment on constitutional questions when making a decision as to whether he should sign or veto proposed enactments.[30]

The veto message was a political document of first importance. It was dealt with as such. The Jacksonians circularized it all over the country, using it as a basis of appeal to support the administration in its struggle with a predatory financial institution. Daniel Webster, on the floor of the United States Senate, made a powerful attack on the administration in reply to the message. The president of the Bank of the United States thought so highly of the Webster speech that he sent many thousands of copies to people all over the country at the expense of the bank. This institution, one-fifth of which was owned by the United States government, was in effect aiding in financing the campaign for the election of a President. The resources of the bank aided in other ways in securing political support. Webster and others received extensive loans from the bank, some of which were only nominally paid off through the transfer of property of lesser value. In still other ways the bank made its influence felt. For many months preceding the summer of 1832 it expanded its loans, thereby increasing the number of persons dependent upon it and stimulating the expansion of business. After the veto of the bill to renew its charter, it contracted its loans rapidly and put pressure upon state banks which were debtors to it. In so doing it created great financial distress throughout the country, justifying its action on the ground that, in view of the action of Congress, it must prepare to wind up its affairs when its charter expired in 1836. That this justification was not offered in good faith was indicated by the fact that, after the election was over, the bank resumed the expansion of its loans. Its purpose had been to create distress which would bring about the election of Henry Clay instead of Andrew Jackson.

The struggle over the bank represented, by and large, a great social and financial cleavage throughout the country. The investor groups, other than that which was closely connected with the state banks, the large propertied interests of the country, the "respectable" element in society, and the people with inclinations corresponding to those of the old Federalist party, aligned themselves with the party of Clay and Webster and with the Bank of the United States in opposition to the popular movement led by Jackson and utilized by the

[30] For the veto message see *Messages and Papers of the Presidents*, III, 1139 ff.

representatives of the state banks in their opposition to the national institution.

Jackson was elected for a second term in spite of the opposition of the bank and its friends. Thereafter, instead of continuing its preparations to wind up its business at the expiration of its charter, the bank again expanded its business, evidently in preparation for another financial and political struggle to prolong its life. The administration countered with an attempt to weaken the bank by depriving it of the strength which flowed from its position as holder of the money deposited by the government. The Secretary of the Treasury, William Duane, assuming that under the law he had the right to exercise his own judgment as to the placement of revenues collected by the government, refused to remove the government deposits as requested by the President. Jackson asserted his own authority by removing Duane from office and appointing Taney, who within the administration had taken the lead in the struggle against the bank. Taney chose certain state banks located at various points throughout the country as depositories of federal funds.

A terrific struggle ensued. Congress was not in session when the removal of the deposits was ordered, but at the session which began in December, 1833, it gave almost all of its attention to issues directly or indirectly related to the Bank of the United States. The friends of the bank bitterly denounced the removal of the deposits, sought to bring about their restoration, and in every possible way attempted to discredit the administration. The Bank of the United States contracted its loans with even greater rapidity than the circumstances required and so managed its affairs as to put tremendous pressure upon the state banks selected as depositories. The assault was so effective that some of those banks were compelled to beg for mercy from the national bank and to refuse to receive deposits from the federal government.

The system established by Taney survived in spite of the attacks of the national bank, but Taney himself was driven from office. His appointment had been made while the Senate was in recess. Doubtless expecting that the Senate would take its revenge by refusing confirmation, Jackson did not send in the nomination until near the end of the ensuing session, when the groundwork for the establishment of the new deposit system had been done. Thereupon the Senate, true to expectations, rejected the nomination. It was the first time that a nomination of a head of a department had been rejected.

The administration succeeded in preventing a renewal of the charter of the Bank of the United States at its expiration in 1836. The bank then secured from the state of Pennsylvania a charter for the central office at Philadelphia, and continued in operation for some time.    Persons connected with the bank and others continued to lobby for a new federal charter for that or some other institution, but without avail.    The political activities of the Bank of the United States, initiated to prolong its life, had resulted in its demise, and had the continuing result of preventing the establishment of any national bank until, in the midst of the Civil War, Congress found it necessary to provide for the chartering, not of a single monopoly national bank, but of many national banks under a general law.

In the meantime, in 1837, near the beginning of the administration of Martin Van Buren, whom Jackson had chosen as his successor, the country suffered one of the severest depressions of its history.    The banks of the country suspended specie payments, including the state banks chosen as government depositories.    The financial system of the country was greatly embarrassed.    The notes issued by the state banks depreciated in value.    As had always been true, but now to a greater extent, the notes depreciated still further in value as they circulated at a distance from the issuing bank.    Since it could agree upon no banking system which seemed adequate to its purposes, the government ultimately established what was called the subtreasury system, made up of units throughout the country, in which the revenues of the country were deposited.    That system was inadequate in that it took money out of circulation for a time and in the fact that it did not provide an adequate medium of exchange or mode of transferring revenues from one part of the country to another.    It did provide, for the period of its operation, a measure of safety for the funds of the government.

In view of the experience of the times, it is quite clear that the Jackson administration was overoptimistic in placing its reliance upon state banks which were inadequately managed and inadequately supervised under inadequate state laws.    This fact, however, does not necessarily lead to the conclusion that the decision to block the renewal of the charter of the Bank of the United States was unwise.    In the bitter struggle which took place from 1832 to 1836 and was continued to some extent for a time thereafter, the bank demonstrated its capacity for the ruthless use of power.    Had it been able to secure the prolongation of its life for a considerable period of years, it might have been able to oppress or to destroy, not merely many of the state banks of the country, but other institutions as well. As was said above, it was a small institution in comparison with many powerful corporations of today. For its own time, however, it was so powerful that it had no real competitor of its own kind. In view both of its financial manipulations and of its attempts to control elections, the possibility that the federal government would have been brought under its sway is not inconceivable.

The threat has never been completely forgotten. Until recent years the history of the struggle with the second bank has been written largely by people sympathetic with the theoretical program of that institution. With the theoretical program few people have any basic quarrel. The point of difference is that the opponents of a strongly centralized system have a keener awareness of the political dangers involved in the accumulation of too much financial power in the hands of a single institution. The national banks provided for by the act of 1863 were competing institutions as have been all those created under subsequent legislation. The federal reserve system of the United States, adopted in 1914, represents a compromise between a highly centralized banking system and one completely decen-tralized.[31]

[31] For further discussion of the subject of banking see chapter 16.

# CHAPTER 10

# THE CONTROL OF COMMERCE

ONE OF THE MAJOR PURPOSES of the convention which met in Philadelphia in 1787 to form "a more perfect Union" was to promote interstate and foreign commerce by giving powers of regulation to the federal government and by placing a curb upon state activities which interfered with the free flow of commerce. Many provisions included in the Constitution were conducive to that end. The hand of the federal government was strengthened by a series of provisions. Congress was given power to collect taxes, duties, imposts, and excises. This power not only strengthened the federal government generally, but enabled it to regulate commercial activities by the selection of subjects to be taxed and by the determination of the amounts to be levied. Immediately after government under the new Constitution was organized, Alexander Hamilton secured provision for an excise tax on the manufacture of alcoholic beverages. The importance of the tax lay not in the amount of revenue raised, but in the establishment of the precedent of requiring the internal business of the country to provide a portion of the revenue. The Jefferson administration opposed this interference with internal business and sought to eliminate this form of taxation. It was resumed when expenditures of the War of 1812 required it. The power to levy duties on imports was not merely a power to raise revenue, but a power to determine in part the extent to which foreign producers should be allowed to sell their goods in the United States in competition with American products.

Extensive possibilities for control over commerce lay in the power given to the federal government to borrow money on the credit of the United States and to coin money and regulate the value thereof, as well as to punish counterfeiting. Some thinkers of the time regarded a national debt as by no means an evil, since the paper issued as evidence of debt might provide a circulatory medium. Among other things, the national debt provided part of the basis for the establishment of the first Bank of the United States. That institution and its successor exerted a tremendous influence over commercial activities in the United States. Various other provisions of the Constitution gave the federal government direct or indirect control over commercial activities. The most important was the one now known as the commerce clause, which gave Congress power "to regulate commerce with foreign nations, and among the several states, and with the Indian tribes." [1]

A number of the powers given to Congress had corollaries in prohibitions against the states. The states were forbidden to enter into treaties, alliances, or confederations. They were forbidden to make anything but gold and silver a tender in payment of debt. They were forbidden to make any law impairing the obligation of contracts. The states, like Congress, were forbidden to levy duties on exports, and they were also forbidden to levy duties on imports. Although the Supreme Court ultimately decided that the term "imports" did not include the movement of merchandise from another state,[2] it was assumed by Chief Justice Marshall as late as 1827 that the term did include what he called "importations from a sister state." [3] Since this was probably the prevailing interpretation generally given during the earlier years, the prohibition against the states in the matter of imports must have been regarded as forbidding discriminatory measures such as were being enacted by a number of states prior to the adoption of the Constitution.

For many years the commerce clause remained in the background as a source of power of federal regulation and as a barrier against regulation by the states. It was supposed to provide at least a partial basis for the laying of embargoes. It was discussed in connection with the power of the federal government to participate in the construction of internal improvements. Some state courts indulged in speculation as to its meaning. In 1820, in a circuit court case, Chief Justice Marshall indicated that in his mind the commerce clause was an independent source of broad power. "I have contended," he said in a sweeping generalization, "that the power of Congress to regulate commerce, comprehends, necessarily, a power over navigation, and

[1] Article I, Section 8. For discussion of the clause see Felix Frankfurter, *The Commerce Clause under Marshall, Taney, and Waite* (1937), and F. D. G. Ribble, *State and National Power over Commerce* (1937).

[2] American Express Co. v. Iowa, 196 U.S. 133, 146 (1905).

[3] Brown v. Maryland, 12 Wheaton 419, 449 (1827).

warrants every act of national sovereignty which any other sovereign nation may exercise over vessels, foreign or domestic, which enter our ports."[4] It was not until 1824, however, in the case of Gibbons *v.* Ogden,[5] that he worked out a careful interpretation of the clause in an opinion for the Supreme Court.

### GIBBONS *v.* OGDEN

The case arose in connection with a new instrument of commerce, the steamboat. At the time when the Constitution was adopted, the foreign commerce of the United States, and much of the interstate commerce as well, was conducted in sailing vessels. After the invention of the steam engine, a few imaginative people leaped to the conclusion that the engine could be used as a source of motive power on the water, more reliable than wind and sails. Some of them undertook experiments. A common mode of encouraging invention was the offer of special privileges connected with its use after development. Robert R. Livingston and Robert Fulton secured from an amused legislature the exclusive right for a period of years to operate steamboats on the waters of the state of New York.[6] In 1807, Livingston and Fulton succeeded in making their first trip on the Hudson River; and the following year, now realizing the value of the invention, the legislature enacted a new measure giving monopoly privileges of steamboat navigation. Additional steamboats were rapidly built and put into operation. Other states, in order likewise to stimulate the expansion of commercial enterprise, gave exclusive privileges of such navigation in their own waters. Steam-propelled vessels were soon in operation in most of the commercial states of the Atlantic coast and in states along the Ohio and Mississippi Rivers.

The monopoly laws soon caused trouble. The owners of steamboats wished to use them, not merely within particular states, but between ports of different states. Yet states required out-of-state owners to secure new licenses by the payment of substantial fees before admitting their boats. The enforcement of these laws provoked retaliation, and the commercial interests of some states were almost at the point of warfare as they had been prior to the adoption of the Constitution. The case of Gibbons *v.* Ogden involved the question whether New York could constitutionally require the acquisition of a

[4] Wilson *v.* United States, Federal Cases No. 17846, p. 245.

[5] 9 Wheaton 1.

[6] Albert J. Beveridge, *The Life of John Marshall* (4 vols., 1916-1919), IV, 399-401.

New York license for the operation of a steamboat operating regularly between New York and New Jersey.

In the light of present-day understanding of the commerce clause, it is clear that the answer was "No." In 1824, however, there was real doubt as to the meaning and application of the clause. Although, in the circuit-court opinion cited above, Chief Justice Marshall had said that commerce included navigation, it seems not to have been generally understood that the commerce clause applied to agencies of transportation as distinguished from the things transported. An attempt to discriminate against goods being imported from New Jersey would probably have fallen afoul of the commerce clause. The mere operation of the vessel, however, which was the point of contact made by the law in this case, did not, in the minds of some people, constitute commerce at all.

Furthermore, even though the mere act of navigation between New York and New Jersey was a commercial activity, it was argued that the states were not necessarily forbidden to regulate it. Although the states were directly forbidden to levy duties on imports, they were not directly forbidden to regulate interstate and foreign commerce. Such a prohibition could be derived only by implication from the clause giving Congress that power. At that time and for many years thereafter, lawyers took various positions on the subject. Some argued that Congress had exclusive power over interstate and foreign commerce, and that, because of the existence of the federal power, the states had no power over interstate commerce. Others argued that the states had the power to regulate interstate commerce until Congress acted on the subject. Still others argued that the states might continue to regulate even after Congress had acted, as long as there was no conflict between state and federal laws. There was no principle of constitutional interpretation by which it could be determined clearly that any one of these principles was correct. It was true that the existence of the taxing power of the federal government did not prevent the states from collecting taxes. The Supreme Court had held that the mere existence of the power of Congress to establish uniform laws on the subject of bankruptcy did not prevent the states from enacting such laws if Congress did not choose to exercise its power.[7] The Court had also held that the existence of the federal power to call state militia into federal service did not prevent the states from punishing men who refused to serve in the militia when

[7] Sturges *v.* Crowninshield, 4 Wheaton 122 (1819).

called into the federal service.[8] In no case, however, did the Supreme Court go so far as to say that the states might exercise every power given to Congress until Congress chose to act in the matter, or that the states might continue to act in every instance as long as there was no conflict between their own legislation and that of the federal government.

As counsel in the case, Daniel Webster, at the height of his intellectual powers, delivered a powerful argument against the claims of the steamboat monopoly. He denied that the state and federal governments had concurrent power to regulate interstate commerce. The very object intended, he declared, more than any other, was to take away such power from the states. If it had not so provided, the Constitution would not have been worth accepting.[9] In establishing the Constitution, the people intended to transfer to the general government "those high and important powers over commerce, which, in their exercise, were to maintain an uniform and general system." He contended that from the very nature of the case these powers had to be exclusive; that is, "the higher branches of commercial regulation must be exclusively committed to a single hand." What was it that was to be regulated? he asked.

> Not the commerce of the several states, respectively, but the commerce of the United States. Henceforth, the commerce of the states was to be a unit; and the system by which it was to exist and be governed must necessarily be complete, entire, and uniform. Its character was to be described in the flag which waved over it, *e pluribus unum.*[10]

In short, Webster came close to a conception of interstate commerce used more and more frequently in recent years; namely, that commerce is not single transactions or movements across state lines, but is a network of interacting business relationships extending across state lines, of which each unit is an important component part. Under this conception, many matters which ordinarily would be viewed as items of intrastate rather than interstate commerce are drawn into the area of federal control. In further elaboration of his point that the Constitution did not intend to leave to the states any portion of the regulation of interstate commerce as such, Webster declared that, if Congress refrained from exercising all the power given to it under the Constitution, the self-restraint might be explained by the belief that it had done all that it deemed wise. "All

[8] Houston *v.* Moore, 5 Wheaton 1 (1820).     [9] 9 Wheaton 13.     [10] *Ibid.*, p. 14.

useful regulation does not consist in restraint; and that which Congress sees fit to leave free, is a part of its regulation, as much as the rest." [11] The argument was used many times in the years ahead.

These several questions were threshed over endlessly by the several counsel in the case. The decision of the Supreme Court was announced by Chief Justice Marshall in an opinion which, says his biographer, "has done more to knit the American people into an indivisible nation than any other one force in our history, excepting only war." [12] Marshall rejected the contention that the powers expressly granted to the federal government ought to be construed strictly. There was no sentence in the Constitution which prescribed that rule. He would agree to the principle that words should not be construed beyond their natural and obvious import. He would not agree that in support of some theory not to be found in the Constitution a narrow construction ought to be given which would cripple the government and render it unequal to the objects for which it was instituted.

In this case the subject to be regulated was commerce. It was contended by counsel on one side that the term was limited to traffic, to buying and selling, or the interchange of commodities, and did not comprehend navigation. This interpretation would restrict to one of its meanings a general term applicable to many objects. Commerce, undoubtedly, was traffic, but it was something more. It was intercourse. It described the commercial intercourse between nations and parts of nations in all its branches, and it was regulated by prescribing rules for carrying on that intercourse. He reached the conclusion that "the word used in the Constitution, then, comprehends, and has been always understood to comprehend, navigation within its meaning; and a power to regulate navigation is as expressly granted as if that term had been added to the word 'commerce.'" [13]

Included in the commerce which Congress might regulate was that which was "among the several states." What was the extent of this commerce? The word "among," said Marshall, meant "intermingled with." A thing which was among others was intermingled with them. Commerce which was among the states could not stop at the external boundary line of each state, but might be introduced into the interior. The term was restricted to that commerce which concerned more states than one. It did not comprehend the completely internal commerce of a state, which might be considered as reserved for the

[11] *Ibid.*, p. 18.    [12] Beveridge, *op. cit.*, IV, 429-430.    [13] 9 Wheaton 193.

state itself. On the other hand, in regulating commerce with foreign nations the power of Congress did not stop at the jurisdictional lines of the several states. Every district of the United States utilizing the chief streams which penetrated into the heart of the country participated in foreign commerce. The power of Congress to regulate such commerce could be exercised wherever the subject existed. Just as foreign commerce might be regulated even within the territory of the several states, so might interstate commerce likewise be regulated by the federal government.[14]

Marshall found it unnecessary to answer the question whether the states were denied the right to regulate interstate commerce merely by the grant of power to Congress, even though Congress failed to exercise its power. Congress had enacted a law concerning the coasting trade, and the vessel involved in this case had been licensed under that statute. He found that the license gave the right of navigation between New York and New Jersey. The New York law conferring monopoly rights in steamboat navigation as applied in this case was therefore in conflict with the federal law, and must fall for that reason. Even though he avoided the broader question, however, he discussed the respective powers of the state and federal governments in a way which reflected the opinions expressed by Webster. He noted the argument that Congress might assert its will concerning portions of interstate commerce quite as much by leaving them untouched as by enacting provisions concerning them. "There is great force in this argument," he said, "and the Court is not satisfied that it has been refuted." [15] Justice Johnson, an appointee of Thomas Jefferson, had by this time become so nationalistic in his thinking that he wrote a concurring opinion, in which he held that the right of free navigation in this case would continue to exist under the Constitution even though the federal licensing act were repealed.

Much of the importance of the decision lay in the fact that Marshall included in the power to regulate commerce the power to control the instruments of commerce, whatever they might be. Had he not done so, the question of the power to control such instruments would have arisen again and again. It would have arisen in connection with railroads, telegraph, telephones, motor cars, airplanes, and radio. As Marshall interpreted the power, however, it included all of commerce across state lines and with foreign nations and Indian tribes, whatever the means by which it was carried on. The statement of principle

[14] *Ibid.*, pp. 194-196.     [15] *Ibid.*, p. 202.

was so broad and so clear that, although litigation inevitably arose with respect to other instrumentalities, the application of the commerce power to those instrumentalities was accepted almost as a matter of course. At the time of the decision, the controversies between the several states over the control of steamboat navigation had provoked hostility similar to that which prevailed prior to the adoption of the Constitution. The decision of the Supreme Court knitted together permanently the torn web of the Constitution even though it left certain important constitutional questions undecided.[16] So irksome were the restrictions of the several state laws upon commerce by means of steamboat navigation that the decision in Gibbons v. Ogden, unlike many other of Marshall's decisions striking down state laws, was generally popular. It did much to establish the prestige of the Supreme Court with the people generally.

Incidentally, it seems to have been the first important Supreme Court decision against a strong business monopoly. Another institution which might be regarded as a monopoly in the field of finance had been involved in McCulloch v. Maryland, which had to do with the constitutionality of the Bank of the United States; but in that case the monopoly received the protection of the Court. It should be remembered, however, that Gibbons v. Ogden, like most of the important cases decided by Chief Justice Marshall, involved, not the assertion of the power of the federal government over interstate commerce, but acted rather as a prohibition against state activity. Apart from granting coasting licenses, the federal government was not interested in the commerce involved. The decision was an act in defense of laissez-faire rather than of positive federal control.

### BROWN v. MARYLAND

The next important commerce case decided by the Supreme Court had to do with the power of the state to enact legislation which infringed upon foreign commerce and which could be interpreted as providing for the taxation of imports. It was the case of Brown v. Maryland,[17] decided in 1827, three years after Gibbons v. Ogden. In 1819, the legislature of Maryland had passed an act requiring retail dealers in foreign merchandise to take out licenses. The constitu-

---

[16] In addition to avoiding certain questions as to the commerce power, Marshall found it unnecessary to discuss the bearing of the patent clause of the Constitution upon the case. *Ibid.*, p. 221.

[17] 12 Wheaton 419.

tionality of this act seems not to have been questioned. In 1822, the legislature passed a supplemental measure requiring the purchase of licenses by wholesalers of drygoods, alcoholic beverages, and other commodities, including, incidentally, those which had been shipped in interstate and foreign commerce. The latter act was challenged as a tax on imports and as a regulation of foreign commerce. The act was defended by two eminent lawyers, Roger B. Taney, later Chief Justice of the United States, and Reverdy Johnson, of Baltimore.[18]

Chief Justice Marshall again wrote the opinion of the Court. He held the Maryland law unconstitutional, both as a duty on imports and as a regulation of foreign commerce. In seeking to discover the point at which federal control over goods imported gave way to state control over goods within the borders of the states, Marshall announced the famous "original-package" doctrine, which was used thereafter as a guide in a long line of decisions. He stated the doctrine as follows:

> When the importer has so acted upon the thing imported that it has become incorporated and mixed up with the mass of property in the country, it has, perhaps, lost its distinctive character as an import, and has become subject to the taxing power of the state; but while remaining the property of the importer, in his warehouse, in the original form or package in which it was imported, a tax upon it is too plainly a duty on imports to escape the prohibition in the Constitution.[19]

Marshall admitted that the state might control imported goods to such an extent as, for example, to require the removal of gunpowder from a place of danger, or to require the removal or destruction of infectious or unsound articles. Inspection laws or health laws as such, however, were not in themselves regulations of imports or of commerce, even though interstate or foreign commerce might be involved incidentally.

Towards the close of his opinion, Marshall stated that "we suppose the principles laid down in this case, to apply equally to importations from a sister state."[20] In later years, however, the Court took the position that the term "imports" applied, not to goods moved from one state to another, but only to importations from a foreign country.[21] As interstate and foreign relationships became more complex,

[18] See *ibid.*, p. 429.     [19] *Ibid.*, pp. 441-442.     [20] *Ibid.*, p. 449.
[21] American Express Co. *v.* Iowa, 196 U.S. 133, 146 (1905).

the "original-package" doctrine more and more frequently proved inadequate as a means of determining the line between commerce which was intrastate and that which was interstate or foreign. Only by a highly attenuated form of reasoning can an original package of natural gas or of electricity or of any relevant unit in radio be discovered. Necessity has, therefore, compelled the development of other lines of reasoning for the determination of the dividing line between state and federal power.

A dissenting opinion by Justice Thompson in Brown v. Maryland and an opinion by Chief Justice Marshall in a later case [22] showed that the members of the Court were not agreed on a clear line of demarcation between federal and state powers affecting interstate and foreign commerce. The case of New York v. Miln,[23] first argued before the Supreme Court in 1834, revealed sharp disagreement. The port cities on the eastern seaboard were having difficulty in absorbing the mass of immigrants then coming to the United States. Large numbers were penniless and were unable either to get jobs or to secure transportation westward to points at which work might be found. The port cities had the alternative of supporting paupers or seeing them starve. To protect itself, the state of New York passed a law requiring masters of incoming ships to make a detailed report concerning each immigrant brought in, and authorizing the city of New York to require masters of vessels to give bond to insure that immigrants would not become a charge upon the city. A case contesting the first provision was taken to the Supreme Court. The opposing parties in the case disagreed as to whether the regulation, which applied to passengers after the voyage had ceased but before they disembarked, was a regulation of foreign commerce. It was contended that the carrying of passengers, as distinguished from commodities, was not commerce at all; and even if it could be classified as commerce, the commerce was said to have ceased at the time when the regulation became effective. It was contended that the regulation was a local matter for the preservation of the health and welfare of people within an area over which the state had jurisdiction. To describe such legislation, counsel were now using the term "police powers," a term which became highly important in future years in determining the lines of jurisdiction between state and federal powers. The master of the vessel contended, on the other hand, that the law had a direct bearing upon the handling of foreign commerce,

[22] Willson v. Blackbird Creek Marsh Co., 2 Peters 245 (1829).    [23] 8 Peters 120.

and that it burdened that commerce. For that reason it should be held unconstitutional.

Of the membership of the Court in 1834, Justice Thompson and two Jackson appointees, McLean and Baldwin, thought the New York law constitutional. Chief Justice Marshall and Justices Story, Duvall, and Johnson, all older members, believed it unconstitutional.[24] Duvall and Johnson were absent at the time the case was argued and could not participate in the decision. The three justices who thought the law constitutional, therefore, made a majority of those who sat in the case. Instead of allowing the case to be decided in this manner, Chief Justice Marshall announced the rule that, except in cases of absolute necessity, it was the practice of the Court not to deliver judgments in constitutional cases unless four justices concurred in the opinion, thus making the decision that of a majority of the whole Court. Since four justices did not concur in this case, it was to be reargued at the next term under the expectation that a larger number of justices might then be present.[25]

Had the membership of the Court remained the same and had all justices been present at the ensuing term, the decision would have been that approved by Marshall — that the New York law was unconstitutional as an infringement of the power of the federal government to regulate foreign commerce — and Justices Thompson, McLean, and Baldwin would have dissented. The period was one of rapid transition in Court personnel, however, and a number of justices, including Marshall himself, died before the case was reargued. When in 1837 the case was taken up before Chief Justice Taney, only Justice Story remained of the old Marshall Court. By a vote of six to one the reconstituted Court held the New York law constitutional. In his dissenting opinion Story took a position never officially taken by Marshall; namely, that the power of Congress to regulate interstate and foreign commerce was exclusive. He thought also that existing federal legislation had, in fact, authorized the immigration of passengers into the country and that the New York law therefore violated a federal statute as well as the federal Constitution. He concluded by saying:

> In this opinion I have the consolation to know that I had the entire concurrence, upon the same grounds, of that great constitutional jurist, the late Mr. Chief Justice Marshall. Having heard the former arguments, his deliberate opinion was that the act of New York was

[24] Beveridge, *op. cit.*, IV, 583.  [25] 8 Peters 122.

unconstitutional, and that the present case fell directly within the principles established in the cases of Gibbons *v.* Ogden . . . and Brown *v.* the State of Maryland.[26]

Although six justices agreed that the New York law was constitutional, they did not agree on the arguments by which it was to be upheld. The task of writing the opinion of the Court was assigned to Justice Thompson. He wrote an opinion which seems to have been acceptable to his brethren in so far as it justified the New York law as a legitimate police regulation. Thompson believed, however, that even though the measure was a regulation of foreign commerce, it was nevertheless legitimate in the absence of conflicting federal legislation, and he apparently insisted on saying so. Some of his brethren refused to support an opinion which took the position that the commerce power was concurrent between the federal government and the states. Thompson refused to delete the objectionable language. The task of writing the opinion of the Court was therefore allotted to Justice Barbour, a Virginia Democrat appointed by Jackson, leaving Thompson's opinion to be filed as a statement merely of his own position. Barbour wrote an opinion upholding the New York law as a legitimate police regulation. He specifically avoided any discussion of the question whether the power to regulate commerce was exclusive, contending that, since the law was a police regulation, it was not a regulation of commerce at all.

Barbour ran into difficulties of another kind in the course of the opinion, which was delivered on the last day of the term when the justices were involved in preparations to leave Washington and evidently had not much time to examine written opinions. He included the statement that persons were "not the subject of commerce." Since they were not imported goods, he declared, they could not fall within a train of reasoning founded upon the construction of a power given to Congress to regulate commerce and upon the prohibition to the states from imposing a duty on imported goods.[27] On this point it seems that only two of the justices were agreed. Four of them, including Justice Story, thought that the carrying of passengers did constitute interstate commerce. Justice Thompson refused to express an opinion on the subject.[28]

The subject was important, not merely because of its relation to

---

[26] New York *v.* Miln, 11 Peters 102, 161 (1837).    [27] *Ibid.*, pp. 136-137.

[28] For a statement of the positions of the several justices see Passenger Cases, **7 Howard** 283, 431 (1849).

the control of white immigrants, but because of its bearing upon the transportation of slaves and, perhaps, of free Negroes, in interstate and foreign commerce. Some of the justices were highly indignant when it was discovered that by sanctioning an opinion of the Court they had unwittingly given support to a doctrine in which they did not believe, and had stored up embarrassment for themselves when other cases on related constitutional questions were to be decided. Justice Baldwin published an opinion of his own the following year, in which he clarified his position.[29] Other justices waited until the decision of other cases, when they had to explain their earlier position and reject Barbour's argument in order to maintain consistency.[30]

## ENTANGLEMENT WITH THE ISSUE OF SLAVERY

The controversy over the interpretation of the commerce power was resumed in the slavery case of Groves v. Slaughter.[31] The case involved a provision in the constitution of the state of Mississippi intended to prevent the purchase of Negroes from other states. The provision reflected no hostility to slavery as such. It represented, rather, an attempt on the part of the state to prevent the injurious withdrawal of capital from the state to purchase Negroes of other states instead of local products. The case was decided on a technicality. It proved unnecessary to discuss the questions whether the movement of slaves across state lines constituted interstate commerce, and whether the state had the constitutional power to prevent such movement. One member of the Court insisted on discussing these questions, however, and other members, who evidently feared the influence of his discussion, proceeded to state their own opinions. The opinions revealed almost complete chaos of interpretation. Justice McLean, for example, who grew closer in doctrine to Justice Story with the passing of the years, took the position that the power of Congress over interstate commerce automatically excluded the state from the exercise of any such power. In addition to being a nationalist, he was also an abolitionist, however, and he was quite willing to sanction principles which would prevent the interstate movement of slaves. He therefore held that Mississippi had the power to prevent the importation of slaves from other states, basing his argument, not on the

---

[29] See the document published as a supplement to 11 Peters at page 181.

[30] See the statements of Chief Justice Taney and Justice Wayne in Passenger Cases, 7 Howard 283, 429-436, 487-490 (1849). For discussion see Carl Brent Swisher, *Roger B. Taney* (1935), pp. 374-376, 394-396, 404-405.

[31] 15 Peters 449 (1841).

power of a state to regulate interstate commerce, but on the police powers of a state. Justice Baldwin took the consistent position that the power of the federal government over interstate commerce was exclusive, and that a state had no power to prevent the importation of slaves from other states. Chief Justice Taney and Justice Thompson avoided full commitment in this case, but in the light of positions taken in other cases it seems that they maintained a consistency directly opposed to that of Justice Baldwin. They thought the power of Congress over interstate commerce was not exclusive and that the state, therefore, had the power to prevent the importation of slaves from other states.[32]

The decision emphasized the lack of a consistent body of doctrine in the Supreme Court with reference to important issues and the absence of a dominating personality such as that of Marshall, which had molded judicial doctrines in earlier years. Chief Justice Taney seemed never to have sought any such personal power as that exercised by Marshall. The domination of the Court by the Chief Justice was opposed to his conception of democratic procedure. Furthermore, even if he had desired to dominate the work of the Court, he probably lacked the forcefulness which would have made success possible. Justice Story, the lone disciple of Marshall, was too much outmoded to have influence over any of his brethren except Justice McLean. McLean himself was not without influence, but it was probably limited by the fact that too much of his judicial work was done with an eye upon party politics and the prospect of winning the presidency.

## THE LICENSE CASES

The next important decision on the commerce power, handed down in 1847, showed some development of the thinking of individual justices, but pointed to no solution of their differences. It included the decision of three cases, which are usually known as the License Cases.[33] The cases, decided together, had to do with the licensing of the sale of liquor in Massachusetts, Rhode Island, and New Hampshire. The continuation of judicial chaos was demonstrated by the fact that, although all justices agreed that the licensing provisions in the three state laws were valid, six justices, nevertheless, wrote nine opinions, no one of which had the full concurrence of a majority of the Court.

[32] For a chart of the positions of the several justices see Swisher, *op. cit.*, p. 400.
[33] Thurlow *v.* Massachusetts, Fletcher *v.* Rhode Island, Peirce *v.* New Hampshire, 5 Howard 504 (1847).

The Massachusetts and Rhode Island cases were much alike. In so far as they dealt with liquor brought from outside the state, they dealt, not with original packages, but with retail sales of smaller quantities, or broken packages. The Massachusetts law forbade the unlicensed sale of alcoholic beverages in quantities of less than twenty-eight gallons. It did not require that a license be issued to every person applying for it, with the result that in temperance areas the law might have the effect of prohibiting retail sales altogether. One of the questions involved, therefore, was whether interference with retail sale of liquor brought from other states constituted such a barrier to interstate commerce as to violate the commerce clause of the Constitution. The "original-package" doctrine, announced by Chief Justice Marshall in Brown v. Maryland, was clearly applicable here. Chief Justice Taney accepted it, even though he had been counsel on the losing side in the case in which the doctrine was first announced. Other justices relied on that doctrine, on the doctrine of concurrent jurisdiction over interstate commerce, and on the doctrine of police powers.

The New Hampshire case, in contrast with the other two cases, had to do with the sale of liquor in the packages in which it had been brought into the state. The regulation was, therefore, harder to justify. Chief Justice Taney, in order to uphold the measure, took the position that a state might regulate interstate commerce in the absence of federal regulation. Justice McLean, on the other hand, continued to insist that the federal power over interstate commerce was exclusive, but contended that the New Hampshire law was valid, not as a regulation of commerce, but as an exercise of the police powers of the state.

The doctrine of police powers is thought of in modern times as one used primarily to justify state legislation which without the aid of the doctrine might be held to exceed the constitutional powers of the state. It is of interest that the doctrine was evolved primarily not by the advocates of state rights, but by the nationalists on the Supreme Court who sought a doctrinal excuse for deviating at times from the implications of their nationalism, as, for example, when they happened to be advocates of temperance and abolition as well as of nationalism. In this case, it was Justice McLean, of the nationalists, who aided in the development of the doctrine of police powers. Chief Justice Taney, who is usually identified with the school of state rights, argued that the power to regulate interstate commerce was concurrent, and thought there was little significance in the development of the doctrine of police powers. What were the police powers of the state? he asked.

> They are nothing more or less than the powers of government inherent in every sovereignty to the extent of its dominions. And whether a state passes a quarantine law, or a law to punish offenses, or to establish courts of justice, or requiring certain instruments to be recorded, or to regulate commerce within its own limits, in every case it exercises the same power; that is to say, the power of sovereignty, the power to govern men and things within the limits of its dominion. It is by virtue of this power that it legislates; and its authority to make regulations of commerce is as absolute as its power to pass health laws, except in so far as it has been restricted by the Constitution of the United States. And when the validity of a state law making regulations of commerce is drawn into question in a judicial tribunal, the authority to pass it cannot be made to depend upon the motives that may be supposed to have influenced the legislature, nor can the Court inquire whether it was intended to guard the citizens of the state from pestilence and disease, or to make regulations of commerce for the interest and convenience of trade.[34]

In future years, as the power of the federal government was extended farther and farther by interpretation, it proved convenient, if indeed it was not absolutely necessary, to resort to the doctrine of police powers in the states to justify state legislation which infringed in one way or another upon matters which the federal government was also entitled to regulate on the basis of the commerce power or some other power delegated by the Constitution. With the development of the concept of due process of law as a restriction upon legislation which the states might enact, the concept of police powers, to be used in justifying their authority, became even more important. In short, the states, which in earlier years were regarded as the residuaries of powers not granted to the federal government or not denied to the states, have been juggled into the position of governments possessing only delegated powers; that is, of powers, for example, which fall within the judicial concept of police powers. This shift in the position of the states, the disappearance of their residual authority, which can be traced from the time of the commerce decisions discussed in this chapter, has been one of the most important trends in the development of the federal Constitution.

[34] *Ibid.*, p. 583.

As to interstate commerce as such, the judges in the License Cases varied all the way from the argument of McLean, that the states could never regulate interstate commerce, to that of Daniel, that states might regulate any business within their borders, the "original-package" doctrine to the contrary notwithstanding. The cases did not directly touch the subject of slavery, but that subject was in the background. In an early argument in the Massachusetts case, Daniel Webster had called attention to the laws in the South restricting the rights of free Negroes from other states, and declared it high time the Court gave an opinion on the basic questions involved.[35]

## THE PASSENGER CASES

The next important commerce decision likewise avoided the slavery issue, but came closer to it, since the subject involved was the carrying of passengers rather than inanimate commodities. The decision was announced in 1849 in what were known as the Passenger Cases.[36] The cases had to do with laws of New York and Massachusetts laying a tax on each passenger brought into the ports of the states. The money collected was to be spent for the support of foreign paupers or of hospitals, or for other purposes connected with the care of the indigent. There were federal laws and treaties dealing with the subject of immigration, but the cases, nevertheless, provided further opportunities for discussion of the question whether the power of Congress over foreign commerce was exclusive. The cases raised again the question whether the carrying of passengers was commerce within the meaning of the Constitution, about which the Court was sharply divided. Counsel seeking to maintain the validity of the laws contended, furthermore, that in any event the laws were health laws which the state had the power to enact and did not rest upon any power to regulate commerce.

The cases were argued three times before the Supreme Court arrived at a decision. Daniel Webster, now approaching the end of his career, participated in each argument, contending that the laws were unconstitutional. He deplored privately the passing of the Court of Marshall, and of Story, who had died recently. He was tired of these constitutional questions, he said. This was no Court for them.[37] He

[35] Swisher, op. cit., p. 399.

[36] Smith v. Turner, Norris v. Boston, 7 Howard 283 (1849).

[37] Charles Warren, The Supreme Court in United States History (rev. ed., 2 vols., 1926), I, 177.

feared the judges were too much inclined to find apologies for irregular and dangerous acts of state legislatures. The Court lacked a strong and leading mind. John Van Buren, counsel for the opposition, urged the Court to be responsive to the will of the people, and congratulated the justices on the overthrow of the "mastodon of construction" by which during an earlier period the rights of sovereignty of the states had been trampled underfoot. Webster chose to understand Van Buren as congratulating the Court for yielding to the popular impulses of the day. This, he declared, was a compliment he would not address to any court for which he entertained a feeling of respect.[38]

Various types of interest were felt in the decision of the Court. Some people were concerned about the welfare of impoverished immigrants who were unable to take care of themselves in the New World. Some favored any source of revenue which caused no pain to native Americans. Some favored the use of a taxing measure to discourage immigration, because many petty criminals were included among the immigrants, who for this as well as other reasons were regarded as objectionable neighbors. Some thought then, as always, that the country would be better off if no more foreigners were admitted. On the other hand, some were opposed to any measure which might check the flow of cheap labor. Southern slaveowners and traders were concerned about the fate of these laws because of the bearing which the decision might have on southern laws providing for the inspection of vessels and the checking of immigration of free Negroes. Others concerned about the decision were those persons who as a matter of principle favored or opposed the centralization of power in the federal government.

The Court finally decided the cases, but it settled no matters of doctrine. By a vote of five to four it held the state laws unconstitutional. Each of the majority justices, however, and three of the minority justices wrote opinions discussing the cases and the several issues involved in the interpretation of the commerce clause and of the powers of the states. The eight opinions illuminate the history of the Supreme Court and throw light on the efforts of the justices to work out constitutional principles. Many things said by individual justices harmonized well with decisions reached in later years, but the opinions in the Passenger Cases, taken alone, did nothing to systematize interpretations upon which the members of the Court had long been unable to agree.

[38] Swisher, op. cit., p. 403.

In spite of the diversity among the opinions, the decision had the effect of striking down the state laws immediately involved and of indicating the unconstitutionality of similar laws in other states, as well as the southern laws prohibiting the importation of free Negroes. Yet the decision turned on the vote of one man. A slight change in the personnel of the Supreme Court might bring about a reversal. For this reason the outcome was unsatisfactory, even to those who had won a technical victory. Constitutional law was made to depend obviously upon the counting of heads on the Supreme Court, rather than upon general agreement as to the meaning of the Constitution. In such a situation the prestige of the Supreme Court was inevitably impaired.

## THE PILOT CASE

It was in the case of Cooley v. The Board of Wardens of the Port of Philadelphia,[39] decided in 1852, that a majority of the Supreme Court agreed upon a rule for the interpretation of the commerce power which seemed to dispel some of the confusion. The first Congress which met after the adoption of the Constitution had enacted a measure providing that all pilots in the bays, inlets, rivers, harbors, and ports of the United States should continue to be regulated in conformity with the existing laws of the states, or with such laws as the states might thereafter enact, until further legislative provisions should be made by Congress. By implication, therefore, the statute asserted the jurisdiction of Congress over the subject, and at the same time recognized the power of the states to legislate on the subject if the power of Congress was dormant. It was not assumed that Congress could delegate to state legislatures its own legislative power over commerce. The provision that pilots should be governed by measures which state legislatures might subsequently enact, was apparently merely a statement that Congress did not intend to regulate the subject merely by inaction and that the subject was left open for state regulation as an exercise of residual state power.

A Pennsylvania law, passed after the date of the federal statute, provided that all vessels of certain description coming into port should employ pilots, or, if they refused to do so, should nevertheless pay half the established fee, for the use of the quaintly named Society for the Relief of Distressed and Decayed Pilots. Cooley refused to pay the fee. He contended that the state law was a regulation of foreign

[39] 12 Howard 299.

commerce, which was subject only to federal control, a control which Congress could not delegate to the states.

A new justice, Benjamin R. Curtis, of Massachusetts, had been appointed to the Supreme Court since the decision of the Passenger Cases. He seems to have brought to the Court no new ideas on the subject of the interpretation of the commerce power — a fact easily understandable in view of the length at which the subject had already been discussed — but he provided a medium through which a compromise doctrine of a majority of the Court could be stated. Commerce, he declared, embraced many subjects quite unlike in their nature. Some of them imperatively demanded a single uniform rule, operating equally on the commerce of the United States at every point. Others, like the subject now in question, just as imperatively demanded diversity of regulation in terms of the local necessities of navigation.

> Either absolutely to affirm, or to deny, that the nature of this power requires exclusive legislation by Congress, is to lose sight of the nature of the subjects of this power, and to assert concerning all of them, what is really applicable but to a part. Whatever subjects of this power are in their nature national, or admit only of one uniform system, or plan of regulation, may justly be said to be of such a nature as to require exclusive legislation by Congress.[40]

It was plain, however, he said, that this could not be affirmed of laws for the regulation of pilots and pilotage. The subject required diverse local regulations. It was not to be assumed that the grant of commerce power in the Constitution did not take into account the nature of the subject, and permit the types of regulation which were necessary. It was "the opinion of a majority of the Court that the mere grant to Congress of the power to regulate commerce did not deprive the states of power to regulate pilots, and that, although Congress had legislated on this subject, its legislation manifests an intention, with a single exception, not to regulate this subject, but to leave its regulation to the several states." [41]

Out of this case, therefore, evolved the general rule that Congress had exclusive jurisdiction over aspects of interstate and foreign commerce that required uniform regulation, whereas Congress might leave to the states the enactment of regulations of such commerce where diversity rather than uniformity was required. Three justices

[40] *Ibid.*, p. 319.      [41] *Ibid.*, p. 320.

refused to concur in the opinion of the Court. Two of them, McLean and Wayne, continued to insist that the power of Congress was always exclusive, and that the states had no power of regulation. Justice Daniel, on the other hand, although he concurred in the judgment of the Court, refused to support an opinion which interpreted so narrowly the powers of the states.

The principle of interpretation of the commerce clause sanctioned by a majority of the Supreme Court in the Pilot Case remained in good standing for many decades, and has never been directly repudiated. It eliminated some of the chaos in judicial decisions on the subject. On the other hand, it left many problems unsolved. It provided no means of determining in other cases what phases of commerce required uniform regulations and what required diverse local regulations. On the whole, the tendency has been to expand the interpretations of the responsibility of Congress and to restrict the responsibility of the states. Few state regulations of interstate or foreign commerce are now sanctioned as legitimate exercises of power over commerce as such. They are sanctioned, rather, as manifestations of the police power of the states of which the effect upon commerce is but incidental.

The fact should be kept in mind that most of the important commerce cases decided before the Civil War had to do, not with federal regulations of commerce, but with state laws encroaching on the field of federal power. It was not until after the Civil War that the commerce clause became a most fertile source of federal regulations of private enterprise. In the earlier period southern slavery interests and other groups, although not powerful enough to control the federal government, were sufficiently powerful to act as a check upon the expansion of federal activity. Examples of the attitudes of southern statesmen toward the expansion of federal power may be found in debates on the measure enacted in 1849 to establish the Department of the Interior.[42] The new department, referred to as a Home Department, was intended to bring together from the older departments of the government a number of agencies having to do with the internal affairs of the United States, such as the Patent Office, the General Land Office, the commissioner of Indian affairs, the commissioner of pensions, and the commissioner of public buildings. The establishment of the department was opposed, however, as a measure to increase the power of the federal government and to bring the internal

[42] 9 Stat. 395.

affairs of the states under federal control. John C. Calhoun found something ominous in the title, "The Secretary of the Interior." He prophesied that the bill would turn over to the federal government the whole interior affairs of the country. It was one of the greatest steps that had been made in his time, he proclaimed, to absorb all the remaining powers of the states.[43] Actually the bill provided no such express opportunity for the centralization of power, although it may, perhaps, be said to mark the beginning of a trend. The debates are important chiefly in indicating the sentiment of a powerful group in the country.

One important fact must be kept in mind for an understanding of the interpretation of the commerce power during the period under discussion and, to some extent, for many years thereafter. Since Congress at that time made no effort at broad regulation of enterprise throughout the country on the basis of the commerce power, the advocates of the doctrine of exclusive federal power were not seeking to justify federal regulation, but rather were using constitutional doctrine as a means of avoiding all governmental control. If the states could not regulate, the prospect was that there would be no regulation at all. Nationalism and laissez-faire were then twin doctrines. In later years, with the growth of federal regulation based on the commerce clause, opponents of regulation shifted their arguments, as convenience and objectives dictated, to oppose federal regulation as encroachment on the powers of the states. They were consistent only in their opposition to regulation from **any source, whether state** or federal.

[43] Warren, *op. cit.*, II, **137.**

# CHAPTER 11

# THE CONTROL OF CORPORATIONS

THE GROWTH OF THE CONSTITUTION is usually studied largely in terms of the development of constitutional doctrines and interpretations. The meaning of the Constitution, whether original or acquired, is presented via such items as the doctrine of separation of powers, the theory of implied powers, and the meaning of the contract and the commerce clauses of the Constitution. Yet constitutional doctrines and interpretations do not develop in a vacuum, and they can be fully understood only if they are studied in relation to conflicts and controversies among the people, and particularly those conflicts and controversies which are economic in character. The interplay of such forces was illustrated above, for example, in the chapters dealing with contracts, the Bank of the United States, and the commerce clause. It dominated constitutional development with reference to the tariff and slavery, which will be discussed in subsequent chapters. It was basic in many phases of constitutional interpretation with respect to corporations, the focal point of this chapter.

The New World possessed great riches in natural resources and little capital for their exploitation. Development had to be undertaken either by government or by corporations which brought together the limited savings of many individuals. The building of roads and canals and bridges, the clearing of rivers and harbors, and the operation of ferries were enterprises of major importance, each of which, in the early years, required a separate legislative act erecting a corporation if the work was to be done by private enterprise. To provide the necessary credit, the privilege of engaging in banking was given oftentimes to the same corporations, usually with little restriction upon the exercise of the privilege. The use of corporations developed rapidly as the country sought to achieve a degree of independence of foreign production by the development of its own industries. Due to lack of experience with corporations, none of the states had an adequate body of law concerning them. Protection was needed if they were to attract capital, and restraint was needed if they were to be kept from trampling upon the rights of individuals and other corporations. A body of law developed gradually upon the basis of common-law doctrines, but with modifications in terms of the needs of a new era. Corporations grew rapidly in numbers and in size, and the growth of large corporations in terms of size and power continues even to the present day.

Constitutional questions inevitably arose as the corporation found its place in the legal system of the country. One of the first problems, the power of Congress to charter a corporation, has already been discussed. The use of the contract clause of the Constitution to prevent a state from impairing the charter of a corporation was illustrated in the Dartmouth College case, in connection with which the doctrine was first announced. The question of the power of a corporation to sue and to be sued in federal courts rather than in state courts where it might be subject to local prejudice, was mentioned briefly and left to further discussion in a subsequent chapter.

### THE INTERPRETATION OF CHARTERS

The Supreme Court never questioned the rule, announced in the Dartmouth College case, that a charter was a contract which could not be impaired by subsequent state action. Counsel for corporations quickly entrenched themselves behind that interpretation, and sought further concessions. They argued that in determining what was given by a charter the Court should interpret its meaning broadly; that is, the charter of a corporation, like a constitution, was to be regarded as a statement of principle, and all powers which might reasonably be implied were to be read into the charter. Adoption of this principle of interpretation was sought at a time when charters were being granted in increasing numbers by legislatures which oftentimes failed to scrutinize carefully their provisions, or adopted provisions as a result of political pressure or bribery. Corporate powers, once acquired, were exercised with a ruthlessness which obscured the fact that some element of public welfare was supposed to be promoted by the granting of every charter. Public hostility to corporations developed quickly, and made itself felt along with the popular urge for the creation of still more charters for the building of roads, canals, railroads, and other forms of enterprise. Additional court decisions were necessary to establish the scope of the rights of corporations which were given by charter and protected by the contract clause.

The beginning of a trend toward narrow rather than broad interpretation was indicated by the Charles River Bridge case,[1] decided in
1837.   The case had to do with an act of the legislature of Massachusetts which chartered a company to build a bridge across the Charles
River, under such circumstances as to provide destructive competition
with another bridge previously erected by a company chartered by the
state.   It was argued that the authorization to build the second bridge
impaired the charter of the company which had built the one first
erected.   The first company was chartered in 1785.   It was empowered to erect a bridge and collect tolls from passengers for a period
of years.   The bridge was built at considerable financial risk, was
opened to traffic, and proved extremely profitable.   Whereas the
original capitalization was $50,000, the bridge company claimed in
1823 that the value of its property was $280,000.[2]   Much of the profit
was made, not by the original holders of the shares, but by subsequent
purchasers.   The public continued to pay tolls even though the cost
of the bridge had been paid many times over.

The management of the Charles River Bridge monopoly, like the
management of Dartmouth College, became involved in party politics.
In 1828 the legislature of Massachusetts chartered a company to build
what came to be known as the Warren Bridge, a few rods from the
old bridge.   The new bridge was to be surrendered to the state as
soon as sufficient tolls had been collected to pay for its construction,
or at the end of a maximum period of six years.   No tolls were to be
charged thereafter.   It was obvious that the old toll bridge would get
little or no traffic in competition with a neighboring bridge, which
was to be open to the public free of charge.   The old bridge company
contested the validity of the act chartering the Warren Bridge Company, contending that it unconstitutionally impaired the contract in
the charter of the Charles River Bridge Company by setting up a
competitor which prevented it from earning the tolls it was authorized
to collect.

The supreme judicial court of Massachusetts decided against the
Charles River Bridge Company, and the case was appealed to the
Supreme Court of the United States, where it was argued for the first
time in 1831.   The Court failed to reach a decision at that term, and
Justice Story subsequently wrote an opinion in the case reversing the

---

[1] Charles River Bridge v. Warren Bridge, 11 Peters 420 (1837).  The discussion herein
follows that of Carl Brent Swisher, *Roger B. Taney* (1935), pp. 361 ff.
[2] See Charles Warren, *History of Harvard Law School* (3 vols., 1909), I, 510-513.

Massachusetts court, in the hope thereby of convincing some of his doubtful brethren. He failed to convince them; and, because of the absence of one or more justices and the disagreements among others, the decision was further postponed.[3]

Because of further absences of members and changes in the personnel of the Court, it was not until 1837, six years after the date of the first argument, that the case was decided. In the meantime the Warren Bridge had been erected, the tolls collected had equaled the cost of construction, and the bridge had been thrown open to the public, toll-free. Passengers who might otherwise have paid for the privilege of crossing the Charles River Bridge now crossed the Warren Bridge instead, entirely without cost to themselves. The outcome was hailed as a victory for the traveling public against what were loosely called vested rights.

The Supreme Court of 1837 was very different from that of 1819, which had decided the Dartmouth College case. Five of the seven judges had been appointed by Andrew Jackson, and the position of Chief Justice was now occupied by Roger B. Taney, of Maryland. Taney had been a leading Federalist in Maryland as long as the Federalist party had survived, but his conception of the Constitution was very different from that of Marshall. He was more steeped in localism than was Marshall, and more fearful of the growth of powerful units of economic enterprise. He was one of the most effective opponents of the Bank of the United States. It is quite probable that his struggle with that institution had much to do with his distrust of corporations and with the emphasis which he gave to the rights of the people which might be imperiled by the growth of great economic units. He was not a state-rights doctrinaire in the narrow sense of the term, but in his interpretation of the commerce clause and of legal principles having to do with the institution of slavery he at least avoided a nationalist alignment. The leanings of the other justices varied considerably, but only Justice Story could be expected to echo the sentiments of his former chief.

In a series of opinions previously written, either as counsel for private parties, or as Attorney General of the United States, or as confidential adviser of the President, Taney had made statements which were ominous for the Charles River Bridge Company. He had contended that the grant of peculiar privileges in the charters of corpo-

[3] See Charles Warren, *Supreme Court in United States History* (rev. ed., 2 vols., 1926), I 773, note 2.

rations must be presumed to rest upon some public interest. He had questioned whether one legislative body might by contract restrict the powers of its successors unless specifically authorized to do so by the constitution of the state. He challenged the conception of vested rights in a way which must have been as disturbing to the business-men of the country as was his opposition to the Bank of the United States. Those who knew of Taney's attitude toward corporations and their obligation to the public doubtless expected that the Charles River Bridge Company would have to make a very clear case if Taney was to sanction its right to provide exclusive access to and from Boston at a particular point and to collect high tolls from the traffic which brought in, again and again, amounts equal to the cost of construction and operation of the bridge.

Counsel reminded the Court that it was not merely the property of the Charles River Bridge Company that was at stake, declaring that the principles to be established by the judgment in the case would decide the title to more than ten million dollars in the state of Massachusetts alone.[4] Taney took account of this fact in the opening paragraph of the opinion of the Court. The Court, he said, was fully sensible of its duty "to deal with these great and extensive interests with the utmost caution; guarding, as far as they have the power to do so, the rights of property, and at the same time carefully abstaining from any encroachment on the rights reserved to the states."[5]

The decision in this case turned upon the interpretation of the charter of the Charles River Bridge Company. Taney rejected the contention that rights conferred by charter were to be interpreted broadly. He found his rule of interpretation in a case in which a court in England had said, "This, like many other cases, is a bargain between a company of adventurers and the public, the terms of which are expressed in the statute; and the rule of construction in all such cases is now fully established to be this — that any ambiguity in the terms of the contract must operate against the adventurers, and in favor of the public, and the plaintiffs can claim nothing that is not clearly given them by the act."[6] Since we had borrowed our system of jurisprudence from the English law, said Taney, and had adopted in every other case its rules for the construction of statutes, there was

[4] 11 Peters 460.
[5] *Ibid.*, p. 536.
[6] Proprietors of the Stourbridge Canal *v.* Wheely, 2 Barn. and Adol. 793, quoted by Taney, 11 Peters 544.

no reason which should lead us to depart from the principle where corporations were concerned.

It would present a singular spectacle if, while the courts in England are restraining, within restricted limits, the spirit of monopoly, and exclusive privileges in the nature of monopolies, and confining corporations to the privileges plainly given to them in their charters; the courts of this country should be found enlarging these privileges by implication; and construing a statute more unfavorably to the public, and to the rights of the community, than would be done in a like case in an English court of justice.[7]

Even though he doubtless knew that John Marshall would have disagreed with him in the case now being decided, Taney also found support in one of Marshall's decisions. Relying on the principle announced by Marshall in McCulloch *v.* Maryland that the power to tax involves the power to destroy, a bank chartered by the legislature of Rhode Island had contended, first, that exemption from taxation ought to be implied from the fact that the state had granted the charter, and second, that state taxation of the bank constituted impairment of the obligation of contract. Marshall had rejected the contention. The community was interested in retaining the taxing power undiminished, he explained, and the community had a right to insist that the abandonment of the taxing power ought not to be presumed in a case in which the deliberate purpose of a state to abandon it did not appear.[8]

The rule of construction announced by Marshall in the Rhode Island case, said Taney, was not confined to the taxing power:

But the object and end of all government is to promote the happiness and prosperity of the community by which it is established, and it can never be assumed that the government intended to diminish its power of accomplishing the end for which it was created. And in a country like ours, free, active, and enterprising, continually advancing in numbers and wealth; new channels of communication are daily found necessary, both for travel and trade, and are essential to the comfort, convenience, and prosperity of the people. A state ought never to be presumed to surrender this power, because, like the taxing power, the whole community have an interest in preserving it undiminished. And when a corporation alleges that a state has surrendered for seventy years its power of improvement and public accommodation, in a great and important line of travel, along which

---

[7] 11 Peters 545-546.    [8] Providence Bank *v.* Billings, 4 Peters 514 (1830).

a vast number of its citizens must daily pass; the community have a right to insist, in the language of this Court above quoted, "that its abandonment ought not to be presumed, in a case in which the deliberate purpose of the state to abandon it does not appear." The continued existence of a government would be of no great value, if, by implications and presumptions, it was disarmed of the powers necessary to accomplish the ends of its creation, and the functions it was designed to perform transferred to the hands of privileged corporations.[9]

No one would question, said Taney, the interests of the great body of the people of the state in the curtailment of the right of free transit which was involved. He stated thereupon this significant doctrine:

While the rights of private property are sacredly guarded, we must not forget that the community also have rights, and that the happiness and well-being of every citizen depend on their faithful preservation.[10]

Having announced and justified the rule of construction, Taney applied it to the charter of the Charles River Bridge Company. The charter contained no language giving exemption from competition by other bridges that might be built. He said:

It would, indeed, be a strong exertion of judicial power, acting upon its own views of what justice required, and the parties ought to have done, to raise, by a sort of judicial coercion, an implied contract, and infer it from the nature of the very instrument in which the legislature appear to have taken pains to use words which disavow and repudiate any intention on the part of the state to make such a contract.[11]

He closed his opinion with a practical consideration. The building of canals and railroads had rendered valueless the franchises of turnpike corporations granted before the new methods of transportation were developed. If the principle were established that the charters of the turnpike companies carried implied exemption from competition, the old corporations would awake from their sleep and call upon the Supreme Court to put down the improvements which had taken their place. The millions invested in railroads and canals would be put in jeopardy.

We shall be thrown back to the improvements of the last century, and obliged to stand still until the claims of the old turnpike corporations shall be satisfied, and they shall consent to permit these states to avail themselves of the light of modern science, and to partake of

[9] 11 Peters 547-548.    [10] Ibid., p. 548.    [11] Ibid., p. 551.

the benefits of those improvements which are now adding to the wealth and prosperity, and the convenience and comfort of every other part of the civilized world.[12]

Furthermore, the Court would find itself compelled to fix by some arbitrary rule the territorial extent of the monopoly rights of these corporations. It had no light for guidance, unless it was prepared to decide that, when a turnpike road from one town to another had been made, no railroad or canal between these two points could afterward be established. The Court was not prepared to sanction principles which might lead to such results.

Justice McLean dissented on the ground that the Supreme Court had no jurisdiction. Justice Story dissented on the merits of the case. The new arguments, he declared, had not shaken his confidence in the conclusion he had reached when the case was first argued. He gave less weight to modern cases than did Taney. He said:

> I stand upon the old law, upon law established more than three centuries ago, in cases contested with as much ability and learning as any in the annals of our jurisprudence, in resisting any such encroachment upon the rights and liberties of the citizens, secured by public grants. I will not consent to shake their title deeds by any speculative niceties or novelties.[13]

Daniel Webster, one of the defeated counsel in the case, assured Story that his opinion left the opposition not a foot nor an inch to stand on. The intelligent part of the profession would all be with him. Webster lamented the overthrow by the majority of the Court of a great provision of the Constitution.[14] As late as 1845 he characterized the opinion of the Court as "an ingenious, elaborate, and sometimes half-shamefaced apology for what is wrong," and staked his reputation as a lawyer that the decision could not stand.[15]

He was right, in part, as to the opposition of the bar to the decision of the Court, but he was wrong as to the future of the decision. Conservative members of the bench and bar and the Whig leadership throughout the country denounced the decision in language similar to that of Webster and Story. The spokesmen of Jacksonian democracy hailed the new trend in constitutional development. The decision was never overruled, nor was its import interpreted away. It

---

[12] *Ibid.*, p. 553.    [13] *Ibid.*, p. 598. Thompson concurred in Story's opinion.
[14] W. W. Story (ed.), *Life and Letters of Joseph Story* (2 vols., 1851), II, 269.
[15] Charles Warren, *History of Harvard Law School* (3 vols., 1909), I, 540.

remained permanently as a restriction upon the rights claimed by corporations on the basis of grants in their charters. The decision survived, not as an initial step in a calculated plan to break down the rights of property, but as an effort on the part of the Court to determine equitably the rights both of the various parties to contracts of this kind and of the community as well. Interpretation was never carried to such an extreme as to deny to corporations rights clearly intended to be conferred by their charters. In order to insure that the rights of a corporation would be protected, it was necessary for the legislature merely to specify clearly the rights which it intended to create.

STATE BANKING CORPORATIONS

Corporations of tremendous importance to the states, to the business interests of the country, and to the people in general were those created for banking purposes. Except for the two Banks of the United States, each of which was chartered by Congress for a period of twenty years, the banks of the country between the time of the adoption of the Constitution and the Civil War were chartered by the states. They made loans and issued notes which circulated as money. They had a flexibility in financial matters which the states themselves did not possess. Some of them were so intimately related to state governments as to constitute in effect almost branches of the governments. It took many years, indeed, to determine the exact legal position of some of the state banks with reference to the sovereign bodies by which they were created.[16]

A number of important Supreme Court decisions were connected directly or indirectly with the Bank of the Commonwealth of Kentucky. That bank had been incorporated under an act of 1820. The capital of two million dollars belonged exclusively to the state, and the profits of the bank became a part of the revenue of the state. The bills and notes of the bank were made receivable in payment of taxes and other demands of the state. The institution was managed by a president and the twelve directors chosen annually by the state legislature. A Kentucky law enacted soon after the bank was chartered sought to compel the acceptance of the notes of the bank in payment of debts. Since the bank was obviously nothing more than an arm of the state, the effect of the law was to avoid the intention of

---

[16] One of the important cases was Bank of the United States v. Planters' Bank, 9 Wheaton 904 (1824).

the Constitution that no state should issue bills of credit or make anything but gold and silver coin a legal tender in payment of debts.

The attempt to enforce acceptance of the notes of the bank in payment of debts was made in connection with rules concerning court procedure in suits for the recovery of debts, rules intended to apply to federal as well as state courts. The federal district court in Kentucky took the position that the state had no power to legislate concerning its procedure and, in spite of the state law, it continued to require that payments be made in gold and silver. An appeal was taken to the Supreme Court, where it was held that the procedure of the federal court was beyond the control of the state.[17] The result was that, whereas suits brought in the state court resulted in judgments that might be satisfied with notes of the state bank, which were greatly depreciated, suits brought in the federal court resulted in a requirement of payment in specie. The decision was a victory for creditors outside the state, particularly one powerful creditor, the Bank of the United States.[18]

In the meantime, a suit was brought to attempt to compel the state bank to redeem its notes with gold or silver. The holder of several thousand dollars of the notes of the bank deposited them in the bank. Soon after making the deposit, he sought to withdraw it and demanded payment in gold or silver. His demand having been refused, he brought suit in the United States circuit court. The bank denied the jurisdiction of the court, on the ground that the suit was in effect a suit against the state, which was forbidden by the Eleventh Amendment. An appeal to the Supreme Court resulted in a decision against the bank on the basis of the decision in the Georgia case. Justice Johnson, who spoke for the Court, quoted the relevant portion of Marshall's opinion in the Georgia case, and added "that if a state did exercise any other power in or over a bank, or impart to it its sovereign attributes, it would be hardly possible to distinguish the issue of the paper of such banks from a direct issue of bills of credit; which violation of the Constitution, no doubt the state here intended to avoid." [19]

Although the state banks issued notes to circulate as money, and although for many years these notes made up almost the entire cir-

[17] Wayman v. Southard, 10 Wheaton 1 (1825).

[18] For discussion see Charles Warren, *Supreme Court in United States History* (rev. ed. 2 vols., 1926), I, chapter XVI.

[19] Bank of Kentucky v. Wister, 2 Peters 318, 324 (1829).

culatory medium apart from gold and silver, it was widely contended that the notes were bills of credit, within the meaning of the Constitution. The framers of the Constitution, knowing the disastrous effects of inflation which had resulted from the undisciplined issue of paper money by the states during and after the Revolution, had included a provision that no state should issue bills of credit. If a state could not issue such bills, could a corporation chartered by a state do what its creator could not do? Some of the banks were privately owned and operated, but others were state-owned and state-operated, so that persons not accustomed to legal pictures could see no distinction between the banks and the chartering states.

The meaning of "bills of credit" had been discussed in Craig v. Missouri,[20] decided in 1830 by a vote of four to three. The Missouri case had to do with the issuing of bills, not by a state bank, but by the state itself, which were intended to circulate as money. When Missouri became a state in 1821, there was virtually no money in circulation within its borders. To provide a circulatory medium, the legislature established loan offices where citizens, in return for promissory notes, could purchase loan certificates issued by the state in denominations running from fifty cents to ten dollars. The certificates were receivable for taxes and other public debts, and for salt from the state salt mines. Redemption of the certificates was pledged by the state. Missouri defended the arrangement as a legitimate device for borrowing money, but it was challenged as the issuing of bills of credit in violation of the Constitution. In writing the opinion of the majority of the Court, Marshall sought to define the term "bills of credit." In its larger sense, he thought, the term might comprehend any instrument by which a state engaged to pay money at a future day, thus including certificates given for money borrowed. But the language of the Constitution contemplated a narrower meaning. In that language the emission of bills of credit "conveys to the mind the idea of issuing paper intended to circulate through the community for its ordinary purposes, as money, which paper is redeemable at a future day." [21] Since the Missouri notes were intended to circulate as money, they were bills of credit, and the statute authorizing their issue was unconstitutional, even though it had not attempted to compel their acceptance by making them a legal tender in payment of debts. In working out his definition, he examined at length the experience of the states and of the United States in the Revolutionary

[20] 4 Peters 410.     [21] Ibid., p. 432.

period and thereafter which had resulted in the inclusion of the clause in the Constitution.[22]

The dissenting opinions of three justices in the Missouri case reflected the unwillingness of a portion of the Court to follow Marshall's doctrines to their logical conclusion, an unwillingness which had been shown three years earlier in the bankruptcy case of Ogden v. Saunders.[23] The dissenting justices contended that the Missouri notes represented a justifiable exercise of the borrowing power of the state. Justice Thompson contended that, if they were to be classified as bills of credit, it would be difficult to escape the conclusion that state bank notes, which they closely resembled, likewise fell within the prohibition of the Constitution:

> and if being used as a circulating medium, or substitute for money, makes these certificates bills of credit, bank notes are more emphatically such. And not only the notes of banks directly under the management and control of a state (of which description of banks there are several in the United States), but all notes of banks established under the authority of a state, must fall within the prohibition. For the states cannot certainly do that indirectly which they cannot do directly. And, if they cannot issue bank notes because they are bills of credit, they cannot authorize others to do it.[24]

Although Marshall did not discuss the logic of Thompson's argument as to the likeness of state bills of credit and state bank notes, he evidently accepted it,[25] but whereas Marshall thought both kinds of notes barred by the Constitution, Thompson thought neither was barred.

It was inevitable that the question should be brought before the Supreme Court in a case dealing with the validity of the issue of state bank notes. The case involved notes of a Kentucky bank which was owned by the state and operated by officers chosen by the state. It was argued before Chief Justice Marshall and others in 1834, but the decision had to be postponed until all members of the Court could be present. It was reargued in 1837, before a reconstituted Court headed by Chief Justice Taney. The Bank of the United States had recently been dissolved as a national institution so that state bank notes were badly needed as currency. Instead of holding their issue unconstitu-

---

[22] See *ibid.*, at pages 437-438, Marshall's rejection of the argument that to submit to the jurisdiction of the Supreme Court was beneath the dignity of a sovereign state.

[23] Discussed in chapter 8.

[24] 4 Peters 449.

[25] See Albert J. Beveridge, *Life of John Marshall* (4 vols., 1916-1919), IV, 582-583.

tional as bills of credit, the Court found a line of distinction and in effect sanctioned their use.[26]

Justice McLean spoke for the Court in a six-to-one decision. His opinion revealed an obvious effort to find constitutional arguments to avoid the disastrous results which would flow from holding state bank notes to be bills of credit. Although the state could not issue bills of credit, he said, it might "grant acts of incorporation for the attainment of those objects which are essential to the interests of society. This power is incident to sovereignty; and there is no limitation in the federal Constitution on its exercise by the states, in respect to the incorporation of banks." [27]

He mentioned the fact that a few state banks were in operation when the Constitution was adopted. He was convinced that the framers of the Constitution did not intend to inhibit the notes of these banks by classifying them as bills of credit within the meaning of the Constitution. On the basis of somewhat tenuous arguments he drew a distinction between the state and the artificial, intangible being created by it in the form of a corporation.

In reaching his conclusion, McLean had to face a powerful dissenting argument by Justice Story. The state bank notes, Story said, were "bills of the state issued by the agent of the state, on the exclusive bondages of the state, for the benefit and profit of the state; to circulate as currency within the state, and without any other responsibility than that of the state. In what respect, then, do they differ from bills of credit of the state? I can perceive none." [28]

When the case was first argued, Story said mournfully, a majority of the justices who heard it were decidedly of the opinion that the act of Kentucky establishing the bank was unconstitutional and void as amounting to an authority to emit bills of credit. "Among that majority was the late Mr. Chief Justice Marshall — a name never to be pronounced without reverence." [29] He had a strong motive for expressing his sentiment in the case —

> my profound reverence and affection for the dead. Mr. Chief Justice Marshall is not here to speak for himself, and knowing full well the grounds of his opinion, in which I concurred, that this act is unconstitutional, I have felt an earnest desire to vindicate his memory from the imputation of rashness, or want of deep reflection. Had he been living, he would have spoken in the joint names of both of us. I am

[26] Briscoe v. Bank of the Commonwealth of Kentucky, 11 Peters 257 (1837).
[27] Ibid., p. 317.     [28] Ibid., p. 344.     [29] Ibid., p. 328.

sensible that I have not done that justice to his opinion which his own great mind and exalted talent would have done. But with all the imperfections of my own efforts, I hope that I have shown that there were solid grounds on which to rest his exposition of the Constitution.[30]

The decision of the majority of the Court meant essentially that the dead hand no longer ruled. In terms of legal precedents, Story seems to have had much the best of the argument. Expediency lay in the path chosen by McLean and the other members of the Court.

Amidst ups and downs of boom periods and panics or depressions, which caused the value of the notes to fluctuate and destroyed the value of some through the collapse of the banks which issued them, the notes of state banks provided most of the circulatory medium of the country until the complete inadequacy of a medium resting upon such an unsound foundation was demonstrated by the experience of the Civil War. The federal government then enacted a measure to charter and regulate national banks which would pay out notes to circulate as money. The constitutionality of the national bank notes was not questionable on the same ground as that of the state bank notes, since only the states were prohibited from issuing bills of credit. State bank notes thereafter were virtually driven from circulation by a federal taxing provision, which was intended to eliminate competition with the notes of national banks.[31] The Supreme Court decision as to the constitutionality of state bank notes ceased thereafter to be a matter of importance. In the interim period, however, between 1837 and 1863, it played a vital part in molding the economic experience of the country.

### THE EXTRATERRITORIAL POWERS OF CORPORATIONS

In the Dartmouth College case, Chief Justice Marshall had defined a corporation as "an artificial being, invisible, intangible, and existing only in contemplation of law." [32] He was not called upon in that case to define "the law," or to define the limits of the area throughout which the force of "the law" might be exercised. Corporations were formed at that time by specific enactments of state legislatures. The time inevitably came when the Court had to decide whether by law of the creating state or by any other authority a corporation of one

[30] *Ibid.*, p. 350.
[31] For discussion of the Civil-War experience see chapter 16.
[32] 4 Wheaton 636.

state could do business in another.    Such a case reached the Supreme Court in 1839.

Many persons interested in particular corporate activities or in the growth of business enterprise in the United States contended that a corporation of one state, like a citizen of that state, had complete freedom to go into another state and to do business there.    Other persons, jealous of the competition of corporations of other states or fearful of the growth of corporate power, contended that the activities of a corporation were restricted to the territory of the state by which it was created or, at least, that it could do no business in another state without the consent of the latter.    The issue, like many others involving the powers of corporations, arose in connection with banking activities.    The state of Alabama had found it advisable to assume ownership or management of most of the banks within its borders.    It had sought to protect its own banks by forbidding banks chartered elsewhere to do business in the state.    The law did not say whether or not the monopoly of banking activities included the buying and selling of bills of exchange.    That business was important, since bills of exchange were used extensively in transferring credit from one section of the country to another.    They greatly facilitated the sale of cotton produced in Alabama and the purchase of goods imported into the state.    The Alabama banks declared that the business was banking, and that they had a monopoly of it.

A suit was brought in the United States circuit court in Alabama before Justice John McKinley, a member of the Supreme Court who had been appointed from that state.    The justice held that a corporation created in one state had no power to make a contract or, apparently, to act in any matter in any other state, either directly or by an agent.    The decision, if upheld by the Supreme Court, threatened with disaster the development of business enterprise throughout the United States by means of corporations.    Justice Story remarked that it "frightened half the lawyers and all the corporations of the country out of their proprieties." [33]    Story wrote to Justice McLean that, if the decision were established, it would have a ruinous effect upon corporations throughout the Union.    He thought it both bad law and bad economics.    He believed that powerful banking institutions operating across state lines were essential for the good of the country, and thought nothing could be more mischievous than the existing system of little banks.    He obviously feared that the Jackson Democrats,

[33] Warren, *Supreme Court in United States History* (rev. ed., 2 vols., 1926), II, 50.

composing a majority of the Supreme Court, would not agree with him.[34]

The Supreme Court decision is cited as Bank of Augusta v. Earle.[35] That title, however, actually applied to only one of three cases argued at the same time. Another of the three, entitled Bank of the United States v. Primrose, involved the Bank of the United States or, as Daniel Webster, its counsel before the Supreme Court, called it, the United States Bank, not now a federal institution, but a state bank under charter from Pennsylvania. The antagonisms of the struggle over the Bank of the United States carried over into this litigation. The banks involved in the three cases had to face a combination of hostility to the Bank of the United States and to corporations generally, and state-rights sentiment which was based on a number of political, economic, and social issues.

Counsel for the banks demanding the right of doing business in Alabama predicted national disaster if McKinley's decision were upheld. It would inflict a deep wound upon the commercial business of the United States. It would break up the harmony which had so long prevailed among the states and the people of the Union. Webster, referring to the constitutional provision that citizens of each state should be entitled to all the privileges and immunities of citizens of the several states, argued that a corporation of Pennsylvania might lawfully do in Alabama anything which a citizen of Pennsylvania might do. Pushed to its logical conclusion, his argument would have made effective state control over corporations a virtual impossibility.

Justice McKinley, as a member of the Supreme Court, heard the arguments of counsel for out-of-state banks, as he had heard them in the court below, but he remained unconvinced. He insisted that corporations of other states had no power to do business in Alabama. Justice Baldwin, on the other hand, went most of the way with Webster in contending that a state could not prevent business activity by a corporation of another state. Chief Justice Taney, writing the opinion of the Court, took an intermediate position. He admitted that "a corporation can have no legal existence out of the boundaries of the sovereignty by which it is created. It exists only in contemplation of law, and by force of the law; and where that law ceases to operate, and is no longer obligatory, the corporation can have no existence. It must dwell in the place of its creation, and cannot migrate to another sovereignty." Yet its existence might be recog-

<hr>

[34] Swisher, op. cit., pp. 381-382.   [35] 13 Peters 519 (1839).

nized in other places, and its residence in one state created no insupportable objection to its power of contracting in another. "It is, indeed, a mere artificial being, invisible and intangible; yet it is a person, for certain purposes in contemplation of law, and has been recognized as such by the decisions of this Court." [36] Natural persons through their agents continually made contracts in countries in which they did not reside and where they were not personally present when the contracts were made. Nobody doubted the validity of these agreements. By the same principle an artificial person, by its agent, might make contracts in a sovereignty in which it did not reside if its charter gave it the power to do so, and if such contracts were not prohibited by the laws of the country in which the contract was sought to be made.

Taney found that in the field of international relations, by a rule or doctrine of comity of nations it was customary for the courts of one country to give effect to the laws of another, provided that the law was not repugnant to the laws or policy of their own country. Contracts made in one country, for example, were ordinarily enforced in another. If such a practice prevailed among nations bound together by no political ties, the "intimate union of these states, as members of the same great political family; the deep and vital interests which bind them so closely together; should lead us, in the absence of proof to the contrary, to presume a greater degree of comity, and friendship, and kindness toward one another than we should be authorized to presume between foreign nations." [37]

Taney admitted that a state had the power to prevent a corporation of another state from doing business within its borders. He rejected Webster's contention that a corporation was entitled to the privileges and immunities which were attached to the citizenship of the members of the corporation. By the principle of comity it would be assumed that a corporation had a right to do business in the second state unless the laws of that state forbade the doing of such business. The state could enact such laws, but the intention to exclude corporations would not be presumed in the absence of clear evidence of such intention.

The opinion defined the position of so-called foreign corporations in American constitutional law for many years to come. In practice, corporations continued to do business in other states than those in which they were created. Since the states had the power to exclude

---

[36] *Ibid.*, p. 588.    [37] *Ibid.*, p. 590.

foreign corporations, they were held to possess also the lesser power of prescribing conditions under which such corporations might do business within their borders.  Through the prescribing of conditions, they regulated the activities of foreign corporations in such a way as to prevent abuses which might otherwise have arisen.  Ultimately, however, the Supreme Court extended further protection to corporations by holding unconstitutional certain types of restrictions, even though the restrictions were less drastic than complete exclusion from the state would have been.  In cases dealing with "unconstitutional conditions" the lines of Taney's doctrine became somewhat blurred.  The case of Bank of Augusta v. Earle remains, however, as a landmark in American constitutional law as well as in constitutional history. [38]

### CORPORATIONS AND THE FEDERAL COURTS

For many years the Supreme Court was hesitant in its definition of the power of corporations to sue and be sued in the federal courts on the basis of what is called diversity of citizenship.  It will be recalled that under Article III of the Constitution the judicial power of the United States extends, not merely to cases arising under the Constitution, laws, and treaties of the United States, but also to cases "between citizens of different states," even though the law to be applied in such cases is the common law or statute law of a state.  The purpose of extending federal judicial power to cases of this kind was to prevent the discrimination which might take place if the courts of one state were to pass upon the rights of a citizen of another.  The Constitution did not say whether corporations might sue and be sued in the federal courts under similar circumstances.  It spoke only of citizens.  A corporation was regarded as a person, even though artificial in character, but legal fiction had not characterized it as a citizen.  If citizens of one state could not get justice in the courts of another, the difficulty was apt to be even greater in securing justice for the corporations of one state in the courts of another.  Corporation counsel, therefore, quite naturally searched for some legal analogy by which the rights of citizens as to suits in federal courts could be extended to corporations.  The Supreme Court decided that the power of a corporation to sue in a federal court depended upon the citizen-

---

[38] For discussion of the origin and development of the doctrine of unconstitutional conditions see Gerard C. Henderson, *The Position of Foreign Corporations in American Constitutional Law* (1918), chapter VIII.

ship of the individual stockholders. For many years it took the position that the federal courts had jurisdiction only when all the stockholders were citizens of a state other than the state of the opposing party to the suit.[39] As corporations grew in size, however, and as the sale of stock became more widely dispersed throughout the several states, this limitation stood as a bar to federal jurisdiction in many corporation cases. It produced an increasing amount of dissatisfaction. Many litigants preferred to have their rights determined in courts presided over by federal judges, who were appointed for life and who were supposed to possess the detachment of federal officials, rather than in courts established locally and subject, politically and otherwise, to the sway of local sentiment.

In 1844, in the case of Louisville, Cincinnati and Charleston Railroad Company v. Letson,[40] the question of jurisdiction was carefully reargued and was reconsidered by the Supreme Court. As a result, Justice Wayne, speaking for the Court, announced that "a corporation created by a state to perform its functions under the authority of that state, and only suable there, though it may have members out of the state, seems to us to be a person, though an artificial one, inhabiting and belonging to that state, and therefore entitled, for the purposes of suing and being sued, to be deemed a citizen of that state." [41] It was assumed thereafter, in diversity of citizenship cases, that the stockholders of a corporation were citizens of the state in which a corporation was formed, and that by virtue of their citizenship federal courts might take jurisdiction of cases between the corporations of one state and citizens or corporations of other states. If, perchance, some of the stockholders of a corporation happened to be citizens, not of the state in which the corporation was formed, but of the state of the other party to the litigation, the courts refused to take cognizance of this fact.

Although the Letson case appears in the record as a unanimous decision, it is said that only six justices participated. One of these later dissented from the doctrine, while another sought to limit its interpretation.[42] The opposition seems to have rested in part on hostility to corporations as such and in part on southern agrarian hostility to corporations of the North. Justice Peter V. Daniel, of

---

[39] See Strawbridge v. Curtiss, 3 Cranch 267 (1806); Hope Insurance Co. v. Boardman, 5 Cranch 57 (1809); and Bank of the United States v. Deveaux, 5 Cranch 61 (1809).

[40] 2 Howard 497.    [41] Ibid., p. 555.

[42] See Justice Campbell dissenting, Marshall v. Baltimore and Ohio Railroad Co., 16 Howard 314, 349 (1853).

Virginia, who was committed to doctrines of state rights, laissez-faire, and slavery, hotly criticized this mode of interpretation of the Constitution to give protection to corporations.[43] He contended that the word "citizen" as used in the Constitution applied only to men, "material, social, moral, sentient beings." He contended that the interpretation given by the Court was carrying the provision of the Constitution "beyond either its philological, technical, political, or vulgar acceptation."[44] He deplored the tendency to trench upon the barrier by which the states had sought to protect themselves against the encroachment of the federal government. He deplored particularly the interference of federal authorities with the governments of the several states under the strange pretext of guarding the people of the states against their own governments. The effect of this practice was to reduce the people of the states and their governments to an habitual subservience to federal power.

Justice John A. Campbell, of Alabama, also deplored the destruction of constitutional landmarks. He regarded the decision concerning the rights of corporations as a decision in the interest of the commercial states; and evidently as in the interest of the North as against that of the South. He said:

It may be safely assumed that no offering could be made to the wealthy, powerful, and ambitious corporations of the populous and commercial states of the Union so valuable, and none which would so serve to enlarge the influence of those states, as the adoption, to its full import, of the conclusion, "that to all intents and purposes, for the objects of their incorporation, these artificial persons are capable of being treated as a citizen as much as a natural person."[45]

In spite of the opposition, the principle announced in the Letson case continued to govern the decisions of the Supreme Court. It gave protection to corporate enterprise, and no doubt stimulated its development.[46]

[43] See Rundle v. Delaware and Raritan Canal Co., 14 Howard 80, 95-102 (1852).

[44] Marshall v. Baltimore and Ohio Railroad Co., 16 Howard 314, 339 (1853).

[45] Ibid., p. 353.

[46] The Supreme Court successfully averted one of the evils which dissenting justices had foreseen. Justice Catron had remarked that, on the assumption that a corporation was a citizen of the state where it was incorporated, a company, such as a railroad company, having charters in two or more states, might avoid the jurisdiction of the courts of each state by claiming citizenship in another. When a case came to the Supreme Court involving a corporation having a charter both from Ohio and Indiana, the Court held, in effect, that a legal entity had been created in each state so that in suits between the corporation and citizens of each of the two states, the federal courts had no jurisdiction at all. Multiple incorporation, therefore, instead of aiding the corporation in securing access to the federal courts, constituted a barrier. See Ohio and Mississippi Railroad Co. v. Wheeler, 1 Black 86 (1862).

## HOSTILITY TO CORPORATIONS

In the meantime, hostility to corporations sprang up at various points for various reasons, giving rise to other constitutional decisions than those having to do with the jurisdiction of federal courts. Railroad corporations and others used blatantly unscrupulous methods of securing from state legislatures the charter and legislative provisions which they sought. Corporations were managed oftentimes with callous disregard for the welfare of the people whom their activities affected. The body of corporation law in each of the states was not yet adequate for the protection of the rights of stockholders, with the result that many of them were defrauded or otherwise suffered at the hands of the management. It is not surprising that people who had sanctioned loans or grants from the states, or grants of exemption from taxation, sought to have those privileges withdrawn.

The result was a series of new cases having to do with the contract rights of corporations.[47] The Supreme Court adhered to the position, which it had taken in the Dartmouth College case, that a charter was a contract and was protected by the contract clause of the Constitution. It adhered also, however, to the position taken in the Charles River Bridge case that the rights conveyed by charter were to be interpreted narrowly. In applying the principles to particular cases, the justices disagreed widely. They varied all the way from the position of Justice Daniel, who was hostile both to the development of corporate enterprise and to the broad interpretation of the Constitution, to that of Justice McLean, who had become the successor to Justice Story in his advocacy of broad interpretation of the Constitution. Certain cases came up from Ohio, where, in order to encourage the business of banking, various privileges, including exemption from taxation, had been given by the legislature. The legislature had subsequently sought to exercise the power of taxation, and counsel for the state contended that a legislature had no power to bar its successor from the exercise of the taxing power. The Supreme Court had to examine, not merely the constitutional principle, but also the question whether the exemptions from taxation were in such a form as to constitute contracts. The positions of the justices differed from case to case. The constitutional argument was well phrased by Chief Justice Taney:

> There are, undoubtedly, fixed and immutable principles of justice, sound policy and public duty, which no state can disregard without

---

[47] For discussion see Warren, *Supreme Court in United States History* (rev. ed., 2 vols., 1926), II, 250-256; Swisher, *op. cit.*, pp. 391-392.

serious injury to the community, and to the individual citizens who compose it. And contracts are sometimes incautiously made by states as well as individuals; and franchises, immunities, and exemptions from public burdens improvidently granted. But whether such contracts should be made or not, is exclusively for the consideration of the state. It is the exercise of an undoubted power of sovereignty which has not been surrendered by the adoption of the Constitution of the United States, and over which this Court has no control. For it can never be maintained in any tribunal in this country that the people of a state, in the exercise of the powers of sovereignty, can be restrained within narrower limits than those fixed by the Constitution of the United States, upon the ground that they may make contracts ruinous or injurious to themselves. The principle that they are the best judges of what is for their own interest is the foundation of our political institutions.[48]

Corporations continued to multiply in number and in size. More and more of the business enterprise of the country was conducted by them. State legislation was enacted for their government and protection and for the purpose of restrictive regulation. While seeking every economic and legal advantage, they resisted control in the interest of society, as well as legislation that was obviously discriminatory against them. Prior to the Civil War, the power of the federal government to protect them from state interference was limited. Afterward the adoption of the Fourteenth Amendment provided a constitutional basis for a broad extension of federal protective power through the judiciary. The utilization of the constitutional amendment for this purpose is a part of the constitutional story of the later years.

[48] Ohio Life Insurance and Trust Co. *v.* Debolt, 16 Howard 415, 428-429 (1854).

# CHAPTER 12

# PROBLEMS OF SLAVERY

No SUBJECT in the constitutional history of the United States has received more attention than that of slavery. The reason is not far to seek. Concern for the preservation of slavery furnished the driving power back of theories of state rights and of limitation upon the power of the federal government which for many decades hampered the expansion of federal power. Concern for the protection of slavery entered into the interpretation of the commerce clause of the Constitution, of clauses having to do with the rights of citizenship, and of other important constitutional provisions. The clash of interest between slavery and non-slavery groups brought on the crisis of a civil war which threatened the complete destruction of the American constitutional system.

Although clashes of interest have been perennial in American history, and many groups have worked out constitutional theories to justify their programs, the slavery controversy was unique in that the existence of a powerful interest coincided also with territorial cleavages. Struggles between capital and labor, between rural and urban interests, and between producers and distributors take place throughout the entire country. Slavery, however, proved profitable only in the South. Only in the South were conditions such that slaves could be used profitably as a means of large-scale production. Only in the South, therefore, was a major segment of property represented by ownership in slaves. Differences in property are accompanied inevitably by differences in ways of life and in moral conduct. The steady expansion of the area of the United States in which slavery was not likely to prove profitable made it clear that people from slave areas were to be in the minority as far as the United States as a whole was concerned. A minority with interests likely to be affected almost inevitably distrusts the expansion of the powers of the federal government and clamors for the rights of local areas where the interests involved can mold the activities of government. It is not surprising that, as the conflict sharpened between slavery and non-slavery interests, spokesmen of the South picked up the doctrines of the Virginia and Kentucky Resolutions and the secessionist attitude manifested by New England states from time to time, and worked out doctrines of the powers of the states to nullify actions of the federal government encroaching upon what were alleged to be the spheres of state authorities.

In connection with the drafting of the Constitution, the subject of slavery was involved at four important points. Southern representatives feared that by the levying of poll taxes the federal government might discriminate against slavery and against the South. In measuring representation in the federal government, they wished slaves to be counted along with citizens. They objected to interference with the importation of slaves into the United States. They sought a constitutional provision which would make possible the recapture of slaves who had fled to other states.

As to the levying of direct taxes, a compromise was worked out. It was provided that such taxes must be apportioned among the several states according to population.[1] This solution made it impossible to raise any major proportion of federal revenue by taxing a kind of property which existed in only one section of the country. The arrangement was somewhat less than a complete victory for the South, however, since by compromise it was provided that, in determining the basis of representation and taxation, only three-fifths of the slaves were to be counted.[2] As to fugitive slaves, the Constitution provided that no state into which they had fled might set them free, but that they should be delivered up on claim of the owners.[3] As to the fourth point, it was provided that the importation of slaves should not be prohibited prior to the year 1808.[4]

A Fugitive-Slave Act was passed in 1793 with little opposition.[5] The act prescribed the procedure for the recovery of fugitive slaves and punishment for persons aiding such slaves to escape. Pursuant to the act, many fugitives who had reached free territory were recaptured and taken back to their owners, but abolitionists, individually or through organized machinery which came to be known as the Underground Railroad, continued to aid fugitives to escape northward. There was abuse in the other direction in that, under the cover of

[1] Article I, Section 2, Clause 3.     [2] *Ibid.*     [3] Article IV, Section 2, Clause 2.
[4] Article I, Section 9, Clause 1.     [5] 1 Stat. 302.

recapturing fugitive slaves, many free Negroes in the northern states were seized and taken southward as slaves. In 1842, as discussed below, the Supreme Court held that the state had the power to withhold all governmental facilities from use in connection with the recapture of fugitive slaves, thereby necessitating a further development of federal machinery for that purpose.[6]

In his annual message of December, 1806, President Jefferson called attention to the approach of the time when Congress might constitutionally prohibit "all further participation in those violations of human rights which have been so long continued on the unoffending inhabitants of Africa, and which the morality, the reputation, and the best interests of our country have long been eager to proscribe."[7] The proposal gave rise to the first bitter congressional controversy over legislation affecting slavery. For varied reasons, a majority of the members of Congress favored the prohibition of the importation of slaves. For equally varied reasons, however, they could not agree as to what should be done with Negroes illegally landed within the territory of the United States. Negro savages from the heart of Africa might create serious problems if turned loose among the free inhabitants of the United States. On the other hand, abolitionists objected to an arrangement, as originally contemplated, whereby these Negroes were to be forfeited to the United States and sold into slavery. Returning them to Africa seemed highly impracticable.[8] Congress compromised by enacting a measure that prohibited the slave trade, but directed that federal officers should "be governed by the provisions of the laws, now existing, of the several states prohibiting the admission or importation of any Negro, mulatto, or other person of color."[9]

The trade was profitable, and it continued in spite of the prohibitory statute. Congress enacted amendatory measures, one of which defined the trade as piracy and prescribed the penalty of death.[10] Even so, daring raiders continued to capture able-bodied members of African tribes and smuggle them into the United States under grossly brutal conditions. Evidence sufficient to bring about conviction was hard to secure. It was not until 1862, in the midst of

[6] Prigg v. Pennsylvania, 16 Peters 539 (1842).

[7] Messages and Papers of the Presidents, I, 396.

[8] For discussion see Henry Adams, History of the United States of America (9 vols., 1889-1891), III, 356 ff.

[9] 2 Stat. 205, 206.

[10] 3 Stat. 600.

the Civil War, that a man was convicted and hanged for participation in the importation of slaves.[11]

## THE MISSOURI COMPROMISE

Important and irritating as they were, the problems of the importation of slaves and of the control of the slave trade in other parts of the world than in the United States were not fundamental matters. They could not compare in importance, for example, with the question whether the exclusion of slavery should be made a condition of admission of particular states into the Union. The admission of new states to the Union might easily determine the balance of control in the federal government. For this reason eastern and northern interests vainly opposed the admission of new states from the Louisiana Purchase.

The state of Louisiana was created in that area in 1812. The second to seek admission was Missouri. The total number of states in the Union at the time of the contest over Missouri was twenty-two, of which eleven were slave and eleven were free. The contest, therefore, became a major political battle in American history. It began in 1818 with the petition of Missouri for admission to statehood.[12] Representatives from the North insisted that Missouri should be admitted only under condition that slavery should be forbidden. Southern representatives contended that Congress had no power to place discriminatory restrictions upon any new state admitted to the Union. If a state was admitted, it possessed thereafter all the powers possessed by the original states. The question was closely related to the question of the power of Congress over slavery in the territories. At this time it seems to have been generally believed that, whatever the power of Congress over slavery in the states, its power over the subject in the territories was not to be doubted. The division in Congress was close, and Missouri might have faced an indefinite deadlock had not Maine also sought admission to the Union at this time, under conditions which made haste desirable from the point of view of northern interests. Southern representatives opposed the admission of Maine until Missouri was admitted without restriction as to slavery.

[11] John G. Nicolay and John Hay, *Abraham Lincoln, A History* (10 vols., 1909), VI, 99.
[12] For an account of the controversy see James A. Woodburn, "The Historical Significance of the Missouri Compromise," *Annual Report of the American Historical Association for 1893*, pp. 251 ff.

Congress finally reached what was known as the Missouri Compromise.  Maine was admitted to the Union, obviously to join the
ranks of the free states.  Missouri was to be admitted without restriction as to slavery with the result of providing an additional slave
state.  In the remainder of the territory purchased from France, however, which lay north of the southern boundary of Missouri, slavery
and involuntary servitude were declared to be forever prohibited.[13]
The compromise quieted the turbulence of the struggle, but left the
alignment of slavery and anti-slavery forces clearer than ever before.
On its face, it seemed to have solved the problem.  Actually it merely
postponed the conflict.  Missouri was the only state then ready for
admission from the territory purchased from France.  As to the exclusion of slavery from the northern part of the territory, the South
made its concession with reference to territory not yet settled.

The agreement seems to have been thought of as something in the
nature of a compact; yet it had no status beyond that of an ordinary
statute which was subject to change by Congress at any time.  Furthermore, although the statute provided that slavery should be forever prohibited in the territory described, it did not solve the problem as to whether Congress had power to enforce the restriction
upon any portion of the territory admitted to the Union as a state.
Many people were convinced that Congress had no such power, and
they argued along lines that the Supreme Court of the United States
subsequently followed.  In a sense, therefore, the Missouri Compromise meant a victory for the North in the admission of Maine and
for the South in the admission of Missouri, with an armistice as to
the admission of other states.  It was not until the crisis became
really acute that the more extreme southern representatives began to
insist that Congress had no power to exclude slavery even from the
territories.[14]

## NULLIFICATION

Southern statesmen insisted that the problems of slavery were local
problems and ought not to be discussed in the national forum.  This
attitude accounts in part, no doubt, for the fact that the theory of
nullification, worked out by South Carolina spokesmen, was announced in terms of the struggle over the tariff rather than in con-

[13] 3 Stat. 545, 548.

[14] For an account of the discussion of the Missouri Compromise in the Monroe cabinet
see *Memoirs of John Quincy Adams* (12 vols., 1874-1877), V, 5 ff.

nection with slavery.   Calhoun and other southern leaders had been for a time friendly toward the protective tariff as a method of securing the entrenchment of American industry.   After 1816, however, the level of protection was increased from time to time, throwing heavy burdens upon consumers of goods produced abroad or of goods produced in successful competition with foreign-made goods.   The anti-protection faction gained control in South Carolina politics, and Calhoun shifted his ground to retain his position of leadership.   Calhoun worked out a body of constitutional doctrine justifying the right of the states, through conventions, to nullify acts of the federal government.[15]   The doctrine was accepted by the government of his state. It was given wide publicity and became the center of the Webster-Hayne debate of 1830 in the United States Senate.[16]   The discussion was recognized, not as a matter of abstract doctrine, but as carrying a threat of actual disunion.   The Tariff Act of 1832 made no important concession to the South.   South Carolina organized a convention to consider the relation of the state to the new law.   In November, 1832, the convention passed the famous Nullification Ordinance.   The ordinance declared the tariff laws of 1828 and 1832 unconstitutional and not binding on the state.   It prohibited appeal to the Supreme Court of the United States in cases arising under the ordinance and required state officials to take an oath of obedience to the ordinance.   It took the position that an attempt at coercion on the part of the United States would absolve the state from allegiance to the Union and leave it a separate sovereign state.

Andrew Jackson denounced the doctrine of nullification, calling attention to the fact that the government of the United States was a government based on a confederation of perpetual Union which was made "more perfect" by the present Constitution.[17]   There was doubt as to the exact method to be followed if nullification was to be met by force, but it was clear from the beginning that submission was out of the question.   On December 10, 1832, Jackson issued his famous Proclamation on Nullification.[18]   He declared that the doctrine of a

[15] See Calhoun's "Exposition" in *The Works of John C. Calhoun* (Crallé ed., 6 vols., 1854-1861), VI, 1 ff.   See also Charles M. Wiltse, "Calhoun's Democracy," *Journal of Politics*, III (May, 1941), 210-223, Andrew C. McLaughlin, *A Constitutional History of the United States* (1935), chapter XXXIII, and Homer C. Hockett, *The Constitutional History of the United States*, II (1939), chapters II and III.

[16] For discussion of the Webster-Hayne debate see Claude M. Fuess, *Daniel Webster* (1930); Henry Cabot Lodge, *Daniel Webster* (1883), chapter VI.

[17] For the story of Jackson and nullification see John Spencer Bassett, *Life of Andrew Jackson* (rev. ed., 2 vols., 1916), II, chapter XXVI.

[18] *Messages and Papers of the Presidents*, III, 1203.

state veto upon the laws of the Union carried with it internal evidence of its impracticable absurdity and that, as our constitutional history proved abundantly, it would have been repudiated with indignation had it been proposed as a feature of our government.   When South Carolina continued preparations to prevent the enforcement of the federal revenue laws, Jackson asked Congress to enact supporting legislation to make their enforcement possible.   Congress passed the so-called "force bill," but enacted at the same time a compromise measure for the gradual reduction of the tariff.   Accepting the compromise, the South Carolina convention reassembled and repealed the ordinance nullifying the tariff laws, while at the same time it attempted to save face by the enactment of another ordinance nullifying the force bill.

The compromise averted the necessity of using the military power of the federal government to combat the nullifying efforts of a state. Although the intention of the administration to use such force, if necessary, was apparent, spectators did not forget that South Carolina's threat had the effect of bringing about modification of objectionable federal legislation.   If such a threat might be successful once, it might be successful again.   Whatever the attitude toward the finespun doctrines of Calhoun, the experience provided an object lesson in terms of which one or more states were able to force their will upon the whole.   The issue did not again become important as far as the tariff was concerned, but the groundwork was laid for resistance to federal policy with respect to slavery which might be offensive to southern interests.

### FUGITIVE SLAVES — PRIGG *v.* PENNSYLVANIA

It was inevitable that many problems connected with slavery should find their way to the Supreme Court.   Among the important cases was that of Prigg *v.* Pennsylvania,[19] decided in 1842, which had to do with a law of Pennsylvania concerning the recovery of fugitive slaves. Although Congress had passed a fugitive-slave law in 1793, the federal act did not cover all the details of recapture.   In states where abolitionist sentiment was strong, it often proved difficult to recover fugitives even where title was clear.   Local legislation was administered in such a way as to give aid to escaping Negroes.   Jury trial was required in some instances to determine whether or not the owner was entitled to the property in question.   If the members of

---

[19] 16 Peters 539 (1842).

the jury were opposed to slavery, it was often exceedingly difficult for the owner to make a case.   On the other hand, abuses were often committed at the opposite extreme, and free Negroes in free states were kidnapped into slavery under the cover of recapturing fugitive slaves. People from the slave states had complained of the difficulty of getting their property out of Pennsylvania.   In 1826, the Pennsylvania legislature enacted a law intended to prevent the capture of Negroes not legally owned, but to provide machinery whereby lawful owners might make their claims effective.   Evidence of ownership was to be presented to a magistrate, who was to direct that the Negro be brought before him.   If the magistrate was convinced that the claim was well founded, he was to issue a certificate authorizing the removal of the Negro from the state.

The case which reached the Supreme Court involved a Negress who had escaped from her owner in Maryland and fled into Pennsylvania.   The owner sent Edward Prigg to capture her and a child born to her after her escape.   Pursuant to the Pennsylvania law, Prigg took the Negroes before the magistrate.   The magistrate, whether because of abolitionist sympathies or inadequacy of the proof of ownership, refused to authorize the removal, whereupon Prigg seized the Negroes and took them into Maryland without a certificate. Both Pennsylvania and Maryland were eager to remove the friction between the two states.   Amicable arrangements were made for a suit to determine the constitutionality of the Pennsylvania law.   Prigg submitted to trial.   He was found guilty; and the case was brought before the Supreme Court of the United States.

The Supreme Court held the Pennsylvania law unconstitutional. In so far as the holding was based on the fact that the Pennsylvania law was in some respects in conflict with the federal fugitive-slave law, all members of the Court were agreed.   The majority of the Court went further, however. Justice Story, speaking for the Court, declared that since the Constitution gave to the federal government the power to deal with fugitive slaves, that power was thereby withdrawn from the states.   The states could not pass laws on the subject even if no conflict with federal laws was involved.   They could not even take action in aid of the federal program.   All this was exceedingly embarrassing to the slavery interests, who were nominal beneficiaries of the decision.   Story went further to express doubt as to whether state officers could be required to enforce federal fugitive-slave laws and whether the states were required to provide the means for making such laws effective. If this was true, the federal government might be compelled to provide, for the enforcement of its legislation, full equipment all the way from police officers and magistrates to places of incarceration.

A minority of the Court rejected this contention. Chief Justice Taney wrote a concurring opinion which held that the Constitution did not prohibit state legislation protecting property rights in fugitive slaves. The federal fugitive-slave law assumed the co-operation of state officers, he declared, and would be ineffective without it, since there were not enough federal officers available for the execution of its provisions. He argued in favor of the constitutionality of such state laws as those of Maryland which provided for the arrest and detention of Negroes passing through the state if they were unable to give a proper account of themselves. The purpose of the laws was the protection of the property rights of the owners, which, he contended, was by the Constitution enjoined upon the state as a duty. If Maryland were rendered unable to enforce such laws, her territory must soon become an open pathway for fugitives escaping from other states.

Justice Thompson wrote an opinion agreeing that the burden of responsibility for enforcing the fugitive-slave provision of the Constitution rested on the federal government. He agreed with Taney, however, that the states might legislate concerning fugitive slaves as long as their laws did not conflict with those of Congress. McLean wrote a long opinion concurring with Story on many points, but emphasizing the power of states to prevent the seizure of free Negroes under the pretense of capturing fugitive slaves. He agreed with Story that state officers were under no obligation to aid in enforcing the federal act. Wayne also agreed with Story, but wrote a long opinion of his own, emphasizing the fact that much state legislation nominally in aid of the recovery of slaves actually operated as a hindrance. Daniel wrote an opinion largely in agreement with that of Taney.

THE COMPROMISE OF 1850

When the northern states learned from the Supreme Court in the Prigg case that they were under no obligation to aid in the enforcement of the fugitive-slave law, a number of them enacted "personal-liberty laws" by which the support of state officials and the use of state jails and other property were denied to the federal government and to the alleged owners of fugitive slaves. The southern states immediately started agitation for amendments which would make the federal fugitive-slave law adequate to their needs. The movement for such legislation was entangled with the controversy over the acquisition of new territory and the admission of new states to the Union. After much controversy, Texas, a slave area, was admitted as a state in 1845 by joint resolution of Congress, after failure to secure approval of a treaty by two-thirds of the Senate. The resultant war with Mexico brought to the Union an additional expanse of territory reaching from Texas to the Pacific Ocean. Oregon Territory was acquired in 1848. The new acquisition carried the threat of conflict by disturbing the balance between the slave and the free states sanctioned by the Missouri Compromise. Northern interests supported what was known as the Wilmot Proviso to the effect that no territory acquired from Mexico was to harbor the institution of slavery. The South refused to accept any such arrangement. California, a part of the Mexican acquisition, was ready for admission to the Union almost immediately after the termination of the war. However, the question of the status of slavery in that state and in other acquired territory blocked action by Congress. Southerners who thirty years earlier had admitted that Congress had full power over slavery in the territories were now contending that Congress had no power to exclude slavery from them.

After a series of bitter struggles, Congress reached what came to be known as the Compromise of 1850.[20] Among its provisions was an arrangement that California should at once be admitted into the Union. Territorial governments were to be established for New Mexico and Utah, comprising the remainder of the territory acquired from Mexico, without inclusion of the Wilmot Proviso. The District of Columbia was no longer to be used as a slave market as hitherto, but slavery within the District was not to be prohibited. Perhaps most important of all, a more effective fugitive-slave law was to be enacted.[21]

The new fugitive-slave law did not attempt to coerce states or state officers into participation in the capture of fugitive slaves, but attempted rather to set up complete federal machinery for the purpose. It provided for appointment, by the federal circuit courts, of commissioners with authority to exercise the powers of any justice of the

[20] James Ford Rhodes, *History of the United States* (8 vols., 1893-1917), I, 172-173.
[21] 9 Stat. 462.

peace or other magistrate of the United States and with jurisdiction in cases involving fugitive slaves. It required federal marshals and deputies to aid in enforcement of the law. The proceeding was to be so devised as to avoid technical difficulties in the way of the removal of the slaves. The testimony of the fugitive was not to be admitted. Abolitionists of the North were angered at the adoption of the new fugitive-slave law and at attempted coercion by the federal government such as they had never before experienced. Their anger on this subject merged with resentment on another subject; namely, the repeal of the Missouri Compromise.

## THE KANSAS-NEBRASKA ACT

That part of the Louisiana Purchase to the west and north of Missouri, which in 1820 had been largely uninhabited, acquired considerable population in the third of a century which followed. When the organization of territorial governments and the admission of new states became imminent, Southerners who had accepted the Missouri Compromise that slavery should be forever excluded from the area underwent a change of heart. They insisted that a slaveowner had a right to take and hold his property in any part of the United States, and that Congress had no power to exclude slavery from the territories. By the Compromise of 1850, the territories of Utah and New Mexico had been established without reference to slavery, the subject being left to the determination of the territorial governments. The principle, variously called non-intervention, squatter sovereignty, and popular sovereignty, was warmly supported by southern statesmen as the principle which ought to rule in determining whether slavery should exist in the remaining territories within the Louisiana Purchase. Soon after the Compromise of 1850 had been adopted, Stephen A. Douglas and others started a movement for the adoption of the principle in connection with a bill for establishment of the territories of Kansas and Nebraska. Northern statesmen denounced as a shameful display of bad faith the attempt to repeal the Missouri Compromise. Although it stood only in the form of a statute, legally alterable by Congress at any time, they claimed for it the character of a sacred compact forever binding upon the two sections of the country. Under the skillful leadership of Douglas, the act was passed. By this act, therefore, as well as by the new fugitive-slave law, the political power of the South was flaunted in the face of the North and the hated southern institution was put on obnoxious display. A bloody struggle between slavery and anti-slavery interests for the colonization of Kansas, and the attempt of Southerners to use the newly established federal machinery for the recapture of fugitive slaves, brought the country nearer and nearer to the "irrepressible conflict."

The South won many victories in struggles over congressional policies related to slavery. In administration after administration the South was successful in maintaining in the presidency men not wholly unsympathetic toward the southern cause. Yet, in spite of the enforcement of the principle of popular sovereignty upon the territories, the time was in prospect when anti-slavery states and anti-slavery people would outnumber the sponsors of slavery. At some time, sooner or later, an anti-slavery Congress would be chosen and an abolitionist would occupy the office of President. What would happen then? Sober statesmen of the Old South longed for assurance that, once the South became the object of majority aggression from the North, the section would leave the Union. There was much talk of secession when, in 1856, the election of John Charles Frémont, the presidential candidate of the newly organized Republican party, was in prospect. Chief Justice Taney, doubtless reflecting the sentiment of many southern leaders, lamented the probability that the South would not secede to save itself. He predicted that the Constitution would be trampled underfoot through the dominance of the minority by the majority. The Union would be one of power and weakness, like the union of England and Ireland, or Russia and Poland. The South was doomed to sink to a state of inferiority; and the predatory power of the North would be exercised to gratify cupidity and evil passions without regard to the principles of the Constitution. Although many bold and brave men of the South would doubtless stand to their arms if Frémont was elected or if aggression took place under Fillmore, the candidate of the Know-Nothing or American party, they could do nothing because of the infiltration of the enemy into their midst. "I grieve over this condition of things," he wrote, "but it is my deliberate opinion that the South is doomed, and that nothing but a firm united action, nearly unanimous in every state, can check northern insult and northern aggression. But it seems this cannot be." [22]

JUDICIAL ACTION

It was inevitable that the Supreme Court should be dragged into

[22] Carl Brent Swisher, *Roger B. Taney* (1935), p. 493.

the slavery controversy again and again, and that it should be denounced as partisan by persons on both sides.  In 1847, in Jones v.
Van Zandt,[23] the Court upheld the power of the federal government
as expressed through the fugitive-slave law of 1793.  The last two
paragraphs of the opinion, written by Justice Woodbury of New
Hampshire, reflected the slavery controversy as follows:

> Before concluding, it may be expected by the defendant that some
> notice should be taken of the argument, urging on us a disregard of
> the Constitution and the act of Congress in respect to this subject, on
> account of the supposed inexpediency and invalidity of all laws recog-
> nizing slavery or any right of property in man.  But that is a political
> question, settled by each state for itself; and the federal power over
> it is limited and regulated by the people of the states in the Constitu-
> tion itself, as one of its sacred compromises, and which we possess no
> authority as a judicial body to modify or overrule.
> Whatever may be the theoretical opinions of any as to the ex-
> pediency of some of those compromises, or of the right of property in
> persons which they recognize, this Court has no alternative, while they
> exist, but to stand by the Constitution and laws with fidelity to their
> duties and their oaths.  Their path is a straight and narrow one, to
> go where that Constitution and the laws lead, and not to break both,
> by traveling without or beyond them.[24]

In spite of the obvious effort of the Court to perform its functions
properly in the case, it was bitterly denounced by the abolitionists.
Justice McLean deemed it necessary to write a public letter defending the members of the Court against the accusations poured out upon
them.[25]

Another important case, Strader v. Graham,[26] was decided in 1851.
Strader, a citizen of Kentucky, enabled certain slaves to escape from
Kentucky, and was made the subject of a damage suit under Kentucky
laws by Graham, the alleged owner.  Strader contended that the
Negroes were not slaves, and that the state law, therefore, did not
apply to his conduct.  The Negroes involved had on earlier occasions
been taken from Kentucky into Ohio, where they served as minstrels.
Strader claimed that because of these visits to Ohio, which had been
part of the territory covered by the Ordinance of 1787 forbidding

[23] 5 Howard 215.          [24] Ibid., p. 231.
[25] Charles Warren, The Supreme Court in United States History (rev. ed., 2 vols.,
1926), II, 156-158.
[26] 10 Howard 82.

the existence of slavery in the Northwest Territory, the slaves had become free; and that the Ordinance of 1787 conferred jurisdiction upon the Supreme Court in this case. The Court held that, whatever the status of the Negroes while outside of the state of Kentucky, they were subject to the laws of that state after their return. There was nothing in the Constitution of the United States that could in any degree control the law of Kentucky upon this subject. The condition of the Negroes, therefore, as to freedom or slavery after their return, depended altogether upon the laws of Kentucky and could not be influenced by the laws of Ohio. The principle announced was an important one, and might have prevented a great deal of strife had the Court adhered to it in the famous Dred Scott case decided six years later.

The Court sought to clarify the situation in another respect. The Ordinance of 1787, it contended, had been supplanted by the Constitution. It had no existence save as its provisions were given new life by subsequent acts of Congress. In the states formed in the territory such provisions of the ordinance as were still observed owed their validity and authority to the Constitution of the United States and the constitutions and laws of the respective states, and not to the authority of the ordinance of the old Confederation.

The decision bore evidence of sound judgment, and it seemed an eminent display of self-restraint on the part of judges, some of whom felt as deeply on the issue of the times as did the most ardent patriots of the North or of the South. Yet again the Court was criticized by northern spokesmen for a decision that had the immediate effect of supporting the cause of the defenders of slavery.

## THE DRED SCOTT CASE

The Supreme Court decision which achieved the greatest notoriety and had the greatest effect upon the course of events was that handed down in the Dred Scott case. The case is discussed at length in every American history covering the period, in every history of the Constitution and of the Supreme Court, in every biography of the Supreme Court justices of the period, and in most biographies of other statesmen of the time. Little can be brought to the story in the way of sound interpretation or factual statement that has not been presented already. Yet the decision played such an important part in the sequence of events that the constitutional history of the period cannot be summarized without it.

Stripped of many interesting details, the factual background was as follows:   A Negro named Dred Scott was held in slavery in Missouri. The owner took him to reside for a time in the free state of Illinois, which was part of the territory originally covered by the Ordinance of 1787 prohibiting slavery in the Northwest Territory.   The owner then took him to reside for an additional period in what is now Minnesota, a part of the territory purchased from France in 1803, in which, according to the Missouri Compromise, slavery was not to exist.   Thereafter the owner brought the Negro back to Missouri.

Subsequently, after a change of ownership had taken place by inheritance, Dred Scott brought suit for his freedom in a local Missouri court, claiming to be entitled to it because of periods of residence in free territory.   Scott obtained a verdict.   The owner appealed to the state supreme court, which reversed the decision of the lower court, following the recent Supreme Court decision in Strader v. Graham. According to that decision, the status of the Negro was determined by the law of the state where he now resided, rather than by the fact that he had previously spent some time in free territory.

Persons aiding Dred Scott in the matter refused to accept defeat with this decision.   They devised a method to bring a new case before a federal court to determine there the question of the Negro's right to freedom.   They sought to establish the jurisdiction of the United States circuit court in Missouri by arranging a fictitious sale of the Negro to a citizen of the state of New York.   They hoped that Scott, bringing a suit as a citizen of Missouri against a citizen of New York, would be heard on the assumption that the case was between citizens of different states — a constitutional ground for the exercise of federal jurisdiction.   Counsel for the alleged owner filed in the case what was known technically as a plea in abatement to the jurisdiction of the court, a plea which was the subject of endless discussion in the ensuing months and years.   It was contended that the court had no jurisdiction in the case because a Negro who had been a slave could not be a citizen of a state in the sense in which the term "citizen" was used in the Constitution to give the federal court jurisdiction in suits between citizens of different states.   The inability to be a citizen was said to be due, not merely to the fact that the Negro had been a slave, but also to the fact that Negroes in the United States were as a whole a degraded people who had not been generally accepted as a part of the body of citizens.   The federal court in Missouri overruled the plea in abatement, however, and the case was argued on its merits before a jury. The judge instructed the jury that on the facts the Negro was not entitled to his freedom, and the jury so decided. A writ of error was sued out in the Supreme Court of the United States.

The Dred Scott case was first argued before the Supreme Court in February, 1856. Rumors and speculation varied considerably as to the decision likely to be reached. Some thought the Court would take a safe position, following the precedent established in Strader *v.* Graham, and hold that, whatever the status of Dred Scott while outside the state of Missouri, his status after his return to that state was dependent upon Missouri laws as interpreted by Missouri courts. Others hoped that the Supreme Court would go farther. Abolitionists continued to denounce what they regarded as bad faith on the part of the South in bringing about repeal of the Missouri Compromise. Some statesmen argued, in reply, that Congress had no constitutional power to exclude slavery from the territories and that the Missouri Compromise was therefore unconstitutional. They thought a Supreme Court decision to that effect would have a most salutary influence upon public sentiment. They hoped that the Supreme Court would utilize the occasion to announce that the Missouri Compromise had been unconstitutional.

The several justices were divided on a number of questions. It seemed likely that almost every member of the Court would write an opinion differing in some respects from the opinions of his brethren. These opinions, if announced at the time when the case was argued, would be utilized by the various factions interested in the campaign of 1856, adding to partisanship and sectional chaos instead of quelling it, and dragging the Supreme Court into the campaign. Fortunately, in view of this prospect, one of the justices asked that the case be reargued. It was returned to the calendar for that purpose.

Before the case was reargued, the nation chose James Buchanan for the presidency. Buchanan planned to restore peace to the distracted country, not by destroying slavery, but by destroying agitation over slavery.[27] Hoping to co-ordinate his inaugural address with the decision of the Supreme Court, Buchanan wrote to a member of the Court, Justice Catron, asking him whether the Dred Scott case would be decided before the date of the inauguration. The interest of the President-elect had the effect of speeding consideration of the case, but, even so, the Court was slow in arriving at a decision. The

[27] Swisher, *op. cit.,* p. 493.

justices still disagreed widely on a number of points. A majority finally came to the conclusion that the case ought to be decided on the analogy of the Strader case, leaving the more highly controversial questions undiscussed. Justice Nelson was appointed to write an opinion of the Court to that effect.

Had the Court adhered to this decision, the case would have had little importance in the annals of American jurisprudence. Only the dissenting opinions would have given it notoriety. Unfortunately, before the decision was announced, the majority of the Court learned that Justices McLean and Curtis, both of whom were ardent abolitionists, were determined to discuss in dissenting opinions the power of Congress over slavery in the territories, and to argue that Congress had power over the subject. Southern sympathizers on the Court were determined that such arguments should not be expressed in judicial opinions without an answer from the other side. A change of plans was made, therefore, whereby Chief Justice Taney took over the task of writing the opinion of the Court, dealing at length with the controversial issues involved, leaving the Nelson opinion to be filed as the opinion of Nelson alone.

Having learned that the Supreme Court would probably hold the Missouri Compromise unconstitutional, Justice Catron gave Buchanan advice on strategy. He suggested that Buchanan say in his inaugural address that the question of the constitutionality of the Missouri Compromise had been presented to the appropriate tribunal, the Supreme Court of the United States, and it was due to the high and independent character of the Court to suppose that it would decide and settle a controversy which had so long and seriously agitated the country. In asking for confidence in the Supreme Court, Buchanan would in effect be uniting the executive and judicial departments of the government in support of the southern cause. In spite of pressure from Buchanan and from colleagues, some justices were slow in making up their minds in the case; they did not formulate their opinions until after the date of the inauguration. Buchanan knew, however, what the decision was to be. As advised by Catron, he made political use of his information. He approved the extension of the principle of majority rule to the subject of slavery in the territories. As to the constitutionality of the exercise of power in this field, it was a judicial question which legitimately belonged to the Supreme Court of the United States and which was now pending before that Court, and would, it was understood, be speedily and finally settled. To the decision of the Court he would, in common with all good citizens, cheerfully submit, whatever it might be.[28]

The decision of the Court was announced on March 6, 1857.[29] The strategy of Taney's argument can be presented in terms of three seemingly simple points:

1. Since Negroes had been regarded as persons of an inferior order at the time when the Constitution was adopted and not as "citizens," the Constitution did not include them in the term "citizens," and did not intend to give them power to sue in the federal courts through the clause which gave jurisdiction in suits between citizens of different states.

2. In any event, no Negro while a slave could be at the same time a citizen with the power to sue in a federal court. Dred Scott had been a slave. He had not become a free man by virtue of the Missouri Compromise, since the Missouri Compromise was unconstitutional. Unless he had some other claim to freedom, he was still a slave and not a citizen and not entitled to sue in a federal court.

3. Whatever Dred Scott's status had been while he was a resident of Illinois, he had returned to Missouri, where his status was determined by Missouri law. The Missouri courts had held that under that law he was still a slave. Therefore, he was not a citizen, and could not sue in a federal court. The case must be dismissed for want of jurisdiction.

Each of the three lines of argument led to a denial of jurisdiction in the circuit court — an arrangement quite satisfactory to the slavery interests, since, if the court had no jurisdiction, it could do nothing toward gaining Dred Scott his freedom. In order to demonstrate in these three ways that the court had no jurisdiction, Chief Justice Taney discussed and took a position on the controversial questions involved in the case. He made statements which were either misunderstood or grossly misinterpreted by abolitionist critics. He declared, for example, that at the time of the adoption of the Constitution Negroes were considered as a subordinate and inferior class of beings, who, "whether emancipated or not, yet remained subject to their authority, and had no rights or privileges but such as those who held the power and the government might choose to grant them." He stated that it was not the province of the Supreme Court to decide upon the justice or injustice, the policy or impolicy, of these laws.[30]

[28] *Messages and Papers of the Presidents,* VI, 2962.
[29] Dred Scott *v.* Sandford, 19 Howard 393 (1857).     [30] *Ibid.,* p. 405.

Elsewhere he rephrased his statement about the status of Negroes at the time when the Constitution was adopted, unfortunately without repeating his comment that justice or injustice, policy or impolicy, were not questions for the Court to decide. Negroes had been deemed so far inferior, he said, "that they had no rights which the white man was bound to respect." [31] The phrase was torn from its context by critics of the decision and published as a statement by Taney that the Negro had no rights which the white man was bound to respect. The error found its way into the history of the period, was repeated in the classrooms of the country, and persists to the present day for proclamation over radio by alleged experts in public information. The persistence of the misinterpretation illustrates the fact that, once an error has fastened its tentacles upon the textbooks and schoolrooms of the country, it achieves a reasonable prospect of immortality in spite of the concerted efforts of scholars to destroy it.

The argument that Negroes could not now be citizens within the meaning of the Constitution because they had not been so regarded at the time of the adoption of the Constitution was not a new argument. It had been used by other southern statesmen, and Taney had used it in an opinion as Attorney General of the United States twenty-five years before the date of the Dred Scott decision.[32] In spite of the historical research of Taney and his colleagues and of historians of later years, it is no easy matter to decide whether Taney was right or wrong. As to his assumption, however, that the meaning of the words of the Constitution is fixed and unchanging, and does not adjust itself to the changing conceptions of other years, the Constitution would long since have had to be abandoned had it lacked the flexibility which Taney failed to find in it. In this instance a constitutional amendment was required to change the definition of citizenship. The great mass of constitutional changes, however, have come about through interpretation rather than formal amendment.

Taney's second point was a rejection of the contention that Dred Scott had become a free man by virtue of residence in territory covered by the Missouri Compromise. The Missouri Compromise, he held, was unconstitutional. Congress had no power to interfere with the property of a slaveowner in the process of governing territory. Any territory acquired by the United States was acquired for the benefit of the people of the several states who created it. The federal government had the duty, as well as the power, to provide for the

[31] *Ibid.*, p. 407.          [32] Swisher, *op. cit.*, pp. 152 ff.

government of the territory acquired, not on the basis of the constitutional provision authorizing the establishment of rules and regulations for the government of territory — which applied only to territory held by the United States at the time of the adoption of the
Constitution — but on the basis of the power to acquire territory.
The power to govern, however, was not an absolute power. In the
government of territory, Congress was limited by the provisions of
the Constitution. Congress could not interfere with freedom of
religion or freedom of speech. It could not deny the right to keep
and bear arms or the right to trial by jury. It could not compel anyone to be a witness against himself in a criminal proceeding. It
could not impair the rights of private property.

> Thus the rights of property are united with the rights of person,
> and placed on the same ground by the Fifth Amendment to the Con-
> stitution which provides that no persons shall be deprived of life,
> liberty, and property, without due process of law. And an act of
> Congress which deprives a citizen of the United States of his liberty
> or property, merely because he came himself or brought his property
> into a particular territory of the United States, and who had com-
> mitted no offense against the laws, could hardly be dignified with the
> name of due process of law.[33]

The prohibition of congressional interference with property, Taney
contended, was not confined to the area of the states, but extended to
the whole territory over which the Constitution gave it power to legislate, including those portions remaining under territorial government. He denied the relevance of the contention that under international law there was a difference between property in slaves and
other property. The question involved was not one of international
law, but of the law of the Constitution of the United States. The
Constitution in certain provisions recognized the right of property of
the master in a slave. Congress had no power to take away that
right.

The logic of this argument led to the same result as that of the
argument based on the alleged inability of a Negro to be a citizen.
Dred Scott had not become free by virtue of residence in territory in
which it was provided by an unconstitutional act of Congress that
slavery should not exist. Since he had not become free, he remained
a slave; and, since he was a slave, he could not be a citizen within
the meaning of the Constitution. Since he was not a citizen, the fed-

[33] 19 Howard 450.

eral circuit court had no jurisdiction in a suit brought by him on the basis of diversity of citizenship.

Taney's third point, dealing with the effect of Scott's residence in Illinois, was essentially the point made in Strader v. Graham; namely, whatever the temporary effect of residence in Illinois upon his status, the laws of Missouri determined his status after his voluntary return to that state. Since the courts of that state had decided that he was a slave, the federal circuit court must accept that decision. Since he was a slave, he could not bring a suit in the federal court on the basis of diversity of citizenship.

The latter point, it will be recalled, was the one on which the Supreme Court originally planned to decide the entire case. Unquestionably the case could have been decided in this manner without discussion of the controversial matters dealt with under other headings. Furthermore, since under his first point Taney had taken the position that no Negro could be a citizen within the meaning of the Constitution, it was not necessary to decide the further question whether Congress had the power to provide that slavery should not exist in territories of the United States, thereby incidentally giving freedom to a slave taken by his master into such territory.

Northern people and the Northern press denounced Taney for deciding questions not necessary to the decision of the case. In the light of history it is clear that Taney made a strategic error. By handling the case in this manner, he hoped he could do something toward suppressing anti-slavery agitation and ward off the conflict between the two sections of the country. The decision had the opposite effect. As for the discussion and the decision of questions that did not have to be decided, however, there was nothing unique about what he did. He followed a precedent established by Chief Justice Marshall and followed by other justices throughout the course of American history. Some of the landmark decisions of the Marshall period would be completely unknown today had Marshall limited his opinions to statements which were essential to the decision of the cases. The same can be said of important decisions from the period of Marshall all the way to that of Harlan F. Stone. The important fact, or one of the important facts, is that Marshall succeeded in molding the course of events through the strategic construction of his opinions — just as Taney succeeded, for example, in some of his outstanding opinions affecting corporations — whereas Taney, in the Dred Scott case, failed altogether in the achievement of his purpose.

Justices McLean and Curtis wrote long dissenting opinions. They attempted both to answer Taney's arguments and to condemn him for the decision of questions not necessary to the decision of the case. Of the other members of the Court, Justices Wayne, Nelson, Grier, Daniel, and Catron also wrote opinions. As is usually true, the additional opinions weakened rather than strengthened the position of the majority. This effect was heightened because some members agreed that certain points discussed by the Chief Justice were not properly before the Court. The northern press of the country made full use of the dissenting opinions and of disagreements among the majority and of unfortunate phrases in Taney's opinion to discredit the decision and the Supreme Court itself. It is safe to say that no decision in American history has done more to injure the reputation of the Supreme Court. Skillfully used by abolitionist propagandists, it played an important part, not in postponing the conflict between the North and the South, but in bringing on the crisis.

### THE BOOTH CASES

The controversy over the Dred Scott decision still raged in 1859, when the Supreme Court had to pass upon the conduct of a state which approached the verge of nullification on a slavery issue. The case arose, not in South Carolina, which had learned well the principles of nullification under the tutelage of Calhoun, but in the northern state of Wisconsin. Many abolitionists were determined that the fugitive-slave law of 1850, which provided for the punishment of persons aiding in the escape of slaves, should not interfere with the movement of the Underground Railroad. In 1854, Sherman M. Booth, editor of an abolitionist paper, the *Milwaukee Free Democrat,* was ordered held for trial for violating the fugitive-slave law by aiding the escape of a Negro from a United States deputy marshal. He was held by federal authorities, but was incarcerated in a local jail because there was no federal prison available. He applied for a writ of habeas corpus, not to the federal court in the district, but to a judge of the state supreme court. The judge issued the writ, and directed that Booth be released, taking the position that the fugitive-slave law was unconstitutional. On appeal to the full membership of the state supreme court, the order of release was confirmed. The United States marshal then sued out a writ of error in the Supreme Court of the United States.

In the meantime, Booth was brought to trial in the federal district

court at Milwaukee. He was found guilty and given sentence including a fine and imprisonment. He was again lodged in a local
prison. Again the Wisconsin supreme court ordered his release on
the ground that the fugitive-slave law was unconstitutional. This
case was likewise appealed to the Supreme Court of the United
States, in spite of efforts of the state court to prevent the appeal. The
two Booth cases were argued together.

Perhaps because of a lesson learned from experience with the Dred
Scott case, the Supreme Court carefully kept from the public all evidence of differences of opinion among the justices. In a unanimous
opinion, characterized by the historian of the Court as "the most
powerful of all his notable opinions," [34] Chief Justice Taney proclaimed the unqualified power of the federal government to enforce
its laws without state interference. This was the first time, he declared, that the supremacy of the state courts over the courts of the
United States had been judicially asserted.

> It would seem to be hardly necessary to do more than to state the
> result to which these decisions of the state court must inevitably lead.
> It is, of itself, a sufficient and conclusive answer; for no one will sup-
> pose that a government which has now lasted nearly seventy years,
> enforcing its laws by its own tribunals, and preserving the Union of
> the states, could have lasted a single year, or fulfilled the high trusts
> committed to it, if offenses against its laws could not have been pun-
> ished without the consent of the state in which the culprit was found. [35]

The Constitution was not formed, Taney contended, merely to
guard the states against danger from foreign nations, but mainly to
secure union and harmony at home. To accomplish this purpose,
those who framed and adopted the Constitution saw the necessity of
ceding to the general government many of the rights of sovereignty
hitherto possessed by the states. They saw the necessity that in the
sphere of action assigned to it the general government should be
supreme and strong enough to execute its own laws by its own tribunals without interruption from a state or from state authorities. It
was evident that anything short of this would be inadequate to the
main objects for which the government was established.

To secure the purposes of the general government it was likewise
necessary "that a tribunal should be established in which all cases
which might arise under the Constitution and laws and treaties of the

[34] Warren, *op. cit.*, II, 336. Ableman *v.* Booth, 21 Howard 506 (1859).
[35] 21 Howard 515.

United States, whether in a state court or in a court of the United States, should be finally and conclusively decided." [36] In defending the appellate power of the Supreme Court, Taney was answering in part, no doubt, the supreme court of Wisconsin, which denied the right of appeal. Probably he was doing more than that, however. Before the case was argued before the Supreme Court, abolitionist members of Congress had tried to secure the enactment of legislation to withdraw the appellate jurisdiction of the Supreme Court in cases of this kind. Taney sought to demonstrate, not merely the legality of appeals as the law now stood, but to show also the necessity that such right of appeal exist if the federal system was to be preserved. He did not deny that Congress had the power to limit the appellate jurisdiction of the Court, but his opinion was so written as to give the impression that the jurisdiction in question was necessary to the survival of the government. He appraised the Supreme Court in the following eloquent paragraph:

> In organizing such a tribunal, it is evident that every precaution was taken, which human wisdom could devise, to fit it for the high duty with which it was entrusted. It was not left to Congress to create it by law; for the states could hardly be expected to confide in the impartiality of a tribunal created exclusively by the general government, without any participation on their part. And as the performance of its duty would sometimes come in conflict with individual ambition or interests and powerful political combinations, an act of Congress establishing such a tribunal might be repealed in order to establish another more subservient to the predominant political influences or excited passions of the day. This tribunal, therefore, was erected, and the powers of which we have spoken conferred upon it, not by the federal government, but by the people of the states, who formed and adopted that government, and conferred upon it all the powers, legislative, executive, and judicial, which it now possesses. And in order to secure its independence, and enable it faithfully and firmly to perform its duty, it engrafted it upon the Constitution itself, and declared that this Court should have appellate power in all cases arising under the Constitution and laws of the United States. So long, therefore, as this Constitution shall endure, this tribunal must exist with it, deciding in the peaceful forms of judicial proceeding the angry and irritating controversies between sovereignties, which in other countries have been determined by the arbitrament of force. [37]

[36] *Ibid.*, p. 518.
[37] *Ibid.*, p. 521.

Since he had taken the position that no state court had the power to release any prisoner held under the authority of the United States, Taney could have avoided all discussion of the constitutionality of the fugitive-slave law. Nevertheless, he stated the position of the Court on the subject, asserting briefly in conclusion that the law was fully authorized by the Constitution in all its provisions. Although, by the addition of this *obiter dictum,* Taney left himself vulnerable to the criticism directed at his decision of the Dred Scott case, wherein he was denounced for deciding questions not necessary to the decision of the case, he was not in this instance subjected to any serious attack. The reason might have been that the opinion had the concurrence of Justice McLean, who held the strongest abolitionist sentiment of any person now on the Court. The opinion as a whole, analyzing as it did the relation between the state and federal governments, was one that in normal times would have been hailed as an outstanding work of statesmanship. The times, however, were far from normal. After his Dred Scott opinion, nothing that Taney could say was likely to receive general approbation in the North. The South quite naturally approved of the decision in the Booth cases, but nothing that Taney could say about fundamental principles of government was likely to curb the trend toward nullification when the South came into the position of a minority section in a country subject to an expanding degree of federal control.

INTERSTATE RENDITION

Early in 1861, the Supreme Court figured in one more important controversy closely connected with the slavery issue. In violation of the laws of Kentucky, a free Negro aided a slave to escape from that state. The free Negro himself then fled to Ohio to escape punishment. The Constitution provided that "A person charged in any state with treason, felony, or other crime, who shall flee from justice, and be found in another state, shall, on demand of the executive authority of the state from which he fled, be delivered up, to be removed to the state having jurisdiction of the crime." [38] Kentucky demanded that the governor of Ohio surrender the free Negro for trial in Kentucky; but the Ohio governor failed to act, whereupon Kentucky sought from the Supreme Court a writ of mandamus directing Governor Dennison to return the fugitive.

The Supreme Court was of the opinion that Kentucky had a right

[38] Article IV, Section 2, Clause 2.

to demand the return of the fugitive, and that it was the duty of the executive of Ohio to surrender him, but it faced the practical problem of attempting to coerce the highest executive official of a state. Such coercion was opposed to the political conceptions of most judges. For a unanimous Court, therefore, Taney held that the provision that it should be the duty of the executive authority of the state to deliver the fugitive did not mean that obedience might be coerced.[39] He said:

> Looking to the subject matter of this law and the relations which the United States and the several states bear to each other, the Court is of opinion the words "it shall be the duty" were not used as mandatory and compulsory, but as declaratory of the moral duty which this compact created, when Congress had provided the mode of carrying it into execution. The act does not provide any means to compel the execution of this duty, or inflict any punishment for neglect or refusal on the part of the executive of the state; nor is there any clause or provision in the Constitution which arms the government of the United States with this power. Indeed, such a power would place every state under the control and dominion of the general government, even in the administration of its internal concerns and reserved rights. And we think it clear that the federal government, under the Constitution, has no power to impose on a state officer, as such, any duty whatever, and compel him to perform it; for if it possessed this power, it might overload the officer with duties which would fill up all his time and disable him from performing his obligations to the state, and might impose on him duties of a character incompatible with the rank and dignity to which he was elevated by the state.[40]

There is reason for believing that the governor of Ohio would have refused to obey this writ of mandamus had it been issued. By deciding the case as it did, therefore, the Supreme Court averted a clash which would have added to the chaos of the period and probably would have further discredited the Supreme Court. The decision had importance beyond the period when it was announced, however, in that it established a precedent for future interpretation. It remains true that the governor of a state, for any reasons satisfactory to himself, may refuse to fulfill the duty prescribed in the Constitution to surrender fugitives sought by other states for violation of their laws.

[39] Kentucky v. Dennison, 24 Howard 66 (1861).     [40] Ibid., pp. 107-108.

## FROM POLITICS TO WAR

When Congress had committed itself to the principle of popular sovereignty, slavery and anti-slavery forces speeded the colonization of Kansas by seeking to locate there people who would determine the slavery issue.  The two factions each presented constitutions for acceptance by Congress.  Congress engaged in a long series of stormy debates, raising all the manifold questions as to the status of slavery in the territories and in the states and utilizing the Dred Scott decision in praise or condemnation, as suited the point of view of the speaker.  The Buchanan administration, which accepted at first the principle of popular sovereignty, shifted to support of slavery when the chaos in Kansas made action necessary, thereby alienating Stephen A. Douglas and other advocates of compromise.

In the debates with Douglas in 1858, and subsequently in his campaign for the presidency, Abraham Lincoln moved forward as the leader of the North.  He did not commit himself to the abolitionist cause, but he opposed the extension of slavery, and he predicted that the nation could not survive half-slave and half-free.  He did not propose overt disobedience to the law as prescribed by the Supreme Court in the Dred Scott case, but he made it clear that he thought the decision should be overruled, and he committed himself to the achievement of that end.  He did not advocate the impeachment of the judges who had announced the decision; but it was clear that, if he became President, he would use all opportunities to appoint judges reflecting a contrary view.  If he were elected, therefore, the South for the first time would find in the presidency a man hostile to its "peculiar institution," with the prospect of losing its majority on the Supreme Court within a relatively short time.  The growing population of the North promised the loss of the House of Representatives.  The South, in spite of its victory in the enactment of the new fugitive-slave law and the Kansas-Nebraska Act, was threatened with eclipse as far as its control over the federal government was concerned.

Down to the beginning of military hostilities, attempts were made to secure constitutional amendments which might avert the conflict.  It was thought by some, for example, that the South might be placated if an amendment was adopted insuring no encroachment upon the institution of slavery.  The efforts were vain.  On December 20, 1860, a South Carolina convention adopted an ordinance of secession.  President Buchanan sought advice from his Attorney General as to his powers of coercion in the face of nullification.  His attention was called to the force act, passed at the request of Andrew Jackson in 1833, and he was advised that he might use the militia and the land and naval forces to protect federal property, such, for example, as that established in the several states for the collection of customs. Apart from such activity, he took the position that Congress could not declare war on a state or direct general hostilities against it. The Buchanan administration expired while engaged in futile speculation as to its powers, without taking any action to prevent secession which had any prospect of success.

# CHAPTER 13

# ON THE EVE OF THE CIVIL WAR

CONSTITUTIONAL DEVELOPMENT is a gradual process. No periods in history mark absolute and final breaks with the past. Transitions are constantly being made, overlapping one another in continuing sequences. Yet more changes seem to originate or take on acceleration in some periods than in others. In the field of American constitutional development the Civil War marks one of the periods of sharpest transition. The eve of that period, therefore, is the obvious point from which to survey briefly such general changes, not yet discussed, as had taken place since the Constitution had been in operation.

Certain facts as to population and territorial change and change in communication and transportation were inseparably linked with constitutional development. The mere statement of figures indicates the sweeping governmental adjustments required. The population was slightly less than 4,000,000 in 1790. In 1830 it was nearly 13,000,000; while in 1860 it was more than 31,000,000. The total area of the United States in 1790 was a little more than 820,000 square miles, of which less than a third was settled. By 1830 the gross area had been more than doubled because of the Louisiana and Florida Purchases, while by 1860 it was slightly less than 3,000,000 square miles, of which nearly 1,200,000 square miles were settled. The original number of states had been thirteen. By 1830 there were twenty-four; and by 1860 there were thirty-three. Instead of comprising merely a line of states along the Atlantic coast, they now included Maine at one extreme and California at the other.

When the Union had been formed, many people believed that some of the states were so far from the others, transportation difficulties so great, and common interests so few that the Union could not survive. Yet it was not until the population had increased more than eight times over, the total area more than three times, and the number of states two and a half times that a concerted attempt was made to break the Union into two parts.

The fact that one government had been able to hold together such a large area had been due in part to changes in transportation and communication since the adoption of the Constitution. Travel on water, which in 1789 was principally in sailboats, was expanded both on the sea and on the inland waters of the United States by the development of the steamboat. Many miles of turnpikes were built during the early years, and within a short period the construction of canals greatly facilitated transportation. Although there were only twenty-three miles of railroad in 1830, there were more than thirty thousand miles in 1860, of which eighty-six hundred miles were in operation east of the Mississippi and south of Maryland.[1] The use of the telegraph, an invention of the middle of the century, was expanding rapidly. A line extending all the way across the country was completed in 1862. The varied improvements in travel, transportation, and communication linked the several distant sections of the country together so that, in effect, notwithstanding the vast increase in area and in population, the people of the United States were closer together in 1860 than they had been seventy years before. Had it not been for the specific issue of slavery and irritating problems of the protective tariff, arising out of conflict of interest between the North and the South, there would have been less reason for the dissolution of the Union in 1860 than ever before.

## CONGRESS

With the varied changes mentioned above went many changes in the political institutions of the country. The number of United States senators was increased by two with the addition of each new state. By 1830 there were forty-eight senators, while in 1860 there were sixty-six. Although in 1789 the Senate was small enough to have functioned as an advisory body to the President, had politics made such an arrangement feasible, it was too large in 1860 to function successfully in any such capacity. The membership of the House of Representatives had likewise greatly increased — by 1830 from sixty-five to two hundred and thirteen; because the body was growing so large as to be unwieldy, the ratio of representation was changed so as to prevent such rapid expansion, and in 1860 the number stood

[1] R. E. Riegal, "Federal Operation of Southern Railroads During the Civil War," *Mississippi Valley Historical Review*, IX (September, 1922), 127.

at two hundred and thirty-seven.[2]    The House was already becoming too large to function effectively as a legislative body; and the transfer of much of its real work to committees was in prospect.

Many men of high caliber served in one or the other of the houses of Congress.    Among them were Webster, Clay, Calhoun, Douglas, Davis, Chase, and others.    Not all members were of the same high caliber; but it was always possible to find extremely able men in Congress, whereas, with few exceptions, the occupants of the presidency were mediocre men as far as executive leadership was concerned.

Something, but not too much, can be made of the fact that over a long period of years in which effective leadership in the presidency was lacking, there were extremely able men in Congress.    It indicates that the work of Congress was sufficiently important to draw real talent.    The fact should be kept in mind, however, that most of the outstanding men in Congress aspired toward the presidency.    It might well have been something in the electoral process which prevented the choice of outstanding men for the executive position.    Webster, Clay Calhoun, and other prominent men tried time and again to win the highest executive office.    In a sense, perhaps, they were too prominent; they had too many rivals and enemies, and they had expressed themselves on so many public questions as to have antagonized large numbers of people who disagreed with one or another of their positions.

Although prior to the Civil War, Congress made no attempt to enact social and economic legislation affecting the welfare of all the people, such as that enacted in relatively recent years, the subjects of legislation were, nevertheless, of sufficient importance to justify the selection of able men for the legislative body.    The tariff on imports was always a vital matter.    Throughout the entire period a major portion of the income of the federal government was derived from customs.    Internal revenue provided a modest supplement until largely abandoned by the Jefferson administration.    The same source was utilized extensively for a period of six or seven years as a result of expenditures for the War of 1812.    Thereafter, however, internal-revenue collections dwindled over a long period of years, and finally dried up altogether, until begun again during the period of the Civil War.    Direct taxes provided important sums in 1800 and for some

---

[2] Of this total, only eighty-nine were from states which seceded, together with the border states of Maryland, Kentucky, and Missouri, where strong southern sympathies prevailed.

years thereafter, and particularly for the period of the War of 1812, whereafter that source, too, was abandoned. The sale of public lands provided the only continuous and important addition to customs. In 1860 the revenue from customs amounted, in round numbers, to $53,187,000, while the revenue from the sale of public lands amounted to $1,756,000. The proportion from the latter source had at times been greater, but customs provided always the major source.

Varied interest groups were represented in the perennial conflicts to determine the source of federal revenue. Every group naturally sought to have the necessary money raised in the manner least injurious to itself. Certain commercial interests were opposed to high tariffs because of the adverse effect on the carrying trade. The growing industries of the United States sought all the protection they could get against foreign competition. The South, which as a section was a consumer rather than a producer of manufactured goods, opposed legislation which would increase the cost of such goods. Producers in the United States tried, for many years successfully, to escape the burden of internal-revenue taxation. Such escape, however, meant inevitably that the costs of government had to be borne by levies of other kinds.

The question of the disposition of public lands was a related problem. From the point of view of revenue, it had an importance similar to that of tariff and internal revenue. The policy of the government in the disposal of public lands was important, furthermore, in that it governed the speed with which western lands were settled, new states admitted to the Union, and new products made available. The handling of these subjects called for the best talents of legislators.

The various issues arising out of the slavery controversy likewise kept problems perennially before Congress. Part of the task of southern legislators was essentially negative in character. It was to prevent the enactment of federal statutes interfering with what they labeled as a purely local institution, subject only to the operation of local laws. The controversy penetrated into many fields. In the matter of fugitive-slave legislation, the South sought and secured positive action from Congress. In the matter of the admission of new states, the South struggled continuously to preserve a balance or, at least, an equality of slave states in the Union. The question of the legality of slavery in the territories was constantly in the minds of members of Congress.

The subject of internal improvements was of perennial importance.

The extent to which the federal government should give aid or should take the lead in the building of roads, canals, and railroads was always a matter of controversy. The government participated in various ways in many projects. Even though the ultimate turn was in the direction of construction and financing by private corporations, the aid given directly and indirectly by the federal government was vital to many projects. The government made surveys for prospective developments, it bought stock in companies, it made outright grants, it gave subsidies indirectly through payment for the carrying of mail, and in other ways it played a part in the development of the network of transportation and communication facilities throughout the country. It was subject constantly to pressure from the varied groups developing the several enterprises and from the communities seeking their development. The several interest groups and the several localities found it to their advantage to be represented as fully as possible on the floors of Congress. Whether or not federal aid was given in particular circumstances, each application provided the occasion for parliamentary conflict. The grants to railroads of right of way through public lands and the grants of tracts of land to aid in the construction of railroads, together with the prospect of speeding the settlement of new areas into which the roads were built, related the railroad policy of the country to the public-land policy, and involved it also in the rivalry between the North and the South. The question whether transcontinental railroads should be constructed first in southern or in northern regions was vitally related to the efforts of each section to establish permanent and binding connections with the Far West.[a]

THE EXECUTIVE

Although the issues which occupied the attention of Congress were also important to the President, Congress was usually regarded as the policy-making organ of the government. Even Jackson, the most independent occupant of the presidency during the period, felt free to veto a bill only when a question of constitutionality was involved. No President exerted powerful leadership over Congress. True, the President was not without influence. Jackson, in particular, was able to appeal to the people over the head of Congress to prevent legisla-

[a] For discussion of the railroad problems of the period see B. H. Meyer, Caroline E. MacGill, et al., History of Transportation in the United States before 1860 (1917), and L. H. Haney, A Congressional History of Railways in the United States to 1850 (1908).

tion to which he was opposed and to secure support for his vetoes. The position was that of coercion, however, more than one of accepted leadership. Each President exerted some control through his power over appointments, and, since constitutional questions could be imported into most legislative controversies, each had a check upon legislation through the instrumentality of the veto. None of them proposed broad legislative policies, however. They were predominantly passive, leaving to Congress the making of policy.

For strength and vigor the administration of Jackson stood out among those which preceded and followed it. He made ringing use of the veto power. He challenged policies sponsored by Congress, as, for example, in connection with the Bank of the United States and with federal expenditures on public works. He defied the sponsors of nullification with the effective threat to make use of all the powers of the federal government to defeat it. He showed an attitude of independence toward the Supreme Court which shocked the reverent admirers of that institution.[4] Altogether, he provided a landmark in the development of presidential authority to which strong Presidents of later years have looked back with warm approval.

Although the formal machinery for the election of President remained the same, certain important informal changes took place. Nominations, which were originally made by caucus of the majority party in Congress, passed to national nominating conventions. Around the end of the first third of the century, furthermore, effects of the expansion of the electorate through the abolition of property and other qualifications in the several states, together with the stream of votes from the unlettered pioneer population of new states in the West, made themselves felt. The changes may have had some effect upon the character of the persons chosen to the presidency. The fact that three of the Presidents — Jackson, Harrison, and Taylor — had been military heroes indicates the tendency to nominate figures marked by the aura of romance, without reference to executive ability in civil affairs. There is significance in the prevailing belief that almost any honest person, even though possessed of no special qualifications, could fulfill the duties of almost any political office. This attitude coincided with the feeling that public office was something that ought to be passed around rather than retained by individuals of outstanding qualifications.

[4] See Charles Warren, *The Supreme Court in United States History* (rev. ed., 2 vols., 1926), I, 757 ff.

In the light of the subsequent experience of the Civil War and of the first and second World Wars, it is of interest that the War of 1812 and the war with Mexico did not bring the temporary centralization of power in the Executive which characterized the later wars. Even though the first of the two approached a major tragedy for the United States, it did not bring the approximation of temporary dictatorship which has characterized other crises of the kind. The country was divided into many factions, and the President lacked the personality to stir the imaginations of the people. The times provided no other figure, military or civilian, who could unify the country and create eagerness for the surrender of popular rights into his hands. As for the Mexican War, perhaps the crisis lacked the seriousness necessary to precipitate major internal changes. The war did not disturb the civilian life and the productive machinery of the entire country. The glory and the power, such as there were, went to military officials exclusively, and modified little, if at all, the executive authority of the President.

Superficially, the executive departments remained much as they were when first established. They had grown somewhat, but they bore little resemblance to the huge establishments of today. The salaries of department heads stood at a uniform figure of $8000. In addition to the Secretary of State, the *American Almanac* for 1861 listed for the Department of State an assistant secretary with a salary of $3000, a chief clerk with a salary of $2200, and a dispensing agent and a superintendent of statistics, each of whom received $2000. The items suggest nothing more than the embryo of the present establishment. The Treasury Department was larger. It had an assistant secretary and a chief clerk with salaries identical with those of the corresponding officers of the State Department. Under the heading of comptrollers, it listed four officials receiving salaries of from $2000 to $3500. Under the heading of auditors, it listed twelve officials with salaries ranging from $2000 to $3000. It had two commissioners of customs, receiving $3000 and $2000 respectively. Six officials listed as appraisers general received salaries of $6000. Two persons in the treasurer's office received $3000 and $2000 respectively. Seven assistant treasurers received salaries of from $2500 to $4000 Two persons in the registrar's office received $3000 and $2000 respectively. Two persons in the solicitor's office received $3500 and $2000 respectively. One person in the coast survey received $6000.

This detailed statement concerning the Treasury Department indicates the range of salaries and the number of officials in what were at the time among the most important positions in the federal government. The War Department listed no assistant secretary. In addition to the Secretary, the *American Almanac* for 1861 listed for that department nine officers, one of whom received $2200, while the others received $1800 each. The Navy Department listed no assistant secretary. In addition to the Secretary, it listed eight officials with salaries ranging from $2200 to $3500. The Department of the Interior had no assistant secretary. Most of its officials were grouped under subordinate headings, including the General Land Office, the Indian Office, the Pension Office, the Patent Office, and the Penitentiary. The salaries of most of the persons listed ranged from $1800 to $2500. The Post Office Department listed three assistant postmasters general, each of whom received $3000. Three other officials were listed with salaries ranging from $2000 to $3000.

There was as yet no Department of Justice. The Attorney General, like other members of the cabinet, received a salary of $8000. He was provided with an assistant at $3000 a year, largely because of the burden of work placed upon his office by California land claims. The total in salaries authorized June 23, 1860, for the Attorney General, the assistant attorney general, and the clerks and messenger in his office was $17,500.[5] The duties of the Attorney General remained largely those involved in handling litigation in the Supreme Court and in giving legal advice to the President and the heads of the departments. The United States attorneys and marshals throughout the country were not yet under his supervision except in special situations such as those involved in litigation arising out of California land claims. He was largely a professional rather than an administrative or executive official.

In comparing the federal establishment of 1860 with that of the present day, the change in price-levels and salary scales generally must be taken into account. Although in terms of dollars the salaries were much lower than those now paid, it seems probable that officials of that time were adequately compensated and that the offices attracted men with ability comparable to that of employees of later years. As for the size of the organizations, however, and the complexity of duties to be performed, there is almost no comparison. The government of New York City today is an incomparably more complicated and expensive affair than was the government of the

[5] 12 Stat. 91, 101.

United States in 1860.    As a matter of fact, the annual expenditure on the New York Police Department alone approaches the amount of the entire annual expenditure on the government of the United States in 1860.

THE JUDICIARY

Down to 1860 the judicial branch of the government had undergone few important changes.    The Supreme Court consisted of nine members.    The work of the courts had increased to the point where the Supreme Court was constantly behind with its docket.    The annual term of the Court now began in December of each year instead of January.    Each member was assigned to a circuit, and continued to perform circuit-court duty in addition to his duties on the Supreme Court.    The country was divided into nine circuits, to each of which a Supreme Court justice was allotted.    An additional circuit had been created in California.    It was not served by any Supreme Court justice, but was presided over by a circuit judge appointed for that purpose.    Because the circuits were already so large as to exhaust the capacity of the Supreme Court justices for travel and professional work, the states of Florida, Iowa, Minnesota, Oregon, Texas, and Wisconsin had not yet been attached to any circuit.    The circuit-court work in those states was performed by the district judges.    There was a local circuit court in the District of Columbia.    The number of district courts had increased from thirteen to fifty.    The work of these courts was done by forty-three district judges.    United States attorneys and marshals were provided for the several district courts.

Most of the important work of the Supreme Court during the chief justiceships of Marshall and Taney, save as the latter extended into the Civil-War period, has been discussed in earlier chapters.    Large numbers of the cases then coming before it had little importance except to the litigants.    As indicated in earlier chapters, it decided from time to time important cases involving the constitutionality of state laws.    Federal laws were applied on rare occasions.    None was held unconstitutional between the dates of Marbury v. Madison in 1803 and the Dred Scott case in 1857.    The explanation lay, not necessarily in the leniency of the Court, but in the fact that Congress enacted no laws which crowded the limits of the Constitution.    It was only in later years, when the field of federal legislative activity was being extended, that much of the important work of the Court consisted in curbing the exercise of federal power.

In 1848, in deciding the case of Luther *v.* Borden,[6] the Supreme Court exercised notable self-restraint in dealing with the scope of its jurisdiction with reference to the powers of Congress and of the Executive. Early in the decade, two rival governments had existed for a time in the state of Rhode Island. The suit was expected to determine which of the two governments was the lawful government of the state. Chief Justice Taney, speaking for the Court, held that the question was not one which the Court was in position to determine. It depended upon facts which a court was not equipped to accumulate. Moreover, he said, the Constitution of the United States, as far as it had provided for an emergency of this kind, had treated the subject as political in its nature, and had placed the power in the hands of the political branches of the government, and not in those of the judiciary. Under the article of the Constitution which provided that the United States should guarantee to every state in the Union a republican form of government and protect each of them against invasion, it rested with Congress to decide what government was the established one in a state. Congress must necessarily decide that question before it could determine whether the government was republican. When the senators and representatives of a state were admitted into the councils of the Union, the authority of the government under which they were appointed, as well as its republican character, was recognized by the proper constitutional authority. Its decision was binding on every other department of the government and could not be questioned in a judicial tribunal.

As to the clause of the Constitution providing for cases of domestic violence, there again it rested with Congress to determine upon the means proper to be adopted to fulfill this guarantee. By a statute enacted in 1795, Congress had authorized the President to call forth militia to suppress insurrections against a state. The power of deciding whether the exigency had arisen upon which the government of the United States was bound to interfere was given to the President. He was to act upon the application of the legislature or of the executive, and consequently he must determine what body of men constituted the legislature, and who was the governor, before he could act. With this exercise of judgment on the part of the President, the Court could not interfere. As to the possibility that the President might abuse his power, all power might be abused if placed in unworthy hands. Taney could think of no place where it might

[6] 7 Howard 1.

better be lodged. Rapid decision and decisive action were often necessary.

> The ordinary course of proceedings in courts of justice would be utterly unfit for the crisis. And the elevated office of the President, chosen as he is by the people of the United States, and the high responsibility he could not fail to feel when acting in a case of so much moment, appear to furnish as strong safeguards against a willful abuse of power as human prudence and foresight could well provide. At all events, it is conferred upon him by the Constitution and laws of the United States, and must therefore be respected and enforced in a judicial tribunal.[7]

The doctrine of political questions, adopted in this case and utilized in many others, has enabled the Supreme Court oftentimes to avoid the necessity of giving decisions in cases in which it was not equipped either to discover the facts on which the decisions ought to be based or to enforce the decisions once they were made. Practical considerations often lie back of the resort to the doctrine. It has saved the Supreme Court embarrassment from time to time, and has left responsibility in the hands of other branches of the government better equipped to exercise it.[8]

All this is not to suggest that the Supreme Court sought to utilize the doctrine of political questions as a means of avoiding decisions in all cases having important political implications. The Court never went so far. It must have been clear then as now that most decisions of importance have strong repercussions in the field of politics. In the Dred Scott case, both the minority and the majority of the Court seem to have sought deliberately to influence the course of political events. It is one of the major tragedies of American history that they failed to exercise in that case the restraint which would have limited the decision to the point necessary to be decided. The prestige of the Court was virtually destroyed in the wrangling which followed the decision, and it was not restored until some years had passed and extensive changes in Court personnel had taken place.

If the Supreme Court exercised self-restraint where political questions were involved, it was less modest in another field. Many cases decided in the federal courts were not based directly on federal law. They were based on state statutes or on the common law as applied in

---

[7] *Ibid.*, p. 44.

[8] For discussion see Charles Gordon Post, Jr., *The Supreme Court and Political Questions* (1936).

the states respectively. The jurisdiction of the federal courts rested solely on the fact that the litigants were citizens of different states. Some judges were disturbed by the fact that the common law was developing differently in different states. Cases essentially alike might be decided one way in New York, another way in Massachusetts, and still another in Virginia. The federal courts, therefore, had to know, not merely the relevant state statutes, but the decisions of state courts, in order to decide cases properly.

In 1842, the Supreme Court sought to avert the disparity of decisions by holding, in Swift v. Tyson,[9] that the federal Judiciary Act did not require that local interpretations of general commercial law be followed in the federal courts. The language of the statute was not wholly clear, and there seemed some ground for this conclusion, worked out by Justice Story, who was a firm believer in fundamental principles of natural law as the basis of the common law. It was believed that if the federal courts, guided by the Supreme Court, exercised independent judgment in interpreting general commercial rules of the common law, the state courts would follow, thereby producing uniformity rather than diversity in legal development. As a matter of fact, the states continued to follow their own interpretations. The result of the Swift case, therefore, was to add a federal version to the chaos of state interpretations rather than to promote order. Historical investigation of a later period showed that Justice Story had probably been incorrect in his interpretation of the Judiciary Act.[10] In 1938, nearly a century after the Swift case had been decided, the Supreme Court reviewed and reversed the decision, holding that under the Constitution the law to be followed was the law of the state in question as interpreted by the state courts.[11] Over that long period, therefore, the federal courts had exceeded their jurisdiction by creating law instead of following state decisions as the Constitution required.

The personnel of the Supreme Court, as, no doubt, of the lower federal courts as well, included a few eminent men and many of average ability. With the exception of Justice Story, no member of the Court in this period or later produced while in office distinguished works of scholarship, apart from his work as a judge. Story's Com-

[9] 16 Peters 1.

[10] Charles Warren, "History of the Federal Judiciary Act of 1789," *Harvard Law Review*, XXXVII (November, 1923), 49-132.

[11] Erie Railroad Co. v. Tompkins, 304 U.S. 64 (1938).

*mentaries on the Constitution of the United States,* published in 1833, probably had greater influence in molding the institutions of the United States than did his judicial opinions.   Others of his books were likewise entitled to high rank.   Chief Justice Marshall, on the other hand, made his significant contribution almost exclusively through his judicial opinions.   His biography of Washington had a measure of value, but it was not a distinguished piece of work.   Chief Justice Taney wrote nothing of importance apart from his opinions. The same is true of the associate justices of the period.

Of the two Chief Justices, Marshall, no doubt, exerted the greater influence.   The explanation lies in the fact that he presided over the Court at a time when a series of important constitutional questions had to be decided, or, at any rate, when there was an opportunity to decide them unencumbered by earlier decisions of the Court.   Marshall took full advantage of the opportunity to establish the major principles of American constitutional law.   By the use of persuasively phrased *obiter dicta* he was able to lay down pronouncements of the Court in most of the important fields of controversy.   His dominance of other members of the Court down until the later years of his term of service resulted in a continuity and uniformity of statement which would not have been possible in a Court of strong personalities in which each justice exercised the privilege of justifying his own line of reasoning.

Taney, by contrast, found many important principles already established, and many precedents standing as limitations upon the work which he and his Court had to do.   Whether or not he desired to do so — and apparently he had no such desire — he did not dominate the Court as Marshall had done.   Divisions among the members were more frequent in important cases, both as to the decisions to be handed down and as to the method of justifying them.   These divisions impaired to some extent the prestige of a Court which was supposed to stand as a single mouthpiece of the law of the Constitution. The prestige of the Court depended, it is true, not merely upon unanimity, but also upon the persuasive justification of principles which the people were willing to accept.   When the people became hopelessly divided on certain issues, as, for example, those connected with slavery, the prospect was disastrous for the Court.

### POLITICAL PARTIES

Although in his first inaugural address Thomas Jefferson professed to believe that all Americans were Republicans and all were Federalists, political parties had by that time come to be institutions of major importance in the American constitutional system. They lost none of that importance during the period under discussion, in spite of the vicissitudes through which they passed. The Federalist party dwindled away and disappeared. Drastic political realignment took place in the eighteen-twenties and thirties. In spite of the varied changes, the so-called Jackson party was the successor to the party of Jefferson, known as Republican, and the forerunner of the Democratic party of today. The Whigs, seizing power only for two brief periods, were in a sense successors to the Federalists. They gave way, in turn, to a new alignment represented by the Republican party, organized in 1854.

For many years the Democratic and Whig parties each succeeded in maintaining unity across sectional lines between the North and South. The Whig party maintained its existence after the formation of the new Republican party, but a major portion of its anti-slavery element in the North shifted to the ranks of the Republicans. The Republican party was definitely sectional. It had no strength at all in the South until after the Civil War. The Democratic party maintained continuity across sectional lines until 1860. The ties between its northern and southern membership lasted even longer than the ties between the northern and southern wings of important church organizations. In 1860, however, the Democrats broke apart and nominated rival candidates for the presidency. The rift in the party made more glaring the developing chasm between the two sections. It aided, furthermore, in bringing about the election of the Republican candidate, Abraham Lincoln, even though the popular vote received by him was far less than a majority of all the votes cast. The Republican party being a party largely without membership in the South, the newly elected President, according to the sentiment of Southerners, was the President of the North and of the West and of the anti-slavery people of the country, but not the President of the South. His inauguration as President was to be the inauguration of the beginning of northern oppression of the South. To avert such domination it was adjudged worth while to secede from the Union and form a new union of states having a common bond of interest.

NO FOURTH BRANCH OF GOVERNMENT

Because of the tendency to view government in the past as a replica of the government of today, the fact should be emphasized that certain modern institutions were altogether lacking in the federal establishment in 1860.   Many years were to pass before federal regulation of private enterprise led to the establishment of independent regulatory commissions and other agencies having a conglomerate of legislative, administrative, and judicial powers.   The so-called fourth branch of the government existed not even in the imagination of the statesmen of the time.   The government consisted only of Congress as originally designed, of an executive branch which as yet had undergone no great expansion, and of a system of courts organized largely according to the pattern originally established.   The country was steeped in the laissez-faire ideas of Adam Smith, which were well adapted to the internal economy of a country largely agricultural, with industrial enterprise operating in isolated units and on a small scale.   If regulation was to be indulged in, it was regarded as the function of the states, and not of the federal government.   As to the attitude of businessmen and their counsel toward the regulation of private enterprise, it should be remembered that their strongest arguments in justification of broad constitutional powers in the federal government were aimed at preventing regulation by the states.   They did not assert the existence of federal power because they desired federal regulation, but because of the hope that, if they demonstrated the existence of federal power, that fact would lead the Court to invalidate state laws providing for the exercise of state power in the same field.   It was only after the grip of the state-rights doctrinaires of the South was broken, and after further expansion of business and industrial enterprise, that the demand for federal regulation brought an expansion of the scope of federal activity — brought it in spite of the opposition of the interests to be regulated and of the theorists who opposed regulation as a matter of principle.

# CHAPTER 14

# THE MAELSTROM OF CIVIL WAR

THE CONSTITUTIONAL ASPECTS of the Civil War are manifold. Because of their number and complexity and their interrelations with matters not directly constitutional in character, their delineation is most difficult. The determination of emphasis is further complicated by the fact that, whereas the solutions adopted for some of the constitutional problems had significance for constitutional development in future years, others were significant only in terms of the crisis then existing. As to the latter, for example, cleavages among the American people are not likely again to follow territorial lines to such an extent as to result in attempts at actual secession or in the attempt to build up a body of constitutional doctrine justifying the right to secede. Cleavages continue, as they will in the future, but, without disasters to the Union as yet undreamed of, the United States is not likely to face again the task of preventing the secession of a portion of its territory.

On the other hand, much of the experience of the government in handling Civil-War problems had relevance for the years ahead. The assumption by the federal government of powers of unprecedented breadth, even though nominally for the period of the war crisis only, established a precedent and conditioned the minds of the people for the similar exercise of broad powers in later years, whether in war crises or otherwise. Within the government the assumption of unprecedented powers by the President and his strategy of putting Congress in position where, instead of determining governmental policy, it could not do otherwise than sanction policies already initiated by the President, provided a handbook for those of his successors who in future years sought to escape the domination and avert the interference of Congress. The problem of dealing with dissenters and people suspected of disloyal activities at a time when unanimity of national action is desired is a critical problem in every time of crisis. The extent to which the government shall assume control of private property during these emergencies is hardly less important. The mode of selecting the man-power for the conduct of a war affects directly or indirectly the lives of all the people. The mode of financing the war and the currency and credit policies adopted are intimately related to all other problems of economic welfare. In connection with all these problems the experience of the Civil War marks the continued unfolding of the American constitutional system.

## BEGINNINGS OF LINCOLN'S ADMINISTRATION

In his inaugural address President Lincoln dealt cautiously but firmly with the problems before him. He participated briefly in the now futile debate as to the constitutional right of a state to secede from the Union. He, of course, took the position that the right of secession did not exist.

> I hold that in contemplation of universal law and of the Constitution the Union of these states is perpetual. . . . The Union is much older than the Constitution. It was formed, in fact, by the Articles of Association in 1774. It was matured and continued by the Declaration of Independence in 1776. It was further matured, and the faith of all the then thirteen states expressly plighted and engaged that it should be perpetual, by the Articles of Confederation in 1778. And finally, in 1787, one of the declared objects for ordaining and establishing the Constitution was *to form a more perfect Union.*[1]

Lincoln declared it his firm intention to preserve the Union and enforce the laws of the United States. He sought to convince the South that he would make no attack upon the institution of slavery as it then stood and that he would enforce the laws giving it protection, but would not participate in its extension. He emphasized the fact that, physically speaking, the two sections of the country could not separate.

> They cannot but remain face to face, and intercourse, either amicable or hostile, must continue between them. Is it possible, then, to make that intercourse more advantageous or more satisfactory *after* separation than *before?* Can aliens make treaties easier than friends can make laws? Can treaties be more faithfully enforced between aliens than laws can among friends? Suppose you go to war, you cannot fight always; and when, after much loss on both sides and no gain on either, you cease fighting, the identical old questions, as to terms of intercourse, are again upon you.[2]

[1] *Messages and Papers of the Presidents*, VII, 3208.     [2] *Ibid.*, VII, 3211.

From the very beginning, the difficulties of presidential leadership proved greater than those faced in earlier years by most of his predecessors. The Union seemed on the point of dissolution. In spite of the hopelessness of the prospects, he was under obligation to make every effort to hold it together. Throughout the ranks of federal employees, from top to bottom, were large numbers of ardent southern sympathizers. In the event of civil war they had to be weeded out and replaced by loyal persons. As the leader of a political party which had never been in office, the new President must listen to the clamor of thousands of people who demanded a share of the spoils of office. The party lacked unanimity of policy and program. Its leaders had come from various sections of the field of politics. They were ambitious and determined men. In the selection of his cabinet he had to decide whether he would choose men who were acquiescent in their make-up and who would be easily subservient to his will or take, on the other hand, men who had been his competitors for the presidency and who were doubtless still convinced that they, rather than he, ought to have been placed at the head of the nation in the crisis.

He chose the latter alternative. He placed in his cabinet such strong characters as William H. Seward and Salmon P. Chase and, later, Edwin M. Stanton. It was apparently his belief that it was better to have the assistance of these men, and to compel them to share a portion of the responsibility for the administration, than to have them acting as critics from without the administration. They disapproved of much that Lincoln did and they were violently critical of each other, but Lincoln demonstrated an unusual capacity for getting the best out of individual men. He had, on the whole, an unusually strong cabinet, in spite of the difficulties involved in their divergent personalities.

Faced with the imminent dissolution of the Union, Lincoln also had to decide whether he would call Congress into immediate special session. He looked back over a period during which Congress had been the primary policy-making institution of the federal government. In so far as his predecessors had had programs to carry out, Congress oftentimes proved more of a hindrance than an aid. The necessity of calling a special session at the very beginning of an administration was regarded by most Presidents as in the nature of a disaster. A number of Presidents had found such sessions the cause of the breakdown of their own administrations. So generally known was this fact that the month of May, during which some of these sessions met, came to be regarded as a symbol of political misfortune. When the necessity of calling Congress was finally forced upon Lincoln, Seward is said to have warned him that in no event should he have the session begin in May.[3]   Lincoln avoided issuing the call until it was clearly his public duty to issue it, and even then he postponed the date of meeting until the fourth of the ensuing July.   The call was issued on the fifteenth day of April as a part of the proclamation in which the President called out seventy-five thousand militia to suppress combinations obstructing the enforcement of federal laws in South Carolina, Georgia, Alabama, Florida, Mississippi, Louisiana, and Texas.   The law applicable to calling the state militia into the federal service provided that no member should be compelled to serve more than three months.[4]   The date set for the assembling of Congress was early enough to give Congress time to enact a new measure providing for the continuation of the militia in the federal service, but it was hardly too early to give the President the necessary time for the consideration of such legislation.   It may be that this factor had much to do with the selection of the date.

On April 19, Lincoln took another drastic step which might be expected to be taken only with congressional sanction or in anticipation of the earliest possible consideration by Congress.   To deal with the insurrection "until Congress shall have assembled and deliberated on the said unlawful proceedings or until the same shall have ceased," he proclaimed that he had deemed it advisable to set on foot a blockade of the ports of the states in insurrection, in pursuance of the laws of the United States and of the law of nations.[5]   By a proclamation of May 3, he issued a call for more than forty-two thousand volunteers to serve for the period of three years, to be mustered into service as infantry and cavalry.[6]   Although the President of the United States was commander-in-chief of the army and navy, it was highly questionable whether he had the power in this manner, without authorization by Congress, to increase the personnel of the army.

## IMPAIRMENT OF CIVIL RIGHTS

Among the most drastic steps taken by President Lincoln without

---

[3] James G. Blaine, *Twenty Years of Congress* (2 vols., 1884, 1886), II (1886), 55.

[4] 1 Stat. 424. For the proclamation see *Messages and Papers of the Presidents*, VII, 3214.

[5] *Messages and Papers of the Presidents*, VII, 3215.          [6] *Ibid.*, VII, 3216-3217.

authorization by Congress was that of empowering military commanders to suspend the privilege of the writ of habeas corpus. The Constitution provided that "The privilege of the writ of habeas corpus shall not be suspended, unless when in cases of rebellion or invasion the public safety may require it."[7] The constitutional provision was in the passive voice and was stated negatively, but it implied that the privilege of the writ might be suspended when in cases of rebellion or invasion the public safety might require it. Unfortunately, it did not say whether it was Congress or the President who might authorize such suspension. Since it was included in a section devoted exclusively to placing limitations on the power of Congress, the implication was that Congress was the rightful agency to act in the matter. The President was not influenced by this line of argument. There were no judicial decisions to indicate whether he was right or wrong.

The privilege of the writ of habeas corpus was protected by the Constitution to prevent persons from being arrested and held unlawfully, and to insure that persons arrested should not be held indefinitely, but should be brought to trial within a reasonable period of time. Suspension of the privilege of the writ made it possible to arrest suspicious characters against whom evidence to secure conviction was lacking and hold them throughout the period during which they might be dangerous without the embarrassing necessity of bringing them to trial. In most of the states of the Union, and particularly in the border states, there were large numbers of southern sympathizers. Some of them were eager to aid the southern cause. They were dangerous, not because of offenses already committed, but because of those which they might commit. Pending the time when the control of the government of the United States could be firmly established, it was important that these persons be got out of the way. If the privilege of the writ of habeas corpus were not suspended, it would be the duty of federal judges, on due application, to order the release of persons against whom no charges of illegal activity had been made. Furthermore, some of the federal judges were themselves southern sympathizers. It was fully expected that these judges would use their power to order the release even of southern sympathizers who were lawfully held.

Some of the greatest difficulties with reference to southern sympathizers arose in Maryland. It was feared for a time that the state

[7] Article I, Section 9, Clause 2.

might formally proclaim secession.    On April 25, 1861, the President wrote to Lieutenant General Scott that the Maryland legislature would assemble on the following day and, not improbably, would take action to arm the people of the state against the United States. The question had been raised as to whether the general-in-chief of the army should not arrest or disperse the members of that body. The President opposed such action.    The legislature had a clear, legal right to assemble, and it could not be known in advance that their action would be unlawful.    Furthermore, he said, "We cannot permanently prevent their action.    If we arrest them, we cannot long hold them as prisoners, and when liberated they will immediately reassemble and take their action; and precisely the same if we simply disperse them — they will immediately reassemble in some other place."    He asked the commanding general to be watchful, even to bombard the cities of Maryland if necessary, and he authorized, "in the extremest necessity, the suspension of the writ of habeas corpus." [8] Two days later, the President authorized the commanding general of the army to suspend the writ of habeas corpus for the public safety, through himself or through the officer in command at the point of resistance, if he should find resistance which rendered it necessary in the vicinity of any military line used between Philadelphia and Washington.[9]    On subsequent occasions he authorized the suspension at other points.

The question of power was raised almost immediately in the federal courts.    One of the first instances occurred in Baltimore, where southern sympathizers were so strong that the government found it expedient to put the city under military control.    A writ of habeas corpus was presented to the commander of Fort McHenry for the release of a minor who had enlisted in the army without his parents' consent.    The commander refused to surrender the man.    He and the judge engaged in spectacular but futile newspaper correspondence over the rights in the matter.    Power was in the hands of the commander, and, whatever the law, he continued to exercise his authority.[10]

This case, brought as it was before a federal district judge who was not generally known outside the area of the controversy, received little general attention.    It provided a local background, however, for the more important case of *Ex parte* Merryman, which was

[8] *Messages and Papers of the Presidents*, VII, 3218-3219.    [9] *Ibid.,* VII, 3219.
[10] Carl Brent Swisher, *Roger B. Taney* (1935), pp. 548-550.

brought soon afterward, not before the district judge, but before Chief Justice Taney. John Merryman, a man of considerable prestige in his own state and an officer in a secessionist company operating in Maryland, was arrested by order of federal military authority and confined in Fort McHenry. On May 25, 1861, he petitioned for a writ of habeas corpus. The petition was presented to Taney, who seems to have gone to Baltimore chiefly for the purpose of receiving it, perhaps with the thought of giving to his decision the prestige of his high office, which of course was far greater than that of the office of a district judge. Taney issued a writ of habeas corpus directing General George Cadwalader to bring Merryman before the Chief Justice of the United States on the following day at the circuit court room in Baltimore. Instead of obeying the order of the court, the general sent a statement to be read by an aide-de-camp. The statement reviewed the facts of the case, stated the President's authorization for the suspension of the writ of habeas corpus, and requested that the case be postponed until the President could be consulted. Taney sternly refused to make any concession. The general having disobeyed his order, he issued the necessary process directing that the general be brought before him on the following day. The general ignored the order of the court. Upon his failure to appear, Taney read his opinion in the famous Merryman case.[11]

No official notice had been given to the courts of justice or to the public, Taney declared, by proclamation or otherwise, that the President claimed the power of suspension of the writ of habeas corpus and had exercised it. "And I certainly listened to it with some surprise, for I had supposed it to be one of those points of constitutional law upon which there was no difference of opinion, and that it was admitted on all hands that the privilege of the writ could not be suspended, except by act of Congress." [12] He sought to demonstrate the correctness of this constitutional interpretation by an analysis of the powers conferred by the Constitution. Even if the privilege of the writ were suspended by act of Congress, he continued, and a party not subject to the rules and articles of war were afterward arrested and imprisoned by regular judicial process, he could not be detained in prison or brought to trial before a military tribunal because of the provision in the Sixth Amendment to the Constitution that "in all criminal prosecutions, the accused shall enjoy the right to a speedy and public trial by an impartial jury of the state and district wherein

[11] *Ex parte* Merryman, Federal Cases No. 9487.          [12] *Ibid.*, p. 148.

the crime shall have been committed, which district shall have been previously ascertained by law; . . . " The Constitution required that the President should take care that the laws should be faithfully executed. "It is thus made his duty to come in aid of the judicial authority, if it shall be resisted by a force too strong to be overcome without the assistance of the executive arm; but in exercising this power he acts in subordination to judicial authority, assisting it to execute its process and enforce its judgments." [13] The President certainly was not faithfully executing the laws if he took upon himself legislative power by suspending the writ of habeas corpus and the judicial power also by arresting and imprisoning a person without due process of law.

In this case, Taney continued, the military authority had gone far beyond the mere suspension of the privilege of the writ of habeas corpus. It had thrust aside the judicial authorities and officers to whom the Constitution had confided the power and duty of interpreting and administering the laws, and had substituted a military government in its place, to be administered and executed by military officers. The civil officers in Maryland were performing their duties. There had been no resistance or obstruction to the process of any court or judicial officer of the United States in Maryland except by the military authority. If a military officer had evidence that the prisoner had violated the laws of the United States, it was his duty to bring the facts to the attention of a civil officer so that the offender might be prosecuted according to law.

The Constitution forbade the taking of life, liberty, or property without due process of law. It prohibited unreasonable searches and seizures. It prohibited search by warrant except on probable cause. It called for speedy and public trial of the accused in a court of justice.

These great and fundamental laws, which Congress itself could not suspend, have been disregarded and suspended, like the writ of habeas corpus, by a military order, supported by force of arms. Such is the case now before me, and I can only say that if the authority which the Constitution has confided to the judiciary department and judicial officers may thus, upon any pretext or under any circumstances, be usurped by the military power, at its discretion, the people of the United States are no longer living under a government of laws, but every citizen holds his life, liberty, and property at the will and

[13] *Ibid.*, p. 149.

pleasure of the army officer in whose military district he may happen to be found.[14]

He had himself exercised all the power which the Constitution and laws conferred upon him, Taney said in conclusion, but that power had been resisted by a force too strong for him to overcome. He filed his opinion, therefore, with an order that a copy be transmitted to the President of the United States. "It will then remain for that high officer, in fulfillment of his constitutional obligation to 'take care that the laws be faithfully executed,' to determine what measures he will take to cause the civil process of the United States to be respected and enforced." [15]

Taney's opinion in the Merryman case has come to be regarded as an eloquent defense of civil liberties against the usurpation of power by executive authority, and particularly by military authority. Many of its principles were sanctioned by the Supreme Court after the termination of the war, in an opinion written by a judge who was a close friend of President Lincoln.[16] Immediate reactions to the opinion, however, were the partisan reactions which were to be expected. Friends of the South were enthusiastic about it. To northern sympathizers it merely represented part of the strategy of a secessionist judge in aiding the cause of the South.[17] It was a time of inflamed passions when few people could view developments with the objectivity necessary for the just enforcement of law. The era was characterized by the reign of politics rather than by the reign of law — politics upon which depended the survival of the Union, the Constitution, and the legal structure which Taney, through his opinion, was seeking to defend.

The President made an indirect answer to Taney in his message to Congress of July 4, 1861. The legality and propriety of the suspension of the privilege of the writ of habeas corpus had been questioned, he said, and the attention of the country had been called to the proposition that one who was sworn to take care that the laws be faithfully executed should not himself violate them.

The whole of the laws which were required to be faithfully executed were being resisted and failing of execution in nearly one-third of the states. Must they be allowed to finally fail of execution, even had it

[14] *Ibid.*, p. 152.    [15] *Ibid.*, p. 153.    [16] *Ex parte* Milligan, 4 Wallace 2 (1866).
[17] For an opinion in another district involving the same kind of case see *In re* McDonald, Federal Cases No. 8751.

been perfectly clear that by the use of the means necessary to their execution some single law, made in such extreme tenderness of the citizen's liberty that practically it relieved more of the guilty than of the innocent, should to a very limited extent be violated? To state the question more directly, Are all the laws *but one* to go unexecuted and the government itself go to pieces lest that one be violated?

In any event, he did not believe that any law had been violated. The Constitution was silent as to the agency by which the privilege of the writ of habeas corpus was to be suspended.

As the provision was plainly made for a dangerous emergency, it cannot be believed the framers of the instrument intended that in every case the danger should run its course until Congress could be called together, the very assembling of which might be prevented, as was intended in this case, by the rebellion.

He left the further argument of the question, however, to an opinion to be presented by the Attorney General. Whether there should be legislation on the subject was submitted to the better judgment of Congress.[18]

Nearly two years passed before Congress took action in the matter. Meanwhile, the President extended from time to time his orders authorizing the suspension of the writ of habeas corpus. Large numbers of arrests were made by military authorities in centers of danger, particularly in the border states. In Maryland the government took into custody members of the state legislature, officials of the government of Baltimore, and other prominent persons suspected or known to be in sympathy with the rebellion. Some of the persons arrested were sent to Fort McHenry. Most of them were shipped later to Fortress Monroe, in Virginia, and then to other places of confinement in the North as expediency required. They were not charged with particular offenses and no attempt was made to bring them to .rial. So reticent was the administration as to its reasons for making arrests in particular instances that when the House of Representatives, by resolution, asked for the grounds, reasons, and evidence upon which the police commissioners of Baltimore were arrested and were detained at Fort McHenry, the President replied, "I have to state that it is judged to be incompatible with the public interest at this time to furnish the information called for by the resolution."[19]

[18] *Messages and Papers of the Presidents*, VII, 3226. For the opinion of the Attorney General see 10 *Opinions of the Attorneys General*, 74.

[19] *Messages and Papers of the Presidents*, VII, 3234.

In February, 1862, over the signature of Secretary of War Stanton, an executive order was issued relating to political prisoners which outlined the history of the activities of the government on that subject. At the beginning of the insurrection, said Stanton, every department of the government was paralyzed by treason. Defection appeared in the Senate, in the House of Representatives, in the cabinet, in the federal courts and among other groups of government officials. The government was not prepared to meet the crisis. The judicial machinery "seemed as if it had been designed, not to sustain the government, but to embarrass and betray it." In the crisis the President deemed it necessary, among other things, to suspend the writ of habeas corpus in various places. He caused persons who were represented to him as being engaged or about to engage in disloyal and treasonable practices to be arrested by special civil as well as military agencies and detained in custody when necessary to prevent them and deter others from such practices. The government now had the situation well in hand. Examinations of many individual cases had been made. Arrangements were being made to release large numbers of persons on their subscribing to a parole to render no aid or comfort to the enemies of the United States. Exceptions would be made when it was deemed necessary.[20]

As a result of this policy, considerable numbers of persons who had been imprisoned at various points throughout the United States were released and allowed to return, fuming and sputtering, to their homes. The process of summary arrest and imprisonment continued, however, when the authorities in Washington and the military authorities deemed it necessary.

An extension of authority was granted by presidential proclamation in September, 1862, to deal with persons encouraging resistance to the draft. The proclamation provided in part as follows:

> That during the existing insurrection, and as a necessary measure for suppressing the same, all rebels and insurgents, their aiders and abettors, within the United States, and all persons discouraging volunteer enlistments, resisting militia drafts, or guilty of any disloyal practice affording aid and comfort to rebels against the authority of the United States, shall be subject to martial law and liable to trial and punishment by courts-martial or military commissions; second, that the writ of habeas corpus is suspended in respect to all persons arrested, or who are now or hereafter during the rebellion shall be

[20] *Ibid.,* VII, 3303-3305.

imprisoned in any fort, camp, arsenal, military prison, or other place of confinement by any military authority or by the sentence of any court-martial or military commission.[21]

It was not until March, 1863, that Congress enacted a measure authorizing the suspension of the writ of habeas corpus. The legislation had an interesting history. The legality of the suspension by the President or by persons to whom he gave authorization continued to be seriously questioned. If the action taken proved to be illegal, the several officials who had obeyed the order of the President by arresting and detaining political prisoners might ultimately pay dearly for their conduct as a result of damage suits brought against them. To avert such an outcome, Thaddeus Stevens introduced in the House of Representatives in December, 1862, a bill to protect government officers against any such liability. It cited the fact that "there is not entire unanimity of opinion as to which branch of the government possesses the constitutional power to declare such suspension." It provided that

all such suspensions, arrests, and imprisonments, by whomsoever made or caused to be made, under the authority of the said President, shall be confirmed and made valid; and the said President, Secretaries, heads of departments, and all persons who have been concerned in making such arrests, or in doing or advising any such acts as aforesaid, are hereby indemnified and discharged in respect thereof, and all indictments, and information, action, suits, prosecutions, and proceedings whatsoever commenced, or to be commenced, against the said President, or any of the persons aforesaid in relation to the acts and matters aforesaid, or any of them, are hereby discharged and made void.

It provided further that during the existence of the rebellion the President should be "invested with authority to declare the suspension of the privilege of the writ of habeas corpus, at such times and in such places, and with regard to such persons, as in his judgment the public safety may require."[22] The bill was passed by the House within an hour of its introduction without having been printed or referred to any committee and without opportunity for consideration or discussion.[23] A minority submitted a resolution of protest, denouncing the encroachment upon the guarantees of individual liberty and objecting to the indiscriminate validation of the actions of

---

[21] Ibid., VII, 3299-3300.    [22] 33 Congressional Globe 529.    [23] See ibid., p. 165.

government officials, whether justifiable or not. The Senate made drastic changes in the bill, and it was changed still further in conference committee, but, as passed, it authorized the President to suspend the privilege of the writ of habeas corpus and provided that any order made by or under the authority of the President should be a defense to any action for any search, seizure, arrest, or imprisonment. Provision was made for the removal of suits of this kind from state courts to federal courts.[24]

In one important respect the act attempted to curb the infringement of personal liberties. It provided that the Secretary of State and Secretary of War should submit to federal judges lists of the persons held as prisoners. If, after the adjournment of the succeeding session of the grand jury in each area, any prisoner remained unindicted, the judge was to discharge him from imprisonment on his taking an oath of allegiance to the United States. Prisoners under indictment were to be admitted to bail pending trial pursuant to law. These provisions represented concessions to those members of Congress who denounced the usurpation of power by the President. In practice, the provisions seem to have had little effect. They interfered but little with the activities of the administration.[25]

### MILITARY POWER EXPANDED

Most of the persons arrested and held as political prisoners without attempts to bring them to trial were from beginning to end in the custody, not of civil, but of military authorities. In his proclamation of September 24, 1862, concerning the treatment of persons interfering with the draft, the President sought greatly to expand the military power over civilians. He admitted that disloyal persons were "not adequately restrained by the ordinary processes of the law." He therefore prescribed by proclamation offenses which were not enumerated in any law of the United States. He took it upon himself to forbid the discouraging of volunteer enlistment. He ordered that persons charged with this and other offenses should be subject, not to trial in the civil courts in the area where those courts were open and functioning, but that the offenders should be "subject to martial law and liable to trial and punishment by courts-martial or military

---

[24] 12 Stat. 755.

[25] James G. Randall, *Constitutional Problems Under Lincoln* (1926), pp. 166-168. For the proclamation of general suspension, issued pursuant to the statute, see *Messages and Papers of the Presidents*, VII, 3371-3372.

commissions." [26] With respect to the offenses prescribed by the President, the proclamation appeared to be the extension of martial rule throughout the entire area of the United States, however distant the area in question might be from the centers of military conflict.[27]

The requirement that trial should be before a military tribunal rather than in a civil court was regarded as an invasion of personal rights no less serious and perhaps even more serious than arrest and imprisonment by military authorities. The Habeas Corpus Act of March 3, 1863, implied or seemed to imply the intention of Congress that persons held by military authorities should be surrendered for trial in the civil courts.[28] The use of military commissions was continued, nevertheless, for the trial of prescribed offenses by civilians. Military commissions much like courts-martial were set up. They were not authorized by statute. They tended to follow the code of courts-martial, but they were under no obligation to do so. They were not restrained by the traditions of the civil judicial system. The bias of the members of the commission could be given free rein without prospect of reversal by appeal to a civil court.[29]

One of the important cases involved Clement L. Vallandigham, a congressman from Ohio, who was highly critical of the war policies of the government. In a public address delivered at Mount Vernon, Ohio, on May 1, 1863, he declared, among other things,

> that the present war was a wicked, cruel, and unnecessary war, one not waged for the preservation of the Union, but for the purpose of crushing out liberty and to erect a despotism; a war for the freedom of the blacks and the enslavement of the whites, and . . . if the administration had not wished otherwise, . . . the war could have been honorably terminated long ago; that peace might have been honorably made by listening to the proposed intermediation of France; that propositions by which the southern states could be won back and the South guaranteed their rights under the Constitution, had been rejected the day before the late battle of Fredericksburg, by Lincoln and his minions.[30]

Major General Burnside, commanding the military department of Ohio, had issued an order some two weeks earlier, saying that all per-

[26] *Messages and Papers of the Presidents*, VII, 3299.

[27] For discussion of martial rule in the United States see Charles Fairman, *The Law of Martial Rule* (1930), chapter VIII.

[28] 12 Stat. 755.     [29] For discussion see Fairman, *op. cit.*, chapter X.

[30] *Ex parte* Vallandigham, 1 Wallace 243, 244-245 (1864).

sons found within his lines who should commit acts for the benefit of the enemies of the country should be tried as spies or traitors and, if convicted, should suffer death. Persons declaring sympathy for the enemy should be arrested either to be tried or to be sent outside the jurisdiction of General Burnside and within the line of the Confederacy. For the offense of delivering his public address, Vallandigham was arrested and brought to trial before a military commission.

Vallandigham contended that he had committed no offense against the laws of the United States and that, since he was a member of neither the land nor naval forces of the United States, a military commission had no power to try him. He was convicted and sentenced to be kept in close confinement in some fortress of the United States during the period of the war. The United States circuit court at Cincinnati refused to disturb the sentence, and the Supreme Court of the United States avoided entanglement in the controversy by holding that, since a military commission was not a court, the jurisdiction of the Supreme Court as defined by statute did not authorize the issuing of a writ which would make it possible for the Supreme Court to review the decision of the commission. It was fortunate for the Court, already badly discredited because of the supposed attachment of a number of judges to the southern cause, that it was able to escape conflict with the Executive over the extent of military powers during the period of the war. As for Vallandigham, Lincoln tempered severity with humor by ordering him banished within the Confederate lines.

## THE MILLIGAN CASE

It was not until 1866, after the war was over, that the Supreme Court passed upon the power of military commissions to try civilians in areas, not in the immediate theater of war, where the civil courts were open and functioning. In this case the Court, speaking through Justice Davis, a Lincoln appointee, laid a restraining hand upon the exercise of military power. The case involved Lambdin P. Milligan, a citizen of Indiana who apparently participated in a conspiracy against the United States much more serious than the public address delivered by Vallandigham. Milligan was arrested by military authorities and was tried by a military commission and sentenced to death. He petitioned the United States circuit court in Indiana for release, contending that he was unlawfully imprisoned.

Superficially the case was much like that of Vallandigham. As to procedure, however, it was different in one important respect. In Vallandigham's case there was no way of taking an appeal from the decision of the military commission to a federal court. In the Milligan case, the situation was such that the Habeas Corpus Act of March 3, 1863, seemed to require that the circuit court order Milligan's release. That act provided that, where a grand jury had met after a prisoner was taken into custody and had terminated its session without finding an indictment, it should be the duty of the judge of the court to order the prisoner discharged. It happened that a grand jury having jurisdiction over the area had met and adjourned while Milligan was in the hands of military authorities, without taking any action against him. Pursuant to the law, therefore, the court had to consider the question of his release. The judges of the circuit court, being divided as to their duty in the matter, certified the question to the Supreme Court so as to get instructions from it. Said Justice Davis, giving the opinion of the Court:

> During the late wicked rebellion the temper of the times did not allow that calmness in deliberation and discussion so necessary to a correct conclusion of a purely judicial question. Then, considerations of safety were mingled with the exercise of power, and feelings and interests prevailed which are happily terminated. Now that the public safety is assured, this question, as well as all others, can be discussed and decided without passion or the admixture of any element not required to form a legal judgment. We approach the investigation of this case fully sensible of the magnitude of the inquiry and the necessity of full and cautious deliberation.[31]

It was essential to the safety of every government, he declared, that, in a crisis like that through which the United States had just passed, there should be a power somewhere of suspending the writ of habeas corpus. This did not mean, however, that martial law could be proclaimed throughout the entire country. "Martial law cannot arise from a threatened invasion. The necessity must be actual and present; the invasion real, such as effectually closes the courts and deposes the civil administration."[32] Such had not been the case in Indiana. "Martial rule can never exist where the courts are open and in the proper and unobstructed exercise of their jurisdiction."[33]

All members of the Supreme Court were agreed that the military commission in Indiana had no power to try Milligan. The logic of Justice Davis's opinion went farther, to the conclusion that, even if it chose to do so, Congress could not authorize trial by military commis-

---

[31] *Ex parte* Milligan, 4 Wallace 2, 109 (1866).    [32] *Ibid.*, p. 127.    [33] *Ibid.*, p. 127.

sion in cases of this kind. Four justices, with Chief Justice Chase as their spokesman, refused to go so far. They contended that there were circumstances in which, the privilege of the writ of habeas corpus being suspended, trial and punishment by military commissions in states where civil courts were open might be authorized by Congress. They maintained that, "when the nation is involved in war, and some portions of the country are invaded, and all are exposed to invasion, it is within the power of Congress to determine to what states or districts such great and imminent public danger exists as justifies the authorization of military tribunals for the trial of crimes and offenses against the discipline or security of the army or against the public safety." [34] Although in Indiana the judges and officers of the courts were loyal to the government, it might have been otherwise. "In times of rebellion and civil war it may often happen, indeed, that judges and marshals will be in active sympathy with the rebels, and the courts their most efficient allies." [35] The minority of the Court refused to deny to Congress the power needed to deal with a situation of this kind.

The decision in the Milligan case had a continuing importance and the point on which the Court divided may have to be examined in the light of modern circumstances. During the period of the first World War it was contended that, since modern wars are fought, not merely by military forces, but also by all the industrial and commercial equipment of nations, enemy activity in any locality may be so dangerous as to render advisable resort to military tribunals. It was contended by certain senators and by an assistant attorney general of the United States that, because of the slowness with which the civil courts performed their functions and the lightness of the penalties applied, the safety of the nation depended upon the trial of certain types of offenders by military tribunals and the administering of the severe penalties which such tribunals were likely to prescribe. No such measures were taken, and it was widely contended that the Milligan decision stood in the way. The possibility remains, however, that in a future military crisis resort to military tribunals might be regarded as necessary to national safety, and, if judicial review were secured, the doctrine presented in the Milligan decision might be modified.[36]

[34] *Ibid.,* p. 140.          [35] *Ibid.,* p. 141.

[36] For discussion of the issue during the first World War see chapter 26. The saboteur case, *Ex parte* Quirin, 317 U.S. 1 (1942), decided during the second World War, seemed to give a possible opening for modernizing the Milligan decision, but the Supreme Court cautiously avoided elaboration upon the doctrines involved. See chapter 38.

CENSORSHIP

During the period of the Civil War, Congress enacted no measure comparable to the Espionage Act of the first World War. It enacted no measure comparable to those of the World-War period concerning exclusion of materials from the mails. It provided no direct authorization for censorship of any kind. The statutes of the period make no mention of censorship. Yet, obviously, divided as the country was, with enemy sympathizers within close range of government departments and with military establishments eager to collect and convey information likely to have value to the enemy, it was necessary to establish some degree of control over communications.[37] An attempt was made, with some success, to work out between military authorities and representatives of the press an understanding as to the information of military significance which might be published. At the beginning of the war the government took over telegraph lines going out of Washington and proceeded to censor dispatches through an official responsible at various times to one or another of the government departments. The censor, like most censors, seems to have performed his task with excessive zeal. An investigation by a committee of the House of Representatives disclosed the fact that censorship extended, not merely to military items, but also to many items of news commenting on the activities of the government in Washington and criticizing high officials.[38] The control exercised was irritating because it interfered with the sending of information that ought not to have been restricted. On the other hand, it was in part ineffective, because shrewdly phrased dispatches conveyed important information in spite of the scrutiny of the censor and, furthermore, because it was possible for some time to send from Baltimore and other points in the country dispatches which could not be sent from Washington.

In January, 1862, Congress enacted a measure authorizing the President to take possession of railroads and telegraph lines in the United States.[39] Soon afterward the government took military possession of all the telegraph lines in the United States. The order of the Secretary of War stated that all telegraphic communications in regard to military operations not expressly authorized by the War Department, the commanding general, or the generals commanding armies in the field in the several departments were absolutely forbidden. All

[37] For discussion see Randall, *op. cit.*, chapter XIX, and materials cited.
[38] See House Report No. 64, 37th Cong., 2d sess.        [39] 12 Stat. 334.

newspapers publishing military news not authorized by the prescribed official authority were to be excluded thereafter from receiving information by telegraph or from transmitting their papers by railroad.[40] The order was broad enough to throttle any publication the government sought to eliminate, if a single offense of the type mentioned could be discovered.

Apart from these provisions for control, the government dealt with disloyal newspapers in two ways. First, military authorities sometimes arrested disloyal editors and imprisoned them indefinitely, or suppressed their papers, or both. Such measures, like many others taken by military authorities with reference to civilians and civilian activities, were not authorized by statutes. If they had a legal basis, it was in the exercise of the war powers of the government. The constitutionality of the military suppression of newspapers was not passed upon by the Supreme Court. In the light of the Milligan case, however, constitutionality was doubtful, to say the least.

The other device for dealing with newspapers opposing the war and urging that peace be made with the Confederate government was exclusion from the mails by order of the Postmaster General. That official dealt with a number of papers in this fashion, explaining, "To await the results of slow judicial prosecution was to allow crime to be consummated, with the expectation of subsequent punishment, instead of preventing its accomplishment by prompt and direct interference."[41] He phrased his constitutional justification as follows:

> The freedom of the press is secured by a high constitutional sanction. But it is freedom and not license that is guaranteed. It is to be used only for lawful purposes. It cannot aim blows at the existence of the government, the Constitution, and the Union, and at the same time claim its protection. As well could the assassin strike his blow at human life, at the same time claiming that his victim should not commit a breach of the peace by a counter-blow. While, therefore, this department neither enjoyed nor claimed the power to suppress such treasonable publications, but left them free to publish what they pleased, it could not be called upon to give them circulation. It could not and would not interfere with the freedom secured by law, but it could and did obstruct the dissemination of that license which was without the pale of the Constitution and law. The mails established by the United States government could not, upon any known principle of law or public right, be used for its destruction. As well

[40] *Messages and Papers of the Presidents*, VII, 3309-3310.
[41] House Misc. Doc. No. 16, 37th Cong., 3d sess., p. 2.

could the common carrier be legally required to transport a machine designed for the destruction of the vehicle conveying it, or an innkeeper be compelled to entertain a traveler whom he knew to be intending to commit a robbery in his house.[42]

The House committee on the judiciary approved of the action of the Postmaster General, even though it had been taken without specific congressional authorization.[43]   Said the committee:

> Every government, unless by its constitution restricted, has the most ample power of self-preservation, and it is by no means essential to that power that it should be enumerated among its expressly granted powers.  It springs from the essential elements of government itself, and the exercise of a power or means of the destruction of the government is as effectually prohibited by the very nature and character of our institutions as if it had been expressly written in the Constitution.[44]

Presumably, these sentiments had the approval of most loyal persons at the time.   No suit was brought in which the Supreme Court had to pass upon the constitutional and other legal questions involved. Many years later, however, at the beginning of the first World War, it seems to have been recognized that, whatever the legality and constitutionality of the exercise of sweeping powers by the Postmaster General, it was better policy to provide specifically by law for the exercise of these powers.   In this field, as in others, the coverage by statute was much broader during the first World War than during the Civil War.   The reason, or one of the reasons, was that in the early period the tradition of presidential guidance of legislative policy, even at a time of crisis, had not yet been worked out.   It was recognized, however, that in such a crisis speedy action under executive guidance was necessary for the winning of the war.   To a limited extent, therefore, amid the clamor of the minority about the usurpation of power and the suppression of the rights of the people, Congress abdicated in favor of the Executive, paving the way for further abdication in other crises, military or otherwise.

CONSCRIPTION

The provision of man-power for military purposes was one of the major tasks of Lincoln's administration.   Lincoln's first step was to issue a call for seventy-five thousand militia.   In calling out the

---

[42] *Ibid.,* p. 2.          [43] *Ibid.,* p. 10.          [44] *Ibid.,* p. 12.

militia he was clearly within the scope of powers given by the Constitution and laws. He went further, however, and issued calls for volunteers to serve three years in the regular army and navy. In the message subsequently delivered to Congress, he admitted tacitly that he had gone beyond his own powers, although he had done nothing that Congress was not competent to authorize. "These measures," he said, "whether strictly legal or not, were ventured upon under what appeared to be a popular demand and a public necessity, trusting then, as now, that Congress would readily ratify them. It is believed that nothing has been done beyond the constitutional competency of Congress." [45] Congress did ratify the action of the President and made further provision for the use of the militia.

The need for additional men forced Congress to consider conscription. The United States had never before resorted to compulsory military service. A measure had been close to enactment during the War of 1812, but had not been passed. Conscription had been opposed as contrary to the principles of liberty embodied in our political institutions. Some believed that it was not authorized by the Constitution. In any event, the belief was firmly ingrained that conscripts were poor soldiers in comparison with volunteers.

By an act of July 17, 1862, Congress cautiously approached the subject of compulsory military service. [46] The act gave the President power to reach down into the states and supervise the enrollment of man-power in the militia, which was to be called into the federal service. The measure proved inadequate. By an act of March 3, 1863, Congress provided for the conscription of men directly into the national forces. [47] So powerful was the criticism of the act that Lincoln drafted an address in its defense, intended to be used as an appeal to the people. Although it was not published, its language is significant as a revelation of the position of the President. The Constitution, he pointed out, declared that Congress should have power to raise and support armies.

> They tell us the law is unconstitutional. It is the first instance, I believe, in which the power of Congress to do a thing has ever been questioned in a case where the power is given by the Constitution in express terms. Whether a power can be implied when it is not expressed has often been the subject of controversy; but this is the first

[45] *Messages and Papers of the Presidents*, VII, 3225.     [46] 12 Stat. 597.
[47] 12 Stat. 731. For discussion of conscription during the Civil War see Randall, *op. cit.*, chapter XI.

case in which the degree of effrontery has been ventured upon, of denying a power which is plainly and distinctly written down in the Constitution.[48]

The Constitution gave Congress the power to raise armies, but it did not prescribe the mode. In such a case Congress must prescribe the mode or relinquish the power.

> Congress could not exercise the power to do the thing if it had not the power of providing a way to do it when no way is provided by the Constitution for doing it. In fact, Congress would not have the power to raise and support armies if even by the Constitution it were left to the option of any other, or others, to give or withhold the only mode of doing it. If the Constitution had prescribed a mode, Congress could and must follow that mode; but, as it is, the mode necessarily goes to Congress, with the power expressly given. The power is given fully, completely, unconditionally. It is not a power to raise armies if state authorities consent; nor if the men who compose the armies are entirely willing; but it is a power to raise and support armies given to Congress by the Constitution, without an if.[49]

Another unpublished manuscript of a very different kind was prepared on the Conscription Act. Chief Justice Taney, now greatly enfeebled, but still at the head of the Supreme Court, wrote drafts of opinions on a number of subjects connected with the war which might possibly come before the Supreme Court. One of them was entitled "Thoughts on the Conscription Law of the U. States." In this opinion Taney pronounced the Conscription Act unconstitutional. He emphasized again the division of powers between the federal and state governments, as he had done in the Booth cases. Although two separate governments exercised powers of sovereignty over the same territory and the same people at the same time, each of them was altogether independent of the other within its own sphere of action. The Conscription Act was an encroachment by the federal government upon the sovereignty of the states. In the Constitution the right of the states to maintain their own militia was clearly recognized. Yet under the Conscription Act the officers and men in the state militia might be taken by the federal government; with the effect of destroying the militia as such. The civil officers of the states, with the exception of the governor, might under the Conscription Act be taken in the same way and the state government thereby virtu-

---

[48] John G. Nicolay and John Hay, *Abraham Lincoln, A History* (10 vols., 1909), VII. 51.
[49] *Ibid.*, p. 52.

ally destroyed. The Constitution, Taney believed, allotted to the federal government no such power.[50]

The question of the constitutionality of this measure never reached the Supreme Court. It was dealt with in some state courts and lower federal courts, but without eliciting definitive answer. Not until after the enactment of a conscription measure in 1917 did the Supreme Court express itself unanimously in an opinion holding that the federal government had the constitutional power to raise armies by conscription.[51]

## THE LEGAL STATUS OF THE CIVIL WAR — THE BLOCKADE

By proclamations of April 19 and April 27, 1861, the President gave notice of the blockade of southern ports "in pursuance of the laws of the United States and of the law of nations." [52]  The proclamation of the blockade raised a number of delicate questions. In international law the right to establish a blockade existed only in conditions of war. War implied the existence of at least two belligerent parties. American statesmen took the position that the Confederacy was not a belligerent party in the full sense of the word and that the persons conducting hostilities against the United States were merely lawless bands of individuals engaged in an insurrection — individuals entitled to be treated, not as belligerents under the laws of war, but as traitors to the United States. The first proclamation of the President, indeed, declared that any person who should molest a vessel of the United States would "be held amenable to the laws of the United States for the prevention and punishment of piracy." Taking this position as to the relation between the United States and the southern rebels, the government objected to the proclamations of neutrality issued by Great Britain and other foreign nations. It struggled hard, and in this case successfully, to prevent general recognition of the Confederate States by foreign nations. In other words, the United States claimed, on the one hand, the benefit of war conditions when there was benefit to be derived, as in resort to the law of nations to justify the establishment of a blockade; but, on the other hand, where the United States would be injured by the recognition of a full-fledged war between two belligerents, it sought to classify the conflict as the

---

[50] See Swisher, *op. cit.*, pp. 570-571.
[51] Selective Draft Law Cases, 245 U.S. 366 (1918). For discussion see chapter 26.
[52] 12 Stat. 1258-1259.

suppression of an insurrection within the country and as a matter which was of no concern to foreign nations.

The questions of law were complicated by the fact that the proclamation had been issued at a time when Congress was not in session and prior to the time when any act was passed indicating the existence of a state of war. Under the Constitution the power to declare war was lodged in Congress. It was widely assumed that war could not exist in a legal sense until Congress made a formal declaration. In his message of July 4, 1861, to the newly assembled Congress, the President told of the establishment of the blockade and said that the action was believed to be strictly legal.[53] Congress did not issue a formal declaration of war. It passed no measure authorizing a blockade of southern ports on the basis of the laws of war. Almost immediately, however, it enacted a measure of July 13, 1861, which authorized the closing of the ports of the collection districts in which the collection of the revenue of the United States was obstructed. It provided, among other things, that "if, while said ports are so closed, any ship or vessel from beyond the United States, or having on board any articles subject to duties, shall enter or attempt to enter any such port, the same, together with its tackle, apparel, furniture, and cargo, shall be forfeited to the United States."[54] The act did not mention the blockade, but, apparently relying heavily upon the revenue powers of the federal government, it included provisions covering many of the activities hitherto supported only by the proclamation of the blockade issued by the President. By an act of August 6, 1861, as if to avoid difficulties from the possible illegality of orders issued by the President after March 4, 1861, Congress provided that all acts, proclamations, and orders issued by the President after that date, "respecting the army and navy of the United States, and calling out or relating to the militia or volunteers from the United States, are hereby approved and in all respects legalized and made valid, to the same intent and with the same effect as if they had been issued and done under the previous express authority and direction of the Congress of the United States."[55]

Although many legal questions arising out of the war either did not reach the Supreme Court at all or were not decided until the war was at an end, the power of the President to establish a blockade was

[53] *Messages and Papers of the Presidents,* VII, 3225.
[54] 12 Stat. 255, 257.
[55] 12 Stat. 326.

passed upon in the Prize Cases,[56] decided in 1863, and important questions as to the status of the war were discussed. All members of the Court agreed that the blockade was legal after the enactment of the measure of July 13, 1861, in which Congress in various provisions recognized the existence of a state of war and authorized the closing of southern ports.

On other important matters, the Court divided five to four. The majority, speaking through Justice Grier, upheld the legality of the blockade from the date of the presidential proclamation. To constitute a war, said Justice Grier, it was not necessary that both parties should be acknowledged as independent nations or sovereign states. It was not less a civil war because it might be called an insurrection by one side, the insurgents being considered as rebels or traitors. It was not necessary that the independence of the revolted province or state be acknowledged in order to constitute it a belligerent according to the law of nations. Although by the Constitution Congress alone had the power to declare a national or foreign war, a civil war was never publicly proclaimed. The Constitution required the President to take care that the laws be faithfully executed. He was commander-in-chief of the army and navy of the United States and of the militia of the several states when called into the actual service of the United States. He had no power to initiate or declare a war against a foreign nation or a domestic state; but he was authorized to call out the militia and use the military and naval forces of the United States in case of invasion by foreign nations and to suppress insurrection against the government of a state or of the United States. If war was made against the United States, the President was bound to resist by force. He did not initiate the war, but was bound to accept the challenge without waiting for any special legislative authority.

This greatest of civil wars was not gradually developed by popular commotion, tumultuous assemblies, or local unorganized insurrections. However long may have been its previous conception, it nevertheless sprung forth suddenly from the parent brain, a Minerva in the full panoply of war. The President was bound to meet it in the shape it presented itself, without waiting for Congress to baptize it with a name; and no name given to it by him or them could change the fact.[57]

[56] 2 Black 635.
[57] *Ibid.*, pp. 668-669.

The proclamation of the blockade, said the justice, was itself official and conclusive evidence to the Court that a state of war existed which demanded and authorized a recourse to such a measure under the circumstances peculiar to the case.

Even if it were necessary to the technical existence of a war that it should have a legislative sanction, the majority of the Court found that sanction in almost every act passed at the special session of Congress which met on July 4, 1861. That session was concerned almost exclusively with legislation that would enable the government to prosecute the war with vigor and efficiency. In addition to other measures, furthermore, the Court called attention to the act of August 6, sanctioning acts, proclamations, and orders of the President as if they had been issued and done under the previous express authority and direction of Congress. Without admitting that such an act was necessary under the circumstances, the majority of the Court indicated that, if the President had in any manner assumed powers for which congressional sanction or authority was necessary, this ratification had operated to cure the defect.

The four dissenting justices, speaking through Justice Nelson, admitted that the conflict became a war in the sense of the law of nations and of the Constitution upon the enactment of the law of July 13, 1861, but denied it that status before the date of the statute. Nelson contended that civil war, like any other war, could exist only by act of Congress, which required the assent of two of the great departments of the government — the executive and the legislative. True, the President had the power to suppress insurrection and repel invasion, but it did not become a war in the sense that a blockade might be authorized until action was taken by Congress.

Nelson scorned the idea that the ratifying measure of August 6, 1861, might be an *ex post facto* law, making illegal and providing punishment for the carrying on of trade which prior to that time had not violated any law. It is to be remembered, of course, that Nelson was speaking only for a minority of the Court. Yet it should also be remembered that, in dealing with this point, Justice Grier, for the majority, was considering what he regarded as nothing more than a hypothetical situation. He took the position that the proclamations of the President were valid without any supporting statute. While he remarked that, if the proclamations had originally exceeded the power of the President, the effect had been cured by a subsequent statute, he made no admission that any such defect existed. He did not find it necessary, therefore, to demonstrate at length the power of Congress to give validity to presidential orders by retroactive legislation. The extent of that power is not yet clear.[58]

## TREASON

Throughout the North all persons participating in and sympathizing with the rebellion were loosely classified and denounced as traitors and their punishment for the crime of treason was demanded.[59] The Constitution provided that "treason against the United States shall consist only in levying war against them, or in adhering to their enemies, giving them aid and comfort."[60] By the statutes in force when the war began, the death penalty was prescribed. Obviously, in spite of the hysteria of the times, not all the persons connected with the rebellion who fell into the hands of the federal government could be prosecuted and convicted of treason. Although the federal government never officially recognized the existence of the Confederate States, it did tacitly permit the application of the laws of war in the disposition of prisoners taken on either side and in other ways. Although the members of the southern forces were regarded as citizens of the United States engaged in war against the United States, it was utterly impracticable on a variety of grounds to make any attempt to convict them of treason. Most of the political prisoners who, by virtue of the suspension of the privilege of the writ of habeas corpus, were kept in prisons by military authorities were called traitors, but little attempt was made to prosecute them for treason.

Persons who burned railroad bridges and in other ways attempted sabotage of the government program were indicted in considerable numbers, for treason and allied offenses. In view of his attitude toward the war, there was much curiosity as to what Chief Justice Taney would do with the cases in his circuit. The United States attorney in Baltimore realized that the cases would have to be made very plain

---

[58] In the case of United States v. *The Francis Hatch*, Federal Case No. 15158, decided in 1864, District Judge Giles took a position very similar to that of Justice Grier in the Prize Cases. The case involved the confiscation of a vessel under regulations issued by the Treasury Department, alleged to be made pursuant to an act of Congress of July 13, 1861. The judge thought that the regulations were supported by the statute, but took the position that, even if they were not so supported, they were given validity by a subsequent act of July 2, 1864. In 1933 and 1934, in enacting banking legislation to deal with crisis conditions, Congress included provisions approving and confirming actions, regulations, rules, licenses, orders, and proclamations previously taken, promulgated, made, or issued by the President or the Secretary of the Treasury under the somewhat questionable color of earlier legislation. 48 Stat. 1, 343.

[59] For discussion see Randall, *op. cit.*, chapter IV.       [60] Article III, Section 3.

and conclusive if a conviction was to be expected. Taney postponed the cases from term to term without permitting them to be brought to trial. He explained his reasons in a letter to Justice Nelson. The official orders issued by military authorities and the arrest of civilians without assignment of cause, he said, showed that Maryland was under martial law and that the civil authority was powerless. A fair and impartial trial would be utterly impossible, since witnesses and jurors would feel that they might be imprisoned for anything they said displeasing to the military authority. If that happened, the Court would be unable to protect them. If the person on trial were acquitted, he might nevertheless be rearrested and imprisoned, and the Court could neither protect him nor punish the offenders. Taney refused to permit the degradation and disgrace of the judicial power in this manner. When the war came to an end, the persons indicted had not been brought to trial and the indictments were eventually dismissed.[61] The attitude of Justice Grier was somewhat similar in cases involving Confederate privateers who were brought to trial in Pennsylvania.[62] It is probable that the judiciary in various sections of the country prevented the application of extreme penalties. In no case was the death penalty applied for treason against the United States. Even though the law of treason was modified so as to permit the substitution of fine and imprisonment for the penalty of death,[63] it seems that most persons punished for giving aid to the rebellion were convicted for other offenses than that of treason.

EMANCIPATION

The significance of the steps taken during the war toward the emancipation of slaves [64] is apparent only in terms of the politics of slavery during the earlier years. A radical element in the North had long been spreading propaganda for the complete abolition of slavery. The more moderate Northerners, however, had opposed any attempt on the part of the federal government to interfere with the peculiar institution of the South. They sought only to prevent the spread of slavery into new territory. In order to keep peace within the Union, they insisted on making broad concessions to the South where southern interests were involved. While apparently convinced that the

---

[61] See Swisher, op. cit., pp. 557-560.     [62] See Randall, op. cit., pp. 92-93.

[63] 12 Stat. 589, 590.

[64] For an account of the steps toward emancipation see Randall, op. cit., chapters XV — XVI.

nation could not permanently exist half-slave and half-free, Lincoln made it clear on entering the presidency that he had no intention of interfering with slavery where it was already established. After the war had begun, the war aims of the federal government, as he saw them, involved, not necessarily the abolition of slavery, but the preservation of the Union.

When the South seceded in spite of northern forbearance toward slavery, however, many northern statesmen could see no reason why forbearance should continue. If the Union was now to be saved, it would be saved by force and not by respecting an institution they detested. Prevailing attitudes were changed, furthermore, by the fact that Southerners disappeared from the councils of the federal government and that uncompromising abolitionists gained influence in increasing numbers, both in civil and military positions. Federal legislation dealing with the conduct of the war, and providing, among other things, for the seizure of property used by the South in its war activities or owned by "rebels," provided in various ways for the confiscation or liberation of slave property. The enforcement of fugitive-slave legislation lapsed completely as far as slaves escaping from the seceding states were concerned. With the passage of time the doing away with slavery became more and more an integral part of the program of the federal government in its war to preserve the Union. Both at home and abroad, the war was portrayed as a great moral crusade to do away with an evil institution.

The President and many members of Congress favored at first a long-discussed plan to have the government share in the property loss involved in emancipation. By an act of April 16, 1862, Congress provided for the release of slaves in the District of Columbia and for compensation to loyal owners from the government up to three hundred dollars for each person liberated.[65] The amount was far less than the market value of the slaves, but the loss was nevertheless substantially reduced. In his annual message of December 1, 1862, the President recommended that Congress adopt a constitutional amendment as a part of a plan whereby the federal government would give financial aid to states abolishing slavery and provide a compensation to the owners.[66] By the time the war was over, however, the intolerance for slavery was so great that the government made no attempt to reimburse owners who lost their property.

While the proposition was pending for aiding the states to liberate

[65] 12 Stat. 376.     [66] *Messages and Papers of the Presidents,* VII, 3337.

slaves within their borders, the President, after due warning, issued his proclamation that "all persons held as slaves within any state or designated part of a state, the people whereof shall be in rebellion against the United States, shall be then, thenceforward, and forever free; and the executive government of the United States, including the military and naval authority thereof, will recognize and maintain the freedom of such persons and will do no act or acts to repress such persons, or any of them, in any efforts they may make for their actual freedom." [67]  The legality of the proclamation, issued without any pretense of congressional authorization, has been much discussed.  It had no support in the Constitution except in the war powers of the President.  There was question whether it could have any practical effect, since it applied only to the area in rebellion.  It did have an important propaganda effect abroad, and within the rebel states it may have encouraged some slaves to leave their masters, thereby disrupting the social order and hastening the final breakdown.  From a practical point of view, the legality of the Proclamation of Emancipation had little importance because of the later adoption of the Thirteenth Amendment, providing that "neither slavery nor involuntary servitude, except as a punishment for crime whereof the party shall have been duly convicted, shall exist within the United States or any place subject to their jurisdiction."

## THE PARTITION OF VIRGINIA

At the beginning of the war, the state of Virginia extended from the Atlantic Ocean to the Ohio River.  The vast level or rolling section to the eastward, which was or had been a fertile crop-producing area, was linked politically with a huge rugged tract west of the mountains where modes of living were strikingly different and where interests were far more closely linked with the western country than with the eastern part of the state.  The division of Virginia into two states must have seemed a logical possibility for many years before the division took place.  Yet a state seldom surrendered territory willingly.  The Constitution provided that "no new state shall be formed or erected within the jurisdiction of any other state . . . without the consent of the legislatures of the states concerned as well as of the Congress." [68]

Although sentiment in western Virginia, as in all the border states, was divided, the people, who owned few slaves, were predominantly

---

[67] *Ibid.*, pp. 3358-3359.     [68] Article IV, Section 3.

out of sympathy with the rebellion. When Virginia seceded, therefore, the western area formed a new Virginia government, which for the most part was treated by the federal government as the true government of Virginia during the period of the war. That government, made up predominantly of westerners, took advantage of the occasion to give formal consent to the separation of the western counties from the state of Virginia, to form the new state of West Virginia.

Although only in fiction had the Virginia known to history given its consent to the creation of West Virginia out of its territory, Congress, believing that the admission of the new state would aid in the suppression of the rebellion, passed an act admitting West Virginia into the Union. Although the cabinet was divided and the Attorney General submitted an opinion that it was unconstitutional and inexpedient,[69] the President reluctantly signed the measure, and West Virginia was admitted into the Union. The feeble and largely fictitious government of Virginia continued to function throughout the period of the war, whereafter it disappeared in the new régime of Reconstruction.[70]

## CONGRESS AND THE CONDUCT OF THE WAR

By delaying until July 4, 1861, the meeting of the special session of Congress, the President entrenched himself firmly in a position of war leadership, so that he was able to continue in control in spite of the competition of Congress. The calls for militia and volunteers, the proclamations of blockade, and other important steps connected with the war were taken as a result of policy made by him rather than by Congress. Large sections of the North were so whole-heartedly back of him and many members of Congress were so ardently in favor of the policies he had initiated that, in spite of criticism by a minority of dissenters and by persons jealous of legislative prerogatives, Congress on the whole gave the President support. It sanctioned directly many of the steps he had taken on his own initiative, and enacted measures to expand the personnel and equipment of the armed forces, to eliminate commerce between the seceding states and the outside world, and in other ways to promote the vigorous prosecution of the war to suppress the rebellion.

The President, as commander-in-chief of the army and navy, kept

[69] 10 *Opinions of the Attorneys General* 426.

[70] For discussion of the partition of Virginia see Randall, *op. cit.*, chapter **XVIII** and materials cited.

in his own hands and in those of his subordinates the choice of military personnel and the management of military operations. In December, 1861, looking back upon a period of military disasters, Congress began an indirect encroachment upon the management of the war. At that time Senator Zachariah Chandler proposed the creation of a committee to investigate disasters at Bull Run and at another point. The idea quickly expanded into a broader plan.[71] A senator objected that such inquiries reflected, "not upon military officers, but upon civil officers — upon the highest civil officer of the government. I say that these investigations lead in that direction, and therefore we ought not to appoint such committees."[72] Another held that, if an inquiry was to be made, it should be made by military authorities rather than by Congress. "I believe in letting the military authorities manage the army. If they manage it badly, we shall make a bad matter worse by tampering and interfering, and that is all that will grow out of our action. If it is badly managed now, I am sorry; I do not believe it is; but if it be, in Heaven's name do not let us make it worse by tampering, for worse we shall make it, and only worse."[73]

Senator William P. Fessenden disagreed, rejecting the doctrine

> that Congress has nothing in the world to do but pass appropriations and leave other public agents to dispose of the money at their pleasure, no matter what may be the opinion of the country and the opinion of us, as senators, as to the manner in which the means placed at the disposal of those agents have been or shall be used.[74] . . . We are not under the command of the military of this country. They are under ours as a Congress; and I stand here to maintain it.[75]

He professed friendship for the administration, but he thought it time for a gentle hint that the representatives of the people deemed it their duty to keep a watchful eye over the proceedings of executive agents, whatever they might be called and whatever might be their position. Senator John Sherman agreed, saying, "In my judgment, this ought to be a committee of inquiry into the general conduct of the war."[76]

The resolution was revised and passed to provide "that a joint committee of three members of the Senate and four members of the

[71] 32 *Congressional Globe* 16-17.    [72] Senator Samuel C. Pomeroy, *ibid.*, p. 29.
[73] Senator Lafayette S. Foster, *ibid.*, p. 30.    [74] *Ibid.*, p. 30.
[75] *Ibid.*, p. 31.    [76] *Ibid.*, p. 31.

House of Representatives be appointed to inquire into the conduct of the present war, and that they have power to send for persons and papers and to sit during the sessions of either house of Congress." [77] The members originally chosen from the Senate were Benjamin F. Wade, Zachariah Chandler, and Andrew Johnson. The House members were George W. Julian, John Covode, Daniel Gooch, and Moses F. Odell. The committee was active throughout the period of the war, under the domination of men whose sentiments were characterized as radical. It sharply criticized military officers chosen by the President; it criticized excessive caution on the part of military leaders; it was intensely abolitionist in its attitude; and it was ready to suspect and to discover the worst as far as charges of southern misconduct were concerned. It made large numbers of investigations and presented voluminous reports of its findings. [78]

The committee went far beyond the mere investigation of military disasters. How far was indicated on January 21, 1862, when it reported in the Senate through Senator Wade, its chairman, a bill "to authorize the President of the United States, in certain cases, to take possession of railroad and telegraph lines." [79] Under the bill all properties and facilities of telegraph and railroad lines could be taken over by the President for the period of the war. Officers, agents, and employees could be placed under military control. Any attempts at obstruction of the lines "in any state or district in which the laws of the United States are opposed" which were "too powerful to be suppressed by the ordinary course of judicial proceedings" or any attempts to injure or destroy the property were to be "punished as a military offense, by death, or such other penalty as a court-martial may impose." [80] Three commissioners were to be appointed by the President, by and with the advice and consent of the Senate, to assess and determine damages and compensation. Administration was to be under the supervision of the Secretary of War.

The purpose of the measure was not, as later, in the period of the first World War, to provide for unified control of all the railroads of

[77] *Ibid.*, p. 32.

[78] For discussion of the committee see William Whatley Pierson, Jr., "The Committee on the Conduct of the Civil War," *American Historical Review*, XXIII (April, 1918), 550-576, and T. Harry Williams, "The Committee on the Conduct of the War," *The Journal of the American Military Institute*, III (fall, 1939), 139. For the reports of the committee see Senate Report No. 108, 37th Cong., 3d sess., and Senate Report No. 142 and Supplement thereto, 38th Cong., 2d sess.

[79] 32 *Congressional Globe* 427. For debate see *ibid.*, pp. 506 ff.    [80] 12 Stat. 334.

the country in the interest of efficiency.  Senator Wade stated that it would not disturb any road the owners of which were willing to let it come into the use of the government and to do the business of the government to the best of their ability.  It was evident, he said, that it would be necessary for the government to seize and take possession of some roads, but they would be few in number.

> Indeed, it will be done in no case unless it becomes absolutely necessary to do it in order to carry on the business of the government for the purposes of the war.  There are probably but very few railroads in the loyal states where this would be refused, the government paying them as much as anybody else.  The fact is that the bill is more radical and sweeping in its terms than it ever will be in its operation.[81]

Perhaps because of this statement, the debate turned, not upon the invasion of rights of property, but upon the extent of the war powers over individuals and the responsibility of Congress in connection with the exercise of the war powers.  Senator Garrett Davis thought that to punish interference with the railroads as a military offense was palpably unconstitutional.  He reminded the Senate of the constitutional provision that the trial of all crimes except in cases of impeachment must be by jury.  He thought the provision applied to every citizen except when the offense arose in the military or naval service of the United States.  Senator Wade replied that employees of railroads engaged in carrying soldiers, provisions, and armaments ought to be governed by military law as were other civilian functionaries, such as teamsters, who were closely connected with the armed forces.[82]  Senator Trumbull sought vainly to narrow the bill to apply to insurrectionary districts, where he thought it wholly legitimate.[83]

Senator Wade argued that this bill merely regulated the exercise of powers already held by the government.  This regulatory power belonged in Congress.  "I hold that every power that the government may rightfully exercise in time of war may be regulated and restricted by Congress if we see fit to do it."[84]  It was not only the right, but the duty of Congress to prescribe the rules upon which war should be declared, and pursuant to which it should be conducted.  "The representatives of the people, clothed with all power, have a right to say precisely upon what principles that war shall be conducted from the beginning to the end."[85]

[81] 32 *Congressional Globe* 506.     [82] *Ibid.*, p. 507.     [83] *Ibid.*, p. 508.
[84] *Ibid.*, p. 509.     [85] *Ibid.*, p. 513.

After additional important debate,[86] the measure was adopted, but the constitutional controversy as to the line of jurisdiction between the President and Congress in the conduct of a war remained, and still remains, unsettled. Throughout the period of the Civil War, Congress enacted no measures placing important restrictions upon the powers of the President. The joint committee on the conduct of the war seems, at least during the earlier years, to have co-operated with and given aid to the administration. Military authorities resented its interference and protested against the investigations which followed upon military disasters and embarrassed commanders in whom the committee lacked confidence. The President at times acted upon the advice of the committee, both in matters of military organization and in the choice of commanders.[87]

The committee, made up from the first of radical members of Congress, seems to have become steadily more radical as the war progressed. It co-operated closely with the radical Secretary of War, Edwin M. Stanton, and therefore became linked with a contentious faction in the executive branch of the government. By 1864 its sentiments were so far different from those of the President as to make it virtually an anti-administration organization, and two of the leading members, Wade and Chandler, delivered acrimonious criticism of the President.[88] The committee constituted a mechanism by which Congress could make itself felt in the management of the war so as to avoid relegation to the position of a mere appropriating agency.

The relation which ought to exist between the two branches of the government in a war crisis is an extremely important governmental problem. Unfortunately, the experience with the joint committee on the conduct of the war gives too little information to provide a solution of the problem. During the first World War, President Wilson let it be known that he would brook no interference by such a committee.[89] Even in the period which preceded the second World War, President Franklin D. Roosevelt took the position that full powers should be placed in his hands. It is usually assumed that the efficiency supposed to result from centralization of power in the President is worth its cost in the surrender of legislative prerogative and in the possible perversion of national policy as interpreted by the

[86] *Ibid.*, pp. 515-516.
[87] Pierson, *op. cit.*, p. 568.
[88] *Ibid.*, p. 559. See also Nicolay and Hay, *op. cit.*, X, 316.
[89] For discussion see chapter 26.

legislative representatives of the people.  It is assumed, furthermore, that a war constitutes a national emergency, an aberration in national experience, in which it may be safe to suspend restrictions on national power because of the infrequency of such emergencies.  The tone of congressional debate during the Civil War suggests that some legislators preferred to overlook the assumption of arbitrary powers for the period of the emergency rather than regulate them and give them the sanction of legislative support.  In view of the frequent recurrence in later years of emergencies of various sorts, whether military or otherwise, it is highly questionable whether this attitude represents a farsighted view of sound national policy.

### THE REGULATION OF PRIVATE ENTERPRISE

Private enterprise underwent no such regimentation during the Civil War as that which it experienced during the first and second World Wars.  War was less highly mechanized.  The co-ordination of the industrial production of the entire country was less essential to success at arms than in the later periods.  Vast areas of the farming section of the country and large numbers of plants and mercantile establishments were affected but little.  The production of supplies for the forces of the Union brought profitable business to many establishments without bringing a corresponding degree of regulation.  The unsettled currency and banking situation, to be discussed in a later chapter, provided disturbance, the shifting value of the currency made exchange unstable, and the legal-tender provision with reference to the irredeemable paper currency issued by the government created uneasiness; but private enterprise continued to function in spite of the disturbances.  Commerce was restricted mainly as restriction was necessary to prevent trade which might be helpful to the Confederacy.

It was only in connection with railroad and telegraph lines that the assumption of broad governmental control of private enterprise was threatened.  After the enactment of the statute of January 31, 1862, authorizing the President to take possession of railroad and telegraph lines, a military supervisor of telegraph messages throughout the United States and a military superintendent of all telegraph lines and offices in the United States were appointed.  The War Department announced that it was taking military possession of all the telegraph lines in the United States, adding, however, that "this possession and control of the telegraph lines is not intended to interfere in any respect with the ordinary affairs of the companies or with private business." [90] The operation of telegraph lines was supervised wherever such supervision was deemed necessary for military purposes. In the border states and in the South many hundreds of miles of telegraph lines were constructed. The construction of new lines by private companies was encouraged, at times with the provision that the United States should have priority in their use. [91]

As to railroads, the following order was announced on May 25, 1862:

By virtue of the authority vested by act of Congress, the President takes military possession of all the railroads in the United States from and after this date until further order, and directs that the respective railroad companies, their officers and servants, shall hold themselves in readiness for the transportation of such troops and munitions of war as may be ordered by the military authorities, to the exclusion of all other business. [92]

For military purposes the government constructed many miles of railroads in the South, and repaired and reconstructed previously existing lines which had been destroyed by the southern armies. At the close of the war the government held more than seven and a half million dollars' worth of railroad property in the southern states. The property was disposed of to private railroad companies. [93]

As to lines in the North, only in a few instances did the government take actual control. A line in Pennsylvania was taken over for some three weeks during the summer of 1863 for the transportation of wounded soldiers. [94] There may have been other instances. In any event, the authorization to take control operated as an effective threat against companies suspected of doing less than their best in aiding the government. It was thought, indeed, that one reason for the enactment of the statute was the need for some form of possible coercion over the Baltimore and Ohio Railroad, [95] which had not given all the service desired.

Railroad services into Washington were at best inadequate during

[90] *Messages and Papers of the Presidents*, VII, 3309-3310.
[91] See for example 13 Stat. 373-374.
[92] *Messages and Papers of the Presidents*, VII, 3314.
[93] Lewis Henry Haney, *A Congressional History of Railways in the United States, 1850-1887* (1910), p. 165.
[94] Herman King Murphey, "The Northern Railroads and the Civil War," *Mississippi Valley Historical Review*, V (December, 1918), 329.
[95] Festus P Summers, *The Baltimore and Ohio in the Civil War* (1939), p. 212.

the military crisis.   The problem of building additional lines, either through private companies or through the government itself, was much discussed.   On March 3, 1863, a select committee of the House of Representatives reported favorably on a project for construction of a railroad line between New York and Washington.   The committee professed no doubt as to the authority of the government to create the important arm of its service "as a means for providing for the common defense and the general welfare of its people."   The establishment of post roads was one of the powers of Congress expressly enumerated in the Constitution, as was also the authority to make all laws which should be necessary and proper for carrying into effect all other powers vested by the Constitution in the government of the United States.   "The narrowest possible construction of these powers will hardly deny the government the right to provide for the protection of its capital and for the transporting with utmost dispatch of military forces and munitions of war in times of national peril such as now, unhappily, confronts us." [96]

The proposed line was to be constructed by a private company pursuant to a right given by the federal government to construct a military and postal route.[97]   The government was to give its patronage to the new road, to have extensive powers of regulation, and to enjoy priority and preference in all cases requiring haste in transportation. The road was to be subject to the proper control of the government, which was to be officially represented in its management and have a supervisory direction of its location and of the basis of its finances and the character of its securities.[98]

The competing lines had friends in Congress who were able to keep the bill from being reported.   Other proposals for competing lines in certain sections of the East were subsequently made, but they likewise were unsuccessful.   The constitutional questions were not fully discussed.   Those favoring the establishment of new lines took the position that the federal government had the power to authorize them in the exercise of its military powers and its powers to establish post roads, while the opposition contended that the federal government had no power to invade the jurisdiction of the states by authorizing the establishment of competing lines which the states themselves were unwilling to authorize.   They referred back to the extended debates over internal improvements during the eighteen-twenties and thirties

[96] House Report No. 63, 37th Cong., 3d sess., p. 2.     [97] Summers, *op. cit.,* p. 216.
[98] House Report No. 63, 37th Cong., 3d sess., p. 4.

and emphasized the apparent decision of the federal government, whatever its reasons, to withdraw from competition with the states in providing internal improvements.[99]

In the western part of the United States the situation was very different. Throughout vast areas there was no problem of competing lines. For military purposes as well as others the government deemed it expedient to grant large tracts of land and to make extensive loans in order to link the West with the East by railroad. Congress chartered the companies that were to build the great lines of the Union Pacific and the Northern Pacific during the period of the war and made extensive grants to other companies holding state charters.[100] The important lines provided for were not completed until the war was at an end and they would doubtless have been built had the war not taken place. Yet the efforts of Congress to bring about the building of a number of the lines was an integral part of a far-reaching military program. The development merged almost imperceptibly with the period of expansion which followed the war. While it cannot be said that the war brought any striking changes in the relations of the federal government to private enterprise, it seems, nevertheless, to have created some awareness of the possibilities of government control, both in the minds of those interested in using the government as an instrument for the expansion of business and industry for private profit and in the minds of others who had no desire to submit to federal regulation any more than to state regulation of their vested interests.

[99] See 35 *Congressional Globe* 911-914.     [100] Haney, *op. cit.*, pp. 19-20.

# CHAPTER 15

# RECONSTRUCTION

THE SERIES OF EVENTS normally grouped under the term "Reconstruction" are infinite in their number and in their interconnections. It is necessary here to deal only with those directly bearing upon the Constitution and to emphasize those having permanent rather than temporary significance. Two struggles stand out in the events of the period: the struggle between the President and Congress over the control of Reconstruction and the struggle for and against the extension of the protection of the Constitution over the varied civil and political rights of individuals. Their history provides the content of this chapter.

## CONGRESS AND THE PRESIDENT

In the prosecution of the war, President Lincoln had been less venomous toward the enemy than the radical members of Congress had desired. The joint committee on the conduct of the war had grown hostile to him because of the mildness of his policy. The radicals were gratified at the change in the presidency made possible by the death of Lincoln. In a political caucus held a few hours after his death they expressed themselves in favor of an entire change in the cabinet and of a line of policy less conciliatory toward the South than that of Lincoln. The new President, Andrew Johnson, had been one of the original members of the joint committee on the conduct of the war. Although he had left the Senate to serve as military governor of Tennessee, the committee seems to have assumed for various reasons that his sentiments were still in harmony with their own. The committee called on him and expressed its sentiments through Senator Wade as follows: "Johnson, we have faith in you. By the gods, there will be no trouble now in running the government." [1]

The expected harmony was not achieved. Except in his attitude

[1] John G. Nicolay and John Hay, *Abraham Lincoln, A History* (10 vols., 1909), X, 316.

toward those responsible for the assassination of Lincoln, Johnson was much less vindictive toward the South than were the radicals. Furthermore, he lacked the discipline necessary for an Executive who must compete for power with a Congress jealous of its own prerogatives. The situation would have been difficult for any occupant of the presidency. Apart from the specific issues of Reconstruction, Congress was determined to return to its position as the policy-making agency of the government. If the President sought to retain the position of leadership taken by his predecessor, a clash with Congress was probably inevitable, whatever his attitude toward the methods of Reconstruction.

During the summer of 1865, the President made surveys of conditions in the South and proceeded with plans for restoration of the southern states to the Union. In his annual message to Congress in December of that year, he reported that provisional governors had been appointed for the states, conventions called, governors elected, legislatures assembled, and senators and representatives chosen to the Congress. As far as possible the federal courts in the South had been reopened. The blockade had been removed and custom-houses reestablished in ports of entry for the collection of federal revenues.[2]

Congress refused to accept the program. It was opposed both to the acceptance of presidential leadership in general and to the specific policy adopted. The radicals insisted that the class of people hitherto dominant in the South could not be trusted to defend civil and political rights of persons whom they had hitherto owned as slaves. It was true that five of the states had ratified the constitutional amendment abolishing slavery and involuntary servitude. One had refused to ratify on the ground that in the states hitherto under control of the Confederacy slavery had already been abolished by presidential proclamation. Other steps had been taken by the states themselves toward a return to their old position in the Union, but with recognition of the fact that the institution of slavery no longer existed.

In spite of a degree of acquiescence in the results of the war, however, the enactment of the so-called "black codes" by southern states made it clear that the freedmen were to be dealt with as a separate class and that from the beginning they were to be denied civil privileges enjoyed by white people. The victorious radicals of the North were determined to secure and guarantee complete equality of rights for the freedmen. They suspected Southerners of plans for re-

[2] *Messages and Papers of the Presidents*, VIII, 3555.

enslaving the Negroes. With the development of the controversy over the mode of Reconstruction, the radicals became more and more firmly convinced that they must avert a realignment between dominant political groups in the South and northern Democrats by which southern statesmen might again be able to control policies of the federal government. They were concerned about the problem of the reapportionment of representation in Congress. In determining apportionment in earlier years, each Negro held as a slave had counted as only three-fifths of one person. Since slavery had been abolished, Negroes would be counted in the same way as white persons, and southern representation in Congress would be greatly increased. If that representation was dominated by the traditional leadership of the South, it might constitute an effective threat to the continuation of northern control. For political reasons, therefore, as well as on humanitarian grounds, the radicals were determined to bring about the enfranchisement of southern Negroes and to give them full protection against domination by the former owners.

At the time when Johnson's first annual message to Congress was delivered, the ratification of the Thirteenth Amendment was almost complete — it was announced two weeks later — but this fact was insufficient to persuade Congress that the southern states were back in the Union and that the representatives they sent to Congress should be admitted. A joint committee on Reconstruction was appointed, consisting of six members from the Senate and nine from the House of Representatives. It proceeded to make a survey of conditions in the South for the purpose of offering recommendations to Congress.[3]

While the committee held hearings and worked on a draft of an additional constitutional amendment and other measures, Congress developed a variety of theories as to the position of the states which had joined the Confederacy. It was contended by some that they were in the position of conquered provinces and were subject completely to the control of the conquerors. Others argued that the southern states had in effect committed suicide, and still others that the offending states had temporarily forfeited their rights as members of the Union, but that those rights should be restored by congressional action. Among the influential leaders of Congress few

[3] For the report of the committee see House Report No. 30, 39th Cong., 1st sess. For the journal see Senate Doc. No. 711, 63d Cong. 3d sess., and Benjamin B. Kendrick, *The Journal of the Joint Committee of Fifteen on Reconstruction* (1914). For a detailed account of the history of Reconstruction see William A. Dunning, *Essays on the Civil War and Reconstruction* (1898).

believed that the President alone could restore the states to their former position in the Union.

In February, 1866, Congress sent to the President a Freedmen's Bureau bill providing for the continuation of a Freedmen's Bureau, previously established to take care of black refugees. It attempted further to protect the rights of newly emancipated Negroes by directing the President to give military protection in all cases where the civil rights and immunities accorded to white people were denied to former slaves. Pending the restoration of the southern states to the Union, officials of the Freedmen's Bureau were to have jurisdiction over the cases mentioned. The bill was passed as a war measure, but the President vetoed it, taking the position that the war was now at an end.[4] The bill failed to pass over the veto. Five months later, however, after a series of clashes between Congress and the President, another Freedmen's Bureau bill was enacted and became a law in spite of a veto.[5]

In the meantime, on Washington's Birthday, 1866, a few days after his first veto of a Freedmen's Bureau bill, Johnson made a violent public attack on the radical leaders in the Senate. This action notably widened the breach between the President and the radical leaders, who more and more were guiding the policies of Congress. In spite of efforts made at various points to bring about co-operation between the President and Congress, a condition of warfare was gradually developing.

The next important measure enacted was the Civil-Rights Act. It went beyond the authorization of the Thirteenth Amendment and provided that all persons born in the United States, with certain exceptions, were citizens of the United States. As citizens they would have the same rights to make and enforce contracts, to sue, to give evidence, to inherit, purchase, lease, sell, hold, and convey real and personal property, and would enjoy the same benefits of all laws and proceedings for the security of persons and property as in the case of white citizens, being subject only to the same pains and penalties, in spite of any law, statute, ordinance, regulation, or custom to the contrary. Penalties were provided for depriving any person, because of color or race, of the rights protected by the act. The whole purpose of the act was to insure to Negroes equality of civil rights. The declaration concerning citizenship was instrumental to that end. It disregarded the contention of the Supreme Court in the Dred Scott case

[4] *Messages and Papers of the Presidents*, VIII, 3596.     [5] *Ibid.*, p. 3620; 14 Stat. 173.

that within the meaning of the Constitution a Negro could not be a citizen of the United States.

The President vetoed the bill. He agreed that the freedmen must be protected to the full extent compatible with the Constitution, but he thought the details of the bill fraught with evil. The two races in the South had hitherto lived together under the relation of master and slave — capital owning labor. Now suddenly that relation was changed. Each party had equal power in settling the terms of their relation. If left to the laws that regulated capital and free labor, it was confidently believed that the problem would be worked out satisfactorily. The bill frustrated the adjustment which would otherwise take place.[6] Furthermore, he said, the provisions of the act

> interfere with the municipal legislation of the states, with the relations existing exclusively between a state and its citizens, or between inhabitants of the same state — an absorption and assumption of power by the general government which, if acquiesced in, must sap and destroy our federative system of limited powers and break down the barriers which preserve the rights of the states. It is another step, or rather stride, toward centralization and the concentration of all legislative powers in the national government. The tendency of the bill must be to resuscitate the spirit of rebellion and to arrest the progress of those influences which are more closely drawing around the states the bonds of union and peace.[7]

The opposition in Congress was now strong enough to bring about the enactment of the Civil-Rights Act over the President's veto.[8] Many persons doubted its constitutionality, however, and their doubts were in part responsible for the fact that the Fourteenth Amendment was submitted to the states — a matter to be discussed more fully in ensuing pages. Congress had won the upper hand and was able to keep it. By an act of March 2, 1867, entitled "An Act to provide for the more efficient government of the rebel states," [9] it divided the South into five military districts to be governed by military commanders. Civil tribunals continued to function only on the sufferance of the military authorities. Under the supervision of these authorities, new governments were to be established through the votes of an electorate described in such a way as to prevent control by the class formerly dominant in the South. After these states had ratified the Fourteenth Amendment and after that amendment had become a part of the

[6] *Messages and Papers of the Presidents*, VIII, 3610.
[7] *Ibid.*, p. 3611.      [8] See 14 Stat. 27.      [9] 14 Stat. 428.

Constitution, the states should be declared entitled to representation in Congress.

The bill was supported as a war measure, in spite of the fact that the end of the rebellion had been proclaimed more than a year earlier. The President vetoed the bill, denouncing the establishment of military rule in time of peace. It was passed over the veto. The provisions of the act, supported by supplementary legislation, were carried out. The South was subjected to military control, pending the establishment of new state governments with the aid of Negro suffrage exercised under the influence of carpetbagger immigrants from the North. Reconstruction was carried on nominally under the direction of the President as commander-in-chief of the army. Actual control was in the hands of Congress and of Edwin M. Stanton, Secretary of War, whom Congress attempted to keep in office in spite of the determination of the President to remove an officer who refused to take orders from his chief.

IMPEACHMENT

If under the cover of the necessities of war, President Lincoln had encroached upon the field belonging to Congress, the situation was now reversed. Perhaps the culminating act of congressional encroachment was the "Act regulating the tenure of certain civil officers." [10] The effect of that act was that any civil officer of the United States appointed by the President by and with the advice and consent of the Senate was to hold office until a successor had been appointed in like manner. The President vetoed the bill [11] as an unconstitutional encroachment upon his powers. [12] It was repassed over the veto. The act provided that, during a recess of the Senate, the President might, with certain exceptions, suspend officers whom he deemed guilty of misconduct, appointing other persons to fulfill their functions. After the Senate had reassembled and the President had explained his action, an officer must be reinstated if the Senate did not concur in his removal. During the summer of 1867, Johnson asked for Stanton's resignation as Secretary of War. Stanton refused. The President suspended him, authorized General Grant to act as Secretary of War *ad interim*, and, as if in recognition of the validity of the Tenure-of-Office Act, made a report of his action to the Senate at the begin-

[10] 14 Stat. 430.        [11] *Messages and Papers of the Presidents*, VIII, 3690.
[12] For early discussions of the constitutional question see chapter 3, pp. 51 ﬀ. For recent discussion see chapter 30.

ning or the ensuing session. The Senate refused to concur in the suspension, Grant withdrew, and Stanton reassumed the duties of his office. Soon afterward the President ordered Stanton's removal. Stanton refused to surrender the office, and the man appointed to exercise the duties of the office of Secretary of War was temporarily placed under arrest. The incident provided the long-sought-for occasion for impeachment of the President. For the first time — and thus far the only time — the House of Representatives impeached (that is, formally accused) the President of the United States of high crimes and misdemeanors and brought him to trial at the bar of the Senate, the Chief Justice of the United States presiding.

It has been well said that "the trial stands today as the most regrettable and shameful exhibition of personal spite and ruthless partisanship in American history."[12] The legal grounds for action against the President were shadowy indeed. Although Johnson had vetoed the several Reconstruction measures, he had not attempted to interfere with their enforcement. It could not be shown that his removal of Stanton was for the purpose of blocking the administration of those acts. Furthermore, the language of the Tenure-of-Office Act was such that, although it barred the removal of a cabinet officer appointed by him unless the Senate could be persuaded to concur, it was not clear that it barred the removal of such an officer who had been appointed by his predecessor. Stanton had been appointed by Lincoln and not by Johnson.

The President escaped conviction by the narrow margin of one vote. From the point of view of the immediate consequences to the country, the issue was perhaps not highly important. Had the President been removed, the radicals in Congress would have dominated the government throughout the remainder of his administration; but less than a year of the presidential term remained, and it is improbable that policies would have been sufficiently different to have any great effect upon the public welfare. As a precedent, however, conviction and removal of the President from office would have been a major disaster. It would have meant that any President who antagonized the requisite number of members of the Senate and the House of Representatives would face the threat of removal from office. While it is true that the law remained the same, whatever the action taken as to President Johnson, precedents have real importance in molding the conduct of the future. They would have been no less

[12] Andrew C. McLaughlin, *A Constitutional History of the United States* (1935), p. 675.

important in the whittling-down of the powers of the President than they have been in recent years in expanding the powers of that officer in his relations to Congress.

When the trial was over, Stanton surrendered the office of Secretary of War. At the beginning of the next administration he was rewarded for faithful service by appointment and confirmation as an associate justice of the Supreme Court — although he died before taking his position on the bench. In the meantime, for the remainder of his administration Johnson appointed another man to the position of Secretary of War "in place of Edwin M. Stanton, removed." The Tenure-of-Office Act was modified during the administration of President Grant and was later repealed without judicial determination of its constitutionality. It was not until 1926, in connection with another statute, that the Supreme Court dealt with the issues involved. The Court held that Congress could not make the concurrence of the Senate a condition of the removal of a political officer appointed by the President by and with the advice and consent of the Senate.[14] It can be said in summary, therefore, that President Johnson came near to being removed for violation of an unconstitutional statute, even though, because of the vagueness of the language of the statute itself, the fact of its violation was not clearly established. The impeachment trial represented the low point in American history for the office of President in its relation to Congress.

### THE SUPREME COURT AND RECONSTRUCTION

With the decision in the Dred Scott case the Supreme Court fell upon evil times. Its prestige in the North was largely destroyed and in the South was hardly an asset. Because of clashes over the Dred Scott decision and for other reasons, Justice Curtis, one of the two dissenters, resigned from the Court soon after the decision was announced. Justice Campbell resigned to align himself with the South, and Daniel and McLean died on the eve of the Civil War. President Buchanan filled one vacancy by the appointment of Nathan Clifford, of Maine, but three positions were left to be filled by Lincoln. He appointed Noah H. Swayne, of Ohio, Samuel F. Miller, of Iowa, and David Davis, of Illinois.

The importance of the issues involved in the Prize Cases once again called to the attention of the country the strategic importance of the Supreme Court. There was uneasiness lest the Court hold

[1] Myers v. United States, 272 U.S. 52 (1926)

that the Civil War was not a war at all in the international sense, and that the blockade of southern ports was illegal.[15] While these cases were illustrating the importance of the loyalty of members of the Supreme Court, the attention of Congress was also fixed upon the problem of linking the Far West more closely to the federal government as a bar to secession. One of the considerations was the establishment on the Pacific coast of a full-fledged judicial circuit to which a justice of the Supreme Court would be allocated. Between the time of the argument and of the decision of the Prize Cases, Congress passed an act creating a tenth circuit and a tenth position on the Supreme Court. The President filled the position by the appointment of Stephen J. Field, a member of the supreme court of California. The death of Chief Justice Taney toward the end of 1864 enabled President Lincoln to appoint Salmon P. Chase as presiding officer of the Court. When Justice Catron died in May, 1865, his position was left unfilled, the membership of the Court being reduced to nine, where it had stood from 1837 to 1863. Five of the nine justices were Lincoln appointees. Only three remained who had participated in the Dred Scott decision. It was virtually a new Court, therefore, that was to pass upon the questions arising out of the Civil War.

The change in the membership of the Court did not bring full acquiescence in the war program of the administration. The decision in the Milligan case, holding unconstitutional the trial of civilians by military tribunals outside the theater of war, was greeted with a virulence reminiscent of that produced by the Dred Scott decision.[16] Northern radicals were angered still further by decisions in two so-called Test-Oath Cases, announced in January, 1867. One case, Cummings v. Missouri,[17] arose under a state law, and the other Ex parte Garland,[18] arose under an act of Congress. The Missouri law required that, before any person in the state could perform any of a long list of functions, he must take an oath, not merely that he would support the Constitution and laws of the United States, but also that he had always been loyal to the United States. It was necessary to take such an oath before he could vote at any election, hold an office, be a candidate for office, serve as a juror, practice as an attorney or counselor-at-law, be an officer of any corporation, teach in any school, public or private, hold property in trust for any religious organization, act as a bishop, priest, deacon, minister, elder, or other clergy-

[15] See chapter 14.　　　[16] See *ibid.*　　　[17] 4 Wallace 277.　　　[18] 4 Wallace 333

man of any religious denomination, or preach or teach or solemnize marriages. Penalties were prescribed for performing any of these functions without taking the oath, and for swearing falsely. The effect of the statute, therefore, was to exclude from a great variety of activities persons who had at any time gone even so far as to express sympathy for the rebellion. The case involved legal action against a priest of the Roman Catholic Church who was indicted and convicted of the crime of teaching and preaching without having taken the test oath.

The Supreme Court divided five to four   Justice Field, an ardent individualist, deserted the other four Lincoln appointees to join the four justices appointed prior to the Lincoln administration in holding the state law unconstitutional. Said Justice Field:

> The theory upon which our political institutions rest is, that all men have certain inalienable rights — that among these are life, liberty, and the pursuit of happiness; and that in the pursuit of happiness all avocations, all honors, all positions, are alike open to everyone, and that in the protection of all these rights all are equal before the law. Any deprivation or suspension of any of these rights for past conduct is punishment, and can be in no other wise defined.[19]

A statute providing punishment for activities not hitherto punishable under any law, or increasing the penalties over those prescribed at the time the offense was committed, fell within the category of *ex post facto* laws and was therefore unconstitutional. This statute fell within that category. Furthermore, said the justice, it was unconstitutional in that it was a bill of attainder; that is, a legislative act inflicting punishment without a judicial trial.

The federal statute involved in the Garland case prescribed a test oath that the deponent had never voluntarily borne arms or in other ways committed offenses against the United States. No person was to be permitted to practice before any court of the United States without taking the oath. A. H. Garland, an active participant in the rebellion, had received a pardon from the President of the United States, and now sought the privilege of practicing as an attorney and counselor of the Supreme Court without taking the oath required. He contended that the statute as it affected him was unconstitutional, and that, even if it was constitutional, he was released from compliance with it by the pardon of the President. Justice Field, again

[19] 4 Wallace 321-322.

speaking for a majority of the Court, admitted that Congress might prescribe qualifications for practitioners before the Court. The question in this case, he said, was whether that power had been exercised as a means for the infliction of punishment against the prohibitions of the Constitution. Since the enactment of *ex post facto* laws and bills of attainder was denied to Congress as well as to the states, he held that the reasoning in this case should follow that of the case just decided. Furthermore, he concluded, since Garland had lawfully received a full pardon from the President, the test oath could not in any event be exacted from him.

Justice Miller wrote for himself and his three brethren a dissenting opinion covering the two cases. He sought to narrow Justice Field's definition of bills of attainder and to demonstrate the fact that the state and federal laws involved were not acts providing punishment, and were, therefore, not *ex post facto* laws. He remarked that

> the history of the time when this [federal] statute was passed — the darkest hour of our great struggle — the necessity for its existence, the humane character of the President who signed the bill, and the face of the law itself, all show that it was purely a qualification, exacted in self-defense, of all who took part in administering the government in any of its departments, and that it was not passed for the purpose of inflicting punishment, however merited, for past offenses.[20]

The cleavage in the Supreme Court was similar to the cleavage in the country itself over the question of the severity to be used in dealing with former sympathizers and participants in the rebellion. The Milligan decision led to a demand for curbing the appellate jurisdiction of the Supreme Court.[21] The Test-Oath decisions accentuated the demand.[22] Many people believed that the Reconstruction Acts, dividing the South into military districts and providing for the trial of cases by military tribunals, were unconstitutional on the basis of the Milligan case. In that case the Supreme Court had taken a stand against military tribunals for the trial of civilians outside the theater of war. The area in the South now governed by military authority had been in the theater of war; but the end of the war had been proclaimed by the President and the states had sought to re-establish their civil tribunals. The parallel between the situations was, there-

[20] 4 Wallace 396.

[21] Charles Warren, *The Supreme Court in United States History* (rev. ed., 2 vols., 1926), II, 448-449.

[22] *Ibid.*, pp. 453-454.

fore, clear. To secure a Supreme Court decision on the Reconstruction Acts, the state of Mississippi asked leave to file a bill, in the name of the state, seeking an injunction to prevent the President of the United States and the general commanding in the districts of Mississippi and Arkansas from executing the measures in question. The Attorney General of the United States took the position that the Court should not allow the filing of a bill which sought an injunction to restrain the President from the performance of his duties. The Court avoided the broader question, whether under any circumstances the President could be enjoined from the performance of ministerial duties on the ground that their performance violated the Constitution. In this case, said Chief Justice Chase for a unanimous Court, the duties were not ministerial, but were executive and political. He gave a practical argument for refusing to issue injunctions against the President in cases of this kind:

> If the President refuse obedience, it is needless to observe that the Court is without power to enforce its process. If, on the other hand, the President complies with the order of the Court and refuses to execute the acts of Congress, is it not clear that a collision may occur between the executive and legislative departments of the government? May not the House of Representatives impeach the President for such refusal? And in that case could this Court interfere in behalf of the President, thus endangered by compliance with its mandate, and restrain by injunction the Senate of the United States from sitting as a court of impeachment? Would the strange spectacle be offered to the public wonder of an attempt by this Court to arrest proceedings in that court? [23]

He thought these questions answered themselves. The Court was fully satisfied that it had no jurisdiction over a bill to enjoin the President in the performance of his official duties and that such a bill ought not to be received.

The opponents of the Reconstruction machinery established by Congress made another attempt to have the Court pass upon the constitutionality of the Reconstruction Acts. The states of Georgia and Mississippi brought suits, not against the President, but against Stanton as Secretary of War and against General Grant and the generals commanding in the respective districts, seeking an injunction against the enforcement of provisions of the Reconstruction Acts which threatened to subvert the government of the states and subject their

[23] Mississippi v. Johnson, 4 Wallace 475, 500-501 (1867).

people to military rule. The Court decided, however, that these questions were political questions. The rights involved were not rights of persons and property.

> The rights, for the protection of which our authority is invoked, are the rights of sovereignty, of political jurisdiction, of government, of corporate existence as a state, with all its constitutional powers and privileges. No case of private rights or private property infringed, or in danger of actual or threatened infringement, is presented by the bill, in a judicial form, for the judgment of the Court.[24]

Once again, therefore, the South failed to secure a determination of the constitutional question, and the Supreme Court avoided the assaults which would have been inevitable had the Reconstruction Acts been held unconstitutional.

In the famous case of *Ex parte* McCardle the enemies of Reconstruction made a further attempt to get the question settled.[25] This case involved a question of purely private right. A southern editor, William H. McCardle, had been arrested under the Reconstruction Acts. He was held for trial by a military commission. He petitioned for a writ of habeas corpus in the United States circuit court in Mississippi. The petition was denied. A recent act of Congress, enacted, oddly enough, for the protection of federal officials and other loyal persons against actions by courts and officials in southern states,[26] defined the right of appeal to the Supreme Court so broadly as to include the action in the McCardle case.[27]

The Supreme Court decided unanimously that it had jurisdiction. A date was set for argument. Congress and the press of the country engaged in anxious speculation as to the outcome. Reactions to the arguments of counsel seemed to indicate that the Court was divided, but it was widely believed that the Reconstruction Acts would be held unconstitutional. The impeachment trial of President Johnson was initiated during the period of the argument of the McCardle case. If Congress would go so far as to impeach the President of the United States in order completely to dominate the course of Reconstruction, it seemed highly improbable that it would permit a decision of the Supreme Court to stand in its way. Yet, at the very least, such a decision would have done much to discredit the radical program.

---

[24] Georgia *v.* Stanton, 6 Wallace 50, 77 (1867, 1868).
[25] 6 Wallace 318 (1868), 7 Wallace 506 (1869).
[26] Warren, *op. cit.*, II, 464-465.      [27] 14 Stat. 385, 386-387.

To avert the embarrassment which would flow from a Supreme Court decision against the Reconstruction Acts, radicals in Congress quietly inserted in a bill then pending a provision withdrawing the appellate jurisdiction of the Supreme Court in cases of the type of that of McCardle, and prohibiting the Court's exercise of jurisdiction on appeals which had already been taken. The bill was passed without a frank discussion of the purpose of the amendment. The President realized the purpose, and vetoed the bill. It was not in harmony with the spirit and intention of the Constitution, he declared. It established a precedent which might eventually sweep away every check on arbitrary and unconstitutional legislation. He continued:

> Thus far during the existence of the government, the Supreme Court of the United States has been viewed by the people as the true expounder of their Constitution, and in the most violent party conflicts its judgments and decrees have always been sought and referred to with confidence and respect. In public estimation it combines judicial wisdom and impartiality in a greater degree than any other authority known to the Constitution, and any act which may be construed into or mistaken for an attempt to prevent or evade its decision on a question which affects the liberty of the citizens and agitates the country cannot fail to be attended with unpropitious consequences. It will be justly held by a large portion of the people as an admission of the unconstitutionality of the act on which its judgment may be forbidden or forestalled, and may interfere with that willing acquiescence in its provisions which is necessary for the harmonious and efficient execution of any law.[28]

The veto message brought the purpose of the bill out into the open. Nevertheless, it was passed over the veto.[29] This is apparently the only instance in American history in which Congress has rushed to withdraw the appellate jurisdiction of the Supreme Court for the purpose of preventing a decision on the constitutionality of a particular law.

Although the Supreme Court had ample time in which to decide the McCardle case before the act withdrawing the jurisdiction of the Court had been passed over the President's veto, it waited, over the protest of two of its members, until the amending act had become a law. Then it had to face the question whether Congress had the

[28] *Messages and Papers of the Presidents*, VIII, 3845-3846.
[29] 15 Stat. 44. See Warren, *op. cit.*, II, 478-480; John W. Burgess, *Reconstruction and the Constitution* (1902), pp. 196-197.

power to withdraw the jurisdiction of the Court in a case which had
already reached the stage of formal argument.    Counsel asked the
privilege of arguing this question before the Court.    In order to give
time for the arguments, the case had to be postponed until the following term.    Justice Grier, with the concurrence of Justice Field,
protested bitterly against the whole proceeding.    The case had been
fully argued, he declared.    It involved the liberty and rights, not only
of the appellant, but also of millions of his fellow citizens.    All had
the right to expect the immediate attention of the Court.    By postponing the case, the Court would be subject to the imputation of
evading the performance of a duty imposed on it by the Constitution
and waiting for legislative interposition to supersede its action and
relieve it from responsibility.    He was ashamed that such opprobrium
should be cast upon the Court.[30]

A year later the constitutionality of the amending act was argued.
The Court upheld the power of Congress to withdraw its appellate
jurisdiction.    "We are not at liberty to inquire into the motives of
the legislature," said Chief Justice Chase for a unanimous Court.
"We can only examine into its power under the Constitution; and
the power to make exceptions to the appellate jurisdiction of this
Court is given by express word." [31]    Since the Court no longer had
jurisdiction over the appeal, it could not proceed to pronounce judgment in the case.    He ended on a note of piety, declaring that
"judicial duty is not less fitly performed by declining ungranted jurisdiction than in exercising firmly that which the Constitution and
the laws confer." [32]

The Supreme Court seems to have acted on the principle that discretion was the better part of valor.    No admirer of the Court would
wish to see it rush to a decision for the purpose of getting itself on
record as to the constitutionality of particular laws.    On the other
hand, it did itself no great credit in postponing action until Congress
relieved it of the embarrassment of deciding a case likely once more
to make the Court the object of radical hostility.    In justification of
the policy adopted by the Court, it should, of course, be remembered
that, had it held the Reconstruction Acts unconstitutional, Congress
might have retaliated in such a way as to do it serious injury.    Much
of the objectionable machinery of Reconstruction was done away with
as soon as new state governments were established in harmony with
the policy laid down by Congress.    It is doubtful if judicial interven-

[30] Warren, *op. cit.*, II, 482.          [31] 7 Wallace 514.          [32] *Ibid.*, p. 515.

tion could have done much to alleviate the discomfort of persons who suffered from Reconstruction policies. It may have been advisable for the Court to retreat in this instance in order that it might continue the unimpeded performance of its functions in connection with less highly controversial issues.

The Supreme Court never passed upon the constitutionality of military Reconstruction. In the case of Texas v. White,[33] however, decided in April, 1869, it threw some light upon the constitutional position of the states which had passed ordinances of secession. The case was an original suit in the Supreme Court, brought by Texas, to recover certain United States bonds owned by Texas before the war, but disposed of during the war for war purposes. Defendants contended that Texas no longer existed as a state in the Union, and that it therefore had no right to bring suit in the Supreme Court. The contention that Texas no longer existed as a state, or was in no position to exercise its powers as a state, was in harmony with the varied "suicide" and "suspended-animation" theories of the radicals in Congress. Yet the most ardent of radicals no doubt favored the recovery of state bonds disposed of in return for materials to be used in war against the Union.

Chief Justice Chase, for a majority of the Court, decided in terms of constitutional law the question which had already been determined by force of arms; namely, that no state could leave the Union. The Union had begun among the colonies, he said, where it grew out of common origin, mutual sympathies, kindred principles, similar interests, and geographical relations.

> It was confirmed and strengthened by the necessities of war, and received definite form, and character, and sanction from the Articles of Confederation. By these the Union was solemnly declared to "be perpetual." And when these Articles were found to be inadequate to the exigencies of the country, the Constitution was ordained "to form a more perfect Union." It is difficult to convey the idea of indissoluble unity more clearly than by these words. What can be indissoluble if a perpetual Union, made more perfect, is not? . . . The Constitution, in all its provisions, looks to an indestructible Union, composed of indestructible states.[34]

The Chief Justice distinguished, however, between the state and its government. There was in Texas at the close of the war no government in constitutional relations with the Union. It became the duty

[33] 7 Wallace 700.        [34] *Ibid.*, p. 725.

of the United States to provide for the restoration of such a government. In describing the steps taken by the federal government, he refused to pass upon their constitutionality, but he went so far as to indicate his opinion that Reconstruction was the function of Congress rather than of the President. The action of the President, he said, must be considered provisional, as it seemed to have been regarded by Congress. Citing the opinion of Chief Justice Taney in Luther v. Borden,[35] he declared that the power to guarantee to each state a republican form of government was primarily a legislative power, and resided in Congress.

In spite of the transitions through which the government of Texas had passed, the Court was of the opinion that, as to the action in this case, it had the power to bring suit in the Supreme Court. The question, therefore, must be decided whether the disposal of the bonds to aid the rebellion had been valid. The Court reached the conclusion that such disposition of the bonds was not legal, and that the state had the right to recover them.

The decision was not unanimous. Justices Grier and Swayne rejected the fiction that Texas had not been out of the Union. Justice Grier asked:

> Is Texas a state now represented by members chosen by the people of that state and received on the floor of Congress? Has she two senators to represent her as a state in the Senate of the United States? Has her voice been heard in the late election of President? Is she not now held and governed as a conquered province by military force? [36]

He did not consider himself bound to express any opinion judicially as to the constitutional right of Texas to exercise the rights and privileges of a state in the Union or the power of Congress to govern Texas as a conquered province, to subject it to military domination, and to keep it in tutelage.

> I can only submit to the fact as decided by the political position of the government; and I am not disposed to join in any essay to prove Texas to be a state of the Union when Congress have decided that she is not. It is a question of fact, I repeat, and of fact only. Politically, Texas is not a state in this Union. Whether rightfully out of it or not is a question not before the Court.[37]

The decision of the majority of the Court in the Texas case came nearer to supporting than to denying the contentions of the radicals.

[35] 7 Howard 1, 45 (1849). See chapter 13.    [36] 7 Wallace 738.    [37] Ibid., p. 739.

Yet a considerable group in Congress remained suspicious of the Court, and for some time they discussed methods of further reducing the appellate jurisdiction of the Supreme Court so as to prevent the handing-down of embarrassing decisions.

## THE FOURTEENTH AMENDMENT

The Thirteenth Amendment, of which ratification was completed toward the end of 1865, represented the first formal change in the Constitution in a period of more than sixty years. The problems of reorganization and reconstruction which the country faced after the war led to the proposal of large numbers of constitutional amendments dealing with the civil and political rights of Negroes, with problems of representation in the federal government, and with related matters. Two of these amendments, known respectively as the Fourteenth and Fifteenth, were added in 1868 and 1870 — the text of the Constitution thereafter being left unchanged until the addition of the Sixteenth Amendment in 1913.

The Fourteenth Amendment was worked out through a long period of evolution in the joint committee on Reconstruction. The first section of the amendment dealt with civil rights. Because of the interpretations given to that section and the use to which it has been put down through the years, it has achieved an importance out of all proportion to that of other sections of the article. For that reason a major portion of the space allotted herein for the discussion of the amendment is devoted to the first section. The other sections had contemporary importance, however, and are discussed here in advance of the first section.

Thaddeus Stevens, the leader of the radicals in the House of Representatives, characterized the second section as the most important in the article.[38] It provided that representatives should be apportioned among the several states according to their respective populations, counting the whole number of persons in each state, excluding Indians not taxed. In effect it eliminated the three-fifths clause of Article I, Section 2, of the Constitution, which was rendered obsolete by the abolition of slavery. It provided, however, that, if the right to vote for federal and state officers were denied or abridged, except for participation in rebellion or other crime, the basis of representation therein should be reduced in proportion to the number of adult male citizens who were excluded. The purpose of the section was to com-

[38] 36 *Congressional Globe* 2459.

pel states to grant universal suffrage or incur the penalty of loss of representation. (The section proved ineffective for the purpose for which it was adopted, and the Fifteenth Amendment had to be added later to provide the Negro with a constitutional guaranty of non-discrimination in matters of suffrage.)

The third section provided that, without removal of the disability by a vote of two-thirds of each house of Congress, no person should become a state or federal official who had participated in the rebellion after previously having taken an oath to support the Constitution of the United States as a state or federal official. The fourth section gave constitutional sanction to the validity of the public debt of the United States and provided, on the other hand, that neither the United States nor any state should be responsible for any debts incurred in aid of insurrection or rebellion against the United States. The fifth and last section empowered Congress to enforce the provisions of the article by appropriate legislation.

The broad outlines of the story of the adoption of the Fourteenth Amendment have been matters of common knowledge for many years.[39] Although the famous first section underwent many changes in the process of evolution, much can be discovered as to its intended meaning from the comments of Senator John A. Bingham, who sponsored it.[40] Bingham was an ardent defender of civil rights, not merely of Negroes, but of all the people. He was also a conscientious lawyer. He apparently favored the provisions of the Civil-Rights bill, but believed a constitutional amendment necessary to give it validity. He opposed the bill, therefore,[41] and concentrated his efforts on bringing about the necessary constitutional change.

It will be recalled that the first eight amendments to the Constitution, commonly referred to as the Bill of Rights, gave broad protection to life, liberty, and property. In Barron v. Baltimore,[42] decided in 1833, and in other cases the Supreme Court had decided that these

---

[39] See, for example, Horace E. Flack, *The Adoption of the Fourteenth Amendment* (1908). The relatively recent controversy as to whether the word "persons" in the Fourteenth Amendment was used in order to extend the protection of the Constitution to corporations will be discussed in a later chapter.

[40] For materials on Bingham's position see Louis B. Boudin, "Truth and Fiction about the Fourteenth Amendment," *New York University Law Quarterly Review*, XVI (November, 1938), 19; and Howard Jay Graham, "The 'Conspiracy Theory' of the Fourteenth Amendment," *Yale Law Journal*, XLVII (January, 1938), 371; XLVIII (December, 1938), 171. For an appraisal of these articles see A. C. McLaughlin, "The Court, the Corporation and Conkling," *American Historical Review*, XLVI (October, 1940), 45-63.

[41] Flack, *op. cit.*, p. 30.

[42] 7 Peters 243. See also Livingston v. Moore, 7 Peters 469 (1833).

amendments protected the rights involved only against infringement by the federal government. It did not protect them against actions of the state governments. Bingham wished by constitutional amendment to extend the protection of what he called "this sacred bill of rights" [43] to people who might be oppressed by the states.[44]

On February 26, 1866, before the draft of the Fourteenth Amendment was presented to Congress, Bingham offered an amendment containing the essence of what later became the first section of the Fourteenth Amendment. It provided:

> The Congress shall have power to make all laws which shall be necessary and proper to secure to the citizens of each state all privileges and immunities of citizens in the several states, and to all persons in the several states equal protection in the rights of life, liberty, and property.[45]

On the following day, to demonstrate the fact that his proposed amendment was not limited to the protection of the rights of Negroes, he made the following statement:

> It is due to the committee that I should say that it is proposed as well to protect the thousands and tens of thousands and hundreds of thousands of loyal white citizens of the United States whose property, by state legislation, has been wrested from them under confiscation, and protect them also against banishment.[46]

Bingham was of the opinion that the amendment, as then drafted, conferred upon Congress a general power of legislation for the purpose of securing to all persons in the several states protection of life, liberty, and property, subject only to the qualification that that protection should be equal.[47] He said again:

> I have advocated here an amendment which would arm Congress with the power to compel obedience to the oath [to support the Constitution], and punish all violations by state officers of the bill of rights, but leaving those officers to discharge the duties enjoined upon them as citizens of the United States by that oath and by that Constitution.[48]

[43] 36 *Congressional Globe* 1090.

[44] *Ibid.,* pp. 1089, 1090, and 44 *Congressional Globe,* Appendix, 84.

[45] 36 *Congressional Globe* 1034.     [46] *Ibid.,* p. 1065.

[47] *Ibid.,* p. 1094. He seems to have had doubts, however, as to the relation of the amendment to rights in real estate which were dependent on state law except when granted by the United States.

[48] *Ibid.,* p. 1292.

The Bingham amendment, like many others, gave way before that
reported by the joint committee on Reconstruction. The first section of the latter amendment in its original form provided as follows:

> No state shall make or enforce any law which shall abridge the
> privileges or immunities of citizens of the United States; nor shall any
> state deprive any person of life, liberty, or property without due
> process of law; nor deny to any person within its jurisdiction the equal
> protection of the laws.[49]

Except for a sentence later inserted at the beginning of the section,
providing that "All persons born or naturalized in the United States,
and subject to the jurisdiction thereof, are citizens of the United
States and of the state wherein they reside," the section was later
adopted in the form reported. It is to be noted that, instead of
stating positively that Congress should have the power to enact legislation protecting the rights in question, the amendment was worded
merely in the form of a prohibition against state action. Bingham
seems to have believed, however, that the authorization was the same,
even though the language was different. He justified the first section
of the amendment proposed by the committee in the following
manner:

> There was a want hitherto, and there remains a want now, in the
> Constitution of our country, which the proposed amendment will
> supply. What is that? It is the power in the people, the whole people
> of the United States, by express authority of the Constitution to do
> that by congressional enactment which hitherto they have not had
> the power to do, and have never even attempted to do; that is, to
> protect by national law the privileges and immunities of all the
> citizens of the Republic and the inborn rights of every person within
> its jurisdiction whenever the same shall be abridged or denied by the
> unconstitutional acts of any state.[50]

Bingham believed that the amendment, even though phrased to the
effect that "no state shall . . .," carried authorization for federal legislation protecting the rights of citizens, just as if it had been phrased
in his earlier language, "The Congress shall have power . . ." On a
subsequent occasion he explained the change from positive to negative

---

[49] *Ibid.*, p. 2542. Senator Howard took the position that congressional legislation was
authorized, not by the first section of the Fourteenth Amendment, but by the fifth
section. See Flack, *op. cit.*, p. 86.

[50] *Ibid.*, p. 2542.

phrasing by saying that after re-examination of the decision in the case of Barron *v.* Baltimore, he had recast the phrasing so as to make it conform with the language of the Fifth Amendment, which was under discussion in that case.[51] The fifth section of the amendment provided, "The Congress shall have power to enforce, by appropriate legislation, the provisions of this article.' He had no idea at all that the change made in the language of the first section would withhold from Congress the power to legislate for the protection of civil rights against state action. This question was soon to be raised in Congress, however, and to result in Supreme Court decisions of basic importance.

Although the amendment as reported from the joint committee on Reconstruction provided, "No state shall make or enforce any law which shall abridge the privileges or immunities of citizens of the United States," it made no attempt to define either privileges and immunities, on the one hand, or citizenship, on the other. The House of Representatives gave its approval to the amendment in this form, apparently assuming that "citizens" included Negroes. The Senate, no doubt remembering the argument of Chief Justice Taney in the Dred Scott case — although the case was not mentioned — deemed it advisable to add a sentence stating who were citizens of the United States. It therefore appended at the beginning of the first section the sentence providing, "All persons born in the United States, and subject to the jurisdiction thereof, are citizens of the United States and of the state wherein they reside." There was mild resistance to the adoption of the provision because of its applicability to Chinese, who were already proving an unassimilable element in California, gypsies in Pennsylvania, and, to an undefined extent, Indians in the United States.[52] An important effect of the amendment was to determine, not merely who were citizens of the United States, but also to determine, as an exercise of federal rather than of state jurisdiction, much of the content of state citizenship as well.

No provision was inserted defining the privileges and immunities protected by the first section of the amendment. The senator who introduced the provision defining citizenship was of the impression that the amendment protected against the states all the privileges and immunities protected against the federal government by the so-called Bill of Rights.[53] The failure to include in the amendment a state-

[51] 44 *Congressional Globe,* Appendix, p. 84.
[52] 36 *Congressional Globe* 2890-2897.          [53] *Ibid.,* pp. 2765, 2766.

ment to that effect was unfortunate; for the Supreme Court, in an important case to be discussed below, came to a different conclusion.[54]

## THE FIFTEENTH AMENDMENT

For some years the enforcement of the Fourteenth Amendment as it related to the rights of Negroes was closely connected with the enforcement of the Fifteenth Amendment. The Fifteenth Amendment, proposed in Congress in 1868, became effective in 1870. At the time of the formulation of the Fourteenth Amendment, it had been assumed that the South could be coerced into giving the suffrage to Negroes by the threat of curtailment of representation in Congress as a result of their disfranchisement. It soon became apparent that such a threat would not have the desired results. The race problems of the South were formed around deep social cleavages. To the white people, who in times past had not merely governed the sections of the country in which they lived, but had owned the Negroes as property, it was unthinkable that these Negroes, without having had experience in owning and governing themselves, should participate as equals with their former owners in the government of their respective communities and of the United States. With all the intensity of their belief in state rights, furthermore, they resented this interference of the federal government with local determination of the right of suffrage.

Since the Fourteenth Amendment failed to achieve the desired end, Congress, by a process of compromise, worked out another constitutional amendment. It provided, "The right of citizens of the United States to vote shall not be denied or abridged by the United States or by any state on account of race, color, or previous condition of servitude." A second section provided, "The Congress shall have power to enforce this article by appropriate legislation." The amendment was supported by a number of groups. Among them were those who believed that an approach to universal suffrage was an approach to a panacea for all the political ills of the country. The faction in the North which was bent upon controlling southern politics sought the enfranchisement of the Negro as a means of ousting from politics the southern class formerly in control.[55] In no small degree the simpleminded Negro of the South was made the instrument for the achievement of the predatory ends of carpetbagger politicians.

[54] Slaughterhouse Cases, 16 Wallace 36 (1873).
[55] John Mabry Mathews, *Legislative and Judicial History of the Fifteenth Amendment* (1909), p. 22.

Soon after the amendment was ratified, Congress passed the so-called Enforcement Act,[50] to make the amendment effective. The Negro, seeking to exercise his franchise, had found innumerable barriers in the way. The technicalities of registration and voting machinery were utilized to confuse and exclude him. Intimidation was utilized all the way from mild threats and commands to the gross outrages perpetrated by the Ku Klux Klan. It was assumed in some instances, furthermore, that the constitutional amendment was intended to protect only the right to vote for federal officers, and did not extend to the election of officers of the states. The statute enacted to enforce the Fifteenth Amendment sought to insure to the Negro the right to vote in all elections, whether state or federal. It attempted to prohibit the use of election machinery in such a way as to disfranchise voters because of race and color. It provided severe penalties for state election officials who should violate the provisions of the act. It penalized interference with the franchise either by bribery or by threats, whether of violence or of economic discrimination. The act authorized the President "to employ such part of the land or naval forces of the United States, or of the militia, as shall be necessary to aid in the execution of judicial process issued under this act." Provision was made for the enforcement of the act in the courts of the United States, even though the offenses might have been committed in connection with local elections. One section, based, no doubt, on the Fourteenth rather than the Fifteenth Amendment, re-enacted the Civil-Rights Act of 1866, which had been of doubtful constitutionality because of the fact that the provisions of the Fourteenth Amendment had not yet been added to the Constitution when the earlier measure was passed.

The statute did not confine itself strictly to the punishment of discrimination at elections because of race, color, or previous condition of servitude. Rather, evidently for the purpose of insuring the right of suffrage to the Negroes, it covered the broad field of electoral procedure and penalized acts which, although they might have the effect of preventing Negroes from voting, might, nevertheless, have a much more general application. The measure was drastic, not merely in that it attempted to secure voting privileges to large numbers of people not competent for an intelligent exercise of the franchise, but also because it attempted to govern procedure which by tradition and law in the United States had been prescribed by the states. Both as

[50] 16 Stat. 140. See also amending act of February 28, 1871, *ibid.*, p. 433.

to policy and constitutionality, it was a highly questionable measure.

Before the courts had an opportunity to pass upon the act to enforce the Fifteenth Amendment, Congress found it necessary to enact another measure to enforce the Fourteenth Amendment — a measure known usually as the Ku Klux Klan Act.[57] The denial of the right to vote was one of the least of the troubles of the freedmen. The hooded bands of the Ku Klux Klan struck terror among the simple-minded people by whipping, shooting, hanging, and otherwise making examples of colored people who had the temerity to stand upon their newly acquired civil rights. State machinery proved wholly inadequate for the preservation of order under local laws. By the act of Congress the federal government undertook to punish acts of violence against persons of the colored race. The President was authorized to utilize the militia or the land and naval forces of the United States if they were needed, with the proviso that persons arrested were to be turned over to the federal civil authority to be dealt with according to law. If resistance to law reached the stage of rebellion, the President was authorized to suspend the privilege of the writ of habeas corpus.

In short, this measure and the measure to enforce the Fifteenth Amendment represented the determination of Congress that both civil and political rights in the South should be exercised pursuant to the standards set by Congress rather than by standards worked out by internal negotiations within the several southern communities. This determination to govern the South in terms of standards projected from without made necessary, not merely the expansion of civil machinery for law enforcement, but the maintenance of federal troops in the several states which were under the control of Reconstruction governments. It was only gradually, after the passing of a period of years, that Congress decided against the permanent maintenance of an army of occupation and withdrew it to permit the course of southern politics to find pretty much its own channel.

JUDICIAL INTERPRETATION

The language of the Fourteenth and Fifteenth Amendments and of the measures enacted to enforce them was the result of compromises in Congress, worked out amid heated debates over purposes and interpretations. To a high degree, however, their meanings were determined, not by the legislators responsible for the words used, but by the Supreme Court. The decisions through which the Court laid

[57] 17 Stat. 13.

down the broader outlines of interpretation were handed down over a considerable period of years. Their history is complicated by inter-relationships among decisions based directly upon the two amendments and decisions interpreting related statutes. It is further complicated by changing attitudes on the part of justices reflecting changes in the personnel of the Court. One effect of judicial interpretation, to be shown more at length below, was to determine that the Fifteenth Amendment could not be used as authorization for a broad scheme of federal regulation of elections and electoral machinery in the South. As to the Fourteenth Amendment, important parts of the legislation based upon it were also swept away. Certain of its provisions were largely devitalized by judicial interpretation, while others, after a period of years, were interpreted so broadly as to make the history of the Fourteenth Amendment, with its restrictions upon the powers of the states, one of the most significant aspects of constitutional development since the Civil War. The cases outlined below indicate more at length the nature of the work done by the Court.

The Fourteenth Amendment received its first interpretation by the Supreme Court in the Slaughterhouse Cases,[58] decided in 1873. The cases arose, not under a federal statute, but under a measure enacted in 1869 by the carpetbag legislature of Louisiana. The act regulated the business of slaughtering livestock in New Orleans. It required that such activities for the city and for a vast area surrounding it should be restricted to a small section below the city of New Orleans and provided that the slaughtering should be done in the houses of one corporation. The effect was virtually a monopoly grant of the business, even though the corporation was required to permit other butchers to have access to their facilities. While some such police legislation may have been needed in the interest of the health and welfare of the city, there seems to have been no reason why the regulation should cover such a large area or why monopoly rights should have been conferred. The butchers of the city who were deprived of their callings appealed to the courts on a number of grounds. The cases were brought to the Supreme Court on the ground that, in having their businesses taken away from them, they were deprived of privileges and immunities as citizens of the United States which were guaranteed to them by the Fourteenth Amendment.

The Supreme Court rejected the contention by a vote of five to four. Neither Justice Miller, who spoke for the majority of the

[58] 16 Wallace 36.

Court, nor Justices Field, Bradley, and Swayne, who wrote dissenting opinions, looked into the speeches of Senator Bingham or other members of Congress to discover whether or not rights of doing business such as those of the butchers of New Orleans were intended to be included among the privileges and immunities protected by the amendment. The debates would have revealed the fact that the first section of the amendment, according to the design of its sponsor, would protect against state interference the great body of rights which a man had as a citizen under a free government, including apparently the ordinary right to do business. It is a significant commentary on the judicial processes of the time that neither the justices who took opposing positions as to the rights in question nor counsel before the Court deemed it relevant to discuss the intention of Congress as revealed by the contents of the *Congressional Globe.* The several justices approached the subject, not from the point of view of detailed information concerning the framing and adoption of the amendment, but from broad conceptions of the recent history of the relations between the nation and the states and of the fundamental rights of man.

Justice Miller declared that a most cursory glance at the Thirteenth, Fourteenth, and Fifteenth Amendments disclosed a unity of purpose. That purpose was the achievement of the freedom of the slave race, the security and firm establishment of that freedom, and the protection of the new freemen and citizens from oppression by their former owners.

> We do not say that no one else but the Negro can share in this protection. Both the language and spirit of these articles are to have their fair and just weight in any question of construction. . . . But what we do say, and what we wish to be understood, is, that in any fair and just construction of any section or phrase of these amendments, it is necessary to look to the purpose which we have said was the pervading spirit of them all, the evil which they were designed to remedy, and the process of continued addition to the Constitution until that purpose was supposed to be accomplished, as far as constitutional law can accomplish it.[59]

The main purpose of the first section of the Fourteenth Amendment, he continued, was to establish the citizenship of the Negro. In addition, however, it made clear a distinction between citizenship of the United States and citizenship of a state. The two types of citizenship were distinct from each other. He thought it significant that

[59] *Ibid.,* p. 72.

the amendment forbade the impairment of privileges and immunities of persons as citizens of the United States, but did not in this connection speak of their rights as citizens of the states. He drew a sharp line of distinction between rights which were derived from state citizenship and those which were derived from citizenship of the United States. The great mass of civil rights possessed by an individual, he believed, were derived from state and not from federal citizenship. That being true, these rights were not protected against state action by the clause forbidding the impairment of privileges and immunities which were derived from federal citizenship. He held it unnecessary to list the privileges and immunities to be classified in the latter group, but suggested that among them were the right of the citizen to go to the seat of government, to transact business with the government, to seek its protection, to have free access to its seaports, and to demand the care and protection of the government over his life, liberty, and property when on the high seas or within the jurisdiction of a foreign government. He listed still others, most or all of them being rights to which the individual would presumably have been entitled without the inclusion of the privileges-and-immunities clause in the Fourteenth Amendment. The effect of his interpretation was to devitalize the clause as far as the giving of additional protection to individuals was concerned.

As for the due-process clause of the same section of the amendment, the clause through which much of the vitality of the amendment has made itself felt in recent years, Justice Miller said the plaintiff had not emphasized the point of deprivation of property without due process of law. On the basis of previous judicial interpretation of the due-process clause of the Fifth Amendment, he considered it sufficient to say that under no construction of that provision hitherto made or now deemed admissible could the restraint imposed by the state of Louisiana upon the exercise of the trade of butchers in New Orleans be held to be a deprivation of property.

Neither had the argument been much pressed that the rights of plaintiffs were protected by the provision in the same section of the amendment that no state should "deny to any person within its jurisdiction the equal protection of the laws." Justice Miller thought the clause intended solely for the protection of the rights of Negroes. He made an astonishingly inaccurate prediction concerning it, saying: "We doubt very much whether any action of a state not directed by way of discrimination against the Negroes as a class, or on account of their race, will ever be held to come within the purview of this provision." [60]

The dissenting opinions in these cases are of unusual importance. Although the decision of the majority of the Court with reference to the narrow interpretation of the privileges-and-immunities clause was never reversed, the insistence of the minority that the fundamental rights of citizens were protected by the amendment against state encroachment later made itself effective through broadened interpretation of the due-process and equal-protection clauses. Justice Field declared that in his judgment the Fourteenth Amendment afforded protection of the common rights of citizens of the United States against deprivation by state legislation, "and was so intended by the Congress which framed and the states which adopted it." [61] Like Justice Miller, he based his conclusion on general interpretation rather than on a detailed study of the intentions of the framers of the amendment. The amendment was adopted, he explained, to obviate objections to the validity of the Civil-Rights Act which had been raised and pressed with great force, and to place the common rights of American citizens under the protection of the national government. On the basis of the Civil-Rights Act and of the interpretation of the words "privileges and immunities" as they appeared elsewhere in the Constitution, he asserted that

> The privileges and immunities designated are those which of right belong to the citizens of all free governments. Clearly among these must be placed the right to pursue a lawful employment in a lawful manner, without other restraint than such as equally affects all persons. In the discussions in Congress upon the passage of the Civil-Rights Act, repeated reference was made to this language of Mr. Justice Washington [in Corfield v. Coryell [62]]. [63]

Referring in another connection to rights of citizens of Louisiana, he stated that the Fourteenth Amendment

> secures the like protection to all citizens in that state against any abridgment of their common rights, as in other states. That amendment was intended to give practical effect to the Declaration of 1776

[60] Ibid., p. 81. For a discussion of Justice Miller in connection with the decision see Charles Fairman, Mr. Justice Miller and the Supreme Court (1939), pp. 179 ff.

[61] 16 Wallace 89. For discussion of the position of Justice Field see Carl Brent Swisher, Stephen J. Field, Craftsman of the Law (1930), pp. 416 ff.

[62] Federal Cases No. 3230. This reference indicates that Justice Field was not unfamiliar with the contents of the debates. Why he failed to use other materials in the debates which gave direct support to his argument is not clear.

[63] 16 Wallace 97.

of inalienable rights, rights which are the gift of the Creator; which the law does not confer, but only recognizes.

He said again that equality of right among citizens in the pursuit of the ordinary avocations of life was a distinguishing privilege of citizens of the United States.

> This is the fundamental idea upon which our institutions rest, and unless adhered to in the legislation of the country our government will be a Republic only in name. . . . That only is a free government, in the American sense of the term, under which the inalienable right of every citizen to pursue his happiness is unrestrained, except by just, equal, and impartial laws.[64]

In this manner Justice Field sought to read into the Constitution broad protection of individual rights and of a laissez-faire order in which he believed with all the depth of his being. He had ample company in the holding of such beliefs, but he as an individual played an outstanding part in reading these conceptions into the constitutional law of the land. Justice Bradley held much the same beliefs. He concurred in the Field opinion and added one of his own. He admitted, as did Field, the right of a state to enact necessary regulations, but he contended that there were fundamental rights which the regulations could not infringe. Furthermore, he called attention, as Field did not, to the fact that the amendment prohibited any state from depriving any person of life, liberty, or property without due process of law. He stated briefly that, in his opinion, the Louisiana statute did deprive the plaintiffs of liberty as well as property without due process of law. He went no further than to state his view, however, leaving to subsequent decisions the working-out of a broadened interpretation of the due-process clause. Justice Swayne concurred in the opinions of Field and Bradley, saying that the privileges and immunities of a citizen of the United States included, among other things, "the fundamental rights of life, liberty, and property, and also the rights which pertain to him by reason of his membership of the nation." [65] He said again, "By the Constitution, as it stood before the war, ample protection was given against oppression by the Union, but little was given against wrong and oppression by the states. That want was intended to be supplied by this amendment." [66] Chief Justice Chase also dissented, but without giving reasons.

In spite of the vigor of the dissenting opinions, the official interpretation of the privileges-and-immunities clause remained the narrow

[64] *Ibid.,* pp. 105, 110-111.  [65] *Ibid.,* p. 126.  [66] *Ibid.,* p. 129.

interpretation given by Justice Miller. Just after the Slaughterhouse
Cases were decided, the Court held that the right to practice law in
state courts was not a privilege or immunity of a citizen of the United
States guaranteed by the Fourteenth Amendment to a woman who
was a citizen of the United States. Justices Field and Swayne sanctioned a concurring opinion by Justice Bradley, in which he said:
"The paramount destiny and mission of woman are to fulfill the
noble and benign offices of wife and mother. . . . And the rules of
civil society must be adapted to the general constitution of things, and
cannot be based upon exceptional cases." [67]    He thought it the prerogative of legislators to prescribe regulations of common callings
which were based upon knowledge of such facts. The following year
the Court held that a man who was deprived by state law of the right
to sell liquor was not thereby deprived of a privilege or immunity of
a citizen of the United States. The decision was unanimous, but
three judges again found it necessary to explain their concurrence on
other grounds than on the basis of Justice Miller's opinion.[68]    In 1875,
speaking through the new Chief Justice, Morrison R. Waite, the
Court held unanimously that the right to vote was not given to
women who were citizens of the United States by means of the privileges-and-immunities clause.[69]    In 1876, the Court held that trial by
jury in suits at common law in the state courts was not a privilege or
immunity of national citizenship.[70]    In like manner, down through
the years, the Supreme Court has persistently refused to expand the
privileges-and-immunities clause to give substantial protection in any
field.[71]

### JUDICIAL CONSTRUCTION OF ENFORCEMENT LEGISLATION

The line of judicial decisions under the Fourteenth and Fifteenth
Amendments now shifts back to the interpretation of enforcement
legislation. The statutes provided the basis for federal military
patrols in the South wherever they were deemed necessary. They
authorized close scrutiny of state and local electoral machinery for the
detection of discrimination against Negroes. Their broad provisions

[67] Bradwell v. Illinois, 16 Wallace 130, 141-142 (1873).

[68] Bartemeyer v. Iowa, 18 Wallace 129 (1874).

[69] Minor v. Happersett, 21 Wallace 162 (1875). See Bruce R. Trimble, *Chief Justice Waite, Defender of the Public Interest* (1938), pp. 160-161.

[70] Walker v. Sauvinet, 92 U.S. 90 (1876).

[71] See Colgate v. Harvey, 296 U.S. 404, 445 (1935), note 2, for a list of cases. The meaning of the clause was slightly expanded in the Colgate case, but that case was overruled
a few years later. James Stewart & Co. v. Sadrakula, 309 U.S. 94 (1940).

gave, or seemed to give, general protection of civil rights against the Ku Klux Klan and other marauding groups. The Department of Justice made strenuous efforts to break up the Ku Klux Klan and restore order generally by vigorous prosecution of offenders. The task was difficult; and, although the formal organization of the Klan was broken up, the government failed to achieve an orderly society in which former slaves exercised unimpeded the civil and political rights of freemen.[72]

Cases involving questions of the constitutionality of the legislation did not reach the Supreme Court until 1875, and were not decided until 1876. Lower courts gave conflicting interpretations. A forecast of the position on civil rights to be taken by the Supreme Court was given in connection with the attempt to punish persons involved in a massacre of Negroes in Louisiana in 1873. A number of persons were indicted under the Enforcement Act of 1870. The act prescribed punishment for persons who should conspire "with intent to violate any provision of this act, or to injure, oppress, threaten, or intimidate any citizen with intent to prevent or hinder his free exercise and enjoyment of any right or privilege granted or secured to him by the Constitution or laws of the United States, or because of his having exercised the same." Justice Bradley participated in the case in the United States circuit court. Although, as demonstrated in his dissenting opinion in the Slaughterhouse Cases, he thought that the Fourteenth Amendment was intended to protect all of the fundamental rights of citizens of the United States against state action, he was of the opinion that the amendment operated merely as a prohibition against the state, and did not authorize Congress to legislate generally for the protection of those rights. In this respect, as in others, he seems not to have taken the trouble to discover the meaning which the framers of the amendment intended it to possess. He reasoned directly from the language of the Constitution, which used the words "no state shall," and not the words "Congress shall have power." True, he said in his circuit-court opinion in the Louisiana case, Congress was given the power to enforce the provisions of the constitutional amendment by appropriate legislation, but enforcement by appropriate legislation meant legislation appropriate to prevent the state from interfering with the rights in question.

The power of Congress, whether implied or expressed, to legislate for the enforcement of such a guaranty, does not extend to the passage

[72] For discussion see Homer Cummings and Carl McFarland, *Federal Justice* (1937), chapter XII.

of laws for the suppression of ordinary crime within the states. This would be to clothe Congress with power to pass laws for the general preservation of social order in every state. The enforcement of the guaranty does not require or authorize Congress to perform the duty which the guaranty itself supposes it to be the duty of the state to perform, and which it requires the state to perform.[73]

The opinion was, therefore, a forerunner of another limitation on the scope of the first section of the Fourteenth Amendment which was not contemplated by the sponsors of the amendment in Congress. In 1876, the Supreme Court decided the case on appeal, agreeing that the indictments in the case were bad, with the result that the persons held should not be prosecuted.[74] Later, in 1883, in writing the opinion of the Supreme Court in another case, Justice Bradley himself stated for the Court the doctrines he had expounded in 1874 in the United States circuit court in Louisiana.[75]

In another case, decided in 1876, the Supreme Court limited the meaning of the Fifteenth Amendment and held unconstitutional two important sections of the Enforcement Act. The amendment, the Court held, did not confer the right of suffrage upon anyone. Its purpose was to prevent the states or the United States from discriminating in matters of suffrage on account of race, color, or previous condition of servitude. The "appropriate legislation" which the amendment authorized Congress to enact was merely legislation calculated to prevent the forbidden discrimination. It did not extend, as in the statute of 1870, to the whole field of discriminations and obstructions. Since the provisions of the statute went beyond the scope of the powers of Congress, the courts could not enforce the statute, even within the limited field over which Congress was empowered to legislate.[76]

These cases, decided at a time when the federal government was growing weary of the task of policing the South and when the ineffectiveness of its efforts was becoming clear to the country, undoubtedly had the effect of discouraging the remaining sponsors of radical Reconstruction. With the change of administration from Grant to Hayes, in 1877, federal troops were withdrawn from the South; and the federal government in large part acquiesced in return of the control of local government in the South to the hands of local white

---

[73] United States v. Cruikshank, Federal Cases No. 14,897, p. 710.
[74] United States v. Cruikshank, 92 U.S. 542 (1876).
[75] The Civil-Rights Cases, 109 U.S. 3 (1883).
[76] United States v. Reese, 92 U.S. 214 (1876).

citizens. A few important cases carried over for decision in later years. In one of them the Supreme Court held unconstitutional sections of the act of 1871 which sought to punish conspiracy to deprive any person of the equal protection of the laws. The Court quoted with approval the language of Justice Bradley in the Louisiana case in the United States circuit court to the effect that the Fourteenth Amendment gave protection only against state action and that the power of Congress to legislate did not extend to the passage of laws for the suppression of crime within the states.[77]

Meanwhile, in 1875, Congress had enacted a new Civil-Rights Act,[78] calculated to guarantee to Negroes equal accommodation in inns, public conveyances, and places of amusement. In December, 1883, in the Civil-Rights Cases,[79] Justice Bradley wrote the opinion of the Supreme Court, holding important provisions of the act unconstitutional and restating his argument that the Constitution did not authorize the enactment of general legislation for the protection of civil rights.

In spite of the emasculation which they suffered from the Supreme Court, some provisions survived among those enacted to enforce the recent amendments to the Constitution. Certain important provisions dealing with elections were justified by the Supreme Court, not on the basis of the amendments, but on the basis of provisions of the original Constitution. In the case of *Ex parte* Siebold,[80] decided in 1880, the Supreme Court upheld federal regulation of elections at which both state and federal officers were chosen. It upheld the provision requiring state election officials to observe both state and federal laws in the conduct of elections at which members of Congress were chosen. It justified the exercise of such power on the basis of the constitutional provision that "The times, places, and manner of holding elections for senators and representatives shall be prescribed in each state by the legislature thereof; but the Congress may at any time by law make or alter such regulations, except as to the places of choosing senators."[81] One of the constitutional difficulties in the way of the legislation was the position taken by the Supreme Court in Prigg v. Pennsylvania[82] that the federal government could not compel state officers to enforce federal laws. As to elections at which federal officers were chosen, however, the Court now held that in the performance of their functions state officers had federal as well as state

[77] United States v. Harris, 106 U.S. 629 (1883).　[78] 18 Stat. 335.
[79] 109 U.S. 3 (1883).　[80] 100 U.S. 371.　[81] Article I, Section 4.
[82] 16 Peters 539 (1842). Discussed in chapter 12.

duties to perform, and, therefore, were subject to control by the United States. The decision was broad enough to justify extensive federal control of all state elections at which votes were cast for members of Congress.

In 1884, again relying upon the provisions of the original Constitution, the Supreme Court upheld provisions of enforcement legislation on the basis of which men had been indicted for outrages perpetrated upon a Negro to prevent his participating in an election at which votes were cast for a member of Congress.[83] The Court held that the right to vote for members of Congress was based upon the federal Constitution and was not intended to be left within the exclusive control of the states. If the federal government had within its constitutional domain no authority to protect the election of its representatives, said Justice Miller,

> if the very sources of power may be poisoned by corruption or controlled by violence and outrage, without legal restraint, then, indeed, is the country in danger and its best powers, its highest purposes, the hopes which it inspires and the love which enshrines it, are at the mercy of the combinations of those who respect no right but brute force, on the one hand, and unprincipled corruptionists on the other.[84]

### THE SOLID SOUTH

The Reconstruction program contemplated the return of the southern states to the Union, the former slaves being transformed into free citizens and endowed with all the civil and political rights of their former owners. The program was successful as far as the achievement of legal freedom was concerned. Sporadic attempts to place particular Negroes in conditions of peonage have been frustrated. Large numbers of them have been subjected to economic domination by white landlords, but in that respect their position has differed little from the condition of the so-called poor whites of the South. As to civil rights, Negroes have achieved only nominal equality with their white neighbors. If through the Fourteenth Amendment the states are prevented from enacting discriminatory legislation, the amendment does not prevent discrimination by individuals and private organizations on such a scale as to make the color line a line of sharp demarcation between the rights to be exercised by different groups.

As to the political rights of Negroes, they are exercised to a limited degree, but in many areas they exist in theory rather than in fact.

[83] *Ex parte* Yarbrough, 110 U.S. 651 (1884).    [84] *Ibid.*, p. 667.

The carpetbag governments in the several states, run by white and colored officers on the basis largely of colored votes, collapsed as soon as the federal government withdrew military support. To the white people of the South those governments symbolized to a high degree, and perhaps continue to symbolize, the Republican party. The great mass of southern white people for that and other reasons have maintained their connection with the Democratic party. By methods direct or indirect, legal or illegal, white people so limited Negro voting as to control all important elections and, incidentally, to keep the Democratic party supreme. By "the Solid South" people meant an area solidly dominated by white members of the Democratic party.

Varying methods have been used to prevent Negroes from voting. Intimidation has always played a part. The technical requirements of registration and other aspects of electoral machinery have been used to debar voting by illiterate and simple-minded people. The requirement that poll taxes be paid — oftentimes long before the date of the election — has helped perpetuate disenfranchisement of large numbers of impecunious colored people along with some white people as well. The requirement of literacy tests for voting, in which leniency is used toward white people and barred toward people of color, has been the means of rejecting large numbers of would-be voters and of discouraging others to the point of their neglecting even to take the test. Over a long period of years the so-called "grandfather clauses" were used in a number of states to bar Negroes from the polls. In essence, these clauses gave voting privileges to persons and descendants of persons who had done military service in wartime or who had been legal voters, at some date, such as January 1, 1866, which preceded the adoption of the Fifteenth Amendment. Other persons, including of course all Negroes in the states enacting such laws, had to submit to prescribed tests, which could be administered in such a way as to eliminate undesirable voters. In 1915, the Supreme Court looked behind the general language of certain of the clauses and held them unconstitutional as a denial of rights guaranteed by the Fifteenth Amendment.[85] Other devious methods apparently continue to be used.

As white people dominated party nominating conventions, so they dominated the primary elections which to a considerable extent replaced conventions. In areas in which nomination in Democratic

[85] Guinn and Beal *v.* United States, 238 U.S. 347 (1915); Myers *v.* Anderson, 238 U.S. 368 (1915).

primaries was tantamount to election, exclusion from the primaries was tantamount to denial of the right to vote. As recently as 1935 the Supreme Court held that although the power to exclude could not be derived from the state itself, the practice of excluding Negroes by the party acting as a private organization did not violate the Constitution.[86] The question of the relation of party primaries to government then became entangled with that of the power of the federal government to exercise authority over them. In 1941 the Court held that the power of the federal government over elections extended to party primaries in states in which the primaries were determining factors in the election of federal officers.[87] Finally, in 1944, the Court decided a case in such a way that all or almost all party primaries must be classified as instruments of the state,[88] with the result that party action with respect to them is limited by constitutional provisions with respect to due process and equal protection and discrimination based on race. So it is that Congress may regulate and so prevent racial discrimination in primaries at which federal officers are chosen, and state and party officers are forbidden to effect such discrimination. In a formal sense, therefore, and to some extent actually, the political position of the Negro is improved, but the long-time process of Reconstruction remains yet to be completed.

[86] Grovey v. Townsend, 295 U.S. 45 (1935). For cases holding that constitutional rights were violated when the party derived its power of exclusion from the state see Nixon v. Herndon, 273 U.S. 536 (1927) and Nixon v. Condon, 286 U.S. 73 (1932).

[87] United States v. Classic, 313 U.S. 299 (1941). For the earlier position of the Court on this subject see Newberry v. United States, 256 U.S. 232 (1921).

[88] Smith v. Allwright, 321 U.S. 649. For the extremes to which the Court will go in interpreting group action as party action see Terry v. Adams, 345 U.S. 461 (1953).

# CHAPTER 16

# BANKS AND MONEY

THE CIVIL WAR raised again banking and currency controversies which had raged during and after the administration of Andrew Jackson. The renewal of the charter of the Bank of the United States had been prevented, with the result that banking business, including the issuing of bank notes to circulate as money, was left thereafter to banks chartered by the several states. Use of selected state banks, the so-called "pet banks," as depositories of funds of the federal government and as sponsors of notes acceptable to the government in financial transactions had proved disastrous in the depression of 1837. The government had then established a sub-treasury system for the deposit of public funds, and refused to accept in payment of debts to the government anything except gold or silver or United States notes, which were put out in limited issues. Except for the payment of duties on imports and other obligations to the government, most of the business of the country involving the use of money was transacted by means of state bank notes. State regulations of banking were somewhat more carefully drafted in 1861 than in 1837; new banks were chartered, as a rule, under general law rather than by specific enactment; and the business of banking was better understood than in the earlier period. Nevertheless, the notes of the several institutions continued to fluctuate in value in terms of many factors, including the distance between the bank of issue and the place where the notes happened to circulate. The notes issued were far from uniform, and large numbers of them were counterfeited. The several banks, being well entrenched in the business life of the country, were in position to secure any needed political protection. The likelihood of the establishment of a single national bank, such as the Bank of the United States, to issue notes in competition with the state banks and exert a strong measure of control over them, such as had been exerted in the early eighteen-thirties, was extremely slight. The series of events which took place in the field of banking and currency in 1861 and the years immediately thereafter was the product of the war crisis and the disturbances which followed.

LEGISLATIVE CHANGES

During the period of the Civil War, Congress increased the revenue from customs duties, provided for a direct tax, and raised substantial sums by a return to internal-revenue taxation. The flow of revenue did not increase greatly until 1862, however; whereas war expenditures began in 1861 and grew by leaps and bounds. The Treasury Department resorted to borrowing, but it quickly approached the limits of government credit, and the interest rate became prohibitive. Most borrowed funds came out of the specie reserves of the state banks. The drain on the banks resulting from this and other factors pointed to a banking crisis of disastrous proportions.

In his report to Congress in December, 1861,[1] the Secretary of the Treasury, Salmon P. Chase, recommended, not merely increased taxation and provisions for additional borrowing, but also fundamental changes in the currency system of the country.[2] He discussed two plans. The first contemplated the gradual withdrawal from circulation of the notes of private corporations and the substitution of United States notes, payable in coin on demand. The second plan contemplated the printing of notes by the government and their delivery for distribution through banks, guaranteeing their redemption by a pledge of United States bonds. Although, in harmony with the first plan, Congress at the special session in the summer of 1861 had authorized the issue of United States notes to be paid out as money in connection with government expenditures, Chase opposed this mode of providing a circulatory medium. He feared the temptation to issue such notes without adequate provision for redemption, since such a course would result in all the evils of monetary inflation.

His discussion of his second plan, though veiled as to its implications, provided a background for the ultimate establishment of a national banking system. He made no mention of a national bank, or of many national banks, as such. He placed emphasis on the value of a currency everywhere receivable, backed by a common security in United States bonds and distributed through banking institutions

---

[1] *Report of the Secretary of the Treasury*, 1861, p. 17.

[2] In his discussion of constitutional questions he ignored the important case of Briscoe v. Bank of Kentucky, 11 Peters 257 (1837). See chapter 11.

located all over the country. He spoke of the change as one brought about "through the voluntary action of the existing institutions," hoping, no doubt, to avert organized opposition on the part of state banks throughout the country. He avoided discussion of the fact or the possibility that the state banks would have to be reorganized under federal law and thereby subjected, perhaps, to more stringent regulations than those hitherto applicable to them if they were to perform the function of the distribution of the new uniform currency. As to constitutionality, he said, no argument was necessary to establish the proposition that the powers to regulate commerce and the value of coin included the power to regulate the currency of the country or to establish the collateral proposition that the power to effect the end included the power to adopt the necessary and expedient means.

At the end of December, before the desired legislation had been enacted,[3] the banks of the country responded to the drain on specie in their vaults by suspending specie payments. In order to avoid the loss of its own supply of gold, the federal Treasury had to take the same step. It was necessary, therefore, that a substitute currency be provided immediately or that the law with reference to the currency which could be used by the federal government should be changed, since the use of state bank notes by the government was forbidden. Recognizing the need for haste, a bill was introduced providing for the issue of legal-tender notes. The federal government, unlike the states, was not forbidden to issue bills of credit, and there was no question of the constitutional power of the government to issue paper intended to circulate as money. There was a serious constitutional question, however, of the power of the government to make these notes a legal tender for the satisfaction of all debts between all parties whatsoever. The House committee of ways and means was divided on the question. The chairman of the committee asked Attorney General Edward Bates for a legal opinion. An established custom of the Office of the Attorney General forbade him to give a formal and official answer, but he obliged by giving an informal opinion that the measure would be constitutional.[4]

The measure was reported favorably and was eventually passed in a form authorizing the issue of $150,000,000 in legal-tender notes.[5] A bill introduced to provide for the issuing of currency through bank-

[3] For an account of the drafting of the bill see Elbridge G. Spaulding, *History of the Legal Tender Paper Money issued during the Great Rebellion* (1869), pp. 11-13.
[4] *Ibid.*, pp. 15-16.    [5] 12 Stat. 345.

ing institutions was not reported at all during that session. The debates in Congress show that in the minds of certain legislators the banking measure was a co-ordinate part of the financial plan as a whole. The legal-tender notes to be issued immediately would provide a temporary currency. The permanent currency would be provided by the notes ultimately to be issued through a national banking system.[6] The legal-tender bill was accepted in spite of objections based on constitutional arguments, and in spite of the fear of inflation and other abuses which might result. Because of the uncompromising hostility of state banks, coupled perhaps with the fact that the national banking measure was conceived as a permanent measure rather than merely as a device for dealing with the current crisis, action on the banking bill was postponed. A measure authorizing the issue of an additional $150,000,000 in legal-tender notes was passed by the same session of Congress,[7] while the banking bill remained in the stage of its first printing.

Because of necessity and with obvious reluctance, the Secretary of the Treasury supported the legal-tender measure.[8] "My whole plan," he said at a later date, "has been that of a bullionist and not that of a mere paper-money man. I have been obliged by necessity to substitute paper for specie for a time, but I never have lost sight of the necessity of resumption; nor, to use a military phrase, have I ever suffered my communications with my base of operations to be broken."[9]

In his report to Congress in December, 1862, Chase repeated his recommendation for the establishment of a sound national currency to be issued through banking associations organized under national legislation with a backing in United States bonds. As to the constitutionality of such a measure, he said that it was

proposed as an auxiliary to the power to borrow money; as an agency of the power to collect and disburse taxes; and as an exercise of the power to regulate commerce, and of the power to regulate the value of coin. . . . If Congress can prescribe the structure, equipment, and management of vessels to navigate rivers flowing between or through different states as a regulation of commerce, Congress may assuredly

[6] See, for example, the statement of Samuel Hooper, of Massachusetts, 32 *Congressional Globe* 615.

[7] 12 Stat. 532.

[8] Spaulding, *op. cit.*, pp. 26-27. See also J. W. Schuckers, *The Life and Public Services of Salmon Portland Chase* (1874), pp. 243-245.

[9] Schuckers, *op. cit.*, p. 402.

determine what currency shall be employed in the interchange of their commodities, which is the very essence of commerce.[10]

Chase urged upon Congress the necessity for legislation [11] and he used his influence with prominent bankers to secure their support for, or allay their opposition to, a national banking bill.[12] Through his influence or by some other means, a body of favorable sentiment was developed and a bill was passed.[13] The measure provided for a Bureau of Currency and for an officer called comptroller of the currency in the Treasury Department. It provided for the formation of banking associations under the supervision of the comptroller of the currency. Such associations were to transfer United States bonds to the treasurer of the United States and receive therefor the new currency notes to be issued by them. Any lawfully existing bank was authorized to become an association under this act. Such an arrangement as far as this statute was concerned was voluntary, however. No attempt was made as yet to coerce state banks into the national banking system, or to interfere with the issuing of notes by the state banks.

Congress passed three legal-tender measures, the last bearing the date of March 3, 1863.[14] Among the reasons why further issues were not needed were the increase in taxation and the expanding stream of revenue, and the improved credit of the government, making possible the continuation of borrowing. In his report to Congress in December, 1863, Chase attributed important salutary results to the establishment of the national banking system. Many state banks transferred to the national system and new national banks were organized. After a year of experience, Congress enacted a supplementary measure making recommended modifications in the system.[15]

As the national banking system became established and national bank notes were put into circulation, Congress moved to complete the task of substituting national bank notes for state bank notes. It provided for a ten-per-cent tax on any state bank notes thereafter put into circulation.[16] Such a tax was obviously prohibitive. If it was con-

---

[10] *Report of the Secretary of the Treasury*, 1862, pp. 20-21.

[11] 33 *Congressional Globe* 485.

[12] For an account of the legislation see Andrew McFarland Davis, *The Origin of the National Banking System* (Senate Doc. No. 582, 61st Cong., 2d sess., 1910).

[13] 12 Stat. 665.

[14] 12 Stat. 709. For discussion of the subject of the legal-tender notes see Wesley C. Mitchell, *History of the Greenbacks* (1903), and Don C. Barrett, *The Greenbacks and Resumption of Specie Payments, 1862-1879* (1931).

[15] 13 Stat. 99.    [16] 13 Stat. 469, 484, and 14 Stat. 98, 146.

stitutional, the further circulation of state bank notes was now effectively prohibited by law. It did not mean that state banks could no longer receive deposits and make loans, but it cut off a profitable source of revenue in that, on the basis of a limited specie reserve, the state banks could no longer create by note issues a much larger amount of currency which brought in substantial interest returns when paid out on interest-bearing loans.

In 1869, the Supreme Court decided the case of Veazie Bank v. Fenno,[17] in which it passed upon the constitutional power of Congress to levy the prohibitive tax on state bank notes. Salmon P. Chase had resigned as Secretary of the Treasury before the end of President Lincoln's first administration and had been appointed Chief Justice. In that position he wrote the opinion of the Supreme Court on the constitutionality of a measure which, although not enacted until after he left the Treasury Department, was but a logical extension of his plan for a uniform currency of national bank notes. The constitutionality of the tax measure was challenged on the ground, first, that it was a direct tax, but was not apportioned among the states as a direct tax must be apportioned, and, secondly, that it was a tax on a franchise granted by a state which Congress had no power to impair. Chase rejected both contentions. He thought that Congress had the unquestioned power to issue notes to circulate as money — without reference to the question of its power to make such notes a legal tender. Since in the exercise of undisputed constitutional powers, Congress had undertaken to provide a currency for the whole country, it could not be questioned that Congress might constitutionally secure the benefit of it to the people by appropriate legislation. To this end, Congress might restrain by suitable enactment the circulation as money of any notes not issued under its own authority. "Viewed in this light," he concluded, "as well as in the other light of a duty on contracts or property, we cannot doubt the constitutionality of the tax under consideration." [18]

In 1875, the Supreme Court held that the National Banking Act rested on the same principle as the act creating the second Bank of the United States. The reasoning of Alexander Hamilton, and of the

---

[17] 8 Wallace 533.

[18] Ibid., p. 549. Justice Nelson dissented in an opinion in which Justice Davis concurred. He regarded the statute as an impairment of the powers of the states to create banks. He contended that the principle involved affected the power to create any other description of corporations, such as railroads, turnpikes, manufacturing companies, and others.

Supreme Court in McCulloch *v.* Maryland [19] and in Osborn *v.* Bank of the United States,[20] applied to the later statute. "The national banks organized under the act," said the Court, "are instruments designed to be used to aid the government in the administration of an important branch of the public service. They are means appropriate to that end. Of the degree of the necessity which existed for creating them, Congress is the sole judge." [21]

The national banking system established during the Civil War continued in operation without fundamental changes for approximately half a century, when in 1913 it was superseded by the federal reserve system.[22] Until that time the currency of the country consisted of the notes of the national banks, together with a substantial quantity of legal-tender United States notes issued during the Civil War and subsequently reissued, some other similar notes issued later, and a limited supply of silver certificates issued also at a later date. It seemed for a time as if the elimination of state bank notes from circulation would result in the elimination of the state banks themselves, leaving the business of banking exclusively in the hands of national banks. State banks survived, however, for a number of reasons. They could be formed with smaller amounts of capital than were required for the establishment of national institutions. The reserve requirements of many of the states were lower than federal requirements. Many state banks were able to lend on real estate, whereas such loans could not be made by national banks. In other respects, state regulations were less rigid than those of the federal government. Furthermore, the percentage of the business of the country transacted through the exchange of currency was gradually reduced, giving way to the use of checking accounts. The federal government did not presume to interfere with the deposit and checking activities of the state banks. As a result of the various factors, the national banks controlled, at the time of the establishment of the federal reserve system, only slightly more than half of the total banking resources of the country.[23]

In summary, the national banking system established during the eighteen-sixties differed fundamentally in many respects from that

---

[19] 4 Wheaton 316 (1819).          [20] 9 Wheaton 738 (1824).

[21] Farmers' and Mechanics' National Bank *v.* Dearing, 91 U.S. 29 (1875).

[22] For the establishment of the federal reserve system, see chapter 25.

[23] For a summary, see Thomas J. Anderson, *Federal and State Control of Banking* (1934), chapter III.

overthrown during the presidency of Andrew Jackson. It consisted of many banks, each independent of the others, rather than of a central institution with subordinate and subservient branches. State banks could join the system, and in doing so could retain most of their independence. The federal government enforced regulations which were of the nature of police measures, but they were uniform and known to all, and were similar to the regulations enforced in the same field by the more enlightened state governments. The federal government had no membership on any board of directors. Except for the restrictions prescribed by statute, the management of the national banks was left completely in the hands of private individuals.

### THE LEGAL-TENDER CONTROVERSY

By the three Legal-Tender Acts Congress authorized the issue of a total of $450,000,000 in United States notes which were to be a legal tender for the payment of debts, public and private, with the exception of duties on imports and interest on the public debt. The notes constituted obligations of the United States, but the government did not bind itself to redeem them in coin. The notes, or greenbacks, as they were called, depreciated greatly in terms of gold prices. To require their acceptance in payment of debts, therefore, had the effect of fulfilling contracts with a currency of substantially less value than that which had been the basis of the contracts. Creditors who had counted on payment in terms of gold values suffered in the process. In the minds of many persons, the legislation constituted an impairment of the obligation of contracts. The federal government, unlike the states, was not directly forbidden by the Constitution to impair the obligation of contracts, but no power of impairment was given directly by the Constitution, and on that ground it was widely contended that the acts were unconstitutional.

Since the use of gold and silver was no longer possible, it was absolutely essential that the federal government provide a circulatory medium or accept the notes of state banks which had suspended specie payments if it was to continue war operations or even normal peacetime operations. Its power to issue notes intended to circulate as money was unquestioned. Mere intention to have the notes circulate, however, was not enough. Confidence in the government was already at such an ebb that further borrowing could be carried on only at rates almost prohibitively high. There was no reason to expect that issues of United States notes would be generally accepted as money unless receivers were authorized to require their own creditors to receive the notes at their face value in payment of debts.

Having agreed to the necessity of the legal-tender enactments, Chase used such influence as he had to see that their constitutionality was upheld. When in 1863 a test case was made up in New York, Chase designated two able lawyers to argue in favor of the constitutionality of the act on behalf of the Treasury Department, bringing from George T. Curtis a protest as to "the improper effort on the part of the administration to influence the court of the state." [24] Judges in New York and Pennsylvania obligingly sent word to Chase that they had found the law constitutional.[25] Justice Miller said in 1870 that fifteen state courts had passed upon the question and all but one had expressed their belief in the constitutionality of the legislation.[26] A study of twelve of the courts considering the measure has indicated a division along political party lines. Of the judges participating in the decisions every Democrat held the legislation invalid, and every Republican but one held it constitutional.[27]

The war came to an end without a decision by the Supreme Court of the United States. Hugh McCulloch, as Secretary of the Treasury, sought to bring about as speedily as possible the retirement of the irredeemable paper money and a return to specie payments. The policy of contraction of the currency met with strong opposition. The people had become accustomed to the use of the greenbacks, which they were able to appraise principally in contrast with the notes of state banks. By comparison with these notes, the greenbacks constituted a relatively sound currency. Most debtor groups, furthermore, were opposed to any contraction in the quantity of currency in circulation. Contraction, by comparison with inflation, meant that the debtor must give greater rather than less value in the satisfaction of his debts. The debtor category included large numbers of people. The conditions of the war period had stimulated speculation. Rapid developments based on credit and hopes for the future were taking place in the West. That development was accompanied by, or even led by, the expansion of railroad systems, which were themselves prominent among the debtor groups. Under pressure from debtor groups acting upon Congress, the Treasury Department was compelled to suspend its program of contraction. Among creditor groups

[24] Quoted in Albert Bushnell Hart, *Salmon P. Chase* (1869), p. 389.
[25] *Ibid.*, p. 389.     [26] Hepburn *v.* Griswold, 8 Wallace 603, 638 (1870).
[27] Charles Fairman, *Mr. Justice Miller and the Supreme Court 1862-1890* (1939), p. 153.

and the persons who, as a matter of policy, were advocates of a currency based upon specie the trend was ominous. They began looking to the courts to save the country from a régime of unsound finance by holding the Legal-Tender Acts in conflict with the Constitution.

The first legal-tender case in which the Supreme Court accepted jurisdiction was that of Hepburn v. Griswold.[28] After the first argument in the case, which was one between private parties, a reargument was ordered because of the contention of the Attorney General of the United States that the great public importance of the question required fuller consideration.[29] While the case was pending, the Court decided a number of other cases dealing with subordinate aspects of the question. In Lane County v. Oregon[30] it held unanimously that the Legal-Tender Act involved did not require a state to accept legal-tender notes in payment of taxes. In Bronson v. Rodes[31] and Butler v. Horwitz[32] the Court further narrowed the meaning of the legislation by holding that it did not require the acceptance of legal-tender notes in satisfaction of contracts that called specifically for payment in coin. Chief Justice Chase wrote the opinions of the Court. A dissenting opinion by Justice Miller and cautious concurring opinions by Justices Davis and Swayne indicated, however, that the Court was reaching a point of division on currency questions. In Veazie Bank v. Fenno[33] the Court cleared the way for the new currency of national bank notes by upholding the prohibitive tax on state bank notes, thereby providing a circulatory medium which would render the United States notes unnecessary for exchange purposes. These decisions indicated that Chase and a majority of the Court were in sympathy with the plan for a permanent currency of national bank notes which he had advocated as Secretary of the Treasury, and were interested in limiting the interpretation of legal-tender measures to which he had given his support reluctantly because of absolute necessity. It remained to be seen whether he and his brethren would hold unconstitutional measures which a few years earlier he had found it necessary to defend.

At the time when the Hepburn case was decided in conference, the Supreme Court consisted of eight members. Five of them held the

[28] 8 Wallace 603 (1870).

[29] Charles Warren, *The Supreme Court in United States History* (rev. ed., 2 vols., 1926), II, 498-499.

[30] 7 Wallace 71 (1869).     [31] 7 Wallace 229 (1869).     [32] 7 Wallace 258 (1869)

[33] 8 Wallace 533 (1869), discussed above.

Legal-Tender Acts unconstitutional in so far as they sought to enforce the acceptance of legal-tender notes in satisfaction of debts incurred before the acts were passed. One of the five was Justice Grier, whose mental powers were by this time so enfeebled that as a result of the way in which he handled himself in connection with this case a committee of his brethren called on him and persuaded him to resign.[34] The majority opinion in the Hepburn case was written by Chief Justice Chase and was read and agreed to in conference on January 29, 1870. It would have been delivered two days later but for the fact that the dissenting opinion was not ready. For that reason it was postponed until February 4. In the meantime, on February 1, Grier's resignation became effective, leaving the alignment of the Court at four to three at the time when the decision was made public.

Although both Chase, spokesman for the majority, and Miller, spokesman for the dissenters, accepted without question the doctrine that some powers might be implied even if not specifically stated in the Constitution, they disagreed on the contention that the power to make United States notes a legal tender in payment of debts previously incurred could be implied. Chase took the position that the only possible justification of the legal-tender measures was in the war power, and he found no justification there. Miller defended the acts on the ground that they were necessary and proper to the exercise of the war power. Both justices labored under difficulties in that they were unable to demonstrate what the effect of the legal-tender enactments had been upon the circulatory medium and what effect they had had upon the conduct of the war. In discussing the operations of the so-called laws of money, Chase resorted to such language of opinion as "All modern history testifies," and, "It is denied, indeed, by eminent writers."[35] Miller made a point with equal assurance in a declaration beginning with the statement that "All experience shows."[36] The division between the two groups of justices was not so much a division as to the meaning of the language of the Constitution as it was a division based upon conflicting economic ideas. The question to be decided was fundamentally a question as to the kind of currency which the United States was to have. In essence it was not a question for a judicial body at all, but one to be decided by the

[34] See Joseph P. Bradley, *Miscellaneous Writings*, edited by Charles Bradley (1902), pp. 73-74. See also Charles Evans Hughes, *The Supreme Court of the United States* (1928), p. 75, and Carl Brent Swisher, *Stephen J. Field, Craftsman of the Law* (1930), pp. 175-176.

[35] Hepburn *v.* Griswold, 8 Wallace 603, 620 (1870).       [36] *Ibid.*, p. 633.

policy-making branches of the government after careful investigation.

Three justices were of the opinion that the legal-tender measures had saved the federal government from a collapse of credit and had prevented the loss of the war and the impoverishment of the people. Miller called attention, furthermore, to the virtual unanimity of sentiment during the war as to the constitutionality of the measures among the two houses of Congress, the President, and fifteen state courts. In the face of this weight of authority, he asked:

> Are we to reverse their action, to disturb contracts, to declare the law void, because the necessity for its enactment does not appear so strong to us as it did to Congress, or so clear as it was to other courts? Such is not my idea of the relative functions of the legislative and the judicial departments of the government.[37]

Chase, on the other hand, speaking for the majority, could find no evidence that the measures had had any important effect on the conduct of the war. He held that they impaired the obligation of contracts. Although the Constitution did not specifically forbid the federal government to impair the obligation of contracts, he stated that "we cannot doubt that a law not made in pursuance of an express power, which necessarily and in its direct operation impairs the obligation of contracts, is inconsistent with the spirit of the Constitution." [38] Furthermore, he said, the Constitution forbade the taking of private property for public use without compensation. If it could not be taken for public use, he found it difficult to understand how it could be taken for private use as in this case. Again, he said, the Constitution forbade the taking of private property without due process of law. It was quite clear to him that due process of law made no part of such a legal-tender measure as was then before the Court. He did not allude directly to his support of the Legal-Tender Acts when he was Secretary of the Treasury, but he phrased a general justification in the following manner:

> It is not surprising that amid the tumult of the late civil war, and under the influence of apprehensions for the safety of the Republic almost universal, different views, never before entertained by American statesmen or jurists, were adopted by many. The time was not favorable to considerate reflection upon the constitutional limits of legislative or executive authority. If power was assumed from patriotic motives, the assumption found ready justification in patriotic

[37] *Ibid.*, pp. 638-639.        [38] *Ibid.*, p. 623.

hearts. Many who doubted yielded their doubts; many who did not doubt were silent. Some who were strongly averse to making government notes a legal tender felt themselves constrained to acquiesce in the views of the advocates of the measure. Not a few who then insisted upon its necessity, or acquiesced in that view, have, since the return of peace, and under the influence of the calmer time, reconsidered their conclusions, and now concur in those which we have just announced. These conclusions seem to us to be fully sanctioned by the letter and spirit of the Constitution.[39]

The holding in the Hepburn case was that the Legal-Tender Acts were unconstitutional in so far as they required the acceptance of greenbacks in fulfillment of contracts made before the acts were passed. Furthermore, the reasoning of the Chief Justice was such as to cast doubt on the constitutionality of the requirement that the notes be accepted in payment of debts subsequently incurred. Since the business of the country had been adjusted to the use of the greenbacks, a holding that they were not adequate for the satisfaction of current debts would create disturbance and, incidentally, would enrich creditors beyond all reasonable expectation. Debtor groups, therefore, began to urge the reargument of the question.

The reversal of the Hepburn decision was quite within the range of possibilities. On the date of the announcement of the decision, the Court consisted of seven members, divided four to three. By a recent statute the President was authorized to increase the membership to nine. Should the two new members align themselves with the three justices dissenting in the Hepburn case, a reversal could be brought about. On the day on which the decision was announced, the President sent to the Senate nominations of two new justices. They were William Strong, of Pennsylvania, who as a judge of a Pennsylvania court had upheld the constitutionality of the Legal-Tender Acts, and Joseph P. Bradley, of New Jersey, a prominent and able lawyer who had included the Camden and Amboy Railroad among his clients. He was thought to believe the Legal-Tender Acts constitutional. It was freely asserted at the time that railroad interests wanted the legal-tender decision reversed to protect the right of the corporations to pay their debts in cheap money.[40] It was thought that Bradley's railroad connection might have something to do with his opinion on the constitutional question.

As a matter of fact, in the light of subsequent events, it was widely

[39] *Ibid.*, pp. 625-626.    [40] See Schuckers, *op. cit.*, p. 260.

charged that President Grant deliberately packed the Supreme Court to secure a reversal of the position of the Court on the legal-tender question.[41] Much time has been spent discussing the question whether the President knew or could have known in advance what the decision of the Court was to be. Since, two weeks before the decision was announced, Chase informed the Secretary of the Treasury confidentially concerning what was about to happen, so that the Treasury Department might be in position to protect itself in the event of financial disturbance,[42] there is no reason for doubting that the President, too, had the information. Evidence has not been produced, however, to prove that he selected the two men for the deliberate purpose of securing a reversal of the legal-tender decision, and there is reason to believe that they made no advance commitments on the subject. Little is known beyond the fact that the two men were appointed, that they did participate in the reversal of the decision, and that they were able lawyers quite apart from questions of currency and finance.

When the Hepburn case was decided, two other cases, Latham v. United States and Deming v. United States,[43] both of which involved the Legal-Tender Acts, were on the calendar of the Supreme Court. When the Chief Justice was about to assign a date for hearing argument in one of them, Justice Miller requested postponement until the matter could be taken up in conference. In the conference room he pointed out that the legal-tender question was involved and expressed a hope that the cases would not be taken up until the two vacancies on the bench had been filled. Chase said he thought the legal-tender question was settled; but the cases were postponed, nevertheless, until after Strong and Bradley had taken their seats. When the cases were set down for argument, a bitter controversy took place among the justices over the question whether the reargument of the legal-tender issue was to be permitted. Chase and other justices who had been in the majority in the Hepburn case took the position that an order had previously been issued that the cases now before the Court would be determined in the same manner as the Hepburn case

[41] For discussion see Warren, *op. cit.*, II, 517 ff., and materials cited; Swisher, *op. cit.*, pp. 181-182; Leon Sachs, "Stare Decisis and the Legal Tender Cases," *Virginia Law Review*, XX (June, 1934), 856-865; Sidney Ratner, "Was the Supreme Court Packed by President Grant?" *Political Science Quarterly*, L (September, 1935), 343-358; Charles Fairman, "Mr. Justice Bradley's Appointment to the Supreme Court and the Legal Tender Cases," *Harvard Law Review*, LIV (April and May, 1941), 977-1034, 1128-1155.

[42] George S. Boutwell, *Reminiscences of Sixty Years in Public Affairs* (2 vols., 1902), II, 209.

[43] 9 Wallace 145 (1870).

as far as the legal-tender issue was concerned. The justices previously in the minority denied knowledge of any such order.[44]

For reasons not directly connected with the issue, these two cases were dismissed prior to argument, but the bitterness provoked by the controversy carried over to other cases in which the same questions were raised. After a series of delays and recriminations, two cases, Knox *v.* Lee and Parker *v.* Davis, known usually as the Legal-Tender Cases,[45] were argued. Each of the seven justices who had participated in the Hepburn decision remained of the same mind as before on the legal-tender question. The two new justices joined the three who had been in the minority in the Hepburn case, with the result that the Hepburn decision was reversed, and, by a vote of five to four, the Legal-Tender Acts were now held constitutional.

The majority opinion was written, not by Miller, who had been spokesman for the minority in the Hepburn case, but by Strong. Bradley agreed with Strong's opinion and added a concurring opinion. Chase, Clifford, and Field wrote long dissenting opinions. In these cases, as in the Hepburn case, the opinions turned on conceptions of the laws of money rather than on constitutional law. All the justices were in essential agreement as to the constitutional doctrine of implied powers. They disagreed as to the constitutionality of the Legal-Tender Acts because they disagreed as to the effect of those measures upon the conduct of the war and the welfare of the people. Strong, speaking for the Court, found that the measures were reasonably adapted to the winning of the war. He believed that they were not merely reasonable means toward that end, but that they had been necessary to that purpose.

In his concurring opinion, Justice Bradley advanced a doctrine that was important for constitutional development in later years in reference to the reissue of legal-tender notes and other aspects of the expansion of governmental powers. The United States was not only a government, he declared, it was a national government. It was the only government in the country that had the character of nationality. It had jurisdiction over all those general subjects of legislation and sovereignty which affected the interests of the whole people equally and alike and which required uniformity of regulations and laws. He

[44] For accounts of the controversy, see Warren, *op. cit.,* II, 519-523; Schuckers, *op. cit.,* chapter 28; Bradley, *op. cit.,* pp. 63-70; Swisher, *op. cit.,* pp. 180-187; Fairman, *op. cit.,* pp. 169-172.

[45] 12 Wallace 457 (1871).

thought it a self-evident proposition "that it is invested with all those inherent and implied powers which, at the time of adopting the Constitution, were generally considered to belong to every government as such and as being essential to the exercise of its functions." [46] He thought that the power to issue bills of credit and to make them a legal tender was an essential national power. Broad control was particularly necessary in times of crisis.

> It is absolutely essential to independent national existence that government should have a firm hold on the two great sovereign instrumentalities of the sword and the purse, and the right to wield them without restriction on occasions of national peril. In certain emergencies government must have at its command, not only the personal services — the bodies and lives — of its citizens, but the lesser, though not less essential, power of absolute control over the resources of the country.[47]

He would not say that the power to issue legal-tender notes was a war power, or that it was to be called into exercise only in time of war, for other public exigencies might arise in the history of a nation to make its use expedient and imperative. Decisions in the matter were to be made by the legislative department of the government.[48]

Strong and Bradley justified the questioning and overthrow of the Hepburn decision in part on the ground that the Court had lacked a full membership at the time when that case was decided. The minority opinions reflected the indignation of the justices who had been in the majority in the Hepburn case. They encouraged, no doubt, the criticism of the Court that prevailed for many years because of the coincidence of the change in constitutional interpretation with the change in Court personnel. Probably no decision prior to that time, with the exception of the Dred Scott decision, had done more to injure the reputation of the Supreme Court as an impartial tribunal. Like the Dred Scott decision, it was based on political beliefs and conceptions of public welfare on which the people of the country were sharply divided. The question involved was one which ought to have been settled by the policy-making branches of the government. In deciding the question, or in reversing a decision previously made, the Court demonstrated the fact that it had taken upon itself the task of molding important national policies.[49]

---

[46] *Ibid.*, p. 556.    [47] *Ibid.*, p. 563.    [48] *Ibid.*, p. 567.

[49] For the legal-tender cases subsequently decided, see Trebilcock *v.* Wilson, 12 Wallace 687 (1872); Dooley *v.* Smith, 13 Wallace 604 (1872); "The *Vaughan* and *Telegraph*," 14 Wallace 258 (1872); Norwich and Worcester Railroad Co. *v.* Johnson, 15 Wallace 195 (1873); Maryland *v.* Baltimore and Ohio Railroad Co., 22 Wallace 105 (1874).

CIRCULATION OF LEGAL-TENDER NOTES

Although the printing of a total of $450,000,000 in legal-tender notes had been authorized, the act of June 30, 1864, contained the pledge that the issue of United States notes should never exceed $400,000,000, with an addition of not more than $50,000,000 which might be temporarily required for the redemption of temporary loans.[50] The largest amount of notes listed for any year by the treasurer of the United States was $447,300,203.10, for 1864. Gradual redemptions were made until in 1868 the figure of $356,000,000 was reached. In that year, in response to sentiment against further deflation of the currency, Congress passed an act suspending the authority of the Secretary of the Treasury to make any reduction of the currency by retiring or cancelling United States notes.[51] The advocates of a return to specie payments continued to urge upon Congress the necessity of speedy retirement of the so-called irredeemable notes. Congress compromised in 1869 by passing a measure under which the United States solemnly pledged its faith to make provision at the earliest practicable period for the redemption of the United States notes, but without suggesting the probable date of that "earliest practicable period."[52]

From 1869 to 1873, the government made substantial payments on the national debt, the credit of the government improved, and the value of United States notes steadily increased in comparison with coin. The panic of September, 1873, precipitated a long period of business depression and stimulated a demand for the increase rather than decrease of the amount of United States notes in circulation. Sponsors of so-called hard money made a counter-move to bring about the immediate resumption of specie payments. The Senate committee on finance, dominated by this group, reported a measure to fix the maximum limit of United States notes at $382,000,000, a figure to which the Secretary of the Treasury had recently raised the amount in circulation in order to pay the expenses of the government; and to redeem the notes gradually in coin or in five per cent bonds, at the option of the Secretary of the Treasury.[53] The opposition in the Senate won control of the measure, abandoned plans for early retirement of the notes, and raised to $400,000,000 the amount of notes authorized. The revised measure was passed, but the President de-

[50] 13 Stat. 218, 219.     [51] 15 Stat. 34.     [52] 16 Stat. 1.
[53] See John Sherman, *Recollections of Forty Years in the House, Senate and Cabinet* (2 vols., 1895), I, 495.

nounced it as a movement toward inflation and vetoed it.[54] The veto was sustained. Subsequently, by a compromise act of June 20, 1874, the amount of notes outstanding was fixed at a maximum of $382,000,000, with no provision for their redemption.[55]

When the "lame-duck" session of Congress assembled in December, 1874, the country faced the prospect of a Democratic majority in the House of Representatives at the ensuing term. Republicans wished to keep the subject of currency control as much as possible in their own hands. Republican leaders, therefore, set about the formulation of an additional compromise measure on which the party could agree, and secured support for it through the exercise of party discipline. It passed both houses with little debate. It provided for a gradual contraction in the volume of greenbacks to $300,000,000, with a compensating expansion in the circulation of national bank notes. It provided that some four years hence, on January 1, 1879, the government would begin the redemption of United States notes in coin. The date set for resumption was sufficiently far ahead to make possible a change in plans in the meantime, should the country desire such a change. The measure gave Republicans credit for good intentions without making them responsible for the discomfort which immediate contraction of the currency might bring about. In some degree the measure was acceptable both to the advocates of resumption of specie payments and to those who opposed such resumption. Some congressmen wanted the greenbacks destroyed as they were redeemed, without power in the government to reissue them. Others insisted that the government should have the power to reissue them. The statute was drawn so vaguely as to leave undetermined the question whether or not the power of reissue existed.[56]

Cheap-money sentiment remained strong, but it was not strong enough to bring about the repeal of the Resumption Act. A measure of May 31, 1878, however, entitled "An act to forbid the further retirement of United States legal-tender notes,"[57] did substantially change the situation. Instead of permitting the continued retirement of United States notes until a maximum of $300,000,000 was reached, as provided by the earlier statute, it forbade the Secretary of the Treasury to retire or cancel additional notes. The amount of notes

[54] *Messages and Papers of the Presidents,* IX, 4222.     [55] 18 Stat. 123, 124.

[56] 18 Stat. 296; Sherman, *op. cit.,* chapter XXVI; Ellis Paxson Oberholtzer, *History of the United States since the Civil War* (5 vols., 1917-1936), III (1925), 119-122.

[57] 20 Stat. 87.

outstanding was left, therefore, at $346,681,016. The act provided, furthermore, that when any of the notes were redeemed or received into the Treasury, they should not be retired, cancelled, or destroyed, but should be reissued and paid out again and kept in circulation. Resumption of specie payments, therefore, was not to result in any contraction of the currency.

The United States notes increased steadily in value for a period of years, so that by January 1, 1879, the date of resumption, they were worth almost their face value in gold. No substantial sums were returned to the Treasury for redemption. Pursuant to instructions from Congress, the notes were put out into circulation again as rapidly as they were received. Debtors continued to use them in payment of debts, assuming that, even though they had been redeemed by the government and then paid out again, they were still a legal tender. Their status was questioned, however, and the Supreme Court had to determine whether a measure hitherto justified as necessary and proper to the exercise of the war powers of the United States could be extended in time of peace without reference to war powers.

By 1884, the personnel of the Supreme Court had changed greatly from that of thirteen years earlier when the original legal-tender decision had been reversed. The Court now, in the case of Juilliard v. Greenman,[58] upheld the power of Congress to make notes a legal tender without reference to the war power. The arguments used by Justice Gray were similar in part to those used earlier in the concurring opinion of Justice Bradley. He said:

> The power, as incident to the power of borrowing money and issuing bills or notes of the government for money borrowed, of impressing upon those bills or notes the quality of being a legal tender for the payment of private debts was a power universally understood to belong to sovereignty, in Europe and America, at the time of the framing and adoption of the Constitution of the United States.[59]

Since the exercise of the power to issue bills of credit was not prohibited to Congress by the Constitution, it could be included in the powers expressly granted to borrow money on the credit of the United States. This position was fortified by the fact that Congress was vested with the exclusive power to coin and regulate the value of money and with the paramount power of regulating foreign and interstate commerce. Under the powers of coinage and borrowing, taken

[58] 110 U.S. 421.  [59] *Ibid.*, p. 447.

together, Congress was authorized to establish a national currency, either in coin or in paper, and to make that currency lawful money for all purposes.  Furthermore,

> the power of making the notes of the United States a legal tender in payment of private debts, being included in the power to borrow money and to provide a national currency, is not defeated or restricted by the fact that its exercise may affect the value of private contracts. If, upon a just and fair interpretation of the whole Constitution, a particular power or authority appears to be vested in Congress, it is no constitutional objection to its existence or to its exercise that the property or the contracts of individuals may be incidentally affected.[60]

Justice Field, the only member of the Court now remaining from the majority of four in the Hepburn case, wrote a vigorous dissent. The decision by which the Hepburn case had been reversed, he declared, had never been entirely accepted and approved by the country.  Nor, he thought, should this excite surprise, for

> whenever it is declared that this government, ordained to establish justice, has the power to alter the condition of contracts between private parties and authorize their payment or discharge in something different from that which the parties stipulated, thus disturbing the relations of commerce and the business of the community generally, the doctrine will not and ought not to be readily accepted.  There will be many who will adhere to the teachings and abide by the faith of their fathers.[61]

The original measure had been passed, he said, as one of overruling necessity in a perilous crisis of the country.  Now it was no longer advocated as one of necessity, but as one that might be adopted at any time.

> Never before was it contended by any jurist or commentator on the Constitution that the government, in full receipt of ample income, with a treasury overflowing, with more money on hand than it knows what to do with, could issue paper money as a legal tender.  What was in 1862 called the "medicine of the Constitution" has now become its daily bread.  So it always happens that whenever a wrong principle of conduct, political or personal, is adopted on a plea of necessity, it will be afterwards followed on a plea of convenience.[62]

[60] *Ibid.*, p. 448.
[61] *Ibid.*, p. 451.
[62] *Ibid.*, p. 458.

### THE CONTROL OF INFLATION

The fears of Justice Field were not realized during the half-century which followed his predictions of disaster. The government did not attempt to pay its bills through the simple process of printing huge quantities of money and making it legal tender. The suspension of specie payments was not again necessary until nearly half a century after the Juilliard case was decided. True, the restraint of inflationary sentiment was at times no easy matter. The Greenback party, the Populist party, and other groups of people, representing usually debtor classes in society, sought to render their economic lot easier by inflationary movements.

The demand for cheap money included, not merely the demand for the issue of additional paper currency, but also that for additional coinage of silver. Until 1873, the government had maintained a bimetallic base for its currency. Gold and silver had provided jointly the official money of the United States. The linkage of the two metals had created difficulties, however, because of fluctuations in their respective values. In 1873, silver was demonetized. Soon afterward, however, the price of silver began to go down. The advocates of cheap money, therefore, fought hard over a period of a quarter of a century to shift the currency back to a silver base, or at any rate to provide for unlimited coinage of silver as money. Cheap-money advocates had the support of silver interests and of other groups affected. They succeeded in bringing about the purchase of substantial quantities of silver and the printing of an additional supply of United States notes for the purchase of silver bullion. The period of the eighteen-nineties witnessed a bitter struggle between the hard-money and the cheap-money groups. The former was for the most part successful. The issue merged with other financial issues of the period and the lines of conflict were redrawn, leading ultimately to the conflict over the establishment of the federal reserve system in 1913.

................................................................................

# CHAPTER 17

# SUPPORT FOR AGRICULTURE

UNTIL THE CIVIL WAR, and only to a slightly lesser degree for many years thereafter, farming constituted the principal occupation of the people of the United States. Most of them lived close to the soil, deriving their income directly from it. A seemingly inexhaustible supply of land, fertile with the accumulations of centuries, covered throughout vast areas by tall timber and underlain in sections by minerals varying from coal to gold, awaited exploitation. So great was the supply that timber was destroyed and the cream of soil fertility was skimmed away quite without reference to the needs of future generations. If within his own generation a man's farm was so exhausted as no longer to yield fertile crops, he had only to move westward to virgin tracts.

Although the cost of new land was never so high as to be prohibitive to people who were not virtually penniless, it is true that large numbers of farms were established by people having little in the way of financial resources. The policy of the government as to the distribution of land from the public domain was, therefore, of great importance to the streams of people moving steadily westward. Many families established farms and homes on land to which they had no legal claim and succeeded in remaining there, whether illegally or on the basis of pre-emption rights subsequently granted by the government. The tide of the westward movement, however, was made up largely of law-abiding people who sought the privilege of legal ownership.

The land policy of the federal government was never at any time thoroughly settled and completely consistent. The desires and interests of the people were in conflict, and the conflicts were reflected by the government in Washington. Some thought that the land should be distributed freely to settlers. Some regarded it as a source of revenue to the federal government. Others wished to see title to public land surrendered to the states in which such land was located. Particular interests in the eastern section of the country favored postponing the distribution of public land in order to slow down the movement of population. The question became entangled with the slavery conflict between the North and the South in such a way that the South was aligned in opposition to the free distribution of land to farmers advocated by the rural people of the North and West. Substantial tracts were set aside to yield revenue for purposes of education. Incomes were provided for people who had rendered military service to the United States. Large tracts were donated to railroads in order to stimulate the building of transportation lines into areas hitherto unsettled. Even though prices were low, enough land was sold to yield a substantial income. The annual figure rose to slightly less than $25,000,000 in 1836, dropped to slightly less than $900,000 in 1843, rose to nearly $11,500,000 in 1855, and declined to slightly more than $150,000 in 1862.

EARLY LEGISLATIVE PROPOSALS

Farmers clamored for many decades for the distribution of farm land without cost to settlers. Beyond the acquisition of the land itself and such matters as protection from Indians, they sought little from the federal government. Agricultural education and improvement in the techniques of farming and conditions of farm living were deemed local matters, and were handled locally. Farmers did little in the way of organizing in their own interest except through non-political agricultural societies. The period of the eighteen-fifties, however, witnessed the beginnings of change. The free-soil movement represented in part organization in the interest of free land for bona-fide settlers. A service built up in the Patent Office of the Interior Department, through which senators and representatives secured seeds for distribution to farmers, was developing a demand for the expansion of governmental organizations for services of this kind. The sale of quantities of public land to secure income to provide for agricultural education in the several states became an important issue. The several movements were blocked prior to the secession of the southern states, but in 1862, within a period of less than two months, three important measures were passed. One provided for the establishment of a Department of Agriculture; one provided for the free distribution of homesteads; and another donated public lands to states and territories to support colleges for the benefit of agriculture and the mechanic arts.

The issues involved in the homestead and land-grant college measures had been fully debated at earlier sessions. In 1854, President Franklin Pierce had vetoed a bill "making a grant of public lands to the several states for the benefit of indigent insane persons." [1] The bill, said Pierce, proposed that the federal government should make provision to the amount of the value of ten million acres of land for an eleemosynary object within the several states to be administered by the political authority of the same. It presented at the threshold the question whether any such act on the part of the federal government was warranted and sanctioned by the Constitution. If Congress had the power to make provision for the indigent insane, it had the same power to provide for indigent who were not insane, and thus to transfer to the federal government the charge of all the poor in all the states. He could not find any authority in the Constitution for making the federal government the great almoner of public charity throughout the United States. He contended that the expenditure could not be justified on the basis of the general-welfare clause, assuming the narrow interpretation of that clause and arguing that it justified expenditures only for purposes otherwise authorized in the Constitution. As for the provision in Article IV, Section 3, of the Constitution, saying, "The Congress shall have power to dispose of and make all needful rules and regulations respecting the territory or other property belonging to the United States," he contended that it did not authorize the donation of land for charitable purposes.[2] Pierce took the position that from the point of view of constitutionality it was wholly immaterial whether the appropriation was in the form of money or in land. He viewed the subject broadly and took a firm stand against the beginning of what in recent years has become a vast grant-in-aid program whereby the federal government shapes the course of activities in the states through the distribution of federal funds.[3]

The measure to provide federal aid to the states for the benefit of indigent insane persons was not passed over the President's veto; but

---

[1] *Messages and Papers of the Presidents*, VI, 2780.

[2] Later in the same year Pierce wrote a long veto message in connection with an internal-improvements bill, in which he elaborated the same narrow interpretation of the Constitution. *Ibid.*, VI, 2790.

[3] See, for example, Austin F. MacDonald, *Federal Aid* (1928); Jane Perry Clark, *The Rise of a New Federalism* (1938); Henry J. Bitterman, *State and Federal Grants-in-Aid* (1938); V. O. Key, Jr., *The Administration of Federal Grants to States* (1937); Walter Thompson, *Federal Centralization* (1923).

in December, 1857, Justin S. Morrill introduced in the House of Representatives a somewhat similar measure to donate public lands to the several states and territories which might provide colleges for the benefit of agriculture and the mechanic arts. He presented statistics to show a startling decline in acreage yield throughout the older states in the Union. His evidence pointed to a widespread deterioration of the soil. "The great, irreversible law of American agriculture appears in the constant and increasing diminution of agricultural products, without any advance in prices. It follows, just in proportion, that capital is disappearing and that labor receives a diminishing reward. Our country is growing debilitated, and we propagate the consumptive disease with all the energy of private enterprise and public patronage." [4] Although we brought forth new states by the litter, he continued, and when we wanted more, we, like our Norman ancestors, committed grand larceny and annexed them, the bitter fact appeared that these new states in half a century would become depleted and stationary.

Although in other nations concerted effort was being made to educate whole peoples for the promotion of their agricultural welfare with governmental aid in the lead, no such effort was being made in the United States. Colleges were needed through which the preservation of the natural heritage could be taught. There was need for experimentation such as could be done only at thoroughly scientific institutions. There was need for the testing of the capability of soils and the power of different fertilizers, of the relative value of different foods for farm animals, of the effects of different depths of plowing and of drainage upon agricultural yield, of the vitality and the deterioration of seeds, of the characteristics and value of different breeds of animals, and of remedies for many crop diseases.

The government had been generous, Morrill said, in meeting the demands of commerce and manufacture. Agricultural men dwelt apart. They could not combine to secure general improvements or to make their complaints heard. He urged this project upon Congress to meet their great need.

As for the constitutionality of the measure, he remarked that, when there was a lack of arguments to be brought against the merits of a measure, the Constitution was fled to as an inexhaustible arsenal of supply. All he asked was "that the Constitution may not be strained and perverted to defeat a measure no less of public good than of pub-

[4] 27 *Congressional Globe* 1693.

lic justice — just politically, just to all the states, and just, above all, to the manhood of our country."[5]  This was not a proposal of legislation for the benefit of a class, "for here is one where four-fifths of all the people are directly, and all the rest indirectly, interested."[6]  He thought the measure was authorized by the constitutional provision empowering Congress to dispose of, and make all needful rules and regulations respecting, the territory or other property belonging to the United States.   During and since 1850, he said, more than twenty-five million acres of land had been granted to ten states and one territory to aid in the construction of more than fifty railroads.   Down to June 30, 1857, Congress had ungrudgingly donated to different states and territories more than sixty-seven million acres for schools and universities.[7]  If such donations were constitutional as to the states in which the public lands were found, how could they be unconstitutional, he asked, merely because donations went to other than those in which the lands were located?[8]

The measure passed the House of Representatives by a bare majority, without the reporting of any clear constitutional arguments in opposition.   A member of the Senate quoted in full the Pierce veto of the bill to grant lands to the states for the benefit of indigent insane persons, and rephrased the same arguments.[9]  Another senator said:

> If we give lands to states for colleges and extend to them the franking privilege, how long will it be before they will ask for every object, and come to rely entirely upon the general government even for the expenses of their own, until they have become so dependent on the national Treasury that they will have but a shadow of sovereignty left, and be mere suppliants at the doors of Congress for anything that the general government may have at its disposal?[10]

The bill passed the Senate, but it was vetoed by President James Buchanan.[11]  He deemed the bill both inexpedient and unconstitutional.   As to constitutionality, he assumed as "undeniable" the proposition "that Congress does not possess the power to appropriate money in the Treasury, raised by taxes on the people of the United States, for the purpose of educating the people of the respective states."[12]  Should Congress exercise such a power, he contended, the

---

[5] *Ibid.,* p. 1692.          [6] *Ibid.,* p. 1695.          [7] *Ibid.,* p. 1696.
[8] *Ibid.,* p. 1696.          [9] 28 *Congressional Globe* 714-717.
[10] *Ibid.,* p. 717.   For additional constitutional argument see *ibid.,* pp. 851-857.
[11] *Messages and Papers of the Presidents,* VII, 3074.          [12] *Ibid.,* p. 3078.

result would be the destruction of barriers carefully constructed in the Constitution to separate state from federal authority. The collection by the federal government of revenue for the use of the states as well as the federal government "would be an actual consolidation of the federal and state governments so far as the great taxing and money power is concerned, and constitute a sort of partnership between the two in the Treasury of the United States, equally ruinous to both." [13]

He contended that the constitutional authorization to dispose of the property of the United States did not include the power to give the land away. To show the true intent of the provision, he quoted from Chief Justice Taney's opinion in the Dred Scott case. He admitted that Congress had in numerous instances granted land for the purposes of education. But these grants, he said, had been chiefly made to the new states as they successively entered the Union and consisted at first of one section and afterward of two sections of the public land in each township for the use of schools, as well as of additional sections for a state university. Such grants were not, in his opinion, a violation of the Constitution. He justified them as speculation by the federal government for the purpose of enhancing the value of adjacent land still owned by the government. On the other hand, he said, no one would contend that donations of land to all the states of the Union for the erection of colleges within the limits of each could be embraced by this principle. It could not be pretended that an agricultural college in New York or Virginia would aid the settlement or facilitate the sale of public lands in Minnesota or California.

The agricultural college bill was not passed over the President's veto. In June, 1860, he applied the same constitutional arguments in a veto message on a homestead bill. [14] This bill proposed to give, for a mere twenty-five cents an acre, homesteads of one hundred and sixty acres to persons residing thereon for five years. It ceded to states public lands within their respective limits which had been subject to sale at private entry and remained unsold after the lapse of thirty years. The latter provision was an outright donation, and the charge of twenty-five cents an acre was so low that the grant of homesteads was virtually in the same class. Buchanan quoted from his earlier veto message to justify his contention that Congress had no power to donate land either to individuals or to states. The bill was not passed

[13] *Ibid.*, p. 3078.　　　[14] *Ibid.*, p. 3139.

over the veto, but Buchanan's attitude provided a focal point of attack on the policies of his administration and helped drive the advocates of free homesteads into the ranks of the Republican party.

## THE CIVIL-WAR MEASURES

Early in the first regular session of the first Republican Congress new homestead and agricultural college bills were introduced, and also a bill to establish a Department of Agriculture. The new party was pledged to the support of agriculture, and southern opposition had largely withdrawn by way of secession. All three measures were passed in spite of preoccupation with the war.

The Department of Agriculture bill was the first enacted, perhaps in part because of the impetus which it received through the first annual message of President Lincoln.

> Agriculture, confessedly the largest interest of the nation, has not a department nor a bureau, but a clerkship only, assigned to it in the government. While it is fortunate that this great interest is so independent in its nature as not to have demanded and extorted more from the government, I respectfully ask Congress to consider whether something more cannot be given voluntarily with general advantage.
>
> Annual reports exhibiting the condition of our agriculture, commerce, and manufactures would present a fund of information of great practical value to the country. While I make no suggestion as to details, I venture the opinion that an agricultural and statistical bureau might profitably be organized.[15]

The clerkship mentioned by the President had a long history. American consuls and other representatives abroad had long taken an interest in the acquisition of seeds and cuttings for the introduction of new plants and trees into the United States. In 1836, the commissioner of patents received from government representatives abroad and from others considerable quantities of seeds and plants, which he distributed to farmers throughout the country. He acted without government authority and with no aid except the use of the franks of congressmen who were his personal friends. He urged, however, that the government should officially take up the work of aiding agriculture in this and other ways. In 1839, Congress made its first appropriation to the extent of one thousand dollars for the purpose of collecting and distributing seeds, prosecuting agricultural investigations, and procuring agricultural statistics. The work was to be done under

---

[15] *Ibid.*, pp. 3253-3254.

the commissioner of patents, who at that time was an official of the Department of State. The work expanded steadily and new and larger appropriations were made. When, in 1849, the Patent Office was transferred to the newly established Department of the Interior, the work was further expanded.[16] By 1862, when the independent agency was created, some sixty thousand dollars a year was being spent on agriculture.

One or more bills to provide for a Bureau of Agriculture in the Interior Department were introduced in the House of Representatives. The committee on agriculture, to which they were referred, reported instead a bill to establish a Department of Agriculture. The department was to be headed, not by a secretary, but by a commissioner, and was clearly intended, for a time at least, to occupy a subordinate status with reference to the other departments of the government. No additional appropriation was to be made beyond the sixty thousand dollars already being allocated annually to agricultural work.

The report of the committee said that the establishment of an agricultural bureau or department had been discussed more or less for the last twenty years. It noted the recommendation of President Taylor for the establishment of an agricultural bureau to be connected with the Department of the Interior [17] and quoted the recommendation of President Lincoln set forth above. It quoted also a recommendation in the current report of the Secretary of the Interior for the creation of an agricultural bureau.

The committee remarked that farmers were numerous and were worthy and had votes, and for this reason had had much eulogistic language bestowed upon them by public men; but that "soft words butter no parsnips." Many pleasing things had been said about farmers, but very little had been done for them. A small appropriation for the distribution of seeds and plants was, indeed, made annually, but it was placed under the supervision of the commissioner of patents, whose leading and engrossing business was in another direction. The work of agriculture had been tolerated rather than fostered, and had suffered often from neglect and mismanagement. The committee proposed to rescue the work from undeserved subordinate obscurity and from hurtful mismanagement by transforming it from

[16] Charles H. Greathouse, *Historical Sketch of the United States Department of Agriculture* (1907), pp. 8-9. For a contemporary study of the department see John M. Gaus and Leon O. Wolcott, *Public Administration and the United States Department of Agriculture* (1940).

[17] See *Messages and Papers of the Presidents*, VI, 2556.

a clerkship to the grade of commissioner, and by attaching to it a salary which should command talent and integrity above mediocrity and above suspicion. It proposed to develop the new department into an instrument for the collection of a wide variety of information needed by the farmers of the country.[18]

The bill passed the House of Representatives with but little debate. In the Senate attempts were made, on the one hand, to expand the functions of the proposed department beyond those provided for in the bill and, on the other hand, to restrict it to a mere bureau in the Department of the Interior. Senators supporting the measure in the form in which it came from the House of Representatives urged its adoption as an obligation owed to farmers, and showed that it had the support of the national agricultural societies. Senator John P. Hale, of New Hampshire, an opponent of the bill, remarked that

> the great anxiety to have agriculture elevated to a department of this government, and finally to a seat in the cabinet, for that is what it looks to, does not come from the men of whom my excellent friend from Rhode Island speaks, that lean upon their plow handles; but it comes from the men who want them to take their hands off the plow handle and vote for them at the ballot-box. . . . If the genius of agriculture could be impersonated and could come here today, its prayer to the American Congress would be, "for God's sake, let us alone." . . . If you make a separate department of this, you will have it with a cabinet minister before long. Go into the President's room in this Capitol and you will see painted upon the walls, first Washington, and then on the panels around five heads of departments, a part of whom only constituted his cabinet. Now there are seven heads of departments, with places in the cabinet. The Navy Department and the Department of the Interior have been created since the administration of Washington, other heads of existing departments have taken place in the cabinet, increasing it from three to seven, and this agricultural department will soon furnish another. Such is the growth of the cabinet. . . . I think the time is inopportune for creating a new department of this government. I think it had better remain as it is.[19]

Senator Edgar Cowan, of Pennsylvania, challenged the bill on constitutional grounds. He outlined his philosophy of government as follows: "That the various departments of industry only desire from the government to be let alone; that the true governmental function

[18] For the report see 32 *Congressional Globe* 855-856.
[19] 32 *Congressional Globe* 2014.

is to protect the people, furnish to them security in their lives, their liberty, and their property, so that every man may have what he earns and may be enabled to keep it after he has got it; and the less government meddles with it the better." [20] He found in the Constitution the power "to promote the progress of science and useful arts," but only by the method of "securing for limited times to authors and inventors the exclusive right to their respective writings and discoveries." He quoted Story's *Commentaries* to show that the Constitutional Convention had rejected a provision authorizing Congress "to establish public institutions, rewards, and immunities for the promotion of agriculture, commerce, and manufactures." [21]

The situation was such, however, that it was hard to make effective the argument against the constitutionality of the bill. It could not be said that the Constitution forbade the placement of a representative of agriculture in the cabinet, since the Constitution made no mention of the cabinet as such. Furthermore, even though the sponsors of the bill may have looked forward to the time when the head of the Department of Agriculture would enter the cabinet, they had no expectation of his doing so immediately since they gave the head the rank only of commissioner. It was hard to attack the bill on the ground of unconstitutional expenditures, because, whatever the intent as to the future, it provided for no immediate increase in expenditures. Few senators were willing to agree that the appropriation gradually built up from one thousand dollars to sixty thousand dollars for the distribution of seeds to farmers and for related purposes had been made year after year in violation of the Constitution.

Because of the difficulty of presenting effective constitutional arguments, senators who were unwilling to go beyond the establishment of a Bureau of Agriculture in the Department of the Interior had to rely largely on arguments from expediency. Senator Fessenden, who favored such a bureau, discussed probable developments as follows:

A head of a bureau is nobody without clerks, and he must have a certain number. Then we shall find that there are new experiments to be tried. We shall have recommendations at once for a little more science here and a little more science there, and that costs money. In the first place, we must have the scientific men, and then we must have money for the experiments. Thus it will go on; it is only a

[20] *Ibid.*, p. 2015.
[21] See Joseph Story, *Commentaries on the Constitution of the United States* (3 vols., 1833), III, sec. 1150, pp. 50-51.

question of time.   If we begin with a department, what is the head of a department without bureaus and without clerks?  Nobody.   The thing enlarges; and my word for it, it will not be many years before a similar proposition to that of the honorable senator from Indiana will be adopted or strongly urged — a department with bureaus, and, necessarily, clerks; and we shall have a hundred clerks in that department, too.[22]

The bill to establish a Department of Agriculture was passed in spite of the opposition and was approved on May 15, 1862.[23]   The be-ginning of the fulfillment of Senator Fessenden's prophecy was indi-cated the following year, when appropriations for agriculture were made to the extent of $118,000,[24] nearly twice the amount appropri-ated in any year before the establishment of the department.

Before continuing with the story of the expansion of the Depart-ment of Agriculture, it is well to turn to the other two agricultural measures enacted in 1862.   The Homestead Act, called "An act to secure homesteads to actual settlers on the public domain," [25] re-sembled the measure vetoed by President Buchanan.   In spite of the constitutional arguments hitherto made by the former President, the new Congress paid little or no attention to constitutional questions. The debate was brief, and the opposition concerned itself largely with questions of expediency, such as the curtailment of federal revenue by giving away public lands instead of selling them, and the failure to discriminate adequately in favor of persons who had ren-dered military service to the United States.   Special concessions were made in the act to soldiers and their families.

An important purpose of the act, as indicated by the title, was to transfer ownership of public land to actual settlers rather than to speculators who, without improving it, might hold it for sale in later years after increases in value.   Homesteads of one hundred and sixty acres each could be secured by residence on the land for a period of five years and by the payment of small fees.   A way was left open to large-scale ownership, however, in that homesteaders could secure immediate possession by the payment of the low prices per acre hitherto charged, and could sell the land thereafter to any purchaser. Land other than the public domain, such as areas taken over from Indians, continued to be offered for sale.   The income of the govern-ment from the sale of public lands continued substantial for many

[22] 32 *Congressional Globe* 2016.
[23] 12 Stat. 387.          [24] 12 Stat. 682, 691.          [25] 12 Stat. 392.

years. Extensive grants were made to railroads, furthermore, which were often consolidated into large holdings in spite of the efforts of the government to promote landholding by actual settlers.

For many years, in spite of additional legislation and varied expedients, the government found law enforcement difficult with reference to the public domain. People having no legal claim to land settled upon and exploited it. Timber and minerals in tremendous quantities were stolen outright. There being little public sentiment against such exploitation, prosecution proved difficult. It was only after most of the valuable land had passed into private hands, or had been set aside as forest reserves, that the government established anything like adequate control.[26]

Congress also passed an agricultural colleges bill,[27] similar to that vetoed by President Buchanan. The measure, approved on July 2, 1862, was entitled "An act donating public lands to the several states and territories which may provide colleges for the benefit of agriculture and the mechanic arts," and is commonly known as the Morrill Act. The act provided for the apportionment of thirty thousand acres of public lands to each state for each senator and representative in Congress to which the state was entitled by the apportionment under the census of 1860. A state having public land within its borders was to make its selection from such land. States having no public land within their borders were to receive scrip from the federal government which could be sold by the state to persons wishing to use it to acquire public land in other states. The proceeds from the sale of land or of scrip were to be invested in state or federal bonds.[28] Only the income from the funds was to be used. The states accepting the provisions of the statute were to use the income for

> the endowment, support, and maintenance of at least one college where the leading object shall be, without excluding other scientific and classical studies, and including military tactics, to teach such branches of learning as are related to agriculture and the mechanic arts, in such manner as the legislatures of the states may respectively prescribe, in order to promote the liberal and practical education

[26] See, for example, Benjamin Horace Hibbard, *A History of the Public Land Policies* (1924); Paul Wallace Gates, "The Homestead Law in an Incongruous Land System," *American Historical Review*, XLI (July, 1936), 652-681; Fred A. Shannon, "The Homestead Act and the Labor Surplus," *ibid.*, pp. 637-651. See also Homer Cummings and Carl McFarland, *Federal Justice* (1937), chapter XIII.

[27] 12 Stat. 503.

[28] The statute used the word "stocks" in place of "bonds."

of the industrial classes in the several pursuits and professions in life.[29]

The act prescribed few details as to the administration of the funds. Only after the state legislatures had assented to certain conditions would the grants be available. Diminutions of the funds were to be made up by the states. The act included no requirement that the states should participate in expenditures on the colleges, but provided that no portion of the federal funds should be applied to buildings — with the result that a certain amount of expense was inevitably incurred by some other agency than the federal government. Each college must make an annual report, sending it to other colleges and to the Secretary of the Interior. The governor of each accepting state must make an annual report to Congress concerning the sale of land and scrip and the use made of the proceeds. This measure, like the Homestead Act, was passed by both houses of Congress without any comprehensive discussion of constitutional questions. Many of the states immediately accepted the conditions of the act, and made use of the funds either in connection with colleges already doing a certain amount of agricultural work or in connection with newly established institutions.[30]

GROWTH OF THE DEPARTMENT OF AGRICULTURE

The expansion of the Department of Agriculture fulfilled prophecies. New functions and personnel were added and annual appropriations were increased. The initial appropriation of sixty thousand dollars in 1862 had risen by 1880 well above three hundred thousand dollars. Additional increases were allowed in succeeding years. In 1876, the National Grange started a movement to give the Department of Agriculture full status as an executive department of the government, with a Secretary who would join the heads of other departments as a member of the President's cabinet.[31]

The first glimpse of success in advancing the status of the department was gained in February, 1881, an attempt then being made to secure a two-thirds vote of the House of Representatives necessary under the rules to permit consideration of a bill for the purpose. The chairman of the committee on agriculture opposed the bill, prophesy-

[29] 12 Stat. 504.
[30] For one of the many accounts of agricultural developments see Alfred Charles True, *A History of Agricultural Education in the United States, 1785-1925* (1929), Part III.
[31] Solon J. Buck, *The Granger Movement* (1913), pp. 117-118.

ing that if it was enacted into law, the department would become a political engine rather than a department of the government intended to foster and promote the interests of agriculture. He held that there was absolutely no warrant in the Constitution for the creation of an executive department of that character.[32] Friends of the measure declared that the bill violated no provision of the Constitution and pointed to the "necessary-and-proper" clause as sufficient justification. Action on the measure had to be suspended, however, because of failure to secure the necessary two-thirds vote to authorize consideration.

From 1881 until 1889, when success was finally achieved, bills to advance the status of the Department of Agriculture were before Congress in some form, and were considered either in committee or on the floor. Decision was complicated by the efforts of groups of legislators to secure departmental organization for other interests than agriculture. A Department of Industry, or of Industries, was proposed many times. It was to include bureaus representing agriculture and commerce, and provision for a labor bureau was subsequently added. No such department was created, but labor interests secured independent action. The Knights of Labor had been instrumental in the creation of labor bureaus in each of many states, to collect statistics and perform other functions in the interest of labor.[33] The organization now sought the creation of a Department of Labor in the federal government. In 1884, it succeeded in securing the establishment of a bureau in the Department of the Interior.[34] Not content with a mere bureau, the interests involved continued agitation until 1888, when a Department of Labor comparable to the existing Department of Agriculture was established.[35] It was headed by a commissioner. Its status was comparable to that of a bureau except for the fact that it was responsible to no department.

The several efforts to merge governmental organization for agriculture with that for labor and commerce having failed, the agricultural group continued its independent struggle to secure full-fledged department status for the Department of Agriculture. In 1889, a bill was passed making it an executive department headed by a Secretary.[36] The Secretary of Agriculture received a place in the cabinet along with the heads of the other major departments.

[32] 11 *Congressional Record* 1318.
[33] Terence V. Powderly, *Thirty Years of Labor* (1890), pp. 313-316.
[34] 23 Stat. 60.     [35] 25 Stat. 182.     [36] 25 Stat. 659.

## FUNDS FOR AGRICULTURAL EDUCATION

Persons critical of the original grants of land to the states for the establishment of agricultural colleges, on the ground that the original expenditure would be but the beginning, proved to have been sound in their reasoning. The next important step in that direction was taken in 1887. Congress then passed the Hatch Act for the establishment and maintenance of agricultural experiment stations in connection with the agricultural colleges.[37] The experiment stations were provided for "in order to aid in acquiring and diffusing among the people of the United States useful and practical information on subjects connected with agriculture, and to promote scientific investigations and experiments respecting the principles and applications of agricultural science." Senate debate on the bill revealed opposition all the way from the position of persons who thought that the original establishment of the Department of Agriculture had been unconstitutional down to mere objections with reference to detailed features of the bill. Senator John J. Ingalls, of Kansas, characterized the bill as

> one of that great category of measures which have been presented to us in times past in obedience rather to the clamor of a certain select class of self-constituted reformers of all the institutions of the earth, and it is based upon an entirely mistaken apprehension of the theory of this government. It illustrates the tendency of this class of agitators to demand the continual interposition of the national government in state and local and domestic affairs, with the result, as I believe, of absolutely destroying the independence and freedom of individual conduct, and subverting the theory on which the government is based and in the conduct of which hitherto it has reached such great results.[38]

He objected especially to a provision "that in order to secure, as far as practicable, uniformity of methods and results in the work of such stations," it was to be the duty of the United States commissioner of agriculture to provide forms for tabulating and reporting results and in other ways to give aid to the experiment stations. This looked to the senator like the beginning of coercion by the general government over colleges which existed as state institutions. He had no objections to making appropriations to assist agricultural experiment

---

[37] 24 Stat. 440. The funds appropriated were to be paid out of money in the Treasury proceeding from the sale of public lands.

[38] 18 *Congressional Record* 723-724. For the same argument by Joseph R. Hawley, of Connecticut, see *ibid.*, pp. 722-723, 728-729.

stations in the several states, but he insisted that the federal government relinquish control over the funds appropriated, as the original grants of land for agricultural colleges had been made without any right whatever of federal control except in the matter of restrictions laid upon the states in connection with their acceptance of the grant. Senator George G. Vest, of Missouri, declared that there was "no power to grant money in the Treasury for the purposes of education in the states, whether it be agricultural education or education in its general features." [39] He asserted that some of the best lawyers in the United States had doubted the constitutionality of the establishment of the Department of Agriculture.[40]

The Senate faced a dilemma in the matter of control. It wished to avoid trespassing beyond the constitutional line of jurisdiction of the federal government. Yet, if federal funds were to be appropriated in large amounts, it was the duty of Congress to see that the funds were not misused. The bill as passed was apparently a compromise worked out in the light of the two seemingly conflicting obligations. One section of the act provided "that nothing in this act shall be construed to impair or modify the legal relation existing between any of the said colleges and the government of the states or territories in which they are respectively located." The section requiring the commissioner of agriculture to take certain steps to promote the purposes of the act was retained. He was given no power of direct coercion, however; and, although each station was required to make to him as well as to the Secretary of the Treasury an annual report of its operations, including a statement of receipts and expenditures, he was not empowered to question the expenditures that were made. The states were in full control after they had assented to the purposes of the grant and after the appropriations had been made. In the way of coercion the federal government retained only the power to refuse the annual appropriations in succeeding years.

Yet, in spite of the limited degree of supervision to be exercised by the federal government, it was greater than any provided for by the Morrill Act under which the land-grant colleges were established. In 1906, a new measure, known as the Adams Act, added to the annual expenditures on the experiment stations. This measure extended federal control, limited the types of research to be done, and placed in the hands of the Secretary of Agriculture responsibility for the proper

[39] *Ibid.*, p. 726.
[40] *Ibid.*, p. 727.

administration of the law.[41] The development was along a line that has come to seem inevitable. If the federal government is to make huge expenditures in the states for agricultural and other purposes, it may be expected to insist more and more on the right to supervise the use of the funds appropriated, even though in doing so it appears to encroach upon a governmental area hitherto thought to be within the exclusive jurisdiction of the states.

In 1890, Congress added to the annual expenditures of the federal government on the agricultural colleges through what was known as the second Morrill Act.[42] Each state was to receive fifteen thousand dollars for the first year covered and that amount plus an additional thousand dollars each year thereafter until a total yearly appropriation of twenty-five thousand dollars was reached. The payments were to be made out of money in the Treasury not otherwise appropriated, "arising from the sale of public lands." It defined more fully and more narrowly the character of the education on which the money might be spent, thereby giving rise to fears that the federal government was encroaching on the power of the states to control education. "If the desire is to aid the agricultural colleges of the states," said Senator Reagan, "I have no objection to the appropriation proposed, but if the object is to make a pretext for taking the control and supervision of that education away from the states, then I think it is very seriously objectionable."[43] Senator John C. Morgan, of Alabama, thought certain features of the bill implied that Congress was to take control of education in the states where the colleges were situated and that the schools were to be regulated by administrative procedures prescribed by Congress. He said:

> I do not believe in the Congress of the United States undertaking the scheme of educating the young men of this country, but I do believe, and I believe heartily and earnestly, in complying with the great trust under which the public lands are held under the deeds of conveyance to the government of the United States for the benefit of the states by placing these funds in the control of the states and letting them regulate education according to their best judgment.[44]

Senators discussed here, as they had done in connection with other educational measures not directly connected with agriculture, the

---

[41] 34 Stat. 63. For the Purnell Act of 1925, adding further to the funds allotted to the experiment stations, see 43 Stat. 970.

[42] 26 Stat. 417.

[43] 21 *Congressional Record* 6086. See also p. 6333.　　　　[44] *Ibid.*, p. 6333.

problem of differentiating between funds in the Treasury derived from the sale of public lands and funds coming from taxation and other sources. The issue in connection with this measure was not clearly stated. Yet it is evident that Congress felt a greater freedom in making use of funds arising from the sale of public lands than of funds arising from taxation. It was in part, no doubt, for this reason that the source of the funds was emphasized.[45]

In the House of Representatives, one member, in lieu of an address on the subject, had printed in the *Congressional Record* President Buchanan's veto message of February 24, 1859, in which he held a land-grant colleges bill both unconstitutional and inexpedient.[46] Another representative apparently sought to show that no constitutional question was involved in the new measure by reprinting the first Morrill Act and the Agricultural Experiment Station Act. "How is there any question of constitutionality involved?" he asked. "How does there arise any question as to the propriety of this general policy? The acts referred to have already been passed; these colleges and agricultural stations have been established." [47]

The act as passed contained one rigid restriction. No money could be paid to any state which failed to provide the education in question to any person on account of race, although such education might be provided in separate institutions. The Secretary of the Interior was made responsible for enforcing this condition. As under the first Morrill Act, none of the money appropriated could be spent on buildings. The states must accept the terms of the act before receiving the money and, furthermore, must replace funds found to have been misapplied. The federal government, however, established no extensive machinery of administration or of inspection for the control of the use of the funds. Apart from dealing with gross abuses, administration remained in the educational institutions themselves. Even in later years with the addition of further appropriations, when money from the sale of public lands was no longer available to meet the payments,[48] the federal government exercised more restraint upon itself as to the control of general educational institutions than in connection with obviously professional organizations such as the agricultural experiment stations. The gradual drift, however, in education

[45] See *ibid.*, pp. 6340-6341, 8839.
[46] *Ibid.*, pp. 8832-8833.
[47] Congressman James H. Blount, of Georgia, *ibid.*, pp. 8838-8839.
[48] See 31 Stat. 179; 49 Stat. 436.

as elsewhere, was the infiltration of federal policy into activities financed by the federal government.

As for expenditures on the Department of Agriculture, they continued to increase until the department became the largest in the government. Although the Supreme Court did not pass directly upon the constitutionality of such appropriations, the long-established custom, coupled with more recent constitutional interpretations in other fields, has resulted in general acceptance of the belief that the making of such expenditures does not violate the Constitution.[49]

[49] For recent decisions as to the power of the federal government over agriculture see chapter 37.

# CONTROL OF RAILROADS

ALTHOUGH THE HISTORY OF RAILROADS in the United States between 1860 and 1900 is constitutional history only to a limited degree, it involves a great variety of interrelated constitutional questions. The following, in brief enumeration, are some of the factors involved. The many important statutes dealing with railroads represented a sweeping expansion of the exercise of legislative power by Congress. The enactment of such measures accustomed Congress and the people to a régime wherein Congress exercised authority over fields of industrial and commercial enterprise. By chartering companies, making grants of land, and lending money, Congress stimulated the construction of railroads, and, in seeking to protect the interests of the public in railroads built partly by means of public credit, it sought to exercise over such railroads control broader in scope than that then exercised over other railroads. In doing so it accumulated a body of experience preparatory to the exercise of general regulatory powers. For the first time since the lapsing of the charter of the second Bank of the United States, in 1836, the government competed for power with corporations able effectively to challenge its authority.

The extent of permissible governmental interference with private property gave rise to argument in Congress and state legislatures and in state and federal courts. The attitudes of the times were predominantly laissez-faire. The chaos of a changing order and the abuses perpetrated by buccaneering businessmen provoked demands for governmental control. By contrast the courts began to broaden the interpretation of "due process of law" in order to protect private property against what many judges and other persons regarded as undesirable governmental interference. The concept of "business affected with a public interest" was established in American constitutional law to justify price control in exceptional fields only, just as the doctrine of police power, heretofore described, was developed to justify other types of regulation as exceptions from the principle that business was, in general, to be left unhampered by government.   Legislatures and courts wrestled with the question of the extent of state power over railroad business which extended beyond the lines of the regulating state; the courts so hedged that power as to render the states virtually impotent as to interstate business.   Congress and the federal courts were concerned about the extent of the power of the federal government over interstate commerce — whether it was limited to preventing obstruction or extended to positive legislation — and about the extent of the commerce power of Congress over business which was intrastate but inseparably linked with interstate business.

Federal regulation of railroads during the early years was based on a variety of powers.   The war powers provided the basis for important steps taken during the Civil War, including temporary control of certain lines, authorization of new lines, and loans for construction.   The postal powers provided an important supplementary source of power over railroads which carried mail.   The commerce power came into its own gradually, becoming the major source of federal regulation of railroads in 1887 with enactment of the broad measure pursuant to which the Interstate Commerce Commission was created.   The establishment of that commission, a new kind of agency in the federal government, was important as a source of constitutional controversies.   All these and other items of constitutional development were involved in the railroad history of the period.   Those of outstanding importance are discussed more fully in the following pages.

### THE PACIFIC RAILROADS

On July 1, 1862, President Lincoln approved "An act to aid in the construction of a railroad and telegraph line from the Missouri River to the Pacific Ocean, and to secure to the government the use of the same for postal, military, and other purposes." [1]   Pursuant to this act and an amending act of July 2, 1864, [2] Congress provided for the first transcontinental railroad, chartering the Union Pacific Railroad Company and making grants of public land and loans of federal bonds, and making similar grants to the Central Pacific Railroad Company, a California corporation already in existence.   The Union Pacific, connecting with eastern lines, was to build westward to meet the Cen-

[1] 12 Stat. 489.
[2] 13 Stat. 356.

tral Pacific building eastward. The two lines met near Ogden, Utah, in 1869. The Northern Pacific Railroad was incorporated by an act of July 2, 1864,[3] to make a northern connection with the Pacific coast. Subsequently, other lines received charters.

The establishment of the first transcontinental connection was undoubtedly a great achievement for its time. It was engineered by men who were energetic, daring, individualistic, and — some of them — ruthless and predatory. Little concern for the public interest marked the use of government funds. The method of construction frequently followed was to let liberal contracts to companies in which the railroad managers themselves had substantial interests. In this manner they enriched themselves without reference to the fate of the lines under construction.[4] The outstanding instance was the organization of the so-called Crédit Mobilier, a construction company which operated, under the domination of the brother of the man at the head of the Union Pacific, to drain away the financial resources of the railroad company. As a member of Congress, the head of the Crédit Mobilier was in position to look out for the legislative welfare of his organization. When threatened with congressional investigation, he undertook to distribute shares of the Crédit Mobilier stock among his fellow legislators for a small part of their value, with payments sometimes deferred until the obligations could be liquidated by dividends of the organization. The scandals were ultimately exposed; and the Attorney General was directed to investigate and determine whether or not the charter and franchises of the Union Pacific and Central Pacific had been forfeited by illegal conduct. To the Attorney General, as to others, the paramount consideration was that the railroad should be built rather than that the builders and the financiers should act scrupulously within the law. Although a suit was instituted at the direction of Congress, the government was unable to repair the damage that had been done.[5]

The government loans to the railroads were to be made in installments paid over on completion of portions of the line. They were to be repaid in thirty years with interest computed semiannually. The companies made every effort to secure loans as quickly as possible, but they resisted every effort of the government to bring about the management of their finances in such a way as to insure the repayment

[3] 13 Stat. 365.
[4] Stuart Daggett, *Chapters on the History of the Southern Pacific* (1922), pp. 70 ff.
[5] United States *v.* Union Pacific Railroad Co., 98 U.S. 569 (1879).

of principal and interest.[6]  One of the most important steps taken by Congress to protect the interests of the government was the passage in 1878 of the so-called Thurman Act,[7] which required twenty-five per cent of the net earnings of the Union Pacific and Central Pacific to be paid into a sinking fund for the retirement of the debt.  While including no such provision, the original statute did empower Congress to alter, amend, or repeal the act at any time.  The companies challenged the constitutionality of the sinking-fund measure.  The Supreme Court, speaking through Chief Justice Waite, sustained it as "a reasonable regulation of the administration of the affairs of the corporation and promotive of the interests of the public and the corporators."[8]  The legislation oppressed no one and inflicted no wrong, contended the Chief Justice.  Furthermore, it was warranted under the authority, by way of amendment, to change or modify the rights, privileges, and immunities granted by the charter.

Three justices dissented.  Justice Strong contended that the sinking-fund measure was an attempt at the exercise of judicial rather than of legislative power.  The statute, he said, "singles out two corporations, debtors of the government, by name and prescribes for them as debtors new duties to their creditor.  It thus attempts to perform the functions of a court.  This, I cannot but think, is outside of legislative action and power."[9]  Justice Bradley contended, "The law virtually deprives the companies of their property without due process of law; takes it for public use without compensation; and operates as an exercise by Congress of the judicial power of the government."[10]  He denounced it on grounds of policy and morality, saying that it had the effect of declaring to the world that the government did not consider itself bound by its engagements.  It set the example of repudiation of government obligations.  It struck a blow at the public credit.  It asserted the principle that might made right.  It sapped the foundations of public morality.  "Perhaps, however," he concluded, "these are considerations more properly to be addressed to the legislative discretion.  But when forced upon the attention by what, in my judgment, is an unconstitutional exercise of legislative power, they have a more than ordinary weight and significance."[11]  Justice Field introduced a vigorous dissent by saying, "The decision

---

[6] For an account of the subject see Homer Cummings and Carl McFarland, *Federal Justice* (1937), chapter XIV.

[7] 20 Stat. 56.        [8] Sinking Fund Cases, 99 U.S. 700, 726 (1879).

[9] *Ibid.*, pp. 738-739.        [10] *Ibid.*, p. 745.        [11] *Ibid.*, p. 750.

will, in my opinion, tend to create insecurity in the title to corporate property in the country." [12]

Although the decision was never overruled, the dissenting opinions were important. They reflected the laissez-faire attitude of what was soon to be that of a growing proportion of the members of the Supreme Court. They revealed the concern of the justices for the development of law in such a way as to avoid interference with corporate enterprise. The Bradley opinion, furthermore, showed the persistence of the idea that the due-process clause had capacity hitherto unused, for the protection of the rights of property.

Because of gross mismanagement of the Union Pacific and the Central Pacific, much of which was undoubtedly deliberate and for fraudulent purposes, the net earnings of the companies were so low as to render the sinking-fund measure ineffective as a means for providing payment of the railroad debt to the government. The companies apparently hoped to avoid payment altogether, either through outright cancellation of the debt or through postponement of the date of collection. Growing public hostility to the abuses characteristic of railroad management prevented Congress from taking any such step. Many newspapers and other railroad critics demanded a thorough investigation and full publicity concerning the management of the railroads that had received loans from the government. The demand became overwhelming early in 1887 when the New York *World* exposed the fact that in a little more than a decade Collis P. Huntington and Leland Stanford, as heads of the Central Pacific, had spent in Washington more than two million dollars without an accounting.[13] The indication was that the money had been used for wholesale bribery. As a result of the disclosure, Congress passed the act of March 3, 1887, providing for a thorough investigation into the workings and financial management of all the railroads that had received aid from the government in bonds.[14]

The investigating commission collected a tremendous quantity of evidence.[15] It disclosed the systematic lootings of the railroads in question over a considerable period of years. Huntington, Stanford, Jay Gould, and many other prominent railroad men who had some

[12] *Ibid.*, p. 750.
[13] Allan Nevins, *Grover Cleveland: A Study in Courage* (1933), pp. 352-353.
[14] 24 Stat. 488.
[15] *Report of the Commission and of the Minority Commissioner of the United States Pacific Railway Commission*, Senate Ex. Doc. No. 51, 50th Cong., 1st sess.

connection with the lines in question, gave testimony.  But in spite
of the facts disclosed by the testimony, witnesses were extremely
reticent as to matters likely to prove embarrassing.  Memories failed
at convenient points, and records were conveniently missing.

Leland Stanford was quite unable to remember the use that had
been made of some one hundred and seventy thousand dollars in
Sacramento, California, some eight years earlier.  The commission
asked him directly if any part of the money had been used for the
purpose of influencing legislation.  Stanford's counsel objected to the
question.  "We are perfectly willing," he declared, "to account to
the government for its proportion of any voucher that is produced, or
any entry upon the books of the company that is unexplained, and
therefore we cannot see that it will make any difference what we did
with the money — whether we threw it into the sea or wasted it in
any manner or form." [16]  Stanford took the same position, saying,
"Whether the money was expended or wasted or anything of the
kind, it can make no possible difference, because if it went into the
sea, if I had used this money improperly or thrown it away, I might
be accountable to the stockholders for my trust, but the government
cannot have any more than the money, and the company is willing to
account for that, if you are not satisfied with the action." [17]  He denied
that he had ever corrupted a member of the legislature and did not
know that any of his agents ever did, but he was unable to explain
past expenditures because he had destroyed the stubs of his check-
book every time when he went away and had kept "only such papers
as, in case I never returned, I cared that other people might see." [18]

Congress had attempted to give the investigating commission sufficient power to compel the submission of all the evidence and testimony needed.  The statute provided that a witness should not be
excused from testifying on the ground that testimony or evidence
might tend to incriminate him.  To prevent conflict with the provision in the Fifth Amendment against compulsory self-incrimination,
however, the statute further provided that such evidence or testimony
should not be used against such person on the trial of any criminal
proceedings. [19]  The statute provided that the circuit or district courts
of the United States might issue orders requiring persons to testify

[16] *Ibid.*, p. 3164.        [17] *Ibid.*, p. 3164.        [18] *Ibid.*, p. 3166.

[19] 24 Stat. 488, 491.  For discussion of this item in the House of Representatives, see
18 *Congressional Record* 2279-2280.  For a case decided as to compulsory self-incrimination the year before the enactment of the statute, see Boyd *v.* United States, 116 U.S. 616
(1886).

and produce books and papers. Any failure to obey such order of the court might be punished by the court as contempt.

The commission, evidently convinced that Stanford knew more of the answers to questions than he was revealing, sought an order from the United States circuit court in California to compel him to give the desired information. The court consisted of Stephen J. Field, a member of the Supreme Court of the United States, Lorenzo Sawyer, United States circuit judge in California, and George M. Sabin, United States district judge for Nevada. Justice Field was a close personal friend of Leland Stanford and of other men prominently connected with the Central Pacific Railroad Company.[20] None knew better than Field the contribution made to the economic life of California by the building of the railroad. Few knew better than he the difficulties that had had to be overcome in the building of the road. The fact that the builders were his intimate friends and associates contributed, no doubt, to harmonize his thinking with theirs. As a matter of principle, furthermore, he was opposed to government interference with private enterprise. Sawyer's philosophy was very similar to that of Field. The commission faced a severe handicap, therefore, in arguing against persuasive railroad lawyers that the court ought to issue an order to compel Stanford to give testimony he had not been able or had not seen fit to give.

The court reached a unanimous decision refusing to grant the desired order.[21] The provision of the act authorizing the courts to aid in the investigation in the manner indicated, said Field, must be adjudged void. "The federal courts, under the Constitution, cannot be made the aids to any investigation by a commission or a committee into the affairs of anyone. If rights are to be protected or wrongs redressed by any investigation, it must be conducted by regular proceedings in the courts of justice in cases authorized by the Constitution."[22] Referring to the fact that the commission did not regard itself bound by the ordinary rules of evidence, but would receive hearsay and *ex parte* statements, surmises and information of every character, Field remarked, "It cannot be that the courts of the United States can be used in furtherance of investigations in which all rules of evidence may be thus disregarded."[23]

[20] For a discussion, see Carl Brent Swisher, *Stephen J. Field, Craftsman of the Law* (1930), especially chapter IX. See also Bruce R. Trimble, *Chief Justice Waite, Defender of the Public Interest* (1938), pp. 261-262; and Howard Jay Graham, ed., "Four Letters of Mr. Justice Field," *Yale Law Journal*, XLVII (May, 1938), 1100-1108.

[21] *In re* Pacific Railway Commission, 32 Fed. 241 (1887).

[22] *Ibid.*, p. 258.          [23] *Ibid.*, p. 259.

Field could not see that the disposition of the money about which Stanford had been questioned was any concern of the United States. He regarded the proceedings as an unjustifiable intrusion. He declared:

> Of all the rights of the citizen, few are of greater importance or more essential to his peace and happiness than the right of personal security, and that involves, not merely protection of his person from assault, but exemption of his private affairs, books, and papers from the inspection and scrutiny of others. Without the enjoyment of this right, all other rights would lose half their value.[24]

The compulsory production of the private books and papers of a party otherwise than in the course of judicial proceedings or a direct suit for that purpose was

> the forcible intrusion into, and compulsory exposure of, one's private affairs and papers, without judicial process, or in the course of judicial proceedings, which is contrary to the principles of a free government, and is abhorrent to the instincts of Englishmen and Americans.[25]

Although judges in more recent years may continue to quote Field's general defense of the rights of individual liberty,[26] his application of the principle to the railroad men of his time was more extreme than any now likely to be given. At that time it had the effect of limiting the power of the government to investigate the management of the railroads. Even so, the disclosures were sweeping, and the difficulty of Congress in collecting the money due the government lay, not in lack of knowledge of abuses by the companies, but in the financial difficulty of collecting huge sums of money from corporations already on the verge of bankruptcy. The Union Pacific was thrown into receivership; and the property was eventually sold to a new Union Pacific Railway Company created under the laws of the state of Utah, and the debt to the federal government was liquidated.[27] As for the Central Pacific, it resisted payment by every possible device, and foreclosure seemed inevitable as the only method of collection. The people in control of it, however, were also in control of the Southern Pacific lines. If the Central Pacific were to pass out of their hands, the Central Pacific-Union Pacific combination might provide costly

[24] *Ibid.*, p. 250.     [25] *Ibid.*, p. 251.

[26] For a summary of the position taken by the Supreme Court down through the years on the power of the government to compel testimony which might be used in connection with legislation, see Sinclair v. United States, 279 U.S. 263 (1929).

[27] See Cummings and McFarland, *op. cit.*, pp. 287-288.

competition for the Southern Pacific. Rather than permit such a development, they agreed to issue bonds, guaranteed by the Southern Pacific, which would enable the government to clear its books of the debt.[28]

## BUSINESS AFFECTED WITH A PUBLIC INTEREST

For an understanding of relations between government and the railroads and other business and industrial enterprises from 1860 to 1900, it is necessary to keep in mind a fact frequently mentioned hitherto; namely, that according to prevailing ideas government was to interfere with business as little as possible. Its duties ended with the performance of police functions. The only legitimate regulator of business enterprise was competition. As to the consumer of the products and services offered for sale, the accepted principle was *caveat emptor,* let the buyer beware. Under a régime of free competition, all the shrewdness, ingenuity, and energy of producers, salesmen, and consumers were supposed to be brought into play. Government interference beyond the mere preservation of order was believed to destroy the proper balance of the competitive system, thereby injuriously affecting the welfare of society as a whole.

Unfortunately, the principle of free competition at times met obstructions in practice. Obstructions were particularly prevalent in railroad transportation. There were many sections of the country in which railroad competition did not exist. In such sections the local companies usually measured their transportation rates by what they thought the traffic would bear. The rates were oftentimes exorbitant. Severe competition might result in the bankruptcy of one or more lines. A company operating partly in a competitive area and partly in a section where there was no competition adjusted its rates accordingly, with corresponding complaints from shippers of the section where no competition existed. When local lines were built through particular sections to compete with powerful companies already in existence, the latter oftentimes reduced their rates deliberately to figures far below cost, and kept them there long enough to drive the competing line out of existence, after which rates were again raised to high levels.[29]

It was only natural, therefore, that the farmers of the affected areas, in spite of the traditional individualism of their beliefs, came to the

[28] *Ibid.,* pp. 290-293.
[29] See Carl Brent Swisher, *Motivation and Political Technique in the California Constitutional Convention, 1878-1879* (1930), chapter IV.

conclusion that state regulation of railroad rates was necessary. The National Grange, a secret order that flourished particularly in the period of the eighteen-seventies, educated the farmers to a demand for state regulatory legislation. Within a decade after the close of the Civil War, the concerted efforts of farmers brought about the enactment of regulatory measures in a considerable number of states. The railroad companies challenged the legislation; but the state courts, responsive to the same sentiment that had provoked legislative action, upheld the measures. If the railroads were to receive judicial protection against interference with their rate schedules, it would have to come from the Supreme Court. From October, 1875, to January, 1876, five cases coming from a number of different states were argued before the Supreme Court, to determine the constitutionality of state laws regulating railroad rates.[30]

The railroad cases were not decided until more than a year after the dates of argument. During the interim period, the Court heard arguments in a case involving state regulation of rates of grain elevators. This case, coming up for argument when it did, had an important effect upon the form of the decisions in the railroad cases.

The grain elevator case grew out of peculiar conditions in the Chicago area. Most of the grain produced in the West for sale in eastern or European markets passed through Chicago, and much of it had to be unloaded and reloaded there. Some fourteen warehouses or elevators had been constructed to meet the needs of the market. Their control was chiefly in the hands of nine business firms. These firms, acting in co-operation, were in position to determine for themselves the extent of the toll they would take from the product of a vast farming area. To prevent abuse of the economic position of these business firms, the legislature of Illinois enacted a measure prescribing maximum charges for the storage of grain. The challenge to the constitutionality of this interference with the rights of private property was brought before the Supreme Court.

The grain elevator case, Munn v. Illinois,[31] was considered along

---

[30] Chicago, Burlington and Quincy Railroad Co. v. Iowa, 94 U.S. 155; Peik v. Chicago and Northwestern Railway Co., 94 U.S. 164; The Chicago, Milwaukee and St. Paul Railroad Co. v. Ackley, 94 U.S. 179; The Winona and St. Peter Railroad Co. v. Blake, 94 U.S. 180; Stone v. Wisconsin, 94 U.S. 181. These cases were all decided on March 1, 1877.

[31] 94 U.S. 113 (1877). For discussion of the development of the doctrine of "business affected with a public interest," see Breck P. McAllister, "Lord Hale and Business Affected with a Public Interest," Harvard Law Review, XLIII (March, 1930), 759-791; Walton H. Hamilton, "Affectation with Public Interest," Yale Law Journal, XXXIX (June, 1930), 1089-1112; and Carl Brent Swisher, Stephen J. Field, Craftsman of the Law (1930), chapter XIV.

with the railroad cases, or Granger cases as they were called, and the doctrine applicable to all the cases was worked out at the same time. A majority of the Court saw the advisability of allowing the states to exercise the regulatory power in question. Yet the Court had no intention of sanctioning similar regulation of all property. The task, therefore, was to work out a distinction between property subject to rate regulation and property not subject thereto.

Chief Justice Waite found his principle in the writings of Sir Matthew Hale, published in the latter half of the seventeenth century. He found, in the words of Lord Chief Justice Hale, that, when private property was "affected with a public interest, it ceases to be *juris privati* only." Property became clothed with a public interest, said Chief Justice Waite in his own words,

> when used in a manner to make it of public consequence, and affect the community at large. When, therefore, one devotes his property to a use in which the public has an interest, he, in effect, grants to the public an interest in that use, and must submit to be controlled by the public for the common good, to the extent of the interest he has thus created. He may withdraw his grant by discontinuing the use; but, so long as he maintains the use, he must submit to the control.[32]

In accordance with this principle, Waite found that at common law many franchises had been subject to regulation. They had included the operation of ferries, public wharves and warehouses, common carriers, and the like. Down to the time of the adoption of the Fourteenth Amendment, it had not been supposed that statutes regulating the use, or even the price of the use, of private property necessarily deprived the owner of his property without due process of law. The amendment, he said, did not change the law in this particular. It simply prevented the states from doing that which would operate as such a deprivation.

He turned now to the business of grain elevators in the city of Chicago, to see if it fell within the concept of businesses affected with a public interest. Employing the words of counsel, he found that the managers of the elevators stood in the very gateway of commerce and took toll from all who passed. Their business, he said, most certainly tended to a common charge and had become a thing of public interest in use. Certainly, if any business could be clothed with a public interest and cease to be *juris privati* only, this was a

[32] 94 U.S. 126.

business of that kind. True, it could not be made a business of this kind by the constitution or statute of the state. But rather it was made so by the facts. He admitted that such a power of regulation might be abused, but held this no argument against its existence.

He found it unnecessary to discuss further the due-process clause of the Fourteenth Amendment. It had been shown that the regulation of other types of business affected with a public interest was within the law. The same principle applied here. As to the relation of the law to the power of Congress to regulate interstate commerce, he found that the regulation applied exclusively within the state, and that it did not encroach upon the exclusive domain of Congress in respect to interstate commerce.

The importance of Waite's opinion lies principally in the establishment of the doctrine of "business affected with a public interest" as a segment of the field of business enterprise in which government might regulate prices without depriving owners of their constitutional rights. "We know," he said, "that this is a power which may be abused; but that is no argument against its existence. For protection against abuses by legislatures the people must resort to the polls, not to the courts." [33]

Such ideas were highly objectionable to Justice Field. "The principle upon which the opinion of the majority proceeds," he declared, "is, in my judgment, subversive of the rights of private property, heretofore believed to be protected by constitutional guaranties against legislative interference, and is in conflict with the authorities cited in its support." [34] It would seem from the opinion, he added, "that the Court holds that property loses something of its private character when employed in such a way as to be generally useful." [35] He held that the due-process clause of the Fourteenth Amendment protected, not merely the title to property, but the use of property as well. Legislation which had the effect of impairing the use of property took it without due process of law and violated the Constitution. Justice Strong concurred in this dissent.

Having established the principle that a state might regulate the rates of a business affected with a public interest, Chief Justice Waite applied the principle briefly to each of the railroad cases, classified the business as one affected with a public interest, and held that the state might fix the rates. Justice Field again dissented, deploring the fact that the railroad companies had been practically placed at the

[33] *Ibid.*, p. 134.    [34] *Ibid.*, p. 136.    [35] *Ibid.*, p. 139.

mercy of the legislature of every state. The decision in the Munn case, he said,

> practically destroys all the guaranties of the Constitution and of the common law invoked by counsel for the protection of the rights of the railroad companies. Of what avail is the constitutional prohibition that no state shall deprive any person of his property except by due process of law, if the state can, by fixing the compensation which he may receive for its use, take from him all that is valuable in the property? To what purpose can the constitutional prohibition upon the state against impairing the obligation of contracts be invoked, if the state can, in the face of a charter authorizing a company to charge reasonable rates, prescribe what rates shall be deemed reasonable for services rendered? That decision will justify the legislature in fixing the price of all articles and the compensation for all services. It sanctions intermeddling with all business and pursuits and property in the community, leaving the use and enjoyment of property and the compensation for its use to the discretion of the legislature.[36]

## DEVELOPMENT OF THE PUBLIC-INTEREST DOCTRINE

Field's dissent was important because of the influence of his position upon future decisions. The doctrine of businesses affected with a public interest survived, but continued pressure soon resulted in the acceptance of limitations upon the regulatory power of the state. In a case decided in 1886, Waite stated for the Court that the power of regulation was a power of government, continuing in its nature, and that, if it could be bargained away at all, it could be only by words of positive grant or its equivalent in law. If there was a reasonable doubt, it must be resolved in favor of the existence of the regulatory power. Instead of reiterating his statement in the Munn case that the victims of legislative abuse must resort to the polls and not to the courts for the preservation of their rights, he now stated his position as follows:

> From what has thus been said it is not to be inferred that this power of limitation or regulation is itself without limit. This power to regulate is not a power to destroy, and limitation is not the equivalent of confiscation. Under pretense of regulating fares and freights, the state cannot require a railroad corporation to carry persons or property without reward; neither can it do that which in law amounts

[36] Chicago, Burlington and Quincy Railroad Co. *v.* Iowa, 94 U.S. 155, 186-187.

to a taking of private property for public use without just compensation, or without due process of law.[37]

The reference to due process of law seems to indicate the increased attention being given to that concept as a restriction upon state legislation. It was now apparent that the Supreme Court would keep a watchful eye over abuses which it had previously threatened to ignore, and would give protection if necessary.

For a decade after the decision in the Munn case, Justice Field dissented in the various cases in which the doctrine of business affected with a public interest was applied. In 1888, however, shortly after the death of Chief Justice Waite, he found that the position of the majority of the Court had grown sufficiently conservative to enable him to vote with the Court and to stand as its spokesman. The Court upheld a Georgia statute conferring powers of rate regulation and other powers upon a railroad commission. The incorporation of the company, said Field for the Court, the grant to it of special privileges, particularly the authority to exercise the state's right of eminent domain, and the obligation assumed by the acceptance of its charter to transport all persons and merchandise upon like conditions and upon reasonable rates, affected the property and employment with a public use. Where property was thus affected, the business in which it was used was subject to legislative control. The power extended to the prevention of extortion by unreasonable charges and of favoritism by unjust discrimination. "This is not a new doctrine," he said, "but old doctrine, always asserted whenever property or business is, by reason of special privileges received from the government the better to secure the purposes to which the property is dedicated or devoted, affected with a public use."[38]

The doctrine of public use as stated by Field was much narrower than the doctrine of public interest as stated by Waite. Waite's doctrine was capable of application to any business which vitally affected the public. Field's doctrine was limited to those businesses which had incurred obligations to the public in return for concessions made by the states.

In 1890, the Supreme Court further invaded the doctrine of public interest as originally announced by Chief Justice Waite. It held unconstitutional a Minnesota statute which provided that the ruling of a state commission as to the reasonableness of rates should be final,

---

[37] Stone *v.* Farmers' Loan and Trust Co., 116 U.S. 307, 331 (1886).

[38] Georgia Railroad and Banking Co. *v.* Smith, 128 U.S. 174, 179-180 (1888).

and that no appeal to the courts should be allowed. Said Justice Blatchford for the Court:

> It deprives the company of its right to a judicial investigation, by due process of law, under the forms and with the machinery provided by the wisdom of successive ages for the investigation judicially of the truth of a matter in controversy, and substitutes therefor, as an absolute finality, the action of a railroad commission which, in view of the powers conceded to it by the state court, cannot be regarded as clothed with judicial functions or possessing the machinery of a court of justice.[39]

Justice Bradley dissented. This case, he said, practically overruled Munn *v.* Illinois and the several railroad cases that were decided at the same time. The governing principle of those cases, he explained, was that the regulation and settlement of the fares of railroads and other public accommodations was a legislative prerogative and not a judicial one. It was urged in the case now before the Court that the reasonableness of a charge was a judicial question. Bradley contended that the question was pre-eminently legislative.[40] Two justices agreed with him, but their position never became the position of a majority of the Court.

In arrogating to the judiciary the final determination of reasonableness in government price-fixing, the Supreme Court transferred tremendous powers to that branch of the government. The next logical step was the holding that in order to be reasonable the rates fixed must be such as to yield to owners a fair return on a fair value of the property involved. The word "fair" and the word "value," like the word "reasonableness," were terms of extremely indefinite content. The content was left to be determined by the courts in each case. In 1898, in the case of Smyth *v.* Ames,[41] the Supreme Court announced the following extremely indefinite rule for guidance:

> The basis of all calculations as to the reasonableness of rates to be charged by a corporation maintaining a highway under legislative sanction must be the fair value of the property being used by it for the convenience of the public. And, in order to ascertain that value, the original cost of construction, the amount expended in permanent

[39] Chicago, Minneapolis and St. Paul Railroad Co. *v.* Minnesota, 134 U.S. 418, 457 (1890).

[40] *Ibid.,* p. 462.

[41] 169 U.S. 466.

improvements, the amount and market value of its bonds and stock, the present as compared with the original cost of construction, the probable earning capacity of the property under particular rates prescribed by statute, and the sum required to meet operating expenses, are all matters for consideration, and are to be given such weight as may be just and right in each case. We do not say that there may not be other matters to be regarded in estimating the value of the property.[42]

The content of the various items included in the so-called rule, and the amount of emphasis to be given to each, were so vague as to leave to the courts, for separate determination in every instance, the fairness of rates contested.

A tremendous amount of litigation took place in the years following the announcement of the rule. The courts were never able to agree upon a scheme of valuation sufficiently definite to make "fair value" clearly determinable apart from appeals to the courts. Determinations of value required many months of investigation. Shrewd corporation attorneys were able to get particular valuations set aside and rate schedules postponed through the strategy of perpetual litigation. Judges differed in social philosophies and expressed those differences in their appraisals of highly complicated economic facts. Down through the years, for example, judges warmly sympathetic with the interests of the corporations being regulated sought to emphasize reproduction cost as a true measure of value in periods in which the cost of reproduction of a given plant would have been high, whereas they sought to emphasize original cost in periods in which reproduction would have been less expensive than the original cost of construction.[43]

There was much doubt for a time whether or not a corporation was a person within the meaning of the constitutional provision that no state should deprive any person of life, liberty, or property without due process of law nor deny to any person within its jurisdiction the equal protection of the laws. It had long been understood that corporations were persons for certain purposes, but not for others. In 1882, in the argument of a case before the Supreme Court,[44] Roscoe Conkling made his famous, if not altogether authentic, presentation of facts to show that an important purpose of the Fourteenth Amend-

---

[42] *Ibid.*, pp. 546-547.

[43] For further discussion see chapter 31.

[44] San Mateo County *v.* Southern Pacific Railroad Co., 116 U.S. 138 (1885).

ment had been to protect the rights of corporations.[45] Four years later, in connection with the argument of another case, Chief Justice Waite made the following statement: "The Court does not wish to hear argument on the question whether the provision in the Fourteenth Amendment to the Constitution, which forbids a state to deny to any person within its jurisdiction the equal protection of the laws, applies to these corporations. We are all of the opinion that it does." [46]

The proposition was reiterated thereafter from time to time as the settled conclusion of the Court that the word "person" in the Fourteenth Amendment did include corporations. As recently as 1938, Justice Black, who had little tolerance for the expansion of constitutional doctrines to give broad protection to the rights of corporate property, took the position that the Court had been erroneous in its holding that corporations were included by the word "person" and were entitled to receive the protection given by the amendment.[47] Whatever the validity of his argument as a matter of history, the intervening decades of consistent decisions probably outweigh it. In any event, it has been contended that, even if corporations had not been accepted as persons within the meaning of the amendment, the courts could take jurisdiction over the subject matter through suits brought in the name, not of the corporation, but of stockholders and bondholders.[48] Furthermore, the social philosophy of the judges of the period, and their concern for the preservation and promotion of economic enterprise which could be carried on only through corporations, were such as to lead to the conclusion that, if one channel was closed, another would be found through which the courts could give protection to corporate interests.

As to the public-interest doctrine, it is not to be inferred, in spite of the judicial evolution of an extremely protective attitude toward business enterprise, that price regulation was to be limited thereafter exclusively to common carriers and other agencies receiving grants of privileges from states. The regulation of the rates charged by

[45] See Louis B. Boudin, "Truth and Fiction about the Fourteenth Amendment," *New York University Law Quarterly Review,* XVI (November, 1938), 19; Howard Jay Graham, "The 'Conspiracy Theory' of the Fourteenth Amendment," *Yale Law Journal,* XLVII (January, 1938), 371; XLVIII (December, 1938), 171; Andrew C. McLaughlin, "The Court, the Corporation, and Conkling," *American Historical Review,* XLVI (October, 1940), 45-63.

[46] Santa Clara County *v.* Southern Pacific Railroad Co., 118 U.S. 394, 396 (1886).

[47] See, for example, his dissenting opinion in Connecticut General Life Insurance Co. *v.* Johnson, 303 U.S. 77 (1938).

[48] Boudin, *op. cit.,* pp. 64-65.

grain elevators, for example, was continued. The Supreme Court again upheld such regulation in a case decided in 1892.[49] Justice Field concurred in a dissenting opinion written by his nephew, Justice Brewer. Brewer restated Field's criticism of the doctrine of public interest, and urged that price regulation by the government should be limited in terms of "public use," a much narrower category. Government interference with a monopoly was justified only if monopoly rights were given by law. Monopolies not created by law could be broken by effective competition. Therefore, there was no necessity for legislative interference.

The case was decided in the period of the Populist movement. There was widespread discontent over the unequal distribution of wealth. There was much talk of socialism — an ominous term for the wealthy and for their defenders. Edward Bellamy had recently contributed to social unrest by the publication of his Utopia called *Looking Backward,* a dream of an ideal socialized world as seen in the year 2087, in which private enterprise had completely disappeared. In his dissenting opinion in the elevator case, Justice Brewer delivered a ringing statement of the conservative position:

> The paternal theory of government is to me odious. The utmost possible liberty to the individual, and the fullest possible protection to him and his property, is both the limitation and duty of government. If it may regulate the price of one service which is not a public service, or the compensation for the use of one kind of property which is not devoted to a public use, why may it not with equal reason regulate the price of all service, and the compensation to be paid for the use of all property? And if so, "Looking Backward" is nearer than a dream.[50]

**REGULATION**

During the early years of railroad-building, little government regulation was assumed to be necessary. As abuses and disorder demonstrated the necessity for some degree of control, the state legislatures took up the task. Various types of police measures were enacted. It was discovered, however, that penal laws applicable to particular abuses were not enough. Soon after the Civil War the states turned to a new device, the regulatory commission. The principal functions

---

[49] Budd *v.* New York, 143 U.S. 517 (1892).

[50] *Ibid.,* p. 551. For an additional elevator case decided two years later, see Brass *v.* North Dakota, 153 U.S. 391 (1894).

of the commissions first established were to investigate and give publicity to facts concerning the operations of the railroads. It was thought that giving adequate publicity to the abuses of railroad corporations would result almost automatically in the elimination of the abuses. To some extent the desired result was achieved, but, by and large, men of the type of Jay Gould, the Vanderbilts, and Huntington and Stanford were not greatly disturbed by publicity concerning their buccaneering methods. When some of the states attempted to fix maximum railroad rates by law, they discovered that a state legislature, made up of people of highly diverse interests and meeting at only infrequent intervals, was not sufficiently flexible as an agency for the regulation of prices. Gradually, therefore, such rate-making functions as were assumed by the states were turned over to the regulatory commissions. This allotment of powers to the commissions represented the merging of legislative, executive, and judicial functions in a single agency. It came about so gradually as to attract little attention; yet it culminated in the development of what has been called the fourth branch of the government. The development was significant in terms of the government of the states alone. It took on added significance in that it marked the way for subsequent and more far-reaching developments in the federal government.

The regulatory activities of the states were limited by decisions of the Supreme Court marking the periphery of state powers. During the period of Chief Justice Chase, who served from 1864 to 1873, the Court is said to have taken a pronounced stand in favor of state regulation.[51] The most important case having an effect upon business generally was that of Paul v. Virginia,[52] in which the Court held that the negotiation of insurance policies and contracts and the business of insurance did not constitute commerce of such a nature that the states were forbidden to regulate it, even though the business was performed across state lines.

However, in the period of Chase's successor, Chief Justice Waite, who served from 1873 to 1888, the Court revealed a greater concern about the exercise of state regulatory power over business which had extensions across state lines. The decisions were coincident with the growth of state laws curbing and regulating the activities of railroads.[53] The degree to which states might, in the absence of federal regula-

[51] Charles Warren, *The Supreme Court in United States History* (rev. ed., 2 vols., 1926), II, 626.

[52] 8 Wallace 168 (1869).        [53] See Warren, *op. cit.*, II, 625 ff.

tions, interfere with the interstate commerce activities of railroads remained undetermined for some time. Chief Justice Waite left the subject obscure in one of the Granger cases, in which he upheld a Wisconsin law on the ground that it was confined to state commerce or such interstate commerce as directly affected the people of Wisconsin.

> Until Congress acts in reference to the relations of this company to interstate commerce, it is certainly within the power of Wisconsin to regulate its affairs, etc., so far as they are of domestic concern. With the people of Wisconsin, this company has domestic relations. Incidentally, these may reach beyond the state. But certainly, until Congress undertakes to legislate for those who are without the state, Wisconsin may provide for those within, even though it may indirectly affect those without.[54]

Railroad counsel and others generally opposed to state regulation of railroads objected to the interpretation permitting states incidentally to regulate interstate commerce in the absence of federal statutes on the subject. They won a victory in the Wabash case,[55] decided in 1886, when the Court shifted its grounds and held that a state might not regulate even that portion of interstate commerce which took place within its borders. Since the railroad companies were in continual process of extending their lines and linking them with other lines, to add to the network of interstate commerce in constant movement throughout the United States, the decision had the effect of leaving an important and growing portion of the railroad business of the country free from any regulation whatsoever, pending the time when the federal government might assume control. The decision speeded the coming of federal regulation.

It is not easy to discover whether or not the several members of the Supreme Court, in curbing the power of the states, favored the development of federal regulation. Speaking for the Court in 1875, Justice Bradley remarked that in the field of maritime transportation relief from exorbitant transportation charges was found in the existence or fear of competition. The same kind of relief, he thought, should avail in reference to land transportation. Much thought had been given, he said, as to whether Congress could counteract impediments by taking positive action to establish and facilitate the means of communication between the different parts of the country. The power

[54] Peik v. Chicago and Northwestern Railway Co., 94 U.S. 164, 177-178 (1877).
[55] Wabash, St. Louis and Pacific Railway Co. v. Illinois, 118 U.S. 557.

had been exercised in the construction of the Cumberland Road and other similar works, and through the establishment of railroad communication with the Pacific coast. He added:

> But it is to be hoped that no occasion will ever arise to call for any general exercise of such a power, if it exists.[56]

He thought, however, that if companies chartered by the state

> should so combine or become so consolidated and powerful as, under cover of irrevocable franchises already granted, to acquire absolute control over the transportation of the country and should exercise it injuriously to the public interest, every constitutional power of Congress would undoubtedly be invoked for relief. . . . Commercially, this is but one country, and the intercourse between all its parts should be as free as due compensation to the carrier interest will allow. This is demanded by the "general welfare," and is dictated by the spirit of the Constitution at least. Any local interference with it will demand from the national legislature the exercise of all the just powers with which it is clothed.[57]

It may be that, with the passage of time, some of the judges grew more sympathetic toward the idea of federal regulation of railroads, although it is apparent that many of the new appointments were made from among lawyers who were firmly opposed to the idea of regulation in general. The need for federal regulation grew steadily more apparent. The need resulted, not merely from judicial decisions limiting the power of the states, but also from the obvious inability of a state to inquire into facts and regulate matters at a distance having repercussions on its own welfare and from the ineffectiveness of state political bodies in competition with powerful railroad corporations. So effective were the corporations in dealing with state regulatory commissions that the corporations were at times better off when nominally governed by commissions which were subject to their influence than when no such body existed to take responsibility.

The beginnings of federal power over railroads were made largely on the basis of other constitutional powers than that to regulate interstate commerce. Grants of land to states for building railroads or grants directly to the railroad companies, for example, did not necessarily involve interstate commerce. The measure enacted in 1862 authorizing the government to take over and operate the railroads

[56] Baltimore and Ohio Railroad Co. *v.* Maryland, 21 Wallace 456, 474 (1875).
[57] *Ibid.*, pp. 474-475.

was enacted in pursuance of the war powers.   Postal powers and war powers were taken heavily into account in chartering the Pacific Railroads and in providing them with land and loans of money.   Federal regulations covering the carrying of the mails and federal expenditures for the purpose had important influences in the matter of railroad administration.

The enactment of federal legislation to regulate railroads began very gradually.   In 1873, the House of Representatives considered, but did not pass, a bill to provide for the creation of a board of commissioners of commerce consisting of five heads of executive departments.   The purpose of the board was to be largely that of accumulating information about commerce by land and water.   Presumably the function of the proposed board was to promote commerce rather than to regulate it.[58]   In March, 1873, a law was somewhat hesitantly enacted on the basis of the commerce power to require more humane treatment of livestock transported by railroads.[59]   A year later, the House of Representatives passed a bill "to regulate commerce by railroads among the several states."   The bill was designed to regulate transportation rates through a board of nine railroad commissioners. It proposed to give the board compulsory powers for the collection of information and authorized a bureau of railway statistics in the Department of the Interior to compile the data for the ascertainment of reasonable rates.   It did not pass the Senate.[60]   The Senate also rejected a bill "to establish a national railroad bureau and for the general government of railroads."   This bill provided for a board of three railroad commissioners.[61]   A number of statutes affecting railroads were enacted during the period, but most of them had to do with the Pacific railroads, to which the government had made grants of land and loans of money.   An act approved in 1878 created the position of auditor of railroad accounts[62] in the Department of the Interior. The title was subsequently changed to office of commissioner of railroads, but the functions remained principally the accumulation of information about railroads in which the federal government had a financial stake.

During the second half of the eighteen-seventies, a movement began

[58] 46 *Congressional Globe* 1331-1338.

[59] 17 Stat. 584.

[60] *Report of the Auditor of Railroad Accounts in the United States Department of the Interior, Annual Report*, 45th Cong., 3d sess., 1878-1879, p. 864.

[61] *Ibid.*, p. 864.          [62] 20 Stat. 169

which resulted in the enactment of the Interstate Commerce Act a decade later. In May, 1878, John H. Reagan, of Texas, reported from the House committee on commerce a bill to regulate interstate commerce and to prohibit unjust discriminations by common carriers.[63] The bill made no provision for a commission, but it established federal penalties calculated to curb serious abuses. It sought to secure equality of freight rates and facilities for all shippers. To this end it prohibited the granting of rebates and drawbacks such as were granted at times to shippers of large quantities of goods in order to secure business which might otherwise go to a competing line. It sought to eliminate evils in what was known as the long-and-short-haul situation by prohibiting greater gross charges for short hauls than for long ones. The evil grew out of the fact that a company often reduced its through rates in order to meet competition from a parallel line or from transportation by water, but recompensed itself by charging excessive rates to intermediate points on its own line where it suffered no competition. It might be cheaper, for example, to ship goods from Omaha to San Francisco than from Omaha to a point on the same line in Nevada or eastern California. The bill required the posting of rates and, where rates were fixed on local commerce by the state, required the posting of the schedules of state rates and prohibited charging more per ton-mile for shipments in interstate commerce than for shipments in state commerce.[64]

An opponent of the bill contended that the framers of the Constitution had never intended to give to Congress any such power over interstate commerce. The commerce clause, he argued, "was aimed at the states, so as to prevent one state from imposing any impost, duty, burden, or hardship upon the exports or imports of any other state which might be passing through its borders."[65] Although most of the Supreme Court decisions cited were decisions curbing state interference with interstate commerce rather than upholding federal regulatory measures, and although constitutional arguments were interspersed throughout the debates, the legislators seem to have been more deeply concerned with the expediency than with the constitutionality of the bill. The bill passed the House of Representatives,[66] but the Senate failed to act. The bill died with the Congress by which it was considered.

[63] 7 *Congressional Record* 3096-3097.
[64] For a summary of the bill, see *ibid.*, p. 3275.
[65] *Ibid.*, p. 3393.    [66] 8 *Congressional Record* 101-102.

Reagan reintroduced his bill in the next Congress, but was embarrassed by the competition of another bill. Railroad attorneys and some congressmen argued that the federal legislation needed was provision for a fact-finding commission to assemble significant data concerning railroad transportation. The House committee on commerce, of which Reagan was chairman, rejected his bill in favor of one providing for a board of commissioners of interstate commerce as a bureau of the Interior Department. The commission was to have little authority beyond that of accumulating data about railroad operations and making reports as to operations and as to violations of law. One of its purposes was stated to be that of amassing the information necessary to the development of a system of federal legislation on the subject. In addition to providing for the commission, the bill outlawed certain abuses, but it was a much milder measure than that proposed by Reagan.[67]

Neither of these bills was passed, but the controversy continued year after year between advocates of penal legislation to cope with abuses and advocates of a commission with limited powers. Establishment of a railroad commission was favored by Thomas M. Cooley, chief justice of Michigan and author of the highly influential *Treatise on the Constitutional Limitations Which Rest upon the Legislative Power of the States of the American Union.* The personnel of the commission, according to one view, should consist of such men as Judge Cooley and Charles Francis Adams, Jr., whose *Railroads: Their Origin and Problems* was much quoted throughout the debates.

In March, 1885, near the beginning of the term of the Forty-Ninth Congress, Senator Shelby M. Cullom, of Illinois, the sponsor of a bill to create a railroad commission, secured adoption of a Senate resolution providing for a select committee of five senators to investigate and report upon the subject of the regulation of transportation by railroad and water routes in the United States. An extended investigation was held, giving publicity to the issues and leading to their further discussion, and in January, 1886, the committee made what was known as the Cullom Report.[68] It analyzed the subject at length and presented much testimony. In October, 1886, the Supreme Court made more obvious the need for federal regulation by its decision in the Wabash case,[69] denying to the states all power to regulate

[67] For discussion of the bills, see 10 *Congressional Record* 4019-4032.

[68] *Report of the Committee on Interstate Commerce*, Senate Report No. 46, 49th Cong., 1st sess., 2 vols., 1886.

[69] Wabash, St. Louis and Pacific Railway Co. *v.* Illinois, 118 U.S. 557 (1886).

interstate commerce by railroad.  The Cullom bill was again introduced.  The Senate passed the bill by a vote of 47 to 4.[70]

In the House of Representatives the Reagan bill was offered as a
substitute.  Both bills prohibited unreasonable charges, rebates, drawbacks, special rates, and unjust discrimination, and both required the
railroads to publish and keep posted their schedules of rates.  Both
contained long-and-short-haul clauses, although the Cullom bill
authorized the commission to modify the restriction under certain
circumstances.  A congressman supporting the Cullom bill made the
following comparison between the modes of enforcement:

> Both these bills aim at the same thing, but by different methods;
> one is to be enforced by five commissioners at the public expense for
> the public good; the other by lawsuits brought by individuals against
> the railroads — a method that people in our region, especially poor
> men, do not feel encouraged by their experience to undertake.
>
> The Cullom bill enables the poorest man, the tenant as easily as the
> rich farmer or mercantile house, to present his complaint in a plain
> way and if he has a fair case to set in motion all of the machinery of
> the courts with able counsel and without any expense or risk to him-
> self, and secure redress for his wrongs as quickly and completely as
> the richest.   Under the Reagan bill he must take the risk of a lawsuit
> that may wear him out and beggar him of what little he had.   Is it
> likely that such men will readily try such a contest?  Is it not more
> likely that these severe provisions of law will be abused by rival
> interests, rich and powerful, to foment and instigate lawsuits to harass
> competitors, and the law merely made an instrument in the struggles
> of the strong to weaken and exhaust the weaker roads? [71]

The House of Representatives accepted the Reagan bill as a substitute
by a vote of 134 to 104,[72] and passed the bill by a vote of 192 to 41.[73]
The bill went to conference for a revision that would make it acceptable to the two houses.  Cullom and Reagan headed the deputations
from the Senate and House respectively.  They agreed on a bill containing as fully as possible the provisions of the two competing bills.
Most of the activities prohibited by the Reagan bill were prohibited
in the compromise draft, and action against offenders was authorized
without the necessity of resort to a commission.  On the other hand,
Reagan yielded to the demand for a commission.  It was to have the
powers hitherto proposed, including the power of investigating al-

[70] 17 *Congressional Record* 4423.          [71] *Ibid.*, p. 7290.
[72] *Ibid.*, pp. 7752-7753.          [73] *Ibid.*, pp. 7755-7756.

leged offenses on complaint, issuing cease-and-desist orders against
offenders, and seeking court action if its orders were disobeyed.

Each house gave considerable attention to the conference report.
Much of the debate had to do with pooling and long-and-short-haul
provisions. Quite incidentally at various points the question of the
rate-making powers of the commission was discussed — a question of
great importance in view of the court decisions handed down within
a few years after the establishment of the commission. The bill gave
the commission no power to establish schedules of rates initially, but
it seemed to confer the power to disestablish existing rates under certain circumstances. Section 4 of the bill, for example, prohibited
charging more for a short distance than for a long distance on the
same line, but empowered the commission to modify the rule, stating
that it might "from time to time prescribe the extent to which such
designated common carrier may be relieved from the operation of
this section of the act." Such a provision seemed to authorize rate-
making in so far as it was related to the long-and-short-haul provision.
Section 1 of the bill, furthermore, incorporated the common-law
principle that all rates should be reasonable and just. Section 15
provided that the commission should investigate alleged violations of
the act and should issue cease-and-desist orders against violations. If
offenses were continued, the commission could petition a United
States circuit court for an injunction. In the light of these widely
separated provisions, it seemed possible that the commission, in issuing cease-and-desist orders against the charging of unreasonable rates,
should be able to fix alternative rates which it regarded as reasonable.

Such seems to have been the interpretation given by Senator John
R. McPherson, of New Jersey. He said:

> The bill confers upon a commission of five members the determina-
> tion of the question as to whether a rate is a reasonable rate or not.
> The railway company may fix such rate as they please, but the com-
> mission have the revision of that rate, and they may make it such rate
> as in their view is reasonable. This, I take it, the commission will
> do; in short, the power to make reasonable within a certain limit is
> the power to make rates.[74]

Other senators emphasized the fact that the bill did not say what was
reasonable, and that the question of the measure of reasonableness
would go to the courts.[75]

The debate disclosed the fact that many legislators were in doubt

[74] 18 *Congressional Record* 528.        [75] *Ibid.,* pp. 566, 576-577.

as to the meaning of many provisions of the bill. Opinions often differed sharply. The Senate was reminded that "the true meaning of this measure, as of every other law, is bound to be settled by the courts, and in arriving at the true meaning of the act it is a fundamental canon of statutory construction that the court will not look at the opinions expressed by the members of the legislature who voted for and against it as to its meaning. The meaning of the act will be determined by a consideration alone of its language." [76] The comment is significant in view of the subsequent judicial history of the statute.

The bill was denounced by some legislators down to the final stage of enactment. Senator George F. Hoar, of Massachusetts, declared that the passage of the bill would create a panic. The creation of the commission with the powers attributed to it seemed to him utterly indefensible legislation. The commissioners were given powers half-legislative and half-judicial. "You give these men power over the business of great towns and great cities and great classes of investments — a power which no Persian satrap or Roman proconsul was ever entrusted with — at a salary of seventy-five hundred dollars a year, with an exposure to temptation in the way of corruption which would not stand at millions and hundreds of millions of dollars." [77] Furthermore, he said, if the commission was to deal with all the cases to be brought before it, it needed a membership, not merely of five, but of five hundred or five thousand men. [78]

A congressman continued to insist that the bill was unconstitutional because it blended in the commission legislative, executive, and judicial powers. Once the commission was established, however wrong the law might prove in many respects, he did not believe that it would ever be repealed. "I do not believe in commissions; I prefer to have the rights of the people adjudged by the regular constitutional courts and juries of the country." The history of legislation and the course of administration of the government, he said, proved that, whenever an office was created, it was never abolished, but rather that those who were appointed to execute it were increased in number if any change whatever was made. "I freely confess, sir," he proclaimed, "that I am jealous of this eternal tendency to the enlargement and centralization of federal power." [79]

[76] Senator James Z. George, of Mississippi, *ibid.*, p. 577.
[77] *Ibid.*, p. 639.     [78] *Ibid.*, p. 640.
[79] Congressman William C. Oates, of Alabama, *ibid.*, p. 847.

The two houses accepted the report of the conference committee and "An act to regulate commerce" was approved by President Cleveland on February 4, 1887.[80]

## THE INTERSTATE COMMERCE COMMISSION

Section 11 of the act to regulate commerce provided for an Interstate Commerce Commission of five members, to be appointed by the President by and with the advice and consent of the Senate. Members were to serve for six years, but the terms of the first appointees were so arranged that they would expire unevenly. No more than three of the commissioners were to be appointed from the same political party.

Realizing that the effectiveness of the commission would depend very largely upon the selection of personnel, President Cleveland made his choices carefully. The dominating figure during the early years was Thomas M. Cooley, of Michigan, who brought to the chairmanship of the commission a body of experience acquired on the supreme bench of his state and some experience with railroads acquired as receiver of the Wabash line, as well as a reputation as a writer in the field of jurisprudence. One of his colleagues said in praise of him that he had laid the foundations of the commission broad and strong and "made it what its creators never contemplated, a tribunal of justice, in a field and for a class of questions where all was chaos before."[81]

The first decade of the life of the commission was a stormy period.[82] The railroads, even though they had favored the establishment of a fact-finding commission as an alternative to the restrictive provisions of the Reagan bill, were determined not to be governed by any agency. They modified those of their practices which were more obviously in violation of the statute, but beyond that point they prepared to block any interference by the commission. However intelligently the commission might set about the performance of its functions, its success depended upon the co-operation of the courts, not merely for the enforcement of the orders of the commission, but

[80] 24 Stat. 379. The statute is referred to hereafter by its modern title, "The Interstate Commerce Act."

[81] A. C. McLaughlin, "Thomas McIntyre Cooley," *Dictionary of American Biography* (1930), IV, 392-393.

[82] See I. L. Sharfman, *The Interstate Commerce Commission* (4 vols. in 5, 1931-1937), I, 19-35; Carl McFarland, *Judicial Control of the Federal Trade Commission and the Interstate Commerce Commission, 1920-1930* (1933), chapter IV, and materials cited; and Robert E. Cushman, *The Independent Regulatory Commissions* (1941), chapter III.

for the interpretation of the vague provisions in the statute. In spite of the prestige of its chairman, the commission had reason to expect judicial hostility on two grounds. First, many of the judges of the federal courts were committed to laissez-faire doctrines. They were opposed to more than a minimum of governmental interference with private enterprise. The time had come when many of the ablest lawyers of the country were corporation attorneys; and federal judges were often chosen from the ranks of such attorneys. It was only natural that they should carry into the courts the legal doctrines previously sponsored in defense of their clients. In the second place, the commission had reason to expect judicial hostility because of the nature of its own organization. Even though it had little of the authority of the modern independent regulatory commission, it clearly marked the beginning of an anomalous organization in the federal government. Feeble as it was, it showed evidence of the merging of legislative, executive, and judicial powers. The courts were by tradition hostile to any broad encroachment on the principle of the separation of powers, and were particularly hostile to the exercise of what they regarded as judicial functions by any organization other than the courts. It was a foregone conclusion, therefore, that they would greet with suspicion and possible hostility this strange addition to the aggregation of governmental agencies.

One of the earliest difficulties encountered by the commission was that of compelling testimony in connection with its investigations. The power to compel testimony was provided by statute, and the constitutionality of the provision was supposed to be protected by an act forbidding the use of the testimony in criminal actions against the witness, so that there was no violation of the provision of the Fifth Amendment of the Constitution that no person in a criminal case could be compelled to be a witness against himself. In 1892, however, the Supreme Court found that full protection against self-incrimination was not given, and therefore denied the power of the government to compel testimony in instances where it might have the effect of criminating the witness.[83] The Interstate Commerce Commission asked for the enactment of new legislation which would make it possible to secure evidence from persons who had themselves been offenders. Congress enacted a new statute to give full protection to such witnesses,[84] but a lower federal court subsequently held it likewise to be unconstitutional. The Supreme Court did not pass upon it

[83] Counselman v. Hitchcock, 142 U.S. 547 (1892).　　[84] 27 Stat. 443.

until 1896. Down to that time the Interstate Commerce Commission had the greatest difficulty in securing important items of evidence because of the refusal of witnesses to testify. In the year mentioned, however, the Supreme Court found the statute adequate for the preservation of constitutional rights, since it gave full personal exemption from legal action flowing from the testimony. Said Justice Brown for the Court:

> It is entirely true that the statute does not purport, nor is it possible for any statute, to shield the witness from the personal disgrace or opprobrium attaching to the exposure of his crime; but, as we have already observed, the authorities are numerous and very nearly uniform to the effect that, if the proposed testimony is material to the issue on trial, the fact that the testimony might tend to degrade the witness in public estimation does not exempt him from the duty of disclosure. A person who commits a criminal act is bound to contemplate the consequences of exposure to his good name and reputation, and ought not to call upon the courts to protect that which he has himself esteemed to be of such little value.[85]

This decision eliminated one of the barriers met by the commission in collecting evidence. Others were harder to eliminate. It will be recalled that, if a railroad refused to obey an order of the commission, the order could be enforced only by an appeal to a United States circuit court. Some railroads withheld information in commission investigations. When the commission appealed to a court to enforce an order, the offending company would then produce a mass of additional evidence to show that the order should not have been issued and to discredit the commission. Since the statute did not restrict the courts to the evidence previously presented before the commission, there was no legal way of preventing the presentation of such evidence. Apparently the Supreme Court could do no more than express its disapproval of this technique of heckling the commission and forcing the complete determination of all issues in the courts. It took such a step in a case decided in 1896:

> We think this a proper occasion to express disapproval of such a method of procedure on the part of the railroad companies as should lead them to withhold the larger part of their evidence from the commission, and first adduce it in the circuit court. The commission is an administrative board, and the courts are only to be resorted to

---

[85] Brown v. Walker, 161 U.S. 591, 605 (1896). See also Interstate Commerce Commission v. Baird, 194 U.S. 25 (1904), and Hale v. Henkel, 201 U.S. 43 (1906).

when the commission prefers to enforce the provisions of the statute by a direct proceeding in the court, or when the orders of the commission have been disregarded. The theory of the act evidently is, as shown by the provision that the findings of the commission shall be regarded as prima facie evidence, that the facts of the case are to be disclosed before the commission. We do not mean, of course, that either party, in a trial in the court, is to be restricted to the evidence that was before the commission, but that the purposes of the act call for a full inquiry by the commission into all the circumstances and conditions pertinent to the questions involved.[86]

The evil was not eliminated, however, until some years had passed and sentiment in favor of regulation by the commission had grown strong enough to secure the enactment of legislation limiting the courts to action based exclusively upon facts presented before the commission.

The case mentioned above was of much greater importance for another reason. The Court stated that it did not find any provision of the Interstate Commerce Act that expressly or by necessary implication conferred upon the Interstate Commerce Commission the power to fix rates.[87] The commission had never assumed that it had the power initially to provide schedules of rates and require railroads to accept them. But when rates established by carriers were challenged before the commission and were known to be unreasonable, the commission had assumed that it had the power to prescribe the alternative rates which would be reasonable. It had exercised this power for more than ten years when the Supreme Court held that the power did not exist at all.

This decision and other decisions bearing upon various powers of the commission so devitalized it that in its annual reports it was compelled to make plea after plea for amending legislation to enable it to perform the functions it was intended to perform.[88] A number of years were required to build up sufficient sentiment to enforce the enactment of legislation materially strengthening the commission. Such legislation was passed, however, after the turn of the century; and the commission gradually developed into one of the most powerful agencies in the federal government.[89]

[86] Cincinnati, New Orleans, and Texas Pacific Railway Co. *v.* Interstate Commerce Commission, 162 U.S. 184, 196 (1896).

[87] *Ibid.*, p. 196.

[88] See, for example, the *Annual Report of the Interstate Commerce Commission for 1897*.

[89] The discussion is resumed in chapter 25.

................................................................................

# CHAPTER 19

# THE MENACE OF MONOPOLY

MUCH OF THE PUBLIC HOSTILITY toward powerful corporations between the Civil War and 1900 was directed at railroad corporations. That hostility gave much of the necessary political support for the adoption of the Interstate Commerce Act and such enforcement of that act as proved possible.[1] The same period saw the development of similar hostility toward corporations of other kinds. The period of depression in the middle of the decade of the eighteen-seventies brought about the collapse of many loosely built business structures, with a tendency toward absorption of smaller units by larger ones. With the gradual return of prosperity, larger units retained their comparative advantage over smaller ones and continued to grow at an accelerated pace. They defeated smaller units through successful competition and drove them out of business or absorbed them by ruthless methods. The tendency in each of many fields was toward the development of monopoly control. Monopoly was opposed, as a matter of principle, by all who believed that the survival of competition was necessary to the health of the economic order. Businessmen ruined by monopolistic organizations added to the hue and cry against monopoly, as did those consumers who had to pay higher prices for goods as a result of the elimination of competition.

The development of monopoly proceeded, not merely through the growth of large integrated units and the elimination of small-scale competitors, but also through the formation of what were known as trusts. A trust was a combination of independent firms, through which the several firms acted as a unit. Each member of the combination submitted to the direction of the trustees and received in turn all the benefits of large-scale organization without the complete loss of independent identity. The combination was formed through the placement of a majority of the voting stock of each of the

[1] See chapter 18.

member firms in the hands of trustees. The trustees acquired thereby full power of control over all the member organizations. Through the formation of the trust the members were relieved of the necessity of engaging in business wars with one another, being able to pool information and inventions for mutual benefit, to crush competitors who refused or were not invited to join the combination, and, within limits, to control the amount of production and the selling prices of goods. Toward such combinations, therefore, including the Standard Oil trust, the whiskey trust, the sugar trust, and many others, was directed all the hostility that characterized the attitudes of the public and of defeated competitors toward monopolies and large-scale business organizations in general.[2]

The accusations against trusts were formally phrased as follows:

(1) That they tend to build up monopolies and drive small capitalists out of business;

(2) That they destroy competition, the great minimizer of profits and equalizer of prices;

(3) That they amass fortunes at the expense of the community by increasing the price of commodities;

(4) That they tend to build up an oligarchy which controls legislation in its own interest against that of the community, thereby undermining personal and political freedom, and endangering the existence of democratic institutions.[3]

While it was clear to some economists that trusts and other forms of large-scale business organizations were not unmitigated evils, the prevailing belief of large numbers of people that they constituted such evils was a driving force toward controlling legislation. Opposition to monopoly developed into something in the nature of a crusade under the leadership of such men as Henry D. Lloyd, subsequently the author of an influential volume entitled *Wealth Against Commonwealth*.[4] In newspaper editorials and in highly influential articles published during the eighteen-eighties he presented dramatic evidence of the predatory and anti-social activities of the big business organizations of the time.[5] The anti-monopoly movement was closely

[2] For evidence as to the formation and operation of trusts, see House Report No. 4165, 50th Cong., 2d sess.

[3] George Gunton, "The Economic and Social Aspect of Trusts," *Political Science Quarterly*, III (September, 1888), 387.

[4] Published in 1894. For an account of his life see Caro Lloyd, *Henry Demarest Lloyd* (1912).

[5] See, for example, his "Story of a Great Monopoly," *Atlantic Monthly*, XLVII (March, 1881), 317-334, and "Lords of Industry," *North American Review*, CXXXVIII (June, 1884), 535-553.

related to the movements for cheap money and for railroad control which were fostered in the agricultural sections of the country. The evils disclosed constituted propaganda for a search for Utopia in the form of a world dominated by socialism.[6] The struggle of the eighteen-nineties for the equalization of economic benefits by the collection of a federal graduated income tax from people and corporations receiving incomes above certain levels developed out of the same general background.[7]

Combinations clearly in restraint of trade, like unreasonable rates on railroads, were illegal at common law. The states were able to deal with some abuses, therefore, without legislation. In a number of instances they supplemented the common law by the enactment of anti-trust legislation, even before the enactment of federal legislation on the subject. Five states, with interests that were predominantly agricultural, enacted such legislation in 1889; and two others in 1890, prior to the date of the federal law. Many of the combinations dealt with extended across state lines, however, and for this and other reasons could not be effectively controlled by the states.

Party platforms during the eighteen-eighties attacked the growth of monopoly as well as railroad abuses, and demanded remedial legislation from the federal government. In his annual message of December 3, 1888, President Cleveland made the following statement:

> As we view the achievements of aggregated capital, we discover the existence of trusts, combinations, and monopolies, while the citizen is struggling far in the rear or is trampled to death beneath an iron heel. Corporations, which should be the carefully restrained creatures of the law and the servants of the people, are fast becoming the people's masters.[8] [He spoke of an arrogance which] appears in the sordid disregard of all but personal interests, in the refusal to abate for the benefit of others one iota of selfish advantage, and in combinations to perpetuate such advantages through efforts to control legislation and improperly influence the suffrages of the people.[9]

Although none of them was passed by either house, a considerable number of anti-trust bills were introduced in Congress in 1888, a presidential election year. Prominent among them was a bill introduced by Senator John Sherman, of Ohio, whose name was attached to the measure finally passed in 1890. As first introduced, his bill

---

[6] See, for example, Edward Bellamy's *Looking Backward,* first published in 1888.
[7] See chapter 20.          [8] *Messages and Papers of the Presidents,* XI, 5359.
[9] *Ibid.,* p. 5360.

merely provided that certain forms of combinations were illegal, that injured parties might sue for damages in the federal courts, and that any corporation taking part in the illegal combination should forfeit its franchise. The Senate committee on finance rephrased the bill and added a section providing penalties of fine and imprisonment for participation in an illegitimate combination.

No debate of importance took place before the date of the election at which Benjamin Harrison was chosen to the presidency. Between that date and the end of the session of Congress the following March, enough discussion took place to indicate lines of cleavage among legislators favoring some kind of anti-trust legislation. It appeared that some, like Senator Sherman, were concerned principally with the enactment of a federal statute incorporating the principle of the common law against combinations, trusts, and the like which affected the value of articles necessary to human life. Others, like John H. Reagan and Shelby Cullom, sought, not merely to establish the principle of illegality so as to permit damage suits and make possible the voiding of contracts, but also to provide severe penalties to be enforced by the federal government. Reagan's attitude toward the enforcement of penalties resembled somewhat his attitude toward legislation for the control of railroads. Apparently none of his colleagues, however, considered seriously the establishment of an independent federal agency to investigate, exercise control over, and recommend legislation concerning corporations other than railroads which were engaged in interstate commerce.

Debate on anti-trust measures was resumed in February, 1890, and continued through June of that year, when a measure was enacted. From the beginning there was doubt as to the constitutionality of any measure that could be made completely effective. The Sherman bill was referred to the Senate committee on finance. The first justification of it given by Senator Sherman rested upon the taxing power rather than upon the commerce power.[10] The subject of corporation control had a close connection with revenue and tariff legislation. It was argued, for example, that tariff legislation which had the effect of restraining the competition of foreign producers made possible the restriction of supply and the raising of prices by local combinations in restraint of trade. Throughout most of the debate, however, it was generally agreed, by Sherman as well as by others, that the proper basis of federal legislation was the commerce power. That being

[10] 19 *Congressional Record* 7513.

true, the drafting of constitutional legislation was extremely difficult. Among the difficulties was the fact that the combinations to be restrained took place oftentimes in terms of production or manufacure rather than of transportation. The power of the federal government was assumed to begin only with actual interstate commerce. The Sherman bill as introduced on December 4, 1889, dealt with combinations which prevented full and free competition in the importation, transportation, or sale of articles imported into the United States "or in the production, manufacture, or sale of articles of domestic growth or production, or domestic raw materials that competes with any similar article upon which a duty is levied by the United States, intended for and which shall be transported from one state or territory to another." [11] Other types of phrasing were devised, but, in so far as they dealt with production, there was always a serious question whether the proposed control extended beyond the constitutional power of Congress.

Sherman reminded the Senate that the interstate commerce bill for the regulation of railroads had been hooted and jeered at in the Senate and had faced constitutional objections without number in the House of Representatives. The arguments were of the same class as those directed against the anti-trust bill. He declared:

> The power of Congress is the only power that can deal with these corporations. The power of Congress is the only one that can regulate the internal commerce of this country. The power of Congress is the only one that can bring all the parties to combinations before a tribunal, and have that tribunal pronounce judgment, not in a criminal suit, but in a civil suit. [12]

He emphasized his position that a provision for criminal suits against the agents of corporations was unimportant.

> They could give up at once one or two or three of their servants to bear this penalty for them. But when you strike at their powers, at their franchises, at their corporate existence, when you deal with them directly, then they begin to feel the power of the government. So in regard to interstate commerce by rail. All those corporations and organizations opposed that law, but when it went into force it produced enormously good effects, and everybody appreciates it, and nobody proposes to dispense with the Interstate Commerce Commission, which was organized to enforce the interstate commerce law. [13]

[11] *Bills and Debates Relating to Trusts,* Senate Doc No. 147, 57th Cong., 2d sess., p. 71
[12] 21 *Congressional Record* 2569.        [13] *Ibid.,* p. 2569.

One senator advanced what seems to have been an unusual idea for the time; namely, that the proper method of dealing with powerful corporations was not to interfere with them through governmental means, but to organize counter-combinations. He said:

> I believe that the true remedy against such trusts is that of counter-combinations among the people. I believe in co-operation. . . . These evils of combination, of course, are great, but the question is, do they not grow out of civilization itself, the foundation of which is organization, and without organization men would be savages? Should we not rather encourage organizations among the people to meet the grasping disposition of the favored few? The great trouble from the beginning of civilization has been that the few have combined against the many, being more competent, and that the few in various ways secure to themselves special privileges against the masses. I say let the masses combine.[14]

Opponents of the bill in general and critics of particular phrasing objected on the ground that it would curb labor organizations and organizations of farmers. Amendments were adopted at one stage to prohibit such applications of the statute.[15] Unfortunately, so many other amendments were adopted as to leave the bill in the form of a hodgepodge. The condition of the bill and questions as to the constitutionality of its various provisions resulted in its reference to the Senate committee on the judiciary, where it was completely rewritten. The constitutional difficulties were less glaring in the committee's new draft, although subsequent events showed that they had not been eliminated. The provisions exempting labor and farm organizations were not retained. The question was left unsettled whether the act was intended to apply to these organizations or whether in the rewriting of other provisions of the bill the committee had intended to exclude such an application.[16]

The act was approved by President Harrison on July 2, 1890. It was entitled "An act to protect trade and commerce against unlawful restraints and monopolies." [17] It made illegal every contract, combination, or conspiracy in restraint of trade or commerce in the inter-

[14] *Ibid.*, pp. 2565-2566. See also p. 2606.

[15] See Edward Berman, *Labor and the Sherman Act* (1930), pp. 21-22.

[16] On this subject see Berman, *op. cit.*, chapters II and III; Alpheus T. Mason, *Organized Labor and the Law* (1925), chapters VII and VIII; and James A. Emery, "Labor Organizations and the Sherman Law," *Journal of Political Economy*, XX (June, 1912), 599-612.

[17] **26 Stat. 209.**

state or foreign field. It made no mention of manufacture or production as such, leaving to the courts the determination whether combination in that field was included in "restraint of trade or commerce
among the several states." It provided that persons who monopolized,
or attempted to monopolize, or to combine or conspire with other
persons to monopolize, any part of the trade or commerce among the
several states or with foreign nations should be guilty of a misdemeanor. Property transported across state lines in the course of such
illegal acts might be seized by the United States. For the enforcement of criminal penalties the district attorneys, under the direction
of the Attorney General, should substitute suits in equity in the federal circuit courts. Private parties were authorized to sue for three
times the damages they sustained at the hand of anyone who violated
the statute.

ENFORCEMENT OF THE SHERMAN ACT

Apart from giving to the federal courts necessary jurisdiction and
to the district attorneys authority to institute actions to restrain violations of the law, no machinery was prescribed for the enforcement of
the Sherman Act. The Attorney General at the time of the adoption
of the act, William H. H. Miller, seems to have been conscientious
and energetic in connection with matters on which he was well informed. He seems to have known little about the content of the
Sherman Act, however, or about the unpopular phenomena known
as trusts. There is no evidence that he was consulted on the drafting
of the bill or that the President referred it to him before signing it.
He had no clear idea as to how the measure was to be enforced, and
during the first year he took no initiative, in spite of the provision
that equity proceedings were to be instituted by district attorneys
"under the direction of the Attorney General."

Neither the Attorney General nor the solicitor general, William
Howard Taft, showed enthusiasm about instituting the case in which
the government won its first anti-trust victory. Credit was due, not to
them, but to the United States attorney in Tennessee who handled the
case. It was a suit to enjoin the maintenance of the Nashville Coal
Exchange, a combination between coal-mining companies operating
mostly in Kentucky, though to a limited extent in Tennessee, on the
one hand, and persons and firms dealing in coal at Nashville, on the
other. The court undertook no positive defense of the Sherman
Act, but applied it to this case, saying, "A court, especially an inferior

one, should hesitate long and consider carefully before it should declare an act of Congress, passed after deliberation and debate, and approved by the President, unconstitutional." [18]

The case was decided nearly eleven months after the Anti-Trust Act was approved. On the first anniversary of the act, the Attorney General notified United States attorneys throughout the country that the circuit court had held the law constitutional, and gave his first general instructions as to its enforcement. He said:

> It is my desire that you examine that law carefully, lay it alongside any combinations or trusts within your district, and if, by such measurement, it is found that those trusts or combinations are infractions of the law, prosecute vigorously. They are great abuses, and if the law can be made to reach them, it is the duty of the law officers of the government, as I doubt not it will be their pleasure, to do everything possible within the law to suppress them, and to punish the wrongdoers.[19]

The United States attorneys replied variously that they had little or no information as to anti-trust violations, but would give the matter their attention. When one of them wrote of a plan to seek indictment, the Attorney General replied that the plan met his approval. The trouble in this business, he said, seemed to be that, while there was a very general feeling that trusts existed and antagonized public interests, no one seemed to have, or to be willing to present, definitive evidence in reference to their acts. He continued to advise caution. He wrote to a United States attorney:

> We do not want to undertake a prosecution and fail, especially a criminal indictment. It is always unfortunate to make a charge of crime against a person of otherwise good standing and subject him to the humiliation of making a defense, even though in the end he may be acquitted. At the same time, we cannot ignore our duty to enforce the penalties of this law, the same as any other, and parties must, of course, take their chances if they get over the border line, even though it may be somewhat difficult to define that line.[20]

In doubtful cases he advised resort to injunction proceedings rather than to criminal trials, in order to get the benefit of the judgment of

---

[18] United States v. Jellico Mountain Coal and Coke Co. et al., 46 Fed. 432, 434 (1891).

[19] Department of Justice Instruction Book No. 13, p. 389. See Homer Cummings and Carl McFarland, Federal Justice (1937), pp. 319-320.

[20] Department of Justice Instruction Book No. 19, pp. 324-325.

the court without the embarrassment connected with criminal prosecutions.

At the end of the Harrison administration, on March 4, 1893, only seven anti-trust cases had been instituted, and of these only two had been concluded during the period. The Tennessee coal case had ended in victory. A whiskey trust case had ended when the indictment was held insufficient. The second Cleveland administration brought no enthusiasm to the task of enforcement. The new Attorney General, Richard Olney, entered the cabinet without anti-monopoly sentiment of any kind and with the record of having appeared against the government in the whiskey trust case. Soon after he took office, he wrote the Secretary of the Treasury that the bankers, merchants, and others of Boston were willing to put some work and money into the repeal of the Sherman law. He asked for a list of senators "who might be persuaded to see the thing in the right light." [21] The act was not repealed, but Olney insisted always on a narrow interpretation.

In his first annual report Olney praised a circuit-court decision by Judge Howell E. Jackson, who at the time of the writing of the report had become a member of the Supreme Court of the United States. The decision interpreted the Anti-Trust Act narrowly, holding among other things that the contracts, combinations, and conspiracies in restraint of trade that the act forbade were only those hitherto illegal at common law.[22]

Olney instituted no new anti-trust cases during his two years as Attorney General, but he carried up one case to secure a test before the Supreme Court. He chose for the purpose a case against the sugar trust. The American Sugar Refining Company had purchased, with shares of its own stock, the stock of four Philadelphia sugar refineries, acquiring thereby nearly complete control of the manufacture of refined sugar in the United States. The government instituted, not a criminal action, but an equity suit to secure the cancellation of the agreements under which the stock was transferred, on the ground that the contracts constituted combinations in restraint of trade in violation of the Sherman Act. The important question was whether monopoly for the purposes of manufacture, with the probable result of the control of supply and of prices, involved interstate com-

[21] Richard Olney to John G. Carlisle, July 5, 1893, Olney Letter Book, Library of Congress.
[22] *In re* Greene, 52 Fed. 104, 111 (1892).

merce to such an extent as to come within the provisions of the Anti-Trust Act and to be subject to federal control on the basis of the commerce power. Government counsel have been criticized for their inadequate presentation of the case on the ground that they did not sufficiently show the relation between the local manufacture of sugar and the interstate distribution of sugar to consumers. Their brief indicates that the relation was not as clearly stated as it might have been, but an attempt was made to show it, and a court seeking a way to apply the Anti-Trust Act to the situation would not have lacked a guide. The opinion of the Supreme Court was written by Chief Justice Melville E. Fuller.[23] With only Justice Harlan dissenting, the Court announced a narrow interpretation of the commerce power, differentiated between manufacture on the one hand and commerce on the other, and held that the Anti-Trust Act did not extend to combinations for the control of manufacture as distinguished from the control of commerce. The interpretation of the act, therefore, went aground on the shoals that its sponsors in Congress had sought to avoid. The Chief Justice said:

> Doubtless the power to control the manufacture of a given thing involves in a certain sense the control of its disposition, but this is a secondary and not the primary sense; and although the exercise of that power may result in bringing the operation of commerce into play, it does not control it, and affects it only incidentally and indirectly. Commerce succeeds to manufacture, and is not a part of it. The power to regulate commerce is the power to prescribe the rule by which commerce shall be governed, and is a power independent of the power to suppress monopoly. But it may operate in repression of monopoly whenever that comes within the rules by which commerce is governed or whenever the transaction is itself a monopoly of commerce.[24]

The regulation of commerce applied to the subjects of commerce, he held, and not to matters of internal police.

> Contracts to buy, sell, or exchange goods to be transported among the several states, the transportation and its instrumentalities, and articles bought, sold, or exchanged for the purpose of such transit among the states, or put in the way of transit, may be regulated, but this is because they form part of interstate trade or commerce. The fact that an article is manufactured for export to another state does not of itself make it an article of interstate commerce, and the intent

[23] United States *v.* E. C. Knight Co., 156 U.S. 1 (1895).      [24] *Ibid.*, p. 12.

of the manufacture does not determine the time when the article or product passes from the control of the state and belongs to commerce.[25]

The decision was not illogical. Yet, until it was gradually interpreted away by the Supreme Court, it destroyed much of the hoped-for effectiveness of the anti-trust statute. The decision was bitterly criticized by enemies of monopoly, such as the New York *World*. Olney was not surprised, however, and gave evidence of being pleased. "You will have observed that the government has been defeated in the Supreme Court on the trust question," he wrote to his secretary. "I always supposed it would and have taken the responsibility of not prosecuting under a law I believed to be no good — much to the rage of the New York *World*." [26]

The replacement of Olney by Judson Harmon in 1895 brought a change of atmosphere to the enforcement of the Anti-Trust Act. Harmon gave advice to Congress as to the strengthening of the legislation, recommended additional appropriations to aid enforcement, and stimulated the efforts of United States attorneys to make the law effective.

Harmon took charge of one important case before the Supreme Court. A suit had been brought in 1892 in the United States district court in Kansas to enjoin a contract and combination among eighteen western railroads to maintain freight rates. The district court held that the Anti-Trust Act did not apply to railroads, arguing that they were exclusively regulated by the Interstate Commerce Act. By a different line of reasoning the circuit court of appeals reached the conclusion that the combination did not violate the Sherman Act. The Supreme Court, dividing five to four, held that the Anti-Trust Act did apply to combinations of railroads as well as combinations of other kinds and that the act had been violated in this case.[27] The Court rejected the contention of the railroads that the Anti-Trust Act did not apply to the continuation of combinations formed before the act was passed. It held also that the fact that the rates fixed by the combination were reasonable did not establish the legality of the combination. In other words, the act forbade all combinations in restraint of trade, and not merely those that were unreasonable.

The dissenting minority, speaking through Justice Edward D.

[25] *Ibid.*, p. 13. He cited at this point the important cases of Coe *v.* Erroll, 116 U.S. 517 (1886), and Kidd *v.* Pearson, 128 U.S. 1 (1888).

[26] Olney to Miss Straw, January 22, 1895; Olney Papers, Library of Congress.

[27] United States *v.* Trans-Missouri Freight Association, 166 U.S. 290 (1897).

White, denounced the contention that a combination to fix reasonable rates violated the statute:

> The theory upon which the contract is held to be illegal is that even though it be reasonable, and hence valid under the general principles of law, it is yet void, because it conflicts with the act of Congress already referred to. Now, at the outset, it is necessary to understand the full import of this conclusion. As it is conceded that the contract does not unreasonably restrain trade, and that if it does not so unreasonably restrain, it is valid under the general law, the decision, substantially, is that the act of Congress is a departure from the general principles of law, and by its terms destroys the right of individuals or corporations to enter into very many reasonable contracts. But this proposition, I submit, is tantamount to an assertion that the act of Congress is itself unreasonable. The difficulty of meeting, by reasoning, a premise of this nature is frankly conceded, for, of course, where the fundamental proposition upon which the whole contention rests is that the act of Congress is unreasonable, it would seem conducive to no useful purpose to invoke reason as applicable to and as controlling the construction of a statute which is admitted to be beyond the pale of reason. The question, then, is, Is the act of Congress relied on to be so interpreted as to give it a reasonable meaning, or is it to be construed as being unreasonable and as violative of the elementary principles of justice? [28]

The dissenting judges or their successors continued to insist on their point in case after case down through the years until 1911, when White, now Chief Justice, rephrased his line of reasoning as a part of the opinion of the majority of the Court in the Standard Oil case.[29]

The Trans-Missouri Freight Association case, discussed above, although decided in the Supreme Court by the narrow margin of one, through an opinion written by Justice Peckham, a recent appointee to the Court, seemed to mark a new trend in the line of Supreme Court decisions on the Anti-Trust Act. The case was followed by another railroad combination case, decided in similar fashion.[30] In 1899, the Court handed down unanimously a decision concerning a combination of manufacturers of cast-iron pipe, which had the effect of limiting the decision in the sugar trust case and restoring to the Anti-Trust Act some of the vitality which seemed to have been taken from it.[31] The government had been defeated in the court of original

---

[28] *Ibid.*, p. 344.    [29] Standard Oil Co. *v.* United States, 221 **U.S. 1** (1911).
[30] United States *v.* Joint-Traffic Association, 171 **U.S. 505** (1898).
[31] Addyston **Pipe and** Steel Co. *v.* United States, 175 **U.S.** 211 (1899).

jurisdiction, but in the circuit court of appeals William Howard Taft had written an opinion distinguishing this case from the sugar trust case and showing that here the combination to control the manufacture of cast-iron pipe had extended to the control of prices in interstate commerce. The Supreme Court accepted the interpretation given by Taft. The difference between the two decisions was due in part, no doubt, to the difference in the language of the two agreements in the matter of showing price control in interstate commerce. There seems also to have been a difference, however, in the vigor with which government counsel demonstrated the effect of combinations for the purpose of manufacture upon sale and delivery in interstate commerce.

Another aspect of the decision in the pipe case is important. Justice Peckham, who wrote the opinion of the Court, was in many respects an ardent believer in laissez-faire in relations between government and the individual. In an important insurance case, decided in 1897, he had announced the principle that the right to make contracts was a part of the liberty guaranteed in the Constitution by due-process clauses.[32] The decision marked the development of a doctrine to be used for many years as a check upon the activities of government in such matters as the regulation of wages and hours of labor. Freedom of contract did not extend so far, however, the justice held, as to protect the making of contracts which would result in violation of otherwise valid acts of Congress. He said:

> On the contrary, we think the provision regarding the liberty of the citizen is, to some extent, limited by the commerce clause of the Constitution, and that the power of Congress to regulate interstate commerce comprises the right to enact a law prohibiting the citizen from entering into those private contracts which directly and substantially, and not merely indirectly, remotely, incidentally, and collaterally, regulate to a greater or less degree commerce among the states.[33]

In spite of success in the cases mentioned, the first decade of the history of anti-trust activity came to an end without evidence of any prospect that the growth of business combinations was at an end. The period around the turn of the century was one of unprecedented amalgamation of railroads and corporations of other kinds. This development of big business was logical in view of the growing possi-

[32] Allgeyer v. Louisiana, 165 U.S. 578 (1897).
[33] Addyston Pipe and Steel Co. v. United States, 175 U.S. 229.

bilities of efficient and profitable production and distribution of goods and services on a large scale by standardized processes. It was welcomed and defended by those who prospered directly as a result of it and by others who hailed the development of the United States as a powerful industrial nation. Yet it created discomfort and fear by disturbing the traditional course of small-scale production and sale under competitive conditions, and made enemies who flooded the Department of Justice with petitions that this or that malevolent trust be investigated and destroyed. New developments in anti-trust activities against corporations awaited the crusading spirit of Theodore Roosevelt.[34]

## COMBINATIONS OF LABOR

The limited use of the Sherman Act to curb the growth of corporate power was hardly less important in the tide of constitutional development than its use to curb the growing power of organized labor. The latter use began in 1892, with a strike by the Workingmen's Amalgamated Council and other unions in the city of New Orleans which tied up interstate and other business in the city. The United States attorney asked for directions, whereupon Attorney General Miller instructed him to institute proceedings under the Anti-Trust Act if in his judgment a case could be made. He instituted an equity suit, but the strike was terminated, and he applied for further instructions under circumstances which led many to believe that the case was kept pending as a threat against further labor disturbances. Counsel for the unions said, in a letter to the Attorney General:

> There are those in this community who believe that that cause was not instituted to be tried, but was on the contrary to be held *in terrorem* over the heads of the workingmen of this city, with the hope that it would alarm and disintegrate them. However this may be, the government of the United States should not be a party to any such juggling Chinese warfare.[35]

The Attorney General apparently agreed that the case should not be kept pending merely as a threat to the union, but he thought that, even though this particular strike was over, the continued threat of further interference with interstate commerce justified proceeding with the case. The federal district court granted the injunction, re-

---

[34] See chapter 23.
[35] M. Marx and A. H. Leonard to the Attorney General, December 17, 1892, Department of Justice File 8247 B—1890. See Cummings and McFarland, *op. cit.*, p. 437.

jecting the contention that the anti-trust law did not apply to labor. Said the judge:

> I think the congressional debates show that the statute had its origin in the evils of massed capital; but, when the Congress came to formulating the prohibition which is the yardstick for measuring the complainant's right to the injunction, it expressed it in these words: "Every contract or combination in the form of trust, or otherwise in restraint of trade or commerce among the several states or with foreign nations, is hereby declared to be illegal." The subject had so broadened in the minds of the legislators that the source of the evil was not regarded as material, and the evil in its entirety is dealt with. They made the interdiction include combinations of labor, as well as of capital; in fact, all combinations in restraint of commerce, without reference to the character of the persons who entered into them.[36]

Miller's successor, Attorney General Olney, who was generally hostile to the statute, regarded the decision as a perversion of it. It was a matter of public notoriety, he said, that the provisions of the Sherman Act were aimed at public mischief of a wholly different character. Furthermore, for the federal government to proceed against labor under the Anti-Trust Act put the whole power of the federal government on one side of a civil controversy between employers and their employees. He regarded such a proceeding as eminently unfair.[37]

Later, however, when, as a result of the panic of 1893, large groups of unemployed people, known variously as "Commonwealers" and "Coxey's Army," organized to move on Washington to secure redress of grievances, Olney agreed to the use of the Anti-Trust Act as a basis for injunction suits against seizure of railroad trains and other disturbances by the so-called marchers. When the famous Pullman strike spread through the railroads of the country, Olney directed the use of injunctions and other devices for its suppression. "Let the act of July 2, 1890, be strictly enforced against all violators and transportation companies," he commanded in one instance.[38] Yet, when his subordinates interpreted his instructions to authorize a suit against the railroad company suspected of postponing the resumption of transportation in order to persuade the government completely to break up the strike, Olney declared that such action went beyond the

---

[36] United States *v.* Workingmen's Amalgamated Council, 54 Fed. 994, 996 (1893).

[37] Cummings and McFarland, *op. cit.*, p. 438.

[38] Olney to George J. Denis, July 14, 1894, Pullman Strike Folder File Box 3, Olney Papers.

limits of his instructions and directed the dismissal of the suit.[39] He never reached the stage of willingness to use the statute against employers.

The sweeping injunction secured in Chicago against the strike leaders was based in part on the Anti-Trust Act. It was upheld in a contempt case in the United States circuit court in Chicago against Eugene V. Debs, president of the American Railway Union.[40] Debs sued out a writ of habeas corpus in the Supreme Court. Olney participated in the argument of the case, but he left the discussion of the Sherman Act to his associates, telling the Court that, if possible, he desired the case decided on general equity grounds "and not by reason of an experimental piece of legislation like the act of 1890." [41] In the main, the Supreme Court accepted Olney's contention, holding that the relations of the federal government to interstate commerce and the transportation of the mails were such as to authorize direct interference by injunction to prevent forcible obstruction. Justice Brewer for the Supreme Court said:

> We enter into no examination of the act of July 2, 1890 . . . upon which the circuit court relied mainly to sustain its jurisdiction. It must not be understood from this that we dissent from the conclusions of that court in reference to the scope of the act, but simply that we prefer to rest our judgment on the broader ground which has been discussed in this opinion, believing it of importance that the principles underlying it should be fully stated and affirmed.[42]

The activities of the various Attorneys General, the decisions of such lower federal courts as passed upon it, and the passive acquiescence of the Supreme Court indicated clearly that, whatever the intention of Congress had been, the Anti-Trust Act was to be applied against combinations of labor as well as combinations of capital. In 1908, the Supreme Court confirmed this impression by holding unanimously that the Sherman Act applied to labor combinations.[43] The desire of labor to escape the toils of the Sherman Act had much to do with its support of the Clayton Anti-Trust Act of 1914 [44] and the Norris-La Guardia Anti-Injunction Act of 1932.[45]

[39] Olney to Denis, August 1, 1894, *ibid.*
[40] United States *v.* Debs, 64 Fed. 724 (1894).
[41] Olney Memorandum, Box H, I, J, Olney Papers.
[42] *In re* Debs, 158 U.S. 564, 600 (1895).     [43] Loewe *v.* Lawlor, 208 U.S. 274 (1908).
[44] 38 Stat. 730.     [45] 47 Stat. 70.

# CHAPTER 20

# THE INCOME TAX

MOST OR ALL METHODS of securing funds for the support of the federal government reflect theories, not merely as to the feasibility of extracting the desired sums of money, but also of social and economic policy apart from the collection of revenue. The collection of substantial sums from the sale of public land reflected down through the years a compromise between those who thought more should be charged for the land and those who preferred to charge less or nothing at all. The tariff, from the time of the enactment of the first act of the kind, has been intended to favor production in the United States as well as to provide revenue, and has been justified in part in terms of a belief that the bill is paid by the foreign exporter rather than by the American people. The first internal-revenue duty collected on the manufacture of whiskey reflected a judgment as to the comparative social value of certain products, as have most subsequent excise measures. The constitutional provision that direct taxes must be apportioned among the several states according to population was intended largely to prevent the burdening of certain kinds of sectionally owned property by high direct taxes for the benefit of other sections or of the country as a whole.

The first use of the income tax by the federal government was made during the Civil War and for half a decade thereafter. The first income-tax measure placed the burden on persons receiving larger incomes, by wholly exempting annual incomes of six hundred dollars or less. The act of 1864 extended the principle by graduating the rate of taxation in terms of the amount of income. The rate was five per cent on incomes up to five thousand dollars, seven and one-half per cent on the excess over five thousand up to ten thousand dollars, and ten per cent on the excess over ten thousand dollars. Wealthy people were naturally opposed to this form of taxation, and its early termination was a foregone conclusion.[1]

[1] Edwin R. A. Seligman, *The Income Tax* (1911), chapter III.

No fundamental attack was made on the constitutionality of the legislation, but certain constitutional limitations were indicated. In paying the salaries of federal judges, the Secretary of the Treasury deducted the amount of the income tax. In a letter to the Secretary of the Treasury, written in February, 1863, Chief Justice Taney denounced as unconstitutional and void the provisions of the statute authorizing such a reduction in the salaries of the judges. The Constitution, he pointed out, provided that federal judges should "receive for their services a compensation, which shall not be diminished during their continuance in office." "The act in question," he said, "as you interpret it, diminishes the compensation of every judge three per cent; and if it can be diminished to that extent by the name of a tax, it may, in the same way, be reduced from time to time at the pleasure of the legislature." [2] All the judges of the courts of the United States had an interest in the question, he continued, and could not therefore with propriety undertake to hear and decide it.

> I am, however, not willing to leave it to be inferred, from my silence, that I admit the right of the legislature to diminish, in this or any other mode, the compensation of the judges when once fixed by law; and my silence would naturally, perhaps necessarily, be looked upon as acquiescence, on my part, in the power claimed and exercised under this act of Congress, and would be regarded as a precedent establishing the principle that the legislature may at its pleasure regulate the salaries of the judges of the courts of the United States, and may reduce their compensation whenever Congress may think proper. [3]

The Secretary of the Treasury, then Salmon P. Chase, forwarded the letter to Attorney General Edward Bates, saying that a number of judges of the Supreme Court and other federal courts had claimed the tax on their salaries was unconstitutional. Bates endorsed Chase's letter with the notation "No reply to be given" and, with Taney's letter, tucked it away in the official files of his office. [4] When it was clear that no reply would be forthcoming, Taney filed a copy of his letter with the records of the Supreme Court. In 1872, when Taney was in his grave, another Secretary of the Treasury, coming to the conclusion that the tax on salaries of federal judges had been illegally collected, refunded the amounts paid. [5]

[2] Samuel Tyler, *Memoir of Roger Brooke Taney, LL.D.* (1876), p. 432.
[3] *Ibid.*, pp. 433-434.     [4] Carl Brent Swisher, *Roger B. Taney* (1935), **p. 569.**
[5] *Ibid.*, p. 569, and Tyler, *op. cit.*, p. 435.

The tax was also collected on the incomes of state judges.   Joseph M. Day, a state judge in Massachusetts, brought a suit against the federal collector in Massachusetts for the tax paid, contending that it had been collected in violation of the Constitution.   The case was taken to the Supreme Court.   Day's counsel placed much emphasis on the case of Dobbins v. Erie County,[6] decided in 1842, in which the Supreme Court had held that a state had no power to tax the office, or the emoluments of the office, of an officer of the United States. This, he declared, was the precise converse of the present case.   With one justice dissenting, the Supreme Court agreed with the contention. The means and instrumentalities employed for carrying on the operation of the state governments should be left free and unimpaired, declared Justice Nelson for the Court, saying that they "should not be liable to be crippled, much less defeated by the taxing power of another government, which power acknowledged no limits but the will of the legislative body imposing the tax."[7]   Without the judicial power, he continued, no one of the states could long preserve its existence under the form of government guaranteed by the Constitution.   The judicial power was, therefore, one of the sovereign powers vested in the states by their constitutions which remained unaltered and unimpaired; and in respect to it the state was as independent of the general government as that government was independent of the state.   He admitted that there was no express provision in the Constitution that prohibited the general government from taxing the means and instrumentalities of the states; nor was there any prohibiting the states from taxing the means and instrumentalities of the federal government.   In both cases, the exemption rested upon necessary implications and was upheld by what he called "the great law of self-preservation."   His decision rested back upon the principle announced by Chief Justice Marshall in McCulloch v. Maryland,[8] that the power to tax involved the power to destroy.   To demonstrate the validity of the principle, he called attention to the way in which the federal taxing power had been used to destroy the note issues of state banks.[9]

This case, known as Collector v. Day, became a landmark in American constitutional history.   It closed to the federal government certain important sources of revenue.   The difficulties were indicated

[6] 16 Peters 435.
[7] Collector v. Day (Buffington v. Day), 11 Wallace 113, 125-126 (1871).
[8] 4 Wheaton 316 (1819).            [9] Citing Veazie Bank v. Fenno, 8 Wallace 533 (1869)

in the dissenting opinion of Justice Bradley, who objected to the exemption of the income of a United States citizen from taxation merely because he happened to be employed by a state. He asked:

> Where are we to stop in enumerating the functions of the state government which will be interfered with by federal taxation? If a state incorporates a railroad to carry out its purposes of internal improvements, or a bank to aid its financial arrangements, reserving, perhaps, a percentage on the stock or profits for the supply of its own treasury, will the bonds or stock of such an institution be free from federal taxation? [10]

He was correct in predicting the difficulties soon to arise.

In 1881, long after the federal income-tax law had expired, the Supreme Court dealt with a direct challenge to its constitutionality in the case of Springer v. United States.[11] Counsel for Springer resisted collection of the tax on the ground that it was a direct tax and therefore could be constitutionally collected only if distributed among the several states according to population. The Supreme Court unanimously rejected the contention. Examining the direct-tax measures passed by Congress, Justice Swayne remarked:

> Whenever the government has imposed a tax which it recognized as a *direct tax,* it has never been applied to any objects but real estate and slaves. The latter application may be accounted for upon two grounds: (1) in some of the states, slaves were regarded as real estate . . .; and (2) such an extension of the tax lessened the burden upon the real estate where slavery existed, while the result to the national Treasury was the same, whether the slaves were omitted or included. The wishes of the South were, therefore, allowed to prevail. We are not sure that the question of the validity of such a tax was ever presented for adjudication. Slavery having passed away, it cannot hereafter arise. It does not appear that any tax like the one here in question was ever regarded or treated by Congress as a direct tax.[12]

He cited the case of Hylton v. United States,[13] decided in 1796, in which the Supreme Court had held that a tax upon pleasure carriages was not a direct tax, and some of the judges had expressed the opinion that within the meaning of the Constitution the only direct taxes were capitation taxes and taxes on land. The line of precedents in the courts and in Congress led to the conclusion that an income tax

[10] 11 Wallace 129.       [11] 102 U.S. 586.       [12] *Ibid.,* p. 599.       [13] 3 Dallas 171.

was not a direct tax, and therefore did not need to be apportioned among the several states according to population.

## THE INCOME TAX OF 1894

Although the federal government was without income-tax legislation for more than two decades, interest in the subject was not wholly lost. Income-tax bills were introduced in Congress at session after session.[14] The National Grange, the Farmers' Alliance, and the Knights of Labor favored the tax, as did such minority parties as the Greenback party, the Anti-Monopoly party, and the Populist party.[15] The late eighteen-eighties saw a growing rift between the hard-pressed farmers of the country and labor groups on the one hand and business, industrial, and financial groups on the other. The period was that of the so-called Populist Revolt,[16] in which people who were economically hard-pressed organized in support of various measures for the improvement of their lot, including measures widely condemned as socialistic. The income tax was among the measures advocated in the platform of the Populist party in 1892.

The Democrats ousted Republicans from control and returned to power under the leadership of Grover Cleveland in his second administration, but the Populists polled a vote so heavy as to demonstrate the political wisdom of making some concessions to their policies. In many localities, furthermore, the Democratic party itself sponsored a program hardly distinguishable from that of the Populists. In a sense, indeed, the movement toward Populism might be called a nonpartisan movement. The sentiment which had aided in the enactment of the Interstate Commerce Act and the Anti-Trust Act and which gave rise to the Populist party and to the movement of what was known as "Coxey's Army" in 1894, following the increase of hard times as a result of the panic of 1893, demanded broad governmental concessions on behalf of the less-favored people of the land.

In the campaign of 1892, the Democrats blamed the ills of the country on the Tariff Act of 1890. Large sections of the population were persuaded that the protective tariff, through the encouragement given to trusts and to the establishment of high prices generally, had a large responsibility for their ills. Early in the session of Congress beginning in December, 1893, a measure was introduced which became the Tariff Act of 1894. In January, 1894, Benton McMillin, of

---

[14] Roy G. Blakey and Gladys C. Blakey, *The Federal Income Tax* (1940), p. 9.
[15] *Ibid.*, pp. 10-11.        [16] See John D. Hicks, *The Populist Revolt* (1931).

Tennessee, introduced an income-tax bill and secured its adoption as an amendment to the tariff bill. Its subsequent history, therefore, was a part of an exciting struggle for and against the adoption of the measure as a whole. Although President Cleveland had cautiously supported a plan for "a few additional internal-revenue taxes, including a small tax upon incomes derived from certain corporate investments," [17] he did not favor including a broad income-tax program in the tariff bill.[18] Sentiment in favor of the income tax was strong enough, however, to carry it through without presidential support.

The measure was advocated, not merely because it pointed to a rich source of revenue, but because it provided a means for equalizing the tax burden in terms of ability to pay. The House committee on ways and means set the tone of the argument by the following statement in its report on the income-tax bill:

> Here we have "a government of the people, by the people, and for the people." We boast that our motto is "Equal rights to all and special privileges to none." Here we claim that the burdens of government ought to be borne in proportion to the ability of each citizen who is protected by it. Yet under our peculiar system there are citizens of great wealth who, by our method of taxing what we must consume rather than what we have accumulated, pay little more to the support of the government than is paid by the day laborer, who has nothing.[19]

Democrats from the industrial states in the East and many Republicans denounced the measure as socialistic and confiscatory. "I am especially opposed to an income tax such as this which is now offered for our consideration," said a congressman, "an income tax which arbitrarily selects for confiscation the property of a limited class in this country, which designates as its victims but eighty-five thousand out of sixty-five million." [20] He declared that the bill was not a democratic measure, but was populistic instead, supported by the same people who had advocated unlimited coinage of silver on behalf of cheap currency. On the other hand, a friend of the measure defended it as follows:

> My friends, I see gentlemen from New York and the eastern states here opposing this measure. Had I the naming of this bill, had I the

---

[17] *Messages and Papers of the Presidents,* **XII,** 5892.

[18] *Letters of Grover Cleveland* (edited by Allan Nevins, 1933), p. **357.**

[19] House Report No. 276, 53d Cong., 2d sess., p. 5.

[20] Congressman Franklin Bartlett, of New York, 26 *Congressional Record* **1642.**

naming of any income-tax bill of a kind like this, I would denominate it a measure to kill anarchy and keep down socialists. I believe, in my humble way, I have passed through as many states, mingling with the people, as any man no older than myself. I know that I have heard expressions from the mouths of ten thousand of the laboring classes all over this country. I know there never has been a meeting of the National Grange, of the National Alliance, of the National Federation of Labor, or the Knights of Labor, where this question was presented, that they have not called with one voice for an income tax. I say if we go to the people of the United States and say to the laboring masses, "We are ready, willing, and anxious to put upon you a great burden of taxation laid down in the customs duties, but we are unwilling to lay a feather's weight upon the great wealth of this country," that is an argument in favor of demagoguery and socialism, without righteousness for its warp and woof, and it will come back and curse us in the future.

We are called demagogues and socialists, because we advocate this measure. My friends, I hate to call names back; it is not the way to discuss great national legislation; but were I to define a man who is a friend of the demagogue, I would say he is the man who advocates legislation that will build up demagoguery. If I were called upon to define a friend of socialism, I would call him the man who advocates principles that will build up socialistic tendencies in this country.[21]

William Jennings Bryan, of Nebraska, advocate of cheap money and thereafter three times a presidential candidate, defended the income-tax bill as follows:

> The gentlemen who are so fearful of socialism when the poor are exempted from an income tax view with indifference those methods of taxation which give the rich a substantial exemption. They weep more because fifteen millions are to be collected from the incomes of the rich than they do at the collection of three hundred millions upon the goods which the poor consume. And when an attempt is made to equalize these burdens, not fully, but partially only, the people of the South and West are called anarchists.
>
> I deny the accusation, sirs. It is among the people of the South and West, on the prairies and in the mountains, that you find the staunchest supporters of government and the best friends of law and order.
>
> You may not find among these people the great fortunes which are accumulated in cities, nor will you find the dark shadows which these fortunes throw over the community, but you will find those willing to

[21] Congressman Uriel S. Hall, of Missouri, *ibid.*, p. 1609.

protect the rights of property, even while they demand that property shall bear its share of taxation. You may not find among them so much of wealth, but you will find men who are not only willing to pay their taxes to support the government, but are willing whenever necessary to offer up their lives in its defense.[22]

Bryan cited figures to show the unequal distribution of wealth, and asked if it was unfair or unjust that the burden of taxation should be equalized between these two classes. Who was most in need of a navy? he asked. Was it the farmer who plodded along behind the plow upon his farm, or was it the man whose property was situated in some great seaport where it could be reached by an enemy's guns?

Republican leaders opposed the Democratic-Populistic measure. Senator Sherman opposed it as not needed as a revenue measure, even though many years earlier he had defended the constitutionality of the Civil-War measures and urged continuation of taxation of this kind. Senator Cullom, who had been sponsor of the Interstate Commerce Act in the Senate, declared that "an income tax of the character outlined in this bill is a sandbagging proposition, the device of the highwayman, the equivalent of the tithing system of Mormondom, and the successor and congener of the ecclesiastical system formerly in vogue in Great Britain." [23]

The names of many economists were dragged into the discussion to attack or defend the proposed measure. Among them were John Stuart Mill, Adam Smith, David A. Wells, William Graham Sumner, Henry George, Amasa Walker, Arthur Latham Perry, Frederick C. Howe, and others. Economic doctrines were used, however, primarily to support pre-established alignments.

Constitutional arguments were used in the same fashion. Democrats in the South were traditional defenders of state rights. The pending measure authorized the taxation of incomes from state and municipal bonds and from corporations chartered by the states. Yet southern Democrats were complaisant about it. Senator David C. Hill, of New York, a vigorous opponent of the measure, quoted the following statement of a prominent Georgian: "We are all for an income tax down in our part of the country; and so is Senator Walsh, who represents us, because none of us have four thousand-dollar incomes, and somebody else will have to pay the tax." [24]

As if taking his cue from Justice Bradley's dissenting opinion in Collector v. Day, Senator Hill challenged the power of the federal

[22] *Ibid.*, p. 1657.          [23] *Ibid.*, p. 4168.          [24] *Ibid.*, p. 6617.

government to tax the income of state-chartered corporations. "The lawful right and power to tax largely involves the power to destroy," he declared. "Can the general government lawfully destroy these agencies or instrumentalities of the state — these corporations which virtually constitute a part of its state system of government, a part of its scheme of administration, a part of its financial system?" [25] He contended also that state and municipal bonds were instrumentalities of the state governments and therefore not subject to federal taxation. He vainly sought the adoption of an amendment to the bill to exempt them from its provisions.[26]

Senator Hill offered another argument that is highly significant in view of the position subsequently taken by the Supreme Court. He called attention to the fact that Congress could not tax land without apportionment of the tax among the several states according to population. He contended that a tax on rentals from land was essentially identical with a tax on the land itself, and would therefore not be constitutional unless apportioned as a direct tax.[27]

Discussion of particular constitutional issues led to implied references to the probable attitude of the membership of the Supreme Court. Said Hill:

> I have hoped that with the Supreme Court as now constituted this income tax will be declared unconstitutional. . . . The times are changing; the courts are changing, and I believe that this tax will be declared unconstitutional. At least I hope so.[28]

What did this mean? asked Senator William V. Allen, of Nebraska.

> Are we to understand that the Supreme Court of the United States is packed upon this question? Are we to understand that any man before he went upon the bench of the Supreme Court of the United States prejudged this question and that his prejudging it was a condition precedent to his promotion? Do seventy million people of the United States hold their constitutional and property and personal rights by a tenure so uncertain as this?

No one had doubted that the question was settled and put at rest, he said, until the senator from New York introduced into the debate a

[25] *Ibid.*, p. 6621. On page 6804, *ibid.*, Senator Hill distinguished the power of the federal government to tax state bank notes out of existence, contending that the power had been upheld in Veazie Bank *v.* Fenno (8 Wallace 533), not merely as an exercise of the taxing power, but as an exercise of the power of the federal government over the currency.

[26] *Ibid.*, pp. 6804 ff.        [27] *Ibid.*, pp. 6826-6827.        [28] *Ibid.*, p. 6637.

suspicion that at least a difference of opinion might be expected from the Supreme Court as then constituted. It was not a question of court practice that could be changed at will without doing injury to anyone or any interest, he declared. It was the settlement of the constitutional right that for nearly one hundred years had been imbedded in the very foundation of our Republic. Yet the Senate was gravely informed that the Supreme Court of the United States as now constituted might possibly overturn a constitutional ruling that had been so frequently made. To him the remark showed that "the power which is dominating legislation today, the power which shows its hand in the Senate every once in a while and in the other branch of Congress, is not satisfied with reaching out its long bony fingers through the legislation of Congress, but that it is seeking to fasten itself upon the supreme tribunal of the land." [29]

### THE INCOME TAX ON TRIAL

In spite of constitutional and economic objections, the income-tax measure was passed as a part of the Wilson Tariff Act [30] and was allowed to become a law without the President's signature. It was drastic in its classification of wealth, in that it exempted incomes up to four thousand dollars, but placed a tax of two per cent on incomes above that amount. The masses of the people, therefore, hailed it as a panacea for their ills, while the well-to-do minority flew to arms to defend themselves against its operation.

The act was to go into effect January 1, 1895. In spite of the well-established principle that the collection of federal taxes would not be restrained by the courts, and that the rights of persons from whom they were unjustly collected might be protected only by suits to recover the taxes after they had been paid, a host of eminent lawyers set out to prevent the original collection from being made. The device used was not that of an injunction to prevent the government from the collection of the tax, but an equity suit brought against a corporation by a stockholder to prevent a threatened breach of trust by the illegal payment of taxes from the treasury of the corporation. The test case, Pollock v. Farmers' Loan and Trust Company,[31] was hurried to the Supreme Court, where it was argued in March, 1895

[29] *Ibid.*, p. 6707.

[30] For the history of the process of enactment, see Seligman, *op. cit.*, chapter IV and materials cited; especially George Tunell, "The Legislative History of the Second Income-Tax Law," *Journal of Political Economy*, III (June, 1895), 311-337.

[31] 157 U.S. 429

The array of counsel was imposing, with the preponderance of weight on the side of the opposition to the income tax.[32] The briefs belied their names by running to large volumes. They dealt with constitutional and other legal problems and with intricate matters of economic theory and economic history. The opponents of the statute contended that the income tax was a direct tax, and could be levied constitutionally only if apportioned among the several states according to population. Even if the taxation of some kinds of income did not constitute direct taxation, they contended, levies on income from land most certainly fell within that category. As to taxation of incomes from state and municipal bonds, they contended that it was unconstitutional, not merely because not properly apportioned, but because it was levied on instrumentalities of the state. They contended finally that the invalidity of certain sections of the income-tax law so destroyed the balance of the scheme of taxation as to invalidate the law as a whole, apart from the question of the constitutionality of remaining provisions.

Former United States Senator George F. Edmunds, in attacking the constitutionality of the income-tax law, challenged previous Supreme Court decisions as to what constituted a direct tax within the meaning of the Constitution. As to the carriage-tax case, he said, "there is no escape from the proposition that the Supreme Court of the United States made a mistake when it said, doubtfully and with hesitation, that a tax upon carriages fell over into the region of indirect taxes." [33] He asked the Court to reconsider the Springer case and "to come back again to the true rule of the Constitution." [34] By resort to dictionaries of the time of the adoption of the Constitution and to other authorities, he attempted to demonstrate that taxes on income fell within the description of direct taxes rather than indirect taxes. Because of the exemption of incomes up to four thousand dollars he predicted that at least ninety-five per cent of all the money that was raised from this tax would be paid by less than two per cent of the taxable inhabitants of the United States. "And this," he expostulated, "we call free government, a government of equal protection of the laws; we call it constitutional government. . . . What will become of a country, and how long will it last, where taxation and all its burdens and expenses are

---

[32] See Carl Brent Swisher, *Stephen J. Field: Craftsman of the Law* (1930), chapter XV.
[33] Edmunds's argument as reported in vol. 39 of the Lawyers' Edition of the United States Reports, p. 784.
[34] *Ibid.*, p. 785.

imposed, by those who pay nothing, upon a very small minority of their fellow citizens?" [35] It was a fundamental principle, he maintained, that the burdens of taxation should bear equally. The Fourteenth Amendment forbade the denial of equal protection of the laws. True, it did not say that Congress should not deny such equal protection, but he believed it was now understood by the Supreme Court and everybody in the land that the principle and the substantial application of the provisions of the Fourteenth Amendment were just as binding upon Congress as they were upon the states. "It appears to me that it is the grand mission of this Court of last resort, independent and supreme, to bring the Congress back to a true sense of the limitations of its powers." [36]

Joseph H. Choate, another eminent lawyer, stated that in the last year of collections under the earlier income-tax law, when the exemption was only two thousand dollars, collections were such that four states, New York, Pennsylvania, Massachusetts, and New Jersey, paid four-fifths of the entire tax. With the exemption raised to four thousand dollars he predicted that these states would pay not less than nine-tenths of the entire tax. If this "communist march" went on, a new statute might be enacted with an exemption of twenty thousand dollars and a tax of twenty per cent upon all having incomes in excess of that amount. The principle would be the same. If the Supreme Court was ever to give protection, it must do it now. One of the fundamental objects of all civilized government, he contended, was the preservation of the rights of private property. "I have thought that it was the very keystone of the arch upon which all civilized government rests, and that this once abandoned, everything was at stake and in danger." [37]

On its face, the defenders of the income-tax law had the easier task, for the judicial precedents were on their side. Yet at the close of his argument, Attorney General Olney showed awareness of the fact that he was opposing, not merely legal arguments, but the combined power of the wealth of the country. He said:

> An income tax is pre-eminently a tax upon the rich, and all the circumstances just adverted to prove it is the immense pecuniary stake which is now played for. It is so large that counsel fees and costs and printers' bills are mere bagatelles. It is so large and so stimulates the efforts of counsel that no legal or constitutional principle that stands in the way, however venerable or however long and universally acquiesced in, is suffered to pass unchallenged. [38]

[35] *Ibid.*, p. 786.   [36] *Ibid.*, p. 788.   [37] *Ibid.*, p. 799.   [38] *Ibid.*, p. 793.

James C. Carter admitted that the income-tax law had been enacted
as a result of conditions in which the rich had succeeded in leaving
most of the burden of taxation upon the poor.   He admitted that the
tax would fall upon about two per cent of the population, but he
reminded the Court that, apart from the income tax, this segment of
the population, which probably received more than fifty per cent of
the national income, was paying little more than two per cent of the
nation's taxes.   He admitted that the act was both class and sectional
legislation, but declared it to be so because wealth had become class
and sectional.   He reminded the Court that it would be transgress-
ing the limits of its own powers if it sought to invalidate an act of
Congress merely because the judges disagreed with the economic
theories involved.   Furthermore, it would be dangerous to attempt
to baffle and defeat a popular determination through the device of a
judgment in a lawsuit.   He concluded as follows:

> When the opposing forces of sixty millions of people have become
> arrayed in hostile political ranks upon a question which all men feel
> is not a question of law, but of legislation, the only path of safety is
> to accept the voice of the majority as final.   The American people
> can be trusted not to commit permanent injustice; nor has history
> yet recorded an instance in which governments have been destroyed
> by the attempts of the many to lay undue burdens of taxation on the
> few.   The teachings of history have all been in the other direction.[39]

Choate countered in rebuttal.   He believed that no member of the
Court had ever heard or would ever hear a case involving a question
more important than this.   It involved

> the preservation of the fundamental rights of private property and
> equality before the law and the ability of the people of these United
> States to rely upon the guaranties of the Constitution.   If it be true,
> as my learned friend said in closing, that the passions of the people
> are aroused on this subject, if it be true that a mighty army of sixty
> million citizens is likely to be incensed by this decision, it is the more
> vital to the future welfare of this country that this Court again
> resolutely and courageously declare, as Marshall did, that it has the
> power to set aside an act of Congress violative of the Constitution,
> and that it will not hesitate in executing that power, no matter what
> the threatened consequences of popular or populistic wrath may be.[40]

The battle continued in the conference room of the Supreme
Court.   Justice Jackson had been absent from the argument of the

[39] 157 U.S. 531-532.        [40] 39 Law. ed. 809.

case because of illness and therefore did not participate in the decision. A majority of the Court agreed on certain questions, but left certain others undecided because the justices were divided four to four. Six of them, speaking through Chief Justice Fuller, re-examined the history of the tax provisions of the Constitution and, in spite of a long line of judicial utterances down through the years, reached the conclusion that a tax on income from land must be apportioned among the several states according to population in order to be constitutional. It was clear that a tax upon land itself would not be constitutional unless apportioned. Said the Chief Justice:

> Unless, therefore, a tax upon rents or income issuing out of lands is intrinsically so different from a tax on the land itself that it belongs to a wholly different class of taxes, such taxes must be regarded as falling within the same category as a tax on real estate *eo nomine*. . . . An annual tax upon the annual value or annual user of real estate appears to us the same in substance as an annual tax on the real estate, which would be paid out of the rent or income.[41]

The Court also found unconstitutional the provisions of the act authorizing taxation of the income from municipal bonds. It was obvious, said the Court, that such a tax would operate on the power to borrow before it was exercised, and would have a sensible influence on the contracts, and that the tax in question was a tax on the power of the states and their instrumentalities to borrow money, and was consequently repugnant to the Constitution.

On three important questions the eight justices were equally divided; namely, whether the void provisions invalidated the whole act, whether the taxes on income from personal property were unconstitutionally levied because they, too, constituted direct taxes, and whether the act was invalid for want of uniformity. Accordingly, on these matters there was not a majority of the Court to express an opinion.

The opinion written by the Chief Justice was highly legalistic in form and packed with citations of other cases. It reflected little of the emotional drive of counsel on either side of the case. Justice Field wrote a concurring opinion, in which he boldly proclaimed the unconstitutionality of the act in all its provisions and denounced the Populistic movement. He asked in closing:

> If the provisions of the Constitution can be set aside by an act of Congress, where is the course of usurpation to end? The present

[41] 157 U.S. 580-581.

assault upon capital is but the beginning. It will be but the stepping-stone to others, larger and more sweeping, till our political con-
tests will become a war of the poor against the rich; a war constantly
growing in intensity and bitterness. . . . There is no safety in allowing
the limitation [of the income to be taxed] to be adjusted except in
strict compliance with the mandates of the Constitution, which require its taxation, if imposed by direct taxes, to be apportioned among
the states according to their representation, and if imposed by indirect
taxes, to be uniform in operation and, so far as practicable, in proportion to their property, equal upon all citizens. Unless the rule
of the Constitution governs, a majority may fix the limitation at such
rate as will not include any of their own number.[42]

Justice White, Justice Harlan concurring, dissented from the decision of the Court except as to the taxing of income from municipal
bonds. It was a mistake, at this late date, he declared, to go back to the
founders to discover what they had meant by a direct tax. The value
of the Court to the government and to the people lay in the consistency and orderliness with which it pursued its work of interpretation. If the Court was to go back to the original sources of our
political system or appeal to the writings of economists in order to
unsettle established principles, he regarded the result as disastrous.
If the belief in judicial continuity were broken down so that on great
constitutional questions the Court might be expected to depart from
the settled conclusions of its predecessors and to determine the cases
merely according to the opinions of those who temporarily filled the
bench, he feared that the Constitution would be bereft of value and
become a most dangerous instrument to the rights and liberties of the
people.

The friends of capital, while lauding the decision, regretted that
the Supreme Court had not disposed of the entire law. Even so, they
thought it pretty well wrecked. A jubilant newspaper remarked that
the Supreme Court was a great sticking point for Populist legislation,
and predicted that the income-tax law would be almost as effective as
the Interstate Commerce Act, which was already being whittled down
by judicial interpretations.[43]

Justice Jackson returned to the bench and the case was reargued
to determine the questions on which the Court had been equally
divided. By a vote of five to four the Court held that taxes on income
from personal property, like taxes on income from land, were direct

[42] *Ibid.*, p. 607.        [43] New York *Sun*, April 9, 1895.

taxes and could not be constitutionally levied without apportionment.[44] The whole taxing scheme was therefore invalidated. The opinions were delivered amid great excitement. It was said that Justice Harlan, in delivering his dissenting opinion, "pounded the desk, shook his finger under the noses of the Chief Justice and Mr. Justice Field, turned more than once almost angrily upon his colleagues of the majority, and expressed his dissent from their conclusions in a tone and language more appropriate to a stump address at a Populist barbecue than to an opinion on a question of law before the Supreme Court of the United States." [45]

The victors were jubilant, but the defeated masses of the people denounced the Supreme Court for its surrender to the moneyed interests. As in the Dred Scott case and the legal-tender cases, the Court was accused of playing politics rather than deciding cases according to the law. That the decision had been won by a margin of only one vote called embarrassing attention to the fact that it rested on the accidental composition of the Court rather than on principles of judicial reasoning. Another circumstance heightened the embarrassment: It was not Justice Jackson whose vote killed the income-tax law, but some one of the four judges who at the time of the earlier decision had thought the law constitutional except as to taxes on income from land and from state and municipal securities. Justice Jackson voted with the minority. For many years Justice Shiras suffered the odium of criticism for surrendering to the blandishment of counsel of the rich and changing his vote for their benefit. Charles E. Hughes, after a period as associate justice in which he learned the traditions of the Court, let it be known that Justice Shiras was not the offender,[46] but did not disclose the name of the man who had changed his mind.

The income-tax cases were decided at the same term at which the Supreme Court refused to apply the Sherman Anti-Trust Act to the sugar trust and upheld the conviction of Eugene V. Debs for activities violating an injunction in the Pullman strike. The Court came to be widely regarded, therefore, as a tool of the corporations and the wealthy businessmen of the country.

As to the Anti-Trust Act, the Court redeemed its reputation in

[44] Pollock *v.* Farmers' Loan and Trust Co., 158 U.S. 601 (1895).

[45] New York *Sun*, May 13, 1895.

[46] Charles Evans Hughes, *The Supreme Court of the United States* (1928), p. 54. For discussion of the subject, see Allan Nevins, *Grover Cleveland* (1932), Appendix II.

some degree by other decisions announced before the end of the
decade; but many years were to pass and a constitutional amendment
was to be required before the results of the income-tax decisions were
done away with.[47]    In the words of Hughes, "There was not the
slightest ground for criticism of the integrity of the judges who participated in the decision." [48]    The several decisions of the period indicated, however, that at a time of sharp cleavage among the people in
terms of economic interests the thinking of the Court was grooved
along the lines of that of one faction in society, and was completely
out of sympathy with the attitudes of vast multitudes of people who
demanded the alleviation of their economic ills.

[47] See chapter 23.  The decision of the Supreme Court in Knowlton *v.* Moore, 178
U.S. 41, handed down in 1900, may be regarded as an important limitation on the
possible implications of the income-tax decisions.  In that case the Court upheld a
provision of the war-revenue act of 1898 providing for a graduated inheritance tax,
holding that the tax was not a direct tax and did not have to be apportioned.

[48] Hughes, *op. cit.,* p. 53.

••••••••••••••••••••••••••••••••••••••••••••••••••••••••••••••••••••••••••••••••••••••••••••••••••••••

# CHAPTER 21

# IMPERIALISM

THE HISTORY OF THE UNITED STATES down to 1900 witnessed the periodic acquisition of large sections of new territory and their settlement and development into statehood.   The vast area acquired in the Louisiana Purchase, Florida, Texas, Oregon, California and adjacent territory, Alaska, Hawaii, and the several island possessions acquired as a result of the Spanish-American War were the principal areas added to the original United States.   With the insignificant exception of the Guano Island, appropriated by right of discovery because of need for the fertilizer located on it, all the areas acquired before the Civil War were contiguous with land already held.   Jurisdiction was assumed over them with the expectation that they would become states or parts of states in the Union, populated by like people and governed in the same manner as the older states.

The areas acquired after the Civil War were not contiguous.   They were located in climates either near-arctic or torrid.   The near-arctic area, including only Alaska, was largely unpopulated except for Indians and deemed unlikely ever to support extensive population.   Acquisitions in the torrid zone included extensive island possessions already thickly populated with natives and with Spanish and other aliens who were unfamiliar with Anglo-Saxon traditions and methods of government.

The difference of kind and location of territory acquired later raised new problems as to the course of American national development.   Chief Justice Taney had said in the Dred Scott case that the federal government had the power to acquire new territory only for the purpose of admission to statehood.   Yet the possibility of admitting Alaska as a state was not discussed at the time it was purchased.   It was not expected that Hawaii or Puerto Rico would be admitted to statehood.   The acquisition of these and other territories, therefore, seemed to imply that the United States was at last entering upon a program of imperialism of the type hitherto carried on by a number of European nations. It seemed as if the areas acquired were to be held, not for the peaceful government and perhaps economic enrichment of the native population, but as areas of exploitation for the benefit of continental United States.

If such was the program of the United States, governmental machinery would have to be adjusted to new types of control. Did the Constitution follow the flag? Did all or none, or some but not all, of the provisions of the Constitution extend to the population of the newly acquired territories? Were their products now to be admitted into continental United States freed from the barriers of protective tariffs? Were the inhabitants entitled to the protection of Anglo-Saxon due process of law and to guarantees of jury trial and freedom of speech? These were some of the many questions raised by territorial expansion. Closely allied were knotty questions as to what authorities of the federal government had the power to decide what territory was to be acquired and how and by what means the price was to be paid.

## ALASKA

The purchase from Russia of Alaska, then known as Russian America, was arranged by treaty in 1867. Little was known about the territory. It was largely uninhabited except for a few thousand natives. It was supposed to consist principally of rocks and ice, and little was known of any possible yield in minerals, furs, or fish. Russia wished to sell, realizing its inability to hold the land should its rival, England, decide to take it. Russia's friendliness toward the United States during the Civil War provided an incentive for the purchase. William H. Seward, Secretary of State, handled negotiations for the United States in almost complete secrecy. The treaty was ready for signature on March 30, 1867, the last day of the current session of Congress. In the effort to secure the concurrence of the Senate, Seward called in Charles Sumner, chairman of the Senate committee on foreign relations. Although a bitter enemy of the Reconstruction policies of President Johnson, Sumner agreed to support the purchase. The President called a special session of the Senate to pass upon the treaty, and Sumner made an elaborate study of the situation in preparation of his defense of the treaty.[1] Since his aim was ratification of the treaty, he was not in position to be too critical

---

[1] For the Sumner speech, see *The Works of Charles Sumner* (15 vols., 1870-1883), XI, 181-349.

of the procedure by which it had been evolved.  Something of the current hostility between the legislative and executive branches of the government was reflected, however, in his suggestion that the Senate ought to have been consulted in advance.   "Let me add," he continued, "that, while forbearing objection now, I hope that this treaty may not be drawn into a precedent, at least in the independent manner of its negotiation.   I would save to the Senate an important power justly belonging to it." [2]

The purchase price was $7,200,000 in gold.   It was the equivalent of roughly ten million dollars in the paper money then providing most of the circulatory medium.   The country had recently incurred the expenses of a major war, and there was opposition to the addition of a substantial sum to the national debt at this time.   The treaty was approved with only two dissenting votes, however, and the formal transfer of title was made almost immediately, although the purchase price could not be paid until both houses of Congress had met and made an appropriation.   The immediate transfer may well have been brought about for the purpose of committing the United States so completely that the House of Representatives would feel bound to collaborate.

The first formal evidence of the attitude of the House of Representatives was made known at a brief session in November, 1867.  Certain members had heard the rumor that Seward was negotiating for the purchase of St. Thomas, one of the Danish West Indian islands, for a substantial sum.  A resolution was passed to the effect that in view of the financial condition of the country any further purchases of territory were then inexpedient and that the House would hold itself under no obligation to vote money for any such purpose.[3]

At the ensuing session a bill was introduced appropriating the agreed amount for the purchase of Alaska.   The purchase was criticized day after day as a waste of money and as a commitment to the management of territory that would yield little or nothing to the United States and would require the expenditure of added millions of dollars if police functions were to be performed   It was contended that we already had enough Indians to supervise without paying for the privilege of supervising more of them.   Apart from references to control of the Indians, not much was said about problems of government, presumably because it was assumed that few white people would ever inhabit the country.   The Stars and Stripes had been

[2] *Ibid.*, p. 232.            [3] 38 *Congressional Globe* 792-793.

raised in place of the Russian flag at Sitka, a post office had been established, and a general with a portion of the United States Army was in possession of the territory.[4] There was little evidence that addi- tional government would be needed.

The major objection to the transaction, made in speech after speech, was that the President and the Senate had committed the gov- ernment to the payment of a huge sum of money for territory of doubtful value without consulting the House of Representatives. The appropriation of money was a legislative act that could be performed only with the co-operation of the House of Representatives. Yet other agencies of the government had made a commitment of such a nature that the House could exercise its proper discretion only in the face of the fact that failure to make the appropriation would result in serious international embarrassment. The President and the Senate had no right to place the House under this form of indirect coercion. It was contended in rebuttal, on the other hand, that the Constitution left the treaty-making power exclusively in the hands of the President and the Senate, and that the House had no constitu- tional right to participate in the process. The debate resembled that of 1796, which followed the adoption of the Jay Treaty.[5] On that occasion, the House had sought to demonstrate its authority with re- spect to treaties which called for the appropriation of money by a request to the President for information concerning the negotiation of the treaty. The President had flatly refused to recognize any right of the House to participate in the treaty-making process.

In making appropriations to carry out the treaty for the purchase of Alaska, the House used a different method of asserting its authority. It passed the appropriation bill with a "whereas" clause relating the facts of the case, and including the following statement:

> And whereas the subjects thus embraced in the stipulations of said treaty are among the subjects which by the Constitution of the United States are submitted to the power of Congress, and over which Con- gress has exclusive jurisdiction; and it being for such reason necessary that the consent of Congress should be given to the said treaty before the same can have full force and effect . . .[6]

The Senate refused to accept any such doctrine and substituted for the House bill another containing a single sentence making the neces-

[4] 39 *Congressional Globe* 1871.　　　　[5] See chapter 4.
[6] 39 *Congressional Globe* 3621, 4159.

sary appropriation. The House refused to accept the substitute. Thereupon the conference committee worked out, and the two houses accepted, a compromise containing the following limited recognition of the authority of the House of Representatives:

> Whereas said stipulations cannot be carried into full force and effect except by legislation to which the consent of both houses of Congress is necessary . . . [7]

The phrase recognized the power clearly belonging to the House of Representatives, but it permitted no encroachment on the treaty-making prerogatives of the President and the Senate.

No single statute enacted at the time of the purchase of Alaska dealt comprehensively with the government to be established and the rights of the inhabitants to be protected. Various phases of the subject were dealt with, specifically or incidentally, in separate statutes. Among others, the act making appropriations for the purchase gave tacit sanction to the following provision of the treaty:

> The inhabitants of the ceded territory . . . with the exception of uncivilized native tribes, shall be admitted to the enjoyment of all the rights, advantages, and immunities of citizens of the United States, and shall be maintained and protected in the free enjoyment of their liberty, property, and religion.[8]

By another act the internal-revenue laws were extended to Alaska,[9] and by another, the laws relating to customs, commerce, and navigation.[10]

Other laws, such as those dealing with the sale of liquor to Indians, were made applicable to Alaska, but on the whole the new acquisition received little attention. It was widely characterized as "Seward's Folly." The census of 1880 showed a population of 33,426, including only 430 white persons. Congress had taken no steps to give to the Russian inhabitants remaining in the country the rights, advantages, and immunities of citizens of the United States and the free enjoyment of liberty, property, and religion promised in the treaty of acquisition. Said a Senate report made in December, 1883, "Sixteen years have elapsed since the treaty of purchase, and during all of that time the inhabitants have been absolutely without the pale of the law, and without any protection of life or property, except such as resulted from the temporary presence of some army detachment or the occa-

---

[7] *Ibid.*, p. 4392; 15 Stat. 198.        [8] 15 Stat. 542.
[9] 15 Stat. 167.        [10] 15 Stat. 240.

sional visit of a vessel of war or a revenue cutter." The enactment of a law providing a civil government for Alaska was recommended.[11]

Debates on the proposed bill raised, but did not deal conclusively with, questions of territorial government that were to constitute serious problems in later years with the acquisition of island possessions in the tropics. It was suggested that, since the Constitution required that all duties, imposts, and excises should be uniform throughout the United States, the taxes collected in Alaska must correspond to those collected in the United States proper.[12] Although it was not denied that Congress had the power to regulate or prohibit the sale of liquor to Indians, it was contended that Congress had no power to prohibit commerce between the states and Alaska by prohibiting the shipment of liquor.[13] Justice Story was cited to the effect that the District of Columbia and the territory west of the Missouri were not less within the United States than Maryland or Pennsylvania.[14] It was assumed in debate that Alaska was as much a part of the United States as had been other United States territory before admission to statehood.

Legislators moved slowly, giving repeated evidence of the continued belief that the acquisition of Alaska had been a mistake. In at least one instance the bill was supported, not because of any interest in Alaska itself, but because of a belief in the inevitability of further territorial expansion. Said Senator Ingalls, of Kansas:

> Mr. President, if I were not in favor of the unification of this continent under American dominion, I should be willing to relinquish Alaska to any power that would undertake to carry on its government and provide for its future welfare. But the Monroe Doctrine is written on the map; that is our first lesson in geography, and "manifest destiny" indicates that our northern shore is to be washed by the Polar Sea, and that our southern boundary will be the interoceanic canal that connects the Atlantic and Pacific.[15]

The "act providing a civil government for Alaska" was passed in 1884.[16] It provided for a governor, a district court, and other officers; but not for a complete territorial government such as had been customarily set up in territories on the way to statehood. Since the small population of Alaska could not justify establishment of a territorial

---

[11] Senate Report No. 3, 48th Cong., 1st sess.

[12] 15 *Congressional Record* 632.          [13] *Ibid.*, p. 658.

[14] Joseph Story, *Commentaries on the Constitution of the United States* (1833), II, sec. 996, p. 463.

[15] 15 *Congressional Record* 566.          [16] 23 Stat. 24.

legislature, the act provided specifically that "there shall be no legislative assembly in said district, nor shall any delegate be sent to Congress therefrom." It met the needs of Alaska by arranging "that the general laws of the state of Oregon now in force are hereby declared to be the law in said district, so far as the same may be applicable and not in conflict with the provisions of this act or the laws of the United States."

In December, 1899, President McKinley reminded Congress that the act of 1884 was substantially the only law providing a civil government for the territory of Alaska. This, he said, was meager in its provisions and fitted only for the administration of affairs in a country sparsely inhabited by civilized people and unimportant in trade and production. The recent increase in population consequent upon the discovery of gold had produced such a condition as required more ample facilities for local government and more numerous conveniences of civil and judicial administration.[17] The act passed pursuant to the recommendation of the President [18] was drafted in the same period in which consideration was being given to the government of Hawaii, Puerto Rico, and other newly acquired island possessions.

## HAWAII

The United States had long been interested in the somewhat unstable tropical kingdom of Hawaii in the middle of the Pacific Ocean. As an American possession, Hawaii would become an important outpost for the protection of our commerce. To some Americans its early acquisition seemed desirable because European nations were suspected of having designs upon it and because the rapid infiltration of Japanese and other Asiatics caused great concern. Although imperialism and manifest destiny were supposed to represent the policies of the Republican rather than of the Democratic party, the Cleveland administration in 1887 acquired a naval base for the United States at Pearl Harbor, near Honolulu.

As early as 1875 a treaty had been made admitting Hawaiian sugar to the United States free from tariff duty. The giving of this advantage over other foreign producers resulted in a rapid development of the sugar industry in the islands and the building of huge fortunes for American producers there. The McKinley Tariff Act of 1890,

---

[17] *Messages and Papers of the Presidents*, XIII, 6400-6402.

[18] 31 Stat. 321. For a study of the government of Alaska, see George W. Spicer, *The Constitutional Status and Government of Alaska* (1927).

however, changed the situation by placing foreign sugar on the free list and giving a bounty to home producers.   Consequently, Hawaiian producers lost the tremendous advantage they had hitherto held.[19] These producers, most of them Americans, engaged in a concerted movement to bring about the annexation of the islands to the United States, so as to secure again special advantages for their products. The American minister seems to have worked closely with them. They stimulated or took advantage of a revolution against the constitutional authorities, used United States troops to support the revolution, aided in the establishment of a provisional government, and brought about the drafting of a treaty of annexation to the United States.   In February, 1893, shortly before his retirement from office, President Benjamin Harrison sent the treaty to the Senate and recommended its approval.[20]

Grover Cleveland returned to the presidency before action had been taken by the Senate.   By contrast with many leading Republicans, he was anti-imperialistic and he had no attachment to the plan of annexation concocted by sugar producers and Republican politicians. He recalled the treaty from the hands of the Senate, therefore, and investigated the Hawaiian revolution.   In a special message to Congress, approximately a year after Harrison had submitted the treaty to the Senate, he disclosed the results of his investigation and denounced the encroachment upon Hawaiian sovereignty.[21] "I regarded, and still regard," wrote Cleveland early in 1898, "the proposed annexation of these islands as not only opposed to our national policy, but as a perversion of our national mission.   The mission of our nation is to build up and make a greater country out of what we have, instead of annexing islands."[22]

On March 4, 1897, the Republican party returned to power under William McKinley.   In June of that year the President sent to the Senate a new treaty of annexation.   Union of the Hawaiian territory to the United States was no new scheme, he said, but was the inevitable consequence of the relation steadfastly maintained with that Pacific domain for three-quarters of a century.   Annexation was not a change; it was a consummation.   The organic and administrative details of incorporation were left to Congress, to be dealt with after the ratification of the treaty.[23]

---

[19] Allan Nevins, *Grover Cleveland: A Study in Courage* (1933), p. 555.
[20] *Messages and Papers of the Presidents*, XII, 5783.        [21] *Ibid.*, pp. 5892 ff.
[22] *Letters of Grover Cleveland* (edited by Allan Nevins, 1933), pp. 491-492.
[23] Senate Report No. 681, 55th Cong., 2d sess., p. 65.

When on December 6, 1897, McKinley delivered his first annual message, the Senate had not yet acted on the treaty. He again called attention to it, saying that the complete absorption of the islands into the domain of the United States awaited only favorable action of the American Senate   He continued:

> What the conditions of such a union shall be, the political relation thereof to the United States, the character of the local administration, the quality and degree of the elective franchise of the inhabitants, the extension of the federal laws to the territory or the enactment of special laws to fit the peculiar condition thereof, the regulation if need be of the labor system therein, are all matters which the treaty has wisely relegated to the Congress.[24]

Failure of the Senate to vote on the approval of the treaty was evidently due to the belief of administration leaders that the necessary majority of two-thirds was not available. The Senate committee on foreign relations, therefore, approached the subject from another direction. It was recalled that the annexation of Texas had been brought about by joint resolution when it proved impossible to secure Senate approval of a treaty. The passage of a joint resolution, while involving action by both houses of Congress, required no more than a mere majority. The committee on foreign relations recommended the use of the same device for the annexation of Hawaii, making a detailed and persuasive report to justify immediate action.[25]

Having shown administration leaders in the two houses a method of avoiding the requirement of a vote of two-thirds of the Senate in order to secure annexation, the Senate left the initiative to the House of Representatives. The House resolution was reported after the declaration of war against Spain and after Dewey's victory in the battle of Manila Bay. Expansionist sentiment being now rampant, it was easy to visualize the Hawaiian Islands as a necessary outpost for the defense of American possessions and as a possible stepping-stone to other possessions farther beyond. Although the debates were limited largely to issues already under discussion for a period of years, wartime emotion seems to have speeded the enactment of the joint resolution.[26]

The Democratic minority of the House committee on foreign affairs objected to the joint resolution. The people of Hawaii had not been

[24] *Messages and Papers of the Presidents*, XIII, 6264.

[25] Senate Report No. 681, 55th Cong., 2d sess.

[26] For the report of the House committee on foreign affairs, see House Report No. 1355, 55th Cong., 2d sess.

consulted upon the proposed annexation, they said. Nor had the people of the United States been consulted. In fact, "the only hope for Hawaiian annexation, and therefore the desire of the annexationists, is to consummate their scheme under the cry of 'war emergency' before the American people can be consulted." [27]   Furthermore, they contended, annexation in the manner proposed was unconstitutional. There were two constitutional methods of increasing the domain of the country. One was the treaty-making power. This method had been tried here and had failed. The other was the power to admit new states. This power applied only to states, not to territory avowedly not wanted for purposes of statehood. It did not apply to colonies or to military or naval stations.

The minority objected also on the ground of the remoteness of the islands and the fact that they furnished too much additional coastline to be defended. The population, they said, was not racially nor religiously nor otherwise homogeneous with our own. Political dominion over the islands was not necessary to our commerce, or to our defense from a naval or military standpoint. The one harbor that, under foreign control, could menace the United States was already in our possession. They did not believe there was danger to the United States in the possible seizure of the islands by some other power.

On the floor of the House accusations as to the continued influence of sugar interests were made. Said Champ Clark, of Missouri, "The propaganda which has been carried on openly in this city for the last five or six years by the agents of the Hawaiian sugar kings in favor of annexation is a disgrace to this government and has lowered us in the eyes of ourselves and the rest of the world. It has no parallel in all history." [28]   Ministers from Hawaii and even the president under the new government had appeared in Washington to exercise their influence.

As for "manifest destiny," about which much was heard, it was a charming phrase, Clark continued. It tickled the ears of men. It pandered to human vanity. It fed the lurid flames of ambition. It whetted the sword of conquest. It was an anodyne for the troubled conscience, but it lured to destruction. It was formulated, he said, quoting incorrectly, by that eminent annexationist Rob Roy in the following plain blunt language:

> The good old rule, the simple plan,
>     That they should take who have the power,
>   And they should keep who can.

[27] *Ibid.*, Part 2, p. 1.          [28] 31 *Congressional Record* 5794.

Moses had placed his veto on this convenient theory of manifest destiny when he wrote the stern command, "Thou shalt not covet thy neighbor's land." The doctrine of manifest destiny had been the specious plea of every robber and freebooter since the world began, and would continue to be until the elements should melt with fervent heat. Hawaii, he declared, was "a blind for our eyes, a snare for our feet, a bait for our cupidity, the will-o'-the-wisp which will lead us into the Slough of Despond, the bewitching, scheming, treacherous Delilah destined to shear our Samson of his leonine locks and to deliver him bound hand and foot into the power of the Philistines." [29]

The western states had such interest in Pacific Ocean commerce that Senator Francis G. Newlands, of Nevada, even though a Democrat, supported the joint resolution. He thought there was danger of the occupation of the islands by other foreign powers, and that the establishment of a mere protectorate would not be sufficient. He said:

> We are confronted by the statement that the acquisition of the Hawaiian Islands means colonial expansion, territorial expansion, empire. I regard it as an unfortunate thing that this question is to be considered in the public mind in connection with the Philippine question. None of us know how that question is to be determined. For one I trust it will not be so determined as to involve colonial expansion. [30]

He did not believe in owning islands all over the globe; he did not believe in a system of colonial extension like that of England.

The joint resolution passed the House of Representatives by a vote of 209 to 91. [31] Consideration in the Senate began with a hostile speech by Senator Morrill, a Republican from Vermont. He would trespass upon the time of the Senate, he said,

> only to state why the annexation of the Hawaiian Islands in time of war is more inopportune than in time of peace, and also to state some of the reasons why I am unable to concur with the learned committee on foreign relations in regard to such an annexation, whether by treaty, by joint resolution, by flagrant executive usurpation, or in any manner which leaves an open door for their admission into the Union as a state. [32]

---

[29] *Ibid.*, p. 5795. For a penetrating study of manifest destiny see Albert K. Weinberg, *Manifest Destiny: A Study of Nationalist Expansionism in American History* (1935).
[30] 31 *Congressional Record* 5830.
[31] *Ibid.*, p. 6019.    [32] *Ibid.*, p. 6141.

He had a long list of objections to annexation, and he was particularly opposed to statehood for Hawaii and to a policy of annexing distant islands that might create a necessity for further enlargement of our naval force. He thought that the policy of the United States should be grounded in the words of perennial wisdom in Washington's Farewell Address.

Senator Bacon, a Democrat from Georgia, denounced the device of substituting a joint resolution for procedure by treaty. A treaty had been recognized as the proper mode of procedure by both parties and had been acted upon. Therefore, the failure of the Senate to ratify the treaty was the same as the failure of an attempted passage of a statute law. The subterfuge violated the Constitution, and it struck a blow at one of the fundamental and most important prerogatives of the President and the Senate.[33] In spite of this argument, however, most senators seem to have been concerned almost exclusively with the expediency or inexpediency of annexing the islands. Few of them seemed concerned about the resort to procedure establishing a precedent for encroachment upon their treaty-making power.

Since the joint resolution, like the treaty that had been presented, did not deal with the details of the government to be established over the Hawaiian Islands, little attention was given to that subject at this time. The question arose incidentally, however, in connection with the status of contract-labor laws. Large numbers of the laborers on the sugar plantations of Hawaii were Asiatic people, imported under contract. The question arose whether, under the Constitution of the United States, with its prohibition of forced labor, these contract-labor laws would remain valid. To what extent would the Constitution and laws of the United States extend over the newly acquired territory? No conclusion was reached, but it was contended by the opposition that the presence of a labor population almost exclusively alien in character created such problems as to constitute a strong argument against the annexation.[34]

The joint resolution passed the Senate by a vote of 42 to 21, with 26 not voting. For the enactment of a joint resolution the vote was much more than sufficient. Had the vote on the treaty been the same, it would have been barely sufficient. It is possible, however, that had the issue of the treaty been forced to a vote, enough opponents would have been found among the twenty-six non-voters to have prevented the adoption of the treaty. It may be, on the other

[33] *Ibid.*, pp. 6150-6151.          [34] *Ibid.*, pp. 6484-6486.

hand, that war sentiment had by this time so affected the personnel of the Senate that even the treaty would have received the necessary number of votes for approval.[85]

### THE SPANISH-AMERICAN WAR

In 1895, the last of a series of destructive insurrections broke out in Cuba against the unjust and incompetent rule of Spain. The war was conducted ruthlessly on both sides with widespread destruction of life and property. Technically the struggle was one merely between Spain and its Spanish colonial possessions, and did not concern the United States in any direct fashion. No authority in the United States claimed any right over Cuba. Yet the closeness of the island to the United States and the development of commercial relationships created interconnections so strong as to seem likely ultimately to involve the United States unless Spain could bring the struggle to an end. In his annual message to Congress in December, 1896, President Cleveland estimated that from thirty to fifty million dollars of American capital were invested in sugar plantations and in various types of other enterprises on the island. The volume of trade between the United States and Cuba in 1894, the year before the outbreak of the insurrection, had amounted to nearly ninety-six million dollars. Much of the property was being destroyed by warfare, and much of the trade had been cut off. Furthermore, although the government of the United States was eager for the restoration of peace in Cuba, much of the resistance to Spanish control had been plotted in the United States by Cubans or others, and many expeditions had been fitted out in the United States for use against the Spanish government in Cuba. Said Cleveland:

> The result is that this government is constantly called upon to protect American citizens, to claim damages for injuries to persons and property, now estimated at many millions of dollars, and to ask explanations and apologies for the acts of Spanish officials whose zeal for the repression of rebellion sometimes blinds them to the immunities belonging to the unoffending citizens of a friendly power. It follows from the same causes that the United States is compelled to actively police a long line of seacoast against unlawful expeditions, the escape of which the utmost vigilance will not always suffice to prevent.[86]

[85] *Ibid.*, p. 6712.
[86] *Messages and Papers of the Presidents*, XIII, 6150-6151.

On various grounds, various forms of intervention, reaching all the
way to a recognition of Cuban independence, were being urged on the
United States. Cleveland resisted any such interference, but he suggested that it would be wise for Spain to offer Cuba genuine autonomy, a measure of home rule which, while preserving the sovereignty
of Spain, would satisfy all rational requirements of her Spanish subjects. Spain, however, was willing to make peace only after complete
suppression of the insurgents. Interventionists in Congress and elsewhere continued their clamor for action by the United States. The
enactment of a joint resolution recognizing the independence of Cuba
was threatened. The Secretary of State, Richard Olney, announced
indignantly that recognition of a foreign state was a prerogative of the
executive branch of the government. The effect of the enactment of
the resolution would be merely to inflame popular passions in the
United States and Spain, endanger the lives and property of American
citizens, and complicate the conduct of American foreign relations.[37]

Strife in Cuba continued through the first year of the McKinley
administration. On February 15, 1898, occurred the destruction of
the United States battleship *Maine,* by a submarine mine, during a
friendly visit in the harbor at Havana. This event, although not
traced to deliberate design, incited new demands for American intervention. In a special message delivered on April 11, 1898, President
McKinley summarized the history of the struggle and made the following request:

> ... I ask the Congress to authorize and empower the President to
> take measures to secure a full and final termination of hostilities be-
> tween the government of Spain and the people of Cuba, and to secure
> in the island the establishment of a stable government, capable of
> maintaining order and observing its international obligations, in-
> suring peace and tranquillity and the security of its citizens as well
> as our own, and to use the military and naval forces of the United
> States as may be necessary for these purposes.[38]

Events moved rapidly. By joint resolution of April 20, 1898, Congress declared that the people of the island of Cuba were and of right
ought to be free and independent. It demanded that Spain at once
relinquish her authority and withdraw her land and naval forces from
Cuba and Cuban waters. The President was directed and empowered
to use the entire land and naval forces of the United States and to call

[37] Allan Nevins, *Grover Cleveland* (1933), p. 718.
[38] *Messages and Papers of the Presidents,* XIII, 6292.

out the militia to make its purposes effective.   As a disclaimer of the charge of imperialism, a statement was added "That the United States hereby disclaims any disposition or intention to exercise sovereignty, jurisdiction, or control over said island except for the pacification thereof, and asserts its determination, when that is accomplished, to leave the government and control of the island to its people." [39]   Spain declined to withdraw, the President proclaimed a blockade of Cuban ports, and on April 25, 1898, war was formally declared.[40]

The Spanish-American War was in few respects comparable to the major wars in which the United States has participated.   A complete victory was won within a few months.   Both the loss of life and the cost were negligible.   Although there was opposition to the war, the people were not sharply divided over it.   The economic and industrial life of the country was not reorganized for war purposes.   People thrilled to the accounts of Roosevelt's charge up San Juan Hill and Dewey's victory over the Spanish fleet in the harbor of Manila, but the period of war activity was too brief to arouse super-patriotic emotions.

With the cessation of military hostilities the United States found itself in control of Cuba, Puerto Rico, the Philippines, and other islands formerly held by Spain.   The capture of the Philippines had been no part of the original plan of the government.   Commodore George Dewey, in command of an American squadron at Hong Kong at the time of the outbreak of the war, had been ordered to go to Manila to destroy the Spanish fleet located there, in order to prevent the fleet from preying upon the western coast of the United States. The destruction of the fleet and the capture of the harbor led to military control of the surrounding area so that with the termination of the war the United States was faced with the question of the permanent disposition of the Philippines.   For reasons not clearly disclosed, President McKinley concluded that they could not be returned to Spain at the end of the war, since such a return would be "cowardly and dishonorable."   It would be bad business and discreditable to turn them over to France or Germany, our commercial rivals in the Orient.   They could not be left to themselves because they were as yet unfit for self-government.   The conclusion reached, therefore, was that the United States should hold the islands in temporary possession, educate, uplift, civilize, and Christianize the Filipinos, and prepare them for ultimate self-government.[41]

[39] 30 Stat. 738, 739.        [40] 30 Stat. 364.
[41] Charles S. Olcott, *Life of William McKinley* (2 vols., 1916), II, 111.

By the treaty [42] Spain relinquished to the United States all claims of sovereignty over and title to Cuba. During its period of occupation the United States was to assume such obligations under international law as arose from the fact of occupation. Spain ceded to the United States the island of Puerto Rico and other islands in the West Indies, and also the island of Guam. Spain also ceded the Philippines, in return for the sum of twenty million dollars to be paid by the United States.

The treaty was signed at Paris on December 10, 1898. Many congressmen and others welcomed the reaching-out for new territory, the inevitable expression of manifest destiny. Others, opposed to territorial expansion, began the building-up of sentiment to prevent the ratification of the treaty. On December 6, 1898, Senator George G. Vest, of Missouri, introduced a joint resolution that under the Constitution the federal government was given no power to acquire territory to be held and governed permanently as colonies. The colonial system of European nations could not be established under the Constitution, but all territory acquired, except for coaling stations, correcting of boundaries, and the like, must be acquired and governed with the purpose of ultimately organizing such territory into states suitable for admission into the Union.[43] To prove his point he relied heavily on the several opinions in the Dred Scott case.[44] He denied that territory could be acquired "to be held as colonies, peopled by millions of subjects not citizens, with no hope or prospect of its ever becoming a state of the Union." He would not insult his brother senators by supposing that they would

> evade the spirit and letter of the Constitution, and, when believing that the colonial system is not possible in this country, would vote to take in vast tracts of land inhabited by barbarians, intending never to allow this territory to come in as a state, but to hold it for commercial advantages alone, in violation of the fundamental law of the land. . . . The colonial system destroyed all hope of republicanism in the olden time. It is an appanage of monarchy. It can exist in no free country, because it uproots and eliminates the basis of all republican institutions, that governments derive their just powers from the consent of the governed.[45]

The answer to Senator Vest was delivered by Orville H. Platt, of Connecticut, who in August, 1898, had made a survey of his state and

[42] 30 Stat. 1754.          [43] 32 *Congressional Record* 20.
[44] *Ibid.*, pp. 93-94.          [45] *Ibid.*, p. 96.

had found the people overwhelmingly in favor of retaining possession of the Philippines.[46] He delivered an eloquent, able, and well-documented address to demonstrate that the federal government had the unrestricted power to govern territory.[47] The gist of his argument was the contention, not that the acquisition of territory was among the powers delegated by the Constitution, but that the United States was a sovereign nation, and had all the powers of sovereignty not withheld by the Constitution. He said:

> I propose to maintain that the United States is a nation; that as a nation it possesses every sovereign power not reserved in its Constitution to the states or the people; that the right to acquire territory was not reserved, and is therefore an inherent sovereign right; that it is a right upon which there is no limitation, and with regard to which there is no qualification; that in certain instances the right may be inferred from specific clauses in the Constitution, but that it exists independent of these clauses; that in the right to acquire territory is found the right to govern it; and as the right to acquire is a sovereign and inherent right, the right to govern is a sovereign right not limited in the Constitution, and that these propositions are in accordance with the views of the framers of the Constitution, the decisions of the Supreme Court, and the legislation of Congress.[48]

He found support for his argument in certain important Chinese cases. The cases involved, not imperialist expansion on the part of the United States, but federal legislation to discontinue the penetration of the United States by Chinese laborers. By a federal statute violating a treaty with China, certain Chinese were forbidden to re-enter the United States after departure therefrom. Justice Field, speaking for the Supreme Court in a case arising under the statute, held that treaties were of no greater legal obligation than an act of Congress and that, in an instance of conflict between the two, the one most recently enacted must control.[49] In justifying the power of exclusion he declared that the United States, in relation to foreign countries and their subjects or citizens, was one nation, invested with powers which belonged to independent nations. The powers to declare war, make treaties, suppress insurrection, repel invasion, regulate foreign commerce, secure republican governments to the states,

[46] Louis A. Coolidge, *An Old-Fashioned Senator: Orville H. Platt of Connecticut* (1910), pp. 287-288.

[47] The debate is summarized, *ibid.,* pp. 296-300.

[48] 32 *Congressional Record* 287-288.

[49] Chae Chan Ping *v.* United States, 130 U.S. 581, 600 (1889).

and admit subjects of other nations to citizenship were all sovereign powers, restricted in their exercise only by the Constitution itself and considerations of public policy and justice which controlled more or less the conduct of all civilized nations.[50]  Field quoted Chief Justice Marshall as saying:

> In war, we are one people.  In making peace, we are one people. In all commercial regulations, we are one and the same people.  In many other respects, the American people are one; and the government which is alone capable of controlling and managing their interests in all these respects is the government of the Union.  It is their government, and in that character they have no other.  America has chosen to be in many respects, and to many purposes, a nation; and for all these purposes her government is complete; to all these objects it is competent.  The people have declared that in the exercise of all powers given for these objects it is supreme.[51]

Field also quoted from the important section of Justice Bradley's concurring opinion in the legal-tender cases, beginning with the statement that "The United States is not only a government, but it is a national government, and the only government in this country that has the character of nationality." [52] The statement contributed directly to Senator Platt's argument.  The senator also found support in another Chinese exclusion case in which Justice Gray, speaking for the Court, said:

> The United States are a sovereign and independent nation, and are vested by the Constitution with the entire control of international relations, and with all the powers of government necessary to maintain that control and to make it effective.  The only government of this country, which other nations recognize or treat with, is the government of the Union; and the only American flag known throughout the world is the flag of the United States.[53]

Defending the power of Congress to acquire and govern territory other than for purposes of statehood, Platt said that up to the time when Alaska was acquired from Russia, every treaty under which new

[50] *Ibid.*, p. 604.          [51] Cohens *v.* Virginia, 6 Wheaton 264, 413 (1821).

[52] Knox *v.* Lee, 12 Wallace 457, 555 (1871).

[53] Fong Yue Ting *v.* United States, 149 U.S. 698, 711 (1893).  For an account of many of the problems arising out of the presence of Chinese in the United States, see Carl Brent Swisher, *Stephen J. Field: Craftsman of the Law* (1930), chapter VIII.  Senator Platt dealt with the power of Congress to govern territory in terms of a recent case, The Late Corporation of the Church of Jesus Christ of the Latter-Day Saints *v.* United States, 136 U.S. 1 (1890).

**territory** was acquired contained a clause that the inhabitants, as soon as they were fitted for it, should be incorporated into the Union. That, he supposed, meant that a state was to be created. But in the instance of Alaska no such provision was included.

> The parties making the treaty, the Senate ratifying it, and the House voting the money to put it into effect industriously and studiously excluded the clause which provided that the inhabitants should be incorporated into the Union. . . . It was not the intention of the framers of that treaty, it was not the intention of the Senate when the treaty was ratified, nor of the House when the money was appropriated, that it should be understood that there was any obligation on the part of the United States, by treaty or otherwise, at any time in the future either to give them self-government or to admit them as a state.[54]

He pointed out that no government had been organized for Alaska down until 1884, and that only a government much limited in form had existed since that date. Thirty-one years had passed since the territory was acquired, and no man had yet voted in Alaska. It had no delegate in the House of Representatives. It resembled the District of Columbia, where the people neither voted nor had a delegate in the House of Representatives. Unless there was a stipulation in a treaty, he denied the existence of any legal or moral obligation to fit for statehood or ever to admit as a state territory that might be acquired.

The argument was impressive, but Senator Hoar challenged it. Did Senator Platt believe that governments derived their just powers from the consent of the governed? It was assumed that no senator would dare publicly reject this principle of the Declaration of Independence. But Senator Platt replied, "From the consent of some of the governed."

> Does the senator from Connecticut seriously claim [challenged Senator Hoar] that the great doctrine which is at the foundation of our Revolution and Declaration of Independence is a falsehood; that it should be qualified by saying governments derive their just powers from the consent of some of the governed, and that the violation of that principle in regard to ten million people, without any discrimination between ignorance and intelligence, is justified by the reading and the writing clause of some of our state constitutions?[55]

He did not deny those principles, Platt replied, but all sorts of qualifications for voting had been adopted, including age, sex, literacy,

[54] 32 *Congressional Record* 296.     [55] *Ibid.*, p. 297.

property rights, and others.   No votes were cast in the District of
Columbia; yet this condition was not challenged as a violation of the
doctrine of the Declaration of Independence.   He could understand
neither the sentiment nor the motive of those who were unwilling to
concede that our government was a nation and who feared to see it
clothed with every element of sovereignty which a nation should
possess and did possess.   Why, he asked, should any man, especially a
senator, wish to detract from, to diminish or belittle the power of his
government?   "For this," he said, "is the people's government; the
government of a great people, a liberty-loving people, a people that
can be trusted to do right, and to guarantee to all men who shall come
under its beneficent sway and be subject to its jurisdiction the largest
measure of liberty consistent with good order and their general well-
being." [56]

The debate on the Vest resolution continued day after day.   Senator Hoar reiterated in a long address his charge that Senator Platt
denied the principle of the Declaration of Independence.[57]  A southern
senator congratulated Platt on his discussion of the right to vote, contending that it justified the South in disfranchising the Negroes, who
were not yet equipped for the exercise of the right.[58]   Senator Henry
Cabot Lodge, of Massachusetts, stated flatly the belief that "the power
of the United States in any territory or possession outside the limits
of the states themselves is absolute, with the single exception of the
limitations placed upon such outside possessions by the Thirteenth
Amendment." [59]

GOVERNMENT OF THE NEW POSSESSIONS

Although, in spite of the length of debate on the Vest resolution
and similar proposals, no formal action was ever taken, the discussion
clarified the issues, and the sentiments of the Senate were revealed by
the approval of the treaty with Spain by the narrow margin of one
vote.   The task was now that of providing peaceful methods of control over the territories that had been taken by conquest.   President
McKinley sent word to Elihu Root, prominent New York lawyer, that
he wanted him to come to Washington as head of the War Department.   When Root replied that he knew nothing about war or about
the army, he was told that the President was not looking for anyone
who knew about these subjects, but that he had to have a lawyer to
direct the government of the Spanish islands and that Root was the

[56] Ibid., p. 297.        [57] Ibid., pp. 493 ff.        [58] Ibid., p. 639.        [59] Ibid., p. 958.

lawyer he wanted.[60] Root accepted the position; and, since for the time being all the possessions were under military control, he supervised generally their management.

The intention of the United States as to the future status of Cuba had been defined in part by the joint resolution of April 20, 1898, in which the United States had disclaimed any disposition or intention to exercise sovereignty, jurisdiction, or control over the island except for the pacification thereof, and had asserted its determination to leave the government and control of the island to its own people.[61] It seems clear that neither Cuba, Spain, nor the rest of the world expected the United States to adhere to this policy.[62] There was strong sentiment within the United States for retaining control. There was likewise sentiment against it, however, sentiment which went so far as to bring about the enactment of a provision "that no property, franchises, or concessions of any kind whatever shall be granted by the United States, or by any military or other authority whatever, in the island of Cuba during the occupation thereof by the United States." [63]

As a matter of fact, the driving interest toward intervention in Cuba had not been a desire to extend the sovereignty of the United States over the island, but a desire to restore order, protect American property, and re-establish conditions under which Americans could resume a profitable business. If Congress was to be dominated by sentiment of such high moral tone as that which prevented the granting of franchises and concessions during the period of occupation, there were business arguments for terminating American occupation as soon as possible rather than making it permanent. In view of the type of government likely to be established in Cuba, it might be easier for enterprising businessmen to secure concessions from the Cuban government than from that of the United States.

American businessmen followed the American flag to Cuba, but it was at once apparent that difficulties lay in the way of the establishment of order under an independent Cuban government. Under American direction, therefore, organized efforts were made to improve sanitary conditions, to terminate lawlessness, to begin the processes of education, and to lay the groundwork generally for a stable society. During two years of military occupation many American authorities reached the conclusion that a government of such stability as to justify complete independence could not be established

---

[60] Philip C. Jessup, *Elihu Root* (2 vols., 1938), I, 215.
[62] Leland H. Jenks, *Our Cuban Colony* (1928), pp. 70-71.

[61] 30 Stat. 738.
[63] 30 Stat. 1074.

at all, and that the right of the United States to extend protection should be preserved. In the army appropriation act of March 2, 1901, therefore, Congress inserted what became known as the Platt Amendment, modifying the earlier resolution as to the intentions of the United States toward Cuba. Among other things, the government of Cuba could never grant rights permitting any foreign power to impair its independence. It must recognize the right of the United States to intervene for the preservation of Cuban independence and the maintenance of a government adequate for the protection of life, property, and individual liberty and for the discharge of obligations to be assumed toward the United States. The Cuban government was to permit the United States to establish coaling or naval stations on the island. It was to ratify the acts of the United States in Cuba during its military occupancy and execute sanitary measures to prevent the recurrence of epidemic and infectious diseases.[64]

Cuba reluctantly included these provisions in its new constitution and also in a treaty with the United States.[65] In 1902, the control of the island was turned over to a government established under the new constitution. Now and then down through the years the United States found it necessary to intervene under the Platt Amendment to restore order, although political interference was not on a scale comparable with economic penetration carried on by American businessmen. The Platt Amendment was for many years a source of irritation to the Cubans, standing as it did as a limitation upon their sovereignty. By a treaty proclaimed in 1934, the amendment was abrogated.[66] Cuba now stands "as a fully accepted member of the family of nations."[67] American imperialism in terms of economic influence, however, goes on unabated and is not likely to be seriously curbed.

As for the Philippines, American control was not completely established with the ratification of the treaty with Spain. The Filipinos had no desire to be governed by the United States. An insurrection broke out early in 1899 and lasted until 1902, conducted by men who were fighting a losing fight for independence. It was put down only after intensive warfare and resort to cruel measures on both sides. The proceedings in the Philippines were a far cry from war for the independence of Cuba. Ultimately, under the leadership of William Howard Taft and others, the establishment of a civil government was

[64] 31 Stat. 897-898.　　[65] 33 Stat. 2248.　　[66] 48 Stat. 1682.
[67] Russell H. Fitzgibbon, *Cuba and the United States, 1900-1935* (1935), p. 252.

begun and civil rights and political privileges were extended as circumstances seemed to permit.

The Philippine Islands never accepted American control with complete willingness, and many Americans had no real desire to assert or
to maintain American sovereignty over them. The Democratic party
became a partisan of Philippine independence. A federal statute of
1916 announced the policy of granting independence as soon as a
stable form of government should be established.[68] In 1934, another
statute provided for independence after a period of ten years, following establishment of a commonwealth government.[69] A commonwealth
government was established and arrangements were made for the termination of American control in 1946.

DOES THE CONSTITUTION FOLLOW THE FLAG?

Although the debate over the power of the United States to acquire
territory not intended for statehood ended with the ratification of the
treaty with Spain, important controversies as to the government of the
acquired territory still remained. They were discussed in hundreds
of pages of debate dealing with the establishment of a government for
Puerto Rico and provisions with reference to customs duties. Many
of the advocates of the acquisition of new areas took the position that
acquisition did not make the areas an integral part of the United
States, but left them to be governed by the United States according to
the will of Congress. Many of the opponents of the original acquisition, on the other hand, took the position that, since territory had
been acquired, it was to be treated as a part of the United States, and
that all the provisions of the Constitution automatically extended to
it. In general, the former group consisted of Republicans and the
latter of Democrats, although the division was not completely along
party lines. "The difference between the imperialists and the anti-
imperialists on this question," said Senator Newlands, of Nevada, "is
that the imperialists wish to expand our territory and to contract our
Constitution. The anti-imperialists are opposed to any expansion of
territory which, as a matter of necessity, arising from the ignorance
and inferiority of the people occupying it, makes free constitutional
government impracticable or undesirable." [70]

The question was much discussed in connection with an issue that
has lost its importance with the passing years; namely, the collection
of import duties on goods shipped into continental United States from

[68] 39 Stat. 545.        [69] 48 Stat. 456.        [70] 33 *Congressional Record* 1996.

island territories.   Although American interests in some of the acquired territories sought to bring about annexation to the United States in order to break down barriers, competitors in the United States opposed the leveling of these barriers.   They sought, therefore, to have the collection of customs duties continued, even though the United States now owned the territories from which the imports were shipped.   Opponents of such duties declared that their collection was now unconstitutional.   The Constitution provided that duties should be uniform, and prohibited taxes on exports from any state.   Commerce between the territories of the United States must, therefore, move without discriminating hindrance.   They enforced their arguments with seemingly interminable compilations of Supreme Court decisions and other materials.   The so-called imperialists, on the other hand, contended that, although the territories had been acquired under the Constitution, the provisions of the Constitution did not extend to them automatically, but only as provided by Congress. They enforced their arguments with similar compilations of legal and historical materials.

Behind the tariff question lay the more important one of the general applicability of all the provisions of the Constitution to the territories.   It was assumed by unprejudiced thinkers that there must be some assurance of the protection of fundamental rights of life, liberty, and property.   On the other hand, such guarantees as those of jury trial and the provision that no criminal trial should proceed except on indictment called for a familiarity with Anglo-Saxon institutions not possessed by the inhabitants of the newly acquired territories.   To enforce these and other types of machinery upon the people of the islands might be expected to interfere with justice rather than promote it.

The enactment of a measure to provide revenues and a civil government for Puerto Rico [71] represented a victory for those who denied that the Constitution in all its fullness followed the flag.   Provision was made for the collection of duties on goods shipped from Puerto Rico to the United States and from the United States to Puerto Rico. The principle was not altered by the fact that the duties to be collected were only fifteen per cent of the duties to be collected on imports from other countries and that no duties at all were to be collected after March 1, 1902.

If the constitutional question was settled in Congress by a counting

[71] 31 Stat. 77.

of heads after a struggle between economic interests which rationalized their views in terms of constitutional arguments, the people of the country seem to have accepted the decision with equanimity. The Republican party, which sponsored the imperialist position, was victorious in the elections of 1900. In May, 1901, the Supreme Court decided a series of cases, known as the Insular Cases, in which it passed upon the same constitutional issues. The members of the Court divided in a bewildering fashion and reached conclusions only by votes of five to four, but, like Congress and the voters, they upheld the imperialist policy. Finley Peter Dunne, a humorist of the time, writing as Mr. Dooley, confessed continuing bewilderment as to whether the Constitution followed the flag or not, but he was sure of one thing, that "th' Supreme Court follows th' illiction returns." [72]

The several cases illustrate the complexity of the judicial process when the Constitution is so indefinite as to provide no guide for action and when it is necessary for the Supreme Court in effect to make constitutional law in the process of announcing a decision.[73] The three cases in which opinions were written, and the other cases decided along with them on May 27, 1901, involved questions as to the applicability of the existing customs laws of the United States to Puerto Rico after the island had been ceded to the United States and as to the constitutionality of a more recent measure for the collection of duties on imports from Puerto Rico. In the case of De Lima v. Bidwell [74] the Court held by a vote of five to four that, after the cession to the United States, Puerto Rico ceased to be foreign country, and that a customs law providing for the collection of duties on imports from foreign countries was inapplicable to imports into the United States from Puerto Rico after the date of the cession. In the case of Dooley v. United States [75] the Court, again by a vote of five to four, held that, on the basis of the phrasing of recently existing law, duties could not be collected on goods imported into Puerto Rico from the United States. In the case of Downes v. Bidwell,[76] however, the Court, still by a vote of five to four, but with an interesting shift

---

[72] Charles B. Elliott, *The Philippines, to the End of the Military Régime* (1916), p. 496, note 16.

[73] For two excellent articles on the subject, see Frederic R. Coudert, "The Evolution of the Doctrine of Territorial Incorporation," *American Law Review*, LX (November-December, 1926), 801-864, and J. W. Burgess, "The Decisions in the Insular Cases," *Political Science Quarterly*, XVI (September, 1901), 486-504. For an account of the government of American territorial possessions as of 1905, see William Franklin Willoughby, *Territories and Dependencies of the United States* (1905).

[74] 182 U.S. 1.          [75] 182 U.S. 222.          [76] 182 U.S. 244.

in the personnel of the two groups of justices, upheld the constitutionality of the new measure providing for the collection of duties on goods imported into the United States from Puerto Rico. Four justices maintained consistently that duties could not be collected on goods imported into the United States from Puerto Rico under either old or new legislation. Four others maintained with equal consistency that the duties could be collected under both old and new legislation. A shift in position by Justice Brown accounted for the different judgments of the Court, and accented the fact that, in these cases, the positions of particular individuals on the Court, rather than fundamental principles of law, determined the decisions. As among the several cases, the Downes case was most important, since it was not limited by the interpretation of a statute enacted before the acquisition of the island, but turned upon the constitutionality of legislation enacted with territorial government in mind.

As among the positions taken on the Court, that of the four, including Chief Justice Fuller and Justices Harlan, Brewer, and Peckham, was most easily understood. They contended that, when the United States acquired Puerto Rico, the island became an integral part of the United States. They stressed constitutional requirements that duties must be uniform and that no duties should be laid on articles exported from any state. The uniformity required by the Constitution, they said, was geographical uniformity, and it was only attained when the tax operated with the same force and effect in every place where the subject of it was found. The correct interpretation of the clause forbade the collection of duties on goods imported from one part of the United States into another. To summarize in terms of the slogan of the time, "the Constitution followed the flag," and applied uniformly in all parts of the United States, however and whenever acquired.

Justice Brown, whose shifting alignments determined the judgments in the several cases, joined these four justices in the De Lima case and wrote the opinion by which the judgment of the Court was announced. Their point of union seems to have been in the fact that foreign territory, once acquired, ceased to be foreign territory. It was unnecessary to go much beyond that point for the decision in that particular case and in the Dooley case.

In the Downes case, however, Justice Brown aligned himself with the other four members of the Court to uphold the measure specially enacted to lay a tariff on imports from Puerto Rico into the United

States. His position is not easily understood. Apparently it was that, although the territory was no longer foreign, not all the provisions of the Constitution extended to it unless specifically extended by act of Congress. The revenue provisions, for example, had not yet been extended to Puerto Rico. That being the case, the limitations on the taxing power on which the minority relied did not stand in the way of the collection of duties on imports from Puerto Rico into the United States.

Justices Gray, White, Shiras, and McKenna aligned themselves with Justice Brown in the Downes case, but they used different reasonings, in a concurring opinion written by Justice White. That opinion is perhaps the most important in the series, because its doctrine ultimately became the doctrine of the Court with respect to the constitutional status of territories acquired by the United States. Justice White developed the doctrine of "incorporation," a doctrine not previously found in American constitutional law. By exercise of the military power or the treaty-making power the United States might acquire new territory. The territory acquired could also be governed, but it did not become a part of the United States, in the sense that all the provisions of the Constitution applied to it, until it had been incorporated into the United States by act of Congress. The power of Congress to levy local taxes for local purposes within the territory was derived, not from the general power to tax, which was limited by the constitutional rule of uniformity, but from broader principles resulting from the power to govern territory. The requirement of uniformity, therefore, did not limit the power to tax in the unincorporated territory. If a territory was incorporated into the United States, on the other hand, then the rule of uniformity must govern. Puerto Rico had not been incorporated into the United States. As to Puerto Rico, therefore, the rule of uniformity as to customs duties did not apply.

Unfortunately for the clarity of constitutional law, Justice White did not explain precisely what constituted incorporation. Like other legal terms, its content is to be discovered through its application in case after case. In a case decided in 1903,[77] it was held that Hawaii had not been incorporated into the United States by the joint resolution of 1898 which had provided for its annexation as a part of the territory of the United States and subject to the sovereign dominion thereof. That being true, it was not unconstitutional to continue the

[77] Hawaii v. Mankichi, 190 U.S. 197 (1903).

use of existing criminal procedure in the Hawaiian Islands instead of substituting therefor procedure by grand juries and trial juries as prescribed by the Constitution. By the organic act for the territory, enacted in 1900, Hawaii was incorporated into the United States, although the mere act of organizing a government does not constitute incorporation. As for Alaska, the Supreme Court held in 1905 that by the treaty of acquisition and subsequent acts of Congress the territory had been incorporated into the United States so as to render repugnant to the Constitution the provision of the Alaska organic act of 1900 that provided for a jury of six persons for the trial of misdemeanors instead of a common-law jury of twelve.[78] The Court held in 1904 that the Philippine Islands had not been incorporated into the United States so as to require the extension of trial by jury.[79] In 1922, although Congress had in 1917 adopted a new and more complete organic act for Puerto Rico, the Supreme Court held that the island had not been incorporated into the United States with the result of establishing the constitutional requirement of jury trial.[80]

Resort to the doctrine of incorporation did not mean that a territory might be governed without reference to the Constitution. Congress may not deny fundamental rights as by passing bills of attainder or *ex post facto* laws. There are doubtless other fundamental rights that may not be violated, but the Court has not chosen to list and define them. As noted in connection with the cases mentioned above, the requirements that indictment by grand jury must precede a criminal trial and that the trial must be by a common-law jury of twelve are not held to be necessary to the protection of fundamental rights in unincorporated territory. There are apparently many rights in the non-fundamental group, but here again the Supreme Court has not chosen to enumerate and define them. The situation is complicated by the fact that Congress may extend a non-fundamental right to an unincorporated territory.[81]

It seems, in short, that the Supreme Court worked out the doctrine of incorporation as a rationalization of policy which the nation had seen fit to adopt. It justifies the protection of all constitutional rights

[78] Rassmussen *v.* United States, 197 U.S. 516 (1905).

[79] Dorr *v.* United States, 195 U.S. 138 (1904).

[80] Balzac *v.* Porto Rico, 258 U.S. 298 (1922).

[81] See Kepner *v.* United States, 195 U.S. 100 (1904). The discussion of fundamental rights in this connection bears some resemblance to discussion of the same subject in connection with the meaning of "due process of law." See, for example, Twining *v.* New Jersey, 211 U.S. 78 (1908).

in territories wherein education and standards are sufficiently similar to those of continental United States to justify the same constitutional order in the fullest sense. On the other hand, it justifies exceptions in the case of territories occupied by people not familiar with such institutions as jury trial. The announcement of the doctrine cleared the way for such policies as the administration in power might see fit to adopt.

At the time of the decision of the Insular Cases the imperialists of the country regarded the recent acquisitions as but the beginning of the renewed expansion of American territory. The expectations were not fulfilled. To be sure, the revolution in Panama which made possible the acquisition of a perpetual lease of territory for the Panama Canal had American encouragment. The Virgin Islands were purchased from Denmark in 1917. On the whole, however, imperialism in the United States proceeded, not in terms of the establishment of American sovereignty over new areas, but of the extension of what was called "dollar diplomacy." As American investments in Central and South America and in other parts of the world flowed in a steadily increasing stream, pressure grew for the use of both the civil and military power of the United States to protect those investments. The question became not so much whether the Constitution followed the flag as whether the flag followed the dollar. The United States did intervene from time to time, in Nicaragua, Haiti, and other countries, where the right of such intervention had no recognition in any such document as the Platt Amendment — or intervention preceded any such formal agreement as that which authorized intervention in Cuba. The continuation of forcible intervention was held in check, however, not merely by anti-imperialist sentiment, but by recognition of the fact that interference in the affairs of proud, though impecunious, neighbors stirred so much ill-will as to constitute bad business diplomacy.

In recent years the pattern of United States relations with other countries has substantially changed. The "good-neighbor" policy initiated by the Franklin D. Roosevelt administration played a part in developing good will toward us in Central and South American countries. Our loans and expenditures made in these regions and in other parts of the world to aid in prosecuting World War II, and the acquisition and development of air and naval bases in countries over which we did not have or seek sovereign control, brought an interrelatedness among peoples some of which has been continued.

Establishment of the United Nations and the building up thereunder of the previously established Organization of American States has tightened the structure of international relations in the western hemisphere and reduced the likelihood of imperialistic practices on the part of any great power. Our influence continues to be felt, it is true, but it is felt along legitimate lines, and it is subject to the formal discipline of international machinery.

# CHAPTER 22

# EXPANSION OF THE GOVERNMENT

No CONSTITUTIONAL AMENDMENT worked any direct change in the form of the federal government between 1860 and 1900. Superficially, it would appear that no fundamental changes of any sort took place. Yet the various organizations within the government, old and new, were in process of growth, new functions being assigned to them and new relations developing among them. The continued growth of the country, with the addition of new states and the acquisition of new territorial possessions, made varied adjustments necessary. Incidental though many of the changes appear when viewed in isolation, the total represents substantial addition to constitutional development.

CONGRESS

By the end of the nineteenth century, the total number of states in the Union had increased to forty-five. The membership of the United States Senate, therefore, had increased to ninety. The House of Representatives had grown to an unwieldy body of three hundred and fifty-seven members. Because of the increased membership, the House, and the Senate to a slightly lesser degree, did much of the important work of legislation through standing committees. There was no systematic preparation of a legislative program and there was little leadership of any kind except partisan control exercised in the interest of political parties. In describing the operation of the committee system during the period, James Bryce, who wrote a significant commentary on American political institutions, remarked, "The most abiding difficulty of free government is to get large assemblies to work promptly and smoothly either for legislative or executive purposes." [1] Woodrow Wilson, writing in 1885 as a fellow in history at the Johns Hopkins University, sharply criticized legislation by committee as it

[1] James Bryce, *The American Commonwealth* (2 vols., 2d ed., 1889), I, 150.

was practiced in the United States, contrasting it unfavorably with parliamentary government in England.[2]

Rules of procedure were so complicated as to bar effective action by all except experienced members and were susceptible of use by parties and cliques for partisan purposes. It was said that, from the time when the slavery issue became important, the rules of the House of Representatives were framed with a view to rendering legislation difficult. By means of them southern congressmen were able to stop measures detrimental to their cherished institution.[3] Speaker Thomas B. Reed, often referred to as "Czar" Reed, succeeded in establishing new rules of such a nature as to make possible the defeat of dilatory tactics, but which added greatly to the power of the speaker's office.[4] The strength of the speaker lay in his power to appoint committees, to determine who should be permitted to speak on the floor of the House, and to change the rules through the committee on rules, of which he was a member. Bryce remarked that the speaker was not merely permitted, but was expected, to use the power of his office in the interests of his party.[5]

Rivalry between political parties oftentimes had the effect of preventing action on legislation. During the period after the Civil War the Democratic party did not win a majority in either house until 1875, when it won control of the House of Representatives; but between that date and 1900, there were six congressional terms in which the Senate was organized by one political party and the House by the other. Some tendency on the part of each to obstruct the legislative program of the other was inevitable. President Grant had the House of Representatives against him during his last two years in office. President Hayes was faced with a Democratic House throughout his term, and a Democratic Senate in the second half. In the Garfield-Arthur administration the Democrats controlled the House during the second two years, while during the first two years the Senate was equally divided. Cleveland lacked a majority in the Senate throughout his first presidential term; Harrison, in the House during his last two years. Cleveland had both Senate and House against him during the last two years of his second term.

[2] See Woodrow Wilson, *Congressional Government* (1885).

[3] See Paul D. Hasbrouck, *Party Government in the House of Representatives* (1927), p. 1, note 1.

[4] For a study of Reed, see William A. Robinson, *Thomas B. Reed, Parliamentarian* (1930). For general discussion of problems of procedure in Congress, see Robert Luce, *Legislative Procedure* (1922).

[5] Bryce, *op. cit.*, I, 135.

Yet, in spite of barriers to effective action, Congress enacted a great deal of extremely important legislation, including measures marking the extension of federal power into important new fields. Among the measures were those enacted in exercise of the war powers, railroad legislation (including the Interstate Commerce Act), monetary legislation, Reconstruction legislation, the Sherman Act, tariff and income-tax measures, and others. The legislation represented in part release of Congress from the restraining control hitherto exercised by the South. It represented in part also, however, the inevitable extension of the power of the federal government with the growth of the nation and the beginning of industrialism.

After the unprecedented enhancement of presidential power during the Civil War, Congress reversed the trend and drove it to the opposite extreme in the impeachment of President Johnson. No other President was dragged down to the same level; but, on the other hand, no President before the turn of the century succeeded in establishing, or even apparently attempted to establish, effective control over Congress. The Senate remained obstreperous in the making of treaties and appointments to office. James Bryce remarked that the requirement of a two-thirds vote for approval of a treaty gave great power to a vexatious minority and increased the danger that the Senate, or a faction of it, might deal with foreign policy in a narrow, sectional, electioneering spirit.

> When the interest of any group of states is, or is supposed to be, opposed to the making of a given treaty, that treaty may be defeated by the senators from those states. They tell the other senators of their own party that the prospects of the party in the district of the country whence they come will be improved if the treaty is rejected and a bold aggressive line is taken in further negotiations. Some of these senators, who care more for party than for justice or the common interests of the country, rally to the cry, and all the more gladly if their party is opposed to the President in power, because in defeating the treaty they humiliate his administration.[6]

Presidential difficulties as to treaties are illustrated by experience with treaties for the acquisition of Hawaii.[7]

As for appointments, the Tenure-of-Office Act, discussed above in connection with Reconstruction problems,[8] required Senate approval for the removal of officers appointed by the President by and with the advice and consent of the Senate. It was not repealed until 1886.

[6] *Ibid.*, I, 104.        [7] See chapter 21.        [8] See chapter 15.

In considering nominations to office covered by this and other statutes, the Senate frequently called on the President for information as to whether confirmation of the new appointment would have the effect of ousting another person from office. There were frequent struggles between the President and the Senate over particular appointments, and many were rejected in spite of all the pressure the President could apply.[9]

As to the personnel of Congress for the period under discussion, it is hard to make comparisons with the earlier period. There may be significance in the fact that almost every moderately well-educated schoolboy will be able to identify Webster, Clay, Calhoun, John Quincy Adams, Jefferson Davis, and Stephen A. Douglas, whereas he will have little information, or, more probably, none at all, about Fessenden, Blaine, Conkling, Sherman, Cullom, and Reagan. Yet the illustration should not be taken to prove too much. The earlier period has been much more dramatized in the writing and teaching of history than the later one. Much more attention has been given to it, year for year, and personality for personality. The odor of scandal, such as that connected with Reconstruction, with the Hayes-Tilden election, with the Crédit Mobilier, and with other contacts between government and the rising world of industry, no doubt did much to restrain the flight of historical imagination. The period is closer to the present day, furthermore, and therefore lacks some of the enchantment which distance lends.

Nevertheless, in a relative sense at least, it may be that the quality of personnel had declined. In the earlier period it is hard to think of leaders in any other walks of life who stand out on a level with or above the congressional leaders mentioned. In the later period, on the other hand, the names of a great many business leaders signify more extensive power and influence than the names of the congressional leaders mentioned. Whatever may be thought of their business ethics or public spirit, it will not be questioned that Jay Gould, the Vanderbilts, John D. Rockefeller, Leland Stanford, Collis P. Huntington, James J. Hill, and others of the type achieved greater eminence than the outstanding members of the Senate and the House of Representatives.[10] The time had come when other walks of life offered opportunities for distinction and for the exertion of personal influence as great or greater than could be exerted in legislative halls.

[9] See Carl Russell Fish, *The Civil Service and Patronage* (1905), chapter IX.

[10] It is true, of course, that Stanford served for a time as a member of the United States Senate — without adding anything to his reputation.

THE EXECUTIVE

Except for Lincoln, no President during the period added particularly to the stature of his office. Johnson was thoroughly discredited. Grant lost the glamour that had been attached to his name as a victorious military leader. Hayes was honest and competent, but nothing more. Garfield was not above the level of his fellows. Arthur was regarded as an ordinary, spoils politician. Cleveland was a courageous, but unimaginative, leader. Harrison was wholly lacking in distinction. McKinley was perhaps an honest, but not much more than mediocre, member of the Republican ruling clique. They were doubtless not below the level of James Monroe or Martin Van Buren or James K. Polk or Millard Fillmore or James Buchanan, but they did not challenge the imagination of the people as Jefferson, Jackson, and Lincoln had done. It was necessary to await more determined and more glamorous personalities before definite presidential leadership of legislative policy was to be established.

A crisis in the election of a President arose in connection with the campaign of 1876, in which Rutherford B. Hayes and Samuel J. Tilden were the candidates of the Republican and Democratic parties respectively. The Democrats had not elected a President since the administration of James Buchanan, but a reaction to Republican Reconstruction policies was setting in and economic depression had created widespread discontent. They had a chance at victory. Tilden won a majority of the total popular votes. It seemed at first that a majority of the electoral votes was also his. The election was close in certain states, however, and Republicans laid claim to votes that had been declared for Tilden. Both parties claimed Louisiana and Florida, and there were violent disagreements over elections in South Carolina and Oregon. There seems to have been ample evidence of intimidation and fraud on both sides. Rival sets of returns were sent to Washington, resulting in disputes as to who had the power to determine which returns should be counted. A majority of the Senate was Republican and a majority of the House was Democratic. If the selection of votes was made by the president of the Senate, it was expected that Hayes would be elected, while, if disagreement threw the election into the House of Representatives, it was clear that Tilden would be victorious.

The Constitution was disappointingly vague on the matter. The Twelfth Amendment provided that the electors should meet in their respective states, vote by ballot, make distinct lists of all persons voted for as President and Vice-President, sign and certify the lists, and transmit them sealed to the president of the Senate. That officer should, "in the presence of the Senate and House of Representatives, open all the certificates and the votes shall then be counted." Nothing was said, unfortunately, as to whether the counting should be done by the president of the Senate, or by representatives of both houses, or by some person or persons chosen by them. Nothing was said about the determination of the validity of votes transmitted to the president of the Senate.

In the midst of great excitement both houses appointed committees to work out solutions. The committees met many times, both separately and together. The House committee worked toward a solution that would lead to the election of Tilden and the Senate committee sought to bring about the election of Hayes. Every decision turned on grounds of partisanship. From the very beginning there was some talk of having the question decided by the members of the Supreme Court. Legislators affected to believe that the justices would not be swayed by partisanship, but each party fought for the selection of a group of the justices including a majority of Republicans or Democrats respectively.[11]

On recommendation of the committees, Congress enacted what has been called "the most extraordinary measure in American legislative history." [12] The statute [13] prescribed in detail the method of counting the votes. To decide which of the two rival slates of votes to accept from each of the states in which conflict had arisen, an electoral commission was appointed. It was to consist of fifteen persons, including five from the Senate, five from the House, and five from the Supreme Court. It was expected that the Republicans would have a majority of one in the Senate delegation and the Democrats a majority of one in the House delegation. Four of the Supreme Court justices were chosen, not by name, but in terms of the judicial districts over which they presided, on the theory that there was value in having territorial representation in the matter. Actually, however, the choice was made in such a way as to provide for two Republicans and two Democrats. These four members of the Court were to choose a fifth. The result was an arrangement wherein seven Republicans and seven Democrats

---

[11] Milton H. Northrup, "A Grave Crisis in American History," *Century*, LXII (October, 1901), 923-924.
[12] Edward S. Corwin, *The President: Office and Powers* (1940), p. 45.
[13] 19 Stat. 227.

would be chosen.   If each of them voted in terms of his party alignment, the decision in each instance would be left with the fifth justice.
It had been expected originally that Justice David Davis, of Illinois,
would be chosen.   He had so vacillated in his party affiliations that
no one knew just where he stood.   "In the ponderous Illinois jurist
was centered the hopes of Democracy, the apprehensions of Republicanism." [14]   Then, to the dismay of the Democrats, Davis was elected
to the United States Senate by the legislature of his state, whereupon
he submitted his resignation as a member of the Court.   Since he was
not to leave the Court until March 4, 1877, three of the four justices
were said to have preferred to carry out the plan of selecting him for
the commission and the position was said to have been offered, in spite
of the belief of Justice Miller, a Republican, that Davis had disqualified himself.   He declined to serve, however, whereupon Justice
Bradley, a Republican, was chosen.[15]   The Supreme Court membership on the commission, therefore, consisted of Clifford and Field,
Democrats, and Miller, Strong, and Bradley, Republicans.[16]

The ballots were opened in the presence of the two houses and the
votes from the disputed states were referred to the electoral commission.   The Republicans had to have all the electoral votes if Hayes
was to win the presidency.   They objected, therefore, to examining
into the conditions of voting in the states to discover irregularity or
fraud.   The interest of the Democrats, on the other hand, lay in
inquiring into the circumstances under which the electoral votes were
cast.   Thus the usual positions of the two parties as to the rights of
the states were reversed.   The Republican party became for the occasion the great defender of state rights.   Public attention was fixed on
the justices who were members of the commission, particularly Justice
Bradley.   On minor points he and others at times seemed to side with

---

[14] Northrup, *op. cit.*, p. 933.

[15] See Carl Brent Swisher, *Stephen J. Field: Craftsman of the Law* (1930), p. 272.

[16] For an account of Miller in connection with the electoral commission, see Charles
Fairman, *Mr. Justice Miller and the Supreme Court* (1939), chapter XII.   For Bradley,
see Charles Bradley, ed., *Miscellaneous Writings of the late Hon. Joseph P. Bradley*
(1902), pp. 165-223.   For general works on the electoral commission, see Paul L. Haworth,
*Disputed Presidential Election of 1876* (1906); Henry L. Stoddard, *It Costs to be
President* (1938); J. Hampden Dougherty, *Electoral System of the United States* (1906),
chapter V.   For special articles, see J. S. Black, "The Electoral Conspiracy," *North
American Review*, CXXV (July-August, 1877), 1-34; George F. Edmunds, "Presidential
Elections," *American Law Review*, XII (October, 1877), 1-20.   For the records of the
activity of the commission, see *Proceedings of the Electoral Commission and of the
Two Houses of Congress in Joint Meeting relative to the Count of Electoral Votes Cast
December 6, 1876 for the Presidential Term Commencing March 4, 1877* (1877).

opponents, but on the decision of vital questions each of them remained loyal to his party.   It was said that Bradley was pale and
trembling when he gave his opinions,[17] but he voted with the Republicans.

The result was the election of Hayes.   The country accepted the
decision, although Democrats were bitter in their denunciation of the
Republican justices, particularly Justice Bradley.   The constitutionality of the method adopted to settle the dispute was not contested in
the courts.   Presumably such a contest would have been futile, since
only two members of the Supreme Court were Democrats.   The
meaning of the relevant provision in the Twelfth Amendment has
never been judicially determined.   If saying that the ballots shall be
opened by the president of the Senate in the presence of the two
houses and shall be there counted means that the counting shall be
done by the president of the Senate, the establishment of such a commission as that provided for by Congress probably violates the Constitution, in taking away from the president of the Senate powers given
to him.   It is by no means clear, however, that such is the intention
of the Constitution.   If the power belonged to the two houses jointly,
there seems nothing unreasonable in the establishment of machinery
for the performance of the joint function.

The Hayes-Tilden controversy did not go so far as the verge of civil
war, but it was a major controversy in American politics.   Although
it turned on questions part of which were constitutional, it might not
have arisen, or, at any rate, might not have reached such proportions,
had Congress previously enacted detailed legislation concerning the
counting of electoral votes.   Nevertheless, a decade passed after the
period of the crisis before such legislation was enacted.   Within that
period the Senate three times passed a bill for the purpose, but the
House of Representatives withheld its approval.[18]   Finally, in 1887, a
measure was enacted prescribing procedure in some detail.[19]   No controversy such as that between the forces of Hayes and Tilden has
arisen to test its effectiveness.

At the time of the assassination of President Garfield, in 1881, Congress renewed debate on the much-discussed subject of the occupancy
of the office of President should some mishap occur to both the President and the Vice-President.   Article II, Section 1, of the Constitution provided that "the Congress may by law provide for the case of

[17] S. S. Cox, *Three Decades of Federal Legislation* (1885), p. 653.
[18] See Dougherty, *op. cit.*, chapter IX.          [19] 24 Stat. 373.   See also 48 Stat. 879.

removal, death, resignation, or inability, both of the President and Vice-President, declaring what officer shall then act as President, and such officer shall act accordingly until the disability shall be removed or a President shall be elected." By a statute of 1792, Congress provided that in such an event the president of the Senate *pro tempore* should act as President, or, in case there should be no president of the Senate, then the speaker of the House of Representatives should occupy the position until the disability of the President should be removed or a successor should be elected. The act provided further for a special election for the choice of a new President.[20] James Madison opposed the arrangement, contending, among other things, that the president *pro tempore* of the Senate and the speaker of the House of Representatives were not officers in the constitutional sense and therefore could not be chosen. As a matter of expediency, he argued that, if one of these persons occupied also the office of President, he would neglect either his legislative or executive duties.[21] It was widely assumed that the person in question would occupy both the executive and the legislative positions at the same time.

Events of the Reconstruction period indicated a mode by which, under existing law, majorities in both houses of Congress hostile to a Vice-President succeeding to the presidency might oust him by process of impeachment, and put the president *pro tempore* of the Senate in his place. Had Andrew Johnson been convicted on the impeachment charges brought against him, Benjamin F. Wade, leader of the radicals in the Senate, would have taken over the duties of the President. Such an event would have removed all hindrance to the legislative program of the radicals. Such an outcome was clearly in mind of some of the enemies of the President.[22]

There were other difficulties in the way of permitting the presidential office to devolve upon persons holding either of the legislative positions. There seem to have been occasions on which there was no president *pro tempore* of the Senate. There were frequent periods in which there was no speaker of the House of Representatives, as for example the period between March 4 of each odd-numbered year and the meeting of the December session of Congress in that year — if a

[20] 1 Stat. 239, 240-241.

[21] House Report No. 26, 49th Cong., 1st sess., p. 2. For discussion of the Vice-President as the occupant of the presidency see Herbert W. Horwill, *The Usages of the American Constitution* (1925), chapter III.

[22] David Miller Dewitt, *The Impeachment and Trial of Andrew Johnson* (1903), pp. 174-177.

special session had not been called for that period.   In the event that neither such position happened to have an occupant no arrangement existed for a head of the executive branch of the government prior to the time when a new President was elected.

Finally, in 1886, Congress enacted a new measure.[23]   It provided that, in the case of vacancies in the offices of President and Vice-President, the order of succession should be the Secretary of State, the Secretary of the Treasury, the Secretary of War, the Attorney General, the Postmaster General, the Secretary of the Navy, and the Secretary of the Interior.   If Congress was not in session at the time when any such person should take over the duties of the President, a special session of Congress was to be called.   No requirement was included, however, that a special election was to be held and the constitutional question as to whether Congress had the power to provide for such a special election was left undetermined.   A number of eventualities were left unprovided for.   As a matter of fact, however, there has never been a time at which both the President and Vice-President have been for any reason unable to perform the duties of the presidential office.[24]

### ADMINISTRATIVE PERSONNEL AND ORGANIZATION

The establishment of the United States Civil Service Commission and of the beginnings of a merit system represented an important development during the period.   It represented the reaching of a stage of maturity in the federal government in which systematic attention now had to be given to efficient operation within the government itself.   Prior to the Civil War the principle that the spoils belong to the victor largely governed the filling of political positions.   In large part it was assumed that almost any person of ordinary competence was able to fill almost any position.   Loyalty to party and to party principles — if such principles could be identified — was considered an adequate basis for the measurement of qualifications.   Rapid turnover in the government, furthermore, had its healthful aspects.   It brought fresh blood into the government, and it prevented the permanent entrenchment of people whose concern would be more for the protection of their own interests than for the efficient conduct of pub-

[23] 24 Stat. 1.

[24] For a discussion of constitutional problems left unsolved by the act of 1886, see Charles S. Hamlin, "The Presidential Succession Act of 1886," *Harvard Law Review*, XVIII (January, 1905), 182-195. The subject has been further dealt with in the Twentieth Amendment and in legislation enacted pursuant thereto.

lic affairs. The spoils system was bad for morals and morale, however; it interfered with the retention of able personnel with capacity enlarged through experience; and it absorbed time and energy of both the executive and legislative branches of the government. The conviction was developing even before the Civil War that the system was a luxury that a mature nation could not well afford.

Movements for the improvement of methods of selecting government personnel spread rapidly during the years immediately after the Civil War. The principle of a merit system was lauded by Presidents and by many federal legislators who sought relief from the burden of patronage without incurring the ill-will of mobs of people seeking political appointments. An early achievement was the enactment of a rider to an appropriation bill of March 3, 1871, authorizing the President to prescribe rules and regulations for the admission of persons into the civil service of the United States. He was authorized to employ suitable persons to conduct inquiries and establish regulations.[25] President Grant appointed an advisory board of seven members, but in the process of filling offices he found it impossible to live up to the standards which the board set for him. Congress showed little enthusiasm and cut off appropriations from the board.[26] Agitation continued, however, for the establishment of a commission with real powers and for a definite classified system.[27] James A. Garfield, long an advocate of civil-service reform, died at the hands of a disappointed office-seeker. His death added impetus to the movement.

The Constitution provided in Article II, Section 2, that the President should appoint certain specified officers by and with the advice and consent of the Senate and that other officers not otherwise provided for should be appointed in the same manner. But, the section continued, "the Congress may by law vest the appointment of such inferior officers as they think proper in the President alone, in the courts of law, or in the heads of departments." Civil-service reformers in the earlier period were concerned primarily with the mass of "inferior officers." The constitutionality of the establishment of the merit system was questioned on the ground that it interfered with provisions for appointment by the President alone, the courts of law, and the heads of departments.[28] The constitutional argument was

[25] 16 Stat. 495, 514.

[26] See Carl R. Fish, *The Civil Service and the Patronage* (1905), pp. 213-214.

[27] For a history of the movement see Frank M. Stewart, *The National Civil Service Reform League* (1929).

[28] See 14 *Congressional Record* 470-471. See also pp. 563-564.

met, at least in part, by leaving to the appointing officer a certain amount of discretion in making appointments, as, for example, in selecting each appointee from any of the three highest on the list of qualified persons. It was contended also, although perhaps not too seriously, that to give to a commission a power to make rules and regulations as to government personnel resulted in an unconstitutional delegation of legislative power.[29] In January, 1883, Congress passed what is commonly known as the Pendleton Act, entitled, "An act to regulate and improve the civil service of the United States." [30]

The development of a scheme of politically neutralizing large numbers of federal employees was so novel as to be understood but dimly by large numbers of people. The illusion existed for a time that the commission was itself a dispenser of patronage.[31] Politicians resented the interference of the new system with their own prerogative of finding jobs for constituents. The extent of the classified service, subject to recruitment by merit, was kept limited, however, leaving large numbers of positions to be filled by political appointment. The annual report of the commission published in 1900 stated that the number of positions in the classified service was about ninety thousand, whereas there were probably more than one hundred thousand unclassified positions.[32] The expansion of the merit system has been gradual down through the years.

Growth in the size of the administrative establishment was a perennial phenomenon. In 1870, the office of the Attorney General was formally expanded into a department of the government under the name of the Department of Justice. The change represented an attempt to bring together under one head the varied types of legal work performed for the federal government. With additions to his administrative duties, the Attorney General tended to become predominantly an administrative officer instead of a professional craftsman, leaving the details of legal work to be handled by his subordinates.[33] The establishment of the Department of Agriculture, first as an inferior organization and then as an executive department of the government, has been discussed, as has also the establishment of a socalled Department of Labor, an agency somewhat of the character of

[29] *Ibid.*, pp. 497, 596.  [30] 22 Stat. 403.

[31] *First Annual Report of the United States Civil Service Commission, 1883-1884*, pp. 29-30.

[32] *Seventeenth Annual Report of the United States Civil Service Commission, 1899-1900*, p. 25.

[33] See Homer Cummings and Carl McFarland, *Federal Justice* (1937), chapter XI.

an independent bureau.[34] The growth of units within the several departments illustrated less spectacularly the process of all-around enlargement. The establishment of the Civil Service Commission and, in a different way, of the Interstate Commerce Commission and other independent regulatory commissions marked the approaching maturity of the federal establishment.

## THE JUDICIARY

With the appointment of Justice Field in 1863 the Supreme Court was enlarged to a total of ten. The membership remained at that figure until 1865, when the death of Justice Catron occurred. After some months of delay, President Johnson nominated Henry Stanbery, then Attorney General of the United States, for the vacancy. Johnson had by this time made himself so unpopular with the Senate through his opposition to radical Reconstruction policies that confirmation of any appointment to the Supreme Court made by him would have been extremely difficult. While the appointment was pending, Congress passed an act providing that no vacancy in the office of associate justice of the Supreme Court should be filled by appointment until the number of associate justices should be reduced to six.[35] The obvious purpose of the statute was to prevent the filling of any vacancies by an unpopular President.[36] By the death of Justice Wayne in the summer of 1867, the membership of the Court was reduced to eight. In April, 1869, soon after a new President had taken office, a new act was passed providing that the Supreme Court should consist of a Chief Justice and eight associate justices.[37] No change has been made since that time. The caliber of the justices on the Court during the period under discussion has been much criticized, even from within the Court itself.[38] The Court was constantly behind in its work, and the situation grew rapidly worse.

It is questionable, however, that responsibility for the overloaded state of the docket of the Supreme Court was rightfully to be attributed to the justices. The mass of cases appealed from lower federal courts and state courts increased with the growth of the country and the expansion of the activities of the federal government. Shortly after the Civil War a renewed effort was made to relieve the justices

[34] See chapter 17.      [35] 14 Stat. 209.

[36] See Charles Warren, *The Supreme Court in United States History* (rev. ed., 2 vols. 1926), II, 422-423.

[37] 16 Stat. 44.      [38] See, for example, Fairman, *op. cit.*, at chapter XVI.

of their circuit duties.   The argument was continued, however, that the justices needed to travel throughout the circuits and to participate in the handling of original cases if they were to understand fully the task of deciding cases appealed to them.   Congress compromised by lightening the burden somewhat through the appointment of a circuit judge for each of the circuits and the requirement that each Supreme Court justice should attend at least one term of the circuit court in each district of his circuit during every period of two years.[39]   Circuit court could be held thereafter by the Supreme Court justice, or the circuit judge, or a district judge, or two or more of them in combination.

In 1875, Congress added greatly to the burden of the circuit courts and, indirectly, of the Supreme Court, by greatly expanding their jurisdiction.   It will be recalled that, in the establishment of the system of federal courts, Congress gave to them only a part of the jurisdiction based on the federal Constitution, laws, and treaties which might have been given under the Constitution, leaving to the state courts the exercise of the remainder of that jurisdiction.[40]   The act of 1875 shifted from the state courts to the federal courts a great mass of litigation hitherto left to the former.[41]

The jam of pending litigation in the Supreme Court was so great as to be the subject of continued discussion.   In 1890, a concerted move was made to reorganize the whole system of federal courts to lighten the burden.   The system then consisted of the Supreme Court, nine circuit courts, and a much larger number of district courts.   The circuit courts ranked higher than the district courts, and had appellate jurisdiction in some cases coming up from the district courts, but they exercised original jurisdiction also, and the differentiation between the circuit courts and the district courts was often confused.   There were certain types of cases in each of the courts from which there was no right of appeal at all.   On the other hand, in the great mass of cases there was a right of appeal to the Supreme Court, even though the questions involved had no general public importance.

The plan of reform proposed in the House of Representatives [42] was to transfer to the district courts all the original jurisdiction previously

---

[39] 16 Stat. 44.      [40] See chapter 3.

[41] 18 Stat. 470.   For an important application of the statute, see Pacific Railroad Removal Cases, 115 U.S. 1 (1885).   For discussion of the business of the federal court during the period, see Felix Frankfurter and James M. Landis, *The Business of the Supreme Court: A Study in the Federal Judicial System* (1927), chapter II.

[42] House Report No. 1295, 51st Cong., 1st sess.

exercised by the circuit courts and to transform the circuit courts into appellate tribunals, adding two judges to each of them for the purpose. A right of appeal was to be given from the district courts to the circuit courts in minor cases in which there had hitherto been no right of appeal, and also in a great mass of cases in which the Supreme Court had hitherto had appellate jurisdiction. In large numbers of cases involving no important federal questions the decisions of the circuit courts were to be final, no access at all to the Supreme Court being given. The Supreme Court justices were to be relieved of the circuit-riding requirement. By these arrangements the burden of Supreme Court activities was to be so reduced as to enable the Court to keep up with its docket.

The bill passed the House of Representatives, but met severe opposition in the Senate. A Senate minority objected to the curtailment of access to the Supreme Court, contending that the work of the Court could be speeded by dividing it, as was done in a number of state courts, so that it might hear cases in sections.[43] The Court was never sympathetic with the idea of deciding cases in division, and no such arrangement was made. The friends of the circuit-court system as it then existed, however, succeeded in preventing its abolition. It remained in operation, and an additional circuit judge was provided for each circuit. To perform the function originally planned for the circuit courts in the House bill a circuit court of appeals of three judges was created in each circuit. The original plan was carried out to cut off appeals from these courts to the Supreme Court in a great mass of cases not generally important except to the litigating parties. The statute as enacted provided that the Supreme Court justices and circuit and district judges should be competent to sit as judges of the circuit courts of appeals within their respective circuits, but the Supreme Court justices were not actually required to par ticipate. With the enactment of this measure, dated March 3, 1891,[44] the court work of the Supreme Court justices in the circuits to which they continued to be assigned came virtually to an end.

Criticism of the Supreme Court during the period was not limited to charges of delay or mediocrity or failure of the justices to resign after their period of usefulness had expired. The justices were ac-

---

[43] Senate Report No. 1571, 51st Cong., 1st sess.

[44] 26 Stat. 826. In 1911, the circuit courts were abolished (36 Stat. 1167). Since that time the federal judicial hierarchy has consisted of the Supreme Court, the circuit courts of appeals, and the district courts. For further discussion see chapters 24 and 31.

cused of improper intervention in politics, and of using the Court as a means of injecting their own social and economic views into the laws of the land. The legal-tender cases provided outstanding illustrations. The faithfulness with which the Supreme Court members of the electoral commission voted in terms of their party alignment emphasized the fact that they acted as partisans rather than as judicious statesmen. The income-tax cases of 1895 and the sugar-trust case and the Debs labor-injunction case of that year emphasized the alignment of the Court with the more conservative interests of the country. It was viewed, not as an unbiased tribunal, but as an instrument of conservative interests to be used in opposition to reforms demanded by the masses of the people. The Insular Cases demonstrated the efforts of particular justices to develop in terms of their own conceptions trends in the law not clearly derived from the Constitution. Decisions of this kind prepared the ground for criticism of the Court during the ensuing decade, and for demands that justices be more carefully selected and for limiting development of judge-made law.

The Court incurred additional criticism by its broad interpretation of certain provisions of the Constitution with the effect of curbing the extent of state and federal legislation. The doctrine of liberty of contract, as something protected by the due-process clauses of the Fifth and Fourteenth Amendments, was injected into constitutional law to prevent governmental interference with property of various kinds, particularly in relations between employers and employees. The concept of due process of law was expanded to restrict substantive legislation as well as the items of procedure to which it had been in earlier years held to apply.[45] After the turn of the century, due process of law flowered out in all directions, laying a protective covering over matters not subject to governmental interference in a régime of laissez-faire. By 1900, judges talked but infrequently of natural law and natural rights as bases for judicial decisions. Examinations of large numbers of opinions, however, demonstrate the fact that "due process of law" had been substituted for the older terminology as a means of translating the fundamental-law concepts of the judges into the supreme law of the land. To use one of many examples, the rates of common carriers fixed by government had to be reasonable in order to avoid the prohibitions of due-process clauses. The judges themselves were the final authorities on the subject of reasonableness.

[45] For development of the concept, see Rodney L. Mott, *Due Process of Law* (1926).

Under the cover of deciding what was reasonable, they read into their decisions their own conceptions of the relations that ought to exist between government and the enterprises to be controlled.

Since the Constitution had been in operation more than a century, a period wherein political, economic, and social conditions had changed immeasurably since the meeting of the Constitutional Convention in 1787, the meaning to be found in the Constitution had to be determined by broad lines of reasoning rather than merely by careful examination of the language of the Constitution. The process of reasoning left the Supreme Court in the position of what has been called a continuous constitutional convention. It could not legislate positively and establish new controls over the economic order, but, in terms of the conservative theories of justices opposed to radical governmental interference with the rights of property, it placed curbs upon the activities of other branches of the government.[46]

Before the end of the nineteenth century, the federal courts saw the development of other tribunals also exercising powers which were judicial in character. The attitude of the courts toward the Interstate Commerce Commission has already been mentioned. A very different tribunal, the Court of Claims, had been organized shortly before the Civil War. Until 1855 Congress itself investigated the great mass of claims against the federal government and made appropriations to satisfy those claims which appeared to be valid. Such machinery was, however, cumbersome, dilatory, and subject to political influence. In 1855, Congress passed "An act to establish a court for the investigation of claims against the United States." [47] The court was to hear and determine claims against the United States and make reports to Congress for action of that body. At that stage it was nothing more than an advisory tribunal organized to give aid to Congress for the more equitable settlement of claims against the government. In 1863, Congress seemed to make the Court of Claims a bona-fide judicial tribunal by giving it the power to render final judgments. One section of the act provided, however, that no money should be paid out of the Treasury for any claim passed upon by the court until after an appropriation therefor had been estimated by the Secretary of the Treasury.[48] As a result of this provision the Supreme Court found the Court of Claims to be still an administra-

---

[46] For discussion, see Charles Grove Haines, *The Revival of Natural Law Concepts* (1930).

[47] 10 Stat. 612.     [48] 12 Stat. 765, 768.

tive or advisory body rather than an actual court, and refused to hear appeals from it.[49]

Congress at once repealed the limiting provision, and subsequently, in 1887, greatly broadened the jurisdiction of the Court of Claims.[50] "By these provisions," said the Supreme Court in later years, "it is made plain that the Court of Claims, originally nothing more than an administrative or advisory body, was converted into a court, in fact as well as in name, and given jurisdiction over controversies which were susceptible of judicial cognizance." [51]

The court was classified, however, not as one of the "constitutional courts" provided for by Article III of the Constitution, but as a "legislative court," such as the territorial courts discussed by Chief Justice Marshall in 1828.[52] That is, it was a court organized by virtue of legislative powers derived from other provisions of the Constitution than those of Article III. Another tribunal of this kind, a court of private land claims, was organized in 1891.[53] Others were established after the turn of the century. As to the performance of their functions, they differed little from ordinary courts established pursuant to Article III. Their duties were limited usually to special types of activities; for example, passing upon claims or upon appeals in technical fields such as customs and patents. They indicated the growing complexity of the types of tasks to be performed through the judicial process.[54] The position of such courts was little different from that of other federal courts except for such matters as the terms and salaries of the judges. The judges did not enjoy the constitutional guarantee of life tenure; nor were their salaries protected from reduction as in the case of salaries of judges employed under Article III.

The history of the federal judiciary during the period was one of increasing complexity and growing power. It followed a natural line of growth along with other governmental agencies with which its operations were connected.[55] It was a powerful conservative influence, holding liberal developments in check until support for them had solidified. In spite of the criticism poured out upon it, it could look forward to additional growth of power in the decades ahead.

[49] See Gordon v. United States, 2 Wallace 561, 117 U.S. 698 (1865).

[50] 24 Stat. 505.        [51] Williams v. United States, 289 U.S. 553, 565 (1933).

[52] See American Insurance Co. v. 356 Bales of Cotton, 1 Peters 511 (1828).

[53] 26 Stat. 854.

[54] See Wilbur G. Katz, "Federal Legislative Courts," Harvard Law Review, XLIII (April, 1930), 894; also in Selected Essays on Constitutional Law (1938), IV, 1211-1237.

[55] For exercise of the power of the President to protect members of the judiciary see In re Neagle, 135 U.S. 1 (1890). For discussion of the background of the case see Carl Brent Swisher, Stephen J. Field: Craftsman of the Law, chapter XIII.

# CHAPTER 23

# THEODORE ROOSEVELT AND THE SQUARE DEAL

THE IMPORTANT CONSTITUTIONAL ISSUES of the period between 1900 and 1909 were the issues of the preceding decade, magnified by the conditions of business and industrial expansion and dramatized by the energetic and picturesque personality of Theodore Roosevelt. Most of the issues involved problems of government control over corporations. Related problems were the conservation of the natural resources of the country, the preservation of public health, the protection of labor, the promotion of business enterprise, and the external protection of the nation through the building of the Panama Canal. Corporations had felt assured of protection at the hands of the administration in power at the turn of the century. William McKinley had been elected to the presidency in 1896 as a high-tariff, sound-money Republican, in a campaign of reckless expenditure of money collected by the systematic assessment of large corporations.[1] He was re-elected in 1900 on a platform reaffirming the principles of his administration. He was a sincere and unimaginative believer in the order he had been chosen to preserve.

Behind the promises of stability and continued emphasis on the protection of growing business and industrial enterprise, however, surged much of the discontent that had given rise to the Populist movement in the preceding decade. True, business conditions had improved sufficiently to allay the worst of hard times, but the Populist movement had had a profound educational effect, and it was obvious that, even though the depression had passed, the abuses then too frequently connected with large-scale corporate enterprise still remained to be curbed. A period of governmental readjustment awaited only a leader in a position of power. Such a leader came into power in the autumn of 1901 through the assassination of President McKinley and the succession of Theodore Roosevelt.

[1] Earl R. Sikes, *State and Federal Corrupt-Practices Legislation* (1928), pp. 188-189.

Even in a constitutional study, the outstanding characteristic of the period from 1901 to 1909 is the personality of Roosevelt. As opposed to McKinley, who sought primarily to preserve political and economic stability, Roosevelt was a crusader. He demanded a "square deal" for all the people. He operated no less shrewdly in political matters than McKinley, but he was by nature a reformer, intolerant of precedents and, at times, even of law. With probably a great deal more fanfare than his achievements justified, he entered upon a varied program of reforms. He carried forward plans for the establishment of a Department of Commerce, for example, adding to the plans variations of his own that would provide for the use of the department to prevent abuses by corporations. He poured enthusiasm into the enforcement of the Anti-Trust Act. He supported amendments to strengthen the Interstate Commerce Act. He advocated legislation to prevent the use of corporation money in federal elections. He engaged in a campaign for the conservation of natural resources. He advocated pure-food and drug legislation, legislation for the protection of workers, and other reform measures. He was concerned about the appointment to the Supreme Court of men who would protect the policies and program in which he believed. In re-establishing the presidency as a position of genuine national leadership, he followed in the footsteps of Jefferson, Jackson, and Lincoln, and paved the way for the strong leadership of Woodrow Wilson and Franklin D. Roosevelt.

THE DEPARTMENT OF COMMERCE AND LABOR

The Department of Agriculture had been the first executive department established to promote the welfare of a particular interest group.[2] An agency with that name had been established in 1862 and had been given official departmental status in 1889, with a Secretary who sat as a member of the President's cabinet. Labor, too, had sought representation. A bureau for the collection of labor statistics had been created in the Interior Department in 1884. The bureau had been made independent in 1888 with the title of Department of Labor, but it was headed only by a commissioner and was really little more than an independent bureau with power to assemble and publish facts on matters of interest to labor. Labor was eager for cabinet representation. In connection with debates on agriculture and labor representation, the establishment of a Department of Industries had

[2] See chapter 17.

been proposed, to give representation to the whole field of commerce as well as to agriculture and labor. Commercial interests continued to lobby for the establishment of a department to represent them.

The Democratic platform for 1900 recommended the creation of a full-fledged Department of Labor, to uplift the workingman as the cornerstone of the prosperity of the country.[3] The Republican platform, while not mentioning a labor department, contained this plank: "In the interest of our expanding commerce we recommend that Congress create a Department of Commerce and Industries, in the charge of a Secretary with a seat in the cabinet."[4] The Senate began consideration of the establishment of such a department while McKinley was still in office. Roosevelt supported the project in his first annual message. It should be the province of a Secretary of Commerce and Industries, he declared, to deal with commerce in its broadest sense, including, among other things, whatever concerned labor, and all matters affecting the great business corporations and the merchant marine.[5] In his annual message of 1902 he renewed his recommendation in the following language:

> The rapid multiplication of questions affecting labor and capital, the growth and complexity of the organizations through which both labor and capital now find expression, the steady tendency toward the employment of capital in huge corporations, and the wonderful strides of this country toward leadership in the international business world justify an urgent demand for the creation of such a position. Substantially all the leading commercial bodies in this country have united in requesting its creation. It is desirable that some such measure as that which has already passed the Senate be enacted into law. The creation of such a department would in itself be an advance toward dealing with and exercising supervision over the whole subject of the great corporations doing an interstate business; and with this end in view, the Congress should endow the department with large powers, which could be increased as experience might show the need.[6]

It was proposed to incorporate the existing Department of Labor in the new Department of Commerce, without recognition of the labor interest except for the continuance of a labor bureau to perform the

[3] Kirk H. Porter, *National Party Platforms* (1928), p. 215; Thomas Hudson McKee, *The National Conventions and Platforms of All Political Parties, 1789 to 1900* (1900), p. 337.

[4] Porter, *op. cit.*, p. 233; McKee, *op. cit.*, p. 345.

[5] *Messages and Papers of the Presidents*, XIV, 6649.     [6] *Ibid.*, pp. 6716-6717.

functions already being performed.  Labor groups objected to being submerged in a commercial organization.  After prolonged conflict, a compromise was worked out by which the new agency was given the title of Department of Commerce and Labor.

Another difficulty in the way of the enactment of the measure was the fact that the President and some members of Congress viewed the proposed department, not merely as an agency for promoting commercial enterprise, but also as a vehicle for bringing about publicity and establishing control over recalcitrant corporations.  To that end the bill as passed by the House of Representatives provided for a Bureau of Corporations in the proposed department.  The commissioner of corporations, as the head of the bureau, was to have power to investigate the organization, conduct, and management of corporations doing business in interstate commerce.  The information obtained, or as much of it as the President might direct, was to be made public.

The Senate, inspired, it is said, by corporation opposition, at first refused to accept this part of the bill.  Roosevelt, in support of it, capitalized the public hostility to corporations and wealthy businessmen by personalizing it in terms of John D. Rockefeller.  He authorized newspapermen to write, without quoting him, that six members of the Senate had received telegrams from Rockefeller saying he was opposed to any anti-trust legislation, that it must be stopped, and that his counsel would see them.  Roosevelt later said, "I got the bill through by publishing those telegrams and concentrating the public attention on the bill."  The strategy was effective, even though, one of his biographers [7] believes, Roosevelt veered from the truth in that the telegrams were signed, not by Rockefeller, but by a Standard Oil attorney, whose name would have carried little weight with the public in comparison with the name of Rockefeller.  The Department of Commerce and Labor was established pursuant to an act of February 14, 1903.[8]

The new department concerned itself in the main with promotion of the welfare of the business interests of the country, an activity which reached its peak in the Coolidge and Hoover administrations in the nineteen-twenties.  The Bureau of Corporations, established within it, had a measure of independence.  It concerned itself pri-

---

[7] Henry F. Pringle, *Theodore Roosevelt* (1931), pp. 340-342.  See also L. White Busbey, *Uncle Joe Cannon* (1927), pp. 220-222.

[8] 32 Stat. 825.

marily with abuses committed by large corporations. In the appendix to his first annual report the commissioner of corporations discussed the possibility of establishing federal control over corporations doing interstate business by requiring them to incorporate under federal law or to secure from the federal government a license for interstate operations.[9] No such legislation was adopted, but the proposal has been revived from time to time down through the years.[10] In spite of opposition to its collection of information, the Bureau of Corporations made and published a number of revealing studies of the activities of corporations. It continued to function until 1914, when it was merged in a more powerful independent agency, the Federal Trade Commission. It paved the way for use of the commerce clause of the Constitution as the basis for more effective policing of corporate enterprise.

### THE HEPBURN ACT AND THE RAILROADS

The Interstate Commerce Act of 1887 had proved inadequate as a means of controlling the railroads. As the first experiment in taking over vast regulatory functions hitherto performed only by the states, if performed at all, it reflected a legislative attitude of caution and uncertainty. The original inadequacy of the act became more pronounced as the courts narrowed its meaning by interpretation.[11] Roosevelt advocated legislation to strengthen the powers of the Interstate Commerce Commission. He said in his annual message of December, 1904:

> In my judgment the most important legislative act now needed as regards the regulation of corporations is this act to confer on the Interstate Commerce Commission the power to revise rates and regulations, the revised rates to at once go into effect, and stay in effect unless and until the court of review reverses it.[12]

From the time of the delivery of the message until 1906, Congress struggled with the enactment of a new measure. Opponents urged

[9] See Report of the Commissioner of Corporations, December, 1904, House Doc. No. 165, 58th Cong., 3d sess.

[10] For a summary and bibliography on the subject see Report of the Federal Trade Commission, No. 69 A, Senate Doc. No. 92, Part 69 A, 70th Cong., 1st sess. (1934). See also Final Report and Recommendations of the Temporary National Economic Committee, Senate Doc. No. 35, 77th Cong., 1st sess., pp. 24-29.

[11] See chapter 18. See also Carl McFarland, *Judicial Control of the Federal Trade Commission and the Interstate Commerce Commission* (1933).

[12] *Messages and Papers of the Presidents,* XV, 6902.

that Congress had no power to regulate railroad rates, and repeated the argument that the organization of the commission was unconstitutional because it ignored the principle of the separation of powers, merging legislative, executive, and judicial powers in one agency. Legislators disagreed over provisions for judicial review of the proposed legislation. Because of the way in which the courts had whittled down the powers of the commission, some friends of regulation sought to cut off the right of appeal to the courts, ignoring the fact that such a procedure would doubtless have been held unconstitutional. Opponents of regulation, at the opposite extreme, sought to open so wide the pathway to the courts that the commission itself would have received little additional power.

The resulting measure, known as the Hepburn Act,[13] was a compromise. As to judicial review, for example, it left substantial power in the commission without taking the unconstitutional step of denying the right of review. As to fixing rates, the statute did not authorize the commission to establish schedules of rates initially, but it did authorize it not merely to condemn existing rates as unjust or unreasonable, but also to substitute just and reasonable maximum rates for those annulled. The act included also the famous commodities clause, designed to divorce the operation of railroads from the operation of businesses, such as coal-mining, which produced important commodities for shipment.[14] With the enactment of these and other provisions of the Hepburn Act began the effective regulation of railroads by the commission. With it began also the accumulation of experience which has led to the establishment of other commissions to exercise similar powers in other fields, bringing about an adjustment of the doctrine of the separation of powers to the necessities of our national life.[15]

[13] 34 Stat. 584.

[14] For discussion of the clause and its interpretation see I. L. Sharfman, *The Interstate Commerce Commission* (5 vols., 1931-1937), I, 42-43.

[15] The year 1906 saw the enactment of another law affecting railroad operations. Railroad employees were still subject in many states to the common-law fellow-servant and contributory-negligence doctrines, whereby the employer could not be required to compensate for injuries to an employee if incurred as a result of his own negligence or that of a fellow worker. Labor representatives had agitated for many years against the application of doctrines they believed to be obsolete under modern conditions of employment by great corporations. As a result, Congress passed an act largely doing away with the operation of the doctrines on interstate railroads. (34 Stat. 232.) Two years later, however, the Supreme Court held the act unconstitutional, by a vote of five to four, because it seemed to apply to the employees of interstate railroads even when engaged in intrastate business. (Employers' Liability Cases, 207 U.S. 463 [1908].) Congress clarified the act soon afterward, making it applicable only to interstate activities,

## THE ANTI-TRUST ACT IN OPERATION

Roosevelt demanded some degree of federal supervision of all corporations doing business in interstate commerce. He believed that ultimately a law must be enacted requiring incorporation by the federal government of such corporations, and that control must be exercised through some such body as the Bureau of Corporations in the Department of Commerce and Labor. Some combinations were good, he contended, while others were bad. Discretion must be used in law enforcement. He remarked in 1901, "Much of the legislation directed at the trusts would have been exceedingly mischievous had it not also been entirely ineffective." [16] He remarked in 1908, "The anti-trust law, though it worked some good, because anything is better than anarchy and complete absence of regulation, nevertheless has proved in many respects not merely inadequate but mischievous." [17]

Until 1903 the Department of Justice lacked adequate funds for enforcement of the Anti-Trust Act. In that year an appropriation of five hundred thousand dollars was made for the enforcement of this statute and the Interstate Commerce Act,[18] and the office of assistant to the Attorney General was established to handle anti-trust work.[19] A measure was enacted to avoid court delay in cases brought under the Interstate Commerce and Anti-Trust Acts by providing that equity cases in which the United States was the complainant might be advanced ahead of other cases. Such cases were to be heard, not before individual judges, but before courts of three judges.[20]

Because of Roosevelt's conviction that not all combinations in restraint of trade were bad, and apparently also because of his unwillingness at times to stir up political enemies, relatively few anti-trust cases were instituted while he was in office. The smallness of the

and in this form it was subsequently upheld. (Second Employers' Liability Cases, 223 U.S. 1 [1912].)

Another step in the enlargement of federal control was taken in 1907 in the enactment of the Hours-of-Service Act for railroad employees. (34 Stat. 1415.) It was enacted to protect passengers, freight, and other employees from injuries resulting from fatigue due to employment over too long a period. It marked another advance in government interference with contracts between employers and employees, interference in the interest of the public making use of a great public utility. It suggested a line of advance to be employed in later years in connection with business not classified as a public utility, but so large in scope and influence as to make its activities of concern to the public. For discussion see the relevant portions of Robert E. Cushman, *The Independent Regulatory Commissions* (1941).

[16] *Messages and Papers of the Presidents*, XIV, 6647.
[17] *Ibid.*, XV, 7192    [18] 32 Stat. 903-904.
[19] Homer Cummings and Carl McFarland, *Federal Justice* (1937), p. 329.
[20] 32 Stat. 823

number instituted, however, was compensated for by the spectacular quality of some of them.   The outstanding case of the period was the suit brought to dissolve the Northern Securities Company, a holding company organized to control a majority of the stock of the Northern Pacific Railway Company and the Great Northern Railway Company, two hitherto competing lines.   The case was initiated under Roosevelt's direction and was carried forward under the pressure of his enthusiasm.   It involved such prominent industrialists and financiers as J. Pierpont Morgan, James J. Hill, Daniel S. Lamont, and George F. Baker.

The government won the case and the combination was ordered dissolved, although the vote in the Supreme Court was five to four.[21] The majority opinion was written by Justice Harlan, who believed that the Anti-Trust Act prohibited all combinations in restraint of interstate trade, whether reasonable or unreasonable.   In this and in former cases, he said, discussing the activities of monopolies, "they seek shelter behind the reserved rights of the states and even behind the constitutional guaranty of liberty of contract.   But this Court has heretofore adjudged that the act of Congress did not touch the rights of the states, and that liberty of contract did not involve a right to deprive the public of the advantages of free competition in trade and commerce." [22]

Justice Brewer, although voting with the majority, deserted his position in former cases and aligned himself with those who said that only unreasonable combinations were prohibited by the law.   He voted to dissolve the combination because of his finding that the Northern Securities combination was unreasonable.   Technically, therefore, although Justice Harlan spoke for a majority of the Court in announcing the judgment, he spoke for a minority of four in the matter of doctrine.   Justice Holmes, one of the dissenters, remarked, "I am happy to know that only a minority of my brethren adopt an interpretation of the law which, in my opinion, would make eternal the *bellum omnium contra omnes* and disintegrate society so far as it could into individual atoms." [23]   The question of interpretation was not yet formally settled, however, and some years were to pass before the "rule of reason" was formulated.

Business interests criticized the decision, but Roosevelt hailed it as

---

[21] Northern Securities Co. *v.* United States, 193 U.S. 406  (1904).          [22] *Ibid.*, p. 351.
[23] *Ibid.*, p. 411.   For contemporary application of the Sherman Act in a case of lesser note between private parties see Montague & Co. *v.* Lowry, 193 U.S. 38  (1904).

evidence that great corporations could be controlled by the government. He regarded it as a reversal of the Knight case, a sugar-trust case decided in 1895, in which the Supreme Court gave a narrow interpretation to the Anti-Trust Act.[24] "This decision I caused to be annulled by the Court that had rendered it," he said in his autobiography.[25] Actually he claimed too much. Other cases had already weakened the interpretation of the Knight case, but it was not directly overruled even by the Northern Securities case. Furthermore, if Roosevelt influenced the decision, he did it otherwise than through the appointment of new men to the Court. He had appointed only two justices at the time when the case was decided, and one of these dissented. The Roosevelt contribution seems to have been limited to pushing the case with vigor and creating an atmosphere favorable for a victory.

Some of the most anti-social abuses of corporations were committed by an aggregation of meat-packers in Chicago, commonly known as the beef trust. The government attacked the trust variously by seeking to enjoin combinations in restraint of trade by criminal action, by investigation through the Bureau of Corporations, and by the enactment of sanitary regulations. Justice Holmes, although in general a sharp critic of the Anti-Trust Act, wrote the opinion of a unanimous Supreme Court in Swift and Company v. United States,[26] affirming the issuing of an injunction. He gave significant breadth to the commerce clause. He said:

> Commerce among the states is not a technical legal conception, but a practical one, drawn from the course of business. When cattle are sent for sale from a place in one state, with the expectation that they will end their transit, after purchase, in another, and when in effect they do so, with only the interruption necessary to find a purchaser at the stockyards, and when this is a typical, constantly recurring course, the current thus existing is a current of commerce among the states, and the purchase of the cattle is a part and incident of such commerce.[27]

The conception of a "current of commerce" paved the way for increasingly broad interpretations of the subject in later years.

The attempt to secure criminal convictions of individual offenders

[24] United States v. E. C. Knight Co., 156 U.S. 1 (1895). See chapter 19.
[25] Theodore Roosevelt, *Autobiography* (1913), p. 465.
[26] 196 U.S. 375 (1905). See also Kelley v. Rhoads, 188 U.S. 1 (1903).
[27] *Ibid.*, pp. 398-399.

met an insuperable obstruction from an unexpected source. The
Bureau of Corporations had investigated the beef trust, requiring a
number of important witnesses to testify under a law which gave them
immunity from prosecution for the offenses disclosed by their testimony.   The federal district court in Chicago reached the conclusion
that the giving of testimony for the bureau conferred immunity from
punishment under the anti-trust law.[28]  The immunity was given to
individuals and not to the corporations they served, but criminal
action against a corporation was not likely to be highly effective in
preventing future misconduct.   The Attorney General of the United
States, in a vein of irony, predicted that Washington would soon become a great watering place for wealthy men eager to give information to the government concerning their doings in order to obtain
immunity from punishment — to take "immunity baths."   He could
imagine Swift, Armour, and others gathering there and saying, "Good
morning, Brother Rockefeller, have you had your immunity bath
this morning?"[29]  Fortunately, the immunity-bath privilege was not
carried as far as the Attorney General predicted,[30] but it had the effect
of giving immediate protection to the principal individuals in the
beef trust.

While the Department of Justice was struggling with anti-trust
cases involving the beef trust, Upton Sinclair was gathering information for his novel, *The Jungle,* in which he described the utterly filthy
condition of the great packing houses in Chicago.   Roosevelt saw the
book in manuscript and immediately appointed men to investigate
the facts.[31]  The disclosures moved Roosevelt to horrified action.[32]  In
1906, his friend Senator Albert J. Beveridge introduced and secured
the adoption of a meat-inspection bill in the face of the opposition of
a powerful lobby of packers and cattlemen.   It constituted in effect
drastic police-power legislation, based on the commerce clause of the
Constitution.[33]

The dramatic disclosure of unhealthful conditions in the stockyards

---

[28] United States *v.* Armour & Co., 142 Fed. 808 (1906).

[29] New York *World,* March 21, 1906.  See Cummings and McFarland, *op. cit.,* p. 335.

[30] On the subject of constitutional immunity from compulsory self-incrimination the
Supreme Court in 1908 decided the important case of Twining *v.* New Jersey, 211 U.S.
78.   The Court, with only Justice Harlan dissenting, held that exemption in the states
from the necessity of giving testimony resulting in self-incrimination was not among the
privileges and immunities of United States citizenship guaranteed by the Fourteenth
Amendment, nor was the requirement of such testimony a denial of due process of law

[31] Claude G. Bowers, *Beveridge and the Progressive Era* (1932), p. 228.

[32] Henry F. Pringle, *op. cit.,* p. 428.          [33] 34 Stat. 674.

gave final impetus to the enactment of another measure that had been long pending. Commonly known as the Pure-Food and Drug Act, it was formally labeled "An act for preventing the manufacture, sale, or transportation of adulterated or misbranded or poisonous or deleterious foods, drugs, medicines, and liquors, and for regulating traffic therein, and for other purposes." [34] These statutes marked the entrance of the federal government into the broad field of national health protection. They took their places beside the Interstate Commerce Act, the Sherman Anti-Trust Act, and other measures extending the power of the federal government to the protection of the public welfare in matters over which the states, for various reasons, were unable to exercise adequate control.

Against the Standard Oil Company, long the outstanding example of a ruthless and undisciplined monopoly, no anti-trust action was completed during the period of the Roosevelt administration. A case was tried under the Elkins Act of 1903, [35] an amendment to the Interstate Commerce Act intended to put an end to the abuse of railroad rebates. Judge K. M. Landis, sitting in a federal district court in Chicago, won notoriety by fining the company the tremendous sum of $29,240,000, [36] but the circuit court of appeals reversed the decision. [37] Roosevelt wrote to his Attorney General concerning the action of the latter court:

> I feel pretty ugly over that decision. The reduction of the fine would have been all right, but the action of the court amounts precisely and exactly to saying that the biggest criminals in this country should be shielded and the law of Congress nullified and that it should be done in the most adroit and meanest of ways; that is, that it should be done by so deciding that the law becomes really ineffective instead of declaring it unconstitutional. [38]

## CONSERVATION OF NATURAL RESOURCES

The period around the turn of the century witnessed a change in attitude on the part of the people and of the government toward natural resources. The traditional boast of the nation's spokesmen

[34] 34 Stat. 768.

[35] 32 Stat. 847.

[36] United States *v.* Standard Oil Co. of Indiana, 155 Fed. 305 (1907).

[37] Standard Oil Co. of Indiana *v.* United States, 164 Fed. 376 (1908).

[38] Roosevelt to Charles J. Bonaparte, July 25, 1908, Personal Letter Book, Roosevelt Papers, Library of Congress.

had been that these resources were inexhaustible. If they were inexhaustible, there was no point in attempting to conserve them. The growth of the nation had depended, not merely on the possession, but on the development, of resources. If the development of some depended upon the destruction of others — if, for example, the destruction of forests was necessary to the operation of farms — such destruction was hailed as an achievement. The cutting and burning of millions of feet of timber was a creditable performance. The timber had stood in the way of civilization.

With the development of the country, the demand for various resources for consumption purposes increased rapidly. Some businessmen wastefully exploited the resources. For example, from areas of the standing timber that remained, the timber was removed without reference to effect upon the soil and upon watersheds. Vast areas fit only for the growth of timber were wholly denuded. The hitherto timber-covered soil washed away with storms, and drainage areas were subjected to disastrous floods because there was no growth to hold the moisture. It gradually became apparent that the timber supply was not inexhaustible after all, and that the mode of exploitation was producing unconscionable waste in terms of the country as a whole. Minerals, likewise, began to seem less than inexhaustible, and their appropriation by corporations and syndicates, even if wholly within the law, began to stir deep resentment. While the masses of the people and the exploiters continued to assume that the good of the nation lay in rapid utilization of resources and that a measure of waste was no cause for concern, a growing minority insisted on a fundamental change in attitude. Hence arose a conflict, almost a moral conflict, between the advocates of exploitation and the leaders of the conservation movement. In a narrow sense, the issue was usually not a constitutional issue. In a larger sense, it was definitely constitutional, marking the beginning of a new trend and new activities on the part of the government which derived its powers from the Constitution.

Roosevelt, while governor of New York, had become interested in some aspects of conservation. As President he gave energetic support to a number of conservation measures and movements. He supported the reclamation bill, enacted by Congress in 1902, setting aside money from the sale of public lands to irrigate and to make habitable great tracts of arid land in the West.[39] Extensive developments were

[39] 32 Stat. 388.

initiated, and in 1908 the reclamation service was established in the Department of the Interior to carry on the work.

Roosevelt showed immediate concern also about some millions of acres of timberland, known as forest reserves, that had been withdrawn from homestead entry. The purpose of the withdrawal had been the permanent preservation of remaining tracts of virgin forests. They were in the custody of the General Land Office of the Department of the Interior, from which they received little attention. "The national-forest idea ran counter to the whole tradition of the Interior Department," wrote Gifford Pinchot, who, when Roosevelt became President, was chief of the Bureau of Forestry in the Department of Agriculture. "Bred into its marrow, bone, and fiber was the idea of disposing of the public lands to private owners." [40]

The Bureau of Forestry was engaged mainly in the scientific study of forestry and the promotion of forestry on private lands. It had nothing to do with the nation's forest reserves, which were under the control of another department. The President brought about a measure of temporary co-operation between the two organizations, but urged that jurisdiction over the reserves be transferred to the Bureau of Forestry. Publicity from timber scandals of the period brought him popular support. In 1905, the forest reserves, renamed national forests, were transferred to a strengthened Bureau of Forestry, which in turn was renamed the Forest Service. Under the leadership of Gifford Pinchot the Forest Service set about the improvement of conditions in the national forests and engaged in a campaign of education which made the people forest-conscious and conservation-conscious as never before.

The setting aside of new national-forest areas provoked a great deal of opposition. Potential exploiters resented being barred from timber lands. Local interests in the habit of pasturing livestock on the public domain free of charge, and excluding rivals therefrom, resented the curtailment of privileges. Local governments, furthermore, were denied the revenue, or the prospect of revenue, which would be available if the resources were developed.

In 1907, the opposition proved strong enough to secure the enactment of an appropriation-bill rider prohibiting the establishment of new national forests in six states except with the consent of Congress. Roosevelt was opposed to the rider, but he did not like to veto the

[40] Gifford Pinchot, "How the National Forests Were Won," *American Forests and Forest Life*, October, 1930.

appropriation bill. He therefore postponed signature while personnel of the Forest Service speeded surveys. He issued proclamations setting aside some sixteen million acres of new reserves and then, having achieved his purpose, signed the bill. Failure to issue the proclamations, he said in a memorandum filed with his papers, would have meant that immense tracts of valuable timber would have fallen into the hands of lumber syndicates before the consent of Congress to the establishment of particular reserves could be secured. His attitude toward what Congress doubtless regarded as a high-handed performance was perhaps well expressed in the following comment, made at an earlier date: "If there is any human being in this country with whom I do not sympathize, it is the type of office individual who has a roll of red tape in place of a gizzard." [41]

Prior to this event, Roosevelt had become much concerned about the rapidity with which coal lands in possession of the government were passing into private hands, oftentimes the hands of great monopoly interests. The Attorney General was asked whether or not coal lands could be withdrawn from entry under the land laws in the same way that timber lands could be withdrawn. His subordinates were of the opinion that, while lands could be withdrawn for public purposes, it was doubtful whether withdrawal of coal lands for conservation constituted a public purpose. Some suggested that the right of entry could be suspended pending investigation of frauds said to have occurred, and that during this period permanent withdrawal might be authorized by Congress. Perhaps to avoid embarrassing the President in what he was determined to do, the Attorney General failed to submit an official opinion. Gifford Pinchot submitted an opinion, arguing confidently that the lands might be permanently withdrawn. Whatever his authority, the President withdrew some sixty-eight million acres of coal lands in seven states, and about eight million in Alaska. When Congress refused the request to ratify this action, he restored to entry about two-thirds of the lands set aside. [42]

The coal-land controversy carried over to make one of the most bitter struggles of the Taft administration. Roosevelt in the meantime withdrew, not merely forest and coal lands, but areas containing phosphate deposits, areas within reclamation tracts, and others which would protect watersheds and preserve to the government sites for reservoirs and potential sources of electric power. He and Pinchot

---

[41] Roosevelt to W. A. Richards, April 21, 1904, Roosevelt Papers. See Cummings and McFarland, *op. cit.*, p. 387.

[42] Cummings and McFarland, *op. cit.*, pp. 389-390.

brought about the publication of report after report to spread the gospel of conservation. The two men were largely responsible for the organization and activities of the Public Lands Commission, the Inland Waterways Commission, the Conference of Governors of May, 1908, the National Conservation Commission, the Joint Conservation Congress of December, 1908, the North American Conservation Congress of February, 1909, and the Commission on Country Life. In every possible way they sought to make the country conservation-conscious. They succeeded as few men could have succeeded in so short a period. Never again would the public view with the same indifference the waste of natural resources, or the disposal of those owned by the government for the benefit of monopoly interests.

The Supreme Court had no occasion in this period to pass directly upon any phase of the conservation program. It might or might not have considered the program a threat to the province of the states. Two decisions involving the powers of states do show awareness of the capacity of a sovereign state to defend its resources for the public benefit, as distinguished from the benefit of individual owners. One case was a suit by Georgia seeking an injunction to prevent a copper company in Tennessee from discharging fumes which threatened damage to forests and other vegetation in Georgia. The injunction was issued. Said Justice Holmes for the Court, "It is a fair and reasonable demand on the part of a sovereign that the air over its territory should not be polluted on a great scale by sulphurous acid gas, that the forests on its mountains . . . should not be further destroyed or threatened by the act of persons beyond its control, that the crops and orchards on its hills should not be endangered from the same source." [43]

In the second case the Court upheld an injunction to prevent a riparian owner of water in New Jersey from transporting it through mains to New York. The public interest in the maintenance of the rivers of a state, said Justice Holmes, again speaking for the Court, "is omnipresent wherever there is a state, and grows more pressing as population grows. It is fundamental, and we are of the opinion that the private property of riparian proprietors cannot be supposed to have deeper roots." [44] The doctrines expressed in these two opinions

[43] Georgia v. Tennessee Copper Co., 206 U.S. 230, 238 (1907).
[44] Hudson County Water Co. v. McCarter, 209 U.S. 349, 356 (1908). For additional discussion of lands and water rights see Kansas v. Colorado, 206 U.S. 46 (1907). For a case in which the Supreme Court, Justice Holmes dissenting, denied that West Virginia had a prior right over other states to natural gas produced in West Virginia see Pennsylvania v. West Virginia, 262 U.S. 553 (1923).

were in harmony with the doctrines of the conservationists. In 1910, the Supreme Court passed upon one aspect of the conservation program. It held that the supervision of the national forests, through rules and regulations issued by the Department of Agriculture, was not an unconstitutional delegation of legislative power.[45]

## THE PENNSYLVANIA COAL STRIKE OF 1902

In various other situations the Roosevelt temperament dominated the course of events and established precedents for vigorous leadership in the presidency. In 1902, a coal strike took place throughout the anthracite region of Pennsylvania, under circumstances in which the public sympathized generally with the miners. The lack of coal caused great inconvenience in some sections, and carried the threat of political repercussions. The President was said to have asked the Attorney General to see if the Anti-Trust Act could be used against the combination of coal and railroad companies whose conduct had forced the strike, and the operators, on the other hand, were said to have been indignant at the unwillingness of the Attorney General to bring an anti-trust suit against the miners' union.[46]

The President called John Mitchell of the miners' union and representatives of the operators to a conference in Washington. Mitchell agreed to the appointment of a commission to pass upon the issues, but the operators refused to concur. They denounced the President for negotiating with the miners and for failure to use the force of the law to settle the strike. Roosevelt, as a last resort, contemplated asking the governor of Pennsylvania to call for federal troops to suppress an internal disturbance — even though there had been little violence, and none with which the state could not cope. Thereupon he, the President, would send Major General Schofield with federal troops, with directions to take over the mines and run them.[47]

Such treading upon the fringes of the Constitution was averted largely as a result of a personal conference between Elihu Root, then Secretary of War, and J. P. Morgan. The operators, while refusing to negotiate with organized labor, agreed to leave settlement to a commission which the President should appoint and which should include, with others, a practical miner, a sociologist, and a banker. Roosevelt settled the dispute over union representation by appoint-

[45] United States v. Grimaud, 220 U.S. 506; Light v. United States, 220 U.S. 523.

[46] Pringle, op. cit., pp. 264-272.

[47] Ibid., pp. 272-275. For the use of federal troops to quell civil disorders see Bennett Milton Rich, The Presidents and Civil Disorder (1941).

ing a leading labor man as "an eminent sociologist"! Negotiations brought the strike to an end.[48] No use of the Sherman Act was made against either the operators or the miners.[49]

### THE PANAMA CANAL

The tactics used in securing the Panama Canal concession likewise illustrate the daring and self-confidence of Roosevelt's leadership. He welcomed, if he did not encourage, a revolution which made it possible to get from Panama that which Colombia had refused to yield. "I took Panama without consulting the cabinet" and "I took the Canal Zone and let Congress debate," [50] were probably overstatements, as was his assertion that he had had a Supreme Court decision reversed; but they were probably not highly erroneous. He had expressed privately the belief that taking the territory was "certainly justified in morals, and therefore justified in law." [51] The country as a whole was not entirely convinced that the high-handed methods had been justified, however, and in 1914, to Roosevelt's indignation and disgust, Secretary of State Bryan negotiated a treaty with Colombia offering an apology and an indemnity of twenty-five million dollars for the secession of Panama.[52]

Roosevelt's attitude toward foreign affairs generally was in harmony with the imperialism of the preceding decade. He ostentatiously carried the "big stick." He dealt firmly with Central and South American countries. In 1905, when the Senate refused to approve a treaty with Santo Domingo whereby the collection of customs in that country was to be taken over by the United States, he avoided senatorial obstruction by an executive agreement to carry out the same plan. In doing so he established incidentally a precedent for the use of his successors in office when Senate co-operation in international negotiations was refused. Roosevelt himself made further use of the executive-agreement device in 1908 through a gentleman's agreement

[48] Pringle, *op. cit.*, pp. 273-278; Philip C. Jessup, *Elihu Root* (2 vols., 1938), I, 271-276; Roosevelt, *Autobiography* (1913), pp. 501-516.

[49] Another strike going on at the same time, however, coupled with what is known as a secondary boycott, resulted in a private suit against a labor union for damages under the Sherman Act. In that case, usually known as the Danbury Hatters case (Loewe *v.* Lawlor, 208 U.S. 274 [1908]), the Supreme Court for the first time, and by a unanimous vote, held the Sherman Act applicable to labor combinations. (For discussion of the case see Edward Berman, *Labor and the Sherman Act* [1930], pp. 77-87.)

[50] Pringle, *op. cit.*, p. 330.

[51] Roosevelt to Mark Hanna, October 5, 1903, Roosevelt Papers. For a detailed account see Pringle, *op. cit.*, pp. 301 ff.

[52] Pringle, *op. cit.*, p. 581. The Senate rejected the treaty.

with Japan, whereby Japan was to take responsibility for stopping the movement of Japanese laborers into the United States. Such agreements have been assumed to be valid, but they represent a measure of encroachment upon the treaty-making power. As a matter of fact, the executive agreement with Santo Domingo, made in 1905, was superseded in 1907 by a treaty embodying substantially the same terms.

### THE SUPREME COURT

A number of current Supreme Court decisions in important cases resting on alignments of five to four emphasized the fact that major constitutional questions were settled oftentimes, not by basic principles, but by a process of counting heads on the Court, the heads of members who differed sharply as to what principles ought to control. If cases were to be decided in this manner, the selection of new justices to fill vacancies constituted a real responsibility. In the matter of Supreme Court decisions as well as on other subjects, Roosevelt had sublime confidence in his own judgment. He knew when decisions were right and when they were wrong. He was eager, therefore, to make appointments from men who had the "right" views. He had the opportunity to fill three vacancies, appointing Oliver Wendell Holmes, Jr., in 1902, William Rufus Day in 1903, and William Henry Moody in 1906.

In weighing the appointment of Holmes, he wrote a much-quoted letter in which he considered a variety of qualifications. He mentioned Holmes's character, his father's name, his career as a soldier, and the prestige connected with his position as Chief Justice of Massachusetts. He mentioned Holmes's labor decisions, which were criticized by railroads and other corporations.

> The ablest lawyers and greatest judges are men whose past has naturally brought them into close relationship with the wealthiest and most powerful clients, and I am glad when I can find a judge who has been able to preserve his aloofness of mind so as to keep his broad humanity of feeling and his sympathy for the class from which he has not drawn his clients. I think it eminently desirable that our Supreme Court should show in unmistakable fashion their entire sympathy with all proper effort to secure the most favorable possible consideration for the men who most need that consideration.[53]

[53] Roosevelt to H. C. Lodge, July 10, 1902, *Selections from the Correspondence of Theodore Roosevelt and Henry Cabot Lodge* (2 vols., 1925), I, 517.

He was concerned, however, about a speech by Holmes which showed a lack of appreciation of John Marshall. Marshall, said Roosevelt, was a partisan in the highest and proper sense, as every judge ought to be. He was a "statesman of the national type." Taney, on the other hand, belonged to and served the wrong party, and was "a curse to our national life." Of the present Court the majority had rendered a great service to mankind and to the nation by upholding the policies of President McKinley and the Republican party in Congress. The minority had stood for reactionary folly.[54] He would like to know that Judge Holmes was in sympathy with "our views." [55]

Soon after he took his place on the Court, Holmes dissented in the Northern Securities case, which represented one of Roosevelt's major efforts. Roosevelt was so offended that he was said to have contemplated excluding Holmes from the White House thereafter.[56]

In 1906, before he had finally decided on the appointment of Moody, then his Attorney General, Roosevelt wrote to Senator Lodge as follows: "Nothing has been so strongly borne in on me concerning lawyers on the bench as that the *nominal* politics of the man has nothing to do with his actions on the bench. His *real* politics are all-important. . . . I have grown to feel most emphatically that the Supreme Court is a matter of too great importance for me to pay heed to where a man comes from." [57] He was considering Horace H. Lurton, of Tennessee, whose appointment was desired by his two former associates on the bench, Taft and Day — and whom Taft himself appointed to the Supreme Court in 1910. Lurton was "right" on the important questions of the day. He was in closer touch with the right policies than even White, who was wrong on corporations.[58] He thought he might appoint Lurton, nominally a Democrat and an ex-Confederate soldier, to counterbalance the later appointment of Moody as a second judge from Massachusetts.[59]

The appointment, before it was finally awarded, was first offered to Taft, who rejected it in anticipation of a nomination for the presidency, as he had rejected the appointment later given to Day in order

---

[54] Referring evidently to the Insular Cases, discussed in the preceding chapter.

[55] *Roosevelt-Lodge Correspondence*, I, 518-519.

[56] Mark A. DeWolfe Howe, ed., *Holmes-Pollock Letters: The Correspondence of Mr. Justice Holmes and Sir Frederick Pollock, 1874-1932* (2 vols., 1941), II, 63-64.

[57] Roosevelt to Lodge, September 4, 1906, *Roosevelt-Lodge Correspondence*, **II, 228.**

[58] White had dissented in the Northern Securities case.

[59] *Roosevelt-Lodge Correspondence*, II, 228-229.

to complete his work as governor of the Philippines.[60] Lurton was passed over for some reason, and Moody, who had gained reputation through anti-trust cases, was named.

The Roosevelt influence on the Supreme Court through appointments was doubtless less than he had hoped and expected. Moody proved an able judge, but he served less than four years, and was in poor health during that time. Day served nearly twenty years, but he does not stand out in the history of the Court. Holmes virtually began his career on the Court by dissenting in the famous Northern Securities case which Roosevelt had set out to win. Furthermore, although it was in Holmes that Roosevelt found a great judge, perhaps the greatest teacher of law from the bench ever to sit on the Supreme Court, there is little evidence of the effects of his influence in the early years after his appointment. It was in later years, when a generation of followers had arisen and when he had been joined by colleagues who agreed with him that "The Fourteenth Amendment does not enact Mr. Herbert Spencer's *Social Statics,*" [61] that his leadership and influence became apparent.

### LABOR CASES IN THE SUPREME COURT

Three important labor cases illustrate the issues of property rights and human rights involved in the struggle between capital and labor during the period. They were Lochner v. New York,[62] decided in 1905, and Adair v. United States [63] and Muller v. Oregon,[64] decided in 1908. The Lochner case showed the rigid conservatism of a majority of the Court where liberty of contract was involved. The case had to do with the validity of a New York statute limiting employment in bakeries to sixty hours a week and ten hours a day. By divided votes the New York courts which had passed upon the measure had upheld it as a legitimate exercise of the police power for the purpose of protecting the health of bakeshop workers. The Supreme Court, on the other hand, dividing five to four, held that the act was not a legitimate exercise of the police power, and that it interfered with the liberty of contract protected by the Fourteenth Amendment.

In writing the opinion of the Court, Justice Peckham had to distinguish the case of Holden v. Hardy,[65] decided in 1898, in which the

[60] James Ford Rhodes, *History of the United States* (9 vols., 1892-1922), IX, 208-211; Henry F. Pringle, *Life and Times of William Howard Taft* (2 vols., 1939), I, 236, 314.

[61] Lochner v. New York, 198 U.S. 45, 75 (1905).

[62] 198 U.S. 45.   [63] 208 U.S. 161.   [64] 208 U.S. 412.   [65] 169 U.S. 366.

Court had upheld a Utah statute prescribing an eight-hour day for workers in underground mines and in ore refineries. The Court, Peckham and Brewer dissenting, had recognized in that case the danger to health involved in working long hours amid the conditions of the industry. In bakeries, on the other hand, said Peckham in the Lochner case, there was no sufficient danger flowing from long hours of work to justify special interference by the legislature. It was not a legitimate subject for the exercise of the police power. There was no justification for interference with the right of the employer to hire whom he would under contracts to which workers were willing to agree, or with the constitutional right of employees to accept contracts for working long hours if they saw fit. Neither party was under any compulsion. Both were legally free. If there was economic coercion of the worker to accept whatever work he could find, under whatever conditions the employer might prescribe, so that his bargaining power was in effect unequal, the Court deemed that fact irrelevant. It handed down a decision which, if scrupulously followed, would prove an effective barrier to future legislation in the interest of workers.

The decision was illuminated by the dissenting opinions of Justices Harlan and Holmes. Harlan did not attack the doctrine of liberty of contract — upon which he later rested his opinion in the Adair case. Rather, he sought to produce evidence that working in a bakery, like working in a mine, was an unhealthful occupation, so that interference with liberty of contract was justified to the extent of limiting the number of hours of employment. The disagreement of Justice Holmes was more fundamental. He said:

> This case is decided upon an economic theory which a large part of the country does not entertain. . . . I think that the word "liberty," in the Fourteenth Amendment, is perverted when it is held to prevent the natural outcome of a dominant opinion, unless it can be said that a rational and fair man necessarily would admit that the statute proposed would infringe fundamental principles as they have been understood by the traditions of our people and our law. It does not need research to show that no such sweeping condemnation can be passed upon the statute before us.[66]

In its defense of laissez-faire principles and of the property rights acquired by more prosperous groups, the Lochner decision is to be classified with income-tax, labor-injunction, and anti-trust decisions

[66] Lochner v. New York, 198 U.S. 45, 75, 76.

of the middle of the preceding decade. As an obstruction to legislation for the betterment of the conditions of labor, it marked the judicial outpost for many years to come.

The other two cases mentioned were related to the Lochner case in different ways. The Adair case reflected much the same conservative attitude toward interference with contracts between employers and employees. The Muller case marked a limitation of the principles presented in the Lochner case. The Adair case had to do with the constitutionality of a provision in the Erdman Act of 1898.[67] The act, passed as a result of the Pullman strike and other labor disputes of the period, was an attempt to provide for the arbitration of labor disputes involving railroad employees. To insure the right of workers to resort to labor unions as bargaining units, the act prohibited what were commonly called "yellow-dog" contracts. That is, it forbade railroads to require as a condition of employment an agreement not to join a labor union and forbade discrimination against union employees and threats of loss of employment because of union membership. The case arose when an employee was discharged for membership in the Order of Locomotive Firemen.

The federal district judge not only considered the section mentioned, dealing with so-called "yellow-dog" contracts, but studied the statute as a whole. It had been known in Congress as a voluntary arbitration bill. Its purpose had been to provide for the settlement of labor disputes by negotiations with the contending parties, labor being represented by its own organization. The provisions calculated to prevent discrimination against union employees were included in order that labor might have responsible representation of its own choosing. The judge found that the statute was given unity by an idea. "That idea is a common purpose, and that common purpose an avoidance of an interruption to interstate commerce arising from a resort by employees to strikes, lock-outs [sic], or boycotts, to redress their real or fancied wrongs."[68] He found the statute constitutional as a legitimate exercise of the commerce power.

The Supreme Court, on the other hand, showed less understanding of the problem as a whole. It approached the subject narrowly. By a vote of six to two it held the provision in question to be unconstitutional. Its grounds were that the restrictions on the making of labor contracts interfered with the liberty of contract protected by the due-process clause of the Fifth Amendment and that such labor contracts

---

[67] 30 Stat. 424.     [68] United States *v.* Adair, 152 Fed. 737, 742 (1907).

were not sufficiently a part of interstate commerce to justify regulation by the federal government on the basis of the commerce clause. As to the application of the Fifth Amendment, Justice Harlan, speaking for the Court, found the provision of the statute

> an invasion of the personal liberty, as well as of the right of property, guaranteed by that amendment. Such liberty and right embrace the right to make contracts for the purchase of the labor of others, and equally the right to make contracts for the sale of one's own labor; each right, however, being subject to the fundamental condition that no contract, whatever its subject matter, can be sustained which the law, upon reasonable grounds, forbids as inconsistent with the public interests, or as hurtful to the public order, or as detrimental to the common good.[69]

As to interstate commerce, "what possible legal or logical connection is there between an employee's membership in a labor organization and the carrying on of interstate commerce?" asked the justice — somewhat naïvely, it now seems, in the light of decisions of later years. "Such relation to a labor organization cannot have, *in itself* and in the eye of the law, any bearing upon the commerce with which the employee is connected by his labor and services."[70] He held that there was no relation sufficient to justify the statute. Yet the district court had found such a relation by viewing the statute as a whole, and Justice McKenna did so, in a dissenting opinion.

Justice Holmes, dissenting, remarked that he would think the relation of unions to interstate commerce at least as close as safety couplers on railroad cars and as the liability of master to servant — matters which it was admitted Congress might regulate. He supposed it would hardly be denied that some relations of railroads with unions were closely enough connected with interstate commerce to justify regulation by Congress, and he thought this statute fell within that class. As for liberty of contract, he thought that the Court had already stretched to its extreme the right to make contracts at will, which had been derived from the word "liberty" in the amendments to the Constitution.[71]

For many years the decision stood in the way of legislation calculated to prevent labor strife by protecting the right of labor to unionize for negotiations with employers. More generally, it indicated the great caution with which federal and state governments must move in any attempt to adjust the constitutional system to the

[69] 208 U.S. 172.     [70] *Ibid.,* p. 178.     [71] *Ibid.,* pp. 190-191.

conditions of an increasingly complex industrial civilization.[72]   It showed that the Supreme Court of 1908 was not essentially different in its philosophy from the Court of 1905 and of the preceding decade.

The Muller case, likewise decided in 1908, resembled the Lochner case of 1905 in that it prescribed maximum hours of employment.   It dealt, not with men employed in bakeshops, however, but with women employed in laundries.   The difference as to sex proved basic in the decision of the case.   The opinion of the Court was written by Justice Brewer, a firm believer in laissez-faire doctrines.   Louis D. Brandeis, counsel for the state, had submitted an unusual brief illustrating the fact that the effect of hard labor upon the physique of women was peculiarly injurious and, through its effect upon mothers, was a menace to the race as a whole.   Justice Brewer paid tribute to this presentation.   There was little or no discussion of the constitutional question involved therein, he said; yet the materials were significant of a widespread belief that woman's physique and the functions she performed in consequence thereof justified special legislation restricting or qualifying the conditions under which she should be permitted to toil.   He continued:

> Constitutional questions, it is true, are not settled by even a consensus of present public opinion, for it is the peculiar value of a written constitution that it places in unchanging form limitations upon legislative action, and thus gives a permanence and stability to popular government which otherwise would be lacking.   At the same time, when a question of fact is debated and debatable, and the extent to which a special constitutional limitation goes is affected by the truth in respect to that fact, a widespread and long-continued belief concerning it is worthy of consideration.   We take judicial cognizance of all matters of general knowledge.[73]

Having recognized the need for the legislation, he held that it did not infringe the liberty of contract guaranteed by the Fourteenth Amendment.

In deciding the Muller case, Justice Brewer made it clear that the Lochner decision was not being questioned.   Yet for some years thereafter it was the philosophy of the Muller case, supported by factual briefs of the type presented by Brandeis, the so-called Brandeis brief, that stood out in decisions having to do with hours and wages of labor.

[72] See for example Coppage v. Kansas, 236 U.S. 1 (1915), in which the Supreme Court held unconstitutional a state law prohibiting "yellow-dog" contracts.
[73] 208 U.S. 420-421.

In the period of the "return to normalcy" after the World War, how-ever, the Lochner decision again became dominant,[74] after some mem-bers of the Court had assumed that it had been overruled *sub silentio.*

JUDICIAL VARIETY

Many Supreme Court decisions handed down within a given period have no necessary relationships to each other, but are nevertheless im-portant in constitutional development. In 1903, for example, the Court decided the case of Champion *v.* Ames,[75] upholding by a vote of five to four a federal statute for the suppression of interstate com-merce in lottery tickets. Many states had tried to do away with lot-teries, but they were handicapped by their inability to control the subject where interstate commerce was involved. To compensate for this handicap the federal government assumed responsibility for the suppression of this aspect of the business. The statute enacted marked an early step in what has subsequently become a broad movement for the exercise of federal regulatory power over matters not subject to effective regulation under the police powers of the states.[76]

In McCray *v.* United States,[77] decided in 1904, the Court upheld an act of Congress placing upon artificially colored oleomargarine an excise tax so heavy as to be prohibitive. The statute was designed ostensibly to raise revenue, but the actual purpose was to protect dairy interests from competition. Since the tax was so heavy as to destroy business in colored oleomargarine, it was hard to find justification for it as a revenue measure. The act could not be justified as a health measure in the sense of preventing the distribution of an unhealthful product, since oleomargarine was not subject to condemnation on that ground. Perhaps the most that could be said for it was that decep-tion might be used in the sale of oleomargarine to customers for but-ter, giving them thereby an article with less food value than butter contains. The Court refused to consider motives, however, and re-fused even to concern itself with the fact that the tax would ultimately defeat its alleged purpose of raising revenue. The act was on its face a revenue measure and as such it was upheld. The act paved the way

[74] See Adkins *v.* Children's Hospital, 261 U.S. 525 (1923). For discussion see chapter 32.

[75] 188 U.S. 321.

[76] The Champion case dealt with lottery tickets when shipped by express. In Public Clearing House *v.* Coyne, 194 U.S. 497 (1894), the Court, with but one dissenting vote, sanctioned the exclusion of lottery tickets from the mails.

[77] 195 U.S. 27.

for the further use of the taxing power for purposes other than taxation, and the Court ultimately found it necessary to restrain the practice.[78]

The need for revenue expanded with the growth of the United States and the enlargement of the functions performed by the federal government. By the income-tax decision of 1895, the Supreme Court had protected the receivers of large incomes from discriminatory levies on the ground that income taxes must be classified as direct taxes and could be collected constitutionally only if apportioned among the several states according to population. Thereafter, other tax measures, particularly the war-revenue act of 1898, were challenged in the hope that still other taxes would be classified as direct. The Supreme Court refused to expand the concept, however, classifying the taxes challenged as excises, which did not have to be apportioned.[79]

By a vote of six to three the Court took a step calculated to prevent the loss of federal revenue in situations in which states took over businesses normally left in private hands. The Court did not reject the Marshall assumption that "the power to tax involves the power to destroy," nor did it then challenge the doctrine that the federal government was forbidden to tax instrumentalities of the states. It drew a distinction, however, between the necessary governmental powers of a state, on the one hand, and proprietary powers, on the other hand, which a state might assume. In South Carolina v. United States,[80] a case involving taxes on the dispensing of liquor by a state agency, the Court upheld the tax, taking the position that, "whenever a state engages in a business which is of a private nature, that business is not withdrawn from the taxing power of the nation." [81] The distinction drawn by the Court was important in future years, but its application was often hard to make. Functions that are not governmental functions at all in one period seem essentially governmental in another. Here, as in other fields, change in circumstances stands in the way of certainty in the law.[82]

[78] See chapter 33.

[79] See Patton v. Brady, 184 U.S. 608 (1902); Thomas v. United States, 192 U.S. 363 (1904); and Spreckels Sugar Refining Co. v. McClain, 192 U.S. 397 (1904).

[80] 199 U.S. 437 (1905).

[81] Ibid., p. 463.

[82] Another important aspect of federal-state relations — the jurisdiction of federal courts as limited by the Eleventh Amendment in matters involving states — was dealt with in Ex parte Young, 209 U.S. 123 (1908), in which the Court clarified the subject of the power of a federal court to enjoin a state officer from enforcing an unconstitutional state

Other cases decided in the same period were important,[83] but those already discussed indicate the character of the work of the Supreme Court. The Court revealed much of the conservatism of the preceding decade, yet no group of decisions blocked as directly the current of new social trends as did decisions of the middle eighteen-nineties affecting income taxes, labor injunctions, and the enforcement of the Anti-Trust Act. Furthermore, touches of liberalism and evidence of careful self-examination appeared here and there in opinions.

On the whole, however, the judiciary showed less evidence of change than did the other branches of the government. Congress was sharply divided on issues of new legislation, but under pressure from the President it enacted measures reflecting the continued expansion of the powers of the federal government. The presidency took on new life, under the direction of a man who, by contrast with most of his predecessors, exercised its powers to the uttermost. Roosevelt wrote to a friend in 1908:

> While I have been President I have been President, emphatically. I have used every ounce of power there was in the office and I have not cared a rap for the criticisms of those who spoke of my "usurpation of power"; for I know the talk was all nonsense and that there was no usurpation. I believe that the efficiency of this government depends upon its possessing a strong central Executive, and wherever I could establish a precedent for strength in the Executive, as I did for instance as regards the external affairs in the case of sending the fleet around the world, taking Panama, settling affairs in Santo Domingo and Cuba; or as I did in internal affairs in settling the anthracite-coal strike, in keeping order in Nevada this year when the Federation of Miners threatened anarchy, or as I have done in bringing the big corporations to book — why, in all these actions I have felt, not merely that my action was right in itself, but that in showing the strength of, or in giving strength to, the executive office, I was establishing a precedent of value.[84]

law, in spite of the constitutional prohibition against entertaining suits against a state. Another important case involving suits against states in federal courts was South Dakota *v*. North Carolina, 192 U.S. 286 (1904). A private owner of North Carolina bonds which the state failed to redeem, realizing that he had no power to bring suit against a state, donated the bonds to the state of South Dakota. Since states were not similarly barred from bringing suit, South Dakota brought an original suit and won judgment in the Supreme Court. Since certain property had been pledged for the redemption of the bonds, the Court left undetermined the mode of forcible collection of a judgment against a state under other circumstances.

[83] See, for example, United States *ex rel*. Turner *v*. Williams, 194 U.S. 279 (1904) and United States *v*. Ju Toy, 198 U.S. 253 (1905).

[84] Joseph B. Bishop, *Theodore Roosevelt and His Time* (2 vols., 1920), II, 94.

# CHAPTER 24

# TAFT AND THE ROOSEVELT POLICIES

THEODORE ROOSEVELT fixed upon William Howard Taft, his Secretary of War, as the man most likely to carry forward the Roosevelt policies. By use of patronage, publicity, and his own personal popularity, Roosevelt persuaded his party to nominate Taft and persuaded the people to elect him. The parallel with Jackson's selection of Van Buren was too close to escape comment. Republicans had been wont to say that Jackson had no policies worthy of the name and that Van Buren had no principles, and they cringed at the comparison with Roosevelt and Taft and sought to show differences. Nevertheless, a parallel remained. A strong President with a dominating personality selected a man of milder temperament, who had served congenially as his subordinate, to become his successor and carry out his program.

The contrast between the administration of Roosevelt and that of Taft was in large part a contrast of personalities. Roosevelt was an energetic crusader. He had the magnetism of a popular leader. He stormed his way through opposition. He scorned red tape and legal technicalities. He carried banners in the cause of righteousness, even though he was deft in compromising with the "malefactors of great wealth" when compromise seemed politically desirable. His reasoning was in terms of morality rather than of law, and he was inclined to assume that whatever he believed right was also legal.

Taft, on the other hand, was first of all a lawyer and a jurist. In contrast with Roosevelt, it is hardly too much to say that for him whatever was legal was also right, at least until the law could be changed. He was not the type of man to act first and seek legal justification afterward. He was not a man on parade with a big stick. He lacked the ability to thrill people with glittering teeth, a clenched fist, and denunciations of the doers of evil. He was a combination of geniality, stubbornness, and willingness to compromise. He profited for a time by the contrast with his predecessor, in that Congress, which had at last refused to be driven by Roosevelt, worked with Taft long enough to put through a quantity of legislation in enviable contrast with the output of the preceding administration. He was handicapped by lack of the qualities of political leadership needed to hold together the dividing wings of his party and pave the way for another term in office. Both the presidency and Congress, therefore, were strikingly different under the guidance of the two men.

### ECONOMIC AND POLITICAL BACKGROUND

If personality is of major importance in explaining events of the Taft administration, however, the inexorable sweep of economic change is likewise entitled to attention. The change was similar to that of preceding decades, but the point of advancement had moved farther across the map of time. The concentration of wealth in the hands of a minority of the people continued steadily. The outstanding business activities were carried on by means of corporations. More and more of the total of profitable business was being done by large corporations. Although production of automobiles had not yet developed far enough to demonstrate possibilities, mass production of identical units of goods was on the horizon, with profits depending on widespread advertising and the sale of large numbers of identical units at prices which large numbers of purchasers could pay. The individual laborer was being lost in the crowd of his fellow workers employed by the artificial, intangible, invisible being called a corporation. If the number of jobs increased with the development of industry, the concentration of production in the hands of few, though larger, corporations tended to reduce the number of employers from whom the worker could seek employment. He possessed legal freedom of contract, but he was under economic compulsion to seek employment with particular employers who were concerned with men as mass man-power, or as instruments possessing particular skill, rather than as individuals. He was driven inevitably toward unionization as a mode of protecting his rights in bargaining with powerful employers.

The building of a great industrial nation was the boast and pride of most of the leaders of the people. Men in all walks of life hailed the production and use of so-called labor-saving machinery, which was making great changes in the conditions of employment on farms and in factories. But, if the people approved of the basic trends, they bit

inadequate, new kinds of taxation must be adopted, and recommended a graduated inheritance tax as correct in principle and certain and easy of collection.[6] He did not at once challenge the conservative leaders of his party by demanding an income tax, but Attorney General Wickersham, with the co-operation of the President and others, drafted a measure providing for an excise tax on the privilege of doing business in the corporate form, the tax to be measured by the net income of the corporation. When conservative leaders came to Taft for support against the coalition of Democrats and insurgent Republicans seeking the adoption of a graduated income-tax law, he required acceptance of the corporation excise-tax bill and of a joint resolution providing for an income-tax amendment as a condition of his support.[7] He then sent a message to Congress announcing his program. The income-tax decision of 1895, he said, had deprived the government of a taxing power it had hitherto been supposed to possess, and one it ought to possess, especially for use in times of crisis. Although he had not considered a constitutional amendment necessary to the exercise of the power to levy taxes on certain kinds of income, he recommended the adoption of such an amendment as the only proper course for establishment of the power to the full extent. He contended that to re-enact a statute once declared unconstitutional on the assumption that the Court would reverse itself would tend to destroy popular confidence in the stability of judicial construction of the Constitution. Pending the adoption of the constitutional amendment, he recommended resort to a corporation excise tax in lieu of a general income tax.[8]

Senator Elihu Root endorsed Taft's opposition to enactment of a new income-tax law without constitutional amendment. This was not an ordinary case of a suitor asking for a rehearing, he contended.

It is that the Congress of the United States shall deliberately pass, and the President of the United States shall sign, and that the legislative and executive departments thus conjointly shall place upon the statute books as a law a measure which the Supreme Court has declared to be unconstitutional and void. And then, Mr. President,

[6] *Messages and Papers of the Presidents*, XV, 7370.

[7] Pringle, *op. cit.*, I, 434-435.

[8] One of the merits of the proposal, said Taft, was the federal supervision which would have to be exercised over accounts and transactions of corporations in order to collect the tax. The purpose of the statute would be the collection of revenue, but it would have the desirable incidental effect of producing much-needed regulation. *Messages and Papers of the Presidents*, XV, 7389 ff.

what are we to encounter? A campaign of oratory upon the stump, of editorials in the press, of denunciation and imputation designed to compel that great tribunal to yield to the force of the opinion of the executive and the legislative branches. If they yield, what then? Where then would be the confidence of our people in the justice of their judgment? If they refuse to yield, what then? A breach between the two parts of our government, with popular acclaim behind the popular branch, all setting against the independence, the dignity, the respect, the sacredness of that great tribunal whose function in our system of government has made us unlike any republic that ever existed in the world, whose part in our government is the greatest contribution that America has made to political science.[9]

Some senators disagreed with Root, contending that to re-enact a measure and secure a new judicial determination of its validity was similar to the legitimate action of a litigant who sought the rehearing of a case already decided. Some, on the other hand, claimed that Congress was constitutionally bound by the Supreme Court decision on the earlier measure and had no right to pass another like it. Others contended that the Court had no power to restrain Congress in the enactment of legislation, even though the measures enacted were like others previously held unconstitutional. Restrained, perhaps, by popular belief in what Root called "the sacredness of that great tribunal," legislators did not criticize the Supreme Court with the same bluntness as that used toward the President. The President had offended by encroaching upon legislative prerogatives in having the Attorney General draft the corporation excise-tax measure and send it to Congress for enactment.[10] The debate ended, nevertheless, in the enactment of a compromise tariff measure with provisions for the corporation excise tax as an integral part.[11]

In March, 1910, fifteen cases involving the constitutionality of the corporation excise tax were argued together before the Supreme Court. A number of changes took place in the personnel of the Court before a decision was reached, and the cases were reargued in January, 1911. Corporations attacked the measure on many grounds, including the charge that it was in reality an income tax and therefore a direct tax, which under the Constitution must be apportioned among the several states according to population. By contrast with the Pol-

[9] 44 *Congressional Record* 4003.

[10] For a discussion of the debates see H. M. Bowman, "Congress and the Supreme Court," *Political Science Quarterly*, XXV (March, 1910), 20.

[11] 36 Stat. 11.

lock case of 1895, the Supreme Court reached a unanimous decision.[12] Justice Day, speaking for the Court, classified the act with excise-tax measures that had already been upheld, refusing to follow the analogy of the income-tax cases.    Even though the tax was measured by net income, he explained, it was levied upon the privilege of doing business as a corporation and was therefore an excise measure, which did not have to be apportioned among the states according to population. Since it was based, not upon income, but upon the exercise of a privilege, the measure was not unconstitutional because some of the income by which it was measured was not itself subject to taxation.    As to the impairment of franchises granted by the states, the tax did not affect the essential functions of the states in such a way as to render it unconstitutional as an interference with state instrumentalities.

The decision did not constitute a reversal of the Pollock decision. Yet by resort to the device — or the subterfuge — of an excise tax measured by income instead of a tax on the income itself, the government was able to do with respect to corporations what it could not do in the name of an income tax itself.    There are certain differences between the collection of a tax on the privilege of doing business and the collection of a tax on income.    Yet these differences do not fully account for the fact that whereas the income-tax measure of 1894 was held unconstitutional by a vote of five to four, the corporation excise-tax measure of 1909 was  unanimously upheld.    The Court was no doubt fully aware of the loss of prestige it had suffered from the income-tax decision.    The members doubtless knew of the growing sentiment that accumulations of wealth should be required to yield their just share of the cost of government through new forms of taxation.    They knew also that an income-tax amendment was on its way through the ratifying process in the states and that ultimately the collection of income taxes was close to inevitable.    Whatever the attitude of individual judges, continued obstruction would eventually be futile.

## THE INCOME-TAX AMENDMENT

President Taft took credit for the adoption of the corporation excise tax and the launching of the income-tax constitutional amendment.    Said Archie Butt, his military aide, "Senator Aldrich and Senator Lodge thought they had him weaned away from the income-tax proposition, but when they thought themselves safe from this

[12] Flint v. Stone Tracy Co., 220 U.S. 107 (1911).

menace he slipped his message, when they were entirely unprepared for it." [13]    Taft said privately that he preferred an income-tax law to the corporation tax, but feared the discussion which might follow its enactment and the criticism of the Supreme Court that would ensue if there were another serious division on the subject of the income tax.

> Nothing has ever injured the prestige of the Supreme Court more than the last decision, and I think that many of the most violent advocates of the income tax will be glad of the substitution in their hearts for the same reason.   I am going to push the constitutional amendment, which will admit an income tax without question, but I am afraid of it without such an amendment. [14]

Congress proposed the amendment to the states in the following language:

> Article XVI.  The Congress shall have power to lay and collect taxes on incomes, from whatever source derived, without apportionment among the several states and without regard to any census or enumeration. [15]

Ratification met severe opposition, some of it from unexpected sources.   Governor Charles E. Hughes, of New York, who was talked of for the Supreme Court and was soon to be appointed, advised against ratification of the amendment as it was phrased.   Although he favored an amendment giving Congress power to lay and collect income taxes without apportionment among the states, he was opposed to the language "from whatever source derived," which seemed to him to open the way to federal taxation of state and municipal bonds.   "To place the borrowing capacity of the state and of its governmental agencies at the mercy of the federal taxing power," he said in a message to the New York legislature, "would be an impairment of the essential rights of the state which, as its officers, we are bound to defend." [16]

The discussion of the amendment in Congress had been such as to indicate that little or no thought was given to the question whether the amendment would authorize federal taxation of income from state and municipal bonds.   Clearly, the major concern was with the aboli-

---

[13] Archie Butt, *Taft and Roosevelt* (2 vols., 1930), I, 123-124.

[14] *Ibid.*, p. 134.        [15] 44 *Congressional Record* 3900.

[16] Department of Justice, *Taxation of Government Bondholders and Employees* (1938), p. 165.

tion of the requirement of apportionment among the states according to population, with respect to income already subject to taxation if so apportioned.   After the publication of the Hughes message, Senators Borah, Root, and others expressed the opinion that the only effect of the amendment would be to abolish the requirement of apportionment for income already taxable, and that income from state and municipal bonds, which was not now taxable even with apportionment, could not be taxed as a result of the amendment.[17]

The subject was widely discussed, but the point was too technical for general understanding, and the amendment became a part of the Constitution without clarification.   To the people its adoption meant that men with huge annual incomes would now be required to pay toward the support of the government in proportion to those incomes. Details of subsequent legislation could be left to Congress, and interpretation of the finer shades of meaning could be left to the courts. The amendment was proclaimed a part of the Constitution on February 25, 1913.   During the period of the Wilson administration federal income-tax legislation was enacted pursuant to the amendment, and the courts were given the opportunity to pass upon the meaning of the new Article in the Constitution.

RAILROAD REGULATION

To redeem the platform pledges of the Taft administration, Attorney General Wickersham submitted to Congress a bill extending the authority of the Interstate Commerce Commission over the railroads of the country.   The measure was drastically changed by Congress and passed as the Mann-Elkins Act.[18]   It authorized the commission to suspend changes in railroad rates pending examination of their reasonableness, and strengthened the long-and-short-haul clause which had been whittled away by court decisions.[19]   It extended the jurisdiction of the commission to telephone, telegraph, and cable lines engaged in transmitting messages in interstate or foreign commerce.

Important procedural changes were made.   In discussing the Interstate Commerce Act, President Taft called attention to the fact that the Interstate Commerce Commission itself initiated and defended litigation in the courts by means of its own attorneys. "This blending of administrative, legislative, and judicial functions," said the President, "tends, in my opinion, to impair the efficiency of the commis-

[17] *Ibid.*, pp. 167-172.       [18] 36 Stat. 539.
[19] See William Z. Ripley, *Railroads: Rates and Regulation* (1913), pp. 560-561.

sion by clothing it with partisan characteristics and robbing it of the impartial judicial attitude it should occupy in passing upon questions submitted to it." He thought all litigation affecting the government should be under the direct control of the Department of Justice, and that proceedings affecting the orders of the commission should be brought by or against the United States in its own name, and not in the name of the commission.[20]

The recommendation raised the old questions as to whether an independent regulatory commission could be established without violation of the doctrine of the separation of powers, and whether a political agency of the government, such as the Department of Justice, could be trusted to administer the law fairly where powerful interests were involved. Opponents of the recommendation deplored the concentration of power in the Attorney General. It was said that railroads would throw their support to a presidential candidate in terms of his probable choice for Attorney General.[21]

The recommendation was adopted, but with qualifications. It was provided that proceedings should be in the name of the United States and under the control of the Attorney General, but the Interstate Commerce Commission was given the right to intervene by its own counsel. Since the commission usually chose to exercise that right, the result was that in most cases the United States was represented by two sets of counsel, one from the Department of Justice and the other from the Interstate Commerce Commission, and the two were not always in agreement. The duplication and rivalry continued until President Taft became Chief Justice Taft, when at his suggestion the two agencies adopted an arrangement for co-operation in preparation of briefs and for division of the cases for argument.[22]

THE COMMERCE COURT

Taft advocated the establishment of a commerce court intended, among other things, to centralize and speed the completion of railroad litigation. It was to have jurisdiction over cases involving the validity of orders of the Interstate Commerce Commission and other types of cases involving the enforcement of the Interstate Commerce Act. As a precedent for the establishment of a court having such a highly

[20] *Messages and Papers of the Presidents,* XVI, 7443-7444.

[21] See Senator Bacon, 45 *Congressional Record* 7363.

[22] See Carl Brent Swisher, "Federal Organization of Legal Functions," *American Political Science Review,* XXXIII (December, 1939), 973-1000.

specialized jurisdiction, he referred to the establishment of the Court of Customs Appeals by the Tariff Act of 1909 to hear appeals in customs cases.[23] The insurgent or progressive group in Congress which had opposed the establishment of the Court of Customs Appeals, objected to the new measure also. The Court of Commerce, they predicted, would build up a vested interest in harmony with the interest of the railroads, which would result in decisions not properly judicial. It would be another anomaly within the judicial system.[24]

The plan for the Commerce Court was included in the Mann-Elkins Act, in spite of considerable opposition. The court was to consist of five judges with the rank of circuit judges. The status of each judge was to be permanent, but at the end of his five-year period he was to be transferred to circuit-court work and was not to be reassigned to the Commerce Court until after the passage of one year. This personnel arrangement indicated confusion of purposes. The court was established in order to bring together in a single court judges who would have, or would acquire, specialized knowledge of the complex problems of the railroad control. The benefit of spe-

---

[23] *Messages and Papers of the Presidents,* XVI, 7442-7443. The Court of Customs Appeals, as its name indicates, was to be a court with a highly specialized jurisdiction, in contrast with the courts of general jurisdiction comprising the basic structure of the federal judicial system. The chief precedent for its establishment was the Court of Claims, which likewise dealt solely with cases in a very limited field.

The purpose of establishing the new court was to relieve the courts of general jurisdiction from a class of highly technical and difficult cases in which a background of specialized knowledge was necessary or highly desirable for the proper disposition of cases. It was thought that a single appellate court, staffed with men possessing such knowledge, could expedite the work and relieve existing courts from a heavy burden. Congress had made an attempt in 1890 to relieve the courts of some of the work arising out of customs disputes by creating a board of general appraisers. The circuit courts so duplicated the work of the board as to render it largely worthless until Congress intervened. When the Court of Customs Appeals was established, the board was left in the position of a court of original jurisdiction in customs cases, and appeals from it were taken only to the Court of Customs Appeals. In 1926 its name was changed to United States Customs Court. *United States Code,* 1934, Title 19, sec. 405a.

The creation of the appellate court was opposed by the insurgent group in Congress. Senator Borah suggested that, if there was difficulty in the interpretation of congressional enactments, Congress ought to clarify the laws rather than create a specialized court to interpret them. The fact was, he said, "that for the last five or six years there has been growing up in this country a tendency to regard the federal court as a kind of emergency hospital for defective legislation. In my judgment, this is only another evidence of that tendency." (44 *Congressional Record* 4191.) For discussion of the establishment of the Court of Customs Appeals see Felix Frankfurter and James M. Landis, *The Business of the Supreme Court* (1927), pp. 148-162. It was believed that the creation of specialized courts was likely to lead to biased decisions, and that the tendency was contrary to the nature of our constitutional system. The controversy provided background for discussion of the creation of a Commerce Court.

[24] See for example Senator Borah, 45 *Congressional Record* 7364.

cialized knowledge was lost in part by the provision for rotating judges. The plan for rotation was adopted, it seems, as a concession to those who feared that the court would develop a bias in favor of railroad corporations.

The Commerce Court had a little less than three years of stormy existence. It lacked the active support of the legal profession; no body of public sentiment in its favor had been built up; and the political administration to which it owed its creation was fighting for its own survival.[25] The legislative expansion of the powers of the Interstate Commerce Commission was the result of widespread anti-railroad sentiment. When the Commerce Court decided against the commission, as it often did, it seemed to justify the prediction that it would be a railroad court. When it decided in favor of the commission, the decisions were regarded as no more than right, and as demonstrating no particular merit in the court. The fact that it decided chiefly railroad cases isolated it for criticism in a way in which most other federal courts were not isolated. Its jurisdiction was not clearly defined, and it had to interpret and apply statutes that were far from clear. When the Supreme Court reversed important decisions of the Commerce Court, the result brought more discredit than was probably warranted.

At the 1911-1912 session, Congress added to an appropriation bill a rider abolishing the Commerce Court. A point of sharp disagreement among the legislators was the question of what to do with the judges of the abolished court. It resulted in a revival of the old question whether judges appointed for good behavior could be deprived of their offices by abolition of the court on which they were appointed to serve. Perhaps as a result of constitutional doubts, combined with political discretion, Congress decided to retain the judges as ambulatory circuit judges.

The device of attaching the repeal measure to an appropriation bill failed of the intended purpose of averting a presidential veto. Said President Taft, "I am utterly opposed to the abolition of a court because its decisions may not always meet the approval of a majority of the legislature. It is introducing a recall of the judiciary, which, in its way, is quite as objectionable as the ordinary popular method proposed."[26] He defended the court, saying, for example, that the

---

[25] See Frankfurter and Landis, *op. cit.*, pp. 162 ff.

[26] *Messages and Papers of the Presidents*, XVI, 7757. On August 22, 1911, President Taft had vetoed the joint resolution for admission of New Mexico and Arizona into the Union because the proposed constitution of Arizona provided for the recall of judges. *Ibid.*, XVI, 7636.

average delay of two years before orders of the Interstate Commerce Commission could become effective had been reduced to six months. It was in the interest of the shippers, and therefore of the public, that an agency thus reducing the time of making remedial legislation effective against railroads should be preserved. The bill was not passed over the veto.

The Commerce Court continued to function, but its prestige was further injured by the impeachment of one of its members. The judge was said to have used his influence to secure from litigants before the court contracts favorable to business associates. The Senate voted to remove him from office. While his dishonesty did not necessarily reflect upon the Commerce Court as such, it added weight to the feeling that the creation of that tribunal had been a mistake. When the Democratic party came into power in 1913, no official support for the court was left. Congress terminated its existence as of December 31, 1913.[27] Once more an extended debate took place over the termination of the offices of the judges. No new light was shed on the constitutional question. By a narrow margin it was decided to retain the judges for the circuits.[28]

The unfortunate experience with the Commerce Court no doubt had a deterring effect upon the establishment of other federal courts of specialized jurisdiction. In 1929, the Court of Customs Appeals was given appellate jurisdiction in patent cases and its name changed to Court of Customs and Patent Appeals, but the step marked no important departure in the development of the judicial system. The problem of adapting the system to the handling of intricate and technical problems in many specialized fields remains yet to be solved.

### THE SUPREME COURT AND RAILROAD REGULATION

The Interstate Commerce Commission was slow in acquiring the respect of the Supreme Court. As late as 1910, Justice Holmes expressed his disbelief that the commission was a fit body to be entrusted with rate-making, even in the qualified manner in which the power was then given. The commission was always trying to extend its power, he said, and he remarked, evidently with satisfaction, that he had written some decisions limiting that power.[29] The enlargement

---

[27] 38 Stat. 208, 219.

[28] For important segments of the debate see 50 *Congressional Record* 5409 ff.

[29] Mark A. DeWolfe Howe (ed.), *Holmes-Pollock Letters: The Correspondence of Mr. Justice Holmes and Sir Frederick Pollock, 1874-1932* (2 vols., 1941), I, 163.

of the powers of the commission by statute, however, restrained somewhat the interference of the Supreme Court with the commission's
orders. In a case decided against the Illinois Central Railroad Company, for example, the Court, while reserving authority to pass upon
all questions of constitutional power and of jurisdiction, disclaimed
the power exercised in earlier years of redetermining the facts as well
as the law and of substituting judicial judgment for that of the commission in the making of administrative orders. The existence of
recognized judicial powers, said Justice White for the Court, lent "no
support whatever to the proposition that we may, under the guise of
exerting judicial power, usurp merely administrative functions by
setting aside a lawful administrative order upon our conception as to
whether the administrative power has been wisely exercised." [30]

In other words, while the power to make an administrative order
was a matter into which the Court might inquire, the expediency of
making a lawful order under given circumstances was to be determined by the administrative body. The Supreme Court would not
attempt to insert its own conception of policy. The statement of
principle was clear. In practice, the line to be drawn between the
mandate of law and the area of administrative discretion was often
hard to find. For the time being it was of great importance that the
Supreme Court recognized the existence of a line beyond which it
should not go in interfering with the judgment of an administrative
body. [31]

[30] Interstate Commerce Commission v. Illinois Central Railroad Co., 215 U.S. 452, 470
(1910). For discussion of this and other cases, see I. L. Sharfman, *Interstate Commerce
Commission* (4 vols. in 5, 1931), I, 48, 68.

[31] Railroad litigants used the development of effective federal regulation of interstate
railroads as a weapon of attack upon state regulation of intrastate railroads. In the
Minnesota rate cases of 1913, Simpson v. Shepard, 230 U.S. 352 (1913), it was contended
that the existence of federal interstate regulation was a bar to state-wide intrastate
regulation even though the state rates were reasonable. The Court held that the Interstate Commerce Commission had not been authorized to establish uniform rates over all
railroads, whether interstate or intrastate, and that the state regulation was therefore
valid in the absence of conflict with the regulation of interstate rates by the Interstate
Commerce Commission.

A year later, in the Shreveport cases, Houston E. & W. Texas Railway Co. v. United
States, 234 U.S. 342 (1914), the Court upheld the power of the Interstate Commerce
Commission to interfere with state-established rates for intrastate commerce where such
rates had a bearing upon the establishment of interstate rates by the Interstate Commerce Commission. Due process required that rates yield a fair return on a fair value.
Since the return on some roads came from the two forms of commerce combined, it was
necessary in such cases that there be some degree of centralized control.

A basic constitutional and legal difficulty in connection with railroads and with public
utilities generally was the establishment of the value of the property on which rates
were to be based. So diverse were the factors to be considered pursuant to the decision

## THE CONTROL OF CORPORATIONS

Taft, like Roosevelt, gave much thought and effort to the control of corporations. He repeated the attempt previously made by Roosevelt to secure the enactment of a national incorporation law. The constitutionality of such a measure was not to be doubted, he argued, as far as it dealt with corporations engaged in interstate commerce. He continued to urge such a measure throughout his term in office, but without success. Control through enforcement of anti-trust legislation was an important part of his program. Before he became President, he talked in terms of bringing about closer co-operation among the Department of Justice, the Bureau of Corporations, and the Interstate Commerce Commission in the enforcement of an amended anti-trust law.[32] He discussed anti-trust legislation at length in a special message to Congress, rejecting the distinction between good trusts and bad trusts and the argument that so-called good trusts should be "permitted to organize, suppress competition, control prices, and do it all legally if only they do not abuse the power by taking too great profit out of the business." [33]

So many anti-trust cases were instituted and carried to completion by Taft's administration that the work of his predecessor in this field was completely overshadowed. They included both equity cases and criminal prosecutions. The Roosevelt enthusiasm and moral indignation had brought the Anti-Trust Act to life, but the establishment of routine enforcement was left to Taft and his Attorney General, Wickersham. This is not to say that the government stopped the expansion of business and the merging of smaller units into larger ones. It is doubtful if any administration could have stopped that seemingly inevitable process. The government did, however, check some of the grosser abuses in the treatment of smaller competitors, and break up, at least temporarily, some of the larger combinations. Success was achieved, in spite of the lukewarm attitudes of some judges. Justice Holmes, for example, expressed privately the belief

of the Supreme Court in Smyth v. Ames, 169 U.S. 466 (1898), that disagreement and obstructive litigation were always possible. In 1913, Congress passed an act authorizing the Interstate Commerce Commission to make an investigation and establish the valuation of all common carriers subject to the provisions of the Interstate Commerce Act. (37 Stat. 701.) So difficult was the task, however, that a long period of years was required for its completion. In the meantime business conditions became such that it was impossible to collect charges fixed high enough to yield a fair return on a fair value. Sharfman, op. cit., I, 119.

[32] Homer Cummings and Carl McFarland, *Federal Justice* (1937), p. 338.

[33] Message of January 7, 1910, *Messages and Papers of the Presidents*, XVI, 7454.

that the Sherman Act was a humbug based on economic ignorance and incompetence.[34]

Prominent among the cases won were the Standard Oil[35] and the tobacco trust cases,[36] in which two great combinations were broken up, although the dissolution in neither case was as complete as was hoped for. In the Standard Oil case, Chief Justice White, now spokesman for the majority of the Court, read into the Anti-Trust Act the so-called "rule of reason," the interpretation that only unreasonable restraints were prohibited by the law. Reasonableness was to be determined by the courts. In an annual message to Congress, President Taft stated that there had been no change in the rule of decision, but only in the form of its expression. The Court had merely adopted common-law terminology. "A reasonable restraint of trade at common law is well understood and is clearly defined."[37] Nevertheless, the language of the opinion created the impression that the Court was arrogating power to itself by enlarging its own discretion in the interpretation of an important statute. Indeed, the Court seemed to be assuming by judicial legislation powers that Taft had objected to giving it by statute on the ground that the judicial burden would be too great.

No changes were made in the Sherman Act during the Taft period. One of the last of his official acts, however, was to veto an appropriation bill which forbade the use of any of the appropriated money for anti-trust actions against labor or farmer organizations. The provision, said the President, was "class legislation of the most vicious sort."[38]

## CONSERVATION OF NATURAL RESOURCES

A part of the Taft heritage from his predecessor was the Roosevelt conservation policy. "I rejoice in my heritage," he said in 1910.[39] In 1908, he had said, "As a people, we have the problem of making our forests outlast this generation, our iron outlast this century, and our coal the next; not merely as a matter of convenience or comfort, but as a matter of stern national necessity."[40] The Taft attitude toward

[34] Howe (ed.), *op. cit.,* I, 163.
[35] Standard Oil Co. *v.* United States, 221 U.S. 1 (1911).
[36] United States *v.* American Tobacco Co., 221 U.S. 106 (1911).
[37] Message of December 5, 1911, *Messages and Papers of the Presidents,* XVI, 7646.
[38] *Messages and Papers of the Presidents,* XVI, 7865.      [39] *Ibid.,* p. 7556.
[40] Quoted, *Investigation of the Department of the Interior and of the Bureau of Forestry,* Senate Doc. No. 719, 61st Cong., 3d sess., p. 1160.

conservation, however, as toward other matters, was essentially different from that of Roosevelt. In analyzing speeches made by the two men at the National Conservation Congress, held at St. Paul in September, 1910, a farm paper said that Taft discussed conservation as a great jurist, while Roosevelt discussed it as a preacher of righteousness.[41] On that occasion Taft deplored the emotionalism in terms of which the subject was usually discussed:

> I am bound to say that the time has come for a halt in general rhapsodies over conservation, making the word mean every known good in the world; for, after the public attention has been roused, such appeals are of doubtful utility and do not direct the public to the specific course that the people should take, or have their legislators take, in order to promote the cause of conservation.[42]

Even though he refused to indulge in "general rhapsodies over conservation," and even though he differed from Roosevelt in being unwilling to act without legal warrant, Taft was responsible for important achievements. He secured the enactment of a measure retaining in the government the title to coal on land subject, under the homestead laws, to entry for agricultural purposes, thereby preventing the passing of a valuable resource into private hands for nominal compensation.[43] He secured the enactment of another statute authorizing him to withdraw from entry lands to be used for water-power sites, irrigation, and other purposes.[44] He made extensive withdrawals pursuant to the statute, and promoted classification of lands in the public domain to discover what ought to be retained by the government. The work was important, although accomplished without evangelistic flourishes.

It was only within the decade that the immensity of the nation's wealth in water-power was coming to be realized. With the realization, it was only natural that business interests rushed to gain control of the most valuable power sites, and that they criticized attempts of the federal government to retain control of a portion of this wealth rather than permit it to pass into private hands. State-rights doctrines were employed to show that the federal program was unconstitutional. Said one writer on the subject:

> The underlying motive of the proposed conservation legislation, and particularly the measures which concern the water-power sites, is

---

[41] *Wallaces' Farmer*, September 23, 1910.
[42] *Messages and Papers of the Presidents*, XVI, 7573.
[43] 36 Stat. 583.　　　[44] 36 Stat. 847.

a profound distrust of the capacity of the state governments to govern their internal affairs with wisdom and justice, and an assumption of superior wisdom and virtue on the part of the national government. But whether or not this distrust is well founded, the ends sought to be accomplished are not fairly or legitimately within the scope of the Constitution, and the means proposed for their attainment are repugnant to its letter and spirit.[45]

Taft questioned the validity of objections of this kind. Where the government owned the land which must be utilized for the development of water-power, the government could determine the conditions under which such lands might be used. He thought it the plain duty of the government to see that conditions were imposed by which the development of water-power on what were now public lands would not lead to monopoly and extortionate charges.[46] Except for permission to withdraw water-power sites from entry, no effective legislation was secured during the Taft administration, but the messages of the President, coupled with the report on water-power development made, in 1912, by the Bureau of Corporations,[47] added to the public understanding and resulted in action later on. It is to be noted that the President concerned himself only with power sites on public lands, and not those where federal jurisdiction could be claimed only on the basis of control of navigation. Much thought remained to be given to the whole subject before a program of federal control was worked out.

For oil and gas lands Congress passed an act giving the right of agricultural entry upon the surface, as in the case of coal lands, without the acquisition of title to subsurface wealth.[48] The government had great difficulty in conserving publicly owned oil and gas because of drainage to wells on privately owned lands. This was particularly true along railroad rights of way where alternate sections had been given to the railroad companies. The subject provided sweeping opportunities for graft, and the government was engaged for years in extensive litigation to protect its rights.

Because public lands in the eastern part of the country had long since passed into private hands, the first national forests established by

---

[45] William B. Bosley, "Conservation and the Constitution," *Yale Law Journal*, XX (November, 1910), 18, 27.

[46] *Messages and Papers of the Presidents*, XVI, 7571.

[47] *Report of the Commissioner of Corporations on Water-Power Development in the United States* (1912).

[48] 37 Stat. 496.

the government were all in the western states.   The conservationists
urged restoring some of the cut-over lands of the East to their prim-
eval condition through intervention of the federal government.  Bills
to that end were introduced in Congress from time to time over a
period of years, in the face of serious constitutional difficulties.   It was
believed that the restoration of some of the forests of the East would
promote the public welfare, but the Supreme Court had never
decided the question whether Congress could tax and spend for the
public welfare save through the exercise of some other granted power.
The Constitution said nothing about the purchase of lands to establish national forests, nor did the power seem easily derived from other
powers which were granted.

In his annual message of December 3, 1907, President Roosevelt
had made the following recommendation:

> We should acquire in the Appalachian and White Mountain
> regions all the forest lands that it is possible to acquire for the use of
> the nation.   These lands, because they form a national asset, are as
> emphatically national as the rivers which they feed, and which flow
> through so many states before they reach the ocean.[49]

Such a conception of nationalism was much broader than that held
by many of Roosevelt's contemporaries.   This portion of his message
and two bills introduced to carry out its recommendations were referred to the House committee on the judiciary, with a request for an
opinion on the powers of the government in the matters.   The committee replied in the following resolution:

> That the committee is of the opinion that the federal government
> has no power to acquire lands within a state solely for forest reserves;
> but under its constitutional power over navigation the federal govern-
> ment may appropriate for the purchase of lands and forest reserves in
> a state, provided it is made clearly to appear that such lands and
> forest reserves have a direct and substantial connection with the con-
> servation and improvement of the navigability of a river actually
> navigable in whole or in part, and that any appropriation made there-
> for is limited to that purpose.[50]

After this resolution was published, bills on the subject were
drafted in such a way as to show a connection between the purchase of
lands and the navigability of streams.   This task had its difficulties.

[49] *Messages and Papers of the Presidents*, XV, 7099.
[50] 45 *Congressional Record* 9000.

Some experts claimed that a forest coverage at the headwaters of streams created a bed of humus and a soil knitted together with the roots of trees which provided a natural reservoir for rainfall, from which water flowed with comparative evenness to maintain the flow of navigable streams. By contrast, if the forest coverage was removed, the rain which fell on hard ground flowed quickly off to flood the streams for a temporary period, after which the streams dried up and failed to provide navigable waters down below. The argument sounded persuasive and was used to the fullest extent to justify authorization to purchase denuded lands on watersheds for reforestation. The difficulty was that other experts found no such difference between the flow of water from forested and deforested areas, and could see no such connection between reforestation and navigability as to provide a constitutional basis for purchase of lands. In any event, it was claimed, and not vigorously denied, that the navigation argument was but a subterfuge to give constitutional justification for action desired on other grounds.

A measure having the support of the President, which came to be known as the Weeks Act, was passed in 1911.[51] It did not go far enough to please the most ardent conservationists, but it was regarded as the entering wedge for additional legislation. Said Senator Newlands, "It establishes and applies a constitutional principle of vast importance, which is that the regulation of the flow of rivers by the protection of the watersheds from denudation and erosion, and the preservation of forests as sources of water supply, is a proper function of the national government under its power to maintain the navigability of rivers."[52] The act provided for a National Forest Reservation Commission, to be made up of the Secretaries of War, Interior, and Agriculture, and two members each from the Senate and House of Representatives. Provision was made for the purchase of lands by the commission over a five-year period. The measure, as predicted, marked the beginning of much more extensive developments in the years ahead.

In spite of his efforts and achievements in the field of conservation, Taft ended his four years in office with the reputation of an opponent of the conservation movement and with the opposition of most of its strong advocates. The explanation lay in the results of the Pinchot-Ballinger controversy and in the fact that Roosevelt split the Republican party in 1912 by assuming leadership of the radical conservation

[51] 36 Stat. 961.    [52] 46 Congressional Record 2589.

faction and other discontented groups. The Pinchot-Ballinger controversy began when Gifford Pinchot, chief of the Forest Service in the Department of Agriculture, sponsored the cause of Louis R. Glavis, a subordinate in the Interior Department, who accused Secretary of the Interior Richard A. Ballinger of improper disposal of coal lands in Alaska. The traditional attitude of the Interior Department was that the interests of the country were best served by the transfer of public lands and minerals to private possession. Pinchot, an ardent conservationist, was interested, not merely in preventing the waste of resources, but also in keeping ownership in the government for the benefit of the people. Glavis gave unauthorized publicity to charges against his superior officer and was dismissed for his pains. Pinchot, supporting Glavis, went over the head of his own immediate superior officer, the Secretary of Agriculture, and over the head of the President, in a letter to a member of the Senate, to appeal for the support of Congress. The letter was made public. For his act of insubordination Pinchot, too, was dismissed from office.

With the dismissal of Pinchot the conservationists of the country swarmed in upon Washington to demand an investigation. Congress investigated at great length.[53] Although differences in philosophy as to the conservation of natural resources were disclosed, no evidence of fraud was produced. It is questionable whether even the term "misconduct" could be legitimately applied to anything done by the Secretary of the Interior. The controversy had the effect of labeling him as an anti-conservationist, however, and Taft, who stood by him, paid the price of his support.[54] The effect of the controversy brought on by the misplaced ardor of conservationists was to injure a President who did much in the interest of conservation, and it may also have had the effect of slowing down the conservation movement.

"WHITE-SLAVE" LEGISLATION

The period saw the extension of the control of the federal government over matters hitherto assumed to be subject to the control only of the states. One of the subjects dealt with was sexual immorality. It seemed obviously a matter of local concern, yet such was the corruption of a number of local governments and the incompetence of local officials that vice flourished openly. There was as yet no federal

---

[53] See Senate Doc. 719, 61st Cong., 3d sess.

[54] For discussion of the controversy see Pringle, op. cit., I, chapters XXVI and XXVII. See also Alpheus T. Mason, *Bureaucracy Convicts Itself* (1941).

income-tax law which the federal government might use, as it did use such a law in later years, to hamper by indirection the business of prostitution. The first attempts at federal regulation were based on the power to regulate foreign and interstate commerce.

For many years Congress had sought, through immigration laws, to exclude from the country aliens who came for immoral purposes. Since the prospect of immoral conduct was not easy to determine, the laws were only mildly effective. By an act of 1907, Congress sought to extend its control by providing for the punishment of any person who harbored an alien woman for immoral purposes within three years after her arrival in the country.[55] The keeping of houses of prostitution was normally subject only to the jurisdiction of the states, but Congress was here attempting to extend the operation of the immigration laws to punishment of the offense.

The Supreme Court, in Keller v. United States,[56] held the act unconstitutional, by a vote of six to three. Said Justice Brewer for the Court:

> While the keeping of a house of ill-fame is offensive to the moral sense, yet that fact must not close the eye to the question whether the power to punish therefor is delegated to Congress or is reserved to the states. Jurisdiction over such an offense comes within the accepted definition of the police power. Speaking generally, that power is reserved to the states, for there is in the Constitution no grant thereof to Congress.[57]

The decision seemed to stand in the way of further federal legislation of this kind. In 1910, however, under the stimulus of disclosures of gross immorality carried on by use of women kept under conditions of actual slavery, in what came to be known as the "white-slave" traffic, Congress turned to a new measure. The purpose was to punish any person who in any way brought about the transportation of a woman in interstate or foreign commerce for immoral purposes, or induced a woman to travel in interstate or foreign commerce for such purposes. The opposition pointed to the Keller case as evidence that the measure was an unconstitutional encroachment on the police powers of the states. The congressman from a state in

---

[55] 34 Stat. 898.    [56] 213 U.S. 138 (1909).

[57] Ibid., p. 144. The Court subsequently upheld the deportation of aliens found practicing prostitution within three years after admission to the United States. (Zakonaite v. Wolf, 226 U.S. 272 [1912].) The act was held not unconstitutional because the findings of fact of the Department of Commerce and Labor were made conclusive.

which such immorality prevailed, said Representative Adamson, ought to appeal to the people of his own state to put an end to it.

> That course is far more patriotic and more in conformity with his oath of office than to come here confessing to such pusillanimous dereliction in his own state in the performance of its duty as a state of this great Union and seeking to cast on Congress the unnatural, improper, unconstitutional, and wholly unnecessary burden of legislating to do the work which his people at home ought to do.[58]

Friends of the measure, on the other hand, argued that, whereas the Keller case had dealt with the harboring of prostitutes, an essentially local matter, the proposed measure dealt with actual transportation in interstate and foreign commerce, which was not within the jurisdiction of the states. As demonstrated by the enforcement of lottery legislation, pure-food and drug legislation, and other acts, Congress had power to purify the stream of interstate commerce by prohibiting that commerce which resulted in evils at the end of the line. Furthermore, said one congressman, "when this Congress offers to pass legislation to prevent a horror which the devil would be ashamed of, why should we higgle over a doubtful question of possible constitutional construction by the courts in the future?"[59]

The measure, known as the Mann Act, was passed and was approved on June 25, 1910.[60] On February 24, 1913, the Supreme Court in Hoke v. United States[61] held it constitutional by a unanimous vote without mentioning the Keller case. Surely, said Justice McKenna for the Court, "if the facility of interstate transportation can be taken away from the demoralization of lotteries, the debasement of obscene literature, the contagion of diseased cattle or persons, the impurity of food and drugs, the like facility can be taken away from the systematic enticement to and the enslavement in prostitution and debauchery of women, and, more insistently, of girls."[62]

### THE WEBB-KENYON ACT

One of the more important regulatory measures enacted during the Taft administration, the Webb-Kenyon Act, was passed over his veto. It had to do with the interstate shipment of liquor. For several decades a number of states or parts of states had attempted to control

---

[58] 45 *Congressional Record* 1032.      [59] *Ibid.*, p. 812.

[60] 36 Stat. 825.      [61] 227 U.S. 308 (1913).

[62] *Ibid.*, p. 322. See also Athanasaw v. United States, 227 U.S. 326 (1913). Once the statute had been upheld, its application was extended far beyond the original purpose of curbing organized vice. It was applied to individual acts of immorality, largely without reference to circumstances. Because of this development it became a fruitful source of blackmail conspiracies.

or prevent the sale of liquor within their borders. They had been handicapped by their inability to interfere with interstate commerce to the extent of preventing the inflow of liquor from other states. Congress had passed the Wilson Act of 1890 to authorize the states to prevent the sale of liquor in original packages which had been shipped in interstate commerce. As interpreted by the courts, however, that act did not allow the state to assert jurisdiction until the delivery of packages to consignees. As the dry area of the country expanded, a huge mail-order business in liquor developed, to the extent of some twenty million gallons a year.[63]

"Dry" forces urged Congress to enact laws to make prohibition effective, but "wet" forces were strong enough to prevent more than nominal prohibition of the shipment of liquor in interstate commerce. By compromise, legislation was drafted that would allow the exercise of state jurisdiction when liquor crossed the state line. If the states had the right to capture the goods in transit, they could do serious damage to the business. The measure agreed upon stated briefly that the shipment of intoxicating liquor into a state in violation of any law thereof was prohibited. No federal penalty was provided. The theory of the act was expressed in the curiously phrased enacting clause — "An act divesting intoxicating liquors of their interstate character in certain cases." It was apparently assumed that, if interstate shipment was forbidden by federal law, shipment in violation of the law would not be interstate commerce, and the states could, therefore, assert jurisdiction at their borders.

Senator Root, an administration adviser in many matters and the member of the Senate most likely to be the purveyor of administration sentiments, opposed the bill on the ground of unconstitutionality. He believed the effect of the bill

> will be that the courts of the United States will have to say that it is beyond the constitutional power of Congress. I think they will have to say that or stultify themselves, and when they say that, they will concentrate upon themselves a measure of unpopularity, of public censure, and of public impatience with the judicial establishment which we will have shifted from our shoulders when we vote for the bill, believing it to be unconstitutional. I think I shall be the better satisfied to take that burden on my own shoulders, and therefore I shall vote against the bill, because I think it is not permitted by the Constitution.[64]

[63] See Interstate Commerce Commission opinion, quoted 49 *Congressional Record* 700.
[64] 49 *Congressional Record* 2914.

Senator George Sutherland, a constitutional lawyer of repute, who in 1922 was to be appointed to the Supreme Court by President Harding, made a devastating analysis of the bill, and found it unconstitutional. The purpose of including the commerce clause in the Constitution, he argued, had been to secure commerce among the states against conflicting and discriminating regulations of the states, such as would be authorized by this statute, which was made specifically dependent on the laws of the several states. The constitutional powers of the states were defined, not by Congress, but by the Constitution. Apparently, in his mind interstate commerce was still interstate commerce, even though power over it was surrendered by Congress, and a congressional surrender of power was not sufficient to give the states control over it. Whatever the action of Congress, the Constitution had put the control of interstate commerce in the hands of the federal government and had thereby taken it away from the states. He believed, furthermore, that Congress could not prevent the shipment of liquor in interstate commerce because of its alleged harmful effects unless the prohibition was made general and not rested upon the separate actions of particular states or parts of states.[65]

The bill was passed by both houses, with admission on the part of its advocates that there were grounds for doubt as to its constitutionality. Attorney General Wickersham prepared for the President an opinion that the bill was unconstitutional.[66] The President sent to the Senate a copy of the opinion and a veto message, saying of the bill:

> I believe it to be a violation of the interstate commerce clause of the Constitution, in that it is in substance and effect a delegation by Congress to the states of the power of regulating interstate commerce in liquors which is vested exclusively in Congress. . . . I cannot think that the framers of the Constitution, or that the people who adopted it, had in mind for a moment that Congress could thus nullify the operation of a clause whose useful effect was deemed so important and which in fact has contributed so much to the solidarity of the nation and the prosperity that has followed unhampered, nation-wide trade.[67]

Part of the President's message followed the lines of Sutherland's argument. One significant paragraph was a development of an idea expressed by Root:

> But it is said that this is a question with which the Executive or

[65] *Ibid.*, pp. 2904 ff.     [66] 30 *Opinions of the Attorney General* 88.
[67] 49 *Congressional Record* 4291-4292.

members of Congress should not burden themselves to consider or decide. It is said that it should be left to the Supreme Court to say whether this proposed act violates the Constitution. I dissent utterly from this proposition. The oath which the Chief Executive takes, and which each member of Congress takes, does not bind him any less sacredly to observe the Constitution than the oaths which the justices of the Supreme Court take. It is questionable whether the doubtful constitutionality of a bill ought not to furnish a greater reason for voting against the bill, or vetoing it, than for the Court to hold it to be invalid. The Court will only declare a law invalid where its unconstitutionality is clear, while the lawmaker may very well hesitate to vote for a bill if of doubtful constitutionality because of the wisdom of keeping clearly within the fundamental law. The custom of legislators and executives having any legislative function to remit to the courts entire and ultimate responsibility as to the constitutionality of the measures which they take part in passing is an abuse which tends to put the Court constantly in opposition to the legislature and executive, and, indeed, to the popular supporters of unconstitutional laws. If, however, the legislators and the executives had attempted to do their duty, this burden of popular disapproval would have been lifted from the courts, or at least considerably lessened.[68]

The Taft administration had almost reached the end of its life, and its influence over Congress was now negligible. The bill, which came to be known as the Webb-Kenyon Act,[69] was passed over the veto. Four years later, while expressing deference to the opinions of Wickersham and Taft, the Supreme Court held the measure constitutional by a vote of seven to two.[70] Disagreeing with Taft, who had appointed him Chief Justice and was later to succeed him in that office, and with Sutherland who was later to be Taft's colleague on the Supreme Court, Chief Justice White argued that the act did not delegate power to the states, but was an exercise of federal power. The act was uniform, he said. The lack of uniformity was in the conditions amid which it was to be applied. Furthermore, the Constitution did not require that federal commercial regulations be uniform throughout the United States. As a regulation of commerce, the Webb-Kenyon Act was but an extension of the Wilson Act, of which the purpose had been to regulate by divesting shipments of their interstate character and stripping them of the right to be sold in the original package, which otherwise would have obtained. The Wilson

[68] *Ibid.*, p. 4292.        [69] 37 Stat. 699.
[70] Clark Distilling Co. *v.* Western Maryland Railway Co., 242 U.S. 311 (1917).

Act had been held constitutional, and this decision must follow precedent.[71]

Shortly before the Supreme Court decided this case, former President Taft, as if fearing that the Court would reject his argument as to the unconstitutionality of the act, again set forth his theory discussed above.[72] His thinking may have been colored by the fact that the issue involved in the Webb-Kenyon Act had arisen in a situation where Congress was acting under pressure of a powerful lobby rather than where the government was taking the lead in planning for the public welfare. His reasoning, in any event, was fundamentally that of a jurist, of a man whose concern was first of all with the law, rather than with taking positive action for the public welfare. It assumed, furthermore, a static quality in the law. It ignored the fact that constitutional adaptation to new circumstances has usually taken place through legislative enactment and executive and judicial acceptance of legislation of somewhat doubtful constitutionality. His argument would have been inconceivable as coming from Theodore Roosevelt. It was at opposite poles from the theory of Franklin D. Roosevelt, expressed in 1935 when he wrote to the chairman of a congressional committee, "I hope your committee will not permit doubts as to constitutionality, however reasonable, to block the suggested legislation." [73]

### THE RECALL OF JUDGES AND ADMISSION OF ARIZONA

Taft's essential conservatism and his interest in the preservation of judicial institutions without fundamental change were further revealed in the struggle to secure the admission of Arizona into the Union. For some years Congress had considered the admission of New Mexico and Arizona, the last of the contiguous territories yet

[71] The Chief Justice did not deal with the contention, present or implied in the Sutherland argument, that interstate commerce was a matter of fact and not merely of law, a condition which could not be changed by act of Congress. The difficulty apparently lay in the uncertainties of the doctrine that Congress may leave to the states regulation of aspects of interstate commerce requiring to be governed by local rather than general rules.

For application of the principles of the Wilson Act and the Webb-Kenyon Act in the field of prison-made goods see Whitfield v. Ohio, 297 U.S. 431 (1936), and Kentucky Whip and Collar Co. v. Illinois Central Railroad Co., 299 U.S. 334 (1937). Congress again resorted to "divesting legislation" in 1940 when it made prize-fight films shipped into a state subject to the laws of the state in spite of the interstate shipments (54 Stat. 686). This device might conceivably become one of great importance in decentralization of control over matters on which attitudes differ in the several states.

[72] William Howard Taft, Our Chief Magistrate and His Powers (1916), p. 21.

[73] 79 Congressional Record 13449.

awaiting admission to statehood. The difficulty as to Arizona lay in the terms of the constitution submitted for approval. The prospective state had succumbed to the then current progressive influence, and had made constitutional provision for the initiative, the referendum, and the recall, the latter including judicial as well as legislative and executive officers.

The initiative and the referendum were generally unpopular in most of the states then represented in Congress, while the recall of judges was subject to hysterical condemnation. Although there was some question as to whether a state which resorted to judicial recall had the republican form which the federal government was to insure to the states, it was not seriously contended that such a procedure violated the federal Constitution.[74] It was said, however, that, if Congress and the President approved the state constitution in its present form, such an act would constitute overt approval of the plan for recall.

Positive support for the governmental innovations in the proposed constitution was given by Senator Bourne, of Oregon, whose state led in what was known as the popular-government movement. Senator Borah opposed the recall of judges, but thought the state ought to be admitted with a constitution of its own choosing. He favored the amended joint resolution which approved the constitution with the provision that the people of the state were to vote on a constitutional amendment to eliminate the recall of judges. That amendment had been proposed because of the known disapproval of recall on the part of President Taft. It left the choice with the people of the state, but the hope was that the people would eliminate the device after the criticism directed at it.

Senator Root opposed acceptance of the constitution prior to removal of the provision for recall, saying, "It is a move backward to those days when human passion and the rule of men obtained rather than the law and the rule of principles, for it ignores, it sets at naught the great principle of government and of civilized society, the principle that justice is above majorities."[75]

Senator Sutherland denounced the questioned provisions of the proposed constitution in a colorful address. He said:

> During the last few years the United States of America has become the field of operation for an amiable band of insurgent soothsayers,

[74] In discussion of the initiative in this connection see Pacific States Telephone and Telegraph Co. *v.* Oregon, 223 U.S. 118 (1912).

[75] 47 *Congressional Record* 3691.

who have been going up and down the land indulging in cabalistic utterances respecting the initiative, the referendum, the recall, and divers and sundry other ingenious devices for realizing the millennium by the ready and simple method of voting it out of its present state of incubation.[76]

Although he thoroughly disapproved the initiative and the referendum, he could subordinate his judgment to that of the people of Arizona in these matters.   But

the power to recall a judge who renders an unpopular judgment is to my mind so utterly subversive of the principles of good government that I can never get my own consent to withhold my condemnation and disapproval of it.

Its theory, he contended, rested on the false assumption that a judge represented a constituency.

A judge has no constituents; he is only in a restricted sense a representative officer at all.   The people who elect him can with propriety make known their wishes only through the laws which they enact. The judge is the mouthpiece of the *law*.   His constituents are the *statutes* duly made and provided.   If his decisions are wrong, the remedy is to appeal to a higher court — not to the people.[77]

The controversy was linked with the growing rift in the Republican party, and with the cleavage developing between Taft and Roosevelt.   Taft's opposition to innovations with respect to the judiciary was well known.   Roosevelt, on the other hand, was making speeches and writing editorials for the *Outlook* sharply critical of the courts, and developing the line of thought which culminated in his advocacy of the recall of judicial decisions in the ensuing presidential campaign.   While the admission of Arizona was being considered by Congress, he stated that under normal circumstances he did not think it advisable to have the principle of the popular recall applied to the judiciary, but to keep Arizona out of the Union merely because of the recall provision would be a grave injustice and "an assault upon the principles which underlie our whole system of free popular government." [78]

[76] *Ibid.*, pp. 2793-2794.        [77] *Ibid.*, p. 2801.

[78] *The Outlook,* June 24, 1911.   Reference to another presidential candidacy appeared in the debates.   Sutherland quoted Woodrow Wilson as saying in his *Congressional Government* that a government "can no more make laws through its voters than it can through its newspapers."   When reminded that Wilson had subsequently approved of the idea of legislation by initiative, Sutherland characterized the revised opinion as "the fevered hallucinations of the hopeful presidential candidate."   47 *Congressional Record* 2798.

The Roosevelt opinion had no deterring effect upon Taft. The resolution of admission was adopted by Congress, coupled with the provision that the people of Arizona were to vote on an amendment to eliminate judicial recall from their constitution. Taft vetoed the resolution of admission, saying, "If I sign this joint resolution, I do not see how I can escape responsibility for the judicial recall of the Arizona constitution." [79] In arguments similar to those of Root and Sutherland he contended that judges were not representatives of majorities of the people as were legislators and executives. The recall, acting quickly on bursts of popular sentiment, would give control to unscrupulous political bosses. Self-respecting men would hesitate to accept judicial office. Independent judicial office would become a thing of the past. He denied that the recall was needed to bring judges into harmony with the popular will and the progress of ideas among the people. "The righteous and just course for a judge to pursue is ordinarily fixed by statute or clear principles of law, and the cases in which his judgment may be affected by his political, economic, or social views are infrequent." [80] Even in these cases the opinions of judges were in the long run colored by the influence of popular opinion. "Individual instances of a hidebound and retrograde conservatism on the part of courts in decisions which turn on the individual economic or sociological views of judges may be pointed out; but they are not many, and do not call for radical action." [81]

Apart from giving the President an opportunity to express his distaste for the recall of judges, the veto was futile. Congress, it is true, passed an amended resolution providing for the admission of Arizona after the constitution had been amended to eliminate the recall.[82] The amendment was adopted. Admission followed, whereupon the state immediately reamended its constitution to provide for the recall of judges. Since it was now on an equal footing with other states, there was no question of its right to take such action. While Congress was discussing the issue, the Supreme Court, in connection with Oklahoma, which had been admitted in 1907, reaffirmed the principle that Congress in admitting a new state could not impose conditions which would deprive it of equality with other states.[83]

[79] *Messages and Papers of the Presidents,* XVI, **7637.**
[80] *Ibid.,* p. **7643.**        [81] *Ibid.,* p. 7643.
[82] 37 Stat. 39.
[83] Coyle *v.* Smith, 221 U.S. 559 (1911).

THE DIRECT ELECTION OF SENATORS

In accepting the Republican nomination for the presidency in 1908, Taft expressed his personal approval of the proposed constitutional amendment whereby United States senators would be elected by the people instead of by the state legislatures. It was not a party question, he said, pointing to the fact that a resolution providing for such an amendment had passed a Republican House of Representatives a number of times, but had been rejected in a Republican Senate by votes of senators from both parties.[84] The question had come up many times. As early as 1826, dissatisfaction with the election of United States senators by state legislatures led to introduction of a resolution providing for a constitutional amendment changing the mode of election.[85] From that time onward the proposal was made again and again. From 1893 to 1902 the House of Representatives five times adopted resolutions for such a constitutional amendment.[86] In each instance the Senate failed to act. The introduction of resolutions was continued in both houses year after year thereafter.

The system of election by state legislatures was defective in a number of ways. Deadlocks in legislatures occurred from time to time over the choice of senators, wasting time and money and delaying the business of the states. There were intervals in which vacancies were not filled at all, leaving states without full representation in the Senate. Bribery and corruption entered into political transactions and were suspected, to the injury of legislative reputation, even when they did not occur. State legislators were sometimes chosen on the basis of their attitudes toward federal senatorships rather than in terms of their capacity to handle local legislative business.

In 1866, acting under its power to legislate concerning the times and manner of choosing senators,[87] Congress attempted to prevent deadlocks between the two houses of legislatures. It provided that if no person secured a majority in separate actions by the two houses, then the houses should meet in joint session and vote as a body in the effort to secure a majority vote for some candidate.[88] Delays continued because of frequent difficulties in securing majority votes even under these circumstances.

Important as were the specific abuses connected with the old method of electing senators, some reasons for the struggle for the con-

[84] 45 *Congressional Record* 7112.     [85] 2 *Register of Debates in Congress* 1348-1349.
[86] George H. Haynes, *The Election of Senators* (1906), p. 104.
[87] Constitution, Article I, Section 4.     [88] 14 Stat. 243.

stitutional amendment lay rather in the growing distrust of representative institutions and traditional forms of government which found expression in the popular-government movement. Popular election of United States senators fitted well into the movement. What amounted to popular election, indeed, was worked out in many northern states before the constitutional amendment was adopted through the pledging of state legislators to vote for senatorial candidates supported by the people in primary or general elections.[89]

The amendment was opposed by the entrenched interests, the party leaders and bosses, who stood to lose by any change in machinery they had learned to control. It was opposed also by conservative persons like Elihu Root, who thought any change likely to create doubt about the stability of our institutions. He said:

> It is not wise that the people of the United States should contract the habit of amending the Constitution. Stability in our government is a matter of vital concern. . . . In our Constitution we have embodied the eternal principles of justice; we have set up a barrier against ourselves. . . . Reverence for that great instrument, the belief of mankind in its perpetuity, the unwillingness of our people to tamper with it or to change it, the sentiments that are gathered around it — these, constituting the basis of stability in our government, are the most valuable of all the possessions of the nation that inhabits this rich and fertile land.[90]

Root argued that the proposed amendment would change the fundamental design of the Senate. The Senate was intended to be a body more secure in tenure, different in the manner of its election, different in its responsibility, more conservative, more deliberative than the other house. It was intended to be a body which would stand firm in the face of the tides of restlessness which swept the country from time to time. The change would result in the election of a type of person more responsive to the current desires of the people. It would exile from the Senate men who now accepted membership as a patriotic duty, but who would not subject themselves to the incidents of the type of political campaign necessary to election by the people.

The voice of Root was the voice of a dying philosophy. It apparently carried less weight against the amendment than did the

---

[89] Arthur N. Holcombe, "Popular Government and Current Politics," *American Yearbook,* 1912, p. 59.

[90] 46 *Congressional Record* 2241.

objections of Southerners who feared that the amendment might interfere with white supremacy in southern elections.    White Democrats were now, through various devices, determining the choice of United States senators in states with large colored populations.  Northern sympathizers with Negroes never ceased to grumble about the abridgement of the rights of Negroes, however, and Southerners feared that a constitutional amendment might be followed by federal legislation prescribing embarrassing regulations for elections.

The proposed amendment in one form met southern views by providing that "the times, places, and manner of holding elections for senators shall be as prescribed in each state by the legislature there of." [91]    By this language the power which Congress had always had over the election of senators and representatives would have been withdrawn as to the election of senators while leaving the election of representatives unaffected.    Opponents of the curtailment of federal powers in this manner secured the elimination of the sentence from the resolution as passed by the Senate.    Its advocates maintained supremacy in the House of Representatives for a period of months, bringing about a deadlock which threatened the defeat of the resolution.    They finally surrendered, however, and the resolution was passed without any restrictive provisions, so that the control of Congress over the election of senators remained the equivalent of its power over the election of representatives.    The joint resolution adopted bore the date of May 15, 1912.[92]    Ratification of the Seventeenth Amendment was proclaimed on May 31, 1913.[93]

As is true of most adjustments in the machinery of government, the adoption of the amendment did not bring the sweeping changes which were hoped for by some and feared by others.    The changes that have taken place, furthermore, are the result of so many factors that responsibility is hard to place.    The white population remains in control of elections in the southern states.    It cannot be demonstrated that state legislatures have lost prestige and declined in caliber because they no longer have responsibility for the election of United States senators.    On the other hand, the removal of this distraction has not resulted in such assiduous attention to the legislative business of the state as to demonstrate an outstanding achievement for the constitutional amendment.    For some reason, the average age of United

[91] The quotation is from Senate Joint Resolution 134, sponsored by Senator Borah, 46 *Congressional Record* 847.
[92] 37 Stat. 646.        [93] 38 Stat. 2049.

States senators is said to have increased.[94]  As is true in most professions, the amount of formal education possessed by senators has increased.  The amount of previous legislative experience has decreased.[95]  Wealth has decreased perceptibly,[96] perhaps as a result of the change of method of election.  As for the number of persons re-elected for ensuing terms, there seems to have been no drastic change in either direction.[97]

### ADMINISTRATIVE CHANGES

One of the final measures enacted during the presidency of Taft was that establishing a Department of Labor with status equivalent to that of other executive departments and consequently with representation in the cabinet.[98]  It marked the end of a long struggle on the part of labor organizations for equality of representation.  The period was one of fruitful discussion of other changes that were not brought about until later years or were not brought about at all.  Monetary reforms were much under discussion.  The establishment of machinery for more effective regulation of corporations was considered.  Taft secured an appropriation for a committee on economy and efficiency, which made the first detailed study of the operations of the federal government.  The heterogeneous assemblage of offices in Washington had grown by accretion, apparently largely without discernible pattern.  Various causes of inefficiency needed to be weeded out. There was an obvious need for a budget system to eliminate waste in expenditures.  Appropriations, then under almost complete control of Congress, were made without reference to a co-ordinated plan.  On the basis of the evidence accumulated, Taft devised the first executive budget of the federal government and submitted it to Congress as a pattern for similar budgets to be submitted annually by the Executive. Congress disregarded the proposal, largely for political reasons, but it had an almost immediate influence on the reorganization of state governments and it was an important step toward the ultimate adoption of the plan for an executive budget in the federal government.[99]

Taft also recommended the adoption of legislation providing seats

---

[94] George H. Haynes, *The Senate of the United States* (2 vols., 1938), II, 1044.
[95] *Ibid.*, p. 1045.          [96] *Ibid.*, pp. 1046-1048.
[97] See E. Earle McClendon, "Re-election of United States Senators," *American Political Science Review*, XXVIII (August, 1934), 636-642.  For analysis of the membership of a recent Congress see Madge M. McKinney, "The Personnel of the Seventy-Seventh Congress," *ibid.*, XXXVI (February, 1942), 67-74.
[98] 37 Stat. 736.          [99] For more complete discussion see chapter 30.

for the heads of executive departments in each house of Congress and giving them the opportunity to take part in all discussions and to answer questions. The rigid holding apart of the executive and the legislative branches of the government, he maintained, had not worked for the great advantage of either. There had been much lost motion in the machinery due to the lack of co-operation and interchange of views, face to face, between the representatives of the executive and the members of the two legislative branches of the government. The functions of the two branches of government needed to be co-ordinated. He thought the presence of the members of the cabinet on the floor of each house would contribute greatly to the enactment of beneficial legislation.[100]

The proposition was hoary with age when presented by Taft and it was restated on subsequent occasions, but Congress never seriously considered its adoption. As a matter of fact, however, although members of the cabinet do not have access to the floors of the two houses, they appear frequently and testify at length before congressional committees, in which much of the important work of legislation is done. So adequate are their facilities for presenting information and opinions concerning pending legislation that there is probably little desire on their part for the opportunity Taft sought to secure for them.

### THE JUDICIARY

Inefficiency existed in the judiciary as well as in the executive branch of the government. In 1911, Congress passed an act "to codify, revise, and amend the laws relating to the judiciary." [101] An important change made by the same statute was the abolition of the circuit courts. There had been duplication of work between the circuit courts and districts courts, and the line of jurisdiction between them was poorly defined. The records of the circuit courts and the suits pending before them were transferred to the district courts. Thereafter the federal judicial system proper consisted of the Supreme Court, the circuit courts of appeals, and the district courts.

An important controversy took place over the scope of the jurisdiction of the Supreme Court to hear appeals from state courts. When the highest state court having jurisdiction upheld a state law alleged by one of the parties to violate the federal Constitution, that party had a right to appeal the constitutional question to the Supreme

---

[100] *Messages and Papers of the Presidents*, XVI, 7811-7813.      [101] 36 Stat. 1087.

Court, by a process technically known as a writ of error. If, on the other hand, the state court held that the state law violated the federal Constitution, the defeated party had no right of appeal to the Supreme Court. One result was the considerable disparity among the states as to liberal legislation that might be enforced. A regulatory measure might be upheld in the highest court of one state, for example, whereupon the case might be taken to the Supreme Court of the United States for redetermination. In another state, on the other hand, a more conservative court might hold an identical statute a violation of the federal Constitution. From such a decision there was no right of appeal.

The Progressive party took up this question in the midst of discussions of related issues, such as the recall of judicial decisions, and embodied in its platform the statement that there should be the same right of Supreme Court review of cases held unconstitutional by the state courts as of those held not to violate the Constitution. The statement called for a measure similar to one previously passed by the Senate with the active support of Senator Root, who had little in common with the Progressives.[102] The consideration of the subject, coupled with certain specific examples of extremely conservative interpretation of the Constitution by state courts,[103] resulted in 1914 in the enactment of a remedial measure.[104] The statute did not give the defeated party a full right of review in all cases in which state courts held state laws in conflict with the federal Constitution. It did give the Supreme Court the right to review such cases at its discretion by a process called the writ of certiorari. By the exercise of its discretion thereafter the Supreme Court was able to eliminate the most obvious disparities in interpretation of the federal Constitution by state courts.

SUPREME COURT PERSONNEL

Five members of the Supreme Court were replaced during the period of the Taft administration, an unusually large number for four years. Justice Brewer died after twenty years of staunch defense of the rights of liberty and property, in most matters a loyal counterpart of his uncle, Justice Field. Justice Moody resigned because of ill

---

[102] For contemporary discussion see W. F. Dodd, "Social Legislation and the Courts," *Political Science Quarterly*, XXVIII (March, 1913), 1.

[103] See for example Ives *v.* South Buffalo Railway Co., 2101 N.Y. 271 (1911), 94 N.E. 431.

[104] 38 Stat. 790.

health, before serving long enough to establish his influence. He seems to have provided Roosevelt with some of his materials for criticizing the conservatism of the courts.[105] Chief Justice Fuller died after twenty-two years on the Court, without bringing either distinction or discredit to himself or to the Court. Justice Harlan died after nearly thirty-four years in office. He had written seven hundred and three opinions for the Court, and dissented in three hundred and sixteen cases.[106] He had a religious reverence for the Constitution and supreme confidence in his own interpretation of it. He delivered sharp dissenting opinions with great vigor in many cases. Justice Holmes seems to have regarded him as something of a relic of the past: "He is the last of the tobacco-spittin' judges." [107]

The Taft appointments to the Court, taken as a whole, were neither better nor worse than those of most of his predecessors. As might be expected, none of the five new members was radical in his leanings. All except Charles E. Hughes, then and thereafter the most distinguished of the group, had had judicial experience. The first of the Taft appointees, Horace H. Lurton, of Tennessee, had been a Confederate soldier; a professor of law at Vanderbilt University; and later, as a federal circuit judge, one of Taft's associates. The President appointed him, even though he was sixty-six years of age, the most advanced age at which a man had ever been appointed to the Supreme Court. He served less than five years. It is said that he had little sympathy with the adjustment of law to changed conditions through judicial interpretation.[108]

Hughes had won favorable notoriety as counsel for the Armstrong Investigating Committee in New York, which revealed great abuses in the life-insurance field, and had served two terms as governor of New York. He was considered a possibility for the presidency as well as for the Supreme Court. Henry Cabot Lodge thought the appointment excellent, remarking that "he takes the Marshall and not the Taney view of the Constitution." [109] Roosevelt, then in Africa, also thought the nomination excellent. He said further:

> I only hope that he has awakened to the fact that unless we are content to face disaster to the judiciary in the future, there must be

[105] See *Roosevelt-Lodge Correspondence*, II, 391.

[106] *Dictionary of American Biography*, VIII, 269-272.

[107] Silas Bent, *Justice Oliver Wendell Holmes* (1932), p. 19.

[108] *Dictionary of American Biography*, XI, 509-510; Pringle, *op. cit.*, I, 530-531.

[109] *Roosevelt-Lodge Correspondence*, II, 378.

a very radical change in the attitude of our judges to public questions. I verily believe that the conduct of the bench, in failing to
move with the times, and in continually sticking on minor points of
the law rather than turning to broad principles of justice and equity,
is one of the chief elements in producing the present popular discontent. I do hope Hughes will realize this.[110]

Hughes's first period on the Supreme Court was to terminate in 1916
when he resigned to become the Republican candidate for the presidency.

Willis Van Devanter had been chief justice of the Wyoming
supreme court, a law officer in the Department of the Interior, and a
United States circuit judge. He served until 1937, aligning himself
with the most conservative faction on the Court. Joseph R. Lamar,
of Georgia, had been a member of the legislature and of the supreme
court of his state. He sat on the Supreme Court of the United States
from 1910 until 1916, a period too short for him to win distinction
even had there been prospect of his winning it. Perhaps his most
discussed opinion was in the case of Gompers *v.* Bucks Stove and
Range Company,[111] in which the enjoining of a boycott was upheld,
but Samuel Gompers and other labor leaders were relieved on procedural grounds from punishment for disobedience.

Mahlon Pitney, of New Jersey, had been a member of Congress, the
state legislature, and the state supreme court, and chancellor of the
state. His leanings, during more than ten years on the Supreme
Court of the United States, were strongly conservative.

Chief Justice Fuller died in the summer of 1910, before Hughes
had taken his seat as a member of the Court. Hughes had been
selected with the thought that he might be promoted to the chief
justiceship.[112] Members of the Court preferred Justice White.[113] For
this and perhaps other reasons Taft disregarded the precedent of selecting the Chief Justice from without the Court and elevated White to
the position of leadership.[114]

While Hughes was of Taft's own party, White was a Democrat with
a record of Confederate military service. It has been suggested that
the appointment was in the nature of an attempt to break the solid
hold of the Democratic party upon the South. However that may be,

---

[110] *Ibid.*, p. 380.        [111] 221 U.S. 417 (1911).

[112] Pringle, *op. cit.*, I, 532-533.        [113] *Ibid.*, pp. 534-535.

[114] Justice William Cushing had been offered the position of Chief Justice in 1796, but
had declined. Charles Warren, *The Supreme Court in United States History* (rev. ed.,
2 vols., 1926), I, 139-140.

the position was put in the hands of a man essentially conservative in his thinking, whose literary style was so indirect and difficult that large numbers of Court opinions written by him are intelligible only after intense and detailed scrutiny. The course of history might have been greatly different had Taft done otherwise. White lived just long enough to permit another Republican President to appoint Taft himself as White's successor. Had Hughes been appointed originally, and found the office so attractive as to preclude resignation to become a candidate for the presidency, Taft himself would have had no chance at the office. Had Hughes resigned from the chief justiceship, as he did resign as associate justice, it is hardly probable that President Wilson would have made Taft Chief Justice in his place.

# CHAPTER 25

# WOODROW WILSON AND THE NEW FREEDOM

THE TEMPORARY SECESSION of the progressive element from the Republican party, along with Theodore Roosevelt himself and a substantial portion of his personal following, helped to make Woodrow Wilson President. The party rift had been developing since the period of the Roosevelt administration. Roosevelt, as President, had known how to use both the conservative and the progressive elements in Congress without fully committing himself to either. Taft, on the other hand, had allowed himself to be driven into the conservative camp, and he ceased, in effect, to be the leader of the party as a whole. His inability to maintain picturesque and effective leadership doubtless had much to do with the fact that his party lost control in Congress. When it lost that control, it was unable to enact party measures, while the rift within the party stood in the way of any program of important social significance. When he was unable to resume leadership of the party, Roosevelt sought to recapture the presidency by assuming leadership of the newly organized Progressive party, whose original leaders were La Follette, Cummins, and others, rather than Roosevelt. He carried with him enough votes to crowd Taft into third place in the presidential race, without being able to win for himself. In effect, Wilson owed his election to Roosevelt.

It was clear that Wilson, like Roosevelt, with whom he had formerly been on friendly terms and whom he had admired, would be a strong President. In his *Congressional Government,* published in 1885, he had deplored the growth of congressional despotism and the gradual eclipse of the presidency. He was disposed to think "that the decline in the character of the Presidents is not the cause, but only the accompanying manifestation, of the declining prestige of the presidential office. That high office has fallen from its first estate of dignity because its power has waned; and its power has waned because the power of Congress has become predominant." [1] His concep-

[1] Woodrow Wilson, *Congressional Government* (1885), p. 43.

tion of the kind of man needed in the presidency was indicated in his *Constitutional Government in the United States,* published in 1908:

> A man who will be and who will seem to the country in some sort an embodiment of the character and purpose it wishes its government to have — a man who understands his own day and the needs of the country, and who has the personality and the initiative to enforce his views both upon the people and upon Congress.[2]

As president of Princeton University he had been a dominant, driving executive, with complete confidence in his own ideas and in his program.   The same was true of him as governor of New Jersey. It was to be no less true of him as President of the United States.   In 1915, recalling in a Jackson Day address that Andrew Jackson had thought every man who disagreed with him an enemy of the country, Wilson remarked, perhaps facetiously, but yet with an element of truth, "I have never got quite that far in my thought, but I have ventured to think that they did not know what they were talking about." [3]   As a recent precedent for vigorous leadership in the presidency, he had the experience of Roosevelt.   He would have been a strong leader, however, even if there had been no such precedent.

As a token of the type of leadership in prospect, he revived a custom, defunct since its abandonment by Thomas Jefferson, of appearing before Congress in person to deliver messages at the beginning of each session.   This calm departure from the customs of the intervening century, in which the separation of the presidency and the legislature had been emphasized by the formality of their relations, served to focus the eyes of the nation upon him.   He made it the occasion of a friendly gesture toward the legislative body from which he was to ask sweeping measures.   He said:

> I am very glad indeed to have this opportunity to address the two houses directly and to verify for myself the impression that the President of the United States is a person, not a mere department of the government hailing Congress from some isolated island of jealous power, sending messages, not speaking naturally and with his own voice — that he is a human being trying to co-operate with other human beings in a common service.[4]

The gesture made a good impression.   Mrs. Wilson remarked that it was the kind of thing Roosevelt would have liked to do had he

---

[2] Woodrow Wilson, *Constitutional Government in the United States* (1908), p. 65.
[3] *Messages and Papers of the Presidents,* XVII, 8033.        [4] *Ibid.,* XVI, 7871.

thought of it. "Yes," said the President, "I think I put one over on Teddy." [5]

The program of the Wilson administration was organized in terms of his conception of the "New Freedom." [6] The conception seems never to have been clearly defined. It apparently applied to a régime wherein the small and weak lived and acted without fear and without danger in the presence of the great and powerful. It meant an end of special privilege for the strong. It implied a reduction of tariffs and the enactment of laws to curb predatory activities of great corporations, without necessarily destroying corporations or breaking them up merely because they happened to be large. An appraisal of the policy obviously had to depend on the specific measures supported under it. Except, perhaps, for indicating broader interference of government with the use of property, it was not essentially different from the "Square Deal" of Theodore Roosevelt. It was much less drastic than the later "New Deal" of Franklin D. Roosevelt. Apart from tariff legislation, three important statutes enacted during the first two years of the Wilson administration reveal the outlines of the program. They were the Federal Reserve Act,[7] the Federal Trade Commission Act,[8] and the Clayton Anti-Trust Act.[9]

### THE FEDERAL RESERVE ACT

In the narrow sense of the word the enactment of the Federal Reserve Act did not involve important questions of constitutionality. Rather, perhaps, it should be said that the measure did not involve important questions of unconstitutionality.[10] In a broader sense, however, the subject involved important problems of constitutional development. More and more, the money power of the country was

[5] Ray Stannard Baker, *Woodrow Wilson, Life and Letters* (8 vols., 1927-1939), IV (1931), 109.

[6] See Woodrow Wilson, *The New Freedom* (1913).

[7] 38 Stat. 251.    [8] 38 Stat. 717.    [9] 38 Stat. 730.

[10] It had long since been determined that Congress had the power to establish national banks and, pursuant to their charters, to regulate their operations. It had been established that Congress had the power to authorize the issue of paper money and to make it legal tender in the payment of debts. It had been established that Congress, pursuant to its power to establish banks and regulate the currency, might by taxation drive issues of state bank notes out of existence. (See chapter 16.) The great need remaining was for co-ordination among the national banks and for greater flexibility in note issues so that the needs of business could be met in times of strain and so that money might not lie idle in particular communities when not needed there or when needed elsewhere. It was not doubted that Congress had the constitutional power to modify the national banking system in such a way as to bring about the greater flexibility if workable means could be discovered.

centering in New York. Should Congress enact a measure which would further strengthen the hold of Wall Street over the credit facilities of the country? Should Congress bring about co-ordination of the national banks by creating a superbank, a great bankers' bank, controlled nominally by all national banks, but in effect by the most powerful of such banks? In attempts to secure the efficiencies achieved in European countries by strong centralization, should Congress return to something resembling the early Banks of the United Stat:s, which had shown up well in theory, but had gone aground because of seemingly inevitable entanglements with politics? Could and should Congress establish central control of banking, not by banking interests, but by government? Free as they were from issues of unconstitutionality, these questions were fundamental in any inquiry as to the direction in which the Constitution was to develop. For more than two decades the government had been attempting under the commerce clause to curb the abuses of great corporations, and to break up the trusts or, at any rate, the "bad" ones. Yet a great money trust, so-called, had been created, which, though not a formally organized trust within the meaning of the Sherman Act, extended its control over credit and the circulatory medium. Should government attack the money trust? Should it go farther than merely negative action and establish positive control in the banking field, as it was beginning to do over the railroads of the country? These were real and vital constitutional questions.

In 1908, after the brief panic period of 1907, Congress enacted the Aldrich-Vreeland Act,[11] which somewhat expanded the power to issue currency by allowing issue by associations of national banks known as National Currency Associations. Because it was understood that this and related provisions did not go to the heart of the problem, however, the same act provided for a National Monetary Commission including members of both houses of Congress. The commission, presided over by Senator Aldrich, of Rhode Island, was to explore the subject thoroughly. It made extensive studies at home and abroad and presented to Congress the Aldrich bill, proposing the establishment of a central bank with little government control.

The conservative faction in Congress was in eclipse toward the end of the Taft administration, and the House had come under Democratic control. The Aldrich bill suffered the unpopularity of its sponsors. Many other monetary measures were proposed during the

[11] 35 Stat. 546.

same period. The Pujo investigation of the money trust, for the House of Representatives, aided in stimulating popular interest. The platform of the Democratic party opposed the Aldrich plan for a central bank, but carried no definite statement of program. The measure to be supported by the administration, therefore, remained to be worked out after it had come into power.

On June 23, 1913, President Wilson made his second personal appearance before the two houses of Congress, to ask the enactment of banking legislation. It was absolutely imperative, he said, "that we should give the businessmen of this country a banking and currency system by means of which they can make use of the freedom of enterprise and of individual initiative which we are about to bestow upon them." Businessmen were about to be set free through removal of the trammels of the protective tariff.

> What will it profit us to be free if we are not to have the best and most accessible instrumentalities of commerce and enterprise? What will it profit us to be quit of one kind of monopoly if we are to remain in the grip of another and more effective kind? . . . The tyrannies of business, big and little, lie within the field of credit.

He stated as follows the principles to govern action:

> We must have a currency, not rigid as now, but readily, elastically responsive to sound credit, the expanding and contracting credits of everyday transactions, the normal ebb and flow of personal and corporate dealings. Our banking laws must mobilize reserves; must not permit the concentration anywhere in a few hands of the monetary resources of the country or their use for speculative purposes in such volume as to hinder or impede or stand in the way of other more legitimate, more fruitful uses. And the control of the system of banking and of issue which our new laws are to set up must be public, not private, must be vested in the government itself, so that the banks may be the instruments, not the masters, of business and of individual enterprise and initiative.[12]

In this statement of principles is the essence of the federal reserve system that was soon to be established.[13] Congress did not provide for one bankers' bank, a central bank which might have been dominated from New York, but for twelve regional bankers' banks. To these regional banks, called federal reserve banks, was transferred the func-

---

[12] *Messages and Papers of the Presidents*, XVI, 7879-7881.
[13] 38 Stat. 251. See William O. Weyforth, *The Federal Reserve Board* (1933).

tion, which the national banks had hitherto possessed, of putting into circulation notes to be used as money.   The federal reserve banks were to promote elasticity of credit by rediscounting the sound securities on which member banks had made loans, thereby liberating the resources of the national banks for making further loans.   By raising or lowering the rate for rediscounting the securities held by member banks, it was expected that the federal reserve banks would be able to stimulate business through low interest rates when stimulation was needed, and to bring about contraction by means of high interest rates when overexpansion was threatened.   By open-market operations — purchase and sale of rediscountable paper and other securities in the open market — the federal reserve banks were to be further able to influence the amount of money in circulation at a given time.

A Federal Reserve Board was created to supervise the activities of the federal reserve banks, the issue of federal reserve notes, and many other matters.   Whereas the federal reserve banks were owned by the member banks, in the sense that the capital was subscribed by them, the Federal Reserve Board was a government agency.   It consisted of five members, appointed by the President with the advice and consent of the Senate, and the Secretary of the Treasury and the comptroller of the currency as members *ex officio*.   The board of directors of each federal reserve bank was to select a member of a Federal Advisory Council, which was to have the power to confer with and advise the board and to call for information concerning banking and monetary activities over which the board had control.

The establishment of the Federal Reserve Board, with its wide powers over banking and currency matters, marked another significant development, both of government powers and of government agencies, for exercising constitutional powers.   The position of the board was similar in some respects to that of the Interstate Commerce Commission.   It was a powerful regulatory agency not directly connected with any government department.   To a lesser degree than the commission, it cut across the traditional lines of separation of powers.   It represented the adaptation of government to a régime wherein the control of business activity arose above the level of private management and centered in government hands.   Although the system had to be strengthened in later years, its establishment at the time was a most fortunate event, for it enabled the credit structure of the country to undergo without injury the strain of World-War disturbance.

THE FEDERAL TRADE COMMISSION ACT AND THE CLAYTON ACT

On January 20, 1914, President Wilson appeared before the two houses of Congress to ask additional legislation for the control of trusts and monopolies. Among other things he asked that the meaning of anti-trust legislation be clarified, that an interstate trade commission be created, and that interlocking directorates and other corporation abuses be prohibited.[14] Strong sentiment in favor of such legislation already existed. In spite of the assertion of former President Taft and others that common-law definitions provided the courts with a certain guide as to what conduct was in unreasonable restraint of trade, it was widely felt that the concept of reasonableness left too much power of interpretation in the hands of the courts and that Congress ought to give specific content to the law.

There had also been for some years sentiment for the creation of some kind of interstate trade commission. Reasons and contemplated purposes varied greatly. An indefinite, but nevertheless probably very real, reason for interest in the subject was the fact that an independent regulatory commission seemed now to be working out well in the domain of railroad corporations, and it was felt, whether logically or not, that an agency adequate for handling the railroads would also be a good thing for the regulation of other corporations engaged in interstate commerce. Advocates of federal incorporation or federal licensing of interstate corporations thought there should be a commission to handle the business. When it was discovered that the decrees entered in the oil and tobacco cases had not resulted in the restoration of competition and the reduction of prices as contemplated, a commission was advocated to aid in working out satisfactory decrees and to superintend their subsequent enforcement. For effective regulation more facts of various kinds about the activities of corporations were needed. A commission was thought to be the proper agency for finding the facts.

True, established departments of the government were already trying to do much of the work contemplated. The Bureau of Corporations in the Department of Commerce had proved an efficient fact-gathering agency, and its reports on the several industries and on the effectiveness of present regulation were received with respect. The bureau had not the prestige of an independent regulatory commission, however, and had no powers beyond the finding of facts. Furthermore, its position in a department caused some jealousy during

[14] *Messages and Papers of the Presidents*, XVII, 7913-7918.

the Roosevelt administration which prevented effective co-operation with the Department of Justice. The latter department was also engaged extensively in gathering facts bearing upon violations of the Anti-Trust Act and in working out and studying the operations of decrees intended to prevent future violations. Like other departments, it was a political organization, however, and was supposed to be subject to political influence in the enforcement of law. Its politically chosen officials held office for only short periods of time, so that continuity of policy was hard to maintain. It was thought that a non-political commission, of officials chosen for long terms, would function better and have more prestige than the department.

The Wilson message was followed by the enactment of two measures, the Federal Trade Commission Act and the Clayton Anti-Trust Act. The former provided for an independent regulatory commission bearing superficially a strong resemblance to the Interstate Commerce Commission. It was to be composed of five commissioners, appointed by the President with the advice and consent of the Senate. Not more than three were to be members of the same political party. The Bureau of Corporations was abolished and its functions and equipment were transferred to the commission, which was empowered to make investigations on its own initiative, and at the request of Congress, or the President, or the Attorney General. The courts might call on it for aid in working out decrees. The power did not extend to banks and common carriers, which were subject to the jurisdiction of the Federal Reserve Board and the Interstate Commerce Commission respectively.

The principal innovation of the act appeared in section 5. This section outlawed unfair methods of competition, and empowered the Federal Trade Commission to issue cease-and-desist orders against such methods and to seek enforcement of the orders in the courts. The first World War delayed the development of the commission's work in this field, and the story of the development of administrative law and the whittling-down of the commission's powers by the courts belongs to a later period. The investigatory work was greatly expanded because of the war, however. Elaborate cost-of-production studies were made, particularly in connection with commodities subject directly or indirectly to price regulation. A member of the commission was a member of the price-fixing committee of the War Industries Board, and the commission had a share in the formulation of economic policies during the war.

The Clayton Act prohibited interlocking corporation directorates under certain circumstances, and a number of specific practices, such as tying agreements and price discriminations, many of which the courts had already held illegal under the Sherman Act.   The Federal Trade Commission was given certain powers of enforcement under the act.   No attempt was made to enumerate all the types of conduct which might constitute anti-trust violations or to define unreasonable restraint of trade.   The courts, therefore, retained broad powers for determining the conduct which constituted violations of the laws. The new legislation yielded much less than had been hoped for it in some quarters.[15]

ANTI-TRUST LAW ENFORCEMENT

The first Attorney General under President Wilson was James Clark McReynolds, of Tennessee.   He resigned in 1914, when he was appointed to the Supreme Court.   He had been an assistant attorney general during the Roosevelt administration, and subsequently special counsel in the tobacco-trust cases.   His connection with Wilson liberalism seems to have been his effectiveness in anti-trust prosecutions. He assumed direction of the Department of Justice without notable change in policy.   Wickersham, his predecessor, had developed the procedure of curtailing anti-trust prosecutions by means of consent decrees, framed in terms satisfactory to the department and agreed to by those accused of violating the anti-trust laws.   These decrees were submitted to federal courts to be entered as if they were the outcome of actual litigation.   Both parties thereby avoided long periods of expensive litigation.   McReynolds continued to make use of consent decrees.

He also settled cases by informal agreements not submitted to courts for sanction.   Perhaps the most notable of these was the Kingsbury Agreement, as a result of which the American Telephone and Telegraph Company divested itself of control of the Western Union Telegraph Company and the government dropped an anti-trust action.   Such agreements were binding upon the Attorney General only in a moral sense, and were perhaps not binding on his successors at all.

[15] Additional legislation during the Wilson administration affecting the anti-trust law enforcement included the anti-dumping provisions of the Revenue Act of 1916 (39 Stat. 756, 798); the Shipping Act of 1916 (39 Stat. 728, 733); and the Webb Export Trade Act of 1918 (40 Stat. 516), which exempted from the anti-trust laws certain forms of combination in export trade.

Some observers thought the technique of the consent decree had possibilities approaching blackmail, in that the Attorney General, working behind closed doors, could coerce corporations by threat of costly litigation.   Philander C. Knox, a former occupant of the office, thought it a radical and dangerous power that the Attorney General was now exercising in relation to the business of the country, "that of accepting confessions and granting indulgences upon his own notions of the meaning and purposes of the law." [16]   William A. Day, who had been an assistant attorney general under Knox, wrote:

> I know Mr. McReynolds to be an able and honest man; but no man can be trusted with such vast autocratic powers.   In the nature of things perspective is gradually lost, because the exercise of power intoxicates.   The consideration of the probable ultimate effect of the establishment of such power in the hands of an administrative, non-judicial officer should give rise to grave concern.   He holds his confessional in secret; the public knows nothing of the crimes condoned or the duress to which he subjects men of property.[17]

[16] Philander C. Knox, in a draft of an opinion addressed to H. C. Frick, January 12, 1914, Knox Papers, Library of Congress.

[17] Day to Knox, January 13, 1914, *ibid.*
The resort to informal agreements as to future conduct, as a result of which prosecution for past offenses would be abandoned, did not result in the anticipated developments.   Further use of the technique may have been prevented by sharp criticism, or by the retirement of Attorney General McReynolds.   The resort to formal consent decrees has been subject to a measure of criticism of the same kind.   Although they are court decrees, they are worked out by the Department of Justice and accepted by the organizations to which they apply, and the courts accept them without hearing formal arguments on the issues.   Acceptance of the decrees is often the alternative to expensive litigation in either injunction or criminal cases.   See Carl Brent Swisher (ed.), *Selected Papers of Homer Cummings* (1939), pp. 240 ff.; *New York Times*, January 12, 23, 25, 26, 31, February 16, 1938.
On the other hand, because of the vagueness of the law, corporations are often ignorant as to the legality or illegality of their conduct, and welcome a technique by which their rights may be discovered.   A consent decree is negative in action and does not tell what may be done, but practically, when the Department of Justice has joined with corporation counsel in working out a consent decree in lieu of litigation, counsel at least gets a fair idea as to what may be done pending a change in administration. Throughout the period of serious attempt to enforce the anti-trust laws there has been demand for a technique or a special agency from which the legality of a proposed line of conduct could be determined in advance.   Some thought, indeed, that the Federal Trade Commission might perform such a function.   Unfortunately, it has not been possible to work out satisfactory formal arrangements.   The Department of Justice has feared to grant assurance as to the legality of formally presented schemes, because a line of conduct must be seen in action rather than on paper before all its implications are clear.   Furthermore, as a result of a variety of experience, the department has learned the ability of private counsel to conceal hidden conduct behind innocent phrases.   The only concession thus far made by the government has been to agree informally to resort only to suits in equity and refrain from criminal actions against firms which present proposed combinations to the Department of Justice for advance consideration.

The Taft administration had left on the dockets of the federal courts large numbers of anti-trust cases. The Wilson administration prosecuted and instituted others. Henry Cabot Lodge accused the Department of "assaulting corporations without any distinction as to whether they are good or bad; whether they are violating the law or trying to live up to it," and of "hitting at everything in an unintelligent way." [18] What the outcome would have been had there been no world war, it is impossible to predict. Except for ineffectual attempts to curb the activities of profiteers, anti-trust activity was largely suspended during the period of the war. A motion was made in the Supreme Court to suspend action in cases involving combinations in shoe machinery, farm machinery, steel, kodaks, and other products. The reason given was that, if the government won the cases, a great deal of private financing of the defeated corporations would be required, and this financing would compete with the flotation of government loans for war purposes.[19]

## THE RIGHTS OF LABOR

President Wilson had the warm support of organized labor. It was fortunate that this was true, for a number of important labor problems, some of them of constitutional significance, arose during the period of his administration. A full-fledged Department of Labor was established, with William B. Wilson, a former labor leader, as Secretary. President Wilson advocated and signed the Newlands Act,[20] to provide for a board of mediation as an aid in settling the disputes of railroad labor. Unlike his predecessor, he signed an appropriation bill with a provision forbidding the use of funds for enforcement of anti-trust laws against labor. As a result of agitation by labor interests, important provisions were included in the Clayton Act which were thought to relieve labor in large measure from the operation of the anti-trust laws. Samuel Gompers, the outstanding labor leader of the time, called the measure "the industrial Magna Charta upon which the working people will rear their structure of industrial freedom." [21] Unfortunately for labor, court decisions in the post-war period greatly narrowed the interpretation of the act.[22]

A controversy over the use of federal troops to suppress disorder in a labor dispute arose in Colorado in 1913 in a serious strike against

[18] *Roosevelt-Lodge Correspondence* (2 vols., 1925), II, 446.
[19] Homer Cummings and Carl McFarland, *Federal Justice* (1937), p. 347.
[20] 38 Stat. 103.    [21] Cummings and McFarland, *op. cit.*, p. 445.    [22] See chapter 32.

the Colorado Fuel and Iron Company, which was controlled by the Rockefeller family.   The strike was over union recognition, hours and wages, and other matters.   Violence became so widespread that Colorado militia proved unable to cope with it.   On April 28, 1914, at the request of the governor of the state, President Wilson sent federal troops into the area, acting pursuant to the provision of the Constitution that the United States should protect the states against domestic violence, on application of the executive of the state made when the legislature could not be convened.[23]   Wilson informed the governor that the action was only temporary and that the state must assume the burden of preserving order.   He wrote to Rockefeller that it was "not the duty of the United States to take the place of the state authorities as a police force, but merely its duty to secure the state against insurrection until the state sees its way clear to resume its sovereign authority."[24]   Under orders from Washington the troops set out to disarm both the miners and the privately employed mine guards and to prevent the importation of strike-breakers.   The attitude was very different from that of the Cleveland administration at the time of the Pullman strike, when suppression of the strike was the chief aim.[25]   President Wilson saw the necessity of putting an end to armed strife, but he was evidently determined that federal troops should not be used to defeat the strike itself.

When the state proved slow to assume the difficult and expensive task of preserving order, Wilson notified the governor that the troops were there only until the state could resume sovereignty and control.   "I cannot conceive that the state is willing to forego her sovereignty or to throw herself entirely upon the government of the United States, and I am quite clear that she has no constitutional right to do so when it is within the power of her legislature to take effective action."[26]   He said later that the troops had been sent with the expectation that their stay would be brief, adding, "I am very doubtful of my constitutional right to maintain them there indefinitely."[27]   Early in 1915, state troops began the replacement of federal troops, and the latter were gradually withdrawn.   In 1916, after a long period of unsuccessful efforts, mediators selected by the federal government were able to bring about the termination of the strike.

In other connections than in the use of troops the federal government guarded itself against becoming a partisan of employers in con-

[23] Article IV, Section 4.        [24] Baker, *op. cit.*, IV, 389.        [25] See chapter 19.
[26] Baker, *op. cit.*, IV (1931), 389-390.        [27] *Ibid.*, IV, 390.

troversies with labor. It refused to prosecute contempt cases in which private litigants had secured injunctions against labor. "Is it not better," asked the solicitor general, "that reliance should be placed in the future as in the past upon the readiness of parties in interest to bring to the attention of the court any acts of disobedience and the willingness of the judges to do their duty by enforcing the orders which they enter?" [28] In spite of protests, the Department of Justice persisted in its refusal to take responsibility for contempt cases except where criminal contempts were involved.[29] Closely related was the matter of the appointment of federal deputy marshals to preserve order where injunctions had been issued by federal courts. Many employers and some judges felt that the government should provide staff to enforce court orders, even when not issued at the request of the government. The Department of Justice took the position that it had no constitutional power to appoint deputies to protect private property merely because a federal court had issued an injunction against interference with such property, explaining that the government had no right to protect property unless it was in some sense *in custodia legis,* as in the instance of a federal receivership.[30]

### THE ADAMSON ACT

A serious labor struggle was threatened in 1916 when the railroad brotherhoods made a drive for an eight-hour day, with time and a half for overtime.[31] The increase of business due to the war in Europe and the consequent scarcity of labor added strength to labor's bargaining power, but the employers refused to yield. Realizing the disastrous results likely to flow from a nation-wide railroad strike, President Wilson intervened. The railroads agreed to arbitrate, but the employees refused. Wilson then urged the adoption of the eight-hour day, but the railroads refused. When the strike was announced for Labor Day, September 4, 1916, they prepared to defend them-

[28] Davis to A. Leo Weil, November 25, 1913, Department of Justice File 169497.

[29] Cummings and McFarland, *op. cit.,* pp. 445-446.

[30] The files of the Department of Justice indicate that in some cases receiverships were resorted to as a means of securing government protection for property involved in labor controversies. Of course the subterfuge aggravated the controversies.

In one important controversy, mine-owners sued the United Mine Workers for triple damages under the anti-trust laws. After thirteen years the litigation resulted in an agreement to pay a relatively small sum. The case established the fact that incorporated organizations such as labor unions could be sued in federal courts. United Mine Workers *v.* Coronado Coal Co., 259 U.S. 344 (1922). See Edward Berman, *Labor and the Sherman Act* (1930), pp. 119 ff.

[31] See Berman, *Labor Disputes and the President* (1924), pp. 106 ff.

selves.  Roads in good financial standing and the receivers of roads in the custody of federal courts alike appealed for the appointment of federal deputy marshals for the protection of property, or for the deputizing of trusted employees in order that they might have the sanction of the government back of their defense of railroad property.  The government refused to take such action.  Marshals, on making inquiry, were told that they were not police officers, and it was no part of their duty to guard private property, railroad or otherwise, within a state.  Their only duties in such cases arose on definite orders from courts having receivership property in custody, when protection might be given through the appointment of deputies strictly responsible to the marshals and paid by the courts out of the property held.[32]

The President made a personal appeal to Congress.  Discussing the sweeping character of the threatened strike, he warned that

> cities will be cut off from their food supplies, the whole commerce of the nation will be paralyzed, men of every sort and occupation will be thrown out of employment, countless thousands will in all likelihood be brought, it may be, to the very point of starvation, and a tragical national calamity brought on, to be added to the other distresses of the time, because no basis of accommodation or settlement has been found.[33]

An emergency measure, somewhat narrower than that advocated by Wilson, was quickly introduced and passed.  The measure, known as the Adamson Act,[34] provided that after January 1 ensuing, eight hours should be deemed a day's work on railroad common carriers, with certain limited exceptions.  The President was to appoint a commission to observe for from six to nine months the effect of the establishment of the eight-hour day.  During that period the same wage was to be paid for eight hours as had previously been paid for ten hours, and overtime was to be paid for on a *pro-rata* basis.

Congress had no opportunity for careful consideration of the bill.  Most congressmen supporting it could have subscribed fully to the succinct statement of Senator Owen, "I shall support the House bill because it appears to be the most convenient means by which we may avoid the strike on Monday." [35]  Added reasons were pressure from the President and the fact that conduct would have to be accounted

[32] Cummings and McFarland, *op. cit.*, p. 452.
[33] *Messages and Papers of the Presidents*, XVII, 8145.
[34] 39 Stat. 721.        [35] 53 *Congressional Record* 13630.

for at the ensuing general election. There were outbursts of protest, such as that by Representative Bennett, of New York, who said,
"By this act today we take the first step away from the old democracy
of Thomas Jefferson and the federal policy of Alexander Hamilton to
the socialism of Karl Marx." [36]

A case was rushed up to the Supreme Court to test the constitutionality of the Adamson Act. It was argued on January 8, 1917.
Apparently the Court was unable to come to a decision. Railroad
labor, tired of waiting, again threatened to strike. On March 19,
under pressure from the President based on the imminence of war, the
railroads conceded the demands of labor.[37] On the same day the
Supreme Court handed down its decision in Wilson v. New.[38] By a
vote of five to four it held the Adamson Act constitutional. The
majority of the Court stated that the power to establish the eight-hour
day was beyond dispute. The difficulty was with the subject of fixing wages — for, in spite of the government's contention, the Court
held that the act was a wage-fixing measure in so far as it required
the payment of ten-hour wages for eight-hour employment.

The Court carefully avoided the position that wages generally, as
well as hours, might be fixed by the government. The wage relation
was "primarily private," said Chief Justice White, and the standard
was not "subject to be controlled or prevented by public authority." [39]

[36] *Ibid.*, p. 13580. As is usually true of emergency legislation enacted under pressure,
the constitutional issues were inadequately discussed. One representative did call attention to Coppage *v.* Kansas, 236 U.S. 1 (1915), decided a year and a half earlier, in which
the Supreme Court, three members dissenting, curbed the power of a state to interfere
with conditions of employment. A Kansas statute forbade employers to require as a
condition of employment an agreement not to become or remain a member of a labor
union. The Court held that the statute interfered with the liberty and property of
employers, in violation of the due-process clause of the Fourteenth Amendment. The
decision was based on Adair *v.* United States, 208 U.S. 161 (1908) — discussed in chapter
23 — in which a similar federal statute with reference to railroad employment was held
to violate the due-process clause of the Fifth Amendment. Neither of these cases was
in point as far as the Adamson Act was concerned, except as they showed the willingness
of a majority of the Court to use the Constitution to curb some types of government
interference with conditions of employment. Justice Holmes expressed his consistent
opposition to these decisions and to the Lochner decision which preceded them.

Senator Brandegee sought to distinguish rate regulation — which might be based on
the commerce clause because the business of the railroads was charged with a public
use — from regulation of wages. He suggested that wages, as distinguished from transportation rates, did not fall within the public-use concept. (53 *Congressional Record*
13614.) No adequate answer was made. Attention was called to the fact that regulations of conditions of employment had already been upheld by the courts, such as
employers'-liability, safety-appliance, and hours-of-service acts. The peculiar sanctity
thought by some to inhere in liberty of contract as to wages was not clearly discussed.

[37] Berman, *Labor Disputes and the President* (1924), pp. 118-119.
[38] 243 U.S. 332 (1917).       [39] *Ibid.*, p. 347.

But in an emergency in which the failure of employers and employees to agree upon a standard resulted in a dispute threatening to disrupt interstate commerce, Congress might establish a temporary standard as a legitimate regulation of interstate commerce. Justice McKenna, in a concurring opinion, remarked that the law might require permission to readjust wage rates. He thought the permission would be given if necessary. If not, "the law might encounter constitutional restriction." [40]

Justices Day and Pitney wrote long dissenting opinions, holding among other things that the act violated the due-process clause of the Fifth Amendment. Justice Van Devanter agreed with them. Justice McReynolds, until recently Wilson's Attorney General, wrote a brief dissent, saying he did not think such a measure a regulation of commerce "within the fair intendment of those words as used in the Constitution." [41] Voting silently with the majority were Justices Brandeis and Clarke, Wilson appointees, and Justice Holmes. The case was important beyond the immediate controversy both for its connection with the subject of wage-fixing and for its use of the indefinite conception of emergency as justifying resort to powers which could not otherwise be exercised. The country was now on the brink of war. Both subjects were soon again to be important.

STATE REGULATION OF HOURS AND WAGES

In the meantime two labor cases, one involving the power of a state to limit employment to ten hours a day in factories and mills and the other involving power to establish minimum wages for women and minors, were about to be decided by the Supreme Court. The laws were enactments of the state of Oregon, then the center of a great deal of liberal legislation. They had been upheld in the highest state court and the cases were argued before the Supreme Court of the United States early in 1916. Evidently the Court was divided on the cases. They were restored to the docket for reargument, perhaps in part because of an intervening change in personnel, involving the appointment of Justice Brandeis. Before the cases were reached again, another change in personnel took place, with the appointment of Justice Clarke.

The cases were reargued in January, 1917, some ten days after the argument of the validity of the Adamson Act in Wilson v. New, and, because of the similarity of issues with reference to hours and wages,

[40] *Ibid.*, p. 364.     [41] *Ibid.*, p. 388.

they must have been in mind when the Adamson-Act case was decided. They were formally decided three weeks after the Adamson-Act decision. Justice Brandeis had participated in the preparation of the briefs in the cases [42] and therefore did not participate in their decision. Felix Frankfurter, who more than twenty years later was himself appointed to the Court, took over the task of compiling the immense factual briefs used to demonstrate the need for the legislation. The briefs were of a type shown to be valuable in 1908 in the Muller case, which had to do with the regulation of hours for women only. [43]

The case involving hours of labor, Bunting v. Oregon, [44] created difficulties in that to a limited extent it also involved wages. It limited the day to ten hours, except that employment might run for thirteen hours on payment of time and a half for overtime. Opponents of the law urged that, even if there were justification for a limitation of hours, there was none for interference with wages. The Court upheld the law by a vote of five to three. Justice McKenna, for the Court, contended that the law was a bona-fide regulation of hours. Instead of following the Lochner case of 1905, which invalidated a law establishing a ten-hour day for work in bakeries, he ignored that case altogether, taking the position that persons challenging the law had not presented facts to rebut the presumption that the Oregon law was a legitimate police-power measure. Since no opinion was written by the dissenters, Chief Justice White and Justices Van Devanter and McReynolds, he was not required either to distinguish or to overrule the Lochner case. [45] The emphasis on the presumption of constitutionality until a measure was proved unconstitutional seemed to suggest a trend definitely more liberal than that followed by the Court a score of years earlier.

Stettler v. O'Hara, [46] involving minimum wages for women, was argued much as the Muller case had been, with the presentation of a great deal of factual evidence to show why it was necessary that women, as mothers of the race and as people in positions of unequal bargaining power, should have government aid in enforcing the right to a minimum wage if employed at all. The Court divided four to four. Although no record was published, it seems clear that the three

[42] Alpheus T. Mason, *Brandeis and the Modern State* (1936), p. 142.
[43] See chapter 23. This type of brief is often called a "Brandeis brief."
[44] 243 U.S. 426 (1917).　　　[45] For discussion of the Lochner case, see chapter 23.
[46] 243 U.S. 629 (1917).

justices who had thought the maximum-hours law unconstitutional also thought the minimum-wage law for women unconstitutional, and that they were joined by one justice who favored upholding the hours law. The particular case was affirmed by an equally divided Court, but the general issue of the constitutionality of minimum-wage legislation for women was left for determination after the "return to normalcy" in 1923,[47] and for redetermination in one of the New-Deal decisions of 1937.[48]

CHILD LABOR

The Congress which passed the Adamson Act passed about the same time an act to prohibit the shipment in interstate commerce of goods produced by child labor.[49]   In contrast with the Adamson Act, the provisions of the child-labor measure had been under discussion for many years and constitutional issues were debated at length. Most of the states already had laws which limited hours of employment of children or employment at night, but there was great lack of uniformity as among the states and enforcement was often lax.   A strong argument against more drastic legislation in each state was the fact that goods produced under this handicap must compete in the interstate market with goods produced in other states where such legislation did not exist.   Only uniform action by the states — which at the time seemed wholly impracticable — or action by the federal government could solve the problem.

The first serious effort to secure federal legislation was made by Senator Albert J. Beveridge, in 1906-1907.[50]   He presented a dramatic exposé of the evils of child labor in the United States, and urged that the sweeping power of Congress over interstate commerce was an adequate basis for federal legislation.   He faced economic opposition to interference with child employment, doctrinaire opposition to what was regarded as a socialistic measure, and constitutional arguments that the commerce clause did not justify legislation interfering in this manner with conditions of employment in manufacture.   He was hopelessly defeated in his attempt.   The House committee on the judiciary made a scathing report, criticizing the proposed bill on grounds of unconstitutionality.   It was not until 1916 that the report

[47] See chapter 32.
[48] See West Coast Hotel Co. *v.* Parrish, 300 U.S. 379 (1937), discussed in chapter 36.
[49] 39 Stat. 675.
[50] See Claude G. Bowers, *Beveridge and the Progressive Era* (1932), pp. 250-255, 264-266.

was discredited to some extent by the discovery that the chairman of the committee had been in consultation at the time with an officer of the National Association of Manufacturers with reference to campaign funds to bring about his re-election.[51]

Similar bills were introduced in Congress year after year thereafter,[52] and discussion of merits and constitutionality continued. People theretofore convinced that the Constitution provided no support began to have doubts.    Supreme Court decisions involving interstate commerce in lottery tickets, impure food and drugs, and women transported for immoral purposes suggested that analogies might be found for supporting prohibition of interstate shipment of goods produced by child labor, since in this case, as in the others, the cessation of commerce would at least reduce the extent of the evil.

In lectures delivered at Yale University, however, former President Taft took a contrary position:

> Bills have been urged upon Congress to forbid interstate commerce in goods made by child labor.  Such proposed legislation has failed chiefly because it was thought beyond the federal power.  The distinction between the power exercised in enacting the pure-food bill and that which would have been necessary in the case of the child-labor bill is that Congress in the former is only preventing interstate commerce from being a vehicle for conveyance of something that would be injurious to people at its destination, and it might properly decline to permit the use of interstate commerce for that detrimental result.  In the latter case Congress would be using its regulative power of interstate commerce not to effect any result of interstate commerce.  Articles made by child labor are presumably as good and useful as articles made by adults.  The proposed law is to be enforced to discourage the making of articles by child labor in the state from which the articles were shipped.  In other words, it seeks indirectly and by duress to compel the states to pass a certain kind of legislation that is completely within their discretion to enact or not.  Child labor in the state of the shipment has no legitimate or germane relation to the interstate commerce of which the goods thus made are to form a part, to its character, or to its effect.  Such an attempt of Congress to use its power of regulating such commerce to suppress the use of child labor in the state of shipment would be a clear usurpation of that state's rights.[53]

[51] 53 *Congressional Record* 3044-3045.

[52] See Raymond G. Fuller, *Child Labor and the Constitution* (1923), pp. 236 ff.

[53] William Howard Taft, *Popular Government* (1913), pp. 142-143, quoted, 53 *Congressional Record* 12066.

The Taft argument provided effective ammunition for the opposition.

The issue was sectional as well as economic and constitutional.   In many of the northern states legislation was adopted in spite of the opposition of employers, whereas in the South child-labor laws were less drastic or non-existent, and factories, unaffected by restrictive legislation, were springing up to compete with the factories of the North.   Perhaps because of the growth of southern competition under these circumstances, many of the northern conservatives withdrew their opposition to legislation that would tend to equalize the conditions of employment in favor of their constituents.   Southern congressmen led the opposition, contending that the measure was sectional and a violation of state rights.

As to the constitutional argument, Senator Borah contended that Congress could enact police regulations in any reasonable way connected with interstate commerce.[54]   Senator Works, in opposition, raised again and again the question, discussed by former President Taft, whether police regulations could be made to apply to conditions which preceded shipment in interstate commerce.   Most of the debaters, indeed, maintained a particularistic view of interstate commerce.   They talked in terms of the manufacture and shipment of particular articles rather than of the network of commercial relationships, and they thought of manufacture as something begun and completed before shipment began.   They did not discuss clearly the fact that the possibility of shipment provided stimulus for manufacture. Senator Cummins, for instance, answered Taft, not in terms of this fact, but by saying, "I can only suggest that the environment in which he lived and moved may have had something to do with his view respecting the power of Congress to enact a national child-labor law." [55]

Judge Cooley, whom Senator Overman called "one of the greatest lawyers and greatest text-writers who ever lived in this country," [56] was quoted again and again as saying that the legislature must never pass an act of which it had doubt as to the constitutionality.[57]   Senator Brandegee thought it unfair to the Supreme Court to vote for measures of doubtful constitutionality or probable unconstitution-

[54] 53 *Congressional Record* 12080 ff.      [55] *Ibid.*, p. 12276.      [56] *Ibid.*, p. 12196
[57] See Thomas M. Cooley, *Principles of Constitutional Law in the United States* (4th ed., 1931), pp. 198-199.   The position taken was essentially that taken by Taft and Root in connection with the admission of Arizona.   See chapter 24.

ality. The Court was deprived of its right to support from a coordinate branch of the government when it was forced to pass upon unconstitutional legislation, enacted in response to popular clamor. When the courts set aside such a measure, "All the journals of the country, the magazine writers and the 'uplifters,' a great many of whom deal in language and not in brains, who know nothing about the law, but are very versatile with epithets, denounce the Supreme Court and say it is time to haul it off the bench and have referendums and recalls and all that sort of thing." [58]

Senator Cummins scoffed at the professions of reluctance to pass this particular measure because of constitutional scruples. The real encroachments upon the Constitution, he contended, lay in the extension of the power of the President over Congress. "There has not been a single important measure passed by the Congress of the United States since the 4th day of March, 1913, that Congress has not felt his heavy hand upon it." It was generally known, he said, that "the Chief Executive has attempted, through every influence of which he is possessed, to absorb the legislative power of the government and to exercise it in connection with the administrative or executive power." By comparison he had no sympathy with forebodings about the constitutionality of a measure to curb child labor. [59]

The act was passed and was signed on September 1, 1916, to become effective a year later. Early in 1918, a case involving its constitutionality came up to the Supreme Court from the cotton-mill region of western North Carolina. By a vote of five to four the Supreme Court decided, in Hammer v. Dagenhart, [60] that the act was unconstitutional. Justice Day, speaking for the Court, followed the Taft argument that, in the cases where the prohibition of interstate commerce had been upheld, the purpose was to prevent the transportation from accomplishing harmful results. Here, in contrast, the goods to be shipped were harmless. [61] As for the need for uniform rules among the states, "the commerce clause was not intended to give to Congress a general authority to equalize such conditions." [62] The act attempted to regulate conditions of manufacture, which were under the control of the states and not of Congress. [63]

Justice Holmes wrote a vigorous dissenting opinion. The regula-

[58] 53 *Congressional Record* 12092-12093.

[59] *Ibid.*, p. 12276. President Wilson, like a number of other persons, had changed his mind about the constitutionality of federal child-labor legislation. For his earlier position see his *Constitutional Government in the United States* (1908), p. 179.

[60] 247 U.S. 251 (1918).     [61] *Ibid.*, pp. 271-272.     [62] *Ibid.*, p. 273.     [63] *Ibid.*, p. 276.

tion of interstate commerce, he demonstrated, could be carried even to the extent of prohibition. As for interference with the powers of the states, "I should have thought that the most conspicuous decisions of this Court had made it clear that the power to regulate commerce and other constitutional powers could not be cut down or qualified by the fact that it might interfere with the carrying out of the domestic policy of any state." [64]

The five-to-four decision again brought sharp criticism of the Court. It was said that the Department of Labor was flooded immediately thereafter with inquiries from employers as to whether they were now free to employ children in mines and factories.[65] Congress sought some new way to prevent the evil. Various expedients were suggested, such as prohibiting shipment of child-made goods into states which prohibited such labor, on the analogy of the Webb-Kenyon Act; denying the use of the mails to persons and concerns employing child labor; prohibiting child labor, under the war powers, for the period of the war; placing a heavy tax on child-made products; and initiating a constitutional amendment which would authorize the prohibition of child labor.

The decision made was to levy a tax on goods knowingly produced by child labor.[66] That act reached the Supreme Court in 1922, when Taft was Chief Justice. Although a number of regulatory tax measures had already been upheld by the Court, he viewed this measure as a regulation only, and not as a tax. "The case before us," he said, "cannot be distinguished from that of Hammer v. Dagenhart." [67] The act was a regulation of matters which were solely within the province of the state. Congress, giving up as hopeless the regulation of child labor without constitutional change, proposed to the states a child-labor amendment.[68] The process of ratification proved extremely slow, and in 1941 the Supreme Court rendered the amendment superfluous by overruling the case of Hammer v. Dagenhart.[69]

INCOME TAXES

Another element in the New Freedom was the shifting of tax burdens to the shoulders of those most able to pay. The Sixteenth Amendment, authorizing taxes on incomes from whatever source de-

---

[64] *Ibid.*, p. 278. Justices McKenna, Brandeis, and Clarke concurred in this dissent.
[65] 56 *Congressional Record* 7692.    [66] 40 Stat. 1057, 1138.
[67] Bailey *v.* Drexel Furniture Co., 259 U.S. 20, 39 (1922). Only Justice Clarke dissented.
[68] 43 Stat. 670.    [69] For discussion of the amendment, see chapter 29.

rived and without apportionment among the states, became a part of the Constitution in 1913. At the special session of that year, Congress enacted a measure "to reduce tariff duties and to provide revenue for the government, and for other purposes." [70] That act provided for a graduated income tax beginning at one per cent on incomes of single persons above three thousand dollars and of married persons above four thousand dollars.[71] The rates were increased in subsequent years, so that the income tax aided greatly in carrying the financial burdens of the war period.

The constitutionality of the act was attacked on various grounds, among them being the contention that the amendment dealt only with taxes on "incomes from whatever source derived," a term said not to describe the present law, which taxed some incomes but not others. In Brushaber v. Union Pacific Railroad Company[72] the Supreme Court unanimously upheld the act.[73]

TAXING SALARIES OF FEDERAL JUDGES

In 1920, the Court passed upon the constitutionality of an income tax on the salaries of federal judges. Article III, Section 1, of the Constitution provided that the compensation of federal judges should not be diminished during their continuance in office. Speaking for the Court in Evans v. Gore,[74] Justice Van Devanter quoted and cited widely to show the need for strict independence in the judiciary. He concluded that a tax on the salary of a judge, even though non-discriminatory, was a diminution of his salary, and therefore unconstitutional. He denied that the Sixteenth Amendment authorized the tax. Citing other cases decided since the amendment had become effective, he declared that it did not extend the taxing power to subjects not taxable before. Incomes "from whatever source derived" did not mean incomes from any and all sources. The language was intended merely to prevent consideration of the source of the income in deciding whether or not a tax should be classified as a direct tax.

---

[70] 38 Stat. 114.  [71] Ibid., p. 166.  [72] 240 U.S. 1 (1916).

[73] For judicial interpretation of "income" see Towne v. Eisner, 245 U.S. 189 (1918), and Eisner v. Macomber, 252 U.S. 189 (1920). For discussion of the latter case see Thomas Reed Powell, "Stock Dividends, Direct Taxes, and the Sixteenth Amendment," Columbia Law Review, XX (May, 1920), 536. The issues involved in taxing corporation surpluses and undivided profits are exceedingly complex, involving as they do a weakening of the profit motive and a possible cessation of business on which the prosperity of the country and the revenues of the government depend. See, for example, the corporate surplus taxes levied during the Franklin D. Roosevelt administration.

[74] 253 U.S. 245 (1920).

Alluding to the fears of Governor Hughes in 1910 that the amendment would extend the taxing power to new sources, specifically to income from state and municipal bonds, he referred to statements of persons who declared that such was not the purpose of the amendment.[75]

Justice Holmes dissented, with Justice Brandeis concurring. He thought that "To require a man to pay the taxes that all other men have to pay cannot possibly be made an instrument to attack his independence as a judge."[76] Furthermore, he thought the Sixteenth Amendment covered the case. "I do not see how judges can claim an abatement of their income tax on the ground that an item in their gross income is salary, when the power is given expressly to tax incomes from whatever source derived."[77] Nearly twenty years later the Court accepted the Holmes argument that such a tax was not an unconstitutional diminution of the salary of a federal judge. The decision turned on the interpretation of the original clause in the Constitution, however, and did not involve the Sixteenth Amendment.[78]

APPOINTMENTS TO THE SUPREME COURT

The criticism of the judiciary of the country as a barrier to social progress, which had been personalized and imbued with political emotion by Theodore Roosevelt and others during the period of the Taft administration, carried over into the Wilson administration as well.[79] Roosevelt and other writers continued their criticisms of the judiciary after the election of 1912, while more conservative spokesmen came to its defense. Like most argumentative discussions of the position of the courts in society, the controversy damaged the halo with which the judiciary had been endowed and emphasized the human character of the institution.[80] In 1912, Gustavus Myers shocked conventional admirers of the Supreme Court by the publication of a

[75] These statements are not such as to carry conviction that Congress or the people gave much thought to the matter, one way or another. See chapter 24.

[76] 253 U.S. 265.

[77] *Ibid.*, p. 267.

[78] O'Malley *v.* Woodrough, 307 U.S. 277 (1939).

[79] For citation and discussion of some of the important criticisms of judicial review in that period see Charles A. Beard, *The Supreme Court and the Constitution* (1912), pp. 1 ff.

[80] For a collection and somewhat biased interpretation of materials published see the report of a New York Bar Association committee "upon the duty of the courts to refuse to execute statutes in contravention of the fundamental law," Senate Doc. No. 941, 63d Cong., 3d sess.

socialist history of that institution,[81] picturing it as the staunch defender of the interests of leading capitalists. Charles A. Beard published in 1913 a book entitled *An Economic Interpretation of the Constitution of the United States.* His thesis, resembling that of the tenth article of *The Federalist,* was that at the time of the adoption of the Constitution a number of important economic interests existed in the country, such as real property, shipping, slaves, currency, and so on, and that, to preserve order and protect property, representatives of the varied property interests met and adopted a Constitution under which the federal government was established.

The discussion brought to the fore the fact that problems of constitutionality were not merely problems of law, but of economics and politics as well. It concentrated attention upon judicial personnel, which was regarded more and more as composed of statesmen, good or bad, rather than, as Senator Sutherland would have it,[82] passive mouthpieces of the law. Critics of judicial appointments, as well as the officials making them, began to stress more heavily the economic and social views of appointees.

In lectures published in 1908, before this particular period of controversy had begun, Woodrow Wilson praised the judiciary of the United States, including the practice of judicial review. He thought that in the main the choice of personnel had been well made. True, he said, "Every government is a government of men, not of laws, and of course the courts of the United States are no wiser or better than the judges who constitute them." [83] He expected judges to participate in the adaptation of law to new conditions. He seemed as much concerned lest they go too fast as that they might not move rapidly enough in making adjustments.

> What we should ask of our judges is that they prove themselves such men as can discriminate between the opinion of the moment and the opinion of the age, between the opinion which springs, a legitimate essence, from the enlightened judgment of men of thought and good conscience, and the opinion of desire, of self-interest, of impulse and impatience.[84]

Wilson's first opportunity to make an appointment to the Supreme Court came with the death of Justice Lurton in the summer of 1914. There is little evidence to show why he filled the position by moving

[81] Gustavus Myers, *History of the Supreme Court* (1912).     [82] See chapter 24.
[83] Wilson, *Constitutional Government in the United States* (1908), p. 165.
[84] *Ibid.,* p. 172.

his Attorney General, James Clark McReynolds, to the Supreme Court. McReynolds held few of the tenets of Wilson liberalism and immediately, and consistently thereafter, aligned himself with the most conservative element on the Court. Wilson said later that the appointment had been a great mistake.[85]

He weighed his second appointment more carefully. The opportunity came with the death of Justice Lamar, in January, 1916. He nominated Louis D. Brandeis, and secured confirmation of the appointment, though only after one of the hardest struggles that ever took place over the filling of such a position.

Brandeis was born in Louisville in 1856, the son of a Jewish manufacturer of Prague who had come to the United States at the time of the revolution of 1848. He worked his way through Harvard Law School, and graduated with first honors, when the authorities suspended the age rule to allow him to graduate at the age of twenty. By the time he was thirty he had a large and prosperous law practice in Boston, and was an intimate associate of the wealthy and cultured element in Boston society, and was well on the way to becoming a wealthy man himself.

Unlike his associates and his prosperous clients, however, he concerned himself with various movements in the public interest. He worked out and secured the establishment of a system of savings-bank insurance for people of low incomes; he interfered with the plans of public-utility magnates for acquiring wealth at the expense of the public; he fought railroad monopolies; he criticized the inefficiencies of big business; he gave his support to the passage of anti-trust legislation, and in other ways made himself obnoxious to conservative interests. On this aspect of his career, he was quoted as saying in 1915 that as a result of it: "If my wife had social ambitions, or if I wanted to join a club, or if I needed to borrow money at the bank, or if I should run for office, they would get me. Fortunately, we don't care for society; I am already a member of the clubs I like, I seem to be able to earn more money than I need, and I shall never seek public office." [86]

Both before and after becoming President, Wilson sought the counsel of Brandeis on trust legislation, currency, and labor problems. He wanted him for Attorney General, but found the opposition too

[85] Baker, *op. cit.*, VI (1937), 113.
[86] Hamilton Holt, "Just the Man for Judge," *Independent*, LXXXV (February 7, 1916), p. 185.

H. A. IRONSIDE
MEMORIAL LIBRARY

great.[87]  He may well have considered him for the first Supreme Court appointment, with the same result.   When the opportunity came for a second appointment, he sent the nomination to Congress.

The Brandeis prediction, that "they would get me" if he sought public office, proved to have foundation.  A flood of propaganda began with a protest from sixty-one prominent persons, many of them leading lawyers and citizens of Boston and vicinity, urging that Brandeis did not have the confidence of the bar or the public and that he was not fit for the position.[88]  Critics submitted petitions, letters, and personal testimony to the subcommittee of the Senate committee on the judiciary having the nomination in charge.   They accused Brandeis of mismanaging the affairs of clients and of damaging the interests of former clients through activities which he claimed to be in the public interest.   Trickery of various sorts was charged or implied. Fundamentally, the opposition boiled down to the charge that he was guilty of unprofessional conduct, and that, being an advocate in social causes and a crusader, he lacked judicial temperament.

After the specific accusations of misconduct failed to stand up under examination, the committee received a communication from six former presidents of the American Bar Association, William Howard Taft, Elihu Root, Joseph H. Choate, Simeon E. Baldwin, Francis Rawle, and Moorfield Storey, saying that in their opinion Brandeis was "not a fit person to be a member of the Supreme Court of the United States." [89]  According to the New York *World,* this communication was "assumed to set forth with unmistakable clarity the opposition to him among nearly all of the judges on the Supreme Court bench." [90]

Too rarely a note of judicious consideration crept into the proceedings.   Roscoe Pound, of Harvard Law School, wrote that it seemed to him that the friends of Brandeis made a mistake in urging as his chief qualifications his views upon social questions and his services in the public interest.   Important as these matters were, he did not think they lay immediately in the direction of qualification for the bench.   What was not so generally known, he said, "is that Mr Brandeis is in very truth a very great lawyer. . . . So far as sheer legal

[87] Baker, *op. cit.,* III (1931), 398; IV (1931), 163, 357-358, 366; VI (1937), 113-114.

[88] *Nomination of Louis D. Brandeis,* Hearings, Senate Committee on the Judiciary, Senate Doc. No. 409, 64th Cong., 1st sess., I, 319.

[89] *Ibid.,* p. 1226.

[90] New York *World,* March 15, 1916.   One of the senators opposing confirmation was George Sutherland, later to be one of Brandeis's colleagues on the Supreme Court.

ability is concerned, he will rank with the best who have sat upon the bench of the Supreme Court." [91]

Considerations of sheer legal ability, however, though brought forth on other occasions, evidently had little to do with either support or opposition or with the confirmation which finally took place. The President used so much pressure in support of the nomination that it was confirmed, approximately by a party vote.

The appointment placed on the bench a man who was at once a brilliant lawyer and a brilliant and adroit liberal. In spite of many differences between them, he quickly took his place beside Justice Holmes, whose dissents against the use of the Constitution to block social legislation were slowly making themselves felt. The two friends became great educators in the adaptation of law to the conditions of the times.

Early in 1916, Justice Hughes began to be considered seriously as the Republican presidential candidate. Largely from Democratic sources, he was criticized for not terminating the movement on his behalf, on the ground that the Supreme Court should not be dragged into politics. He was compared to Justice McLean, who before the Civil War had been a perennial candidate for the presidency. One congressman, arguing that no member of the Court should ever be nominated for the presidency, remarked as follows: "Suppose four years hence an agitation is started to nominate Justice Louis D. Brandeis. Does anyone doubt, even though he keep his mouth closed, the 'spasms' into which certain interest-serving publications would be thrown by the very suggestion of his nomination?" [92]

Hughes resigned from the Court immediately after his nomination, leaving another vacancy to be filled by President Wilson. The President chose John H. Clarke, of Ohio, because, as he expressed it, Clarke could be depended upon for a liberal and enlightened interpretation of the law. [93] Wilson had appointed Clarke as a federal district judge two years earlier, so that, like all but one of the Taft appointees, but unlike McReynolds and Brandeis, he had judicial experience before going to the Supreme Court. This fact helped to make him acceptable to the bar. The *New York Times* remarked cautiously that Clarke was known as a progressive Democrat, and that, although his progressivism was perhaps not greatly to be feared, it would be likely to be received with some misgivings by the conserva-

[91] Hearings, *op. cit.*, II, 251.    [92] 53 *Congressional Record* 9357.
[93] Baker, *op. cit.*, VI (1937), 116.

tive part of the public, coming so soon after the Brandeis appointment.[94] The nomination was confirmed with but little opposition. On most social issues during the six years he served on the Court, Clarke stood with Holmes and Brandeis, in sharp contrast with McReynolds, with whom he found nothing in common.

[94] *New York Times,* July 15, 1916.

# CHAPTER 26

# THE NATION AT WAR

THE CONFLICT originally known as the World War, which because of its successor is being renamed the First World War, or World War I, developed new possibilities for the extension of federal power without conflict with the Constitution. Military operations provided the focal point of activity, but control extended far into the economic, civic, and personal affairs of the people. In varying degrees the government regimented industries necessary to the conduct of the war. It fixed many prices. It handled labor with diplomacy, but resorted to indirect coercion. It sharply curtailed civil liberties. It launched, with government capital and under government management, enterprises necessary for the conduct of the war. It created new agencies in the form of government corporations and regulatory and managerial commissions and greatly expanded established agencies. It took up boldly, for the first time, the molding of public opinion as a function of government. The experience of the First World War was like that of the Civil-War period in that controls first exercised for war purposes were continued or later revived and justified under peacetime constitutional powers.

The broad expansion of governmental activity during the war and the accompanying regimentation of people and property were encouraged by popular enthusiasm for winning the war, which was in part stimulated externally and in part created by the government itself. In their zeal for victory, people tended to forget their traditional belief in a minimum of government. They accepted tolerantly the edicts of administrators under circumstances that would have provoked revolt but for the unifying sentiment as to the war. If it is too much to say that the absolutist character of military institutions penetrated and colored civil government wherever the conduct of the war was involved, it is at least true that the distinction between civil and military authority became temporarily less sharp and less significant.

To some extent, perhaps, the tendency to let down the barrier between civil and military government was due to change in the military establishment through the infusion of non-professional personnel. The United States had never maintained a large standing army. The traditions of the country had opposed the maintenance of a military force greater than the minimum needed for protection and the preservation of order. To prevent the concentration of too much military power in one organization, a substantial share of the funds expended on military training had been appropriated, not to the standing army, but to the National Guard, which consisted of the militia of the several states, and remained under state control until called into the federal service in time of emergency.

Because of the inadequacy of the trained military forces for handling a major war, therefore, the professional soldiery was virtually submerged by the civilian population drafted into the army. To the masses of the people the army lost its character as an alien body within an area rightfully ruled by civil government; and it became an aggregation of the boys from home, organized to "avenge the rape of Belgium," "defeat the Huns," and "hang the Kaiser." In fact, while the men put into uniform learned military tactics, they never developed any love of military rule. Essentially they were civilians. This fact may have made possible a cross-filtration of ideas and tactics between the wartime military and civil establishments that would not have been possible under other circumstances.

There is another and perhaps more important explanation of the change in the organization and activities of the government during the war. Under normal conditions the federal government, like the state governments, had been chiefly a policing and facilitating agency. Apart from the preservation of order externally and among the states, its function had been the promotion of private enterprise in commerce, industry, and agriculture. The government existed for the service of the individual citizens.

In time of war, however, the situation was strikingly different. The task of overwhelming importance to the government and to the people was that of winning the war completely and in the shortest possible time. In theory, and to a large extent in practice, all the national resources of wealth and man-power were dedicated to that end. It was to be achieved finally, not through private enterprise, but through governmental activity. The government ceased to be merely a policeman and became an entrepreneur, a business manager for the nation, with all the national resources at its command for the production of victory. The individual, even when not engaged in military operations, lost much of his peacetime civilian status. It ceased to be true that the government existed merely for his service. His service belonged to the government as well, even if it cost him inconvenience, his property, or his life. The government never became what in terms of European experience is called totalitarian, but it moved a long way in that direction.

### THE UNITED STATES ENTERS THE WAR

When Woodrow Wilson first became President of the United States, his principal interest was in the internal affairs of the country. Unsettled conditions in Mexico, however, quickly embroiled him in problems of foreign relations. The beginning of the war in Europe gave rise to a new series of critical problems in the foreign field, even though the initial policy of the government was the maintenance of strict neutrality. As always, the solution of problems of foreign relations was the peculiar task of the President. Since he was by temperament a strong leader in whatever field he acted, it is not surprising that his is the dominant personality in the story of American relation to and participation in the war.

To general American history rather than to constitutional history belongs the account of various prewar events such as the following: original aloofness from the war; expansion of foreign trade with, and foreign loans to, the Allies; spreading of war propaganda; peace efforts and the re-election of the President who had "kept us out of war"; frightfulness at sea; and transition to the armed neutrality which preceded entry into the war. In the midst of these events came the enactment of two important measures under pressure from the President. Of these the first was the National Defense Act [1] of 1916, which reorganized and enlarged the military establishment. The second was the Shipping Act [2] of 1916, which set up a United States Shipping Board to aid in creating a naval auxiliary and a merchant marine and to regulate marine commerce.

Perhaps the constitutional story may be said to begin with the request made by the President to Congress on February 26, 1917, for authority to supply merchant ships with defensive arms so that they might defend themselves against submarine attacks. He said:

> No doubt I already possess that authority without special warrant of law by the plain implication of my constitutional duties and

[1] 39 Stat. 166.    [2] 39 Stat. 728.

powers; but I prefer, in the present circumstances, not to act upon general implication. I wish to feel that the authority and the power of the Congress are behind me in whatever it may become necessary for me to do.[3]

Moved by popular resentment at the Zimmermann note, which revealed a German attempt to provoke a war between the United States and Mexico, the House of Representatives passed the President's bill by an overwhelming majority. In the Senate, however, a small group of men was opposed to any step that might involve the United States in war and thought that a special session of Congress should be called to keep watch over the situation. Under the leadership of Senators La Follette and Norris, a filibuster was organized to prevent the passage of the bill to arm merchant ships before the date of adjournment of the regular session on March 4. The filibuster succeeded. Seventy-five senators signed a manifesto saying they favored the bill, but were prevented by a small minority from expressing their support.

On March 4, the President issued a statement making a bitter attack on the "little group of eleven Senators." "A little group of willful men," he said wrathfully, "representing no opinion but their own, have rendered the great government of the United States helpless and contemptible." He saw but one remedy, a change in the rules of the Senate which would terminate the unlimited right of debate.[4]

The language was that of a President thwarted by a small minority in Congress who refused to accept the Executive as the principal leader in national policy. It was also the language of the author of *Congressional Government* driving home his conception of the inefficiency of poorly co-ordinated legislative action in contrast with the efficiency of control by a responsible executive. The attack upon the rules of the Senate was daring, but in this case he was able to amass the sentiment of the country back of him, a sentiment further inflamed by the discovery that Germany had proposed to embroil us in war with a neighbor in our own hemisphere.

Along with the President's statement, a White-House comment was issued to the effect that the situation had become more serious because of the discovery of an old statute which seemed to withhold from the President the power to arm merchant ships.[5] George W. Wickersham remarked, "The ill-considered and unpatriotic act of the small group of senators in having prevented the passage of the bill giving the

[3] *Messages and Papers of the Presidents*, XVII, 8211.
[4] *Ibid.*, pp. 8217-8218.     [5] *New York Times*, March 6, 1917.

President power to arm merchant ships has had as its immediate consequence the probable destruction of the last real deliberative assembly in our government." [6]

As a result of public and private pressure, the Senate, on March 8, 1917, adopted a mild closure rule. The rule was intended to prevent the defeat of a bill by a very few senators unless the bill were presented very near the end of the session. It did not constitute a real limitation on freedom of debate, such as was feared.[7] In the meantime the President's advisers decided that he had the authority to arm merchant ships without further action by Congress. Initial steps to that end were taken, but the program of armed neutrality was quickly lost in a war program. On April 2, after further depredations on American shipping by German submarines, President Wilson appeared before a special session of Congress to ask formal recognition of the existence of a state of war with the imperial German government. Admitting defeat, the small group of dissenting senators made no serious attempt to postpone action by futile debate. On April 6, ignoring such protests as that of Senator Norris that "We are going into war upon the command of gold," and "I feel that we are about to put the dollar sign upon the American flag," Congress voted a declaration of war.[8]

## CONSCRIPTION

The character of the war as a grim, businesslike, national enterprise was quickly revealed by plans of the government to raise its armed forces largely by conscription rather than by calling for volunteers. Conscription had been used in the Civil War only after the volunteer system proved inadequate. The belief prevailed widely that conscripts were cowardly or at least lacked the enthusiasm necessary for successful combat. It was argued that brave and patriotic men should be allowed to demonstrate their bravery and patriotism through volunteering and ought not to be herded together ignominiously with men who fought only under compulsion. But experience abroad taught otherwise. England had entered the war with a volunteer system, and had quickly lost at the front thousands of courageous youths who ought to have been reserved for both military and indus-

[6] George W. Wickersham, letter of March 5, 1917, *New York Times,* March 6, 1917.

[7] For discussion see George H. Haynes, *The Senate of the United States* (2 vols., 1938), I, 402 ff.

[8] For the President's speech see 55 *Congressional Record* 102-104; for Norris's remarks see *ibid.,* p. 214.

trial leadership. Ultimate resort to conscription had been necessary after a costly lesson. With an eye on the experience of the Allies, the United States War Department, before the declaration of war, had prepared plans for the systematic selection and training of men from the entire population and with a minimum of disturbance to necessary internal enterprise. In his war message the President advocated resort to conscription. With difficulty and after a long period of congressional debate, he succeeded in getting the desired legislation.

Many government officials were uneasy as to whether the mass of eligible men would register for draft purposes. The strategy of the Secretary of War was to have registration day made a day of festivity and celebration. The Attorney General, on the other hand, let it be known that all violations of law would be punished. Although some agitators had to be taken into custody, the draft machinery worked with more smoothness than might have been expected. There was little disturbance of the peace, and there were no draft riots such as those which took place during the Civil War.

The constitutional power of the federal government to raise an army by conscription had never been passed upon by the Supreme Court. Some doubt existed on the subject, although not in the same degree as during the Civil War. On July 10, 1917, a United States district court in Michigan held that the power to draft or conscript an army was a necessary incident to the constitutional power to raise an army.[9] On August 20, 1917, a United States district court in Georgia upheld the Conscription Act, denied that conscription fell within the meaning of "involuntary servitude" as used in the Thirteenth Amendment, and held that the power of Congress extended to raising an army to be used abroad.[10] The opinion was given wide publicity through the ordinary press and through the *Official Bulletin,* the publicity and propaganda magazine of the government. In a speech on "War Powers Under the Constitution," delivered before the American Bar Association on September 5, 1917, Charles E. Hughes, a former associate justice of the Supreme Court and Republican candidate for the presidency the preceding year, maintained that the powers being exerted in the emergency were constitutional, including that of conscription. The Bar Association voted to distribute the opinion widely throughout the country.[11]

[9] United States *v.* Sugar, 243 Fed. 423 (1917). For the action of the United States circuit court of appeals in the case see 252 Fed. 74, 79 (1919).

[10] Story *v.* Perkins, 243 Fed. 997 (1917).

[11] *New York Times,* September 6, 1917; September 7, 1917.

A long list of cases, involving persons who had sought to avoid the draft or had conspired to persuade others to avoid the draft, came up from lower federal courts for argument in the Supreme Court in December, 1917.[12] It was a significant fact that all the cases had been decided for the government. A clue to the attitude of the Supreme Court was found in the fact that Chief Justice White reprimanded counsel in one of the cases when he remarked that the Conscription Act required men to take part in a war which had never received the approval of the people. "I don't think your statement has anything to do with the legal arguments," said the Chief Justice sharply, "and should not have been said to this Court. It is a very unpatriotic statement to make." [13]

In an omnibus opinion in what came to be known as the Selective Draft Law Cases, Chief Justice White, for a unanimous Court, held that the power of conscription was included in the constitutional power to raise armies.[14] The power was not limited, said the Court, by the fact that other powers of Congress over state militia were narrower in scope than powers over the regular army. Furthermore, in reply to contentions of counsel, the Court held that the statute did not unconstitutionally delegate power to state officials or unconstitutionally vest legislative powers or judicial discretion in administrative officers. The exemption of certain persons on religious grounds did not violate the constitutional provision prohibiting the establishment of a religion. Compulsory service in the army was not "involuntary servitude" within the meaning of the Thirteenth Amendment.[15]

[12] See the comment of Robert Morss Lovett, "A Task for Pacifists," *New Republic,* XII (August 25, 1917), 106.

[13] *New York Times,* December 14, 1917.

[14] Selective Draft Law Cases, 245 U.S. 366 (1918). See also Jones *v.* Perkins, 245 U.S. 390 (1918), and Goldman *v.* United States, 245 U.S. 474 (1918). In Ruthenberg *v.* United States, 245 U.S. 480 (1918), the Court held that Socialists who had been brought to trial for failure to register were denied no constitutional or statutory right because of the fact that grand and trial juries were composed exclusively of members of other political parties.

[15] Four months later, in another case, the Court went over much of the same ground — Cox *v.* Wood, 247 U.S. 3 (1918). A man called into military service petitioned for a writ of habeas corpus, seeking discharge from further service on the ground that, although compulsory service might be required for the purposes specified in the militia clause of the Constitution, "to execute the laws of the Union, suppress insurrections, and repel invasions," it could not be required for military duty in a foreign country. The Court reiterated its conclusion that the militia clause placed no restrictions on the broader power to raise armies.

In 1912, Attorney General Wickersham had written an official opinion that the President could not send the organized militia of the states into a foreign country with the regular army as a part of an army of occupation. (29 *Opinions of the Attorney General*

ESPIONAGE AND SEDITION

Of great importance was the effect of the war upon traditional liberties of the people, the subject of the remainder of this chapter.[16] President Wilson had no illusions about the fate of civil liberties in the United States, once the nation had plunged into war. The people would forget there was ever such a thing as tolerance, he predicted. The spirit of ruthless brutality would enter into the very fiber of national life, infecting Congress, the courts, administrative officers, and the people at large. Freedom of speech and of the press would go, in spite of protective constitutional provisions.[17]

The difficulty, as always, lay not in any malignant desire of the people or their political officers to destroy liberty, but in the necessity for united action in protecting life and property and in winning the war. The shadow of coming events was visible for a considerable time before the United States entered the war. The United States produced great quantities of goods for sale to the Allies. Trade with the Central Powers was drastically reduced as a result of the Allied blockade. In aid of their own cause, therefore, German agents committed sabotage in American factories, and interfered, wherever possible, with production and sale to their enemies.

The mass of criminal legislation at this time was state legislation. The federal government had not enacted laws nor set up machinery to deal with the type of offenses being committed. In the summer of 1916, the Department of Justice asked for the enactment of a number of measures that would enable it to deal with espionage and other activities of undesirable aliens. An omnibus measure passed the Senate in February, 1917, but failed to pass the House. Churches

322.) To make the personnel of the militia available at all times for all national military purposes the National Defense Act of 1916 provided that members of the National Guard, as the militia were now called, should be discharged from the militia when called into the service of the United States, and should thereafter be subject to the laws applicable to the regular army. (39 Stat. 211.) On July 9, 1917, President Wilson issued a call for the militia, pursuant to the statute. (*Messages and Papers of the Presidents*, XVII, 8306.) At no time, apparently, did anyone seriously sponsor the position privately taken by Chief Justice Taney during the Civil War that conscription by the federal government was unconstitutional if it prevented the maintenance of the state militia provided for in the Constitution. (See chapter 14.)

[16] Part of the materials of this chapter were presented by the author in "Civil Liberties in War Time," *Political Science Quarterly*, LV (September, 1940), 321-347. For the work of the Committee on Public Information see James R. Mock and Cedric Larson, *Words that Won the War: The Story of the Committee on Public Information, 1917-1919* (1939).

[17] Ray Stannard Baker, *Woodrow Wilson: Life and Letters* (8 vols., 1927-1939), VI (1937), 506-507.

and pacifist and humanitarian institutions strongly opposed the enactment of restrictive and inquisitorial provisions in what was called the "Spy Bill."

In spite of the lack of adequate legislation the Department of Justice accumulated detailed information about the activities of some hundreds of suspected aliens, preparatory to taking action immediately upon the outbreak of war. Those thought to be dangerous were interned as soon as war officially began. The government, while restricting the activities of all enemy aliens, was chiefly concerned with cases of actual misconduct. Through the Department of Justice it sent out a circular to be given publicity by United States attorneys and marshals saying that aliens not hitherto engaged in plotting against the United States had nothing to fear. The circular carried the peremptory warning, "Obey the law; keep your mouth shut." [18] Thereafter many enemy aliens were made intensely uncomfortable by the scrutiny of the government and the hostility of the people, but on the whole they fared much better here than in most belligerent countries.

The omnibus measure extending the criminal jurisdiction of the federal government, which had failed of enactment just before war was declared, was brought up again and enacted in a revised form. It came to be known as the Espionage Act. [19] It was passed without certain important censorship provisions which it had formerly contained, but two sections of the act were so phrased that they might interfere seriously with freedom of speech and of the press. [20] One section [21] provided punishment for (1) making or conveying false reports for the benefit of the enemy, (2) seeking to cause disobedience in the armed forces of the United States, and (3) willfully obstructing the recruiting or enlistment service. The first clause was used rarely by enforcement officers, the second more often, and the third constantly, [22] to curtail the activities of persons not in sympathy with the conduct of the war.

Another section of the act, mild in its phrasing but drastic in its result, closed the mails to any item which violated any provision of

[18] Homer Cummings and Carl McFarland, *Federal Justice* (1937), p. 418.

[19] 40 Stat. 217.

[20] For broad discussion of censorship during the World War see James R. Mock, *Censorship, 1917* (1941).

[21] Title I, Section 3.

[22] John Lord O'Brian, "Civil Liberties in War Time," *Report of the New York State Bar Association*, XLII (1919), 301.

the act.[23] A newspaper or magazine, for example, which carried an article or item deemed in violation of some general provision of the act, might be virtually barred from circulation by an administrative decision that it was not mailable.

The Espionage Act did not provide for censorship of mail which was not otherwise open for inspection. However, the Trading-with-the-Enemy Act, of October 6, 1917, included provisions for censorship of mail or any other kind of communication with a foreign country.[24] On May 16, 1918, the Sedition Act [25] was passed as an amendment to the Espionage Act. It prohibited activity with intent to obstruct the sale of United States bonds, and it specified intent to obstruct as well as outright obstruction covered in the earlier measure. The Sedition Act further provided as follows:

> Whoever, when the United States is at war, shall willfully utter, print, write, or publish any disloyal, profane, scurrilous, or abusive language about the form of government of the United States, or the Constitution of the United States, or the military or naval forces of the United States, or the flag of the United States, or the uniform of the army or navy of the United States, or any language intended to bring the form of government of the United States, or the Constitution of the United States, or the flag of the United States, or the uniform of the army or navy of the United States, into contempt, scorn, contumely, or disrepute, or shall willfully utter, print, write, or publish any language intended to incite, provoke, or encourage resistance to the United States, or to promote the cause of its enemies, or shall willfully display the flag of any foreign enemy, or shall willfully, by utterance, writing, printing, publication, or language spoken, urge, incite, or advocate any curtailment of production in this country of any thing or things, product or products, necessary or essential to the prosecution of the war in which the United States may be engaged, with intent by such curtailment to cripple or hinder the United States in the prosecution of the war, and whoever shall willfully advocate, teach, defend, or suggest the doing of any of the acts or things in this section enumerated, and whoever shall by word or act support or favor the cause of any country with which the United States is at war or by word or act oppose the cause of the United States therein, shall be punished by a fine of not more than ten thousand dollars or imprisonment for not more than twenty years, or both.

The statute provided a basis for sweeping regimentation of speech and publication. It was so broad that it might be subject to gross

[23] Title XII, Section 1.    [24] 40 Stat. 411, 413.    [25] 40 Stat. 553.

abuse at the hands of administrative and judicial officers.　The right to interfere with mail to be delivered in the United States was extended.　If the Postmaster General found evidence, satisfactory to himself, that any person or concern was using the mails in violation of any provision of the act, he might refuse to allow delivery of any mail of any kind to that person or concern.　Mail, when held up, was to be returned to the sender with the words stamped upon it, "Mail to this address undeliverable under Espionage Act."　The business of any person or concern which was dependent upon use of the mail might thus be destroyed in peremptory fashion by an administrative decision of the Postmaster General.

### THE SEARCH FOR DISLOYALTY

Since much of the language of the statutes bearing upon civil liberties was exceedingly general, effects would depend much upon interpretation and mode of enforcement.　Information concerning illegal activities was gathered by the Bureau of Investigation of the Department of Justice, the Secret Service of the Treasury Department, the military-intelligence section of the War Department, and the postal, internal-revenue, customs, immigration, and naval-intelligence services, many of which pooled their information to promote speed and efficiency in detection.

The Bureau of Investigation had some three hundred agents scattered throughout the country before the United States entered the war, and added another hundred by the following June.　In addition, shortly before the declaration of war the bureau had organized the American Protective League, made up of private citizens eager to help capture spies and other criminals.　By the middle of June, 1917, the league had branches in almost six hundred cities and towns, and a membership of between eighty and a hundred thousand.　In the following year the membership reached approximately two hundred and fifty thousand.[20]　At the Washington headquarters of the league, the Department of Justice allowed the use of its own postage-free envelopes to carry the voluminous correspondence of the league, and United States attorneys were instructed to allow the use of their own envelopes for the same purpose.

Members had no power to make arrests, but they performed a variety of services for the Department of Justice.　The league assigned investigators to draft-exemption boards to locate and apprehend delin-

[20] See Cummings and McFarland, *op. cit.*, p. 421.

quents. It investigated the antecedents and loyalty of employees and applicants for important government positions connected with the war. It performed like services for the Red Cross. It aided in running down facts in the thousands of cases of suspicious activities reported by people throughout the country in response to appeals for vigilance in detecting spies and persons guilty of sabotage.

Inevitably, however, the league membership was untrained and undisciplined. Almost any person could join, and at the cost of a dollar or less could provide himself with a badge which often created the impression that he was a member of the official Secret Service. Intimidation and gross violations of privacy often occurred, leading to bitter protests from Secretary of the Treasury McAdoo, who finally persuaded the Department of Justice to change the form of the badge provided for its unofficial agents. "One unpleasant fact continually impressed on my associates and myself," said John Lord O'Brian, head of the War Emergency Division of the Department of Justice, and who was also to become general counsel of the principal emergency agency in the next World War more than twenty years later, "was the insistent desire of a very large number of highly intelligent men and women to become arms of the Secret Service and to devote their entire time to the patriotic purpose of pursuing spies." [27] Actually the spy menace was not a serious matter for any length of time.

When they realized the excessive zeal which they had aided in stirring up for prosecuting even the mildest instances of nonconformity, officials of the Department of Justice sought to restrain their agents. The Sedition Act was a dangerous weapon to put into the hands of vindictive or fanatical prosecutors. The difficulty, said John Lord O'Brian, was that it covered all degrees of conduct and speech, serious and trifling alike, "and, in the popular mind, gave the dignity of treason to what were often neighborhood quarrels or barroom brawls." [28] In a circular to all United States attorneys the Attorney General gave instruction that the statute

should not be permitted to become the medium whereby efforts are made to suppress honest, legitimate criticism of the administration or discussion of government policies; nor should it be permitted to become a medium for personal feuds or persecution. . . . Protection of loyal persons from unjust suspicion and prosecution is quite as important as the suppression of actual disloyalty.[29]

[27] O'Brian, *op. cit.*, p. 280.       [28] *Ibid.*, p. 304.
[29] *Annual Report of the Attorney General*, 1918, p. 674.

Such a variety of interpretations was placed on the provisions of the Espionage Act by United States attorneys and commissioners that large numbers of persons, who were charged with making comments hardly more than trivial, were haled into court and, if convicted, were given heavy sentences of fine and imprisonment. Shortly before the termination of the war, the United States attorneys were directed to submit each case to the Department of Justice for instructions before submitting it to a grand jury.[30] The order was not always obeyed, but it resulted in checking the stream of prosecutions.[31]

UNREASONABLE SEARCHES AND SEIZURES

Enforcement officers were impatient of constitutional procedures when they stood in the way of desired results. The Fourth Amendment, prohibiting unreasonable searches and seizures, was said to have been violated on September 5, 1917, when Department of Justice agents in Chicago and a number of cities farther west raided the offices of the Industrial Workers of the World and seized files of correspondence and other documents. As a result, William D. Haywood and other leaders were arrested for activities intended to impede the conduct of the war. A United States circuit court of appeals said:

> The affidavits, on which the search warrants issued, failed to describe the property to be taken except by reference to its general character, and failed to state any facts from which the magistrates could determine the existence of probable cause. If the proper parties had made prompt application, it may be assumed that they would have obtained orders quashing the writs and restoring the property.[32]

Constitutional rights were not asserted at the proper time, and many persons were convicted and given heavy sentences as a result of

[30] *Ibid.*, p. 674.

[31] The following, gleaned from charges to juries and court opinions, are some of the expressions for which persons were haled into court with the possibility of heavy fines and long imprisonment: "I cannot see how the government can compel troops to go to France. If it was up to me, I would tell them to go to hell." "Men conscripted to go to Europe are virtually condemned to death and everybody knows it." "The Attorney General of the United States is so busy sending to prison men who do not stand up when the Star-Spangled Banner is played that he has no time to protect the food supply from gamblers." "This is a poor man's fight and a rich man's war. President Wilson and Congress ought to be assassinated. My boy and I will take to the woods and die there before we would go to war." "The Christian may not go to 'the front' to repel the foe - for he is required to kill men." One man was haled into court because in the privacy of his home he explained his failure to buy Liberty Loan bonds by saying that he wanted neither side to win, but hoped the war would end in a draw, and believed Germany would meet the United States and agree to just terms if overtures were made.

[32] Haywood *v.* United States, 268 Fed. 795, 801 (1920).

the evidence gathered in the raids. The government regarded the I.W.W. as an obstructionist organization and believed it to be influenced and perhaps financed by the enemy. President Wilson spoke of it as "worthy to be suppressed."

Investigation during the summer of 1918 showed that several thousand men previously registered under the Conscription Act were delinquent and at large. Partly to provide an example before the date of the new registration, which was scheduled for September 12, the Department of Justice instituted a series of so-called "slacker" raids throughout the country. The method used was to surround a given area and take into custody all men seemingly of the draft age and hold them until it was discovered that they were not subject to detention. The innocent and the guilty alike were herded together throughout the period of the inquiry.

A raid conducted in New York City was handled with particularly objectionable methods. Soldiers and sailors and members of the American Protective League were used in making the arrests and in forcing the prisoners to give an account of themselves, by procedures which bore little resemblance to due process of law. A reputable New York newspaper took the risk of bitterly criticizing this invasion of the rights of the people, in an editorial entitled "Department of Injustice." [33] The President asked the Attorney General for an explanation. "The arrests have aroused so much interest," he wrote, "and are likely to give rise to so much misunderstanding that I would be very much obliged to you if you would let me know all the facts and circumstances."

The Attorney General took responsibility for the dragnet process as the only effective method. The use of soldiers and sailors and members of the American Protective League, however, he declared, had been in violation of his repeated instructions.[34] Since the war was then almost at an end, it is impossible to say whether, from this time on, a resort to more acceptable procedures was to be expected.

## DECISIONS IN LOWER FEDERAL COURTS

No cases involving the constitutionality of the war measures which affected civil liberties were decided by the Supreme Court during the period of active hostilities, but lower federal courts upheld constitutionality and interpreted provisions in many cases. The Espionage

[33] New York *Evening World*, September 6, 1917.
[34] Cummings and McFarland, *op. cit.*, pp. 426-427.

Act, said the courts, did not violate freedom of speech or of the press as guaranteed by the First Amendment. It was not unconstitutional in making criminal in times of war statements which might be within the constitutional rights of the citizen in times of peace. It was not unconstitutional as providing punishment for conduct which was treasonable, and which was punishable as treason or not at all.

The courts interpreted the Espionage Act broadly, and held it applicable to a wide variety of offenses, particularly those having to do with the recruitment of armed forces. They did not, however, go as far as some prosecutors. For instance, the act was held to apply, not to all disloyal utterances, but only to those affecting military or naval forces. The act was applied in connection with a statement that anyone enlisting for service in France would be used for fertilizer. It was applied in connection with a motion picture showing atrocities committed by British soldiers during the Revolutionary War. It was not applied in the case of a school officer who said he would rather see a pair of old trousers hanging over the schoolhouse than the United States flag. It was not applied in the case of a man who explained in his own home that he had not bought Liberty Loan bonds because he hoped neither side would win the war and that it would end in a draw.

The Postmaster General exercised freely his power to exclude from the mails publications containing materials which he deemed in violation of the law. In some instances his rulings extended not merely to issues containing objectionable matter, but to subsequent issues as well, however innocent their contents. In the case of *The Masses,* a revolutionary journal published in New York, a federal district judge interpreted the act more narrowly than did the Postmaster General and issued a preliminary injunction against the order barring an issue from the mails; but he was reversed by a higher court.[35] The Postmaster General exercised his power of censorship with a high hand, excluding from the mails publications which only by far-fetched lines of reasoning could be held to be in violation of the statute.[36] No other court sought to block his action, and no court held the statute unconstitutional in the form in which he applied it.

SUPREME COURT DECISIONS

No espionage cases were argued before the Supreme Court until

[35] See Masses Publishing Co. *v.* Patten, 244 Fed. 535; 245 Fed. 102; 246 Fed. 24 (1917).
[36] See Zechariah Chafee, Jr., *Freedom of Speech* (1920), pp. 108-109.

after the cessation of military hostilities. The first decision was reached in Schenck v. United States,[37] which was argued on January 10, 1919, and decided on March 3. The case involved conspiracy to violate the Espionage Act by stimulating insubordination in the armed forces, obstructing the recruitment and enlistment service, and illegal use of the mails in connection therewith. It was clear from the record that documents had been prepared and sent through the mails which were calculated to achieve these unlawful ends. Justice Holmes wrote the opinion, in which the Court weighed the Espionage Act in terms of the freedom of speech and press guaranteed by the First Amendment. He admitted that in ordinary times the defendants would have been within their constitutional rights in saying all that was said in the circular in question, but "the character of every act depends upon the circumstances in which it is done." [38]

With this principle in mind, Justice Holmes phrased the "clear-and-present-danger" doctrine, to govern the interpretation of the First Amendment:

> The question in every case is whether the words used are used in such circumstances and are of such a nature as to create a clear and present danger that they will bring about the substantive evils that Congress has a right to prevent. It is a question of proximity and degree. When a nation is at war, many things that might be said in time of peace are such a hindrance to its effort that their utterance will not be endured so long as men fight, and that no court could regard them as protected by any constitutional right.

The principle stated was clear, and in the Schenck case the Supreme Court agreed unanimously as to its application. The Court also agreed unanimously in the case of Frohwerk v. United States,[39] wherein Justice Holmes added the comment:

> We venture to believe that neither Hamilton nor Madison, nor any other competent person then [when the First Amendment was adopted] or later, ever supposed that to make criminal the counseling of a murder within the jurisdiction of Congress would be an unconstitutional interference with free speech.[40]

The Court again agreed unanimously in the Debs case.[41] Eugene V. Debs, the well-known Socialist leader, was accused of, and had been convicted by a trial court for, inciting disobedience in the armed

---

[37] 249 U.S. 47.     [38] *Ibid.*, p. 52.     [39] 249 U.S. 204 (1919).
[40] *Ibid.*, p. 206.     [41] Debs v. United States. 249 U.S. 211 (1919).

forces and obstructing recruitment and enlistment. In a speech dealing principally with the growth of socialism, Debs had praised the conduct of persons who had been convicted for obstructing enlistment and for other offenses. Said Justice Holmes, "If a part or the manifest intent of the more general utterances was to encourage those present to obstruct the recruiting service, and if in passages such encouragement was directly given, the immunity of the general theme may not be enough to protect the speech." [42] The judgment of the lower court was affirmed.

It was not until the decision in Abrams v. United States,[43] on November 10, 1919, that difference of opinion was revealed among the justices of the Supreme Court as to conduct creating a clear and present danger of bringing about substantive evils which Congress had the power to prevent. The case involved the publication of two articles which denounced the efforts of capitalist nations to interfere with the Russian Revolution, criticized the President and the "plutocratic gang in Washington" for sending American troops to Russia, and urged workers producing munitions in the United States not to betray their Russian comrades. Justice Clarke, speaking for the Court, came to the conclusion that "the plain purpose of their propaganda was to excite, at the supreme crisis of the war, disaffection, sedition, riots, and, as they hoped, revolution, in this country, for the purpose of embarrassing, and if possible defeating, the military plans of the government in Europe." [44] Conviction was upheld.

Justice Holmes dissented, with the concurrence of Justice Brandeis. He belittled the influence of a silly leaflet surreptitiously published by an unknown man, and thought intent to violate the law was not shown. Sentences of twenty years' imprisonment had been imposed, he said, "for the publishing of two leaflets that I believe the defendants had as much right to publish as the government has to publish the Constitution of the United States now vainly invoked by them." [45] He made an eloquent plea for "free trade in ideas." He had thought the United States had shown its repentance for the Sedition Act of 1798 by repaying the fines it had imposed. "Only the emergency that makes it immediately dangerous to leave the correction of

[42] Ibid., pp. 212-213.    [43] 250 U.S. 616.
[44] Ibid., p. 623. For relatively recent illumination of the clear-and-present-danger test of freedom of speech sponsored by Justice Holmes and the so-called bad-tendency test, sponsored by Justice Clarke, see Herndon v. Lowry, 301 U.S. 242 (1937), and Bridges v. California, 314 U.S. 252 (1941).
[45] Ibid., p. 629.

evil counsels to time warrants making any exception to the sweeping command, 'Congress shall make no law abridging the freedom of speech.' " [46]

On March 1, 1920, the Court again divided, in Schaefer v. United States,[47] over the interpretation and application of the Espionage Act. A German-language newspaper in Philadelphia secured its materials by reprinting, often in digested form, materials already published elsewhere. In the estimation of the Court, many of the items were derisively contemptuous of the war activities of the United States, and certain changes in the articles as republished added to the damaging quality of their criticism. By a vote of six to three the Supreme Court upheld the conviction of a number of the persons involved. Justice McKenna, speaking for the Court, referred scornfully to persons who, to their country's peril, deliberately violated the law and then sought defense behind the constitutional guarantee of free speech. He had no difficulty in upholding restrictions on freedom of speech which interfered with the conduct of the war.

In dissent for himself and Justice Holmes, Justice Brandeis made a plea for the "clear-and-present-danger" principle. Correctly applied, he said, it would "preserve the right of free speech both from suppression by tyrannous, well-meaning majorities, and from abuse by irresponsible, fanatical minorities." It could be applied only by the exercise of good judgment, which demanded a mood of calmness.[48] He held the publications relatively innocuous, and thought their suppression marked new perils for the constitutional liberty of the press in peacetime as well as in war. In time of peace an intolerant majority might be prone "to stamp as disloyal opinions with which it disagrees. Convictions such as these, besides abridging freedom of speech, threaten freedom of thought and of belief." [49]

Holmes and Brandeis again disagreed with a majority of the Court when it upheld the Postmaster General in excluding from second-class mail a newspaper which systematically published materials which violated the Espionage Act. The case was that of the *Milwaukee Leader,* a Socialist paper published by Victor L. Berger, which printed rabid criticism of the war policies of the government. "Freedom of the press may protect criticism and agitation for modification or re-

[46] *Ibid.*, pp. 630-631.
[47] 251 U.S. 466.
[48] *Ibid.*, pp. 482-483. Justice Clarke also dissented.
[49] *Ibid.*, p. 494. Justice Clarke dissented in a separate opinion.

peal of laws," said Justice Clarke for the Court, "but it does not extend to protection of him who counsels and encourages the violation of the law as it exists. The Constitution was adopted to preserve our government, not to serve as a protecting screen for those who, while claiming its privileges, seek to destroy it." [50] The dissenting justices contended that the question was one of statutory construction, and that the statute did not confer upon the Postmaster General the privilege of denying second-class privileges to all issues of a newspaper of which some issues contained "non-mailable" materials. [51]

### STATE ESPIONAGE LEGISLATION

A number of states enacted their own espionage laws and other measures intended to preserve order in the midst of wartime disturbances. These measures likewise vitally affected civil liberties and raised important constitutional problems. A number of the problems were dealt with in a case arising under a Minnesota statute which contained provisions similar to those of the Espionage Act. The offender had made statements such as the following:

> We are going over to Europe to make the world safe for democracy, but I tell you we had better make America safe for democracy first. ... If this is such a good democracy, for Heaven's sake why should we not vote on conscription of men? We were stampeded into this war by newspaper rot to pull England's chestnuts out of the fire for her. [52]

The defendant contended that the statute encroached upon the powers of Congress and that it violated rights of free speech protected by the Fourteenth Amendment. The Supreme Court, through Justice McKenna, denied both contentions. The welfare of the states, as well as that of the nation, was involved in the war. The Constitution did not prevent the state from making national purposes its own purposes, to the extent of exerting its police powers to prevent local obstruction of the achievement of such purposes. The Court held, furthermore, that the law did not infringe freedom of speech as guaranteed by the Constitution. Justice Holmes concurred in the result. Chief Justice White dissented on the ground that Con-

---

[50] United States *ex rel.* Milwaukee Social Democratic Publishing Co. *v.* Burleson, 255 U.S. 407, 414 (1921).

[51] As to cases in which he wrote the opinions of the Court, Justice Holmes regretted the results as to the convicts and hoped the President would pardon them. See Mark A. DeWolfe Howe (ed.), *Holmes-Pollock Letters: The Correspondence of Mr. Justice Holmes and Sir Frederick Pollock, 1874-1932* (2 vols., 1941), II, 7, 11, 15, 32.

[52] Gilbert *v.* Minnesota, 254 U.S. 325, 527 (1920).

gress had exclusive power of legislation in the field. Justice Brandeis wrote a long dissenting opinion criticizing the invasion of civil liberties.

### THREAT OF MILITARY TRIALS FOR CIVILIANS

The curtailment of civil rights was threatened in other ways. The efficiency of the peacetime machinery of government was impaired by the disturbances of war. This was true of the courts as well as of other agencies. Personnel of the judicial establishment was affected, masses of additional cases were added, and morale and good judgment were subjected to the vibration of military conflict. In one respect the normal mode of operations of the criminal courts failed adequately to protect society amid war conditions. According to custom, bail was granted to all but the most serious offenders pending trial and appeal, so as to minimize the inconvenience suffered by persons accused, but not finally convicted, of crime.

From one point of view the need for granting bail was greater during the war than at other times because of the overloaded condition of many dockets and the consequent delays. On the other hand, when persons accused of obstructing the conduct of the war were released on bail, it was possible for them to continue, and they often did continue, the type of activities for which they were awaiting trial.

Such cases were numerous. The most picturesque, if not the most serious, was that of Victor L. Berger, editor of the Socialist *Milwaukee Leader,* who was indicted in February, 1918, for conspiracy to violate the Espionage Act. Shortly before his indictment, he became the Socialist nominee for a seat in the United States Senate, and thereafter, on bail, he carried on his campaign on a platform demanding, among other things, an immediate armistice and the withdrawal of United States troops from France. He was defeated, but he polled over one hundred thousand votes and doubtless had considerable influence on popular attitudes toward the war. He was found guilty of the offense charged, but, while his case was being appealed, he won an election to the House of Representatives. The fact that the House denied him a seat presumably did nothing to remedy any injury to the country of which he may have been guilty in the meantime.[53]

People concerned about this problem looked enviously at the speedy and effective procedure by which the government dealt with spies, in the accepted legal sense of a person lurking about the military

[53] See Chafee, *op. cit.,* pp. 315-319.

establishment to secure information for transmission to the enemy. The relevant Article of War, as it was phrased in the 1916 revision, read as follows:

> Any person who in time of war shall be found lurking or acting as a spy in or about any of the fortifications, posts, quarters, or encampments of any of the armies of the United States, or elsewhere, shall be tried by a general court-martial or by a military commission, and shall, on conviction thereof, suffer death.[54]

In their zeal for winning the war, the people of the United States gave little thought to the preservation of the civil procedures which, over a period of centuries, had been worked out to protect persons accused of crime, and they were not particularly fearful of the arbitrary aspects of military rule. They were not generally aware, as after the war they were made aware, of the despotic nature of the system of law and procedure by which the military forces were governed.[55]

People not trained in law usually failed to distinguish between spies in the narrow sense — those persons guilty of military espionage — and persons otherwise guilty of sedition, sabotage, or aid to the enemy. They felt that all such offenders should be treated alike. As an example of popular attitudes, a petition signed by thousands of citizens of Wyoming, doubtless not otherwise of bloodthirsty tendencies, was sent to the Department of Justice urging that every individual found to be a spy or traitor by a competent court be compelled to pay the penalty of death.

Even a prominent official in the Department of Justice, Assistant Attorney General Charles Warren, became convinced that persons guilty of a wide range of offenses involving interference with the progress of the war should be turned over to the military for summary trial before military courts and the application of drastic penalties. He prepared a bill to that effect and sent it to Senator George E. Chamberlain, chairman of the Senate committee on military affairs, together with an explanatory document entitled "Who are Spies? A Memorandum of Law on the Power of Congress to Subject Civilians to Trial by Courts-Martial."

---

[54] 39 Stat. 619, 663.

[55] Criticism of the operation of military law by returning soldiers who refused to be indoctrinated with the professional-soldier point of view resulted in a statute making many changes in court-martial procedure. 41 Stat. 759. See "The New Articles of War," *Columbia Law Review*, XXI (May, 1921), 477.

Warren's approach to the subject is indicated in the following language of the bill:

> . . . owing to changes in conditions of modern warfare, whereby the enemy now attempts to attack and injure the successful prosecution of the war by the United States, by means of civilian and other agents and supporters behind the lines spreading false statements and propaganda, injuring and destroying the things and utilities prepared or adapted for the use of the land and naval forces of the United States, thus constituting the United States a part of the zone of operations conducted by the enemy . . .[56]

The bill provided that any person guilty in a variety of ways of sedition, sabotage, or propaganda for the cause of the enemy should

> be deemed to be a spy and be subject to trial by general court-martial, or by a military commission of the army, or by a court-martial of the navy, and, on conviction thereof, shall suffer death or such other punishment as such general court-martial, or military commission, or court-martial shall direct.

In introducing the bill, Senator Chamberlain predicted that the military would provide a speedy disposition of offenders. "The moral effect of one man arrested and tried by court-martial for spy activity would be worth a hundred convictions in the criminal courts."[57]

At an executive session of the committee on military affairs, Warren presented a plausible argument for the constitutionality of the bill, in spite of the case of *Ex parte* Milligan,[58] which in his estimation dealt, not with a situation such as this, but rather with the power of the President to set up military tribunals outside the military zone in places where the civil courts were open and functioning. Many senators were not convinced, however, and an attempt was made to have the Senate judiciary committee report whether or not the bill violated the Constitution.[59]

In the meantime, Senator Lee S. Overman wrote to President Wil-

---

[56] S. 4364, 65th Cong., 2d sess. For a copy of the bill see the *New York Times,* April 17, 1918.

[57] *New York Times,* April 17, 1918.

[58] 4 Wallace 2 (1866). For Warren's position see his "Spies, and the Power of Congress to Subject Certain Classes of Civilians to Trial by Military Tribunals," *American Law Review,* LIII (March-April, 1919), 195. See also "Spies and Plotters," *New York Times,* April 28, 1918.

[59] See 56 *Congressional Record* 5401-5402, 5471-5472.

son asking his position on the bill. Wilson replied with a stinging letter of criticism, which read in part as follows:

> I am wholly and unalterably opposed to such legislation, and very much value the opportunity you give me to say so. I think it is not only unconstitutional, but that in character it would put us upon the level of the very people we are fighting and affecting to despise. It would be altogether inconsistent with the spirit and practice of America, and, in view of the recent legislation, the espionage bill, the sabotage bill, and the woman spy bill, I think it is unnecessary and uncalled for.[60]

As a result of the President's opposition the bill was withdrawn.

Warren's action was repudiated at the Department of Justice. Attorney General Gregory wrote to a member of the House of Representatives that Warren, though an assistant attorney general, had prepared and sent the bill and brief to Senators Overman and Chamberlain without the knowledge of his superior officer. "The general policies therein urged and sought to be enacted into law are exactly contrary to those approved by the assistant to the Attorney General in charge of the problems involved [61] and by the Attorney General himself." He entirely disapproved of the action taken by Mr. Warren, he said, and would not have permitted it had he known it was contemplated.[62]

This is not to say that the issue was determined for all time. There was cogency in the argument of Warren and others that war was no longer just a matter of military hostilities, but that it reached far back into the industrial structure of the country as well. Industrial espionage and kindred offenses might help the enemy and injure the United States quite as much as espionage in the military zone. It may yet become a practical necessity in wartime that industrial spies and persons suspected of sabotage be kept isolated while awaiting trial and while cases are being appealed, however great the inconvenience to alleged offenders, including those who ultimately prove not to be

---

[60] Wilson to Overman, April 20, 1918, *New York Times,* April 23, 1918.

[61] John Lord O'Brian.

[62] Gregory to William Gordon, April 20, 1918, *New York Times,* April 23, 1918; 56 *Congressional Record, Appendix,* 307-308. The constitutional issue was raised again during the same year, when an alleged spy for Germany was arrested in Nogales, Arizona, immediately upon entering the United States from Mexico. For an account of the case see 31 *Opinions of the Attorney General* 356, 357 (November 25, 1918); Edmund M. Morgan, "Court-Martial Jurisdiction Over Non-Military Persons Under the Articles of War," *Minnesota Law Review,* IV (January, 1920), 79; and De Lacey *v.* United States, 249 Fed. 625 (1918).

guilty. In that event, if military trial is the only acceptable device, constitutional interpretation may be adjusted to it.

If constitutional interpretation has to be adjusted to the necessities of the situation, however, less drastic steps might be taken than requirement of trial before military tribunals. Effort could be made to speed the action of civil courts. Bail could then be denied altogether or fixed so high as to constitute denial in effect. The Eighth Amendment prohibits the fixing of excessive bail, but the interpretation of the word "excessive" is left to the courts. If the penalties hitherto applied are deemed inadequate, they may be changed by statute. The prohibition of cruel and unusual punishments, in the Eighth Amendment, is also subject to judicial interpretation. In view of the patriotic emotions stirred by a foreign war, it is hardly to be expected that juries will refuse to convict because of the drastic character of the punishment to be applied. Indeed, a review of cases made by the Department of Justice after the first World War had come to an end indicated that the zeal of prosecutors, juries, and judges had been excessive rather than lax in dealing with offenders under war statutes.

### THE RIGHTS OF LABOR

Attempts were made to include in the Espionage Act provisions to prevent obstruction of shipment of goods abroad. Such provisions might well have been used to prevent strikes or to punish strikers. Labor representatives maneuvered successfully to prevent their enactment.[63] While the sabotage bill was pending, an amendment was introduced to provide punishment for persons who, with intent to interfere with the prosecution of the war, should conspire to prevent the production of war materials. Thereupon, at the insistence of labor leaders, another amendment was introduced providing that the act should not be construed to prevent employees from agreeing together to stop work or to refuse to accept work "with the sole and bona-fide purpose of securing better wages or conditions of employment." [64]

The controversy over these provisions held up the bill for a period of weeks. Many strikes had occurred during the first six months of the war.[65] The Industrial Workers of the World and other organizations were stirring up labor troubles in many places. The war stim-

---

[63] 56 *Congressional Record* 4903.       [64] *Ibid.*, p. 4901
[65] See National Industrial Conference Board Research Report No. 3, *Strikes in American Industry in Wartime, April 6 to October 6, 1917* (March, 1918)

ulated the demand for labor and greatly curtailed the supply. The increased cost of living brought agitation for higher wages. Congress was sensitive to labor opinion; but there was also resentment over labor's taking advantage of the emergency to better its position. The Senate for a time refused to approve the bill with the provision excepting labor and the House refused to approve it without the provision. Both houses finally agreed to eliminate it, together with the other amendment applying to types of interference which might include strikes.

The Lever Food-Control Act,[66] which among other things was intended to prevent combinations to limit supply and raise prices, contained provisions which might be interpreted to apply to labor activities. The president of the American Federation of Labor claimed to have received from Attorney General Gregory assurance that the act would not be applied to labor. Gregory's successor made use of it against labor, however, in the post-war period.

The strikes which took place interfered with the conduct of the war and endangered the military forces by limiting the supply of munitions and other necessary equipment. Some legislators favored the outright drafting of labor for necessary industries. It was one thing to draft men for direct service to the government, however, and quite another to compel them to work for fixed wages in industries said to be fattening on war profits.[67] A less objectionable and more effective device than the conscription of labor was the "work-or-fight" order issued by the War Department.[68] In terms of the order, persons in deferred classifications lost their deferment or exemption privileges unless they engaged in what the government considered useful employment. This strategy, although less drastic than the draft, had a pronounced coercive effect. The war ended too soon to show the operation of the order in detail, but it might have been used effectively to dispose of troublemakers in the ranks of labor as well as persons who failed to secure employment at all.

A number of states approached the subject of coercion more directly. In June, 1917, the Maryland legislature passed an act enabling the governor to require the registration of every able-bodied and unemployed man in the state between the ages of eighteen and

[66] 40 Stat. 276; 41 Stat. 297.

[67] For discussion of the conscription issue see Francis Hoague *et al.,* "Wartime Conscription and Control of Labor," *Harvard Law Review,* LIV (November, 1940), 50-104.

[68] *Official Bulletin,* May 24, 1918.

fifty years. Persons registered were to be provided with positions in public or private employment, and they were to be subject to severe penalties if they did not work.[69] A system of registration and placement was put into effect. West Virginia, Delaware, Rhode Island, New York, and other states enacted similar laws.[70] A New Jersey court held that such a measure did not impose involuntary servitude when enacted as a war measure. The states, the court declared, had the power to enact measures beneficial to the federal government while it was at war with a foreign country.[71] A West Virginia court, on the other hand, held unconstitutional a statute to punish as a vagrant any able-bodied male resident of the state between the ages of sixteen and sixty years who did not work at least thirty-six hours a week.[72]

The state laws reached some age groups not covered by the work-or-fight requirement of the federal government. They had the advantage and the disadvantage of depending upon local arrangements and local officials for enforcement. The several statutes differed greatly, and many states had no such legislation. On the whole, within the limits which it covered, the federal requirement was probably more equitable than were the state laws.

## PROHIBITION

Prohibition of the manufacture and sale of alcoholic beverages represented the wartime curtailment of personal liberty which had the most drastic extension into the post-war period. For many years temperance and prohibition forces had struggled to limit or prohibit altogether the sale of intoxicating drinks. At the beginning of the war, some nineteen states were listed as dry,[73] while in the summer of 1918, a total of twenty-eight states were said to have laws limiting the use of intoxicating beverages.[74] Congress had aided the states in the exercise of their powers through the Wilson Act [75] and the Webb-Kenyon Act,[76] by permitting regulation even when interstate ship-

[69] Maryland Acts of 1917, chapter 33.

[70] See West Virginia Acts of 1917, chapter 12; Council of Defense Law of Delaware, approved April 8, 1918; Public Laws of Rhode Island, 1917-1918, chapter 1661; Laws of New York, 1918, chapter 625.

[71] State v. McClure, 7 Boyce, 265, 105 Atlantic 712 (January 7, 1919).

[72] Ex parte Hudgins, 86 W. Va. 526, 103 S.E. 327 (May 20, 1920).

[73] See the Literary Digest, May 26, 1917, p. 1576.

[74] See "The Problem of Prohibition in War Time," The Outlook, CXIX (July 31, 1918), 515.

[75] 26 Stat. 313.      [76] 37 Stat. 699.

ments were involved. The subject had until this time been assumed to be a matter of state and local rather than national concern. The industrial states were definitely opposed to prohibition, however, and unanimous action throughout the entire United States seemed extremely improbable.

The war gave a new turn to events. Since the earliest days of the conflict, the various belligerents had sought to control the drink problem as a measure of defense. Lloyd George was quoted as saying, "We are fighting Germany, Austria, and Drink; and, as far as I can see, the greatest of these deadly foes is Drink. If we are to settle with German militarism, we must first of all settle with Drink." [77] Prohibition advocates cited European experience as an argument for national prohibition in the United States as a war measure. They stressed the need for efficiency in the armed forces and in the manufacture of war materials. They called attention to the huge quantities of food supplies which might be saved for use as food if the stream going into the manufacture of alcoholic beverages was cut off. They condemned the use of transportation facilities for delivery of such beverages when those facilities were already clogged with cargoes of war materials.

Prohibition organizations and the prohibition lobby in Congress had tremendous political power. They took advantage of the war sentiments of the people to advance their program. Some aspects of the program had the sympathy of administrative leaders, but, unlike other movements that secured the support of Congress during the war, it did not command the support of President Wilson.

The first step was taken in the Selective Draft Act, which prohibited the sale of intoxicating or spirituous liquors at any military post or to members of the military forces while in uniform. [78] A more drastic step was taken in the Lever Food-Control Act of August 10, 1917. The use of food materials in the production of distilled spirits for beverage purposes and the importation of such distilled spirits were prohibited. The President was authorized to commandeer stocks of distilled spirits if needed for alcohol in the production of munitions, and to limit the food products consumed in the production of wine or beer if such limitation should be necessary to the conservation of the food supply. [79]

It was found unnecessary to commandeer distilled spirits. No

[77] In the New York *Sun*, quoted, *Literary Digest*, May 26, 1917, p. 1573.
[78] **40 Stat. 76, 82.**      [79] 40 Stat. 276, 282.

action was taken with respect to wines, since grapes were not otherwise extensively consumed.   The amount of foodstuffs manufactured
into beer was limited to seventy per cent of the amount used the preceding year.   The prohibition lobby tried to force the President to
prevent the use of cereals and fruits for the production of beer and
wine.   Their strategy was to forbid the use of certain appropriated
funds until the desired proclamation to that effect was issued.   They
failed in their effort.   The Fuel Administration, to conserve the fuel
supply, aided the prohibition movement by limiting breweries to half
the average amount of fuel consumed during 1915, 1916, and 1917.[80]

While striving zealously for greater restraint in the use of alcoholic
beverages in time of war, prohibition forces capitalized the situation
to launch a constitutional amendment providing for permanent prohibition.   Giving manufacturers a year in which to liquidate their
businesses, the amendment was to place a complete ban upon the
liquor traffic for beverage purposes.   Fearing that the assumption of
federal jurisdiction would be interpreted as a bar to the enforcement
of state laws on the subject, advocates of the amendment insisted on
a provision giving the states concurrent power to enforce the article.

Opposition to the amendment was poorly organized.   Critics
stressed the fact that it was not a war measure, since it was expected
that the war would be over before it could become effective.   They
denounced the invasion of personal liberties and the insertion in the
Constitution of a provision legislative rather than properly constitutional in character.   They issued warnings against federal invasion of
the province of the states.   On the whole, however, the issues were
inadequately discussed.   Action on the amendment was speeded in
Congress and in the ratifying state legislatures as if it were badly
needed emergency legislation.[81]   Ratification was completed in less
than thirteen months.   The Eighteenth Amendment became a part
of the Constitution in January, 1919, some two months after military
hostilities had ceased with the signing of the armistice.   It became
effective a year later, long after it could have any appreciable effect on
the conduct of the war.

In the meantime, Congress enacted other wartime prohibition
measures.   An act of September 12, 1918, authorized the President

[80] "The Problem of Prohibition in War Time," *The Outlook*, CXIX (July 31, 1918),
p. 516.

[81] President Wilson allowed himself to be carried along with the movement, saying,
without clear explanation of the statement, that "It is a war measure as deeply as it is
a peace measure." *Current Opinion*, LXIV (February, 1918), 84.

to prevent the sale of liquor in zones to be established around "coal mines, munition factories, shipbuilding plants, and such other plants for war material as may seem to him to require such action." [82]     An act approved on November 21, 1918, ten days after the armistice was signed, provided that from June 30, 1919, until the completion of demobilization no distilled spirits or beer or wine should be sold in the United States for beverage purposes.   Such intoxicating liquors were not to be imported after the approval of the act and prior to the completion of demobilization. [83]

Cases were quickly instituted and hurried on their way to the Supreme Court to test the constitutionality of this measure, which was known as the Wartime Prohibition Act.   It was urged that the war was now ended and that restrictive measures could no longer be enacted on the basis of war powers.   Statements of President Wilson were quoted to the effect that the war had ended and peace had come. The Supreme Court found ample evidence that the official termina-tion of the war had not yet taken place, however, and the act was up-held as a war measure. [84]

After the Eighteenth Amendment became a part of the Constitu-tion, Congress turned to the enactment of permanent legislation to carry out its purpose.   Controversy raged over a period of months before the Volstead Act [85] was agreed upon.   That measure provided for more drastic enforcement of prohibition under the Eighteenth Amendment than had been provided for under the Wartime Prohi-bition Act, but also strengthened the wartime measure to provide for rigid enforcement prior to the date when the constitutional amend-ment was to become effective.   President Wilson vetoed the measure because it merged enforcement based on war powers with that based on the constitutional amendment, [86] but it was passed over his veto. Soon afterward the Supreme Court, dividing five to four, held consti-tutional the amendment of the war measure. [87] War and peace enforce-m°nt were merged indelibly.   The federal government took up the task of enforcing a type of legislation which became increasingly un-popular with the years, and which in 1933 was swept away by a re-pealing amendment after enforcement in certain sections of the United States became virtually impossible. [88]

[82] 40 Stat. 958.          [83] 40 Stat. 1047-1048.

[84] Hamilton v. Kentucky Distilleries and Warehouse Co., 251 U.S. 146 (1919).   See also United States v. Standard Brewery, 251 U.S. 210 (1920).

[85] 41 Stat. 305.          [86] 58 Congressional Record 7607.

[87] Ruppert v. Caffey, 251 U.S. 264 (1920).

[88] For resumption of the history of prohibition see chapter 29.

# CHAPTER 27

# ORGANIZATION AND CONTROL IN TIME OF WAR

GOVERNMENTAL REGIMENTATION of the lives of people and curtailment of civil liberties constituted but one segment of constitutional development during the first World War. Equally important were the competitive struggles for power between the President and Congress and the creation of administrative organizations to exercise unprecedented control over private property. A seemingly endless chain of committees, commissions, boards, councils, and administrations sprang into being to administer the war economy. They fumbled at their tasks and fought each other over jurisdiction as they got under way. President Wilson worked for their establishment and their independence from congressional control, and struggled to bring order among them. In so doing he established precedents for extension of presidential authority and paved the way for permanent changes in relations between government and private enterprise.

In spite of Wilson's early insistence that Americans should be neutral even in thought, many observers foresaw immediately the possible involvement of the United States in the war. English and American commentators urged the government to avoid the condition of unpreparedness that had resulted in tragic floundering in England during the first year of the war. Late in 1915, Professor Graham Wallas, of the London School of Economics, a scholar of repute among jurists and political scientists in the United States, published an account of some of the unfortunate experiences of Great Britain, in the hope that the United States might profit from them if it entered the war. He thought it obvious that "a nation which believed that war is a real possibility should set some of the best brains among its citizens to imagine war during peace, and so to secure that all the course of action which war will make necessary shall as far as possible have been thought out before war begins." [1]

[1] Graham Wallas, "Mobilizing the Administration," *New Republic,* V (November 6, 1915), 12.

The British Treasury, he wrote, had not been ready with a finance program for war. Had the war finance of the United States been thought out? Until the spring of 1915, England had not come to realize that the war required mobilization of industry and commerce beyond the scope of the powers of the military-minded officials of the War Office. Had the United States thought out plans for the exercise of such control in time of war? England had had to improvise censorship after the war began. By what agency, and by what authority, could such powers be exercised in the United States? England had been driven to the adoption of conscription. Had the United States a plan for the mobilization of man-power? [2]

### ORGANIZATION AND PLANNING BEGIN

The relationship between the federal government and the industrial and commercial life of the country was not such as to make possible an easy transition to centralized and co-ordinated control for war purposes. The control exercised in wartime was sporadic and diverse. Some industries received protection through the tariff. Traffic on railroads and communications by telephone and telegraph were regulated by the Interstate Commerce Commission. The government gathered some information about corporations in the process of collecting excise taxes and through investigations by the Federal Trade Commission. It decentralized rather than co-ordinated commercial and industrial activities through enforcement of anti-trust legislation. As for industry itself, it had no plans for a swift transition to the production of war materials; and neither industry nor government knew the capacity of the country for the production of such materials beyond the scope of production already achieved in supplying the Allies. From warnings and from direct observation it became gradually apparent that involvement in war would render necessary the mobilization and carefully planned utilization of all the

---

[2] Wallas also thought the nation ought to face in advance the war problems arising from relations between the nation and the states. He had sometimes thought that, if he were an American, he would concentrate all his own political efforts "on a proposal for a constitutional amendment having the single purpose of making more easy the carrying within a reasonable time of other constitutional amendments desired by a substantial majority of the people."

The assumption that preparation for conducting a major war would require amendment of the Constitution proved erroneous. The prohibition amendment, which was initiated during the war period, was in no real sense a war measure, even though wartime prohibition was authorized by statutes based on war powers. The woman-suffrage amendment, which occasioned much discussion during the war period, was not a genuine war measure. No other amendment was seriously considered during that period.

resources of the country if the United States was to participate successfully.

Examination of the equipment of the United States began as preparation for national defense rather than for war. Naval expansion represented the first step in actual preparation. In that connection a naval consulting board was appointed to give to the naval establishment the benefits of modern science. Within the board a committee on industrial preparedness was organized. That committee made a survey of the industrial plants of the country, to measure capacity for the production of war equipment. It then made plans for the allotment of small orders for munitions to large numbers of plants to develop experience in the production of war materials.[3] As war clouds grew heavier, it became apparent that broader planning was needed than could be done through such a committee in such a subordinate position. Accordingly, in the Army Appropriation Act of 1916, Congress provided for a Council of National Defense.[4] It was to consist of the Secretaries of War, Navy, Interior, Agriculture, Commerce, and Labor. On nomination of the council the President was to appoint an advisory commission of not more than seven members, each of whom should have some special qualification, such as knowledge of some industry, or public utility, or the development of some natural resource. The council was to make investigations of industry and transportation as related to national defense, and make recommendations to the President and the heads of the executive departments. In effect, therefore, the function of the committee on industrial preparedness was taken over, and the chairman of the committee was appointed to the Advisory Commission.

The Council of National Defense was an important emergency organization throughout the period of the war. Its work was done largely, not by the department heads who comprised its membership, but by the Advisory Commission, and by subordinate fact-finding and advisory committees. Perhaps the most important achievements of the council and the Advisory Commission were the creation of other agencies, some of which were severed largely or completely from the Council of National Defense and given independent status by executive order or by statute. All emergency organizations, and to a lesser extent the permanent organizations of the government, were

[3] See Howard E. Coffin, "Organizing Industry for National Defense," *World's Work*, XXXII (May, 1916), 23.

[4] 39 Stat. 619, 649.

in process of change throughout the period of the war. Viewed as a whole, much of the process seems meaningless in terms of any general principle, save that it represented constant adaptation to new conditions as they arose. Superficially, since constructive changes in organization stopped with the termination of military conflict, it may be assumed that the changes represented struggles toward the stage of organization arrived at by the later months of 1918. Had the war lasted longer, however, the modification of organization would doubtless have continued, although perhaps at a slower pace. Frequent changes and adjustments are essential characteristics of adequate organization in time of war, and the flexibility which makes them possible is an essential characteristic of an adequate constitutional system.[5]

The organizations growing out of the Council of National Defense, or those created separately, could not take on definite outlines until some agreement had been reached as to the functions to be performed. Many interest groups were concerned lest war measures become pretexts for permanent changes in governmental functions. Producers of alcoholic beverages feared — with ample reason — that the war might be used as an excuse for instituting national prohibition.[6] Businessmen feared that price-fixing for war purposes might establish a precedent for price regulation in time of peace. Both labor and capital were concerned about the establishment of precedents in the regulation of labor relations.

To lull suspicion, the President in some instances drew a distinction between normal government functions which were to continue in the hands of established agencies and emergency functions which were to be performed by emergency agencies. By leaving the latter functions in the hands of organizations which were to last only for the period of the war, the danger in the establishment of precedents would be eliminated or at least reduced. Concerning the food-control program, for instance, the President made the following statement:

[5] At the beginning of the war, to provide for mobilization of the resources of the nation, the Advisory Commission of the Council of National Defense divided among its seven members the following groupings of subject matter: transportation and communication; munitions, manufacturing, and industrial relations; supplies, including clothing; raw materials, minerals, and metals; engineering and education; labor, including the conservation of the health and welfare of workers; and medicine and surgery, including general sanitation. The topics dealt directly or indirectly with all phases of industrial and commercial life. Subordinate organizations were set up to deal with the several topics.

[6] Charles Merz, "War as a Pretext," *New Republic*, XI (June 2, 1917), 129. See chapter 26.

It is proposed to draw a sharp line of distinction between the normal activities of the government represented in the Department of Agriculture in reference to food production, conservation, and marketing, on the one hand, and the emergency activities necessitated by the war in reference to the regulation of food distribution and consumption, on the other. All measures intended directly to extend the normal activities of the Department of Agriculture in reference to the production, conservation, and the marketing of farm crops will be administered, as in normal times, through that department, and the powers asked for over distribution and consumption, over exports, imports, prices, purchase, and requisition of commodities, storing, and the like which may require regulation during the war will be placed in the hands of a commissioner of food administration, appointed by the President and directly responsible to him.[7]

PRESIDENTIAL CONTROL

The strong hand of the President reached down into all phases of governmental organization and activity.[8] He kept a close watch over the War and Navy Departments, the permanent agencies having most to do with the conduct of the war. He participated in the establishment of new agencies and in defining their jurisdiction. It was inevitable that some groups in Congress should be jealous of the increased powers of the President, suspecting him of the desire to exercise dictatorial powers, and that they should seek to curb his authority. Experiences connected with legislation to regulate the food and fuel industries provide clear illustrations and are therefore presented at length in the following pages.

Some regulation in those fields seemed essential. The food supply had already been curtailed by shipments abroad and by unfavorable weather conditions. Wilson decided that the subject should be allotted to a food administrator, who should serve under the direction of the President. The administrator, Herbert Hoover, was chosen long before Congress enacted the regulatory statute sought by the President. In requesting the legislation, Wilson asked for power to fix prices, both to encourage production and to secure consumers against extortion. He noted Hoover's belief that administration could be worked out through voluntary co-operation, but asked, nev-

[7] Statement, May 19, 1917, *Messages and Papers of the Presidents*, XVII, 8262.

[8] Part of the contents of this chapter were published under the title of "The Control of War Preparations in the United States," *American Political Science Review*, XXXIV (December, 1940), 1085-1103.

ertheless, for full powers of enforcement, saying, "It is absolutely necessary that unquestionable powers shall be placed in my hands." He gave assurance that the regulation was to continue "only while the war lasts" and that it was to be a demonstration of democracy at its best. "The last thing that any American could contemplate with equanimity would be the introduction of anything resembling Prussian autocracy into the food control in this country." [9]

In spite of administration pressure for hasty enactment, the measure was debated over a period of several weeks, with a minority bitterly opposing it. Even before the bill, known as the Lever bill, had passed the House of Representatives, Senator James A. Reed, of Missouri, had it printed in the *Congressional Record* [10] and voiced his condemnation. The bill, as then phrased, declared that "necessaries" and the processes, methods, and activities connected therewith were "affected with a public interest." This, said the senator, was a false statement, made "to afford some kind of shadow of pretense of the exercise of a constitutional power." [11] The things included, he insisted, were not affected with a public interest within the legal meaning of the term. He declared:

> The power demanded is greater than has ever been exercised by any king or potentate of earth; it is broader than that which is exercised by the Kaiser of the Germans. It is a power such as no Caesar ever employed over a conquered province in the bloodiest days of Rome's bloody despotism. [12]

He particularly denounced the plan to put the exercise of dictatorial power in the hands of Herbert Hoover. Hoover, he said, was a mining engineer who for many years had sought his fortunes in other lands. He had only recently come to public attention through his work in Belgium. "It is proposed to give to this man, whom the American people have heard of through the newspapers only in the last few months, the power to say to every housewife what she shall feed her babe, her children, her husband, or herself." [13] Throughout the debate he continued his attacks on the bill and on the plan to centralize authority in Herbert Hoover.

The bill passed the House of Representatives by an overwhelming majority. The measure was handicapped in the Senate by the oppo-

[9] *Messages and Papers of the Presidents,* XVII, 8263-8264.
[10] 55 *Congressional Record* 3594-3596.
[11] *Ibid.,* p. 3596.   [12] *Ibid.,* p. 3597.   [13] *Ibid.,* p. 3597.

sition of Senator Thomas P. Gore, chairman of the committee on agriculture, who denounced the plan for one-man control. "I maintain it is unconstitutional legislation," he said. "It would turn over the business of our country to one individual." [14] The Constitution ought to be cherished in times like these, lest in other times of crisis it be needed to protect us against a dictator, "and to protect us against subserviency of a Congress that might be willing to lick the dust at the feet of such a dictator." [15]

Senator Henry Cabot Lodge announced that he expected to support the bill, but he thought Congress was going "some distance beyond that once venerated instrument, the Constitution of the United States, in creating crimes." He doubted the wisdom of giving the President, or his agents, the power to fix prices. [16]

The constitutionality of the measure was defended on the ground that the business regulated was "affected with a public interest," and on other grounds. [17] Senator J. Hamilton Lewis thought that in time of war the Constitution was "more or less suspended." [18] He saw a difference between the written Constitution and an unwritten constitution which was being built up. As he saw it, "The time has gone by when the people of this country are so much concerned about the Constitution as they are about their institutions; and I for myself announce as my creed that I will not permit the obsolete provisions of a paper constitution to prevent the preservation of the human constitution." [19] Other legislators were in doubt whether the Constitution was, in the words of Senator Lewis, "more or less suspended" during war, or whether the war powers in the Constitution justified the exercise of drastic powers not granted in time of peace.

The consideration of a number of proposed amendments delayed the enactment of the food-control measure. Some of them had to do with the curtailment or prohibition of the use of food materials for the production of alcoholic beverages. [20] Most of them, however, grew out of the feeling of legislators that too much power was being transferred to the hands of the President and officers whom he chose without senatorial confirmation. One proposed amendment, which was rejected without a recorded vote, provided for an "official" court to

---

[14] Quoted, Edward M. Sait, "The Sixty-Fifth Congress," *The American Yearbook*, 1917, p. 13.

[15] 55 *Congressional Record* 4459.     [16] *Ibid.*, p. 4405.

[17] See the speech of Senator William S. Kenyon, *ibid.*, pp. 3910-3933.

[18] 55 *Congressional Record* 4459.     [19] *Ibid.*, p. 4560.     [20] See chapter 17.

try government officials who were accused of abuse of the sweeping powers given them.[21]

Other proposals received more support. The bill, as sponsored by the Senate, provided, not for an administrator, but for three commissioners, to be appointed by the President by and with the advice and consent of the Senate.[22] The selection of a chairman from among the three was left to the President, but the bill, as approved by the Senate, deprived him of the one-man agency which he sought. Mr. Hoover, as chairman, would be subject to check by the other two commissioners. Taking advantage of the fact that, because of his long absence from the United States, Hoover was not a qualified elector in any state, Senator Reed tried vainly to exclude him altogether by amendments providing that the commissioners should be qualified electors of the United States.[23] A proposal to return to the President's plan for a single administrator received the support of only 10 votes, as against 63 votes in the negative.[24] A second consideration resulted in a vote of 60 to 23 against the President's plan.[25]

The Senate included in the bill another provision which was calculated to limit or provide a check upon the powers of the President, and which was highly objectionable to him. It provided for a joint committee on expenditures in the conduct of the war. The relation of Congress to the conduct of the war had been a matter of discussion among members since the war began. A minority, at least, showed uneasiness about the lack of adequate check by Congress upon the expenditure of huge appropriations being voted for war purposes. It was recalled that during the Civil War Congress had established a joint committee on the conduct of the war.[26]

A proposal for such a committee had been presented to the Senate on April 9, 1917, three days after the declaration of war, when Senator John W. Weeks, a Republican from Massachusetts, offered a plan for a joint committee to be known as "the joint committee on the conduct of the war." The committee was to "make a special study of the problems arising out of the war" and to "confer and advise with the President of the United States and the heads of the various executive departments." Senator Weeks explained that he was recommending the general course followed during the Civil War. The committee would furnish a direct connecting link between the exec-

---

[21] See 55 *Congressional Record* 4708, 5363.

[22] *Ibid.*, p. 5261.  [23] *Ibid.*, pp. 5256, 5259.

[24] *Ibid.*, p. 5265.  [25] *Ibid.*, p. 5366.  [26] See chapter 14.

utive and legislative branches of the government. Its establishment would be no reflection on the President or the heads of departments. It was part of the duty of Congress to have some knowledge of methods by which the five or six billions of war appropriations would be expended and to determine whether expenditure was being made in accordance with the purpose of Congress.[27] The Democratic majority on the committee of rules rewrote the proposed resolution to limit it more specifically to consideration of expenditures, and changed the title to "the joint committee on expenditures in the conduct of the war." On August 4, 1917, however, quite possibly after learning the sentiments of the President in the matter, the committee made an adverse report, and no further action was taken on that particular bill.[28]

In the meantime, on July 18, 1917, Senator Weeks offered the proposal in its original form as an amendment to the food-control bill.[29] When it came up for consideration, Senator Owen, a Democrat, asked the substitution of the draft as reported out of the committee on rules, and Senator Weeks accepted the substitute.[30] With no debate whatsoever a vote was taken, and the amendment was adopted, 53 to 31.[31] The Senate passed the food-control bill as amended, by a vote of 81 to 6.[32]

The bill was sent to conference committee to iron out differences in the measure as passed by the two houses. In the meantime, the Senate again discussed the proposed joint committee, in connection with a resolution calling for facts about the Committee on Public Information which the President had established by executive order.[33] Senator Lodge, Senator Weeks's colleague from Massachusetts, brought up the subject by a reminder that Congress as well as the President was part of the government.

> That seems an amazing statement to make, but we are part of the government under the Constitution, and I believe we have a right to know how the public money is spent. I say to you, the money that is being wasted in Creel's bureau [34] is perhaps a little thing, but nothing

[27] 55 *Congressional Record* 459. An identical measure was introduced in the House of Representatives on the same day by Representative Madden, *ibid.*, p. 497.

[28] Senate Report No. 102, 65th Cong., 1st sess.

[29] 55 *Congressional Record* 5231.

[30] *Ibid.* p. 5363.        [31] *Ibid.*, p. 5364.        [32] *Ibid.*, p. 5367.

[33] Senate Resolution 101, 65th Cong., 1st sess. See 55 *Congressional Record* 4811, 5414-5424.

[34] George Creel was chairman of the Committee on Public Information.

could be done more helpful to the President and the administration than a strict watch of the expenditures by Congress. If these vast sums of money, vast beyond anything that was ever dreamed of before, are to be poured out by agents, many of whom are utterly unknown except perhaps for personal admiration wisely bestowed, or for petty political services, agents with no public responsibility, you are laying up a day of reckoning which we shall all deplore.[35]

The discussion ended after some debate as to whether the Civil War committee had interfered with the conduct of the war by the administration.

When the conference committee took up the food-control bill, the President hurled the weight of his opposition against the two objectionable amendments. The plan for the joint committee, he wrote to Representative Lever, would render his task of conducting the war almost impossible. "The constant supervision of executive action which it contemplates would amount to nothing less than an assumption on the part of the legislative body of the executive work of the administration." He referred to the Civil-War experience as an ominous precedent, wherein President Lincoln had suffered distressing harassment. The proposed co-operation of Congress with the President was not practicable. "The responsibility rests upon the administration. There are abundant existing means of investigation and of the effective enforcement of that responsibility."[36] He asked a friend in the Senate to aid in preventing his management of the war from "being put under an espionage committee."[37]

Wilson also refused to accept the defeat of his plan for a food administrator. "If I can help it," he wrote to a friend, "'there ain't going to be no food-control *board*.' I think that it will come out in conference. It makes the bill practically unworkable."[38] Under pressure from him a majority of the conferees voted to eliminate the provisions to which he objected. They had "received their orders," said Senator Gore, who refused to fall into line.[39]

Administration leaders sought to force the immediate acceptance of the report of the conference committee. "The lash, forever and eternally the lash, is laid across the legislative back," shouted Senator Reed in protest. "More and more we cringe. More and more we

[35] 55 *Congressional Record* 5420.      [36] *New York Times,* July 24, 1917.

[37] Ray Stannard Baker, *Woodrow Wilson: Life and Letters* (8 vols., 1927-1939), VII (1939), 186, note.

[38] *Ibid.,* p. 191.      [39] *New York Times,* July 31, 1917.

whine and crawl between the legs of those who master us." [40] Senators examined again the records of Civil-War experience to see whether the joint congressional committee had interfered unwisely in the conduct of the war and to speculate whether the proposed committee would so interfere.[41] The controversy over the proposal for a food-control board was discussed sporadically. The conference report was agreed to by a vote of 66 to 7.[42] The President was complete victor on the points clearly at issue between himself and Congress.

## THE LEVER ACT

The statute, known usually as the Lever Act,[43] was one of the most important war measures enacted for the control of the internal economy of the United States. The following were some of the more important provisions with reference to the food supply: It prohibited the destruction, waste, or hoarding of necessaries. It provided for the licensing of the handling of necessaries. Licenses were to be revoked for making excess charges or profits, and penalties were prescribed for handling without such licenses. Necessaries might be requisitioned for public use connected with the common defense, and plants might be taken over for the production of such necessaries. The President was empowered to buy and sell necessaries. To stimulate the production of wheat, he was authorized to fix a minimum price, which for the 1918 crop was not to be less than two dollars a bushel. He was authorized to make the guarantee effective by direct purchases.

These authorizations of drastic interference with a free economy were made only for the period to end with the termination of the war. Although no definite statement was made, the act seemed to rest solely upon war powers. It did not retain the reference to "business affected with a public interest" which appeared in an early draft of the Lever bill.

The act left to the President the choice of agencies to carry out its provisions. He formally sanctioned the creation of the United States Food Administration, which had already been in process of organization, with Herbert Hoover at its head. This agency sought by propaganda methods to stabilize prices at reasonable levels and to conserve

---

[40] 55 *Congressional Record* 5802.
[41] *Ibid.*, pp. 5838-5846, 5864-5866.      [42] *Ibid.*, p. 5927.
[43] 40 Stat. 276. It was known also as the Food-Control Act, in contrast with the Food-Production Act, 40 Stat. 273, which was approved at the same time, and which gave broad powers to the Department of Agriculture.

supply by appeals to the patriotism of producers, processors, dealers, and consumers. It co-operated with state and local agencies interested in the conservation of food. The meatless days, the wheatless days, and the consumption of flour with other ingredients than those usually included were accepted as essential factors in the winning of the war. To stimulate the production of wheat, guarantees fixing minimum prices above the two-dollar level were established. Prices to consumers could not be fixed directly in any field, but such price-fixing was approached indirectly. Processors and dealers were licensed, and reasonable charges for their services were proclaimed. The threat to revoke licenses stood in the way of higher charges. Dealers were required to post lists of prices which the Food Administration regarded as fair. The patriotic sentiment of the people, supplemented by the threat to licensees, was effective in most cases in holding prices to a level regarded as reasonable for war conditions.[44]

For the acquisition of grain and related purposes, the President issued an executive order directing the formation of the United States Grain Corporation, under the laws of Delaware, with stock-ownership in the United States except for the number of shares necessary to qualify directors.[45] The grain corporation was the first corporation owned by the federal government to be formed under the laws of a state. The purpose, evidently, was to approximate as closely as possible the methods of modern business in commercial dealings in agricultural supplies, while retaining control in the hands of the government. This step, unheralded though it was at the moment, was important in constitutional development in marking the beginning of the use of a device for the extension of government operation into fields hitherto managed exclusively by private enterprise. At a later date, with the consent of the President, the Food Administration formed under the laws of Delaware another corporation, called the

[44] For discussion of price-fixing see F. W. Taussig, "Price-Fixing as Seen by a Price-Fixer," *Quarterly Journal of Economics*, XXXIII (February, 1919), 205; C. F. Stoddard, "Price-Fixing by the Government During the War," *Monthly Review of the United States Bureau of Labor Statistics*, X (May, 1920), 1095; Lewis H. Haney, "Price-Fixing in the United States During the War," *Political Science Quarterly*, XXXIV (March, June, September, 1919), 104, 262, 434; Charles O. Hardy, *Wartime Control of Prices* (1940).

[45] For discussion see Harold Archer Van Dorn, *Government-Owned Corporations* (1926), pp. 81 ff. The government-owned corporation was a little-used device in the federal government at that time. A railroad acquired with the Panama Canal Zone gave the first experience. The Shipping Act of 1916 (39 Stat. 728, 731) authorized the creation of the Emergency Fleet Corporation, under the laws of the District of Columbia, to acquire, build, and control ships for a merchant marine, and the corporation had been formed a few months before the enactment of the Lever Act.

United States Sugar Equalization Board, to deal with specialized problems connected with that commodity.[46]

## THE FUEL ADMINISTRATION

Adequate production and distribution of coal provided one of the most difficult industrial problems faced by the country at the beginning of the war. The Federal Trade Commission reported that production was held in check by low prices, disturbed labor conditions, and chaos in distribution resulting from inadequate and poorly coordinated railroad facilities. On June 19, 1917, the commission recommended that the production of coal and coke be conducted through a pool in the hands of a government agency, and that producers be paid cost of production plus a uniform profit. Regarding the problem as inseparable from that of transportation, the commission also recommended that transportation agencies be similarly pooled.[47]

The Council of National Defense had already established a committee on coal production. In a conference with operators, that committee had worked out a price to be paid for coal, but it was reminded that its duties were purely advisory and that it had no actual power to fix prices.[48] To give the necessary powers to the government, a section dealing with coal and coke was included in the Lever Act. It authorized the President, through an agency to be designated by him, to fix prices and enforce strict regulations of production and distribution, with power to take over and operate plants and to require that the coal and coke produced be sold to the United States. The Federal Trade Commission was to make the necessary investigations as to cost.[49] Pursuant to the act the President established the United States Fuel Administration, with Doctor Harry A. Garfield, president of Williams College, as administrator.

The Fuel Administration developed a huge organization with branches and connections throughout the coal-producing areas of the country. It performed detailed and complicated tasks of price-fixing, to stimulate production and at the same time secure the delivery of products at reasonable costs. It dealt with the problem of labor rela-

[46] Van Dorn, *op. cit.*, pp. 170 ff. The War Finance Corporation and the United States Housing Corporation were similar emergency organizations in other fields.

[47] *Anthracite and Bituminous Coal*, Senate Doc. No. 50, 65th Cong., 1st sess., pp. 20-21.

[48] William F. Willoughby, *Government Organization in War Time and After* (1919), p. 295.

[49] 40 Stat. 276, 284-286.

tions in the coal industry, which was one of the major problems of production. It secured agreements from capital and labor to clear the way for uninterrupted production, or at any rate for production less disturbed than theretofore by labor controversies. It had no direct control over transportation agencies, but it co-operated with those having such control to bring order out of shipping chaos, and it aided in devising priorities for the still insufficient supply.

As the Food Administration sponsored meatless and wheatless days, so the Fuel Administration sponsored heatless days and Sundays without gasoline, making the program effective through public opinion. As for price-fixing, acceptance was secured in much the same way, with occasional resort to pressure or threats of pressure. The fuel administrator remarked in his final report, "Most of us who were called upon to deal with the fixing of prices of commodities during the war had been trained in a school totally opposed to the principle of government interference with price arrangements between buyers and sellers." [50] Economic and political dogmas gave way before the necessities of war, however, in the minds of administrators and of the public. The courts, to the limited extent to which they were involved, also fell into line for the most part. The following is one of the few clear expressions of a federal court on the constitutionality of price-fixing under the Lever Act.

> While the war created no new powers in Congress, it undoubtedly required the exercise of powers latent in times of peace. . . . The right to regulate business, including the fixing of prices for essential commodities, in furtherance of a constitutional power of the United States, exists when the business sought to be regulated is one in which the public has an interest beyond that of the persons who participate in the individual transactions therein. . . . Businesses which are purely private in times of peace may become matters of vital public concern in times of war. The late war was a marshaling, not only of the man-power of the nations engaged, but of their total resources and economic strength. The production and distribution of coal, the chief source of industrial energy, was a business in which the public had a vital interest over and above that of the individuals engaged in the particular transactions; therefore, it was a business which Congress had the right to regulate. [51]

[50] *Final Report of the United States Fuel Administrator* (1921), p. 23.

[51] United States *v.* Ford, 265 Fed. 424-425 (1920). The Supreme Court reversed the decision, holding that the order of the President which was involved did not apply to the transaction, which had been begun before the order was issued. If the order

One somewhat vague provision of the Lever Act as subsequently amended was held unconstitutional by the Supreme Court. It provided punishment for making "any unjust or unreasonable rate or charge in handling or dealing in or with necessaries." The Court held that the provision violated the Fifth and Sixth Amendments, which required that Congress prescribe an ascertainable standard of guilt and secure to accused persons the right to be informed of the nature and cause of accusations against them. The mere existence of a state of war, said the Court, could not suspend or change the operation of these constitutional amendments upon the power of Congress.[52] The decision came too late to have any important effect on economic control during the war. Moreover, the evil passed upon by the Court could have been cured by more careful and detailed phrasing of the statute.

### THE CONTROL OF RAILROADS

The control of railroads provided another example of the extension of governmental powers for war purposes, with particular enhancement of executive powers. In its report of June 19, 1917, the Federal Trade Commission had recommended the actual operation of the coal industry and the transportation lines of the country by the government.[53] Although the Fuel Administration exerted a tremendous amount of influence over the coal industry through price-fixing, zoning, licensing, and granting priorities, it did not assume direct responsibility for the operation of mines. As for the railroads, the government was slow in admitting necessity for taking them over and operating them. It was not until December 26, 1917, that such a decision was announced by presidential proclamation.[54] Reluctance to assume control, in contrast with early action by Great Britain and France, was due partly to uneasiness about a current movement for permanent government ownership and operation. The field was one of many in which it was feared that the war might be used as a pre-

---

were otherwise construed, said Justice McReynolds for a unanimous Court, "we must decide a grave constitutional question, not necessary to consider if another view be accepted. Under the existing circumstances, did Congress have the power to fix prices at which persons then owning coal must sell thereafter, if they sold at all, without providing compensation for losses? If this difficulty can be eliminated by some reasonable construction of the order, it should be accepted." (Matthew Addy Co. *v.* United States, 264 U.S. 239 [1924].) Critical though some of its implications are, it is to be noted that the Court avoided an adverse action on the war measure, in a decision handed down more than five years after the cessation of hostilities.

[52] United States *v.* L. Cohen Grocery Co., 255 U.S. 81, 88 (1921).

[53] See note 47 above.      [54] 40 Stat. 1733.

text for bringing about permanent changes which could not be instituted without such a pretext.

The railroad companies, however, recognized the necessity of co-ordination of transportation for war purposes. The leading railroad executives of the United States met in Washington on April 11, 1917, pursuant to the request of the Council of National Defense, and established their own co-ordinating agency in the form of a committee called the Railroads' War Board.[55] A member of the Advisory Commission of the Council of National Defense and a member of the Interstate Commerce Commission were made *ex-officio* members of the board. Throughout the remainder of 1917 the board sought to bring about the maximum of co-operation among agencies which had theretofore been denied the privilege of any high degree of co-operation.

The Railroads' War Board undoubtedly did much to alleviate the congestion and chaos of transportation, but they grew worse. Competitive psychology could not be uprooted with a mere declaration of new policy. It was hard to secure an over-all picture of the struggle for transportation facilities going on all over the country, which resulted in a stampede in the direction of eastern ports so sweeping that empty cars, as well as loaded equipment, were hopelessly clogged on eastern sidings. Anti-trust laws and anti-pooling provisions of the Interstate Commerce Act still stood in the way. Priority orders, issued pursuant to an emergency statute,[56] often added to the confusion. It was reported that priority orders were issued indiscriminately by the War and Navy Departments and the Food and Fuel Administrations, not only through principal officers in Washington, but through minor officials scattered throughout the country. In addition, government officials gave priority cards to manufacturers to use on products shipped for the government, with the result that they sometimes applied to private shipments with which the government had no direct or indirect connection.[57] For a time the whole purpose of priority orders was defeated and the chaos in transportation increased.

The financial situation of the railroads also created serious problems. Many of them needed heavy loans for upkeep and new equipment. The European market for new securities was cut off. The government was floating several billion dollars of loans and could ill afford to face the competition of huge quantities of railroad securities.

[55] See I. Leo Sharfman, *The American Railroad Problem* (1921), p. 77.
[56] 40 Stat. 272.     [57] 56 *Congressional Record* 2016-2017.

Since transportation facilities had to be maintained, the alternative was for the government itself to raise the money needed both by the government and by the railroads as well, and then to allot funds as seemed best.

On December 5, 1917, the Interstate Commerce Commission made a special report to Congress on the railroad situation. It recommended that the government take active steps to remove barriers to unification in private hands and give financial aid from the federal Treasury, or take over the railroads and operate them as a unit during the period of the war.[58] On the following day William Gibbs McAdoo, Secretary of the Treasury, urged the President to assume control of the railroads on the basis of his existing authority and seek additional legislation after taking that step.[59]

Existing legislation on the subject consisted of the following paragraph in the Army Appropriation Act of 1916:

> The President, in time of war, is empowered, through the Secretary of War, to take possession and assume control of any system or systems of transportation, or any part thereof, and to utilize the same, to the exclusion as far as may be necessary of all other traffic thereon, for the transfer or transportation of troops, war material and equipment, or for such other purposes connected with the emergency as may be needful or desirable.[60]

The paragraph had been inserted in the bill without extended consideration. No committee hearings were held on it. It had been drafted after the experience of the government in sending troops to the Mexican border, a time when the threatened strike for the eight-hour day seemed likely to tie up the transportation system of the country. The chairman of the Senate committee on military affairs said the reason for it was

> the complaint that was generally being made that these young men of the National Guard who were being sent from Chicago and other points in the Middle West to the border were herded on cattle cars, and so with the young men, I think, from other parts of the country. . . . The committee formulated this provision thinking it might have the effect of letting the railroad companies understand that if they could not handle these things in time of war or if they could [not] do

[58] J. P. Blair, "The Federal Railway Control Act of March 21, 1918," *Southern Law Quarterly*, III (May, 1918), 97, 101. For the Interstate Commerce Commission report see 56 *Congressional Record* 1941-1942.

[59] Baker, *op. cit.*, VII, 394.  [60] 39 Stat. 619, 645.

it in time of peace or when war threatened, they might expect the government to take charge.[61]

In the language of another senator, spoken after the President had assumed control of the railroads:

> No man in either chamber of the Congress at the time the legislation was passed thought for one moment that it was giving power to the government of the United States to take over the entire railroad systems of this country. It was passed for a purpose, and a single purpose, and that purpose was to enable the government to mobilize its troops on the Mexican border.[62]

Since the measure provided no machinery for governing or managing the railroads, made no provision for determination of rates or of compensation to the owners, and left unmentioned the important subject of the ultimate return of the property to private hands, the normal procedure would have been to ask Congress for additional legislation before taking action. The administration evidently feared that Congress, faced with anything less than a *fait accompli,* would bog down in a discussion of the respective merits of public and private ownership and operation, so that disastrous chaos in transportation and finance would result before the desired legislation was enacted.

Action was weighed for nearly three weeks. Then, on December 26, 1917, when Congress had adjourned for the Christmas holidays, the President issued a proclamation taking possession and assuming control of the railroads as of December 28, 1917.[63] Administration was vested in the Secretary of the Treasury, William Gibbs McAdoo, not in his secretarial capacity, but as director general of railroads. Existing statutes and orders of the Interstate Commerce Commission affecting railroads were to continue in operation, but, said the President's proclamation, "any orders, general or special, hereafter made by said director, shall have paramount authority and be obeyed as such." [64] The director was to negotiate with the companies concerning compensation. A statement, issued along with the proclamation, explained the problems of transportation and finance which made the step necessary and gave assurance that property rights would be respected. As soon as Congress reassembled, said the President, he would recommend legislation giving definite guarantees.[65] On Janu-

---

[61] Senator Chamberlain, 53 *Congressional Record* 11492.
[62] 56 *Congressional Record* 2372.      [63] 40 Stat. 1733.      [64] 40 Stat. 1734.
[65] *Messages and Papers of the Presidents,* XVII, 8412-8413.

ary 4, 1918, he appeared before Congress to repeat his explanation and ask that the promised guarantees be given.[66] Administration bills to achieve the desired ends were introduced simultaneously in both houses.

Although there were indications of muffled resentment in Congress at the President's strategy in assuming control when the legislators were not in session, there was no outburst of criticism. The action was generally supported by government agencies, including the Interstate Commerce Commission, and, apparently, by the railroad companies themselves. Congress made no effort to secure participation of the Senate in the selection of the director general or his subordinates, or to determine the type of organization to be set up for operation of the railroads. The managerial arrangements already worked out by the administration were assumed to be permanent for the period of government operation, subject to modification as the President and his subordinates saw fit. In general, the authority sought by the administration was granted. The statute gave the President power to fix rates. It authorized the Interstate Commerce Commission to inquire into their reasonableness, but did not authorize suspension during the period of inquiry. Actually there was little likelihood of interference by the commission. A scheme of generous compensation to the railroads was included. Federal control was to end not later than a year and nine months after the ratification of a treaty of peace. The statute, as approved on March 21, 1918, concluded with a section reading as follows:

> That this act is expressly declared to be emergency legislation enacted to meet conditions growing out of war; and nothing herein is to be construed as expressing or prejudicing the future policy of the federal government concerning the ownership, control, or regulation of carriers or the method or basis of the capitalization thereof.[67]

The director general divided the country into regions for administrative purposes. He appointed railroad presidents or other high officers of the railroads as federal managers. They were required to resign from positions they had theretofore held and to accept lower salaries, representing oftentimes adjustment from a level of seventy-five thousand down to twenty-five thousand dollars a year.[68] With a generosity more characteristic of governmental paymasters than of

[66] *Ibid.*, XVIII, 8418.        [67] 40 Stat. 451, 458.
[68] Walker D. Hines, *War History of American Railroads* (1928), p. 27.

private employers, the director general raised wages to avert labor controversies. Equipment of the several roads was pooled, and the attempt was made to manage the railroads of the entire country as if they were a part of one integrated system. The director general worked with the War Industries Board, the Fuel Administration, and other agencies in bringing order out of chaos. Before the war was over, he had eliminated much of the congestion which had made centralized management a necessity. A number of inland water-transportation lines were likewise brought under his control and integrated into the system.[69]

CONTROL OF TELEPHONE AND TELEGRAPH LINES

The extension of governmental power can be illustrated from a number of other fields. The statute books contained no prewar enactment giving the President authority to take over telephone, telegraph, and cable lines as he had taken railroads. A threatened telegraphers' strike in the summer of 1918 led to a movement for enabling legislation. The President made no direct request for the legislation, as he had done in other instances. Through Joseph Tumulty, his secretary, he replied to an inquiry by saying he thought the legislation should be enacted as soon as possible.[70] He sent to the chairman of the House committee on interstate and foreign commerce a brief note endorsing a letter from Postmaster General A. S. Burleson which urged the enactment. The Burleson letter said in part:

> At this moment the paralysis of a large part of the system of electrical communication is threatened with possible consequences prejudicial to our military preparations and other public activities that might prove serious or disastrous. We are reminded that there is not a nation engaged in the war that intrusts its military or other communications to unofficial agencies.[71]

Many senators were suspicious of presidential advocacy which came only through subordinate officials or as confirmation of positions taken by subordinates. They knew that, in a number of annual reports, the Postmaster General had advocated government ownership of the agencies of electrical communication and their consolidation under the control of the Post Office Department.[72] They had no desire to see the war used to bring about the success of Mr. Burleson's

[69] Willoughby, op. cit., pp. 180-181.    [70] 56 Congressional Record 8743.
[71] Ibid., p. 8744.    [72] See Post Office Department Annual Report, 1917, p. 79.

aspirations or to give to him or others drastic powers of censorship. Some of them believed that, if government control was a war necessity, it could be exercised without legislative action. On this point as on others, however, there was no way to discover the limits of the powers of the President and the point at which legislative support was necessary. A concisely phrased joint resolution was passed, giving the President the desired powers until the ratification of a treaty of peace. Just compensation was to be paid for the use of the property.[73]

The President immediately vested control over telegraph and telephone lines in the Postmaster General.[74] The latter established a wire-control board and other agencies through which he exercised his authority. The public seems never to have been thoroughly convinced that government control was necessary or to have regarded the administration of the act favorably. Burleson advocated legislation to extend the period of control, and evidently believed that the lines would never be returned to private hands. Without waiting for a treaty of peace, Congress, on the advice of the President, terminated government control at the end of a year.[75] In his report on government operation, Burleson said that, when the properties were taken over, it was generally assumed that control would be for at least three years, "one additional year of war, one year before the proclamation of peace, and one year allowed for adjustment and settlement should Congress at the close of the war require the return of the properties."[76] The statement showed how little attention he had given to the enabling statute, which provided that government control should "not extend beyond the date of the proclamation by the President of the exchange of ratifications of the treaty of peace."[77]

## MARITIME COMMERCE, AND ENEMY TRADE

Control over common carriers on the seas had been vested in the United States Shipping Board, which was created by the Shipping Act of 1916.[78] The board was intended to have regulatory functions somewhat similar to those of the Interstate Commerce Commission. In addition, it was intended to build up the merchant marine of the

---

[73] 40 Stat. 904.

[74] 40 Stat. 1807. Control over marine cable systems was given on November 2, 1918, 40 Stat. 1872.

[75] 41 Stat. 157.    [76] Senate Doc. No. 152, 66th Cong., 1st sess., p. 6.

[77] 40 Stat. 904.    [78] 39 Stat. 728.

country through the purchase and construction of ships. For this purpose the board, pursuant to the statute, formed the government-owned Emergency Fleet Corporation under the laws of the District of Columbia. By means of this corporation the government carried on throughout the war period a huge shipbuilding program. The corporation was in part under the control of the Shipping Board, but the bylaws gave its management some degree of independence. Conflicts of jurisdiction between the two agencies interfered with operations. A true hierarchy of authority was eventually established, placing responsibility in the president of the board of trustees of the corporation, who was also chairman of the Shipping Board.[79]

Pursuant to the Trading-with-the-Enemy Act,[80] the President established by executive order a War Trade Board, consisting of representatives of the Secretaries of State, Treasury, Agriculture, and Commerce, and the heads of the Food Administration and the United States Shipping Board. Trade with persons in enemy countries could be carried on only under license from the board. By means of the supervision provided for, a certain amount of trade beneficial to the United States was continued, while transactions injurious to the United States were prohibited.

The office of alien property custodian was created pursuant to the same act, to hold and manage property in the United States which belonged to citizens or nationals of enemy countries. Money seized was invested in government bonds, to aid the United States in winning the war. It was contemplated that the property held, or the proceeds from it, would ultimately be restored to the private claimants when satisfactory relationships had been re-established with the enemy countries. The custodian began the making of payments after treaties of peace with enemy countries had been ratified. Some claims of Germans, however, remain unsettled because of failure of Germany to fulfill certain financial obligations to the United States. There was no attempt at wholesale confiscation of enemy property, such as had been advocated by many people during the Civil War.

THE CONTROL OF FINANCE

The federal reserve system established in 1914 was now in good working order. It provided a flexibility which greatly aided the United States in waging a major war without the suspension of specie payments. Through various agencies, however, the government

---

[79] Van Dorn, *op. cit.*, pp. 47-50.    [80] 40 Stat. 411.

found it necessary to exert unprecedented controls. If billions of dollars were to be available for borrowing by the government, it was necessary that borrowing for non-governmental purposes be curtailed. The raising of capital for private agencies necessary to the conduct of the war, such as the railroads, needed to be handled in such a way as to avoid competition with the government. This need provided one of the arguments for assuming complete governmental control over the railroads. The Federal Reserve Board established a capital issues committee to inspect the borrowing plans of local governments and private agencies and to discourage the marketing of loans not connected with the management of the war or necessary to the public welfare.[81] The committee was highly influential in drying up the stream of capital flowing into ordinary private business. Its functions were regarded as so important that an act of April 5, 1918, gave it independent status with the provision that at least three of the members of the committee should be members of the Federal Reserve Board.[82] Machinery was needed, on the other hand, by which the necessary capital could be provided for industries essential to the conduct of the war. By the statute mentioned, Congress created the War Finance Corporation, with the Secretary of the Treasury as chairman of the board of directors. The corporation was equipped with five hundred million dollars of government-owned capital. It was authorized to make loans to banking institutions, which in turn made loans to establishments whose operations were necessary or contributory to the prosecution of the war. The establishment of the War Finance Corporation, like many other wartime expedients, was important, not merely because of its effectiveness as a war measure, but because it constituted a precedent for other agencies, such as the Reconstruction Finance Corporation, which was created to make loans to business in later years.[83]

## EMERGENCY HOUSING

Experience in the field of emergency housing was similar to that in many other fields. Private enterprise was not equipped to bring about the rapid construction of the dwellings that were needed. Part of the difficulty lay in the extent to which finance, men, and materials were being absorbed for other war purposes. The government, there-

[81] See Woodbury Willoughby, *The Capital Issues Committee and War Finance Corporation* (1934), chapter I.

[82] 40 Stat. 506, 512.    [83] For discussion see Van Dorn, *op. cit.*, pp. 121-138.

fore, found it necessary to undertake the construction of single dwellings and apartment houses in areas congested with war workers. The
Emergency Fleet Corporation built homes for the workers brought to
its shipyards. A great deal of residential construction in other areas
was turned over to the United States Housing Corporation, which
was formed by the Secretary of Labor under the laws of New York.[84]
The corporation completed twenty-eight major projects and had
many others under way when the termination of the war made their
continuation unnecessary.[85] The difficult constitutional question
whether the federal government had the power to requisition land for
housing purposes was answered in the affirmative by a federal district
court,[86] but did not reach the higher federal courts.

### LABOR

In labor relations, as in other fields, governmental organization had
to adjust itself to the war emergency. The war depleted the supply
of available workers and increased the demand, thereby putting labor
in a strategic bargaining position. The rise in the cost of living, the
prevalence of profiteering, and the faulty distribution of labor for war
purposes gave rise to large numbers of disputes which threatened to
curtail production in the midst of the war crisis. Conditions were
particularly bad in the copper, oil, and timber industries of the West,
with the seditious influence of the Industrial Workers of the World
playing a prominent part.

During the autumn of 1917, the President's Mediation Commission,
headed by the Secretary of Labor, made a survey of the areas in which
labor troubles were reported and submitted a series of recommendations. It urged elimination of profiteering to the utmost extent, acceptance of collective bargaining, establishment of continuous administrative machinery for the settlement of disputes, acceptance of the
eight-hour day, a single-headed government administration for dealing with wartime labor problems directly affecting the government,
surrender by labor of practices restricting efficiency, and education
concerning labor's relation to the war.[87]

In co-operation with the Council of National Defense a War Labor
Administration was established in the Department of Labor. A group

---

[84] For authorizing statute see 40 Stat. 550 and 595.
[85] For discussion see Van Dorn, *op. cit.*, pp. 139-169.
[86] United States *v.* Stein, 48 F. (2d) 626 (1921).
[87] *Report of the Department of Labor*, 1918, p. 28.

of representatives of employers and workers was called together to advise on program and methods. This group became the National War Labor Board, one of the more important agencies for dealing with labor disputes during the war. Recognizing the difficulty of choosing a chairman of the group satisfactory to both factions, the Secretary invited each faction to choose a chairman, and it was arranged that each chairman was to preside on alternate days. William Howard Taft was chosen by the employers and Frank P. Walsh by the workers. When the board was given official status by the President, the two chairmen were designated as representatives of employers and employees.[88] They worked together harmoniously throughout the war.

The National War Labor Board helped to settle many serious labor disputes. It protected the right of labor to organize, without aiding the establishment of the closed shop. As an aspect of war policy it took a stand against the enforcement of "yellow-dog" contracts, even though the Supreme Court in the same period, in the Hitchman case,[89] held that rights secured by such contracts were entitled to protection. When the Western Union Telegraph Company refused to re-employ men discharged for union membership, the government took over the lines and operated them itself. When a manufacturer of rifles refused to accept the mediation or adopt the rules of the board, the War Department took charge of the operation of the plant. When members of a machinists' union went on strike in violation of an agreement rather than accept an award made through the War Labor Board, the President assured them that, unless they returned to work, they would be barred from any war industry in the community for one year. The United States Employment Service would refuse to find them work in any war industry and employment in all government agencies would be cut off from them. Draft boards would be instructed to reject exemption claims based on their alleged usefulness for war production. The men returned to work.[90]

The federal government itself had become the greatest employer in the country. To co-ordinate labor policies in the several government agencies the War Labor Policies Board was established. It consisted of representatives of the Departments of Labor, War, Navy, and Agri-

[88] *Ibid.*, pp. 99-100.

[89] Hitchman Coal and Coke Co. *v.* Mitchell, 245 U.S. 229 (1917). "Yellow-dog" contracts made abstention from union membership a condition of employment.

[90] Baker, *op. cit.*, VIII (1939), 401-402.

culture, and of the Shipping Board, the Emergency Fleet Corporation, the Food and Fuel and Railroad Administrations, and the War Industries Board. The new board did much to establish uniform standards for labor throughout the field of government employment.[91]

Many employers took the position that state laws governing labor conditions could not be enforced in plants producing goods under contract for the government. The federal government had no code of labor law to apply to private industry. To secure adequate protection for labor, therefore, the War Labor Policies Board secured the insertion in contracts of clauses requiring full compliance with state labor laws in carrying out the contracts.[92]

A different kind of state legislation threatened to embarrass the federal government. Because workers were being drawn away by news of jobs elsewhere at better wages and under better conditions, a number of states, many of them in the South, enacted laws taxing the solicitation of labor or forbidding outright the enticement of workers away from employers whom they were serving under contract. Attempts were made to enforce these laws against agents of the federal government and of corporations producing materials for the government. The Department of Justice took the position that the laws could not be enforced to embarrass the federal government and instructed United States attorneys to defend persons prosecuted. The invalidity of the laws was particularly clear, it was said, in such a case as that of the Du Pont Engineering Company, where the company was under contract to erect a plant and operate it for the government. It was even more clear as to the government-owned corporation operating the nitrate plant at Muscle Shoals.[93]

A federal court issued an injunction against a strike in a plant engaged primarily in manufacture of goods for the government, in a building erected at government expense, with raw materials provided by the government. The company, said the judge, was "to all intents and purposes an instrumentality or agency of the government itself created and existing under national laws." [94] Other employers would have liked to use government contracts as a means of escape from unpleasant labor involvements. Usually, however, the government did not support the use of government contracts to secure injunctions

---

[91] *Report of the Department of Labor,* 1918, pp. 115-118.     [92] *Ibid.,* p. 121.

[93] LaRue Brown to Hooper Alexander, June 26, 1918, Department of Justice File No. 191906. See Homer Cummings and Carl McFarland, *Federal Justice* (1937), p. 454.

[94] Wagner Electric Mfg. Co. *v.* District Lodge, 252 Fed. 597 (1918).

against strikes. Curtailment of the right to strike came through such agencies as the War Labor Board, which compensated for loss of the right by securing many of the privileges for which strikes might otherwise have been undertaken.

## THE COMMITTEE ON PUBLIC INFORMATION

A unique expansion of federal powers for war purposes was the creation — one might almost say the manufacture — of public sentiment favorable to measures necessary for the conduct of the war. National leaders saw the necessity of cutting off the flow to the enemy of information that might injure the United States and the Allies and of checking the spread of enemy propaganda in the United States; but from the beginning it was recognized that something other than, or in addition to, mere censorship was needed. Furthermore, England's blundering experience with censorship at the beginning of the war had not been particularly happy. It was hoped that by combining censorship with a positive publicity program, which would give out a maximum of war information not injurious to the country and which would stimulate enthusiasm for vigorous prosecution of the war, a maximum of good would be achieved with a minimum of evil.

On April 13, 1917, a week after the date of the declaration of war, the Secretaries of State, War, and Navy addressed to the President a letter advising the creation of a Committee on Public Information, to consist of the three Secretaries, or persons designated by them, and a civilian chairman, "preferably some writer of proved courage, ability, and vision, able to gain the understanding co-operation of the press and at the same time rally the authors of the country to a work of service." The three Secretaries believed the President had the power to create such a committee without waiting for further legislation. The President created it by executive order of April 14, 1917, with George Creel, a magazine writer and former newspaperman, as chairman.[95] A news item said that administration officials were considering the draft of a simple bill to be recommended to Congress with the object of giving the committee statutory authority to carry out its rulings.[96]

Under Creel's direction, the Committee on Public Information

[95] *Official Bulletin*, May 10, 1917, p. 4. See also James R. Mock and Cedric Larson, *Words that Won the War: The Story of the Committee on Public Information, 1917-1919* (1939), pp. 48-51.

[96] *New York Times*, April 15, 1917.

operated as a loosely knit and ever-changing, but always powerful, organization, spreading information and propagating beliefs for the American people. It prepared articles, editorials, and cartoons for the use of newspapers. Beginning May 10, 1917, it published an *Official Bulletin* by which public documents and digests of information were circulated among the departments, bureaus, and offices of the government, and displayed in post offices; and it was sent to such subscribers as would pay the price. Casualty lists lent grim attraction to this daily publication. The committee provided advertisements and posters for Liberty Loan drives and other purposes, speeches and "four-minute men" to deliver them before public assemblies, and motion pictures, not yet vocal, with propaganda displays and appropriate scripts.[97]

Although the committee had no power of censorship in the nature of direct authority to punish the publication of any kind of material, it had indirect power through reliance of the administration on its judgment as to the giving-out of information. Furthermore, the chairman became a member of the censorship board established under the Trading-with-the-Enemy Act, to deal with foreign communications, and was in such close contact with the Postmaster General and other government officials as to make it unwise for any publication to flout his policies.

During the weeks following the creation of the Committee on Public Information, Congress debated the provisions of the omnibus measure which came to be known as the Espionage Act. Censorship was discussed at length, under the suspicious eyes of the press of the country. Drastic proposals were rejected, and Congress included no provisions concerning an agency to control public information. Bills introduced thereafter to provide for a war information commission died in committee.[98]

The Committee on Public Information continued to function, therefore, purely on the basis of the executive order which created it. It was watched with suspicion by the press and by anti-administration politicians. A dispute over the handling of one item of information led to the proposal of a Senate resolution asking the Secretary of the Navy to provide the relevant facts, and asking him further "to furnish the Senate with the names of all persons employed by such Committee on Public Information, and the salaries received by them,

[97] For discussion see generally Mock and Larson, *op. cit.*
[98] 55 *Congressional Record* 3589, 3745, 4058.

and the character of the duties performed by each, together with a full statement of the rules regulating press censorship and the reasons for the frequent changes in the same, especially concerning cable messages." [99] The resolution was debated, but no further action was taken. It was disclosed that expenses of the committee were paid out of a fund of one hundred million dollars allotted to the President for use at his discretion for general purposes of defense. Senator Lodge remarked that Congress had refused to give power to Mr. Creel, and added sarcastically that "Mr. Creel, apparently, is part of the general defense of the country; and the little government publication which he is publishing, and the scores of people whom I am told he has employed to do what might be done by a stenographer and a couple of clerks, are being paid for out of that fund." [100]

Other measures were introduced in Congress to provide statutory authorization for a publicity organization, but none of them were enacted. The Committee on Public Information continued to function and exerted a tremendous amount of influence. It worked alongside the Food Administration, the Fuel Administration, the Department of Agriculture, and the many other agencies pouring out publicity and propaganda material. It also worked alongside or with the Post Office Department and other agencies restricting publication and circulation of news and propaganda. It achieved its results in spite of lack of monopoly powers and in spite of the fact that no statute provided for its existence. [101]

CO-ORDINATION

The number, size, and complexity of agencies operating in the federal government during the first World War were unprecedented. The problems of co-ordination were overwhelming, both because of the lack of experience with agencies of such size and complexity and because of the novelty of the purposes for which they were created. No scheme was worked out for the complete co-ordination of the entire governmental establishment as it had to do with the war, except through the hands of the President. The beginnings of co-ordination were made in the summer of 1917 when two agencies set up under the Council of National Defense, the Munitions Standards Board and the General Munitions Board, were merged in the War Industries

[99] *Ibid.,* p. 5414.    [100] *Ibid.,* p. 5421.

[101] By an appropriation act of July 1, 1918, 40 Stat. 634, 646, Congress recognized the existence of the Committee on Public Information by making an appropriation for its expenses.

**Board.** The new board was to supervise the acquisition of supplies by the War and Navy Departments and act in many ways as an intermediary between government and industry. It ultimately drew together in its own hands many lines of control. Throughout 1917, however, it remained subordinate to the Council of National Defense and was therefore subordinate to agencies which needed at times a measure of regimentation in order to eliminate conflicts.

Before the end of the year a considerable amount of dissatisfaction developed concerning the progress of war preparations. Confusion was much in evidence. Plans went awry, programs of production and distribution bogged down, frantic agencies got in each other's way, and competing government purchasing agencies fought for the possession of the same materials. Materials were said to have been carried to Europe and then carried back again for want of ballast in otherwise empty ships. Men trained for battle were sent abroad and had to be provided with clothing and guns by the Allies whom they went to assist. Hearings before the Senate committee on military affairs disclosed gross inefficiency at critical points. In spite of the fact that criticism of the government was denounced as giving aid and comfort to the enemy, such criticism was voiced in Congress and given publicity by the press.

The great need was not for more agencies but for over-all supervision, co-ordination of activity from the top. The President, it was said time and time again, was already burdened with more responsibility than any man could possibly carry. He should be provided with right-hand assistance in managing the mass of organizations subject to his control. The committee on military affairs did not return to the plan for a joint congressional committee to aid the President, but proposed the creation of a ministry of munitions and of a war cabinet of three men.

Senator Chamberlain, chairman of the committee on military affairs, and Senator Hitchcock, a member of the committee, called on the President to discuss means of co-ordinating and speeding-up the military program, and Senator Chamberlain mentioned a bill which he had in mind for the creation of a munitions ministry. On January 11, the President wrote to Senator Chamberlain opposing the plan for such a ministry. He said in part, "I have had in the last few months a great deal of experience in trying to co-ordinate things, and upon every fresh co-ordination delay inevitably results, and not only delay, but all sorts of cross-currents of demoralization which are very serious impediments to the effective conduct of business." He spoke of evidence that munitions ministries on "the other side of the water" had not fulfilled expectations, and added that "the structure of those governments is so utterly different from our own that we could not, if we would, create any such parity of power and influence between the head of such a bureau and the heads of the permanent departments as can be created under such political arrangements as the French and English." [102]

Senator Chamberlain was not convinced. In a speech delivered in New York on January 19, 1918, he declared that the military establishment had fallen down and had almost stopped functioning because of inefficiency in every bureau and department of the government. Congress was trying to centralize in one man the power of supplying the army.

> We have reported a bill, following the experience of Great Britain and France, creating a director of munitions for this purpose. We have gone one step further, and we have provided a bill for the creation of a cabinet of war, whose duty it shall be to lay out what we never have had, and have not now — a program to carry on this war to a successful conclusion. My friends, this is not an administration measure; it is an American measure, and comes from Republicans and Democrats both. [103]

The President wrote to ask if the senator's statement about the condition of the military establishment had been reported correctly. [104] Chamberlain verified the report, whereupon the President gave to the press a pronouncement that the statement of the senator was "an astonishing and absolutely unjustifiable distortion of the truth." There had been delays and disappointments, but the War Department had performed a great and difficult task with extraordinary promptness and efficiency. Congressional investigations had merely contributed to such delay and confusion as had already arisen. Reorganization measures based on experience had already been worked out, and were "much more likely than any others to be effective, if the Congress will but remove a few statutory obstacles of rigid departmental organization which stand in their way. The legislative proposals I have heard of would involve long additional delays and turn our experience into mere lost motion." [105]

---

[102] 56 *Congressional Record* 1207.
[103] *New York Times*, January 20, 1918, quoted, 56 *Congressional Record* 1195.
[104] 56 *Congressional Record* 1195.
[105] *Washington Herald*, January 22, 1918, quoted, 56 *Congressional Record* 1196.

In the meantime, on January 21, 1918, Senator Chamberlain introduced the war cabinet bill. The war cabinet was to consist of "three distinguished citizens of demonstrated executive ability," to be appointed by the President with confirmation by the Senate. It was to work out and execute plans for the effectual conduct of the war and to supervise, co-ordinate, and direct the functions of other executive agencies of the government for that purpose. Although the activities and decisions of the cabinet were to be subject to the review of the President, it seemed clear that, if the bill were enacted, it would delegate to the cabinet many of the reins of authority which the President had hitherto jealously kept in his own hands.[106]

Publication of Chamberlain's speech, the exchange of correspondence between him and the President, the President's statement to the press, and the senator's comment resulted in angry discussion of the bill and the issues. On February 4, Senator Hitchcock made a speech to the Senate in which he disclosed many of the findings of the investigating committee, including the "confusion of authority, red tape, circumlocution, and incapacity" found in the War Department.[107] Senator James A. Reed, although often a critic of the administration, opposed the bill. It was unconstitutional, he believed, in that it established an agency to exercise the powers conferred on the President as commander-in-chief of the army and navy. Furthermore, it added to the multiplicity of agencies by providing one not desired by the President, in the hope of promoting efficiency by co-ordinating lines of authority running from the President.[108] It was argued by some that final authority was still vested in the President and that the bill merely provided machinery for the exercise of his powers. The issue was never completely clarified.

Wilson was apparently concerned about the possibility that the bill might be passed and about the criticism of governmental inefficiency. As the debate was getting under way, therefore, he had a bill prepared authorizing him to co-ordinate or consolidate executive agencies for the period of the war, and to transfer functions and create new agencies by executive order. Postmaster General Burleson took the bill to Senator Martin, of Virginia, Democratic floor leader, who thought it went too far and refused to introduce it.[109] It was introduced by Senator Overman, chairman of the Senate judiciary committee, and referred to his committee.

[106] S. 3583, 56 *Congressional Record* 1077-1078.     [107] 56 *Congressional Record* 1807 ff.
[108] *Ibid.*, pp. 1618-1621.     [109] *New York Times,* February 7 and 8, 1918.

The presentation of the administration bill created excitement in the Senate and in the press. Senator Hitchcock declared that its enactment "would mean nothing but an abdication by Congress of its lawmaking power." [110] Senator Reed Smoot thought there would be nothing left but to make the President a king. [111] Other senators sputtered about the proposed congressional abdication of power. The *New York Times* said of the bill, "It outstrips in its delegation of power the authority contemplated in the war cabinet bill and the measure for a director of munitions together." [112] One effect, in any event, was to prevent further consideration of the latter measures.

The committee eliminated the important provision of the Overman bill authorizing the President to create new agencies by executive order and "to vest therein the performance of such functions as he may deem appropriate." Other changes of lesser importance were made, and information was circulated that the principal desire of the President was to have unrestricted power for effective co-ordination of the work of the War Department. President Wilson conferred with individual senators from time to time and urged the enactment of the measure. On the last day of February it came to a vote in the judiciary committee, and the vote was a tie. Three weeks passed before the tie was broken and the measure was reported favorably.

Formal debate began early in April. It was more than six weeks before the bill was ready for the signature of the President. Friends of the measure demonstrated that reorganization of government agencies to promote efficiency was not the product of the war emergency. It had been vigorously advocated by President Taft, for example, when there was no war on the horizon. The need was a continuing need which was merely accentuated by the war. Opponents suggested that the bill was a device for taking powers and functions from independent agencies, including the Interstate Commerce Commission, the Federal Trade Commission, and the Federal Reserve Board. Another ground of criticism was the fact that the President had asked for the enactment indirectly through intermediaries rather than by a formal request stating his grounds for advocating the measure.

Debate on the Overman bill, as on other measures, showed disagreement as to the line drawn by the Constitution between the powers of the President and those of Congress. Senator Knox, who in earlier years had been Attorney General and then Secretary of State, argued that the President, not as war chief, but as the Chief

[110] *Ibid.*, February 7.  [111] *Ibid.*, February 8.  [112] *Ibid.*, February 7.

Executive of the United States, "could distribute the executive functions as he saw fit and compel such co-ordination as he saw fit" without the enactment of legislation to that effect. He thought it a mistake for the President to call upon Congress for authority to do what he already had the power to do.[113]

In contrast, Senator Cummins, of Iowa, thought the bill unconstitutional because it attempted to delegate legislative power to the President:

> The difficulty of the question we have before us is that there are some people who harbor the delusion that in time of war all the power of the government which it may properly exercise in defense or in aggression must be exercised by the President. That is the point of divergence. The President has vast war powers under the Constitution. In the very nature of things his authority as commander-in-chief of the army and navy is immensely widened in the event of war. But, after all, the war powers which can be justly exercised by the President under the Constitution are but a tithe of the powers which we must employ in order to carry on the war successfully; and those further powers are to be employed by Congress and not by the President.[114]

As in many other debates, the discussion here did little to clarify the constitutional question. The bill was ultimately passed by both houses of Congress and was approved by the President.[115] No serious attempt was made to secure the enactment of the competing measures.

### THE WAR INDUSTRIES BOARD

Under the Overman Act the President brought about a number of changes in governmental organization. The principal change was decided upon and actually initiated some weeks before the act was passed. The powers of the War Industries Board, or of its chairman, were expanded and its position was strengthened as a co-ordinating agency. The board had originally been in the form of a committee under the Council of National Defense, by which it had been organized. It was in no position to give orders to the Secretary of War or to other members of the council. On March 4, 1918, while the Senate judiciary committee was deadlocked over the bill, the President wrote a letter to Bernard M. Baruch asking him to accept the chairmanship of the War Industries Board. The letter gave full power and responsibility to the chairman in most matters over which

[113] 56 *Congressional Record* 4581.  [114] *Ibid.*, p. 5015.  [115] 40 Stat. 556.

the board had jurisdiction. With the important exception of price-fixing, it left the remaining members chiefly as advisers to the chairman. The President outlined the functions of the board and the duties of the chairman as if it were now independent of the Council of National Defense. To all intents and purposes it became independent immediately after the Overman Act was passed, when the President issued an executive order establishing the board as "a separate administrative agency to act for me and under my direction." [116]

In separating the War Industries Board from the Council of National Defense and establishing it as an independent administrative agency, the President may have violated the spirit of the Overman Act, since the authorization to create new agencies and transfer powers and functions to them had been stricken from the bill. However that may be, the board, through Chairman Baruch, became an extremely powerful agency during the last months of the war. Grosvenor B. Clarkson, the historian of the board, has said that through it the United States "had in the end a system of concentration of commerce, industry, and all the powers of government that was without compare among all the other nations, friend or enemy, involved in the World War." [117]

A great deal of the power of the War Industries Board was exercised through the establishment of priorities, in connection with both production and distribution. It "said what should be produced and where, and it said who should have the product." [118] The chairman of the board and a price-fixing committee worked out in co-operation with industry the prices which the government was to pay for commodities. The prices fixed were high, allowing substantial profits to industry, but they were not as high as they would have been without control through negotiation. Taxes on incomes and on excess profits operated further to make industry the servant of the government for the purpose of winning the war, even though they did not prevent the growth of a crop of war millionaires. No attempt was made to test the limits of the legal authority of the board. Some thought that such authority was broad; others thought it was narrow. Much of its control was exercised through co-operation with industry and with the government agencies it was authorized to co-ordinate. In terms

[116] Executive order of May 28, 1918. The letter of March 4, 1918, was included as a part of or an appendix to the order. *Messages and Papers of the Presidents*, XVIII, 8518-8519.

[117] Grosvenor B. Clarkson, *Industrial America in the World War* (1924), p. 63.

[118] *Ibid.*, p. 154.

of results, it smoothed out many of the tangles of production and purchase and delivery, so that by the date of the armistice the nation
had relatively smoothly functioning supply machinery for war purposes.

Such were the major forms of organizational adjustment for the
conduct of the war. There were others of importance. The Department of Agriculture girded itself for the stimulation of agricultural
production. The Department of Justice organized a War Emergency
Division and enlarged its Division of Investigation. Investigatory
and detecting agencies in other departments were expanded. The
high degree of compartmentalization in the War Department was
modified. The military establishment itself had to adjust its organization to the practical experience of preparation for and conduct of
war in a foreign field.

CONCLUSION

The experience with problems of organization and control during
the first World War demonstrated the fact that the federal structure
of the government and the principle of the separation of powers provided no real hindrance to efficient conduct of war. State-rights issues
caused little friction of any importance. By the enactment of new
laws and by law enforcement the several states gave full support to
the federal government. On the other hand, the extension of the
power of the federal government over commerce and industry speeded
the perennial process by which the federal government assumed control over matters which, if subject to control at all, were supposed to
be within the exclusive province of the states.

As to relations between Congress and the President, the outstanding characteristic was presidential dominance. The illustrations presented above, and many others not enumerated here, show that for
the most part the President was able to secure the organizational
set-up he wanted for the conduct of the war. In some instances, as in
the establishment of the Council of National Defense, he found clear
authorization in statutes previously enacted. In other instances, as
in the case of railroad control, he found statutes which gave at least a
certain amount of plausible authority for doing what he wanted to do.
In some instances legislation was speedily enacted at his request. In
others, as in the matter of selecting Herbert Hoover to be food administrator and as in the matter of making Bernard Baruch virtual director of the War Industries Board with augmented powers, he acted in

advance of legislation which was finally enacted. He had struggles with Congress from time to time, but in each case he finally won his point.

Wilson achieved for the presidency far more power than the office had ever held down to that time. The resources subject to his command were incomparably greater than those available during the Civil War. To a much greater extent than President Lincoln, he laid down a legislative program for enactment by Congress. The subordination of Congress to his will was much more in evidence than during any preceding administration. For the period of the war he went a long way toward establishing the relation between the President and Congress which he regarded as permanently desirable. In spite of the temporary and partial revolt against such a relation during a period of years after the end of military hostilities, Wilson paved the way for the powerful administration of Franklin D. Roosevelt.

Another fact is important; namely, that organizational patterns created for war purposes provided the technical basis for subsequent control of economic life when war powers could not be relied upon as the constitutional basis. Experience with wartime organization helped to determine the course of constitutional development, as knowledge of previously used patterns of control and desires for the achievement of particular results combined to overcome constitutional scruples about the legitimacy of a given program.

The following are outstanding examples of the carry-over: Former members of the War Industries Board aided in shaping the National Recovery Administration of 1933 in its image and in attempting to re-create the co-operative atmosphere in which the board functioned. The War Finance Corporation established a pattern for the Reconstruction Finance Corporation and for other government lending agencies. The Fuel Administration provided background for the National Bituminous Coal Commission and its successor, the Bituminous Coal Division in the Department of the Interior, as well as for organization in the Interior Department for control of the oil industry. The Food Administration provided background for subsequent activities of the Department of Agriculture. The housing agencies of the war period were succeeded, a quarter of a century later, by other housing agencies in the New-Deal period. The director general of railroads had his counterpart in the federal co-ordinator of transportation. The labor boards of the war period provided experience for other labor boards established in later years, including the National Mediation Board set up pursuant to the Railway Labor Act of 1926, and the National Labor Relations Board. The United States Shipping Board passed through a series of changes and culminated in the United States Maritime Commission. Many obvious parallels exist between the war organization of 1917-1918 and the period of national defense beginning in 1939 and of war beginning in 1941.[119]

Other illustrations might be given, but those listed demonstrate the point. It is true that many of the succeeding organizations differed somewhat from their predecessors when they were created and differed still more as experience with changed conditions showed the desirability of change. The fact remains, however, that the patterns carried over and served as a guide for the establishment of new organizations, and therefore to some extent for the shaping of national policies.[120]

[119] See chapter 38.

[120] For further discussion see ensuing chapters, particularly those covering the New Deal period.

••••••••••••••••••••••••••••••••••••••••••••••••••••••••••••••••••••••••••••••••••••••••••••••••••••••••••••••••••••••••••••

# CHAPTER 28

# BETWEEN WAR AND PEACE

THE PERIOD between the signing of the armistice in November, 1918, and the formal termination of war between the United States and Germany some three years later was one of bitter conflict within the American government and among the American people over the methods to be adopted to achieve and maintain permanent peace. Amid the heat of the military conflict, President Wilson had committed himself to the creation of a league of nations which would do away with the approximate condition of anarchy among nations, a condition which culminated in the catastrophe of modern war. The conception was not essentially different from that in terms of which the American states had united under the Articles of Confederation. The plan had support among statesmen of both political parties, but it had opposition as well in a high degree from Republicans and to a lesser degree from Democrats. Without reference to partisanship, furthermore, many vigorous participants in the war effort continued opposed to involvement of the United States in more than a minimum of foreign entanglements. They were hostile to any conception of a super-government which might in any way limit the sovereignty and the freedom of action of the United States. This chapter deals with the constitutional aspects of the struggle for and against the embodiment of the Covenant of the League of Nations in the treaty of peace. It deals extensively with the efforts of the President to preserve his dominance over a Congress increasingly resentful of presidential domination and his effort to coerce the Senate into ratifying the Treaty of Versailles.

## PARTISAN CONTROL OF CONGRESS

During the first two years of President Wilson's second administration, his own party held a majority in both houses of Congress. Although most Republicans had given loyal support to the war program,

Wilson naturally desired the continuation of Democratic majorities in the post-war period, when the patriotism of Republicans would no longer compel them to accept his leadership. He decided upon an appeal to the people to avert the possibility that Republicans might gain control of one or both houses. Accordingly, on October 25, 1918, he issued a request that the people return Democratic majorities if they approved of his leadership and wished him to continue as their unembarrassed spokesman in affairs at home and abroad. He said:

> The leaders of the minority in the present Congress have unquestionably been pro-war, but they have been anti-administration. At almost every turn since we entered the war they have sought to take the choice of policy and the conduct of the war out of my hands and put it under the control of instrumentalities of their own choosing.

This was no time, he urged, for divided counsel or divided leadership.

> The return of a Republican majority to either house of the Congress would, moreover, be interpretative on the other side of the water as a repudiation of my leadership.[1]

Up to this point during the war the masses of the people had been persuaded to support the President as the leader of a unified nation, rather than as the head of a victorious political party. Wilson's appeal was a call back to partisanship. Though indignant at his strategy, Republican leaders were delighted to be able once more to fight election battles openly along party lines. Two Republican ex-Presidents, Roosevelt and Taft, put aside their differences with each other to make a joint appeal for the election of a Republican Congress to put a check on one-man power,[2] Taft saying that the President demanded power equal to that of the Hohenzollerns.[3] Charles E. Hughes said Republicans had supported Wilson, not as a party President, but as head of the nation.[4] He criticised the administration for capitalizing the patriotism of the people for party purposes.[5]

The elections gave Republicans a majority in both houses, although their control of the Senate was precarious. What the election results would have been had the Wilson appeal not been issued is beyond prediction. The Republicans were now in power in Congress — or rather, would be in power when the newly elected Congress assembled after March 4, 1919 — and feeling of partisanship was as

[1]*Messages and Papers of the Presidents,* XVIII, 8627-8629.
[2] *New York Times,* November 1, 1918.          [3] *Ibid.,* November 2, 1918.
[4] *Ibid.,* October 30, 1918.          [5] *Ibid.,* November 1, 1918.

bitter as if the people had never been asked to forget party and think only of the nation. The result was not serious as far as the direction of military activities was concerned, since the armistice was announced a few days after the election was held, but it meant divided leadership in working out the terms of peace. In view of the President's interest in achieving a peace which would do more than provide a breathing period to prepare for another war, and of his plans for a league of nations which would prevent future wars, his defeat in the election seemed disastrous.

### THE PRESIDENT'S TRIPS TO EUROPE

The defeat was irrevocable, but the President could hardly do otherwise than continue with his plans for a new world order after the war, as if no such defeat had taken place. On November 18, 1918, one week after the armistice was announced, he stated briefly his intention to sail for France immediately after Congress assembled, "for the purpose of taking part in the discussion and settlement of the main features of the treaty of peace." [6] Such a step involved a drastic departure from precedent. Other Presidents had ventured into Mexico, Cuba, and Canada, but only for brief visits,[7] and not for the purpose of conducting in person the official diplomatic business of the government.

Wilson's purpose in going abroad was clearly the achievement of justice in the establishment of peace along the lines of his famous Fourteen Points, and the establishment at this strategic moment of a league of nations to prevent future wars. He never published a clear statement of his reasons for believing that these ends could be achieved better if he went in person than if he followed precedent and sent representatives to negotiate for him. His decision indicated his belief that a meeting of principals rather than of subordinates was more likely to be effective.

Whatever the reasons for the decision, the public was at best not more than lukewarm toward it, and Republican leaders and other critics challenged the constitutionality of the plan. They contended, for example, that, if the President went abroad for a prolonged stay, he would be unable to discharge the powers and duties of his office,

---

[6] *Messages and Papers of the Presidents*, XVIII, 8649.

[7] See Harry J. Cole, "To What Extent Can the President of the United States Perform the Duties of His Office While Abroad?" *Massachusetts Law Quarterly*, IV (February, 1919), 180; 57 *Congressional Record* 25 ff.

and these duties, under the Constitution, would therefore devolve on the Vice-President.[8] George Wickersham, formerly Attorney General in the Taft administration, enumerated presidential duties which could not be performed adequately by a President absent from the country, stressing those connected with bills passed by Congress. The President was to consider such bills and approve and sign them, or return them to the house of origin with his objections, after which they might be passed over his veto. If he did not return a bill within ten days (Sundays excepted) after it was presented to him, it became a law as if he had signed it, unless Congress adjourned in the meantime. It seemed to Wickersham that the mere mechanical operation of this machinery required the presence of the President in his own country while Congress was in session. Furthermore, he said:

> The power and duty of acting on the bills are not conferred upon the President that they may be exercised without regard to public sentiment, and he can only properly exercise that power and discharge that duty by being in a position where he can feel the pulse of public sentiment, receive observations respecting the bill from those who may be affected by it, and give to considerations for and in opposition to it impartial and thorough consideration. If he is not within the country, he cannot fitly discharge those duties.[9]

Under those circumstances Wickersham thought the duties should devolve upon the Vice-President, but he was in doubt as to the measures necessary "to set the Vice-President in motion." Some thought, he said, that a joint resolution of Congress would be the proper method. Others thought a mandamus would lie to compel the Vice-President to act. Wickersham agreed that a mandamus might lie,[10] but thought it would be an unsatisfactory remedy because of the great amount of time required.[11]

The *New York Times* rushed an interview with Vice-President Thomas R. Marshall on the Wickersham speech. Marshall declared that he would not assume presidential duties of his own volition when President Wilson went to the peace conference. He was unable to

---

[8] See the part of Article II, Section 1, of the Constitution which reads as follows: "In case of the removal of the President from office, or of his death, resignation, or inability to discharge the powers and duties of the said office, the same shall devolve on the Vice President, and the Congress may by law provide for the case of removal, death, resignation, or inability, both of the President and Vice President. . . ."

[9] *New York Times*, November 27, 1918.

[10] Citing Attorney General *v.* Taggart, 66 N.H. 362.

[11] *New York Times*, November 27, 1918.

say what he would do if Congress adopted a joint resolution to "set the Vice-President in motion." On the other hand, he would assume the presidential duties if a court having jurisdiction directed him to do so. He did not commit himself on the difficult constitutional problem as to the power of a court to control the actions of the Vice-President by mandamus, when the question involved was what might be called a political question.[12]

Taking no direct notice of the criticism and of the discussion of his powers and duties, the President, on December 2, 1918, announced at the opening of the "lame-duck" session of Congress his intention to go to Europe and discuss there the main features of the treaty of peace, saying that the peace settlements "are of transcendent importance both to us and to the rest of the world, and I know of no business or interest which should take precedence of them."[13] He sailed on December 4, with a retinue notably lacking in representatives of the Senate and of Republican statesmen. Former President Taft stood virtually alone among Republican leaders in approving the President's trip.[14] Democratic leaders were not too convincing in their support of it.

Republicans in Congress heckled the President in terms of constitutional questions. A representative introduced a joint resolution declaring the absence of the President from the United States an inability to discharge the duties of the office and providing that the powers of the office should devolve upon the Vice-President.[15] A senator introduced a concurrent resolution with a series of explanatory "whereas" clauses, providing that the President's departure be declared to constitute an inability to discharge the powers and duties of his office and that these powers and duties immediately devolve upon the Vice-President, who should serve until a President should be duly elected.[16] The resolution was hotly debated.[17] A letter from Hannis Taylor, a constitutional lawyer of some repute, was presented in support of the Republican contention.[18]

The criticisms of the President for leaving the country were taken so seriously that Taft, an ardent advocate of a league of nations, pub-

[12] For discussions of political questions see Index.

[13] Messages and Papers of the Presidents, XVIII, 8647.

[14] New York Times, November 27, 1918.

[15] 57 Congressional Record 19.      [16] Ibid., p. 23.      [17] Ibid., pp. 24 ff.

[18] Ibid., pp. 27-28. See David Hunter Miller, "Some Legal Aspects of the Visit of President Wilson to Paris," Harvard Law Review, XXXVI (November, 1922), 51. See also Henry E. Davis, "Inability of the President," published as Senate Doc. No. 308, 65th Cong., 3d sess.

lished a defense in a Washington newspaper,[19] which was reprinted in the *Congressional Record.*[20] It read in part as follows:

> There is no constitutional inhibition, express or implied, to prevent the President's going abroad to discharge a function clearly given him by the Constitution. That instrument says that he shall make treaties by and with the consent of two-thirds of the Senate. It is a curious error to assume that the President himself may not attend a conference to which he can send a delegate. . . . There is certainly no express restriction of this sort in the Constitution, and it is difficult to see why it should be implied. . . .
>
> The President can by cable perform all his executive duties from Paris. If his duty abroad is more important than his duty here in connection with a session of Congress, Congress may well wait until his return, or, if the public exigency requires, may invite the Vice-President to do these things as Acting President which the absence of the President on foreign duty prevents his doing.
>
> Our Constitution is great in its elastic character and in its adapting itself to the changing and varying needs of the unseen future. No other executive is forbidden to leave the country. Kings do it, premiers do it; why should we infer such a restriction when it is not expressed?

Taft recognized the fact that most critics were interested less in accurate constitutional interpretation than in heckling the President, and remarked, "The disposition of some to nag the President . . . by urging the adoption of resolutions inviting the Vice-President to act for the President meets with no popular favor."[21] His interpretation of public sentiment may have been correct and his comments may have played a part in checking the discussion. In any event, the Democrats were in control of Congress for the period of the current session and in position to prevent the adoption of either of the proposed resolutions.

While in Paris, during that session, the President performed varied duties in relation to Congress. He approved a number of bills which had been sent to him for that purpose.[22] He cabled the Secretary of

[19] *Washington Post,* December 5, 1918.

[20] 57 *Congressional Record* 119-120.     [21] *Ibid.,* p. 120.

[22] See Lindsay Rogers, "American Government and Politics," *American Political Science Review,* XIV (February, 1920), 87-88, note 7; Lindsay Rogers, "Power of the President to Sign Bills After Congress Has Adjourned," *Yale Law Journal,* XXX (November, 1920), 4, note 6. The ten-day period began to run when the bills reached the President for signature. Notice of the signature of a number of bills was not received by Congress until well beyond the expiration of the ten-day period. In the meantime, therefore, Congress must have been in ignorance whether the statutes achieved validity by virtue of the presidential signature or because of being held by the President beyond the ten-day period.

the Treasury to seek from Congress an appropriation to feed the starving people in Europe.[23]  He asked chairmen of congressional appropriation committees to speed the enactment of the measure.[24]  He appointed Walker D. Hines director general of railroads, to succeed William G. McAdoo.[25]  He issued a proclamation permitting the use of grain in the manufacture of non-intoxicating beverages.[26]  He returned to the United States doubtless in part to be in position to decide on the disposition of a large number of bills enacted in the later days of the expiring Congress,[27] but, however inconvenient he may have found it to dispose of domestic business while abroad, he seems to have had no difficulty with constitutional or other legal inhibitions.

He went abroad a second time, and while there he issued proclamations and executive orders.  He called an extra session of Congress,[28] now to be controlled by Republicans.  He sent a message for the opening session of Congress, discussing needed legislation.[29]  He approved a number of bills.[30]  No real attempt was made to interfere with his authority or to have the Vice-President perform his functions.  While the Vice-President presided at cabinet meetings,[31] represented the President at the funeral of Theodore Roosevelt,[32] and doubtless took care of other minor matters, he never became an Acting President in any real sense, as Taft had suggested that he might do.

### THE SENATE AND THE TREATY-MAKING POWER

Prospects of controversy between the President and the Senate over the work of the peace conference were accentuated by the tradition of conflict over treaties submitted for senatorial approval.  The treaty to be negotiated was not only to terminate the most sweeping war in world experience, but was also to provide machinery for the settlement of future international disputes without recourse to war.  Treaties for the pacific settlement of such disputes had received rough

---

[23] *Messages and Papers of the Presidents,* XVIII, 8684.

[24] *Ibid.,* p. 8685.      [25] *Ibid.,* p. 8686.      [26] *Ibid.,* p. 8687.

[27] See Josephus Daniels, *The Life of Woodrow Wilson* (1924), p. 308.

[28] *Messages and Papers of the Presidents,* XVIII, 8709.

[29] *Ibid.,* p. 8712.

[30] Lindsay Rogers, "American Government and Politics," *American Political Science Review,* XIV (February, 1920), 87-88.

[31] *New York Times,* January 1, 1919.

[32] *Ibid.,* January 8, 1919.

handling by the Senate during the two preceding decades.[33]  That
body took the substance out of a group of arbitration treaties negotiated by Secretary of State John Hay.  Its attitude had much to do
with the limited character of other arbitration treaties negotiated by
Elihu Root.  It so effectively devitalized the Taft-Knox arbitration
treaties of 1911 that the President refused thereafter to resubmit them
to the other parties.

The experience of the Taft-Knox arbitration treaties, negotiated
with Great Britain and France, is illuminating.  They provided that
controversies between the parties not otherwise terminated, and
which were justiciable in their nature by reason of being susceptible
of decision by the application of the principles of law or equity,
should be submitted to an arbitral tribunal.  Any question as to the
justiciable character of a dispute was to be decided by a joint high
commission of inquiry.  In a report submitted by Senator Henry
Cabot Lodge, the Senate committee on foreign relations condemned
this arrangement, on the ground that the question whether a matter
was justiciable was itself a matter to be determined by treaty-making
machinery, of which action by the Senate was a part.

> The committee believes that it would be a violation of the Consti-
> tution of the United States to confer upon an outside commission
> powers which, under the Constitution, devolve upon the Senate. . . .
> To take from the Senate, in any degree or by any means, the power
> of saying whether a given question is one for arbitration or not is to
> destroy the power of the Senate on the most important point to be
> decided in connection with differences arising with any other nation.[34]

The report reveals the Senate's deep distrust of treaties which might
limit its powers.  Hostility to these particular treaties was deepened
by the rift in the Republican party, for Theodore Roosevelt, who was
close to Senator Lodge, was one of the most vociferous critics of the
treaties sponsored by Taft.  The attitude went deeper, however, than
any temporary political struggle.  True, William J. Bryan, as Wilson's Secretary of State, was successful in securing Senate approval of
twenty of his thirty conciliation treaties, which were limited chiefly to
providing a period of delay between the time of a dispute and the
beginning of military hostilities.  Senator Lodge, who was absent at
the time the Bryan treaties were approved, referred to them later as

---

[33] See Royden J. Dangerfield, *In Defense of the Senate* (1933), pp. 185 ff.; and W.
Stull Holt, *Treaties Defeated by the Senate* (1933); pp. 178 ff.

[34] Senate Doc. No. 98, 62d Cong., 1st sess., pp. 5-7.

"fatuous," saying that, if he had been present, he would have resisted them.[35] When the period is viewed as a whole, there is little evidence showing any tendency of the Senate to forego any of its treaty-making prerogatives.[36] On the other hand, as had been true after the Civil War, the Senate, like the House of Representatives, was in a mood to take back from the President control of policy which the exigencies of war had placed in his hands.

### EARLY DISCUSSION OF THE TREATY AND THE LEAGUE

President Wilson was aware that difficulties with the Senate lay ahead. His strategy was to secure from the nations at war the acceptance of a peace treaty as just as possible in its provisions for immediate settlement, and to include in the treaty a covenant for a league of nations which would bring about peaceably the just settlement of future international disputes. He evidently expected to be able to coerce the Senate into accepting the treaty by using public pressure from two sources: he would capitalize the desire of the people for a return to conditions of peace and the devotion of many of the people to himself and to the ideals for which he stood.

On February 15, 1919, while the contents of the peace treaty were still highly tentative, Wilson left Europe for the United States, to take care of an accumulation of business at home and to be in Washington during the last days of the Sixty-Fifth Congress. On that day American newspapers published a draft of a covenant providing a "constitution of the League of Nations." In a manner which to unsympathetic senators doubtless reflected the methods of a stern and unbending schoolmaster, the President had sent to the foreign relations committees of both houses of Congress a cablegram reading in part as follows:

> Each article was passed only after the most careful examination by each member of the committee. There is a good and sufficient reason for the phraseology and substance of each article. I request that I be permitted to go over with you, article by article, the constitution before this part of the work of the conference is made the subject of debate of Congress. With this in view, I request that you dine with me at the White House as soon after I arrive in the United States as my engagements permit.[37]

[35] *Roosevelt-Lodge Correspondence*, II, 453.
[36] See Holt, *op. cit.*, pp. 244-248.
[37] *New York Times*, February 16, 1919.

Some senators heeded the request for delay in discussing the proposed league of nations. Others, regarding it as an unwarranted attempt to muzzle the opposition while the President marshaled sentiment in his support, began the delivery of opposition speeches. Except for persons such as Senators Borah and Fall, who declined to attend, the members of the foreign relations committees met the President at dinner on February 26, and discussed at length the plans for the peace treaty. The discussion probably had little effect upon individual attitudes. Some senators were willing to accept any treaty advocated by the President. Others would approve no treaty which included provision for a league of nations. Others agreed as to the desirability of some kind of international organization, but insisted on modifications, either because they were interested in particular items or because they wanted their own stamp or the stamp of their political party on the final product.

Only a week remained between the date of the President's dinner with the legislators and the end of the session of Congress. Within that period varied efforts were made by Republican senators to obstruct the plans of the President and discredit them with the people. Although no treaty was as yet before the Senate, a number of speeches were delivered attacking the provisions of the proposed treaty, particularly those dealing with a league of nations. Senator Lodge, who at the next session would be chairman of the Senate committee on foreign relations, was judicious in his mode of attack, evidently seeking to retain the support of those Republicans who favored some kind of association of nations to preserve world peace. He disapproved of a number of commitments made by the United States in the proposed treaty and suggested a number of reservations. He thought that a treaty to restore peace with Germany ought to be concluded without delay, whereas plans for a league of nations ought to be worked out with care and deliberation. He contended, therefore, that plans for such an organization must be divorced from the treaty of peace.[38]

Senator Knox denounced the scheme to create a United States of the World and condemned the proposed league as futile and as a menace to peace and freedom. Other senators attacked, and some defended, the program of the President. The debate constituted one of the many wedges that gradually separated the United States from the program to which the President sought to commit it.

[38] For discussion see Denna Frank Fleming, *The United States and the League of Nations, 1918-1920* (1932), pp. 136-140.

Another device was adopted for the same purpose and to demonstrate the fact that the President must take the Senate into account in making decisions on items of major policy. A minority group of Republican senators worked out a resolution declaring it the sense of the Senate that

> the constitution of the league of nations in the form now proposed to the peace conference should not be accepted by the United States; and . . . that the negotiations on the part of the United States should immediately be directed to the utmost expedition of the urgent business of negotiating peace terms with Germany satisfactory to the United States and the nations with whom the United States is associated in the war against the German government, and that the proposal for a league of nations to insure the permanent peace of the world should be then taken up for careful and serious consideration.[39]

When Senator Lodge offered the resolution on the last day of the session, the unanimous consent necessary for its consideration was denied. Thereupon he submitted a list of thirty-seven senators and senators-elect who declared that they would have supported the resolution had they had the opportunity.[40] This action gave notice that the peace treaty as planned by the President would not receive the support of two-thirds of the members of the Senate. It provided additional argument for separating the proposed league of nations from the treaty of peace.

The President appeared unperturbed. In a speech delivered in New York on the evening of the same day, he declared that, when the treaty came back, "gentlemen on this side will find the covenant not only in it, but so many threads of the treaty tied to the covenant that you cannot dissect the covenant from the treaty without destroying the whole vital structure." [41] He did not admit the possibility that the treaty as a whole might be rejected.

### AGITATION FOR A SPECIAL SESSION OF CONGRESS

Certain Republican senators resorted to another device to embarrass or place a check upon the activities of the President. They wanted him to call immediately a special session of the next Congress,

---

[39] 57 *Congressional Record* 4974.

[40] Two additional names were received the following day from senators not present. See Henry Cabot Lodge, *The Senate and the League of Nations* (1925), 118-120; and Fleming, *op. cit.*, p. 155.

[41] *New York Times*, March 5, 1919.

in which the Republican party would have a majority. Wilson made
it clear that he planned to return to Europe to complete negotiations
already begun, and that he did not intend to call a special session. A
number of important measures, including certain appropriation bills,
needed to be passed at once. A deficiency appropriation bill contained an allotment badly needed by the Railroad Administration.
Bills making appropriations for the army, the navy, the Emergency
Fleet Corporation, and other important agencies had to be dealt with
immediately or not at all. Republican party leaders, including Senators Lodge and Knox, refused to assume responsibility for blocking
the bills, but Senators Sherman, La Follette, and France were less
cautious. Without formal party sanction they closed the session with
a filibuster, deeming the calling of a special session inevitable as a
result.

Wilson refused to surrender and call a special session. He issued
a statement saying that a group of men in the Senate had deliberately
chosen to embarrass the administration of the government, imperil
railroad finances, and make arbitrary use of their powers. They
must assume responsibility for the results. It was plainly his duty to
attend the peace conference in Paris. It was also his duty to be in
close contact with public business when Congress was in session. He
concluded that "It is not in the interest of the right conduct of public
affairs that I should call the Congress in special session while it is
impossible for me to be in Washington, because of a more pressing
duty elsewhere, to co-operate with the houses." [42] On March 5, Wilson sailed from New York, en route to France.

DRAFTING THE TREATY

Upon his return to the peace conference, President Wilson found
that sentiment for the League of Nations had greatly cooled, and that
a number of statesmen were in a mood to drop it and resort merely to
a conventional treaty of peace. The outlines of the controversy are
not clear, nor are they more than incidentally relevant in the story of
the development of the Constitution of the United States. One mode
of procedure, which was seriously considered and which might have
impeded the establishment of the League, was resort to a preliminary
treaty to include part, but not all, of the terms of peace, leaving the
remainder to be worked out at leisure. Presumably provision for the
League would not have been included in the preliminary treaty.

[42] Messages and Papers of the Presidents, XVIII, 8697-8698.

Wilson had considered the extension of the armistice and the broadening of its terms. He had thought not so much in terms of a preliminary treaty as of "a sort of exalted armistice," the terms of which would be reincorporated in the formal treaty.[43] Others, however, thought of the preliminary treaty as final and conclusive on the matters with which it dealt. The argument for such an arrangement was that matters capable of immediate settlement should be settled as quickly as possible, leaving others to be dealt with at leisure. Wilson called attention to the probability that any arrangement which had the status of a treaty would have to be referred to the Senate for action. In such an event, because of the slow processes of legislatures, the plan for speedy settlement of the questions involved in the preliminary treaty would be frustrated.[44] The discussion of a preliminary treaty was dropped.

Wilson was faced with a difficult task. On the one hand, he had to secure phraseology in the treaty which would satisfy Americans suspicious of foreign entanglements. On the other hand, he had to convince the Allies, France in particular, that the treaty, including the Covenant of the League of Nations, provided adequate protection against attack from Germany, so that provisions in harmony with his Fourteen Points might be safely adopted. The amendments needed to satisfy American criticism had been enumerated by Senator Hitchcock under four headings: First, there must be specific recognition of the Monroe Doctrine. Second, there must be provision for withdrawal of the United States from the League. Third, certain domestic questions must be excluded from the jurisdiction of the League. Fourth, the United States was not to be compelled to accept mandates.[45] Former President Taft sent a cablegram urging specific recognition of the Monroe Doctrine and other reservations, saying that, if they were made, "the ground will be completely cut from under the opponents of the League in the Senate."[46] In a later cablegram he warned that without an amendment safeguarding the Monroe Doctrine "Republican senators will certainly defeat ratification of treaty,

---

[43] David Hunter Miller, *The Drafting of the Covenant* (2 vols., 1928), I, 89.

[44] Ibid., pp. 89-92. (For a different version see Robert Lansing, *The Peace Negotiations; A Personal Narrative* [1921], pp. 206-207.) As justification for the belief that a preliminary agreement might settle a number of non-military questions, reference was made to the protocol signed at the close of the Spanish-American War. See *ibid.*, p. 90.

[45] Ray Stannard Baker, *Woodrow Wilson and World Settlement* (3 vols., 1922), I, 323.

[46] *Ibid.*, p. 324.

because public opinion will sustain them.    With such amendment, treaty will be promptly ratified." [47]

Wilson succeeded in keeping the Covenant of the League of Nations in the treaty of peace.   He won specific recognition of the Monroe Doctrine and secured other changes likely to make the treaty less objectionable to honest critics at home.   He fought for a maximum of equity in the settlement of territorial questions in many parts of the world, winning on some points and losing on others.   On such matters he accepted the results as the best obtainable, deeming undesirable arrangements compensated for by the new order to be created under the League of Nations.   He went to a dangerous extreme in accepting a separate treaty by which the United States would go to the defense of France if the latter should be attacked by Germany.   It was provided therein that "The present treaty will be submitted to the Senate of the United States at the same time as the Treaty of Versailles is submitted to the Senate for its advice and consent to ratification." [48]

### THE TREATY BEFORE THE SENATE

Wilson returned to the United States on July 8, 1919.   In the meantime, on May 7, he had found it necessary to issue a call for a special session of Congress, to assemble May 20, to enact important appropriation bills which had been blocked by filibuster at the end of the preceding regular session.   A number of these bills were passed immediately — for the filibuster had been directed, not at the bills themselves, but at the determination of the President not to have Congress in session while completing negotiation of the peace treaty.   The willingness of Republicans to support non-controversial measures was not to be interpreted as susceptibility to presidential influence, particularly in such matters as the peace treaty and the League of Nations.

The President faced a critical audience when, on July 10, he appeared before the Senate to present the Treaty of Versailles for approval.   Part of his address called to mind his prediction of March 4 that the Covenant of the League of Nations would be so embedded in the treaty as to make it inseparable.   He told the Senate:

> Examine the treaty of peace and you will find that everywhere throughout its manifold provisions its framers have felt obliged to turn to the League of Nations as an indispensable instrumentality

[47] *Ibid.,* p. 325.
[48] For a copy of the proposed treaty see Lodge, *op. cit.,* pp. 152-155.

for the maintenance of the new order it has been their purpose to set up in the world — the world of civilized men.[49]

Analyzing the work of the peace conference, he declared that the people of the world demanded the complete destruction of the old order of international politics.

A war in which they had been bled white to beat the terror that lay concealed in every balance of power must not end in a mere victory of arms and a new balance. . . . The League of Nations was not merely an instrument to adjust and remedy old wrongs under a new treaty of peace; it was the only hope for mankind. . . . Dare we reject it and break the heart of the world? [50]

Our isolation had ended twenty years earlier, with the war with Spain. There could be no question of our ceasing to be a world power.

The only question is whether we can refuse the moral leadership that is offered us, whether we shall accept or reject the confidence of the world.[51]

The President did not discuss the League of Nations in relation to the Constitution of the United States, but that relation was important. If the United States was to become a member of the League, it would be going farther than ever before toward putting its conduct under the guidance of a body over which it did not have control. The analogy of the Articles of Confederation as a basis of a loosely knit union of states, a union which was later made "more perfect" by the bonds of the Constitution, was one not to be forgotten by the American people. True, the word "constitution" had been eliminated from the organic act of the League. The union provided for was not "perpetual," since a member might withdraw from it. It had less power than was provided for under the Articles of Confederation. Yet the resemblance existed, and it was recognized.

If the Constitution of the United States was being changed, it was being changed, not by the prescribed amending procedure, but by the exercise of the treaty-making power. The League, for example, was expected to restrain the action of member states when they were predatory in character; it was to call upon them for positive action in coercing rebels into obedience; and it was to have the right of financial support from member states. Under the Constitution the power to declare war was lodged in Congress. The power to make

[49] *Messages and Papers of the Presidents,* XVIII, 8733.
[50] *Ibid.,* p. 8735.  [51] *Ibid.,* p. 8737.

appropriations was lodged in the same body, with the restriction that measures to raise revenue must be initiated in the House of Representatives. If the United States became a member, therefore, the League might legitimately advise on the performance of functions which had hitherto been left to the discretion of Congress. The League could only request action on the part of a member and it could not impose legal sanctions for non-performance. In this respect again, however, the resemblance to the Articles of Confederation should not be forgotten.

This would not be the first time that commitments had been made by treaty which could be carried out only if Congress made appropriations or took other action. We had acquired territory on the pledge of sums in payment. We had guaranteed the territorial integrity of nations on this hemisphere, with the knowledge that action of Congress would be necessary if we were to support our guarantees. Other types of commitments in treaties could be enforced only if both houses of Congress took action in support of them. Yet, if the commitments in the Covenant of the League of Nations were not essentially different in character from those made in the past, they were nevertheless different in degree. Joining the League would be recognition of a new era, in which the over-all supervision of international affairs underwent a definite shift in its center of gravity. It was questionable whether such a fundamental shift should be made by treaty rather than through the prescribed forms of constitutional change.

Various constitutional issues were debated in the struggle over approval of the treaty. The struggle was in part a personal conflict between Woodrow Wilson and senators whose ill-will he had incurred. It was in part a conflict between the President as leader of the Democratic party and a group of Republican leaders. In some respects, however, it was like conflicts in other administrations over arbitration treaties, in which the Senate refused to grant sweeping powers over international affairs. Now, as on other occasions, the overt program of the opposition was not the outright rejection of the treaty, but the devitalization of the treaty by amendments or reservations.

The Senate committee on foreign relations held hearings over a period of weeks,[52] at which they sought information and opinion about the drafting of the treaty of peace and its probable operation. Debate on the floor of the Senate was conducted through the same period.

[52] *Treaty of Peace with Germany*, Senate Doc. No. 106, 66th Cong., 1st sess.

Grounds of opposition multiplied with discussion. Presentation of the treaty of alliance with France [53] made matters worse. The committee on foreign relations met with the President and gave him the opportunity to explain and defend the treaty, but he was unable to turn the tide.

Before the committee reported to the Senate, the President decided upon a desperate expedient, a tour of the country in defense of the treaty, in the hope that public sentiment would compel the Senate to approve it. He found the people less responsive than he had hoped. His health had already been impaired by months of strain. It collapsed before the completion of his tour, and he returned to Washington an invalid no longer capable of active political leadership.

The opposition in the Senate had resented the obvious purpose of the President's tour. During his absence the committee on foreign relations reported a recommendation that the treaty be approved, but with a list of devitalizing amendments and reservations. One drastic reservation had to do with Article 10 of the Covenant of the League of Nations, which President Wilson regarded as "the heart of the Covenant." Under that article the members of the League undertook, on the advice of the Council of the League, "to protect and preserve as against external aggression the territorial integrity and existing political independence of all members of the League." Under the reservation recommended by the committee the United States declined to assume

> any obligation to preserve the territorial integrity or political independence of any other country or to interfere in controversies between other nations, members of the League or not, or to employ the military or naval forces of the United States in such controversies, or to adopt economic measures, for the protection of any other country, whether a member of the League or not, against external aggression or for the purpose of coercing any other country, or for the purpose of intervention in the internal conflicts or other controversies which may arise in any other country. . . . [54]

After a number of weeks of additional debate, the Senate prepared to vote on the treaty with a number of reservations, including a modified version of that quoted above. Loyal Democrats sought advice from the President as to how they should vote. In a letter to Senator Hitchcock he replied that in his opinion "the resolution in that form does not provide for ratification, but, rather, for the nullifica-

[53] *Messages and Papers of the Presidents*, XVIII, 8762.  [54] Lodge, *op. cit.*, p. 173.

tion of the treaty. I sincerely hope that the friends and supporters of the treaty will vote against the Lodge resolution of ratification." [55]

A number of loyal Democrats, therefore, joined with irreconcilable Republicans in opposition to the treaty as limited by the reservations. Thirty-nine senators voted for approval and fifty-five against it. A vote was then taken on unconditional approval. The alignment of persons shifted, but the numerical result was much the same. Thirty-eight voted for approval of the treaty as submitted to the Senate by the President and fifty-three opposed it. The result was a long way from the majority of two-thirds which was necessary before the treaty could be ratified.

Even after this decisive action, it was still possible that the Treaty of Versailles might be ratified in some form. It was taken up again at the session of Congress which began in December, 1919, not with the expectation that Republicans would surrender in their demand for reservations, but with the thought that they might recede from their extreme position and that Democrats might then vote for the treaty as limited by the reservations. In a letter to Senator Hitchcock, the President again asserted his uncompromising opposition to the proposed reservations. He said in part:

> I have given a great deal of thought to the whole matter of reservations proposed in connection with the ratification of the treaty, and particularly that portion of the treaty which contains the Covenant of the League of Nations, and I have been struck by the fact that practically every so-called reservation was in effect a rather sweeping nullification of the terms of the treaty itself. I hear of reservationists and mild reservationists, but I cannot understand the difference between a nullifier and a mild nullifier. [56]

Accepting the advice of their leader against a ratification which was a mere pretense, many Democrats again refused to support the treaty with the reservations. Forty-nine senators, a number which was less than the requisite two-thirds majority, voted to approve the treaty with the reservations. Thirty-five opposed. On March 19, 1920, the treaty was returned to the President without advice and consent to ratification. [57]

### THE QUESTION OF MANDATES

Early in the summer of 1920, a controversy involving the United

[55] 58 *Congressional Record* 8768.
[56] 59 *Congressional Record* 4052.       [57] *Ibid.*, p. 4600.

States with the League of Nations, which had been simmering for more than a year, reached the boiling point. It had to do with a proposed mandate which the United States was being asked to take over Armenia, where chaos prevailed and where Armenians had been slaughtered in large numbers by their Turkish enemies. President Wilson was from the beginning apparently in favor of accepting the mandate. The subject was discussed intermittently throughout 1919. In August, 1919, an American military mission, which for some reason was known as the American Mission of Transportation and Economic Specialists, was sent to make a study of Armenia and surrounding countries. It was instructed to "investigate and report on political, military, geographical, administrative, economic, and other considerations involved in possible American interests and responsibilities in that region." [58] The mission was under the direction of Major General James G. Harbord, of the United States Army. On October 16, 1919, he made a report to the Secretary of State, summarizing the results of his investigations. The personnel of the mission was evidently divided as to the acceptance of a mandate by the United States, and the report was non-committal. In favor of acceptance was the argument that, as one of the chief contributors to the formation of the League of Nations, the United States was morally bound to accept the obligations and responsibilities of a mandatory power. Another argument was expressed as follows: "Intervention would be a liberal education for our people in world politics; give outlet to a vast amount of spirit and energy and would furnish a shining example." [59] On the other hand, it was suggested that the United States had greater obligations closer home. Furthermore, "This region has been a battle-ground of militarism and imperialism for centuries. There is every likelihood that ambitious nations will still maneuver for its control. It would weaken our position relative to the Monroe Doctrine and probably eventually involve us with a reconstituted Russia." [60]

The contents of the report were not revealed until the following April, after the Senate had passed a resolution requesting its submission. [61] In the meantime the United States was repeatedly urged to

---

[58] Senate Doc. No. 266, 66th Cong., 2d sess., p. 3. Printed also in 59 *Congressional Record* 7877.

[59] *Ibid.*, p. 26.    [60] *Ibid.*, pp. 25-26.

[61] *New York Times*, March 7, 1920. The special study of the mandate question, made for Major General Harbord by Brigadier General George Van Horn Moseley, was presented to the Senate May 29, 1920, Senate Doc. No. 281. 66th Cong., 2d sess.

accept the mandate. On May 24, 1920, Wilson sent to Congress a message requesting that "the Congress grant the Executive power to accept for the United States a mandate over Armenia." [62] He stated, "for the information of the Congress," that he had already undertaken to arbitrate the difficult question of the boundary between Turkey and Armenia. He did not discuss the constitutional or other difficulties in the way of assuming the mandate, but based his plea upon humanitarian grounds.

On May 27, 1920, the Senate committee on foreign relations revealed its sentiments toward the President's request by reporting in a single sentence the following concurrent resolution: "That the Congress hereby respectfully declines to grant to the Executive the power to accept a mandate over Armenia, as requested in the message of the President, dated May 24, 1920." [63] The resolution passed the Senate four days later by a vote of 52 to 23.[64] It was asserted that Congress had no constitutional power to authorize the President to accept the invitation to govern Armenia, which was tendered to him by the prime ministers of the Old World. It was argued in reply that, since the United States had the power to acquire complete sovereignty over territory, it must therefore have the lesser power to exercise limited sovereignty,[65] but the argument was not pressed. Indeed, the majority of the Senate was so bitterly opposed to further involvement in the affairs of the Old World that acceptance of the mandate would have been unthinkable. The House failed to pass the resolution, but only because of the fact that it adjourned almost immediately after the resolution was reported. However, the failure of Congress to authorize acceptance of the mandate, together with the disapproval expressed by the Senate and by the House committee on foreign affairs,[66] destroyed all hope that the mandate would ever be accepted.

### THE RESTORATION OF PEACE

As month after month went by after the armistice was signed, trade with Germany was gradually resumed, but under severe handicap, since technically a state of war still prevailed. Persons interested in that trade united with opponents of the Treaty of Versailles in attempt to have peace restored by act of Congress. There was doubt

---

[62] House Doc. No. 791, 66th Cong., 2d sess., p. 3.

[63] 59 *Congressional Record* 7714.   [64] *Ibid.*, p. 8073.   [65] *Ibid.*, p. 8058.

[66] House Report No. 1101, 66th Cong., 2d sess.; *New York Times*, June 4, 1920; June 5, 1920.

whether Congress had the power to terminate war. The Constitution did not specifically give the power, and it had been said at times that only a treaty could restore peace with a surviving belligerent.[67] On April 9, 1920, the House of Representatives passed a joint resolution declaring the war to be at an end and terminating the operation of the several war statutes. The resolution included a penalty provision to the effect that trade and financial aid would be cut off from Germany unless Germany declared a termination of the war with the United States and waived all claims against the United States that would have been waived had the Treaty of Versailles been signed.[68] The Senate, doubtless aware of the opposition of business interests to any curtailment of trade with Germany, redrafted the resolution to include much milder penalty provisions than those originally proposed. The question of the constitutional power of Congress to restore peace by joint resolution was debated at length, but inconclusively.[69] The alignment was largely partisan. The joint resolution was passed on May 15, 1920, by a vote of 43 to 38.[70] The House accepted the Senate draft.

On May 28, 1920, the President vetoed the joint resolution.[71] He did not discuss the constitutional question. He had not felt at liberty to sign the joint resolution, he explained,

> because I cannot bring myself to become party to an action which would place an ineffaceable stain upon the gallantry and honor of the United States.

Notwithstanding our professions upon entrance into the war, he said:

> we have now in effect declared that we do not care to take any further risks or to assume any further responsibilities with regard to the freedom of nations or the sacredness of international obligations or the safety of independent peoples. Such a peace with Germany — a peace

[67] Edward S. Corwin, "The Power of Congress to Declare Peace," *Michigan Law Review*, XVIII (May, 1920), 669-675; Manley O. Hudson, "The Duration of the War Between the United States and Germany," *Harvard Law Review*, XXXIX (June, 1926), 1020-1045; Forrest Revere Black, "The Power of Congress to Declare Peace," *Kentucky Law Journal*, XIX (May, 1931), 327-335; John M. Mathews, "The Termination of War," *Michigan Law Review*, XIX (June, 1921), 819-834; Charles S. Thomas, "The Power of Congress to Establish Peace," *American Law Review*, LV (January-February, 1921), 86-104.

[68] 59 *Congressional Record* 5480-5481.

[69] See, for example, the speeches of Senator Knox, 59 *Congressional Record* 6556-6566, and Senator Hitchcock, *ibid.*, pp. 6895-6899.

[70] *Ibid.*, p. 7102.

[71] House Doc. No. 799, 66th Cong., 2d sess.

in which none of the essential interests which we had at heart when we entered the war is safeguarded — is, or ought to be, inconceivable, is inconsistent with the dignity of the United States, with the rights and liberties of her citizens, and with the very fundamental conditions of civilization.

In attempting to have the joint resolution passed over the President's veto, its sponsor in the House of Representatives emphasized the fact that nowhere in the President's message appeared an intimation that the resolution was unconstitutional. He was unable to secure a sufficient majority for his purpose.

### TERMINATING OPERATION OF WAR STATUTES

The official termination of the war was desired partly to render inoperative provisions of a large number of war statutes under which the country continued to be governed in spite of the cessation of military hostilities. These statutes provided for regimentation of life, in many ways not familiar to the United States except in time of war, by officials not trained in the self-restraint necessary to acceptable regimentation by government under conditions of peace. The policy of enforcing war legislation that restricted civil liberties and rights of property was complicated by the fact that the post-war or post-armistice period was one of general unrest. Both labor and capital had been restive during the war, but in most important controversies they had submitted to mediation or control provided by the several wartime agencies. After the conflict was over, each group sought to retain any advantages it had won and to capture others in the process of readjustment to peacetime economy. While each group struggled for advantage, prices of consumers' goods continued to rise and the business outlook grew more and more uncertain. The radical element in the country, encouraged by the success of Bolshevism in Russia, clamored for sweeping changes in the American economic and political system, creating terror in the minds of conservative people and causing demand for drastic suppression of disloyal factions.

In the latter part of 1919, the United Mine Workers had called a strike to secure better conditions as to hours and wages in an industry which during the war had experienced one of the few prosperous periods in its history. Various agencies of the federal government sought to prevent the strike. Attorney General A. Mitchell Palmer secured in a federal district court an injunction against union leaders to prevent the strike. The court acted on the basis of the Lever

Food-Control Act,[72] a war measure which, among other things, had been intended to prevent profiteering in necessities and also to prevent combination to restrict supply and raise prices. The American Federation of Labor had acceded to the enactment of the measure only after its leaders were persuaded that it would not be used to interfere with labor activities which would otherwise be legitimate. They claimed that Attorney General Gregory had given assurance that the district attorneys would be instructed not to enforce the measure against labor.[73] The injunction played a part in the termination of the strike, but it did nothing to smooth out the swelling tide of unrest.

Other types of war legislation were used as a basis of governmental action in other types of situations. Violence accredited to radicals occurred in many cities of the United States. Terrified people demanded protection from the government. Said Attorney General Palmer, "I was shouted at from every editorial sanctum in America from sea to sea; I was preached upon from every pulpit; I was urged — I could feel it dinned into my ears — throughout the country to do something and do it now, and do it quick, and do it in a way that would bring results to stop this sort of thing in the United States." [74] A general intelligence division was created in the Department of Justice to investigate radical activities. Within a short period of time it gathered and indexed a history of some sixty thousand radicals, laying a foundation for deportation or for prosecution if illegal acts had been committed.[75] The department conducted sweeping raids to collect alien radicals at various centers throughout the country.[76] Referring to deportations of undesirable aliens, Attorney General Palmer told the Women's Democratic Political League of New York that the people of the city would soon be treated to the spectacle of "second, third, and fourth Soviet Arks sailing down their beautiful harbor." [77]

A growing minority of the people, however, criticized the Depart-

[72] 40 Stat. 276, 1 Stat. 297.

[73] Homer Cummings and Carl McFarland, *Federal Justice* (1937), pp. 455-456. See 55 *Congressional Record* 5828 ff. See also 60 *Congressional Record* 295-297, for understanding at the time the act was passed.

[74] U.S. Congress, Senate committee on the judiciary, *Hearings on Charges of Illegal Practices of the Department of Justice*, 66th Cong., 3d sess., p. 580.

[75] Senate Doc. No. 153, 66th Cong., 1st sess., p. 10.

[76] See for example the *New York Times*, January 3, 1920. See also Frederick Lewis Allen, *Only Yesterday* (1931), chapter III.

[77] *New York Times*, February 29, 1920.

ment of Justice for deliberately provoking the prevailing anti-radical hysteria. The National Popular Government League published a pamphlet entitled *A Report upon the Illegal Practices of the United States Department of Justice.* It was sponsored by twelve prominent lawyers, including Zechariah Chafee, Felix Frankfurter, Ernst Freund, Roscoe Pound, and Frank P. Walsh. It charged that

> wholesale arrests both of aliens and citizens have been made without warrant or any process of law; men and women have been jailed and held incommunicado without access of friends or counsel; homes have been entered without search warrant and property seized and removed; other property has been wantonly destroyed; workingmen and workingwomen suspected of radical views have been shamefully abused and maltreated. Agents of the Department of Justice have been introduced into radical organizations for the purpose of informing upon their members or inciting them to activity; these agents have even been instructed from Washington to arrange meetings upon certain dates for the express object of facilitating wholesale raids and arrests. In support of these illegal acts, and to create sentiment in its favor, the Department of Justice has also constituted itself a propaganda bureau and has sent to newspapers and magazines of this country quantities of material designed to excite public opinion against radicals, all at the expense of the government and outside the scope of the Attorney General's duties.[78]

The abuse of war powers and the extension of the drastic methods of wartime enforcement into the handling of peacetime problems was beginning to disturb Congress. The situation was summarized by Senator France after the President's veto of the joint resolution which would have terminated the state of war between the United States and Germany and would, therefore, have rendered war statutes inoperative. The President, who was elected on the slogan that "he kept us out of war," said the senator, now stubbornly and against the will of the overwhelming majority of the people persisted in keeping us out of peace. By means of war powers, which he still refused to relinquish, more than a year and a half after the war had actually ended, he had built up the most powerful autocracy in the entire world. He continued as follows:

> The author of the "New Freedom" has sat unmoved in the White House, while American citizens have, in violation of the law protect-

---

[78] National Popular Government League, *Report Upon the Illegal Practices of the Department of Justice* (1920), p. 3. See also Louis F. Post, *The Deportations Delirium of Nineteen-Twenty* (1923).

ing inherent natural rights, been hurled into dungeons for disagreeing with the views of the majority, while the Postmaster General, renegade from the principles of Jeffersonian democracy, seized and censored the mails and wires in his autocratic clutch, while spies and secret service agents from a department which disgraces the very name of justice have prowled about as they did in the old days in Russia seeking whom they might destroy. Intimidation, search, and seizure without warrant, brutality, torture, perjury, provocation of crime, the holding of prisoners without sentence and the sentencing of prisoners without sense or the sanctions of justice, bloodshed, and, if we can credit rumors current in New York, which I cannot verify, even murder, these have been their methods.[79]

Although the session was near its end, a joint resolution was introduced in the House of Representatives to declare that certain acts of Congress, joint resolutions, and proclamations should be construed as if the war had ended and the present or existing emergency had expired. The measure was considered for a few minutes and passed by a vote of 326 to 3.[80] Certain statutes relating to war situations which were not yet resolved were exempted from the effect of the joint resolution. Along with them the Food-Control Act was exempted. Its potential use as a check upon labor activities and as a corresponding check upon profiteering was too important to be dispensed with in short order. The Senate passed the repealing measure without debate and without a record vote. The President killed it with a pocket veto!

A similar joint resolution was introduced in the House of Representatives at the ensuing short session. The committee on the judiciary reported it favorably, saying that a number of the war statutes were not only unnecessary, but a burden and a menace.[81] Both houses passed it, and this time the President signed the measure.[82]

## WAR OFFICIALLY TERMINATED

The termination of the war itself had to await the administration of President Harding. In his message to a special session of Congress on April 12, 1921, Harding stated that the United States alone among the Allied and Associated Powers continued in a technical state of war against the Central Powers. This condition, he said, ought not

---

[79] 59 *Congressional Record* 7918.
[80] *Ibid.*, p. 8416. For a copy of the resolution see *ibid.*, pp. 8412-8413.
[81] House Report No. 1111, 66th Cong., 3d sess.  [82] 41 Stat. 1359.

to be permitted to continue. "To establish the state of technical peace without further delay, I should approve a declaratory resolution by Congress to that effect, with the qualifications essential to protect all our rights." [83]  A resolution to that effect was passed by both houses. Most of the Democratic leaders opposed the resolution in committee and on the floor, but without avail. The minority members of the Senate committee on foreign relations charged that it was an attempt by act of Congress to usurp the treaty-making power of the President and the Senate, and listed many practical objections. [84] As reported in the Senate, the resolution repealed the declaration of war and declared the state of war to be at an end. The House committee on foreign affairs provided a substitute which declared the state of war to be at an end, without repealing the act declaring it. Said the committee, the Constitution vested in Congress all the war powers, among which was the power to declare war and, by necessary implication, the power to declare a state of peace. Both declarations were findings of fact. They were separate and distinct acts; and it was unnecessary and perhaps unwise to repeal the declaration of a state of war, for such a step might raise the inference that we had disavowed and repudiated the war and be construed as a mild apology for our participation in it. The substitute fully recognized that the Constitution vested in the President the exclusive power to make a treaty with our late enemies, subject to ratification by the Senate. [85] The minority of the committee thought that the resolution as modified was still in the nature of a contract, and argued that under the Constitution we could not, by an act of Congress, enter into a contract with another government. It was an invasion of the treaty-making power, which was a constitutional prerogative of the President by and with the advice and consent of the Senate. [86]

The joint resolution as finally agreed upon and approved by the President followed the House plan of declaring the state of war at an end. It reserved to the United States and its nationals all rights which accrued under the armistice and from other sources, including the Treaty of Versailles. [87] Its constitutionality was not thereafter seriously questioned. Before the end of the year, a separate treaty of peace with Germany was proclaimed. [88]

[83] 61 *Congressional Record* 173.
[84] Senate Report No. 2, Part 2, 67th Cong., 1st sess.
[85] House Report No. 148, 67th Cong., 1st sess.        [86] *Ibid.*, Part 2.
[87] 42 Stat. 105, 106.        [88] 42 Stat. 1939.

## THE UNITED STATES IN INTERNATIONAL AFFAIRS

In the years which followed the establishment of peace with Germany, the United States was an active participant in international affairs. It worked strenuously to bring about the limitation of armaments. It tried to aid in the solution of the problem of reparation payments. It participated in the Kellogg Pact (Pact of Paris) and other international agreements. Until its position with reference to the League of Nations was understood, however, it maintained an attitude of ostentatious aloofness from that organization.

For many years after the struggle over the ratification of the Treaty of Versailles, the United States dallied over the possibility of submitting to the jurisdiction and joining in the support of the Permanent Court of International Justice, an adjunct of the League of Nations. Many persons who distrusted a political league strongly favored the establishment of a tribunal to expound and apply principles of law applicable among nations. Elihu Root did much toward devising the organization of the court. Presidents Harding, Coolidge, Hoover, and Franklin D. Roosevelt advocated participation by the United States.

Although it appears that formal participation would have been possible without involvement with the League of Nations, many people, including a substantial number of United States senators, feared the relationship between the two agencies. On each of the several occasions on which the Senate dealt with the question, drastic reservations and understandings were agreed upon to guarantee aloofness almost to the extent of non-membership. The debates further illustrated the rivalry between the President and the Senate in the handling of foreign affairs and the unwillingness of the Senate to entrust any agency beyond its control with decisions affecting American interests. The Senate voted its consent to adherence in 1926, but with reservations which were not fully accepted by the powers represented in the League of Nations. Advocates of American affiliation therefore suffered another defeat. The Senate definitely refused adherence in 1935, and the question was apparently settled permanently. The fact that American citizens aided in the nomination of members of the court, and that three American judges sat successively on the court, did not materially alter the fact that the United States government, as such, does not formally share in the work of the court or submit to its decisions.[80]

[80] For continuation of the story of participation in international affairs see chapter 38.

# CHAPTER 29

# RECENT AMENDMENTS TO THE CONSTITUTION

SO MUCH CONSTITUTIONAL CHANGE takes place through gradual evolution in interpretation that the possibility of change by formal amendment often tends to be forgotten.   Long periods have occurred, indeed, in which the Constitution has undergone no formal changes at
all.   Amendments have seemed to come in groups, in periods in
which drastic and speedy readjustments have been demanded.   Of
the twenty-one amendments adopted, it will be recalled that the first
ten were approved immediately after the adoption of the Constitution itself.   The Eleventh and Twelfth Amendments were adopted
at the turn of the century as a result of defects which were quickly
disclosed.

Then passed a period of more than sixty years without additional
formal changes.   At its end, after the Civil War, the Thirteenth,
Fourteenth, and Fifteenth Amendments were adopted at the culmination of the long struggle over the position of the Negro in American
life.   Another period of more than forty years had elapsed when, in
1913 after prolonged debate over the income tax and the direct election of senators, the Sixteenth and Seventeenth Amendments were
adopted.   The first World War hastened the adoption of the
Eighteenth and Nineteenth Amendments, dealing respectively with
prohibition and suffrage for women.   Finally, in 1933, the Twentieth
Amendment abolished the "lame-duck" session of Congress, and the
Twenty-First Amendment reversed the position on prohibition taken
in the Eighteenth.

The adoption of all but three of these amendments has been discussed in earlier chapters.   This chapter deals with the remaining
three, with the stormy career of the short-lived attempt to legislate
national prohibition by constitutional amendment, and with other
amendments recently proposed but not adopted.   The period covered is short.   The background is in the first World War and its

aftermath, and in conditions of economic disturbance which stimulate desire for constitutional change.[1]

## THE WOMAN-SUFFRAGE AMENDMENT

From the time when the American states became independent until the adoption of the Nineteenth Amendment, struggles were in progress to win suffrage for some group hitherto disfranchised. Religious qualifications for voting were gradually abolished. The abolition of property qualifications came more slowly. The enfranchisement of the Negro came only as part of the aftermath of a major war. The most prolonged struggle, and the one concerned with the largest group of non-voters, was the movement for the enfranchisement of women, which reached its goal in 1920.

Early attempts to win voting privileges were directed exclusively at state action. The reason lay principally in the fact that federal suffrage depended upon state constitutions and laws. The Constitution provides that electors in each state for members of the federal House of Representatives should "have the qualifications requisite for electors of the most numerous branch of the state legislature." [2] Presidential electors in each state were to be chosen "in such manner as the legislature thereof may direct." [3] When the election of United States senators was transferred from the legislatures to the people, the Seventeenth Amendment provided that electors in each state "shall have the qualifications requisite for electors of the most numerous branch of the state legislature."

Since the matter was left to state control, little effort was made before the Civil War to secure federal action to extend suffrage privileges. When the Fourteenth Amendment was under discussion, however, with the purpose in mind of extending citizenship to Negroes,

---

[1] The amending process has itself been the subject of controversy. Some critics contend that the process is too easy. Others point to the small number of amendments which have been approved since the adoption of the Constitution and contend that the amending process is already too difficult and should be simplified. The latter have perhaps been more effective in getting their views before Congress in recent years. One proposal which has received attention calls for an amendment to Article V to allow ratification of amendments by popular vote. This proposal has been opposed as not needed, since "all delay and difficulty in the amendment of the Constitution has arisen in the field of the proposal of amendments and not of their ratification." It was pointed out that "The adoption of amendments to the Constitution has been characterized by celerity rather than by delay." Of twenty-six amendments submitted for ratification, twenty-one have been ratified within an average period of one and one-third years. Only five received unfavorable action. Testimony of Bainbridge Colby, Senate committee on the judiciary, 75th Cong., 3d sess., *Hearings on S. J. Res. 134*, p. 53.

[2] Constitution, Article I, Section 2.     [3] *Ibid.*, Article II, Section 1.

women leaders began to urge the use of language which would aid persons of their sex, along with the colored race. The Fourteenth Amendment did not grant directly a right to vote. It did, however, provide for reduction of representation in the House of Representatives in proportion as "male inhabitants" who were generally qualified were denied the right to vote. Advocates of woman suffrage tried vainly to secure the elimination of the word "male." [4] Had they succeeded, they would have created an entering wedge for universal suffrage.

When the Fourteenth Amendment proved insufficient to guarantee the voting privilege to Negroes, the Fifteenth Amendment was adopted forbidding the denial of the right to vote "on account of race, color, or previous condition of servitude." Again the propagandists for woman suffrage sought a modification, urging that sex be included along with race, color, and previous condition of servitude as a forbidden ground of discrimination in the matter of voting. Again they failed.[5] Thereafter they started a campaign to incorporate such a provision in a Sixteenth Amendment. They kept up the fight until victory was achieved in 1920, not in the Sixteenth Amendment, but in the Nineteenth. The amendment for which they clamored was introduced in the Senate in 1878 and was reintroduced, session after session, until it was adopted.

In the meantime, as the movement for a constitutional amendment was being started, suffragists pursued for a time the forlorn hope that the Fourteenth Amendment or some other provision of the Constitution already gave them the right to vote. Susan B. Anthony, a crusading leader of the group, succeeded in getting her vote accepted in a federal election in New York. She was arrested and tried for violation of the Enforcement Act of 1870.[6] The statute had been enacted principally to protect the rights of Negroes and prevent illegal practices in elections by persons who had participated in the rebellion, but the relevant provision was general in its language. It forbade voting in federal elections by persons who had no legal right to vote.[7] Miss Anthony claimed that the state of New York had no right to deny to women the privilege of voting, because of the provisions in the Fourteenth Amendment which created and defined citizenship of the United States and forbade the states to make or enforce any law which

---

[4] Elizabeth Cady Stanton, Susan B. Anthony, and Matilda Joslyn Gage (eds.), *The History of Woman Suffrage* (6 vols., 1887-1922), V, 619-620.
[5] *Ibid.*, p. 620.     [6] 16 Stat. 140.     [7] 16 Stat. 144.

should abridge the privileges or immunities of citizens of the United States. The United States circuit court in New York, however, which was conducted by Justice Ward Hunt, a member of the Supreme Court of the United States, rejected her argument. "The right of voting, or the privilege of voting," he said, "is a right or privilege arising under the constitution of the state and not under the Constitution of the United States." [8]

Virginia L. Minor, wife of a lawyer in St. Louis, who believed that women were enfranchised by the Fourteenth Amendment, sued a registering officer who refused to register her as a lawful voter. The trial court and the highest court in Missouri decided against her, whereupon she took an appeal to the Supreme Court of the United States. The Supreme Court said: "Sex has never been made one of the elements of citizenship in the United States. In this respect men have never had an advantage over women. The same laws precisely apply to both." [9] The right to vote, however, the Court held, was not a privilege or immunity of citizens of the United States which was protected by the Fourteenth Amendment. The Court met other arguments of counsel for Mrs. Minor by holding that state laws denying the voting privileges to women did not constitute a denial of a republican form of government which the federal government was under obligations to guarantee to the state. Nor did such state laws constitute bills of attainder which the states were forbidden to pass. [10]

Victories for the woman-suffrage movement were achieved gradually, not in Congress, but in state and local governments. State laws enacted by male legislators made concessions to women from time to time concerning grievances used as arguments for woman suffrage. Their rights to own and inherit property, to keep control over children, and to assert independence of tyrannical husbands were given protection. Wyoming gave the privilege of voting for territorial officers in 1869, and continued it in 1890 when statehood was achieved. Colorado followed its example in 1893, Utah in 1895, and Idaho in 1896.

After a decade of no additional achievements, the movement picked up again. It was co-ordinated with a popular-government movement or progressive movement which aimed at putting more power in the hands of the people. The other reforms advocated included the initiative, the referendum, the recall, the direct primary, the presi-

[8] United States *v.* Anthony, Fed. Case No. 14459, p. 830 (1873).
[9] Minor *v.* Happersett, 21 Wallace 162, 170 (1875).     [10] *Ibid.,* pp. 176-177.

dential primary, and the direct election of senators. The movement was in the nature of a reaction to corruption and inefficiency which pervaded existing methods. The campaign for and the adoption of the Sixteenth and Seventeenth Amendments paved the way for further constitutional changes by attacking the position that the Constitution must not be subject to additional modification.

By 1914 the number of equal-suffrage states was raised to eleven. The movement met defeat in some states in which strong efforts were made, but in 1917 it succeeded in New York, which was regarded as an eastern stronghold of opposition. In the meantime a number of other states had extended to women local voting privileges and the privilege of voting for presidential electors.

The occasional victories which were won in states from time to time strengthened the national movement. The votes of enfranchised women had to be taken into account by representatives from states in which suffrage had been granted when considering action on the national amendment. An argument much used against the Susan B. Anthony amendment was the contention that it represented interference with the prerogatives of the states. Suffrage was a state matter; any state, if it so desired, could give the privilege of voting in state and federal elections to any group; the federal government had no right to interfere. The argument was used by those who sincerely believed in it and also by those who sought any plausible excuse for opposing the federal amendment. It was employed by representatives of both major political parties, although it was perhaps more consistent with the philosophy of the state-rights Democratic party than with that of the Republicans. The answer usually given to the argument was that in many of the states the process of amending state constitutions was so difficult as to make victory virtually impossible. Only through federal intervention could the difficulties be overcome.

The platforms of the two major political parties in 1916 advocated woman suffrage by state action. Charles E. Hughes, the Republican candidate, announced in addition his approval of the woman-suffrage amendment, but President Wilson adhered to his position, stated many times, that the matter was one for determination by the states. By this time a faction of the women propagandists for suffrage was taking a more militant attitude, based on the experience of English "suffragettes." They tried to organize a protest vote against President Wilson because of his failure to support their amendment. In 1917, in the midst of the war crisis, a number of swashbuckling extremists picketed the White House, created disturbances, got themselves thrown into jail, engaged in hunger strikes, and made themselves nuisances generally, on the assumption that these were the tactics necessary to achieve the desired results. They embarrassed the more conventional leaders of their cause and antagonized politicians who favored it. Nevertheless, the publicity which they won through their melodramatic activities may have had some favorable effects toward the achievement of their goal.

It was feared for a time that public disgust with picketing and the disturbance of the peace in Washington would endanger success of the women's movement in the New York election, which represented a major struggle for their cause. To show his continued support of suffrage won through state action, President Wilson expressed publicly to Mrs. Carrie Chapman Catt, one of the more conservative leaders, the hope that bad effects would not result from the unfortunate methods used.[11] The victory won in New York added greatly to the number of representatives to be elected with the support of women voters and added to the national significance of the movement. The time had come when Congress would have to weigh carefully the political force back of it.

On September 15, 1917, the Senate committee on woman suffrage reported favorably, but without discussion, a woman-suffrage amendment.[12] On December 15, 1917, the House committee on the judiciary gave its support to the same kind of amendment. This committee did not discuss the amendment, but proposed the addition of a new section, like the one included in the Eighteenth Amendment, providing that the article should be inoperative unless fully ratified within seven years.[13] On January 8, 1918, the House committee on woman suffrage took a stand in favor of a woman-suffrage amendment and discussed the issues at length.[14] The committee found that, when women had the right to vote, they did so in about the same proportion to their numbers as men. Voting had wrought no mysterious, unfeminizing influence upon them. It had not overturned political parties or the social order. With the advocates of woman suffrage the only question remaining was, how should it be written into the law of the land? Although planks in the Democratic and Republican platforms of 1916

[11] *New York Times,* October 17, 1917.
[12] Senate Report No. 130, 65th Cong., 1st sess.
[13] House Report No. 219, 65th Cong., 2d sess.
[14] House Report No. 234, 65th Cong., 2d sess.

declared for state action, they did not declare against federal action. Recent events, including the election in New York, indicated the movement of public opinion in the direction of a federal constitutional amendment. During 1917, said the report, the number of electoral votes cast by equal-suffrage states grew to one hundred and ninety-three. "These voting women as well as the millions of non-voting petitioners, are certain to be deeply incensed if the same Congress which referred prohibition to the states refuses equally fair treatment to woman suffrage." [15]

The report closed with a brief discussion of the amendment as a war measure.

> It must be borne in mind that it was the nation, not the states, which declared war, conscripted men, voted a necessarily huge war tax, and has taken over the control of food and fuel. It is the nation which has appealed to women to take the places of men, to give their money, their labor, their sons. All these things which but a few months ago seemed impossible have happened and the nation is engaged in the greatest war of its history — a war for democracy.
>
> This crisis of our nation calls for bolder action than would have been necessary a year ago. We cannot consistently profess to lead in a war for democracy and be the last nation to establish it at home. Nor can we claim that the nation is fighting for democracy abroad and leave the states to demonstrate our understanding of democracy at home. The loyal votes of women who would vote in the places of absent men are a national concern. The war has made woman suffrage a national question. The Congress should treat it as such. [16]

Action on the measure was rushed. The Republican caucus in the House of Representatives announced its support. Democrats were in danger of being put in a position of opposition to a measure which was backed by an increasing number of voters. A delegation was sent to confer with the President. Wilson changed his position and announced his support of the amendment. He gave a number of reasons why Democratic congressmen should support it. The party platform, he said, which declared the matter one to be settled by each state for itself, had been drafted before the present exigencies arose. Strict adherence to it could not now be expected. He now held the matter of suffrage to be primarily a national question and a constitutional question, as distinguished from prohibition which was a legislative question and not necessarily national. He favored this amendment,

[15] *Ibid.*, p. 6.  [16] *Ibid.*, p. 6.

therefore, while continuing to oppose the prohibition amendment. He remarked that, since Great Britain was granting the franchise to women, and since the Allies were recognizing the patriotic services of women in the war, this country could do no less than follow their example.[17]

The *New York Times* said that the President, in changing his position, "sacrificed what seemed to be a reasoned conviction to political expediency; to save his party from defeat in the congressional elections he disregarded its platform and his own belief that suffrage is a matter for state decision." [18] Whatever his true reason, the weight of the President's influence was now thrown in favor of the suffrage movement.

The gallery of the House of Representatives was crowded with women when the joint resolution came up for a vote. They had arrived with knitting bags which they had had to surrender because of the rules of the House. Deprived of part of their equipment, they nevertheless sat knitting and listening intently. Their leaders knew in advance the position of almost every congressman on the bill. The whisper had started that defeat was in prospect when a man who had arrived late rushed to the platform and demanded that his vote be counted.[19] The count was 274 to 136,[20] a bare two-thirds victory. One representative had come from a hospital in Washington to vote for the measure and another from a hospital in Baltimore. Another man with a broken shoulder refused to have it set lest the operation make it impossible for him to appear and cast his vote.[21] People in the galleries arose and cheered *en masse* when the result was announced. "Fully a thousand women congregated on the steps outside the House following adjournment and cheered with all the enthusiasm of collegians after a football victory." [22]

It seems to have been assumed that an early victory would follow in the Senate. Many months passed, however, while efforts were being made to secure commitments from enough senators to make it safe to bring the issue to a vote. President Wilson made personal appeals for the support of particular senators.[23] More Republicans than Democrats were committed to the measure, but it was impossible to assure enough Republican votes to make up the two-thirds majority

[17] *New York Times,* January 10, 1918.    [18] *Ibid.,* January 11, 1918.

[19] *Ibid.,* January 11, 1918.    [20] 56 *Congressional Record* 810.

[21] Elizabeth Cady Stanton *et al., The History of Woman Suffrage,* V, 637.

[22] *New York Times,* January 11. 1918.    [23] *Ibid.,* July 31, August 3, 1918.

necessary for enactment. The alignment was embarrassing to Democratic leaders, who feared that failure to pass the joint resolution would discredit the Democratic party with those women who were already enfranchised or who would be enfranchised in time to vote at the ensuing general election.

The difficulty in the Democratic party was not merely the traditional state-rights position of the party. Nor was it the conservative attitude of those members who regarded women as ornaments not to be soiled by contact with a sordid political world. It was rooted in the possibility that change might disturb the delicate subject of control of Negroes in the South. Senator Hardwick, of Georgia, discussed the subject in the debate which began on September 26, 1918, and ended five days later with a Senate vote on the issue. He expected the war itself, apart from any new constitutional amendment, to stir up trouble in the South. Negroes had been drafted into the army along with white men. When they returned, "honest but impracticable men" in the North and West would insist that the black men of the South who risked their lives in their country's cause were entitled to the same rights as any white man. In a state that had a population half black and half white, he contended, it would be destruction and ruin to carry out that kind of policy.[24]

Senator Williams, of Mississippi, sought to limit the amendment to white citizens of the United States.[25] His amendment meant, he said,

> that we enfranchise every white woman in the United States, and that we do not enfranchise any Japanese, Chinese, or Negro woman in the United States, but that we leave to each state the question as to whether or not it shall do that. If California wants to enfranchise the Chinese and Japanese women, let her do it; if Mississippi wants to enfranchise the Negro women, let her do it; but do not force upon California and Mississippi the enfranchisement of those women who are not of our race, who are not of our aspirations, who are not of our ideals, who are not of anything that makes an essential part of us.[26]

[24] 56 *Congressional Record* 10778-10779.     [25] *Ibid.*, p. 8346.

[26] *Ibid.*, p. 10981. Representative Clark, of Florida, said on May 21, 1919:

"While the great masses of the Negroes in the South are contented with existing conditions, some of the alleged leaders of the race are agitators and disturbers and are constantly seeking to embroil their people in trouble with the white people by making demands for social recognition which will never be accorded them; and the real leaders in these matters are the Negro women, who are much more insistent and vicious along these lines than are the men of their race.

"Make this amendment a part of the federal Constitution and the Negro women of the southern states, under the tutelage of the fast-growing socialistic element of our common country, will become fanatical on the subject of voting and will reawaken in the Negro men an intense and not easily quenched desire to again become a political factor." 58 *Congressional Record* 90.

The opposition cf Southern senators was so intense that the amendment seemed likely to be defeated unless some unusually strong influence was brought to bear. On September 30, 1918, President Wilson made a surprise appearance before the Senate to urge the passage of the amendment. He regarded it, he said, "as vitally essential to the successful prosecution of the great war of humanity in which we are engaged."[27] Its adoption was "clearly necessary to the successful prosecution of the war and the successful realization of the objects for which the war is being fought." This was a people's war. If Americans were Democrats and wished to lead the world to democracy, they must demonstrate their sincerity by their actions. If measures like this were rejected, people of the world who were looking to us for leadership would cease to believe in us, would cease to follow or trust us. The war could not have been fought without the services of women. "I tell you plainly that this measure which I urge upon you is vital to the winning of the war and to the energies alike of preparation and of battle."[28]

The message carried a ring of insincerity for those senators who disapproved of the amendment. They did not deny or question the services of women in the war, but they did not regard suffrage as necessary to those services. Some of them lacked the belief in America's moral leadership of the world which the President expressed then and later in connection with his struggle for the League of Nations. They were concerned with the hard problems of government at home. The President's speech made no converts. The vote cast on October 1, 1918, was 53 to 31.[29] The majority was less than the necessary two-thirds.

At the elections held in November, 1918, three more states fully enfranchised women, and enough additional advocates of woman suffrage were elected to the Senate and the House of Representatives to insure ultimate success for the amendment. If action were left to the new Congress, however, credit for the amendment would go to Republicans who would dominate that Congress rather than to the Democrats who would remain in power until the ensuing March 4. In his annual message to Congress on December 2, 1918, the President urged that the least tribute that could be paid to women was to make them the equals of men in political rights as they had proved themselves equals in every field of practical work they had entered.[34]

[27] *Messages and Papers of the Presidents*, XVIII, 8600.
[28] *Ibid.*, pp. 8600-8602.     [29] *56 Congressional Record* 10987.
[30] *Messages and Papers of the Presidents*, XVIII, 8639.

The vote was taken in the Senate on February 10, 1919. The count was 55 to 29.[31] The measure had failed again.

A joint resolution providing for the amendment was introduced at the special session of Congress which met on May 19, 1919. It passed the House of Representatives May 21 by a vote of 304 to 90.[32] It passed the Senate on June 4, 1919, by a vote of 56 to 25.[33]

The techniques of securing ratification by the several states have been described as follows:

> Long before the federal suffrage amendment passed the Congress, the National American Woman Suffrage Association had its ratification campaign formulated to the last detail.
>
> Every legislature had been polled, governors had been interviewed, the press kept informed of the necessary procedures of the campaign, and an expectant, eager army, thoroughly well equipped and trained, was waiting for the next move. Before the sun set on June 4, telegrams had been sent to all governors where special legislative sessions would be necessary, urging that such sessions be called. Instructions for still more intensive campaigns with governors, legislators, and the press were wired to state auxiliaries to the National Suffrage Association, and when the sun rose on June 5 the campaign was already under full speed.[34]

A number of state legislators were called into special session in order that women might have the privilege of voting in the presidential election of 1920. Ratification was proclaimed on August 26, 1920.[35] The southern states were notably absent from the list of those approving the amendment.

A number of futile attempts were made in the courts to secure holdings that the woman-suffrage amendment could not become a part of the Constitution. Two cases reached the Supreme Court. In one, a suit was brought to restrain the Secretary of State from issuing a proclamation declaring that the amendment had been ratified, and to restrain the Attorney General from enforcing the amendment. The Supreme Court held that a person who had no interest in the matter beyond that of any private citizen had no right to bring a suit to secure by indirection a determination whether a constitutional amendment would be valid if adopted.[36]

---

[31] 57 *Congressional Record* 3062.  [32] 58 *Congressional Record* 93-94.  [33] *Ibid.*, p. 635.
[34] Carrie Chapman Catt and Nettie Rogers Shuler, *Woman Suffrage and Politics* (2d ed., 1926), p. 343. By permission of Charles Scribner's Sons.
[35] 41 Stat. 1823.      [36] Fairchild v. Hughes, 258 U.S. 126 (1922).

The other case was instituted by Oscar Leser, a representative of the Maryland League for State Defense, an organization which was opposed both to the woman-suffrage and the prohibition amendments. Maryland had refused to ratify the woman-suffrage amendment. Leser attempted to prevent the registration of two women, one white and one colored, for voting purposes. In the subsequent litigation he gave a long list of reasons why the woman-suffrage amendment was not a part of the Constitution. Although he was defeated all the way along the line, the litigation aided in clarifying a number of points in the amending process. Leser contended that so great an addition to the electorate as would be made by the woman-suffrage amendment without the consent of the state would destroy the autonomy of the state as a political body. The Supreme Court replied, however, that the language of this amendment was precisely similar to that of the Fifteenth Amendment and that the Fifteenth had been held valid. Leser contended that the constitutions of a number of the states whose legislatures had been listed as ratifying the amendment contained provisions forbidding such drastic legislative action as the ratification of an amendment of this kind. The Supreme Court replied that the function of a state legislature in ratifying a proposed amendment to the federal Constitution was a federal function derived from the federal Constitution and that it transcended any limitations thought to be imposed by the people of a state. It was further contended that the ratifying resolutions of two states were inoperative because adopted in violation of the rules of procedure prevailing in the respective states. The Court replied, however, that official notices of ratification received by the Secretary of State were binding upon him, and said that, since the Secretary of State had proclaimed the amendment in effect, that fact was conclusive upon the Court.[37] This decision virtually settled the question of the validity of the Nineteenth Amendment.

As is often the case with innovations, universal woman suffrage has justified neither all the hopes nor all the fears to which it gave rise prior to its adoption.[38] The South has remained under the control of the white population. It seems clear that the women of the country who were not otherwise masculine and coarse in tendency have not become so by virtue of the privilege of voting along with men. On

[37] Leser v. Garnett, 258 U.S. 130 (1922).
[38] For a summary and interpretation of information about the effects of woman suffrage see Edward M. Sait, American Parties and Elections (third ed., 1942), pp. 96-106.

the other hand, politics has not been greatly purified by the presence of women at the polls. Boss rule still prevails in many localities. The enactment of social legislation has continued with the support of the votes of some women, but the movement was begun long before equal suffrage was granted, and presumably would have continued in some degree without the votes of women.

No separate records are kept of the votes of men and women, but it is generally believed that women vote much as men do. It is true that certain of their organizations, such as the League of Women Voters, have done much to educate women voters, and men as well, on important voting issues. They have doubtless had more influence because of the fact that women vote as well as educate, but women were not without educational and political influence before they became voters, as witness the part which they played in the prohibition movement. In a sense, it may be true that the important results of the woman-suffrage movement, were those achieved before the enactment of the constitutional amendment, in that many of the legal discriminations against women were removed by the several states, and special protection desired by women was gained in maternity and labor legislation.

Since the adoption of the woman-suffrage amendment, most women's groups engaged in education and lobbying on behalf of their sex have concentrated on legislation to be enacted by the state and federal governments. The Woman's party, however, which included most of the more vociferous personnel, the people who engaged in picketing, hunger strikes, and other melodramatic performances, has sought an additional constitutional change known as the equal-rights amendment. The usual form of the proposed amendment is as follows:

> Men and women shall have equal rights throughout the United States and every place subject to its jurisdiction.
> Congress shall have power to enforce this article by appropriate legislation.

The argument for the amendment is based on the fact that many states have laws discriminating in one way or another in terms of sex. The great bulk of these laws constitutes a heritage from the distant past. Some of them, however, represent more recently enacted legislation intended for the protection of women, such as that fixing maximum hours and minimum wages for their employment and prohibiting their employment altogether at certain times, usually at night. Such laws, say the proponents of the amendment, have the unfortunate result of bringing about the employment of men for work which women might otherwise be allowed to do.

Other organized groups of women oppose the amendment. They defend the legislation already enacted in their interest. They say that, since they now have the vote, further changes should be limited to those that can be secured by legislation. They argue that the amendment as phrased creates uncertainty in many fields of law, in that it does not state whether the equality to be achieved is to be on the level of present legislation affecting men or that affecting women. Furthermore, they contend that the amendment places sweeping powers in the hands of the federal government, going much farther as an invasion of substantive state rights than did the woman-suffrage amendment. The equal-rights amendment has been introduced at each session of Congress since 1923. Extensive hearings have been held, but, with the exception of one unfavorable report, it has never been reported out of committee. Since the organizations sponsoring it have no widespread following among the masses of the voters, there seems no great likelihood that it will be adopted.[39]

## THE PROHIBITION AMENDMENT

The Eighteenth Amendment to the Constitution had an unusual history. It was enacted with the impetus given by war conditions.[40] Its validity was attacked in the courts on every possible ground Friends of prohibition brought about the enactment of drastic legislation for its enforcement, while opponents prevented the appropriation of adequate funds and the establishment of necessary machinery for enforcement. Concurrent power of enforcement between the federal government and the states resulted in confusion as to responsi-

---

[39] For the several arguments see "Equal-Rights Amendment and the Constitution," House judiciary committee, *Hearings on H. J. Res. 197,* March 16, 1932, 72d Cong., 1st. sess.

A number of legal authorities, both men and women, oppose the proposed amendment. They differentiate this proposed amendment from the Eighteenth and Nineteenth Amendments, each of which stated a broad rule but related to a specific object. They claim that the equal-rights amendment would cause chaos in almost all fields of law. See statements by Joseph P. Chamberlain, Richard R. Powell, and Albert C. Jacobs, professors of law at Columbia University. Senate committee on the judiciary, 75th Cong., 3d sess., *Hearings on S. J. Res. 65,* Part 2, pp. 188-191. For the unfavorable report see Senate Report No. 1641 on S. J. Res. 65, 75th Cong., 3d sess., 83 *Congressional Record* 5684.

[40] See chapter 26.

bility. The amendment, and legislation under it intended to restore order in a society corrupted by the open saloon, resulted in the establishment of a bootleg industry and in organized gangster activities which surpassed, or seemed to surpass, all previous experience for lawlessness. Finally, with the depression of 1929 and afterward, came a revulsion of sentiment, resulting in repeal of the constitutional amendment. Repeal was justified in part to permit the re-establishment of the liquor industry in order that taxes raised from it might be used to balance the budget of the federal government. The following pages tell somewhat more elaborately the story here summarized.

The Eighteenth Amendment read as follows:

> Section 1. After one year from the ratification of this article the manufacture, sale, or transportation of intoxicating liquors within, the importation thereof into, or the exportation thereof from, the United States and all territory subject to the jurisdiction thereof for beverage purposes is hereby prohibited.
>
> Section 2. The Congress and the several states shall have concurrent power to enforce this article by appropriate legislation.
>
> Section 3. This article shall be inoperative unless it shall have been ratified as an amendment to the Constitution by the legislatures of the several states, as provided in the Constitution, within seven years from the date of the submission hereof to the states by the Congress.

By January 16, 1919, the necessary three-fourths of the states had ratified the amendment. It was to become effective a year later.[41] Organizations of distillers, liquor dealers, hotel keepers, and other opponents of prohibition continued their opposition. They contended that, in states providing for referenda on acts of their legislatures, there was still time to block the amendment by having the people reject the act of ratification.[42]

After the legislature of Ohio had ratified the amendment, the proceedings necessary for a referendum were begun. Prohibition forces countered with a petition for an injunction to prevent the secretary of state from spending public money on a referendum. The legal question involved was whether, under Article V of the Constitution of the United States, a state could substitute action by referendum

---

[41] Dillon v. Gloss, 256 U.S. 368 376 (1921). The case determines the fact that a constitutional amendment becomes a part of the Constitution when ratified by the requisite number of states, whatever the date of the formal proclamation.

[42] See *The American Year Book,* 1919, p. 55.

for an act of a legislature ratifying a constitutional amendment. The liquor interests lost the fight all the way along. "The proposed change," said the Supreme Court in Hawke *v*. Smith, "can only become effective by the ratification of the legislatures of three-fourths of the states or by conventions in a like number of states." [43] As between these two methods, the choice was left to Congress. It was clear that within the meaning of the Constitution the legislature of Ohio was its bicameral assembly, and not the electorate at large which might participate in a referendum. The Supreme Court did not question its earlier decision that the state might resort to the referendum in connection with its own laws. The act of ratifying a federal constitutional amendment, however, said the Court, derived its authority from the provisions of the federal Constitution and not from the constitution of the state. The effect of the decision was to eliminate direct action by the people as a mode of ratifying or passing upon federal constitutional amendments. It closed the door to opposition to the Eighteenth Amendment by this route.

One week after its decision in this case, the Supreme Court decided, in one group, seven other important cases contesting the validity of the Eighteenth Amendment and of the National Prohibition Act, or Volstead Act. [44] Two of the cases were original suits brought by states, Rhode Island and New Jersey, to enjoin the Attorney General of the United States from enforcing the law. "Not since the Milligan case was argued in 1866," said a commentator, "has a more notable array of counsel stood up before the Court, while the *amici curiae* filing briefs in the cases comprised precisely half the state attorneys general of the Union." [45] Prominent among the counsel were Elihu Root and William D. Guthrie.

The amendment was attacked on what seemed like every conceivable ground. The Supreme Court, in Rhode Island *v*. Palmer,

[43] 253 U.S. 221, 226 (1920). An amendment to Article V was introduced in the Sixty-Eighth Congress after this discussion. It contained a provision "that any state may require that ratification by its legislature be subject to confirmation by popular vote." It also reserved the right of a state to change the vote before an amendment had been finally ratified or defeated. The adoption of such a proposal would have saved litigation in later cases. (See Coleman *v*. Miller, 307 U.S. 433 [1939].) This resolution was reported in both houses and debated in the Senate, but not brought up for a vote. Senate Report No. 202 on S. J. Res. 4 and House Report No. 944 on H. J. Res. 68, 68th Cong., 1st sess. See also Senate Report No. 1235 on S. J. Res. 40, 67th Cong., 3d and 4th sess.

[44] 41 Stat. 305.

[45] Edward S. Corwin, "Constitutional Law in 1919-1920," *American Political Science Review*, XIV (November, 1920), 635, 651.

unanimously upheld the validity of the amendment, but the several justices disagreed as to reasons for doing so and as to interpretation of the amendment.  Five justices concurred in a concise statement of eleven points made by Justice Van Devanter concerning the amendment and the enforcement legislation, but left their reasons unstated, evidently because of inability to reach agreement.  "The Court declares conclusions only," said Justice McKenna, in ironic comment, "without giving any reasons for them.  The instance may be wise — establishing a precedent now, hereafter wisely to be imitated.  It will undoubtedly decrease the literature of the Court if it does not increase its lucidity." [46]

Chief Justice White thought reasons should be given for certain positions taken, and proceeded to state his own.  Justice McReynolds cautiously limited himself to the statement that he did not dissent from the disposition of the cases as ordered by the Court.  He thought it impossible to say what construction should be given to the Eighteenth Amendment.  "Because of the bewilderment which it creates," he said, "a multitude of questions will inevitably arise and demand solution here.  In the circumstances I prefer to remain free to consider these questions when they arrive." [47]

The *New York Times* remarked, "The effect of the decision is to put into Congress and undoubtedly into politics for some years to come a fight for the repeal or liberalization of the Volstead Act." [48] The prediction was correct, but the struggle also continued in the courts, even if based on somewhat far-fetched arguments.  In May, 1921, a year after the decisions discussed above, the Supreme Court handed down its decision in Dillon *v.* Gloss, based on the third section of the constitutional amendment.  The section provided that the article should be inoperative unless ratified within seven years. A man who was in custody for violating the Volstead Act contended that this contingent provision invalidated the amendment.  He argued that Congress had no power to base ratification of an amendment on a condition as to the time in which it might be ratified by the states.

Speaking for the Supreme Court. Justice Van Devanter discussed the history of constitutional amendments previously proposed. Twenty-one amendments, he said, had been proposed by Congress down to that time; seventeen of them had been ratified by legislatures of three-fourths of the states within periods of not more than

---

[46] 253 U.S. 350, 393 (1920).  [47] *Ibid.,* p. 392.          [48] June 8, 1920.

four years. Each of the remaining four had been ratified in some states, but not in a sufficient number. He found nothing in the Constitution, however, which suggested that an amendment, once proposed, was to be open to ratification for all time, or that ratification in some of the states might be separated from that in others by many years and yet be effective. The Court had no doubt of the power of Congress to fix a reasonable definite period for the ratification of an amendment. It concluded that there was nothing unreasonable about the selection of a period of seven years, and held, therefore, that the validity of the amendment was not affected by the provision as to ratification.[49]

Apart from questions as to the validity of the amendment itself, the Eighteenth Amendment gave rise to constitutional questions in a number of fields. Important among them were those in cases in which it was argued that the government indulged in unreasonable searches and seizures in violation of the Fourth Amendment.[50] Investigations to detect manufacture, storage, transportation, and sale of liquor in violation of the Volstead Act required widespread searching in hotels, restaurants, warehouses, offices, automobiles, and other places and equipment. Law enforcement, therefore, verged constantly on the fringes of civil liberty. Investigations were facilitated by tapping telephone wires to obtain relevant information. A culminating case, testing this method of detection, was Olmstead v. United States,[51] in which the Supreme Court upheld the action of government agents and, incidentally, summarized a long line of decisions as to the constitutionality of methods of collecting evidence for use in prosecution. There was no searching and no seizure involved in the process of tapping telephone wires, declared Chief Justice Taft,

[49] 256 U.S. 376. For evidence of confusion of thought on the part of the Court in the case, see Ernst Freund, "Legislative Problems and Solutions," *American Bar Association Journal*, VII (December, 1921), 656. The Court discussed the power of Congress to limit the period of ratification. What Congress did, however, was to incorporate the time provision, not merely in the joint resolution, but in the amendment itself.

In 1939, the Supreme Court heard a case raising the question as to the validity of ratification of a child-labor amendment some thirteen years after the amendment was submitted. The amendment contained no limitation as to the period of ratification. The Court held that the question was not justiciable, but was one for the determination of Congress. Two justices dissented. (Coleman v. Miller, 307 U.S. 433.) For discussion of the proposed child-labor amendment, see below.

For still another attack on the prohibition amendment see United States v. Sprague, 282 U.S. 716 (1931).

[50] For general discussion see Howard Lee McBain, *Prohibition Legal and Illegal* (1928), pp. 77-105.

[51] 277 U.S. 438 (1928).

speaking for the Court. "The evidence was secured by the use of the sense of hearing and that only." [52] Congress could prohibit the use of evidence gathered in this manner, he added, but "the courts may not adopt such a policy by attributing an enlarged and unusual meaning to the Fourth Amendment." [53].

Justices Holmes and Brandeis dissented, the former remarking, "For my part I think it a less evil that some criminals should escape than that the government should play an ignoble part." [54] Elsewhere in his opinion he referred to wire-tapping as "dirty business." His indignant comments were used again and again by the opponents of prohibition in efforts to secure the enactment of legislation to prevent wire-tapping by the federal government. Over a period of several years, bills were introduced in Congress to prohibit the practice. Finally, in an act of March 1, 1933, making appropriation for the Bureau of Prohibition in the Department of Justice, Congress provided that no part of the appropriation should be used for or in connection with wire-tapping to procure evidence of violation of the National Prohibition Act. [55]

In the Federal Communications Act of 1934, passed after the repeal of the Eighteenth Amendment, Congress, without mentioning government officials directly, forbade the divulging of information received by wire or radio by any person not entitled thereto. [56] The Supreme Court has interpreted the act to prohibit the use in federal courts of information which federal agents have acquired by wire-tapping. Said Justice Roberts for the Court in 1937, "Congress may have thought it less important that some offenders should go unwhipped of justice than that officers should resort to methods deemed inconsistent with ethical standards and destructive of personal liberty." [57]

Serious difficulties both of interpretation and administration arose out of the second section of the Eighteenth Amendment, which provided, "The Congress and the several states shall have concurrent

---

[52] Ibid., p. 464.　　　[53] Ibid., p. 466.　　　[54] Ibid., p. 470.

[55] 47 Stat. 1371, 1381.　　[56] 48 Stat. 1064, 1103.

[57] Nardone v. United States, 302 U.S. 379, 383 (1937). See also Weiss v. United States, 308 U.S. 321 (1939); and Nardone v. United States, 308 U.S. 338 (1939). On June 14, 1940, the House committee on the judiciary in House Report No. 2574, 76th Cong., 3d sess., reported favorably H. J. Res. 571, to authorize the Federal Bureau of Investigation of the Department of Justice to resort to wire-tapping, on approval of the Attorney General, "to ascertain, prevent, and frustrate any interference or attempts or plans to interfere with the national defense by sabotage, treason, seditious conspiracy, espionage, violations of the neutrality law, or in any other manner." The measure had the approval of the Attorney General. Other bills were introduced thereafter to permit wire-tapping in connection with the war.

power to enforce this article by appropriate legislation." The language was confusing. It purported, not to protect the exercise of state powers already held, but to give power based on the amendment itself. If this was the effect, the meaning of the word "concurrent" became extremely important. The word was not used elsewhere in the Constitution. It had been widely used in judicial decisions, but with conflicting and varied interpretations. Judges and laymen who sought the meaning of the concurrent provision by textual exegesis found a bewildering number of meanings,[58] of which many were capable of use to embarrass prohibition enforcement. In any event, the confusion itself was embarrassing.

The Supreme Court, after some initial disagreement,[59] clarified the situation in 1922 by accepting the interpretation justified by the history of the drafting of the amendment. Speaking for a unanimous Court, Chief Justice Taft made the following statement:

> To regard the amendment as the source of the power of the states to adopt and enforce prohibition measures is to take a partial and erroneous view of the matter. Save for some restrictions arising out of the federal Constitution, chiefly the commerce clause, each state possessed that power in full measure prior to the amendment, and the probable purpose of declaring a concurrent power to be in the states was to negative any possible inference that, in vesting the national government with the power of country-wide prohibition, state power would be excluded. In effect the second section of the Eighteenth Amendment put an end to restrictions upon the state's power arising out of the federal Constitution and left her free to enact prohibition laws applying to all transactions within her limits. To be sure, the first section of the amendment took from the states all power to authorize acts falling within its prohibition, but it did not cut down or displace prior state laws not inconsistent with it. Such laws derive their force, as do all new ones consistent with it, not from this amendment, but from power originally belonging to the states, preserved to them by the Tenth Amendment, and now relieved from the restriction heretofore arising out of the federal Constitution.[60]

In view of this interpretation, the amendment protected the pre-existing powers of the states, but laid upon them no obligation to

[58] Noel T. Dowling, "Concurrent Power Under the Eighteenth Amendment," *Minnesota Law Review*, VI (May, 1922), 447-479.

[59] Rhode Island *v.* Palmer, 253 U.S. 350 (1920).

[60] United States *v.* Lanza, 260 U.S. 377, 381-382 (1922). See also Hebert *v.* Louisiana, 272 U.S. 312 (1926).

enforce prohibition if enforcement was contrary to their own policy. This interpretation was immensely unpopular with federal administrators and other advocates of prohibition enforcement. They took the position that the states, whether or not they had previously attempted to enforce prohibition, were now legally and morally responsible, jointly with the federal government, for carrying out the purposes of the Eighteenth Amendment. Their concern about the interpretation lay in the fact that the federal government had no adequate machinery for enforcement without the aid of the states. The federal government was not equipped with investigators, marshals, prosecutors, courts, or prisons to take care of the great mass of offenders against the Volstead Act. There was general opposition to building up federal machinery to parallel the police machinery of the states. This fact, coupled with opposition to prohibition itself, was sufficient to prevent the appropriation of sufficient federal funds for the establishment of such machinery.[61]

At the time of the adoption of the Eighteenth Amendment, thirty-three states had prohibition laws of their own. After the adoption of the amendment, twelve other states, caught by the impetus of the movement and perhaps persuaded, by the language of the amendment, that a moral obligation was laid upon them, enacted enforcement legislation. Eighteen states added to or amended their laws to make them correspond with the National Prohibition Act. The impetus of the movement quickly subsided, however. Maryland was never caught by it and never enacted a prohibition law. New York repealed its law in 1923, amid denunciations from prohibitionists for immoral conduct in withdrawing support from the Constitution. Four other states followed suit, and enforcement virtually ceased in still others. Enforcement grew lax even in states in which it had been vigorous prior to the adoption of the constitutional amendment. Cause lay partly in a sweeping increase of public sentiment against the restraints of prohibition. It also lay in the desire of state officials and taxpayers to shift responsibility and expense to the federal government.

Federal enforcement got off to a bad start.[62] By 1922, President Harding found it necessary to say, in his annual message to Congress,

---

[61] For discussion of serious difficulties in the way of enforcement, see J. P. Chamberlain, "Enforcement of the Volstead Act Through State Agencies," *American Bar Association Journal*, X (June, 1924), 391-394.

[62] Charles Merz, *The Dry Decade* (1931), pp. 57-61.

"There are conditions relating to its enforcement which savor of nation-wide scandal. It is the most demoralizing factor in our public life." [63] Neither President Harding nor his successors, however, asked for sufficient funds and organization to make the federal law effective. No Congress undertook the task of its own volition. Minor changes in machinery were made from time to time; and there was much scolding of the states for failure to do their part.

In 1926, probably at the request of the assistant secretary of the treasury, who had charge of the prohibition unit, President Coolidge issued an executive order authorizing the appointment of state, county, and municipal officers as prohibition officers of the Treasury Department at a nominal rate of compensation to enforce the provisions of the National Prohibition Act. The purpose of the order was to secure closer co-ordination between state and federal officers. The order was permissive and not mandatory, and it excepted officers in those states having constitutional or statutory provisions against the holding of federal office by state officers. [64] Since, under the Volstead Act, the commissioner of internal revenue and the Attorney General were authorized to appoint inferior officers, the consent of the President to designate state officers as representatives of the federal government was probably not necessary. The situation was confused, however, by an executive order of 1873 forbidding such appointments. The new executive order sought to clarify the situation by amending its predecessor.

The order produced an uproar of criticism in Congress. The appointment of state officers as agents of the federal government was denounced as a sweeping invasion of state rights. [65] A commentator remarked derisively that the Senate acted from "baffled egoism" in that its concurrence was not required either in making appointments or in making appropriations to carry out a program. [66] After considerable discussion, the controversy died down. [67] It is said that no appointments of state officers to federal positions were made. [68]

Confusion and disorder reached a crisis during the administration of Herbert Hoover. Early in 1928, when, as a potential candidate for the Republican nomination to the presidency, he was asked to state

[63] 64 *Congressional Record* 215.          [64] 67 *Congressional Record* 9923.

[65] *Ibid.*, pp. 9923, 9944, 9989.

[66] John H. Wigmore, "The President, the Senate, the Constitution, and the Executive Order of May 8, 1926," *Illinois Law Review*, XXI (June, 1926), 142-147.

[67] Laurence F. Schmeckebier, *The Bureau of Prohibition* (1929), pp. 18-19.

[68] Merz, *op. cit.*, pp. 192-193.

his position on prohibition, Hoover replied that he did not favor repeal of the Eighteenth Amendment. He stood for the efficient, vigorous, and sincere enforcement of the laws enacted under it. "Our country," he said, "has deliberately undertaken a great social and economic experiment, noble in motive and far-reaching in purpose. It must be worked out constructively." [69]   Soon after he became President, he appointed what came to be known as the Wickersham Commission, pursuant to a statute which appropriated a quarter of a million dollars for "a thorough inquiry into the problem of the enforcement of prohibition under the provisions of the Eighteenth Amendment of the Constitution and laws enacted in pursuance thereof." [70]

The commission made its final report early in 1931.[71] It found that a series of bad features and difficulties stood in the way of enforcement and that an appalling amount of corruption had prevailed throughout the decade. The bad start made with enforcement had affected the entire period. Public opinion, hostile to enforcement, had presented a serious obstacle in many sections of the country. The huge profits to be made out of illicit bootlegging had resulted in widespread violations of the law. Several thousand miles of shore line and other geographical conditions had facilitated illicit manufacture and sale. Overwhelming political difficulties had arisen out of the nature of our federal system. The existence of two sovereigns in the same territory often resulted in situations wherein neither government was both equipped and willing to enforce the kind of legislation authorized by the constitutional amendment. The following paragraph is significant:

> We have a long tradition of independence of administrative officials and systematic decentralizing of administration. In consequence disinclination to co-operate has pervaded our whole polity, local, state, and federal; and for historical reasons since the Civil War there has been more or less latent, or even open, suspicion or jealousy of federal administrative agencies on the part of many of the states. Concurrent state and federal prohibition has shown us nothing new. It has repeated and recapitulated in a decade the experience of one hundred and forty years of administration of nation-wide laws in a dual gov-

[69] Hoover to William E. Borah, February 23, 1928, *New York Times*, February 24, 1928.
[70] 45 Stat. 1613.
[71] United States National Commission on Law Observance and Enforcement, *Enforcement of the Prohibition Laws of the United States*, House Doc. No. 722, 71st Cong., 3d sess.

ernment. In the beginnings of the federal government, it was be-lieved that state officials and state tribunals could be made regularly available as the means of enforcing federal laws. It was soon neces-sary to set up a separate system of federal magistrates and federal enforcing agencies. We had no traditions of concerted action be-tween independent governmental activities and it was not until the World War that we succeeded in developing a spirit of co-operation at least for the time being. In spite of that experience, the Eighteenth Amendment reverted to the policy of state enforcement of federal law, and again there has been not a little falling down of enforcement between concurrent agencies with diffused responsibility. The result was disappointing. Too frequently there has been a feeling, even in states which had prohibition laws before the National Prohibition Act, that enforcement of prohibition was now a federal concern with which the state need no longer trouble itself. Thus there has often been apathy or inaction on the part of state agencies, even where local sentiment was strong for the law. It is true the good sense and energy of some prohibition directors and vigorous action on the part of some state executives have at times brought about a high degree of co-operation in more than one jurisdiction. Sometimes this co-operation is local and fitful, sometimes and in some places it is com-plete, and sometimes it is well organized and co-ordinated. But there are no guaranties of its continuance.[72]

The committee commented on psychological factors, such as public irritation at a constitutional "don't" in a matter where the people saw no moral question. The matter was the more irritating in that the statutory definition of "intoxicating" was fixed much below what was intoxicating in fact. Resentment and irritation had also grown out of incidents of enforcement. There had been obvious discrimination between workers and employers, between rich and poor. Enforce-ment of the National Prohibition Act had shifted to the federal courts a great deal of what was essentially police-court work for which they were not equipped. Lawyers greatly deplored the change in the general attitude toward the federal courts. Formerly they had been of exceptional dignity and had commanded wholesome fear and re-spect through the efficiency with which they had handled their crim-inal business. The huge volume of liquor prosecutions had injured their dignity, impaired their efficiency, and endangered the respect for them which had once obtained. The morale and methods of prosecutors had been affected in the same way.

[72] *Ibid.,* p. 53.

The commission recommended that federal appropriations for enforcement be substantially increased and that various improvements be made in statutes, organization, personnel, and equipment for enforcement. Some members thought the amendment could yet be enforced; others thought it had been proved unenforceable and that it ought to be modified. The suggestion for modification of the amendment was that, instead of flatly prohibiting manufacture and sale of intoxicating liquor, it should authorize Congress either to regulate or prohibit.

President Hoover forwarded the report to Congress, giving support to its recommendations as to statutory changes. He said:

> I do, however, see serious objections to, and therefore must not be understood as recommending, the commission's proposed revision of the Eighteenth Amendment which is suggested by them for possible consideration at some future time if the continued effort at enforcement should not prove successful. My own duty and that of all executive officials is clear — to enforce the law with all the means at our disposal without equivocation or reservation.[73]

Throughout the years in which the Eighteenth Amendment was in force, persistent efforts were made to secure its modification or repeal. Between 1921 and 1933, more than one hundred and thirty amendments were introduced which affected the Eighteenth Amendment in some manner. A considerable number of them provided for outright repeal, while others weakened the amendment in varying degrees. Sentiment in favor of change grew stronger with the coming of the depression of 1929 and the consequent unrest, and with the development of the argument that substantial revenues could be collected if the illicit business, then running into millions of dollars, were legalized, regulated, and taxed. Along with agitation for change in the Constitution ran similar agitation for modification or repeal of the Volstead Act. Prohibition forces resisted changes which would weaken the statute. They were aided by persons who felt that, whatever the merits of prohibition, Congress should not take action which would have the effect of nullifying a provision of the Constitution.

By the time when the Democratic and Republican national conventions met in the summer of 1932, sentiment for repeal of the amendment was so strong that the platform of both parties advocated constitutional change. The Democratic platform advocated repeal of

[73] *Ibid.,* p. iv.

the Eighteenth Amendment. It demanded that Congress propose a repealing amendment, to be acted upon by conventions in the several states. It suggested that the states themselves take action to prevent the return of the saloon and other evils connected with the liquor traffic. Franklin D. Roosevelt, the candidate nominated by the party, was already committed to repeal.

The Republican platform was less clear. It advocated the proposal of an amendment which would retain in the federal government power to preserve the gains already made in dealing with the evils of the liquor traffic, but would also allow the states to deal with the problem as their citizens might determine, subject to the power of the federal government to protect those states desiring to enforce prohibition legislation of their own. In accepting the Republican nomination, President Hoover likewise advocated an amendment giving each state the right to deal with the problem as it saw fit. He wished, however, to preserve the federal power to protect each state from interference and invasion by its neighbors and to prevent a return of the saloon system with its inevitable political and social corruption.

The forthright position of Roosevelt probably contributed to the sweeping victory which he won at the polls in November, 1932. The "lame-duck" session of Congress which assembled in December, 1932, recognized the trend in public sentiment. After additional controversy over phraseology, it proposed to the states the Twenty-First Amendment by which the Eighteenth Amendment was to be repealed. Action was to be taken, not by state legislatures, but by conventions chosen for the specific purpose of dealing with the amendment.

RATIFICATION OF THE TWENTY-FIRST AMENDMENT

There was much speculation as to how ratification by convention would be carried out. Leading authorities on constitutional law debated the question whether the states or the federal government should prescribe procedure. James M. Beck, a congressman who had once been solicitor general, took the position that all details must be left to state legislatures.[74] Former Attorney General Palmer argued that the question of ratifying an amendment was a purely federal question, and that Congress must prescribe the conditions of ratification by the conventions.[75] Other authorities differed similarly on the

[74] 76 *Congressional Record* 124-126.
[75] *Ibid.*, pp. 130-134.

subject.[76] Bills were introduced in Congress concerning the conventions, but none of them were passed. A number of state legislatures thought it possible that Congress might act on the subject. At least twenty-one of them included in their own statutes provisions that state officers should follow procedure prescribed by Congress if a federal statute were enacted. By contrast, one state, New Mexico, asserted the exclusive power of the state in the matter and provided that all state officers should resist to the utmost any attempt at congressional dictation and usurpation.[77] Sixteen of the states acted on the assumption that the matter was one permanently within the scope of state power, and passed laws applicable, not merely to the convention about to assemble, but also to future conventions which might assemble for the same purpose. The other laws passed related only to the amendment at hand.[78]

There was question whether delegates should be elected locally or at large. Since sentiment on the liquor traffic differed sharply between urban and rural areas, it might be possible to gerrymander districts so as to influence the election if members of the conventions were chosen locally. The custom of local election of legislators was deeply engrained throughout the country. In an advisory opinion, the supreme judicial court of Maine stated that the principal distinction between a convention and a legislature was that the former was called for a specific purpose while the latter was called for general purposes. In view of custom as to the choice both of members of legislatures and members of conventions, the court held that it was not permissible for the state to organize a convention wherein the delegates were elected at large.[79] The other states divided as to the

[76] Everett S. Brown, "The Ratification of the Twenty-First Amendment," *The American Political Science Review*, XXIX (December, 1935), 1005, 1007. See Howard Lee McBain, " 'Or by Conventions,' " *New York Times*, December 11, 1932.

On February 15, Senator Hastings, of Delaware, discussed the understanding that party leaders had at the time that they were writing their demands for ratification by convention into the party platform. He said that he pointed out the difficulties in setting up the machinery for conventions by the state legislatures, "and then for the first time I discovered that there was in their minds the determination and the thought that all this could be arranged by the Congress and that there could be but one election on the same day all over the country upon this subject. . . . My own judgment is that on neither side, either in the Democratic convention or in the Republican convention, did those who were advocating this plan know exactly what they were doing with respect to it. From the very beginning they had had the idea that . . . in order to get a majority vote of the people of the nation, one must have a convention method." 76 *Congressional Record* 4167.

[77] Brown, *op. cit.*, pp. 1008-1009.   [78] *Ibid.*, pp. 1009-1010.
[79] *In re* Opinion of the Justices, 167 Atlantic 176 (1933).

mode of choice. Some elected all delegates at large; some elected all locally; and others chose part in one way and part in another.[80] No controversies resulted in suits to determine the constitutionality of the mode of election.

In spite of the fact that a convention was in common parlance a deliberative body, there was little expectation or desire that the conventions chosen to pass upon the Twenty-First Amendment should engage in debate on the subject. They were expected to meet and vote, and nothing more. Most of the states submitted to the people lists of delegates who favored or opposed the ratification of the proposed amendment. The choice of delegates, therefore, in effect constituted a popular referendum on the amendment itself. Some states provided the alternative of voting for unpledged delegates, perhaps in recognition of the tradition that a convention was a deliberative body. Some states held a referendum on the constitutional amendment at the time when delegates were chosen, and required the delegates elected to vote as a majority of the people had voted.[81]

In Ohio, evidently as a forlorn hope of prohibitionists, an attempt was made to secure a referendum, not on the amendment, but on the act of the state legislature providing for the ratifying convention. The supreme court of Ohio expressed the opinion that the calling of such a convention was but a step necessary and incidental to the final action of the convention in registering the voice of the state upon the amendment proposed by Congress. The action of the legislature rested upon the authority of Article V of the Constitution of the United States. It was a federal function which, in the absence of action by Congress, the state legislature was authorized to perform. The court held, therefore, that the statute was not subject to referendum.[82] A similar attempt was made in Missouri to secure a referendum, not on the proposed constitutional amendment itself, but on the act of the state legislature. The supreme court of Missouri, like the Ohio court, concluded that, when a state legislature performed any act looking to the ratification or rejection of an amendment to the federal Constitution, it was acting, not in accordance with any power given to it by the state, but was exercising a power conferred upon it by the federal Constitution. Its action, therefore, was not subject to

[80] Noel T. Dowling, "A New Experiment in Ratification," *American Bar Association Journal*, XIX (July, 1933), 383, 386.

[81] Brown, *op. cit.*, p. 1013. *In re* Opinions of the Justices, 148 Southern 107 (1933).

[82] State *ex rel.* Donnelly *v.* Myers, 186 N.E. 918 (1933).

review by referendum.[83] A suggestion that the Supreme Court of the United States approved of this decision is found in the fact that it declined to review the decision of the state court.[84]

The number of delegates in the conventions varied from three hundred and twenty-nine in Indiana to three in New Mexico.[85] The conventions differed in many other respects. Yet on the whole they functioned with dispatch. They met, voted, and adjourned. By December 5, 1933, less than ten months after the amendment had been proposed to the states, thirty-six conventions had ratified the amendment, and it was proclaimed as a part of the Constitution.[86]

As far as this particular issue was concerned, ratification by convention had proved a speedy and generally satisfactory device for amending the Constitution. Action by state legislatures would doubtless have been almost as rapid, however, in view of the sentiment of the times. Although the legislators were chosen to legislate rather than to vote on a constitutional amendment, the speed with which they provided for the conventions indicated their attitude toward the amendment. Had sentiment been less clearly defined or more strongly opposed to ratification, the legislatures might have been slower in providing for conventions, and there might have been demand for conventions which were in fact deliberative rather than merely reflectors of sentiment previously expressed by the people.

In spite of intense agitation, the Congress which ended with the Hoover administration failed to pass a bill to permit the manufacture and sale of beverages containing more than one-half of one per cent of alcohol. A bill to permit the manufacture of beverages containing more than three per cent of alcohol was reported early in the special session which met in March, 1933, to deal with the depression crisis, and glowing expectations were expressed concerning the prospective

---

[83] State ex rel. Tate v. Sevier, 62 S.W. (2d) 895 (1933).

[84] Tate v. Sevier 290 U.S. 679 (1933).    [85] Brown, op. cit., p. 1006.

[86] 48 Stat. 1720. For additional articles on the process of ratification see William A. Platz, "Article Five of the Federal Constitution," George Washington Law Review, III (November, 1934), 17; "Recent Cases," Harvard Law Review, XLVII (November, 1933), 130; Alexander Lincoln, "Ratification by Conventions," Massachusetts Law Quarterly, XVIII (May, 1933), 287; William D. Mitchell, "Methods of Amending the Constitution," Lawyer and Banker, XXV (September-December, 1932), 265-270; Dumont Smith, "Has Congress Power to Call Conventions in the States to Consider Constitutional Amendments?" Journal of the Bar Association of Kansas, II (August, 1933), 1-7; H. S. Phillips, "Has Congress Power to Call and Regulate Ratifying Conventions?" Florida State Bar Association Law Journal, VI (April, 1933), 573-578: George J. Schaefer, "Amendments to Constitution: Ratification by State Convention,' St. John's Law Review, VII (May, 1933), 375-378.

yield in taxes.[87] On March 13, President Roosevelt recommended the enactment of the legislation, saying that he deemed action at this time to be of the highest importance.[88] The bill was passed and was approved on March 22.[89] The return to pre-prohibition days was, therefore, begun immediately. On December 5, 1933, President Roosevelt proclaimed the repeal of the Eighteenth Amendment. He urged the people to aid in restoring respect for law and order by making purchases only from duly licensed dealers. He called attention to the authority given by the Twenty-First Amendment to prohibit transportation or importation of intoxicating liquors into any state in violation of the laws of such state. He urged that no state should, by law or otherwise, authorize the return of the saloon either in its old form or in some modern guise.[90]

The bootlegging and gangster organizations which had developed in the period of open defiance of the Eighteenth Amendment and prohibition legislation sought to continue their old activities wherever possible and to expand into fields of extortion and kidnapping. The New-Deal administration worked out a co-ordinated program for dealing with these criminal elements, and through that program did much to make the United States once more a law-abiding nation.[91] With the adoption of the Twenty-First Amendment, the concern of the federal government with the liquor industry became predominantly one of revenue. Most of the federal legislation subsequently enacted had to do with facilitating the collection of large sums in federal taxes. A provision of an earlier statute was re-enacted to penalize the shipment of liquor into states forbidding its manufacture or sale,[92] but little or no attempt has been made to enforce the provision.[93]

The Twenty-First Amendment reads as follows:

> Section 1. The eighteenth article of amendment to the Constitution of the United States is hereby repealed.
> Section 2. The transportation or importation into any state, territory, or possession of the United States for delivery or use therein of

[87] House Report No. 3, 73d Cong., 1st sess.; Senate Report No. 3, 73d Cong., 1st sess.
[88] *Public Papers and Addresses of Franklin D. Roosevelt* (5 vols., 1933), II, 66-67.
[89] 48 Stat. 16.
[90] *Public Papers and Addresses of Franklin D. Roosevelt*, II, 510-512.
[91] Carl Brent Swisher (ed.), *Selected Papers of Homer Cummings* (1939), pp. 23 ff.
[92] 48 Stat. 316.
[93] Leonard V. Harrison and Elizabeth Laine, *After Repeal: A Study of Liquor Control Administration* (1936), pp. 21-23.

intoxicating liquors, in violation of the laws thereof, is hereby prohibited.

Section 3. This article shall be inoperative unless it shall have been ratified as an amendment to the Constitution by conventions in the several states, as provided in the Constitution, within seven years from the date of the submission hereof to the states by the Congress.

The first and third sections of the amendment have been the occasion of little controversy. The second section, however, has given rise to a number of Supreme Court decisions. The purpose of Congress in including the provision seems clearly to have been to protect dry or partly dry states from invasion by liquor interests in other states. In effect, it was to give constitutional basis to the provisions of the Webb-Kenyon Act which had been upheld by a narrow margin.

To the surprise of many persons, the Supreme Court interpreted the Twenty-First Amendment solely on the basis of its language and without reference to its history, and gave it force which the earlier law did not possess. The first important case to reach the Supreme Court came from California, which was not a dry state. A California law exacted a license tax for the privilege of importing beer. Prior to the Twenty-First Amendment the law "would obviously have been unconstitutional," because the fee would have been a direct burden on interstate commerce.[94] The liquor dealers involved asked the Supreme Court to give the Twenty-First Amendment the following meaning: "The state may prohibit the importation of intoxicating liquors provided it prohibits the manufacture and sale within its borders; but if it permits such manufacture and sale, it must let imported liquors compete with the domestic on equal terms." [95]

"To say that," however, said Justice Brandeis for the Court, "would involve, not a construction of the amendment, but a rewriting of it." [96] The language of the amendment made no distinction between wet and dry states. It prohibited transportation or importation of liquor into any state in violation of its laws.

The liquor dealers contended, also, that the California law discriminated against them and therefore denied to them the equal protection of the laws guaranteed by the Fourteenth Amendment. The Supreme Court answered briefly, "A classification recognized by the

[94] State Board of Equalization of California v. Young's Market Co., 299 U.S. 59, 62 (1936).
[95] Ibid., p. 62.
[96] Ibid., p. 62.

Twenty-First Amendment cannot be deemed forbidden by the Fourteenth." [97]

The Twenty-First Amendment, as interpreted by the Supreme Court, has encouraged the erection of interstate trade barriers by the several states as far as the liquor business is concerned.[98] There is no evidence in the debates that Congress intended such a result,[99] but the refusal of the Supreme Court to rewrite the amendment by interpretation is understandable.[100] States have enacted laws discriminating against the alcoholic products of other states, whereupon the other states have passed retaliatory measures. The result has been a system of internal protective tariffs. The laws have been upheld as within the protection of the Twenty-First Amendment. Unintentionally, therefore, Congress, in choosing the language of the amendment, restored an evil of the type of those which caused the adoption of the Constitution of the United States with its grant of power over interstate and foreign commerce to the federal government. The direct effect is to burden interstate commerce only with respect to alcoholic beverages. The ill-will produced by discrimination and retaliation doubtless plays a part, however, in producing additional interstate discrimination in other fields.[101]

[97] *Ibid.*, p. 64. In Mahoney v. Joseph Triner Corporation, 304 U.S. 401 (1938), the Supreme Court upheld a Minnesota statute which in the language of the Court clearly discriminated in favor of liquor processed within the state as against liquor completely processed elsewhere. For discussion of these and other cases see Joe de Ganahl, "The Scope of Federal Power over Alcoholic Beverages since the Twenty-First Amendment," *George Washington Law Review*, VIII (March, April, 1940), 819-834, 875-903. See also "Constitutional Discrimination under the Twenty-First Amendment," *Illinois Law Review*, XXXIII (February, 1939), 710-714; R. L. Wiser and R. F. Arledge, "Does the Repeal Amendment Empower a State to Erect Tariff Barriers and Disregard the Equal Protection Clause in Legislating on Intoxicating Liquors in Interstate Commerce?" *George Washington Law Review*, VII (January, 1939), 402-414; *Harvard Law Review*, LII (April, 1939), 1012-1013; *Minnesota Law Review*, XXIII (December, 1938), 87-88; L. A. Goldberg and A. B. Miller, "Liquor Control Returns to the States; Twenty-First Amendment," *Georgetown Law Journal*, XXVII (March, 1939), 612-623; "Retaliation and 'Equal Protection' in State Liquor Regulations," *Virginia Law Review*, XXV (December, 1938), 225-231.

[98] George R. Taylor, Edgar L. Burtis, Frederick V. Waugh, *Barriers to Internal Trade in Farm Products*, U.S. Department of Agriculture (March, 1939), pp. 31-35.

[99] For discussion of power to be conferred upon the states by section 2 of the amendment, see 76 *Congressional Record* 4140-4141, 4143, 4170, 4219, 4225.

[100] For additional Supreme Court decisions on the subject, see Indianapolis Brewing Co. v. Liquor Control Commission, 305 U.S. 391 (1939); Joseph S. Finch & Co. v. McKittrick, 305 U.S. 395 (1939); Ziffrin v. Reeves, 308 U.S. 132 (1939).

[101] See U.S. Department of Agriculture, *Barriers to Internal Trade in Farm Products*, cited above. See also Works Progress Administration, "Comparative Charts of State Statutes Illustrating Barriers to Trade Between States," *The Marketing Laws Survey*, especially section 6 and accompanying chart; *Selected Liquor Laws Affecting Interstate*

Experience with the Eighteenth Amendment stands as a permanent warning against including in the Constitution provisions which are in effect police measures, prohibiting conduct about which the public is sharply divided. No danger lay in authorizing Congress to prohibit the sale of intoxicating beverages, but it was bad policy to direct Congress to take action to which a large portion of the public might become hostile. The potency of the Constitution lies in its general acceptance, and not merely in the text of its provisions. The Constitution must outline the structure, and, on very broad lines, the character, of the government, but it must leave to the functioning of representative institutions the choice of specific measures, in terms of current expressions of popular will. Otherwise, nullification, with its bad effects upon morale and law enforcement generally, becomes next to inevitable.

### THE "LAME-DUCK" AMENDMENT

The Twentieth Amendment, unlike the Eighteenth, Nineteenth, and Twenty-First Amendments, stirred no deep emotions in the people. It included among its friends and enemies no important interests in property, religion, sex, or social welfare. Those in favor of it were largely persons concerned with improving the efficiency of government; those opposed were largely persons by disposition hostile to governmental change. Some thought the proposed change not sufficiently important to justify a constitutional amendment. On the whole, it was lethargy which stood in the way of the amendment rather than overt opposition.

The principal aim of advocates of the amendment was to eliminate the short session or "lame-duck" session of Congress, and put legislators and Presidents into office more promptly after election. The situation which they desired to change developed in the following manner: The Constitution was ratified by the requisite number of states in the summer of 1788. The responsibility for launching the new government rested with the Continental Congress. Congress provided in sequence for the appointments of presidential electors in the several states, for the casting of their ballots for President, and for the commencement of proceedings under the Constitution. The

*Commerce* (May, 1939), pp. 63-71; Ralph Cassady, Jr., "Trade Barriers Within the United States," *Harvard Business Review*, XVIII (Winter Number, 1940), 231-247; F. E. Melder, *State and Local Barriers to Interstate Commerce in the United States*, University of Maine Studies, Second Series, No. 43 (1937); "Trade Barriers Among the States," *Proceedings*, The National Conference on Interstate Trade Barriers, April, 1939.

several dates were evidently based on an estimate as to the time it would take to get the machinery of government into operation. The date chosen for the beginning of operation was March 4, 1789. The terms of senators and representatives, who were expected to serve six years and two years, respectively, began on that date. The terms came to an end in subsequent odd years on the same day. The regular sessions of Congress, however, as provided by the Constitution, began on the first Monday in December unless Congress by law provided otherwise. Many times in the early years of American history, Congress acted to change the date of the regular session, and many special sessions have been called by the President, but the major portion of the legislation enacted by Congress has been enacted at sessions beginning regularly on the first Monday in December.

The difficulty to be met by constitutional amendment lay in the fact that, although representatives were elected to office in November of even-numbered years, they were not entitled to office until after the expiration of the terms of their predecessors in the following March. The Congress which assembled in December following the election was made up, not of persons recently elected, but of those chosen to office two years earlier. They remained the legislators of the country in spite of the fact that the principles for which they stood might have been repudiated at the election which preceded their last session. This session, usually made up in part of members whom the people refused to re-elect, came to be known as the "lame-duck" session.[102] The next Congress, which would be made up of the persons elected the preceding November, would not assemble in a regular session until December of the odd-numbered year, or more than thirteen months after the election was held.[103]

Certain changes were possible without amending the Constitution. It would have been possible to change by statute the dates at which the regular sessions of Congress were to be held so as greatly to abbreviate the thirteen-month period. Congress could have provided, for example, that the regular terms should begin on March 4 rather than on the first Monday in December. Such an arrangement was made,

[102] The term "lame duck" was originally a stock-exchange term applied to persons unable to meet their obligations.

[103] Another situation in at least theoretical need of remedy lay in the fact that, if the election of President were thrown into House of Representatives, the election would be performed, not by recently elected personnel, but by the "lame-duck" session. Since no President had been so elected since 1824, it was hard to create an active interest in the situation.

indeed, for a short period of time, when Congress was bent on remaining in session to keep a watchful eye on the conduct of President Andrew Johnson;[104] but because winter was the traditional period of legislative activity, and because sessions which began in March inevitably continued into summer when legislators did not wish to be in Washington and when they had important business elsewhere, this arrangement was generally unsatisfactory, and was not continued.

The changes that were possible, however, did not meet all needs. If the "lame-duck" session needed more time in which to deal adequately with the business before it, as was frequently the case, there was no way in which an extension of time could be provided, because the terms of the legislators expired as of a given day. The business must be completed by March 4, or must be postponed until the ensuing December, or a special session must be called. This situation seems to have caused some irritation from the very beginning. On the last day of such a session, in March, 1795, Aaron Burr laid before the Senate a motion providing for a constitutional amendment by which the terms of senators and representatives expiring in March should be continued until the first day of the following June.[105] A resolution proposed in 1808, providing that Congress should sit for but one year, contained an added provision that the terms should expire on the first Tuesday in April.[106] In 1840, Millard Fillmore introduced the first resolution providing for a constitutional amendment which, if adopted, would have eliminated the "lame-duck" session. His resolution provided that the terms of senators and representatives should commence on the first day of December instead of the fourth day of March.[107] No action was taken on the proposal.

It was not until the last quarter of the nineteenth century that members of Congress began the frequent introduction of measures to make varied changes in terms of office and dates of sessions of Congress. Some legislators wanted to change the beginning of terms until April or May, so that inauguration day might fall on a day more likely to provide good weather than did March 4. The extension of

[104] Everett S. Brown, "The Time of Meetings of Congress," *American Political Science Review*, XXV (November, 1931), 955, 958.

[105] *Annals of Congress*, 3d Cong., 2d sess., p. 853.

[106] Herman V. Ames, "Proposed Amendments to the Constitution of the United States during the First Century of Its History," *Annual Report of the American Historical Society* for the year 1896, II, 36, published also as House Doc. No. 353, 54th Cong., 2d sess., Part 2.

[107] 9 *Congressional Globe* 44.

the short session so as to leave time for the completion of business was apparently also an item of consideration. Less numerous were other measures providing for the completion of terms at earlier, rather than later, dates so as to eliminate the short session of Congress altogether.[108]

It was not until in the midst of the Harding administration, which began in 1921, that the movement for a so-called "lame-duck" amendment got under way with such vigor as to indicate that enactment was probable. The period was one of more than usual political ferment in Congress. One hundred and three joint resolutions proposing constitutional amendments of various kinds were introduced during the two regular and two special sessions of the Sixty-Seventh Congress.[109] A liberal group, made up largely of western Progressives and members of the so-called farm bloc, interfered with measures supported by the conservative Republican leadership, and urged the enactment of other measures opposed by the conservatives.

The "lame-duck" issue was raised in striking fashion when at the last session of that Congress the administration made use of legislators defeated at the polls the preceding November in an attempt to secure enactment of a ship-subsidy bill for the continued support of an American merchant marine which was opposed by the liberals and, in view of the results of the preceding elections, seems to have been opposed by the people as well.[110] A group of Arkansas farmers, known as the Farmers' Union, irritated by administration strategy, sent to Senator Caraway for introduction a resolution demanding that "lame ducks" desist from voting on anything but routine legislation.[111] There was no prospect that such a drastic resolution would be adopted; but instead of leaving it unreported or making an unfavorable report, Senator George W. Norris presented from the committee to which the proposal had been referred a joint resolution providing for a constitutional amendment to eliminate the "lame-duck" session by providing that the terms of federal legislators should begin on the first Monday in January following their election.[112] Such an amendment could not have become effective soon enough to have any direct bear-

[108] See Ames, *op. cit.*, pp. 36-38; M. A. Musmanno, "Proposed Amendments to the Constitution," House Doc. No. 551, 70th Cong., 2d sess., pp. 1-8.

[109] Lindsay Rogers, "American Government and Politics; The Second, Third and Fourth Sessions of the Sixty-Seventh Congress," *American Political Science Review*, XVIII (February, 1924), 79, 88.

[110] *Ibid.*, pp. 90-91.     [111] Alfred Lief, *Democracy's Norris* (1939), p. 241.

[112] Senate Report No. 933, 67th Cong., 4th sess.; 64 *Congressional Record*, 3505-3507.

ing on the ship-subsidy bill or other measures then pending, but its favorable reception would have some effect in discrediting the parts of the administration program being pressed in spite of the disapproval of the people. It is not surprising, therefore, that the measure was opposed by the President.

Senator Norris's resolution contained a provision for the abolition of the electoral college and the direct election of the President. For strategic reasons he dropped this provision, although in subsequent years he urged its adoption. As modified, the measure was not new to the Senate. Senator Ashurst, of Arizona, had introduced a similar resolution in the same Congress nearly two years earlier,[113] and hearings were being held at the time when the Norris resolution was reported. A committee of the American Bar Association testified in its favor,[114] indicating widespread, intelligent support. After brief debate a vote was taken on the Norris resolution. It passed by a majority of 63 to 6.[115] The experience in the House, however, was different. The resolution was reported favorably, but the administration is said to have prevented it from coming to a vote by effective use of a "lame-duck" floor leader who was awaiting appointment to a new position.[116]

On four subsequent occasions Senator Norris had similar experiences. He secured favorable reports from the judiciary committee, of which he ultimately became chairman, and the Senate passed the resolutions by overwhelming majorities. In the House of Representatives, however, he met skilled and effective opposition from administration forces which were accustomed to use "lame ducks" and "lame-duck" sessions, and filibusters made possible by these sessions, to control the legislative program. In some way or other, the resolution was blocked in each succeeding Congress.

On the last of the four occasions mentioned, the Senate passed the resolution on June 7, 1929. The speaker of the House of Representatives refrained from referring it to a committee until April 17, 1930, some days after the House committee had independently reported a similar resolution.[117] The House passed the resolution reported by its own committee, but before doing so it adopted an amendment, proposed by Speaker Longworth, providing that in even-numbered years sessions of Congress should end on May 4.[118] An argument advanced

---

[113] S. J. Res. No. 8, 67th Cong.    [114] *New York Times,* December 6, 1922.

[115] 64 *Congressional Record* 3540-3541.    [116] Lief, *op. cit.,* p. 243.

[117] Arthur W. Macmahon, "Congress and Its Functions," *The American Year Book,* 1930, pp. 6-7.

[118] F. W. Coker, "Congress and Its Functions," *The American Year Book,* 1931, p. 4.

by politicians in support of the Longworth amendment was that it would give them adequate time to attend political conventions and take care of other political responsibilities. To that portion of the public which felt that business was more secure when Congress was not in session, it promised a respite from legislative activity. The real purpose of the amendment was to provide a deadline at which a congressional session must terminate and thereby provide an instrument of strategy similar to that which was given by the existing short session. The resolutions adopted by the two houses were referred to a conference committee, but both houses refused to make a complete surrender in the matter of the Longworth amendment. The measure, therefore, died in conference.

On January 6, 1932, the Norris resolution was reported in the Senate for the sixth and last time.[119] Senator Bingham, of Connecticut, long an opponent of the resolution, tried vainly to secure the adoption of the Longworth amendment. He quoted a Longworth speech, including a statement that his amendment had the backing of the American Bar Association.[120] The amendment was rejected, however, by a vote of 18 to 47,[121] and the joint resolution was passed by a vote of 63 to 7.[122]

The experience of the resolution in the House of Representatives, now controlled by the Democrats, was very different from that of earlier years. Speaker Longworth had died since his last successful struggle against the measure. His Democratic successor, John N. Garner, gave it his full support.[123] The opposition was of the kind obviously intended to heckle the majority rather than to carry real influence. A New York congressman asked why Congress should waste its time on an insignificant piece of legislation when eight million people were unemployed and hungry. The measure, he declared, was "conceived by crackaloos, propagated by crackpots, and supported by thoughtless demagogues."[124] It passed the House by a vote of 336 to 56.[125] Enactment of the joint resolution was completed on March 3, 1932.[126] The amendment was speedily ratified by the necessary number of states, and was proclaimed as a part of the Constitution on February 6, 1933.[127]

The first section of the Twentieth Amendment, as it was finally

---

[119] 75 *Congressional Record* 1372-1373. Senate Report No. 26, 72d Cong., 1st sess.
[120] *Ibid.*, p. 1374.  [121] *Ibid.*, p. 1383.  [122] *Ibid.*, p. 1384.
[123] Lief, *op. cit.*, pp. 384-385.  [124] 75 *Congressional Record* 3827.
[125] *Ibid.*, p. 4060.  [126] 47 Stat. 745.  [127] 47 Stat. 2569.

adopted, provides that the terms of the President and Vice-President shall end at noon on the twentieth day of January, and the terms of senators and representatives at noon on the third day of January, and that the terms of their successors shall then begin. In each fourth year, therefore, Congress assembles more than two weeks before the incoming President takes office. It has time to organize, count the electoral votes, and, should there be no electoral majorities, vote for the President and Vice-President in House and Senate respectively.

The second section, after having gone through various forms, now provides that the annual meetings of Congress shall take place at noon on the third day of January. To prevent the necessity of meeting on Sunday, Congress is given the power to appoint a different day. Legislators begin their formal work, therefore, some two months after the date of election, instead of thirteen months, as was once the case unless they were called into special session.

The third and fourth sections of the amendment deal with questions of presidential succession which had not previously been dealt with in the Constitution. Congress had provided for the eventuality of the death of both the President and Vice-President, prescribing that the office should be held by heads of departments according to a prescribed arrangement.[128] There was no provision, however, to determine who was to assume the duties of the Presidency if a President-elect failed to qualify. No one knew what action should be taken in the event of the death of any of the persons from whom the House of Representatives was to elect the President or from whom the Senate was to elect the Vice-President if majorities were not achieved in the electoral college. The amendment provided for a number of eventualities, so that the country need not find itself without a President and a known constitutional means of making a selection.

The last section of the amendment carried a provision that, in order to be valid, the amendment must be ratified within seven years. Ratification by convention, however, was not prescribed.

## THE TWENTY-SECOND AMENDMENT

The Twenty-Second Amendment, the last of the amendments thus far adopted, became a part of the Constitution in 1951. It had been proposed by Congress to the state legislatures in 1947 in an atmos-

---

[128] 24 Stat. 1. For discussion see H. H. Sawyer, "The Presidential Succession," *American Mercury*, XVI (February, 1939), 129–135.

phere of protest against the abandonment of the traditional restriction of each President of the United States to two terms. Franklin D. Roosevelt had served three full terms and had been elected to a fourth on which he had embarked at the time of his death. The prevailing discontent was a product both of antagonism to the late President and of concern lest an ambitious President of some future time should seize and hold the reins of power indefinitely by virtue of his ability to bring about his own re-election through the power of the office which he occupied. The basic provision of the amendment is that

> No person shall be elected to the office of President more than twice, and no person who has held the office of President, or acted as President, for more than two years of a term to which some other person was elected President shall be elected to the office of president more than once.

In the text of this amendment, as in three of its predecessors, it was provided that the amendment must be ratified within ten years in order to be valid. Indeed, inclusion of such a provision now seems to have become a permanent part of the procedure of amending the Constitution. Ratification of the amendment was left to state legislatures. Ratification by conventions has been resorted to only once — in connection with the Twenty-First Amendment. It remains to be seen whether that device will be used again.

## AMENDMENTS PROPOSED, BUT NOT RATIFIED

Although only twenty-two amendments to the Constitution have been adopted, many hundreds of others have been proposed in the two houses of Congress. The total number down to about 1927 was said to be some 2670.[129] The stream since that time has continued in full force. Congress has proposed five of these amendments to the states, but they have not been ratified by the necessary number. Of these five, four were proposed prior to the beginning of the Civil War. Only the child-labor amendment, proposed in 1924, has been advocated in recent years.

The resolution for a child-labor amendment provided that Congress should have power "to limit, regulate, and prohibit the labor of persons under eighteen years of age."[130] Although leaving the power of the states unimpaired except for the suspension of laws to

---

129 Musmanno, *op. cit.*, p. v.    130 43 Stat. 670.

the extent necessary to give effect to legislation by Congress, it sanctioned broad invasion of a field of regulation which traditionally had belonged to the states. Circumstances seemed to justify this proposal. Individual states had experienced difficulty in making and enforcing laws against child labor because of the competition of goods produced by child labor in other states. Congress, therefore, had attempted to enact uniform federal laws on the subject; but the Supreme Court had held unconstitutional a statute prohibiting the shipment in interstate commerce of goods produced by child labor [131] and a subsequent statute which attempted to achieve the same results by taxing the products of child labor.[132]

The constitutional amendment was proposed in order to remove the barrier to federal legislation which decisions of the Supreme Court had erected. The opposition, however, was well organized. It made effective use of arguments, based on state rights, family rights, human rights, religion, and other grounds, to defeat the amendment and preserve the twilight zone in which neither the states nor the federal government could regulate effectively.[133] Ratification proceeded slowly. Only four states had acted favorably by the end of 1925. Sixteen, on the other hand, had passed resolutions of rejection, while three others had voted and failed to ratify. By the end of 1931, only six had ratified, while nineteen had passed resolutions of rejection.[134] The prospects that the amendment would ever become a part of the Constitution seemed completely hopeless.

A change in sentiment came in 1933 with the Democratic admin-

---

[131] Hammer v. Dagenhart, 247 U.S. 251 (1918).

[132] Bailey v. Drexel Furniture Co., 259 U.S. 20 (1922).

[133] "The real issue is the old one of state rights," said a contemporary magazine. "The federal government, which alone holds jurisdiction co-terminous with the American business field, is without adequate powers of regulation. The states have sufficient regulatory power, but because they are arbitrary fragments of the national economic unit, they are unable to use it effectively. In the no-man's land between state ineffectiveness and federal incompetence, business may build up an economic state of its own, unhampered by regulation, insured against attack by the constitutional safeguards of property." New Republic, XLI (December 24, 1924), 108, 109. See also "Twentieth Amendment; Symposium," Forum, LXXIII (February, 1925), 278–282; O. R. Lovejoy, C. S. Thomas, "Resolved that the Twentieth Amendment to the Constitution of the United States should be Ratified," Proceedings of the National Conference of Social Work, 1925, pp. 27–52; "Catholics and Child Labor," Nation, CXX (January 21, 1925), 59; N. M. Butler, "New American Revolution," American Bar Association Journal, X (December, 1924), 845–851; "Child Labor Amendments' Defeat," New Republic, XLII (May 20, 1925), 330–331; T. F. Cadwalader, "Defeat of the Twentieth Amendment," The Annals of the American Academy of Political and Social Science, CXXIX (January, 1927), 65–69.

[134] See the chronology of the amendment appended to Coleman v. Miller, 307 U.S. 433, 474 (1939).

istration and its so-called "New Deal." Emphasis was placed on the curtailment of hours and the spreading of employment so as to provide income for the maximum number of persons and families. Industrial codes administered under the National Industrial Recovery Act banned the employment of persons under sixteen years of age. Under the impetus of the movement, more states ratified the child-labor amendment. By the end of 1933, the total number of ratifications was twenty; by the end of 1936, it was twenty-five.[135]

By this time the movement for ratification had slowed down. On January 8, 1937, in a letter addressed to governors of nineteen states which had not ratified, President Roosevelt stated that child labor was increasing, especially in low-paid, under-standardized types of work. He therefore urged that ratification of the amendment be made one of the major items in the legislative program of each state for the year.[136] The request seems to have had little effect. Ratifications stopped with a total of twenty-eight, or eight less than was necessary to complete the process.

In the meantime, ratifications which had already taken place were being challenged. A number of them were certified by states which had previously passed resolutions of rejection. It was argued that, after having passed such a resolution, a state had no power to change its position. Furthermore, by 1937, thirteen years had passed since the amendment was first submitted to the states. Opponents contended that it had lost its vitality by virtue of the length of the period, and that it could not, therefore, in any event, become a part of the Constitution. A case involving these questions was decided by the Supreme Court in June, 1939.[137] The Court refused to take responsibility for what it evidently considered a matter for legislative or executive determination. The questions were political in character, it said, and were to be decided by the political branches of the government. Congress would determine the validity of ratification through the exercise of its control over the promulgation of the adoption of amendments.[138]

The prospects of the completion of ratification seemed so poor that

---

[135] The figures used are those given in the chronology cited above.

[136] *New York Times,* January 9, 1937.

[137] Coleman *v.* Miller, 307 U.S. 433 (1939).

[138] Two justices dissented, arguing that the amendment could not now be ratified because of the lapse of time, and that the Court should so declare. For a discussion of the case see comments on recent decisions in *New York University Law Quarterly Review,* XVII (November, 1939), 122–125; *Southern California Law Review,* XIII (November, 1939), 122–125; *Minnesota Law Review,* XXIV (February, 1940), 393–406.

other amendments affecting child labor were introduced from time to time. One of them was reported favorably in the Senate in 1937.[139] It was drafted to cope with the opposition of groups who believed that the earlier amendment might authorize Congress to control child life in many ways not actually intended by the authors. It reduced the age limit from eighteen to sixteen years, eliminated the provision concerning the regulation of labor, and gave the power to "limit and prohibit the employment for hire of persons under sixteen years of age," so as to make it clear that the amendment dealt only with employment for hire. In spite of the milder character of the amendment, however, it was not proposed to the states for action.

In the meantime, at the request of the President,[140] Congress passed an act concerning fair labor standards which prohibits shipment or delivery for shipment in interstate commerce of any goods produced in an establishment situated in the United States in connection with which "any oppressive child labor" has been employed.[141] Early in 1941, after a complete change of personnel since the decision in the child-labor case of 1918, the Supreme Court reversed that decision and upheld the new measure.[142] The proposed constitutional amendment is, therefore, no longer needed. Agitation for it over a long period of years has served no purpose save that of education.

Other constitutional amendments have been offered on a wide range of subjects during the years since the child-labor amendment was submitted to the states. Senator Norris sponsored for a number of years an amendment for the abolition of the electoral college, and other legislators have introduced similar amendments. Proposals have been made to change the term of the President to six years and prohibit re-election. The repeal of the Seventeenth Amendment has been proposed. Large numbers of resolutions have dealt with the income tax. Many of these would extend the taxing power to cover securities hitherto exempt from taxation. Others, which were particularly numerous in the middle nineteen-thirties, when the Supreme Court was invalidating New-Deal legislation, would have extended the power of the federal government to include broad regulation of industry and agriculture. Still others dealt in a variety of ways with the Supreme Court itself, curbing its powers and limiting the effec-

---

139 Senate Report No. 788, 75th Cong., 1st sess.
140 81 *Congressional Record* 4960–4961.
141 52 Stat. 1060, 1067.        142 United States *v.* Darby, 312 U.S. 100 (1941).

tiveness of its veto upon desired legislation. Many proposals have dealt with war conditions, limiting profits or providing for high taxation or for the conscription of property. Some required a popular referendum before the United States could declare war.

Between 1923, when the Supreme Court held unconstitutional a law establishing minimum wages for women,[143] and 1937, when that decision was reversed,[144] many amendments were introduced to authorize such legislation. Others have sought to bring about uniformity in marriage and divorce laws throughout the United States. Still others have dealt with such miscellaneous purposes as the following: authorizing item vetoes in appropriation bills; abolishing congressional immunity for speeches and debates in either house; providing representation for the District of Columbia; changing the amending process; providing for the election of judges; providing for the independence of the Philippine Islands; prohibiting sectarian legislation; conferring upon the House of Representatives co-ordinate power for the ratification of treaties; defining the right of states to regulate employment of aliens; providing for federal control of banking; providing for congressional regulation of the insurance business; limiting the wealth of individual citizens; providing for legislation by initiative; extending the civil-service merit system; regulating industry; requiring teachers to take an oath of allegiance; prohibiting governmental competition with private enterprise; and prohibiting war loans to any except allies.

These items show the sweeping range of topics on which change is desired by individuals and groups, change usually not possible at the time when the proposals are first made without modification of the Constitution. Judging by past experience, few of the proposals made will be adopted. State constitutions are now amended freely, in some states almost as freely as statutes, but there is still powerful sentiment against formal modification of the federal Constitution except in extreme cases. By the time when sufficient sentiment has been built up to justify a constitutional amendment, furthermore, the change in sentiment may have had its effect upon constitutional interpretation so that formal amendment is no longer necessary.

[143] Adkins v. Children's Hospital, 261 U.S. 525 (1923).
[144] West Coast Hotel Co. v. Parrish, 300 U.S. 379 (1937).

•••••••••••••••••••••••••••••••••••••••••••••••••••••••••••••••••••••••••••••••••••••••••••••••••••••

# CHAPTER 30

# MODERNIZING THE GOVERNMENT

THE GREAT MASS OF TECHNICAL DETAIL involved in the operation of the federal government is infinite in its variety and always in process of change. Only in a most limited degree does it make up the story of constitutional development. Since the broader outlines of organization and the division of functions involve basic issues of the separation of powers, however, there are constitutional implications in such questions as whether financial control of the government shall be in the hands of Congress or the President or both, and whether control of personnel shall be in the hands of the President or of Congress. The adequacy or inadequacy of organization and of administrative techniques, furthermore, may determine whether the constitutional functions of the government are to be performed well or poorly, or not at all. The limitations of administrative efficiency may be just as effective as the decisions of the Supreme Court in marking the operative limits of constitutional development.

At no time has governmental organization been completely static. There has been fluctuation, however, between periods of relative stability and fairly rapid and important readjustment. A period of considerable ferment, for example, was that of the administration of Theodore Roosevelt, with both continuation and reaction in the administration of William Howard Taft.[1] One of the serious problems of that period was the fact that rapidly increasing governmental expenditures were outrunning revenues, so that the government was accumulating a deficit of several million dollars each year and was said to be facing the threat of national bankruptcy.

### THE THEODORE ROOSEVELT INVESTIGATION

In 1905, President Roosevelt appointed a committee to investigate the salaries of government officials, business methods within the gov-

[1] See chapters 23 and 24.

ernment, and questions of economical purchase of supplies. The committee, commonly known as the Keep Commission, found chaotic conditions in all the fields which it investigated. It rectified a number of abuses largely through the publicity given.[2] Politicians resented interference with various forms of graft, however, and Congress was never sympathetic with the President's methods of reform. The work of the committee was done by persons regularly employed in the government. The appropriation of twenty-five thousand dollars to pay salaries and expenses of specialists and experts, which was requested by the President,[3] seems never to have been made.

As the government was organized, the control of revenues and expenditures was largely in Congress rather than in the President. "It is a fundamental principle of constitutional government," said a distinguished writer of the period, "that appropriations are made and that expenditures are controlled by the representatives of the people."[4] The Secretary of the Treasury submitted to the speaker of the House of Representatives each year the estimate of the needs of the government for the ensuing fiscal year. The Secretary had no responsibility for the figures submitted, however. He received them from the federal departments and acted merely as the transmitting agency. The departments, knowing that Congress was likely to appropriate less than was requested, padded their estimates in the hope that even after reductions were made appropriations would be sufficient for their purposes. Although it was generally known that appropriations were exceeding revenues, no department assumed a patriotic responsibility for reducing its own expenditures. Neither the Secretary of the Treasury nor the President had any authority to reduce the estimates. In gathering information about appropriations needed, Congress conferred, not with the President, but with the heads of departments and their subordinates. Policy was made, not by the President, but by Congress.

The situation was further complicated by the fact that neither Congress as a whole, nor either house, nor any single committee in either house, was equipped to deal adequately with the subject of finances as a whole. When the government was first organized, Alexander

[2] Henry Beach Needham, "New Business Methods in National Administration," *World Today*, IX (December, 1905), 1332-1339; C. H. Forbes-Lindsay, "New Business Standards at Washington — Work of the Keep Commission," *American Review of Reviews*, XXXVII (February, 1908), 190-195.

[3] Senate Doc. No. 162, 59th Cong., 1st sess.

[4] Henry Jones Ford, *The Cost of Our National Government* (1910), p. 11.

Hamilton, as Secretary of the Treasury, worked out co-ordinated programs for revenues and expenditures, presented the programs to Congress, and secured intelligent action upon them. Within a few years, however, the committee system developed, and the committee of ways and means of the House of Representatives stood between Congress as a whole and the Secretary of the Treasury. The sending of estimates to Congress then became a purely ministerial function. For many years this single committee was responsible both for taxation and appropriations. As the work became more voluminous, a separate committee on appropriations was established. Gradually, for various reasons, appropriation bills for particular departments were taken away from the committee on appropriations and allotted to committees concerned with the welfare of particular departments. Experience in the Senate was similar to that in the House. The result was that co-ordination in Congress was lacking as completely as in the executive branch of the government.[5] Each committee, however strongly it might favor the general principle that income must balance expenditure, made little effort to reduce expenditures of the agency over which it had jurisdiction. The condition of unbalance was due in no small part to this fact.

THE TAFT INVESTIGATION

While Congress jealously avoided sharing any of its prerogatives with the President, it was not averse to having him share responsibility for mismanagement. In an appropriation bill, approved on March 4, 1909, it provided that if estimates of expenses should exceed estimates of revenues, the Secretary of the Treasury should submit a detailed statement to the President so that he might,

> in giving Congress information of the state of the Union and in recommending to their consideration such measures as he may judge

[5] The following statement made on October 13, 1909, by James A. Tawney, chairman of the House committee on appropriations, is significant: "One of the greatest evils that today exists in our system of submitting estimates and making appropriations for public expenditures is the divided jurisdiction over appropriations. This jurisdiction is divided between eight committees of the House. Seven of these committees have jurisdiction over but one appropriation bill, and that is the bill carrying the appropriations for one particular executive department. The agricultural committee has charge of the agricultural appropriation bill; the naval committee, of the naval appropriation bill; the committee on military affairs, of the army appropriation bill and Military Academy appropriation bill; the post office committee, of the post office appropriation bill; the foreign affairs committee, of the diplomatic and consular appropriation bill; the committee on Indian affairs, of the Indian appropriation bill; and the rivers and harbors committee, of appropriations for river and harbor improvements, except those improvements which are authorized to be made under continuing contracts." *Ibid.*, p. 129.

necessary, advise the Congress how in his judgment the estimated appropriations could with least injury to the public service be reduced so as to bring the appropriations within the estimated revenues or, if such reduction be not in his judgment practicable without undue injury to the public service, that he may recommend to Congress such loans or new taxes as may be necessary to cover the deficiency.[6]

The provision was evidently not intended to give additional power to the President. It was an effort to shift responsibility without giving authority. President Taft welcomed the opportunity, which was given by the statute, to discuss efficiency and economy in government. He applauded the organization of a committee on public expenditures in the Senate, including the chairmen of the several committees having charge of appropriation bills, for the purpose of co-ordinating work in the field.[7] The Secretary of the Treasury hailed developments as pointing toward the establishment of a system under which the executive branch of the government would co-ordinate and harmonize requests for an appropriation in a budget to be dealt with by Congress in a scientific manner.[8]

In 1910, President Taft secured from Congress an appropriation with which to make a study of the government with a view to promoting efficiency and economy.[9] The commission on economy and efficiency that was established made a series of reports and recommendations as to conditions in the government, though it had to make them under the handicap of the declining popularity of the administration and the growing hostility of Congress.[10]

One of the most important reports of the commission recommended an arrangement for a federal budget, to be submitted to Congress by the President. The budget was to harmonize requests for appropriations, provide information about revenues and the needs of the government, and systematize treatment of the whole subject of government finance.[11] The recommendation was received coldly by a hostile

[6] 35 Stat. 945, 1027.

[7] *Messages and Papers of the Presidents*, XVI, 7422-7425.

[8] *Annual Report of the Secretary of the Treasury*, 1909, p. 4.

[9] 36 Stat. 703.

[10] For a list of the reports see President Taft's special message of January 8, 1913. (*Messages and Papers of the Presidents*, XVI, 7829-7834.) See also special message of January 17, 1911 (*ibid.*, pp. 7698-7719); message of March 3, 1911, Senate Doc. No. 859, 61st Cong., 3d sess.

[11] "The Need for a National Budget," *Report of the President's Commission on Economy and Efficiency*, House Doc. No. 854, 62d Cong., 2d sess.

Congress,[12] and a sample budget, prepared for the fiscal year 1914,[13] was ignored.

The report of the commission on economy and efficiency was not submitted to Congress until after the meeting of the Republican national convention. The platform of the Republican party commended the earnest efforts of the Republican administration to secure economy and increase efficiency in the conduct of government business, but made no recommendations as to fundamental changes in procedure. The Democratic platform denounced the profligate waste of money wrung from the people by oppressive taxation, but made no constructive suggestions. The Progressive party promised readjustment of the business methods of the national government and a proper co-ordination of government agencies, but made no mention of a budget. Since 1884, when he had written his *Congressional Government*, Woodrow Wilson, Taft's successor in the presidency, had been a severe critic of unco-ordinated government by congressional committees.[14] Before his inauguration, he wrote to Senator Tillman that he had always insisted upon the absolute necessity of a carefully considered and wisely planned budget and that he expected to hold conferences with his legislative colleagues in Washington, with a view to bringing some budget system into existence.[15] He may have held conferences on the subject as promised; but, whether because of other duties or because Taft had made the issue his own, President Wilson never became an active sponsor of a definite measure for budgetary reform.

Although the adoption of an executive budget for the federal government was not yet in sight, the work of the Taft commission received a great deal of attention in the several states, and a number of them achieved order in their own finances by the adoption of budget systems.[16] By 1916, public education on the subject had spread far enough to compel attention in party platforms. The Republican

[12] Frederick A. Cleveland, "Evolution of the Budget Idea in the United States," *The Annals of the American Academy*, LXII (November, 1915), 15, 23-28.

[13] "Message of the President of the United States Submitting a Budget," *Report of the President's Commission on Economy and Efficiency*, Senate Doc. No. 1113, 62d Cong., 3d sess.

[14] Woodrow Wilson, *Congressional Government* (1885), chapter III.

[15] Ray Stannard Baker, *Woodrow Wilson, Life and Letters* (8 vols., 1927-1939), IV (1931), 212.

[16] See "Digest of Budget Legislation in the Several States," Senate Doc. No. 111, 66th Cong., 1st sess., and W. F. Willoughby, *The Movement for Budgetary Reform in the States* (1918).

platform of 1916 denounced the wasteful appropriations of the Democratic administration, its shameless raids on the Treasury, and its opposition to the Taft proposals. The party pledged itself to the establishment of a simple, business-like budget system. The Progressive party sponsored a national budget and the destruction of "pork-barrel" legislation. The Democratic platform approached the subject more diffidently. It favored a return by the House of Representatives to the control of all appropriation bills by a single committee in order to center responsibility and eliminate waste and duplication. It favored this "as a practical first step toward a budget system." [17]

### THE WILSON ADMINISTRATION

The government gave little attention to the subject during the course of the first World War, even though intelligent management of finance was more important than ever before. In his message, delivered on December 4, 1917, President Wilson warned that

it will be impossible to deal in any but a very wasteful and extravagant fashion with the enormous appropriations of public moneys which must continue to be made, if the war is to be properly sustained, unless the House will consent to return to its former practice of initiating and preparing all appropriation bills through a single committee, in order that responsibility may be centered, expenditures standardized and made uniform, and waste and duplication as much as possible avoided.[18]

Although the reporter noted "applause" after the statement, the House of Representatives made no immediate reform in its procedure.

Without a great deal of support, Representative Swager Sherley, chairman of the House committee on appropriations, had worked throughout the Wilson administration for some degree of budget reform. During his first period at the Paris Peace Conference, President Wilson sent Sherley a cablegram, saying, "I hear you are again endeavoring to work out a budget system plan. I hope that you will succeed." [19] The proposal which Sherley had in mind was introduced as a rider to a deficiency appropriation bill. It provided for a joint commission on financial methods, consisting of six senators and six representatives. The commission was to inquire into the financial methods of the government and recommend such changes as might

---

[17] For the party platforms of the period see Edward Stanwood, *A History of the Presidency* (2 vols., 1928), II, Appendix.

[18] 56 *Congressional Record* 23.     [19] *New York Times*, February 12, 1919.

be deemed necessary. It was to consider the budgetary process all the way from the preparation of estimates to the auditing of disbursements.[20]

The amendment was adopted after brief debate and without any penetrating discussion of a budget system. A speech by Representative Mann, of Illinois, revealed the pressure by which congressmen were being compelled to act. "We cannot afford to have the country believe that Congress is grossly extravagant and careless in its appropriations, unmindful of the public needs," he declared, adding that by propaganda the people had been persuaded to believe that Congress had a very loose and lamentable method of making up its appropriations. It was necessary to make an investigation, "first, to satisfy ourselves and possibly and probably accomplish good, and, second, to satisfy the country that we are not an irresponsible body of looters." [21]

The House passed the appropriation bill providing for the commission; but enactment was prevented by the filibuster against this and other important measures conducted in the Senate to compel the President to call a special session of the next Congress,[22] and the subject was left for treatment by a Republican Congress.

During the summer of 1919, at the special session which President Wilson had been forced to call, the House of Representatives organized a select committee on the budget. Testimony of members of the Taft commission on economy and efficiency and of many other persons was heard. Carter Glass, formerly a member of the House of Representatives and now Secretary of the Treasury, urged the adoption of a budget system. He warned Congress that in view of the financial burden created by the war it would be hazardous to continue in the old way of transacting the public business. "I note that not a little has been said about the constitutional prerogative of Congress," he said, "but I know of no clause in our Constitution that will prevent the Congress exercising self-control." [23]

The committee reported a bill to provide for an executive budget, to be prepared by a bureau of the budget, acting under the direction of the President and to be submitted by the President to Congress. The bill also provided for a comptroller general and an assistant comptroller general of the United States, who were to head an independent establishment known as an accounting department. These

[20] 57 *Congressional Record* 4608.    [21] *Ibid.*, p. 4618.    [22] See chapter 28.
[23] *Annual Report of the Secretary of the Treasury*, 1919, p. 121. The testimony of Secretary Glass before the committee is incorporated in this report, pp. 118-126.

officers were to be appointed by the President by and with the advice and consent of the Senate, and were to serve during good behavior, subject to removal only by a concurrent resolution of Congress on account of inefficiency, neglect of duty, or malfeasance in office. They were to provide Congress with a check on expenditures through control and audit of the accounts of the government. The bill represented no departure from the fundamental political principles of the present government of the United States, said the report.

> It rather seeks to emphasize and make more effective those principles. It thus makes more definite the constitutional obligation that rests upon the President "from time to time to give to Congress information of the state of the Union and recommend to their consideration such measures as he shall judge necessary and expedient," and furnishes him with the means by which he may meet this obligation. It provides for no restriction on the part of Congress to modify the proposals of the President, but on the other hand seeks to have such proposals come before it in such a form, so itemized, classified, and supported by detailed data as will enable it more effectively to perform this function.[24]

The bill passed the House of Representatives on October 21, 1919, by an overwhelming vote of 285 to 3.[25] In the meantime, the Senate had organized its own select committee to deal with the budget question. The House bill remained in the custody of this committee until some months of the ensuing regular session had passed, before action was taken. Meanwhile, the President, in his annual message of December 2, 1919, took a stand in support of the position of the Secretary of the Treasury. During the preceding summer he had said that, until the Senate had acted on the treaty of peace, there could be no properly studied national budget.[26] His concern then was apparently with content rather than with machinery. In the annual message he advocated an executive budget system of the same general nature as that provided for in the House bill,[27] but he made no mention of specific provisions.

On April 13, 1920, the Senate committee reported a substitute differing in some respects from the bill passed by the House.[28] The

[24] House Report No. 362, 66th Cong., 1st sess., pp. 9-10.
[25] 58 *Congressional Record* 7297.
[26] David F. Houston, *Eight Years with Wilson's Cabinet* (2 vols., 1926), II, 8.
[27] *Messages and Papers of the Presidents*, XVIII, 8810-8811.
[28] Senate Report No. 524, 66th Cong., 2d sess.

Senate passed the bill without a record vote,[29] the House and the Senate bills were harmonized in conference committee, and the resulting measure was sent to President Wilson, who at this time was seriously ill. Since it was a finance measure, the bill was referred to David F. Houston, who had succeeded Carter Glass as Secretary of the Treasury. The officers of the government were keenly conscious of the charge that the President had sought to extend his own powers into the areas belonging to other branches of the government. The Secretary of the Treasury saw in this bill evidence of a corresponding attempt at encroachment by Congress. He took the position that it violated the Constitution in denying to the President power to remove the comptroller general and the assistant comptroller general, and in providing that Congress might remove these officers by concurrent resolution. The President agreed, and asked Houston to prepare a veto message.[30]

The veto message [31] was an important document in the development of constitutional interpretation of the power of appointing and removing federal officers. It had always been the accepted construction of the Constitution, said the President, that the power to appoint officers "of this kind" carried with it as an incident the power to remove. He was convinced that Congress was without constitutional authority to limit the appointing power or the power of removal. He questioned, furthermore, the constitutional power of Congress to remove by concurrent resolution an officer appointed by the President with the advice and consent of the Senate. In view of Section 2 of Article II of the Constitution, he said,

> it would have been within the constitutional power of Congress, in creating these offices, to have vested the power of appointment in the President alone, in the President with the advice and consent of the Senate, or even in the head of a department. Regarding as I do the power of removal from office as an essential incident to the appointing power, I cannot escape the conclusion that the vesting of this power of removal in the Congress is unconstitutional and therefore I am unable to approve the bill.[32]

Expressing his entire sympathy with the objectives of the bill, he added the hope that Congress might find time before adjournment to remedy the constitutional defect.

---

[29] 59 *Congressional Record* 6395.    [30] Houston, *op. cit.*, II, 82-83.

[31] 59 *Congressional Record* 8609.

[32] For a contemporary discussion of the opinion see Thomas Reed Powell, "The President's Veto of the Budget Bill," *National Municipal Review*, IX (September, 1920), 538-545.

The sponsor of the bill in the House of Representatives argued that the President had received faulty legal advice as to the constitutional powers of Congress. He thought it very important that the two highest officers of the general accounting office should be placed upon a plane "somewhat comparable to the position occupied by federal judges. The positions are semi-judicial, and it was the opinion of the committee that we should remove them as far as possible from political considerations." In the interest of independence he thought it necessary that the comptroller general be free from the threat of removal by the President. "You will recall that a former President, somewhat miffed because a comptroller of the Treasury had ruled against his contention, sent word to the comptroller that if he could not change the opinion of the comptroller he could change the comptroller." He thought the office should be an arm of Congress rather than an agent of the Executive.[33]

The margin of Republican control in both houses of Congress was narrow, and it proved impossible to override the President's veto. The House passed a new measure eliminating the provision which the President found objectionable, but the Senate failed to act. The Republican party platform of 1920 praised the original enactment and condemned the veto of the President. The Democratic party platform condemned the Republican Senate for adjourning without passing the amended measure initiated in the House of Representatives.

### THE BUDGET AND ACCOUNTING ACT

New measures to provide for a federal budget system were introduced in the special session of Congress called by President Harding to meet on April 11, 1921. In his message to Congress, the President remarked, "It will be a very great satisfaction to know of its early enactment, so that it may be employed in establishing the economies and the business methods so essential to the minimum of expenditure." [34] The measure, known as the Budget and Accounting Act,[35] was approved on June 10, 1921.

The statute placed the Bureau of the Budget in the Treasury Department, but the connection with the President was direct and the relationship with the Treasury Department only nominal. In 1939, the bureau was severed completely from the department and made a

---

[33] 59 *Congressional Record* 8610.      [34] 61 *Congressional Record* 170.
[35] 42 Stat. 20.

part of the Executive Office of the President.[36] As a result of the legislation, the estimates of financial needs made by government agencies are now sent, not to the Secretary of the Treasury for submission to Congress, but to the Bureau of the Budget. The bureau holds hearings on the several estimates, attempts to prevent appropriations which will lead to the duplication of functions at various points in the government, and in every way possible seeks to avoid the waste of government funds. In harmony with the administrative policies of the President, it trims estimates. When the budget has been prepared by the bureau, it is submitted to the President for criticisms, suggestions, or approval. Thereafter, it is sent to Congress as evidence of the needs of the government as seen by the President.

This does not mean that Congress, in enacting the Budget and Accounting Act, has surrendered to the President its control over the finances of the government. It means, rather, that, in place of the chaotic and inaccurate information which Congress once received concerning the activities of the government, it now receives a scientific statement, made up in terms of the policies of the President. Having received the estimates, Congress may revise them upward or downward. It does change them with great freedom; yet the major outlines of the program of the President nearly always remain. The testimony of administrative officers is called for and is given freely; but their responsibility to the President in the matter of budget-making is kept clear. They are forbidden to call for expenditures greater than those recommended by the President. Although there are ways for letting congressmen know that additional funds are desired, the lines of presidential control remain intact.

Centralization took place in Congress as well as in the executive department. In 1920, the House of Representatives changed its procedure so that all appropriation bills were to be handled by a single appropriations committee of thirty-five members. Subcommittees are created within that committee to hold hearings on the several sections of the budget. In 1922, the Senate adopted a similar procedure.[37]

In spite of the constitutional argument of President Wilson's veto message, the statute denied to the President the power to remove the comptroller general or the assistant comptroller general. A concession was granted, in that removal by Congress was to be made, not by concurrent resolution, but by joint resolution. The principal differ-

---

[36] 4 F. R. 2727.
[37] W. F. Willoughby, *The National Budget System* (1927), pp. 35-38.

ence was that the latter form required the approval of the President unless the act of removal was passed over his veto. The change made removal even more difficult than under the earlier arrangement. The statute also differed from the earlier bill, in that, instead of giving tenure during good behavior to the comptroller general and the assistant comptroller general, it provided that they were to serve for fifteen years. The comptroller general was made ineligible for re-appointment.

There has been much discussion of the constitutionality of the statute in so far as it provided for the appointment of the comptroller general by the President with the advice and consent of the Senate, but denied to the President the power of removal.[38] No President has brought the issue to the courts, however, by attempting to remove the comptroller general. That official has been accused of unconstitutional invasion of the powers of the Executive, and the attempt has been made to abolish or greatly change the office by statute, but thus far without success.[39] No one questions the desirability of a careful audit of government expenditures to guarantee fulfillment of the constitutional injunction that "No money shall be drawn from the Treasury but in consequence of appropriations made by law." [40] There was little objection to the establishment of machinery necessary for such an audit and for careful and detailed reports to Congress. In passing the Budget and Accounting Act, Congress expected that these functions would be performed, and that the comptroller general would be of great assistance in showing how money appropriated was being spent.

In practice, however, the work of auditing has not been adequately done, and reports submitted to Congress have not been informative. To determine what expenditures were authorized, the comptroller general made himself a quasi-judicial officer in financial matters. Under cover of interpreting the law, he decided questions of policy which belonged either in Congress or in the Executive. Comptroller General J. R. McCarl, who was in office at the time when the administration of Franklin D. Roosevelt began, was personally hostile to the spending policies inaugurated by the President and Congress. On many occasions he used his position to delay or prevent expenditures

[38] The President's power of removal is discussed elsewhere in this chapter.

[39] For discussion of the comptroller general and the management of the general accounting office see Harvey C. Mansfield, *The Comptroller General: A Study in the Law and Practice of Financial Administration* (1939).

[40] Constitution, Article I, Section 9.

which administrative officers believed to have been authorized by Congress. He substituted his own judgment for that of the administration in matters upon which the successful exercise of administrative responsibility depended.[41] The President, who was elected by the people to manage the affairs of the government, found himself blocked at innumerable points by what he called the comptroller general's "unconstitutional assumption of executive power." [42] Yet the comptroller general, unlike other policy-making officials in the government, could not be removed by the President. He was assured of his fifteen-year term unless Congress saw fit to pass an act removing him. The intricacies of particular financial controversies are so complex that such issues do not lend themselves well to congressional action. The administration, therefore, had to function as best it could, in spite of interference by the comptroller general. When an attempt was made to secure the enactment of a statute to change the office of comptroller general to that of auditor general, and limit the functions of that official to auditing and making reports to Congress, the issues, in spite of extensive debate, were still not clear enough to bring about enactment. They were further complicated by persons hostile to the administration, who favored anything the comptroller general might do to interfere with the administration program.[43]

When the summer of 1936 brought the retirement of the man who had held the office of comptroller general for a full term of fifteen years, President Roosevelt for some time evaded the intent of the statute by leaving the office unfilled and in the charge of an acting comptroller general. The latter could be removed from control of the agency at any time by the simple expedient of appointing a permanent official. When the permanent appointment was finally made,

[41] Mansfield, op. cit., pp. 1-5, 70-73. See also Harvey C. Mansfield, "The General Accounting Office," in President's Committee on Administrative Management, Report of the Committee, with Studies of Administrative Management in the Federal Government (1937), pp. 175-177.

[42] Message of President to Congress, January 12, 1927, in President's Committee on Administrative Management, op. cit., p. iv.

[43] Harvey C. Mansfield, The Comptroller General (1939), pp. 274-288. It seems clear that members of Congress expected the comptroller general to exercise functions of control as well as of audit. See remarks by Representative Good, chairman of the House committee on appropriations, 58 Congressional Record 7131, and 59 Congressional Record 8610.

The President or his advisers seem, therefore, to have been lax in scrutinizing the bill for encroachments on the jurisdiction of his office. As a matter of fact, President Wilson was himself incapable of giving the subject proper attention, and President Harding had no doubt formed his attitude as a senator, which he was during the Wilson administration, rather than as an executive.

the new officer served a short period and then found it necessary to resign because of ill health. The changes left conditions in flux and prevented the maintenance of an agency with the same powers as that which had operated for fifteen years under the control of one man. By various devices the President might continue to keep the office in flux. Since the statute provides that the comptroller general shall not serve beyond seventy years of age, a man approaching that age might be appointed if approval of the Senate could be secured. Such devices, however, are merely schemes of getting around a statute which Congress could change at any time if it saw fit to do so. Legislative change would be much better than executive evasion.

### LEGISLATIVE ATTEMPTS AT EXECUTIVE REORGANIZATION

The question of reorganizing the government to save money and to promote efficiency has come to the fore time and again since the studies of the Taft commission on economy and efficiency were made. Unfortunately, every change that is proposed threatens the security or the interests of some group of employees or other vested interests. Complaints flow into Congress, and political opposition gets in the way of change. Because of the war crisis, President Wilson secured the enactment of the Overman Act in 1918, which authorized him to shift agencies and functions. The power was given, however, only for the period of the war.[44]

The conduct of the war made necessary the multiplication of agencies and employees in Washington. After the armistice, Congress began to think in terms of a national debt of some twenty-eight billions of dollars which had to be liquidated. The reorganization of government on a peacetime basis so as to reduce government costs was one of the important tasks ahead. Congress, which was now under the control of Republicans, was highly jealous of its own prerogatives and was determined to keep control in its own hands. During the summer of 1920, the Senate passed without debate a joint resolution providing for a joint committee on reorganization, consisting of three members of each house to be appointed by the presiding officers of the respective houses.[45] The committee was to make a survey of the administrative services of the government and make recommendations on reorganization. The House postponed action, evidently fearing that the committee would be, in the language of one congressman, "just another smelling committee, to bring out a lot of

[44] See chapter 27.  [45] 59 *Congressional Record* 6794-6795.

bogus facts to use in campaigns on the hustings." [46] The measure was passed, however, at the session which followed the presidential campaign. President Wilson refused to sign it; but, perhaps because he realized that a veto would be futile, he allowed it to become a law without his signature. [47]

The attitude of Congress toward co-operation with the President in reorganizing the government changed greatly as soon as Warren G. Harding, a former senator and a member of the dominant party in Congress, became President. Senator Reed Smoot, who had sponsored the joint resolution providing for the joint committee on reorganization, suggested to Mr. Harding, apparently even before he became President, that it would be well for him to have a representative to work with the committee. Soon after Congress had assembled in the special session called by President Harding, Senator Smoot submitted to him, and secured his approval of, a resolution authorizing the appointment of a representative of the Executive to co-operate with the committee. [48] Without the assistance and complete co-operation of the President, said Senator Smoot, and the co-operation of the heads of the departments, it would be next to impossible to conduct an adequate investigation and to get any legislation through Congress to make the necessary changes. It was recognized, furthermore, that if the program were co-operative, the risk of a veto might be avoided.

The resolution passed the Senate unanimously. Democratic members of the House of Representatives objected to creating an office intended to take care of the President's friend, Walter F. Brown, of Ohio, and to smooth out difficulties in Republican politics in that state. A Democrat said, to the accompaniment of laughter and jeers from Republicans, that, if there was one thing that he was afraid of more than another, it was the domination of the legislative branch of the government by the Executive. [49] The measure passed by a large majority. [50]

Walter F. Brown was appointed as the President's representative and acted as chairman of the joint committee of Congress. Most of the work of investigation was done by administrative officers of the government under his direction. Scores of bureau chiefs and others in the executive branch of the government collected information as to the organization and functions of the several agencies. In collaboration with the President and the heads of departments, Brown

---

[46] *Ibid.*, p. 8437.    [47] 41 Stat. 1083.   See Senate Doc. No. 352, 66th Cong., 3d sess.
[48] 61 *Congressional Record* 396, 431.      [49] *Ibid.*, 942.      [50] 42 Stat. 3.

worked out a program of reorganization. He secured the President's approval of the program and submitted it to the joint committee in February, 1923.[51]

Some of the changes recommended were drastic, and the joint committee wrestled with them for more than a year. It held extensive public hearings, which were concluded in April, 1924. The report was presented the following June.[52] The committee recommended the establishment of a new department, to be known as the Department of Education and Relief. A number of subordinate agencies, dealing with education, pensions, hospitals, and other functions, were to be transferred to the new department. A Bureau of Purchase and Supplies, to centralize and co-ordinate the acquisition of supplies by the government, was to be established. Department solicitors, who were nominally under the Attorney General, were to be transferred to the departments which they served. The Bureau of the Budget was to be taken away from the Treasury Department altogether and placed under the exclusive control of the President. Large numbers of other changes were to be made by transferring agencies from one department to another, in attempt to prevent duplication of function and to reduce expenses. The committee did not recommend that the War and Navy Departments be merged in a Department of Defense as the President himself had recommended.[53] The heads of the two departments were opposed to any such merger, and vested interests in the departments were strong enough to prevent accomplishment of the change.

Congress was about to adjourn at the time when the report was made, and it was not expected that the reorganization bill proposed by the committee would be taken up until the next session. The Republican platform, which was announced a week later, favored reorganization along the line of the plan of the joint committee of Congress, which, it said, had the unqualified support of President Coolidge. The Democratic platform merely opposed the extension of bureaucracy, the creation of unnecessary bureaus and federal agencies, and the multiplication of offices and officeholders.

In his annual message to Congress the following December, President Coolidge said that one way to save public money would be to

[51] *New York Times,* February 16, 1923; see also Harlean James, "Remaking the Federal Administration," *American Review of Reviews,* LXIV (August, 1921), 171-176.

[52] Senate Doc. No. 128, 68th Cong., 1st sess. Also published as House Report No. 937 and House Doc. No. 356.

[53] See *The Outlook,* CXXXIII (February 28, 1923), 386.

pass the pending bill for the reorganization of the various departments. He called the legislation vital as a companion piece to the budget law.[54] On January 5, 1925, through letters sent by his secretary to leading members of Congress, he again attempted to secure action on the bill.[55] In the meantime, however, congressmen had heard bitter opposition to each of large numbers of proposed changes from employees or other persons who were adversely affected. It was clear that a great deal of time would have to be given to debate before a measure could be worked out which would be acceptable to majorities in both houses. It proved impossible, therefore, to secure action at the short session.

### PRESIDENTIAL REORGANIZATION

In his annual message to Congress in December, 1925, President Coolidge again urged the enactment of the measure,[56] but it was becoming more and more apparent that a reorganization prescribed in detail by act of Congress would not be achieved. The alternative was to seek from Congress a grant of power so that the President might prescribe a reorganization and put it into effect. Such a move would involve drastic surrender of congressional prerogatives, but it would also relieve congressmen from innumerable embarrassments. On December 10, it was announced that congressional leaders and Secretary of Commerce Herbert Hoover had conferred with the President and agreed on a compromise measure to create a board of five members to recommend changes in the government service which were to be made effective by the President without further legislation.[57] Bills were introduced in both houses of Congress,[58] but neither of them was ever reported out. Some changes were made in the government which did not require congressional action, but attempts to secure such action appeared futile. Bills to bring about specific changes were introduced from time to time, such as those to create departments of conservation, education, and public works, but none of them was passed.

Herbert Hoover entered the presidency in 1929 from the Commerce Department, where he had proved himself an efficient organizer. He promised full support to the reorganization movement. In his annual

---

[54] 66 *Congressional Record* 55.     [55] *New York Times,* January 6, 1925.

[56] 67 *Congressional Record* 464.

[57] *New York Times,* December 11, **1925.**

[58] 67 *Congressional Record* 613, 684.

message to Congress in December, 1929, he recounted the events of twenty years of unavailing struggle. He said:

> With this background of all previous experience, I can see no hope for the development of a sound reorganization of the government unless Congress be willing to delegate its authority over the problem (subject to defined principles) to the Executive, who should act upon approval of a joint committee of Congress or with the reservation of power of revision by Congress within some limited period adequate for its consideration.[59]

His recommendation bore no fruit, however, until the last year of his administration, when the business depression drove Congress to seek some way of saving money.

On February 17, 1932, President Hoover sent to Congress a special message, saying that the absolute necessity for the most drastic economy made the problem of governmental reorganization one of paramount importance. He declared that a patchwork organization compelled inefficiency, waste, and extravagance, and that economy and efficiency could come only through modernization. He recommended that Congress provide for consolidation and grouping of various executive and administrative activities in terms of certain general principles. Authority to make the changes should be lodged in the President, who was to effect them by executive order, "such executive order to lie before the Congress for sixty days during sessions thereof before becoming effective, but becoming effective at the end of such period unless the Congress shall request suspension of action." [60]

The House of Representatives organized a committee on economy, which drafted a bill calculated to save some two hundred million dollars without impairing the efficiency of the government. In addition to providing for many specific changes affecting salaries and personnel, the bill gave to the President broad powers to group, coordinate, and consolidate government agencies. These powers were drastically limited, however, by the provision that no executive department or agency created by statute could be abolished by the President, and that his power in this field was limited to making recommendations to Congress. As the President had recommended, the bill provided that a reorganization order could not become effective until it had been before Congress for sixty calendar days. Perhaps because the House of Representatives was Democratic, whereas the Senate and

[59] 72 *Congressional Record* 27.
[60] House Doc. No. 254, 72d Cong., 1st sess., p. 2.

the President were Republican, the bill provided that action by one house alone within the sixty-day period might render the executive order ineffective.[61]

The bill was passed with relatively little discussion of the constitutional question of delegation of power to the President or the question of permitting one house of Congress to nullify an order of the President. The significant statement was made in the House of Representatives that Congress could not delegate to the President authority to abolish an executive department or an agency created by statute. "To do so would be to delegate to the President authority to legislate. This clearly cannot be done under the Constitution." [62] The measure became a law as a part of an appropriation bill to which it had been attached as a rider.[63]

Administration of the statute proved almost as difficult as the task of enactment had been. The President assigned to the Bureau of the Budget the task of working out a large number of transfers of agencies within the government to promote efficiency and economy, and on December 9, 1932, he presented to Congress a series of executive orders providing for changes, with an explanation and a justification of his proposals.[64] As was to be expected, many legislators from both political parties were dissatisfied with the proposed changes. A new President had been elected, furthermore, from the party which had been out of power for some years, and was soon to take office. Democratic congressmen took the position that this reorganization had been deferred so long that it ought to wait a little longer, and be supervised by the President who would be responsible for the next administration. It was rumored that many Democrats were opposed to any changes in administration which would curtail the number of appointments to be made when their party came into power. Hearings on the reorganization orders submitted by the President were held by the committee on expenditures in the executive departments in the House of Representatives, which was already under Democratic control. From the hearings and from other sources it became clear that the strategy of the House was to block the orders issued by President Hoover, while enacting a new measure under what was at least a pretense of giving the next President more power than President Hoover had possessed.

---

[61] House Report No. 1126, 72d Cong., 1st sess., p. 11.
[62] 75 *Congressional Record* 9264.
[63] 47 Stat. 382, 413.     [64] 76 *Congressional Record* 233-254.

At a press conference Hoover declared that the opposition to reorganization was not merely partisan, but was the opposition which had defeated every effort at reorganization for twenty-five years. The proposal to transfer the task to his successor was simply a device by which it was hoped that the proposal could be defeated. Congress must either keep its hands off now or must give to his successor much larger powers of independent action than had been given to any President, if there was ever to be reorganization  He added a comment reflecting his own experience with executive orders issued subject to revocation by a house of Congress:

> And that authority to be effective should be free of the limitations in the law passed last year which gives Congress the veto power, which prevents the abolition of functions, which prevents the rearrangement of major departments. Otherwise it will, as is now being demonstrated in the present law, again be merely make-believe.[65]

The House rejected the Hoover executive orders on January 19, 1933,[66] and Congress, driven by the deepening depression, which threatened the collapse of the whole economic system, moved swiftly to enact a measure to empower the incoming President to reorganize the government as a means of reducing costs. President Hoover and Attorney General Mitchell sought indirectly to keep out of the new measure a provision authorizing congressional rejection of executive orders issued under the act. In an official opinion advising the President to veto a deficiency appropriation bill because certain provisions encroached on the authority of the Executive, the Attorney General referred to the reorganization statute under which President Hoover had issued his several orders, only to have them nullified by a resolution of the House of Representatives. Said the Attorney General.

> It must be assumed that the functions of the President under this act were executive in their nature or they could not have been constitutionally conferred upon him, and so there was set up a method by which one house of Congress might disapprove executive action. No one would question the power of Congress to provide for delay in the execution of such an administrative order or its power to withdraw the authority to make the order, provided the withdrawal takes the form of legislation. The attempt to give to either house of Congress, by action which is not legislation, power to disapprove admin-

istrative acts, raises a grave question as to the validity of the entire provision in the act of June 30, 1932, for executive reorganization of governmental functions.[67]

President Hoover sent a copy of the opinion of the Attorney General with his message vetoing the appropriation bill in connection with which it had been prepared.[68] Congress took the constitutional argument into account[69] and eliminated the objectionable provision from the new measure. It preserved the sixty-day period within which orders must be subject to the consideration of Congress, but provided that, in order to reject them, it would be necessary for Congress to pass a joint resolution rather than a concurrent resolution. A joint resolution was subject to the approval of the President. If he continued to support his orders, therefore, a majority of two-thirds in each house would be necessary to pass over his veto a measure rendering the orders ineffective.

Congress strengthened the new measure at another point at which the old one had been criticized by President Hoover. It gave the President the power to abolish agencies and functions as well as to consolidate them, with the exception that he was not to abolish or transfer entire executive departments. The exception, presumably, was to prevent the much-discussed merger of the War and Navy Departments and to curb the proposals being made by many Democrats that the entire Commerce Department, which had been the subject of special favor during the administration of President Hoover, might be abolished or merged in other departments.

Many legislators cringed at the proposal to authorize the President to alter or abolish agencies and functions created by law. It seemed to them clearly to provide for the delegation of legislative power to the President, and such delegation was assumed to be unconstitutional. Some refused to vote for the measures; but others, realizing the impossibility of securing action without some such delegation, sought a means to justify support. Since the period of the first World War, the belief had prevailed widely that legislation not otherwise justified by the Constitution might be upheld if an emergency making it necessary for the public welfare were shown to exist.[70] A provision was

[67] 37 *Opinions of the Attorneys General* 63-64.

[68] House Doc. No. 529, 72d Cong., 2d sess.

[69] See, for example, 76 *Congressional Record* 3538-3539.

[70] See Wilson *v.* New, 243 U.S. 332 (1917); Block *v.* Hirsh, 256 U.S. 135 (1921). For discussion of the doctrine of emergency prior to 1933 see W. W. Willoughby, *The Con-*

therefore incorporated to the effect that "The Congress hereby de-clares that a serious emergency exists by reason of the general economic depression; that it is imperative to reduce drastically governmental expenditures; and that such reduction may be accomplished in great measure by proceeding immediately under the provisions of this title." [71] In harmony with this theory, the authority granted to the President was given for only two years.

The bill was made a part of one of the departmental appropriation bills, and its enactment was not completed until the very end of the session. The addition of other provisions, giving to the President sweeping powers to reduce expenditures at will, was discussed from time to time. Speaker Garner of the House of Representatives said, "I'm for going the limit. The limit is the Constitution of the United States." [72] A veto by President Hoover was rumored as a possibility. The word "dictatorship" was heard in the halls of Congress and paraded in newspaper headlines. "Will Congress abdicate?" asked one of a number of similar editorials in the *New York Times*.[73]

So widespread were the comments about the development of dic-tatorship that Senator Borah found it advisable to give to the press a letter in which he insisted that President-elect Roosevelt had no desire for dictatorial power. "Should Congress undertake to confer upon him dictatorial power, I would hope, I would expect him to fling it back in the chattering teeth of a pusillanimous Congress with the reminder that he was the President of the United States and not its dictator." [74] There was no way by which Congress could confer dictatorial powers without the cowardly betrayal of its constitutional obligations, the senator continued. "And beyond Congress is a Supreme Court which has not yet suffered an attack of this flabby Americanism." There were ample powers available under the Consti-tution, he believed, for dealing with the existing emergency.

Franklin D. Roosevelt became President of the United States just at the time when every bank in the United States was compelled to close its doors and when every business enterprise was threatened

*stitutional Law of the United States* (3 vols., 1929), III, 1795; George W. Wickersham, "The Police Power and the New York Emergency Rent Laws," *University of Pennsylvania Law Review*, LXIX (May, 1921), 301-316; "District of Columbia Rent Laws," *Minnesota Law Review*, V (May, 1921), 472-474; Robert A. Maurer, "Emergency Laws," *Georgetown Law Journal*, XXIII (May, 1935), 671-721; John E. Curry, "Executive Power as Affected by Emergency," *George Washington Law Review*, III (January, 1935), 195-204.

[71] 47 Stat. 1517.  [72] *New York Times*, February 11, 1933.
[73] *Ibid.* See also *ibid.*, February 20, February 23, and February 24.
[74] *Ibid.*, February 23, 1933.

with ruin. Terror-stricken people looked for leadership and reassurance which would give a sense of security against economic disaster. Roosevelt offered that leadership and assurance with a confidence and enthusiasm which seemed to betoken either unparalleled strength and wisdom or equally unparalleled incomprehension of the task before him. "This nation," he said in his inaugural address, "asks for action, and action now." He promised action to the limit of national need and of constitutional power. "It is to be hoped," he added, "that the normal balance of executive and legislative authority may be wholly adequate to meet the unprecedented task before us. But it may be that an unprecedented demand and need for undelayed action may call for temporary departure from that normal balance of public procedure." He would seek to bring about the speedy adoption by Congress of those measures needed by a stricken nation in the midst of a stricken world. If Congress failed to act, "I shall not evade the clear course of duty that will then confront me. I shall ask the Congress for the one remaining instrument to meet the crisis — broad executive power to wage a war against the emergency, as great as the power that would be given to me if we were in fact invaded by a foreign foe." [75]

One after another, in rapid succession, he proposed and brought about the adoption of a series of measures dealing with banking and the currency, economy, the production and taxation of light wines and beer, agricultural relief, unemployment relief, relief of homeowners, development of electric power in the Tennessee Valley, the reorganization of railroads, and industrial recovery.

In connection with a bill drafted to give the President broad powers to institute economies in the government and with other measures, a minority of the legislators protested against the broad delegation of legislative power, the surrender to virtual dictatorship,[76] but the majority gave support. Said one congressman, "As the wandering and abject tribes of Israel in that remote period of almost forgotten centuries called to Moses to lead them from a wilderness of despondency and to free them from shackles which bound them in ruthless subjection to tyranny, so today the American people call to President Franklin D. Roosevelt to lead them from a wilderness of unemployment, suffering, hunger, and despair into the promised land of steady employment, contentment, and economic security." [77] Said another,

[75] 77 *Congressional Record* 5-6.     [76] See *ibid.*, pp. 203, 206, 218, 315, 419, 556.
[77] *Ibid.*, p. 222.

"The people have summoned to their service a leader whose face is lifted toward the skies. We follow that leadership today, and we shall follow that leadership until we stand again in the glorious sunlight of prosperity and happiness in this Republic."[78] "In Roosevelt I trust," proclaimed another.[79]

Congress amended the reorganization measure enacted at the end of the Hoover administration so that an order for reorganization might become effective within sixty days, even though Congress was not in session throughout that entire period.[80] Executive orders were issued providing for a number of readjustments.[81] During the two years covered by the statute, however, the administration found little time for consideration of economy and symmetry in government. Its economic and social program resulted in the forming of an incredible mass of administrations, authorities, commissions, committees, corporations, and boards, which at times seemed utterly lacking in organized relations to one another. The two-year life of the reorganization statute had expired before the President was ready to give attention to scientific reorganization. Indeed, it was not until the beginning of his second administration that he turned the spotlight upon it.

### THE HUMPHREY REMOVAL CASE

In the meantime, during his first administration, another important development took place. President Roosevelt was determined to have the loyalty and full support of every agency in the government, including the so-called independent regulatory commissions. These commissions were set up in such a way as to reduce to a minimum political interference with policies and personnel. The Federal Trade Commission Act, for example, provided for the removal of a commissioner by the President only for inefficiency, neglect of duty, or malfeasance in office. The commission included one member, William E. Humphrey, whom the President wished to remove. Humphrey was a conservative Republican, who had been appointed by President Coolidge and reappointed by President Hoover, and whose sympathies and ideas were completely out of line with the policies of President Roosevelt. If he left the office, he would have to be replaced by another Republican, since the statute forbade the appointment of more than three members from the same political party; but the President thought that he could find another Republican who would co-

[78] *Ibid.*, p. 79.　　　[79] *Ibid.*, p. 227.　　　[80] 48 Stat. 16.
[81] United States Code (1940 edition), Title 5, section 132.

operate with him much more heartily than Humphrey could be expected to do.

Humphrey was informed indirectly that the President desired his resignation. He wrote to the President, asking for a personal interview, saying that he knew of nothing discreditable in his record and that a forced resignation would be a reflection on his career and would injure him in his profession. Roosevelt replied that he had no time for an interview, and said:

> Without any reflection at all upon you personally or upon the service you have rendered in your present capacity, I find it necessary to ask for your resignation as a member of the Federal Trade Commission. I do this because I feel that the aims and purposes of the administration with respect to the work of the commission can be carried out most effectively with personnel of my own selection.[82]

Humphrey asked for time to consult with his friends as to his future action. The President chose to regard the letter as a resignation and replied, "I fully appreciate your desire to have a little time to make arrangements. Therefore I am accepting your resignation, but not to take effect until August 15." Humphrey, evidently after consultation with his friends, replied that he had not resigned and did not intend to do so. Congress, he said, intended that the Federal Trade Commission should be an independent, semi-judicial, continuing body. The very purpose of the statute, he thought, was destroyed by the power assumed by the President to remove a member of that body because he wanted to bring about the replacement by a member of his own selection. Under the statute the President had no such power of removal.[83]

The President made another plea: "You will, I know," he said, "realize that I do not feel that your mind and my mind go along together on either the policies or the administering of the Federal Trade Commission, and frankly I think it is best for the people of this country that I should have full confidence." Humphrey again rejected the plea, and subsequently scolded the President for giving publicity to the controversy.[84]

The President was faced with the alternative of acknowledging defeat or of removing Humphrey in violation of the statute. Since the time of President Wilson's veto of the Budget and Accounting bill because of the removal provision concerning the comptroller

[82] *New York Times*, October 8, 1933.     [83] *Ibid.*     [84] *Ibid.*

general, the constitutional problem of the power of the President to remove appointees had received careful consideration by the Supreme Court. The case, Myers *v.* United States,[85] decided in 1926, had to do with President Wilson's removal in 1920 of Myers, a politically appointed postmaster. An act of 1876 made removal of first, second, and third class postmasters subject to the consent of the Senate.[86] The act was one of a number of its kind which had been passed during the years immediately following the Civil War. They had grown out of controversies between Congress and the President which achieved particular prominence during the presidency of Andrew Johnson. No additional measures of this kind had been enacted for a number of decades, but this particular statute was still in force.

The decision in the Myers case was regarded as a landmark in constitutional history. The Supreme Court divided six to three. The majority and minority opinions took up some one hundred and ninety pages in the official reports. Chief Justice Taft, for the majority, traced in great detail the history of the appointing power under the Constitution and the relations which had prevailed between the legislative and executive branches of the government. The Court had no hesitation, said the Chief Justice, in holding that the original Tenure-of-Office Act of 1867, "in so far as it attempted to prevent the President from removing executive officers who had been appointed by him by and with the advice and consent of the Senate, was invalid and that subsequent legislation of the same effect was equally so." [87] In like manner, he found unconstitutional the act of 1876 by which the unrestricted power of removal of first-class postmasters was denied to the President.

Although it was not necessary to the decision in the Myers case, the Chief Justice added a broader statement which seemed to protect the power of the President to remove at will even such officers as members of the Federal Trade Commission:

> Then there may be duties of a quasi-judicial character imposed on executive officers and members of executive tribunals whose decisions after hearing affect interests of individuals, the discharge of which the President cannot in a particular case properly influence or control. But even in such a case he may consider the decision after its rendition as a reason for removing the officer, on the ground that the discretion regularly entrusted to that officer by statute has not been on the whole

[85] 272 U.S. 52 (1926).      [86] 19 Stat. 80.      [87] 272 U.S. 176.

intelligently or wisely exercised.     Otherwise he does not discharge his own constitutional duty of seeing that the laws be faithfully executed.[88]

Evidently believing that on the basis of the Myers decision the Federal Trade Commission Act would be held unconstitutional in so far as it prevented the President from removing a commissioner except on specified grounds, President Roosevelt, on September 27, 1933, sent Humphrey the following note: "Effective as of this date, you are hereby removed from the office of commissioner of the Federal Trade Commission." [89]

Humphrey contested the removal by bringing suit for his salary. The case reached the Supreme Court and was decided on May 27, 1935,[90] the date of the decision which undermined the National Industrial Recovery Act.[91] Both decisions reflected a hostility toward the aims and methods of the New Deal which was growing in certain sections of the public and had always been felt by certain members of the Supreme Court. The Humphrey decision was unanimous. Justice Sutherland, speaking for eight of the nine members of the Court, found that the Federal Trade Commission acted in part quasi-legislatively and in part quasi-judicially, and could not in any proper sense be characterized as an arm or an eye of the Executive.     The coercive influence of removal by the President would threaten the independence of the commission, which was not only wholly disconnected from the executive department, but was created by Congress as a means of carrying into operation legislative and judicial powers and as an agency of the legislative and judicial departments.     The principle stressed in the Myers decision was limited to purely executive officers.

The Humphrey decision, therefore, denied to the President the power to remove members of the independent regulatory commissions and, perhaps, other undefined officers in agencies not wholly executive

[88] *Ibid.*, p. 135. For discussion of the Myers case see James Hart, *Tenure of Office Under the Constitution* (1930); Edward S. Corwin, "Tenure of Office and the Removal Power Under the Constitution," *Columbia Law Review*, XXVII (April, 1927, 353; also published as "The President's Removal Power Under the Constitution," in *Selected Essays on Constitutional Law* (1938), IV, 1467.     Howard Lee McBain, "Consequences of the President's Unlimited Power of Removal," *Political Science Quarterly*, XLI (December, 1926), 596; Albert Langeluttig, "The Bearing of Myers v. United States upon the Independence of Federal Administrative Tribunals — a Criticism," *American Political Science Review*, XXIV (February, 1930), 59; George B. Galloway, "Consequences of the Myers Decision," *American Law Review*, LXI (July-August, 1927), 481.

[89] *New York Times*, October 8, 1933.

[90] Humphrey's Executor v. United States, 295 U.S. 602 (1935).

[91] A. L. A. Schechter Poultry Corporation v. United States, 295 U.S. 495 (1935).

in character.[92] The decision constituted, or threatened to constitute, a definite obstruction to presidential control in a government that had become a complicated amalgam of agencies of many kinds. There were probably both coincidence and design in the fact that within two years after the decision in the Humphrey case the President made a series of attempts at governmental change, calculated to bring the Supreme Court more nearly under his control and to reorganize the regulatory commissions so that many of their functions would be shifted to the executive establishment.

THE ROOSEVELT REORGANIZATION PROGRAM

The tentative plan to reorganize the independent regulatory commissions was part of a much broader plan to bring order, not merely among the older administrative agencies of the government, but also in the chaotic assemblage of New-Deal organizations. A committee with the title of "The President's Committee on Administrative Management" was created by the President in March, 1936, to make a study of administrative management in the federal government and submit recommendations to the President. In January, 1937, the President sent the report of the committee to Congress with his approval. The report called for the expansion of the White House staff; improvements in connection with the federal budget, including transfer of the Bureau of the Budget to the Executive Office of the President; extension of the merit system upward, outward, and downward, and the replacement of the Civil Service Commission by a responsible administrator; the overhauling of the one hundred independent agencies, administrations, authorities, boards, and commissions to place them within one or the other of twelve major executive departments, including two new departments of social welfare and public works; and the reorganization of functions connected with the comptroller general so that control would be restored to the Executive, and Congress would be provided with a genuine, independent post-audit of all fiscal transactions of the government.[93]

[92] For discussion of the Humphrey case see William J. Donovan and Ralstone R. Irvine, "The President's Power to Remove Members of Administrative Agencies," *Cornell Law Quarterly,* XXI (February, 1936), 215-248; "Removal of Federal Administrative Officers," *Illinois Law Review,* XXX (April, 1936), 1037-1055; "Constitutionality of Limitation by Congress of President's Right to Remove Officers Appointed with the Consent of the Senate," *Columbia Law Review,* XXXV (June, 1935), 936-938; "Congressional Limitation upon the President's Power of Removal," *Harvard Law Review,* XLIX (December, 1935), 330-333.

[93] See President's Committee on Administrative Management, *Report of the Committee with Studies of Administrative Management in the Federal Government* (1937).

Hearings were held before a joint committee of Congress from February to April, 1937, and before a Senate committee on government organization the following August. The first half of 1937 witnessed also the struggle to enlarge or change the membership of the Supreme Court to put an end to judicial nullification of New-Deal measures. That controversy brought charges of attempted dictatorship, and the suspicion created was carried over to the subject of reorganization. The independent regulatory commissions, particularly the Interstate Commerce Commission, had achieved in the minds of the people prestige comparable to that of the Supreme Court. In spite of the probable desires of the President, no bill seriously considered in Congress attempted to carry out the recommendations of the President's committee as they affected the independent regulatory commissions. Yet critics of the bills that were proposed continued for many months to talk as if the independence of the regulatory commissions was in danger.

In the hearings and on the floors of Congress, furthermore, the attempt to relieve the administration of the shackles that the comptroller general had fastened upon it and to establish the office of auditor general to provide for Congress a thorough post-audit of government expenditures was denounced as an effort to facilitate the rash spending of government funds. Similarly, the attempt to invigorate the supervision of government personnel by replacing the bipartisan Civil Service Commission with a single administrator was denounced as the device of a politically minded President to substitute a spoils system for a merit system. The proposal that executive orders of the President should become effective within sixty days unless the Congress nullified them by a joint resolution, which was subject to the disapproval of the President, was denounced by those who favored congressional action by concurrent resolution, even though in 1933 the latter device had been abandoned because of the belief that it was unconstitutional. It was on these three points — the action on the comptroller general, the action on the Civil Service Commission, and the mode of defeating orders of the President — that most of the controversy over the reorganization proposal took place.

The reorganization bills introduced during 1937 went through many changes. The House of Representatives attempted to deal with separate segments of the subject by passing separate bills. The Senate insisted on incorporating all provisions in a single bill, but allowed the regular session to come to an end before taking final action on the bill. At a special session of Congress which met in November, the President renewed his recommendation. He was so bold as to reject one of the principal arguments for reorganization made in earlier years — the argument of economy. The experience of states and municipalities, he said, demonstrated definitely that reorganization of government along the lines of modern business administrative practice could increase efficiency, but it had not proved a method of making major savings in the cost of government. Large savings could be made only by cutting down or eliminating government functions.[94]

Former President Hoover delivered a blast against the plan for reorganization. "It proposes to abolish the Civil Service Commission," he said, "which has for fifty years given fine service and held high standards of training and freedom from politics in public service. The new plan proposes to substitute one-man control. No matter what the words of that bill may purport to mean, it is clear that the plan is to destroy the progress we have made and substitute personal political control." [95] He did not allude to the fact that as President he had recommended the substitution of a personnel administrator for the chairman of the Civil Service Commission.[96]

The special session came to an end without important action. At the regular session, beginning in January, 1938, the President renewed his recommendation.[97] A new Senate measure was drafted to allay concern about dictatorship, but without fundamental modification of the plans of the administration. Voluminous, repetitive, confused, and confusing debates took place, with continued charges that the bill was a step toward dictatorship. Senator Wheeler introduced an amendment which would have thrown back upon Congress full responsibility for the details of any reorganization adopted. It provided, not for a congressional veto of an executive order of the President, but for the enactment of a joint resolution, positively adopting any plan worked out before it could become effective. The senator had no faith in reorganization plotted in the executive branch of the government. The President would not have time for such a task. As to who would do the work, he was of the opinion that "some professor or some clerk in the department is going to do it." [98] The amendment led again to a discussion of congressional rejection of executive orders

---

[94] 82 *Congressional Record* 7.    [95] *New York Times*, November 13, 1937.
[96] 75 *Congressional Record* 4109-4110.    [97] 83 *Congressional Record* 9.
[98] *Ibid.*, p. 3018.

by concurrent resolution and the possible violation of the Constitution involved in such a procedure. The amendment was defeated and, after running the gantlet of innumerable attacks, the bill passed the Senate. It provided, in effect, that executive orders for reorganization should become operative within sixty days unless rejected by joint resolution, which, of course, was subject to presidential veto.

Genuine fears as to the evils which might result from the enactment of the reorganization bill had combined with deliberate misinterpretation by the enemies of the President, to create a wave of popular hysteria in opposition to the measure. The opposition was reflected in a tremendous outpouring of telegrams, addressed to members of the Senate. The margin of victory was narrow, the vote in the Senate being 49 to 42. Roosevelt, jubilant over his victory, made the undiplomatic statement that "it proves that the Senate cannot be purchased by organized telegrams based on direct misrepresentation." [99] The implication was clear that some of the senators who had voted against the measure had been "purchased." The statement was hotly denounced in the Senate and added to hostile feelings on the issue.

The President's statement was followed two days later by one of the oddest documents in the history of presidential diplomacy. In the form of a letter, addressed to a friend whose name was deleted, he gave to the press, at one-forty-five in the morning, a refutation of the charges that he was seeking to make himself a dictator. He had neither the inclination nor the qualifications which would make him a successful dictator, he said. It was the first time that any American President had found it necessary formally to repel the charge. [100] As to reorganization of the government, he said, attempts made by Congress had failed many times, and it was agreed that detailed reorganization by Congress was a practical impossibility. It was necessary, therefore, that the task be done by executive order. The opposition had been deliberately created; it had "planted bogies under every bed." He was opposed to having executive orders blocked by concurrent resolution, first, because of the constitutional question involved in the passage of a concurrent resolution, which was only an expression of congressional sentiment, and, second, because on rare occasions he felt that the President ought to be in position to veto a congressional act of rejection. He gave assurance that, if a joint resolution were passed by Congress disapproving an order, he would in

[99] *New York Times*, March 30, 1938.     [100] *Ibid.*, April 1, 1938.

the overwhelming majority of cases go along with carefully considered congressional action.[101]

The statement apparently made no friends for the reorganization bill. It succeeded chiefly in producing speculation as to why the President had found it necessary to announce to the country, in the middle of the night, that he had no aspirations toward dictatorship. The administration was at first hopeful of securing adoption of the Senate bill in the House of Representatives, where part of the reorganization provisions had already been adopted in separate bills, but the hope speedily declined. An amendment providing for the rejection of executive orders by concurrent resolution was accepted by way of compromise. Other amendments weakened the bill at point after point, but still a majority to enact it could not be secured. In April, 1938, the emasculated bill was killed by being sent back to committee. The President, whose plan to reform the Supreme Court had met a similar fate, had undergone his second major defeat. Although the bill had been whittled down to the point where it was relatively innocuous, many people still regarded it as an embodiment of evil. It was reported that shares in the stock market rose from two to six points on the announcement of the defeat of the bill.[102]

New reorganization bills were introduced at the session of Congress which met in January, 1939. Their range was more limited than that of some of the earlier measures proposed; but, even so, many of the old battles were fought over again. A measure was finally enacted.[103] Under the act the President was forbidden completely to abolish any department, or to transfer all the functions of any department, or to change the name of any department, or to create any new department. A long list of agencies was not to be touched.

The act provided that reorganizations specified in plans worked out by the President should take effect in accordance with the plan "upon the expiration of sixty calendar days after the date on which the plan is transmitted to the Congress, but only if during such sixty-day period there has not been passed by the two houses a concurrent resolution stating in substance that the Congress does not favor the reorganization plan." In effect, this provision of the act differed very little from earlier provisions for congressional rejection of executive orders of the President by concurrent resolution. The language was modified, however, to meet criticisms on constitutional grounds. The President was to submit, not "executive orders" directing reorganiza-

[101] *Ibid.*   [102] *Ibid.*, April 10, 1938.   [103] 53 Stat. 561.

tion, but "plans" for reorganization, which, pursuant to the statue, were to become law in the eventuality that a concurrent resolution rejecting them was not passed. The validity of legislation that would become effective only upon specified contingencies was clearly recognized. Said the House committee which considered the reorganization bill, "The failure of Congress to pass such a concurrent resolution is the contingency upon which the reorganizations take effect. Their taking effect is not because the President orders them. That the taking effect of action legislative in character may be made dependent upon conditions or contingencies is well recognized." Citing a recent decision of the Supreme Court upholding an act of Congress authorizing the Secretary of Agriculture to exercise certain powers in the event that certain action was taken by a referendum of farmers,[104] the committee said, "It seems difficult to believe that the effectiveness of action legislative in character may be conditioned upon a vote of farmers, but may not be conditioned on a vote of the two legislative bodies of the Congress." [105]

Within a few weeks after the statute was enacted, the President submitted two plans making extensive changes in the organization of the government. There was not sufficient opposition to raise any serious questions of rejection by Congress. Instead, Congress with the approval of the President passed an act making both plans effective on the same day, July 1, 1939.[106]

Three other reorganization plans, making changes on a lesser scale, were submitted by the President during the first half of 1940. Only one item, the shifting of the Civil Aeronautic Authority from its position as an independent agency to a position in the Department of Commerce, caused serious controversy. The House of Representatives passed a resolution to reject the shift,[107] but the resolution failed to pass in the Senate.[108]

Nothing was done under the Reorganization Act to justify the fears expressed in connection with the earlier and broader proposed measures. The steps taken did little, if anything, to reduce government expenditures; indeed, although the statute paid lip-service to economy, very little in the way of economy was expected to result from it.

---

104 Currin v. Wallace, 306 U.S. 1 (1939).

105 House Report No. 120, 76th Cong., 1st sess., p. 6.

106 53 Stat. 813. For the text of the orders see United States Code (1940 edition), Title 5, section 133t.

107 New York Times, May 9, 1940.          108 Ibid., May 15, 1940.

REORGANIZATION CONTINUED

The pattern of administrative reorganization which was worked out during the Roosevelt administration was continued under later statutes. When in December, 1941, the United States became a direct participant in World War II, Congress conferred upon the President for the war period broad powers of reorganization for war purposes, and the powers were freely exercised. In 1945, sensing the need for broad governmental changes in readjustment to conditions of peace, Congress enacted a new reorganization measure to run until April 1, 1948. Under it President Truman submitted a number of reorganization proposals, securing congressional acceptance of only part of them.

Extensive reorganization took place as a result of recommendations of Commission on Organization of the Executive Branch of the Government, better known as the Hoover Commission. The Commission, consisting of twenty members under the leadership of Herbert Hoover and operating with the aid of a huge staff, made a survey of the executive branch and published a long list of recommendations on the basis of which the Bureau of the Budget worked out a series of reorganization proposals. Although a few of the more controversial were rejected in Congress, important steps were taken toward eliminating some of the administrative disorder resulting from the war and from the post-war expansion of functions. In 1953 Congress conferred on President Eisenhower powers similar to those previously conferred on Presidents Roosevelt and Truman, whereafter still other organizational changes were made.

The task of reorganization, however, is not one to be performed for all time at any given stage. It is a continuing responsibility. Each major change in the character and scope of governmental activity brings changes in the organization of government itself which interfere with structural symmetry and leave distortions which must be remedied for the sake of efficiency. Determined efforts are required to compress or to eliminate emergency agencies. It is true, as said by a member of the Senate, that "The nearest earthly approach to immorality is a bureau of the federal government." [109] The political influence of government agencies is almost always strong enough to prevent reorganization or elimination on the initiative of Congress. They are at times strong enough to prevent the filing of executive

[109] Senator James F. Byrnes, of South Carolina, 76 *Congressional Record* 3538.

proposals for reorganizations with Congress and to bring about the defeat of proposals that are made.

The dominant trend in administrative change includes growth in the size, cost, and multiplicity of functions of the federal government, and enhancement therein of the power of the President and of the entire executive establishment as the policy-making branch of the government. As later chapters will show, the shift of power from Congress to the Executive and the decline of the relative influence of the judiciary with expansion in the use of administrative processes are matters of grave concern. The assumption as to their inevitability is to be carefully scanned. Certain it is that unless the science of administration can be improved at a rapid rate the trend toward administrative dominance carries the threat both of gross inefficiency and waste and of increasing display of arbitrary rule. The discipline and the containment of administration constitute major constitutional problems of the present day.

·············································································

# CHAPTER 31

# THE SUPREME COURT, FROM THE FIRST WORLD WAR TO THE NEW DEAL

A CENTURY AGO the Supreme Court decided in a single decade only a few cases of general importance. By contrast, in the period between the first World War and the beginning of the so-called New Deal, in 1933, the number was so great and the subjects so diverse as to render all but impossible a treatment at once concise and comprehensive. As always, certain cases are to be understood only in terms of their particular settings in law and fact. The descriptions of those settings, however, tend to get in the way of the unified treatment of groups of cases assumed to belong together under classifications such as police power, interstate commerce, powers of the President, and due process of law. To add to the difficulty of portrayal, the membership of the Supreme Court at a particular time may be extremely important in determining the way in which a particular issue will be decided. Yet a classification of the work of the Court in terms of membership alone would leave unexplained many decisions of constitutional significance.

By way of compromise, various modes of presentation are used in the following pages. The first section of the first of the three chapters on the subject deals predominantly with personnel rather than with cases or groups of cases. It deals generally with conflicts of philosophy which will be illustrated in detail when, in later sections, particular cases are examined. It portrays struggles over judicial appointments which developed in part from the consideration of social attitudes. It deals also with the successful efforts of Chief Justice Taft to have the jurisdiction of the Court narrowed, with the object of enabling it to concentrate on important issues and keep up with its work. The later sections of this chapter, and the two ensuing chapters, deal with groupings of judicial decisions which are more or less closely related to each other. From varied approaches to the subject an attempt is made to give a revealing picture of the important work of the most powerful court in the world during the period mentioned.

SUPREME COURT PERSONNEL

Only three justices who were members of the Supreme Court at the beginning of the Harding administration in 1921 were still in office at the beginning of the Roosevelt administration in 1933. They were Willis Van Devanter, appointed by Taft in 1910, James C. McReynolds, appointed by Wilson in 1914, and Louis D. Brandeis, appointed by Wilson in 1916. A number of changes were imminent at the beginning of the Harding administration. The Chief Justice, Edward D. White, had been a member of the Court since his appointment by Cleveland in 1894 to be an associate justice. He had been Chief Justice since his elevation to that office by Taft in 1910. White was a Democrat, but he was a warm admirer of Taft, to whom, doubtless, he felt grateful for his elevation. He seems to have promised, or at least intimated to Taft, that he would hold the office of Chief Justice until a Republican President had been chosen by whom Taft might be appointed to the chief justiceship.[1] Joseph McKenna, who had been appointed by McKinley to succeed Stephen J. Field in 1898, had completed his best years of service by 1921, and was expected soon to retire. Oliver Wendell Holmes, appointed by Roosevelt in 1902, was still vigorous, but the retirement of William R. Day, appointed by Roosevelt in 1903, was expected soon. Mahlon Pitney, although he had been a member of the Court only since 1912, was also near the end of his period of service. A survey of the Court, therefore, indicated that if President Harding were to serve two terms in office, he might be able almost completely to remake the Court.

To Taft's distress, Chief Justice White did not resign when Harding became President, but he died a few months later. Harding had promised to put Taft on the Court when there was a vacancy, but, when the time came, he hesitated because he had also promised a position to his friend George Sutherland, of Utah, who had been his colleague in the Senate until defeated for re-election in 1916.[2] An arrangement was made to have Sutherland await another vacancy, however, and the Taft appointment was made in the summer of 1921, so that he might be in position to advise Attorney General Daugherty on the filling of vacancies in the lower federal courts.

The new Chief Justice brought to his office a variety of experience. He had served on both state and federal courts. He had been solicitor general, Secretary of War, and President of the United States. He had

---

[1] Henry F. Pringle, *Life and Times of William Howard Taft* (2 vols., 1939), II, 955, 956.
[2] *Ibid.*, p. 957.

been a professor of constitutional law at Yale University. His social philosophy was conservative. His knowledge of men and of public affairs would tend to prevent his acting with reactionary blindness, but he would never see eye to eye with radicals, and seldom even with people generally classified as liberals. He was an intelligent conservative, bent on the preservation of the best in the social order which he knew. In terms of his philosophy he gave tone to the work of the Court throughout his period in office, though oftentimes in the face of the criticism of its more liberal members.

Harding's opportunity to appoint Sutherland came in 1922 with the unexpected resignation of John H. Clarke, a Wilson appointee who had often voted with Holmes and Brandeis in conservative-liberal cleavages on the Court. As a Republican senator and as president of the American Bar Association and, incidentally, as an opponent of the appointment of Louis D. Brandeis to the Supreme Court, Sutherland had demonstrated himself an ultra-conservative, with an excellent capacity for fluent, philosophical justification of his position. There was no question what his alignment on the Court would be.

Upon the resignation of Justice Day, later in the same year, Harding nominated Pierce Butler, a Democrat from Minnesota. As a Catholic, Butler took the place of Chief Justice White. He was a competent railroad attorney, who quite naturally had conducted his professional activities for the benefit of his clients, and who later, as a member of the Court, continued to think in terms of the economic philosophy of his former employers. With Sutherland, Van Devanter, and McReynolds, he remained a staunch defender of conservative interests throughout the remainder of his life.

Upon the resignation of Justice Pitney at the end of 1922, Harding appointed Edward T. Sanford, of Tennessee. Sanford, unlike the other two Harding appointees, had had judicial experience. He had been a United States district judge since his appointment by Roosevelt in 1907. His conservatism was slightly less rigid, and certainly less vigorously expressed, than that of Sutherland and Butler, but he aligned himself with them much more frequently than with the liberal members of the Court.

## THE PROGRESSIVE ATTACK ON THE COURT

During the early years of the nineteen-twenties, the Supreme Court handed down decisions blocking liberal movements in a variety of directions. The subjects included child labor, minimum wages for women, the application of anti-trust legislation to labor, farm problems, and utility-valuation problems. Some of the decisions angered large groups of people. In addition, certain lower federal courts antagonized labor groups by the issuing of injunctions against labor activities.

The discontent to which the decisions gave rise was capitalized by a new Progressive party, which in 1924 nominated Robert M. La Follette for President and Burton K. Wheeler for Vice-President. The platform denounced the recent usurpation of the Court in vetoing acts of Congress and thus nullifying legislative power in defiance of the Constitution. It urged a constitutional amendment which would protect from judicial veto a law re-enacted by Congress after having been nullified by the Supreme Court. It also called for the election of all federal judges for limited terms; the abolition of injunctions in labor disputes; ratification of the proposed child-labor amendment and legislation to make it effective; public ownership of railroads and of water-power; and other policies and measures calculated to benefit farmers, laborers, and the common people of the country.

The leadership of the new movement was furnished by the liberal Republican group in Wisconsin and by the remnant of Progressive leadership in the campaigns of 1912 and 1916. Enough support was drawn from farm and labor groups to constitute a definite threat to the two old parties in the presidential campaign. The candidates and the other leading spokesmen of the Democratic and Republican parties criticized the Progressive plan for the re-enactment of federal statutes held unconstitutional by the Supreme Court. The plan was subjected to devastating criticism by Attorney General Harlan F. Stone, former dean of the Columbia University School of Law, who had taken charge of the Department of Justice after Attorney General Daugherty had retired under a cloud. Stone called attention to the fact that one of the purposes of the Constitution was to make possible the maintenance of a federal system wherein the state and the federal governments functioned side by side without encroachment by either upon the sphere of the other. The Attorney General said:

> When, therefore, we provide by constitutional amendment that Congress may enact a law which the Supreme Court has declared to be unconstitutional, we are not merely attacking the Supreme Court, a group of worthy gentlemen, who hold court in the capital; we are

lodging in Congress the power and authority to wipe out every vestige of state sovereignty and all the reserved powers of the states. With that provision in force, we would cease to be a national federation of states with sovereign powers vested in the federal government for purpose of conducting foreign relations, and those internal and external relations which pertain to a central, national government. . . . It is hardly conceivable that the voters in the several states of the United States would ever take a step which would so completely renounce the rights of citizenship in the states and so wholly subject the states to domination of Congress, truly imperial in character.[3]

The comment has added significance in view of the fact that a few months later Attorney General Stone was himself appointed to the Supreme Court.

The critics of the Progressive plan were joined by Secretary of State Charles E. Hughes, who had once been a member of the Supreme Court, and who, in 1930, was to succeed Taft as Chief Justice. The plan would mean, said Hughes, that Congress could do anything it pleased by re-enacting a statute and its will would be supreme over all other authority. A majority in Congress could decide upon any system of representation it pleased in order to continue its own power.

The right to be secure in your person, in your life, in your property, the right to a fair trial if you were accused, the right to freedom of speech, freedom of the press, freedom to worship God according to your own conscience, would be at the mercy of Congress.[4]

The Supreme Court was a human institution, of course, he admitted,

but it is about as far removed from political influence as any human institution could possibly be. Congress is also a human institution, and one that is exposed to every variety of partisan motives, and every wave of passion that sweeps the country. It is only from the Supreme Court that we can obtain a sane, well-ordered interpretation of the Constitution.[5]

During the same period, Congress discussed the need for some kind of change that would limit the power of the Supreme Court. Much was said about the nullification of legislation through five-to-four decisions. Senator Borah called attention to the fact that under the Constitution the Supreme Court exercised its appellate jurisdiction "with such exceptions and under such regulations as the Congress shall make." In view of this clause, giving Congress the power to make

---

[3] *New York Times*, October 2, 1924.     [4] *Ibid.*, October 16, 1924.     [5] *Ibid.*

regulations, he argued that five-to-four decisions could be eliminated, and he introduced a bill to require the concurrence of seven members of the Court to declare an act of Congress unconstitutional.[6] Few senators, however, even if they favored such action, believed that Congress could constitutionally interfere with the manner of deciding cases which were properly before the Supreme Court. A representative proposed a constitutional amendment to give Congress the power to fix the number of judges who must concur in order to decide cases affecting constitutional questions.[7] Bar associations and other conservative organizations proclaimed their opposition to any interference with the Supreme Court and its proceedings.

In spite of the interest in the subject which prevailed for a number of months, Congress took no action to curb the power of the Supreme Court. The Republican party won the election, and Senator La Follette had no opportunity to carry out his program. To all appearances the attack was abandoned and forgotten. Yet it served as a reminder of similar attacks in earlier years and it provided an additional precedent for criticism a decade later.

### THE STONE APPOINTMENT

Justice McKenna remained in office until the beginning of 1925. To succeed him President Coolidge appointed Attorney General Harlan F. Stone, once a fellow student at Amherst, who had done much already to redeem the Department of Justice from the reputation created by his predecessor and who had defended the Supreme Court against the assaults of the Progressives. Probably to the surprise of the President, Stone frequently aligned himself with Justices Holmes and Brandeis when they dissented on social issues. He clashed hotly with his more conservative brethren and remained one of their severe critics after Holmes and Brandeis had retired from the Court. During the five years immediately following his appointment, the dissenting opinions of one or the other of the three justices commonly classified as liberals, and the repeated comment, "Holmes, Brandeis, and Stone dissenting," created in the minds of the people a keen awareness of the cleavage which prevailed among the justices on social issues.

### THE HUGHES APPOINTMENT

Chief Justice Taft resigned early in 1930 because of illness which culminated soon afterward in his death. For persons concerned about

[6] 64 *Congressional Record* 3959-3960.
[7] *New Republic*, XXXIV (March 14, 1923), 59.

the issues over which the Court had been divided, the choice of his successor was important. Justice Stone was a close personal friend of President Hoover. Many persons in sympathy with the liberal point of view hoped that he would be made Chief Justice. The views of many other people are correctly illustrated by the perhaps apocryphal story that certain members of the Supreme Court not in sympathy with his point of view issued an ultimatum to the President that they would resign if Stone were made Chief Justice. In any event, the appointment went, not to Stone, but to Charles E. Hughes, who had resigned from the Court in 1916 to accept the Republican nomination for the presidency.

Hughes was perhaps the most distinguished jurist available; yet the appointment was subject to attack on two grounds. First, although as a justice he had shown broad-minded attitudes in his decisions, he had in more recent years been the high-paid counsel of great corporations which he had represented before the Supreme Court. It was argued that through this experience his point of view must have been molded to that of his clients. Secondly, he was accused of having dragged the Supreme Court into politics by resigning to seek a political office. It was argued that he ought not to be rewarded by being returned as the presiding officer of the Court. Senator Norris and other liberal senators opposed confirmation on the ground of social philosophy. Senator Glass and other Democrats opposed it on the ground of wishing to keep the Supreme Court out of politics. The debate ended quickly, however, and the nomination was confirmed by a vote of 52 to 26.[8]

The appointment was completed almost before the people of the country realized the issue that was involved. In a subsequent statement the conservative *World's Work* remarked that

> the spectacular battle of words has come to be recognized, not so much as a drive against Mr. Hughes, the man, as the beginning of a campaign intended to liberalize the highest of judicial bodies, which has been conservative throughout all its history. There is recognition, as well, that it was formal notice to President Hoover by the progressive Republicans and liberal Democrats in the Senate that they will contest the appointment of any conservatives whom he may seek to elevate to the bench during his incumbency.[9]

The magazine added that the country should applaud the confirmation of Mr. Justice Hughes because it assured the continuance of the conservative policy at least temporarily.

[8] *72 Congressional Record* 3591.   [9] *World's Work*, LIX (April, 1930), 34.

The liberal *New Republic* said that the significance of the contro-versy over the appointment was heightened by Mr. Hughes's personal integrity, his distinction as a lawyer, and his world-wide eminence. The truth was that the Supreme Court was a great policy-making body which differed from other branches of the government chiefly in that its members held their positions for life and were therefore not responsible to public opinion.

> The only protection for the public welfare against an anti-social policy of the Court is scrupulous examination of nominees to its bench and constant and unrelenting criticism of its decisions. It must not be regarded as a sacrosanct retreat of abstract justice, but as a very mundane body of fallible men, who should be called to account by name and made to justify their opinions. There is no wonder that an outcry arose against Mr. Hughes, who in his law practice has been so closely associated with great corporations who have had and will have favors to seek at the hands of the Court, in view of some of the recent appointments.[10]

### THE PARKER NOMINATION

The majority of the Senate which favored the Hughes appointment shrewdly refrained from taking time to defend the nominee against the accusations made. It forced an immediate vote, thereby denying to opponents the time needed to organize. Another occasion for con-troversy arose, however, when Justice Sanford died suddenly some three weeks later, leaving another position to be filled. The Presi-dent knew that any nominee would have to run a gantlet of criticism from liberal, or insurgent, Republicans in the Senate and that his selection must be made with great care. As usual, many persons were recommended, and the letters of recommendation were turned over to the Attorney General for scrutiny. In framing his advice to the Presi-dent, the Attorney General naturally took into account political con-siderations as well as the qualifications of the particular candidates. His choice was John J. Parker, of North Carolina, a member of the United States circuit court of appeals for the fourth circuit. Both the Attorney General and the President were later embarrassed by the publication of a letter to the President's secretary, written by Joseph M. Dixon, first assistant to the Secretary of the Interior, recommend-ing Judge Parker. North Carolina had given President Hoover a majority of sixty-five thousand in the 1928 election, said Dixon. That state carried more hope of future permanent alignment with the Republican party than any other of the southern states that broke from their political moorings. He believed that the appointment of Judge Parker at this time would be "a master political stroke." [11] It may have been true, as stated by Attorney General William D. Mitchell,[12] that the President knew nothing of the Dixon letter and that it received no particular attention at the Department of Justice, but the consideration which he mentioned and the prospect of securing votes from southern Democratic senators in support of the nomination were undoubtedly taken into account.

Judge Parker's name was sent to the Senate on March 21, 1930. Opposition quickly developed in two important groups. The American Federation of Labor attacked the nomination because of Parker's decision in what was commonly known as the Red Jacket case.[13] In that case he had accepted the validity of what were known as "yellow-dog" contracts, which were intended to interfere with the unionization of employees. He had sustained an injunction, issued in a federal district court, restraining officers and members of the United Mine Workers of America from persuading men employed by a coal company to join the union, in violation of contracts with their employer by which they had agreed not to do so. When publicity was given to Judge Parker's decision in this case, protests against the appointment to the Supreme Court began to pour in from laborers and labor organizations all over the country.

The second opposition group was made up of Negroes. When a Republican candidate for governor of North Carolina in 1920, Judge Parker had made the statement, "The participation of the Negro in politics is a source of evil and danger to both races and is not desired by the wise men in either race or by the Republican party of North Carolina." [14] The National Association for Advancement of Colored People cited the statement and opposed the nomination. The national executive committee of the Socialist party added its voice to the clamor of protest.[15] Senators who ordinarily followed the leadership of the President became concerned about the opposition from the

[11] *New York Times,* May 1, 1930.

[12] *Ibid.,* May 6, 1930. See also 72 *Congressional Record* 8341.

[13] International Organization, United Mine Workers of America, *et al. v.* Red Jacket Consolidated Coal and Coke Co., 18 F. (2d) 839 (1927).

[14] Subcommittee of the Senate committee on the judiciary, *Hearings* on the confirmation of Honorable John J. Parker to be an associate justice of the Supreme Court of the United States, 71st Cong., 2d sess., April 5, 1930, p. 74. See quotation from *Greensboro Daily News,* April 19, 1920.

[15] *New York Times,* April 6, 1930.

colored people. A number of them were to seek re-election a few months hence in states in which the Negro vote might be a decisive factor.[16] The President, however, refused to withdraw the nomination.[17] The Department of Justice prepared a memorandum in defense of Parker's decision in the Red Jacket case. Parker and his two colleagues, it said, had felt bound by the decision of the Supreme Court in the Hitchman case.[18] At no point in the decision had Judge Parker assumed to exercise any independent judgment or opinion.[19]

After a subcommittee had received the testimony of the leading opponents of the nomination, it made an adverse recommendation by a vote of 10 to 6.[20] The President stood by the nomination. A representative of the National Association for Advancement of Colored People announced that attempts were being made to coerce prominent colored people in North Carolina into supporting the nomination.

The Senate debated the nomination from April 28 to May 7, with Senator Borah leading the opposition.[21] It came back again and again to the Red Jacket decision as the principal ground of opposition. The race issue was doubtless important as far as voting was concerned, but it was too complicated and delicate to become the subject of extensive debate. A number of administration spokesmen defended Judge Parker and a letter which he had written in his own defense was read,[22] but in no instance was a clear case made for the appointment as one that would bring great distinction to the Supreme Court. An uproar was raised in the Senate by the assertion of Senator Ashurst that federal judgeships and other appointments were being offered in return for votes in support of the nomination.[23] The several issues were charged with emotion. Newspapers gave prominent headlines and long editorials and published innumerable letters for and against the nomination. Final action came on May 7, when the Senate rejected the nomination by a vote of 39 to 41.[24]

Voluminous comments by the press followed the rejection. They showed that Judge Parker himself had been only an incident in a controversy which went much deeper than the qualifications of any one man. The controversy rested upon a sharp divergence of economic and social philosophies which had revealed itself in the presidential campaign of 1924 and had been revived in connection with

---

[16] *Ibid.*, April 12, 1930.    [17] *Ibid.*, April 13, 1930.

[18] Hitchman Coal and Coke Co. *v.* Mitchell, 245 U.S. 229 (1917).

[19] *New York Times*, April 14, 1930.    [20] *Ibid.*, April 22, 1930.

[21] See 72 *Congressional Record* 7930-7933.    [22] *Ibid.*, p. 7793.

[23] *New York Times*, May 6, 1930.    [24] 72 *Congressional Record* 8487.

the nomination of Chief Justice Hughes. It was a part, also, of the perennial tug-of-war between the President and the Senate over the appointing power.

## THE ROBERTS APPOINTMENT

In the struggle over the Parker nomination, the liberals and the insurgent Republicans won a complete victory over the conservatives and the Senate demonstrated its power to check the President in making appointments. Satisfied with their victory, they showed no evidence of further intentions to flout the will of the President. On May 9, 1930, the President sent to the Senate the name of Owen J. Roberts, of Philadelphia. He was a lawyer who had served wealthy clients. Although he had served the federal government in cases involving the notorious Teapot Dome oil lease scandals, he had shown no particular evidence of liberalism. There was no reason for believing that his philosophy differed greatly from that of Chief Justice Hughes or even that of Judge Parker. Yet, apart from some questions as to his attitude on the Eighteenth Amendment, little criticism was heard of the nomination. Investigation was perfunctory and confirmation quickly given.

In the light of subsequent decisions of the Supreme Court, the Roberts appointment proved to have been a victory for neither the conservatives nor the liberals. In divisions on social and economic questions, he voted on some occasions with the conservatives and on others with the liberals. Like Chief Justice Hughes, he avoided all attempts at easy classification. He moved back and forth between groups with an agility bewildering to those who sought to predict his conduct.

## THE CARDOZO APPOINTMENT

The next change in personnel of the Supreme Court came two years later, in 1932, after the resignation of Justice Holmes. The retirement of this "grand old man of the law" at the advanced age of ninety years was an event of much greater import than most withdrawals from the Court. He was not merely a judge, but from his position on the bench he made himself a great teacher of law. He had hosts of admirers who felt that his position must be filled, not by a rank-and-file lawyer, but by a man worthy of the great tradition. Benjamin N. Cardozo, chief judge of the New York court of appeals, was the almost unanimous choice of the Holmes admirers. He, too, was a great teacher of law, through his books on the judicial process and allied subjects as well as through his judicial opinions. He was recognized as a great lawyer, furthermore, by large numbers of people who would not have classified themselves as liberals. The fitness of the appointment was so obvious that it was virtually forced upon President Hoover. The appointment was confirmed almost immediately.

Justice Cardozo had not the robustness, the physical vigor, and the high spirits of his predecessor, and his intellectual processes were strikingly different from those of Holmes. He was perhaps less close to Justice Brandeis than Holmes had been. Yet in his alignment on social and economic issues he took for the most part the position which Holmes had occupied. Once the liberal group had been Holmes, Brandeis, and Stone; now it was Brandeis, Stone, and Cardozo.

Such were the changes in personnel of the Supreme Court which took place between the first World War and the beginning of the Franklin D. Roosevelt administration. The tendency throughout the period was toward sharpening the division on social and economic issues. The alignments were marked by three justices at one extreme and four at the other. Chief Justice Hughes and Justice Roberts played back and forth between the two extremes and held in their own hands, oftentimes, the determination of important issues argued before the Court.

JURISDICTION OF THE SUPREME COURT

Largely as a result of the efforts of Chief Justice Taft and some of his associates, an important change was made in the jurisdiction of the Supreme Court over cases appealed from other courts during the period of the nineteen-twenties. It will be recalled that during the early years of American history there was not enough work in the Supreme Court to keep the justices busy and that much of their time was spent attending circuit courts. As judicial business expanded, circuit judges were appointed to aid the Supreme Court justices in the circuit work and to relieve them of part of their circuit duties. Then, in 1891, a circuit court of appeals was created in each circuit in attempt to relieve the Supreme Court of some of the burdens of appellate work as well, and the members of the Supreme Court ceased riding circuit.

With the growth of the country the business of all federal courts continued to expand. In 1911, Congress attempted to eliminate confusion by abolishing the old circuit courts so that the hierarchy included only district courts, circuit courts of appeals, and the Supreme Court.   Because state courts were differing sharply in the interpretation of the federal Constitution where their own laws were involved, Congress found it necessary to add to the jurisdiction of the Supreme Court by authorizing it to review cases in which state courts had held state laws to be in conflict with the federal Constitution.   Because of the difficulties of the Court in keeping up with its docket, however, Congress in 1916 passed an act to lighten its burden by shutting off cases of minor importance.[25]   Even so, when Chief Justice Taft took office in 1921 he found that the work of the Court was more than a year behind.

Taft immediately took the lead in a movement for judicial reform. He delegated to a committee of colleagues, which at the time of reporting consisted of Justices Van Devanter, McReynolds, and Sutherland, the task of drafting legislation to be enacted by Congress.   The committee drafted a bill which greatly reduced the obligatory jurisdiction of the Supreme Court.[26]   In spite of the act of 1916, a great stream of cases flowed from state and federal courts on appeal and by writ of error which, under existing law, the Supreme Court was compelled to hear.   They included cases which came into the federal courts only because of diversity of citizenship and criminal cases which might well have been left to final determination in lower courts.   The principal purpose of the new bill was to provide that many of these cases could be brought to the Supreme Court only on writ of certiorari.   Cases brought up by writ of certiorari might be heard or rejected by the Supreme Court at its discretion.   The exercise of discretion would enable the Court to review cases of broad public importance and to reject large numbers of others which were important exclusively, or principally, to the litigants.   The enactment of the bill meant that the Supreme Court was no longer available as the arbiter of all legal rights and that many cases must be determined finally in the circuit courts of appeals and other tribunals.   By such

[25] 39 Stat. 726.   For other discussions herein of the jurisdiction of the several federal courts see index references to the federal judiciary.

[26] For the history of the bill see Felix Frankfurter and James M. Landis, *The Business of the Supreme Court* (1927), chapter VII.   See also the articles by William Howard Taft, "Possible and Needed Reforms in the Administration of Civil Justice in the Federal Courts," *American Law Review*, LVII (January-February, 1923), 1-23; "Three Needed Steps of Progress," *American Bar Association Journal*, VIII (January, 1922), 34-36; "Possible and Needed Reforms in Administration of Justice in Federal Courts," *ibid.*, pp. 601-607.

an arrangement, however, the Supreme Court could better serve the country by conserving its time for the decision of cases involving determination of principles of general importance.

The draft of the bill was referred to the entire membership of the Supreme Court and was approved.  When the bill was introduced in Congress, members of the Court appeared before a subcommittee of the Senate judiciary committee to explain and defend it.  Chief Justice Taft delivered addresses, wrote letters, and lobbied in person to secure the enactment of the measure.  It became law on February 13, 1925.[27] Under the statute the Court was able to limit the number of cases heard to the time which was available for hearing them.  It caught up with the docket, and was able to keep up with it thereafter.

Chief Justice Taft rendered important service likewise in co-ordinating the work of the several federal courts.  In 1924, those courts consisted of the Supreme Court with nine justices, nine circuit courts of appeals with a total of thirty-three circuit judges, eighty-one district courts with one hundred and twenty-two district judges, and a number of territorial and other specialized courts.  The highest state courts were also, in effect, part of the federal judicial system.  Procedure in the several courts and relations among them were highly complex.  So great was the chaos prevailing in the system that the Senate committee reporting on the bill prepared by the justices of the Supreme Court remarked that "there is no civilized country in the world where the path to justice is so hard to find, so long from its beginning to its end, and so expensive to travel as in the United States."[28]  Chief Justice Taft joined with other critics of this condition in seeking a remedy.  He secured the enactment of a measure[29] which provided, among other things, for a judicial conference, made up of the Chief Justice and the senior circuit judges, who were to meet and discuss the problems of efficient handling of the work of the courts of the United States.  The conference was a step in the direction of bringing order out of chaos.[30]

THE SUPREME COURT AND GOVERNMENTAL POWERS — POWERS OF THE
     PRESIDENT

With all the diversity and interrelations of judicial decisions in the period under discussion, some semblance of independent groupings is discernible.  One grouping is of decisions dealing broadly with

[27] 43 Stat. 936.          [28] Senate Report No. 362, 68th Cong., Ist sess., p. 2.
[29] 42 Stat. 837.          [30] For discussion see Frankfurter and Landis, *op. cit.*, chapter VI.

powers of the President and with the functioning of electoral, legislative, and administrative machinery. The decisions discussed below deal in part with questions long pending, but not hitherto answered because no case had arisen to force their determination. They deal in part also with the development of new governmental activities which called for appraisal in terms of constitutionality.

The importance of the appointing and removal power increased with the expansion of federal employment and with the extension of federal regulation of economic affairs. Concerning the removal power, the most important decision during the period was that in the Myers case,[31] discussed in the preceding chapter. In 1932, the Supreme Court decided a case involving an attempt of the Senate to withdraw its confirmation of an appointment after the appointee had taken office and had acted in such a way as to displease a majority of the Senate. The officer, George Otis Smith, was one of three persons appointed members of the Federal Power Commission, after that agency had been reorganized and strengthened to curb the activities of predatory private interests in the field of electric power. One of his first official acts was to aid in removing two employees of the commission who had incurred the hostility of the so-called power trust, nominally on the ground that their removal was necessary to secure harmony among employees.

The removal of the two men caused great indignation and received a great deal of attention from the press. Senator Thomas J. Walsh secured the adoption of motions to reconsider the nominations of the three commissioners and to request the President to return the resolutions of confirmation which had been sent to him. The Attorney General advised the President that the appointments were constitutionally made and had become effective and that the return of the papers to the Senate would serve no lawful purpose because no action which the Senate could now take would disturb or operate to revoke the appointments.[32] The President, therefore, refused the request, saying, "I cannot admit the power in the Senate to encroach upon the executive functions by removal of a duly appointed executive officer under the guise of reconsideration of his nomination."

The Senate took issue with the President and voted again on the nomination of George Otis Smith, who had been designated chairman of the Federal Power Commission. A majority of the senators

[31] Myers v. United States, 272 U.S. 52 (1926).
[32] 36 *Opinions of the Attorneys General* 382.

voted in the negative. The President was notified of the action and a suit was instituted to test Smith's right to hold office. Counsel for the Senate argued that since under the Constitution the Senate had the power to make its own rules, and since the rules provided for reconsideration of an appointment within the two days of actual executive session after the vote was taken, the Senate was within its rights in reconsidering the appointments. Opposing counsel argued that the participation of the Senate in the nomination was completed when notification of confirmation was sent to the President and the Senate had no constitutional power thereafter to act on the nomination.

The Supreme Court found it unnecessary to decide the constitutional question, but held that the rules of the Senate did not provide for reconsideration of the action of the Senate after notice of confirmation had been sent to the President. Technically, since the Senate could change its rules at will, the decision was a victory for the President only in a political sense and in the case immediately at hand. No constitutional principle was asserted which gave protection to his rights in the matter of appointments.[33] The political victory, however, gave support to the President in the perennial struggle with the Senate over the appointing power.[34]

Two decisions clarified the powers of the President in dealing with bills passed by Congress. One of them involved the so-called pocket veto, and the other, the signature of bills after the adjournment of Congress. The pocket-veto case [35] arose over a bill presented to President Coolidge on June 24, 1926. The President had not taken action on the bill when Congress adjourned on July 3, and he did not act

[33] United States v. Smith, 286 U.S. 6, 28 (1932). For discussions of the case see Ernest Scott, "The Constitutional Function of the Senate in Respect to Appointments," *University of Pennsylvania Law Review*, LXXXI (November, 1932), 43-57.

[34] It is significant of trends in public policy that one of the two men dismissed by the newly appointed Federal Power Commission was engaged soon afterward by Governor Franklin D. Roosevelt, of New York, to make surveys for water-power development projects. (*New York Times*, March 13, 1931.) In the summer of 1933, after Roosevelt had become President, George Otis Smith gave up the chairmanship of the Federal Power Commission to another member at the request of the President. (*Ibid.*, July 20, 1933.) Later, also at the request of the President, he resigned from the commission altogether. (*Ibid.*, November 1, 1933.) Unlike Commissioner Humphrey, of the Federal Trade Commission, he made no attempt to enforce a legal right to the office in spite of the desire of the President to have another man in his place. Having been able to hold the office originally only because of the vigorous support of President Hoover, he perhaps thought it futile to remain in office when even the President was against him.

[35] Okanogan Indians v. United States, 279 U.S. 655 (1929).

thereafter, assuming that it was killed by pocket veto. Persons affected by the bill claimed rights under it on the ground that, since the President had not vetoed it, it had become a law.

The relevant provision of the Constitution reads, "If any bill shall not be returned by the President within ten days (Sundays excepted) after it shall have been presented to him, the same shall be a law, in like manner as if he had signed it, unless the Congress by their adjournment prevent its return, in which case it shall not be a law." [36] The Supreme Court accepted the argument of the Attorney General that the word "adjournment" included an interim adjournment, such as that which had taken place in the summer of 1926, as well as the final adjournment at the end of a Congress. The ten-day period was given to the President for the consideration of bills, said the Court, so that he might have time adequately to perform his duties concerning them. This power could not be narrowed or cut down by Congress. It frequently happened that the President was unable to consider properly all of the great mass of bills passed toward the end of a session and take the action necessary for vetoes where vetoes were warranted. [37]

The other case also dealt with bills enacted during the last days of a session of Congress. It involved the powers of the President to approve bills after Congress had adjourned. By the custom of earlier years, the President had gone to the Capitol on the last day of each session to be able to sign immediately the large number of bills passed during the last hours of a session. Action at such speed, however, meant that careful consideration of individual measures was impossible. Presidents had longed for the opportunity to take the full ten-day period to consider the legislative output even though Congress had adjourned. [38] Toward the end of a session in June, 1920, President Wilson asked his Attorney General for an opinion whether he could approve bills within the ten-day period after adjournment. The Attorney General examined the precedents and such historical evidence as was available and expressed the opinion that such approval would be valid. [39] President Wilson then signed a number of

[36] Constitution, Article I, Section 7, Clause 2.

[37] The Court also held that the word "days" meant calendar days and not legislative days. The latter interpretation, if accepted, would have meant that bills presented to the President at one session of Congress could be killed by him only by a veto message sent to the ensuing session of the same Congress.

[38] Lindsay Rogers, "The Power of the President to Sign Bills After Congress Has Adjourned," *Yale Law Journal*, XXX (November, 1920), 1-22.

[39] 32 *Opinions of the Attorneys General* 225.

bills after the adjournment of a Congress which was to assemble again before the expiration of its term. No litigation resulted from the action.

In 1931, at the end, not of a first or intermediate session of the Seventy-First Congress, but of the final session, President Hoover asked his Attorney General if he had the power to approve bills enacted by that Congress after it had adjourned and after its term of service had expired. The Attorney General answered in the affirmative, saying that there was nothing in the Constitution to the contrary and that the public interest would gain by allowing the President time to give careful consideration to all the measures submitted to him.[40] President Hoover approved a measure on March 5, 1931, and a case contesting its validity was taken to the Supreme Court. The Court upheld the contention of the Attorney General, saying, "Regard must be had to the fundamental purpose of the constitutional provision to provide appropriate opportunity for the President to consider the bills presented to him. The importance of maintaining that opportunity unimpaired increases as bills multiply."

The Court cited the statement of the Attorney General that between February 28 and March 4, 1931, two hundred and sixty-nine bills were presented to the President for his consideration, one hundred and eighty-four of which were presented during the last twenty-four hours of the session. There was no reason, based either on constitutional theory or public policy, why the time of the President for the examination and approval of bills should be cut down merely because Congress had adjourned. "No public interest would be conserved by the requirement of hurried and inconsiderate examination of bills in the closing hours of a session, with the result that bills may be approved which on further consideration would be disapproved or may fail, although on such examination they might be found to deserve approval."[41]

---

[40] 36 *Opinions of the Attorneys General* 403.

[41] Edwards *v.* United States, 286 U.S. 482, 493 (1932).

Presidential authority was upheld in two cases involving the pardoning power. In *Ex parte* Grossman, 267 U.S. 87 (1925), a lower federal court had challenged his power to pardon a man guilty of criminal contempt for which that court had sentenced him. It contended that the presidential pardon was an unconstitutional interference with the powers of the judiciary. The Supreme Court refused to recognize such a doctrine. In Biddle *v.* Perovich, 274 U.S. 480 (1927), the Supreme Court held that the President could commute a sentence even though the prisoner objected to the commutation. For general discussion of the pardoning power see W. H. Humbert, *The Pardoning Power of the President* (1941).

CONGRESSIONAL INVESTIGATIONS

As powers of the President were strengthened or confirmed by Supreme Court decisions, so also were some of what might be called the administrative powers of Congress. This was particularly true of the power to collect facts from unwilling witnesses as a basis for legislation. The power of Congress to conduct investigations and require testimony became increasingly important down through the years with the extension of regulatory legislation into diverse fields of business and industry. Only by compulsion, oftentimes, could the necessary data be secured. It was true, however, that many inquisitions conducted by congressional committees had legislation only as an incidental purpose. Investigations of alleged corruption in government agencies frequently served the dual purpose of eliminating the corruption by turning the spotlight of publicity upon it and of embarrassing politicians or political parties with which it happened to be connected. Such investigation was regarded by unsympathetic persons as unjustifiable congressional snooping into matters which were no concern of Congress at all. Since almost any fact might be sought under the pretense of seeking a basis for legislation, the latitude of congressional power to investigate was far from clearly defined.

In the moral and emotional let-down which followed the first World War, the administration of President Harding plunged into a morass of political corruption, involving bad appointments, bribery, and misappropriation of government funds. The malodorous activities of the "Ohio gang" extended even to the Department of Justice. The Attorney General, Harry M. Daugherty, resigned under fire. Early in 1924, before Daugherty resigned, the Senate passed a resolution providing for a committee of five senators to investigate the reason for the failure of the Attorney General and his subordinates to enforce the laws of the United States and to bring about the punishment of criminals. An extended investigation was held. In spite of the convenient scarcity of contemporary records in the Department of Justice, it revealed a disgracefully low order of public administration in the federal government.[42]

One stream of corruption seemed to flow through the Midland

---

[42] Senate select committee on investigation of the Attorney General, *Hearings* on S. Res. 157, 68th Cong., 1st sess., Parts 1-11. For accounts of the governmental scandals of the Harding period see Samuel Hopkins Adams, *Incredible Era, The Life and Times of Warren Gamaliel Harding* (1939); Harry M. Daugherty and Thomas Dixon, *The Inside Story of the Harding Tragedy* (1932); Mark Sullivan, *Our Times* (6 vols., 1900-1925), VI (1935), chapters 11-15.

National Bank of Washington Court House, Ohio, which was under the management of Mally S. Daugherty, a brother of the Attorney General. The Senate committee was eager to question the banker and to get access to the records of the bank. By subpoena it directed him to appear before the committee in Washington. He refused to comply. Thereafter, two members of the committee went to Washington Court House and summoned Daugherty to appear before them at their hotel. This also he refused to do. The committee reported these refusals to the Senate and recommended that a warrant be issued to bring him before the bar of the Senate. The warrant was issued and he was taken into custody. A federal district court ordered his release on the ground that the Senate exceeded its powers under the Constitution in directing the investigation and in ordering his attachment.[43]

The Supreme Court, emphasizing the fact that only the person of Daugherty was involved by the subpoena and not the books, records, and papers of the bank, reversed the lower court and sustained the power of the Senate. The Court was of the opinion that the power of inquiry, with process to enforce it, was an essential and appropriate auxiliary to the legislative function. A legislative body could not legislate wisely or effectively in the absence of information respecting the conditions which the legislation was expected to affect or change. The court below had thought the attempt to compel Daugherty to testify unconstitutional because the investigation was not in aid of the legislative function. The Supreme Court found the administration of the Department of Justice a legitimate subject of legislation. "The only legitimate object the Senate could have in ordering the investigation," it said, "was to aid it in legislating; and we think the subject matter was such that the presumption should be indulged that this was the real object." [44]

There is irony in the fact that former Attorney General Daugherty secured from his brother, and then burned, the relevant records of the bank before the Senate could get them and before they could be used

---

[43] *Ex parte* Daugherty, 299 Fed. 620 (1924).

[44] McGrain *v.* Daugherty, 273 U.S. 135, 178 (1927). For discussion of the case see James M. Landis, "Constitutional Limitations on the Congressional Power of Investigation," *Harvard Law Review*, XL (December, 1926), 153-221; C. S. Potts, "Power of Legislative Bodies to Punish for Contempt," *University of Pennsylvania Law Review*, LXXIV (May, 1926), 691-725, 780-829; "The Power of Congressional Investigating Committee to Issue Subpoena Duces Tecum," *Yale Law Journal*, XLV (1936), 1503, reprinted in *Selected Essays on Constitutional Law*, IV (1938), 1379. For a general discussion of investigating committees see Marshall E. Dimock, *Congressional Investigating Committees* (1929); George Galloway, "The Investigative Function of Congress," *American Political Science Review*, XXI (February, 1927), 47-70.

in a criminal case against him.[45] So much time was consumed by the litigation that his brother was never compelled to testify before the Senate committee. The right of the Senate which the Supreme Court upheld, important as it was for future investigations, proved barren in the case at hand.

The oil scandals of the Harding period produced another case involving the power of the Senate to compel testimony. Interests headed by Harry F. Sinclair had secured from the Interior Department, through the notorious Teapot Dome oil leases, immensely valuable property. The Senate authorized a committee to make a detailed study of the land laws of the United States and of the leases of public property to discover whether additional legislation was necessary. Sinclair appeared before the committee a number of times. On a final occasion, however, he refused to give further evidence. One reason offered was that the questions asked related to his personal affairs. Another was that the facts which would be disclosed by the answers would thereby be made available for use in suits authorized by Congress in connection with the oil leases. Because of his refusal to testify, he was punished under an act of Congress of long standing which made it a misdemeanor to refuse to give testimony sought by either house of Congress.

The Supreme Court unanimously sustained the conviction, while making it clear that, in giving evidence before legislative bodies, private individuals could not be compelled to testify as to matters not pertinent to the powers of legislative bodies. The Court considered the questions that had been asked fully pertinent to the subject of legislation, even though the facts gathered might be used in embarrassing litigation as well.[46] Sinclair spent three months in jail for his refusal to testify. Yet, as far as this case was concerned, the government had won an empty victory. It was in 1924 that the refusal to testify took place. The decision of the Supreme Court was not announced until 1929. During the five-year period Sinclair had been able to withhold from the government evidence necessary to the effective conduct of the investigation.[47]

[45] New York Times, September 25, 1926.

[46] Sinclair v. United States, 279 U.S. 263 (1929).

[47] Robert E. Cushman, "Constitutional Law in 1928-29," American Political Science Review, XXIV (February, 1930), 72-74. For further troubles of Sinclair arising out of the same litigation see Sinclair v. United States, 279 U.S. 749 (1929).

In Barry v. United States ex rel. Cunningham, 279 U.S. 597 (1929), decided at the same term as the Sinclair cases, the Supreme Court upheld the power of the Senate to arrest and bring before it a man whose testimony was desired in connection with the

CONTROL OF ELECTIONS

One of the perennial tasks of representative government is that of protecting elections from corruption.  The language of the Constitution seemed to imply that the control of election of members of the Senate and the House of Representatives was to be exercised predominantly by the states, with corrective powers in Congress.  The specific language is, "The times, places, and manner of holding elections for senators and representatives shall be prescribed in each state by the legislature thereof; but the Congress may at any time by law make or alter such regulations, except as to the place of choosing senators." [48]    After the Civil War, and partly because of conditions connected with that war, Congress enacted a number of regulations of electoral practices.  The power of Congress was upheld,[49] but additional measures were enacted in later years.  One of the problems in determining the extent of the power of Congress over elections lay in the fact that many of the evils to be eliminated existed, not merely in connection with general elections at which federal officers were finally chosen, but also in connection with primary elections.   Originally the latter had been not governmental elections at all, but devices by which privately organized political parties chose the candidates whom they would support at formal elections.  Corruption in primary elections was especially important in states in which political machines in both great political parties, by the use of huge sums of money and resort to corrupt practices, nominated machine candidates, none of whom represented a choice of the people.  Primary elections were of even greater importance in states dominated by a single political party to such an extent that the results of primary elections in effect determined the candidates who would be chosen to office.  The states were finding it necessary to exercise more and more control over proceedings.

The question whether the regulatory power of Congress extended to primary elections at which United States senators were nominated was argued before the Supreme Court in 1921 in connection with the election of Truman H. Newberry to the Senate.  Newberry was accused of violating the Federal Corrupt Practices Act of 1910 by ex-

election of William S. Vare, of Pennsylvania, to the Senate.  The power in this case was based, not on the power to legislate, but on the power of the Senate to judge of the elections, returns, and qualifications of its own members.

[48] Constitution, Article I, Section 4.

[49] See *Ex parte* Siebold, 100 U.S. 371 (1880); *Ex parte* Clarke, 100 U.S. 399 (1880); *Ex parte* Yarbrough, 110 U.S. 651 (1884); *Ex parte* Coy, 127 U.S. 731 (1888).

cessive expenditures in a primary election. Four justices, with Justice McReynolds as their spokesman, took the position that the power of Congress to regulate elections did not extend back to the regulation of the nominating process.[50] Four other justices argued for a much broader power in Congress to reach back to cover the whole process of election, including the machinery of nomination. One justice took a qualified position based on the fact that the mode of electing senators had changed since the statute involved was enacted and refused to pass on the general principle. The question of the extent of the power of Congress was therefore left unsettled, but the impression prevailed that Congress could not regulate primaries until twenty years later, when in United States v. Classic [51] the Supreme Court removed the doubt by holding that primary elections were subject to federal control.[52]

In the Federal Corrupt Practices Act of 1925,[53] Congress extended federal regulation to the choice of presidential electors who had usually been regarded as state officers rather than federal officers. The Supreme Court upheld the statute, denying that it invaded any exclusive power. While presidential electors were not officers or agents of the federal government, they did exercise federal functions. The importance of the election of the President and its relationship to and effect upon the welfare and safety of the whole people could not be too strongly stated.

> To say that Congress is without power to pass appropriate legislation to safeguard such an election from the improper use of money to influence the result is to deny to the nation in a vital particular the power of self-protection. Congress, undoubtedly, possesses that power, as it possesses every other power essential to preserve the departments and institutions of the general government from impairment or destruction, whether threatened by force or by corruption.[54]

[50] Newberry v. United States, 256 U.S. 232 (1921). For background see Spencer Erwin, *Henry Ford vs. Truman H. Newberry* (1935).

[51] 315 U.S. 299. For discussion of the effects of the earlier decision see House Report No. 721, 68th Cong., 1st sess.; Louise Overacker, *Money in Elections* (1932), chapters X and XI; James K. Pollock, Jr., *Party Campaign Funds* (1926), pp. 202 ff.; Thomas Reed Powell, "Major Constitutional Issues in 1920-1921," *Political Science Quarterly*, XXXVI (1921), 472.

[52] For recent cases dealing with race discrimination in party primaries, see the latter part of chapter 15. On the general subject of the Negro in southern politics, see Paul Lewinson, *Race, Class and Party* (1932).

[53] 43 Stat. 1070.

[54] Burroughs v. United States, 290 U.S. 534, 545 (1934).

To go briefly beyond the period here under discussion, the Supreme Court has upheld later statutes, in particular the so-called Hatch Acts of 1939 and 1940, which sought to protect the purity of elections by limiting the political activities of the great mass of workers for the federal government [55] and of workers for states when engaged in expenditure of federal funds.[56] The decisions stress the importance of the issues involved. It is essential for the preservation of democratic government that government workers linked with a particular political party shall not have the power to perpetuate that party in office. On the other hand, it is a serious matter to limit the political privileges of millions of American citizens merely because they are employed by government. The matter is serious both for the workers themselves and for the country which is to some extent deprived of their political services.

To summarize with respect to the period between World War I and the New Deal, appointments were made to the Supreme Court during this period which had a far-reaching impact on the development of our constitutional law. With respect to exercise of powers by executive and legislative branches the Court took for the most part a lenient view, in some instances strengthening the federal government at the expense of the states. It paved the way for broader operations by the federal government, in spite of philosophies held by some of the justices in opposition to the expansion of federal power.

[55] United Public Workers *v.* Mitchell, 330 U.S. 75 (1947).
[56] Oklahoma *v.* United States Civil Service Commission, 330 U.S. 127 (1947).

# CHAPTER 32

# PERSONAL RIGHTS AND LIBERTIES

THE PERIOD between the first World War and the New Deal had its share of cases dealing with personal rights and liberties. Many of the controversies grew in some manner out of the war and the disturbances which followed. A major portion of them involved conflicts between capital and labor. Some of them, particularly those involving the rights of the accused, were connected with the enforcement of legislation based on the prohibition amendment. The social cleavages which the controversies represented were regarded as serious, but not as precipitating an immediate crisis. They represented, or seemed to represent, the varied and perennial struggles by which democracy works itself out. Many of them had repercussions in the ensuing decade, the era of the New Deal, and gave rise to the subject matter of chapters which follow herein. The Supreme Court decisions of the period show the reaching-out of the hand of government both to curtail the liberties of the individual in the interest of society and to protect him against the exercise of arbitrary power. The issues involved were issues both of political and social philosophy and of raw economic interest. A number of decisions in the field widened the area of disagreement between the conservative majority and the liberal minority of the Supreme Court. Because of their emotional content, the decisions aided in drawing the rift in the Court to the attention of the people.

CIVIL LIBERTIES AND DUE PROCESS OF LAW

The series of important civil-liberties cases which arose out of violation of World-War statutes was discussed in an earlier chapter.[1] During or immediately after the war, many states attempted to curb radical, and often criminal, activities by the enactment of what were

[1] Chapter 26.

generally known as criminal syndicalism laws.[2]  A number of these laws resulted in decisions affecting civil liberties and raised the important constitutional question whether the due-process clause of the Fourteenth Amendment prohibited interference with freedom of speech by the states.

The first Supreme Court decision in the field arose, not under one of the criminal syndicalism laws of this period, but under a criminal anarchy law of New York, enacted in 1902, which contained similar provisions.  It placed a ban upon language and publications which advocated the overthrow of organized government by force.  Benjamin Gitlow, a member of the left-wing section of the Socialist party, was indicted for the publication and distribution of what was known as the "Left-Wing Manifesto" and of other allegedly subversive documents.  In passing upon the constitutionality of the state law, the Supreme Court assumed, for the first time in any decision, "that freedom of speech and of the press — which are protected by the First Amendment from abridgment by Congress — are among the fundamental personal rights and 'liberties' protected by the due-process clause of the Fourteenth Amendment from impairment by the states."[3]  Nevertheless, the right was not absolute, said a majority of the Supreme Court, and the New York law was constitutional as applied to Gitlow.  Even though he had indulged in only theoretical advocacy of revolution, "the state cannot reasonably be required to measure the danger from every such utterance in the nice balance of a jeweler's scale.  A single revolutionary spark may kindle a fire that, smoldering for a time, may burst into a sweeping and destructive conflagration."[4]  The Court quoted with approval the statement of another court that "if the state were compelled to wait until the apprehended danger became certain, then its right to protect itself would come into being simultaneously with the overthrow of the government, when there would be neither prosecuting officers nor courts for the enforcement of the law."[5]

As it had done already in two cases arising under federal law,[6] the

[2] See E. Foster Dowell, *A History of Criminal Syndicalism Legislation in the United States* (1939).

[3] Gitlow *v.* New York, 268 U.S. 652, 666 (1925).  For a discussion of the interpretation given in this case see Charles Warren, "The New 'Liberty' under the 14th Amendment," *Harvard Law Review*, XXXIX (February, 1926), 431; reprinted, *Selected Essays on Constitutional Law*, II, 237-266.

[4] *Ibid.*, p. 669.     [5] *Ibid.*, pp. 669-670.

[6] Abrams *v.* United States, 250 U.S. 616 (1919), and Schaefer *v.* United States, 251 U.S. 466 (1920).

Court limited the "clear-and-present danger" doctrine, stated in an earlier case, where it was said that "the question in every case is whether the words used are used in such circumstances and are of such a nature as to create a clear and present danger that they will bring about the substantive evils" [7] which government had the power to prevent. Justice Holmes, who as spokesman for a unanimous Court had phrased that doctrine, dissented in the Gitlow case, with the concurrence of Justice Brandeis, on the ground that the Gitlow decision departed from this criterion. In reply to the statement that the manifesto published by Gitlow was an incitement, he declared that every idea was an incitement. Furthermore, he contended, "If, in the long run, the beliefs expressed in proletarian dictatorship are destined to be accepted by the dominant forces of the community, the only meaning of free speech is that they should be given their chance and have their way." [8]

People who were generally classified as liberals deplored the narrow interpretation of constitutional rights sponsored by the majority of the Court and applauded the dissent of Justice Holmes. On the other hand, the decision was approved by the many people who were concerned about the growth of radicalism among the workers of the country.

The issue was revived some two years later when the Supreme Court decided another case based on the criminal syndicalism law of California. The alleged criminal involved was Charlotte Anita Whitney, a niece of Justice Field who had served on the Supreme Court for more than thirty-four years, and a member of a conservative and wealthy family. Miss Whitney had devoted her life to promoting the welfare of the laboring class and had been intimately involved in the organization of the Communist Labor party of California which advocated governmental change by revolution. The Supreme Court unanimously held that the statute as applied in this case was not unconstitutional. For himself and Justice Holmes, however, Justice Brandeis wrote a concurring opinion, in effect restating the doctrine of clear and present danger. "Those who won our independence by revolution," he declared, "were not cowards. They did not fear political change. They did not exalt order at the cost of liberty." [9] Although he found evidence of criminal conspiracy sufficient to justify upholding the conviction, he could not agree with the majority of the

[7] Schenck v. United States, 249 U.S. 47, 52 (1919).          [8] 268 U.S. 673.
[9] Whitney v. California, 274 U.S. 357, 377 (1927).

Court that merely assembling with a political party that had been formed to advocate the desirability of a proletarian revolution by mass action at some date necessarily far in the future was not a right within the protection of the Fourteenth Amendment. The case terminated in a pardon granted by the governor of California.[10]

In the meantime, in 1923, the Supreme Court held unconstitutional a Nebraska statute which forbade teaching any subject in any school in the state in any language other than English. The man whom the state sought to punish under the act had taught reading in the German language in a parochial school. Mere knowledge of the German language, said Justice McReynolds for the Court, could not reasonably be regarded as harmful. The right of the teacher to teach the language, and of parents to engage him to instruct their children, was within the liberty protected by the Fourteenth Amendment.[11] Similar statutes of Iowa and Ohio were also held unconstitutional. The dissenting justices in the several cases were Justices Holmes and Sutherland, a couple seldom found working together except when the Court was united.[12] Two years later, the Supreme Court relied heavily upon the decisions in the foreign-language cases when it held unconstitutional an Oregon statute which, if enforced, would have destroyed parochial and other private schools in the state through a requirement that all children between the ages of eight and sixteen years should attend the public schools.[13] The decision was unanimous.

One characteristic of the period of social disturbance which followed the first World War was the effort of civilian groups such as the Ku Klux Klan to assume authority by taking the enforcement of law into their own hands and, in effect, by making laws of their own. In some states the government resisted the encroachment of the Klan and other organizations, while in other states officials were themselves active in organizations nominally for the promotion of Americanism. In Arizona, in 1919, a group of people including some American citizens were expelled from the state by a lawless band. The state failed to punish the offenders. An attempt was made to punish them under a federal statute, but the Supreme Court held that under the Constitution the federal government had not the power to protect the de-

[10] For other criminal syndicalism cases decided at the same term of the Supreme Court see Fiske v. Kansas, 274 U.S. 380 (1927), and Burns v. United States, 274 U.S. 328 (1927).

[11] Meyer v. Nebraska, 262 U.S. 390 (1923).

[12] Bartels v. Iowa, 262 U.S. 404, 412 (1923).

[13] Pierce v. Society of Sisters, 268 U.S. 510 (1925).

portees, even though they were American citizens. That power was lodged exclusively in the states.[14]

Those people who feared that Chief Justice Hughes might become the mouthpiece of ultra-conservatism on his return to the bench were reassured in 1931 with respect to freedom of speech and of the press when he wrote opinions of the Court in two important cases. The first had to do with a California "red-flag law," which forbade the display of a red flag, either as a symbol of opposition to organized government or as a stimulus to anarchistic action or as an aid to seditious propaganda. A young woman, Yetta Stromberg, was convicted for violation of the law. As supervisor in a children's camp operated by the Young Communist League, she directed a daily ceremony in which the flag of Soviet Russia and of the Communist party was saluted by children and in which she received a pledge of allegiance in a manner and language approximating the procedure followed by school-children throughout the country in saluting the American flag. The scope of the statute was not properly limited and the Court held it a denial of the liberty guaranteed by the due-process clause of the Fourteenth Amendment. Said Chief Justice Hughes:

> The maintenance of the opportunity for free political discussion to the end that government may be responsive to the will of the people and that changes may be obtained by lawful means, an opportunity essential to the security of the Republic, is a fundamental principle of our constitutional system. A statute which, upon its face, and as authoritatively construed, is so vague and indefinite as to permit the punishment of the fair use of this opportunity is repugnant to the guaranty of liberty contained in the Fourteenth Amendment.[15]

The other important case decided at the same term of the Court turned on the constitutionality of a Minnesota law which provided that a newspaper or magazine publishing malicious, scandalous, or defamatory material might be abated as a nuisance. The measure

[14] United States v. Wheeler, 254 U.S. 281 (1920). In attempt to establish control over the Ku Klux Klan, New York, in 1923, enacted a civil-rights law, requiring organizations like the Klan to file sworn copies of constitutions, bylaws, rules, regulations, oaths of memberships, rosters of membership, and lists of officers. Organizations like those of the Masons, Odd Fellows, and Knights of Columbus were exempted. The Supreme Court held that the law did not unconstitutionally deprive a man of a right to belong to a secret organization or deny him the equal protection of the laws through the exemption of other secret organizations. New York ex rel. Bryant v. Zimmerman, 278 U.S. 63 (1928).

[15] Stromberg v. California, 283 U.S. 359, 369 (1931). Justices McReynolds and Butler dissented. See George Foster, Jr., "The 1931 Personal Liberties Cases," *New York University Law Quarterly Review*, IX (September, 1931), 64-81; reprinted, *Selected Essays on Constitutional Law*, II, 1080-1098.

was said to have been sponsored in the legislature by a member who sought to silence an editor who was attacking him.[16]

The statute was used to stop the publication of a Minneapolis newspaper, evidently a scandal sheet of a low order, which had delivered a series of gross attacks upon local government officials and others. The *Chicago Tribune* and a newspaper publishers' association, realizing the threat of censorship for all newspapers if the statute were upheld, came to the defense of the editor whose paper had been suppressed. The Supreme Court divided five to four on the constitutionality of the law. Chief Justice Hughes, as spokesman for the majority, found it unconstitutional. Summarizing procedure under the statute, he declared that public authorities might call a newspaper to account for conducting a business of publishing scandalous and defamatory matter, and that "unless the owner or publisher is able and disposed to bring competent evidence to satisfy the judge that the charges [made by the newspaper] are true and are published with good motives and for justifiable ends, his newspaper or periodical is suppressed and further publication is made punishable as a contempt. This is of the essence of censorship." [17]

The Chief Justice was concerned primarily, not with the punishment of an editor or publisher for publication of libelous materials, but with the fact that a single violation of the statute invoked the threat of permanent suppression of a periodical, whatever its contents thereafter. The statute as applied, therefore, was held to be an infringement of the liberty of the press guaranteed by the Fourteenth Amendment. Although Justices Van Devanter, McReynolds, Sutherland, and Butler protested against use of the Constitution to give partial immunity to any person guilty of offenses such as those described, the significant fact was that a majority of the Court had taken a vigorous stand in defense of freedom of speech and of the press against state interference.

### RIGHTS OF PERSONS SUSPECTED OF CRIME

Attempts to secure evidence of crimes and to bring about conviction are restrained by constitutional provisions, some of which apply to the federal government and others to the states. Unreasonable

---

[16] *New York Times*, January 12, 1930.

[17] Near *v.* Minnesota *ex rel.* Olson, 283 U.S. 697, 713 (1931). See George Foster, Jr., *op. cit.* See also Harry Schulman, "The Supreme Court's Attitude Toward Liberty of Contract and Freedom of Speech," *Yale Law Journal,* XLI (December, 1931), 262-271; reprinted, *Selected Essays on Constitutional Law,* II, 1098-1106.

searches and seizures, compulsory self-incrimination, jury trial, equal protection of the laws, and due process of law were focal points of constitutional controversy during the period. In 1920, for example, the Supreme Court placed a ban upon arbitrary methods used by the federal government for securing evidence. Two suspects were taken into custody and, while they were detained, representatives of the Department of Justice and the United States marshal, "without a shadow of authority," seized books and papers from their office. Photographs and copies of damaging documents were made, after which, in recognition of the illegality of the seizure, the originals were returned. On the basis of the information gathered, however, subpoenas were then issued lawfully to compel the reproduction of the originals. The Supreme Court refused to accept an interpretation of the search-and-seizures provision of the Fourth Amendment which, it said in the language of Justice Holmes, reduced the Fourth Amendment to a form of words:

> The essence of a provision forbidding the acquisition of evidence in a certain way is that not merely evidence so acquired shall not be used before the Court, but that it shall not be used at all. Of course this does not mean that the facts thus obtained become sacred and inaccessible. If knowledge of them is gained from an independent source they may be proved like any others, but the knowledge gained by the government's own wrong cannot be used by it in the way proposed.[18]

By contrast, when the government found it extremely difficult to cope with the illegal transportation of liquor by automobile, the Supreme Court relaxed the constitutional barrier to searches and seizures without warrant.[19] In a wire-tapping case, decided by a vote of five to four, the Court sanctioned the power of the government to make and use records of conversations over telephones secretly heard for the purpose of securing conviction. Justice Holmes's dissenting characterization of such methods as "dirty business" which the government ought not to employ had no immediate effect upon the majority interpretation of the Constitution.[20]

A number of decisions related to the subject of jury trial. The Court held that a defendant had the privilege of waiving his constitu-

---

[18] Silverthorne Lumber Co. *v.* United States, 251 U.S. 385, 392 (1920). Among others see also the important case of Gouled *v.* United States, 255 U.S. 298 (1921).

[19] Carroll *v.* United States, 267 U.S. 132 (1925).

[20] Olmstead *v.* United States, 277 U.S. 438 (1928). For discussion see chapter 29.

tional right of trial by jury in a federal court. The effect of constitutional provisions, said the Court, was not to establish trial by jury as an indispensable part of the frame of government, but only to guarantee to the accused the right to such a trial.[21] The Court held in another case that driving an automobile at a forbidden rate of speed constituted so serious a crime that one charged with it must be accorded a jury trial on demand rather than dealt with as the perpetrator of a minor violation of law which could be tried summarily without a jury.[22]

The procedural rights of Negroes came up for consideration again and again. The Court held that a Negro on trial for killing a white man was entitled to have jurors asked whether they had racial prejudice which might prevent the giving of a fair and impartial verdict.[23] In what was known as the second Scottsboro case the Supreme Court held that a Negro was denied equal protection of the laws when brought to trial before a jury of white men in a county where there were large numbers of colored inhabitants and where the fact that Negroes were never called to serve on juries demonstrated that they were systematically excluded. The Court did not insist on having concrete evidence of the exclusion of Negroes in this case, but drew its deductions from the fact that Negroes had never been called to serve.[24] The first of the Scottsboro cases, decided three years earlier, had dealt, not with jury trial, but with questions as to whether Negroes on trial for a capital offense had been denied due process of law guaranteed by the Fourteenth Amendment in that they had not been properly represented by counsel. The Supreme Court held that representation by counsel was guaranteed by the Constitution and that the right had been denied.[25] In these cases, and in others decided during the years which followed, the Supreme Court proved a staunch defender of the rights of Negroes in crises in which race prejudice might be expected to operate against them. The principles which the Court announced, however, were applicable, not only to Negroes, but to all persons in like situations.

[21] Patton v. United States, 281 U.S. 276 (1930).

[22] District of Columbia v. Colts, 282 U.S. 63 (1930).

[23] Aldridge v. United States, 283 U.S. 308 (1931).

[24] Norris v. Alabama, 294 U.S. 587 (1935). See "Scottsboro — What Now?" New Republic, LXXXII (April 17, 1935), 270.

[25] Powell v. Alabama, 287 U.S. 45 (1932). For demonstration of the fact that the right is limited, however, see Betts v. Brady, 316 U.S. 455 (1942).

THE RIGHTS OF ALIENS

In any time of national crisis the position of aliens in the country is extremely uncomfortable. This was true of enemy aliens during the first World War and, to a lesser extent, of other aliens who for any reason became the subject of suspicion. After the war, the attitude of hostility originally directed toward the enemy was concentrated upon radicals, many of whom were aliens, who sponsored doctrines of communism or of anarchy. A federal statute of 1920 facilitated the deportation of undesirable aliens by expanding the powers of the Secretary of Labor. A case arising under the statute was taken to the Supreme Court. It involved the deportation of certain aliens whose undesirability was demonstrated by their having been convicted for the violation of certain war statutes. The aliens claimed that the statute of 1920 provided additional punishment for acts which had been committed before the statute was passed and that it was unconstitutional because it fell within the category of *ex post facto* laws. The Supreme Court, through Chief Justice Taft, rejected the contention. It was well settled, he said, that deportation, while it might be burdensome and severe for the alien, was not punishment. "The right to expel aliens is a sovereign power, necessary to the safety of the country, and only limited by treaty obligations in respect thereto, entered into with other governments." [26] The statute did not increase the punishment for the crimes of which the aliens had been convicted. It only sought to rid the country of persons who had shown by their careers that their continued presence here would not make for the safety or welfare of society.

Alien problems of a different kind arose in the western part of the United States, where Chinese and Japanese competed in large numbers with white farmers and white laborers. Congress had long recognized the problem of Chinese competition by statutes and treaties under which the immigration of Chinese laborers was curtailed. By the Immigration Act of 1924 it brought the immigration of Japanese laborers almost to an end, thereby promoting a great deal of ill-will in Japan. Many of the states, not content with such federal control as had been exercised, passed laws to prevent ownership or leasing of land by Oriental aliens. The constitutionality of such laws was challenged as deprivation of due process and of equal protection of the laws.

The first of these measures to be passed upon by the Supreme Court

[26] Mahler *v.* Eby, 264 U.S. 32, 39 (1924).

was a law of the state of Washington which forbade all aliens, except those who had declared their intention to become citizens of the United States, to own or acquire any interest in land within the state. The penalty was forfeiture of the land to the state and criminal punishment of those conveying the title or interest in violation of the law. The law applied to Japanese, Chinese, and other Oriental aliens, since under federal statutes they were not entitled to become citizens and could not file legal declarations of intention to become citizens. The Supreme Court differentiated the right of the alien resident to earn a living by following ordinary occupations, which had been protected in an earlier case,[27] from the right to own land. While Congress had exclusive jurisdiction over immigration, naturalization, and the disposal of the public domain, said Justice Butler for the Court, each state, in the absence of any treaty provision to the contrary, had power to deny to aliens the right to own land within its borders. A law distinguishing between aliens who had declared their intention of becoming citizens and those who had not so declared provided for no new classification, said the Court, and did not deny equal protection of the laws.[28] In other cases the Court upheld legislation enacted in California to prevent the ownership or control of land and the ownership of stock in a corporation holding land for agricultural purposes by aliens ineligible to citizenship, without reference to the right of eligible aliens who had not declared their intention of becoming citizens.[29]

The beliefs of aliens concerning the duties of citizenship when they sought the privilege of naturalization came under the close scrutiny of the federal courts. In 1929, the Supreme Court reviewed a decision denying United States citizenship to a woman, forty-nine years of age, who said that for conscientious reasons she would not take up arms in defense of the country if called upon to do so. She was a woman of considerable intellectual attainment, but she admitted that she was an uncompromising pacifist and that she had no sense of nationalism, but only a cosmic consciousness of belonging to the human family. Although the question was not one of constitutionality, but of administrative interpretation of federal statutes dealing with naturalization, the Court went back to constitutional principles, nevertheless, as a basis for statutory interpretation. Speaking for the

[27] Truax v. Raich, 239 U.S. 33, 42 (1915).

[28] Terrace v. Thompson, 263 U.S. 197 (1923).

[29] Porterfield v. Webb, 263 U.S. 225 (1923); Webb v. O'Brien, 263 U.S. 313 (1923); and Frick v. Webb, 263 U.S. 326 (1923). See also Cockrill v. California, 268 U.S. 258 (1925).

majority of the Court in a six-to-three division, Justice Butler declared that the duty to defend our government against all enemies was a fundamental principle of the Constitution. The common defense was one of the purposes for which the Constitution was ordained and established. Pacifists who lacked a sense of nationalism, he said, were likely to be incapable of the attachment for and devotion to the principles of our Constitution that were required of aliens seeking naturalization.[30]

Justices Holmes, Brandeis, and Sanford dissented. Justice Holmes deplored the rejection of a person who, he thought, was obviously more than ordinarily desirable as a citizen of the United States. He said:

> Surely it cannot show lack of attachment to the principles of the Constitution that she thinks that it can be improved. I suppose that most intelligent people think that it might be. Her particular improvement looking to the abolition of war seems to me not materially different in its bearing on this case from a wish to establish cabinet government as in England, or a single house, or one term of seven years for the President. To touch a more burning question, only a judge mad with partisanship would exclude because the applicant thought that the Eighteenth Amendment should be repealed.[31]

If there was any principle of the Constitution that more imperatively called for attachment than any other, he continued, it was the principle of free thought —

> not free thought for those who agree with us, but freedom for the thought that we hate. I think that we should adhere to that principle with regard to admission into, as well as to life within, this country.[32]

## THE RIGHTS OF LABOR

Supreme Court decisions affected the rights of labor in many fields. An important decision had to do with the power of government to fix minimum wages for women. Some cases involved the use of federal anti-trust legislation to curb the activities of labor organizations.

---

[30] United States v. Schwimmer, 279 U.S. 644 (1929). See Outlook, CLII (June 12, 1929), 250.

[31] Ibid., p. 654.

[32] Ibid., p. 655. In two other cases, United States v. Macintosh, 283 U.S. 605 (1931), and United States v. Bland, 283 U.S. 636 (1931), the Supreme Court, by five-to-four decisions again interpreted the naturalization laws so as to exclude conscientious objectors. In 1946 after sweeping changes in Court personnel, the Schwimmer, Macintosh and Bland cases were all overruled. Girouard v. United States, 328 U.S. 61.

Others dealt with the use of injunctions in labor disputes and still others with federal machinery for solving the problems of railroad labor.

Since the beginning of the twentieth century, many states had enacted laws to protect workers by regulating the conditions of their employment. The measures included workmen's-compensation legislation, safety-appliance legislation, legislation affecting the health of workers, regulation of hours of employment, and, to a limited extent, regulation of minimum wages. The enactment of such legislation involved, not merely political struggles, but struggles all the way along to win judicial sanction in terms of the Constitution. The legislation had to be justified in terms of legitimate exercise of the police powers of the states in order to avoid the prohibition of the Fourteenth Amendment against taking liberty or property without due process of law. The line of constitutional demarcation was never clearly defined. It will be recalled that in the Lochner case,[33] decided in 1905, the majority of the Supreme Court, arguing in terms of liberty of contract, had invalidated a state law establishing the maximum number of hours for which men working in bakeshops might be employed. In 1908, however, in Muller v. Oregon,[34] the Supreme Court upheld an Oregon law restricting the number of hours which women might be required to work in certain forms of employment, basing its decision largely upon the effects which long hours of labor were thought to have upon women and, through them, upon the physical well-being of the race as a whole. In 1917, after many changes in the personnel of the Court, it sustained, in Bunting v. Oregon,[35] a law limiting the hours of labor of any person, whether man or woman, engaged in certain forms of employment. The Lochner case was completely ignored, and it was widely assumed that to all intents and purposes the case had been overruled.

It was then an established principle of American economic and legal thought that governmental regulation of wages, as of other prices, constituted a more serious invasion of the liberty guaranteed by the Constitution than other forms of regulation such as those of hours and conditions of employment. The state of Oregon, however, a leader in this as in other forms of social legislation, sought to enforce

---

[33] Lochner v. New York, 198 U.S. 45 (1905).

[34] 208 U.S. 412 (1908). See Felix Frankfurter, "Hours of Labor and Realism in Constitutional Law," Harvard Law Review, XXIX (February, 1916), 353.

[35] 243 U.S. 426 (1917).

a minimum-wage law applicable only to women, on grounds similar to those successfully urged in the Muller case with reference to maximum hours of employment for women. The highest state court upheld the measure. Before the Supreme Court the case was first argued in 1914, then again in 1916, and a third time in 1917. It was decided at a time when the Court had a full membership of nine, but when only eight members were eligible to vote, Justice Brandeis having been of counsel in the case in earlier years. The Court divided four to four.[36] The effect was to sanction the decision of the state court as far as this case was concerned, but without determining the ultimate policy of the Supreme Court.

In 1923, the Court decided another minimum-wage case, Adkins v. Children's Hospital.[37] The case dealt with an act of Congress establishing minimum wages for women and children in the District of Columbia, but the importance of the decision was nation-wide, in that the principles were applicable to state legislation on the same subject. Felix Frankfurter filed a long, factual brief to demonstrate the alleged effects upon women occasioned by employment for inadequate wages. A number of additional changes in the personnel of the Court had taken place since the four-to-four decision in the Oregon case. With three justices dissenting and Justice Brandeis declining to participate, the Court held the statute unconstitutional. A careful study of the position of various members of the Court on the constitutionality of minimum-wage legislation has convinced one commentator that, had the case come before the Court at almost any other time within a considerable period, the decision would have been in favor of the constitutionality of the law. In his language, "The unconstitutionality of minimum-wage legislation has been dictated by the calendar rather than by the Constitution."[38] Justice Sutherland, almost always an opponent of legislation restricting the freedom of business enterprise, wrote the opinion of the Court. He revived the arguments of the Lochner case and held that women of mature age

[36] Stettler v. O'Hara, 243 U.S. 629 (1917). For further discussion of these several cases see chapter 25.

[37] 261 U.S. 525 (1923).

[38] Thomas Reed Powell, "The Judiciality of Minimum-Wage Legislation," *Harvard Law Review*, XXXVII (March, 1924), 545-548; reprinted, *Selected Essays on Constitutional Law*, II, 716-732. For further discussion of the decision see Edward Berman, "The Supreme Court and the Minimum Wage," *Journal of Political Economy*, XXXI (December, 1923), 852-856; "The Supreme Court Supplants Congress," *Nation*, CXVI (April 25, 1923), 484; "An Appeal from the Supreme Court," *New Republic*, XXXIV (April 25, 1923), 228; Francis Bowers Sayre, "The Minimum-Wage Decision," *Survey*, L (May 1, 1923), 150-151, 172.

had a right to make contracts of employment which could not be limited by legislation fixing minimum wages.

Chief Justice Taft and Justices Holmes and Sanford dissented. Taft had always supposed that the Lochner case had been overruled *sub silentio* by the Bunting case. He saw no reason why wages should have greater freedom from regulation than hours. One was the multiplier, he said, and the other the multiplicand. Holmes said the only objection that could be urged against the present law was found "within the vague contours of the Fifth Amendment," [39] and he considered the enactment clearly within the power of Congress. The earlier decisions upon the liberty guaranteed by the due-process clauses of the Constitution, he argued, went no farther than an unpretentious assertion of the liberty to follow the ordinary callings. Later, "that innocuous generality was expanded into the dogma, liberty of contract." [40] Pretty much all law, he remarked, consisted in forbidding men to do some things that they wanted to do, and contract was no more exempt from law than other acts. Like Chief Justice Taft, he could see no difference in kind or degree of interference with liberty between regulation of hours and regulation of wages.

Liberal groups and reputable lawyers and teachers of law criticized the decision. It gave impetus to the movement to limit in various ways the powers of the Supreme Court to nullify legislation on constitutional grounds. The emptiness of the constitutional guarantee of a woman's freedom of contract was graphically portrayed by Rollin Kirby in the New York *World* in a cartoon depicting Justice Sutherland handing the decision to a woman wage-worker over the caption, "This decision affirms your constitutional right to starve." [41]

The criticism continued without avail for more than a decade. Another case was decided on the basis of the Adkins case as late as 1936.[42] It was only in the midst of the bitter controversy over Supreme Court reform which took place in 1937 that the Supreme Court overruled its decision in the Adkins case and sanctioned governmental establishment of minimum wages for women. The decision even then was handed down on the narrow margin of five to four.[43]

### THE LABOR INJUNCTION

Labor tried to secure limitation of hours, higher wages, and better working conditions for men, not predominantly through legislation,

[39] 261 U.S. 568.     [40] *Ibid.,* p. 568.
[41] Reproduced, *Survey,* L (May 1, 1923), 164.
[42] Morehead *v.* New York, 298 U.S. 587 (1936).
[43] West Coast Hotel Co. *v.* Parrish, 300 U.S. 379 (1937).

but through collective bargaining between employers and representatives of labor unions. Such a method contributed to the strength of the unions and to the maintenance of organizations equipped at all times for the perennial struggle between employers and employees. The weapon of the union was to strike, supported by picketing and by boycotting the products of recalcitrant employers. Employers usually sought to prevent unionization, often requiring workers to sign what were known as "yellow-dog" contracts, by which they agreed not to hold membership in labor unions during the terms of their employment. If unionization seemed inevitable, employers often sought to control the unions by one device or another, including the device of establishing company unions. The most powerful employer weapon used against strikes, picketing, and boycotts was the labor injunction. Employers began to make effective use of injunctions issued by federal courts to curb the activities of labor organizations during the period of the eighteen-nineties.[44] The injunction represented the use of the equity power of courts to prevent injury to property or property rights for which no adequate compensation could be secured by suits brought after the injury had taken place. Even when it was possible to win damage suits against particular workers, they usually lacked the property necessary to pay the damages assessed against them. Since labor unions were usually unincorporated organizations, there was doubt for many years as to whether they were entities suable in the courts. Even after the courts had decided that they were suable, and when they were shown to have had funds in their treasuries upon which levies might be made under the law, making collections from them proved difficult. The injunction, therefore, which sought to prevent the perpetuation of injuries, seemed to most judges and, of course, also to most employers the logical instrument for the protection of the property and the rights of the latter. To labor unions, however, its use meant the alignment of the courts on the side of property in the struggle for advantage between the employers and the employed. The unions denounced "government by injunction" with increasing bitterness as federal injunctions placed drastic restrictions on the civil rights of workers and crippled what seemed to be strictly legitimate effort to resolve labor grievances.

[44] For a history of labor injunctions see Felix Frankfurter and Nathan Greene, *The Labor Injunction* (1930); Edwin E. Witte, *The Government in Labor Disputes* (1932); Thomas Reed Powell, "The Supreme Court's Control over the Issue of Injunctions in Labor Disputes," *Proceedings of the Academy of Political Science*, XIII (June, 1928), 37-77.

The jurisdiction of federal courts in labor cases rested on various grounds, including provisions of anti-trust legislation, the Interstate Commerce Act, and other federal statutes.    Frequently, however, jurisdiction was exercised, not upon the basis of any federal statute, but by virtue of the fact that the parties involved in the labor controversy could be shown to be citizens of different states.    The law involved in such cases consisted usually of fundamental principles of law and equity as interpreted, not by the courts of the states in which the controversies arose, but by the federal judges acting in the cases. Federal judges were appointed for life and were free from some of the restraints of public sentiment which were placed upon most state judges by the periodic necessity of standing for re-election.    In their exertion of restraints upon labor, therefore, they were regarded by exasperated laborers as untouchable associates of and sympathizers with the employer class.

Over a long period of years the friends of labor sought in various ways to eliminate "government by injunction."    Some of them tried vainly to do away with that portion of the jurisdiction of federal courts which depended upon diversity of citizenship.    They argued that all cases should be left to the determination of the state courts except those arising out of the federal Constitution, laws, and treaties. Attempts were made to secure legislation to prevent the use of injunctions for the enforcement of anti-trust, interstate commerce, and other forms of federal legislation.    Other proposals looked to the general elimination of the equity powers of federal courts where labor controversies were involved.    Less sweeping proposals attempted to eliminate some of the more drastic abuses connected with the use of injunctions.

In the Clayton Act, passed in 1914, friends of labor brought about the insertion of provisions which it was hoped would greatly restrict the use of injunctions in labor disputes.    Early in 1921, the Supreme Court, with Justices Brandeis, Holmes, and Clarke dissenting, held that the Clayton Act did not legalize the secondary boycott and immunize workers responsible for it from the operation of the principles of equity.[45]    Soon afterward, the Court confirmed the frustration of the hopes of labor by holding that no new principle was introduced into the equity jurisprudence of the federal courts by the provisions of the Clayton Act.    These provisions, said Chief Justice Taft, were merely declaratory of the practice which had already prevailed in the

[45] Duplex Printing Press Co. v. Deering, 254 U.S. 443 (1921).

courts.[46] Other cases, decided thereafter, sanctioned the continued use of injunctions to curb violations of anti-trust legislation by labor organizations.[47]

Equity procedure did not include jury trial. Persons who violated injunctions were punished for contempt, usually by the judges who issued the injunctions, without the protection that juries would have afforded. To give a measure of protection against arbitrary action by partisan judges, a provision had been inserted in the Clayton Act to the effect that a person accused of contempt of court, if the action committed was of such a character as also to constitute a criminal offense under any statute of the United States or law of any state, was to have the privilege of trial by jury. The Supreme Court upheld the statute but by a decision which greatly restricted its interpretation.[48]

Late in 1921, the Supreme Court decided the important injunction case of Truax v. Corrigan.[49] This case was based upon the laws of the state of Arizona. Striking employees of a restaurant had used all the typical methods of strikes to keep people from patronizing the establishment. The owner sought an injunction in a state court. Provisions of Arizona law, however, were interpreted by the state court to prohibit the issuing of injunctions in situations of this kind. The owner of the restaurant contended that in denying him protection against injury the state took his property without due process of law, in violation of the Constitution of the United States. The case was appealed to the Supreme Court, where Chief Justice Taft, speaking for a majority of the Court, upheld this contention. The legislative power of a state, he said, could be exerted only in subordination to the fundamental principles of right and justice which the guarantee of due process in the Fourteenth Amendment was intended to preserve. He held also that the state statute denied equal protection of the laws.

Four justices dissented, throwing the issue into relief as they did so. Principles which had evolved for the protection of physical property were now being used to protect intangibles such as ways of doing business, including the "good-will" of customers. Justice Holmes remarked that by calling a business "property" it was made to seem like

[46] American Steel Foundries v. Tri-City Central Trades Council, 257 U.S. 184 (1921).

[47] United States v. Brims, 272 U.S. 549 (1926); Bedford Cut Stone Co. v. Journeymen Stone Cutters' Association, 274 U.S. 37 (1927). For a study of the application of anti-trust legislation to labor see Edward Berman, *Labor and the Sherman Act* (1930).

[48] Michaelson v. United States, 266 U.S. 42 (1924). The act was held to apply only to criminal contempt and not to civil contempt.

[49] 257 U.S. 312 (1921).

land, with the resulting conclusion that a statute could not substantially cut down the advantages of ownership existing before the statute was passed. Although an established business might have pecuniary value which was protected by law, he declared, it could not be given definiteness of contour by calling it a thing. It was a course of conduct and, like other conduct, was subject to substantial modifications. He could not understand the notion that it would be unconstitutional to authorize by statute boycotts and the like in aid of the employee's or the employer's interests. After stating other objections, he concluded by saying:

> There is nothing that I more deprecate than the use of the Fourteenth Amendment beyond the absolute compulsion of its words to prevent the making of social experiments that an important part of the community desires, in the insulated chambers afforded by the several states, even though the experiments may seem futile or even noxious to me and to those whose judgment I most respect.[50]

The use of injunctions by workers to protect their own rights was never more than sporadic.[51] It was predominantly an instrument of the employer group. In 1928, the president of the American Federation of Labor submitted a partial list of three hundred and eighty-nine labor injunctions in state and federal courts issued during the preceding decade,[52] some of which were so sweeping as to constitute gross abuses of the rights of the parties restrained. An extreme example was an injunction issued in 1930 in a federal district court in Iowa. Senator Norris described its effect as follows:

> The defendants in this case, it will be observed, were not allowed to tell anyone that a strike was in progress. They were not allowed to give any publicity in any way to the fact that a strike existed. They were not allowed to tell anyone that the complainant required its employees to sign the "yellow-dog" contract. In other words, their mouths were absolutely closed and "free speech" was forbidden. They could not, without violating this injunction, have sought advice from an attorney. The son would not be allowed to seek advice from his own father. And if the defendants violated this severe decree they would be liable for contempt of court, which means that they would be tried for an offense made illegal by the judge — an offense consisting of an act which would be perfectly lawful under the laws of the

[50] *Ibid.*, p. 344.
[51] For one important instance see Texas and New Orleans Railroad Co. *v.* Brotherhood of Railway and Steamship Clerks, 281 U.S. 548 (1930).
[52] Senate Report No. 1060, 71st Cong., 2d sess., Part II, p. 7.

state where the controversy existed. They were not only forbidden to violate this judge-made statute, but, in case they did violate it, they would be tried by the man who made the statute. They would not be allowed a trial before a jury of their peers — a privilege granted to the vilest of criminals.[53]

When successive decisions of the Supreme Court demonstrated that the provisions of the Clayton Act did not bar injunctions in labor disputes, a movement was started for new legislation. Friends of labor sponsored at session after session of Congress a bill to remedy the abuses. The bill made "yellow-dog" contracts unenforceable in any federal court, either in law or equity. It gave the right of jury trial in a wider range of contempt cases than that covered by the Clayton Act. It withdrew from the federal courts the power of issuing injunctions in a wide range of cases involving labor disputes. Opponents of the measure argued that Congress had no constitutional power to curtail the equity jurisdiction of the federal courts. In opposition to this argument, Felix Frankfurter, of Harvard Law School, submitted a persuasive memorandum demonstrating the fact that the extent of the judicial power vested in the inferior courts rested with Congress.[54]

In spite of the dissatisfaction of those for whom the bill went too far and others for whom it did not go far enough, it was passed by substantial majorities in 1932, a presidential election year. Before signing it, President Hoover referred it to the Attorney General for comment. The Attorney General called attention to the argument that the bill was unconstitutional because of its provisions concerning "yellow-dog" contracts and on other grounds, but came to the conclusion that these questions could be settled only by judicial determination. In many respects he thought the bill less clear than it might have been. It was inconceivable, he said, that Congress could have intended to protect racketeering and extortion under the guise of labor-organization activity. The anti-trust division of the Department of Justice had studied the measure and had concluded that it did not prevent injunctions in such cases and in suits by the United States to enjoin unlawful conspiracies or combinations under the anti-trust laws to outlaw legitimate articles of interstate commerce. Somewhat reluctantly, it appeared, he recommended that the President sign the bill.[55] In signing the bill, the President made public the

[53] *Ibid.*, p. 16.

[54] See Appendix to House Report No. 669, 72d Cong., 1st sess., pp. 12-16. For the arguments of the opposition see statement by James M. Beck, 75 *Congressional Record* 5471-5477.

[55] *New York Times*, March 24, 1932.

opinion of the Attorney General. Senator Norris, one of the sponsors of the bill, remarked bitterly that the President dared not veto it, but did everything he could to weaken its effect.[56]

The enactment of the measure, known as the Norris-La Guardia Act,[57] was hailed by labor as the fruit of a definite victory, but not as labor's Magna Charta which the Clayton Act at first appeared to be; and it was not generally believed that the new statute, even if held constitutional in all respects, would be a panacea for all the ills of labor. The constitutionality of the limitation on the powers of the federal courts to issue injunctions was upheld by lower federal courts; but the Supreme Court was able to avoid an official appraisal of the act during the earlier years of its operation.[58] A number of states enacted similar laws, some of them even preceding the federal enactment. As a result of the movement, the abuse of injunctive power by both federal and state courts has been greatly curtailed. Controversies between employers and employees have usually been fought out along other lines.

In summary, the period between World War I and the New Deal was a kind of interim period with respect to personal rights and liberties. The elements of disloyalty to the United States stirred by the war integrated with the disloyalty involved in syndicalist movements and other radical movements of the time to provoke intense controversy. The disturbance reflected itself in decisions about the relation of liberty to the clear and present danger amid which liberty could be limited, about the nature and obligations of American citizenship, about the rights of racial minorities, and about the rights of organized labor in a highly industrialized society. The disagreements among the justices carried into the even more controversial period which followed.

[56] Edwin E. Witte, "The Federal Anti-Injunction Act," *Minnesota Law Review*, XVI (May, 1932), 638–658, 643. For general discussions of the bill see Felix Frankfurter and Nathan Greene, "Congressional Power over the Labor Injunction," *Columbia Law Review*, XXXI (March, 1931), 385–412; J. P. Chamberlain, "The Federal Anti-Injunction Act," *American Bar Association Journal*, XVIII (July, 1932), 477–479; Francis B. Sayre, "Labor and the Courts," *Yale Law Journal*, XXXIX (March, 1930), 682–705.

[57] 47 Stat. 70.

[58] Cinderella Theatre Co. *v.* Sign Writers' Local Union, 6 F. Supp. 164 (1934); Levering and Garrigues Co. *v.* Morrin, 71 F. (2d) 284 (1934); United Electric Coal Companies *v.* Rice, 80 F. (2d) 1 (1935). (The Supreme Court denied certiorari in the last two cases.) New Negro Alliance *v.* Sanitary Grocery Co., 303 U.S. 552 (1938).

......................................................................................

# CHAPTER 33

# JUDICIAL LIMITS OF REGULATORY POWER

SUPREME COURT DECISIONS between the first World War and the New Deal reflected the steady expansion of state and federal regulatory power over economic enterprise and the desires of the judiciary to establish barriers against the overextension of such power all along the line. Cases involving state regulations were so numerous and varied as to discredit gloomy predictions of the decimation of the states in the face of growing federal authority. The principal limitations upon state authority resulted not so much from the expansion of federal regulatory power as from judicial holdings that state regulations violated some provision of the Constitution. The decisions reflected concern of the courts about the increasingly obvious departure of the United States from laissez-faire principles. They had their counterpart in other decisions similarly limiting the powers of the federal government. Both groupings of decisions, together with related decisions in the field of taxation, are discussed in this chapter.

## POLICE POWERS OF THE STATES

Depending upon whether the measures were approved or disapproved, the courts classified most state regulations either as legitimate exercises of the police power or as measures invalid under the Constitution, usually because of violation of the commerce or due-process clauses. The requirement that they fit into the judicially created category of police power put the states virtually in the position of exercising powers delegated by the Constitution, rather than all powers which the Constitution did not confer upon the federal government or prohibit to the states. The Supreme Court became, in great detail, the arbiter of what the states might do.[1]

---

[1] For a detailed discussion of police-power decisions from 1922 to 1930 see Thomas Reed Powell, "The Supreme Court and State Police Power, 1922-1930," *Virginia Law Review*, XVII and XVIII (April, 1931), 529-556; (May, 1931), 653-675; (June, 1931), 765-799; (November, 1931), 1-36; (December, 1931), 131-169; (January, 1932), 270-305;

Many cases discussed hitherto or hereafter in other connections illustrate the relations of state police power to the commerce and due-process clauses. A few examples provide further illustrations as to police power and due process. A Pennsylvania statute was unconstitutional, said Justice Holmes for the Supreme Court, in its prohibition of coal-mining under private dwellings or streets where the right to mine such coal had been reserved in the grant of the property. The general rule, he explained, was that while property might be regulated to a certain extent, if regulation went too far it would be regarded as a taking of property in violation of the Constitution. He thought the regulation went too far in this case.[2]  The Court held that the police power did not authorize a Nebraska statute which established maximum weight for loaves of bread, and, after allowing a certain leeway known as tolerance, provided penalties for selling or for making for sale bread in other weights. The purpose of the statute was to protect customers against fraud involved in selling underweight loaves for loaves of prescribed dimensions.[3]  Some years later, however, the Court upheld another Nebraska statute dealing with the same subject, in which the tolerances were increased and certain of the other regulatory provisions were modified.[4]  To decide each of the cases the Court had to inquire into and reach a decision concerning intricate facts about the baking and the preservation of bread which were quite within the realm of the parties at interest, but had little relation to the specialized training of the members of the Court.

Dividing six to three, the Court invalidated a Pennsylvania statute forbidding the use of shoddy in the manufacture of bedding materials. The Court found it necessary to decide whether or not the material known as shoddy might well contain germs or otherwise constitute a menace to health so as to justify the regulatory measure.[5]  The Court held unconstitutional a Pennsylvania statute requiring that all drugstores of which ownership was thereafter acquired should be owned only by licensed pharmacists. One purpose of the statute was no doubt to prevent the further expansion of drugstore chains. Justice

(February, 1932), 379-414; (March, 1932), 481-509; (April, 1932), 597-640. For a review of police-power cases, 1919-1922, by the same author, see *Michigan Law Review*, XIX (December, 1920), 136-147; XX (January, 1922), 261-287; XXI (January, 1923), 307-333.

[2] Pennsylvania Coal Co. *v.* Mahon, 260 U.S. 393 (1922). Justice Brandeis dissented.

[3] Burns Baking Co. *v.* Bryan, 264 U.S. 504 (1924).

[4] Peterson Baking Co. *v.* Bryan, 290 U.S. 570 (1934).

[5] Weaver *v.* Palmer Brothers, 270 U.S. 402 (1926). Justice Butler spoke for the majority, and Justices Holmes, Brandeis, and Stone dissented.

Sutherland, speaking for the Court, could see no justification for the requirement that all owners should be pharmacists.[6]

Police-power issues in the regulation of property were the counterpart of others in the field of personal rights, discussed in the preceding chapter, as in a decision upholding a Virginia statute which provided for the sterilization of mental defectives confined in public institutions. Said Justice Holmes for the Court:

> We have seen more than once that the public welfare may call upon the best citizens for their lives. It would be strange if it could not call upon those who already sap the strength of the state for these lesser sacrifices, often not felt to be such by those concerned, in order to prevent our being swamped with incompetence. It is better for all the world, if, instead of waiting to execute degenerate offspring for crime, or let them starve for their imbecility, society can prevent those who are manifestly unfit from continuing their kind. . . . Three generations of imbeciles are enough.[7]

Only Justice Butler dissented, and he wrote no opinion.

### BUSINESSES AFFECTED WITH A PUBLIC INTEREST

Many of the decisions on state regulatory measures fell into the well-known category of businesses affected or clothed with a public interest, which was imported into the constitutional law of the United States in 1877 in the case of Munn v. Illinois.[8] According to the reasoning of the Supreme Court in many decisions, prices involved in most business operations were not subject to regulation by government. Efforts to regulate took property without due process of law in violation of the Fourteenth Amendment. In business affected with a public interest, however, prices might be regulated. Grain elevators, railroads, and other types of business were held to be so affected as to justify rate regulation. Unfortunately, the line between businesses affected and those not affected with a public interest was never

---

[6] Liggett Co. v. Baldridge, 278 U.S. 105 (1928). Justices Holmes and Brandeis dissented.

Municipal zoning represents an important field where interference with property was justified as a legitimate exercise of police power. For discussion see M. T. Van Hecke. "Zoning Ordinances and Restrictions in Deeds," *Yale Law Journal*, XXXVII (February 1928), 407-425; J. S. Young, "City Planning and Restrictions on the Use of Property," *Minnesota Law Review*, IX (May-June, 1925), 518-541, 593-637; Newman F. Baker, "The Constitutionality of Zoning Laws," *Illinois Law Review*, XX (November, 1925), 213-248; Euclid v. Ambler, 272 U.S. 365 (1926); Gorieb v. Fox, 274 U.S. 603 (1927); Nectow v. Cambridge, 277 U.S. 185 (1928); Washington ex rel. Seattle Title Trust Co. v. Roberge, 278 U.S. 116 (1928).

[7] Buck v. Bell, 274 U.S. 200, 207 (1927).     [8] 94 U.S. 113. See chapter 18.

clear and the limits of regulatory power were always obscure.[9] The reasoning of the justices was often such as to suggest that the classification of a business as affected or unaffected with a public interest depended, not upon the intrinsic nature of the business, but upon whether the justices, in terms of their own economic philosophies, thought that prices in the field ought or ought not to be subject to governmental regulation.

The vague outlines of the doctrine were still further confused during and immediately after the first World War by the existence of emergency conditions and by the holding of the Supreme Court that the existence of an emergency might have a temporary effect in determining whether a given business was so affected with a public interest as to justify regulation of prices. The cases arose out of the shortage of houses, particularly in the larger cities of the United States, which resulted partly from the cessation of residential building during the war, and the consequent difficulty of finding places of residence at reasonable prices. After military hostilities had ceased, but before the war was technically at an end, Congress passed an act declaring the existence of a housing emergency in the District of Columbia and restricting the right of landlords to raise rents on the threat of eviction of tenants. Dividing five to four, the Supreme Court held the act constitutional. Said Justice Holmes, circumstances might so change in time or so differ in space as to clothe with a public interest what at other times or in other places would be a matter of purely private concern.[10] At the same time, on the same grounds, and by the same vote, the Court upheld a similar emergency statute of the state of New York.[11]

By a later decision, the Supreme Court emphasized the fact that it had no intention of classifying the business of renting homes as permanently affected with a public interest. The act of Congress con-

[9] For general discussions of the doctrines see Dexter M. Keezer and Stacy May, *The Public Control of Business* (1930), chapters V and VI; Walton H. Hamilton, "Affectation with Public Interest," *Yale Law Journal*, XXXIX (June, 1930), 1089-1112; Breck P. McAllister, "Lord Hale and Business Affected with a Public Interest," *Harvard Law Review*, XLIII (March, 1930), 759-791.

[10] Block v. Hirsch, 256 U.S. 135, 155 (1921).

[11] Marcus Brown Holding Co. v. Feldman, 256 U.S. 170 (1921). See also Levy Leasing Co. v. Siegel, 258 U.S. 242 (1922). For discussion of the issues involved see Walter F. Dodd, "Constitutionality of Emergency Rental Regulation," *West Virginia Law Quarterly*, XXVIII (January, 1922), 125-132; Walter F. Dodd and Carl H. Zeiss, "Rent Regulation and Housing Problems," *American Bar Association Journal*, VII (January, 1921), 5-12; Alan W. Boyd, "Rent Regulation under the Police Power," *Michigan Law Review*, XIX (April, 1921), 599-607.

cerning housing in the District of Columbia was extended by two successive acts. A case was taken to the Supreme Court on the argument that the emergency had passed and that there was no constitutional justification for further enforcement of the statute. The Supreme Court admitted that the contention might be correct in spite of the declaration of emergency in the statute, and sent the case back to the lower courts for independent investigation of facts as to whether or not the emergency still existed.[12]

In a decision handed down in 1923 by a unanimous Court, Chief Justice Taft divided into three classes businesses said to be clothed with a public interest and, therefore, subject to some public regulation. His classification was as follows:

> 1. Those which are carried on under the authority of a public grant of privileges which either expressly or impliedly imposes the affirmative duty of rendering a public service demanded by any member of the public. Such are the railroads, other common carriers, and public utilities.
> 2. Certain occupations, regarded as exceptional, the public interest attaching to which, recognized from earliest times, has survived the period of arbitrary laws by Parliament or colonial legislatures for regulating all trades and callings. Such are those of the keepers of inns, cabs, and gristmills. . . .
> 3. Businesses which, though not public at their inception, may be fairly said to have risen to be such, and have become subject in consequence to some government regulation. They have come to hold such a peculiar relation to the public that this is superimposed upon them. In the language of the cases, the owner, by devoting his business to the public use, in effect grants the public an interest in that use, and subjects himself to public regulation to the extent of that interest, although the property continues to belong to its private owner, and to be entitled to protection accordingly.[13]

The first two categories had a measure of definiteness. The third, however, was subject to interpretation pretty much as the Court saw fit. In this case the Court refused to accept the declaration of a state legislature that the preparation of human food was affected with a public interest to the extent that prices might be regulated. It had never been supposed, said the Chief Justice, "that the business of the butcher, or the baker, the tailor, the woodchopper, the mining oper-

---

[12] Chastleton Corporation v. Sinclair, 264 U.S. 543 (1924).
[13] Wolff Packing Co. v. Court of Industrial Relations, 262 U.S. 522, 535 (1923).

ator, or the miner was clothed with such a public interest that the price of his product or his wages could be fixed by state regulation." [14]

As is often true, judges who were able to agree upon a statement of general principles could not agree as to their application. In 1927, dividing five to four, the Court, speaking through Justice Sutherland, held unconstitutional a New York statute declaring the price of theater tickets to be a matter affected with a public interest and forbidding the retail of any ticket at more than fifty cents above the price printed on its face.[15] In 1928, dividing six to three, the Court held unconstitutional a New Jersey statute regulating the rates charged and other aspects of the business of employment agencies. The legislation was the culmination of a long period of effort to deal with serious abuses connected with private employment agencies in finding jobs for clients. The evils affected vitally the welfare of the masses of people who found it necessary to seek employment through such agencies. Yet the majority of the Court, speaking again through Justice Sutherland, found that the business was not affected with a public interest and that rates were therefore not subject to governmental regulation.[16]

Controversies over the extent of the public-interest category continued through a number of important decisions.[17] The majority of the Court continued to limit the regulatory power of the states to fix prices, but, with the deepening of the depression which began in 1929, the contentions of the minority received more and more public attention. People were impressed by the arguments of Justice Brandeis in the Oklahoma ice case that the Court ought not to curtail the power of the states to attempt solutions of their internal problems at a time when they were "confronted with an emergency more serious than war." [18] To stay experimentation in things social and economic was a grave responsibility, he contended. Denial of the right to experiment might be fraught with serious consequences for the nation. It was one of the happy incidents of the federal system that a single courageous state might, if its citizens chose, serve as a laboratory and try

---

14 *Ibid.*, p. 537.

15 Tyson *v.* Banton, 273 U.S. 418 (1927). See Maurice Finklestein, "From Munn *v.* Illinois to Tyson *v.* Banton: A Study in the Judicial Process," *Columbia Law Review,* XXVII (November, 1927), 769-783.

16 Ribnik *v.* McBride, 277 U.S. 350, 373 (1928). Overruled, Olsen *v.* Nebraska, 313 U.S. 236 (1941).

17 Williams *v.* Standard Oil Co., 278 U.S. 235 (1929); Frost *v.* Corporation Commission, 278 U.S. 515 (1929); O'Gorman and Young *v.* Hartford Fire Insurance Co., 282 U.S. 251 (1931).    18 New State Ice Co. *v.* Liebmann, 285 U.S. 262, 306 (1932).

novel social and economic experiments without risk to the rest of the country. The Court had the power to strike down such experiments because the due-process clause had been held applicable to matters of substantive laws as well as to matters of procedure. In the exercise of this high power, he urged, "we must be ever on our guard, lest we erect our prejudices into legal principles. If we would guide by the light of reason, we must let our minds be bold." [19]

By 1934, much additional havoc had been worked by the depression. The federal government, under the guidance of a new administration, had embarked upon its program of social and economic regulation which was characterized as the New Deal. States were enacting similar regulatory measures. At this time the Supreme Court had to pass upon the constitutionality of a New York statute intended to fix maximum and minimum prices at which milk could be sold. Four members of the Court, Justices Van Devanter, McReynolds, Sutherland, and Butler, quite logically contended that nothing in past decisions of the Court could be interpreted to justify price regulation in this industry which had never been held to be affected with a public interest. The majority, however, including Chief Justice Hughes and Justice Roberts along with the three liberals, turned its back upon the doctrine as hitherto interpreted by Justice Sutherland. Justice Roberts, who seems never to have been clearly committed to the public-interest doctrine, spoke for the Court. He cited evidence that the public welfare required price regulation of the milk industry. There was no closed category of businesses affected with a public interest, he said. The phrase "affected with a public interest" could mean no more than that an industry, for adequate reasons, was subject to control for the public good. He called attention to the fact that the Court had in the past upheld legislation to promote free competition by laws aimed at trusts and monopolies, in spite of interference with private property and freedom of contract. If, by contrast, the lawmaking body found unrestricted competition an inadequate safeguard of the consumer's interests, legislation to that effect need not be set aside because it fixed prices reasonably deemed to be fair to the industry and to the consuming public. This was especially so, he continued, where, as here, the economic maladjustment was one of prices which threatened harm to the producer at one end of the series and to the consumer at the other. Taking the position hitherto taken by Justices Stone and Brandeis, he declared that price control, like

[19] *Ibid.,* p. 311.

any other form of regulation, was unconstitutional only if arbitrary, discriminatory, or demonstrably irrelevant to the policies the legislature was free to adopt, and hence an unnecessary and unwarranted interference with individual liberty.[20]

The decision destroyed the effectiveness of the public-interest doctrine as an instrument for the prevention of price regulation. The decision did not mean, however, that state legislatures would thereafter be free to regulate prices in any industry as they saw fit. It preserved ample grounds for continued judicial intervention. Those grounds have subsequently been acted upon many times. The Supreme Court continues to stand as a barrier to such regulation as it deems objectionable. The due-process clause is no less applicable than before, even though the technical language of the public-interest doctrine is now largely obsolete as a justification for judicial determinations. The process of judicial determination has such flexibility as exists in the minds of the judges working out the decisions, and no more. The illusion of definiteness which was given by resort to the public-interest doctrine largely disappeared as a result of the opinion of Justice Roberts. Whether an illusion of non-existent definiteness in the judicial process is worth preserving is a matter upon which legal scholars are likely to continue to disagree.

PUBLIC-UTILITY RATE-MAKING

The Supreme Court was entangled many times in the intricacies of rate-making for public utilities. The problems involved economic theory and economic policy quite as much as matters of law. The conceptions of legally trained judges as to the reasonableness of highly complicated financial arrangements determined decisions on constitutionality. The subject, like many others over which the Court had jurisdiction, was not directly mentioned in the Constitution. Its point of contact was the due-process clause of the Fourteenth Amendment. In the basic case on the subject, Smyth v. Ames,[21] decided in 1898, the Supreme Court had said that rates fixed by government must allow a fair return upon a fair value of the property. It did not say how the fairness of the return was to be measured. As to the fair value, the Court said that original cost, market value, earning capacity, cost of operation, and other factors were to be considered in measure-

---

[20] Nebbia v. New York, 291 U.S. 502 (1934). For a discussion of the case see Irving B. Goldsmith and Gordon W. Winks, "Price-Fixing: From Nebbia to Guffey," Illinois Law Review, XXXI (June, 1936), 179-201.

[21] 169 U.S. 466.

ment, but it gave no indication as to how the several factors were to be weighed. Out of a composite of all of them in each case the courts were to determine whether the regulatory agency had recognized the full value of the property upon which the return was to be based.

Endless public-utility litigation resulted from the indefiniteness of the rules for discovering whether regulatory measures were constitutional. Utility companies disputed governmental findings as to the value of property and secured injunctions against the enforcement of rate schedules prescribed by regulatory agencies. In times of rising prices the companies sought to emphasize reproduction cost as the true measure of value, as against the original cost of the property,[22] reserving, of course, the right to change their position after a reversal in price trends.

The thinking of the conservative members of the Supreme Court was much more in harmony with that of utility counsel than was the thinking of the liberal justices. Justice Brandeis sought a measurement of value in what he called "prudent investment," hoping thereby to eliminate the fluctuations in value which kept all parties in a condition of uncertainty and resulted in endless litigation and re-valuation of property.[23] In fixing railroad rates the Interstate Commerce Commission leaned toward the Brandeis proposal,[24] but the majority of the Court refused to commit themselves to it. The Court remained divided until the decline of prices during the depression made obsolete the earlier estimates of value. Utilities which had developed during the period of high prices shifted their arguments on valuation and after prices had fallen emphasized original cost as against cost of reproduction. The Supreme Court remained without a scientific approach to the problem and without any definite rules.[25] For subsequent developments see Chapter 37.

---

[22] See, for example, McCardle v. Indianapolis Water Co., 272 U.S. 400 (1926).

[23] Southwestern Bell Telephone Co. v. Public Service Commission, 262 U.S. 276 (1923). For other valuation cases decided during the period see United Railways v. West, 280 U.S. 234 (1930); Los Angeles Gas and Electric Corporation v. Railroad Commission, 289 U.S. 287 (1933); Public Service Commission v. Great Northern Utilities Co., 289 U.S. 130 (1939); Wabash Valley Electric Co. v. Young, 287 U.S. 488 (1933); Great Northern Railway Co. v. Sunburst Oil and Refining Co., 287 U.S. 358 (1932).

[24] St. Louis and O'Fallon Railway Co. v. United States, 279 U.S. 461 (1929).

[25] For discussions of the subject see Edwin C. Goddard, "The Evolution and Devolution of Public Utility Law," *Michigan Law Review*, XXXII (March, 1934), 577–623; James C. Bonbright, "The Problem of Valuation: The Economic Merits of Original Cost and Reproduction Cost," *Harvard Law Review*, XLI (March, 1928), 593–622; David E. Lilienthal, "Regulation of Public Utilities During the Depression," *Harvard Law Review*, XLVI (March, 1933), 745–775; Richard Joyce Smith, "The Judicial Interpretation of Public Utility Franchises," *Yale Law Journal*, XXXIX (May, 1930), 957–979.

POLICE-POWER ENDS AND MARTIAL LAW

The rapid development of production in the oil industry and the active competition among producers resulted in tremendous overproduction and in depressed prices. Overproduction was deplored, both because it resulted in waste and because the depressed prices brought about by cut-throat competition reduced or eliminated the profits of production. Some measures restricting production were upheld by the courts,[26] but the judicial barrier remained always a potential threat to regulatory legislation.

A law was enacted in Texas pursuant to which oil wells capable of producing five thousand barrels a day were limited to production of less than two hundred barrels. A federal district court issued a temporary injunction against the enforcement of the order. Thereupon the governor of the state sought to achieve results similar to those intended by the statute by proclaiming martial law in the oil counties, on the ground that they were in a state of riot and insurrection, and ordering that for the purpose of quelling the insurrection the production of oil should be limited to one hundred barrels per day. The question of the proclamation and enforcement of martial law in the United States had been regarded as largely "political" in character and therefore not subject to judicial interference.[27] As a result, martial law in the states had come to be used as "almost a household remedy."[28] In the petroleum controversy, however, a United States district court issued an injunction against enforcement of the governor's proration order. The Supreme Court agreed with the district court that a proration order issued under such circumstances did not constitute a valid exercise of martial law, but took property without due process of law.[29] The decision was important because of the restrictions which it set upon the development of martial law for the settlement of civil controversies.

THE RIGHTS OF FOREIGN CORPORATIONS

In 1839, in Bank of Augusta v. Earle,[30] Chief Justice Taney, for a majority of the Supreme Co rt, had taken the position that a state might exclude from within its borders corporations of other states not

---

[26] See, for example, Champlin Refining Co. v. Corporation Commission, 286 U.S. 210 (1932).

[27] See Charles Fairman, The Law of Martial Rule (1930).

[28] Charles Fairman, "Martial Rule in the Light of Sterling v. Constantin," Cornell Law Quarterly, XIX (December, 1933), 20-34, 29.

[29] Sterling v. Constantin, 287 U.S. 378 (1932).    [30] 13 Peters 519, 274 (1839).

engaged in interstate commerce or might prescribe the conditions under which they would be admitted. Down through the years, the conditions of admission prescribed by the states provided a subject of controversy. As the corporation became more and more important as an instrument of business and industrial enterprise, restrictions placed upon foreign corporations increased in importance to the economic life of the country. Spokesmen for corporations seeking to do business in states other than those in which they were created criticized the doctrine that a state had absolute freedom in laying down the conditions under which a corporation of another state might be admitted to do business.[31] The decisions of the Supreme Court lacked harmony, and the justices divided in handing down a number of decisions.

The matter came before the Court in 1922 in a case involving an Arkansas statute which provided that the license by which a foreign corporation did business in the state should be revoked if, in any suit between it and a citizen of Arkansas, it instituted the action in a federal court or sought to remove the case to a federal court. The statute was evidently enacted as a result of indignation, felt in many states, at corporations which sought to escape local courts by transferring cases to federal courts. Chief Justice Taft announced the decision in terms of what is called the "doctrine of unconstitutional conditions." The sole question presented, he said for a unanimous Court, was whether a state law was unconstitutional which revoked a license to a foreign corporation to do business within the state because, while doing only a domestic business in the state, it resorted to the federal court sitting in the state. He admitted that the cases involving the power of a state to exclude a foreign corporation and those dealing with the right of the corporation to resort to the federal courts could not be reconciled. He announced the overruling of two of the long list of earlier decisions and held that the condition that a corporation should not resort to the federal court was unconstitutionally prescribed. The principle, he said, rested on the ground that the federal Constitution conferred upon citizens of one state the right to resort to federal courts in another; that state action, whether legislative or executive, necessarily calculated to curtail the free exercise of the right thus secured was void because the sovereign power of a state, in excluding foreign corporations, as in the exercise of all

[31] For discussion see Gerard C. Henderson, *The Position of Foreign Corporations in American Constitutional Law* (1918).

other of its sovereign powers, was subject to the limitation of the supreme fundamental law.[32]

Such are many of the important cases involving regulatory powers of the states. Others dealt with state quarantine legislation,[33] farm legislation,[34] and other subjects. On the whole, the powers of the states underwent considerable expansion under the scrutiny of a Supreme Court sometimes divided but always watchful over the rights of property.

### FEDERAL CONTROL — ANTI-TRUST LAWS

The expansion down through the years of state regulation of many matters hitherto left unregulated was accompanied by a similar expansion of regulation by the federal government. Federal regulatory measures, both old and new, gave rise to many Supreme Court decisions during the period under discussion. They dealt with the enforcement of anti-trust laws, Federal Trade Commission activities, the Packers and Stockyards Act, the control of railroads, the control of the sale of grain futures and related farm problems, radio regulation, the tariff, federal grants-in-aid to the states, and many other matters. In many instances the development represented something in the nature of a federal police power analogous to the police power of the states.

The laws calculated to prevent combinations in restraint of trade were enforced in the face of a rapid expansion of large enterprises at the expense of smaller ones. The growth of mass-production enterprise led to greater prosperity and more rapid growth among large organizations than among smaller ones, to the incorporation of separate organizations into larger units, and to the repression of small units which were unable to use mass-production techniques.[35] Supreme Court decisions on the application of anti-trust laws were reached in the midst of this movement, and were undoubtedly colored by it. One of the most important of the decisions was in a long-pending suit against the United States Steel Corporation.[36] The corporation

---

[32] Terral v. Burke Construction Co., 257 U.S. 529 (1922). The case did not remove all questions as to the limits of state power in the field. See Power Manufacturing Co. v. Saunders, 274 U.S. 490, 498 (1927).

[33] See Oregon-Washington Railroad and Navigation Co. v. Washington, 270 U.S. 87 (1926); Mintz v. Baldwin, 289 U.S. 346 (1933).

[34] See Lemke v. Farmers' Grain Co., 258 U.S. 50 (1922).

[35] For discussion see Adolph Berle and Gardiner Means, *The Modern Corporation and Private Property* (1933).

[36] United States v. United States Steel Corporation, 251 U.S. 417 (1920). See also United States v. International Harvester Co., 274 U.S. 693 (1927).

had the largest capitalization of any single unit in the country and was the leading producer in its field. Yet the Supreme Court refused to order the dissolution of the corporation or the separation from it of any of its subsidiaries, holding that its conduct had not been unlawful, and saying that the mere size of a corporation or the mere existence of unexerted power unlawfully to restrain competition did not of itself make a corporation a violator of the law. The Court thereby greatly limited the range of the Sherman Act and doubtless accentuated the amalgamation of small corporations into larger ones.

Decisions in other fields likewise encouraged mergers. Trade associations organized by competitors in particular industries worked out codes of ethics and exchanged information calculated to prevent waste in production and distribution. The associations were capable of performing valuable economic functions, in that through sharing information they might prevent the disturbances consequent upon the glutting of the market by excess production. The sharing of information, however, tended at times to curtail competition, and it led, or was suspected of leading, to co-operative control of prices which was contrary to the anti-trust laws.[37] In a number of cases the Supreme Court found trade-association activities illegal. Yet, in spite of the logic of the decisions, there was an apparent lack of harmony between them and the decisions holding that actual mergers were not illegal in spite of the size of the new organizations created. Harmony in the planning of price policies and other policies was to be expected within a single organization, but when similar concerted action was brought about among separate business entities which together perhaps controlled only a limited portion of the business in its particular field, the combination was banned as illegal. The Supreme Court, therefore, by the line of decision which it adopted, encouraged the merging of corporations as against limited co-operation.[38]

The depression of 1929 and after brought a new trend in trade-association cases. The new trend was announced in a decision in an anti-trust suit affecting a large block of the coal industry. That in-

[37] For discussion see Herman Oliphant, "Trade Associations and the Law," *Columbia Law Review*, XXVI (April, 1926), 381-395; Dexter Keezer and Stacy May, *The Public Control of Business* (1930), pp. 50-57; Milton Handler, "Industrial Mergers and the Anti-Trust Laws," *Columbia Law Review*, XXXII (February, 1932), 179-271; National Industrial Conference Board, *Trade Associations, Their Economic Significance and Legal Status* (1925).

[38] See Justice Brandeis dissenting in American Column and Lumber Co. *v.* United States, 257 U.S. 377, 419 (1921). See also Maple Flooring Manufacturers' Association *v.* United States, 268 U.S. 563 (1925); Cement Manufacturers' Protective Association *v.* United States, 268 U.S. 588 (1925).

dustry had experienced prosperity during the first World War, but the capacity developed at that time was too great for maintenance thereafter in time of peace and in competition with other fuels. It was a sick industry during the middle nineteen-twenties when other forms of business were prosperous. The depression and the growing competition of other fuels made matters worse. For various reasons combinations in the coal industry were not so frequent as to raise the specter of monopoly. Cut-throat competition among units kept it demoralized and interfered with profit for owners and operators and with steady work for laborers.

As a result of these conditions, producers controlling about seventy-three per cent of the commercial production of bituminous coal in four states set up a corporation to act as an exclusive selling agency to market their products at the best prices obtainable. The government brought a suit to enjoin the combination as a restraint of interstate commerce in bituminous coal and an attempt at monopolization of part of that commerce. The United States district court, speaking through Judge John J. Parker, held the proposed selling arrangement illegal.[39]

The Supreme Court reversed the decision. "As a charter of freedom," said Chief Justice Hughes for all members of the Court except Justice McReynolds, "the act has a generality and adaptability comparable to that found to be desirable in constitutional provisions." [40] He found that the limitation of production was not contemplated by the combination and that the end in view was the stabilization of prices in an industry suffering from overexpansion and loss of markets. It seemed apparent to him that the plan would expand rather than curtail business and that the operation of the selling agency would not have the effect of fixing the price of coal in consuming markets, since the agencies would be confronted with effective competition and with the organized buying power of large consumers. The effect of the arrangement, nevertheless, was intended to be the stabilization of prices charged by independent business entities. The decision of Judge Parker was more nearly consistent with the letter of previous Supreme Court decisions than was that of Chief Justice Hughes. The Supreme Court was cautiously reshaping the law in terms of the necessities of the times. The Chief Justice made it clear that future developments would be subject to renewed judicial exam-

---

[39] United States *v.* Appalachian Coals Co., 1 F. Supp. 339 (1932).
[40] Appalachian Coals Co. *v.* United States, 288 U.S. 344, 359-360 (1933).

ination. "If in actual operation," he said, "it should prove to be an undue restraint upon interstate commerce, if it should appear that the plan is used to the impairment of fair competitive opportunities, the decision upon the present record should not preclude the government from seeking the remedy which would be suited to such a state of facts." [41]

In its attitude toward the stabilization of prices by industry in the interest of all the parties involved, the decision in this case is in harmony with the New York milk case of the following year, in which the Court held that price-fixing by government was not prohibited, any more than other types of regulation if necessary to the public welfare.[42] How the selling agency would have operated and what the attitude of the Supreme Court toward the details of its operation might have been remain undisclosed, because of the fact that the National Industrial Recovery Act and other federal legislation led to other forms of experimentation for stabilizing the coal industry and other industries in which similar experiments might have been attempted. However, the changed attitude of the Court toward the immunity of prices from considerable control other than by competition seems to have been permanently established.[43]

## WORK OF THE FEDERAL TRADE COMMISSION

Congress had established the Federal Trade Commission in 1914 for a purpose similar to that of the anti-trust laws, namely, the maintenance of competition. It empowered the commission to investigate business conduct, issue "cease-and-desist" orders against unfair competitive practices, and in other ways seek to promote the normal activities of the capitalistic system. The agency was called an independent regulatory commission, but its independence, like that of other such commissions, was limited: Congress could take away its powers for any reason whatsoever. The President could in time, by a sequence of appointments, change the character of the discretionary work of the commission. As an administrative tribunal with quasi-judicial powers it was subject to the restrictive supervision of the courts.

The commission was not in a position to build prestige for itself by

---

[41] *Ibid.*, p. 378.      [42] Nebbia *v.* New York, 291 U.S. 502 (1934).

[43] For discussion of the coal case see Notes in *Virginia Law Review*, XIX (June, 1933), 851-867; Harry Shriman, "Proposed Modifications of the Anti-Trust Laws," *Illinois Law Review*, XXVII (February, 1933), 671-684; John D. Eldridge, Jr., "The Appalachian Coals Case and the Rule of Reason," *George Washington Law Review*, I (May, 1933), 507-513.

the effective supervision of a single industry, as could the Interstate Commerce Commission in regulating the railroads. Its position was different, in that while it had no broad powers over any one industry, it had a limited policing supervision over almost all business in interstate commerce. Its work was often the thankless job of heckling business which ventured from time to time beyond the borderline of lawfulness.

During the period under discussion, Congress made few changes in the powers of the commission. It did not restrict those powers, but on the other hand it did not come to the commission's support in the controversies in which it was engaged by giving additional authority. It is clear that the Republican Presidents, Harding, Coolidge, and Hoover, had no great enthusiasm for the work of the commission, and that appointments were sometimes made with the idea of restricting its interference with business. As to the judiciary, the significant fact in an account of constitutional development is that the Court whittled down the powers of the commission and insisted on their own right of detailed examination of commission findings. Although the Interstate Commerce Commission had gradually won for itself a considerable area of discretion, no such area was found as far as the Federal Trade Commission was concerned. It performed valuable work as an investigating agency,[44] but its efforts to police industry were so hedged about by judicial supervision and were so unpopular with the business world, and oftentimes with the administrative officers of the federal government, that its achievements could not be regarded as significant.[45] Only in recent years, with the addition of new powers and with a change in the attitude of the Executive and of the courts, has it achieved substantial regulatory effectiveness.

### REGULATION OF THE PACKERS AND STOCKYARDS

The Federal Trade Commission made one of its most important reports in the summer of 1918 while the nation was at war. It dis-

[44] See, for example, the extended investigation of electrical utilities in the United States; *The Report on the Meat Packing Industry*, in six volumes, 1919; *Report on the Grain Trade*, in seven volumes, 1920-1926. Reports have also been made on chain stores, the tobacco industry, the steel industry, the petroleum industry, resale price maintenance, open-price associations, and many other subjects.

[45] For a study of the comparative attitude of the courts toward the Federal Trade Commission see Carl McFarland, *Judicial Control of the Federal Trade Commission and the Interstate Commerce Commission, 1920-1930* (1933). For other accounts of the work of the commission and its relation to the courts see Gerard C. Henderson *The Federal Trade Commission* (1924); Thomas C. Blaisdell, *The Federal Trade Commission* (1932); Myron W. Watkins, "An Appraisal of the Work of the Federal Trade Commission," *Columbia Law Review*, XXXII (February, 1932), 272-289; National Industrial Conference Board, *Public Regulation of Competitive Practices* (1929).

closed the fact that five large meat-packing companies were taking advantage of the war crisis and of their strategic position generally to dominate the meat market at the expense of consumers. The packers owned and operated, not only the packing establishments themselves, but also stockyards, railroads, refrigerator cars, and other vital equipment. In various ways they used their great power to curb competitors and to curb the sale of competing food products. The report showed that the Department of Justice and the Federal Trade Commission had been unable to enforce existing legislation in such a way as to preserve competition.[46]

From 1918 until 1921, Congress struggled with the problem of additional regulatory legislation. During the same period an anti-trust suit was instituted to divorce the packers from control of stockyards, railroads, and other facilities, to eliminate their control over competing products, and in other ways to restore competitive conditions. The packers, evidently partly for the purpose of preventing the enactment of some of the drastic regulatory provisions, joined in a consent decree whereby, without admitting previous guilt, they agreed that as to the future they would refrain from doing many of the things of which they were accused. Congress thereafter passed the Packers and Stockyards Act,[47] taking into account the existence of the consent decree in phrasing the legislation. Having achieved their ends with reference to the legislation, the packers thereafter tried for a decade to prevent the enforcement of the decree. Within that period they were largely successful, but finally, in 1932, the Supreme Court handed down a decision which terminated that phase of the litigation by deciding against the packers.[48]

The Packers and Stockyards Act transferred to the Secretary of Agriculture authority hitherto possessed by the Federal Trade Commission to deal with unfair trade practices in the meat-packing industry. It treated the stockyards as a public utility and gave to the Secretary of Agriculture power over rates and other aspects of the business similar to that possessed by the Interstate Commerce Commission over railroads. Packers immediately sought injunctions against the enforcement of these provisions. They were defeated both in the lower court and in the Supreme Court. Chief Justice Taft, with only

---

[46] Federal Trade Commission, *Report on the Meat Packing Industry,* in six volumes (1918-1920).

[47] 42 Stat. 159.

[48] United States *v.* Swift & Co., 286 U.S. 106 (1932). See comment, *New Republic,* LXXI (May 25, 1932), 33.

Justice McReynolds dissenting, held that the business of the various livestock yards of the country was affected with a public interest so as to be subject to legislative regulation and that they were agencies of interstate commerce.[49]

### TRADING IN GRAIN FUTURES

Soon after the close of the first World War, Congress began to study possible methods of preventing fluctuations in the price of grain brought about by speculation in grain futures on boards of trade. Fluctuations in prices of grain sold for future delivery gave speculators opportunity for greater profits and worked to the disadvantage of both producers and consumers. Extensive hearings gave ample evidence of the need for legislation, but they did not reveal a source of constitutional power. It was doubted whether speculative sales which did not result in the shipment of particular quantities of grain in interstate or foreign commerce could be regulated on the basis of the commerce power. Use of the commerce power for the performance of police functions, hitherto left to the states, had been curbed by the Supreme Court in a recent child-labor case.[50] Congress had subsequently enacted a taxing measure to achieve the same end. The Supreme Court had not yet passed upon it, but the Court had in the past permitted use of the taxing device for some regulatory purposes, and it was hoped that the use would be sanctioned here.

In the end, Congress decided to use the taxing power as a means of control of the sale of grain futures. An act was passed prescribing machinery for detailed regulations and prescribing a prohibitive penalty tax on operations other than those regulated. A case to contest the constitutionality of the act was decided on the same day as the child-labor tax case. The child-labor tax measure was held unconstitutional;[51] and the grain-futures tax measure met the same fate. Speaking for the Court, Chief Justice Taft, quoting with approval his statement in the child-labor case, said:

> Grant the validity of this law, and all that Congress would need to do hereafter, in seeking to take over to its control any one of the great number of subjects of public interest, jurisdiction of which the states have never parted with and which are reserved to them by the Tenth Amendment, would be to enact a detailed measure of complete

[49] Stafford v. Wallace, 258 U.S. 495 (1922). See also Tagg Brothers and Moorhead v. United States, 280 U.S. 420 (1930).

[50] Hammer v. Dagenhart, 247 U.S. 251 (1918).

[51] Bailey v. Drexel Furniture Co., 259 U.S. 20 (1922).

regulation of the subject and enforce it by a so-called tax upon departures from it. To give such magic to the word "tax" would be to break down all constitutional limitation of the powers of Congress and completely wipe out the sovereignty of the states.[52]

The Chief Justice dropped a hint that, although the tax regulations were unconstitutional, others based on the commerce power might be upheld.[53] Congress took the hint and immediately passed another measure which, according to the preamble, was for the prevention of obstructions and burdens upon interstate commerce in grain by regulating transactions on grain-futures exchanges. The Court upheld the new statute as a legitimate regulation of interstate commerce.[54] Chief Justice Taft likened the regulation of the sale of grain futures to the regulation of business conducted in the stockyards, which, although including many individual transactions in intrastate business, were, nevertheless, so integral a part of interstate commerce that the regulation had been upheld.[55]

The cases with reference to grain futures were important, not merely because they marked a somewhat unusual instance of the positive guidance of legislation by the Supreme Court. They were important also as an indication that the Supreme Court was prepared to permit the commerce clause to be used more broadly for regulatory purposes than the taxing power. It was in terms of the commerce power that most of the regulatory measures of the federal government over business enterprise were thereafter enacted.

### THE CONTROL OF RAILROADS

The most obvious form of federal control of enterprise based on the commerce power continued throughout the period to be the regulation of railroads. The desirability of extensive regulation by the Interstate Commerce Commission had by this time been accepted by the Supreme Court even when, in order to regulate the rates and other aspects of the business of interstate railroads, it was necessary to regulate competing railroads doing intrastate business. Decisions in important cases during the nineteen-twenties confirmed the trend which

[52] Hill v. Wallace, 259 U.S. 44, 67-68 (1922).

[53] Ibid., p. 69. See Senate Report No. 871, 67th Cong., 2d sess.

[54] Board of Trade v. Olsen, 262 U.S. 1 (1923).

[55] The case cited was Stafford v. Wallace, 258 U.S. 495 (1922). The argument in that case rested back upon the famous Swift case, 196 U.S. 375, decided in 1905. Legislation affecting grain futures was expanded in 1936 by extension to other commodities. See 49 Stat. 1491.

had already been established. One of the best known was that up-holding the constitutionality of the so-called "recapture clause" of the Transportation Act of 1920. By that statute Congress returned the railroads from public to private hands after the first World War; confirmed broad regulatory powers of the Interstate Commerce Commission; and enacted varied provisions in an attempt to stabilize the industry and protect the public. Chief Justice Taft accepted the following explanation of the statute:

> The Transportation Act adds a new and important object to previous interstate-commerce legislation, which was designed primarily to prevent unreasonable or discriminatory rates against persons and localities. The new act seeks affirmatively to build up a system of railways prepared to handle promptly all the interstate traffic of the country. It aims to give the owners of the railways an opportunity to earn enough to maintain their properties and equipment in such a state of efficiency that they can carry well this burden. To achieve this great purpose, it puts the railroad systems of the country more completely than ever under the fostering guardianship and control of the commission, which is to supervise their issue of securities, their car supply and distribution, their joint use of terminals, their construction of new lines, their abandonment of old lines, and by a proper division of joint rates, and by fixing adequate rates for interstate commerce, and, in case of discrimination, for intrastate commerce, to secure a fair return upon the properties of the carriers engaged.[56]

At the time when the measure was being considered in Congress, the several agencies seeking to influence the language of the statute included, not merely the management of the several railroads and the shippers, but also an association of railroad-security owners. This association brought about the inclusion of a "recapture clause" which was favored by neither of the other groups. The clause was intended to maintain the prosperity and hence the credit of competing railroads in spite of the fact that some railroads normally found it easier to earn a fair return on their fair value than did others. The method used was to maintain the normal flow of transportation by fixing uniform rates and recapturing excess profits of more prosperous roads for the benefit of those which were less prosperous and for other purposes. The Supreme Court found the arrangement constitutional, but it did not work well in practice. In annual reports for 1930, 1931, and 1932, the Interstate Commerce Commission recommended the repeal

---

[56] Dayton-Goose Creek Railway Co. *v.* United States, 263 U.S. 456, 478 (1924).

of the recapture provisions.[57] By an act of June 16, 1933, to "relieve the existing national emergency in relation to interstate railroad transportation," the provisions were repealed.[58]

## THE CONTROL OF RADIO

In 1927, Congress provided for the establishment of a new independent regulatory commission, the Federal Radio Commission. It was given jurisdiction over the allocation of wave-lengths and other matters connected with broadcasting. Speaking for a unanimous Supreme Court in 1933, Chief Justice Hughes sanctioned the lodgment of broad powers in the commission. No state lines divided the radio waves, he remarked, and national regulation was not only appropriate but essential to the efficient use of radio facilities. He upheld the power of the commission to make an equitable allotment of wavelengths among broadcasting stations in the United States even when new arrangements meant the silencing of old stations. He said:

> This Court has had frequent occasion to observe that the power of Congress in the regulation of interstate commerce is not fettered by the necessity of maintaining existing arrangements which would conflict with the execution of its policy, as such a restriction would place the regulation in the hands of private individuals and withdraw from the control of Congress so much of the field as they might choose by prophetic discernment to bring within the range of their enterprises.[59]

Statutory provisions for the control of radio were subsequently expanded and jurisdiction was transferred from the Federal Radio Commission to the newly organized Federal Communications Commission, which exercised supervision over telephone and telegraph as well as over radio.

## THE PROTECTIVE TARIFF

One of the oldest forms of regulation of enterprise by the federal government was the protective tariff. The fixing of protective rates, as against tariffs for revenue only, had been debated since the enactment of the first tariff measure by the First Congress, but protection in varying degrees had always been possible. The constitutionality

[57] See also testimony of Commissioner Joseph B. Eastman before the Senate committee on interstate commerce on April 5, 1933, in *Hearings on S. 843 and S. 844*, 73d Cong., 1st sess.

[58] 48 Stat. 211, 220.

[59] Federal Radio Commission *v.* Nelson Brothers Bond and Mortgage Co., 289 U.S. 266, 282 (1933).

of tariffs established for protection rather than for revenue purposes had usually been assumed, apart from periodic challenges in Democratic national platforms, but, oddly enough, the Supreme Court did not pass upon the question until 1928. In that year it decided a case based on the so-called flexible tariff provisions of the Tariff Act of 1922. It held that a provision authorizing the President to revise tariff schedules in terms of competitive costs of production in other countries was not unconstitutional as a delegation of legislative power to the President. The Court discussed in that connection the constitutionality of duties levied for protection as well as for revenue. It called attention to the fact that Congress, from the very beginning, had deemed it legitimate to lay tariffs for protection, and held that the legislation could be justified under the revenue powers even though other matters than the collection of revenue had brought about its enactment.[60]

There was a measure of inconsistency in justifying the protective tariff in terms of the taxing power, in that if a tariff was completely protective — that is, if it completely excluded the competing products of other countries — it would yield no revenue at all. The Supreme Court took a more realistic approach to the subject in a case decided in 1933. The University of Illinois had been compelled to pay import duties on scientific materials imported for use in its laboratories. The university contended that as a state agency it was immune from taxation by the federal government. A unanimous Supreme Court, speaking through Chief Justice Hughes, held that the import duties in question were imposed by Congress in the exercise of its authority to regulate commerce with foreign nations. Congress had full power to regulate such commerce, even to the extent of prohibiting it altogether. No state had any right to engage in foreign commerce free from the restrictions which Congress might impose.[61] The decision brought constitutional doctrine into harmony with the realities of the situation at a time when the nations of the world were using subsidies, embargoes, and other devices for the control of imports and exports, often without reference to any revenue which might accrue directly to the several governments. The devices used were instruments of foreign policy. Even though such revenues as were derived were accepted with alacrity, they did not constitute the primary purpose of regulation.

[60] Hampton v. United States, 276 U.S. 394 (1928).
[61] University of Illinois v. United States, 289 U.S. 48 (1933).

## CONTROL BY TREATY

The treaty-making power proved an important source of federal regulatory authority over local matters not otherwise subject to federal control. A case decided in 1920 illustrated the point. It dealt with a statute based upon a treaty between the United States and Canada which was intended to protect migratory birds moving back and forth over the two countries, destroying predatory insects and adding to the food supply. Before the treaty was made, Congress had passed an act regulating the killing of certain migratory birds; but a state court and two federal courts held that the act exceeded the powers of Congress.[62] In the debate which preceded the enactment of the earlier measure, some legislators had indicated doubts as to the constitutionality of the proposal and had suggested the advisability of resorting to the treaty-making power. Others seemed to think that the authority over the subject given by the treaty-making power was no broader than that already possessed.[63] The treaty was made with Canada in spite of continuing doubt concerning the authority which might be given by that device. As soon as a statute was enacted on the basis of the treaty, the state of Missouri challenged its validity.

The Supreme Court, speaking through Justice Holmes, drew a distinction between acts of Congress which were based upon treaties and those which were not so based:

Acts of Congress are the supreme law of the land only when made in pursuance of the Constitution, while treaties are declared to be so when made under the authority of the United States. It is open to question whether the authority of the United States means more than the formal acts prescribed to make the convention. We do not mean to imply that there are no qualifications to the treaty-making power; but they must be ascertained in a different way. It is obvious that there may be matters of the sharpest exigency for the national well-being that an act of Congress could not deal with, but that a treaty followed by such an act could, and it is not lightly to be assumed that, in matters requiring national action, "a power which must belong to and somewhere reside in every civilized government," is not to be found.[64]

[62] United States v. Shauver, 214 Fed. 154 (1914); United States v. McCullagh, 221 Fed. 288 (1915).

[63] For a discussion of the statutes, the treaty, and the case, and for the citation of comments, books, and articles see Willard Bunce Cowles, Treaties and Constitutional Law (1941), and Julian P. Boyd, "The Expanding Treaty Power," Selected Essays on Constitutional Law (4 vols., 1938), III, 410-435.

[64] Missouri v. Holland, 252 U.S. 416, 433 (1920).

It has been shown that the purpose of the framers of the Constitution in referring to treaties as "made under the authority of the United States" instead of "pursuant to the Constitution," as in the case of acts of Congress, was to include treaties made prior to the adoption of the Constitution as well as those made thereafter.[65] Justice Holmes, however, gave the distinction a new meaning. He said:

> When we are dealing with words that also are a constituent act, like the Constitution of the United States, we must realize that they have called into life a being the development of which could not have been foreseen completely by the most gifted of its begetters. It was enough for them to realize or to hope that they had created an organism; it has taken a century and has cost their successors much sweat and blood to prove that they created a nation. The case before us must be considered in the light of our whole experience, and not merely in that of what was said a hundred years ago. The treaty in question does not contravene any prohibitory words to be found in the Constitution. The only question is whether it is forbidden by some invisible radiation from the general terms of the Tenth Amendment. We must consider what this country has become in deciding what that amendment has reserved.[66]

He found in this instance a national interest which could be protected only by national action. But for the treaty and the statute based on it, that interest might be destroyed. He found the measures to be constitutional.

The decision provoked much discussion of the possibility of regulating by treaties many other subjects in connection with which Congress was otherwise hampered.[67] It was suggested that labor conditions involving the control of hours, wages, child labor, night work for women, workmen's compensation, and other matters might be made subject to congressional action through the making of treaties on these subjects with other countries. Actual developments of this kind, however, remained in abeyance. One reason, no doubt, was the fact that, with changes brought about by the business depression, Congress found it possible to enact without resort to treaty many types of regulatory measures hitherto thought to be beyond the scope of its powers. The upsurge of international hostilities which took place during the same period and the breaking-down of international co-operation in many fields likewise stood in the way of the development which

[65] Boyd, *op. cit.*, pp. 425-426 and materials cited.
[66] 252 U.S. 433-434.   [67] See Boyd, *op. cit.*, pp. 429 ff. and materials cited.

had been foreshadowed. In the event of the return of international co-operation on a large scale, the treaty-making power might yet become the basis for the further extension of the regulatory power of Congress.

### CONTROL THROUGH GRANTS-IN-AID

For many decades, Congress has exercised a measure of control over affairs within the states by granting money, or land to be converted into money, for projects to be supervised by the states. Education, highways, military training, maternity welfare, and vocational rehabilitation were among the important projects for which grants were made prior to the beginning of the depression. The federal government sees that the money granted is spent on the project for which it is allotted. The grants are often conditioned upon the making of appropriation for the same purposes by the state. No state is under any direct compulsion to accept government funds and to make corresponding appropriations for the purposes for which they are allotted. For political reasons, however, it is not easy to reject offers of tremendous sums from the federal government. Federal funds are raised through taxation all over the country. Every state wishes to share in their distribution. It usually accepts such grants as are offered, therefore, together with the regulations prescribed by the federal government.

Persons opposed to the projects sponsored by the federal government, or opposed to participation of the federal government in such matters, sought to prevent expenditures of this kind. They challenged the constitutionality of the expenditure of federal funds on projects over which the government had no jurisdiction except through making appropriations. The constitutional question was essentially that which had been debated since the time when Hamilton and Madison disagreed as to whether the power to tax "to pay the debts and provide for the common defense and general welfare of the United States" was as broad as the purposes which Congress itself found promotive of the general welfare, or, on the other hand, was limited to the carrying into effect of powers granted by other clauses of the Constitution.

An attempt was made to test the constitutionality of legislation of this kind in connection with a maternity act passed in 1921 by which Congress extended financial aid to such states as would accept and comply with its provisions for the work of reducing maternal and infant mortality and protecting the health of mothers and infants. The Supreme Court decided together two cases challenging the constitutionality of the act. One was an original suit by the commonwealth of Massachusetts to enjoin enforcement of the act. The other was an appeal in a case in which a woman taxpayer likewise sought an injunction against enforcement. Counsel for Massachusetts urged that the appropriations were for purposes which were not national but local, and that they, together with numerous similar appropriations, constituted an effective means of inducing the states to yield a portion of their sovereign rights. The burden of this legislation, they said, fell unequally upon industrial states such as Massachusetts; the act was a usurpation of power not granted to Congress, and was an attempt to exercise the power of local self-government reserved to the states by the Tenth Amendment; and although Massachusetts had not accepted the act, its constitutional rights were infringed by its passage and the imposition upon the state of an illegal and unconstitutional option either to yield or to lose the share which it would otherwise be entitled to receive from the appropriation of federal funds. The Court held, however, that the state could avoid involvement simply by refusing to accept the provisions of the act, and that the state, therefore, lacked a sufficient interest in the matter to entitle it to bring the suit. As for the effect of the act upon citizens of the state, they were also citizens of the United States, and a state had no power to institute judicial proceedings to protect them from the operation of federal statutes.[68]

This portion of the decision closed the path to a determination of the constitutional question through a suit instituted by a state. The woman bringing suit as a taxpayer was no more successful. The Supreme Court held that the interest of any one citizen in the money in the Treasury of the United States was too minute and indeterminable to entitle him to bring a suit in attempt to govern the mode of its expenditure. If a taxpayer could bring such a suit in connection with this statute, said the Court, he could bring it in connection with any appropriation act. If one taxpayer could bring such a suit, so could every other, with chaos the inevitable result.

The decisions in the two cases indicated that, whether or not Congress had the constitutional power to make grants-in-aid of the types being made, there was no manner of bringing about a judicial determination that the acts were unconstitutional. Congress, therefore,

[68] Massachusetts v. Mellon, 262 U.S. 447 (1923).

continued to make appropriations of this kind, largely immune from judicial scrutiny.  The further development of experience with such grants permitted the country, and, unofficially, the courts as well, to observe the operation of projects based on grants-in-aid in advance of the determination of the constitutional question.  Finally, in the midst of the New-Deal period when grants to the states had greatly increased in volume for relief and for social-security purposes, the Supreme Court upheld the broader interpretation of the taxing power of Congress.  It maintained that the power to make appropriations was not limited to the carrying-out of functions authorized by other provisions of the Constitution, but constituted in itself an independent power on the basis of which Congress was authorized to act.[69] Although the decisions left loopholes for continued judicial interference, they had the effect of clearing the way for important expenditures.  The development continued unchecked to the extent of a very real modification of our federal system.[70]

PROBLEMS OF TAXATION

The first World War increased tremendously the expenses of the federal government, not merely for the war years, but for the later years during which the accumulated national debt was being retired. The extension of governmental activities into new fields added to the expenses of both state and federal governments.  Greater expenditures brought higher taxes on sources already being taxed and brought also the search for new sources and forms of taxation.  The income tax became an increasingly important source of federal revenue. Estate taxes, gift taxes, and excise taxes of various kinds brought funds in smaller totals which were, nevertheless, important.  The states, which had hitherto relied predominantly on general property taxes, followed the federal government in taxing incomes and inheritances and added sales taxes and excise taxes of various kinds.

Taxpayers resisted their increased burden on every conceivable legal ground.  The meaning of income, due process of law, equal protection, and the commerce clause were battle-grounds of innumerable constitutional struggles, with the courts as umpires.  Some controveries [71] were so intricate, the decisions so unrevealing of principles

[69] United States v. Butler, 297 U.S. 1 (1936); Helvering v. Davis, 301 U.S. 619 (1937).

[70] For general discussion of grants-in-aid see V. O. Key, Jr., *Administration of Federal Grants to States* (1937); A. F. MacDonald, *Federal Aid; A Study of the American Subsidy System* (1928).

[71] See, for example, Thomas Reed Powell, "Contemporary Commerce Clause Controversies over State Taxation," *University of Pennsylvania Law Review*, LXXVI (May-June, 1928), 773-797, 958-972.

actually followed, and the cases so numerous, that they could be dealt with adequately only in a treatise devoted exclusively to problems of taxation. Other decisions indicate more clearly the development of lines of policy. Certain groupings of them are presented herein.

As already indicated, the Supreme Court frowned on broad use of the taxing device for the performance of functions other than the raising of revenue. Such a position, however, was not universally taken. If scrutinized closely, most tax measures will be found to be framed with some regulatory, discriminatory, or equalizing function in mind besides that of providing revenue. Graduated income and inheritance taxes provide clear examples. The levying of excise taxes on some commodities and not on others has in it an appraisal of social values. The courts accept such graduations and selections for taxation almost as a matter of course. The child-labor and grain-futures cases represented points beyond those to which the Supreme Court was willing to go in permitting regulation by taxation. The Court upheld taxing measures, however, which had the purpose of regulating the sale of narcotics over which the states were unable to exercise adequate control. In 1919, dividing five to four, it sustained the Harrison Narcotic Drug Act despite its obvious regulatory purpose and the lack of concern about revenue. The Court had long held, said Justice Day for the majority, that it would not inquire into the motives that might impel the exercise of federal taxing power. If the legislation enacted had some reasonable relation to the exercise of the taxing authority conferred by the Constitution, it could not be invalidated because of the supposed motives which induced it. Nor was the taxing power of Congress invalidated by the fact that the same business might be regulated by the police power of the states.[72]

A similar controversy was present in the decision of 1936 on the processing-tax provision of the Agricultural Adjustment Act.[73] No clear principle has been worked out in terms of which the layman can predict whether a federal tax measure which also regulates matters otherwise beyond federal control will be upheld as a tax or invalidated because of its regulatory provisions. The Supreme Court remains the final arbiter in each case, with a wide area of discretion in its own hands.

Many state tax measures enacted in part for regulatory purposes

[72] United States v. Doremus, 249 U.S. 86 (1919). See also Nigro v. United States, 276 U.S. 332 (1928), decided after the statute had been amended and after the child-labor tax case had seemed to modify the principle.

[73] See chapter 36.

were challenged in the courts, usually on the ground that they denied the equal protection of the laws guaranteed by the Constitution. Those directed against chain stores provide examples. In response to local sentiment against the rapid rise of chain stores and the effectiveness of their competition, the Indiana legislature enacted a statute requiring the payment of a license tax by all stores. Individual stores each paid the same license fee. Where more than one store was operated under the same management or ownership, however, the amount of the fee increased at an extremely rapid rate. It was high enough to place a real burden upon chain stores, and the principle involved, if accepted, could be carried to even greater extremes. The owner of a chain of grocery stores sought an injunction against enforcement of the act on the ground that it arbitrarily discriminated against him and thereby denied him equal protection of the laws. The Supreme Court upheld the statute by a vote of five to four.[74]

The advocates of the legislation were victors by the narrowest of margins. That the statute went to the limit of the tolerance of certain of the justices who voted in its favor was indicated by a decision handed down two years later concerning a Florida statute. The latter statute was similar to that of Indiana, but provided in addition that the tax on a group of stores should be increased in terms of the number of counties in which they happened to be located. In this case the statute was held unconstitutional by a vote of six to three.[75] The decisions left the principle involved in a state of confusion. It is clear, however, that the taxing power is less safe as a basis of regulation than is the commerce power.

INHERITANCE TAXES

Many of the states and the federal government made the transfer of property at the time of death an occasion for raising substantial revenue. Some states, however, with Florida as the leading example, found it to their advantage to refrain from levying inheritance taxes, in order to attract as residents wealthy, retired persons who wished to have their estates pass to their descendants without sharp curtailments by any government agency. Congress, in addition to regarding transfers at death as a legitimate object of federal taxation, seems to have disapproved of the strategy of those states. It levied a federal estate

[74] State Board of Tax Commissioners v. Jackson, 283 U.S. 527 (1931). Justices Sutherland, Van Devanter, McReynolds, and Butler dissented.

[75] Liggett Co. v. Lee, 288 U.S. 517 (1933). Justices Brandeis, Stone, and Cardozo dissented.

tax on which it allowed a credit up to eighty per cent of the amount of inheritance, legacy, or succession taxes paid to any state.  In states having high inheritance taxes, therefore, the federal government collected only twenty per cent of its own tax, whereas, in states having no such taxes of their own, the federal government collected the full amount of its tax.  Hence the advantage of removing to Florida or to any other state for the purpose of avoiding state inheritance taxes was eliminated.  Florida challenged the constitutionality of the law by an original suit in the Supreme Court, but was told that the statute did not involve any unconstitutional lack of uniformity.[76]

## RECIPROCAL IMMUNITY FROM TAXATION

Another type of question which gave rise to many constitutional controversies was whether particular state taxes placed unconstitutional burdens on the federal government and whether particular federal taxes placed unconstitutional burdens on instrumentalities of state governments.  The principle of the immunity of each government from tax burdens created by the other, which had been recognized long ago in the cases of Collector v. Day [77] and Dobbins v. Commissioners of Erie County,[78] had been reinforced by subsequent decisions down through the years.  By argument in terms of this principle, the owners of property which had any reasonably close connection with either government sought to avoid the payment of taxes to the other.  As to the taxing powers of the states, the following were some of the questions raised.  Could a state, in lieu of all other taxes hitherto levied upon a company except real-estate taxes, levy an omnibus tax on its income, including income from United States bonds?  Could a state tax a company on the net value of its property, including United States bonds?  Could a state tax gross income which included gross receipts of money received from the United States government for carrying mail?  Could a state tax income from royalties derived from patents issued by the federal government?  Could a state levy a franchise tax measured by net income which included income in the form of royalties from motion-picture film copyrights?  Could a state collect an excise tax on gasoline sold to the United States? Could a state tax the sale of gasoline to a contractor working for the federal

[76] For the subject of taxation of the same property by more than one state, usually discussed as "double taxation," see Frick v. Pennsylvania, 268 U.S. 473 (1925), Farmers Loan and Trust Co. v. Minnesota, 280 U.S. 204, 209-210 (1930), and other cases.

[77] 11 Wallace 113 (1871).          [78] 16 Peters 435 (1842).

government? Could a state tax oil which has been produced on lands granted to Indians by the federal government? Could a state tax the property of a company operating under license from the Federal Power Commission?

Similar questions were raised concerning the taxing power of the federal government. Could the federal government tax profits accruing from the sale of county and municipal bonds, even though the bonds themselves and the interest thereon were exempt from taxation? Could it tax income from the sale of oil and gas produced under leases of lands owned by a state? Could it tax the sale of a motorcycle to a municipality for use of the police department? Could it tax the income of a company derived from the development of oil resources leased from a city? Could it collect an excise tax upon the sale of intoxicating liquors by stores owned and managed by a state?

The Supreme Court had to answer these questions in the settings of particular cases. It upheld some of the taxing measures in question and found others unconstitutional. In some cases in both groups the decisions were unanimous. In most of them, however, the Court was divided. Usually, although not always, the division was along the line of the liberal-conservative cleavage in the Court. The conservatives, scrupulous in their concern about the preservation of the rights of property, argued in terms of the absolutist principle, phrased by Chief Justice Marshall, that the power to tax involved the power to destroy, and sought to curb encroachment by taxation upon property which might reasonably be shielded from taxation by connection with any government. The liberals, however — usually Justices Holmes, Brandeis, and Stone, and later Justice Cardozo — were less fearful of governmental inroads upon property having some connection with another sovereign and were more concerned about the obligation of every property-owner to pay his just share of the costs of government. In an important case involving a question of state power, Justice Holmes remarked that in the time of Chief Justice Marshall it had not been recognized, as now, that most of the distinctions of the law are distinctions of degree.

> If the states had any power it was assumed that they had all power, and that the necessary alternative was to deny it altogether. But this Court, which so often has defeated the attempt to tax in certain ways, can defeat an attempt to discriminate or otherwise go too far without wholly abolishing the power to tax. The power to tax is not the power to destroy while this Court sits.[79]

[79] Panhandle Oil Co. v. Mississippi ex rel. Knox, 277 U.S. 218, 223 (1928).

The dissenting opinions of the liberal minority of the Court cast doubt upon the soundness of a principle by which large blocks of property were freed from their share of responsibility for the support either of a state or of the federal government. With the coming of the depression, the tapping of all possible sources of revenue became a matter of increasing importance, while investors, no longer able to find comparatively safe and profitable investments in private industry, turned more and more to the purchase of tax-exempt bonds. New decisions showed increasing doubts on the part of the Supreme Court as to the serviceability of a principle which prevented non-discriminatory taxation of large blocks of property. Finally, in 1939, in a case involving, not government securities, but the salary of a government employee, the Supreme Court overruled the original cases on which the principle was based.[80] The change was a product both of a change in the membership of the Supreme Court and of a recognition of the practical necessity of permitting state and federal governments to have non-discriminatory access to the property from which sustenance could be derived, to the extent, at least, of taxation of official salaries.

STATE TAXATION AND INTERSTATE COMMERCE

As indicated above, the question whether state taxes bore so heavily upon interstate commerce as to be an unconstitutional burden arose perennially. If a generalization is to be made at all, it is perhaps to the effect that the principles involved became less clear with the passing years, and the decisions rested more obviously upon the beliefs of the Court as to what in each case would best serve the public welfare. The lines of the original-package doctrine, which was never used in all its fullness to prevent state taxation of articles of interstate commerce, became increasingly blurred as decisions dealt with such matters as natural gas and electricity which only in a highly figurative sense could be thought of as in packages at all. The principle that state control began when the article shipped in interstate commerce came to rest in the state was likewise blurred because of the fact that so many of the items of interstate commerce could not be thought of as coming to rest. The absence of a clear line marking the taxing jurisdiction of the state resulted, not from any particular line of decisions of the Supreme Court, but from the nature of commerce itself and the nature of the federal system. So long as commerce and the

[80] Graves *v.* New York *ex rel.* O'Keefe, 306 U.S. 466 (1939).

conditions of its operations continue to change, and so long as the federal system survives, the necessity of frequent constitutional decisions in the field will remain.

In summary, although many important cases of the period are left unmentioned, those listed indicate the breadth and variety of the work of the Supreme Court. They show the trends of decisions in important fields and the influence of the personnel of the Court and of external happenings upon those trends. The cases represented day-to-day adjustment of constitutional law to the day-to-day changes in the conditions over which the state and federal governments had jurisdiction. The time was coming, in the virtual social revolution brought about by the depression, when new decisions, some of which are mentioned above, would suggest sharp breaks with the past. Prior to 1933, however, the great bulk of the decisions of the Supreme Court represented the strenuous efforts of its members, or of most of its members, to maintain the constitutional system in terms of established traditions. History may label the period as that of the Indian summer of the old Supreme Court, of that Court at its best, as it sought, in terms of constitutional tradition, to preserve the symmetry of the constitutional structure as traditionally conceived.

# CHAPTER 34

# TOWARD THE NEW DEAL

THE LONG STEP toward socialization of enterprise in the United States which came in 1933 with the New Deal is to be understood only in terms of developments dating back as far as the first World War. The war brought an unprecedented extension of the power of the federal government over the industrial and commercial life of the country. Amid the economic chaos of the post-war period diverse groups made conflicting demands for a return to "normalcy" and for continued extension of governmental control. The conditions of economic strain influencing the course of constitutional development were so intricate and far-reaching that only the presentation of selected illustrations is possible herein. The state of psychological disillusionment of the people is analyzed briefly to show the cynical reaction to government control and also the emphasis on acquisition of wealth as the principal aim of life, which intensified the frustration caused by the defeat of economic aspirations in the depression of 1929. The plight of the farmer in the nineteen-twenties is portrayed, with the successful and unsuccessful struggles for extension of the regulatory hand of the federal government in the interest of the farmer. The Muscle Shoals controversy is used to illustrate the conflict over governmental encroachment on the field of private enterprise. The successful movement for the construction of Boulder Dam is used to illustrate the retreat of laissez-faire before the advocates of the extension of governmental power.

DISILLUSIONMENT

Disillusionment with the idealism of the American war effort began even before the end of the war. President Wilson's request for the election of Democratic majorities in Congress indicated to loyal Republicans that the emergency was being used, not merely to make the world safe for democracy, but also to make the government secure for the Democratic party. The defeat of Democratic hopes by a narrow margin and the ensuing partisan conflicts in houses of Congress that were almost equally divided served further to eclipse idealism with factional strife. One of the results was the return of the Republican party to power in all branches of the government, with a program very different from that of President Wilson. "Normalcy" meant approximate isolation in international affairs and approximate laissez-faire at home.

The apparent inequities of the war settlement emphasized the fact that greed and fear still dominated the councils of European nations and that, in spite of the virtually forcible establishment of democratic forms of government in certain countries, the cause of democracy had not been greatly advanced by a war waged for the alleged purpose of making it safe. Americans who had paid a high price for participation in the war began to suspect that they had been duped. Discovery of the fact that war industries had bred a flock of new millionaires provoked jealousy and added further to disillusionment. A series of studies of the causes of the World War and of the propaganda of the war period led to growing doubt as to the validity of the professions of the statesmen of the Allied and Associated Powers.

The emotions of conflict, whipped to white heat in the United States, found inadequate relief because of the fact that the military conflict ended when active American participation had hardly begun. The pent-up emotions found a new outlet in the movement to suppress radical groups of various sorts. Attorney General Palmer's deportation of radicals who were unlawfully in the United States, the suppression of criminal syndicalism in the several states, and the suppression of liberal sentiment in the schools went to such extremes as to lead once more to cynical reaction. Returning soldiers, the heroes of an hour, reached their homes to find their former positions occupied by men who had never been in uniform. No longer heroes, they found themselves ignored in a nation now operating under the slogan, "Business as usual." The depression of 1921 accentuated the economic pressure. The scandals of the Harding administration accented the tendency on the part of great numbers of the American people to subordinate ideals to the acquisition of property.

Before the formal conclusion of peace, the United States had fixed upon itself the shackles of the Eighteenth Amendment. The reaction against such regimenting of conduct led to wholesale violation of law and to disrespect for law generally. A decline of moral standards resulted from the departure of millions of young men from their homes during the period of the war, with consequent escape from the control of community pressure. The improvement of highways and the increase of travel, particularly by automobile, had a further effect in lessening the control of the community over the conduct of the people. The decade of the nineteen-twenties was one wherein a disillusioned people sought self-satisfaction, with a growing scorn for established standards and for law.

At the end came the depression of 1929. It represented the collapse of an unprecedented orgy of speculation, an orgy wherein millions of people expected to get rich merely through the process of speculative investment. Business, relieved from the controls of the World War, had demanded to be let alone in order that it might continue the enrichment of the American people through the normal operation of the profit system. Three Presidents — Harding, Coolidge, and Hoover — had been firm believers in non-interference of government with business. Commercial and industrial enterprise came first in the allotment of prerogatives; and government was largely the servant of such enterprise. In the laconic language of Coolidge, "The business of the United States is business." With limited exceptions, already discussed or discussed hereafter, the government had refrained from interference. The Federal Trade Commission had been packed with personnel friendly to business enterprise. The Federal Reserve Board had been unable to find a way to control the speculative activity that brought the most disastrous depression in American history. Timid steps toward recovery by special aids to business, such as those involved in the creation of the Reconstruction Finance Corporation, were without avail. After three years of repeated assurance that the economic structure of the country was essentially sound and that prosperity was just around the corner, the American people completed a psychological cycle with reference to the powers of government over economic enterprise and voted out of office the sponsors of the program of non-interference. They were now ready to accept strong personal leadership and to support the enactment of drastic regulatory legislation.

### THE PREDICAMENT OF AGRICULTURE

Agriculture, unlike much of industry, was in a state of chronic depression throughout the period under discussion. The war had created an unprecedented demand for agricultural commodities.

Under the stimulus of high prices, production had been greatly expanded. Land prices rose to new high levels. Because of the demand and because of the scarcity of farm labor, new investments were made in farm machinery. Both land and machinery were bought on credit, with the expectation that payment would be made out of future profits.

Superficially, the war period was one of great prosperity for the farmers of the country. Actually, although prices in terms of money were high, prices of commodities bought by farmers were also high and the net yield was not as impressive as might have been expected. Before the war was formally terminated, farmers found themselves loaded down with debt for land and implements, which they could pay only if they were able to continue production on a large scale. Because of both inability to buy and resumption of local production, the nations of Europe ceased quickly to provide markets for the huge stream of products from the United States. The new tariff law enacted by the Republican Congress made it increasingly difficult for foreign purchasers to pay for American agricultural products. The result was a collapse in the price of farm products and of the land itself. Many farmers were driven into bankruptcy and others were barely able to survive. Farm representatives in the Senate and, to some extent, in the House of Representatives organized to enact legislation to help the farmers of the country out of their predicament.[1]

The early legislation demanded had to do with improvement of the conditions of marketing and with extension of credit to farmers. The first important farm measure enacted was the Packers and Stockyards Act,[2] which gave broad regulatory powers to prevent monopolistic abuses in the meat-packing business and in the use of the stockyards. The measure took regulatory power away from the Federal Trade Commission, which, with its predecessor, the Bureau of Corporations, had struggled for nearly two decades to bring about the enactment of effective regulatory legislation. It vested that power in the Secretary of Agriculture. This step, although weakening the Federal Trade Commission as a policing agency, strengthened the Department of Agriculture as the national representative of farming interests.[3]

Speculation in grain futures, similar to stock-market speculation,

---

[1] See Arthur Capper, *The Agricultural Bloc* (1922). See also V. O. Key, Jr., *Politics, Parties, and Pressure Groups* (1942), pp. 43 ff.

[2] 42 Stat. 159.     [3] For discussion of the constitutionality of the act see chapter 33.

by which huge sums of money were gained and lost, caused fluctuations in the price of grain which were often disastrous to farmers. A few days after the enactment of the Packers and Stockyards Act, Congress passed an act, based on the taxing power, in attempt to remedy the abuse.[4] When the act was declared unconstitutional as an illegitimate exercise of the taxing power, Congress passed another measure, based on the commerce power, to achieve the same end.[5] The latter measure, known as the Grain Futures Act, was upheld. It authorized the Secretary of Agriculture to designate boards of trade as "contract markets" for the conduct of trade. If a board of trade failed to obey prescribed regulations, a commission, composed of the Secretary of Agriculture, the Secretary of Commerce, and the Attorney General, was authorized to suspend or to revoke the designation of the board as a contract market.

Another statute for the promotion of agricultural marketing authorized the association of agricultural producers for marketing purposes.[7] The intent of the act was to prescribe circumstances under which such combinations would be relieved from the restrictions of the antitrust laws. The Secretary of Agriculture was given supervisory power to see that the associations, when formed, did not monopolize or restrain trade in interstate or foreign commerce to such an extent that the price of any agricultural product was unduly enhanced.

To facilitate the export of farm products, Congress revived the War Finance Corporation, added the Secretary of Agriculture to the membership of the board of directors, and authorized the corporation to make loans for the exportation of agricultural surpluses resulting from the war or from the disruption of foreign trade created by the war.[8] Another statute, designed to expand agricultural credit, provided among other things for the establishment of federal intermediate credit banks, to make extensions of credit for intermediate periods between short-term loans, on the one hand, and long-term mortgage-secured loans, on the other.[9]

THE EXPORTATION OF FARM SURPLUSES

These several measures, enacted during the Harding administration, and the amendments added from time to time failed to restore

---

[4] 42 Stat. 159.          [5] 42 Stat. 998.

[6] For discussion of the constitutionality of the two measures see chapter 33.

[7] 42 Stat. 388.          [8] 42 Stat. 181.

[9] 42 Stat. 1451. For discussion see Claude L. Benner, *The Federal Intermediate System* (1926), and Frieda Baird and Claude L. Benner, *Ten Years of Federal Intermediate Credits* (1933).

agricultural prosperity. Surpluses of agricultural products continued to pile up, depressing the prices of the commodities sold and impoverishing producers. Farmers' organizations and farm representatives in Congress demanded additional legislation for the disposal of the surpluses. Over a considerable period of years they urged the enactment of a bill which came to be known as the McNary-Haugen bill. By its provisions a Federal Farm Board with a substantial capitalization was to purchase surpluses in basic agricultural commodities in order to maintain reasonable prices in the United States and to sell these surpluses in the export markets at so-called world prices. The purpose was to enable farmers to produce and sell at a reasonable profit, whether the purchases were made by private consumers in the United States or by the Federal Farm Board. The losses incurred by the board in selling surpluses at prices lower than those paid for them were to be reimbursed by an equalization fee, collected from American farmers in the form of a tax levied upon the producers of the respective products. The tax would take away some of the profits initially made by the farmers, but the operations of the board would prevent the disastrous depression of prices through the dumping of surpluses on the home markets.

This plan for the further extension of federal power over agriculture first appeared in print in 1922.[10] Congress debated it sporadically from time to time, and gave it serious consideration in 1925. The Secretary of the Treasury, Andrew Mellon, who was evidently the spokesman of the administration in the matter, denounced the proposed interference with prices which in his opinion should be governed only by the laws of supply and demand. "We cannot successfully oppose fundamental economic laws," he declared.[11] He was undisturbed by the inconsistency of his position in that his argument could be used as effectively against the protective tariff, of which he was a vigorous defender.[12]

President Coolidge announced his opposition in his annual message in December, 1926,[13] but Congress continued debate on the plan, and early in 1927 passed the McNary-Haugen bill, providing for a Federal Farm Board to purchase and dispose of surpluses in cotton, wheat, corn, rice, tobacco, and swine. President Coolidge referred the bill to the Department of Justice to aid in preparation of the inevitable

[10] For discussion see John D. Black, *Agricultural Reform in the United States* (1929) chapter VII.

[11] 67 *Congressional Record* 11266-11267.

[12] *Ibid.*, pp. 11358 ff.          [13] 68 *Congressional Record* 31.

veto. The Attorney General submitted an opinion holding the bill unconstitutional on a number of grounds. On one ground it was highly vulnerable, and objection might well have been made to it, even by lawyers in sympathy with its general purposes. In order to bring about the selection of members of the board in sympathy with the purposes of the bill, Congress had provided that the President must make nominations from slates of candidates submitted by agricultural organizations. The constitutional power of the President to appoint officers, said the Attorney General, carried with it the duty to exercise his judgment in the selection of higher officers. The Constitution contemplated that appointments should be made by and with the advice and consent of the Senate and not by and with the advice and consent of any other person or official.[14] In view of the broad discretionary powers conferred on the board, furthermore, he contended that the act was unconstitutional as a delegation of legislative power.

He thought the act unconstitutional on a broader ground. The federal government was a government of limited powers. He had been unable to find anything in the constitutional history or in the decisions of the Supreme Court of the United States to justify the belief

> that the power of the federal government to regulate commerce includes the power to establish and maintain or take steps to establish and maintain the price at which merchandise may be bought and sold in interstate commerce, with the necessary consequence of fixing the price at which the commodity in question shall be bought and sold in every place in the land, whether in or out of interstate commerce.[15]

In general, he said, legislation under the commerce power had been directed at carrying out the primary purpose of the clause, which was to prevent undue discriminations against, or burdens or restraints on, interstate commerce. This act, instead of preventing, created burdens and restraints on commerce, as those terms had been understood. He was of the opinion, furthermore, that the tax provided for was not a true tax within the meaning of the Constitution, and that it violated the due-process clause of the Fifth Amendment.[16]

President Coolidge attached the opinion of the Attorney General to a long veto message, using, says one of his biographers, "such emotional language that the message cracked with malicious static." [17] He

---

[14] *Ibid.*, pp. 4776-4777.  [15] *Ibid.*, p. 4777.  [16] *Ibid.*, p. 4778.
[17] William Allen White, *A Puritan in Babylon: The Story of Calvin Coolidge* (1938), p. 262.

found the bill unjustly discriminatory as among sections and as among farm products. He condemned it as giving the proposed federal board almost unlimited authority to fix prices on the designated commodities. It was price-fixing, furthermore, on some of the nation's basic foods and materials. "Government price-fixing, once started, has alike no justice and no end. It is an economic folly from which this country has every right to be spared." [18] The main policy of the bill, he contended,

> is an entire reversal of what has been heretofore thought to be sound. Instead of undertaking to secure a method of orderly marketing which will dispose of products at a profit, it proposes to dispose of them at a loss. It runs counter to the principle of conservation, which would require us to produce only what can be done at a profit, not to waste our soil and resources producing what is to be sold at a loss to us for the benefit of the foreign consumer. It runs counter to the well-considered principle that a healthy economic condition is best maintained through a free play of competition by undertaking to permit a legalized restraint of trade in these commodities and establish a species of monopoly under government protection, supported by the unlimited power of the farm board to levy fees and enter into contracts. For many generations such practices have been denounced by law as repugnant to the public welfare. It cannot be that they would now be found to be beneficial to agriculture. [19]

A revised bill was passed in May, 1928. It brought another veto message, accompanied by another opinion from the Attorney General, holding the bill unconstitutional. [20] Congress failed to enact the measure over the President's veto. No statute was ever enacted providing for the disposition of farm surpluses by means of the proposed equalization fee. Another device, the export-debenture plan, was much discussed and was incorporated in a number of proposed bills. The plan was calculated to encourage the exportation of farm surpluses by giving to exporters debentures, which might be presented to customs officials in payment of duties on imports in lieu of equivalent amounts of cash. Since the scheme would have reduced the amount of money collected by the federal government in the form of tariff duties, the government itself would have borne indirectly the burden of the disposition of the surpluses. None of the bills incorporating the plan was enacted. [21] In 1929, the Senate tried hard to secure the

[18] 68 *Congressional Record* 4771.  [19] *Ibid.*, p. 4775.

[20] 69 *Congressional Record* 9524-9531.

[21] For discussion see Black, *op. cit.*, chapter IX. See also Joseph S. Davis, *The Farm Export Debenture Plan* (1929).

inclusion of the export-debenture plan in the agricultural marketing statute pledged by the Republican party in the national campaign of the preceding year. The plan was included in the bill as passed by the Senate, but the Senate conferees surrendered it when the House of Representatives, in recognition of the opposition of President Hoover, refused to accept it.

### THE FEDERAL FARM BOARD

Although economic conditions improved in the middle nineteen-twenties, so that many branches of industry enjoyed great prosperity, the farm problem remained serious. American farmers continued to overproduce in terms of what they were able to sell. Farmers were not equipped for efficient marketing at home, and increased production in other countries and the inability of other countries to buy American products, owing to impoverishment resulting from the war and to the American protective tariff and to other causes, curtailed export sales. Competition at home from agricultural products produced abroad began to be regarded as a serious matter. Because of these conditions and because of the growth of political organization among farmers, no administration could safely ignore the demand for agricultural reform. In the campaign of 1928 the Republican party pledged the adjustment of the protective tariff to aid the farmer and the enactment of legislation to promote the efficiency of agricultural marketing. Soon after taking office, President Hoover called a special session of Congress to enact the promised legislation.

In his message to this session, the President asked for an effective tariff on agricultural products. He asked for the creation of a Federal Farm Board comparable to agencies created for the benefit of transportation and banking, which would assist farmers to meet each of their varied problems on its own merits. The creation of such an agency, he said, would at once transfer the agricultural question from the field of politics to that of economics and would result in constructive action. The pledged purpose of such a board was the reorganization of the marketing system on sounder, more stable, and more economic lines.

He added a warning, however, characteristic of those who distrusted the intervention of government in private enterprise:

> Certain vital principles must be adhered to in order that we may not undermine the freedom of our farmers and of our people as a whole by bureaucratic and governmental domination and interference.

We must not undermine initiative. There should be no fee or tax imposed upon the farmer. No governmental agency should engage in the buying and selling and price-fixing of products, for such courses can lead only to bureaucracy and domination. Government funds should not be loaned or facilities duplicated where other services of credit and facilities are available at reasonable rates. No activities should be set in motion that will result in increasing the surplus production, as such will defeat any plan of relief.[22]

After considerable controversy over the export-debenture plan and other proposals, Congress passed "An act to establish a Federal Farm Board to promote the effective merchandising of agricultural commodities in interstate and foreign commerce, and to place agriculture on a basis of economic equality with other industries."[23] The board was to consist of eight members, to be appointed by the President by and with the advice and consent of the Senate, "and of the Secretary of Agriculture, *ex officio.*" The addition of the latter novel provision as to the making of appointments, constituting a nominal restriction on the powers given by the Constitution to the President and the Senate, went without challenge. Presumably, it was intended as an item of assurance that representatives of agriculture would be consulted in the selection of members of the board.

Equipped with large sums in federal funds, the federal government set out to encourage the formation of additional farm co-operatives and particularly to bring about sectional and national organization of the large number of small co-operatives already in existence. Through these agencies it tried to promote efficient marketing of agricultural products. Facing the fact that the agricultural predicament was due, not merely to inefficiency in marketing, but also to excessive production, the board sought to use the co-operative organizations, the federal banks organized to extend credit to farmers, and such other agencies as were available for the purpose of persuading farmers to restrict production to quantities which they might reasonably expect to be able to sell. Pursuant to the statute, the board also attempted to deal with those limited surpluses which threatened from time to time to clog the market with particular products and to depress excessively their prices. It authorized stabilization corporations, formed through agricultural co-operatives, to purchase surpluses with government funds in the expectation that they would be returned to the market when conditions made their sale possible without injurious

[22] 71 *Congressional Record* 47.     [23] 46 Stat. 11.

effects. Corporations were organized and arrangements were made for the purchase of surpluses of wheat, cotton, and other commodities. The arrangement was undoubtedly based on a sound principle. Unfortunately, it was put into operation, not at a time when the price-level was roughly horizontal, but at a time when the depression which began in the autumn of 1929 was driving the whole price-level sharply downward. Although quantities of some commodities were purchased and then resold, therefore, the general result was that prices never returned to a level high enough to justify the board or the corporations in selling products they thought they had been justified in purchasing. They had to choose between retaining possession, on the one hand, and selling at a loss to the government, on the other, in competition with the products of harassed farmers. Because of the accident of the times the Federal Farm Board was seriously discredited in the eyes of the people. At the beginning of the ensuing administration, the board was abolished and its functions were transferred in part to the newly established Farm Credit Administration.

## EDUCATION FOR PRODUCTION CONTROL

The limitation of land settlement and the curtailment of agricultural production were foreign to the traditions of the American people. Innumerable social and economic problems had been solved or avoided by the spilling-over of excess population into areas hitherto unsettled. Until recent decades, farming was a relatively self-sufficing mode of life. The sale of agricultural products outside the areas of production raised the standard of living within those areas, but extensive exportation was not essential to survival. In the language of numerous commentators, farming constituted a way of life rather than merely a form of business enterprise. The exhaustion of the supply of good, free land for farming blocked the traditional mode of disposing of the surplus population, and the mechanization and specialization of farming impaired its self-sufficiency, so that the marketing of agricultural products became increasingly essential.

Even so, many people still considered population problems and farm problems in traditional terms. As late as 1916, the Department of Labor was supporting a bill for the creation of a national colonization board, to establish farm colonies on lands of the public domain. Nothing grew directly out of the scheme, but it provided background for the discussion of the various bills subsequently introduced in Congress for the placement of soldiers after the first World War. In 1918,

Franklin K. Lane, Secretary of the Interior, offered a plan for the rural settlement of returning soldiers which was popularized under the slogan, "A million farms for soldiers." [24] He spoke in terms of large available areas of cut-over land, land rich with the accumulated humus of hundreds of years and possessing extraordinary agricultural possibilities. He declared, furthermore, that there were thousands of acres available in the older states, such as Massachusetts, New York, Maryland, Virginia, and Louisiana, which could be used. Vast tracts of arid land were yet to be reclaimed. The United States could support three or four times its present population, he declared, if the people would forego the desire to live in industrial centers.

The enthusiasm of the Department of the Interior was not shared by farm magazines, farm organizations, and the Department of Agriculture. They were quite aware of the fact that if agricultural production were increased beyond the needs of consumers, the prosperity resulting from the war demands would be quickly terminated. They knew the low standard of living of many farmers in so-called reclaimed areas and on cut-over lands, and they realized that the abandonment of large areas of farm land in the East had an economic justification. None of the bills to establish soldiers in co-operative settlements received the general support of agricultural spokesmen and none of them was passed. Private land companies capitalized interest in the subject by buying up tracts of unused land and advertising them in glowing terms for sale to returning soldiers and others seeking to start life anew. Those who settled in these tracts were caught by the depression of 1921 and the continued downward drift of land prices.

In spite of the excess of agricultural production over demand, the Department of the Interior, in which the Reclamation Service was located, continued throughout the nineteen-twenties to advocate projects for the irrigation of arid lands and for the draining of swamps to bring about new settlements and to check the population movement away from the farm.[25] Like the plan for soldier settlements, this scheme to establish new farm settlements was opposed by farmers and farm organizations. The Department of Agriculture opposed it. There had been an overdevelopment of agricultural land in the recent past, declared the Secretary of Agriculture in 1927. and the agricultural depression had been prolonged thereby. New land would come

[24] *Annual Report of the Secretary of the Interior,* 1918, pp. 24-29. See also John R. McMahon, "A Million Farms for Soldiers," *Country Gentleman,* November 9, 1918.

[25] See House Doc. No. 765, 69th Cong., 2d sess., and Senate Doc. No. 45, 70th Cong., 1st sess.

into cultivation without government aid if demand and price justified it. Reclamation projects at this time were justified only for water-power and flood protection.[26]

The results of the depression beginning in 1929 gave weight to the arguments of agricultural spokesmen. In his annual report, made near the end of 1930, the Secretary of Agriculture stated that farm-commodity prices had dropped to the lowest point in fifteen years. Farm production, already above normal requirements, had become disastrously excessive when the depression curtailed purchasing power. He recommended an elaborate program for investigating and dealing with the subject of land utilization in such a way that much of the land not making a profitable yield would be withdrawn from cultivation.[27] Under the auspices of the executive committee of the Association of Land-Grant Colleges and Universities, a national conference on land utilization was held in Chicago in 1931.[28] The speeches delivered at the conference showed that under the pressure of agricultural depression educators in the agricultural field, once the most independent field of American enterprise, had gone far in the direction of advocacy of a planned economy. They discussed the need for a careful survey of all land used for agricultural production, with a program for taking out of production altogether that land which was to be classified as submarginal. They favored the careful planning of land utilization, with the result that, before new land was brought into production, careful account would be taken of the effect on competing areas. The result of the conference, in addition to the public education involved, was the creation of two committees which worked for some time on a revised program for agriculture. The movement, like many others then under way, was merged in the recovery movement of the Franklin D. Roosevelt administration.

The work done under the New Deal, therefore, in the way of restriction of agricultural production, retirement of submarginal land, extension of credit to agriculture, and promotion of efficient marketing and other essential farm activities through co-operative organizations had its preparatory background in the fumblings of the preceding period. Attitudes changed fundamentally concerning governmental interference with private enterprise in agriculture. Even in

---

[26] *Yearbook of Agriculture,* 1927, pp. 25-28.

[27] *Yearbook of Agriculture,* 1931, pp. 24 ff. See also Arthur M. Hyde, "A Land Policy for the United States," *Ohio Farmer,* December 13, 1930.

[28] See *Proceedings of the National Conference on Land Utilization,* Chicago, Illinois, November 19-21, 1931 (May, 1932).

the field of industry there was doubtless some recognition of the need for the solution of the farm problem, rising out of the fact that farmers were important purchasers of industrial commodities. Their continued purchases, and hence the prosperity of industry itself, depended upon the maintenance of a degree of agricultural prosperity.

## GOVERNMENT IN RELATION TO ELECTRIC POWER

While hard times for farmers were breaking down traditional concepts of the relation of government to farm enterprise, the same concepts as they related to industry were the subject of combat in the field of electric power. That relatively new industry was expanding in spectacular fashion. The rapidly growing investment was already tremendous; income was measured in high figures; and costs to consumers were being reduced as service was extended. In spite of the extension of service, the industry was hotly criticized. It was contended, presumably correctly, that, even though costs to consumers were tending downward rather than upward, producers were reaping huge profits from their sales. Partly because of financial and managerial linkages between power companies and other industries, industry paid much lower charges than were paid by domestic consumers. Few companies showed any interest in building transmission lines into agricultural sections of the country and distributing electricity to farmers at prices which they could afford to pay.

Government regulation proved exceedingly difficult. Rates fixed, in order to be constitutional, had to yield a fair return on a fair value. The business of a company in one state was apt to be inextricably entangled with business in another state. It often proved next to impossible to discover the fair value which might be used as a rate base. States had no regulatory jurisdiction beyond their borders, and companies frequently succeeded in upsetting rate structures established by state governments through the process of distributing electricity across state lines and juggling prices to serve their purposes. Public ownership of electrical utilities was proposed by those who despaired of effective regulation of privately owned companies and by others who thought that regulation of privately owned companies would be facilitated if government maintained electrical plants in various communities to serve as a yardstick. The plants would show the cost of producing and distributing electric power and the rates that ought to be charged. Much use was made of the fact that the Hydroelectric Power Commission of Ontario, Canada, had been able to furnish electric power to municipalities in the province at rates far below those charged by private companies in the United States. Private companies, on the other hand, used every conceivable argument against public ownership. Some municipalities did establish their own plants, but they did not engage in the business on a scale great enough to provide an adequate comparison between public and private enterprise.

The disclosure of the predatory activities of oil companies connected with Teapot Dome and other scandals of the Harding period had served to throw suspicion on the activities of corporations in other fields. Early in 1927, Senator Thomas J. Walsh, of Montana, who, as an efficient investigator, had been responsible for important disclosures connected with the oil scandals, proposed that a Senate committee investigate the electrical industry. He cited as matters for investigation the rapid growth of the industry, the long list of mergers taking place among electrical companies, the probable violation of anti-trust laws, and the probable need for regulation of the sale of securities.

The Senate took no immediate action, but an investigation by the Federal Trade Commission,[29] previously requested by the Senate, although given little publicity, indicated that the growth of holding companies in the electrical field, resulting in varied abuses and adding to the difficulties of regulation by the several states, was worthy of further examination. In December, 1927, Senator Walsh introduced a revised resolution. He added a provision that the investigating committee be empowered to report on the expenditure of money for publicity purposes and on efforts made to influence or control public opinion on the issue of public as against private ownership and on attempts to influence or control elections. It was the logical expectation that, if an investigation were authorized, Senator Walsh would be made a member of the committee. He was likely to be thorough to the point of ruthlessness. When the opposition found itself unable to block the investigation altogether, it supported an amendment to have the investigation conducted by the Federal Trade Commission rather than by a committee of the Senate. The Federal Trade Commission was in bad odor with those genuinely interested in having the investigation made. It had been slow in making a preliminary investigation which the Senate had asked for, and its work was

[29] See Senate Doc. No. 212, 69th Cong., 2d sess., and Senate Doc. No. 45, 70th Cong., 1st sess.

suspected of being superficial. By the judicious selection of new members, including William E. Humphrey,[30] the administration was believed to have weakened the Federal Trade Commission as a policing agency. In its annual report for 1927, the commission announced a new policy of co-operation with business, of "helping business to help itself" wherever and whenever it could be done without prejudice to the best interests of the public. The senators desiring the investigation felt that the electrical industry could very well take care of itself without aid from the government and were interested in a fearless inquiry into the conduct of the industry. They were defeated to the extent of being compelled to accept the Federal Trade Commission as the investigating agency. To prevent defeat of the plan by the delay of action on the part of the commission, the resolution required the committee to file hearings and partial reports within each thirty days after the passage of the resolution until the investigation was completed. Detailed examination into the organization and activities of the industry was prescribed.[31] Owing perhaps to the requirement of interim reports, to which the public gave much attention, and to the criticism directed at the Federal Trade Commission because of its alleged unwillingness to take any action that might be detrimental to big business interests, the investigation made was thorough and detailed. It was still in progress when the depression of 1929 began, and its many volumes threw light on the complicated industrial structure, including the so-called Insull Empire, much of which collapsed during the depression.

The evils suspected before the investigation was directed loomed up in greater number and on a grander scale. The holding-company structures proved bewildering networks such that the proper allocation of earnings and allotment of values were virtually impossible. While constituting agencies of real service, in many instances holding companies proved also to be devices whereby regulation could be hindered and the profits of legitimate industry could be channeled into the coffers of the chosen few. On a tremendous scale the industry engaged in the creation of favorable publicity for itself and in the criticism of public ownership. It subsidized portions of the press and brought about the publication of prepared materials in newspapers and magazines all over the country. It provided funds for the

---

[30] See chapter 20.

[31] For the text of the Senate resolution see *Annual Report of the Federal Trade Commission*, 1928, p. 3.

use of universities, subsidized the writing of books for use in the schools, and in various ways sought to influence the content of teaching. Power companies exerted influence as advertisers. They engaged in good-will advertising. They provided public speakers and ghost writers. The director of publicity of the National Electric Light Association remarked that he knew of no means of publicity that had been neglected except that of sky-writing from airplanes.[32]

There was obvious sincerity in the opposition of the publicity managers of the electrical utilities to public ownership. They believed, along with a substantial proportion of the American people, that governmental encroachment upon the field of business enterprise was an evil of the first rank. Presumably, some of them believed that the skillful juggling of language and figures in defensive action against public ownership was wholly justified by the end in view. Some of them were shrewd strategists and knew the effectiveness of symbols and of emotional appeal in carrying conviction. They understood the value of labeling opponents as "Reds" and "Bolsheviks." "My idea," said one of them in discussing a campaign against an advocate of public ownership, "would be not to try logic, or reason, but to try to pin the Bolshevik idea on my opponent." [33] The significance of the situation was that a powerful, wealthy, and, in spots, unscrupulous and predatory industry took upon itself the shaping of public opinion and the prevention of government competition and of effective regulation, so that its leaders might continue to garner wealth by a mixture of good and of anti-social methods.

## MUSCLE SHOALS

It was in the midst of controversies over the control of the electrical industry that major battles were fought in Congress over electric-power developments at Muscle Shoals and Boulder Dam. The potential value of the drive of the water rushing over Muscle Shoals in the Tennessee River had long been recognized when Congress, in the National Defense Act of 1916, arranged to harness electric power for the manufacture of nitrates for use in explosives, if the United States became involved in war, and to manufacture fertilizer and other useful commodities in time of peace.[34] Many millions of dollars were

---

[32] Senate Doc. No. 92, 70th Cong., 1st sess., Part 3, p. 214. For a summary of evidence as to publicity methods see Part 71A.

[33] *Ibid.*, Part 2, Exhibits, p. 9.

[34] 39 Stat. 215.

spent on dams and power plants and other equipment in the period of high prices during the first World War. The resources of Muscle Shoals did not come into use while the war was in progress and much costly experimentation proved to have little value. When the war was over, it was assumed that the development would not be needed for military purposes. Rather than maintain it as a military asset in the event of a possible future war, to produce fertilizers in the meantime for American farmers in competition with private producers and spend additional millions of dollars of money to be raised by taxes, many government officials favored the sale of the government investment to private owners. It was realized that no offer would be made at all commensurate with the amount already spent by the government, but it was deemed better to write off losses already incurred than to incur additional expense in the continuation of the development and operation of the facilities.

When the Harding administration came into power in March, 1921, most of the people were in a mood to liquidate the residue of the World War as quickly as possible. Rather than spend additional millions of dollars completing the work already begun, the administration sought to dispose of the property. The Secretary of War let it be known that he would recommend to Congress the acceptance of any reasonable bid. Henry Ford submitted the first bid and the one most seriously considered. He agreed to pay substantial annual sums on a one-hundred-year lease of the property, including interest on additional sums which the government was to pay for the construction or completion of dams not yet ready for use. Values cannot easily be discovered from the record. It is clear that the Ford offer would by no means have reimbursed the government for its total investment, but it is also clear that part of the investment of the government was worth by no means what it had cost.

The Ford offer was considered seriously but intermittently until October, 1924, when it was withdrawn. The people remained in confusion as to the issue. They were opposed to wasting government money. Many of them were opposed both to government operation and to the sale of property owned by the government for an amount less than it was worth. Advocates of governmental regulation of the electric-power industry objected particularly to leases running as long as one hundred years. Farmers, who had been intrigued with the prospect of the production of huge quantities of cheap fertilizer at Muscle Shoals, were interested in the prospect that Ford would be able to sell fertilizer at approximately half its present cost. Yet many believed that facilities at Muscle Shoals were worth far more than Ford offered to pay for them. They believed also that electric-power developments in the area provided opportunity for a huge governmental experiment in the production of electric power which would demonstrate the capacity of government to operate in the field and at the same time provide a yardstick to measure the performance of privately operated electrical utilities. In 1922, Senator George W. Norris introduced a bill providing for a government corporation to produce electric power and fertilizer at Muscle Shoals. The proposition was kept before Congress almost constantly until the first session in the Franklin D. Roosevelt administration, when it was enacted into law. It received all the support of reformers of various kinds, including believers in public ownership and operation of all public utilities and believers in less drastic devices, who sought to bring about the more effective regulation of privately owned utilities. Farmers who desired the immediate production of cheap fertilizer, but desired also increased production of cheap electric power, were confused and divided in various ways with reference to various propositions.

In his first annual message, delivered in December, 1923, President. Coolidge recommended that the property be sold, subject to the right of recapture in time of war, thereby ending the present burden of expense and returning to the Treasury the largest amount it was possible to secure.[35] In his message of the following year, he emphasized the need for fertilizer to replenish the fertility of the soil, declaring that, in his opinion, the support of agriculture was the chief problem to consider in connection with the Muscle Shoals property. Much costly experimentation was necessary, he said. For that reason, it was a field better suited to private enterprise than to government operation. He favored the sale of the property or a long-time lease. He thought it might be advantageous to dispose separately of the right to surplus power.[36]

In December, 1925, as if irritated at the inability of Congress to arrive at a solution, Coolidge remarked that the problem of Muscle Shoals seemed to him to have assumed a place all out of proportion with its real importance.

> It probably does not represent in market value much more than a first-class battleship, yet it has been discussed in the Congress over a period of years and for months at a time. [He added:] If anything

[35] 65 *Congressional Record* 100.        [36] 66 *Congressional Record* 53.

were needed to demonstrate the almost utter incapacity of the national government to deal directly with an industrial and commercial problem, it has been provided by our experience with this property. We have expended vast fortunes, we have taxed everybody, but we are unable to secure results which benefit anybody. This property ought to be transferred to private management under conditions which would dedicate it to the public purpose for which it was conceived.[37]

He submitted soon afterward majority and minority reports of a committee which he had appointed to look into the matter. The majority favored private operation.[38] He did not deal with the subject directly in his message of 1926, but certain comments with reference to federal regulation might have been taken as an answer to the contention that the federal government should devise means to regulate the electric-power industry. He said:

It is too much to assume that because an abuse exists it is the business of the national government to provide a remedy. The presumption should be that it is the business of local and state governments. Such national action results in encroaching upon the salutary independence of the states and by undertaking to supersede their natural authority fills the land with bureaus and departments which are undertaking to do what it is impossible for them to accomplish and brings our whole system of government into disrespect and disfavor.[39]

In the meantime, electric power in huge amounts ceased to be necessary for fertilizer production because of improvements in techniques of extracting nitrogen from the air. It began to appear that, had no investment already been made at Muscle Shoals, the place would not now be a particularly desirable location either for war purposes or for the production of fertilizer. This fact lent weight to the argument of those opposed to continued government control. In his annual message in December, 1927, President Coolidge called attention to the changes in the methods of producing nitrates. Extensive investigation made by the Department of War indicated, he said, that the nitrate plants on the Muscle Shoals project were of little value for national defense and could probably be disposed of within two years. This left the project mostly concerned with power. In order to promote the interest of agriculture, as originally intended when the development was undertaken, he proposed the disposition of the plant and the allotment of the revenues for research on methods of more

[37] 67 *Congressional Record* 462.

[38] House Doc. No. 119, 69th Cong., 1st sess.     [39] 68 *Congressional Record* 33.

economical production of concentrated fertilizer and for demonstrations and other methods of stimulating the use of fertilizer on farms.[40]

Ignoring the recommendation, Congress passed a bill for operation of the plant by a Muscle Shoals Corporation of the United States. Congress adjourned less than ten days after sending the bill to the President. This fact enabled him to kill the measure merely by withholding his signature and without a veto message. In December, 1928, in his last annual message to Congress, he advocated the division of the Muscle Shoals property into its two component parts of power and nitrate plants, making it possible to dispose of the power, and reserving to any concern that wished to make nitrates the right to use any power that might be needed for that purpose. He said that he would also gladly approve a bill granting authority to lease the entire property for the production of nitrates. He did not wish to incur further public expense in the construction of another dam, which was deemed necessary by those favoring public operation and by some of those contemplating the lease of the property. "Nor," he continued, "do I think this property should be made a vehicle for putting the United States government indiscriminately into the private and retail field of power distribution and nitrate sales." [41] Congress did not choose to accept the advice.

The attitude of President Hoover was like that of his predecessor.[42] The Senate refused to accept Hoover's leadership. Producing evidence that lobbyists of chemical companies and private power companies had used White House connections and connections with an important farm organization to oppose the project, it again passed a bill providing for public operation through a government-owned corporation. The House of Representatives made a drastic change in the bill, but the change was reduced to minor significance in conference committee, and both houses agreed to it.

The pressure of contending groups was now shifted to the President. On February 28, 1931, he issued a preliminary statement. It was obvious from the debate, the press, and the many communications which had been sent to him, he complained, that the Muscle Shoals controversy was no longer a question of disposing of a war activity to the advantage of the people primarily concerned. It had been transformed into a political symbol and was expected to be a political issue.

[40] 69 *Congressional Record* 106.     [41] 70 *Congressional Record* 24.
[42] See his annual message of December, 1929, 72 *Congressional Record* 26. See speeches of Senator Norris and materials incorporated, 72 *Congressional Record* 6365-6377, 7153-7163.

To be against Senator Norris's bill appeared to be cause for denunciation as being in league with the power companies. It was also emerging as the test of views upon government operation and distribution of power and government manufacture of commodities. This happened to be an engineering project, he concluded in crabbed fashion, and, so far as its business merits and demerits were concerned, it was subject to the cold examination of engineering facts.[43]

On March 3 he submitted his veto message. Instead of limiting it to a statement of engineering facts, he, too, resorted to general considerations and the use of political symbols. "I am firmly opposed to the government entering into any business the major purpose of which is competition with our citizens," he declared.[44] While government might temporarily enter the field of business in national emergencies and might construct great dams and reservoirs where navigation, flood control, and reclamation were of dominant importance, it must not go beyond these limits. In these cases power was often a by-product and could be disposed of by contract or lease. For the federal government deliberately to build up the major purpose of power production and manufacturing in its own hands was to break down the initiative and enterprise of the American people. It was destructive of equality of opportunity among the people. It was the negation of the ideals upon which our civilization had been based. He continued:

> This bill raises one of the important issues confronting our people. That is squarely the issue of federal government ownership and operation of power and manufacturing business, not as a minor by-product, but as a major purpose. Involved in this question is the agitation against the conduct of the power industry. The power problem is not to be solved by the federal government going into the power business, nor is it to be solved by the project in this bill. The remedy for abuses in the conduct of that industry lies in regulation and not by the federal government entering upon the business itself. . . . I hesitate to contemplate the future of our institutions, of our government, and of our country if the preoccupation of its officials is to be no longer the promotion of justice and equal opportunity, but is to be devoted to barter in the market. That is not liberalism, it is degeneration.[45]

Friends of the bill were unable to secure enough votes to override the veto. Some time later a commission was appointed, consisting of

---

[43] William Starr Myers and Walter H. Newton, *The Hoover Administration; A Documented Narrative* (1936), p. 469.

[44] Senate Doc. No. 321, 71st Cong., 3d sess., p. 6.  [45] *Ibid.*, p. 6.

persons selected by the President and of representatives of Tennessee, Alabama, and the American Farm Bureau Federation. The commission made a report advocating private operation of Muscle Shoals.[46] The President transmitted the report to Congress, but Congress refused to accept its recommendations. On the other hand, the advocates of public operation were unable to secure the votes that would be needed to enact their bill over a veto. The issue merged in the several issues of the presidential campaign of 1932. The enactment of a measure to provide for public operation and for the continued development of the several Muscle Shoals projects was one of the first important steps of the New-Deal administration.[47]

The Muscle Shoals controversy was "constitutional" chiefly in the larger sense of the expansion of governmental functions to include the conduct of enterprises hitherto left to private operation. The Constitution as such was seldom mentioned in the debates. Conventional constitutional questions were involved, however, in that federal authority was assumed to rest on certain constitutional provisions. Development of Muscle Shoals was provided for under the National Defense Act of 1916, on the basis of the war power. The promotion of navigation on the waters of the United States involved the commerce clause. Since development contemplated flood control, the improvement of transportation, the improvement of the soil, the improvement of the conditions of living through the provision of relatively cheap electric power, and related forms of community betterment, the general welfare could also be said to be involved. The determination of constitutional questions, however, remained for the period after the enactment of legislation in 1933.

BOULDER DAM

The controversy over the Colorado River development, resulting in provision for the construction of Boulder Dam and of an All-American canal to carry water from the river into Imperial Valley in Southern California, took place within the period of the Muscle Shoals controversy. Some of the same issues were involved; yet conditions were sufficiently different that the Colorado River project was authorized in 1928, whereas full development at Muscle Shoals was not authorized until 1933.

Flowing streams had an importance to the arid states of the West not possessed in eastern states, which were served by relatively even

[46] Senate Doc. No. 21, 72d Cong., 1st sess.          [47] See chapter 34.

rainfall. The opportunity to irrigate often made the difference between desert conditions, on the one hand, and luxuriant agricultural production, on the other; and an adequate water supply was necessary to the growth of towns and cities and the operation of industries. The Colorado River was a necessary asset to seven states in the West and Southwest. It was also a liability in certain areas, in that raging torrents of the wet seasons threatened untold damage by flood. Theodore Roosevelt, with his interest in conservation, gave some attention to developments on the Colorado. During the first World War and thereafter, reclamation engineers in the Interior Department showed a renewed interest in the subject. At the same time the states affected, realizing that appropriations from the river might ultimately lead to scarcity and prevent further development for which additions to water supply were necessary, sought to work out an agreement for the allotment of the waters of the Colorado.

Legislatures of the seven states — Arizona, California, Colorado, Nevada, New Mexico, Utah, and Wyoming — passed acts providing for the appointment of commissioners to represent them in negotiating an agreement. The Constitution provided that no state should enter into any agreement or compact with another state without the consent of Congress.[48] The legislatures, therefore, asked Congress to authorize the making of the compact. Since international problems were involved, in that the river ran through Mexico as well as through the United States and in that the question of navigation must be raised, the federal government was asked to appoint a representative to meet with the representatives of the several states. By an act of August 19, 1921, Congress authorized the appointment of the federal representative in the making of the compact, with the reservation that the compact should not be binding until it should have been approved by the legislature of each of the states and by Congress.[49] Herbert Hoover was appointed the representative of the federal government, and in 1922 the commission worked out a compact allocating rights as between the upper and lower basin states. Arizona, a state not yet extensively developed, but with vast tracts of arid land capable of future development if water were available, refused to ratify the compact on the ground that its interests were not adequately pro-

[48] Article I, Section 10. On interstate compacts see Felix Frankfurter and James M. Landis, "The Compact Clause of the Constitution — A Study in Interstate Adjustments," *Yale Law Journal*, XXXIV (May, 1925), 685-758, and Arthur W. Macmahon, "Compacts, Interstate," *Encyclopedia of the Social Sciences* (1931), IV, 109-113.

[49] 42 Stat. 172.

tected. The situation was, therefore, deadlocked. In 1925, the conclusion of a compact by six states, exclusive of Arizona, was suggested, but California, with vast immediate interests involved, threw doubt on the feasibility of such a plan by insisting on certain important conditions.

Engineering developments by the federal government were deemed contingent upon agreement among the states on the allocation of water rights. If such agreement could be made, a project was planned to provide for flood control, irrigation, and electric-power production. A huge dam was to be constructed at Boulder or Black Canyon, between Nevada and Arizona, to hold back the flood waters of the stream and provide for a relatively even flow. Power plants were to be constructed for the production of electric power, and the costs were to be liquidated through the sale of power. Farther down the river, but still within the territory of the United States, a canal was to be constructed to carry water into the fertile Imperial Valley of Southern California. It was to supplement or replace a canal already in use, running from the river at a point in Mexico. The new canal was advocated because of the fear that, in the event of disturbed relations between the United States and Mexico, Mexicans might cut the water life-line of the fertile valley. President Coolidge mentioned the proposed project at some length in his annual message of December, 1925. He spoke of the conflicting rights of the several states and of their inability to agree. It was imperative, he said, that flood control be undertaken for California and Arizona and that preparation be made for irrigation, for power, and for domestic water. He suggested that Congress consider the creation of some agency to determine methods of improvement solely upon economic and engineering facts, and to negotiate and settle, subject to the approval of Congress, the participation, rights, and obligations of each group. Only by some such method, he asserted, could early construction be secured.[50]

A measure known thereafter as the Swing-Johnson bill, introduced in the Senate by Hiram W. Johnson and in the House by Philip D. Swing, was reported in both houses in 1926. It provided for the project which the President had mentioned on conclusion of a satisfactory compact of six states. It was debated, but not passed. It was reintroduced in the succeeding Congress, and final action was taken in December, 1928. In and out of Congress many people, including Secretary of Commerce Herbert Hoover, for example, believed firmly

[50] 67 *Congressional Record* 463.

in private enterprise, but favored, nevertheless, the construction of huge reclamation projects by the federal government, to make possible the utilization of land and other resources of which profitable use could not otherwise be made. As a rule the projects were not intended to yield income to the government, at least not beyond the recovery of their cost and to the extent of making the government a competitor of private enterprise. Even so, the Swing-Johnson bill met severe opposition. Part of it came from representatives of Arizona and scattered representatives of other states, who regarded the project as an encroachment upon the rights of their respective states. Strong opposition was said to have been inspired by power companies in the West and by power interests throughout the country, which were opposed to any degree of governmental encroachment. Their hostility was directed particularly at the provision in the bill which authorized the Secretary of the Interior at his discretion to construct a power plant at the dam for the production of electric power which would be sold at the plant to consumers who built transmission lines to it. It was contended that, even though the government might construct equipment for flood control and irrigation, it had no right to enter the field of private enterprise to the extent of engaging in power production. The strategy was to compel the government to lease water rights to a private power company which would be given the privilege of constructing a plant. Any power going out from the dam would as a result have to go out from the plant of this company, and the right of the government to see that sales were made to various municipalities and other purchasers would be restricted or cut off.[51]

Congress passed the bill with a provision authorizing the Secretary of the Interior to construct the power plant. However much he may have disliked that particular provision,[52] Coolidge signed the bill.[53] Six of the seven states ratified the interstate compact, and the Secretary of the Interior, after having let contracts for the sale of power as provided by the bill, directed the beginning of work on the project. The state of Arizona, which did not agree to the compact, brought a suit in the Supreme Court against the Secretary of the Interior and the six states to enjoin the carrying-out of the Boulder Dam project.

[51] See speech of Congressman Swing, 68 *Congressional Record* 2633-2637. See also Hiram W. Johnson, "The Boulder Canyon Project," *Annals of the American Academy*, CXXXV (January, 1928), 150-156.

[52] For his opposition to governmental operation of power production see 70 *Congressional Record* 24.

[53] 45 Stat. 1057.

The Court found that a portion of the Colorado River had once been navigable and that the construction of the dam would make a portion of it navigable again. It therefore upheld the power of the federal government to construct the dam as a promotion of navigation. "The fact that purposes other than navigation will also be served could not invalidate the exercise of the authority conferred," said Justice Brandeis for the Court, "even if those other purposes would not alone have justified an exercise of congressional power." [54]

The several phases of the Boulder Dam project were carried to completion, not during the Coolidge-Hoover régime, but during the New-Deal period. The project fitted well into the network of government projects carried on for reclamation purposes, for the promotion of the public welfare generally, and for giving employment during the years of depression. The power plant at Boulder Dam was constructed by the government, and it became the center of supply for a vast area throughout the Southwest.

## THE TREND OF THE TIMES

Certain aspects of the farm situation and of the situation with reference to the electric-power industry are given the space allotted to them here, not because they represent the only developments of the kind, but because they illustrate the movement, or the retreat, toward increased governmental control between the first World War and the New-Deal period. Additional illustrations might be given from the same and from related fields. The successful struggle to provide full-time personnel for the Federal Power Commission and expand its authority might be presented at length. The organization of the Federal Radio Commission, to deal with the emerging radio industry, might be described. The story of the continuation and extension of control of railroads might be resumed. Again, the depression, which brought the collapse of foamy holding-company structures in the electrical field, disclosed gross abuses in investment and commercial banking and created demand for revision and extension of machinery and methods of control. The foundation was laid for drastic federal regulation of security issues and for the elimination of holding-company structures in interstate commerce that could not show justification. Need, or the alleged need, for broader regulation of enterprise was not discovered initially with the coming of the de-

---

[54] Arizona v. California, 283 U.S. 423, 456 (1931). For further litigation as to the rights of Arizona see Arizona v. California, 298 U.S. 558 (1936).

pression, but it was impressed upon the minds of the people when they suffered the results, individually and *en masse.*

Inevitably, attempts were made to discover causes. In the midst of the period of alleged prosperity thoughtful students had called attention to the extent to which private enterprise was falling into the hands of great corporations that were managed in the interest of the chosen few without a sense of public morality or civic responsibility.[55] A careful study entitled *The Modern Corporation and Private Property,* by Adolf A. Berle, Jr., and Gardiner C. Means, published in 1932, showed dramatically the rapid extension of the power of corporations over private enterprise and, within the corporate field, the rapid growth of new large corporations at the expense of smaller ones and of partnerships and individual enterprise. It showed accretions of power in gigantic organizations such as to dwarf the power of individual states in the Union. Within these powerful organizations it showed the concentration of power in the hands of the few by the pyramiding of holding-company structures and other devices. It showed a gradual but fundamental change in the character of private property not apparent to the casual observer, and a type of concentration of actual power not revealed by merely formal studies of our constitutional system.

The authors concluded that the modern corporation might be regarded, not simply as one form of social organization, but as the dominant institution of the modern world. Its rise had brought a concentration of economic power which could compete on equal terms with the modern state. Where its own interests were concerned, the corporation even attempted to dominate the state. They suggested that the future might see the economic organism now typified by the corporation, not only on an equal plane with the state, but possibly even superseding it as the dominant form of organization. The law of corporations might be considered as the potential constitutional law for the new economic state.[56]

Whatever the validity of these suggestions, certain facts are clear. A nation founded on principles of individual liberty and of individual rights regarding the use of property had evolved out of a simple and atomistic property organization into one in which the welfare of the

[55] See, for example, William Z. Ripley, *Main Street and Wall Street* (1927). See also H. S. Raushenbush and Harry W. Laidler, *Power Control* (1928).

[56] Adolf A. Berle and Gardiner C. Means, *The Modern Corporation and Private Property* (1933), p. 357.

individual and the property which was nominally his own were caught up in a tide of economic enterprise dominated by huge corporations. If within themselves some of these corporations had achieved a moderately orderly status, resembling in some degree well-arranged political establishments, there was oftentimes little order as among them and there was little or no over-all planning as to economic and social ends to be achieved. The business collapse of 1929 represented an unintentional and tragic achievement of the efforts of the managers of enterprise in its new form. These new and powerful units of economic enterprise were wholly unable to relieve the resulting distress. It was only natural that the people turned once more to government to remedy their ills, and sought through government to establish firm control over the powerful but anarchic units then dominating economic enterprise. Few thoughtful people assumed that it would be easy for government to establish and maintain wise control over the unco-ordinated branches of the huge industrial machine that had evolved in an era of mass production achieved through corporation control. Some over-all supervision, however, seemed the only alternative to intermittent, if not permanent, chaos and disaster. Such was the background of the New Deal.

# CHAPTER 35

# THE NEW DEAL IN OPERATION

THE NEW-DEAL PERIOD is too recent to be viewed in settled perspective. Its final appraisal will depend on the course of events in coming years. This chapter and those which follow attempt a tentative statement of what seem to be the outstanding facts of constitutional significance, on the assumption that, even though a more distant view will unquestionably lead to a modified interpretation, it is worth while to sketch in the relevant happenings of a dramatic decade for the light which they throw upon the happenings of the later years.

## THE SETTING

As indicated in the preceding chapter, the United States experienced after the first World War a reaction against governmental encroachment upon the field of private enterprise. Although certain groups demanded broad governmental action in their own interests on such a scale that the ultimate expansion of the power of the federal government over a number of fields must have seemed inevitable to thoughtful observers, the leaders of the several administrations were spokesmen of rugged individualism. After three years of the worst depression in the history of the country, the masses of the people were tired of being assured that the depression was largely psychological and of being urged to adhere to the economic faith of their fathers. They were quite willing to accept such governmental intervention as might be necessary to still the panic and restore economic order. The morale of the believers in rugged individualism was shattered. Most of their leaders were voted out of elective office in 1932. It is not clear that the philosophy of Franklin D. Roosevelt was well understood at the time of the election, or that strong personal leadership and a definite program of governmental control were expected of him. Republican leadership was repudiated because it had failed. The process of repudiation brought a Democratic administration into power. The credit to which the New-Deal administration is entitled is not so much credit for selling a program to the people at the time of the election as for recognizing in the hour of crisis, and satisfying, a deep, popular desire for strong, positive, and assured leadership. Roosevelt knew how to give assurance and win confidence. Whereas every pronouncement of Herbert Hoover that the country was fundamentally sound and that prosperity was just around the corner seemed to bring new disasters, Roosevelt could relieve the minds of the people with the assurance that the only thing they had to fear was fear itself. He recognized the fact that the people wanted drastic action even though they had little conception of what the action ought to be. He gave them such an avalanche of action as to change the whole face of the economic situation. If his program created problems on a parallel with those which it solved, the people were not immediately disturbed. Old burdens, at any rate, had been thrown off.

Broadly speaking, the purpose of the New Deal was the elimination of poverty in the midst of plenty. The sufferings of the people had not been caused by national inability to produce plentiful supplies of either agricultural or industrial commodities. The embarrassing situation was that the agricultural and industrial plant was equipped to produce more than purchasers both at home and abroad were able to buy. In much of industry and, to some extent, in agriculture as well, efficient and cheap production now depend upon what is called mass production. Profits are made through the sale of large numbers of identical units of each product. The machinery necessary for the production of an article by mechanized devices rather than by hand methods may be tremendously expensive. The sale of thousands or hundreds of thousands of units may be necessary to cover the cost of such machinery. Profits begin to flow in only when the sale of still more units is brought about. The cost of production of additional units is relatively small. The theory of enterprise based on mass production, therefore, is that retail costs must be kept sufficiently low to make sales possible in large quantities. A basic difficulty in the depression period was that consumers were unable to buy the final units of production from which profits were derived. With the loss of income, stockholders failed to fulfill to a normal extent their own functions as purchasers and consumers. The decline in production led to a curtailment in labor supply and hence to a curtailment of the purchasing power of labor. The demand for commodities was thereby still further reduced and the curtailment of production was still further in order, with continued procedure in a descending spiral.

The plan of the New Deal was to reverse the spiral by restoring confidence and purchasing power. "Pump-priming" was a characteristic description. Revivifying credit was to be injected into the veins of a nation in which businesses of every kind were collapsing from anaemia. The fear of bankruptcy was to be removed from well-managed and normally sound enterprise. The funds necessary for survival were to be provided for impoverished families. Emergency projects were to be instituted to create additional employment. Regulation of industry was to be undertaken in such a way as to spread employment to larger numbers of people. Increased purchasing power would create new demand for products. New demand would lead to increased production. Increased production would bring about employment of additional persons and such employment would further stimulate demand. With the spiral turned upward, the major immediate problem would be solved. The more adequate distribution of employment and the increase of wages were expected to start and maintain the spiral in the right direction.

It was deemed necessary that high price-levels be maintained and that the production of surpluses be avoided. The existence of surpluses was apt to result in price-cutting. Price-cutting might destroy the profits, and even the capital, of the producer. The man who lost his profits and his capital was unable to fulfill his normal function as a purchaser of the products of other producers. His condition, coupled with that of other producers in the same situation, might bring about the decline in purchases which would enforce curtailment of production and start the spiral downward once more. Hence, for the first time, apart from the limited experience of the World-War period, the federal government sought to exercise broad control over the whole field of production and distribution, over prices in terms of which exchange was made, and over labor involved in production. Speculation and other evils of the old régime likewise bore upon the situation and called for regulation or elimination. If a broad program of government control meant interference with property rights and privileges hitherto deemed constitutionally exempt from interference, the prevailing attitude was that constitutional problems must await solution in less critical times. When the Franklin D. Roosevelt administration came into office, the banks of the country were all closed. Industrial and commercial activity was approaching stagnation. The times seemed inappropriate for concern about the interpretation given by black-robed justices to a document written a century and a half ago. The nation had to be rescued, even if the Constitution suffered in the process.

The new President approached the subject of the depression as if it were a common enemy of all the people, to be met by disciplined and united action as a military invader would have to be met. If we were to go forward, he said in his inaugural address:

> we must move as a trained and loyal army willing to sacrifice for the good of a common discipline, because without such discipline no progress is made, no leadership becomes effective. We are, I know, ready and willing to submit our lives and property to such discipline, because it makes possible a leadership which aims at a larger good. This I propose to offer, pledging that the larger purposes will bind upon us all as a sacred obligation with a unity of duty hitherto evoked only in time of armed strife.[1]

If Congress failed to enact measures adequate to meet the crisis, he proposed to ask for "broad executive power to wage a war against the emergency, as great as the power that would be given to me if we were in fact invaded by a foreign foe." [2] During the first World War, Roosevelt had been assistant secretary of the navy under Woodrow Wilson. In planning the warfare of his own presidency against the economic enemy, it is clear that much of his thinking was done in terms of World-War analogies. The return to power of a Democratic administration, the first to hold office since the Wilson period, made it only natural that some of the World-War leaders should return to federal office and that others should become unofficial advisers of the administration. They, like the President, thought in terms of the dramatic concentration of power in the federal government which they had helped to bring about for the defeat of a foreign enemy. It is not surprising that modes of procedure were carried over from one period to the other. The propaganda for national unity, for example, was much the same. The use of the symbol of the blue eagle to secure co-operation in the program worked out under the National Industrial Recovery Act was analogous to the method of securing subscriptions to Liberty bonds and co-operation in other phases of the World-War program. The resort to psychological coercion rather than to enforcement at law had characterized many of the activities of the Wilson administration.

At the beginning of the Roosevelt administration, many people

[1] *Public Papers and Addresses of Franklin D. Roosevelt* (5 vols., 1938), II, 14.
[2] *Ibid.*, II, 15.

were convinced that the country must be saved immediately by drastic action or go down to almost irrevocable ruin. Whether for better or for worse, it was believed that the emergency would come to an end in a relatively short period of time. In this they were mistaken. The emergency flattened out into a prolonged experience over succeeding years. Or, to phrase the matter differently, it was succeeded by a series of emergencies, each of which called for new emergency solutions. New-Deal government, therefore, became symbolic of emergency government. Indeed, as the shadow of another world war began to darken upon the nation, what appeared to be a permanent office for emergency management was set up in the Executive Office of the President. A tremendous concentration of power was brought about under the title, indicating the emphasis which emergency continued to play in the minds of the administration. Government in terms of emergencies means oftentimes a disregard of permanent welfare. The accusations of such disregard were punctuated throughout the New Deal period by huge additions to the national debt without plans or prospects for payment.

If the administration was criticized for acting almost exclusively in terms of emergencies rather than in terms of permanent public welfare, it was also criticized for using emergency situations to speed the enactment of measures for permanent reforms. Roosevelt and his advisers were advocates of many of the changes for which there had been agitation during the preceding years. He favored drastic measures for reducing farm surpluses, for increasing farm incomes, for regulating utilities and the sale of securities, and for giving economic security to the less favored members of society. From the time of the first emergency session of Congress in his administration, therefore, his recovery program and his reform program were inseparable. The reforms which he sponsored were advocated, indeed, as essential to permanent recovery.

The institution of a vast program for recovery and reform, involving as it did the broad extension of the powers of the federal government, required a tremendous expansion of the machinery of government. It brought about the establishment of new regulatory commissions, new government corporations, new administrations, new authorities, and new committees and bureaus. It resulted in a complicated and rapidly changing governmental structure, much of which was conceived at first, not as a permanent part of the government, but as organization to meet the needs of the hour. As the continuation of the emergency, or the repetition of emergencies, demonstrated the probability of the continuation of many of the functions assumed for temporary periods, the mushroom structure was recast to some extent and given an appearance of order and stability which it had not possessed hitherto.[3] The liberalization and extension of the program of the federal government with the coming of the Roosevelt administration meant inevitably bringing into the service of the government large numbers of people who had not hitherto undergone the discipline of such experience. In many instances they were the advocates of social reforms which they had not had the privilege of seeing in operation and about which many of their ideas needed revision in terms of experience. Their own discipline, therefore, had to be acquired at the expense of the government, and the defects of their respective programs had to be ironed out in the process of trial and error. This lack of experience and the fact that large numbers of the new employees were lodged in emergency agencies had the advantage of making possible changes that could not have been brought about with older, experienced personnel in permanent establishments with binding procedures and traditions.

An administration with the kind of program, the kind of organization, and the kind of personnel indicated had to have strong leadership if it was to avoid within itself the chaos already suffered by the economic system of the country because of the alleged absence of leadership, planning, and control. Although governmental chaos was by no means completely avoided, President Roosevelt gave the strong leadership which he promised in his inaugural address. From the time of the delivery of that address he was accused of asking for or of seizing dictatorial powers. At the beginning of his administration, when people in all walks of life were impressed with the necessity for immediate and drastic action, statements as to his exercise of dictatorial powers were often made with approval rather than in the form of accusations. The following statement, for example, was attributed to Vice-President Garner: "The President has been given dictatorial powers to straighten out the banks. He has been given dictatorial powers over wages of government employees and veterans' benefits. Why should he not also have dictatorial powers to help the farmers?" [4] Eventually, only the critics of the administration made charges of dictatorship. In connection with his support of a bill to reorganize the executive branch of the government, the President

[3] See chapter 30.          [4] *New York Times,* March 21, 1933.

found it expedient to give to the press the statement that he had neither the desire nor the temperament to be a dictator.[5] Although the use of the term, which took its contemporary meaning from European dictators, was obviously inappropriate as applied to President Roosevelt, he exercised peacetime power without precedent, receiving it by grant from an acquiescent Congress, or receiving it indirectly through his position as Executive charged with the fulfillment of functions of his branch of the government, or assuming it through his own broad interpretation of the powers of his office.

## THE FIRST SPECIAL SESSION

One of the first official acts of President Roosevelt was to call a special session of Congress to meet on March 9, 1933. In the meantime, he proclaimed a bank holiday to last until that date. The banks of the country were already closed. The purpose of the holiday was to maintain the *status quo* until legislation could be worked out and confidence in the sound banks of the country thus sufficiently restored to check the withdrawal of deposits that was rapidly draining the resources of even the strongest banking institutions at the time when they closed their respective doors. The proclamation represented a sweeping exercise of authority on a somewhat doubtful statutory basis. The people of the country had put their trust in their new President, however, and there was little complaint. In his inaugural address he had declared that there must be an end to conduct in banking and in business which too often had given to a sacred trust the likeness of callous and selfish wrongdoing. He had said there must be a strict supervision of all banking and credit and investments, so that there would be an end to speculation with other people's money. There must be provision for an adequate but sound currency. With more confidence than they had felt in many months, the people awaited the initiation of his program.

On March 9, he outlined the program to Congress. The first task, he said, was to reopen all sound banks. To that end he asked Congress to give the executive branch of the government control over banks for the protection of depositors, authority to open such banks as had already been ascertained to be in sound condition, and other banks as rapidly as possible, and authority to reorganize and reopen such banks as might require reorganization. He asked amendments to the Federal Reserve Act to provide for such additional currency,

[5] See chapter 30.

adequately secured, as might be necessary to meet demands for currency.[6] With the message he submitted a bill for speedy enactment.

Congress responded so speedily that the measure was ready for his signature on the same day.[7] To take care of the possible invalidity of steps already taken, the new statute approved and confirmed the relevant proclamations and orders already issued. It based action on the recognized power to provide for the safer and more effective operation of the national banking system and to preserve for the people the full benefits of the currency authorized by Congress and on the power to relieve interstate commerce of the great burdens and obstructions resulting from the receipt, on an unsound or unsafe basis, of deposits subject to withdrawal by check during the emergency period. The statute prescribed machinery to investigate the banking system, arrange for the opening of those banks that might be safely opened, and dispose of those whose doors must remain closed. To re-establish a basis for credit by recapturing the gold and gold certificates that had been withdrawn from banks for hoarding, the statute authorized the Secretary of the Treasury to require their surrender to the government. Machinery was set up for restoring order within the banking system. By assurance of safety, appeals to patriotism, and threats of prosecution, the government produced a flowing stream of gold from hoarders to the United States Treasury. Later in the session, after more time for consideration, Congress enacted another banking bill to remedy serious abuses in the system.[8] One of the important steps taken was the attempt completely to separate commercial banking from investment banking. Commercial banks having investment affiliates were required to divorce them. A Federal Deposit Insurance Corporation was created and provision was made to secure depositors against loss up to certain amounts.

On March 10, 1933, the President sent to Congress a request for authority to effect drastic economies in government. For three long years, he said, the federal government had been on the road toward bankruptcy. It had piled up an accumulated deficit of five billion dollars. He asked for legislation in terms of broad principles authorizing him to make reductions in veterans' benefits and in the amounts paid in salaries to civil and military employees of the government. He asked that the details of expenditure be left to the Executive. "The flexibility of the measures which I am proposing is not only practical but proceeds along the road of constitutional government." [9]

[6] *Public Papers and Aadresses of Franklin D. Roosevelt*, II, 45-47.     [7] 48 Stat. 1.
[8] 48 Stat. 162.     [9] *Public Papers and Addresses of Franklin D. Roosevelt*, II, 51.

The veterans' lobby put up opposition, but the measure proposed by the President was enacted.[10]

On March 13, the President sent to Congress a brief message, recommending the passage of legislation legalizing the manufacture and sale of light wines and beer, to provide a much-needed revenue for the government. This measure also, proposed in partial fulfillment of campaign pledges, was speedily enacted.

On March 16, the President sent to Congress an agricultural reform bill, which he characterized as "the most drastic and far-reaching piece of farm legislation ever proposed in time of peace." [11] It was intended to restrict agricultural production, thereby eliminating troublesome farm surpluses and raising farm prices so as to restore the purchasing power of the farmer and benefit indirectly the industrial producers from whom farm purchases were made. Secretary of Agriculture Henry A. Wallace had held a meeting of representatives of farm organizations and farm co-operatives to discuss plans for farm legislation. An important part of the bill agreed upon was the so-called "domestic-allotment" plan.[12] The plan provided for the reduction of acreage planted for domestic consumption by the allotment to each producer of the right to plant only a given percentage of the acreage hitherto planted with the crops in question. Enforcement of the restriction was to be brought about by cash payments for acreage taken out of production. The money from which the payments were to be derived was to be collected by the government through taxes levied upon the processing of the commodities grown, as, for example, by a tax upon the milling of wheat.

Governmental limitation of agricultural production was a drastic step. The President had to give steady support to see the measure through Congress. One congressman protested that the bill was contrary to the law of God as well as of man. "I contend that we have no right or power to legislate to control or seek to limit the income of a producer, as we are attempting to do in this bill." [13] Congressman James M. Beck, a distinguished constitutional lawyer of the conservative school, took the same position. He contended that the federal government had no constitutional control over agriculture, except in respect to interstate transportation of agricultural products, or foreign

---

[10] 48 Stat. 8.     [11] *Public Papers and Addresses of Franklin D. Roosevelt*, II, 79.

[12] For the origin of the plan see John D. Black, *Agricultural Reform in the United States* (1929), chapter X.

[13] 77 *Congressional Record* 753.

commerce, or legitimate taxation. The only other theory, he said, was the suggestion of an emergency.

> I think of all the damnable heresies that have ever been suggested in connection with the Constitution, the doctrine of emergency is the worst. It means that when Congress declares an emergency there is no Constitution. This means its death. It is the very doctrine that the German chancellor is invoking today in the dying hours of the parliamentary body of the German republic, namely, that because of an emergency it should grant to the German chancellor absolute power to pass any law, even though that law contradicts the constitution of the German republic. Chancellor Hitler is at least frank about it. We pay the Constitution lip-service, but the result is the same.[14]

The Constitution still lived, he said, in so far as it prescribed the mechanics of government and protected and safeguarded the liberties of the individual.

> But the Constitution of the United States, as a restraining influence in keeping the federal government within the carefully prescribed channels of power, is moribund, if not dead. We are witnessing its death-agonies, for when this bill becomes a law, if unhappily it becomes a law, there is no longer any workable Constitution to keep the Congress within the limits of its constitutional powers.[15]

However much impressed his auditors may have been with the eloquence of Congressman Beck and with the general soundness of his constitutional doctrine, the House passed the farm bill by a vote of more than three to one.

A clash of interests in the Senate threatened the dismemberment or defeat of the bill, but most of the opponents were kept in line by the President and his cohorts. In the meantime, the President sent to Congress a message, asking for related legislation to save farm mortgages from foreclosure. This measure was so popular in Congress that in both houses rival committees fought for jurisdiction over it.[16] In the Senate the farm-mortgage bill was added by amendment to the general agricultural bill, thereby greatly increasing the popularity of the latter.

The passage of the farm bill by the Senate was delayed by another, much more controversial, amendment. Competing nations in world markets had abandoned the gold standard and substantially inflated

---

[14] *Ibid.*, p. 754.    [15] *Ibid.*, p. 755.
[16] See *New York Times*, April 5 and 6, 1933.

their currencies. Such inflation had added to the difficulties of marketing American farm products. Spokesmen for American farmers took the position that corresponding changes needed to be made in our own currency system. Farm leaders were reported as saying at a conference at the White House that "reflation" was necessary for farm relief.[17] A number of inflationary amendments, including amendments for the coinage of silver, were introduced. It was announced that the President favored none of the amendments,[18] but he changed his mind or was forced to compromise. On April 19, he took the United States off the gold standard in foreign exchange. (The country was already off the gold standard as far as domestic exchange was concerned, in that holders of gold were required by law to surrender it to the Treasury of the United States, where it was retained.) Administration officials then collaborated with members of the Senate in working out what was called an inflation amendment to the farm bill. That amendment, as adopted, gave the President broad power over the currency whenever he found that the foreign commerce of the United States was adversely affected by reason of the depreciation of the currency of other nations, or when the economic emergency required an expansion of credit, or when an expansion of credit was necessary to secure by international agreement a stabilization of the currencies of various governments at proper levels. The President was authorized to expand credit by open-market operations conducted through the Federal Reserve Board. If such operations proved inadequate, he was authorized to issue up to three billion dollars in United States notes. He was authorized to change the gold content of the dollar, to fix the relation between gold and silver, and to purchase substantial sums in silver.

The farm bill, as approved on May 12, 1933, included the essential provisions of the original bill, the farm-mortgage amendment, and the inflation amendment.[19] On May 26, a measure was introduced, with the backing of the President, to give an unquestioned statutory base to the practices already established of refusing to pay gold in redemption of government bonds or currency containing clauses providing for such payment and of requiring private individuals to surrender gold to the government so that private contracts calling for payment in gold could not be fulfilled in that commodity. The bill prescribed the currencies that should constitute legal tender and required their acceptance in full payment of debts, even though the contracts

[17] *Ibid.*, April 15, 1933.     [18] *Ibid.*, April 18, 1933.     [19] 48 Stat. 31.

called for payment in gold.  Little time was taken for discussion of
the constitutionality of the measure.  Senator Carter Glass, an expert
on banking, was reported as saying that it was unconstitutional and
that the courts would so hold if there was any integrity left in the
courts with regard to sanctity of contracts.[20]  Administration spokesmen argued briefly that all contracts were made subject to the sovereign power of the government.  They contended that creditors
suffered no actual injury from the requirement that they accept legal
tender other than gold in payment of debts due to them.  Opponents
discussed the bill in terms of morality as much as in terms of law.  "I
think this matter before us involves the most serious question of
national dishonor that has arisen in the Congress in my recollection,"
said Senator David A. Reed, of Pennsylvania.  "I think it much more
important to consider this question from the standpoint of national
honesty and national honor than it is to split hairs on constitutional
construction, and the letter of that charter of our liberty to which we
so often refer, and so seldom follow." [21]  He called particular attention to the provision in Section 4 of the Fourteenth Amendment, that
the validity of the public debt of the United States authorized by law
should not be questioned.  He contended that due process of law was
violated, furthermore, in that bondholders entitled by contract to
payment in gold were required to accept debased money in its stead.
The act was passed by substantial majorities in spite of the opposition,[22] and the constitutional question was left to the courts.[23]

In his message of March 21, 1933, the President dealt with the
highly controversial subject of unemployment relief.  In the early
years of the depression period the Hoover administration had contended that relief was a matter of local concern and that the federal
government had no jurisdiction over it.  The states and municipalities
were themselves hard-pressed for funds, however; and in the summer
of 1932, Congress had passed an act providing for federal loans to
states for relief purposes.  Roosevelt asked for enrollment of unemployed workers by the federal government, for grants to states for
relief work, and for a broad public-works, labor-creating program.
Like Theodore Roosevelt, he was an ardent conservationist. He asked
for authority to set up a Civilian Conservation Corps, through which
he would gather up thousands of unemployed young men from the

[20] *New York Times*, May 27, 1933.
[21] 77 *Congressional Record* 4894.                [22] 48 Stat. 112.
[23] For discussion of the issue before the Supreme Court see chapter 36.

streets and highways of the country and put them to work at preventing soil erosion and promoting flood control and at bettering generally the condition of the national forests.[24] Congress speedily enacted the proposed measure.

On March 29, 1933, the President recommended to Congress the enactment of legislation for federal supervision of traffic in investment securities in interstate commerce. Large numbers of the people were still smarting from the results of commercial debauchery wherein high-pressure salesmen had sold to a gullible public large quantities of gilt-edged securities having little more value than the paper on which they were printed. The federal government could not, and should not, create the appearance of approving or guaranteeing that newly issued securities were sound in all respects, said the President, but it had an obligation to insist that every issue of new securities to be sold in interstate commerce should be accompanied by full publicity and information, and that no essentially important element attending the issue should be concealed from the buying public. "This proposal adds to the ancient rule of *caveat emptor,* the further doctrine 'let the seller also beware.' It puts the burden of telling the whole truth on the seller. It should give impetus to honest dealing in securities and thereby bring back public confidence."[25] The proposed bill required that securities, shipped or advertised in interstate commerce or through the mails, should be registered with the Federal Trade Commission and that prescribed information should be made available to the commission and to the public. It represented a broad extension of the regulatory power of the federal government over commercial activities hitherto regulated only by inadequate laws in the several states. The bill was passed,[26] in spite of the opposition of interests to be regulated.

In his message of April 10, 1933, the President took up the subject of Muscle Shoals. The development, he said, if envisioned in its entirety, transcended mere power development. It entered the wide fields of flood control, soil erosion, afforestation, elimination from agricultural use of marginal lands, and distribution and diversification of industry. It led logically to national planning for a complete river watershed, involving many states and the future lives and welfare of millions. He suggested the creation of a Tennessee Valley Authority, "a corporation clothed with the power of government, but possessed

---

[24] See *Public Papers and Addresses of Franklin D. Roosevelt,* II, 80-83.
[25] *Ibid.,* p. 93.        [26] 48 Stat. 74.

of the flexibility and initiative of a private enterprise." He recommended that the authority be charged with the broadest duty of planning for the proper use, conservation, and development of the natural resources of the Tennessee River drainage basin and its adjoining territory, for the general social and economic welfare of the nation.[27] In short order he brought about the enactment of what was essentially the Norris bill, over which Congress had struggled during the past decade. It declared the purpose of the act to be that "of maintaining and operating the property now owned by the United States in the vicinity of Muscle Shoals, Alabama, in the interest of the national defense and for agricultural and industrial development, and to improve navigation in the Tennessee River and to control the destructive flood waters in the Tennessee River and Mississippi River basins."[28] The Tennessee Valley Authority was to be operated by a board of three members. It was to construct additional dams, make other necessary improvements, arrange for the production and sale of electric power, and in a great variety of ways provide for agricultural and industrial development throughout the entire Tennessee River basin.[29] It represented regional planning on a grand scale.

In his message of April 13, 1933, the President asked for legislation to prevent foreclosure of mortgages on homes. The measure was to be along the general lines of the farm-mortgage refinancing bill which was incorporated in the farm bill. He said:

> Implicit in the legislation which I am suggesting to you is a declaration of national policy. This policy is that the broad interests of the nation require that special safeguards should be thrown around home ownership as a guarantee of social and economic stability, and that to protect home owners from inequitable enforced liquidation in a time of general distress is a proper concern of the government.[30]

Congress responded with the enactment of the Home Owners Loan Corporation Act.[31] Thousands of families were enabled to retain possession of their homes by this federal invasion of a field hitherto deemed outside the jurisdiction of the federal government.

On May 4, 1933, the President sent to Congress a message on emergency railroad legislation. Through the Reconstruction Finance

[27] *Public Papers and Addresses of Franklin D. Roosevelt*, II, 122.

[28] 48 Stat. 58.

[29] For a summary of developments down to 1938 see *Public Papers and Addresses of Franklin D. Roosevelt*, II, 123-129.

[30] *Ibid.*, II, 135.          [31] 48 Stat. 128.

Corporation, created by the Hoover administration, financial aid to railroads had already been granted. Pursuant to the request of the President, Congress passed an act providing for the office of federal co-ordinator of transportation and outlining a program for the better co-ordination of the work of the railroads and the improvement of their financial condition.[32]

In a talk over the radio, delivered on May 7, 1933, the President summarized steps taken down to date and announced others then being devised. He was planning to ask Congress for legislation to enable the government to undertake public works, thus stimulating directly and indirectly the employment of many people. "Well-considered and conservative measures will likewise be proposed which will attempt to give to the industrial workers of the country a more fair wage return, prevent cut-throat competition and unduly long hours for labor, and at the same time encourage each industry to prevent overproduction."[33]

During the Hoover administration spokesmen for labor in Congress had brought about committee hearings on the Black-Connery bill to limit hours of labor in industries connected with interstate commerce. The bill was introduced again at the special session. As drafted, it limited hours of labor to thirty a week. Its purpose was not merely to lighten the burden of work upon persons already employed, but to distribute employment to large numbers of additional persons. Industry was opposed to legislation making any such drastic curtailment in hours of labor. Labor unions, furthermore, were lukewarm toward it. Labor officials had discovered that their interests were better served by winning the battles of labor through collective bargaining than through legislation. If achievements could be attributed to union activities, the unions were strengthened thereby. If, on the other hand, government took over the function of protecting all the rights of labor, the need for unionization would be less apparent and membership might be expected to decline. In spite of opposition from industrial and labor groups, it seemed for a time as if the bill might pass. There is little doubt that it could have been enacted had the administration given its support. Administration leaders apparently believed, however, that the device to be employed, namely, the exclusion from interstate commerce of goods produced by persons working more than thirty hours a week, was too rigid. It was not sufficiently adaptable to the complicated needs of the times. The ad-

[32] 48 Stat. 211.   [33] *Public Papers and Addresses of Franklin D. Roosevelt*, II, 163.

ministration withheld its approval, and the bill was slowed down by opposition attributed to industry, while a different mode of control over employment was being evolved.

Closely related to the promotion of employment of workers was the promotion of the welfare of industry itself. The hitherto self-confident leadership of industry, now battered and confused by years of depression, offered no solution except proposals that anti-trust laws and other restrictive legislation be relaxed. Some arguments for the relaxation of anti-trust laws had plausibility. A major purpose of those laws was to preserve such conditions of competition that the attempt of each producer to capture and retain the market would keep prices at a relatively low level for consumers. In so far as the anti-trust program succeeded in isolating producers from each other, however, it interfered with intelligent economic planning in terms of the needs of the nation. In an era of mass production tremendous sums went into the construction of plant. If each producer in a given field equipped himself with sufficient plant to supply the entire market, without reference to his competitors, the waste in expenditure upon plant was tremendous. If each producer turned out a quantity of consumer's goods sufficient to supply the entire market, without reference to the production of his competitors, a surplus of consumer's goods was inevitably produced. In any event, surpluses were likely to be created which had to be sold at a loss or held at a loss, bringing disturbances of the kind that produce the worst features of depression. It was argued that producers in a given field should be permitted to work together, plan intelligently, and allot among themselves the production needed.

Administration leaders recognized the necessity of replacing chaos with order, but they sought to avoid an order wherein monopolies, freed from competitive conditions, defeated the whole purpose by boosting prices and perhaps curtailing production to such an extent as to bring about commercial stagnation and conditions of chaos all over again. They set out to draft legislation to authorize industrial self-government with effective governmental supervision. It was assumed that, if an industry was carefully planned by the people who knew it best, with the plans subject to change by government wherever anti-social aspects were involved, the great evils of excess production and at times of underproduction and of prices that were too high and prices that were too low could be eliminated. The prosperity of commerce and industry would thereby be restored. Both production and employment would be stabilized. If continued prosperity was to be assured, however, not only must prices be kept down to reasonable levels, but employment must be spread among the people at adequate wages so as to create purchasing power and make possible the consumption of the goods produced by industry. Any adequate regulatory measure needed to deal directly or indirectly with wages and hours of employment as well as with the immediate problems of industrial stabilization. It was realized, furthermore, that the restoration of prosperity merely by regulations dealing with private production, private employment, and private consumption would be inadequate to bring about an immediate restoration of prosperity. Plans were made for a huge program of public works, with an allotment of more than three billion dollars in public funds. Emergency expenditures would create new employment, employment would create purchasing power, and purchasing power would start the wheels of industry.

A bill to achieve the several related purposes was in preparation over a period of weeks. President Roosevelt submitted it to Congress on May 17, 1933, with a special message. He requested that Congress provide the machinery necessary for a great co-operative movement throughout all industry to promote re-employment, to shorten hours and increase wages, and to prevent unfair competition and disastrous overproduction. Anti-trust laws were to be retained as a permanent assurance that the old evils of unfair competition should never return. But the public interest would be served, he said, if, with the authority and under the guidance of the government, private industries were permitted to make agreements and codes insuring fair competition. In order to meet rare cases of non-co-operation and abuse, it would be necessary to provide a rigorous licensing power for use by the government. He recommended, furthermore, an appropriation of approximately $3,300,000,000 to be invested in necessary and useful public construction.

The purpose of the proposed statute was stated in the first section in language calculated at once to show the urgent need for the legislation and to indicate its constitutional basis. In its final form it read as follows:

> Section 1. A national emergency productive of widespread unemployment and disorganization of industry, which burdens interstate and foreign commerce, affects the public welfare, and undermines the standards of living of the American people, is hereby declared to exist.

It is hereby declared to be the policy of Congress to remove obstructions to the free flow of interstate and foreign commerce which tend to diminish the amount thereof; and to provide for the general welfare by promoting the organization of industry for the purpose of co-operative action among trade groups, to induce and maintain united action of labor and management under adequate governmental sanctions and supervision, to eliminate unfair competitive practices, to promote the fullest possible utilization of the present productive capacity of industries, to avoid undue restriction of production (except as may be temporarily required), to increase the consumption of industrial and agricultural products by increasing purchasing power, to reduce and relieve unemployment, to improve standards of labor, and otherwise to rehabilitate industry and to conserve natural resources.[34]

The commerce clause provided the only clearly indicated basis for constitutionality. The act was to remove obstructions to the free flow of interstate and foreign commerce. Emphasis was placed on the emergency character of the legislation, doubtless in part to show its necessity, and in part also to gather up any accretions to constitutionality, if such there were, that derived from the existence of a national emergency. The expressions "public welfare" and "general welfare" were also used to show the necessity of the statute and to promote good-will for it, and perhaps also to secure such constitutional support as might be derived from the terminology in the Constitution.

The bill gave the President broad power to create machinery and to delegate functions for the control of industry. It authorized trade or industrial associations or groups to work out and submit to the President codes of fair competition for their government. Such codes, when approved, became legal standards of fair competition. Any violations of such standards was to be deemed an unfair method of competition in commerce within the meaning of the Federal Trade Commission Act. The district courts of the United States were authorized to restrain violations of the code. The President might modify the codes worked out by industries and he might impose a code upon a group unable to work out one of its own. As supplementary means of control, the power was also given to license businesses engaged in interstate or foreign commerce and to impose restrictions in the

[34] 48 Stat. 195. Many of the New-Deal statutes attempted in similar fashion to justify their enactment and demonstrate their constitutionality. The conception of regulating interstate commerce by removing obstructions from it had already been recognized by the Supreme Court. See, for example, United States v. Ferger, 250 U.S. 199 (1919).

process. Suspension of a license because of violation was to have the effect of excluding the offender from interstate or foreign commerce. The importance of the adoption of codes which were to have the force of law stood out in the statute. They were to be made by trade associations or other non-governmental groups, subject to the approval of the President and to the power of the President to modify them. Congress was to authorize a broad scheme for the regulation of industry and to delegate, not merely the administrative power, but the power of making the rules to be administered.

Critics of the bill challenged the constitutionality of the sweeping delegations of legislative power. No federal statute had as yet been held unconstitutional on such a ground, however, and no change resulted from the argument. Accusations of dictatorship were made again and again, and the President and those around him were accused of undermining the Constitution. Congressman James M. Beck, one of the most ardent and most eloquent opponents, made the following statement:

> While I do not see the prospect of any master architects that will be able today to rebuild upon the old foundations of the Constitution a new Constitution with the same wisdom as the master builders of 1787, yet the "brain trust" is ceaselessly at work "undermining" our Constitution, to use Washington's phrase. They work silently but none the less effectually. In this construction of a new form of government — now in progress — Professor Moley takes the place of George Washington, and Professor Tugwell that of Hamilton, and Professor Berle that of James Wilson, and the old architects must yield to these new architects, who, fresh from the academic cloisters of Columbia University, and with the added inspiration of all they have learned in Moscow, are now intent upon rebuilding upon the ruins of the old Constitution a new Constitution, in which, as in the old German Reichstag, this Congress will be merely a debating society, and the Executive will be master of the destinies of the American people.[35]

Other legislators saw great danger in the policy of the act. For many years the government had been attempting, through enforcement of the anti-trust laws, to prevent monopoly and the evils that flowed from it. This bill, contended Senator Borah, was an advanced step toward the ultra-concentration of wealth in the country. The bill would give monopoly something it had been fighting for for

[35] 77 *Congressional Record* 4212-4213.

twenty-five years — the death of the anti-trust laws. It would permit combination as large as the industry itself. If such combination were once permitted, it would not again be resolved.[36] He tried vainly to secure the adoption of an amendment that would constitute an effective curb upon monopoly. The restrictive provisions in the act as adopted provided merely that the President might approve a code of fair competition if he found "that such code or codes are not designed to promote monopolies or to eliminate or oppress small enterprises and will not operate to discriminate against them" and "that such code or codes shall not permit monopolies or monopolistic practices."[37]

The President approved the statute with words of high praise. "History," he predicted, "probably will record the National Industrial Recovery Act as the most important and far-reaching legislation ever enacted by the American Congress. It represents a supreme effort to stabilize for all time the many factors which make for the prosperity of the nation and the preservation of American standards."[38] He stated its goal to be the assurance of a reasonable profit to industry and living wages for labor, with the elimination of the tyrannical methods and practices which had not only harassed honest business but also contributed to the ills of labor.

The National Industrial Recovery Act constituted the last of the series of important measures enacted with record-making swiftness by the special session. Speed was achieved as a result of a number of factors. The President himself evolved a definite program. He made it specific to the extent of submitting drafts of legislation to be enacted. The people of the country were eager to accept his leadership — a fact well known to Congress. Congress itself, in spite of factional revolt on particular measures, also wanted definite leadership. The election of 1932 had brought into power, not merely a new President, but a political party that had been out of office for twelve years. There were many appointments to be made. Roosevelt postponed most of them until after he had secured the enactment of his chosen measures. It was politically dangerous to oppose the program of the man who controlled the fruits of patronage.

### EMERGENCY EFFORTS

Enactment of emergency measures at the special session was followed by organization to give them effect. Although the pace of legis-

---

[36] *Ibid.*, pp. 5162-5163.     [37] 48 Stat. 196.
[38] *Public Papers and Addresses of Franklin D. Roosevelt*, II, 246.

lation slackened, additional important measures were enacted at each of the following sessions. Organizations were created, officials were appointed, and vested interests were created in the new régime. Although the financial condition of the federal government grew steadily worse and efforts to balance the federal budget were virtually abandoned, the business index moved irregularly upward, employment increased, and the physical distress of impoverished people was alleviated. Conflicts in the program developed. The government found itself encouraging production at some points and discouraging it at others without justification for the difference. During the early years it economized in some branches to aid in the effort toward balancing the budget, and expended large sums in other branches for purposes of "pump-priming." Without careful discrimination, spokesmen for the administration encouraged business on the one hand and denounced and discouraged it on the other. Personnel chosen to carry out the program interpreted various phases of it in conflicting ways, with inefficiency as the inevitable result.

Nevertheless, whether acting from something in the nature of instinct or from long-term or short-term conceptions of personal or public welfare, a huge majority of the people voted approval of the New Deal in 1936 by returning the Roosevelt administration to power. The country had experienced more than six years of the New Deal when the outbreak of war in Europe began to change the picture and the New Deal became a domestic basis for preparation for defense against a foreign enemy. The laws enacted, the organizations formed, and the programs carried out during the period are far too numerous for individual presentation. The following pages portray certain segments of New-Deal activities which grooved so deeply into the life of the nation as to represent important trends in constitutional development. The decisions of the Supreme Court with reference to these matters and the sharp deviation in trends on the part of those decisions are left to the ensuing chapter.

## THE NATIONAL RECOVERY ADMINISTRATION

By executive order the President created the National Recovery Administration to administer most of that portion of the National Industrial Recovery Act which had to do with industrial control, while the public-works program, provided for in the same act, was allotted to the Public Works Administration. Since a concerted effort was assumed to be necessary to restore consumers' purchasing power and create a demand for new products, and since the process of drafting codes for the government of each industry would take considerable time, the National Recovery Administration, or NRA, as it was commonly called, urged immediate adherence to the President's re-employment agreement, which was commonly and somewhat inaccurately known as a blanket code. The basic points in the agreement were the elimination of child labor, the limitations of hours of labor to from thirty-five to forty a week, the fixing of minimum wages at from twelve to fifteen dollars a week and thirty to forty cents an hour, equitable upward adjustment of wages generally, limitation of price increases, and, finally, the support of other enterprises which were parties to the agreement.[39] Establishments joining in the agreement were allowed to display the blue eagle symbol. Propaganda for the recovery program was so effective that few establishments interested in doing a profitable business could afford not to use the symbol. The threat of the deprivation of the blue eagle was oftentimes the only mode of coercion needed to compel performance of the agreement and, later, obedience to the industrial codes.

Most of industry that had any close relation to interstate or foreign commerce signed up immediately under the President's re-employment agreement. The drafting of codes proceeded in a more leisurely fashion. By contrast with the agreement, the codes dealt with the whole field of industrial operations. They covered trade practices, employer-employee relationships, prices, and many other matters. They were worked out largely by representatives of the respective industries, were discussed in public hearings, and were refined thereafter and submitted to the President for his approval. As a condition of approval the President required the inclusion in the codes of the content of the President's re-employment agreement and of other conditions intended to prevent the evil features of monopoly and injury to small business.[40]

Since the administration was acting on all fronts at once for the improvement of economic conditions, and since forces beyond the control of the administration were also operating on the economic situation, it is next to impossible to measure the effects of the efforts of NRA.[41] It is clear that, by the limitation on hours of labor, employment was spread to include large numbers of hitherto unem-

[39] Charles L. Dearing *et al., The ABC of the NRA* (1934), p. 62.

[40] See *ibid.*, chapter VI.

[41] For a critical appraisal see Leverett S. Lyon *et al., The National Recovery Administration* (1935). See also Charles F. Roos, *NRA Economic Planning* (1937).

ployed persons. There is reason to believe that there was substantial additional employment and consequently substantial addition to purchasing power. Prices rose considerably; but as the operation of NRA was but one of many factors conducive to that end, the measurement of causes is next to impossible. There was tremendous enthusiasm for the program during the early months; but fears being dispelled as conditions improved, individuals and corporations began to chafe at restrictions placed upon them. Difficulties arose in enforcing code provisions as to price-filing and price-fixing, cost-accounting, production control, and fair-trade practices. Much of industry refused to abide by the provisions of Section 7a of the National Industrial Recovery Act guaranteeing the right of collective bargaining in labor matters. Complaints poured into Washington in large quantities that the codes, worked out actually for the most part by representatives of large industrial and commercial establishments, were placing great hardships on small business enterprises. Senator Borah, convinced of the validity of these complaints, introduced a bill to reinstate the anti-trust laws. NRA officials insisted that small business had been helped rather than injured, contending that complaints had been received almost exclusively from establishments that could survive only by the exploitation of workers.[42] A board was appointed to survey the operation of the codes. It reported that codes in many industries were enforced by code authorities dominated by representatives of larger units and that monopoly was promoted and small enterprises were injured.

NRA became the subject of attack by large establishments which grew restive under regulation, by small establishments which felt themselves oppressed by larger units, and by labor organizations which felt that their interests were not adequately protected. The wholehearted approval and enthusiasm on the part of the people were gradually dispelled so that deprivation of the blue eagle no longer constituted a punishment serious enough to enforce obedience. As the recovery program came to be thought of as a program for an indefinite period rather than merely for the period of an existing crisis, constitutional questions began to be taken more seriously. In the beginning, administration leaders had avoided judicial tests for a number of reasons. Some of them had thought that the emergency would be over relatively soon and that there was no point in getting

---

[42] For a summary account of developments see Frederic Dewhurst, "The National Recovery Administration," *The American Yearbook*, 1934, pp. 15-23.

involved in litigation which might prove embarrassing. It was thought also that enforcement through the creation of public sentiment represented by the blue eagle would be more effective than legal coercion and that resort to litigation might destroy the atmosphere in which coercion by propaganda was possible. The obvious avoidance of litigation, however, led to accusations that the administration was doubtful as to the constitutionality of the law upon which important recovery activities were based. In defense against the charge, it became necessary finally to seek a case in which the constitutionality of the basic activities of NRA could be tested. Unfortunately, because of the informality of procedure during the chaotic period in which the Roosevelt administration got under way, it proved next to impossible for the Department of Justice and the National Recovery Administration to find a case in which the government program could be presented to the courts in a clearly favorable light. Case after case was considered and was dismissed because of legal defects somewhere along the line.[43] Early in 1935, the administration was virtually forced to defend itself before the Supreme Court in a case which was far from suitable for its purposes. The government had secured a conviction and it had no means of preventing the appeal to the Supreme Court. The famous Schechter case,[44] which, along with other important cases of the period, is discussed in the following chapter, virtually wrecked the code structure through which the National Industrial Recovery Act was enforced. Although the administration sputtered wrathfully at the interference of the Supreme Court, it was nevertheless probably somewhat relieved at the termination of a program which was becoming unmanageable. It gave up its plans to secure the renewal of the statute beyond the two-year period previously allotted. The control of industry by the federal government was exercised thereafter in a different manner.

Experience under the NRA should not be discounted too completely merely because administration bogged down and because the Supreme Court found unconstitutional the delegation of legislative power and held that the commerce clause did not authorize the regulations based upon it. In governmental activities, as elsewhere, success is built oftentimes upon experience derived from failure. The plan for industrial control was too broad and too intricate for full

---

[43] See Carl Brent Swisher (ed.), *Selected Papers of Homer Cummings* (1939), pp. 122-128.

[44] A. L. A. Schechter Poultry Corporation *v.* United States, 295 U.S. 495 (1935).

and complete comprehension, either by those charged with administration or by the persons and industries affected. The education of
personnel paid dividends later in the national defense crisis, however,
and it is probable that most of the information acquired about industrial control will be utilized.

## THE AGRICULTURAL PROGRAM

In the meantime the agricultural program was put into operation.
The new farm statute known as the Agricultural Adjustment Act,
upon which the program was based, opened with the following declaration of emergency:

> That the present acute economic emergency being in part the conse-
> quence of a severe and increasing disparity between the prices of
> agricultural and other commodities, which disparity has largely de-
> stroyed the purchasing power of farmers for industrial products, has
> broken down the orderly exchange of commodities, and has seri-
> ously impaired the agricultural assets supporting the national credit
> structure, it is hereby declared that these conditions in the basic in-
> dustry of agriculture have affected transactions in agricultural com-
> modities with a national public interest, have burdened and ob-
> structed the normal currents of commerce in such commodities, and
> render imperative the immediate enactment of title I of this act.[45]

The policy of the statute was declared to be

> to establish and maintain such balance between the production and
> consumption of agricultural commodities, and such marketing con-
> ditions therefor, as will re-establish prices to farmers at a level that
> will give agricultural commodities a purchasing power with respect
> to articles that farmers buy, equivalent to the purchasing power of
> agricultural commodities in the base period.

The base period chosen for agricultural commodities except tobacco
was to be the five-year period, from August, 1909, to July, 1914,
wherein it was assumed that price relations as between agricultural
and other commodities came closest to what they ought to be. The
base period for tobacco was the ten years between August, 1919, and
July, 1929. The plan was to approach equality of purchasing power
by gradual correction of existing inequalities as rapidly as was deemed
feasible. In the interest of the consumer, the statute asserted the
purpose of readjusting farm production at such a level as would not
increase the percentage of the consumer's retail expenditures for agri-

[45] 48 Stat. 31.

cultural commodities, or products derived therefrom, which was returned to the farmer above the percentage which was returned to the farmer in the period from 1909 to 1914.

Pursuant to the Agricultural Adjustment Act, the Agricultural Adjustment Administration, known commonly as the AAA, was established in the Department of Agriculture. Through this agency, with powers and duties conferred in broad language by the original statute and by amending acts passed from time to time, the Secretary of Agriculture made the first comprehensive attempt in American history to limit the total of agricultural production in basic commodities for the purpose of raising the prices of these commodities and enabling the farmer to earn a fair income. The program was described as voluntary. Under the act the Secretary of Agriculture discovered the price-level of the commodities affected during the base period. He estimated the amount of each commodity likely to be sold in the year affected at the price prevailing in the base period. He estimated the acreage needed to be planted in the respective commodities in order to reduce the supply and make arrangements for withdrawing from production all additional acreage likely otherwise to be planted in such crops. The government brought about withdrawal, not by compulsion, but by contracts with each individual farmer. The farmer received compensation in the form of cash payments known as "benefit payments." The money used for the benefit payments was raised by a federal tax on the processing of the respective commodities, as, for example, a tax upon the milling of wheat. The money collected, over and above the cost of collection, was paid in equitable amounts to farmers who signed and carried out contracts with the government to withdraw from production acreage that otherwise would have been planted in wheat. The farmer who refused to sign a contract for the reduction of acreage was at a disadvantage only in that he received no benefit payment, but that disadvantage might be a serious financial matter. In effect, the recalcitrant farmer incurred a financial penalty for refusing to co-operate with the government.

The difficulties and uncertainties of such a program were immense. It was no easy task to calculate the amount of a given commodity likely to be consumed if sold at a given price or the amount to which sales must be limited if prices were to be kept at a given level. Because of variations in the weather, it was next to impossible to estimate the acreage needed to grow a given supply. Since the restrictions exerted no control over the fertility of the soil, it was possible for any farmer to observe his contract with the government and yet add fertilizer to the acreage planted and so improve his methods of cultivation as greatly to increase the yield on the acreage not withdrawn from cultivation. Once the broad estimates as to acreage had been made, the intricate task remained of allotting the local withdrawals of acreage, making and supervising individual contracts, collecting taxes, and making benefit payments.

Agricultural production was curtailed somewhat under the program. Farm prices improved somewhat, although not as much as was desired. It was impossible to tell the extent to which changes were due to the program, on the one hand, and, on the other hand, to currency devaluation, export conditions, weather conditions, and other factors. Farm income was increased to the extent of the higher prices plus the amount received by farmers in benefit payments. The increased income doubtless resulted in increased purchases and contributed to the total effort toward recovery. It is probable that the benefit payments represented a smaller addition to farm income than was generally assumed and that consumers suffered from the burden. Although the taxes collected were paid by processors, the latter presumably passed the tax backward to the farmer in the form of lower prices paid for raw commodities or forward to consumers in the form of higher prices for processed goods — or used the existence of the tax as an excuse for passing it backward and forward at the same time in the form of lower and higher prices respectively.

Because of the complications of the program, the varied interests involved, and the impossibility of exact measurement of its effect, it inevitably made enemies as well as friends. While Congress was extending the number of basic commodities affected and enacting statutes actually penalizing excess production in certain fields, hostile persons were denouncing the whole program and predicting that the courts would find it unconstitutional. When the Supreme Court found basic defects in the National Industrial Recovery Act in unconstitutional delegations of legislative power, the Department of Agriculture speedily prepared amendments to the Agricultural Adjustment Act to eliminate any such defects as might be found therein. The taxing features of the statute, however, remained vulnerable. Large sums due in taxes were tied up in litigation pending a decision of the Supreme Court. The Court held that the tax was not a genuine revenue measure, but was a device whereby the federal government sought to exercise control over matters subject only to the control of the state.[46]   The result was collapse of the whole program of crop control based on the collection and disbursement of processing taxes.

Drastic as was the effect upon the AAA of the exercise of judicial power, it was not as overwhelming as the effect upon NRA.[47]   There was a political difference in that, whereas NRA was largely without organized support either from large or small industry or from labor, the AAA had strong support in well-organized and politically powerful farm groups.   Pressure from farm groups brought about the immediate enactment of legislation to be substituted in part for that invalidated.   The new measure was called the Soil Conservation and Domestic Allotment Act.[48]   Nominally, and in part actually, it was based on a program for conservation of the soil, which had been sponsored by the administration.   The government paid farmers to withdraw acreage from production of basic commodities in order to prevent soil wastage in excess production.   The money was to be paid out of the federal Treasury and not from the proceeds of a special tax.   Since no taxing scheme was connected directly with the expenditure, there was no feasible method by which the constitutionality of expenditures for soil conservation could be contested in the courts.

The new statute contemplated the early transfer of the administration of the crop-control program to the several states, but in 1937 good growing weather contributed to the development of surpluses, which had been kept down hitherto by drought and the government program.   Farmers, therefore, demanded a permanent control program administered by the federal government.   Congress enacted a new measure providing for the continuation of benefit payments for soil conservation.   Control was not complete, however, and had to be supported by other devices.

The Agricultural Adjustment Act of 1938,[49] which provided for the continuation of crop restriction by the making of benefit payments for conservation purposes, provided also a collateral though indirect method of restraining production.   The act empowered the Secretary of Agriculture to establish marketing quotas for the products affected when a surplus was threatened which might clog the channels of inter-

[46] United States v. Butler, 297 U.S. 1 (1936).

[47] For appraisal see Edwin G. Nourse et al., Three Years of the Agricultural Adjustment Administration (1937).

[48] 49 Stat. 1148.              [49] 52 Stat. 31.

state commerce. It prescribed a penalty equal to fifty per cent of the market price on that portion of the commodity offered for sale in excess of the quota allotted to each producer. The provisions of the act were based upon the commerce power rather than upon the taxing power, and they dealt with marketing in interstate commerce rather than directly with production. Yet, since certain commodities, tobacco, for example, had little value to their producers except as they could be marketed in interstate or foreign commerce, the effect of the restriction on marketing must naturally be to restrain production. The Supreme Court accepted the statute as a regulation calculated to keep open the channels of interstate commerce, however, and ignored the consequent restraint of production,[50] over which, in the earlier case, it had held that the federal government had no control. The establishment of marketing quotas became potentially an important technique to be used alongside benefit payments as a mode of restricting production.[51]

In addition to the provisions already discussed, the original Agricultural Adjustment Act authorized the control of the marketing of certain commodities through marketing agreements and orders issued by the Secretary of Agriculture. The decision against the constitutionality of the processing-tax features of the statute left doubt whether the whole statute was invalidated; and it was deemed wise to incorporate the marketing provisions in a new Agricultural Marketing Act.[52] The statute gave the Secretary of Agriculture tremendous power, authorizing him, with the concurrence of certain percentages of the producers and handlers of milk and certain other products, to control prices and the conditions of marketing. With reference to milk, the control was exercised on a broad scale. The Supreme Court upheld the statute, with only three of the nine justices classifying it as an unconstitutional delegation of legislative power to the Secretary of Agriculture.[53] The Supreme Court decisions were the forerunner of further expansion of the power of the federal government over the distribution of essential commodities.

In 1935, important activities for improving the condition of the lowest-income third of American farmers were merged in the Resettle-

[50] Mulford v. Smith, 307 U.S. 38 (1939).

[51] See Donald C. Blaisdell, *Government and Agriculture* (1940), pp. 63-64.

[52] 50 Stat. 246.

[53] United States v. Rock Royal Cooperative, 307 U.S. 533 (1939), and H. P. Hood and Sons v. United States, 307 U.S. 588 (1939).

ment Administration, which subsequently became the Farm Security Administration in the Department of Agriculture. Efforts were made to cope with problems of impoverished owners of submarginal land, farm tenants, relatively immobile farm laborers, and migratory workers.[54] The government in earlier years had cautiously purchased from time to time tracts of cut-over land which could be demonstrated as important for the control of water flowing into navigable streams. Now it boldly acquired large totals of acreage in land not fit to support its residents by means of farming. It planned to return the land to forests, make it into wild-life refuges, or otherwise utilize it in terms of its capacity. The government used funds to resettle the former residents on better farm lands, where they had some prospect for achieving a substantial degree of self-sufficiency. It made loans, established so-called "subsistence" homesteads, constructed labor camps, and utilized other methods of relief and rehabilitation.

The farm program was carried forward for nearly eight years under the leadership of an able Secretary of Agriculture, Henry A. Wallace.[55] Under his direction the Department of Agriculture evolved into an organization of tremendous size, power, and complexity.[56] Early in 1938, on the occasion of congressional hearings on a bill making appropriations for the department, Wallace made the following statement as to a significant change:

> First, I want to call the attention of the committee again to the same point which I emphasized last year — that we now have a new Department of Agriculture which is quite different from the old department. The old department, especially previous to the war, was concerned with research, scientific activities, educational activities. There were some regulatory activities at the time, and later on more regulatory activities were added. There was also the job of custodianship and management of certain lands. Later on, the federal-aid highway program became an important matter.
>
> But the functions of the old Department of Agriculture today represent only a small part of our total activities. These activities have come on especially since 1933, and for the most part have to do with action programs.
>
> The money spent in the older activities represented money spent

[54] See Blaisdell, op. cit., chapter VII. See also Senate Doc. No. 213, 74th Cong., 2d sess.
[55] See his books published while in office, especially New Frontiers (1934) and Whose Constitution? (1936).
[56] See John M. Gaus and Leon O. Wolcott, Public Administration and the United States Department of Agriculture (1940), chapter IV.

largely for personnel, equipment, and the like. In most of the new activities, a smaller share of the money is for personnel; much of it is paid out in the form of grants-in-aid to individual farmers.[57]

Through expenditures made as benefit payments, loans, and otherwise, and through control exercised without the payment of money, the department reaches down to determine the activities of individual farmers — once more restive under control than any other group in the United States. It is rapidly accustoming them to organization and regimentation. So intimately is their welfare related to the continuation of governmental payments and governmental planning that they constitute powerful interest groups which, if handled skillfully, can be mobilized for political purposes. As for the goal of the farm program, the lifting of farm income to the level comparable with other incomes which it had occupied in the years from 1909 to 1914, the decade of the nineteen-thirties passed without its achievement. Improvement took place[58] so that farm purchasing power was substantially increased, but farm income continued to lag far behind non-farm income. Many factors had intervened to make the task difficult. The Supreme Court had seriously crippled crop restriction by invalidating the processing-tax method. War and other disturbances abroad had interfered with the foreign market. Foreign producers provided new competition in the foreign market. Alternating conditions of good and bad weather added to the difficulties of careful planning. The problem of agricultural surpluses remained serious, and the government was expanding its program of purchasing food surpluses and distributing them for relief purposes. Until the initiation of the national defense program, governmental expenditures on agriculture were major contributors to the condition of unbalance in the federal budget.

## LABOR

Problems of labor, like those of industry and agriculture, were multiplied by the depression. The strength of labor unions as measured by membership had declined after 1920,[59] but two important federal statutes affecting labor were enacted before the beginning of the New Deal. The first was the Railway Labor Act of 1926.[60] This act pro-

[57] *Hearings on the Agricultural Department appropriation bill for 1939,* before the subcommittee of the House committee on appropriations, 75th Cong., 3d sess., 1938, p. 1.

[58] See Blaisdell, *op. cit.,* p. 5.

[59] See Lewis L. Lorwin and Arthur Wubnig, *Labor Relations Boards* (1935), p. 19.

[60] 44 Stat. 577.

vided, among other things, that representatives to settle railway labor disputes should be designated by the respective parties as provided by corporate organization or unincorporated association, or by any other means of collective action, without interference, influence, or coercion exercised by either party over the organization or selection of representatives by the other. This guarantee to railway labor of the right of collective bargaining, subsequently upheld by the Supreme Court,[61] was a long step forward in the movement to protect the rights of labor.

The second important labor statute was the Norris-La Guardia Anti-Injunction Act.[62] This measure, enacted in 1932, marked a victory for labor as the culmination of a long struggle to curb judicial interference by injunction with strikes and picketing and other labor activities. The statute contained a statement of purpose wherein it was said that under prevailing conditions the individual unorganized worker was commonly helpless to exercise liberty of contract and protect his freedom to obtain acceptable terms and conditions of employment. Although he should be free to decline to associate with his fellows, it was necessary that he have full freedom of association, organization, and designation of representatives of his own choosing to negotiate the terms and conditions of employment. It was necessary that he should be free from the interference, restraint, or coercion of employers or their agents in organization and in the selection of representatives for collective bargaining. The statute declared so-called "yellow-dog" contracts to be unenforceable in the courts of the United States. As a result, employers could not thereafter rely upon action in any federal court to enforce agreements not to become or remain members of labor unions.

The National Industrial Recovery Act restated the policy of the Norris-La Guardia Act, but the picture was confused somewhat in that the President was empowered to interfere and impose regulations as to hours, wages, and other matters. The President's re-employment agreement prescribed certain basic conditions for labor. In general, the codes of fair competition also dealt with labor problems and incorporated the statutory language guaranteeing the right of collective bargaining.

With the prospect of improvement in business conditions, both capital and labor lost some of their fears; and innumerable conflicts broke

---

[61] Texas and New Orleans Railroad Co. *v.* Brotherhood of Railway and Steamship Clerks, 281 U.S. 548 (1930).

[62] 47 Stat. 70.

out over the interpretation of the President's re-employment agreement and the drafting and interpretation of the codes of fair competition. The National Industrial Recovery Act contained no provision for agencies to protect the rights of labor. By executive order a National Labor Board, replaced later by a National Labor Relations Board, and labor boards in specific fields of industry, were created to solve various labor problems.[63]

Before the National Industrial Recovery Act was declared unconstitutional, progress was made toward the enactment of an independent statute that would incorporate the guarantee of the right of collective bargaining and establish an agency for the protection of that right. The National Labor Relations Act was passed in July, 1935.[64] It restated earlier findings as to the necessity for the unimpaired right of collective bargaining if workers were to deal as equals with their employers. It required employers in interstate commerce to bargain collectively with their employees, and outlawed as unfair labor practices modes of dealing with employees which might interfere with their independence in bargaining.

The members originally appointed to the board undertook their task in a crusading spirit. In their necessarily large subordinate staff they included large numbers of persons with alleged radical tendencies, who by their mode of enforcing the act succeeded in bitterly antagonizing many employers. They were accused of relying upon gossip for evidence of employers' misdeeds and of aligning themselves with radical agitators whose purpose was to make trouble rather than to promote the welfare of labor through orderly collective bargaining. Although the Supreme Court upheld broadly the administration of the act,[65] the controversy grew so bitter that it was necessary eventually to change the personnel of the board and, to some extent, of the subordinate staff.

It is to be noted that the purpose of the National Labor Relations Act was not in itself to deal with hours, wages, working conditions, or other matters of controversy. The purpose was merely to guarantee to labor the right to bargain with employers through representatives selected by labor without any coercion from employers. To that end broad supervisory powers over the selection of representatives was given. It meant, in effect, the right to unionize and the right of each group of workers to select its own union. Many of the controversies

---

[63] See Lorwin and Wubnig, *op. cit.*    [64] 49 Stat. 449.
[65] See chapter 36.

connected with enforcement of the act grew out of, or at least were complicated by, the struggle within the ranks of labor between unions affiliated with the American Federation of Labor and those affiliated with the Congress of Industrial Organizations.

In a sense, it was good political strategy to provide for the solution of problems of employment, not through detailed rule-making by the federal government, but by utilizing the organized power of the persons most affected, the workers themselves, in competition with employers, the opposing parties to labor controversies. Congress was not satisfied, however, to permit minimum conditions of employment to be determined in all instances by the competitive struggle of employers and employees. In 1936, it enacted the Walsh-Healey Act,[66] which laid down certain labor terms for all producers who made contracts with the federal government involving amounts in excess of ten thousand dollars. Such employers were required to pay not less than the prevailing wage rate of the locality, to maintain the eight-hour day and the forty-hour week, and to exclude from employment boys under sixteen and girls under eighteen. The federal government thereby prescribed some of the standards which it hoped to see in operation throughout the field of industry.

Many people were dissatisfied with arrangements which left the regulation of wages, hours, and child labor to the bargaining power of labor representatives, supplemented only by a federal law establishing minimum standards for employers making sales to the federal government. Interest in the Black-Connery bill, introduced in 1933 to limit the work-week to thirty hours, had not completely disappeared. Many administration leaders thought that something should be done to replace the labor machinery which had to be abandoned at the time of the dissolution of NRA. On May 24, 1937, the President initiated a campaign for broader legislation. The time had come, he said in a message to Congress,[67] "to take further action to extend the frontiers of social progress." Such further action was within the common-sense framework and purpose of our Constitution and received beyond doubt the approval of the electorate. He found that "one-third of our population, the overwhelming majority of which is in agriculture or industry, is ill-nourished, ill-clad, and ill-housed." The nation, so richly endowed with natural resources, and with a capable and industrious population, should be able to devise ways and means of insuring to all able-bodied working men and women a fair

---

[66] 49 Stat. 2036.        [67] For the message see 81 *Congressional Record* 4960.

day's pay for a fair day's work. A self-supporting and self-respecting democracy could plead no justification for the existence of child labor, no economic reason for chiseling workers' wages or stretching workers' hours. Enlightened business, he said, was learning that competition ought not to cause bad social consequences, which inevitably reacted upon the profits of business itself. All but the hopeless reactionary would agree that to conserve our primary resources of man-power, government must have some control over maximum hours, minimum wages, the evil of child labor, and the exploitation of unorganized labor. As to the constitutionality of federal restraint upon child labor, he quoted with warm approval from the dissenting opinion of Justice Holmes in Hammer v. Dagenhart,[68] in which the Supreme Court had declared unconstitutional federal regulations based on the commerce power. "But although Mr. Justice Holmes spoke for a minority of the Supreme Court," said the President, "he spoke for a majority of the American people." One of the primary purposes of the formation of our federal Union had been to do away with the trade barriers between the states. To Congress, and not to the states, was given the power to regulate commerce among the several states. Congress could not interfere in local affairs; but, when goods passed through the channels of commerce from one state to another, they became subject to the power of Congress, and Congress might exercise that power to recognize and protect the fundamental interests of free labor. Goods produced under conditions which did not meet rudimentary standards of decency should be regarded as contraband and ought not to be allowed to pollute the channels of interstate trade.

Following the delivery of the President's message, bills were introduced in the Senate and in the House by Senator Black and Representative Connery, respectively, to carry out his program. Minimum wages and maximum hours were to be adjustable within limits from industry to industry and from section to section. In defending the curb on child labor, Assistant Attorney General Robert H. Jackson criticized sharply the decision of 1918. "We owe it to our times," he declared, "to challenge the perversion of our Constitution injected into our law by the child-labor decision. This bill would challenge it. We should give the courts a chance to remove this blemish from our judicial history."[69] He characterized the doctrine of the majority

---

[68] 247 U.S. 251.

[69] *Joint hearings on S. 2475 and H.R. 7200* before the Senate committee on education and labor and the House committee on labor, 75th Cong., 1st sess., p. 5.

in that case as belonging to the same dark era of legal thought as the decision announced in 1923 holding a minimum-wage law for women unconstitutional, a decision which had recently been overruled by the Supreme Court.

Jackson scoffed at the contention that the proposed statute was unconstitutional because of the delegation of power to an administrative agency. "It must be borne in mind," he explained, "that there is nothing whatever in the Constitution that forbids Congress to make a delegation of its power. The prohibition is purely judge-made, not Constitution-made." [70] The Supreme Court, he said, rarely found fault with a congressional delegation of power. There was nothing in the recent decisions of the Court which would justify Congress in abandoning administrative handling of modern complexities too numerous and too diverse to be subjected to a single and inflexible rule directly imposed by Congress. There were only two cases where congressional delegation of power had been adjudged invalid in one hundred and fifty years of constitutional practice. [71]

Much of the opposition was more fundamental than that which dealt with procedure and the exercise of discretion in the enforcement of the act. Industry that was operating without profits protested that wages could not be increased. Southern representatives challenged the bill as an attack upon the South. Many industries in recent years had moved away from the northeastern section of the country, where state labor laws were highly restrictive, to locate in the South, where such restrictions were few and far between. It was believed that the proposed statute would curtail the incipient industrial development in the South and that it was intended to do so.

In his annual message of January, 1938, the President again insisted on the enactment of the measure. After discussing the agricultural program, he declared that to raise the purchasing power of the farmer was not enough. [72] It would not stay raised if we did not also raise the purchasing power of that third of the nation which received its income from industrial employment. We had seen minimum-wage and maximum-hour provisions prove their worth economically and socially under government auspices in 1933, 1934, and 1935. The people were now overwhelmingly in favor of having Congress put a floor below which industrial wages should not fall and a ceiling be-

[70] *Ibid.*, p. 9.

[71] For discussion of those cases, both arising under the National Industrial Recovery Act, see chapter 36.

[72] For the message see 83 *Congressional Record* 8.

yond which the hours of industrial labor should not rise; some of the utterances of opponents sounded like the philosophy of half a century ago. In the long run, he said, profits from child labor, low pay, and overwork inured not to the locality or region where they existed, but to the absentee owners who had sent their capital into exploited communities to gather larger profits for themselves.

The Fair Labor Standards Act was passed in June, 1938.[73] For establishments using the facilities of interstate commerce it sought to bring about by a series of gradual steps the limit of forty cents an hour as a minimum for wages and of forty hours as a maximum period of employment for each week. It outlawed the employment of children under sixteen years of age and such employment under eighteen as was not approved by the chief of the Children's Bureau in the Department of Labor. Except for the latter officer, who was charged with the enforcement of the child-labor provision, the administration of the act was lodged in an administrator, a new officer in the Department of Labor, to be appointed by the President by and with the advice and consent of the Senate.

The constitutionality of the act was passed upon by the Supreme Court early in 1941. Without a dissenting vote the Court held the act constitutional, and overruled the child-labor case of 1918.[74] The decision removed an obstruction in the way of broad federal regulation of industrial and commercial enterprise involving interstate commerce.

It was the policy of the President and of Congress to leave to collective bargaining between employers and employees the fixing of wages of those persons receiving more than the minimum and the hours of those persons working less than the maximum prescribed. Labor spokesmen had at times objected to the fixing of maximum hours and minimum wages by law on the ground that the minimum wage prescribed would thereby tend to become also the maximum for all workers employed and the maximum hours would tend also to become the minimum. The machinery of collective bargaining guaranteed by the National Labor Relations Act was expected to prevent any such outcome. Should collective bargaining prove ineffective, or should labor unions become so unco-operative where the public welfare is concerned as to require the withdrawal of the protection of the fed-

---

[73] 52 Stat. 1060.

[74] United States *v.* Darby, 312 U.S. 100 (1941). See also Opp Cotton Mills *v.* Administrator, 312 U.S. 126 (1941).

eral government, it might be necessary to extend to individual workers additional protection in the form of the regulation of all wages and hours rather than merely of the minimum in the one instance and the maximum in the other.

## SOCIAL SECURITY

Closely related to the betterment of conditions of employment was the problem of caring for the unemployed. For that purpose and for the related purpose of "pump-priming" so that production with all its beneficent consequences might be stimulated, billions of dollars were expended with a lavish hand either for the creation of employment or for direct relief. Even before the New-Deal administration came into power, furthermore, attention was being given to insurance methods which might tide workers over periods of unemployment occurring during the downward swing of business cycles and to take care of them during old age. The Democratic platform for 1932 advocated unemployment and old-age insurance under state laws. The candidate of the party had long been an advocate of such legislation.

Early in 1934, the President expressed warm approval of a House bill levying a federal excise tax upon large employers, but allowing them to deduct from their federal tax amounts contributed under state unemployment-insurance laws. The benefits of such a system, he said, would not be limited to the individual, but would extend throughout our social and financial fabric. There was no reason, he contended, why private charities and public treasuries should assume the entire burden of meeting costs of sustaining the unemployed, which were a foreseeable loss. Major costs ought to be computed and borne like every other cost of a business. He approved of the relationship of the national government to unemployment insurance provided for under the bill. Under our system of government the task of caring for the unemployed fell primarily on the states. If a state could not bear the burden, the United States must be prepared to do so and to collect revenue for that purpose.[75]

The subject was highly controversial, and the bill was not passed. Some months later, the President appointed a committee on economic security and an advisory council to inquire into the problem. In a statement to the advisory council the President again asserted that for the administration of insurance benefits, the states were the most logical units.[76] The reason given was that unemployment insurance

[75] *Public Papers and Addresses of Franklin D. Roosevelt,* III, 161-162.
[76] *Ibid.,* III. 453.

was still untried in this country and there was room for difference in methods which might be put into practice in the several states. Other reasons which may have lain in the background included the fact that the President and his party were already committed to the support of action by the states and doubt whether an exclusively federal program would be upheld by the Supreme Court. The President's concern at the moment was with insurance against unemployment rather than with permanent provision for income for the aged. The organization of the Townsend movement for huge pensions for old people as a mode, not merely of taking care of the persons involved, but of stimulating production and employment, required the giving of attention to that subject as well. Said the President:

> I do not know whether this is the time for any federal legislation on old-age security. Organizations promoting fantastic schemes have aroused hopes which cannot possibly be fulfilled. Through their activities they have increased the difficulties of getting sound legislation; but I hope that in time we may be able to provide security for the aged – a sound and a uniform system which will provide true security.[77]

In January, 1935, the President submitted a social security program to Congress.[78] A statute was enacted in August of that year.[79] The statute made extensive use of the grant-in-aid device. The federal government made grants to states for immediate old-age assistance, administration of unemployment-compensation acts, aid to dependent children, maternal and child welfare, public health, and aid to the blind. Federal control was extended over state activities, however, in that state legislation and machinery and methods of administration had to conform to standards prescribed by the federal statute and approved by the Social Security Board, to be established under the statute. An old-age insurance fund was established. The money paid into the fund was to be derived from income taxes on workers, collected and paid by their employers, and by excise taxes on employers. For unemployment compensation a federal tax was levied upon employers alone. Employers in states which enacted satisfactory unemployment-compensation laws were to receive credit up to ninety per cent of the federal tax. Payments of unemployment compensation were to be made only in states having unemployment-compensation laws. Since a federal tax was to be collected whether or not any such

[77] *Ibid.*, III, 454.
[78] See the several documents, *ibid.*, III, 43, 47, 49.        [79] 49 Stat. 620.

state law existed, pressure was put indirectly upon each state to enact unemployment-compensation legislation, in order that payments might be made to its own people for probable expenditures within its own borders. The money collected under approved state unemployment-compensation laws was to be placed in a trust fund managed by the federal government.

Federal machinery for the administration of the Social Security Act was quickly provided, and most of the states immediately enacted the legislation necessary to make participation possible. In 1937, in the midst of the struggle over court reform, the Supreme Court upheld the constitutionality of the major provisions of the act.[80] The accumulation of immense reserve funds in the United States Treasury began Uneasiness developed as to the safety of such funds. They could not be merely stored away in the form of legal-tender money. Indeed, not enough money had been coined or printed to make up the total if mere storage had been desirable. The only practicable alternative was to invest the money. Since the government itself was the greatest of borrowers, it was only natural that the money collected for social security purposes should be re-expended by the federal government. In effect, the government borrowed from trust funds held by itself instead of, and in addition to, borrowing from the people through normal channels. It was obvious that, when the reserves were needed, they would not be found immediately in the federal Treasury, where in terms of fiction they were deposited, but would have to be collected by the government through borrowing from other sources or through taxation. Dissatisfaction with this arrangement led to arguments against the collection of trust funds in advance as distinguished from a pay-as-you-go method of financing social security. Although needed changes were made in the statute, however, the original financial arrangement was allowed to stand.[81]

Like the Fair Labor Standards Act, the Social Security Act was limited in the extent of its operation, but it established a principle of guaranteeing security which could be expanded as to degree and number of persons affected. On the occasion of the third anniversary of

[80] Charles C. Steward Machine Co. *v.* Davis, 301 U.S. 548 (1937), and Helvering *v.* Davis, 301 U.S. 619 (1937). See chapter 36.

[81] The complicated relations of the federal and state governments for administering the Social Security Act have given rise to serious problems. For a discussion of certain of these problems see V. O. Key, *The Matching Requirement in Federal Grant Legislation in Relation to Variations in State Fiscal Capacity*, Social Security Board, Bureau of Research and Statistics, Monograph No. 46 (1942).

the act, President Roosevelt sought to explain it in its historical and philosophical setting. In the early days of colonization, he said, and through the long years following, the American people had sought security in their family strongholds. As the nation had developed and as industry and commerce had grown more complex, the hazards of life had also grown more complex. The individual could not find the needed security within his own strength. Laws had been enacted to give security to property-owners, to industrialists, to merchants, and to bankers. The "little man" profited by this type of legislation chiefly as a by-product. It was not until workers became more articulate through organization that they were given protection through labor legislation. He continued:

> Because it has become increasingly difficult for individuals to build their own security single-handed, government must now step in and help them lay the foundation stone, just as government in the past has helped to lay the foundation of business and industry. We must face the fact that in this country we have a rich man's security and a poor man's security and that the government owes equal obligations to both. National security is not a half-and-half matter; it is all or none.[82]

## CONTROL OF COMMERCE AND INDUSTRY

Although some of the types of control over commerce and industry exercised under the National Industrial Recovery Act had to be abandoned as a result of the action of the Supreme Court on that statute, the extension of federal control by other methods was continued. In 1934, for example, Congress created a new independent regulatory commission, called the Securities and Exchange Commission. The enforcement of the Securities Act of 1933 was transferred to the new organization, and it was given regulatory powers over stock exchanges selling securities in interstate commerce or through the mails. In 1935, it was given new powers by the Public Utility Holding Company Act. That statute, enacted after the powerful resistance of a utility lobby had been overcome, contained what was called "the death sentence" for kinds of holding companies that had been connected with the most serious abuses at the time of the beginning of the depression. The purpose of the act was to provide for the dissolution of such holding companies as rendered no important financial or managerial services to the operating companies held and as seemed to feed upon

[82] *New York Times*, August 16, 1938.

those companies for the benefit of holding-company stockholders or managers who rendered no adequately compensatory service. Holding-company structures were given time in which to reorganize in conformity with the statute and subject to the approval of the Securities and Exchange Commission. If they refused to reorganize, the commission was empowered to force reorganizing measures upon them. It was authorized to require registration and the presentation of data by companies not hitherto subject even to such control as could be exercised through investigation and publicity. Because of the authority conferred by the three original statutes and by other statutes subsequently enacted, the Securities and Exchange Commission became one of the most powerful agencies in the federal government.

The coal industry seemed to call for special action by the government. Unlike most other industries, it had achieved no genuine state of prosperity since the period of high production during the first World War. There were too many mines; too much capacity for production; and too many miners. The industry was of such a nature that it was unable to combine to restrict production, raise prices, and promote prosperity of such portion of the industry as would be kept in operation. It was shot through with labor troubles. It was unionized in part, but cut-throat competition resulted in bitter labor strife characterized by the efforts of operators to break union control on the one hand, and of labor to strengthen unionism and improve hours, wages, and working conditions on the other.

In 1935, Congress enacted a Bituminous Coal Conservation Act, setting up the National Bituminous Coal Commission, with power to regulate maximum and minimum prices of coal and to regulate the labor engaged in coal production. The Supreme Court declared the act unconstitutional.[83] The statute was re-enacted in 1937 without the labor provision, and was upheld by the Supreme Court after important changes in Court personnel.[84] The National Bituminous Coal Commission set about the tremendous task of collecting through formal hearings and in other ways the information necessary to the establishment of minimum prices. While the work was in progress, the commission was abolished by one of the President's reorganization orders and its functions were transferred to a bituminous-coal division in the Department of the Interior. The work was continued and the

---

[83] Carter v. Carter Coal Co., 298 U.S. 238 (1936). See chapter 36. For discussion of the various constitutional problems involved in regulation see Ralph H. Baker, *The National Bituminous Coal Commission* (1942), chapter X.

[84] Sunshine Anthracite Coal Co. v. Adkins, 310 U.S. 381 (1940).

fixing of prices was begun, but the industry was still in a condition of depression down to the time when the national defense program began to have an effect upon it.

The Tennessee Valley Authority undertook the construction of dams, the building of plants, and the distribution of electricity throughout a vast area. It took charge of flood control, the prevention of erosion, reforestation, the development of park areas, and other functions that elsewhere in the country would have been supervised by various separate agencies in Washington. The authority constituted a planning, and to some extent a managerial, agency for the region over which it had control. The Tennessee Valley project was regarded by many as an experiment to determine the practicability of establishing similar regional authorities throughout the various sec tions of the country, to operate in similar fashion. The development of regional control in many fields has demonstrated interesting possibilities. With the breaking-down of barriers between states, regional areas, in contrast with state areas, were coming more and more to the fore as areas of control.

To regulate common carriers in interstate communication, the Federal Communications Commission was established in 1934. It took over the functions of the Federal Radio Commission and the regulation of telephone and telegraph, hitherto lodged in the Interstate Commerce Commission. The importance of the new agency increased with the increasing importance of the subject over which it had control. A Civil Aeronautics Authority was established to regulate the operation of non-military aircraft. The organization was subsequently transferred to the Commerce Department, where the performance of its functions continued.

Similar regulatory bodies functioned in other fields. The United States Maritime Commission was created to take the place of the old United States Shipping Board, dealing with a variety of marine affairs and regulating shipping on the high seas. The regulatory powers of the Federal Trade Commission were increased, particularly with reference to false or misleading advertising. Railroads required continuing care and assistance in the form of loans and in the extension of bankruptcy privileges. Various changes were made in banking legislation, including a creation of the Board of Governors of the Federal Reserve System to replace the Federal Reserve Board. The Reconstruction Finance Corporation, optimistically scheduled for dissolution at one stage, was continued with expanding powers of government lending.  More and more of the functions hitherto performed by private banks were being handled by the process of government lending.  Government support of house-building and home-ownership continued in various forms.[85]

## THE CONCENTRATION OF ECONOMIC POWER

In spite of or because of the New-Deal program, the drift toward the concentration of ownership and control continued rapidly.  By many the operations under NRA were credited with speeding the trend.  It is difficult to tell whether such was the case, or whether every important change, such as the prosperity of the post-war period, the depression, and the various modes of governmental intervention, merely gave the opportunity for the speeding-up of a fundamental trend.  Discussions continued as to the best method of securing effective control of powerful corporations.  The device of requiring corporations engaged in interstate commerce to secure charters or licenses from the federal government and submit to regulation in the process, which had been discussed down through the years from the time of the Theodore Roosevelt administration, was still being considered in the New-Deal period.[86]  Persons fearful of the growing power of huge corporations returned perennially to enforcement of anti-trust laws as the best mode of dealing with the problem.  After the dissolution of NRA, the administration placed new emphasis on the enforcement of these laws.  The theory announced was not one of antagonism to business, but of elimination of the "bottlenecks of business" created by selfishness or short-sightedness at particular points and injurious to business itself as well as to the country as a whole.[87]

In April, 1938, the President discussed the subject in a special message to Congress.[88]  Unhappy events abroad, he said, had retaught us two simple truths about the liberty of a democratic people.  The first was that the liberty of a democracy was not safe if the people tolerated the growth of private power to a point where it became stronger than their democratic state itself.  That in its essence was fascism — ownership of government by an individual, by a group, or by any other controlling private power.  The second truth was that the liberty of a democracy was not safe if its business system did not

[85] For discussion of the work of important regulating agencies, see Robert E. Cushman, *The Independent Regulatory Commissions* (1941).

[86] For studies down to 1934 see Senate Doc. No. 92, Part 69-A, 70th Cong., 1st sess.

[87] See Thurman Arnold, *Bottlenecks of Business* (1940).

[88] Senate Doc. No. 173, 75th Cong., 2d sess.

provide employment and produce and distribute goods in such a way as to sustain an acceptable standard of living.  He called attention to the growing concentration of economic power, to the extent of the centralization of financial control over industry, to the decline of competition and its effects on employment, and to other matters.  He asked that a thorough study of the subject be made.  He recommended an inquiry into the improvement of anti-trust procedure, into mergers and interlocking relationships, into financial controls, into trade associations, into patent laws, into tax correctives, and into the feasibility of establishing a Bureau of Industrial Economics, to perform for businessmen functions similar to those performed for farmers by the Bureau of Agricultural Economics in the Department of Agriculture.  The program was not intended, he said, as the beginning of any ill-considered trust-busting campaign.  It was a program to preserve private enterprise for profit by keeping it free enough to be able to utilize all our resources of capital and labor at a profit.  It was a program whose basic purpose was to stop the progress of collectivism in business and to turn business back to the democratic competitive order.  It was a program whose basic thesis was not that the system of free private enterprise for profit had failed in this generation, but that it had not yet been tried.  Once it was realized, he predicted, that business monopoly in America paralyzed the system of free enterprise on which it was grafted and was as fatal to those who manipulated it as to the people who suffered beneath its imposition, action by the government to eliminate these artificial restraints would be welcomed by industry throughout the nation.

The investigation by the Temporary National Economic Committee, made at the request of the President, disclosed the facts foreshadowed in his message.  The committee recommended various changes as desirable, but with apparent awareness that they would be slow in coming and would bring about no fundamental adjustment.[89]  The report was made at the time when the New-Deal program was being merged in the program of national defense, which in turn became a program of war.  Although on the whole the influence of the work of the committee will be hard to trace, it is clear that the impetus continued at least in attempts to see that patents were used as the Constitution provided, namely, "to promote the progress of science and useful arts" rather than for the stratification and stultification of industry.[90]  Other influences may be no less important.

[89] See Senate Doc. No. 35, 77th Cong., 1st sess.

[90] See *Hearings on S. 2303 and S. 2491* before the Senate committee on patents, 77th Cong., 2d sess.

# CHAPTER 36

## THE SUPREME COURT IN TRANSITION

"After March 4, 1929," said Franklin D. Roosevelt in a campaign address in 1932, "the Republican party was in complete control of all branches of the federal government — the Executive, the Senate, the House of Representatives, and, I might add for good measure, the Supreme Court as well." [1] The reference to the Republicanism of the Supreme Court presumably had to do, not with party membership in a narrow sense, but with the identification of a majority of the Court with the conservative philosophy of government which the Republican party professed. The conservatism of four of the justices, Van Devanter, McReynolds, Sutherland, and Butler, and the diligence with which they guarded rights of property against the extension of governmental control have been amply illustrated in earlier chapters.[2] It will be recalled that Chief Justice Hughes and Justice Roberts seemed to occupy something of a middle ground, shifting back and forth between liberal and conservative positions. By comparison with their brethren, Justices Brandeis, Stone, and Cardozo could be classified as liberals. Unless positions hitherto staunchly maintained had been shaken by the depression, therefore, the antagonism of four justices toward the New-Deal program was to be assumed, the alignment of two others was highly uncertain, and only three offered any prospect of enthusiasm for the program. There was room for doubt even as to these three. Justice Brandeis, for example, while a stalwart defender of so-called human rights when they came into conflict with property rights and an advocate of governmental intervention for the protection of human rights, was also critical of bigness in any form. His disapproval of the consolidation of wealth in units alleged to be too large for efficient administration did not preclude a corresponding disapproval of establishment of huge and unwieldy governmental organizations, even for New-Deal purposes.

[1] *Public Papers and Addresses of Franklin D. Roosevelt* (5 vols., 1938), I, 837.
[2] See chapters 31, 32, and 33.

Chief Justice Hughes and other members of the Court, furthermore, embodied the traditional distrust held by the judiciary and the bar for non-judicial administrative agencies to which the determination of rights had to be delegated if government was to perform broad regulatory and administrative functions. They knew the impracticability of treating as judicial questions all questions affecting rights and of requiring their determination by already overloaded judicial systems, but they retained the conviction that only the courts could be relied upon for a disciplined settlement of controversial questions. In an address delivered before the Federal Bar Association in February, 1931, Chief Justice Hughes called attention to the fact that overworked legislatures had been unable to keep pace with social demands and had adopted the practice, after the formulation of some very general standards, of turning over the business of regulation to a great variety of administrative agencies. The distinctive development of the era, he said, was one which raised the problem of executive justice, or administrative justice. A host of controversies as to provisional rights were now decided, not in the courts, but by administrators. Administrative authority within a constantly widening sphere of action, and subject only to the limitations of certain broad principles, established particular rules, found facts, and determined the limits of particular rights. This power was of enormous consequence. "An unscrupulous administrator might be tempted to say, 'Let me find the facts for the people of my country, and I care little who lays down the general principles.'" He admitted that this development had been to a great extent a necessary one, but declared that these new methods put us to new tests, "and the serious question of the future is whether we have enough of the old spirit which gave us our institutions to save them from being overwhelmed."[3]

The distrust of Chief Justice Hughes for administrative determinations unchecked by the courts was revealed again less than two weeks later in his opinion in the important case of Crowell v. Benson.[4] By an involved process of reasoning and in the face of a devastating dissent, he recaptured for the courts power to redetermine facts designated as "jurisdictional facts" previously determined by administrative agencies. Unfortunately, almost any set of facts involved in a case could be dragged into the category of jurisdictional facts. The deci-

[3] *New York Times*, February 13, 1931. See James M. Landis, *The Administrative Process* (1938), pp. 135-136.
[4] 285 U.S. 22 (1932).

sion was a long step backward in the movement to lighten the burden of the courts and relieve them of tasks they were not equipped to perform and to build up administrative agencies accustomed to responsibility and equipped for the performance of various kinds of tasks. It reflected the attitude of a Court unlikely to be sympathetic with the flowering-out of a host of new federal administrative agencies, manned by inexperienced personnel who, in the process of the extension of federal control over most of the economic order, were in many instances to take action limiting and shaping the rights of the people.

### JUDICIAL REVIEW OF THE NEW DEAL

For an appraisal of the relation of the courts to the New Deal, it is important to recall the atmosphere and attitudes of the early years of the period.[5] In his inaugural address, President Roosevelt promised vigorous leadership in combating the ills of the depression crisis — "action, and action now." Under the spur of his driving enthusiasm Congress accepted from his hand and enacted a list of drastic and far-reaching measures with a speed unprecedented in American history. Hosts of enthusiastic followers rushed to Washington to aid in saving the nation from economic disaster. They were filled with a sense of mission and a scorn for precedent. New agencies were established, manned, and put into operation virtually overnight for the performance of functions not hitherto considered functions of the federal government at all. Supervision and co-ordination were wholly inadequate. Only zeal for the cause kept machinery moving with any semblance of order. The cause, however, in the face of a threat of economic ruin, was one on which all citizens of every philosophy could unite. For the moment, something approaching unity of sentiment prevailed.

Not much was heard about the Supreme Court as the vast program of the New Deal got under way. Some doubts as to the constitutionality of parts of the program were hesitantly expressed. It was widely believed that the crisis would be over before the Supreme Court could have an opportunity to act, but some uneasiness was felt lest crippling injunctions be issued on constitutional grounds. "All you need do to scare the wits out of any administration leader," said a news commentator, "is to creep up behind him and whisper, 'Injunction.' " [6]

---

[5] Part of this chapter in an abbreviated form was presented in "The Supreme Court in Transition," *Journal of Politics*, I (November, 1939), 349-370. See also Charles A. Beard and Mary R. Beard, *America in Midpassage* (2 vols., 1939), I, chapters VI and VIII.

[6] T. R. B., *New Republic*, LXXVI (August 30, 1933), 71.

Enforcement during the early months was carried on largely by propaganda. Failure to obey New-Deal regulations resulted often-times in public sentiment damaging to the culprit's business. With-drawal of the blue eagle, the stamp of conformity with the President's re-employment agreement and with NRA codes, was a penalty not lightly to be incurred. Scattered judicial decisions of the early period suggest that the courts moved along with the prevailing sentiments. Two decisions, handed down early in 1934, indicated that the Supreme Court, in recognition of what Justice Brandeis, in a minority opinion in 1932, had called "an emergency more serious than war," [7] was at-tempting to find constitutional bases for drastic regulations deemed necessary to meet crisis conditions. In a case dealing with what was called a mortgage moratorium, the Court upheld a Minnesota law severely limiting the rights of creditors.[8] In a New York milk case it apparently abandoned much hitherto rigid doctrine on the subject of price-fixing.[9] Both cases were decided in the face of unrelenting opposition from Justices Van Devanter, McReynolds, Sutherland, and Butler.

The mortgage-moratorium case dealt with an emergency statute enacted in Minnesota in 1933, to postpone foreclosure of mortgages at a time when foreclosures were being made or threatened on such a scale as to disrupt the whole social and economic fabric of the state. The act permitted courts of the state to postpone sales and extend the period in which mortgaged property might be redeemed, a reason-able income or rental being paid in the meantime to the holder. It was challenged as an unconstitutional impairment of the obligation of contracts. Justice Sutherland, as spokesman for the minority, found ample precedents to justify the challenge. A majority of the Court, however, speaking through Chief Justice Hughes, held the act consti-tutional. The Chief Justice did not go so far as to contend that a state might at all times interfere in this manner with contract rights. Nor did he contend that an emergency created new governmental power. "Emergency does not increase granted powers or remove or diminish the restrictions imposed upon power granted or reserved." [10] But, "while emergency does not create power, emergency may furnish the occasion for the exercise of power." [11] The constitutional provi-sions against the impairment of the obligation of contracts was limited

[7] New State Ice Co. v. Liebmann, 285 U.S. 262, 306 (1932).

[8] Home Building and Loan Association v. Blaisdell, 290 U.S. 398 (1934).

[9] Nebbia v. New York, 291 U.S. 502 (1934).          [10] 290 U.S. 425.

[11] Ibid., p. 426.

by the restriction that a state continued to possess authority to safeguard the vital interests of its people, even though contracts were
affected.   The Court concluded that an emergency existed in Minnesota which furnished a proper occasion for the exercise of the reserved
power of the state to protect the vital interests of the community.   It
found that the interference with contracts authorized under the Minnesota statute was legitimate under the circumstances.   In so doing, the
Court seemed by implication to pave the way for the removal of constitutional barriers against the great mass of governmental regulations deemed necessary for dealing with the crisis.

In the New York milk case the Court, speaking through Justice
Roberts, upheld a state statute creating a milk-control board with
power to fix minimum and maximum retail prices to be charged by
stores to consumers of milk.   Justice Roberts admitted that the milk
industry was not a public utility, that it did not constitute a monopoly, and that it did not depend upon any public grant or franchise.
Within the definition of the four dissenting members of the Court, it
was not a "business affected with a public interest."   The Court, in
effect, discarded that conception, however, as a measure for determining whether prices might legitimately be fixed by government.   It
took the position that there was no closed category of businesses actually affected with a public interest and that, where the public interest
required, prices as well as other aspects of a business were subject to
regulation.   The decision represented a sharp break with past decisions in this field.

All in all, the two current decisions justified optimism on the part
of New-Dealers.   It was to be remembered, however, that they were
arrived at by votes of five to four, the narrowest of possible margins,
and that they had to do with the interpretation of state laws rather
than with broad federal statutes, resulting in the creation of a huge
federal bureaucracy.   Furthermore, even though the two statutes were
upheld, the opinions were so carefully phrased that if conditions
changed slightly, or if other statutes to be brought before the Court
varied slightly from those already passed upon, the Court could easily
shift its ground without reversing the decisions.

While economic conditions gradually improved, the complete recovery hoped for was not achieved.   For a number of reasons, public
sentiment in favor of the New-Deal program lost its unanimity.   It
was impossible to maintain indefinitely the emotional pitch which
made possible the administration of the program.   The enforcement

of varied types of emergency regulations became more and more irksome, both to businessmen and to consumers. The unbalanced federal budget and the growing cost of the New-Deal program caused uneasiness. People began to wonder if the multifarious and oftentimes conflicting activities of the government had really been necessary for the achievement of such recovery as had been brought about or for such further improvement as seemed in prospect.

With the growth of doubts came a relaxation of the sentiment which made enforcement possible without resort to the courts. The administration, which had hitherto sought to avoid litigation, now began a search for good cases by which to demonstrate the constitutionality of New-Deal measures and the determination of the government to enforce these measures. The search for test cases disclosed in the records of the government the effects of haste in drafting legislation, executive orders, and codes, and in working out procedures. Every case considered as a possible means of determining the validity of the essential features of the administration program involved legal defects or embarrassing points which threw doubt on the wisdom of using it. One of the serious errors discovered was in the code of fair competition for administration of the petroleum industry. It will be recalled that the National Industrial Recovery Act gave the President power to modify the code. It seems that a change was ordered to be made in the petroleum code and that, in copying the document so as to include a new provision, the penalty provision of the code was inadvertently omitted, thereby leaving the code without any legal sanction whatsoever. The Petroleum Administration, unaware of or ignoring this highly important technical error, proceeded with the enforcement of the code as if penalties were still prescribed. In a case against one J. W. Smith, originally intended by the government as a test case for the National Industrial Recovery Act, it was discovered, in the language of counsel in a later case, that "Smith was arrested, indicted, and held in jail for several days and then had to put up bond for violating a law that did not exist.[12]

Government counsel discovered the error and the case was dropped, for this or other reasons. Two other cases,[13] of which one involved, not merely the petroleum code, but other provisions of the National Industrial Recovery Act dealing with regulation of the petroleum indus-

[12] *New York Herald Tribune,* December 12, 1934.
[13] Panama Refining Co. *v.* Ryan and Amazon Petroleum Corporation *v.* Ryan, 293 U.S 388 (1935). They are commonly known as the hot-oil cases.

try, were taken to the Supreme Court. Counsel for the private parties involved were able to embarrass government counsel in a discussion of the missing provision of the petroleum code; and members of the Court insisted on being told how codes and other executive orders were made available for the use of the government and of the public. It was disclosed that orders having the force of law were being issued at a rapid rate without any systematic mode of making them available. It was oftentimes next to impossible for private parties, and even government officials, to discover the content of the law on a given subject. From the bench and in its subsequent opinion, the Court criticized such disreputable procedure. The disclosures and the criticism had the important effect of bringing success to the movement for the publication of a magazine to be called the *Federal Register,* in which the great mass of orders having the force of law were to be printed. The establishment of the *Federal Register* was followed by the codification of the mass of such orders as existed at that time.

The cases involved in the petroleum litigation, the so-called "hot-oil" cases, are remembered, however, not for their applicability to the petroleum code, but for the decision with respect to a provision in the National Industrial Recovery Act giving certain powers to the President. The provision authorized the President to prohibit the transportation in interstate and foreign commerce of petroleum produced in excess of the amount permitted by any state law or valid regulation. It did not attempt to guide the discretion of the President. He might prohibit shipment or not, as he saw fit. The President issued an executive order prohibiting the interstate or foreign shipment of "hot oil." With only Justice Cardozo dissenting, the Court held that the conferring of this power upon the President, without the prescription of a policy or standard to guide his decision, was an unconstitutional delegation of legislative power. Although the Court had often paid lip-service to the principle that legislative power could not be delegated, it had never before held a federal statute unconstitutional on that ground. Even though the damage done by this particular decision was easily curable by new legislation — which was speedily enacted — the step taken by the Court was ominous.

The next New-Deal cases to be decided were the so-called gold-clause cases. It will be recalled that all gold and gold certificates had been ordered turned in to the United States Treasury and that a joint resolution of Congress declared provisions in public and private contracts for payment in gold contrary to public policy and unenforceable in the courts of the United States. For the purpose of reviving business, the President exercised powers given by Congress to reduce the gold content of the dollar, or, in other words, to reduce the amount of gold by which the value of the dollar was to be measured. Public and private contracts then outstanding to the amount of several billions of dollars were affected. Price-levels were not greatly changed Persons who by contract were entitled to payment in gold could purchase with devalued dollars almost as much in commodities as they could have purchased before the presidential order was issued. They suffered little or no loss by the action of the government, except for the fact that they, like other people, had to forego the right to gold. It was widely contended, however, that these persons had property rights in gold-clause contracts which could not be destroyed by legislation. If the government had the right to call all gold into the Treasury and to refuse to pay it out or to permit private individuals to use it in satisfaction of contracts, it was contended that gold-clause contracts made before the dollar was devalued could be satisfied only by the payment of an additional amount in devalued dollars corresponding to the extent of the devaluation. For example, a contract for payment of a dollar in gold could not be satisfied by a paper dollar representing only about fifty-nine cents as measured by the amount of gold held prior to devaluation.

The question was argued in terms of morals as well as of law. It was regarded as a particularly heinous offense for the federal government to flout its obligations in this manner. On the other hand, it was contended that the obligation to adjust the monetary system in such a way as to promote the welfare of all the people constituted a higher obligation than that to carry out in all their provisions the contracts for the payment of gold. Public contracts, like private contracts, were made subject to the limitation that the performance of their provisions must not be injurious to the public welfare. It was recognized, furthermore, that the national economy had been adjusted to the deflated currency, and that Supreme Court decisions requiring the fulfillment of gold-clause contracts with payments at face value plus amounts to the extent of the devaluation might result in financial chaos. This practical consideration may have had as much to do with the decisions of the Court as did its interpretation either of law or morality.

After keeping the cases under consideration over a period of weeks, during which the people waited tensely for a decision, the Supreme

Court announced opinions in a series of gold-clause cases. The government was the victor by the narrowest of margins. In the first of the cases decided,[14] Chief Justice Hughes, speaking for a majority of the Court, pointed out that the use of gold was closely related to the exercise of important powers which the Constitution conferred upon Congress. Contracts made between private parties could not restrain the exercise of powers, monetary or otherwise, possessed by Congress.

> Contracts, however express, cannot fetter the constitutional authority of the Congress. Contracts may create rights of property, but when contracts deal with a subject matter which lies within the control of the Congress, they have a congenital infirmity. Parties cannot remove their transactions from the reach of dominant constitutional power by making contracts about them.[15]

The Court held that, in exercising its control over gold, Congress had acted within its powers and that private contracts could not be enforced in so far as they were inconsistent with that policy.

The Supreme Court also found that the holder of gold certificates who was required to surrender them to the government for their dollar value in spite of the allegedly high market value of gold was not entitled to further reimbursement from the government, since the certificates were only for gold dollars, and not for gold bullion.[16] Finally, it held unconstitutional the repudiation of gold-clause contracts in United States bonds — giving Chief Justice Hughes an opportunity to scold the administration for the immorality of its conduct — but five justices agreed that the person bringing the suit had lost nothing by the devaluation process, and was therefore not entitled to sue.[17]

The outcome was that the government won technical, though marginal, victories in all cases. Justice Stone wrote a concurring opinion in one case, and four justices joined in an indignant dissenting opinion written by Justice McReynolds to apply to all cases. In delivering his opinion in the courtroom he added extemporaneously the ominous statement, "As for the Constitution, it does not seem too much to say that it is gone." [18]

The reaction of administration leaders to the gold-clause decisions

---

[14] Norman v. Baltimore and Ohio Railroad Co., 294 U.S. 240 (1935).
[15] Ibid., pp. 307-308.     [16] Nortz v. United States, 294 U.S. 317 (1935).
[17] Perry v. United States, 294 U.S. 330 (1935).
[18] See the New York Herald Tribune, February 19, 1935, and other morning newspapers of that day.

was a mixture of relief and indignation. Although not quite believing that the Supreme Court would take the risk of creating the economic chaos that might result from adverse decisions, they had been anxiously searching for methods of softening the blow if it came. To protect the government against suits on its own gold-clause contracts, they had been planning legislation to withdraw the jurisdiction of federal courts to entertain such suits. Even if they had succeeded in this field, however, the effect as to private contracts would have been disastrous. The five-to-four vote of the Court was too close for comfort; and they resented what they regarded as a moral lecture on the part of Chief Justice Hughes with reference to the repudiation of government contracts. It stood to reason that if some of the justices had been virtually coerced into supporting the government against their convictions, because of the disastrous effects which would have resulted from decisions of a different kind, their indignation at New-Deal methods would carry over to the decision of other cases where the results of adverse action would be less dangerous. Even though they had won a technical victory in the gold-clause suits against the government, administration leaders deemed it expedient to bring about the enactment of legislation to cut off additional suits of the kind in the near future.[19] In the meantime, they turned to the defense of the program at points of greater vulnerability.

JUDICIAL DISASTERS FOR THE NEW DEAL

Since late in 1933 a case, known as United States v. Belcher,[20] had been pending in the courts and had been considered by government officials from time to time as satisfactory for use as a test case on code administration under the National Industrial Recovery Act. In response to criticism of the administration for failure to bring about the settlement of the question before the Supreme Court, the public at large and lower federal courts throughout the country were assured that this case, which involved administration of the lumber code, would bring about a definitive judicial test of the recovery statute. After the adverse decision of the Supreme Court in the oil cases, however, the Belcher case seemed exceedingly vulnerable. The government victory in the gold-clause cases was not of such a nature as to build confidence. On April 1, 1935, on the request of Solicitor Gen-

[19] 49 Stat. 938. For additional gold-clause cases see Holyoke Water Power Co. v. American Writing Paper Co., 300 U.S. 324 (1937), and Smyth v. United States, 302 U.S. 329 (1937).
[20] See 294 U.S. 736.

eral Stanley Reed, the Supreme Court dismissed the appeal. As a result, the administration was criticized for bad faith and was accused of admitting tacitly that it doubted the validity of legislation it was seeking to enforce.

In the meantime, without much publicity and evidently without the knowledge of many government officials interested in demonstrating the constitutionality of the National Industrial Recovery Act, government counsel had won, in lower federal courts in New York City, a criminal case that had arisen in connection with the administration of the poultry code. Had the government lost the case in the circuit court of appeals, there would have been no question of an appeal to the Supreme Court and of the use of this case as a test case for the recovery statute before the Supreme Court. When the defeated defendant petitioned for a Supreme Court review, however, the Department of Justice could do little more than make the best of the situation, even though, from a number of angles, the case was a bad one in which to present code administration in its best light.[21]

The so-called live-poultry code applied only to an area in and around New York City in the states of New York, Connecticut, and New Jersey. It regulated hours, wages, and working conditions and various trade practices in the handling and slaughtering of poultry. Although most of the poultry sold in New York City came from states other than New York, the matters regulated seemed, on their face, to be largely local in character. The marketing of diseased and uninspected poultry was forbidden. Buyers were also forbidden to make selections among fowls in particular coops instead of taking them as they came. The purpose of the latter provision was to prevent the practice whereby first-comers selected the best poultry at the market price, whereafter price-cutting, which was of course injurious to the industry and therefore contrary to the purposes of the National Industrial Recovery Act, was necessary to dispose of the remaining, less desirable stock. The administration of these provisions, however, on which the constitutionality of the code structure of the National Industrial Recovery Act was to depend, was discussed in the courtroom in high levity. In response to a question from the bench, counsel for the poultry firm involved explained that "straight killing," which was required by the code, meant, "You have got to put your hand in the

---

[21] In the process of making the best of the situation, the Department of Justice likewise filed in the Supreme Court a petition for a writ of certiorari as to certain aspects of the case in which the government had not been the victor in the court below.

coop and take out whichever chicken comes to you." Thereafter the following colloquy took place:

> "And it was for that your client was convicted?" asked Mr. Justice McReynolds.
>
> "Yes, and fined and given a jail sentence," Mr. Heller replied.
>
> "But if a customer wants half a coop of chickens, he has to take it just like it is," he further explained.
>
> "What if the chickens are all at one end?" inquired Mr. Justice Sutherland. Counsel's answer to that question was lost in the laughter from the bench and the bar which ensued.
>
> As to the charge of selling diseased poultry, Mr. Heller explained that it was based upon the sale of one chicken which had passed federal inspection, but which, upon an autopsy, was found to be "eggbound." [22]

Amid the unfavorable atmosphere indicated, a government counsel had the task of persuading the Court that authorizing the President to make or sanction the rules enforced in the poultry industry did not represent an unconstitutional delegation of legislative power, that the rules constituted legitimate regulations of interstate commerce, and that they did not take liberty or property without due process of law.

The case, known as the Schechter case,[23] or, more informally, as the "sick-chicken" case, was decided on May 27, 1935. Speaking for a unanimous Court, Chief Justice Hughes held that Section 3 of the recovery statute, which authorized the government of industry through codes of fair competition, was unconstitutional because of the sweeping delegation of legislative power. He summarized his conclusion as follows:

> It supplies no standards for any trade, industry, or activity. It does not undertake to prescribe rules of conduct to be applied to particular states of fact determined by appropriate administrative procedure. Instead of prescribing rules of conduct, it authorizes the making of codes to prescribe them. For that legislative undertaking, Section 3 sets up no standards, aside from the statement of the general aims of rehabilitation, correction, and expansion described in Section 1. In view of the scope of that broad declaration and of the nature of the few restrictions that are imposed, the discretion of the President in approving or prescribing codes, and thus enacting laws for the government of trade and industry throughout the country, is virtually unfettered. We think that the code-making authority thus conferred is an unconstitutional delegation of legislative power.[24]

[22] *United States Law Week,* May 7, 1935.
[23] A. L. A. Schechter Corporation *v.* United States, 295 U.S. 495 (1935).
[24] *Ibid.,* pp. 541-542.

Justice Cardozo, the only justice who had dissented in the hot-oil case in which the Supreme Court first exercised its veto on the ground of the unconstitutional delegation of legislative power, concurred vigorously in the Schechter case.   He said:

> The delegated power of legislation which has found expression in this code is not canalized within banks that keep it from overflowing. It is unconfined and vagrant. . . . Here . . . is an attempted delegation not confined to any single act nor to any class or group of acts identified or described by reference to a standard.   Here in effect is a roving commission to inquire into evils and upon discovery correct them.[25]

Government by means of codes of fair competition was very different, he declared, from action against unfair methods of competition, such as that taken by the Federal Trade Commission.   Delegation of the power to discover and denounce unfair practices was obviously necessary in view of the number and diversity of the industries of the country.   Government by codes of fair competition went much farther:

> It is to include whatever ordinances may be desirable or helpful for the well-being or prosperity of the industry affected.   In that view, the function of its adoption is not merely negative, but positive; the planning of improvements as well as the extirpation of abuses.   What is fair, as thus conceived, is not something to be contrasted with what is unfair or fraudulent or tricky.   The extension becomes as wide as the field of industrial regulation.   If that conception shall prevail, anything that Congress may do within the limits of the commerce clause for the betterment of business may be done by the President upon the recommendation of a trade association by calling it a code.   This is delegation running riot.   No such plenitude of power is susceptible of transfer.   The statute, however, aims at nothing less, as one can learn both from its terms and from the administrative practice under it.[26]

The Court also held unanimously that the practices involved in this case were in intrastate commerce and could not be regulated under the commerce clause.   Government counsel had contended that the abuses to be prevented had such an injurious effect upon interstate commerce as to justify federal regulation.   Drawing a distinction between direct and indirect effects upon interstate commerce, the Court rejected the contention.

The devastating result of the decision was that the statutory base,

[25] *Ibid.*, p. 551.          [26] *Ibid.*, pp. 552-553.

not merely for the poultry code, but for all codes formed under the National Industrial Recovery Act, was destroyed.  Furthermore, the interstate-commerce aspect of the decision stood in the way of enforcement of important provisions in this and other codes, even if the codes should be submitted directly to Congress and enacted by it.  The complete collapse of recovery machinery for the control of industry was decreed.  The President told a press conference that the implications of this decision were probably more important than any decision since the Dred Scott case.[27]  From reading the decision he thought that the delegation of power was not an unsurmountable object, and that an act could be written giving definite directions to administrative or quasi-judicial bodies which would be acceptable.  He regarded as more serious the narrow interpretation of the commerce clause.  Although the country had been in "the horse-and-buggy age" when the commerce clause was written, the tendency in recent years had been to view the clause in the light of present-day civilization.  He intimated that the Schechter decision represented a return to the horse-and-buggy age.[28]

Two other important cases were decided against the administration on the day on which the Schechter case was decided.  In one of them the Supreme Court held a federal farm-bankruptcy statute unconstitutional as taking the property of creditors without due process of law.[29]  In the other case, discussed in an earlier chapter,[30] the Court held that the President had no power to remove a member of the Federal Trade Commission other than as prescribed in the Federal Trade Commission Act.

Three weeks earlier, while these cases were awaiting decision, Justice Roberts had joined the four traditional conservatives to make the majority of the Court which wrecked a comprehensive retirement scheme for railroad workers.[31]  The federal statute involved was perhaps not an integral part of the New-Deal program, but it was closely related to it.  It was intended to provide economic security in old age for one class of workers, and it might have reduced the excess of workers seeking employment on railroads by providing a mode of subsistence for those beyond a certain age who had rendered service in earlier years.  The Court not only found defects in this particular

[27] *Public Papers and Addresses of Franklin D. Roosevelt,* IV, 205.
[28] *Ibid.,* p. 209.
[29] Louisville Joint Stock Land Bank *v.* Radford, 295 U.S. 555 (1935).
[30] Humphrey's Executor *v.* United States, 295 U.S. 602 (1935).  See chapter 30.
[31] Railroad Retirement Board *v.* Alton Railroad Co., 295 U.S. 330 (1935).

law, however, but decided the case in such a way as apparently to invalidate any similar scheme sponsored by the federal government.[32] On the whole, in spite of victories for the administration in the gold-clause cases, the 1934-1935 term of the Supreme Court made the prospect for drastic social legislation of any kind seem dismal indeed.

THE 1935–1936 TERM

The New Deal continued to suffer at the hands of the Supreme Court at the term beginning in October, 1935.   In United States v. Butler, the processing-tax provisions of the Agricultural Adjustment Act, on which a major portion of the farm program was based, were held unconstitutional by a vote of six to three.[33]  Justice Roberts spoke for the Court in a complicated and mystifying opinion.  He admitted that Congress had the power to tax in order to provide for the general welfare and to appropriate the money raised for that purpose.   He did not deny the obvious fact that huge sums in revenue were raised by the processing tax.   He did not deny that the taxing device might be used for regulatory purposes, if the purposes themselves were within the power of the federal government.   A tax, however, he said, "in the general understanding of the term, and as used in the Constitution, signifies an exaction for the support of the government.   The word has never been thought to connote the expropriation of money from one group for the benefit of another."[34]  The tax here provided for was not a means of raising revenue for support of the government, but was part of a plan to regulate and control agricultural production, "a matter beyond the powers delegated to the federal government."[35]  He rejected the contention that the plan was not compulsory.   The farmer, of course, might refuse to comply, but the price of such refusal was the loss of benefits.   "The amount offered is intended to be sufficient to exert pressure on him to agree to the proposed regulation.   The power to confer or withhold unlimited benefits is the power to coerce or destroy."[36]

In a dissenting opinion concurred in by Justices Brandeis and Cardozo, Justice Stone by implication accused his colleague of resorting to "a tortured construction of the Constitution," and remarked, "Courts are not the only agency of government that must be assumed to have capacity to govern."[37]  His words had influence, however, only

[32] A revised scheme worked out with the approval of railroad companies was never theless put into operation.   See 50 Stat. 307.

[33] 297 U.S. 1 (1936).          [34] Ibid., p. 61.          [35] Ibid., p. 68.

[36] Ibid., pp. 70-71.          [37] Ibid., p. 87.

in connection with the later attack upon the rigid conservatism of the Supreme Court. Control of agricultural production by the processing-tax device was invalidated for the time being, and it was clear that more obviously compulsory measures for limiting the production of cotton, tobacco, and potatoes were likewise unconstitutional. The statutes in question were accordingly repealed.

Another important decision turned on the constitutionality of the Bituminous Coal Conservation Act of 1935, a statute providing for the control of working conditions in the mining industry and for the fixing of prices for the sale of coal. Congress had been slow in passing the measure, justifying hesitancy on the ground that the constitutionality of such regulations was in doubt. The President sent to the subcommittee in charge of the bill a statement justifying the legislation. He closed with the following significant paragraph:

> Manifestly, no one is in a position to give assurance that the proposed act will withstand constitutional tests, for the simple fact that you can get not ten but one thousand different legal opinions on the subject. But the situation is so urgent and the benefits of the legislation so evident that all doubts should be resolved in favor of the bill, leaving to the courts, in an orderly fashion, the ultimate question of constitutionality. A decision by the Supreme Court relative to this measure would be helpful as indicating with increasing clarity the constitutional limits within which this government must operate. The proposed bill has been carefully drafted by employers and employees working co-operatively. An opportunity should be given to the industry to attempt to work out some of its major problems. I hope your committee will not permit doubts as to constitutionality, however reasonable, to block the suggested legislation.[38]

Opponents of the bill denounced the request of the President for enactment of the legislation in spite of doubts as to constitutionality, "however reasonable." They denounced the cavalier attitude of a President who would advocate legislation without reference to constitutional difficulties, leaving their solution to the Supreme Court. They quoted with approval from a veto message in which President Taft had taken an entirely different attitude. Said Taft:

> The oath that the Chief Executive takes, and which each member of Congress takes, does not bind him any less sacredly to observe the Constitution than the oaths which justices of the Supreme Court take. It is questionable whether the doubtful constitutionality of a bill ought not to furnish a greater reason for voting against the bill, or vetoing it, than for the Court to hold it invalid.[39]

[38] 79 Congressional Record 13449.       [39] Ibid., pp. 13435, 13449.

The Roosevelt statement, however, was written in the knowledge that constitutional arguments were being used against the bill when the real reasons for opposition had little or nothing to do with the Constitution. Furthermore, it seemed to the administration that the Supreme Court, under the cover of interpreting the Constitution, was making itself the arbiter of governmental policy in rivalry with the elected representatives of the people. Rather than to yield passively to judicial opposition to New-Deal policies, officials deemed it better strategy to require the Court to show its hand in as many cases as possible, thereby demonstrating to the people that the Court, and not the administration, was responsible for the ineffectiveness of the program. The act was passed, and the Court responded by its decision in Carter v. Carter Coal Company.[40]

Dividing on different points by votes of six to three and five to four, it held the act unconstitutional. The majority opinion, written by Justice Sutherland, reflected throughout a narrow conception of the powers of the federal government. He argued:

> The proposition, often advanced and as often discredited, that the power of the federal government inherently extends to purposes affecting the nation as a whole with which the states severally cannot deal or cannot adequately deal, and the related notion that Congress, entirely apart from those powers delegated by the Constitution, may enact laws to promote the general welfare, have never been accepted, but always definitely rejected, by this Court.[41]

Federal authority under the statute was supported by means of a taxing device. An excise tax was levied in such a way as to operate as a penalty upon those producers of coal who failed to comply with the provisions of the act. The constitutional basis for the regulatory provisions of the statute, however, had to be found, not in the taxing power, but in the commerce power. Justice Sutherland analyzed the word "commerce" to show that it was the equivalent of the phrase "intercourse for the purposes of trade." Plainly, he said, the incidents leading up to and culminating in the mining of coal did not constitute such intercourse. The employment of workers in mining was not interstate commerce. It might have an effect upon such commerce, but the effect was indirect, however great its magnitude, and was therefore not subject to federal control. The conclusion that working conditions were obviously local conditions over which the federal government had no legislative control implied so drastic a curtail-

[40] 298 U.S. 238 (1936).     [41] Ibid., p. 291.

ment of the commerce power as to threaten the enforcement of other important measures by which the administration sought to restore order in the field of industrial relations and improve the conditions of labor.

Justice Sutherland found also that legislative power was unconstitutionally delegated in the provisions of the statute whereby maximum hours of labor were to be determined by certain percentages of the producers in the industry. He found that provisions as to hours and wages did not accord with the requirement of due process of law. Having held that the labor provisions were defective, he reached the further conclusion that the price-fixing provisions in the statute could not stand alone and that the entire act must be held unconstitutional and void. Justice Cardozo wrote a vigorous dissenting opinion, concurred in by Justices Brandeis and Stone, which served further to portray the majority of the Court as an agency setting out deliberately to use constitutional interpretation as an instrument to curb distasteful governmental policies.

Other federal statutes suffered a similar fate. By a vote of five to four, with Justice McReynolds as spokesman for the majority, the Court invalidated the Municipal Bankruptcy Act of 1934.[42] In an important case involving administrative procedure in connection with the fixing of stockyard rates by the Secretary of Agriculture, Chief Justice Hughes, for a majority of the Court, reasserted the power of the judiciary to inquire into facts already determined by the administrator when constitutional questions turned upon them. When the constitutionality of a regulation depended upon such matters as net income and valuation, even though these matters were essentially factual, the Court held that they were subject to re-examination.[43] The effect of the decision was to broaden the judicial authority over fact-finding previously asserted in Crowell v. Benson in connection with so-called jurisdictional facts. In another case the Court limited the power thought to have been given to the Securities and Exchange Commission.[44]

A decision having to do with the establishment of minimum wages for women, although it concerned a state statute, was regarded also as a New-Deal defeat. In the Adkins case, decided in 1923, the Supreme

[42] Ashton v. Cameron County Water Improvement District No. One, 298 U.S. 513 (1936).

[43] St. Joseph Stockyards Co. v. United States, 298 U.S. 38 (1936). Justice Roberts concurred in the result. Justices Brandeis, Stone, and Cardozo dissented.

[44] Jones v. Securities and Exchange Commission, 298 U.S. 1 (1936).

Court had held that Congress had no power to prescribe minimum wages for women in the District of Columbia.[45]  By a vote of five to four, with Justice Roberts joining the conservatives and Justice Butler speaking for the majority, the Court held that the decision as to a New York law must follow the earlier decision.[46]  The reasoning stood in the way of new federal legislation that might attempt to eliminate the evil of substandard wages.

The administration achieved only one important victory at the term of the Court under discussion.  With only Justice McReynolds dissenting, the Court upheld the constitutional power of the federal government to dispose of electric power generated at Wilson Dam in the Tennessee Valley.[47]  Chief Justice Hughes emphasized the relation to the war power and to the power of Congress to improve the navigability of streams as an incident to the regulation of commerce.  He emphasized also the power of the federal government "to dispose of and make all needful rules and regulations respecting the territory or other property belonging to the United States." [48]

In a sense, the TVA decision, nominally the one bright spot in the Supreme Court record for the term, constituted an embarrassment for the administration.  It indicated that the Court had not set out maliciously to batter every major feature of the New-Deal program, and that, if New-Deal legislation could be brought within the traditional lines of constitutional interpretation, it might be upheld by the Court.  In spite of the conviction of many administration leaders that the Court had set out deliberately to sabotage their program, the line-up of decisions conveyed the suggestion that it was the program and not the Court that was wrong.  Presumably no administration leaders accepted this interpretation, but a number of them realized the persuasiveness of the argument as far as the general public was concerned.

THE ATTEMPT AT JUDICIAL REFORM

In any event, the prospects remained gloomy for the portions of the New-Deal program not yet passed upon.  These included such major statutes as the National Labor Relations Act, the Social Security Act, and the Public Utility Holding Company Act.  Furthermore, the replacement of some of the statutes invalidated was being planned, along with the enactment of new measures of social significance.  It ap-

[45] See chapter 32.
[46] Morehead v. New York ex rel. Tipaldo, 298 U.S. 587 (1936).
[47] Ashwander v. Tennessee Valley Authority, 297 U.S. 288 (1936).
[48] Constitution, Article IV, Section 3.

peared that something would have to be done about the Supreme Court if such enactments were to constitute anything more than futile gestures.

A device much discussed, and actually employed to a limited extent, was to withdraw the jurisdiction of federal courts to entertain suits of a kind likely to embarrass the government. Since the government could not be sued without its own consent, it was an easy matter to secure the enactment of legislation cutting off suits against the government by persons contending that they had been injured by the devaluation of the currency. The device was used again in connection with suits against the government to recover taxes unconstitutionally collected under the Agricultural Adjustment Act of 1933. Such suits were to be entertained by the courts only if the persons bringing them could prove, not only that they had paid the taxes, but that they had not either passed them back to farmers in the form of lower prices paid for raw materials or forward to consumers in the form of higher prices.[49]

Further limitations of jurisdiction were under constant discussion as a means of preventing judicial interference with the New-Deal program, but it was practically impossible to withdraw all constitutional questions from judicial determination. As to the original jurisdiction of the Supreme Court, indeed, it was derived, not from Congress, but from the Constitution itself. Even if, as was not generally believed, the appellate jurisdiction of the Supreme Court could be cut off in cases involving constitutional questions, those questions must inevitably be raised in the lower federal courts. Many of those courts showed a disapproval of the New-Deal program no less ardent than that of the Supreme Court. Furthermore, the disparity of decisions on constitutional questions, if not subject to the unifying influence of the Supreme Court, would result in chaos throughout the several judicial districts.

Constitutional amendments to clear the way for New-Deal measures were also considered. The amending device was opposed because of the difficulty and the time to be consumed in securing amendments. Furthermore, although the Supreme Court was at times unanimous or close to unanimous in its position, a number of decisions made the cleavage among the justices sharply apparent, and suggested that the remedy lay with the Court and not with the Constitution. In May, 1935, after the decision on the Railroad Retirement Act, Attorney

[49] 49 Stat. 771 and 1747. See Anniston Manufacturing Co. *v.* Davis, 301 U.S. 337 (1937).

General Homer Cummings included the following comment in a letter to the President:

> The case was always a difficult one, but the form the opinions took would seem to indicate such a marked cleavage in the Supreme Court that it may be, and probably is, a forecast of what we may expect with reference to almost any form of social legislation that Congress may enact. Apparently there are at least four justices who are against any attempt to use the power of the federal government for bettering general conditions, except within the narrowest limitations. This is a terrific handicap and brings up again, rather acutely, matters we have previously discussed, including a proposed constitutional amendment.[50]

The Attorney General continued to watch the situation and to analyze the possibilities of constitutional amendments and of congressional limitations on the jurisdiction of the Supreme Court. The real difficulty, he wrote to the President in January, 1936, was not with the Constitution, but with the judges who interpreted it. As long as a majority of those who had the final say in such matters were wedded to their present theories, there were but two courses open. The administration must endeavor to find a way to bring helpful national legislation within the explicit terms of the decisions being reached by the Court or it must frankly meet the issue of a constitutional amendment. For the present he preferred the former course. He said:

> If we come to the question of a constitutional amendment, enormous difficulties are presented. No one has yet suggested an amendment that does not do either too much or too little, or which does not raise practical and political questions which it would be better to avoid. If we had liberal judges, with a lively sense of the importance of the social problems which have now spilled over state lines, there would be no serious difficulties; and the existing constitutional restraint when interpreted by such a Court would be very salutary.[51]

He suggested giving serious thought to a constitutional amendment which would require the retirement of all federal judges, or at least all Supreme Court judges, at the age of seventy. It would have the advantage of not changing in the least degree the structure of the government; nor would it impair the power of the Court. It would merely insure the exercise of the powers of the Court by judges less likely to be horrified by new ideas.

[50] Swisher (ed.), *Selected Papers of Homer Cummings* (1939), p. 130.
[51] *Ibid.*, pp. 148-149.

During the presidential campaign of 1936, Republicans and such non-partisan or bi-partisan organizations as the Liberty League lauded the Supreme Court as the defender of the rights of the people against New-Deal encroachments. The President, on the other hand, made no public comment about the Republicanism of the Supreme Court, such as he had made four years earlier, avoiding all attacks upon that institution which might create public antagonism. The administration sought to fix the attention of voters upon its program and not upon governmental machinery. All who thought deeply about the subject knew that for the preservation of the program something would have to be done about the judicial blockade, but most of them were willing to leave the mode of action to future determination.

In the meantime, the office of the solicitor general was secretly making a comprehensive study of the various suggestions "by which the legislature might, to a greater or lesser extent, lessen its vulnerability to the constitutional views of a majority of the Court." The study was made, said the solicitor general in a memorandum for the Attorney General on December 19, 1936, "so that if, as, and when the President brings the matter up again, we would have this background. It was suggested at the first cabinet meeting after the election that we should be thinking on them."

The study analyzed, classified, and appraised the various suggestions having some element of feasibility. The suggestions included the following: Congress should insist on determining such facts as whether a given industry or practice had a direct effect upon interstate commerce; through its control over procedure, Congress should require that the vote necessary to invalidate an act be more than a bare majority of the Court; Congress should withdraw from the jurisdiction of the lower federal courts, and from the appellate jurisdiction of the Supreme Court, the power to pass upon the constitutionality of acts of Congress; the membership of the Supreme Court might be increased to allow the appointment of enough liberal justices to insure a majority; and finally, Congress might adjust retirement compensation progressively so as to make retirement at seventy or at a similarly early age much more attractive than in the later years of life.

From the point of view of the general history of the period, the document was significant. As background for the action taken soon after it was written, however, it served chiefly to clear the air by pointing out impossibilities or pitfalls in the way of achieving the desired ends. The writer or writers were extremely pessimistic about the practicability of any of the proposals, when both legal and political objections were taken into account.

Around the turn of the year 1936-1937, the President and the Attorney General agreed on the outlines of a plan. Without again taking up the subject with his cabinet, the President consulted with the Attorney General from time to time, as the program was worked out with great secrecy in the Department of Justice. Since the difficulty was not with the Constitution, but was with the Court, they agreed that a constitutional amendment was not the appropriate remedy. Both knew, furthermore, that, although the President had carried all but two states in the recent election, as many as thirteen states might fail to sanction a constitutional amendment, in which event the amendment would not become operative.

They concluded that the subject must be dealt with in terms of the retirement of aged justices or the superseding of such justices. Since under the Constitution the justices served during good behavior, there was no way to compel them to retire merely on grounds of age. The device hit upon, therefore, was to assume that justices over seventy years of age were to some extent incompetent and provide for the appointment of an additional justice for each justice who had served for ten years and had not resigned or retired within six months after reaching the age of seventy. The plan was not novel. It was already in effect with respect to circuit and district judges, except that there had to be a finding of mental or physical disability of a permanent character. Its automatic operation in the Supreme Court would have been humiliating to the justices involved, however, and might in fact have coerced them into retirement. Presumably, the President and the Attorney General hoped for such an outcome. If the aged justices did not retire, it was hoped that their conservative votes would be outnumbered by majorities including the votes of the new appointees.

With the mode of attack agreed upon, the sponsors were faced with a further problem of strategy. Should the attack be made with its purpose starkly apparent — the purpose of reversing the trend of Supreme Court decisions on New-Deal measures, or should the issue be merged with issues of other needed judicial reforms? The records of the purely political arguments on this subject are not yet available. This much is known, however. Attorney General Cummings was deeply interested in a whole series of reforms in the federal court system. To him the fact that justices well beyond the retirement age, and out of touch with the problems of the nation, retained Supreme Court positions to the detriment of the public welfare, provided only one example of the antiquated character of the system. He knew that procedure was excessively complicated, that the several federal courts were poorly co-ordinated for the disposition of the judicial burden and for handling the business matters of the courts themselves, and that many positions on the lower federal courts were occupied by men who could fairly be characterized as "dead wood." The problem as he saw it was not simply one of packing the Supreme Court to get specific New-Deal measures held constitutional, but was rather one of renovating the judiciary as a whole. Presumably it was largely on the basis of his persuasion that the attack was made in terms of the aggregate of needed reforms, rather than simply in terms of changing the membership of the Supreme Court.

The President submitted the plan for judicial reform to Congress on February 5, 1937.[52] The story of the ensuing congressional struggle is too long and involved for presentation here.[53] The press and the critics of the administration seized upon the aspect of the plan which had to do with increasing the membership of the Supreme Court and largely ignored the other provisions. Even many friends of the administration were shocked at the thought of laying irreverent hands upon the Court in the manner proposed. Until the middle of the following summer, magazines, newspapers, and the radio spread propaganda for both sides. The Senate committee on the judiciary listened to testimony by deans of law schools, professors, labor leaders, newspaper columnists, and others,[54] the sum total of which added astonishingly little to existing knowledge of our judicial institutions.

To all appearances, the Supreme Court preserved an attitude of judicial calm. While apparently ignoring the battle raging around it, however, the Court, or certain members of it, aided in defeating the plan for its reorganization. In a series of decisions, of which some will be discussed in the following section, it demonstrated that change in personnel was not necessary to secure approval of important social measures. In a new case involving a state minimum-wage law, Justice

[52] House Doc. No. 142, 75th Cong., 1st sess.

[53] For a dramatic account see Joseph Alsop and Turner Catledge, *The 168 Days* (1938) See also Robert H. Jackson, *The Struggle for Judicial Supremacy* (1941), chapter VI.

[54] *Hearings on S. 1392*, Senate judiciary committee, 75th Cong., 1st sess.

Roberts shifted his ground, and the Court overruled the Adkins case and upheld the new statute by a vote of five to four. It upheld unanimously an amended farm-bankruptcy act and a new railway-labor act which extended the right of collective bargaining on interstate railroads. It upheld the National Labor Relations Act and a state unemployment-compensation act, dividing five to four. It upheld the federal Social Security Act, dividing five to four on the unemployment-compensation provisions and seven to two on the provisions as to old-age benefits.

The Court was much in the public eye. Every decision of the type mentioned received attention in the headlines. On April 14, 1937, after the announcement of certain of these decisions, the Attorney General issued the following press release:

> The recent decisions of the Supreme Court make it abundantly clear that President Roosevelt has been right all the time. It was his proposition that there was nothing fundamentally wrong with the Constitution; that the trouble was with the judges who interpreted it along the lines of their economic prejudices. . . .
>
> Gratifying as these recent decisions are, it must be remembered that they are five-to-four decisions, and it is impossible to predict what will be the attitude of the Court in connection with the whole range of necessary legislation dealing with child labor, sweatshops, minimum wages, maximum hours, old-age benefits, and other social matters. . . .
>
> It is not a wholesome situation when an administration, under a mandate to carry out a progressive program, must face a court of nine, with four votes lost to it in advance. The margin is too narrow and the risk is too great.

Even though the Supreme Court was falling into line, apparently because of the coercive threat of reorganization rather than on its own initiative, the fact remained that a majority or more of the justices upheld important social measures. The enactment of the program to reform the Supreme Court seemed less and less necessary.

Justice Van Devanter struck a blow at the reorganization plan when, at a strategic moment, he announced that, as of the end of the term, he would accept the provisions of the newly enacted Retirement Act, whereby Supreme Court justices might retire without resigning, remaining thereafter subject to recall for further judicial duty. The retirement of one member of the group of four conservatives meant that the group must be joined by at least two other justices in order to control future decisions. If President Roosevelt appointed a successor likely to vote with Justices Brandeis, Stone, and Cardozo, both the Chief Justice and Justice Roberts must join the conservatives in order to give them a majority. Many people felt that the coming change would be entirely adequate, and that there was now no need whatsoever for the violation of tradition by openly packing the Supreme Court.

While ignoring the conflict as such, Chief Justice Hughes also struck a blow at the plan of reorganization in a written response to inquiries from Senator Burton K. Wheeler with respect to the work of the Court. In a letter having the approval of Justices Van Devanter and Brandeis, he stated that the Supreme Court was fully abreast of its work. He argued convincingly that adequate attention was being given to the large numbers of petitions for certiorari presented; that is, petitions for review of lower-court decisions which were granted only at the discretion of the Supreme Court. He thought it safe to say that about sixty per cent of the applications for certiorari were wholly without merit and ought never to have been made. If any error was made at all in dealing with these applications, he thought it was on the side of liberality. He declared that an increase in the number of justices of the Supreme Court would not promote the efficiency of the Court. He thought it would impair that efficiency so long as the Court acted as a unit. "There would be more judges to hear, more judges to confer, more judges to discuss, more judges to be convinced and to decide. The present number of justices is thought to be large enough so far as the prompt, adequate, and efficient conduct of the work of the Court is concerned." He believed that a plan to hear cases in divisions would be impracticable. In a large proportion of the cases heard, a decision by a part of the Court would be unsatisfactory. He called attention to the fact also that the Constitution did not appear to authorize two or more Supreme Courts, or two or more parts of a Supreme Court, functioning in effect as separate courts.[55]

Chief Justice Hughes was almost universally respected. His restrained statement of facts undoubtedly had much to do with the molding of sentiment on the reform program.

At one time the President could probably have secured the adoption of a considerable portion of his program if he had been willing to accept definite limitations. He refused to make any compromise. As opposition sentiment developed, Senator Joseph Robinson, who

[55] Senate Report No. 711, 75th Cong., 1st sess., pp. 38-40.

was expected to be appointed a member of the Court, led the struggle in the Senate for a modified court plan which would permit the President to nominate two additional justices instead of six. Even that project was blocked. Senator Robinson died suddenly, and the organization back of the plan collapsed. By a vote of ten to eight, the Senate judiciary committee submitted a scathingly adverse report on the bill.[56] Although a new measure affecting the federal judicial system was introduced and passed,[57] it did not affect the personnel of the Supreme Court or in any way limit its powers. The scheme for changing the trend of decisions by changes in Court personnel other than in the usual manner was completely defeated.

### CASES DECIDED DURING THE COURT FIGHT

Some of the transitional decisions mentioned above require further discussion. As to state laws fixing minimum wages for women, Justice Roberts, in West Coast Hotel Company v. Parrish,[58] abandoned the conservatives with whom he had voted in a similar case the previous year, making it possible for Chief Justice Hughes, as spokesman for the majority, to overrule the Adkins case of 1923 and declare a minimum-wage law valid. The Chief Justice handled the opinion in such a way as to give a moderately plausible excuse for the different positions of Justice Roberts in the two cases, but the feeling of the public, and probably of the bar as well, was that Justice Roberts had deemed it expedient to change his position because of the movement to reorganize the Court. In any event, the decision represented an important step in the extension of governmental control over conditions of employment.

In each case, said Chief Justice Hughes, the violation alleged by those attacking minimum-wage regulation for women was deprivation of freedom of contract. "What is this freedom?" he asked. "The Constitution does not speak of freedom of contract. It speaks of liberty and prohibits the deprivation of liberty without due process of law. In prohibiting that deprivation the Constitution does not recognize an absolute and uncontrollable liberty." [59] He approved warmly of statements made by Chief Justice Taft and Justice Holmes in dissenting opinions in the Adkins case. He found ample justification in the public interest for the protection of women by regulating minimum wages as well as by other methods. He continued:

[56] *Ibid.*
[57] 50 Stat. 751.
[58] 300 U.S. 379.
[59] *Ibid.,* p. 391.

There is an additional and compelling consideration which recent economic experience has brought into a strong light. The exploitation of a class of workers who are in an unequal position with respect to bargaining power, and are thus relatively defenseless against the denial of a living wage, is not only detrimental to their health and well-being, but casts a direct burden for their support upon the community. What these workers lose in wages the taxpayers are called upon to pay. The bare cost of living must be met. We may take judicial notice of the unparalleled demands for relief which arose during the recent period of depression and still continue to an alarming extent despite the degree of economic recovery which has been achieved. . . . The community is not bound to provide what is in effect a subsidy for unconscionable employers. The community may direct its lawmaking power to correct the abuse which springs from their selfish disregard of the public interest.[60]

In a dissenting opinion, with Justices Van Devanter, McReynolds, and Butler concurring, Justice Sutherland restated the essentials of the position he had taken in the Adkins case and offered in addition the argument that the statute constituted a denial of equal protection of the laws, in that it applied to women but not to men. As if in response to much of the criticism being directed at the Court, he incorporated a long statement of his conception of the place of that tribunal in the governmental system:

Under our form of government, where the written Constitution, by its own terms, is the supreme law, some agency, of necessity, must have the power to say the final word as to the validity of a statute assailed as unconstitutional. The Constitution makes it clear that the power has been entrusted to this Court when the question arises in a controversy within its jurisdiction; and so long as the power remains there, its exercise cannot be avoided without betrayal of the trust.

It has been pointed out many times, as in the Adkins case, that this judicial duty is one of gravity and delicacy, and that rational doubts must be resolved in favor of the constitutionality of the statute. But whose doubts, and by whom resolved? Undoubtedly it is the duty of a member of the Court, in the process of reaching a right conclusion, to give due weight to the opposing views of his associates; but in the end, the question which he must answer is not whether such views seem sound to those who entertain them, but whether they convince him that the statute is constitutional or engender in his mind a rational doubt upon that issue. The oath which he takes as a judge is not a composite oath, but an individual one. And in passing upon

[60] *Ibid.*, pp. 399-400.

the validity of a statute, he discharges a duty imposed upon *him,* which cannot be consummated justly by an automatic acceptance of the views of others which have neither convinced, nor created a reasonable doubt in, his mind.  If upon a question so important he thus surrender his deliberate judgment, he stands forsworn.  He cannot subordinate his convictions to that extent and keep faith with his oath or retain his judicial and moral independence.

The suggestion that the only check upon the exercise of the judicial power, when properly invoked, to declare a constitutional right superior to an unconstitutional statute is the judge's own faculty of self-restraint, is both ill considered and mischievous.  Self-restraint belongs in the domain of will and not of judgment.  The check upon the judge is that imposed by his oath of office, by the Constitution, and by his own conscientious and informed convictions; and since he has the duty to make up his own mind and adjudge accordingly, it is hard to see how there could be any other restraint.  This Court acts as a unit.  It cannot act in any other way; and the majority (whether a bare majority or a majority of all but one of its members), therefore, establishes the controlling rule as the decision of the Court, binding, so long as it remains unchanged, equally upon those who disagree and upon those who subscribe to it.  Otherwise, orderly administration of justice would cease.  But it is the right of those in the minority to disagree, and sometimes, in matters of grave importance, their imperative duty to voice their disagreement at such length as the occasion demands — always, of course, in terms which, however forceful, do not offend the proprieties or impugn the good faith of those who think otherwise.[61]

The statement was an eloquent defense by the most fluent and the most scholarly of the four conservatives.  It contains much with which any justice would agree.  When viewed in terms of its application, however, it was the expression of a dying philosophy.  The time had passed when Justice Sutherland and others holding his point of view were to dominate the interpretation of constitutional law.

The decision upholding the Railway Labor Act of 1934 [62] represented only a short step in the extension of governmental control — as is indicated by the fact that the decision was unanimous.  It had already been established that collective bargaining could be required between employers and the interstate employees of railroads.  The importance of this case was largely in the fact that so-called "back-shop" employees, who did not themselves move in interstate commerce or

[61] *Ibid.,* pp. 401-402.
[62] Virginia Railway Co. *v.* System Federation No. 40, 300 U.S. 515 (1937).

participate in the actual movement of trains, but were engaged in necessary shop work, were so classified as to justify control on the basis of the commerce power.

More important were National Labor Relations Board *v.* Jones and Laughlin Steel Corporation[63] and other cases decided under the National Labor Relations Act. The purpose of that act was not directly to regulate conditions of labor, but to guarantee to labor the right of collective bargaining with employers, without coercion as to unionization or the selection of bargaining representatives in any way. The act was based on the commerce power. Its constitutionality was imperiled by the narrow interpretation of the commerce clause given in the Schechter case in connection with the National Industrial Recovery Act, and in the Carter case in connection with the Bituminous Coal Conservation Act.

Counsel for the corporation contended that production at the manufacturing plant at Aliquippa, Pennsylvania, where the labor controversy involved had taken place, was exclusively production in intrastate commerce. Government counsel, on the other hand, showed that the corporation was engaged in a network of activities extending over a number of states. Raw materials of various kinds were brought in from other states and manufacturing products were shipped outward. The attempt was to create an analogy with cases such as Stafford *v.* Wallace,[64] decided under the Packers and Stockyards Act, in which the Court had looked at the entire "flow of commerce," both inward and outward, and had refused to view particular processes in isolation. The Court had found that the stockyards were but a throat through which the current of commerce flowed, and that transactions occurring there could not be separated from the entire movement, which embraced a great deal of activity in interstate commerce. Speaking for the majority in the Jones and Laughlin case, Chief Justice Hughes mentioned the analogy, but stated that the Court did not find it necessary to determine whether the analogy to the "stream-of-commerce" cases was disposed of by certain differences discussed by counsel for the corporation. The congressional authority to protect interstate commerce from burdens and obstructions was not limited to transactions which could be deemed to be an essential part of a "flow" of interstate or foreign commerce. The fundamental principle was that the power to regulate commerce was the power to enact all appropriate legislation for its protection and advancement. Al-

[63] 301 U.S. 1.  [64] 258 U.S. 495 (1922). For discussion see chapter 33.

though activities might be intrastate in character when separately considered, if they had such a close and substantial relation to interstate commerce that their control was essential or appropriate to protect that commerce from burdens and obstructions, Congress could not be denied the power to exercise that control. The close and intimate effect which brought the subject within the reach of federal power might be due to activities in relation to productive industry, even though the industry, when separately viewed, was local. The fact that the employees here concerned were engaged in production was not determinative. The question remained as to the effect upon interstate commerce of the labor practice involved, a question which called for examination in every case involving regulation based on the commerce clause. The Schechter case and the Carter case were not controlling. The Court decided, in brief, that the effect of the unfair labor practice of which the corporation was accused was such as to justify federal interference, via the National Labor Relations Act, to prevent the obstruction of interstate commerce which might take place.

Having established the principle in the Jones and Laughlin case, involving activities of the steel industry, the Court then applied it in a case involving the production of trailers, and in another involving the production of clothing. In all these cases Justice McReynolds wrote a dissent, Justices Van Devanter, Sutherland, and Butler concurring. He asserted that the Court had departed from well-established principles followed in the Schechter case and the Carter case. The dissenting opinion was another swan song of a dying philosophy.

In another labor case the Associated Press challenged the enforcement of an order of the National Labor Relations Board forbidding the discharge of workers for membership in the American Newspaper Guild and for union activities connected therewith.[65] The Associated Press denied that an editorial writer was engaged in interstate commerce to such an extent as to give jurisdiction to the federal government, and contended that compulsory action to enforce the continued employment of the editor was a violation of the freedom of the press safeguarded by the First Amendment. Justice Roberts, speaking for a majority of the Court, upheld the enforcement of the statute. It did not require the employment of anyone, he pointed out, or preclude the discharge of an employee for any reason other than union activities or agitation for collective bargaining with employees. It

[65] Associated Press v. National Labor Relations Board, 301 U.S. 103 (1937).

did not require the retention of an editor who was incompetent or who failed faithfully to edit the news to reflect the facts without bias or prejudice. The business of the Associated Press was not immune from regulation because it was an agency of the press. To show that interstate commerce was involved, he described the vast network of operations of the organization. The opinion of the four dissenters, written by Justice Sutherland, ended on a note of warning and despair:

> Do the people of this land — in the providence of God, favored, as they sometimes boast, above all others in the plenitude of their liberties — desire to preserve those so carefully protected by the First Amendment: liberty of religious worship, freedom of speech and of the press, and the right as freemen peaceably to assemble and petition their government for a redress of grievances? If so, let them withstand all *beginnings* of encroachment. For the saddest epitaph which can be carved in memory of a vanished liberty is that it was lost because its possessors failed to stretch forth a saving hand while yet there was time.[66]

Supreme Court decisions on social-security legislation were eagerly awaited. Early in the term, before the presentation of the plan for reorganization of the federal judicial system, the Court divided four to four on the constitutionality of a New York unemployment-compensation law enacted to secure participation in the social-security system established by the federal government.[67] Because of illness Justice Stone had been unable to participate. It was expected that his return to the Court would give judicial clearance to the social-security program. The expectation was fulfilled. Later in the term, in Carmichael *v.* Southern Coal Company,[68] the Alabama Unemployment Compensation Act was sustained by a vote of five to four.

Justice Stone spoke for the majority. He found relief of unemployment clearly a public purpose. He said:

> For the past six years the nation, unhappily, has been placed in a position to learn at first hand the nature and extent of the problem of unemployment, and to appreciate its profound influence upon the public welfare. Detailed accounts of the problem and its social and economic consequences, to be found in public reports of the expenditures of relief funds and in the studies of many observers, afford a

[66] *Ibid.*, p. 141. For the same alignment of justices, upholding a state law prohibiting the use of injunctions against important labor activities, see Senn *v.* Tile Layers Protective Union, 301 U.S. 468 (1937).

[67] Chamberlain *v.* Andrews, 299 U.S. 515 (1936).      [68] 301 U.S. 495 (1937).

basis for the legislative judgment.   It suffices to say that they show that unemployment apparently has become a permanent incident of our industrial system; that it varies, in extent and intensity, with fluctuations in the volume of seasonal businesses and with the business cycle.   It is dependent, with special and unpredictable manifestations, upon technological changes and advances in methods of manufacture, upon changing demands for manufactured products — dictated by changes in fashion or the creation of desirable substitutes, and upon the establishment of new sources of competition.[69]

The evils of the attendant social and economic wastage, he continued, permeated the entire social structure.   Local agencies were unable to cope with the problem.   The state as a whole, indeed, had contributed only a small fraction of the relief money spent in the state in the years 1933 to 1935 inclusive.   Of more than forty-seven million dollars expended, only a little more than two and a half millions were provided from within the state.

The Court rejected the contention that the state act was invalid because its enactment was coerced by the adoption of the Social Security Act and that it involved an unconstitutional surrender of state power.   Unemployment within the state was a common concern of both the state and federal governments, said Justice Stone.

> Together the two statutes now before us embody a co-operative legislative effort by state and national governments, for carrying out a public purpose common to both, which neither could fully achieve without the co-operation of the other.   The Constitution does not prohibit such co-operation.[70]

On the same day on which the Court passed upon the constitutionality of the Alabama law, it decided the case of Charles C. Steward Machine Company v. Davis,[71] in which it upheld the federal tax on employers authorized by the Social Security Act for use in connection with unemployment compensation.   Justice Cardozo spoke for the five justices constituting the majority.   Justices McReynolds and Butler each wrote dissenting opinions, and Justice Sutherland dissented in part, with the concurrence of Justice Van Devanter.   A large portion of the opinion of Justice McReynolds consisted of a reprint of a message of President Franklin Pierce, sent to the Senate on May 3, 1854, explaining his veto of "an act making a grant of public lands to the several states for the benefit of indigent insane

[69] *Ibid.*, pp. 515-516.        [70] *Ibid.*, p. 526.        [71] 301 U.S. 548 (1937).

persons." [72] Pierce had warned solemnly against the subversion of the states by the making of federal grants and had argued that the making of such grants was unconstitutional. McReynolds declared that the social-security decision just announced opened the way for practical annihilation of the theory of the independence of the states, adding, "No cloud of words or ostentatious parade of irrelevant statistics should be permitted to obscure that fact." [73]

In Helvering v. Davis [74] the Supreme Court upheld the provision of the Social Security Act levying an excise tax which was intended to yield money to be paid out to persons who had reached the age of sixty-five, and the separate provision of the act which authorized that expenditure. The expenditure was justified under the clause in Article I, Section 8, of the Constitution, which authorized Congress to lay and collect taxes to provide for the general welfare of the United States. Said Justice Cardozo for the majority, in support of the statement that Congress might spend money in aid of the general welfare:

> There have been great statesmen in our history who have stood for other views. We will not resurrect the contest. . . . The conception of the spending power advocated by Hamilton and strongly reinforced by Story has prevailed over that of Madison, which has not been lacking in adherents. Yet difficulties are left when the power is conceded. The line must still be drawn between one welfare and another, between particular and general. Where this shall be placed cannot be known through a formula in advance of the event. There is a middle ground or certainly a penumbra in which discretion is at large. The discretion, however, is not confided to the Court. The discretion belongs to Congress, unless the choice is clearly wrong, a display of arbitrary power, not an exercise of judgment. This is now familiar law. [75]

He held that caring for the aged involved fundamental problems of general welfare. The problems were plainly national in area and dimensions. Separate states could not deal with them effectively. Only a power that was national could serve the interests of all. Justices McReynolds and Butler dissented, however, with the brief statement that they considered the provisions of the act here challenged repugnant to the Tenth Amendment.

These several cases, all of which were decided before any changes

[72] See chapter 17.
[74] 301 U.S. 619 (1937).
[73] 301 U.S. 548, 599 (1937).
[75] Ibid., p. 640.

took place in the personnel of the Supreme Court, illustrate the way in which the Court was gradually falling in line with the generally accepted ideas of the New-Deal period. It is possible that some of the statutes here passed upon were better drafted and more carefully administered than those previously held unconstitutional. It is probable, however, that the change in interpretation was due largely to coercion in the form of the movement to reorganize the Supreme Court, backed by popular sentiment which strongly favored the substantive program of the New Deal even if it did not include enthusiasm for direct interference with the Supreme Court. The new trend in constitutional interpretation was to become more obvious with the changes in personnel which took place in ensuing years.

••••••••••••••••••••••••••••••••••••••••••••••••••••••••••••••••••••••••••••••••••••••••••••••••••••••••••

# CHAPTER 37

# EXPANDING AREAS OF CONTROL

ALTHOUGH THE GOVERNMENT CONTROL of enterprise begun with the New Deal contracted in some quarters as need for combatting depression declined, or when as in the instance of the National Industrial Recovery Act the control was held unconstitutional, the contraction was but slight. Government continued to operate in the fields of agriculture, industry, and labor on a scale unprecedented before the nineteen-thirties. The new level of activity brought vast changes in patterns of taxation and in relations between the federal government and the states. The changes, no longer blocked by a Supreme Court convinced of their unconstitutionality, had to be worked into the body of constitutional law as cases arose. The readjustment began with the Parrish case and the Jones and Laughlin case, discussed in the preceding chapter, before there were changes in the personnel of the Supreme Court. Beginning with the summer of 1937, personnel changes came thick and fast. By autumn of 1941 only two members of the old Court remained, Justices Stone and Roberts, and one of them, Justice Stone, had received a token of Roosevelt approval in the form of promotion to the Chief Justiceship. In the place of names hitherto familiar, new decisions and concurring opinions began to appear in the names of Justices Black, Reed, Frankfurter, Douglas, Murphy, Byrnes, and Jackson, and later, of Rutledge, Burton, Vinson, Clark, and Minton. The personnel of the Roosevelt-Truman Court will be discussed more at length in a later chapter. It is enough to say here that the changes gave assurance of judicial support for the expanded program of regulation and that the rapidly changing Court took up the difficult task of working new governmental behavior into the structure of constitutional law.

## THE CONTROL OF AGRICULTURE

There is artificiality in separating into groups the cases dealing with agriculture, business, and labor. The different groups of cases were decided during the same period. They involved many of the same questions as to the scope of the commerce clause, the restrictions of due process of law, and the nature and scope of the taxing power. It is impossible to discuss everything at once, however, and these subject matter groupings are useful in bringing the technicalities of constitutional law into areas of common understanding.

Although general recovery from the depression brought relief to the American farmer, it did not solve the basic problems of agriculture. Farmers still faced the possibility of unintentional over-production of particular products and consequent depression of prices to disastrous levels. They faced difficulties of distribution to available markets and of holding excess products until they were needed. They had no adequate and legal way of combining among themselves to limit production, to restrict marketing, or to determine what distributors should serve particular areas. In varying degrees the federal government, and to some extent the states, entered into these fields.

### PRODUCTION CONTROLS — TOBACCO

In 1936, in United States *v.* Butler, as discussed in the preceding chapter, the Supreme Court had defeated the project of the federal government for restricting production of basic farm products, holding that collection of the processing tax for that purpose was unconstitutional. Only to a limited extent had the government been able to escape the impact of this decision by making soil conservation payments out of the general funds in the treasury for taking land out of production of basic crops. Having been defeated in its attempt to use the taxing power as the basis for control, the administration now turned to the commerce power. In a skillfully drafted statute, the Agricultural Adjustment Act of 1938, Congress noted the fact that much of the tobacco, corn, wheat, cotton, and rice produced in the United States moved in interstate and foreign commerce. It found that such commerce was injured by disorderly marketing in that producers were offering for shipment more of these products than would be purchased at appropriate prices. It authorized control by the Secretary of Agriculture to prevent such disorderly marketing. If by prescribed standards the Secretary found that the supply of a crop available for marketing was excessive, he was to limit the amount marketed during the ensuing year by allotting quotas to the producing states and to farmers within those states.

The statute did not purport to regulate production as had the statute found unconstitutional in the Butler case. It did not prescribe production limits for any state or for any farm. It merely prescribed prohibitive penalties on marketing products in excess of quotas. Producers of tobacco, however, and in large part of other commodities, could make little use of their products apart from selling them in the interstate or foreign market. A major effect of this commerce regulation was therefore to restrict production, a subject which, according to the Butler decision, belonged within the jurisdiction of the states. So it was that the marketing statute was attacked on the basis of the Butler decision.

The Supreme Court passed upon the new statute in Mulford v. Smith,[1] Justice Roberts again acting as spokesman. It upheld the statute as a regulation of marketing, of interstate and foreign commerce, and not as a regulation of production. The majority opinion did not even mention the Butler decision. That decision received attention only in a dissenting opinion by Justice Butler, in which Justice McReynolds concurred.

The Mulford decision did not overrule its predecessor. The Court as constituted in 1939 might still have held direct federal control of agricultural production to be unconstitutional. But here the control of production was only indirect. It was an incidental effect of the power of Congress to regulate interstate and foreign commerce. The decision undoubtedly reflected a trend in judicial attitude toward the exercise of federal regulatory power, but not too much stress should be laid on this point. On numerous occasions the Court has shown a preference for regulations based on the commerce power, which is specifically a regulatory power, rather than on the taxing power where the primary constitutional purpose is to raise revenue rather than to regulate.[2]

WHEAT

Likewise under the commerce clause and under the same statute, the government went still farther toward control of agricultural production. To maintain reasonable wheat prices for producing farmers, the Secretary of Agriculture, with approval of wheat farmers given through a referendum, fixed acreage quotas for wheat planting. In

[1] 307 U.S. 38 (1939). Way was paved for this decision by Currin v. Wallace, 306 U.S. 1 (1939), upholding the Tobacco Inspection Act of 1935.
[2] See Chapter 33.

other words, although the regulation was still a commerce regulation calculated to preserve the flow of interstate and foreign commerce, it extended beyond the range of marketing quotas to quotas for production, or at any rate for acreage. Producers received the benefits of the higher prices maintained by limitation of supply, and were also entitled under certain circumstances to loans and payments from the federal government. Penalties were fixed for excess planting and for marketing more than fixed amounts of wheat from the acreage allotted. The penalties could be avoided by storing the excess wheat under federal regulations or by delivering it to the Secretary of Agriculture. If stored, the excess could be applied on the quota for the succeeding year. The penalties were forcibly collected only when the producer attempted to market his wheat. In order to market any of it in interstate or foreign commerce he had to have a marketing card, and he could get the card only after paying penalties assessed against him.

A test case arose when Roscoe C. Filburn, an Ohio farmer, harvested twenty-three acres of wheat instead of the eleven acres of his allotment, and then applied for a marketing card to enable him to market part of the product. The card was withheld because of nonpayment of the penalty. Filburn challenged the constitutionality of exclusion of any of his wheat from interstate and foreign commerce because of excess production which might never be shipped but might rather be consumed on his own farm. The Supreme Court unanimously upheld the statute. The regulation of production, including that part of the production which might be for local consumption, was justified on the basis of its relation to commerce. Said Justice Jackson for the Court:

> One of the primary purposes of the Act in question was to increase the market price of wheat and to that end to limit the volume thereof that could affect the market. It can hardly be denied that a factor of such volume and variability as home-consumed wheat would have a substantial influence on price and market conditions. This may arise because being in marketable condition such wheat overhangs the market and checks price increases. But if we assume that it is never marketed, it supplies a need of the man who grew it which would otherwise be reflected by purchases in the open market. Home-grown wheat in this sense competes with wheat in commerce. . . . Congress may properly have considered that wheat consumed on the farm where grown if wholly outside the scheme of regulation would

have a substantial effect in defeating and obstructing its purpose to stimulate trade therein at increased prices.[3]

Under this statute Congress went to the extreme of its exercise of the commerce power, in that it regulated not merely commerce and production for that commerce but also production for consumption on the producing farms. It was also true, however, that if interstate and foreign trade was to be promoted by limiting production to raise prices it was necessary to exercise control to the far reaches of wheat production. It may well have been true, as argued above by Justice Jackson, that the regulation provided for was essential to the effective regulation of interstate and foreign commerce.

In addition to challenging the production quota system as a regulation of commerce, Filburn argued that the restriction of production for local use violated the due process clause of the Fifth Amendment. The Court pointed out that both the restrictive and the subsidy features of the program were for the benefit of wheat farmers generally, and could not be invalidated under the due process clause merely because in an individual instance they were regarded as having an inequitable result. In any event

> We can hardly find a denial of due process in these circumstances, particularly since it is even doubtful that appellee's burdens under the program outweigh his benefits. It is hardly lack of due process for the Government to regulate that which it subsidizes.[4]

### MILK

Federal regulation under the commerce clause of production of commodities such as tobacco and wheat, which circulated far and wide, was in some respects simpler than regulation of the marketing of milk and other perishable commodities which circulated less widely. The purpose in each instance was maintenance of production and prices at such levels as to promote the welfare of the community, including producers, marketers, and consumers. There could be flexibility in the marketing of wheat in that excess supplies could be stored for long periods or shipped to markets at a distance. Although there was limited flexibility in the marketing of milk in its uses for cheese or butter, it was on the whole highly perishable, and had to

[3] Wickard v. Filburn, 317 U.S. 111, 128–129 (1942).

[4] Ibid., p. 131. See also Secretary of Agriculture v. Central Roig Refining Co., 338 U.S. 604 (1950), upholding the constitutionality of the Sugar Act of 1948 with an intricate quota system.

be marketed quickly and near the vicinity of production if losses were to be avoided. To a larger extent than in the instance of non-perishable commodities, milk was consumed in the state of production or in adjacent states. Again, more than in connection with non-perishable commodities, conditions of sanitation affecting production and marketing required government regulation. Local sanitation was traditionally regarded as a responsibility of the states rather than of the federal government, yet to the extent that milk was shipped in interstate commerce the responsibility of the federal government was also involved. So it was that with respect to dairy products innumerable conflicts took place to determine the appropriate spheres of governments competing for control.

Legislation for protection of the dairy business began with the states. A landmark statute was that enacted by New York in 1933 to fix maximum and minimum prices for resale of milk. It was a depression product. Dairy prices had declined much more than prices generally. Living conditions for dairy producers, who were victims of declining purchasing power and of cut-throat competition among themselves, had become desperate. The legislature fixed minimum prices to curb such disastrous competition, recognizing the fact that ultimately the consuming public as well as the producers were victims of the prevailing chaos. Dividing five to four in a decision as to the constitutionality of the statute, the Supreme Court held that it did not take liberty or property without due process of law.[5] This decision went a long way toward enabling states to regulate the milk business within their borders.

The constitutional difficulties of state regulation arose from the fact that most large consuming areas buy part of their milk in interstate commerce. When a state fixed minimum prices for sale of milk produced within its borders, that milk was put in an unfavorable market position by milk from other states where prices were not so regulated, unless the importing state could also fix prices of the imported milk. New York attempted to regulate the price paid to Vermont producers, on the ground that to these producers as well as to those in New York reasonable prices must be paid if the producers were to provide the sanitary conditions necessary to protection of the health of consumers. The Supreme Court held this stratagem unconstitutional as a regulation of interstate commerce. If Vermont

---

5 Nebbia *v.* New York, 291 U.S. 502 (1934). For discussion of the case see above, pp. 819–820.

milk were found to be a danger to health it could be dealt with under New York's police powers, but New York could not reach into Vermont to regulate conditions there.[6] The Court also held that New York could not restrict destructive competition by limiting the number of receiving stations in New York to be established for distribution of milk from Massachusetts.[7] It held that as to milk brought from without the state a Madison ordinance violated the commerce clause in requiring that all milk sold in Madison be pasteurized within five miles of the city.[8]

Constitutional limitations on state powers meant that where interstate commerce was extensively involved, and beyond the scope of clearly legitimate health regulations, the milk business had to be regulated by the federal government if regulated at all. Congress authorized such regulation in the Agricultural Marketing Agreement Act of 1937. Under that statute the Secretary of Agriculture fixed the minimum price of milk sold in the New York area, some two-thirds of which moved in interstate commerce. The order of the Secretary extended even to the price at which milk was delivered by a dairy farmer to a country plant in his own state, whereafter it was shipped in interstate commerce. The Supreme Court found even this nominally local transaction within the scope of federal power because of the intermingling of intrastate and interstate commerce.[9] Thus federal and state governments operate side by side in the regulation of the distribution of dairy products, the one operating on the basis of the commerce clause and the other on the basis of state police powers. Jurisdictions overlap, and from time to time the courts must draw distinguishing lines between the two sets of powers.[10]

## CONTROL OF BUSINESSS

As in the field of agriculture, so also in the field of business the Roosevelt-Truman Court upheld broad federal regulation under the commerce power and curtailed the use of due process clauses as retrictions on control by federal and state governments. In other words, the Court sanctioned the broad program of federal and state regulation to stabilize the economic life of the country and coordinate it

6 Baldwin v. Seelig, 294 U.S. 511 (1935).
7 H. P. Hood & Sons v. Du Mond, 336 U.S. 525 (1949).
8 Dean Milk Co. v. Madison, 340 U.S. 349 (1951).
9 United States v. Rock Royal Co-operative, Inc., 307 U.S. 533 (1939).
10 For the power of a state to regulate agricultural marketing with the approval of the federal government, see Parker v. Brown, 317 U.S. 341 (1943).

with the public welfare. The paragraphs immediately following will deal with such regulation in various fields, leaving specifically labor regulations for discussions thereafter.

HOLDING COMPANIES

Through the Public Utility Holding Company Act of 1935, Congress had set up machinery for remedying abuses through holding company devices which had been disclosed during the depression. A holding company was a company which held enough voting stock in other companies to control their operations. It could render services to them by lending machinery and personnel and by giving to them the benefits of laboratory discoveries and developments and other services. On the other hand, often through ownership of a very small minority of the total stock of an operating company, the holding company might control its finances and dictate its purchase and use of property in such a way as to benefit the holding company a great deal and the operating company not at all. Holding company structures might be infinitely complicated. Below the top holding company might be still other holding companies with operating companies still farther down the line, and confusion was added by the fact that a company might operate a business, such as the provision of electricity for municipalities, and at the same time merely hold controlling interests in the stock of other operating companies. Some of the complications are indicated by a single paragraph from a Supreme Court decision affecting relations between a top holding company, the Electric Bond and Share Company, and two subordinate holding companies, American Power and Light Company and Electric Power and Light Corporation:

> Bond and Share holds 20.7% of the total voting stock of American, this holding having a book value of nearly $10,000,000 or 3.68% of American's total capitalization of $270,000,000. Through this investment, Bond and Share controls not only American but American's 21 subsidiaries with a total capitalization of $729,000,000. An investment of $10,000,000 thus controls $729,000,000, a ratio of 1 to 73.[11]

The Public Utility Holding Company Act required all holding companies using interstate commerce or the mails to register with the Securities and Exchange Commission. In connection with

[11] Electric Power & Light Corporation *v.* Securities and Exchange Commission, 329 U.S. 90, 110 (1946).

registration the companies had to provide detailed explanations of their corporate structures. Under the statute the Commission might then order the structures simplified, by requiring companies to divest themselves of certain of their holdings or by requiring their dissolution altogether. Because the enforcement of the statute would curb the profitable activities of powerful interests, it was resisted at every point, but the Supreme Court upheld the measure throughout. It first upheld the registration requirement.[12] It upheld the requirement that holding company systems divest themselves of holdings which had no proper economic relations with them.[13] Finally, it upheld the so-called "death sentence," the dissolution of holding companies which had no adequate economic justification.[14] If the task of reordering corporate structures remained a difficult one, it was difficult because of the intrinsic nature of the task and not on constitutional grounds as seen by the Supreme Court, which found the commerce power an adequate basis for the program Congress had authorized.

PRICE CONTROL

In industry as in agriculture, Congress upheld the fixing of minimum prices when doing so was necessary to protect the country against the evils of cut-throat competition. In upholding federal price fixing for the coal industry the Court said:

> Congress under the commerce clause is not impotent to deal with what it may consider to be dire consequences of laissez-faire. It is not powerless to take steps in mitigation of what in its judgment are abuses of cut-throat competition. And it is not limited in its choice between unrestrained self-regulation on the one hand and rigid prohibitions on the other. The commerce clause empowers it to undertake stabilization of an interstate industry through a process of price-fixing which safeguards the public interest by placing price control in the hands of its administrative representative.[15]

Upholding federal regulatory power under the commerce clause did not imply a judicial policy of shifting the regulatory balance

---

[12] Electric Bond & Share Co. *v. Securities and Exchange Commission*, 303 U.S. 419 (1938).

[13] North American Co. *v.* Securities and Exchange Commission, 327 U.S. 686 (1946).

[14] Electric Power & Light Corporation *v.* Securities and Exchange Commission, 329 U.S. 90 (1946).

[15] Sunshine Anthracite Coal Co. *v.* Adkins, 310 U.S. 381, 396 (1940).

from the states to the federal government. Much more than it would have done in earlier years, the Supreme Court looked sympathetically on state regulation, including price regulation, for conservation and other local purposes, even where interstate commerce was to some extent affected. A single illustration out of many will suffice. The State of Oklahoma had reason for concern about the economic effects of exploitation practices in a huge natural gas field. The field had more than 1,000,000 acres, with 240 producing wells. About ninety percent of the production was consumed outside the state. Over half the production was by the Cities Service Company, which had a pipeline to out-of-state consuming areas, but there were other extensive producers, including the Peerless Oil and Gas Company, who had no pipeline outlets and therefore had to sell to Cities Service in order to find a market. Cities Service, while drawing through its own wells gas which underlay the territory of other producers, refused to buy gas from those producers except at what others alleged to be a too-low price of four cents per thousand cubic feet for the life of the leases. The Peerless Company asked the Oklahoma Corporation Commission to determine the price Cities Service was to pay and to require Cities Service to make connection with the Peerless wells and to take gas ratably from them along with the use of its own wells. After hearing testimony that conservation and the proper use of gas required such action the Commission issued the desired order, fixing the price at seven cents.

Cities Service challenged the order as a denial of due process of law and equal protection of the laws, and as an unconstitutional regulation of interstate commerce. The Supreme Court, in 1950, upheld the commission order. Said Justice Clark for the Court:

> The Due Process and Equal Protection issues raised by appellant are virtually without substance. It is now undeniable that a state may adopt reasonable regulations to prevent economic and physical waste of natural gas. This Court has upheld numerous kinds of state legislation designed to curb waste of natural resources and to protect the correlative rights of owners through ratable taking . . . or to protect the economy of the state. . . . These ends have been held to justify control over production even though the uses to which property may be properly put are restricted.[16]

The challenge based on the commerce clause met the same fate. It

16 Cities Service Co. *v.* Peerless Oil & Gas Co., 340 U.S. 179, 185–186 (1950).

was true that since most of the production was for interstate commerce Congress could have regulated the business had it desired to do so, and that state regulations in conflict with those of Congress would have been invalid. But the commerce, even though largely interstate, had local peculiarities which meant that regulations would have to be adapted to the local situation. Under such circumstances the regulatory power of Congress is not exclusive of state regulation. Said Justice Clark:

> It is now well settled that a state may regulate matters of local concern over which federal authority has not been exercised, even though the regulation has some impact on interstate commerce. . . . The only requirements consistently recognized have been that the regulation not discriminate against or place an embargo on interstate commerce, that it safeguard an obvious state interest, and that the local interest at stake outweigh whatever national interest there might be in the prevention of state restrictions. Nor should we lightly translate the quiescence of federal power into an affirmation that the national interest lies in complete freedom from regulation.[17]

So it was that the regulation of prices and other aspects of business was further entrenched in our constitutional pattern, whether the regulatory government was the federal government or a state.

## THE RIGHT TO A FAIR RETURN

In an era in which property rights had lost much of the sanctity they had posessed before the depression period it was inevitable that the Supreme Court should have to re-examine the dogma that in fixing prices government must permit the earning of a fair return on the fair value of the property.[18] In 1939, with Justice Black concurring, Justice Frankfurter criticized an opinion of the Court because it seemed to give new vitality to the "mischievious formula" for fixing utility rates. "The force of reason," he insisted, "confirmed by events, has gradually been rendering that formula moribund by revealing it to be useless as a guide for adjudication." [19] By 1942 seven members of the pre-New Deal Court had been replaced and a new point of view with respect to property rights was well entrenched. In a rate case decided in that year the Court said that

---

17 *Ibid.*, pp. 186–187.
18 See pp. 403–404, 820–821.
19 Driscoll *v.* Edison Light & Power Co., 307 U.S. 104, 122 (1939).

The Constitution does not bind rate-making bodies to the service of any single formula or combination of formulas. Agencies to whom this legislative power has been delegated are free, within the ambit of their statutory authority, to make the pragmatic adjustments which may be called for by particular circumstances. Once a fair hearing has been given, proper findings made and other statutory requirements satisfied, the courts cannot intervene in the absence of a clear showing that the limits of due process have been overstepped.[20]

Even this broad statement of regulatory power was unsatisfactory to three justices, who thought the Court should disavow the power on its own part to invalidate rate orders as violations of due process clauses on the grounds that the rates were unreasonable. "Price-fixing," they declared, "like other forms of social legislation, may well diminish the value of the property which is regulated. But that is no obstacle to its validity." [21] Substantive due process, as an instrument for limiting government regulation of property, had indeed fallen upon evil times.

Two years later Justice Douglas, one of the three justices taking the extreme position, spoke for the Court when it said that

The fixing of prices, like other applications of the police power, may reduce the value of the property which is being regulated. But the fact that the value is reduced does not mean that the regulation is invalid.[22]

The heart of the matter, Justice Douglas declared, was that the fairness of rates could not be made to depend on the value of the property when the value of the property was itself determined by the rates the operator was permitted to charge. By contrast with the earlier position that constitutional rates had to permit earning a fair return on the fair value of the property, he held that, even under a statute requiring that rates be just and reasonable, nothing more was required than that the total effect of the rate order should be just and reasonable. The method employed in reaching that result was not important.

As far as constitutional protection was concerned, it now appeared, property was pretty much at the mercy of legislatures and administrators, as long as they observed the merely procedural requirements

---

[20] Federal Power Commission v. Natural Gas Pipeline Co., 315 U.S. 575, 586 (1942).
[21] Ibid., p. 603.
[22] Federal Power Commission v. Hope Natural Gas Co., 320 U.S. 584, 601 (1944).

of due process of law. Property rights, instead of being entitled to preference, took their place alongside a variety of other considerations in the making of governmental decisions.

## PROBLEMS OF MONOPOLY

The National Industrial Recovery Act has encouraged cooperation among business corporations to limit production and fix prices, with government supervision to protect the public interest. When that statute was held unconstitutional the Department of Justice resumed attempts at rigorous enforcement of anti-trust acts. In terms of constitutionality most of the cases contained little that was new. The broad interpretation of the commerce power to which the Supreme Court was not committed gave an adequate constitutional base for anti-trust enforcement. The leading decision in this field during the 1940's was United States v. South-Eastern Underwriters Association,[23] in which the Sherman Act was applied against combinations of fire insurance companies. The constitutional difficulty in this case dated back to 1869 when in Paul v. Virginia the Court had said that "issuing a policy of insurance is not a transaction of commerce."[24] If insurance was not commerce, clearly it could not be interstate commerce. If it was not interstate commerce it would seem that the business could not be reached through the Sherman Act, which was based on the commerce power. So argued a group of companies when combinations were challenged under the statute.

The statements that insurance was not commerce had been made by the Court, however, not in connection with any attempt of Congress to regulate insurance, but in answer to companies contending that state laws regulating insurance companies were unconstitutional because the companies operated across state lines. The companies, seeking to escape regulation, had contended that their business was interstate commerce and therefore out of the reach of the states. The Court decided otherwise.[25] The Sherman Act was passed in 1890, after the Court had taken the position that the commerce clause did not prevent state regulation of insurance business done across state lines. Half a century passed before the government attempted to enforce the Sherman Act against abuses by insurance companies doing business across state lines. When that attempt was made, the companies aban-

---

23 322 U.S. 533 (1944).
24 8 Wallace, 168, 183.
25 Hooper v. California, 155 U.S. 648, 654 (1895).

doned the positions of the earlier companies and quoted Court decisions to the effect that insurance was not interstate commerce. If it was not interstate commerce, Congress could not regulate it under the commerce clause. They claimed that, even if in terms of recent interpretations of the commerce clause, insurance could be classified as commerce, the Sherman Act could not apply to insurance because the Constitution as read in 1890 did not permit federal regulation since insurance was not then considered commerce.

In 1944 the Supreme Court, speaking through Justice Black, noted that

> In all cases in which the Court has relied upon the proposition that "the business of insurance is not commerce," its attention was focused on the validity of state statutes — the extent to which the Commerce Clause automatically deprived states of the power to regulate the insurance business. Since Congress had at no time attempted to control the insurance business, invalidation of the state statutes would practically have been equivalent to granting insurance companies engaged in interstate activities a blanket license to operate without legal restraint.[26]

It was quite a different matter, Justice Black contended, to apply this reasoning to strike down an act of Congress regulating the doing of insurance business. He had no difficulty finding in the interstate business aspects which Congress could regulate.

> The modern insurance business holds a commanding position in the trade and commerce of our nation. Built upon the sale of contracts of indemnity, it has become one of the largest and most important branches of commerce. . . . Perhaps no modern commercial enterprise affects so many persons in all walks of life as does the insurance business. . . . Interrelationship, interdependence, and integration of activities in all the states in which they operate are practical aspects of the insurance companies' methods of doing business.[27]

The Court unanimously reached the conclusion that such interstate business could be regulated under the commerce clause. A minority dissented in this case but only on the ground that, in view of the history of the regulation of insurance and of anti-trust legislation, Congress should now affirm its intention to make that legislation applicable to insurance if the Court was so to apply it.

26 322 U.S. 544.
27 *Ibid.*, pp. 540–541.

Whether the statute involved in litigation was enacted by a state or by the federal government, insurance companies selected their constitutional arguments for the purpose of defeating regulation. They found the commerce power broad enough to defeat state regulation and too narrow to support federal regulation. The Supreme Court rejected both contentions. When the Court upheld federal regulation based on the commerce power — regulation limited to the Sherman Act and a few other statutes and by no means covering the whole field of insurance — it was expected that insurance companies would immediately challenge the existing network of state regulatory and tax laws affecting insurance as unconstitutional invasion of the commerce power of Congress. Such a challenge would be a serious matter because of the fact that even if the country had desired enactment of a code of federal regulations to supplant those of the states, years of effort would have been required for the drafting and adoption of such a code, and such a task would have been particularly difficult in the war period. To protect state laws against such attack, Congress passed an act declaring that continued regulation and taxation by the states were in the public interest and that silence on the part of Congress was not to be construed as imposing barriers to such state action. It provided that

> The business of insurance, and every person engaged therein, shall be subject to the laws of the several States which relate to the regulation or taxation of such business.

Although nearly a century had passed since the decision in the Pilot case,[28] doubt still prevailed as to the extent of state power to regulate interstate commerce in areas in which Congress was not regulating. The so-called rule of the Pilot Case had not been abrogated, but its application was difficult. With respect to insurance Congress here formally declared its intention to remain out of certain areas to enable the states to continue to enforce their own regulations. In spite of this precautionary act of Congress, taxation and regulation by states were now challenged as unconstitutional regulation of interstate commerce. The Supreme Court, however, acting in the light of the federal statute, upheld the exercise of state power.[29] The states, in other words, were able to continue regulation and taxation of insurance business operating across state lines as

---

28 See pp. 204–206.
29 Prudential Insurance Co. *v.* Benjamin, 328 U.S. 408 (1946).

they had done prior to the decision that the business was subject to federal regulation under the commerce clause.[30]

## PATENTS

In important cases the courts had the difficult task of drawing a line between the anti-trust laws which forbade monopolies and patent laws which conferred monopoly rights. The Constitution authorizes Congress

> To promote the progress of science and useful arts, by securing for limited times to authors and inventors the exclusive right to their respective writings and discoveries.[31]

Patent laws give this exclusive right. It is assumed that guarantee of the right of use of an invention will stimulate development of new and useful articles, to the ultimate benefit of the American people. It is only natural that from time to time men and corporations sought patents not only for bona fide inventions but also for slight modifications of devices hitherto known or new combinations of old and therefore not patentable devices. It is likewise not surprising that competing industries sometimes developed devices and sought patents for them not so much because of a desire to exploit them as to keep competitors from developing and exploiting them and winning customers thereby. Patent laws therefore were at times used, or attempted to be used, not so much to promote "science and useful arts" as to curb them and to monopolize without the giving of public benefits. During the New Deal period the Supreme Court sensed this fact and scrutinized with great care the rights of claimants to the patents in question. The principle had been voiced long ago when the Court had said

> The design of the patent laws is to reward those who make some substantial discovery or invention, which adds to our knowledge and makes a step in advance in the useful arts. Such inventors are worthy of all favor. It was never the object of those laws to grant a monopoly for every trifling device, every shadow of a shade of an idea, which would naturally and spontaneously occur to any skilled mechanic or operator in the ordinary progress of manufactures. Such

---

[30] Another case, initiated before enactment of the federal statute, upheld the power of the states to exclude from their borders insurance companies doing interstate business who refused to conform to the pattern of regulations adopted by the states. Robertson v. California, 328 U.S. 440 (1946).

[31] Article I, section 8.

an indiscriminate creation of exclusive privileges tends rather to obstruct than to stimulate invention.[32]

During the 1940's the Court frowned on the use of patent claims to justify corporate price fixing and other types of private control which, unless justified by patent laws, were prohibited by anti-trust laws.[33] In 1950 it reasserted that the function of a patent was to add to the sum of useful knowledge and that patents could not be sustained when on the contrary their effect was to subtract from former sources freely available. In a concurring opinion Justice Douglas summarized the problem of administration by saying that

> The attempts through the years to get a broader, looser conception of patents than the Constitution contemplates have been persistent. The Patent Office, like most administrative agencies, has looked with favor on the opportunity which the exercise of discretion affords to expand its own jurisdiction. And so it has placed a host of gadgets under the armor of patents — gadgets that obviously have had no place in the constitutional scheme of advancing scientific knowledge.[34]

In essence the difficulty of drawing a line between the monopoly rights given by patent laws and the monopoly activities prohibited by the anti-trust laws can never be resolved as long as we have both patent laws and anti-trust laws. New cases call for adjudication in terms of established principles, with lines of control shifting somewhat from situation to situation. The overall drift toward bigness continues, but under varying degrees of anti-trust restraint and with varying degrees of leniency in interpretation of rights derived through patents. As for the course of business as a whole, or of government relations with business as a whole, the Roosevelt-Truman Court placed no real barriers in the way of control. The limits observed were the limits established not only by the courts but by Congress, or by the inaction of Congress, which in turn marked roughly the limits of control as envisaged in the minds of the large mass of influential people.

## GOVERNMENT AND LABOR

The separation of labor issues from those of business generally is

---

[32] Atlantic Works v. Brady, 107 U.S. 192, 200 (1883).

[33] See for example United States v. Univis Lens Co., 316 U.S. 241 (1942), and United States v. Masonite Corporation, 316 U.S. 265 (1942).

[34] Great Atlantic & Pacific Tea Co. v. Supermarket Equipment Corporation, 340 U.S. 147, 156 (1950).

largely artificial, since the concern with labor in this discussion has to do with workers as employed by industry and other aspects of business. Yet the interests of labor, or at least its short run interests, are different from those of employers, and they have the backing of powerful organizations which exert pressure upon government. It therefore seems best to treat labor as a separate topic, remembering that labor cases have their inevitable repercussions on employers and that they turn on the same provisions of the Constitution as cases involving regulation in other fields.

In certain important respects Supreme Court decisions affecting labor during the period in question differ from those affecting business. Although the federal government gave aid to business in certain instances by financial assistance through the letting of contracts at profitable rates, and in a variety of other ways, the constitutionality of aid to business was not challenged in important decisions. Government aid to labor, on the other hand, which was newer in our national experience and less well entrenched in custom, was challenged again and again. This was true particularly in connection with the National Labor Relations Act, which guaranteed the right of collective bargaining, and the Fair Labor Standards Act, which authorized the government to fix minimum wages in business in or affecting interstate and foreign commerce. In cases more closely resembling those relating directly to business, the Court also passed on the application of regulatory and resrictive measures to labor and on their constitutionality as applied. Early decisions in a great variety of fields gave protection to the labor interest. Later ones seemed to reflect the trend in Congress, wherein sentiment seemed gradually to turn away from the extension of aid to labor in favor of increased restriction of its power and activity.

THE WAGNER ACT

Many cases turned on the scope and meaning of the Wagner Act, or National Labor Relations Act. The basic constitutionality of that act was established in the Jones and Laughlin case, which was discussed in the preceding chapter.[35] The later cases rested upon its reasoning, extending the conception of the commerce power to reach far down into the area of interstate activity. For example, the National Labor Relations Board was able to regulate relations of the Consolidated Edison Company with its employees even though the

[35] See pp. 949–950

company produced no electricity for consumption outside the state. The Supreme Court found that disruption of the company's production would injure interstate commerce even though the activities involved were immediately local. The electricity produced was necessary for telephone, telegraph, and radio, for illumination which was necessary to interstate commerce, and for such transportation as that carried on at the terminals of great railroads.[36]

The methods by which employers sought to avoid employing or retaining workers who agitated for the strengthening of unions and for use of the power of unions to promote labor welfare were matched only by the strategy of labor leaders in protecting and adding to their power. In many cases the Court upheld the board in its effort to preserve for labor the full right of collective bargaining. However, it refused to enforce collective bargaining for workers who acted illegally by engaging in a "sit down" strike, even though the employer had also violated the law.[37]

## THE FAIR LABOR STANDARDS ACT

A victory for which labor had struggled many years came with the Supreme Court decision in United States v. Darby [38] in 1941. The decision upheld the Fair Labor Standards Act of 1938. By that act Congress had forbidden shipment in interstate commerce of goods produced by workers receiving less than prescribed minimum wages or working longer than a prescribed maximum of hours. These provisions were enacted in the face of the Supreme Court decision in Hammer v. Dagenhart, the child-labor case of 1918, wherein the Court had outlawed similar regulations with respect to goods produced by child labor. A proposed constitutional amendment to get around the decision had failed of adoption, but under the pressure of growing sentiment the Court had whittled down the Dagenhart doctrine in case after case so that its continued potency was in doubt. In the Darby case the Supreme Court flatly overruled the Dagenhart case and upheld the type of commerce regulation which had hitherto been banned. The Darby decision left little room for the doctrine that the power of Congress to regulate commerce or to exercise others of its granted powers was limited by sovereign powers assumed

[36] Consolidated Edison Corporation v. National Labor Relations Board, 305 U.S. 197 (1938).

[37] National Labor Relations Board v. Fansteel Metal Corporation, 306 U.S. 240 (1939).

[38] 312 U.S. 100.

to have been left to the states. It mattered not, said Justice Stone for the Court, that regulation of commerce was attended by the same incidents as those attending exercise of the police power of the states.

> The motive and purpose of the present regulation are plainly to make effective the Congressional conception of public policy that interstate commerce should not be made the instrument of competition in the distribution of goods produced under substandard labor conditions, which competition is injurious to the commerce and to the states from and to which the commerce flows. The motive and purpose of a regulation of interstate commerce are matters for the legislative judgment upon the exercise of which the Constitution places no restriction and over which the courts are given no control.[39]

Later interpretations of the Fair Labor Standards Act showed the Court willing to go a long way in permitting Congress to regulate local matters via the commerce clause. For example, it upheld federal regulation of the hours and wages of janitors, elevator operators, repairmen, and other employees of a landlord who leased a building to manufacturers of clothing to be sold in interstate commerce.[40] It upheld such regulations with respect to employees of an electrical contractor who was engaged in local wiring and local sale of electrical equipment but whose customers were engaged in production for interstate commerce.[41] To justify federal regulation some relation to interstate commerce had to be shown, but the relation sometimes seemed highly tenuous.[42]

### CHANGING ATTITUDES TOWARD LABOR

In the changed atmosphere wherein it seemed that all three branches of the federal government looked with unprecedented favor on the cause of labor, the Supreme Court had to decide additional cases involving the extent of the application of anti-trust laws to labor. Although it had held that the National Labor Relations Act did not protect the rights of labor when labor violated law by engaging in a sit-down strike, it also held that engaging in such a strike did not constitute a combination in restraint of trade in violation of anti-trust laws.[43] It held also that these laws did not reach a second-

---

[39] *Ibid.*, p. 115.
[40] Kirschbaum *v.* Walling, 316 U.S. 517 (1942).
[41] Roland Electric Co. *v.* Walling, 326 U.S. 657 (1946).
[42] See Schulte *v.* Gangi, 328 U.S. 108 (1946).
[43] Apex Hosiery Co. *v.* Leader, 310 U.S. 469 (1940).

ary boycott carried on by a union in support of a jurisdictional strike between two unions.[44] In similar fashion the Court refused to apply to members of a labor union preying on trucks running from New Jersey into New York the Anti-Racketeering Act of 1934.[45]

As a result of administrative support, favorable legislative enactments, and seemingly friendly judicial decisions, labor organizations during the New Deal period achieved unprecedented power. The scarcity of labor during World War II and the necessity of avoiding strikes that might affect war production added to that power. Arbitrary exercise of that power brought a shift in the trend of decisions and enactment of restrictive legislation which in turn received judicial support. The change in the trend of decisions became apparent with the case of the United States v. United Mine Workers,[46] which was decided March 6, 1947. In that case the Supreme Court upheld a decision which had brought assessment of a fine of $3,500,000 against the United Mine Workers and $10,000 against John L. Lewis personally for maintaining a coal strike in violation of a court order when the mines were being operated by the federal government. The Court also upheld a 1946 statute outlawing a labor practice known as "featherbedding" in radio broadcasting. The American Federation of Musicians, concerned about popular resort to radio and other indirect media to music and the consequent lessening of demand for the services of groups of musicians, refused to permit broadcasting of music except under condition that prescribed numbers of musicians be employed in addition to those needed for the broadcasts. Under the impetus of popular resentment at the alleged tyranny of the union and its president, James C. Petrillo, Congress outlawed the practice. The Supreme Court held the measure a legitimate regulation of interstate commerce,[47] and labor found its activities restrained at still another point.

THE TAFT-HARTLEY ACT

The Republican Congress which was elected in 1946 brought into focus a great deal of sentiment hostile to the growing power and alleged arrogance of organized labor in the immediately post-war period. It enacted two restrictive measures, one to get rid of Supreme Court interpretations of the Fair Labor Standards Act from

[44] United States v. Hutcheson, 312 U.S. 219 (1941).
[45] United States v. Local 807, I.B.T., 315 U.S. 521 (1942).
[46] 330 U.S. 258.
[47] United States v. Petrillo, 332 U.S. 1 (1947).

which labor derived irritating wage benefits and the other to replace
the National Labor Relations Act with a measure calculated to protect interests of employers as well as employees. The first of these
measures brought an end to what was known as the portal-to-
portal issue. It terminated the requirement that wages be paid from
the time the worker entered the "portal" of the mine, factory, or
other establishment until his exit from that "portal" at the end
of the day. The second and far more important statute was the
Labor Management Relations Act of 1947, better known as the Taft-
Hartley Act. In repealing the National Labor Relations Act this
measure re-enacted many of its provisions, but it excluded others
and added provisions for protection of employers against excessive
demands of labor. Among other changes it outlawed the closed shop,
jurisdictional strikes, and other devices regarded as detrimental to
the public welfare, changed administrative machinery in order to
eliminate an alleged bias in favor of labor, and took steps to restrict
government support to unions who had not purged communism from
their leadership.

Few of the provisions of the Taft-Hartley Act invited constitutional
challenge. As to one of the most controversial, the Supreme Court
upheld requirement of an anti-communist and anti-subversive oath
of union leaders.[48] Leaders continued to denounce the statute as a
slave-labor measure, however, and President Truman repeatedly
sought its modification or repeal. Although in some instances he
reluctantly made use of its anti-strike provisions, he ignored it in the
crisis of the threatened steel strike in 1952, taking different steps
from those provided in the Taft-Hartley Act. Without authorization
from any statute, and relying on his broad executive powers and particularly on his powers as commander in chief of the army and navy,
he had the Secretary of Commerce take command of major steel
plants to keep production going. His action brought a storm of protest from non-labor groups and court action to enjoin the Secretary
of Commerce from executing the President's order. The litigation was
rushed through the lower courts to the Supreme Court.

The Supreme Court found the President's order unconstitutional.
The power of Congress to authorize such action, said Justice Black,
spokesman for the Court, was beyond question. But Congress had
not authorized it. The President had acted on his own initiative,

[48] American Communications Association *v.* Douds, 339 U.S. 382 (1950). For discussion see Chapter 39.

without constitutional authorization. As for his taking such action as commander in chief, "This is a job for the Nation's lawmakers, not for its military authorities." [49] As for other possible sources of power,

> In the framework of our Constitution, the President's power to see that the laws are faithfully executed refutes the idea that he is to be a lawmaker. The Constitution limits his functions in the lawmaking process to the recommendation of laws he thinks wise and the vetoing of laws he thinks bad. And the Constitution is neither silent nor equivocal about who shall make the laws which the President is to execute.[50]

The trend, therefore, both in Congress and in the Supreme Court, was in the direction of curtailment of the exercise of governmental power to aid organized labor in its competition for power with employers. With the change in administration in 1953 it appeared that the executive also had shifted to a conservative position. Labor, like agriculture and industry, still had the support of government in innumerable ways, but this particular movement involving improvement of its relative position, which had begun with the New Deal, seemed at an end.

## THE NATION AND THE STATES

Superficially the expansion of the exercise of federal power which came with the New Deal and continued thereafter seemed a threat to the power of the states. Justice Roberts made much of this threat in the Butler case, discussed in the preceding chapter, when the Court held unconstitutional the collection of a processing tax to restrict agricultural production. Important New Deal decisions based on federal exercise of commerce power upheld federal regulations which reached far down into the area of local problems. In spite of uneasiness in the matter however — uneasiness often provoked by dislike of regulation from any source rather than by concern about the states — federal competition did not even make a beginning toward putting the states out of business. They collected and spent more money, employed more people, and engaged in more activities than ever before. Part of the expenditure and employment, it is true, was in connection with projects for which the federal government made

---

[49] Youngstown Sheet & Tube Co. *v.* Sawyer, 343 U.S. 579, 587 (1952).
[50] *Ibid.*, p. 587.

grants-in-aid. No doubt the fact that the federal government made grants for some purposes and not for others had some influence on the course of state activity, but it was only through indirection of this kind that the states subordinated themselves to control from Washington.

### THE STATES AND COMMERCE

The states did not stop enactment and enforcement of laws having effects on interstate commerce. The exercise of federal power did not debar the states from the field. Some state statutes it is true, as for example some of those governing the distribution of milk from other states, were found unconstitutional. But the states continued to exercise police powers and taxing powers in a variety of ways which had bearing on interstate commerce. Indeed, the states legislate so extensively with respect to interstate public transportation — with statutes prescribing the conditions of the use of highways, gasoline and other taxes to be paid, and inspection based on health and other considerations — that concern remains as to interstate trade barriers reminiscent of those which gave rise to adoption of the Constitution.

### STATE TAXES

As in the field of direct regulation of commerce, so also in the field of state taxation having some bearing on interstate commerce, there was no clearly defined line to be followed by the courts in determining what was and what was not constitutional. States were not permitted to tax in such a way as deliberately to discriminate against interstate commerce, but measures obviously affecting interstate commerce were at times upheld, perhaps in recognition of the fact that the states had to be permitted to raise adequate revenue if they were to hold their own in competition with a federal government which was steadily expanding its powers. The sales tax and use tax law of the State of Washington provides an example. The law, passed in 1935, levied a tax of two per cent on retail sales in the state. Realizing the fact that collection of the tax would lead some customers to purchase in adjacent states to avoid the levy, and that a sales tax on purchases made in other states would be unconstitutional, the legislature provided also for a two per cent use tax on goods which had been purchased outside the state. The use tax was not collected on goods purchased in the state, and was therefore geared to purchases in interstate commerce. Its purpose was to prevent an increase in interstate commerce at the expense of intrastate commerce as a result of the sales tax law. Recognizing the fact that the purpose was to maintain the status quo with respect to interstate commerce, and not to injure it, the Supreme Court upheld the measure.[51]

It was in recognition of the need of both state and federal governments for access to revenues that the Supreme Court narrowed application of the doctrine of reciprocal immunity from taxation, the doctrine that neither government could tax the instrumentalities of the other. In Graves v. New York ex rel. O'Keefe,[52] the Court overruled earlier decisions protecting government salaries from taxation by the non-employing government [53] and brought reciprocal immunity in this field virtually to an end. Although it did so with the confusion that results from multiple opinions, the Court seemed to extend the scope of the power of the federal government to tax state-owned enterprises, as in the instance of mineral water bottled and sold by the State of New York.[54] While some types of income remained untaxed, such as that from state and municipal bonds, even that immunity may now have derived not from constitutional safeguards but from the policy of the federal government. The tendency was to permit a maximum of access to property and income for tax purposes.

## FEDERAL COURTS AND COMMON LAW

In 1938 the Supreme Court gave up to the states an important area of jurisdiction exercised for a century by the federal courts, overruling Swift v. Tyson [55] which had been decided in 1842. It will be recalled that when suits arise between citizens of different states involving sufficient amounts they may be brought in federal courts, even though the law involved is state law and not federal law. Under the Judiciary Act of 1798 the federal courts were required to follow state interpretations of state statutes when deciding such cases. There was doubt, however, whether this requirement applied to common

---

[51] Henneford v. Silas Mason Co., 300 U.S. 577 (1937). See also Nelson v. Sears, Roebuck & Co., 312 U.S. 359 (1941).

[52] 306 U.S. 466.

[53] For discussion of earlier cases, Dobbins v. Erie County and Collector v. Day, see above, pp. 438–439, 842.

[54] New York v. United States, 326 U.S. 572 (1946).

[55] 16 Peters 1.

law in a state, as distinguished from state statutes. In the Tyson case Justice Story held, for the Court, that when the matter was one of "general law" the federal courts might exercise their independent judgment of what the law was, and need not be bound by state decisions. In so deciding, the Court apparently believed that the state courts would thereafter follow the common law interpretations of the Supreme Court and that harmony would be preserved in the common law instead of the diversity which resulted in differing interpretations in different states.

Justice Story evidently regarded the broad principles of the common law as all-pervasive and as entitled to universal interpretation, whatever the attitude of the judiciary of the particular state in which it was enforced. The law seemed to exist apart from the state. His position is illuminated by a criticism offered by Justice Holmes: "The Common law is not a brooding omnipresence in the sky, but the articulate voice of some sovereign or quasi-sovereign that can be identified. . . . It is always the law of some state." [56]

The strategy of the Supreme Court failed to bring unity in interpretation of the common law. State courts continued to follow their own interpretations, with the result that state courts and federal courts, sitting virtually side by side, were handing down different interpretations. Newly discovered materials on the history of the Judiciary Act of 1789 indicated that Congress had probably intended that the federal courts should follow the state courts instead of acting independently.[57] Finally, in Erie Railroad Company v. Tomkins,[58] the Supreme Court re-examined the entire question. Speaking through Justice Brandeis, it held that the Constitution itself required that in applying the common law of a state a federal court must follow the state's own interpretation of that law and not some independent interpretation. The states were therefore left in position to make their common law mean whatever they wanted it to mean, however much their interpretation of a given common law principle might differ from that of another state and however much federal judges might disagree with it.[59]

---

[56] Southern Pacific Co. v. Jensen, 244 U.S. 205, 222 (1917).

[57] Charles Warren, "New Light on the History of the Federal Judiciary Act of 1789," *Harvard Law Review*, Vol. XXXVII (November, 1923), 49–132.

[58] 304 U.S. 64 (1938).

[59] For sharp criticism of this freeing of state courts from federal judicial control see William W. Crosskey, *Politics and the Constitution in the History of the United States* (1953), Vol. II, Chapter XXVI.

TIDEWATER OIL

Still another important struggle illustrates the indefiniteness of the dividing line between the federal government and the states. It had been discovered that rich oil deposits under privately owned land in California extended far out under the bed of the ocean and that thousands of square miles of submerged lands had a value not hitherto dreamed of. It had long since been settled by the Supreme Court that the states owned in trust for their people tidewater lands within their borders that lay between high and low water mark, the land sometimes submerged by the tides and sometimes exposed. The states apparently assumed that they owned also the permanently sub-merged lands out to the three mile limit, and to any limit beyond that point to which the jurisdiction of any government might extend. If this was true, then the State of California had the right to lease the submerged land off its coast and to collect whatever returns it con-tracted for with exploiting oil companies.

Partly because of the importance of our oil supply for national de-fense, the United States has long been concerned about the ownership and control of oil lands. Noting that the question of the ownership of entirely submerged lands had never been settled, representatives of the federal government instituted an action in the Supreme Court against the State of California to get the lands in controversy declared the property of the United States. Voting six to two, the Court held in favor of the United States.[60] The argument of Justice Black, who spoke for the Court, is too intricate for brief statement. The dissent-ing opinions of Justices Reed and Frankfurter seemed more persua-sive in terms of reasoning from precedents. Yet the decision seemed calculated to keep within the jurisdiction of the nation as a whole a resource enormously important to all the people. It seemed more consistent with a broader justice than with the letter of the law. This distinction seemed even more obvious in later cases dealing with sub-merged lands off the coasts of Louisiana and Texas, where for tech-nical reasons the legal claims of the states seemed even stronger.[61]

The decisions ran counter to powerful interests. Some huge oil companies — although not necessarily all of them — preferred to se-cure drilling rights from the states rather than the federal govern-ment. In times past the states have usually been more amenable to

[60] United States v. California, 332 U.S. 19 (1947).

[61] United States v. Louisiana, 339 U.S. 699 (1950), and United States v. Texas, 339 U.S. 707 (1950).

corporation influence than has the federal government. In addition, the revenue received from the oil companies, even if it were less than it ought to be, would somewhat lighten the tax burdens of the states. So it was that, having failed to win their cases before the Supreme Court, the states, undoubtedly with the backing of interested oil companies, shifted their fight to Congress to secure from Congress a transfer of ownership of submerged lands from the United States to the states adjacent to them. The controversy demonstrated, as has been demonstrated many times before, the difficulties arising from conflicting jurisdictional claims between the federal government and the states. It added little to our knowledge, however, of the place at which jurisdictional lines ought to be drawn. The matter became a political issue in the campaign of 1952, and in the following year Congress passed and the President signed a bill to transfer the oil rights to the states.

# CHAPTER 38

# THE SECOND WORLD WAR

THE OUTBREAK OF WAR in Europe in 1939 marked the beginning of a transition from the New Deal to a war régime. Even apart from the war, the New Deal was destined for a transition of some kind. An operative program which is six years old, whatever its name, is no longer new. By that time its sponsors have either lost the struggle or have developed vested interests and become "conservative" in the sense of devoting much energy to preserving their old program as distinguished from advocating a new one. For a time the task of New-Dealers seemed to be that of protecting their hold on specific reforms already instituted, or about to be put into operation, against a return to power of advocates of the older conservatism. The war provided new goals, without eliminating the goal of preserving the social gains of the New Deal. The new task brought a realignment of program and an influx of new personnel of which only a part was committed to the New-Deal program. With this transition the New-Deal period fades into history and its issues merge with an overpowering tide of alien elements.

Involvement of the United States in the second World War, however, can be understood only in terms of events of the New-Deal period. The processes by which the United States prepared for national defense, made itself the "arsenal of democracy," and then took up active warfare were highly complex. They were influenced, not merely by conflicting attitudes toward the New Deal, but also by diverse sentiments concerning foreign affairs. The population included fanatics at the two extremes of isolationism and internationalism, others less fanatical who were committed to programs less extreme, and a great body of people who had no very definite attitude except a desire to avoid involvement in matters beyond their ken or thought to be none of their concern. It took time, careful strategy, and the action of the enemy to bring about relative unanimity of sentiment.

Confusion of economic interests likewise stood in the way of establishing a harmonious program in the field of foreign affairs. American thought as to international trade evolved around transactions in particular fields rather than around a national program. American producers, whether agricultural or industrial, sought to sell abroad everything they could market and to prevent the sale of foreign competitive products at home. They were interested primarily in immediate profits rather than in economic or political doctrines. Had they been forced to take doctrinaire positions, many of them, no doubt, would have adhered to the concept of the "favorable balance of trade," which involved a belief that the country was in a more favorable position when the value of its exports exceeded the value of its imports. Few of the people engaged in commercial activities for profit concerned themselves about the question of how a creditor nation could continue to maintain indefinitely a favorable balance of trade without ultimate disaster. Since the first World War the United States had bought as little as possible from abroad except in commodities not produced at home and had lent abroad, directly or indirectly, the money with which foreigners were to purchase American products. The participants in international trade had no solution for the problem of repayment of debts. American interests, as commonly conceived and commonly acted upon, were not interests of the nation as a unit, but the separate, and oftentimes short-range, interests of particular individuals, groups, and regions. There was irony in the fact that profits from business promoted by American exports were invested in foreign bonds never likely to be redeemed. At the very best, such practices would have left the United States in a serious predicament. The attack of the depression upon the entire world turned the predicament into a catastrophe.

## HISTORICAL BACKGROUND

### THE FOREIGN POLICY OF THE NEW DEAL

Because ideas and interests were confused, the foreign policy of the Roosevelt administration was also confused. When he took office, the President left no doubt that the domestic situation rather than the world situation was his first concern. The administration at times attempted the solution of world problems from various angles, but the task was made more difficult because of inconsistency with the domestic program and with the interests and ideas of important groups within the United States. Entanglement with war debts, tariffs, and other issues, for example, prevented international agreements for stabilization of currencies. The government abandoned the gold standard and reduced the gold content of the dollar in part to improve the position of the United States in foreign exchange, but the collection of debts to the United States was thereby rendered more difficult. The nations of the world were exchanging goods more and more on the basis of governmental negotiations as to what should be bought and sold in each instance, and were establishing quotas and tariff levels to promote centralized management. The foreign trade of the United States had suffered as a result of the growing control of international trade by governmental bargaining in other countries because the United States had no administrative agency with adequate authority to make tariff concessions and agreements-to-purchase in return for similar concessions and agreements by other nations. Because of the representation of special interests in Congress and their tendency to co-operate with one another to secure protection through the tariff, intelligent reduction of tariff levels was hard to secure.

A limited amount of control of tariff rates was lodged in the President. Since 1922, the President, with the assistance of the Tariff Commission, had been authorized to make investigations into the difference between cost of production in the United States and abroad, and to make such changes in duties as were necessary to equalize the differences. This slight degree of flexibility, however, was by no means sufficient to enable the President to participate in international negotiations for the promotion of foreign trade. In 1934, President Roosevelt secured enactment of a measure authorizing him to enter into trade agreements with foreign nations. To that end Congress authorized him to modify duties and other import restrictions up to fifty per cent of existing rates. It also authorized him to deny the benefits of such lower rates to the products of countries which discriminated against the commerce of the United States. The President directed the Secretary of State to undertake a vast program of international negotiations. The Secretary entered into many agreements whereby the United States reduced duties on goods the importation of which would do a minimum of damage to American producers, in return for similar concessions by the other parties to the agreements. Although on the whole no spectacular reductions of tariff levels were made, the tendency was beneficial.

Many of the reciprocal trade agreements were worked out with Central and South American countries. Their negotiation became a part of the "Good-Neighbor" policy announced by the President toward those countries. Other aspects of the policy were the abrogation of the Platt Amendment in our relations with Cuba, the withdrawal of American troops from Nicaragua and Haiti, and the maintenance of a general attitude of friendliness and cooperation toward Central and South America, as distinguished from the earlier brusque attitude which carried the perennial threat of coercive intervention. The decision to grant independence to the Philippines, after a ten-year period of gradual assumption of self-rule, although brought about in part by the efforts of commercial interests that would profit by severing the Philippines from the United States, reflected, superficially at least, the same attitude of friendliness and the same renunciation of any right to continue the exercise of coercive power.

The middle nineteen-thirties witnessed the preparation of European nations for new wars, along with default on reparations payments and on payments of debts incurred during the first World War. This fact added to disillusionment in the United States and to the development of isolationist sentiment. A series of books and articles disclosed the ruthless activities of munitions makers and financiers in the deliberate promotion of war for the sake of profit.[1] In 1934, the Senate authorized a special committee to investigate problems incident to the private manufacture of arms and munitions of war and the international traffic in such materials. President Roosevelt gave full support to the investigation. The private and uncontrolled manufacture of arms and munitions and the traffic therein, he said, had become a serious cause of international discord and strife. Since international control was necessary, he urged the Senate to ratify a convention of 1925 for the supervision of the international trade in arms, ammunition, and implements of war. He expressed publicly the hope that provision for more far-reaching control would be made at the conference to be held in Geneva in the summer of 1934.[2]

The Senate investigating committee, headed by Gerald P. Nye of North Dakota, uncovered a great deal of malodorous information about the munitions industry. It showed that manufacturers had sold arms simultaneously and indiscriminately to both sides in

---

[1] See, for example, H. C. Englebrecht and F. C. Haneghen, *Merchants of Death* (1935), and Walter Millis, *The Road to War* (1935).
[2] *Public Papers and Addresses of Franklin D. Roosevelt* (1936), III, 239–241.

various wars. In the United States, they had maintained lobbies in Washington to support military and naval appropriations and to oppose arms embargoes. They had shipped arms to warring nations in violation of embargoes. Armament firms in various countries exchanged information and cooperated to stimulate races in armament between friendly nations. The committee examined with mistrust comprehensive plans being worked out in the War Department for industrial mobilization for the next war. Disclosing huge accumulations of profits during the first World War, it advocated machinery to prevent such profits in the future by government operation of industries producing munitions, by taxation, and by price-fixing.[3]

The disclosures of the munitions investigation deepened isolationist sentiment in the United States. The Senate refused to follow the leadership of the President to the extent of approving membership in the Permanent Court of International Justice. It did ratify the Arms Traffic Convention of 1925, on condition that certain other arms-producing nations should also ratify, but negotiations collapsed, the disarmament conference in Geneva disbanded in failure, and the world hurried on its way toward new military conflicts.

## NEUTRALITY LEGISLATION

At this point Congress turned to so-called neutrality legislation as a means of avoiding future military involvements. In the summer of 1935 it enacted a joint resolution providing for

> the prohibition of the export of arms, ammunition, and implements of war to belligerent countries; the prohibition of the transportation of arms, ammunition, and implements of war by vessels of the United States for the use of belligerent states; for the registration and licensing of persons engaged in the business of manufacturing, exporting, or importing arms, ammunition, or implements of war; and restricting travel by American citizens on belligerent ships during the war.[4]

The act prohibited shipments of specified articles to belligerents, directly or indirectly. It set up a National Munitions Control Board to receive registration and prescribed information from munition manufacturers in the United States. It provided that American citi-

---

[3] For the voluminous findings of the committee see Senate Report No. 944, 7th Cong., 1st sess.

[4] 49 Stat. 1081. Neutrality has been a subject of prolific discussion. Among the several volumes see *Neutrality, Its History, Economics and Law* (4 vols., 1935–36), and Charles G. Fenwick, *The Neutrality Laws of the United States* (1913).

zens should travel on the vessels of belligerent nations only at their own risk, if the President proclaimed that they should refrain from traveling on such vessels because of the need for protecting the lives of citizens of the United States or commercial interests of the United States or for preserving the security of the United States. This section of the statute marked the beginning of the renunciation by the United States of rights possessed under international law.

Congress made the act temporary in character, partly because administration leaders thought it should have left discretion in the hands of the President instead of making embargo provisions mandatory, but renewed and extended it in 1936 and 1937. Isolationist leaders were determined to have a measure so inflexible that not even the President would have authority to prevent its operation. They sought to include in neutrality legislation all trade, travel, transportation, and financial activities that might possibly involve the United States in a foreign war. Throughout the years of discussion of the subject, however, a substantial minority insisted that the law should be modified so that embargoes would not have to be applied indiscriminately. The moral issues involved in a particular conflict, or the ultimate safety of the United States from attack, might justify the United States in continuing to exercise its traditional right of trade so as to benefit one of the belligerents. After the former allies of the United States again became involved in war with Germany in September, 1939, opposition to the embargo grew so strong that the President was able to bring about repeal of the prohibition of exports to belligerents.[5] In other respects, however, the new statute continued the policy of restricting the exercise of American rights in order to prevent involvement in war. American shipping was to be excluded from war zones by the proclamation of combat areas in the vicinity of the belligerents, to prevent incidents which might lead to war.

### PRESIDENTIAL LEADERSHIP

The sweeping authority of the President in the field of foreign affairs, as distinguished from the domestic field, was already generally recognized. In 1936, the Supreme Court emphasized the existence of that authority in the important case of United States v. Curtiss-Wright Export Corporation.[6] Congress had enacted a joint resolution

[5] 54 Stat. 4.
[6] 299 U.S. 304.

providing that the sale of arms and munitions of war to the countries engaged in armed conflict in the Chaco in South America should be forbidden if the President proclaimed that such a prohibition might contribute to the re-establishment of peace between the countries involved. The President issued the proclamation, but an American corporation ignored it and sold some machine guns to Bolivia, contending that the statute made an unconstitutional delegation of legislative power to the President. Justice Sutherland, speaking for the Supreme Court, stressed the difference between the external and the internal powers of the federal government.[7] In the external realm, he explained, with its important, complicated, delicate, and manifold problems, the President alone had the power to speak or listen as a representative of the nation. In the case at hand, the Court was dealing, not alone with an authority vested in the President by statute, but with such an authority plus the very delicate plenary and exclusive power of the President as sole organ of the federal government in the field of international relations. Justice Sutherland continued:

> It is quite apparent that if, in the maintenance of our international relations, embarrassment — perhaps serious embarrassment — is to be avoided and success for our aims achieved, congressional legislation which is to be made effective through negotiation and inquiry within the international field must often accord to the President a degree of discretion and freedom from statutory restriction which would not be admissible were domestic affairs alone involved. Moreover, he, not Congress, has the better opportunity of knowing the conditions which prevail in foreign countries, and especially is this true in time of war. He has his confidential sources of information. He has his agents in the form of diplomatic, consular, and other officials. Secrecy, in respect of information gathered by them may be highly necessary, and the premature disclosure of it productive of harmful results.[8]

The opinion has permanent importance because of this emphasis on the broad powers of the President in the management of foreign affairs.

Franklin D. Roosevelt had been in some degree interested in international affairs throughout his life. He had once been an advocate of the League of Nations.[9] While still President-elect, he had con-

[7] For an important earlier statement of his position on this subject see Senate Doc., No. 417, 61st Cong., 2d sess.

[8] 299 U.S. 320.

[9] See Raymond Moley, *After Seven Years* (1939), p. 377.

curred in the policies of Secretary of State Henry L. Stimson in refusing to recognize Japan's aggression in Manchuria in violation of treaties. American foreign policy must uphold the sanctity of international treaties, he announced.[10] This attitude, reminiscent of that of Woodrow Wilson in connection with recognition of the régime in power in Mexico, imported a moral standard into the recognition policy of the country, or at any rate gave greater emphasis to such a standard. It represented deviation from the traditional practice of recognizing whatever government happened to be solidly and effectively in power in a particular state, for a policy colored by the conception that the United States should appraise the moral right of the régime in question to continue in power. Such a policy, if justified, would give the United States a right to exercise pressure upon other nations which those nations completely refused to recognize. They resented the pressure which interfered with predatory plans and, perhaps even more, they resented the moral tone of criticism coming from the United States.

As far as President Roosevelt was concerned, it is true, he did not engage in pontifical moralizing to the rest of the world. He took the broad position that the prosperity of the United States, which could develop only with the expansion of foreign trade in an orderly world, and even the protection of the United States from involvement in future foreign wars, depended upon the preservation of a world order in which international rights, and particularly international agreements, were honored. If he did not now favor something in the nature of a League of Nations for the entire world, he evidently believed that the preservation of international peace depended upon a measure of collective security, promoted by expressions of disapproval of misconduct and backed up by economic sanctions. He approved of neutrality legislation authorizing him to levy embargoes upon materials of war, but he wished discretion left in his hands as to the application of the embargo. In some instances, presumably, he would have applied it to both belligerents and in other instances only to the one which he regarded as the aggressor. In connection with the predatory war of Italy upon Ethiopia, he not only put in force the embargo provisions of the Neutrality Act of 1935, but sought, though vainly, to secure something in the nature of a general economic boycott of Italy.[11] He sponsored the policy pursuant to

10 *Ibid.*, p. 94.
11 See *ibid.*, pp. 320–321.

which Congress, in 1936, passed a joint resolution prohibiting export of arms to the contending factions in Spain. He failed to apply the embargo to the undeclared war between Japan and China, no doubt for a number of reasons, but partly because in some respects China, obviously the victim of aggression, would be injured by it more than would Japan.

Excerpts from speeches delivered from 1937 to 1941 indicate the development of the thinking of the President with the growth of the international crisis. In what came to be known as his "quarantine speech," delivered at Chicago in October, 1937, he delivered a ringing denunciation of those responsible for the present reign of terror and international lawlessness. The peace-loving nations, he proclaimed, must make a concerted effort in opposition to those violations of treaties and those ignorings of human instincts which were creating a state of international anarchy and instability such that escape through mere isolation or neutrality was impossible. "There must be a return to a belief in the pledged word, in the value of a signed treaty. There must be recognition of the fact that national morality is as vital as private morality." [12] There could be no stability or peace, he declared, either within nations or between nations, except under laws and moral standards adhered to by all. International anarchy destroyed every foundation for peace. The epidemic of world lawlessness was spreading. "When an epidemic of physical disease starts to spread, the community approves and joins in a quarantine of the patients in order to protect the health of the community against the spread of the disease. . . . War is a contagion, whether it be declared or undeclared." [13]

In his annual message of January, 1939, he declared that the God-fearing democracies of the world which observed the sanctity of treaties and good faith in their dealings with other nations could not forever let pass without effective protest acts of aggression against sister nations, acts which automatically undermined all of us. Obviously, he said, they must proceed along practical, peaceful lines. Words might be futile, but war was not the only means of commanding a decent respect for the opinions of mankind. "There are many methods short of war, but stronger and more effective than mere words, of bringing home to aggressor governments the aggregate

[12] *Public Papers and Addresses of Franklin D. Roosevelt*, 1937, p. 408. Although the early volumes of the Roosevelt papers are designated by volume numbers (see note 2), the later volumes can be identified only by year or subtitle.

[13] *Ibid.*, pp. 410–411.

sentiments of our own people." [14] One method had proved to be wrong. "We have learned that when we deliberately try to legislate neutrality, our neutrality laws may operate unevenly and unfairly — may actually give aid to an aggressor and deny it to the victim. The instinct of self-preservation should warn us that we ought not to let that happen any more." [15]

He expressed the same sentiment on other occasions. In a commencement address delivered in June, 1940, he characterized as an obvious delusion the belief that we of the United States could safely permit the United States to become a lone island, a lone island in a world dominated by the philosophy of force. "Such an island represents to me and to the overwhelming majority of Americans today a helpless nightmare of a people without freedom — the nightmare of a people lodged in prison, handcuffed, hungry, and fed through the bars from day to day by the contemptuous, unpitying masters of other continents." [16] He denounced the Italian invasion of France as France was giving way before the forces of Germany: "On this the 10th day of June, 1940, the hand that held the dagger has struck it into the back of its neighbor."[17] The United States ought to pursue two obvious and simultaneous courses. It ought to extend to the opponents of force the material resources of the nation and at the same time harness and speed up the use of these resources in order that we ourselves in the Americas might have equipment and training equal to the task of any emergency and every defense.

In his annual message to Congress, delivered on January 6, 1941, President Roosevelt linked his conception of domestic and foreign policy in terms of a statement of four essential human freedoms:

> The first is freedom of speech and expression — everywhere in the world.
> The second is freedom of every person to worship God in his own way — everywhere in the world.
> The third is freedom from want, which, translated into world terms, means economic understandings which will secure to every nation a healthy peacetime life for its inhabitants — everywhere in the world.

[14] *Public Papers and Addresses of Franklin D. Roosevelt*, 1939, p. 3.
[15] *Ibid.*, pp. 3–4.
[16] *Public Papers and Addresses of Franklin D. Roosevelt*, 1940, p. 261.
[17] *Ibid.*, p. 263.

The fourth is freedom from fear, which, translated into world terms, means a world-wide reduction of armaments to such a point and in such a thorough fashion that no nation will be in a position to commit an act of physical aggression against any neighbor — anywhere in the world.[18]

That was no vision of a distant millennium, he declared. It was a definite basis for a kind of world attainable in our own time and generation. That kind of world was the very antithesis of the so-called "new order" of tyranny, which the dictators sought to create with the crash of a bomb.

The war brought many casualties to American governmental institutions. The embargo on the export of war materials to belligerents was among the first. Another, and perhaps ultimately the one to be regarded as the most serious of all, was the tradition that no President should serve more than two terms. The tradition was broken down, not by the process of logical argument, but by the process of ignoring it altogether. Millions of people who had come to trust Franklin D. Roosevelt preferred the continuation of his leadership to a change at a time when his domestic program was not yet completely established and when the international situation was one of turmoil. He yielded to a so-called draft carefully arranged by his political agents, and sought re-election without discussing the value of the tradition being overthrown.

His strategy is explained partly by the way in which he handled other issues in earlier years. Throughout his presidency he showed far more interest in the content of policy than in governmental traditions or machinery. An unbalanced budget, for example, was to him a matter of little importance by comparison with the human welfare to be promoted by the use of government finances. He had no hesitancy in attacking the hallowed institution of the Supreme Court when that tribunal stood staunchly in the way of measures which he deemed essential to the public welfare. The Civil Service Commission, the independent regulatory commissions, and other governmental devices to which the people had emotional attachments, were to him not necessarily symbols of good government. If they proved inadequate, or if they interfered with the promotion of the public welfare, he sought to have them reorganized. So it was with the third-term tradition. If observance of that tradition meant the replacement of the New Deal at a critical period in American

[18] 87 *Congressional Record* 46–47.

history, with the probable result of destroying much of the program which seemed to him vital, he had no hesitancy in overriding the tradition without stopping to discuss it. The goal, as he saw it, was the publc welfare. Government was but a means to an end. He sought justification in the ends to be achieved, regardless of machinery. Although some had more faith in the protective value of traditions than did the President, and believed fervently that the third-term tradition was worth preserving even at the expense of possible immediate losses, there was little genuine debate on the subject. The defenders of the tradition were concerned primarily, not with the tradition, but with election of the opposing candidate.

### PRE-WAR MOBILIZATION AND CONTROL

Although the masses of the people hoped and probably believed that the United States would never again find it necessary to participate in a major war, the War Department and the military leaders of the country had no such illusions. Remembering the chaos of preparation for the equipment of an army after the declaration of war in 1917, and sensing that even to a greater degree the wars of the future would be wars of machines and of whole peoples rather than merely of trained army personnel, they began immediately to plan for rapid mobilization whenever the occasion required. They worked out plans for the conversion of peacetime industrial production to the production of war materials, and arranged for the allotment of so-called "educational orders" for war materials to enable plants to develop valuable preliminary experience. Evidently with the operation of the War Industries Board of the first World War in mind, they worked out plans for emergency governmental machinery to be co-ordinated under centralized leadership. They planned conscription of manpower for military service and effective control of labor in essential industries. Maximum wages were to be fixed and maximum prices were to be regulated, although without fundamental interference with the operation of the profit system. Through power to establish priorities and to commandeer equipment wherever necessary, the government was to maintain effective control over industry. Bills were drafted to be presented to Congress for speedy enactment if an emergency developed.[19] The plan was subjected to much unfavorable publicity during the middle nineteen-thirties when it was

---

[19] For the evolution of plans see Harold J. Tobin and Percy W. Bidwell, *Mobilizing Civilian America* (1940), chapter III.

sharply criticized by the Senate committee investigating the munitions industry. The sentiment of the committee and, evidently, of most of the American people was that the energies of the nation ought to be utilized in solving the problems of peace rather than in preparing for improbable war.

By the summer of 1939, although public sentiment was still divided, war clouds loomed so darkly that, in August of that year, President Roosevelt appointed a War Resources Board with a membership predominantly from eastern industrial and banking circles to act as a civilian advisory committee to the Army and Navy Munitions Board in developing industrial mobilization plans. The board worked behind closed doors for a period of months, during which war broke out in Europe, submitted a confidential report, and then disbanded. For reasons never publicly announced, the President made no further use of that board, but instead, on May 26, 1940, he returned to the device utilized at the beginning of the first World War, and, acting under the National Defense Act of 1916, he created a new advisory commission to the Council of National Defense.[20] The Council of National Defense, consisting of six members of the cabinet, did not again become active as a separate organization, but the Advisory Commission, consisting of seven persons representative of various fields of activity, played an important part in the initial co-ordination of the resources of the country for national defense.

Because the commission was advisory only and possessed little or no authority in its own right, the opposition party in the presidential campaign of 1940 denounced the President's failure to establish machinery such as a War Industries Board or a Munitions Administration in which the administration of the rearmament program would be lodged. The President resisted such demands, however, until the allotment of power for administration could be segregated in a considerable degree from the power to make policy. Gradually, as lines of policy were clearly established, he strengthened the hands of his administrative agents. He co-ordinated newly established agencies for national defense with the program of reorganization carried out under the Reorganization Act of 1939. Pursuant to that act he brought together in what was called the Executive Office of the President a number of agencies including the Bureau of the Budget, the Division of Statistical Standards, the Office of Government Reports, and the National Resources Planning Board. Along

[20] For the experience of the first World War see chapter 26.

with these agencies he made provision for an Office for Emergency Management.[21] The title was unique among permanent government agencies, but its use was understandable in view of the extent to which contemporary government had been government in terms of emergencies and was likely to continue so. Within the Office for Emergency Management, the President created a long line of new agencies for the performance of functions connected with national defense and war, including functions that were new and older ones that had previously been exercised by the Advisory Commission.

In the meantime, although the United States was not yet a formal belligerent, Congress began the enactment of measures reminiscent of or going beyond those of the period of the first World War. It authorized the expenditure of billions of dollars directly for the army and navy, for the equipment of plants for production of war materials, and for aid to nations which later became the allies of the United States. In line with slowly changing public sentiment, it eliminated neutrality legislation forbidding extension of credit to belligerents and other legislation prohibiting loans to nations which had defaulted on their obligation to us. It enacted a so-called Lend-Lease Act whereby the President was given almost unlimited power to transfer to Great Britain and other countries whose defense he considered essential to the United States almost any kind of equipment needed for conduct of the war, on a leasing basis or for any compensation the President might see fit to accept. Congress also enacted the first peacetime conscription act in the history of the United States. It provided for registration of all aliens in the country and strengthened legislation dealing with sedition and espionage. It required registration of propagandists of foreign governments, and enacted other measures for the mobilization of man-power and resources for national defense.

FROM DEFENSE TO WAR

Although both the legislative and executive branches undertook sweeping measures for national defense, operations moved sluggishly until after the disastrous experience at Pearl Harbor on December 7, 1941. That attack brought the speedy enactment of a declaration of war against Japan which was followed by other declarations of war against the other Axis Powers. With a minimum of delay, Congress

21 See William H. McReynolds, "The Office for Emergency Management," *Public Administration Review,* I (Autumn, 1940), 131–138.

thereafter enacted a host of measures desired by the President. The flow of appropriations for war purposes developed into a torrent. "If appropriations could win this war," declared Senator Vandenberg, "victory is 'in the bag.'" [22] Congress reinstated the provisions of the Overman Act of the first World War period, which authorized the President to reorganize the federal government virtually as he saw fit, and of the Trading-with-the-Enemy Act, which gave sweeping control over foreign trade and communications. Other measures strengthened the hand of the government in its control over raw materials, finished goods, transportation, communications, prices, wages, and so on.

In the executive branch of the government, the reorganization of agencies and their interrelationships continued at a rapid rate. Within the Office for Emergency Management an Office for Production Management, headed by two men, had been given authority to supervise the flow of materials which had been allotted to the several fields of military and civilian consumption. Because of need for greater speed and more freedom of action in that agency, the OPM was reorganized under one man as the War Production Board. Its position was similar to that of the War Industries Board of the first World War, but the pressure on it from competing agencies was greater, its powers were greater, and it exercised them on a grander scale. An Office of Price Administration, which was closely co-ordinated with the War Production Board, developed great power over the distribution and the prices of civilian supplies. A director of economic stabilization was given authority in areas of conflict over governmentally controlled prices and priorities. A Lend-Lease Administration sent munitions, food, and other materials to our allies and to countries whose defense the President deemed essential to the defense of our own country, at the rate of some ten billion dollars a year.

The over-all purpose was to speed production and delivery of war materials, secure the proper allotment of raw materials for war and other purposes, and provide for uniform distribution of the limited stock of supplies for civilians. The government had to function under tremendous pressure from the several services for the immediate production and delivery of supplies, while providing for at least a minimum of civilian needs and making replacements in the machinery of production and transportation. It had to deal also with the competitive claims of Great Britain, Russia, China, and other

22 88 *Congressional Record* 964.

allies, whose survival might depend upon a speedy delivery to them of supplies which were sought also by our own military and naval forces. It had to struggle with the seemingly insoluble problems of the proper allotment of man-power between the military and naval forces and the fields of industrial and agricultural production.

Management of the war effort called for a greater degree of executive rule-making and executive supervision of the life of the country than ever before. During 1942 the *Federal Register,* the official journal for publishing proclamations, orders, rules, and instructions of various kinds which have effect beyond the range of the issuing agency, turned out more than eleven thousand pages of what might be called law. The bulk was out of all comparison with that of the legislative output of Congress during the same period. The rulings issued by the Office of Price Administration alone made up a huge code of law, a code of which the contents were in such rapid transition as to acquire constant attention on the part of landlords, tenants, wholesalers, retailers, and consumers. Most rulings had, or were said to have, an ultimate basis in general statutes. Yet their specific provisions and the operations of the administrative machine were determined so completely by agencies in the executive branch of the government that members of Congress were hardly better informed about them than was the general public.

The continued concentration of power in the executive branch of the government is important not merely for the war crisis. It brings quasi-permanent entrenchment of administrative machinery and it grooves more deeply the already speedily developing trend in terms of which an administrative machine determines the nature of governmental operations and molds the life of the country. Furthermore, the decisions made within the administrative bureaucracy for the direction of the war effort will have tremendous influence on the post-war period. There is no possibility that a treaty of peace or federal statutes subsequently enacted can eliminate the post-war influence of such administrative decisions as the following: that war plants would be constructed in certain areas and not in others; that certain firms would receive huge war contracts of certain kinds, while other firms would receive contracts of other kinds, or none at all; and that housing adjustments would be made through the construction of new projects of chosen design, or through the improvement of transportation, or by other means. Whether the work is done well or poorly, what may possibly seem like economic havoc in the post-war period will be the product of administrative decisions during the war period which will have been made under the strain of the crisis, without reference to nationally planned public policy.

The enhancement of executive power is not limited to the home field. As commander in chief of the army and navy in a total war, the President found it not merely possible but necessary to exercise far-reaching powers over foreign affairs. Commitments in plans worked out with our allies for the conduct of the war involved agreements on many matters not strictly military. Executive agreements, made often without publicity and even without the knowledge of Congress, governed matters which under other circumstances might preferably have been taken care of by treaty, in which event the concurrence of the Senate would have been necessary. As was indicated in the hearings and debates early in 1943 on extension of the Lend-Lease Act, the great popularity of that measure was qualified by suspicion that the almost unlimited power to aid allies and friends by distributing to them the resources of the United States was being or might be used to mold international policies which ought to be subject to legislative check. At hearings on the bill, an assistant Secretary of State remarked, "Many aspects of the arrangements made for mutual aid, through lend-lease and lend-lease in reverse, call for extended negotiations with foreign governments vitally affecting our political and economic relations with them." [23] The lend-lease administrator said that "the State Department at the present time is in the process of negotiation with foreign governments on that whole question of the use of air fields after the war." [24] From many other sources comes evidence of the extension of executive agreements as devices for the control of important aspects of American foreign relations.[25] The trend of events may lead ultimately to a mode of procedure whereby most of the details of international arrangements will be determined by executive agreement, leaving the treaty-making power for exercise only in connection with major international compacts.

In his relations with Congress, the President maintained a position of clear dominance throughout the first year of our formal participation in the war. Few legislators voiced the belief, which had been held by some of their predecessors in the Civil-War period, that Con-

[23] *Hearings on H.R. 1501* before the House committee on foreign affairs, 78th Cong., 1st sess., p. 82.

[24] *Ibid.*, p. 16.

[25] On executive agreements generally see Edward S. Corwin, *The President: Office and Powers* (1940), 235–238, 413–415.

gress should control policy and oversee administration of the war. The experience of enacting the President's "must" legislation in the New-Deal period had paved the way for general acceptance of presidential leadership in the war crisis. When, in the autumn of 1942, Congress, under leadership of the farm bloc, showed hostility to enactment of legislation to fix maximum prices of farm products at the parity level, the President declared sternly that, if Congress failed to enact the desired legislation within a specified time, he would take action without the support of new legislation:

> In the event that the Congress should fail to act, and act adequately, I shall accept the responsibility, and I will act. . . . The President has the powers, under the Constitution and under congressional acts, to take measures necessary to avert a disaster which would interfere with the winning of the war.[26]

He explained his position by saying that the responsibilities of the President in wartime to protect the nation were very grave. The use of executive power was far more essential in this war than in any previous war. He could not tell what powers might have to be exercised in order to win. The American people could be sure, he said, that he would use his powers with a full sense of his responsibility to the Constitution and to his country. When the war was won, the powers under which he acted automatically reverted to the people to whom they belonged.[27] Congress enacted the desired legislation in spite of charges of presidential dictatorship.

The Democratic loss of a number of seats in both houses of Congress in the election of November, 1942, although resulting from many causes, marked the beginning of increased congressional resistance to presidential domination. Congress scolded the President for seeking broad grants of power for specified purposes and using the powers thereafter for purposes of which no hint had been given when the legislation was requested. As its term expired, the Seventy-Seventh Congress refused to enact a requested measure authorizing the President to do away with tariff barriers wherever he might deem such action desirable in promoting the conduct of the war. It was apparent that Congress would not refuse to give specific powers that were clearly needed; but its attitude was that the need must be shown and the grant must be specific rather than general.

[26] 88 *Congressional Record* 7054.

[27] For discussion see Edward S. Corwin, "The War and the Constitution: President and Congress," *American Political Science Review,* XXXVII (February, 1943), 18–24.

In December, 1942, the same Congress forced a change in the leadership of the Office of Price Administration by the simple device of withholding appropriations. Early in 1943, using the suspicion of personal and political misconduct as an excuse, the Senate indirectly forced the withdrawal of the name of the President's nominee as minister to Australia. Congress cut off appropriations for the President's official national planning agency and a number of officials in high positions were threatened with similar treatment. Congress brought forward for serious consideration bills in many fields in spite of the fact that the President was known to be opposed to them. None of the proposed measures threatened basic interference with the management of the war, and no substantial group in Congress sought to take the basic control of the war out of the hands of the President; yet the series of petty conflicts between Congress and the administration showed that intra-governmental co-operation was at a low ebb at the time when it was most needed. Commentators who criticized what they regarded as executive usurpation of power watched uneasily the growth of negative criticism and petty sniping on the part of Congress and began to talk of the disastrous usurpation of power by Congress which had followed both the Civil War and the first World War, and in each instance had prevented the satisfactory solution of post-war problems.

It was clear to most critics of the administration both in and out of Congress that the war must be waged for the most part under presidential leadership.[28] The necessities of secrecy and of speedy and flexible action could not be met by an unwieldy body such as Congress. Its basic function seemed likely to be that of continuing to enact legislation desired by the President while scrutinizing and debating both policy and details of administration in such a way as to incite speedier and more effective administration. In spite of presidential criticism of unfavorable analyses of the war effort by congressional committees, Congress continued to bring out information about the errors which clogged the wheels of administration and, incidentally, about laudable administrative achievements. It is questionable whether such problems as have arisen in relations between Congress and the Executive are as much problems of constitutional machinery as of the weaknesses of human beings when operating

[28] For important pre-war studies of the presidency provoked in part by the expansion of the powers of the office, see Harold J. Laski, *The American Presidency* (1940), Pendleton Herring, *Presidential Leadership* (1940), and Edward S. Corwin, *The President: Office and Powers* (1940).

under heavy political pressure and the handicaps of wartime uncertainties, weariness, and strain. Clearer thinking, more self-restraint, and more good-will, together with a self-denying attitude which seldom finds its way into high leadership, are greatly needed in both branches of the government.

## ECONOMIC RIGHTS AND THE CONSTITUTION

Much more than any previous war or other national emergency had done, World War II modified and gave shape to the whole pattern of American life. The armed services assumed jurisdiction over 11,000,000 able bodied men and women. The industries of the country converted to war production and employed therein millions of workers of both sexes, including large numbers who had not previously worked for salaries and wages. The flow of huge quantities of raw materials was channeled into war production, while scarce necessities were rationed to consumers. Some supplies and equipment were rationed for government use. The government made loans to stimulate war production and at times financed construction of plants for operation by private corporations. It limited corporation financing and credit buying, and through its own borrowing power it absorbed billions of dollars of private savings into war production.

Much of the governmental program was carried on co-operatively and without formal coercion. A combination of patriotism and self interest brought men and materials together without the exercise of authority and without resort to the courts to determine the rights involved. So it is that in important areas there are no court decisions to rationalize wartime behavior in terms of our constitutional pattern. There were critical areas, however, in which the courts were called upon for decision and enforcement. These areas included the control of prices, the rights of persons in various categories, and problems involved in the punishment of offenses connected with the war.

### CONTROL OF PRICES TO PRIVATE PURCHASERS

Wartime legislation and administration quickly invaded the semi-sacred field of prices charged for privately owned property. By the Emergency Price Control Act of 1942 Congress gave broad powers for price regulation and provided for a Price Administrator to make the act effective. The purpose was to prevent the rise in prices which had cost the people and the government dearly during World War I and to prevent the destruction of morale by wartime profiteering. The Administrator was given vast leeway for discretion in determining the commodities on which prices would be fixed and the levels of prices to be established. The statute did not require that commodities be sold, but it did require that they be sold at the prices fixed by the Administrator if they were sold at all. To prevent aggrieved property owners from seeking injunctions in courts all over the United States against particular prices, and thereby defeating the price control program in a time of crisis, the statute limited determinations of constitutionality to an Emergency Court of Appeals which was set up in Washington.

However patriotic people in general may be, there are always, even in time of war, those who resist government interference with what they regard as their legitimate property rights. Certain merchants were indicted and convicted for selling beef at prices above the maximum prices fixed by the Administrator. They appealed, in a case known as Yakus v. United States,[29] which reached the Supreme Court early in 1944. Contending that the statute was unconstitutional, Yakus challenged the provisions which gave broad discretionary powers to the Administrator, gave to the Emergency Court of Appeals jurisdiction to determine the validity of any price-fixing order, drastically limited the right of judicial review at any point, and withheld the power to issue injunctions in the course of judicial review.

Deciding the case at a critical point during the war period, the Supreme Court upheld the sweeping exercise of power. Even Justice Rutledge, who dissented on the ground that the jurisdiction of the courts was unduly limited, admitted that

> War such as we now fight calls into play the full power of government in extreme emergency. It compels invention of legal, as of martial tools adequate for the times' necessity. Inevitably some will be strange, if also life-saving, instruments for a people accustomed to peace and the normal working of constitutional limitations. Citizens must surrender or forego exercising rights which in other times could not be impaired.[30]

The Court as a whole upheld the restriction of the power of the courts, and, more important, it held that Congress had not unconstitutionally delegated its own legislative power in giving broad dis-

29 321 U.S. 414.
30 Ibid., p. 461.

cretion to the Administrator to decide what prices were to be fixed and at what levels.

Other provisions of the same statute were challenged by a landlady who contended that it made a grant of unbridled discretion to the Administrator. The Court rejected this contention and also the contention that the landlady was unconstitutionally denied a fair return on the fair value of her rental property.

> Of course, price control, the same as other forms of regulation, may reduce the value of the property regulated. But . . . that does not mean that the regulation is unconstitutional. . . . A nation which can demand the lives of its men and women in the waging of war is under no constitutional necessity of providing a system of price control on the domestic front which will assure each landlord a "fair return" on his property.[31]

These two decisions suggest the extremes to which the Court is willing to go in upholding the delegation of power to administrators and in restricting property rights for war purposes. The opinions indicate also a revision of judicial attitudes generally toward the exercise of sweeping powers in these fields, whether or not a war emergency is involved.

PRICES PAID BY GOVERNMENT

These decisions on price control had to do with prices to private purchasers. Of comparable importance were prices the government had to pay on contracts for war supplies. The letting of war contracts is always a difficult task. There is little time for the inspection of bids on war supplies and the letting of contracts to the lowest bidder. Contracts must often be let for goods not hitherto in production, so that there is no adequate measure of probable cost. On mass production contracts there is seldom or never adequate competition among would-be producers to insure reasonable costs to the government. During World War I the government had made extensive use of cost-plus-fixed-fee contracts, whereby producers received fixed amounts above whatever costs were incurred. Such contracts, however, provided no sufficient incentive to produce economically. They often resulted in wasteful production and in much deplored profiteering at the expense of the government.

During World War II, through the Renegotiation Act, Congress

31 Bowles v. Willingham, 321 U.S. 503, 517–519.

resorted to a different device to curb exorbitant profits on war contracts. Permitting the making of contracts at such figures as were
sufficient to insure production, it set up machinery for the renegotiation of contracts wherever circumstances disclosed that excess profits
were made. By means of this machinery the government recaptured,
or withheld original payment of, amounts which went beyond the
range of reasonable returns on contract jobs. The arrangement by
no means pared profits to the bone or recaptured all profits that
might be deemed excessive but it did eliminate some gross waste.

Although no case reached the Supreme Court until after cessation
of military hostilities, the Renegotiation Act was challenged as unconstitutional on the ground of violation of contract rights by means
of unconstitutional delegation of renegotiation authority to administrative officials. The Supreme Court unanimously upheld the statute.
The purpose of the statute, said Justice Burton, had been

> To enable us to take the leading part in winning World War II on
> an unprecedented scale of total global warfare without abandoning
> our traditional faith in and reliance upon private enterprise and in-
> dividual initiative devoted to the public welfare.[32]

In enacting the measure Congress was exercising its constitutional
power to support armies, which was on a comparable level with its
power to raise armies as exercised in the Selective Service Act.

> Given this mission, Congress then had to choose between possible al-
> ternatives for its performance. In the light of the compelling neces-
> sity for the immediate production of vast quantities of war goods, the
> first alternative, all too clearly evident to the world, was that which
> Congress did not choose, namely, that of mobilizing the productive
> capacity of the nation into a governmental unit of the totalitarian
> model. This would have meant the conscription of property and of
> workmen. It would have meant the raising of supplies for the Armies
> in much the same manner as that in which Congress raised the man-
> power for such armies. . . . Faced with this ironical alternative of con-
> verting the nation in effect into a totalitarian state in order to pre-
> serve itself from totalitarian domination, that alternative was stead-
> fastly rejected. The plan for Renegotiation of Profits which was
> chosen in its place by Congress appears in its true light as the very
> symbol of a free people united in reaching unequalled productive

[32] Lichter v. United States, 334 U.S. 742, 746 (1948).

capacity and yet retaining the maximum of individual freedom consistent with a general mobilization of effort.[33]

The Supreme Court upheld the government in its fixing of prices even when it took over property which owners preferred not to sell at government prices. Owners of property taken by eminent domain were protected by the provision in the Fifth Amendment forbidding the taking of private property for public use without just compensation, but the Court showed inclination to accept administrative judgment as to the compensation that was just. A key case involved a corporation from which the government took by eminent domain 760,000 pounds of black pepper out of a stock of 17,000,000 pounds which the corporation was holding for higher prices than those allowed by OPA ceiling prices. The government paid only the ceiling price. The Court of Claims held that the corporation could not be compelled to sell its property at ceiling prices and set a figure at more than twice the ceiling figure. The Supreme Court overruled that decision, holding that when the government found it necessary to take property by eminent domain the "just compensation" which the Constitution required it to pay could be measured by the standard of fairness employed under the Emergency Price Control Act.[34] Here again the emphasis was on the right of the government to get supplies at reasonable prices rather than on the right of the corporation to make profit in time of war. This emphasis ran through the several cases involving wartime prices.

## THE WAR'S IMPACT ON PERSONAL RIGHTS AND LIBERTIES

### CONSCRIPTION

Educated during World War I to the necessity for conscription of military manpower, the United States resorted to it through the Selective Training and Service Act of 1940, enacted more than a year before the beginning of our formal participation in the war. Lower federal courts upheld the constitutionality of peacetime conscription, and the Supreme Court apparently regarded the issue as so well settled that it refrained from hearing argument on the subject. Exercise of the power was again provided for in the Selective Service Act

---

33 *Ibid.,* p. 766. For discussion of profiteering during World War I when the rights of the people were inadequately protected by appropriate legislation, see United States *v.* Bethlehem Steel Corporation, 315 U.S. 289 (1942).

34 United States *v.* Commodities Trading Corporation, 339 U.S. 121 (1950).

of 1948 and in the Universal Military Training and Service Act of 1951. Most of the litigation over conscription was initiated by conscientious objectors, many of them Jehovah's Witnesses, who were told, as were conscientious objectors during World War I, that they had no constitutional right to immunity from conscription but only such rights as Congress had seen fit to confer by statute.

The power of conscription was directly exercised only in connection with military service. Conscientious objectors, it is true, were required to do non-military work of national importance, and the constitutionality of this requirement was upheld. But, although indirect methods were used to channel civilian workers into employment where they were most needed for war purposes, and to keep them there, the government did not resort to conscription of men to work in privately owned plants which were producing war supplies. The scope of government power in this area is still a matter for speculation. The thought of such conscription is offensive to many people, but so also is the thought of government operation of plants by means of military personnel. Should conscription for civilian employment develop, the attempt would no doubt be made to render it palatable, as in the instance of military conscription, by pension awards, educational benefits, and protection of rights to pre-conscription civilian jobs.

LIMITING RIGHTS OF CITIZENS

During World War II as during other wars, the government found it necessary in various way to limit the rights which citizens were accustomed to exercise. Such limitation, when applied to all citizens without discrimination, was taken as a matter of course. It brought constitutional challenge, however, when it meant discrimination against natural born citizens of the Japanese race only, and when it applied only to citizens by naturalization. Restriction of the rights of Americans of Japanese ancestry resulted from anxiety over the presence of large numbers of such persons on the Pacific coast at the beginning of the war when the coast was vulnerable to attack and when the presence of enemies among them was greatly feared. Additional anxiety in the matter is said to have been stimulated by local anti-Japanese groups seeking excuse to expel people of the Japanese race and to terminate Japanese ownership of local property.

To meet the danger that might lurk among residents of the Japanese race, Congress, the President, and the military commander in the Pacific coast area co-operated to supervise the conduct of dangerous persons in the area and eventually to bring about their removal therefrom. There was no question about the constitutionality of the supervision, detention, or removal of enemy aliens, whether Japanese, Germans, or Italians. There was question, however, about the right to discriminate against American citizens merely on the basis of their race. The first case to reach the Supreme Court arose when Gordon Kiyoshi Hirabayashi, an American citizen, violated a military order requiring all enemy aliens and all persons of Japanese ancestry in certain districts to be within their places of residence each day from 8:00 P.M. to 6:00 A.M. Hirabayashi contended that as an American citizen he was entitled to all the rights and immunities of other American citizens, that his rights were protected by the Fifth Amendment, and that Congress had unconstitutionally delegated to a military commander the power to make such an order.

The Supreme Court, no doubt impressed by the gravity of the military situation, unanimously upheld the constitutionality of the military order, with three concurring opinions expressing the concern of justices for the invasion of liberty involved. Said Chief Justice Stone for the Court:

> We cannot close our eyes to the fact, demonstrated by experience, that in time of war residents having ethnic affiliations with an invading enemy may be a greater source of danger than those of a different ancestry. Nor can we deny that Congress, and the military authorities acting with its authorization, have constitutional power to appraise the danger in the light of facts of public notoriety. We need not now attempt to define the ultimate boundaries of the war power. We decide only the issue as we have defined it — we decide only that the curfew order as applied, was within the boundaries of the war power.[35]

Although the military situation had vastly improved when the Court passed on a more drastic military order, that excluding Japanese-Americans altogether from certain areas, it upheld the constitutionality of the order. Justice Black, speaking for the Court, noted that investigations had indeed disclosed the presence of disloyal persons within the group in question, and that some five thousand persons in the group had refused to swear unqualified allegiance to the United States and to renounce allegiance to the Japanese Em-

---

[35] Hirabayashi v. United States, 320 U.S. 81, 101–102 (1943).

peror. While perhaps hinting that the military situation might have changed far enough that what had previously been an exercise of constitutional power would now be unconstitutional, Justice Black announced cautiously for the Court that

> We uphold the exclusion order as of the time it was made and when the petitioner violated it.[36]

Of the three dissenters, Justice Roberts considered the order a clear violation of constitutional rights, declaring it to be

> The case of convicting the citizen as a punishment for not submitting to imprisonment in a concentration camp, based on his ancestry, and solely because of his ancestry, without evidence or inquiry concerning his loyalty or good disposition toward the United States.[37]

Justice Murphy, who had thought that the curfew order involved in the earlier case had gone to the very brink of constitutional power, found the removal order a

> racial restriction which is one of the most sweeping and complete deprivations of constitutional rights in the history of this nation in the absence of martial law.[38]

Although all the justices were deeply concerned about the line of demarcation between the constitutional rights of citizens and the power of the nation to defend itself against enemies, it was Justice Jackson, the third dissenter, who most fully exposed the predicament in which the Court found itself. Concerned both with protecting constitutional rights and with preserving freedom of military action which might not be easily subject to constitutional tests, he came close to arguing that the waging of war was extra-constitutional and not to be measured by such tests at all. He thought it dangerous and impractical idealism to expect military commands in an area of probable military operations to conform to conventional tests of constitutionality. The paramount requirement of military action, he contended, was that it should be successful rather than that it should be legal. Military orders "may have a certain authority as military commands, although they may be very bad as constitutional law." [39]

[36] Korematsu v. United States, 323 U.S. 214, 219 (1944).
[37] Ibid., p. 226.
[38] Ibid., p. 235.
[39] Ibid., p. 244.

If military orders were not to be confined by the Constitution, Jackson continued, neither would he distort the Constitution to approve all the military might deem expedient — something the Court in this case appeared to be doing. In the very nature of things, military decisions were not susceptible of judicial appraisal.

> Much is said of the danger to liberty from the army program for deporting and detaining these citizens of Japanese extraction. But a judicial construction of the due process clause that will sustain this order is a far more subtle blow to liberty than the promulgation of the order itself. A military order, however unconstitutional, is not apt to last longer than the military emergency. Even during that period a succeeding command may revoke it all. But once a judicial opinion rationalizes such an order to show that it conforms to the Constitution, or rather rationalizes the Constitution to show that the Constitution sanctions such an order, the Court for all time has validated the principle of racial discrimination in criminal procedure and of transplanting American citizens. The principle then lies about like a loaded weapon ready for the hand of any authority that can bring forward a plausible claim of an urgent need. Every repetition imbeds that principle more deeply in our law and thinking and expands it to new purposes. All who observe the work of courts are familiar with what Judge Cardozo described as "the tendency of a principle to expand itself to the limit of its logic." A military commander may overstep the bounds of constitutionality, and it is an incident. But if we review and approve, that passing incident becomes the doctrine of the Constitution. There it has a generative power of its own, and all it creates will be in its own image. Nothing better illustrates this danger than does the Court's opinion in this case.[40]

The discussion is important, not because the Jackson dissenting opinion had any direct effect upon the law but because it points up a dangerous rift between constitutional principles as we have known them and the régime of military necessities in time of war or threatened war. The rift was to appear again in later cases.

As far as treatment of Americans of Japanese ancestry was concerned, the Supreme Court at the same time called a halt to another military expedient. Thousands of Japanese-Americans who were expelled from their homes were detained against their will in relocation centers. Avoiding the question of constitutionality, the Court held that neither the statute nor the executive orders based on it jus-

[40] *Ibid.,* pp. 245–246.

tified the detention.[41] The decision seemed to imply that the statute would have been unconstitutional had it authorized the detention. Two justices, Roberts and Murphy, insisted on saying so.

## RIGHTS OF NATURALIZED CITIZENS

Supreme Court decisions during World War II protected more fully the constitutional rights of naturalized citizens than those of natural born citizens of Japanese ancestry. The rights of naturalized citizens were jeopardized because of abuses by some members of the group. American citizenship, with its attendant rights and privileges, was desired even by persons having no admiration for our institutions. Furthermore, there was reason for believing that members of Fascist, Nazi, and Communist groups in other countries had deliberately applied for American citizenship to enable them with impunity to spread subversive doctrines in this country. It was a well recognized principle that American citizenship, once conferred, could not be taken away from any person remaining in residence in the United States.

As naturalized citizens took advantage of their sheltered position to organize and lead groups in the United States hostile to American institutions, government officials sought ways to put an end to their misuse of American hospitality. The primary effort made was to show that, as proved by the disloyal conduct, the naturalized citizens in question had received their citizenship illegally. If such a showing could be made, citizenship papers could be canceled and the holders could be deported as undesirable aliens.

The first case involving an attempt to cancel citizenship papers because of subversive activities was decided by the Supreme Court in 1943, involving a member of the Communist Party, at a time when the Soviet Union was a military ally of the United States. The government contended that since William Schneiderman had been a member of the Communist Party at the time of his naturalization in 1927 he had not taken the oath of allegiance to the United States in good faith, and his naturalization certificate had been illegally procured. Wendell Willkie, the recently defeated Republican candidate for the presidency, argued that Schneiderman had conformed to all legal requirements and that citizenship, once conferred, could not be taken away.

Six members of the Supreme Court agreed with Willkie. Justice

41 *Ex parte* Endo, 323 U.S. 283 (1944).

Murphy, speaking for the Court, noted the fact that it was for Congress to set up the rules for naturalization but that once citizenship had been conferred by a court in conformity to the rules, a later court could not withdraw citizenship because of a different view of the person's fitness for it. Justice Rutledge, concurring, noted the consideration uppermost in the minds of all the majority justices: although immediately the case involved only one man, indirectly it affected millions. It affected all naturalized citizens. Any one of them might be deprived of his citizenship at any time.

> No citizen with such a threat hanging over his head could be free. If he belonged to "off-color" organizations or held too radical or, perhaps, too reactionary views, for some segment of the judicial palate, when his admission took place, he could not open his mouth without fear his words would be held against him.[42]

The government carried to the Supreme Court another test case involving cancellation of a naturalization certificate, this one involving a German naturalized in 1932 who thereafter became an enthusiast for Hitler and his doctrines of German superiority. The government attempted to show by the man's subsequent conduct that he had never given allegiance to the United States as he had sworn to do, and that he had therefore acquired American citizenship by fraud. The entire Supreme Court agreed that the government had failed to show that blatant sponsorship of Hitler at a later date proved fraud as of the date of naturalization.[43] With this decision the government was compelled to give up hope of coping with spuriously acquired citizenship of the kind involved in war issues by means of denaturalization proceedings, and people who had been naturalized in good faith were left to breathe more easily over their status. They were left, in other words, in the exact position of natural born citizens as far as their conduct was concerned. They could be punished for violation of the laws but they could not be deprived of their citizenship and deported as aliens.[44] If their behavior constituted a menace to their adopted country, they could be punished or restrained only by the means applied to natural born citizens guilty of like conduct.

[42] Schneiderman v. United States, 320 U.S. 118, 167 (1943).

[43] Baumgartner v. United States, 322 U.S. 665 (1944).

[44] In Girouard v. United States, 328 U.S. 61 (1946) the Supreme Court overruled United States v. Schwimmer, 279 U.S. 644 (1929), and other cases in which it had been held that the statutes concerning naturalization required the taking of an oath to participate in defense of the country against its enemies, thereby excluding pacifists from naturalization.

After the beginning of the war crisis in the late nineteen-thirties Congress progressively restricted the rights of aliens to come indiscriminately to the United States and to live here unwatched by government. They were required to register with the government and to give periodic notice of place of residence and activity. Aliens with subversive intentions found entrance into this country increasingly difficult and, if admitted to the country, faced a growing threat of deportation for subversive conduct. Supreme Court decisions during the period dealt with the rights of aliens only at scattered points. Although a majority of the Court always adhered to the position that the government had full power to exclude any and all aliens as it saw fit and to deport aliens already here, members often divided over whether deportation or exclusion had actually been authorized by Congress in certain instances. Minority justices argued that, since aliens in this country were entitled to the constitutional protection of due process of law and equal protection of the laws, their rights in deportation proceedings had to be safely guarded.

An important non-war deportation case that was decided during the war period had to do with Harry Bridges, a highly controversial labor leader from Australia, who was alleged to be promoting the cause of communism among longshoremen in the Pacific area. In a concurring opinion in the case which held that deportation was not authorized by existing statutes Justice Murphy declared that

> Seldom if ever in the history of this nation has there been such a concentrated and relentless crusade to deport an individual because he dared to exercise the freedom that belongs to him as a human being and that is guaranteed to him by the Constitution.[45]

Through his labor union leadership Bridges antagonized conservative interests represented among employers, veterans' groups, police departments and others, interests which found him vulnerable primarily to the charge of communism on which they hoped to get him deported. The existence of communism among longshoremen was well known but affiliation by Bridges was hard to prove. In 1934 and 1935 the Immigration and Naturalization Service cleared him after an extensive investigation. In 1938 he was again cleared for the same agency by Dean James M. Landis of Harvard Law School, who served

[45] Bridges *v.* Wixon, 326 U.S. 135, 157 (1945).

as a special examiner. Then, in the Alien Registration Act of 1940, Congress included a provision widely believed sufficient to authorize Bridges' deportation. It applied to any alien who was or at the time of entry had been a member of or affiliated with an organization advocating the forceful overthrow of the government. The question of the power to deport Bridges under this provision was taken to the Supreme Court in the case mentioned above.

The government had sought to prove that Bridges was or had been a member of the Communist Party or that he had been affiliated with the party within the meaning of the statute in that he had worked closely with the party and supported its candidates for political office. Five members of the Supreme Court, however, speaking through Justice Douglas, held that his conduct did not constitute "affiliation" and that the hearing to prove membership had been unfair, and the attempt at deportation was again defeated.

The prolonged controversy over the deportation of Harry Bridges illustrates the difficulty of defining constitutional issues when for one reason or another the government is unable to collect a goodly share of the relevant facts. After the date of the Supreme Court decision here discussed, naturalization proceedings were completed and Bridges became a United States citizen. But shortly after that step was taken, evidence was brought to light that Bridges had perjured himself in the deportation hearings. He was brought to trial, convicted of perjury and given a heavy jail sentence, whereafter in still another judicial proceeding his certificate of naturalization was canceled. He was now back in the position of an alien who had violated our laws and was subject to deportation. Once again, however, he appealed to the Supreme Court. That Court set aside his conviction, not on the ground of absence of guilt but on the ground that the statute of limitations prevented the government from prosecuting him at this late date.[46] Once again, therefore, the issue of citizenship was back in controversy. The difficulty of the case illustrates the difficulty of many such cases — that of getting sufficient facts about the case for use in court at the right time. Access to the relevant facts as well as knowledge of law is essential to the doing of justice.

During the war, under the Alien Enemy Act of 1798, the Attorney General had the unquestioned power to expel enemy aliens from the United States. Such aliens had no legal right to a hearing before deportation, and they had no right to judicial review. The Supreme

46 Bridges v. United States, 346 U.S. 209 (1953).

Court upheld the exercise of this power as to a German alien even after military hostilities had ceased. Although a hearing had been provided before the order of deportation was issued, the alien involved challenged its fairness. The Court took the position that since there was no constitutional right to a hearing of any kind at all, it could not pass on the fairness of the hearing that was granted.

Here again, however, the Court was divided. Four justices contended that the power of removal without a hearing could not be exercised in the period after the complete collapse and surrender of Germany, and Justice Black, for the group, deplored the fact that "because of today's opinion individual liberty will be less secure tomorrow than it was yesterday." [47] The minority contended that the deportee was entitled to the notice and hearing ordinarily required in administrative proceedings by due process of law.

With the development of the "cold war" with the Soviet Union and the shooting war in Korea, both Congress and the administration used a firmer hand in effort to deport from the country aliens whose conduct indicated that they might be communist agents. In the cases reaching the Supreme Court a majority of the Court upheld the measures taken, with minorities dissenting on the ground of violation of constitutional rights. Communist sympathizers and agents who had in earlier years felt safe in acting openly now found it advisable to go "underground," with the result that it was often difficult to deal with them on the basis of current conduct without disclosing American personnel and methods of espionage. Although current activities were often known to the government, it found it advisable to proceed under provisions of the Alien Registration Act of 1940 which authorized deportation for subversive activities either at the time of entry into the United States or at any time thereafter. Only Justices Black and Douglas challenged the power of the government to deport any alien at any time for any reason.[48] With three justices dissenting on constitutional grounds and one on the ground of statutory interpretation, the Court upheld the power of the government to hold under arrest without bail aliens scheduled for deportation whose temporary freedom was deemed dangerous.[49] Once more the judicial battle took place over location of the line between legitimate govern-

[47] Ludecke v. Watkins, 335 U.S. 160, 183 (1948).
[48] See Harisiades v. Schaughnessy, 342 U.S. 580 (1952). These justices rejected the doctrine of full power to deport aliens which was asserted in Fong Yue Ting v. United States, 149 U.S. 698 (1893).
[49] Carlson v. Landon, 342 U.S. 524 (1952).

ment action for protection of American institutions and the rights of individuals — individuals who in these cases were aliens.

## PUNISHMENT OF CRIME

### TREASON

During World War II, as during other wars, many people were punished for espionage, sedition, and other serious offenses connected with the war. Some, furthermore, were guilty of the ugly crime of treason, one of the most serious of crimes of which any person can be guilty. In keeping with the narrow definition of treason in the Constitution itself — limiting it to levying war against the United States or adhering to our enemies, with guilt proved only by two witnesses to the same overt act or by confession in open court — the Supreme Court restricted narrowly the application of treason statutes. In the case of Cramer v. United States [50] the Court analyzed at length the nature of treason and the kind of evidence necessary to prove it. In a five-to-four decision reversing a judgment of conviction, the majority, through Justice Jackson, traced the history of the law of treason in England and in the United States to show why the framers of the Constitution insisted on a narrow definition of treason and on specific requirements as to the evidence for conviction. The framers had been concerned about the use of treason charges as a method of fighting political opponents and about convictions for treason secured on inadequate evidence or by perjury when public passions were aroused. In the face of criticism from an indignant minority of four justices, Justice Jackson explained that in spite of a complex of evidence as to misconduct on the part of the defendant, the offenses sworn to by two or more witnesses did not in themselves constitute overt acts of treason within the meaning of the Constitution.

However, fears of the minority that the Cramer decision made conviction for treason virtually impossible were stilled in an only slightly dissimilar case wherein the allegedly "overt acts" were more clearly delineated.[51] Convictions for treason, indeed, were secured in a considerable number of war cases in spite of the difficulty of proof, while related offenses, as stated above, were punished under other categories, where prosecution is less restricted by constitutional definitions and requirements as to evidence for conviction.

[50] 325 U.S. 1 (1945).
[51] Haupt v. United States, 330 U.S. 631 (1947).

MILITARY TRIALS FOR CIVILIANS

Since a major war always brings vast expansion of the military establishment, the strict and often harsh rules which govern military activities inevitably reach more people than in time of peace. As military activities extend into zones occupied by civilians, the activities of the latter tend to fall within some kind or degree of military jurisdiction. Our formal participation in World War II began with the dropping of Japanese bombs on Pearl Harbor, which precipitated a régime of military control of civilian life in the Hawaiian Islands. As authorized by the Hawaiian Organic Act, the act of Congress setting up the Hawaiian territorial government, the governor of Hawaii immediately proclaimed martial law and suspended the privilege of the writ of habeas corpus, with the result that much of the government of the territory passed into the hands of the military. The action was approved by the President. Military tribunals took the place of civilian courts for the trial even of civilian offenses, uncontrolled by the rules of evidence and procedure that governed civilian courts. Federal and territorial laws and military orders were enforced swiftly and firmly without resort to procedures deemed necessary to the finer shadings of justice in common law countries. Military government of civilian life continued well beyond the time when the immediate Japanese threat to Hawaii had ceased.

Continuation of military government of civilians was challenged in the case of Duncan v. Kahanamoku,[52] which reached the Supreme Court in 1946, after military hostilities had ceased. The case involved offenses committed by civilians in 1942 and 1944 — embezzlement in one instance and brawling with Marine sentries in the other — for which prison sentences had been given by military courts. The Supreme Court held that in authorizing proclamation of martial law the Hawaiian Organic Act "was not intended to authorize the supplanting of courts by military tribunals." [53] It was clear that some members of the Court believed that Congress could give no such power, at least beyond the period of the military emergency. The decision sharply delimited military power over civilians. It had important implications for any future war in which an attempt might be made to govern danger zones of our own territory exclusively through military agencies. It marked an attempt to preserve the

[52] 327 U.S. 304 (1946). For discussion of military trials during World War I see Chapter 26.
[53] Ibid., p. 324.

protections of civil jurisdiction to the maximum degree consistent at all with public safety.

## MILITARY TRIALS FOR MILITARY PERSONNEL

In a different category were military trials for military personnel. A number of war cases were decided by the Supreme Court dealing with the scope of this military power and with the jurisdiction of the civil courts to define the limits of the military jurisdiction. The first such case, *Ex parte* Quirin,[54] arose early in the war period. It involved the conduct of men who, in June, 1942, landed secretly from German submarines on the coasts of New York and Florida, buried their military uniforms, and departed in civilian dress to destroy war industries and war facilities in the United States. All the men had been born in Germany but had recently been resident in the United States, where they had acquired knowledge of the country which made them peculiarly valuable to Germany. One of them claimed American citizenship by virtue of the naturalization of his father. All of them had returned to Germany for training in a sabotage school. The time had now come to reap the benefits of their training. Their hopes were quickly dashed when they were picked up by agents of the Federal Bureau of Investigation.

The saboteurs, as they were commonly called, had evidently assumed that if they were caught while landing from enemy submarines and while in enemy uniforms they would be made prisoners of war with all the protections commonly accorded to such prisoners. But they had evidently assumed also that if they were caught after donning civilian clothes and engaging in sabotage they would be treated as civilians; as such they would be entitled to the protections involved in indictment by grand jury, trial by jury, and application of the strict rules of evidence required for conviction in civil courts. Instead, the President, as commander in chief of the army and navy, appointed a military commission to try them for offenses against the law of war and the Articles of War — federal statutes dealing with the conduct of war. In the federal district court for the District of Columbia, the saboteurs challenged the power of the President to bring about their trial by military procedures before a military tribunal instead of by procedures with constitutional safeguards before a civil court. The district court rejected their claim and the circuit court of appeals followed suit. The Supreme Court shattered prec-

54 317 U.S. 1 (1942).

edent by convening a special term on July 29, 1942, to hear appeal in the case.

The saboteurs lost by a unanimous decision, including the member of the group who claimed American citizenship. The Supreme Court held that as members of the armed forces of the enemy they were subject to military jurisdiction and could be brought to trial before a military tribunal for military offenses. Had they been captured in uniform they would have been entitled to the protection given to lawful combatants. But having been captured out of uniform and charged with plotting destructive activities connected with the war, they were unlawful combatants, and as such were subject to military trial for violation of the law of war, a kind of international common law with respect to the conduct of war. American citizenship, the court held, gave no protection against such trial to a person who acted as a member of the military forces of the enemy. The military trial was thereafter carried to completion and, with the exception of two who were said to have provided testimony of aid to the prosecution, the saboteurs were put to death. The decision stands as a landmark outlining the scope of the jurisdiction of military tribunals. It stands also as an indication of the one thing the Supreme Court will do on behalf of military personnel held by military tribunals. In the language of Robert E. Cushman,

> What the Court did and held appears to boil down to this: the Court will look at the question of the detention of anybody under circumstances so unusual or suspicious as to raise the question whether he may possibly be entitled to a civilian trial. It is an important protection to civil liberty that the Court, in its discretion, is willing to take this initial look.[55]

Grimly important also were controversies over the scope of the power of military tribunals to try military personnel for military offenses. Outraged citizens of the United States contended that the military leaders of enemy nations were subject to military trial for violations of the law of war and of international conventions concerning the conduct of war. With its allies the United States participated in establishment of an International Military Tribunal to try the leading criminals of the European Axis powers. Justice Robert H. Jackson, of the Supreme Court, was appointed as the representative of the

[55] Robert E. Cushman, "The Case of the Nazi Saboteurs," *American Political Science Review*, Vol. XXX (Dec., 1942), p. 1090.

United States to work with representatives of the British, the French, and the Soviet governments. The charter of the tribunal was based on principles and practices of law in the four countries. An indictment was drawn charging twenty-four persons with conspiracy to wage aggressive war, breaches of international peace, violation of rules of warfare, and wholesale crimes against humanity.

The trial was carried on for a period of 216 days at Nürnberg, Germany, before judges of the four countries. Extensive testimony and huge quantities of war records demonstrated the gross misconduct of German defendants. The outcome was the sentence of death for twelve defendants and imprisonment for seven others. Outraged sentiments throughout the world supported the treatment accorded the defendants, but people concerned about legal institutions were troubled by the trial, conducted as it was by a tribunal set up by the victor nations for prosecution and punishment of the leaders of the vanquished. Gross as were the offenses against the peoples on whom the Axis powers made war, and even against persecuted peoples within their own populations, these offenses were not at this time clearly outlawed by any rule of international law. The United Nations, therefore, with the United States as a leading participant, were setting up a tribunal not only to apply law but also to make the law to be applied to offenses already committed. It is an obvious fact that American courts and other courts to some degree make law, or at least extend law, in the process of applying it, but they do not operate in this sweeping fashion. They move only short step by short step in the development of the legal pattern. At Nürnberg, by contrast, an attempt was made in the process of one series of interlinked decisions to create a vast pattern of law and apply it to offenses antedating not only the decision but also any clear statement of the law as law and antedating the life of the tribunal itself. The process was a process of legislation as well as of adjudication, legislation of the nature of ex post facto law which is anathema to the Anglo-Saxon tradition and for the United States is specifically forbidden in the Constitution.

Although one of its own members participated as organizer and later as prosecutor at Nürnberg, the Supreme Court was not required to express itself in any way about the trial. However, when a similar trial of war criminals was held at Tokyo, resulting likewise in convictions, certain defendants sought in the Supreme Court a review of the right of the Tokyo military tribunal to try them. In Hirota

It refused to follow an American tribunal to foreign soil to inquire into jurisdiction over alien enemies who had never been on American soil. It therefore left to the military and to administration a vast amount of discretion in the application of military justice. It presumably left to Congress and the executive the responsibility for such improvement in military justice as our sentiments of justice in future years may require. As after World War I, so after World War II Congress enacted legislation to improve the safeguards of military justice, enacting in this instance a *Uniform Code of Military Justice* for use by the three armed services. But it remains to be seen whether the ends of justice will be adequately served in mass action by military tribunals without the injection of more in the way of the principles and practices of the civil judiciary.

# CHAPTER 39

# CRISES FOR LIBERTY

BETWEEN THE EARLY 1940's and the present day, cases involving questions of constitutional liberty came thick and fast from many directions. They dealt with freedom of religion, freedom of assembly, and freedom of speech and press in great variety. The cases involved control of education, labor issues of many kinds, postal censorship, peonage, controversies over contempt of court, bills of attainder, defenses against communist interpenetration, problems of racial discrimination, and a host of procedural problems on which the rights of individuals depended. It is hard to find unity among them save in the suggestion that the Supreme Court, having recognized the necessity for retreat from the earlier line of protection of rights of property, attempted to protect the basic principles of American institutions by holding the line or even advancing the line for protection of civil liberties. This suggestion seems to have validity, particularly for the period of the early and middle 1940's when Justices Murphy and Rutledge, the most ardent defenders of civil liberties, were members of the Court.

Yet the defenses of liberty were fragmentary, as they ordinarily have to be in view of the fact that the Court has to deal with issues piecemeal as cases are brought before it. Patterns of judicial thought reveal them in some groups of cases but not in others. Patterns were often obscured by the unprecedented number of divisions among the justices. In advance of the discussion it can be said that the Court never effectively came to grips with the over-all problems of liberty as the conflict between the western and eastern worlds increased in intensity, necessitating more and more restrictions on rights hitherto deemed not subject to restriction. The synthesis on the subject of liberty under the pressures of national defense and war remained for statement in some case or cases not yet decided. The thinking of the justices, as of the people at large, developed gradually without bringing a clear perception of the vast changes necessary to our constitutional pattern if we were to hold ourselves secure in the face of the hostility of vast regions of the world and the jealousy and envy of others. This chapter presents some of the groups of liberty cases to illustrate the work of the Court in this field.

## RELIGION AND EDUCATION

SALUTING THE FLAG

Through the constitutional law of the years in question ran a number of strands of controversy over rights involved in the overlapping of religious belief or desire to be protected against exposure to religious belief, and the machinery of education. Examples were in cases involving the constitutionality of state laws requiring that children in public schools regularly go through the ceremony of saluting the American flag. The flag is a symbol of national unity. Encouragement of such unity is a legitimate function of government and of education. In the language of Justice Frankfurter,

> The ultimate foundation of a free society is the binding tie of cohesive sentiment. Such a sentiment is fostered by all those agencies of the mind and spirit which may serve to gather up the traditions of a people, transmit them from generation to generation, and thereby create that continuity of a treasured common life which constitutes a civilization.[1]

The Supreme Court therefore upheld a Pennsylvania requirement that all children salute the American flag. It did so, however, in the face of an argument that the requirement denied religious freedom to children of Jehovah's Witnesses who were taught by their sect that saluting the flag was a kind of idolatry. Since by state law the children were required to attend school, they were in effect forced to violate their religious principles.

Justice Stone delivered a lone dissent in which he declared that the Pennsylvania statute did more than suppress freedom of speech and prohibit the free exercise of religion. By means of the statute, he contended, the state sought to coerce children to express a sentiment which they did not entertain and which violated their deepest religious convictions.

Certain members of the Court majority seem to have watched the results of the decision as states relying thereon attempted to prosecute as incorrigible delinquents the children of Jehovah's Witnesses

[1] Minersville School District *v.* Gobitis, 310 U.S. 586, 596 (1940).

who refused to salute the flag. The principle of the decision was used to support a requirement of saluting the flag as a condition of distributing literature, which was a technique widely used by this sect in spreading its propaganda. In these and other ways the rite which was intended to build respect for the flag was used to bring disgrace upon it.[2] In a case not directly involving the same issue three justices, Black, Douglas, and Murphy, expressed their belief that the Pennsylvania case had been wrongly decided.[3] When another flag salute case came up from West Virginia the Court overruled the Pennsylvania decision. Justice Jackson for the majority of six noted that the power of the state to foster national unity by persuasion and example was not in question, but he argued that coercive indoctrination was both futile and unconstitutional.

> Those who begin coercive elimination of dissent soon find themselves exterminating dissenters. Compulsory unification of opinion achieves only the unanimity of the graveyard. . . . Freedom to differ is not limited to things that do not matter much. That would be a mere shadow of freedom. The test of its substance is the right to differ as to things that touch the heart of the existing order.[4]

From 1938 through more than half a decade, the same religious sect as that involved in the flag salute cases brought to the Supreme Court a long list of cases turning on their constitutional right to distribute literature and otherwise to propagate their doctrines in the face of efforts of states and municipalities to curb their often irritating activities. Again and again the Court defended freedom of religion — and at times freedom of speech and press — as involved in the cases.[5] The opinions were written in the light of the fact that a denial of religious freedom to a possibly self-deluded sect paved the way for denial of freedom to people of any belief whatsoever. The Court, it is true, limited its defense to operations within the range of decency. It upheld conviction of a member of Jehovah's Witnesses who, when arrested, profanely denounced the arresting officer as a racketeer and a Fascist. Said Justice Murphy for the Court,

---

2 See Victor W. Rotnem and F. G. Folsom, Jr., "Recent Restrictions Upon Religious Liberty," *American Political Science Review,* Vol. XXXVI (December, 1942), 1053–1068.

3 Jones v. Opelika, 316 U.S. 584, 623–624 (1942).

4 West Virginia State Board of Education v. Barnette, 319 U.S. 1, 624, 641–642 (1943).

5 See for example Marsh v. Alabama, 326 U.S. 501 (1946) and cases there cited. See also Niemotko v. Maryland, 340 U.S. 268 (1951), and Kunz v. New York, 340 U.S. 290 (1951).

There are certain well-defined and narrowly limited classes of speech, the prevention and punishment of which has never been thought to raise any constitutional problem. These include the lewd and obscene, the profane, the libelous, and the insulting or "fighting" words — those which by their very utterance inflict injury or tend to incite an immediate breach of the peace.[6]

## AID TO RELIGIOUS EDUCATION

In queer fashion the concept of liberty has in recent years become involved in the issues of governmental aid to religious education. Restrictions are placed on the federal government by the provision of the First Amendment that

> Congress shall make no law respecting an establishment of religion, or prohibiting the free exercise thereof.

The Constitution does not mention religion in connection with its prohibitions against the states, but the Supreme Court has held that the Fourteenth Amendment, which consists primarily of such prohibitions, has the effect of making the First Amendment applicable to the states. The first of three important cases on the subject, Everson v. Board of Education,[7] dealt with a New Jersey law under which officials paid the bus transportation of children not only to public schools but to Catholic parochial schools as well. Payment of transportation to the Catholic schools was challenged as a violation of the prohibition against making any "law respecting an establishment of religion."

In the debates of the Constitutional Convention there is little evidence as to what the framers meant by "an establishment of religion." But the term "establishment" was then used to designate a given church or denomination as the church of the government, which was to receive state support and receive such favors as government conferred upon religious institutions. Although the Constitution refers to "an establishment of religion" rather than to "an establishment of a church," it seems probable that the framers had a specific intention only to prevent the federal government from selecting any church to be the recipient of support and to have the benefit of discrimination against other churches. Surveying the history of the early years, however, the Supreme Court in 1947 unanimously reached the conclu-

6 Chaplinsky v. New Hampshire, 315 U.S. 568, 571–572 (1942).
7 330 U.S. 1 (1947).

sion that the Constitution was intended to forbid all governmental aid to churches whether discriminatory or not, to erect, in the language of Thomas Jefferson, "a wall of separation between Church and State."

This conclusion would seem at first glance to condemn as unconstitutional the provision of state aid to transport children to Catholic schools. A majority of the Court, however, speaking through Justice Black, took the position that the provision of transportation was a service to the children and not to the parochial schools — that it was intended to help children get to institutions where they could receive the education required by the state, and that the fact that religious education was received from the same institution did not invalidate aid to the children. On this point four justices dissented. Justice Jackson remarked that the decision of the Court seemed utterly discordant with the constitutional interpretation agreed upon, adding that

> The case which irresistibly comes to mind as the most fitting precedent is that of Julia, who, according to Byron's reports, "whispering 'I will ne'er consent,' — consented." [7a]

In the next case in the series the Supreme Court did not "consent." It came to the Court in 1948 as Illinois *ex rel*. McCollum *v*. Board of Education.[8] It turned on the constitutionality of what was called a "released time" procedure in an Illinois community. For certain periods during the school day pupils were excused from secular classes in the public schools to attend classes in religious instruction which were given in public school class rooms by teachers provided by religious organizations. Attendance records were kept and children not attending religious classes were required to continue their secular studies. By a vote of eight to one the Court, with the majority again speaking through Justice Black, held that this arrangement gave aid to religion in violation of the Constitution. Only Justice Reed dissented.

The Illinois decision brought an enormous amount of controversy. Critics protested that if religion were to be driven completely from the schools it would mean the outlawing of Bible reading, of the observation of Christian and Jewish holidays, and of many other religious practices hitherto accepted. Religious leaders stressed the need

[7a] *Ibid.*, p. 19.
[8] 333 U.S. 203.

for procedures to preserve the religious strands of our culture. They stressed also the threat implicit in the fact that schools and organized recreation and other activities took so much of the time and attention of the younger generation as to leave little opportunity for the acquisition of religious values.

There was widespread speculation as to whether released time procedures in other states than Illinois, which made less or no use of state facilities, would likewise be found to be unconstitutional. The question was partly answered in 1952 in the case of Zorach v. Clauson,[9] involving a released time program in New York City. The program differed from that of Illinois primarily in that no use was made of public school facilities for the purposes of religious instruction, the instruction being given elsewhere. Six members of the Court, speaking through Justice Douglas, held that the program was not unconstitutional. In explanation it was said that

> We are a religious people whose institutions presuppose a Supreme Being. We guarantee the freedom to worship as one chooses. We make room for as wide a variety of beliefs and creeds as the spiritual needs of man deem necessary. We sponsor an attitude on the part of government that shows no partiality to any one group and that lets each flourish according to the zeal of its adherents and the appeal of its dogma. When the state encourages religious instruction or co-operates with religious authorities by adjusting the schedule of public events to sectarian needs, it follows the best of our traditions. For it then respects the religious nature of our people and accommodates the public service to their spiritual needs. To hold that it may not would be to find in the Constitution a requirement that the government show a callous indifference to religious groups. That would be preferring those who believe in no religion over those who do believe. Government . . . can close its doors as to those who want to repair to their religious sanctuary for worship or instruction. No more than that is undertaken here.[10]

Of the three dissenting justices it is not surprising that Justice Black, spokesman of the Court in the Illinois case, saw little to distinguish the New York case from that of Illinois. He closed his dissenting opinion with the eloquent statement that

> State help to religion injects political and party prejudices into a holy field. It too often substitutes force for prayer, hate for love, and

9 343 U.S. 306 (1952).
10 *Ibid.*, pp. 313–314.

persecution for persuasion. Government should not be allowed, under the cover of the soft euphemism of "co-operation," to steal into the sacred area of religious choice.[11]

Justice Jackson, also dissenting, voiced sarcasm in the statement that

Today's judgment will be more interesting to students of psychology and of the judicial processes than to students of constitutional law.[12]

Arguments of seeming wisdom can be advanced on either side of the question. It seems clear that the last word has not yet been said by justices on either side, partly because the subject has not yet been viewed in all its fullness. There is no doubt that the essence of religious experience must be kept free from governmental interference, and that as far as possible religious conflict must be kept out of the governmental sphere. The complicating fact remains that as government, through schools, military training, and otherwise, takes up more and more of the time of the people, and as more and more non-religious institutions are the beneficiaries of governmental aid, religion which is not similarly aided must suffer in the competition. The people must themselves decide to what extent and by what measures they wish to preserve their religious heritage. When the popular decision begins to make itself felt, the judiciary can draw constitutional lines with greater confidence.

## THE RIGHT OF SELF-EXPRESSION

### VARIETIES IN FREE SPEECH

The freedoms of religion, speech, press, and assembly are linked in the First Amendment and are generally thought of somewhat together even when they are not actually intertwined. In protecting these freedoms against state action the Supreme Court must of course rely on the Fourteenth Amendment, and treat the First Amendment, which in itself is merely a restriction on congressional action, as part of the text of the Fourteenth Amendment which restricts state action. This process of reading the two amendments is not dictated by the Constitution but was evolved by the Supreme Court itself. Having decided that the Fourteenth Amendment included the specific prohibitions appearing in the First Amendment, the Court of the New-Deal period found those specific prohibitions more potent than the general prohibition in the Fourteenth Amendment against tak-

11 *Ibid.*, p. 320.
12 *Ibid.*, p. 325.

ing life, liberty, and property without due process of law. In other words, liberty came to the fore as the subject more specifically protected, as a subject more nearly immune to interference than property, which was not mentioned in the First Amendment. Said Justice Jackson for the Court in the West Virginia flag salute case:

> The test of legislation which collides with the Fourteenth Amendment, because it also collides with the principles of the First, is much more definite than the rest when only the Fourteenth is involved. Much of the vagueness of the due process clause disappears when the specific prohibitions of the First become its standard. The right of a state to regulate, for example, a public utility may well include, so far as the due process clause is concerned, power to impose all the restrictions which a legislature may have a "rational basis" for adopting. But freedoms of speech and of press, of assembly, and of worship may not be infringed on such slender grounds. They are susceptible of restriction only to prevent grave and immediate danger to interests which the state may lawfully protect. It is important to note that while it is the Fourteenth Amendment which bears directly upon the State it is the more specific limiting principles of the First Amendment that finally govern this case.[13]

This concept of liberty as having more constitutional protection against governmental invasion than property fitted in well with the dominant New-Deal philosophy. It was referred to in case after case, usually without repetition of the reasoning based on the two constitutional amendments. When it took the form of the phrase, "the preferred position of freedom of speech in a society that cherishes liberty for all," [14] Justice Frankfurter protested against the uncritical use of the phrase.

> I deem it a mischievous phrase, if it carries the thought, which it may subtly imply, that any law touching communication is infected with presumptive invalidity.[15]

This protest, made in a concurring opinion, may have marked a turning point in judicial attitudes on the subject.

In any event, whether or not they accepted the phrase, justices continued to differ as to how far freedom of speech should be protected against state action. Examples are provided by two cases turning on

13 West Virginia State Board of Education *v.* Barnette, 319 U.S. 624, 639 (1943).
14 Kovacs *v.* Cooper, 336 U.S. 77, 88 (1949).
15 *Ibid.,* p. 90.

municipal restriction of the use of loud speakers. In Saia *v.* New York [16] the Court held unconstitutional a municipal ordinance that forbade the use of sound amplification devices except when used with the permission of the chief of police. The Court found that the ordinance gave the chief of police too much discretion over an issue of free speech. Said Justice Douglas for the Court:

> Loud speakers are today indispensable instruments of effective public speech. The sound truck has become an accepted method of political campaigning. . . . Must a candidate for governor or the Congress depend on the whim or caprice of the Chief of Police in order to use his sound truck for campaigning? Must he prove to the satisfaction of that official that his noise will not be annoying to the people? [17]

Yet four justices dissented, feeling that the mechanical amplification of sound carried such a threat to privacy that a municipality could take this means of limiting it.

In the second case, Kovacs *v.* Cooper,[18] the Court upheld an ordinance forbidding the emission of "loud and raucous noises" by sound trucks, but none of the five opinions written in the case had the support of a majority of the justices. Justice Murphy dissented without opinion. Five opinions spread out in as many directions to attempt different shadings of the right of free speech. Although as a result of the decision Charles Kovacs knew that he could not broadcast loud and raucous noises from a sound truck in violation of the ordinance, little else was known about the scope of the rights involved. The confusion is pointed up by the following statement by Justice Rutledge:

> In effect Kovacs stands convicted, but of what it is impossible to tell, because the majority upholding the conviction do not agree upon what constituted the crime. How, on such a hashing of different views of the thing forbidden, Kovacs could have known with what he was charged or could have prepared a defense, I am unable to see. How anyone can do either in the future, under this decision, I am equally at a loss to say.[19]

The two cases show how difficult is the application of general prin-

---

16 334 U.S. 558.
17 *Ibid.,* pp. 561–562.
18 336 U.S. 78 (1949).
19 *Ibid.,* p. 105.

ciples of freedom of speech to the mixed conditions of modern communication.

Another case further indicates the difficulty of applying principles to actual situations. City authorities in Syracuse, New York, had granted permission to use a public school building for a speech by O. John Rogge, a former Assistant Attorney General of the United States, on the subject of racial discrimination. When on the date set the authorities suddenly withdrew their permission, the Young Progressives, who were sponsoring the address, arranged for a meeting in a hotel and set out to attract an audience. A student, Irving Feiner, standing on a box on a sidewalk and using a loud speaker on an automobile, harangued a mixed white and colored audience, denouncing the city authorities, President Truman, and the American Legion. When Feiner ignored the requests and demands of policemen that he get down from the box, he was taken into custody. He was convicted on a charge of disorderly conduct.

Six Supreme Court justices held that the conviction did not unconstitutionally restrict free speech. Three justices earnestly insisted that it did. The facts were by no means clear enough to determine the danger of a race riot or other disturbance or the extent of interference with normal street traffic. In the judicial opinions the facts seem to be selected and weighted according to the convictions of the justices writing them. Chief Justice Vinson, for the majority, reached the conclusion that

> The findings of the state courts as to the existing situation and the imminence of greater disorder coupled with petitioner's deliberate defiance of the police officers convince us that we should not reverse this conviction in the name of free speech.[20]

Justice Black, on the other hand, deplored the fact that the Court was here abandoning the rule that it would independently examine the facts where denial of federally protected rights was in question.

> Even a partial abandonment of this rule marks a dark day for civil liberties in our Nation.
>
> But still more has been lost today. Even accepting every "finding of fact" below, I think this conviction makes a mockery of the free speech guarantees of the First and Fourteenth Amendments. . . . I will

20 Feiner v. New York, 340 U.S. 315, 321 (1951).

have no part or parcel in this holding which I view as a long step toward totalitarian authority.[21]

Justice Douglas thought the facts were such that police should have protected the speaker instead of arresting him, noting that

> Police censorship has all the vices of the censorship from city halls which we have repeatedly struck down.[22]

### RIGHTS OF LABOR

Important civil liberty controversies in this period had to do with the rights of labor. A leading question was the extent to which peaceful picketing could be classified as speech which was entitled to constitutional protection. In 1940, in Thornhill v. Alabama,[23] the Supreme Court held unconstitutional a state statute which forbade picketing even to the extent of prohibiting "a single individual from walking slowly and peacefully back and forth on the public sidewalk in front of the premises of the employer." [24] Although the Court did not go so far as to sanction all peaceful picketing under all circumstances whatsoever, the impression was created that the decision constituted a great victory for labor. Disillusionment came in later years when the Court refused to defend peaceful picketing in behalf of ends outlawed by a state, as when the purpose was in conflict with the state's anti-trust laws. Said the Court in one such case:

> It rarely has been suggested that the constitutional freedom for speech and press extends its immunity to speech or writing used as an integral part of conduct in violation of a valid criminal statute. We reject that contention now.[25]

Since a state may legitimately forbid combinations in restraint of trade on the part of labor as well as of employers, and other activities as well which labor may consider to its advantage, picketing, however peaceful, may under many circumstances be outlawed. It is of course true that whether or not the ultimate goal of a labor organi-

---

21 *Ibid.*, pp. 322–323.
22 *Ibid.*, p. 331.
23 310 U.S. 88.
24 *Ibid.*, pp. 98–99.
25 Giboney *v.* Empire Storage and Ice Co., 336 U.S. 490, 498 (1949). See also Hughes *v.* California, 339 U.S. 460 (1950), International Brotherhood *v.* Hanke, 339 U.S. 470 (1950), and Building Service E.I.U. *v.* Gazzam, 339 U.S. 532 (1950).

zation is legitimate, the Constitution does not protect it in using threats and violence to intimidate non-conforming workers.[26]

In a reaction against the growing power of labor unions a number of states forbade the making of labor contracts establishing the union shop. That is, they forbade contracts whereby non-union workers were to be denied the right of employment. Labor challenged such prohibitions as unconstitutional deprivation of freedom of speech and assembly and the right to petition for redress of grievances. The Supreme Court denied labor's claim, saying that

> The constitutional right of workers to assemble, to discuss and for-
> mulate plans for furthering their own self interest in jobs cannot be
> construed as a constitutional guarantee that none shall get and hold
> jobs except those who will join in the assembly or will agree to abide
> by the assembly's plans.[27]

Meeting from opposite poles problems involving both labor and liberty, the Supreme Court outlawed state action to compel people to work and upheld state action restricting the right of women to serve as bartenders. The former type of action, taken in Georgia and Florida, was an attempt to compel people, usually impecunious Ne-groes, to pay their debts by working them out. The social fault may have been sometimes on the part of the borrowers and sometimes of the lenders. Certain it is that Negroes often found themselves in great need and had to borrow virtually to survive. Under pressure of circumstances they incurred debts and agreed to work them out. After spending the money they lost their zeal for employment and often failed to fulfill their contracts. On the other hand, if workers could be punished by state law for violating such contracts, em-ployers could insure their labor supply by making loans and then permitting the coercive power of the state to keep workers on the job. Looking at the latter possibility, the Supreme Court held that state laws punishing as fraud the non-performance of such contracts provided for involuntary servitude in violation of the Thirteenth Amendment.[28]

On the other hand, women lost their case when they challenged the power of the State of Michigan to deny them the right to work as barmaids. Said Justice Frankfurter for the Court,

26 Cole *v.* Arkansas, 338 U.S. 345 (1950).

27 Lincoln Federal Labor Union *v.* Northwestern Iron and Metal Co., 335 U.S. 525, 531 (1949).

28 Taylor *v.* Georgia, 315 U.S. 25 (1942) and Pollock *v.* William, 322 U.S. 4 (1944).

The fact that women may now have achieved the virtues that men have long claimed as their prerogatives and now indulge in vices that men have long practiced, does not preclude the States from drawing a sharp line between the sexes, certainly in such matters as the regulation of the liquor traffic.[29]

The fact that exception was made on behalf of wives and daughters of owners of liquor establishments, who presumably operated under the watchful eyes of husbands and fathers, was likewise held to constitute no violation of the equal protection clause.

## LIBERTY AND LOYALTY

In a period of ideological conflict mixed with military conflict it was inevitable that the constitutional defense of freedom should become involved with the issues of loyalty to American institutions. It is not surprising, in view of the tangle of ideas and loyalties among the people themselves, that the Supreme Court, tying in with controversies only sporadically as cases arose, should present anything but a united front. It was not that there were gradations of loyalty on the Court. It was rather that conflicting principles and conflicting interpretations of situations made it hard to measure conduct in terms of loyalty. By the early nineteen-fifties it was hard to remember that the Soviet Union had been our ally in defeating the European Axis Powers, and that millions of honest if perhaps naïve people had believed that it would be possible to live in peaceful and friendly relations with the Soviet Union in the family of United Nations. It was hard to remember the wartime assumption that communist ideology would be softened by friendly association with the Western world, and the possible benefits seemed worth the cost of going more than half way in meeting our uncouth but not necessarily unfriendly competitor. It was hard to remember that some intellectual and political co-operation between American liberalism and economic and industrial development on the one hand and on the other hand communist organization and production for the benefit of the masses had seemed possible. It was hard to remember that we had had a vision of what Wendell Willkie had publicized as *One World*.

Opposed to accepting the picture of "one world" and to belief in friendliness with the Soviet Union were shrewd analysts of communist policy and also the economic and political reactionaries who re-

29 Goesaert *v.* Cleary, 335 U.S. 464, 466 (1948).

sented the social changes of the New Deal period and who believed in a policy of isolation as the only feasible policy for the United States under existing circumstances. As the development of the "cold war" and the shooting war in Korea demonstrated the emptiness of the idealism of the would-be friends of the Soviet Union, the stigma of disloyalty began to attach to their efforts and ideas in spite of the extent to which their ideas had been held throughout the country during the war period. Matters were made worse by disclosure of the fact that some Americans had not been merely mistaken idealists but had engaged in espionage for and had otherwise given aid to the Soviet Union at the expense of the United States. With the deepening of the cleavage between the two worlds, action to give aid and comfort to the Soviet Union smacked more and more of treason to the United States, and intelligent and loyal liberals adjusted their conduct accordingly. Unfortunately it was often impossible to draw a clear line between patriotic ferreting out of disloyal conduct and reactionary and demagogic persecution of liberals. The difficulty is revealed in a number of Supreme Court decisions.

The first Supreme Court case in this field, United States v. Lovett,[30] was decided in 1946 in a controversy which arose in the midst of the war period. The Committee on Un-American Activities,[31] of the House of Representatives, had been searching for disloyalty among government employees. In 1943, in the House of Representatives, the chairman of the committee denounced certain government employees as "irresponsible, unrepresentative, crackpot, radical bureaucrats," who were affiliates of "communist front organizations." He urged that they be removed from the government payroll. After considerable controversy Congress included in an appropriation bill a provision that after a specified date no compensation should be paid to Goodwin B. Watson, William E. Dodd, Jr., or Robert Morss Lovett, "unless prior to such date such person has been appointed by the President, by and with the consent of the Senate." Since there was no prospect of appointment of either of these men to a position requiring senatorial confirmation, the effect of the statute was permanently to exclude them from the payroll.

The statute was widely criticized by authorities on the Constitution even as it was being tested in the courts. Robert E. Cushman, as

---

[30] 328 U.S. 303 (1946).
[31] For a recent careful appraisal of the work of the Committee see Robert K. Carr, *House Committee on Un-American Activities, 1945–50* (1952).

president of the American Political Science Association, denounced the provision as "a dangerous and brutal assault upon the principles of freedom of opinion." He continued:

> Out of the welter of words by which Congress has sought to explain and justify this action, the real truth lies in the cynically frank statement of a member of the House that the men were removed from office "because we didn't like the things they said and the things they wrote." Congress and its committee apply the litmus paper of their own conventional opinions and prejudices to the views and the writings of these federal officials and dismiss them summarily if the resulting reaction looks even faintly pink.[32]

The Supreme Court unanimously held the provision unconstitutional as a bill of attainder. That is, it was a legislative act decreeing punishment without the benefit of a judicial trial, a type of measure forbidden by the Constitution. The Court did not hold that any man had a legal right to a position in the executive branch of the government in opposition to the desire of the government not to employ him or to retain him in employment, but merely that no person might in this fashion be punished for his beliefs by permanent exclusion from employment by act of Congress and without benefit of judicial trial to determine guilt of some offense prescribed by law. The three men were enabled, therefore, to continue to draw their salaries as government employees.

The next important Supreme Court case involving the loyalty issue, American Communications Association v. Douds,[33] was decided in 1950. It involved the provision of the Labor Management Relations Act of 1947 providing that in order to get the support of the federal government in enforcement of the right of collective bargaining each labor union officer must take an oath that

> he is not a member of the Communist Party or affiliated with such party, and that he does not believe in, and is not a member of or supports any organization that believes in or teaches, the overthrow of the United States Government by force or by any illegal or unconstitutional methods.

The purpose of the provision was to eliminate communist leadership in unions which was said to have infiltrated them during the

[32] Robert E. Cushman, "Civil Liberty After the War," *American Political Science Review*, Vol. XXXVIII (February, 1944), 10.

[33] 339 U.S. 382 (1950).

war. Certain union leaders challenged this alleged invasion of their freedom, hurling at it almost every conceivable charge of unconstitutionality. For various reasons three members of the Supreme Court disqualified themselves, leaving only six justices to decide the case. Five of them, speaking through Chief Justice Vinson, upheld the statute as it involved membership in or affiliation with the Communist Party, but of these only three upheld the statute as it involved not party membership but belief in the overthrow of the government. Justice Black dissented entirely, finding the statute an unconstitutional infringement of free speech.

The reasoning of the majority of the Court may be summarized as follows: In exercise of its power to regulate interstate commerce Congress had tried to facilitate relations between employers and employees by legislation on collective bargaining which strengthened the bargaining position of the workers. Later, by the Labor Management Relations Act here under attack, it had tried to remove other restrictions on interstate commerce by limiting the freedom of employees, particularly as the so-called "political strike" was involved. Elimination of communist leadership was directed to that end. Unions whose bargaining power was strengthened by government intervention could not expect their own activities affecting interstate commerce to go unrestrained.

> Because of the necessity to have strong unions to bargain on equal terms with strong employers, individual employees are required by law to sacrifice rights which, in some cases, are valuable to them. . . . The loss of individual rights for the greater benefit of the group results in a tremendous increase in the power of the representative of the group — the union. But power is never without responsibility. And when authority derives in part from Government's thumb on the scales, the exercise of that power by private persons becomes closely akin, in some respects, to its exercise by Government itself.[34]

There was here no denial of the rights guaranteed by the First Amendment but merely regulation of the commerce which Congress had the constitutional power to regulate.

The delicacy of the constitutional questions was revealed by separate opinions in which Justices Frankfurter and Jackson concurred in part and dissented in part from the opinion of the Court. They agreed that the statute could be enforced as to Communist Party

34 *Ibid.,* pp. 401–402.

membership or affiliation, and Justice Jackson presented an analysis to show the fundamental difference between the Communist Party and other political parties in the United States and to show its use as the instrument of a foreign power. But both justices thought that constitutional rights were denied when federal support to unions was conditioned on oaths taken by leaders with respect not to organization and activity but merely to belief concerning the overthrow of government. The statute, in other words, reflected an unconstitutional attempt to control belief. Justice Black, dissenting from the decision of the Court in its entirety, warned that

> Centuries of experience testify that laws aimed at one political or religious group, however rational these laws may be in their beginnings, generate hatreds and prejudices which rapidly spread beyond control. Too often it is fear which inspires such passions, and nothing is more reckless or contagious. In the resulting hysteria, popular indignation tars with the same brush all those who have even been associated with any member of the group under attack or who hold a view which, though supported by revered Americans as essential to democracy, has been adopted by that group for its purposes. . . . Today the "political affiliation" happens to be the Communist Party: testimony of an ex-Communist that some Communist union officers had called "political strikes" is held sufficient to uphold a law coercing union members not to elect any Communist as an officer. Under this reasoning, affiliations with other political parties could be proscribed just as validly.[35]

From the loyalty of labor union officers the chronological story of loyalty cases in the Supreme Court shifts back to the loyalty of government employees. Under pressure of congressional accusations of employment of subversive persons, the administration set up machinery for determining the facts. The program provided for mass investigation of loyalty of government employees and applicants for government jobs, by means of administrative procedures which contemplated a minimum of interference from courts. One wing of the procedure involved the Attorney General's listing of certain organizations as subversive. Members of those organizations were denied government employment. The Attorney General's sources of evidence for branding the organizations as subversive were not disclosed to the organizations themselves, to the government employees affected, or to any court. The organizations were branded in secret, and public

35 *Ibid.*, pp. 448–450.

discredit and dismissal of members who were government workers resulted almost automatically and in large part without judicial determination of rights.

A number of the proscribed organizations challenged in lower federal courts the power of the Attorney General, operating from behind closed doors, publicly to stigmatize them in this fashion and indirectly to penalize their members by excluding them from government employment. The courts dismissed the complaints and appeals were taken to the Supreme Court. In Joint Anti-Fascist Refugee Committee *v.* McGrath [36] that Court, in a wonderland of five opinions which defy summary or clear differentiation and with one dissenting opinion joined in by three justices, held that the proscribed organizations were entitled to relief and sent the cases back to the lower courts for further proceedings. Out of the confusion of opinions we could be sure only that the Supreme Court as constituted in 1951 would not tolerate administrative activities exactly like those here used under these exact circumstances. The Court voiced its disapproval in a babel of criticism without sufficient agreement among the justices to provide guidance for the lower courts in the further handling of these cases and others of the same kind. We can say that, in addition to the restrictions defined in the Lovett case, there are other restrictions on the methods of determining fitness for public employment. We can say that the Supreme Court showed its determination to hold somewhere a line against arbitrary administration, but that it gave so many conflicting clues as to the location of the line as in effect to give almost no clues at all. It remained to be seen, indeed, whether the Court could continue to hold any line at all if it was to continue to speak with such a multiplicity of tongues.

The difficulty in determining the position of the Court on loyalty proceedings was illustrated by another case decided on the same day as that discussed above by an equal division of eight justices, Justice Clark as a former Attorney General not voting. Dorothy Bailey, a government employee, had been deprived of her government job by a loyalty board decision, upheld by the Loyalty Review Board, on the basis of charges that she was a communist and was active in a "communist front organization." The Circuit Court of Appeals for the District of Columbia found that she was denied no constitutional rights. As is customary in cases decided by an evenly divided Supreme Court, no opinions were written in the case, but in the

[36] 341 U.S. 123 (1951).

Joint Anti-Fascist Refugee case, discussed above, Justices Douglas and Jackson took occasion to stress their opposition to upholding the lower court decision in the Bailey case. Justice Douglas noted the fact that counsel for Dorothy Bailey had been denied information as to the names of her accusers or as to their activities. The loyalty board itself lacked this information.

> The Loyalty Board convicts on evidence which it cannot even appraise. The critical evidence may be the word of an unknown witness who is "a paragon of veracity, a knave, or the village idiot." [37] His name, his reputation, his prejudices, his animosities, his trustworthiness are unknown both to the judge and to the accused. The accused has no opportunity to show that the witness has lied or was prejudiced or venal. Without knowing who her accusers are she has no way of defending. She has nothing to offer except her own word and the character and testimony of her friends.[38]

Justice Jackson, comparing the two cases decided by the Supreme Court, professed amazement that it granted judicial review and relief to the group appealing to it, while denying it to the individual.

> So far as I can recall, this is the first time this Court has held rights of individuals subordinate and inferior to those of organized groups. I think that is an inverted view of the law — it is justice turned bottom-side up.[39]

The justices who felt that Dorothy Bailey had been deprived of no constitutional rights nowhere stated their position. They may have felt that since no person has a constitutional right to be employed by government a defendant had no constitutional right to particular procedures governing his removal from such employment. They may have accepted the practical argument that to require disclosure of sources of government information about disloyalty would dry up such sources for future information of the same kind. Justice Douglas, believing that constitutional rights had been denied, nevertheless admitted that the problem of security was real. He would have followed the British practice of transferring to non-sensitive positions those employees accused of disloyalty against whom disloyalty could not be proved without denial of constitutional safeguards.

[37] Quoted from Barth, *The Loyalty of Free Men* (1951), p. 109.
[38] 341 U.S. 180.
[39] *Ibid.*, p. 186.

We meet constitutional difficulties when the Government undertakes to punish by proclaiming the disloyalty of an employee and making him ineligible for any government post.[40]

States and municipalities as well as the federal government became concerned about the loyalty of employees and enacted restrictive measures concerning employment. The measures varied from government to government but included such items as prohibition of employment of members of the Communist party and other agencies advocating the overthrow of government by force and violence and requirement of an oath denying any such membership. Cases reached the Supreme Court involving a Maryland statute prescribing such an oath as a condition of filing as a candidate for public office; [41] a Los Angeles charter provision and ordinance requiring such an oath of city employees;[42] a New York statute prohibiting employment of members of subversive organizations in public schools;[43] and an Oklahoma statute prohibiting employment of teachers unless they took an oath that they were not and for the past five past years had not been members of subversive organizations.[44] The Supreme Court upheld the regulations involved in the first three cases, although it did so unanimously in only the case from Maryland, where the candidate for office was required merely to swear that he was not engaged in the attempt to overthrow the government by force or violence and that he was not knowingly a member of an organization engaged in such an attempt. Four justices dissented in the Los Angeles case, and three in the New York case. In the Oklahoma case, in which the statute was declared unconstitutional, all justices concurred in the result.

It was unfortunate that the majority opinions were written by justices without the felicity of philosophical statement which characterized minority opinions, for there was much to be said on behalf of the right of states and municipalities to employ only people loyal to their country and its institutions, and there was much to be said on behalf of liberty, as in the Oklahoma case, which needed to be said on the authority of the Court as a whole and not merely by concurring justices. The cases illustrated the prime defect of the

40 *Ibid.,* p. 181.
41 Gerende *v.* Board of Supervisors, 341 U.S. 56 (1951). This case was decided by means of a brief Per Curiam opinion.
42 Garner *v.* Board of Public Works, 341 U.S. 716 (1951).
43 Adler *v.* Board of Education, 342 U.S. 485 (1952).
44 Wieman *v.* Updegraff, 344 U.S. 183 (1952).

Supreme Court in recent years in that majority opinions did not become a composite of the best thinking of the several members. The more persuasive statements were made either in concurring opinions or in dissents. Justice Clark, in speaking for the Court in upholding the Los Angeles regulation and striking down the Oklahoma statute, and Justice Minton in upholding the New York statute, provided no such illumination as did Justices Frankfurter, Black, and Douglas in taking their various positions. A thin line differentiated the Oklahoma case from the other three, in that, as distinguished from them, it involved a statute applicable to persons who had been members of organizations later found to be subversive whether or not the members knew them to be subversive at the time. In spite of the Oklahoma decision, the principle still holds that government may require of its employees test oaths based on beliefs and organization memberships. The danger, as seen by Justice Black in the Oklahoma case, is stated as follows:

> The Oklahoma oath statute is but one manifestation of a national network of laws aimed at coercing and controlling the minds of men. Test oaths are notorious tools of tyranny. When used to shackle the mind they are, or at least they should be, unspeakably odious to a free people. Test oaths are made still more dangerous when combined with bills of attainder which like this Oklahoma statute impose pains and penalties for past lawful associations and utterances.
>
> Governments need and have ample power to punish treasonable acts. But it does not follow that they must have a further power to punish thought and speech as distinguished from acts. Our own free society should never forget that laws which stigmatize and penalize thought and speech of the unorthodox have a way of reaching, ensnaring and silencing many more people than at first intended. We must have freedom of speech for all or we will in the long run have it for none but the cringing and the craven. And I cannot too often repeat my belief that the right to speak on matters of public concern must be wholly free or eventually be wholly lost.[45]

Of critical importance also was the case of Dennis v. United States,[46] in which the Supreme Court upheld the conviction of eleven communist leaders for conspiracy to violate the Smith Act of 1940, which forbade organization to overthrow the government by force or vio-

[45] *Ibid.*, p. 220.
[46] 341 U.S. 494 (1951).

lence. The case reflected a bitter fight from the beginning in a United States district court in New York, where some of the counsel for defendants so conducted themselves as to win sentences for contempt of court. In upholding that no constitutional rights were denied in punishing the defendants for organizing the Communist Party the Court left in confusion the clear and present danger doctrine. Once again the Court was badly divided. Four justices found existence of a clear and present danger. One justice concurred in the decision but merely deferred volubly to the judgment of Congress without relating it to the clear and present danger doctrine. Another upheld conviction even though there might be no such clear and present danger. Two justices dissented on the ground that no such danger existed, and one justice did not participate. The convictions were sustained but the law was left in confusion.

## FUNDAMENTALS OF JUSTICE

### RIGHTS OF MINORITIES

Minorities of various kinds sought protection from the Supreme Court. Discussed above are cases affecting Jehovah's Witnesses and Japanese-Americans. Included also are the above mentioned peonage cases affecting Negroes. Other cases affecting Negroes involved both the substance and the procedures of constitutional law. Many times the Court listened to accusations of racial discrimination against Negroes denying equal protection of the laws. As long ago as 1896 the Court had held that equal protection of the laws was not denied by a state statute requiring passenger trains in intrastate commerce to provide separate coaches or separate compartments for Negroes and white people.[47] The Court interpreted the statute as intended to enforce "the absolute equality of the two races before the law," while recognizing fundamental distinctions between them. This expedient of providing "separate but equal" accommodations for white and colored railway passengers was approved again and again. The Supreme Court insisted, however, that the accommodations should be equal. In 1941, for example, it recognized the rightful claim of a Negro member of Congress who, leaving Chicago on a first-class ticket for Hot Springs, Arkansas, was required under an Arkansas statute to leave the sleeping car on which he had begun his trip. The Court found it not sufficient that he had been able to complete his

47 Plessy *v.* Ferguson, 163 U.S. 537 (1896).

journey in a second-class coach. It found no justification in the fact that there was not enough demand for sleeping car accommodations to support operation of separate sleeping cars for Negroes. In order to be constitutional a requirement of separate accommodations also had to provide equal accommodations.[48] In 1950 the Court applied the same rule when Negroes were denied equal dining car facilities.[49]

Negroes and advocates of their equal rights have not been satisfied with application of the "separate but equal" rule. They have been opposed to separation as such, or segregation, and have contended, furthermore, that in most instances the separate facilities provided for colored people are not actually the equal of those provided for white people, even when nominal equality existed. On these questions the field of education became the critical area of legal controversy. As to graduate education and professional education the Supreme Court continued to insist on real equality and rejected subterfuges challenged before it. The Court found lack of equality in a Missouri statute which was intended to dispose of the responsibility for giving Negroes training in law comparable to that given to white students by paying the tuition of Negroes in the law school of some other state.[50] When Oklahoma postponed admission of a Negro woman to its law school the Court held that under the equal protection clause the state must provide equal law training, "and provide it as soon as it does for applicants of any other group."[51] When Oklahoma admitted a Negro to its law school the Court held that the state denied him equal protection of the laws by isolating him from white students in the classroom, the library, and the cafeteria.[52] The Court held that a Negro was denied equal protection of the laws by exclusion from the University of Texas Law School even though a separate and adjacent law school was maintained for Negroes, since facilities for training were not equal. Said Chief Justice Vinson for a unanimous Court:

> In terms of number of the faculty, variety of courses and opportunity for specialization, size of the student body, scope of the library, availability of law review and similar activities, the University of Texas Law School is superior. What is more important, the University of

[48] Mitchell v. United States, 313 U.S. 80 (1941).
[49] Henderson v. United States, 339 U.S. 816 (1950). This case involved only the Interstate Commerce Act and not directly the constitutional provision.
[50] Missouri ex rel. Gaines v. Canada, 305 U.S. 337 (1938).
[51] Sipuel v. University of Oklahoma, 332 U.S. 631, 633 (1948).
[52] McLaurin v. Oklahoma State Regents, 339 U.S. 637 (1950).

Texas Law School possesses to a far greater degree those qualities which are incapable of objective measurement but which make for greatness in a law school. Such qualities, to name but a few, include reputation of the faculty, experience of the administration, position and influence of the alumni, standing in the community, traditions and prestige. It is difficult to believe that one who had a free choice between these law schools would consider the question close.[53]

Insistence of the Supreme Court on actual equality as between services to the two races in professional schools led opponents in segregation to attack it in grade schools and high schools. In December, 1952 the Court heard together arguments in five cases from four states and the District of Columbia. Counsel for Negroes argued that most Negro schools are not equal to white schools and that in any event the very fact of segregation created a sense of inferiority on the part of Negro children and impaired the learning process.[54] In many states, particularly in the South, it was clear that Negro grade schools were not equal to those provided for white children. It was also clear that expenditures of large sums would be required to make them equal, that there would be tremendous protest against making such expenditures, and that if segregation as such were outlawed there would be resort to subterfuge to avoid the import of the Court decision. The record of the argument and the interchange between counsel and the justices provides fascinating evidence of the difficulties involved in dealing with such a basic social problem.[55] Unable to reach a decision, the Court restored the cases to the docket for reargument. The reargument was postponed into the régime of Chief Justice Warren.

Negroes and members of other minority groups have been discriminated against or have been segregated not only in the use of such facilities as those of public transportation and public education but also in the matter of purchase and occupation of residence property. In a series of decisions which began in 1917 [56] the Supreme Court upheld the right of white people to sell residence property to

53 Sweatt v. Painter, 339 U.S. 629, 633–634 (1950).

54 This was argued in the appeal from a case arising in Topeka, Kansas, where the lower court had held that there was equality of educational facilities. See Brown v. Board of Education, 98 Fed. Sup. 757 (1951).

55 For a summary of the arguments and discussion, see United States Law Week, Vol. 21 (December 16, 1952), pp. 3161–3167.

56 Buchanan v. Warley, 245 U.S. 60 (1917).

Negroes and the rights of Negroes to buy such property in spite of state laws to the contrary. Finding that it was unconstitutional as well as at times politically impossible or inexpedient to zone select residential areas against occupation by minority groups, developers of such areas turned to use of restrictive covenants on the sale of property therein. Since no white person can be compelled to sell property to a Negro, it was thought that there was nothing unconstitutional about a restriction on the sale to the white person himself in the form of a prohibition against selling to Negroes. Covenants were therefore included in deeds forbidding such sale.

In the case of Shelley v. Kraemer,[57] however, which was decided in 1948, the Supreme Court rendered the restrictive covenant device partly ineffective. While admitting that private parties had a right to make covenants concerning the persons to whom they would or would not sell property, it held that state courts could not be used to enforce such covenants, since enforcement by a state agency would deny equal protection of the laws in violation of the Fourteenth Amendment. While the decision of the Court has not meant the flooding of exclusive residential districts by minority groups, it has tended somewhat to discredit this form of discrimination.

PROCEDURAL RIGHTS

Questions of the substantive rights of minorities, rights of life, liberty, and property, and of freedom of religion, speech, press, and assembly,[58] merge with questions of procedural rights. Procedure has to do less with the basic content of rights than with the machinery by which rights are to be protected. Procedural questions involve such matters as the composition of juries, the prisoner's right to counsel, the treatment of prisoners, the use of confessions which prisoners have been coerced to make, the use of evidence obtained by search and seizure, and so on. The significance of procedural rights is suggested by the following quotation from Justice Douglas:

> It is not without significance that most of the provisions of the Bill of Rights are procedural. It is procedure that spells much of the difference between rule of law and rule by whim or caprice. Steadfast adherence to strict procedural safeguards is our main assurance that there will be equal justice under law.[59]

[57] 334 U.S. 1.
[58] For reference to the political rights of Negroes see Chapter 15.
[59] Joint Anti-Fascist Refugee Committee v. McGrath, 341 U.S. 123, 179 (1951).

The difficulties experienced in earlier years with trial of Negroes before juries from which Negroes had been excluded carried over into the 1940's and 1950's primarily through exclusion from grand juries by which indictments of Negro defendants were found. Three cases reached the Supreme Court from the State of Texas in less than a decade. In one case the Court found evidence of deliberate exclusion of Negroes in the fact that in a county with a large Negro population no Negro had been on a grand jury list in sixteen years. Under such circumstances conviction of a Negro after indictment by an exclusively white grand jury could not stand. Said Chief Justice Stone:

> Equal protection of the laws is something more than an abstract right. It is a command which the state must respect, the benefits of which every person may demand. Not the least merit of our constitutional system is that its safeguards extend to all — the least deserving as well as the most virtuous.[60]

In a later case the defendant failed to escape merely because the one Negro who appeared on the indicting grand jury did not represent a proportion of the jurors equal to the local proportion of Negro residents to white people.[61] It was not necessary, the Court held, that Negroes be represented on grand juries in proportion to population. In a still later case, however, a conviction was set aside when the absence of Negroes on a grand jury was correlated with the fact that over a period of years representation of Negroes had been less than half the ratio of Negro to white population in the county.[62] It was typical of the Court as of the turn of the half-century, however, that not enough justices could agree on a line of reasoning to enable them to list one opinion as the "opinion of the Court."

In insisting that Negroes should not be excluded from grand juries and trial juries the Supreme Court has adhered to the ideal that persons tried should be subject to trial by their "peers," by their equals, and not exclusively by some different group of people. With division among its members it did uphold the New York practice of using "blue ribbon" juries for cases of special difficulty. "Blue ribbon" panels of jurors are drawn from the general jury panel in such a way as to provide persons of superior intelligence or stamina. They are supposed to be of special use in intricate cases and cases in which

60 Hill v. Texas, 316 U.S. 400, 406 (1942).
61 Akins v. Texas, 325 U.S. 398 (1945).
62 Cassell v. Texas, 339 U.S. 282 (1950). See also Shepherd v. Florida, 341 U.S. 50 (1951).

intimidation may be threatened. By a vote of five to four the Supreme Court held that trial by such a specially selected jury did not deny equal protection of the laws.[63]

An essential characteristic of jury trial as guaranteed by the Constitution is that the jury shall be impartial. In the District of Columbia there has been difficulty in getting an adequate selection of jury personnel if government employees were excluded from the list. On the other hand, it was widely felt that inclusion of government personnel on juries before whom defendants were prosecuted imported a bias against defendants. In 1948 the Supreme Court upheld by a five to four decision a conviction on a narcotics charge, in spite of the fact that all jurors were government employees. One of the jurors, furthermore, and the wife of another, were employees of the department charged with enforcement of the statute. The Court held that in order to eliminate such jurors there had to be a basis for a charge of actual bias, and not merely employment among the millions who worked for the prosecuting government.[64] Justice Jackson, dissenting, thought trial lawyers would be in nearly unanimous agreement that "a jury, every member of which is in the hire of one of the litigants, lacks something of being an impartial jury." [65]

The same question arose again in 1950 in connection with the trial of a member of the Communist Party for contempt of a committee of the House of Representatives. The Court gave the same answer, with two justices dissenting. Justice Jackson went along with the majority since the earlier decision was not to be overruled, noting that he was unwilling to make an exception in favor of Communists. He explained his position in part as follows:

> It is true that Communists are the current phobia in Washington. But always, since I can remember, some group or other is being investigated and castigated here. At various times it has been Bundists and Germans, Japanese, lobbyists, tax evaders, oil men, utility men, bankers, brokers, labor leaders, Silver Shirts, and Fascists. At times, usually after dramatic and publicised exposures, members of these groups have been brought to trial for some offense. I think that

[63] Fay v. New York, 332 U.S. 261 (1947), Moore v. New York, 333 U.S. 565 (1948). In the latter case (p. 570), Justice Murphy contended for the dissenters that "the 'blue ribbon' method of selecting only the 'best' of the general jurors, a method instituted with the highest intentions, does violence to the fundamental precepts of the jury system."

[64] Frazier v. United States, 335 U.S. 497 (1949).

[65] Ibid., p. 514.

none of them at such times ever should be forced to defend themselves against the Government's accusations before the Government's employees. But so long as accused persons who are Republicans, Dixiecrats, Socialists, or Democrats must put up with such a jury, it will have to do for Communists.[66]

TREATMENT OF PRISONERS

A number of cases suggest a kind of running battle between the Supreme Court and local police officers to prevent cruelty to prisoners on the part of those officers. The Department of Justice as a law enforcing agency has pushed to the limit federal civil rights legislation to protect minority groups, and especially Negroes, against undue harshness of treatment,[67] but largely without avail. Actually the Supreme Court can do little more than nullify convictions for crime when convictions have been based on or accompanied by gross abuse of the rights of prisoners.

The Supreme Court receives many appeals from convictions in state courts based on confessions extorted from prisoners. The case of Chambers v. Florida,[68] decided February 12, 1940, received much attention because it was decided on the birthday of Abraham Lincoln, emancipator of slaves, and because the opinion of the Court was written by Justice Black whose appointment to the Supreme Court had been attacked because of his earlier membership in the Ku Klux Klan. Four Negroes had been convicted for murder on confessions extorted before they were brought to trial. Although the record did not conclusively prove the use of physical violence it did show

> the drag net methods of arrest on suspicion without warrant, and the protracted questioning and cross questioning of these ignorant young colored tenant farmers by State officers and other white citizens, in a fourth floor jail room, where as prisoners they were without friends, advisers or counselors, and under circumstances calculated to break the strongest nerves and the stoutest resistance.[69]

Explaining the procedural protection given by due process of law, Justice Black said:

[66] Dennis v. United States, 339 U.S. 162, 175 (1950).
[67] See Screws v. United States, 325 U.S. 91 (1945).
[68] 309 U.S. 227.
[69] Ibid., pp. 238–239.

The testimony of centuries, in governments of varying kinds over populations of different races and beliefs, stood as proof that physical and mental torture and coercion had brought about the tragically unjust sacrifices of some who were the noblest and most useful of their generations. The rack, the thumbscrew, the wheel, solitary confinement, prolonged questioning and cross questioning, and other ingenious forms of entrapment of the helpless or unpopular had left their wake of mutilated bodies and shattered minds along the way to the cross, the guillotine, the stake and the hangman's noose. And they who have suffered most from secret and dictatorial proceedings have almost always been the poor, the ignorant, the numerically weak, the friendless, and the powerless.[70]

In this case the decision of the court below was unanimously reversed.

Protection has been given in a long line of later cases which have involved coerced confessions. Official misconduct which has invalidated convictions has included persistent and protracted questioning, threats of exposure to mob violence, isolation from friends and from counsel, and questioning in isolated places. The justices have disagreed widely over the degree of pressure necessary to invalidate a confession for use in court. Justices Douglas and Black would outlaw all confessions obtained during the period between the time when the prisoner was taken into custody and the time when he was officially arraigned, when he was charged with a specific offense and allowed access to counsel. In the language of Justice Douglas:

> The practice of obtaining confessions prior to arraignment breeds the third degree and the inquisition. As long as it remains lawful for the police to hold persons incommunicado, coerced confessions will infect criminal trials in violation of the commands of due process of law.[71]

These justices hold that when the way is paved for later confessions by confessions coerced in the pre-arraignment period the later ones too may not be used in court. The other justices go less far but differ in varying degrees in protecting the rights of the accused. The differences reveal themselves in cases involving the treatment of prisoners by federal officers as well as by officers of state and local governments.[72]

70 *Ibid.*, pp. 237–238.
71 Stroble *v.* California, 343 U.S. 181, 203–204 (1952).
72 See for example United States *v.* Carignan, 342 U.S. 36 (1951).

THE RIGHT TO COUNSEL

One of the protections widely guaranteed to prisoners is that of the advice of counsel. In federal courts the right is guaranteed in all cases by the Sixth Amendment. In state cases the protection is derived merely from the due process clause of the Fourteenth Amendment. While a minority of the justices have contended that the effect of the Fourteenth Amendment is to incorporate fully the guarantee contained in the Sixth,[73] the majority of the Court insists on looking at the specific situation to see whether due process requires the giving of this protection. The Court, in other words, exercises vast discretion in deciding whether a conviction should be set aside on the ground that the defendant lacked the benefit of the advice and assistance of counsel, in a state prosecution. In arriving at its decision the Court will look into the following considerations: the gravity of the offense, and particularly the question whether life is at stake; the complexity of the legal issues; the age and mental capacity of the accused; his education and experience, particularly his knowledge of law and court procedure; and the degree of protection given by the court during the trial.

In general the Supreme Court required the provision of counsel in capital cases.[74] In other cases it exercised its judgment as to whether due process required that counsel be provided. The standards of measurement were obviously indefinite, and cases turning on this issue were among those on which the Court divided in multiple directions. Unity could have been achieved by holding that provision of counsel was required by the due process clause in all cases, but the Court seemed to feel that such a holding would in some cases unnecessarily handicap state prosecutions. It could have been achieved by holding that the clause never included the right to counsel, but the Court evidently felt that such a holding would in some cases sanction injustice. Between the two poles it seemed impossible to reach agreement on a statement of clear principle.

SELF-INCRIMINATION

Multiple congressional investigations and other inquiries into communist activities and crime in various fields led to new cases dealing with the scope of the power of government to compel testimony.

[73] See for example Bute v. Illinois, 333 U.S. 640, 677–682 (1948).
[74] See Uveges v. Illinois, 335 U.S. 437 (1948).

Federal cases turned on the provision of the Fifth Amendment that no person should be compelled "in any criminal case to be a witness against himself," and state cases turned on the due process clause of the Fourteenth Amendment. In 1950 the Supreme Court held that a witness could not be compelled to testify as to employment by the Communist Party, in view of the provisions of the Smith Act making it a crime to engage in conduct implicit in such employment.[75] It held that where incrimination was involved a husband could not be compelled to disclose the whereabouts of his wife.[76] It held that a witness who admitted her membership and activity as an officer of the Communist Party might not thereafter claim a privilege against self-incrimination to avoid testimony as to the disposition of the books and papers of the party.[77] The privilege must be fully claimed at the right time if it was to be claimed at all. In many investigations and trials witnesses learned to their cost that the extent of the right to refuse testimony on ground of self-incrimination was measured by the courts and not by the witnesses, and that the witness who over-estimated the scope of his right might end up in jail for his refusal to testify.

The Fifth Amendment is not directly applicable to the states, and majorities of the Supreme Court have always denied that the protection given to state prisoners went so far as to include the privilege against self-incrimination. In 1947 a major controversy over this issue took place in Adamson v. California.[78] While no state permits the admitted use of direct coercion to compel a defendant to testify against himself — such coercion, even if attempted, would be held to violate the Fourteenth Amendment — state laws do often embarrass defendants by permitting courts to draw inferences as to guilt from the refusal of defendants to testify in their own behalf. A California defendant in a murder case who already had a criminal record was faced with the dilemma that if he took the witness stand the prosecution was permitted to bring out his previous criminal record, whereas if he did not take the stand the prosecutor and the judge might call to the attention of the jury the implications of his failure to testify. He was therefore under pressure to testify and not to testify. He did not testify, and this fact was stressed before the jury. He was convicted. After conviction he appealed to the Supreme Court on the

75 Patricia Blau v. United States, 340 U.S. 151 (1950).
76 Irving Blau v. United States, 340 U.S. 332 (1951).
77 Rogers v. United States, 340 U.S. 367 (1951).
78 332 U.S. 46.

ground that he had been unconstitutionally compelled to be a witness against himself.

The Court held, as it had in other cases, that the privilege against self-incrimination did not apply in state courts, and further held that the California procedure did not deny due process of law. Justice Black, supported by Justice Douglas and in large part by Justices Murphy and Rutledge, made a major effort to show that the Fourteenth Amendment — apparently the amendment as a whole and not merely its due process clause — made the procedural prohibitions of the first eight amendments applicable to the states.[79] Justice Black was concerned about the use merely of the due process clause for protection against state action, and about the indefiniteness of that clause, which as to self-incrimination, the right to counsel, and other procedural matters was applied with a bewildering number of variations so that neither courts nor defendants could measure their rights in advance of decisions. Such expansion and contraction of "due process" according to the beliefs of judges in individual cases seemed to him a deplorable practice analogous to deciding cases on the basis of natural law. He disapproved of the theory

> that this Court is endowed by the Constitution with boundless power under "natural law" periodically to expand and contract constitutional standards to conform to the Court's conception of what at a particular time constitutes "civilized decency" and "fundamental liberty and justice." [80]

He thought that the "natural" law theory of the Constitution degraded the constitutional safeguards of the Bill of Rights and appropriated for the Supreme Court a broad power which it was not authorized to exercise.

Although the controversy came up in case after case, Justice Black was never able to persuade a majority of the Court to hold that the procedural prohibitions of the first eight amendments applied directly to the states and to abandon its use of a flexible concept of due process. It appeared again in the field of self incrimination in the so-called "stomach pump" case in 1952. Police officers in Los Angeles, invading the room of an alleged narcotic agent, arrived in time to see the man grab and swallow two suspicious-looking capsules. They

79 For disapproving analysis of this position see Charles Fairman and Stanley Morrison, "Does the Fourteenth Amendment Incorporate the Bill of Rights?" *Stanford Law Review*, Vol. 2 (December, 1949), 1–173.
80 332 U.S. 69.

rushed him to a hospital where a doctor forced an emetic solution into his stomach through a tube, and the resultant vomiting brought up the capsules which proved to contain morphine. He was convicted in part on the basis of this evidence. He appealed the decision on the ground of compulsory self-incrimination in violation of the due process clause of the Fourteenth Amendment.

The Supreme Court voted unanimously to reverse the decision. Justices Black and Douglas reiterated their argument that the self-incrimination clause of the Fifth Amendment was applicable, but the majority, speaking through Justice Frankfurter, relied on the due process clause. In an opinion which constituted an essay on due process in the running verbal battle with Justice Black, Justice Frankfurter contended that due process was not to be derided as resort to natural law. Due process was not a matter of judicial caprice.

> In each case "due process of law" requires an evaluation based on a disinterested inquiry pursued in the spirit of science, on a balanced order of facts exactly and fairly stated, on the detached consideration of conflicting claims, . . . on a judgment not ad hoc and episodic but duly mindful of reconciling the needs of both continuity and of change in a progressive society.[81]

The handling of this case, Frankfurter contended, provided an example of the application of due process. The conduct of government agents shocked the conscience and offended even the most hardened sensibilities. Due process forbade basing convictions on coerced confessions. Furthermore:

> To attempt in this case to distinguish what lawyers call "real evidence" from verbal evidence is to ignore the reasons for excluding coerced confessions. Use of involuntary verbal confessions in State criminal trials is constitutionally obnoxious not only because of their unreliability. They are inadmissible under the Due Process Clause even though statements contained in them may be independently established as true. Coerced confessions offend the community's sense of fair play and decency. So here, to sanction the brutal conduct which naturally enough was condemned by the court whose judgment is before us, would be to afford brutality a cloak of law. Nothing would be more calculated to discredit law and thereby to brutalize the temper of a society.[82]

[81] Rochin v. California, 342 U.S. 165, 172 (1952).
[82] Ibid., pp. 173–174.

SEARCHES AND SEIZURES

The problem of indefiniteness of constitutional language carries over from self-incrimination to the subject of unreasonable searches and seizures, where the indefiniteness is unavoidable even as to the work of federal courts. The Constitution forbids unreasonable searches and seizures by the federal government but it does not say what they are. It forbids issuing warrants except upon probable cause but it does not say when arrests or searches may be made without warrants. From the beginning, therefore, courts were compelled to follow the common law pattern of decisions on such matters and, in effect, to make new law as cases arose not covered by precedents.

Of the long line of search and seizure cases decided during the nineteen-forties and early nineteen-fifties, many had to do with the extent of the power to make searches in connection with valid arrests. It was a long-established principle that the arrested person might be searched and that his immediate relevant surroundings might also be searched without a separate warrant, but the scope of the power to search and the scope of things that might be seized was left in doubt. In this area the position of the Supreme Court shifted back and forth from case to case. In 1947, in Harris v. United States,[83] the Court interpreted the power broadly. Harris was arrested, in his apartment, for fraud involving the use of forged checks. The arresting officers, with a warrant of arrest but without a search warrant, searched the entire apartment for canceled checks. In a bedroom bureau drawer an officer found a sealed envelope marked "personal." In the envelope he found not checks but classification cards and other Selective Service documents, of which possession by private parties was illegal. Harris was prosecuted and convicted not for forgery but for possession of these documents. He appealed on the ground of the unreasonableness of the search and seizure, but the Supreme Court, dividing five to four, held that the Constitution had not been violated.

In 1948, in Trupiano v. United States,[84] the Supreme Court made what appeared to be a major shift in position, again voting five to four but with a different arrangement of personnel. An agent of the federal Alcohol Tax Unit, having evidence of the operation of a still, arrested a man whom he saw operating the still when he approached an open door. He and other officers then proceeded to search the

[83] 331 U.S. 145.
[84] 334 U.S. 699.

entire premises, without a search warrant, and a group of defendants were convicted on the basis of the evidence. They challenged the reasonableness of the search. The Supreme Court held that for such a search a warrant was required, since there had been ample time to procure it. Said Justice Murphy for the Court:

> This rule rests upon the desirability of having magistrates rather than police officers determine when searches and seizures are permissible and what limitations should be placed upon such activities. . . . In their understandable zeal to ferret out crime and in the excitement of the capture of a suspected person, officers are less likely to possess the detachment and neutrality with which the constitutional rights of the suspect must be viewed.[85]

In 1949, after the death and replacement of Justices Murphy and Rutledge, the two most ardent defenders of liberty on the Court, the trend shifted back toward the earlier position. In United States *v.* Rabinowitz [86] the Court overruled the Trupiano decision. In connection with a valid arrest for selling and possessing forged and altered government stamps, it upheld an extensive search of an office, files, desk, and safe for evidence without possession of a search warrant. This does not mean that searches may now be made indiscriminately without search warrants and other than in connection with valid arrests. It is clear that they may not.[87] But there seems to be an over-all trend in favor of the admission of seized evidence which parallels the trend concerning admission of testimony. The latter was in 1952 stated as follows by Justice Jackson for the Court:

> The trend of the law in recent years has been to turn away from rigid rules of incompetence, in favor of admitting testimony and allowing the trier of fact to judge the weight to be given to it.[88]

It is also true, however, that the case in which this statement was made was decided by a vote of five to four, and that even if all justices agreed on the generalization they would be apt to divide when applying it in marginal cases. In this group of cases, as in others involving different areas of the conflict over the scope of the rights of the individual, the achievement of judicial unity is an ideal far from realized.

85 *Ibid.,* p. 705.
86 339 U.S. 56.
87 See United States *v.* Jeffers, 342 U.S. 48 (1951).
88 On Lee *v.* United States, 343 U.S. 747 (1952).

# CHAPTER 40

# THE ROOSEVELT–TRUMAN COURT

THE EPOCH-MAKING SHIFT in constitutional interpretation which the Supreme Court made at the 1936–1937 term marked the end of an old era and the beginning of a new one. The three preceding chapters have outlined the trends in interpretation which have taken place during the intervening years. The remaining task is to present in more detail an account of the personnel of the Roosevelt-Truman Court and to bring together the threads of judicial strategy and behavior for a more definitive summary.

## PERSONNEL

The change from the Court which was generally anti-New Deal in its approach to a Court accepting the New Deal as clearly constitutional marked one of the few sharp transitions in our judicial history. While the period of the Court's greatness began with the term of John Marshall as Chief Justice, it was the personality and intellect of Marshall, rather than other changes on the Court calculated to give strength to his point of view, that made his term a memorable one. Indeed, Jefferson and other appointing Presidents of the Marshall period were in general out of sympathy with Marshall's constitutional doctrines, and they assuredly made no effort to give him greater influence by appointing justices who thought as he did. The unique opportunity of President Taft to appoint five justices during a single presidential term brought no significant change in the approach of the Court to constitutional problems. Innumerable other changes had only very gradual effects on the work of the Court.

Indeed, there were only two periods in the early history of the Court in which relatively abrupt personnel changes brought doctrinal changes comparable in impact to those which came with the Roosevelt Court. Of these the first was the period of the eighteen-thirties and the second the period of the Civil War. Even during these periods the transitions were less abrupt than that of a century later. The influence of Chief Justice Marshall had begun to decline before his death in 1835, and even before Andrew Jackson became President in 1829. On the other hand, Jackson's first appointee, John McLean, selected in 1829, belonged hardly less with the Marshall régime than with that of Chief Justice Taney. The same can be said of the appointment of Henry Baldwin, made in 1830. The transition from the Marshall régime, in other words, was a relatively gradual one, and its arrival was punctuated only with decisions affecting the scope of state powers which were handed down in 1837 after the accession of Taney to the Chief Justiceship and after the appointment also of James M. Wayne and Philip P. Barbour. The doctrinal shift of this period, furthermore, while a very real one, was exaggerated in appearance by the fact that Taney apparently did not seek to exert, and certainly was not able to exert, the influence over his brethren that had been exercised by Marshall for a third of a century. As a result, the Taney Court produced far more divided opinions than did the Court of Marshall and seemed to differ from the Marshall Court more than it actually did.

The Civil War transition more definitely resembles that of the nineteen-thirties, although here too important differences are to be seen. While appointments to the Court were not stigmatized as intended to pack the Court with men of the President's views, the size of the Court was increased to ten, the all-time maximum, and the Lincoln appointees were as a matter of course selected from among the persons loyal to the Union. There was little criticism of such selection, and the process was therefore not denounced as "packing." There was no complete break with the past. Yet there was a pronounced change in attitude as the nation abandoned hope of compromise on the sectional issue and as the sentiments of the North became the dominant sentiments of the federal government. The Supreme Court became with new appointments the Court of the Union, which meant in general the Court of the North.

### THE ROOSEVELT JUSTICES

If the Civil War and post-Civil War Court was the Court of the North, the Court of which Franklin D. Roosevelt made the initial appointment in 1937 was the Court of the New Deal. It was a Court committed to getting "back to the Constitution" for a constitutional construction that would support the New Deal program. The pre-

Roosevelt Court had been completely stable for five years. During the four years beginning in 1937, seven members left the Court and successors were appointed, and in the process of change Justice Stone was promoted to the Chief Justiceship. Only Justice Roberts remained without the stamp of New Deal approval at the time of the death of President Roosevelt in the spring of 1945, and he retired the following summer. He was replaced by a Truman appointee, as was Chief Justice Stone after his death in 1946. In short, the old Court virtually disappeared in four years, and in nine years it had disappeared completely. Within that period one Roosevelt appointee left the Court to be replaced by another. In any comparable period, personnel changes of such rapidity would be disturbing to the smooth unfolding of judicial interpretation. Because of the individualism of the newly appointed justices and their lack of traditional reverence for settled law and for the Court itself, the disturbance during this period was particularly great. Some account of each of the new members is therefore relevant to explanation of the work of the renovated Court.

President Roosevelt's first appointee to the Court was Hugo L. Black, then United States senator from Alabama.[1] Black was without judicial experience except for a period in a municipal police court, but he was a skilled practitioner. In the Senate he had proved a brilliant and ruthless investigator in connection with airmail scandals and lobbying by powerful corporations. He was not a passive follower of President Roosevelt but a crusader in his own right for measures in general consistent with the New Deal program. For example, he had been year after year one of the sponsors of the Black-Connery bill to limit the hours of labor. Such activities in the Senate indicated that he was by no means a typical member of Congress from the South, and they made him suspect to typical conservative interests which were well represented in the southern contingent.

Nevertheless it was on grounds of what might be called southern conservatism rather than of liberalism that he proved vulnerable to attack. The Senate followed tradition in confirming the appointment of one of its own members without holding hearings on it. After he had taken the oath of office but before he had taken his seat as a member of the Court, an enterprising newspaper man published evidence to show that Black had been a member of the Ku

[1] For discussion see John P. Frank, *Mr. Justice Black* (1949) and Charlotte Williams, *Hugo Black* (1950).

Klux Klan. Returning from a vacation in Europe to find the country excited over the issue, with a storm of protest against the appointment, Black took the unusual step of delivering an explanatory address over radio. He admitted that he had once been a member of the Klan but insisted that his membership had long since expired and that he had none of the prejudices as to race and creed which such membership implied.

Protest against the appointment continued, and Black began his work on the Court under embarrassing circumstances. A lawyer among his critics asked leave of the Supreme Court to file a petition for an order requiring Black to show cause why he should be permitted to serve as a member of the Court. Two legal grounds were stated, neither of which had anything to do with the real basis of objections to Black. The first ground stated was that Black could not become a justice because of the constitutional provision that no member of Congress should be appointed during his congressional term to a position of which the emoluments had been increasing during that term. Shortly before Black's appointment, Congress had added to the attractiveness of a position on the Court by authorizing members to retire at a specified age without resigning, and therefore without releasing their constitutional right to an undiminished salary. It was contended that this action debarred Black from membership on the Court. The second ground was that since his predecessor, Justice Van Devanter, had merely retired from the Court of nine justices but had not resigned, there was no vacancy on the Court, and therefore no position to which Black could be appointed.

Without discussing either of the grounds, the Court refused to hear argument in the case. In a brief opinion it stated that the petitioning lawyer had not shown that he had a personal stake in the issue other than as a citizen, and that such a limited interest was not enough to make him a party to a suit. It was an established principle that, to enable a private individual to invoke judicial power to determine the validity of legislative or executive action, he must show that he had sustained, or was in immediate danger of sustaining, a direct injury as a result of that action. It was not sufficient that he have merely a general interest common to all members of the public.[2]

In spite of the failure of the challenge to Black's position, it created additional bad odor for the appointment. For a time the new justice remained under observation as a former Klansman who perhaps

[2] *Ex parte* Levitt, 302 U.S. 633 (1937).

ought never to have been appointed, in an office from which he might conceivably have been ousted had the legal question been properly brought before the Court. Gossip, stemming perhaps in part from members of the Court and others who disliked his point of view, had it that he was a poor legal craftsman. Then gradually opinion concerning him began to change, partly for the better and in any event to a substantially different picture. The Ku Klux Klan stereotype was pretty much destroyed by his delivery of an opinion of the Court denouncing procedure by which Negroes were convicted of a capital offense in a state court on the basis of confessions secured by torture.[3] The opinion was announced in 1940 on the birthday of Abraham Lincoln, author of the Proclamation of Emancipation, and received widespread publicity partly because of the anniversary. Although he did not take the extreme positions of Justices Murphy and Rutledge, Black came gradually to be known as one of the most ardent defenders of liberty and of the rights of minority groups and oppressed individuals. He was intensely conscious of the oppressive power of big property and he joined in the movement to deflate "due process of law" as a bulwark for the defense of property when human rights or other interests were involved on the other side. He tried unsuccessfully to get the Supreme Court to reverse its holding that a corporation was a person within the meaning of the Fourteenth Amendment so as to be entitled to the protection given by that amendment.[4] He sensed the possibility of tyranny in government as well as outside it, and even within the area of the judiciary itself. He distrusted "due process of law" as the basis for protection of rights other than those strictly procedural, for the reason that its indefiniteness left it subject to expansion and contraction according to judicial whim. He tried unsuccessfully to persuade the Supreme Court to rely not merely on the due process clause of the Fourteenth Amendment for protection of rights against the states but to hold that the more specific language of the first eight amendments, hitherto found applicable only to the federal government, was made applicable to the states through adoption of the Fourteenth Amendment.[5] At one time as many as four justices took this position, but changes in membership reduced the group to Black and Douglas. In these and other areas, Justice Black proved a strong individualist, refusing to merge his

[3] Chambers v. Florida, 309 U.S. 227 (1940). For discussion see Chapter 39.

[4] See his dissenting opinion, Connecticut General Life Insurance Co. v. Johnson, 303 U.S. 77 (1938).

[5] See Adamson v. California, 332 U.S. 46 (1947).

views with those of differing brethren so as to secure unity of judicial expression.

Stanley Reed, of Kentucky, became the second Roosevelt justice, taking his seat after the retirement of Justice Sutherland in 1938. He was much less of a controversial figure than Black. He had received appointments to office from both political parties. President Hoover had appointed him general counsel for the Federal Farm Board. In the Roosevelt administration he had served first as general counsel for the Reconstruction Finance Corporation and then as solicitor general in the Department of Justice. In the latter position he had argued many important New-Deal cases before the Supreme Court, suffering some grievous defeats at the hands of unsympathetic justices. Under the direction of Attorney General Cummings he had aided in collecting materials for use in the fight to pack the Court, but he had persuaded the Attorney General that his responsibility for argument of government cases made it necessary for him to remain in the background in the Court controversy. By people of differing viewpoints he was well liked and was regarded as a competent lawyer. His nomination was confirmed without opposition.

In a group of nine in which many were highly controversial characters, Justice Reed remained largely uncontroversial. He in general supported New-Deal measures and the New-Deal philosophy, but he wrote opinions conventionally as a justice and not as a crusader for particular theories or practices. In public observation he remained a quiet figure while controversy raged around him. In particular, he engaged but little in the jibes at the beliefs and performances of other justices which characterized the performances of some of his colleagues. He was an old-fashioned justice on a Court with a pronounced new tone.

Felix Frankfurter, a professor of law at the Harvard Law School became the third Roosevelt appointee in 1939 as the successor to Justice Cardozo who had died in office. He was known as an able law teacher with liberal tendencies. He had been a close friend of Justices Holmes, Brandeis, and Cardozo and was expected to take positions on constitutional issues similar to theirs. He was close also to President Roosevelt and was reputed to be influential in molding New-Deal policies. The principal overt opposition to the appointment was on the ground of alleged radicalism. Belief in the taint of radicalism had arisen largely from his efforts on behalf of the defendants in the Sacco-Vanzetti case in 1927 and his efforts to free Tom Mooney from a California prison. Frankfurter appeared at Senate committee hearings on his nomination to explain his activities and to declare that he was not and never had been a communist.

Like Justice Black, although from a different direction, Frankfurter somewhat confounded his critics by the pattern of his Supreme Court decisions. In 1940, with only Chief Justice Stone dissenting, he wrote the opinion of the Court upholding the right of a state to require public school children to salute the American flag as a means of indoctrinating loyalty to the United States.[6] To many of his liberal admirers this decision seemed a threat to principles of liberty which he had hitherto defended. To them the decision seemed an unconstitutional invasion of the freedom of religion due to children whose parents thought saluting the flag the equivalent to the worship of idols which the Scriptures forbade.

The Frankfurter decision in the flag-salute case reflects one of his major judicial tenets — that in cases involving alleged denial of liberty the courts should pay great deference to the judgment of the legislature. He did not himself defend compulsory saluting of the flag as a means of developing patriotism, but thought the courts should defer to the legislature in the matter.

> To stigmatize legislative judgment in providing for this universal gesture of respect for the symbol of our national life in the setting of the common school as a lawless inroad on that freedom of conscience which the Constitution protects, would amount to no less than the pronouncement of pedagogical and psychological dogma in a field where the courts possess no marked and certainly no controlling competence.[7]

The courtroom, he contended, was not the arena for debating issues of educational policy. To the legislature no less than to the courts was committed the guardianship of cherished liberties.

> To fight out the wise use of legislative authority in the forum of public opinion and before legislative assemblies rather than to transfer such a contest to the judicial arena, serves to vindicate the self confidence of a free people.[8]

---

6 Minersville School District *v.* Gobitis, 310 U.S. 586 (1940).

7 *Ibid.*, p. 597.

8 *Ibid.*, p. 600. Since Justice Frankfurter adhered to his position in this case, it is irrelevant to this discussion that a majority of the Court overruled the case in West Virginia State Board of Education *v.* Barnette, 319 U.S. 624 (1943).

It is a complicating factor in appraisal of the Frankfurter position that whereas he was inclined to accept legislative judgment where curtailment of personal liberty was involved, he seemed less inclined to accept it when measuring the power of states to regulate property on the edge of the interstate commerce field.[9] One of the possible implications is that he was more eager to use the power of judicial review in defense of property rights than of personal rights. There is irony also in the fact that he dissented in a case in which the Court upheld collection of a tax on gambling, with the attendant requirement of disclosure of activities which the states might punish on the basis of the disclosure. He would have held the federal act unconstitutional, finding that it sought "enforcement of the formal revenue purpose through means that offended those standards of decency in our civilization against which due process is a barrier." [10]

Admitting that "due process of law" was an exceedingly vague concept, Justice Frankfurter opposed Justice Black's efforts to restrict it to a narrow procedural meaning. Whereas Black sought to narrow the discretion of judges in passing on legal rights, Frankfurter sought to keep that discretion expanded through flexible interpretation of due process.

> Our constitutional system makes it the Court's duty to interpret those feelings of society to which the due process clause gives legal protection. Because of their inherent vagueness the tests by which we are to be guided are most unsatisfactory, but such as they are we must apply them.[11]

His equivocal position on the defense of personal liberty, his demand for due process flexibility, and habit of writing prolific dissenting and concurring opinions made Justice Frankfurter an important factor in preventing the solidification of judicial opinion on the Court.

William O. Douglas, then chairman of the Securities and Exchange Commission and formerly professor of law at Yale School of Law, was appointed to the Court in March, 1939, to succeed Justice Brandeis who had retired. Douglas was an energetic administrator and it was rumored from time to time after his judicial appointment that he might be a candidate for Vice-President or even for President. No

[9] For discussion see Wallace Mendleson, "Justices Black and Frankfurter: Supreme Court Majority and Minority Trends," *Journal of Politics*, Vol. 12 (February, 1950), 66–92.

[10] United States *v.* Kahriger, 345 U.S. 22 (1953).

[11] Haley *v.* Ohio, 332 U.S. 596, 605 (1948).

such nomination came his way, but he developed into a world traveler during the summer periods, and into an author of some distinction with respect to his travels. As chairman of the Securities and Exchange Commission he had worked for the civilizing of modern business practices, reflecting there some of the distrust of bigness in business which had characterized the thinking of Justice Brandeis and had been revealed in Brandeis' book, *The Curse of Bigness*. The Douglas attitude was portrayed in a dissenting opinion in an antitrust suit against big steel companies in 1948:

> We have here the problem of bigness. Its lesson should by now have been burned into our memory by Brandeis. The Curse of Bigness shows how size can become a menace — both industrial and social. It can be an industrial menace because it creates gross inequalities against existing or putative competitors. It can be a social menace — because of its control of prices. Control of prices in the steel industry is powerful leverage on our economy. For the price of steel determines the price of hundreds of other articles. Our price level determines in large measure whether we have prosperity or depression — an economy of abundance or scarcity. Size in steel should therefore be jealously watched. In final analysis, size in steel is the measure of the power of a handful of men over our economy. That power can be utilized with lightning speed. It can be benign or it can be dangerous. The philosophy of the Sherman Act is that it should not exist. For all power tends to develop into a government in itself. Power that controls the economy should be in the hands of elected representatives of the people, not in the hands of an industrial oligarchy. Industrial power should be decentralized. It should be scattered into many hands so that the fortunes of the people will not be dependent on the whim or caprice, the emotional stability of a few self-appointed men. The fact that they are not vicious men but respectable and social-minded is irrelevant. That is the philosophy and the command of the Sherman Act. It is founded on a theory of hostility to the concentration in private hands of power so great that only a government of the people should have it.[12]

Distrusting private government, Justice Douglas also distrusted the exercise of arbitrary power by public government as well. He approved of constitutional restraint on executive power in the federal government. He denied the right of the President to seize the steel industry for government operation without authorization from Congress even though such seizure might be desirable from the point of

12 United States v. Columbia Steel Co., 334 U.S. 495, 536 (1948).

view of speedy production of war materials. He admitted the possibility that executive action was more efficient than legislative action but noted that efficiency was not our sole concern.

> All executive power — from the reign of ancient kings to the rule of modern dictators — has the outward appearance of efficiency. Legislative power, by contrast, is slower to exercise.[13]

He quoted an opinion of Justice Brandeis, however, to the effect that the doctrine of separation of powers was written into the Constitution "not to promote efficiency but to preclude the exercise of arbitrary power, . . . to save the people from autocracy." [14]

In these and other matters Justice Douglas of course differed only in degree from his colleagues, but the difference was often substantial. He stressed the dangers of tyranny whether deriving from government or from concentrations of private power and he was one of the stalwart defenders of individual liberty. More often than with any of the others, he aligned himself with Justice Black in the multiple divisions over important cases.

Frank Murphy, Attorney General since 1937, joined the Court in January, 1940, to succeed Justice Butler who had died some weeks earlier. Like his predecessor he was a Catholic, the only Catholic on the Court during his term. He served until his death in 1949. He had previously been high commissioner to the Philippines, mayor of Detroit, and governor of Michigan. In the latter position he had achieved national prominence by refraining from direct action against sitdown strikers in a situation in which public sentiment was sharply divided, thereby providing a forecast of pro-labor leanings when he became a member of the Supreme Court. One of his achievements in a largely uneventful career as Attorney General was the establishment of a Civil Rights Unit for defense of civil rights in matters over which the United States had jurisdiction.

During his nine years on the Court, Justice Murphy proved an ardent defender of human rights in a great variety of cases. The following statement about the evils of coerced confessions provides illustration.

> One of the fixed principles of due process, as guaranteed by the Fourteenth Amendment, is that no conviction in a state court is valid which is based in whole or in part upon an involuntary confession.

---

[13] Youngstown Sheet and Tube Co. v. Sawyer, 343 U.S. 579, 629 (1952).
[14] Myers v. United States, 272 U.S. 52, 293 (1926).

. . . This principle reflects the common abhorrence of compelling any man, innocent or guilty, to give testimony against himself in a criminal proceeding. It is a principle which was written into the Constitution because of the belief that to torture and coerce an individual into confessing a crime, even though that individual may be guilty, is to endanger the rights and liberties of all persons accused of crime. History has shown that once tyrannical methods of law enforcement are permitted as to one man such methods are invariably used as to others. Brutality knows no distinction between the innocent and the guilty. And those who suffer most from these inquisitorial processes are the friendless, the ignorant, the poor and the despised.[15]

Where such abuses took place, Justice Murphy was not likely to be a stickler for the niceties of legal procedure when those niceties stood in the way of providing a remedy for the abuses — as in the case from which the quotation was taken. To him procedure had to be the servant of justice rather than its master. In the cases which came before the Supreme Court during his membership Murphy was almost always on the side of the person whose liberty was threatened.[16]

As a friend of labor Justice Murphy led in establishing the position that the right of labor to picket peacefully in connection with a labor dispute was part of the freedom of speech guaranteed by the Fourteenth Amendment. In that connection he said for the Court that

Free discussion concerning the conditions in industry and the causes of labor disputes appear to us indispensable to the effective and intelligent use of the processes of popular government to shape the destiny of modern industrial society. . . . The group in power at any moment may not impose penal sanctions on peaceful and truthful discussion of matters of public interest merely on a showing that others may thereby be persuaded to take action inconsistent with its interests. Abridgment of the liberty of such discussion can be justified only where the clear danger of substantive evils arises under circumstances affording no opportunity to test the merits of ideas by competition for acceptance in the market of public opinion.[17]

This defense of peaceful picketing had a measure of staying power even though in later cases the Court recognized the unlawfulness of peaceful picketing to promote ends which Congress or state legislatures had constitutionally forbidden. That is, labor may not peace-

15 Taylor v. Alabama, 335 U.S. 252, 275 (1948).
16 See Thurgood Marshall, "Mr. Justice Murphy and Civil Rights," *Michigan Law Review,* Vol. 48 (April, 1950), 745-766.
17 Thornhill v. State of Alabama, 310 U.S. 88, 103, 104–105 (1940).

fully picket to compel violation of federal or state labor laws which do not violate the constitution, including, for example, laws which prohibit enforcement of the closed shop. Even so, picketing may not be restricted as fully as some states have at times attempted to restrict it. Something, but by no means all, of the Murphy influence remained.

James F. Byrnes, United States senator from South Carolina, joined the Supreme Court after the retirement of Justice McReynolds in 1941. As senator he had been an effective aid of the Roosevelt administration. After appointment to the Court he continued to advise on many administrative matters. He resigned in October, 1942, to accept an administrative position, without having exercised any important influence on the Court. He was the first of the Roosevelt appointees to leave the Court.

Robert H. Jackson, then Attorney General, was appointed to the Court in 1941 when Chief Justice Hughes retired to be replaced as Chief Justice by Justice Stone. Jackson, a New York lawyer, had joined the administration in 1934 as general counsel for the Bureau of Internal Revenue. He had served thereafter as assistant attorney general, solicitor general, and Attorney General. He was an able and energetic lawyer. However, his phenomenal success as solicitor general in winning government cases before the Supreme Court, by contrast with the numerous failures of Solicitor General Reed who had preceded him in that office and then in appointment to the Supreme Court, had been due in part to changes in the attitude in the Court itself. As Jackson expressed it, the Court had become "in general outlook, the most liberal of any court of last resort in the land." [18] He had loyally supported the President's plan to enlarge the membership of the Court and was an ardent New-Dealer.

In general the philosophy propounded in Justice Jackson's judicial opinions proved to be that which he had propounded as a member of the New-Deal administration. He approved of the broad pattern of regulation now in use, based on the commerce power and other powers, and of curtailment of the use of due process and other restrictive devices. It was characteristic of his position on constitutional issues that he could say, in defense of a subsidy program to restrict agricultural production, that "it is hardly lack of due process for the government to regulate that which it subsidizes." [19]

[18] Robert H. Jackson, *The Struggle for Judicial Supremacy* (1941), p. vi.
[19] Wickard *v.* Filburn, 317 U.S. 111, 131 (1942).

Although his choice of words was more felicitous from a literary point of view, Justice Jackson's doctrinal positions were little more unique than those of Justice Reed, whose opinions tended to lack color on a Court where colorful performance was the rule rather than the exception. Jackson's uniqueness showed in matters of alignment among his colleagues and in personal disagreements more than in doctrine. According to his own statement he engaged for a time in a "feud" with Justice Black. Jackson had written a sharp dissent in a five-to-four decision in what was known as the Jewell Ridge case in which Justice Black had voted with the majority.[20] The majority vote was on the side of the case taken by a lawyer who had once been Black's law partner. Although there was no rule governing circumstances under which a justice would not participate in a decision, Jackson thought Black should have withdrawn. When the losing party applied for a rehearing on this ground, Jackson, with the concurrence of Frankfurter, insisted on making a statement which disclosed the question to the public.[21] Jackson asserted that he had done so in the face of a threat from Black that to do so would "mean a declaration of war."

Soon afterward Jackson received a leave of absence from the Supreme Court to aid in setting up an international tribunal for trial of war criminals and to serve as chief prosecutor for the United States at Nürnberg. During his absence from the country Chief Justice Stone died. Although Jackson had been spoken of as a possible successor, the appointment went instead to Fred M. Vinson, in a period in which Washington gossip was carrying stories of the strife among the justices, some of which was believed to be inspired by Justice Black. From Germany Justice Jackson wrote an explosive letter to the chairmen of the Senate and House Judiciary Committees saying that "This feud has been so much and so long publicized that Congress has a right to know the facts and issues involved." [22] He proceeded to tell the story. Although in his official statement about the Jewell Ridge case he had admitted that "it appears always to have been the responsibility of each justice to determine for himself the propriety of withdrawing in any particular circumstances," [23] he was unwilling in this instance to leave discretion in the hands of Justice Black. He believed that for a justice to sit in a case argued by a former law partner would bring the Court into disrepute. He stated bluntly that

20 Jewell Ridge Coal Corporation v. Local, 325 U.S. 161 (1945).
21 Ibid., p. 897.     22 92 Congressional Record 6724.     23 325 U.S. 897.

However innocent the coincidence of these two victories at successive terms by Justice Black's former law partner, I wanted that practice stopped. If it is ever repeated while I am on the bench I will make my Jewell Ridge opinion look like a letter of recommendation by comparison.[24]

Intemperateness of statement found its way into later Jackson opinions. The following, in which he lamented that the Court should "flounder in wordy disagreement" and criticized intemperance of statement on the part of his colleagues, provides an example:

The extravagance of some of the views expressed and the intemperance of their statement may create a suspicion that the decision of the case does not rise above the political controversy that engendered it.[25]

That he somewhat deplored his tendency to rash utterance is indicated by his dissent in a case involving disbarment of a lawyer who, as Jackson stated the case, "was guilty of several unplanned contumacious outbursts during a long and bitter trial." Jackson commented that "Perhaps consciousness of our own short patience makes us unduly considerate of the failing tempers of others of our contentious craft." [26]

Wiley B. Rutledge was appointed to the Court in 1943 to replace Justice Byrnes and served until his death in 1949. He had been dean of the law school at Washington University, St. Louis, and of the college of law of the State University of Iowa. He had been an ardent New-Dealer and a critic of the conservative pre-New Deal Supreme Court. When after the resounding New-Deal victory in the 1936 presidential election the four ultra-conservatives on the Court continued to show hostility to a social security program, Rutledge remarked that "The old four-square block remains intact . . . the Four Horsemen do not know that we had an election." [27] He vigorously supported the President's plan for Court reform. Presumably his support of the administration brought him his appointment to the Court of Appeals for the District of Columbia in 1939 and paved the way for his promotion to the Supreme Court four years later.

Although his opinions were less eloquent than those of Justice Murphy from a strictly literary point of view, Justice Rutledge showed

24 92 *Congressional Record* 6725.

25 Joint Anti-Fascist Refugee Committee *v.* McGrath, 341 U.S. 123, 183 (1951).

26 *Re* Isserman, 345 U.S. 286, 294 (1953).

27 Irving Brant, "Mr. Justice Rutledge — The Man," *Iowa Law Review*, Vol. 35 (Summer, 1950), 554.

a passion for human rights comparable to that of Murphy. The two justices often voted together in positions on liberty issues too extreme for the remainder of the Court, and at times shared the field with Justices Black and Douglas who were next in line on that issue. Along with Murphy and Douglas, Rutledge followed the lead of Black in urging that the Fourteenth Amendment made all the protections of the first eight amendments applicable to the states. Failing to get that position accepted by the majority of the Court, he welcomed such expansion of the Fourteenth Amendment as he could get, remarking that "one should not reject a piecemeal wisdom, merely because it hobbles toward the truth with backward glances." [28]

### THE TRUMAN JUSTICES

As stated above, only Justice Roberts and Chief Justice Stone remained from the pre-Roosevelt Court at the time of President Roosevelt's death in the spring of 1945, and Stone, having achieved his promotion to the Chief Justiceship through Roosevelt, was in effect a Roosevelt justice by adoption. Justice Roberts retired at the end of the 1944–45 term, making the end of the pre-Roosevelt Court and giving President Truman the opportunity to make the first of his four appointments.

By this time, the summer of 1945, conditions had vastly changed from those of the earlier period in which President Roosevelt and his admirers had placed the stamp of the New Deal on the federal government and imprinted its idealism on the minds of large numbers of people. We were at the point of winning a major war that had cost us billions of dollars, tremendous physical effort, and a vast share of our idealism. Although New Deal practices had been institutionalized in the government, the enthusiasms and sentiments that had given rise to them had now paled. Protections for labor, social security, and various restrictions on the power of big business now derived their support more from the political vested interests that had been built around them than from the original idealism. If zeal remained for campaigns for more federal aid for education, for federal financing or insurance of medical care and for the extension of other services to the people, the major crusade for social betterment in the United States was now at an end. The new President, furthermore, lacked the capacity of his predecessor for stirring enthusiasm for social reforms.

28 Wolf v. Colorado, 338 U.S. 25, 47 (1949).

These several factors might have foretold the fact that a new order was in prospect in the selection of Supreme Court justices.

Harold H. Burton, then United States Senator from Ohio, was President Truman's choice for replacement of Justice Roberts. He was a Republican, the first Republican appointee to the Court since the Roberts appointment in 1930. Since Republican membership on the Court had now been reduced to one, Chief Justice Stone, it seemed advisable to make this selection from the opposition party. In matters internal to the United States, Burton was less conservative than Republican senators from Ohio usually are, and he had built a reputation for internationalism as a co-sponsor of the Ball-Burton-Hatch-Hill resolution to commit the United States to continued participation in international affairs in the interest of world peace after the conclusion of World War II. He was well liked personally and was gregarious as most politicians must be, listing in *Who's Who in America* memberships in the following organizations: Mason, Knights of Pythias, Moose, Eagle, and Grange. He was an honorary member of Rotary, Kiwanis, and Exchange. He was an active Unitarian.

These superficial facts concerning Burton's life suggest much more a man who moves easily among his fellows than a legal scholar brooding over problems of law and justice. The suggestion proved more than valid. For some years after his appointment he carried a lighter load than his colleagues in writing opinions of the Court. He participated but little in the questioning of counsel when cases were being argued. His opinions revealed no outstanding competence. Neither did they reveal any dominant personal preoccupation, as with civil liberties or with correctness in judicial procedure. He was seemingly less contentious than most of his colleagues but the absence of contentiousness did not seem to imply depths of wisdom merely undisturbed by personal and at times unedifying contention among other justices. He was a quiet, courteous man going about his business without lending to that business any great mark of distinction.

Fred M. Vinson may have been in a sense a beneficiary of the strife among the justices, including the "feud" between Justices Black and Jackson, in that, instead of choosing a Chief Justice from among them at the death of Chief Justice Stone in 1946, President Truman turned to Vinson as his choice. Vinson, a Kentuckian, had had experience in all three branches of the government. He had been elected to Congress seven times, he had been from 1938 until 1943 a member of the Court of Appeals for the District of Columbia, and he had held im-